INTEGRATED CME PROJECT

Mathematics II

The Center for Mathematics Education Project was developed at Education Development Center, Inc. (EDC) within the Center for Mathematics Education (CME), with partial support from the National Science Foundation.

 Learning transforms lives. **Education Development Center, Inc.**
Center for Mathematics Education
Newton, Massachusetts

 This material is based upon work supported by the National Science Foundation under Grant No. ESI-0242476, Grant No. MDR-9252952, and Grant No. ESI-9617369. Any opinions, findings, and conclusions or recommendations expressed in this material are those of the author(s) and do not necessarily reflect the views of the National Science Foundation.

Taken from:
CME Project: Geometry, Algebra 2, Algebra 1, Precalculus
By the CME Project Development Team
Copyright © 2009 by Education Development Center, Inc.
Published by Pearson Education, Inc.
Upper Saddle River, New Jersey 07458

CME Common Core Additional Lessons: Geometry, Precalculus, Algebra 2, Algebra 1
By the CME Project Development Team
Copyright © 2012 by Education Development Center, Inc.
Published by Pearson Education, Inc.
Upper Saddle River, New Jersey 07458

CME Project Development Team

Lead Developers: Al Cuoco and Bowen Kerins

Core Development Team: Anna Baccaglini-Frank, Jean Benson, Nancy Antonellis D'Amato, Daniel Erman, Paul Goldenberg, Brian Harvey, Wayne Harvey, Doreen Kilday, Ryota Matsuura, Stephen Maurer, Nina Shteingold, Sarah Sword, Audrey Ting, Kevin Waterman.

Pearson Learning Solutions, 501 Boylston Street, Suite 900, Boston, MA 02116
A Pearson Education Company
www.pearsoned.com

Printed in the United States of America

1 2 3 4 5 6 7 8 9 10 V011 17 1 61 51 41 3 12

000200010271656491

CP

ISBN 10: 1-256-69466-5
ISBN 13: 978-1-256-69466-3

Contents in Brief

GAS AHEAD

Introduction to the CME Project

The CME Project, developed by EDC's Center for Mathematics Education, is a new NSF-funded high school program, organized around the familiar courses of algebra 1, geometry, algebra 2, and precalculus. The CME Project provides teachers and schools with a third alternative to the choice between traditional texts driven by basic skill development and more progressive texts that have unfamiliar organizations. This program gives teachers the option of a problem-based, student-centered program, organized around the mathematical themes with which teachers and parents are familiar. Furthermore, the tremendous success of NSF-funded middle school programs has left a need for a high school program with similar rigor and pedagogy. The CME Project fills this need.

The goal of the CME Project is to help students acquire a deep understanding of mathematics. Therefore, the mathematics here is rigorous. We took great care to create lesson plans that, while challenging, will capture and engage students of all abilities and improve their mathematical achievement.

The Program's Approach

The organization of the CME Project provides students the time and focus they need to develop fundamental mathematical ways of thinking. Its primary goal is to develop in students robust mathematical proficiency.

- The program employs innovative instructional methods, developed over decades of classroom experience and informed by research, that help students master mathematical topics.

- One of the core tenets of the CME Project is to focus on developing students' Habits of Mind, or ways in which students approach and solve mathematical challenges.

- The program builds on lessons learned from high-performing countries: develop an idea thoroughly and then revisit it only to deepen it; organize ideas in a way that is faithful to how they are organized in mathematics; and reduce clutter and extraneous topics.

- It also employs the best American models that call for grappling with ideas and problems as preparation for instruction, moving from concrete problems to abstractions and general theories, and situating mathematics in engaging contexts.

- The CME Project is a comprehensive curriculum that meets the dual goals of mathematical rigor and accessibility for a broad range of students.

About CME

EDC's Center for Mathematics Education, led by mathematician and teacher **Al Cuoco**, brings together an eclectic staff of mathematicians, teachers, cognitive scientists, education researchers, curriculum developers, specialists in educational technology, and teacher educators, internationally known for leadership across the entire range of K–16 mathematics education. We aim to help students and teachers in this country experience the thrill of solving problems and building theories, understand the history of ideas behind the evolution of mathematical disciplines, and appreciate the standards of rigor that are central to mathematical culture.

Contributors to the CME Project

National Advisory Board The National Advisory Board met early in the project, providing critical feedback on the instructional design and the overall organization. Members include

Richard Askey, University of Wisconsin
Edward Barbeau, University of Toronto
Hyman Bass, University of Michigan
Carol Findell, Boston University
Arthur Heinricher, Worcester Polytechnic Institute
Roger Howe, Yale University
Barbara Janson, Janson Associates
Kenneth Levasseur, University of Massachusetts, Lowell
James Madden, Louisiana State University, Baton Rouge
Jacqueline Miller, Education Development Center
James Newton, University of Maryland
Robert Segall, Greater Hartford Academy of Mathematics and Science
Glenn Stevens, Boston University
Herbert Wilf, University of Pennsylvania
Hung-Hsi Wu, University of California, Berkeley

Core Mathematical Consultants **Dick Askey,** **Ed Barbeau,** and **Roger Howe** have been involved in an even more substantial way, reviewing chapters and providing detailed and critical advice on every aspect of the program. Dick and Roger spent many hours reading and criticizing drafts, brainstorming with the writing team, and offering advice on everything from the logical organization to the actual numbers used in problems. We can't thank them enough.

Teacher Advisory Board The Teacher Advisory Board for the CME Project was essential in helping us create an effective format for our lessons that embodies the philosophy and goals of the program. Their debates about pedagogical issues and how to develop mathematical topics helped to shape the distinguishing features of the curriculum so that our lessons work effectively in the classroom. The advisory board includes

> **Jayne Abbas, Richard Coffey,**
> **Charles Garabedian, Dennis Geller,**
> **Eileen Herlihy, Doreen Kilday,**
> **Gayle Masse, Hugh McLaughlin,**
> **Nancy McLaughlin, Allen Olsen,**
> **Kimberly Osborne, Brian Shoemaker,**
> and **Benjamin Sinwell**

Field-Test Teachers Our field-test teachers gave us the benefit of their classroom experience by teaching from our draft lessons and giving us extensive, critical feedback that shaped the drafts into realistic, teachable lessons. They shared their concerns, questions, challenges, and successes and kept us focused on the real world. Some of them even welcomed us into their classrooms as co-teachers to give us the direct experience with students that we needed to hone our lessons. Working with these expert professionals has been one of the most gratifying parts of the development—they are "highly qualified" in the most profound sense.

California Barney Martinez, Jefferson High School, Daly City; **Calvin Baylon** and **Jaime Lao,** Bell Junior High School, San Diego; **Colorado Rocky Cundiff,** Ignacio High School, Ignacio; **Illinois Jeremy Kahan, Tammy Nguyen,** and **Stephanie Pederson,** Ida Crown Jewish Academy, Chicago; **Massachusetts Carol Martignette, Chris Martino,** and **Kent Werst,** Arlington High School, Arlington; **Larry Davidson,** Boston University Academy, Boston; **Joe Bishop** and **Carol Rosen,** Lawrence High School, Lawrence; **Maureen Mulryan,** Lowell High School, Lowell; **Felisa Honeyman,** Newton South High School, Newton Centre; **Jim Barnes** and **Carol Haney,** Revere High School, Revere; **New Hampshire Jayne Abbas** and **Terin Voisine,** Cawley Middle School, Hooksett; **New Mexico Mary Andrews,** Las Cruces High School, Las Cruces; **Ohio James Stallworth,** Hughes Center, Cincinnati; **Texas Arnell Crayton,** Bellaire High School, Bellaire; **Utah Troy Jones,** Waterford School, Sandy; **Washington Dale Erz, Kathy Greer, Karena Hanscom,** and **John Henry,** Port Angeles High School, Port Angeles; **Wisconsin Annette Roskam,** Rice Lake High School, Rice Lake.

Special thanks go to our colleagues at Pearson, most notably Elizabeth Lehnertz, Joe Will, and Stewart Wood. The program benefits from their expertise in every way, from the actual mathematics to the design of the printed page.

1 Real Numbers

2 Polynomials

3 Quadratics and Complex Numbers

4 Functions

5

Applications of Probability

Investigation 5A

6 Congruence and Proof

7 Similarity

8 Circles

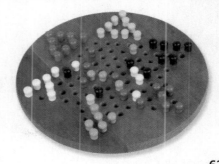

9 Using Similarity

10 Analytic Geometry

Honors Appendix

CME Project
Student Handbook

What Makes CME Different

Welcome to the CME Project! The goal of this program is to help you develop a deep understanding of mathematics. Throughout this book, you will engage in many different activities to help you develop that deep understanding. Some of these instructional activities may be different from ones you are used to. Below is an overview of some of these elements and why they are an important part of the CME Project.

The Habits of Mind Experience

Mathematical Habits of Mind are the foundation for serious questioning, solid thinking, good problem solving, and critical analysis. These Habits of Mind are what will help you become a mathematical thinker. Throughout the CME Project, you will focus on developing and refining these Habits of Mind.

Developing Habits of Mind

Develop thinking skills. This feature provides you with various methods and approaches to solving problems.

You will develop, use, and revisit specific Habits of Mind throughout the course. These include

- **Process** (how you work through problems)
- **Visualization** (how you "picture" problems)
- **Representation** (what you write down)
- **Patterns** (what you find)
- **Relationships** (what you find or use)

Developing good habits will help you as problems become more complicated.

Habits of Mind

Think. These special margin notes highlight key thinking skills and prompt you to apply your developing Habits of Mind.

Minds in Action

Discussion of mathematical ideas is an effective method of learning. The Minds in Action feature exposes you to ways of communicating about mathematics.

Join Sasha, Tony, Derman, and others as they think, calculate, predict, and discuss their way towards understanding.

Minds in Action

Sasha, Tony, and Derman have just skimmed through their Mathematics II book.

Sasha   Did you notice the student dialogs throughout the book?

Derman Sure did!

Tony   They talk and think just the way we do.

Sasha   I know! And they even make mistakes sometimes, the way we do.

Tony   But I like how they help each other to learn from those mistakes. I bet they use the Habits of Mind I saw all over the book, too.

Sasha   That's great! They should help a lot.

Exploring Mathematics

Throughout the CME Project, you will engage in activities that extend your learning and allow you to explore the concepts you learn in greater depth. Two of these activities are In-Class Experiments and Chapter Projects.

In-Class Experiment

In-Class Experiments allow you to explore new concepts and apply the Habits of Mind.

You will explore math as mathematicians do. You start with a question and develop answers through experimentation.

Chapter Projects

Chapter Projects allow you to apply your Habits of Mind to the content of the chapter. These projects cover many different topics and allow you to explore and engage in greater depth.

Chapter Projects
Using Mathematical Habits

Here is a list of the Chapter Projects and page numbers.

Using your CME Book

To help you make the most of your CME experience, we are providing the following overview of the organization of your book.

Focusing your Learning

In *Mathematics II*, there are 10 chapters, with each chapter devoted to a mathematical concept. With only 10 chapters, your class will be able to focus on these core concepts and develop a deep understanding of them.

Within each chapter, you will explore a series of Investigations. Each Investigation focuses on an important aspect of the mathematical concept for that chapter.

The CME Investigation

The goal of each mathematical Investigation is for you to formalize your understanding of the mathematics being taught. There are some common instructional features in each Investigation.

Getting Started

You will launch into each Investigation with a Getting Started lesson that activates prior knowledge and explores new ideas. This lesson provides you the opportunity to grapple with ideas and problems. The goal of these lessons is for you to explore—not all your questions will be answered in these lessons.

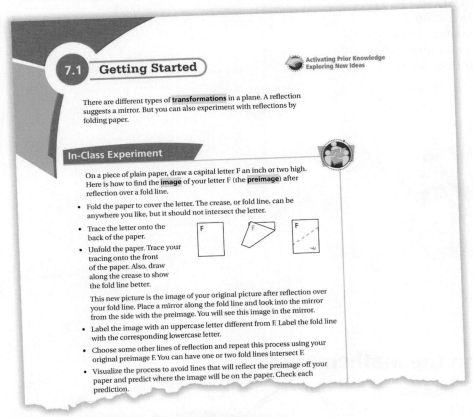

Learning the Mathematics

You will engage in, learn, and practice the mathematics in a variety of ways. The types of learning elements you will find throughout this course include

- **Worked-Out Examples** that model how to solve problems
- **Definitions and Theorems** to summarize key concepts
- **In-Class Experiments** to explore the concepts
- **For You to Do** assignments to check your understanding
- **For Discussion** questions to encourage communication
- **Minds in Action** to model mathematical discussion

Communicating the Mathematics

Student dialogs

By featuring dialogs between characters, the CME Project exposes you to a way of communicating about mathematics. These dialogs will then become a real part of your classroom!

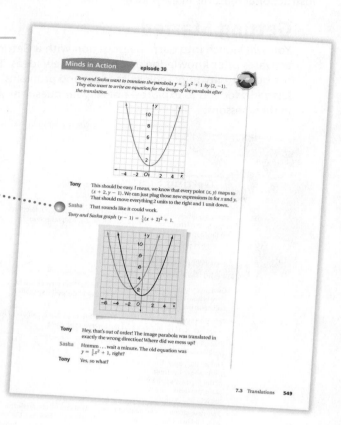

Minds in Action   episode 30

Tony and Sasha want to translate the parabola $y = \frac{1}{2}x^2 + 1$ by $(2, -1)$. They also want to write an equation for the image of the parabola after the translation.

Tony   This should be easy. I mean, we know that every point (x, y) maps to $(x + 2, y - 1)$. We can just plug those new expressions in for x and y. That should move everything 2 units to the right and 1 unit down.

Sasha   That sounds like it could work.

Tony and Sasha graph $(y - 1) = \frac{1}{2}(x + 2)^2 + 1$.

Tony   Hey, that's out of order! The image parabola was translated in exactly the wrong direction! Where did we mess up?

Sasha   Hmmm... wait a minute. The old equation was $y = \frac{1}{2}x^2 + 1$, right?

Tony   Yes, so what?

7.3   Translations   **549**

Reflecting on the Mathematics

At the end of each Investigation, Mathematical Reflections give you an opportunity to put ideas together. This feature allows you to demonstrate your understanding of the Investigation and reflect on what you learn.

Practice

The CME Project views extensive practice as a critical component of a mathematics curriculum. You will have daily opportunities to practice what you learn.

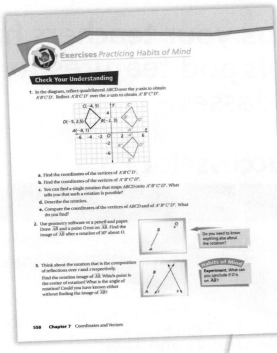

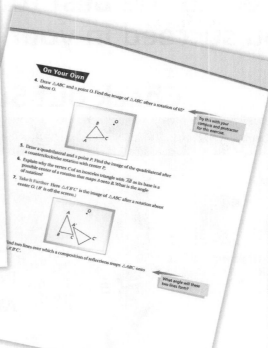

Check Your Understanding

Assess your readiness for independent practice by working through these problems in class.

On Your Own

Practice and continue developing the mathematical understanding you learn in each lesson.

Maintain Your Skills

Review and reinforce skills from previous lessons.

Also Available

An additional Practice Workbook is available separately.

Go Online

With **SuccessNet Plus** your teachers have selected the best tools and features to help you succeed in your classes.

Check out SuccessNet Plus

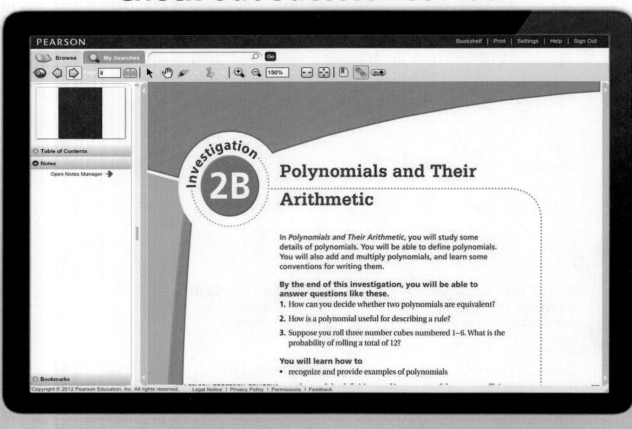

Log-in to www.successnetplus.com to find:

- an online Pearson eText version of your textbook

- extra practice and assessments

- worksheets and activities

- multimedia

Check out the TI-Nspire™ Technology Handbook on p. 990 for examples of how you can use handheld technology with your math learning!

Investigations at a Glance

1A Radicals

1B Working with Exponents

Real Numbers

In the 1930s, Charles Richter developed the Richter scale at the California Institute of Technology. The Richter scale measures the magnitude of earthquakes. Earthquake magnitudes vary widely, from tiny microearthquakes that only sensitive seismographs can detect to catastrophic events that cause widespread destruction.

The wide variation of magnitude led Richter and his colleagues to use the base-10 logarithm in their formula. This limits the possible values of the magnitude to a more manageable and understandable range.

To calculate the magnitude M_L of an earthquake, you measure the maximum amplitude A of the wave pattern that your seismograph records. Richter used the formula $M_L = \log_{10} A - \log_{10} A_0$, where A_0 is a correction value based on the seismograph's distance from the earthquake and local conditions.

A small earthquake can have a negative magnitude. The largest magnitude ever recorded was 9.5, during the Great Chilean Earthquake on May 22, 1960. Instruments detect over a million earthquakes every year. Humans can only feel about one third of these.

Vocabulary and Notation

- arithmetic sequence
- geometric sequence
- irrational number
- negative exponent, a^{-m}
- nth root, $\sqrt[n]{r}$
- radical
- rational exponent
- rational number
- square root
- unit fraction exponent
- zero exponent, a^0

Radicals

In *Radicals*, you will learn the difference between rational and irrational numbers. You will represent some irrational numbers as square roots, cube roots, and fourth roots using radicals. You will learn to express results in simplified radical form.

By the end of this investigation, you will be able to answer questions like these.

1. What is an irrational number?

2. What are the basic moves for multiplying and dividing square roots?

3. What does $\sqrt[3]{7}$ mean?

You will learn how to

- distinguish between rational and irrational numbers

- understand the meaning of radicals, such as square roots, cube roots, and fourth roots

- calculate using square roots, cube roots, and other radicals

- express irrational expressions in simplified form

You will develop these habits and skills:

- Understand the difference between rational and irrational numbers.

- Understand the square root function as the inverse of the function $x \mapsto x^2$.

- Understand the basic rules of radicals.

A quilt square has a side length of 8 in. and a diagonal length of $8\sqrt{2}$ in.

You will explore the relationship between square roots and squares.

For You to Explore

1. Explain how to locate each point on a number line.

a. 7

b. -5

c. 101

d. $\frac{3}{7}$

e. $-\frac{5}{7}$

f. $\frac{101}{7}$

2. There is only one positive number that satisfies the equation $\phi - 1 = \frac{1}{\phi}$. Based on this definition, find the value of ϕ.

> You can pronounce the Greek letter ϕ as "fee" or "fy."

3. Follow these steps.

- Choose an integer a.

- Square the integer.

- Find the prime factorization of the squared integer. How many twos are in the prime factorization?

Repeat this process with at least five integers. Use even and odd integers.

Is it possible to find an integer a, such that the prime factorization of a^2 contains an odd number of twos? If so, find the integer. If not, explain why.

4. Follow these steps.

- Choose an integer b.

- Square the integer.

- Multiply the squared integer by 2.

- Find the prime factorization of the result. How many twos are in the prime factorization?

Repeat this process with at least five integers.

In general, does the prime factorization of $2b^2$ contain an even or odd number of twos, or does it depend on your choice of integer b? Explain.

5. **Write About It** Can a perfect square ever be twice as great as another perfect square? Use your results from Problems 3 and 4 to explain.

Exercises *Practicing Habits of Mind*

On Your Own

6. Here is a list of perfect squares: 4, 9, 36, 49, 64, 100, 144, 400, 900. Find the prime factorization of each number. What do you notice about the factors?

7. Which of the prime factorizations represent numbers that are perfect squares? Which represent numbers that are not perfect squares? Try to find each result without calculating the product of the factors.

    a. $a = 2^3 \cdot 3^2$ **b.** $b = 2^4 \cdot 3^2$ **c.** $c = 3^2 \cdot 5^2 \cdot 7$

    d. $d = 3^2 \cdot 7^2$ **e.** $e = 5^2 \cdot 3^6$ **f.** $f = 2^5 \cdot 7^2 \cdot 5^2 \cdot 11^2$

8. Use this table to find the first two decimal places of $\sqrt{3}$. What kind of table would help you find the third decimal place of $\sqrt{3}$?

9. **Write About It** Suppose you have a calculator with only the four basic operations of arithmetic: $+$, $-$, $\times$, and $\div$. How can you use your calculator to find an approximation of $\sqrt{2}$?

x	x^2	x	x^2
1.65	2.72	1.73	2.99
1.66	2.76	1.74	3.03
1.67	2.79	1.75	3.06
1.68	2.82	1.76	3.10
1.69	2.86	1.77	3.13
1.70	2.89	1.78	3.17
1.71	2.92	1.79	3.20
1.72	2.96	1.80	3.24

Maintain Your Skills

10. Calculate each sum without using a calculator.

    a. $\frac{1}{2} + \frac{1}{4}$ **b.** $\frac{1}{2} + \frac{1}{4} + \frac{1}{8}$

    c. $\frac{1}{2} + \frac{1}{4} + \frac{1}{8} + \frac{1}{16}$ **d.** $\frac{1}{2} + \frac{1}{4} + \frac{1}{8} + \frac{1}{16} + \frac{1}{32}$

    e. Describe a pattern in the results.

11. Express each sum as a fraction and as a decimal.

    a. $\left(\frac{1}{1}\right)\left(\frac{1}{2}\right)$

    b. $\left(\frac{1}{1}\right)\left(\frac{1}{2}\right) + \left(\frac{1}{2}\right)\left(\frac{1}{3}\right)$

    c. $\left(\frac{1}{1}\right)\left(\frac{1}{2}\right) + \left(\frac{1}{2}\right)\left(\frac{1}{3}\right) + \left(\frac{1}{3}\right)\left(\frac{1}{4}\right)$

    d. $\left(\frac{1}{1}\right)\left(\frac{1}{2}\right) + \left(\frac{1}{2}\right)\left(\frac{1}{3}\right) + \left(\frac{1}{3}\right)\left(\frac{1}{4}\right) + \left(\frac{1}{4}\right)\left(\frac{1}{5}\right)$

    e. $\left(\frac{1}{1}\right)\left(\frac{1}{2}\right) + \left(\frac{1}{2}\right)\left(\frac{1}{3}\right) + \left(\frac{1}{3}\right)\left(\frac{1}{4}\right) + \left(\frac{1}{4}\right)\left(\frac{1}{5}\right) + \left(\frac{1}{5}\right)\left(\frac{1}{6}\right)$

    f. Describe a pattern in the results.

Go Online
Video Tutor
www.successnetplus.com

In this lesson, you will learn more precisely what the $\sqrt{}$ symbol means by exploring some definitions, facts, and assumptions.

Minds in Action

Tony and Sasha puzzle over the rules for square roots.

Tony   Does every real number have a square root?

Sasha   I don't think so, because if you take a positive number and square it, you get a positive number. If you take a negative number and square it, you get a positive number. So, I'm pretty sure a negative number can't have a real number as a square root.

Tony   Well, my calculator gives me an error if I try to find $\sqrt{-3}$, so I agree. Do you think all positive numbers have square roots?

Sasha   Yes, I think so. Here, show me the graph of $y = x^2$.

Tony produces the graph on his calculator.

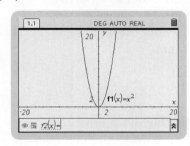

For help graphing an equation on a coordinate plane, see the TI-Nspire™ Handbook, p. 990.

Tony   Can we use the graph to answer my question?

Sasha   Sure. The number $\sqrt{7}$ is the number x such that $x^2 = 7$.

Tony   So, I draw a horizontal line 7 units up from the x-axis and find where it crosses the graph.

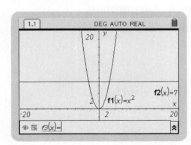

Tony   There are two intersections. So, there are two values for x that make $x^2 = 7$. Which one do we choose?

Sasha   I think we should choose the one with the positive x-coordinate. Every square root I've seen has been positive.

Tony   This might be picky, but how do we know that there isn't a hole in the graph where $y = 7$? Sometimes a calculator just draws over a hole as if it wasn't there.

Sasha   I suppose anything is possible, but I don't think there are any holes. Look, I can use the graph and the calculator to get points whose square is very close to 7. It looks like the x-coordinate where $y = 7$ is about 2.6, so I'll start there.

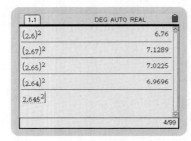

The x-values I'm squaring are getting closer and closer to each other. Also, the squares are getting closer and closer to 7. So, my x-values are getting closer and closer to a number whose square is 7. I can find a number as close to 7 as you want me to. If there were a hole in the graph, I think I could fill it in.

Tony   Sasha, someday I want to borrow your brain.

Sasha and Tony's discussion leads to this formal definition of square root.

Definition

If $r \geq 0$, the **square root** $\sqrt{r}$ is a real number s such that $s \geq 0$ and $s^2 = r$.

> If s satisfies both properties, $s = \sqrt{r}$.

Using calculus, you can prove that there are no holes in the graph of $y = x^2$. For now, you can state the idea as an assumption.

Assumption   *The Square Root Assumption*

If $r \geq 0$, there is exactly one nonnegative real number s such that $s^2 = r$. In other words, every nonnegative real number has exactly one square root.

For You to Do

1. Use the graph $y = x^2$, or other methods, to approximate $\sqrt{5}$. Round to three decimal places.

Because of the above assumption, you can use the "duck principle" to show when one number is the square root of another number.

Habits of Mind

Detect the defining properties. You can describe the duck principle in this way: If it walks like a duck and it quacks like a duck, then it is a duck.

Example

Problem Show that $\dfrac{\sqrt{10}}{\sqrt{2}} = \sqrt{5}$.

Solution To show that a number is equal to $\sqrt{5}$, you need to show that each of the following statements is true.

- The number is not negative.
- The square of the number is 5.

Here is how to show that each statement is true for $\dfrac{\sqrt{10}}{\sqrt{2}}$.

Step 1 $\sqrt{10}$ and $\sqrt{2}$ are both positive, so their quotient, $\dfrac{\sqrt{10}}{\sqrt{2}}$, is also positive.

Step 2 $\left(\dfrac{\sqrt{10}}{\sqrt{2}}\right)^2 = \dfrac{(\sqrt{10})^2}{(\sqrt{2})^2}$ since $\left(\dfrac{a}{b}\right)^2 = \dfrac{a^2}{b^2}$

$\qquad\qquad\quad = \dfrac{10}{2}$ since $(\sqrt{10})^2 = 10$ and $(\sqrt{2})^2 = 2$

$\qquad\qquad\quad = 5$

So, $\dfrac{\sqrt{10}}{\sqrt{2}}$ is a nonnegative number with a square of 5. There is only one such number, $\sqrt{5}$.

For You to Do

2. Show that $\sqrt{18} \cdot \sqrt{2} = 6$.

To apply the duck principle, use the fact that $6 = \sqrt{36}$.

For Discussion

3. Is the conjecture $\sqrt{x^2} = x$ true for all real numbers x?

Why is $(\sqrt{x})^2 = x$ true for all real numbers $x \geq 0$?

Exercises Practicing Habits of Mind

Check Your Understanding

1. For each equation, approximate x to three decimal places.

   a. $x^2 = 10$ **b.** $x^3 = 10$

   c. $x^4 = 10$ **d.** $x^2 = \sqrt{10}$

2. Use the duck principle to show that each equation is true.

   a. $\sqrt{2} \cdot \sqrt{3} = \sqrt{6}$ **b.** $\dfrac{\sqrt{19}}{\sqrt{5}} = \sqrt{\dfrac{19}{5}}$

   c. $\sqrt{11} \cdot \sqrt{7} = \sqrt{77}$ **d.** $\dfrac{\sqrt{12}}{2} = \sqrt{3}$

   e. $\dfrac{10}{\sqrt{10}} = \sqrt{10}$

3. Let $a = \dfrac{1}{\sqrt{2}}$ and $b = \dfrac{\sqrt{2}}{2}$. Find the value of the expression $(a + b)^2$. Simplify your result.

On Your Own

4. Sasha thinks of an integer and gives Tony a few hints. "The square root of my number is between 2 and 3, and my number is prime," Sasha says. Is this enough information to find Sasha's number? Explain.

5. Tony thinks of an integer. Sasha tries to guess this integer. Tony says, "The square root of my number is between 3 and 4, and my number has six factors." Is this enough information to find Tony's number? Explain.

6. Write each expression as the square root of an integer. Let $p = \sqrt{2}$, $r = \sqrt{3}$, and $s = \sqrt{5}$.

   a. pr **b.** ps **c.** rs

   d. Does $p + r = s$?

   e. What is the product of your results for parts (a), (b), and (c)?

7. Find the value of each expression. Let $a = \dfrac{1}{\sqrt{2}}$, $b = \dfrac{1}{2}$, and $c = \dfrac{\sqrt{3}}{2}$.

   a. $2a^2$ **b.** $b^2 + c^2$

8. **Standardized Test Prep** For $x > 0$, which expression is equal to $\sqrt{\dfrac{1}{x}}$?

   A. $\dfrac{\sqrt{x}}{x}$ **B.** $\dfrac{x}{\sqrt{x}}$ **C.** $\dfrac{1}{x}$ **D.** $\dfrac{2}{\sqrt{x}}$

9. The area of a circle is the product of the constant π and the square of the length of the radius of the circle, or $A = \pi r^2$.

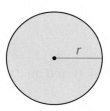

The constant π is the ratio of a circle's circumference to its diameter. The value of π is approximately 3.1416.

Find the radius of each circle with the given area.

a. 4π **b.** 2π

c. 3π **d.** 17π

Maintain Your Skills

10. Determine whether each square root is an integer. For each square root that is *not* an integer, find the two integers it lies between.

a. $\sqrt{2}$ **b.** $\sqrt{3}$ **c.** $\sqrt{4}$

d. $\sqrt{5}$ **e.** $\sqrt{6}$ **f.** $\sqrt{7}$

g. $\sqrt{8}$ **h.** $\sqrt{9}$ **i.** $\sqrt{10}$

j. What is the least positive integer with a square root greater than 4?

A center-pivot irrigation system with a radius of 1000 ft can water $\pi(1000)^2$, or $1,000,000\pi$, ft^2 of farmland.

Go Online
www.successnetplus.com

Historical Perspective

In ancient Greece, Pythagoras (namesake of the Pythagorean Theorem) founded a mystical religious group. Its members came to be called the Pythagoreans. They believed that they could describe everything in the world with integers. They looked for mathematical patterns in nature, music, and art. As a part of their religious beliefs, they investigated mathematics and proved a number of important theorems.

A central belief of the Pythagorean school is that you can express all numbers as integers or ratios of integers. In other words, the Pythagoreans believed that all numbers are rational. It came as a great shock when the Pythagorean Hippasus of Metapontum proved that $\sqrt{2}$ was not a rational number. The existence of an irrational number directly contradicted one of the central Pythagorean beliefs.

Arithmetic with Square Roots

Consider the following calculation. What is the reason for each step?

$$(\sqrt{7} \cdot \sqrt{2})^2 = (\sqrt{7})^2(\sqrt{2})^2$$

$$= 7 \cdot 2$$

$$= 14$$

The product $\sqrt{7} \cdot \sqrt{2}$ is a positive number with a square of 14. Based on the duck principle, the following equation is true.

$$\sqrt{7} \cdot \sqrt{2} = \sqrt{14}$$

This calculation is a specific example of a useful basic rule of square roots.

> **Be careful!**
> $\sqrt{7} + \sqrt{2} \neq \sqrt{7+2}$.
> Explain.

Theorem 1.1

If x and y are nonnegative numbers, then $\sqrt{x} \cdot \sqrt{y} = \sqrt{xy}$.

> You say that the product of the square roots is the square root of the product. Use this basic rule for calculating with square roots.

Proof Use the duck principle as you did in Lesson 1.02. From the definition of a square root, you know that $\sqrt{xy}$ is the unique nonnegative number whose square is xy. To prove that the equation is true, you need to show that the left side of the equation is also a nonnegative number whose square is xy.

Step 1 The product of two nonnegative numbers is nonnegative. Since $\sqrt{x} \geq 0$ and $\sqrt{y} \geq 0$, it follows that $\sqrt{x} \cdot \sqrt{y} \geq 0$.

Step 2 $(\sqrt{x} \cdot \sqrt{y})^2 = (\sqrt{x} \cdot \sqrt{y})(\sqrt{x} \cdot \sqrt{y})$

$$= \sqrt{x}\sqrt{x}\sqrt{y}\sqrt{y}$$

$$= (\sqrt{x})^2(\sqrt{y})^2$$

$$= xy$$

Since the Square Root Assumption in Lesson 1.02 tells you that a square root is unique, both quantities must be equal.

Like all basic rules, this equation is a two-way street. You can use the rule to move from the right side of the equation to the left side of the equation, or from left to right.

For You to Do

Explain how each equation is a consequence of Theorem 1.1.

1. $\sqrt{15} = \sqrt{5} \cdot \sqrt{3}$

2. $\sqrt{2} \cdot \sqrt{\frac{1}{3}} = \sqrt{\frac{2}{3}}$

3. $\sqrt{20} \cdot \sqrt{5} = 10$

4. If $n \geq 0$, then $7n = \sqrt{7} \cdot \sqrt{7n^2}$.

For Discussion

5. Is the square root of the sum of two numbers the same as the sum of the square roots? Explain.

Example

Problem Is the square root of the quotient of two numbers the same as the quotient of the square roots? Explain.

Solution Yes, if the numbers are positive, the square root of the quotient of two numbers is also the quotient of their square roots. In other words, there is another basic rule.

Corollary 1.1.1

If a and b are nonnegative real numbers ($b \neq 0$), then $\dfrac{\sqrt{a}}{\sqrt{b}} = \sqrt{\dfrac{a}{b}}$.

To show that a number is $\sqrt{\dfrac{a}{b}}$, you need to show that each statement is true.

- The number is not negative.
- The number's square is $\dfrac{a}{b}$.

Step 1 If a and b are nonnegative ($b \neq 0$), then $\sqrt{a}$ and $\sqrt{b}$ are both nonnegative. So the quotient $\dfrac{\sqrt{a}}{\sqrt{b}}$ is also nonnegative.

Step 2 Square $\dfrac{\sqrt{a}}{\sqrt{b}}$ and find whether the result is $\dfrac{a}{b}$.

$$\left(\frac{\sqrt{a}}{\sqrt{b}}\right)^2 = \frac{(\sqrt{a})^2}{(\sqrt{b})^2}$$ because when you square a fraction, you square the numerator and denominator

$$= \frac{a}{b}$$ because $(\sqrt{a})^2 = a$ and $(\sqrt{b})^2 = b$

The fraction $\dfrac{\sqrt{a}}{\sqrt{b}}$ is a nonnegative number whose square is $\dfrac{a}{b}$. There is only one such number, $\sqrt{\dfrac{a}{b}}$.

> The duck principle is at work. If the number is nonnegative, and the square is $\dfrac{a}{b}$, then the number must be the square root of $\dfrac{a}{b}$.

The square root of a sum is not, in general, the sum of the square roots. Sometimes you can use the Distributive Property to simplify calculations involving the sum of square roots. Here are some examples.

- $2\sqrt{2} + 5\sqrt{2} = (2 + 5)\sqrt{2} = 7\sqrt{2}$
- $3\sqrt{7} + 19\sqrt{7} = (3 + 19)\sqrt{7} = 22\sqrt{7}$
- $4\sqrt{3} - 2\sqrt{11} - 6\sqrt{3} + 5\sqrt{11} = -2\sqrt{3} + 3\sqrt{11}$

> **Habits of Mind**
>
> **Experiment.** Try it with numbers! Is $\sqrt{2} + \sqrt{3} = \sqrt{5}$?

The rule for finding the sum of square roots is very similar to the rule for combining terms in expressions such as $2x + 4y + 3x + 5y$. You can use the Distributive Property to combine like terms. In the expression above, notice that there is no way to further simplify $-2\sqrt{3} + 3\sqrt{11}$.

Remember...

One version of the Distributive Property states that if a, b, and c are any numbers, then $(a + b)c = ac + bc$.

For You to Do

6. Simplify the expression below by combining like terms.

$$3\sqrt{2} - 6\sqrt{5} - 1.25\sqrt{2} - 2\sqrt{17} + 8\sqrt{5} + 1.25\sqrt{2} + 2\sqrt{6} + \sqrt{6}$$

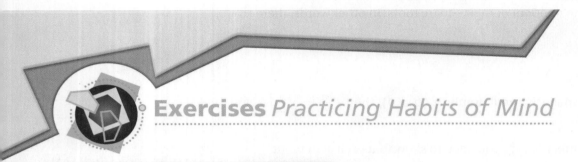

Exercises Practicing Habits of Mind

Check Your Understanding

1. Find the value of each expression. Let $a = \sqrt{5} + 1$ and $b = \sqrt{5} - 1$.

    a. ab
    b. $a + b$
    c. $a - b$
    d. **Take It Further** $a^2 - b^2$

2. For each equation, find the integer k that satisfies the equation.

    a. $\sqrt{8} = k\sqrt{2}$
    b. $\sqrt{12} = k\sqrt{3}$
    c. $\sqrt{45} = k\sqrt{5}$
    d. $\sqrt{500} = k\sqrt{5}$
    e. $\sqrt{27} = k\sqrt{3}$
    f. Why can you find an integer k in each part above?

3. Use the graph of $y = x^4$ to find approximations of all real numbers x that satisfy each equation.

    a. $x^4 = 15$
    b. $x^4 = 16$
    c. $x^4 = 7$
    d. $x^4 = -7$

4. For each group of numbers,
    • find the products of the possible pairs of numbers
    • find the product of the three products

    a. $\sqrt{2}, \sqrt{3}, \sqrt{11}$
    b. $\sqrt{3}, \sqrt{4}, \sqrt{5}$
    c. $\sqrt{5}, \sqrt{7}, \sqrt{11}$
    d. How does the product of the three products relate to the initial three numbers? Explain.

5. **Standardized Test Prep** Simplify the expression $\sqrt{3} \cdot \sqrt{2} + 5\sqrt{6}$.

    A. $6\sqrt{6}$
    B. $\sqrt{5} + 5\sqrt{6}$
    C. $5\sqrt{11}$
    D. 30

On Your Own

6. For each equation, find the integer k that satisfies the equation.

   a. $\sqrt{8} + \sqrt{2} = k\sqrt{2}$ **b.** $\sqrt{12} - \sqrt{3} = k\sqrt{3}$

   c. $\sqrt{500} - 15\sqrt{5} = k\sqrt{5}$ **d.** $\sqrt{605} + \sqrt{5} = k\sqrt{5}$

   e. $\sqrt{275} + \sqrt{11} = k\sqrt{11}$

Go Online
www.successnetplus.com

7. **Take It Further** In general, $\sqrt{x} + \sqrt{y} \neq \sqrt{x + y}$. What statements can you make about the inequality? For example, is the value of one side of the equation always larger than the value of the other side?

   Substitute each of the following values for x and y. Calculate the approximate values of each side of the inequality.

   a. $x = 1$ and $y = 1$ **b.** $x = 2$ and $y = 7$

   c. $x = 3$ and $y = 3$ **d.** $x = 15$ and $y = 10$

8. Use the graph of $y = x^5$ to find approximations of all real numbers x that satisfy each equation.

   a. $x^5 = 15$ **b.** $x^5 = 32$ **c.** $x^5 = 7$ **d.** $x^5 = -7$

9. Sometimes you can simplify square roots by factoring out a perfect square from under the square root symbol. For instance, $\sqrt{12} = \sqrt{4} \cdot \sqrt{3} = 2\sqrt{3}$.

   Using a similar method, simplify each expression.

   a. $\sqrt{50}$ **b.** $\sqrt{40}$ **c.** $\sqrt{2^3 \cdot 5^5}$

10. Order the following expressions from least to greatest.

    $\sqrt{39},\ \sqrt{7},\ \sqrt{9 \cdot 16},\ \sqrt{10} + \sqrt{26},\ \dfrac{\sqrt{12}}{\sqrt{3}}$

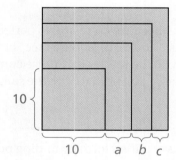

11. In the diagram, there are four squares that share the same lower left corner. The areas of the squares are 100, 200, 300, and 400. Find a, b, c, and $a + b + c$ without using a calculator.

Maintain Your Skills

12. Calculate each difference without using a calculator.

    a. $\dfrac{1}{\sqrt{2}} - \dfrac{\sqrt{2}}{2}$ **b.** $\dfrac{1}{\sqrt{3}} - \dfrac{\sqrt{3}}{3}$

    c. $\dfrac{1}{\sqrt{4}} - \dfrac{\sqrt{4}}{4}$ **d.** $\dfrac{1}{\sqrt{5}} - \dfrac{\sqrt{5}}{5}$

    e. What is the pattern in the differences?

1.04 Conventions for Roots— Simplified Forms

You can express the same number in many different ways. Here are some ways to write the number 2.

$$2 = 1 + 1 = \frac{3+1}{2} = \frac{4}{2} = 6 \cdot \frac{1}{3} = 16 \cdot 0.125 = \frac{10}{5}$$

Your result may be equal to someone else's result, but you may have written the result in a different way.

Because there are many ways to write a result, mathematics uses standard forms for writing numbers and expressions. For example, you write variable letters at the end of terms in expressions. You write $3x$ instead of $x3$, even though both expressions could mean the same thing. The standard form for fractions is to write them in lowest terms, without any common factors in the numerator and denominator. You write the fraction $\frac{90}{50}$ in lowest terms as $\frac{9}{5}$.

There is also a set of conventions for writing square roots. The first convention is to have the smallest possible integer inside the radical. For instance, you can write $\sqrt{50}$ with a smaller integer inside the radical.

$$\sqrt{50} = \sqrt{25 \cdot 2}$$
$$= \sqrt{25} \cdot \sqrt{2}$$
$$= \sqrt{5^2} \cdot \sqrt{2}$$
$$= 5\sqrt{2}$$

These moves are legal because of Theorem 1.1.

The form $5\sqrt{2}$ is standard, because there are no perfect squares that divide 2. Numbers such as 2 and 6 are "square-free" because they have no perfect square factors. Recall the reason that these conventions exist is so that you can recognize that $\sqrt{50}$ and $5\sqrt{2}$ are the same result.

For You to Do

Write each square root in simplified form by finding perfect squares in the number under the $\sqrt{}$ symbol.

1. $\sqrt{32}$ **2.** $\sqrt{92}$ **3.** $\sqrt{20}$ **4.** $\sqrt{1800}$

The second convention is to never leave a square root in the denominator of a fraction. You can rewrite the fraction $\frac{1}{\sqrt{2}}$ by multiplying the numerator and denominator by $\sqrt{2}$.

$$\frac{1}{\sqrt{2}} = \frac{1}{\sqrt{2}} \cdot \frac{\sqrt{2}}{\sqrt{2}} = \frac{1 \cdot \sqrt{2}}{\sqrt{2} \cdot \sqrt{2}} = \frac{\sqrt{2}}{2}$$

Conventions have exceptions. Sometimes it is easier to work with expressions by leaving square roots in the denominator.

For example, suppose you find the result $\frac{\sqrt{2}}{2}$ and a friend finds the result $\frac{4}{\sqrt{32}}$. You both have the same result, but it is hard to know that without using the conventions for simplifying square roots.

For You to Do

Write each fraction in simplified form by eliminating the square root in the denominator.

5. $\dfrac{1}{\sqrt{3}}$

6. $\dfrac{\sqrt{2}}{\sqrt{7}}$

7. $\dfrac{3\sqrt{11}}{\sqrt{11}}$

8. $\dfrac{\sqrt{2}}{\sqrt{6}}$

Facts and Notation

The conventions for simplifying square roots are the following:

- Replace perfect squares inside the square root sign with their square roots outside the square root sign.

- Do not leave a square root sign in the denominator.

Making the number inside the square root sign "square-free" helps identify like terms in square roots. This is useful when you add or subtract radicals. For example, you can simplify the expression $\sqrt{48} - \sqrt{3}$ to a single term.

$$\begin{aligned}
\sqrt{48} - \sqrt{3} &= \sqrt{16 \cdot 3} - \sqrt{3} \\
&= \sqrt{16} \cdot \sqrt{3} - \sqrt{3} \\
&= 4\sqrt{3} - \sqrt{3} \\
&= 3\sqrt{3}
\end{aligned}$$

By factoring out the perfect squares from the number inside the square root sign, you can identify and combine like terms.

Exercises Practicing Habits of Mind

Check Your Understanding

1. The area of a circle is the product of the radius of the circle squared and the constant π. Find the radius of each circle with the given area. Simplify any radicals.

   a. $\dfrac{\pi}{2}$

   b. $\dfrac{\pi}{4}$

   c. $\dfrac{\pi}{31}$

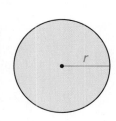

2. Some numbers are larger than their square roots. For instance, $3 > \sqrt{3}$. Other numbers are smaller than their square roots. For instance, $\frac{1}{4} < \sqrt{\frac{1}{4}}$. Find a rule that tells you which values of x satisfy the inequality $x > \sqrt{x}$.

3. In Lesson 1.01, you searched for a number ϕ.

   a. Use the equation $\phi - 1 = \frac{1}{\phi}$ to find the value of $\phi^2 - \phi$.

   b. Use the exact value $\phi = \frac{\sqrt{5} + 1}{2}$ and arithmetic with square roots to confirm the value of $\phi^2 - \phi$.

   > Try rewriting the equation without fractions.

4. **Take It Further** There are different ways to express ϕ using square roots. For example, you can write $\phi = \frac{\sqrt{5} + 1}{2}$ and $\phi = \frac{2}{\sqrt{5} - 1}$.

   a. Show that the expressions for ϕ are equal.

   b. Use the first expression for ϕ to calculate a fraction for $\phi - 1$.

   c. Recall that ϕ has the property that $\phi - 1 = \frac{1}{\phi}$. Use your result from part (b) to show that this property is true.

On Your Own

5. Write each radical in simplified form.

   a. $\sqrt{8}$ **b.** $\sqrt{27}$ **c.** $\sqrt{12}$

   d. $\sqrt{56}$ **e.** $\sqrt{26}$ **f.** $\sqrt{162}$

   g. $\sqrt{55}$ **h.** $\sqrt{121}$ **i.** $\sqrt{200}$

6. Annie, Hideki, and Derman rewrite the fraction $\frac{5}{\sqrt{3} + 1}$ in simplified form.

   Annie says, "We need to multiply by $\frac{\sqrt{3}}{\sqrt{3}}$."

   Hideki replies, "No, we need to multiply by $\frac{\sqrt{3} - 1}{\sqrt{3} - 1}$."

   Derman chimes in, "No, we need to multiply by $\frac{\sqrt{3} + 1}{\sqrt{3} + 1}$."

   Which method produces a number in simplified form?

7. For each right triangle, find the length of the third side. Write your result in simplified form.

   a. legs of 4 in. and 6 in.

   b. legs of $\frac{1}{2}$ in. and $\frac{1}{4}$ in.

   c. a leg of $\frac{1}{3}$ in. and a hypotenuse of $\frac{2}{3}$ in.

8. Calculate the area and perimeter of each rectangle given its side lengths.

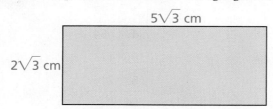

   a. $2\sqrt{3}$ cm and $5\sqrt{3}$ cm

   b. $3\sqrt{5}$ cm and $8\sqrt{2}$ cm

   c. $\frac{\sqrt{7}}{2}$ cm and $4\sqrt{7}$ cm

9. The area of an animal pen is 30 square feet. What are the lengths of the pen's sides if the pen has each given shape? Write your answers in simplified form.

   a. a square

   b. a rectangle with a longer side twice the length of the shorter side

   c. a rectangle with a longer side three times the length of the shorter side

   d. a right triangle with a height five times the length of the base

10. **Standardized Test Prep** What is the height of a triangle with an area of 1 and a base that is six times as long as the height? (*Hint:* The area of a triangle is $\frac{1}{2}$ times the base times the height.)

   A. $\frac{\sqrt{6}}{6}$ **B.** $\frac{1}{3}$

   C. $\frac{\sqrt{3}}{3}$ **D.** $\sqrt{3}$

11. Here is an input-output table of the function $f(x) = x^3$.
Simplify each square root.

x	x^3
1	1
2	8
3	27
4	64
5	125
6	216

   a. $\sqrt{8}$ b. $\sqrt{27}$ c. $\sqrt{64}$

   d. $\sqrt{125}$ e. $\sqrt{216}$ f. What is the pattern?

Historical Perspective

Before people used calculators to compute square roots, they could remember the approximation for a smaller square root, such as $\sqrt{2}$, $\sqrt{3}$, and $\sqrt{5}$. To find $\sqrt{500}$, they could simplify it this way.

$$\sqrt{500} = 10\sqrt{5} \approx 10 \cdot 2.24 = 22.4$$

They used the second convention from page 17 to find the value of $\frac{1}{\sqrt{2}}$ without a calculator. Using long division is a big mess.

$$\begin{array}{r} 0.7 \\ 1.414213562\ldots \overline{)1.00000000000} \\ -0.98999494934\ldots \end{array}$$

Since the decimal expansion of $\sqrt{2}$ is a nonrepeating decimal, it is impossible to find the product $0.7 \cdot 1.414213562\ldots$. How do you calculate $1.00000000000 - 0.98999494934\ldots$?

By eliminating the square root in the denominator, you can always divide by an integer. In the example above, instead of dividing 1 by $\sqrt{2}$, you can divide $\sqrt{2}$ by 2.

$$\begin{array}{r} 0.7071\ldots \\ 2\overline{)1.414213562\ldots} \\ -1.4 \\ \overline{0.014213562\ldots} \\ -0.014 \\ \overline{0.000213562\ldots} \\ -0.0002 \\ \overline{0.000013562\ldots} \end{array}$$

2. Square Roots. 1.00–5.49

N	0	1	2	3	4	5	6	7	8	9	Differences 1 2 3 4 5 6 7 8 9
1.0	1.000	1.005	1.010	1.015	1.020	1.025	1.030	1.034	1.039	1.044	0 1 1 2 2 3 3 4 4
1.1	1.049	1.054	1.058	1.063	1.068	1.072	1.077	1.082	1.086	1.091	0 1 1 2 2 3 3 4 4
1.2	1.095	1.100	1.105	1.109	1.114	1.118	1.122	1.127	1.131	1.136	0 1 1 2 2 3 3 4 4
1.3	1.140	1.145	1.149	1.153	1.158	1.162	1.166	1.170	1.175	1.179	0 1 1 2 2 3 3 3 4
1.4	1.183	1.187	1.192	1.196	1.200	1.204	1.208	1.212	1.217	1.221	0 1 1 2 2 2 3 3 4
1.5	1.225	1.229	1.233	1.237	1.241	1.245	1.249	1.253	1.257	1.261	0 1 1 2 2 2 3 3 4
1.6	1.265	1.269	1.273	1.277	1.281	1.285	1.288	1.292	1.296	1.300	0 1 1 2 2 2 3 3 3
1.7	1.304	1.308	1.311	1.315	1.319	1.323	1.327	1.330	1.334	1.338	0 1 1 2 2 2 3 3 3
1.8	1.342	1.345	1.349	1.353	1.356	1.360	1.364	1.367	1.371	1.375	0 1 1 1 2 2 3 3 3
1.9	1.378	1.382	1.386	1.389	1.393	1.396	1.400	1.404	1.407	1.411	0 1 1 1 2 2 3 3 3
2.0	1.414	1.418	1.421	1.425	1.428	1.432	1.435	1.439	1.442	1.446	0 1 1 1 2 2 2 3 3
2.1	1.449	1.453	1.456	1.459	1.463	1.466	1.470	1.473	1.476	1.480	0 1 1 1 2 2 2 3 3
2.2	1.483	1.487	1.490	1.493	1.497	1.500	1.503	1.507	1.510	1.513	0 1 1 1 2 2 2 3 3
2.3	1.517	1.520	1.523	1.526	1.530	1.533	1.536	1.539	1.543	1.546	0 1 1 1 2 2 2 3 3
2.4	1.549	1.552	1.556	1.559	1.562	1.565	1.568	1.572	1.575	1.578	0 1 1 1 2 2 2 3 3
2.5	1.581	1.584	1.587	1.591	1.594	1.597	1.600	1.603	1.606	1.609	0 1 1 1 2 2 2 3 3
2.6	1.612	1.616	1.619	1.622	1.625	1.628	1.631	1.634	1.637	1.640	0 1 1 1 2 2 2 2 3
2.7	1.643	1.646	1.649	1.652	1.655	1.658	1.661	1.664	1.667	1.670	0 1 1 1 2 2 2 2 3
2.8	1.673	1.676	1.679	1.682	1.685	1.688	1.691	1.694	1.697	1.700	0 1 1 1 2 2 2 2 3
2.9	1.703	1.706	1.709	1.712	1.715	1.718	1.720	1.723	1.726	1.729	0 1 1 1 1 2 2 2 3
3.0	1.732	1.735	1.738	1.741	1.744	1.746	1.749	1.752	1.755	1.758	0 1 1 1 2 2 2 2 3
3.1	1.761	1.764	1.766	1.769	1.772	1.775	1.778	1.780	1.783	1.786	0 1 1 1 1 2 2 2 2
3.2	1.789	1.792	1.794	1.797	1.800	1.803	1.806	1.808	1.811	1.814	0 1 1 1 1 2 2 2 2
3.3	1.817	1.819	1.822	1.825	1.828	1.830	1.833	1.836	1.838	1.841	0 1 1 1 1 2 2 2 2
3.4	1.844	1.847	1.849	1.852	1.855	1.857	1.860	1.863	1.865	1.868	0 1 1 1 1 2 2 2 2
3.5	1.871	1.873	1.876	1.879	1.881	1.884	1.887	1.889	1.892	1.895	0 1 1 1 1 2 2 2 2
3.6	1.897	1.900	1.903	1.905	1.908	1.910	1.913	1.916	1.918	1.921	0 1 1 1 1 1 2 2 2
3.7	1.924	1.926	1.929	1.931	1.934	1.936	1.939	1.942	1.944	1.947	0 1 1 1 1 2 2 2 2
3.8	1.949	1.952	1.954	1.957	1.960	1.962	1.965	1.967	1.970	1.972	0 1 1 1 1 1 2 2 2
3.9	1.975	1.977	1.980	1.982	1.985	1.987	1.990	1.992	1.995	1.997	0 1 1 1 1 1 2 2 2
4.0	2.000	2.002	2.005	2.007	2.010	2.012	2.015	2.017	2.020	2.022	0 0 1 1 1 1 2 2 2
4.1	2.025	2.027	2.030	2.032	2.035	2.037	2.040	2.042	2.045	2.047	0 0 1 1 1 1 2 2 2
4.2	2.049	2.052	2.054	2.057	2.059	2.062	2.064	2.066	2.069	2.071	0 0 1 1 1 1 2 2 2
4.3	2.074	2.076	2.078	2.081	2.083	2.086	2.088	2.090	2.093	2.095	0 0 1 1 1 1 2 2 2
4.4	2.098	2.100	2.102	2.105	2.107	2.110	2.112	2.114	2.117	2.119	0 0 1 1 1 1 2 2 2
4.5	2.121	2.124	2.126	2.128	2.131	2.133	2.135	2.138	2.140	2.142	0 0 1 1 1 1 2 2 2
4.6	2.145	2.147	2.149	2.152	2.154	2.156	2.159	2.161	2.163	2.166	0 0 1 1 1 1 2 2 2
4.7	2.168	2.170	2.173	2.175	2.177	2.179	2.182	2.184	2.186	2.189	0 1 1 1 1 1 2 2 2
4.8	2.191	2.193	2.195	2.198	2.200	2.202	2.205	2.207	2.209	2.211	0 0 1 1 1 1 2 2 2
4.9	2.214	2.216	2.218	2.220	2.223	2.225	2.227	2.229	2.232	2.234	0 0 1 1 1 1 2 2 2
5.0	2.236	2.238	2.241	2.243	2.245	2.247	2.249	2.252	2.254	2.256	0 0 1 1 1 1 2 2 2
5.1	2.258	2.261	2.263	2.265	2.267	2.269	2.272	2.274	2.276	2.278	0 0 1 1 1 1 2 2 2
5.2	2.280	2.283	2.285	2.287	2.289	2.291	2.293	2.296	2.298	2.300	0 0 1 1 1 1 1 2 2
5.3	2.302	2.304	2.307	2.309	2.311	2.313	2.315	2.317	2.319	2.322	0 0 1 1 1 1 1 2 2
5.4	2.324	2.326	2.328	2.330	2.332	2.335	2.337	2.339	2.341	2.343	0 0 1 1 1 1 1 2 2
N	0	1	2	3	4	5	6	7	8	9	1 2 3 4 5 6 7 8 9

Move the decimal point ONE place in $\sqrt{N}$ for every TWO places that it is moved in N.

328

Schoolbooks had tables like this. Can you find the approximate value of $\sqrt{1.34}$ from this table?

Rational and Irrational Numbers

You can think of a positive number as a number that measures a distance from 0 on a number line. The set of real numbers ℝ is the set of all positive numbers, their opposites, and 0. The set ℝ includes all integers and fractions.

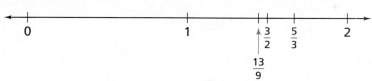

You can write every integer as a fraction. For example, you can write 7 as $\frac{7}{1}$. Positive and negative integers and fractions, along with 0, form the rational number system.

> You use the word *rational* because every rational number is the ratio of two integers.

Definition

A **rational number** is a number that you can express as $\frac{a}{b}$, where *a* and *b* are integers and *b* ≠ 0. You can denote the set of rational numbers with the symbol ℚ for *quotient*.

For You to Do

Write each number as a fraction with an integer in the numerator and the denominator.

1. 1.341   **2.** 1.3 + 2.8   **3.** $5\frac{2}{3}$

> Any decimal that terminates after any number of digits is a rational number. For instance, 17.131 is a rational number, because $17.131 = \frac{17,131}{1000}$. Even some decimals that go on forever are rational numbers. For instance, $\frac{1}{3}$ is a rational number. Its decimal form is 0.333. . . .

The ancient Greeks first believed that every real number was rational. They eventually discovered real numbers that were not rational. Historians believe the first known example of a number that is not rational is $\sqrt{2}$.

In geometry, $\sqrt{2}$ appears as the length of the hypotenuse in a right triangle with legs that both have a length of 1. By the Pythagorean Theorem, where *c* is the length of the hypotenuse, $1^2 + 1^2 = c^2$. So, $c = \sqrt{1 + 1} = \sqrt{2}$.

What is the value of $\sqrt{2}$? If you measure $\sqrt{2}$ units on a number line, you find that its value lies between 1 and 2.

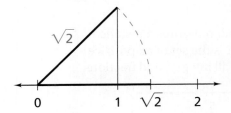

Is $\sqrt{2}$ a rational number? A calculator tells you that $\sqrt{2} \approx 1.414213562$.

The decimal 1.414213562 is a rational number. However, this number is only an approximation of $\sqrt{2}$. No rational number is precisely equal to $\sqrt{2}$. The only way to be sure that this is true is to prove it.

The proof uses contradiction. Assume that $\sqrt{2}$ is rational. Then, work toward developing a false statement. If your assumption results in a statement that is false, you have shown that the initial assumption was false.

Proof Assume that $\sqrt{2}$ is rational.

By the definition of a rational number, you can write $\sqrt{2}$ as a fraction.

$$\sqrt{2} = \frac{a}{b}, \text{ where } a \text{ and } b \text{ are integers.}$$

Now, square both sides of the equation.

$$2 = \frac{a^2}{b^2}$$

Multiply both sides of the equation by b^2.

$$2b^2 = a^2$$

Each step is valid by the basic rules and moves of algebra. If the first equation is true, then the last equation must also be true.

Now, you can apply two facts you verified in Lesson 1.01.

Fact 1 If a is an integer, then the prime factorization of a^2 has an even number of factors of two.

Fact 2 If b is an integer, then the prime factorization of $2b^2$ has an odd number of factors of two.

From the two facts, the expression on the left side of the equation has an odd number of twos, and the expression on the right of the equation has an even number of twos. That cannot happen! You can conclude that the initial assumption, that $\sqrt{2}$ is rational, is false due to this contradiction. Thus, $\sqrt{2}$ is not a rational number.

For Discussion

4. Why can a number not have both an even and an odd number of twos in its prime factorization?

Reflect on this remarkable proof. There are infinitely many fractions that you can make with integers. No amount of computing power can ever find them all. However, if you introduce the variables a and b to form the possible fraction equivalent of $\sqrt{2}$, you deal with all possible cases at once. This reasoning shows the tremendous power and efficiency of algebra.

For You to Do

5. Use a similar argument to show that $\sqrt{5}$ is *not* a rational number.

The proof shows that there are real numbers that are not rational.

Definition

An **irrational number** is a real number that is not a rational number. That is, an irrational number is a real number that you cannot write as a fraction with an integer in both the numerator and denominator.

This diagram shows how the different sets of numbers fit together.

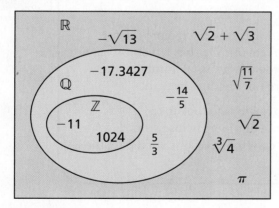

The numbers in $\mathbb{R}$ but not in $\mathbb{Q}$ are the irrational numbers.

According to the diagram, any member of $\mathbb{Z}$ (the integers) is also a member of $\mathbb{Q}$ (the rational numbers). Also, any member of $\mathbb{Q}$ is a member of $\mathbb{R}$ (the real numbers). An irrational number is not a member of $\mathbb{Q}$.

Developing Habits of Mind

Reason about calculations. In Chapter 1, you learned that if you add, subtract, or multiply any two members of $\mathbb{R}$, the real numbers, the result is always a real number. The same is true for any two members of $\mathbb{Z}$: the sum, difference, or product of any two integers is an integer. It makes sense to ask the same questions about rational and irrational numbers.

You can prove that the sum of two rational numbers is rational. By following the process of calculating the sum $\frac{3}{7} + \frac{2}{5}$, you can generalize to calculating $\frac{a}{b} + \frac{c}{d}$. Remember, you can multiply the numerator and denominator of a fraction by the same value to produce an equivalent fraction.

$$\frac{3}{7} + \frac{2}{5} =$$

$$\frac{3 \cdot 5}{7 \cdot 5} + \frac{2 \cdot 7}{5 \cdot 7} =$$

$$\frac{15}{35} + \frac{14}{35} =$$

$$\frac{29}{35}$$

$$\frac{a}{b} + \frac{c}{d} =$$

$$\frac{a \cdot d}{b \cdot d} + \frac{c \cdot b}{d \cdot b} =$$

$$\frac{ad}{bd} + \frac{bc}{bd} =$$

$$\frac{ad + bc}{bd}$$

Habits of Mind

$\frac{a}{b}$ and $\frac{c}{d}$ are used to represent two general rational numbers. It would be incorrect to write $\frac{a}{b} + \frac{a}{b}$, since that would force both numbers to be the same. All of a, b, c, and d must be integers. To prove the sum is rational, write $\frac{a}{b} + \frac{c}{d}$ as the ratio of two integers.

The numerator $ad + bc$ and the denominator bd must both be integers, so the sum has been written as the ratio of two integers—a rational number! Using variables, this proves that if you add *any* two rational numbers (members of $\mathbb{Q}$), the result must be a rational number. Similar proofs show that if you subtract or multiply any two rational numbers, the result is a rational number.

You'll be asked to complete these proofs in the exercises.

What about division? You can divide by multiplying by the reciprocal: for example, $\frac{3}{7} \div \frac{2}{5} = \frac{3}{7} \cdot \frac{5}{2} = \frac{15}{14}$. Every nonzero real number has a reciprocal. You can use this to prove that when you divide two rational numbers, the result is a rational number, as long as you are not dividing by zero.

What about irrational numbers? One way to begin is to look for a counterexample: try to find a pair of irrational numbers whose sum, difference, or product isn't irrational. If you can find even one such pair, the general statement can't be true.

For You to Do

6. Find a pair of irrational numbers whose difference is 0.

7. Find a pair of irrational numbers whose sum is 0.

8. Find a pair of irrational numbers whose sum is irrational.

9. Find a pair of irrational numbers whose product is an integer.

10. Find a pair of irrational numbers whose quotient is an integer.

What is true about x and y if $x - y = 0$?

Now that you know about the sum of two rational or two irrational numbers, what about the sum of one rational and one irrational number? Surprisingly, this sum is always irrational.

Theorem 1.2

The sum of a rational number and an irrational number is irrational.

Proof Let the sum be written as $q + r = x$, where q is rational and r is irrational. Since x is a real number, it is either rational or irrational. Assume that x is rational.

Consider $r = x - q$. If x is rational, and q is rational, then $r = x - q$ must also be rational. Now r is both rational *and* irrational! That cannot happen, so the initial assumption that x is rational must be false. Therefore, x must be irrational.

This is the same tactic used to prove that $\sqrt{2}$ is irrational. If you want to prove that a number is irrational, this is one of only a few ways to do so.

For Discussion

11. Prove that the product of a nonzero rational number and an irrational number is irrational, using a similar argument.

Rational numbers have decimal expansions that either stop or contain a finite string of digits that repeats. For example, $\frac{2}{11} = 0.181818\ldots$ is rational. This repeating decimal has two digits that repeat forever. The decimal is periodic.

> The decimal expansion of every rational number either terminates or repeats.

Suppose that you calculate $\sqrt{2}$ beyond the nine decimal places that most calculators show. The first hundred digits are:

    1.4142135623 7309504880 1688724209 6980785696 7187537694
    8073176679 7379907324 7846210703 8850387534 3276415727...

While some sets of digits may repeat for a while, the decimal form never repeats onward forever.

A famous irrational number is ϕ. An exact value of ϕ is $\phi = \dfrac{1 + \sqrt{5}}{2}$.

In mathematics, you will see many examples in which a precise value is more useful than an approximate value. In this chapter you will learn to handle precise values, such as $\dfrac{1 + \sqrt{5}}{2}$, and approximations, such as 1.618.

> Square roots are only one kind of irrational number. Another famous irrational number is p While many people use $\frac{22}{7}$ for p in formulas, p is not precisely equal to a quotient of integers.

1.05 Rational and Irrational Numbers 25

Exercises *Practicing Habits of Mind*

Check Your Understanding

1. Fill in each blank using the word *all, some,* or *no.* For help, refer to the diagram showing the sets $\mathbb{Z}$, $\mathbb{Q}$, and $\mathbb{R}$.

   a. ___?___ rational numbers are real numbers.

   b. ___?___ integers are rational numbers.

   c. ___?___ rational numbers are integers.

   d. ___?___ integers are irrational numbers.

   e. ___?___ real numbers are irrational numbers.

   f. ___?___ real numbers are either irrational numbers or rational numbers.

2. Identify each number as rational or not rational. Explain.

   a. $\frac{13}{2}$　　　　　b. -19.13　　　　　c. $\sqrt{17}$

   d. $\sqrt{121}$　　　　　e. $\sqrt{36-25}$　　　　　f. $\frac{0.5}{7}$

   g. $\frac{13\pi}{2\pi}$

3. Consider the following unusual definition.
$$f(x) = \begin{cases} 0 & \text{if } x \text{ is rational} \\ 1 & \text{if } x \text{ is irrational} \end{cases}$$

   a. Is f a function? Explain.

   b. **Take It Further** What does the graph of f look like?

> **Remember...**
> A function is a machine that returns a single output for each valid input.

4. Is $0.9999\ldots$ a rational number? Explain.

5. **Take It Further** Is $\sqrt{-1}$ a real number? Explain.

6. a. Determine the difference $\frac{3}{7} - \frac{2}{5}$ by finding a common denominator.

   b. Prove that the difference of any two rational numbers must be a rational number.

> If $0.9999\ldots$ is a rational number, how can you write it as a fraction?

7. a. Find the solution to the equation $\frac{3}{7} \cdot x = 1$.

   b. Given $a \neq 0$ and $b \neq 0$, solve the equation $\frac{a}{b} \cdot x = 1$ for x.

   c. In the equation $\frac{a}{b} \cdot x = 1$, explain why neither a nor b can equal zero.

8. Use the result from Exercise 7 to prove that the reciprocal of a nonzero rational number must be rational.

On Your Own

9. Plot each number on a number line. Decide whether each number is greater than or less than $\sqrt{2}$.

   a. $\frac{29}{21}$ **b.** $\frac{30}{21}$ **c.** $\frac{31}{21}$

   d. $\frac{13}{9}$ **e.** $\frac{37}{27}$ **f.** $\frac{141}{100}$

   > Not every real number is rational, but you can approximate every real number using a rational number.

10. Draw a diagram like the diagram of the sets of $\mathbb{Z}$, $\mathbb{Q}$, and $\mathbb{R}$ in this lesson. Then place each number in the diagram.

    a. $\sqrt{6}$ **b.** $\frac{17}{9}$ **c.** $\sqrt{144}$ **d.** 11.55

    e. $\sqrt{13} + \sqrt{3}$ **f.** $\sqrt{2.5^2}$ **g.** $\frac{91}{7}$ **h.** $1 + \sqrt{6}$

11. **Take It Further** Suppose that for two real numbers x and y, both the sum $x + y$ and product xy are integers. Either prove that x and y must be rational numbers, or find a counterexample.

12. **a.** Determine the product $\frac{3}{7} \cdot \frac{2}{5}$.

    b. Prove that the product of any two rational numbers must be a rational number.

    www.successnetplus.com

13. **What's Wrong Here** Derman had this to say about the square root of 6:

    > *Derman:* $\sqrt{6}$ is rational because it's the product of two irrational numbers, $\sqrt{2}$ and $\sqrt{3}$.

    Describe what is wrong with Derman's argument.

14. Prove that the quotient of any two nonzero rational numbers must be a rational number.

15. Given that the number π is irrational, show that $\frac{1}{\pi}$ must also be irrational.

    > Assume that $\frac{1}{\pi}$ is rational, and then look for a contradiction.

16. **Standardized Test Prep** Which one of these is irrational?

    A. $4 - \sqrt{49}$ **B.** π^0

    C. $(5 + \sqrt{2}) + (5 - \sqrt{2})$ **D.** $-3 \cdot \sqrt{5}$

Maintain Your Skills

17. Determine whether each square root is an integer. For each square root that is *not* an integer, find the two consecutive integers it lies between.

    a. $\sqrt{11}$ **b.** $\sqrt{12}$ **c.** $\sqrt{13}$ **d.** $\sqrt{14}$ **e.** $\sqrt{15}$

    f. $\sqrt{16}$ **g.** $\sqrt{17}$ **h.** $\sqrt{18}$ **i.** $\sqrt{19}$ **j.** $\sqrt{20}$

    k. What is the least positive integer with a square root that is greater than 5?

Roots, Radicals, and the *n*th Root

By definition, the square root of 2 is the nonnegative number x such that $x^2 = 2$.

You can expand this definition. For instance, if y is the number such that $y^3 = 10$, then you can say that y is the "cube root of 10." You can write this as $y = \sqrt[3]{10}$.

You can continue to expand the definition of a root. Consider the number z that satisfies this equation.

$$z^4 = 19$$

So, z is the "fourth root of 19."

$$z = \sqrt[4]{19}$$

The word **radical** refers to roots such as square roots, cube roots, fourth roots, and so on.

There is one slight complication. There are two numbers x that satisfy the equation $x^2 = 3$. From the graph of $y = x^2$, you can see that one of these numbers is positive and one is negative.

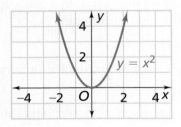

You can define $\sqrt{3}$ as the positive value that satisfies the equation. The number $-\sqrt{3}$ is the negative value.

Notice that while $x^2 = 3$ has two possible real-number results, $x^2 = -3$ has no real-number results. That is because the range is not all real numbers, only nonnegative numbers. Since a horizontal line at $y = -3$ does not intersect the graph of $y = x^2$, there is no real solution to $x^2 = -3$.

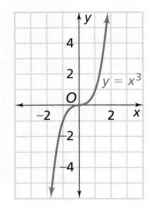

This issue does not arise with cube roots. For example, find the value of x that satisfies the equation $x^3 = 7$. Look at the graph of $y = x^3$.

There is only one value of x whose cube equals 7. So, $\sqrt[3]{7}$ is uniquely defined. Also, notice from the graph of $y = x^3$ that the range of the function $f(x) = x^3$ is all real numbers. Any horizontal line will intersect the graph of $y = x^3$ at one point.

When dealing with fourth roots, however, the issue of no real solutions arises again. Look at the graph of $y = x^4$.

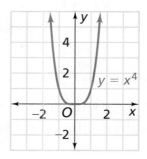

There are two values of x that satisfy the equation $x^4 = 5$. One value is positive and one value is negative. The value $\sqrt[4]{5}$ is defined as the positive of these two values.

Also, notice that the entire graph of $y = x^4$ is in the first two quadrants. So, a horizontal line below the x-axis will not intersect the graph. In other words, $\sqrt[4]{a}$ is not defined if a is negative.

In general, if n is odd, then $\sqrt[n]{a}$ is uniquely defined for any real number a. If n is even, then $\sqrt[n]{a}$ is the positive value of the two possible values if a is nonnegative, and is undefined if a is negative.

Definition

- If n is even, then for $a \geq 0$, the **nth root** $\sqrt[n]{a}$ is the positive value of x that satisfies the equation $x^n = a$.

- If n is odd, then for any real number a, $\sqrt[n]{a}$ is the unique value of x that satisfies the equation $x^n = a$.

For You to Do

Find each value without a calculator.

1. $\sqrt[3]{27}$ 2. $\sqrt[4]{16}$ 3. $\sqrt[6]{1}$ 4. $\sqrt[3]{125}$ 5. $\sqrt[3]{-27}$

You may recall that the function $x \mapsto \sqrt{x}$ cannot take negative inputs. If there was a real number x such that $x = \sqrt{-2}$, then $x^2 = -2$. Since squares of real numbers are never negative, x^2 cannot equal -2.

For Discussion

6. Is there a number w that satisfies the equation $w^3 = -2$?

7. Is there a number y that satisfies the equation $y^4 = -2$?

In Lesson 1.03, you learned some rules for calculating square roots if $x \geq 0$ and $y \geq 0$.

Rule 1   The product of two square roots is the square root of the product.

$$\sqrt{x} \cdot \sqrt{y} = \sqrt{xy}$$

Rule 2   The quotient of square roots is the square root of the quotient.

$$\frac{\sqrt{x}}{\sqrt{y}} = \sqrt{\frac{x}{y}}$$

Rule 3   When adding square roots, you can combine like terms.

$$a\sqrt{x} + b\sqrt{x} = (a + b)\sqrt{x}$$

The same rules apply with any other radical. For instance, these are the rules for cube roots.

Rule 1   The product of two cube roots is the cube root of the product.

$$\sqrt[3]{x} \cdot \sqrt[3]{y} = \sqrt[3]{xy}$$

Rule 2   The quotient of cube roots is the cube root of the quotient.

$$\frac{\sqrt[3]{x}}{\sqrt[3]{y}} = \sqrt[3]{\frac{x}{y}}$$

Rule 3   When adding cube roots, you can combine like terms.

$$a\sqrt[3]{x} + b\sqrt[3]{x} = (a + b)\sqrt[3]{x}$$

Similar rules hold for fourth roots, fifth roots, and so on.

Can you simplify expressions with different radicals such as a fifth root and a square root? For the most part, you cannot simplify these expressions.

Exercises *Practicing Habits of Mind*

Check Your Understanding

1. Graph each equation.

   a. $y = x^2$ **b.** $y = x^3$ **c.** $y = x^4$

   d. $y = x^5$ **e.** $y = x^6$

   f. How can you use the shapes of these graphs to show that $\sqrt[3]{-2}$ exists, but $\sqrt[4]{-2}$ does not exist?

2. The table shows values near 2.2 and the first two digits of the cubes of values near 2.2. Use the table to find the first two decimal places of $\sqrt[3]{11}$.

x	x^3
2.17	10.22
2.18	10.36
2.19	10.50
2.20	10.65
2.21	10.79
2.22	10.94
2.23	11.09

x	x^3
2.24	11.24
2.25	11.39
2.26	11.54
2.27	11.70
2.28	11.85
2.29	12.01
2.30	12.17

3. Is there a way to express radicals using exponents? In other words, can you find a, such that $2^a = \sqrt{2}$? The following questions will help you find a.

a. Explain why $1 < \sqrt{2} < 2$. Use this fact to show that a cannot be an integer.

b. Square both sides of the equation $2^a = \sqrt{2}$. Use 2 as the base on the left side of the equation. What is the result?

c. Both sides of the equation have the same base, so for the expressions to be equal, the exponents must be equal. Write an equation showing that the exponents are equal.

d. Solve the equation in part (c) for a.

e. Until now, your definition of exponents only allows for integer exponents. Since a is not an integer, you will have to extend the definition of exponents while making sure that the rules work. The definition of square root lets you say $\left(\sqrt{2}\right)^2 = 2$. Substitute 2^a for $\sqrt{2}$. Replace a with the value you found in part (d).

> **Remember...**
>
> $(a^b)^c = a^{bc}$

f. Use the same process you used in parts (a)–(e) to find b in the equation $2^b = \sqrt[3]{2}$.

g. Use the same process you used in parts (a)–(e) to find c in the equation $2^c = \sqrt[n]{2}$ in terms of n.

On Your Own

4. Make input-output tables for the functions $f(x) = \sqrt{x^2}$ and $g(x) = \sqrt[3]{x^3}$. Use inputs that include at least a few negative numbers. How are the two functions similar? How are they different? Have you seen either function before, possibly in a different form?

> **Remember...**
>
> To show that some number x is $\sqrt[n]{a}$, you need to show that $x^n = a$. If n is even, you have to show that x is not negative.

5. Use the duck principle to show that each equation is true.

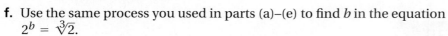

a. $\sqrt[4]{125} \cdot \sqrt[4]{5} = 5$ **b.** $\sqrt[3]{18} \cdot \sqrt[3]{12} = 6$ **c.** $\dfrac{\sqrt[5]{128}}{\sqrt[5]{16}} = \sqrt[5]{8}$

d. $\sqrt[4]{100} = \sqrt{10}$ **e.** $\sqrt[3]{4} \cdot \sqrt[6]{3} = \sqrt[6]{48}$

6. Use the fact that $6561 = 3^8$. Simplify each radical.

   a. $\sqrt{6561}$ b. $\sqrt[3]{6561}$ c. $\sqrt[4]{6561}$ d. $\sqrt[5]{6561}$

   e. $\sqrt[6]{6561}$ f. $\sqrt[7]{6561}$ g. $\sqrt[8]{6561}$ h. $\sqrt[9]{6561}$

   i. Which of the numbers in parts (a)–(h) are integers? Explain.

7. Suppose you need storage space twice the size of your existing storage space that is 10 ft × 10 ft × 10 ft, or 1000 cubic feet.

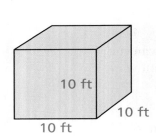
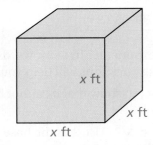

   a. Why can't you double the length of every side of your existing space?

   b. How long does each side of the larger space need to be to make it twice the size of the smaller space?

8. **Standardized Test Prep** Jasper has a cube with a volume of 100 cm³. In which of the following ranges is x, the length of the cube's side, in centimeters?

   A. $4.0 \leq x < 4.5$ B. $4.5 \leq x < 5.0$

   C. $5.0 \leq x < 5.5$ D. $5.5 \leq x < 6.0$

Go Online
www.successnetplus.com

Maintain Your Skills

9. Find the median of each set of numbers.

   a. $\sqrt{5}, \sqrt[3]{5}, \sqrt[4]{5}, \sqrt[5]{5}, \sqrt[6]{5}$ b. $\sqrt{7}, \sqrt[3]{7}, \sqrt[4]{7}, \sqrt[5]{7}, \sqrt[6]{7}$

   c. $\sqrt{31}, \sqrt[3]{31}, \sqrt[4]{31}, \sqrt[5]{31}, \sqrt[6]{31}$ d. $\sqrt{157}, \sqrt[3]{157}, \sqrt[4]{157}, \sqrt[5]{157}, \sqrt[6]{157}$

   e. What is the pattern?

10. Find the value of k that satisfies each equation.

   a. $\sqrt{7}\sqrt{k} = 7$ b. $\sqrt[3]{7}\sqrt[3]{k} = 7$

   c. $\sqrt[4]{7}\sqrt[4]{k} = 7$ d. $\sqrt[5]{7}\sqrt[5]{k} = 7$

   e. $\sqrt[6]{7}\sqrt[6]{k} = 7$ f. What is the pattern?

In this investigation, you distinguished between rational and irrational numbers. You worked with square roots, cube roots, and fourth roots. You also used the basic moves for multiplying and dividing square roots. These questions will help you summarize what you have learned.

1. The prime factorization of a number x is $3^4 \cdot 5^2 \cdot 2^6$.

   a. How do you know that x is a perfect square?

   b. If $x = y^2$, what does y equal?

2. Determine whether each number is rational or irrational.

   a. $\frac{1}{2}$ **b.** $\sqrt{3}$ **c.** 2π

   d. $\sqrt{9}$ **e.** -2.8 **f.** $\frac{3\pi}{4\pi}$

3. Find the integer k that satisfies each equation.

   a. $\sqrt{8} = k\sqrt{2}$ **b.** $\sqrt{300} = k\sqrt{3}$

   c. $\sqrt{20} + \sqrt{5} = k\sqrt{5}$ **d.** $\sqrt{24} + \sqrt{54} = k\sqrt{6}$

4. Use the duck principle to show that each equation is true.

   a. $\sqrt[3]{8} = 2$ **b.** $\sqrt{5} \cdot \sqrt{2} = \sqrt{10}$

   c. $\sqrt[4]{2} \cdot \sqrt[4]{8} = 2$ **d.** $\sqrt[3]{4} \cdot \sqrt[3]{54} = 6$

5. Write each radical in simplified form.

   a. $\sqrt{32}$ **b.** $\sqrt{500}$ **c.** $\sqrt{\frac{1}{3}}$

   d. $\sqrt{72}$ **e.** $\sqrt{720}$ **f.** $\sqrt{\frac{3}{5}}$

The length of a quilt is 14 squares. Each quilt square has a diagonal length of $8\sqrt{2}$ in. What is the length of the quilt?

6. What is an irrational number?

7. What are the basic moves for multiplying and dividing square roots?

8. What does $\sqrt[3]{7}$ mean?

Vocabulary and Notation

In this investigation, you learned these terms and symbols. Make sure that you understand what each one means and how to use it.

- **irrational number**
- **nth root, $\sqrt[n]{r}$**
- **radical**

- **rational number**
- **square root, $\sqrt{r}$**

Working with Exponents

In *Working with Exponents*, you will use the basic rules of algebra to discover the laws of exponents. You will learn how to extend the rules to work with zero, negative, and rational exponents.

By the end of this investigation, you will be able to answer questions like these.

1. What is the Fundamental Law of Exponents? What are some of its corollaries?

2. How do you extend the laws of exponents to define zero, negative, and rational exponents?

3. What are the simplified forms of the expressions 4^0, 7^{-2} and $5^{\frac{27}{3}}$?

You will learn how to

- evaluate expressions involving exponents, including zero, negative, and rational exponents

- find missing terms in a geometric sequence and generate geometric sequences to interpret expressions involving rational exponents

- convert between exponential and radical forms for rational exponents

You will develop these habits and skills:

- Extend the laws of exponents to allow evaluation of zero, negative, and rational exponents.

- Reason logically to verify that a particular interpretation of an exponent follows the laws of exponents.

- Generalize from specific examples to develop and verify identities.

Radiographers use X-rays for medical imaging. X-rays have wavelengths between 10^{-7} and 10^{-10} cm.

Activating Prior Knowledge
Exploring New Ideas

Expressions or equations may contain variables as exponents.

For You to Explore

1. Copy and complete this table for the function $f(n) = 2^n$.

Input, n	Output, $f(n)$
6	64
5	32
4	16
3	8
2	■
1	■
0	■
−1	■
−2	■
−3	■

2. Solve each equation.

a. $2^3 \cdot 2^5 = 2^a$

b. $2^b \cdot 2^8 = 2^{14}$

c. $3^c \cdot 3^c = 3^{12}$

d. $(3^d)^2 = 3^8$

e. $\dfrac{5^7}{5^f} = 5^6$

f. $3^g = 9^5$

g. $5^{3h} = 5^7$

h. $(5^k)^3 = 5^4$

3. Write About It What are some rules of exponents? Give examples.

A *geometric sequence* is a list of numbers in which you get each term by multiplying the previous one by a constant. For example, the sequence below is a geometric sequence, since each term is three times as great as the previous term.

$$4, 12, 36, 108, 324, \ldots$$

For Problems 4 and 5, find the missing terms in each geometric sequence.

4. a. $4, 8, 16, ■, ■, ■, \ldots$

b. $4, -8, 16, ■, ■, ■, \ldots$

c. $2, 2\sqrt{3}, ■, ■, ■, ■, \ldots$

d. $a, 2a, ■, ■, ■, ■, \ldots$

e. $k, 3k, ■, ■, ■, ■, \ldots$

5. a. $1, ■, ■, 8, ■, ■, \ldots$

b. $■, ■, 1, \frac{1}{2}, ■, ■, \ldots$

c. $2, ■, 18, ■, ■, ■, \ldots$

d. $1, ■, ■, ■, 9, ■, \ldots$

Habits of Mind

Look for relationships. What is a closed form for the function g with this sequence of outputs?

Input	Output
0	4
1	12
2	36
3	108
4	324

Exercises Practicing Habits of Mind

On Your Own

Habits of Mind

Experiment.
If the equation is not true for all positive integers, is it true for some values of a, b, and c?

6. Decide whether each equation is true for all positive integers a, b, and c.

   a. $a^b \stackrel{?}{=} b^a$
   b. $a^{b+c} \stackrel{?}{=} a^b + a^c$
   c. $a^{b+c} \stackrel{?}{=} a^b \cdot a^c$

   d. $a^b \cdot a^c \stackrel{?}{=} a^{bc}$
   e. $(a^b)^c \stackrel{?}{=} a^{bc}$
   f. $(a^b)^c \stackrel{?}{=} a^{(b^c)}$

   g. $\dfrac{a^b}{a^c} \stackrel{?}{=} a^{b-c}$
   h. $(ab)^c \stackrel{?}{=} a(b^c)$

7. Determine whether each expression is equal to 2^{12}. Explain.

Try this without a calculator.

   a. $2^{10} + 2^2$
   b. $(2^4)(2^4)(2^4)$
   c. $2^6 \cdot 2^6$

   d. $2^9 + 2^3$
   e. $(2^{10})(2^2)$
   f. $2^{11} + 2^{11}$

   g. $(2^4)(2^3)$
   h. $4(2^{10})$

8. Copy and complete the table for the function $g(n) = 3^n$.

9. Problem 1 shows a table for $f(n) = 2^n$. Exercise 8 shows a table for $g(n) = 3^n$. Consider the function $h(n) = f(n) \cdot g(n)$.

   a. Calculate $h(3)$.

   b. Use the completed tables to calculate $h(0)$, $h(1)$, and $h(2)$.

   c. Find a simple rule for $h(n)$.

10. **Take It Further**

    a. Explain why there are no positive integers a and b such that $2^a = 5^b$.

    b. Find the number x that makes $2^x = 5$. Round to four decimal places.

    c. Find the number y that makes $2 = 5^y$. Round to four decimal places.

    d. What is the relationship between x and y?

Input, n	Output, $g(n)$
5	243
4	81
3	27
2	▪
1	▪
0	▪
−1	▪
−2	▪
−3	▪

Maintain Your Skills

11. Solve each equation.

    a. $3^x = 81$
    b. $3^{x+1} = 81$
    c. $3^{2x} = 81$

    d. $3^{-x} = 81$
    e. $3^{4x-1} = 81$
    f. $3^{x^2} = 81$

1.08 Laws of Exponents

If n is a positive integer, then a^n (read as "a to the n") is the product of n factors of a.

$$a^n = \underbrace{a \cdot a \cdot a \cdots \cdot a}_{n \text{ factors of } a}$$

This lesson develops the rules for working with expressions in the form a^n. These rules are built on the basic rules for multiplication and division.

For You to Do

1. Use a product model like the one above to demonstrate that $a^3 \cdot a^5 = a^8$.

2. How can you use a product model to write out $(a^2)^5$? What is the result?

Remember...

Another name for the any-order property is the commutative property: $3 \cdot 5 = 5 \cdot 3$. Another name for the any-grouping property is the associative property: $(3 \cdot 5) \cdot 7 = 3 \cdot (5 \cdot 7)$.

Multiplication has the any-order, any-grouping properties, but not all operations do. Division and subtraction do not have either property. Neither does exponentiation.

$$2^{20} \neq 20^2 \text{ and } (2^3)^4 \neq 2^{(3^4)}$$

You will review some of the rules for calculating with exponents and look at why they work.

Theorem 1.3 The Fundamental Law of Exponents

If b and c are positive integers, then
$$a^b \cdot a^c = a^{b+c}$$

Proof Use a product model to expand a^b and a^c.

$$(a^b)(a^c) = \underbrace{(a \cdot a \cdots \cdot a)}_{b \text{ factors}} \cdot \underbrace{(a \cdot a \cdots \cdot a)}_{c \text{ factors}} = \underbrace{(a \cdot a \cdots \cdot a)}_{(b+c) \text{ factors}} = a^{b+c}$$

Habits of Mind

Experiment. It may help to work out this proof with numbers. For example, suppose a is 5, b is 3 and c is 7.

It is important to notice that you can use Theorem 1.2 only if the base numbers are the same.
$$7^3 \cdot 7^8 = 7^{3+8} = 7^{11} \text{ but } 6^3 \cdot 7^8 \neq (6 \cdot 7)^{3+8}$$

For Discussion

3. Use Theorem 1.3 to prove that $a^b \cdot a^c \cdot a^d = a^{b+c+d}$.

A second law of exponents follows from Theorem 1.3.

Corollary 1.3.1

If b and c are positive integers such that $b > c$ and $a \neq 0$, then
$$\frac{a^b}{a^c} = a^{b-c}$$

Later in this investigation, you will find a way to remove the restriction $b > c$.

Proof By Theorem 1.3, you have
$$a^c \cdot a^{b-c} = a^{c+(b-c)} = a^b$$

Note that $b - c$ is positive, which allows you to use Theorem 1.3. Since $a^c \neq 0$, you can divide each side by a^c.
$$a^{b-c} = \frac{a^b}{a^c}$$

A third law of exponents applies when you raise an expression with an exponent to another power.

Corollary 1.3.2

For all numbers a and positive integers b and c,
$$(a^b)^c = a^{bc}$$

Proof Write c factors of a^b and then use Theorem 1.3.
$$(a^b)^c = \underbrace{(a^b)(a^b) \cdot \cdots \cdot (a^b)}_{c \text{ factors of } a^b}$$
$$= a^{(b+b+\cdots+b)}$$
$$= a^{bc}$$

In the expression $a^{(b+b+\cdots+b)}$, the exponent is the sum of c values of b.

Developing Habits of Mind

Use a different process to get the same result. These three laws come from the properties you learned for multiplication and division. So, if you are unsure about the rules of exponents while doing calculations, you can rewrite the expressions as products of factors. For example, you can rewrite

$$\frac{(b^4)^2}{b^7} \text{ as } \frac{(b \cdot b \cdot b \cdot b) \cdot (b \cdot b \cdot b \cdot b)}{b \cdot b \cdot b \cdot b \cdot b \cdot b \cdot b}$$

Then, you can cancel the factors of b to get the answer: b^1, or just b.

Remember...

The expression $(b^4)^2$ means b^4 times itself. So, $(b^4)^2 = (b^4)(b^4)$.

For now, these rules apply only to positive integer exponents. The rest of this investigation will focus on how to extend the definition of exponents to zero, negative integers, rational numbers, and real numbers. Some of the exercises in this lesson ask you to work with exponents that are not positive integers. Try them and see what happens.

Exercises *Practicing Habits of Mind*

Check Your Understanding

1. Explain why $(ab)^n = a^n b^n$. It may help to make models similar to the ones at the beginning of this lesson.

2. Use a product model to show that $\frac{3^{11}}{3^5} = 3^6$.

3. Use a product model to prove Corollaries 1.3.1 and 1.3.2.

4. Decide whether each expression equals 3^{15}. Explain.

   a. $3^{14} + 3^{14} + 3^{14}$

   b. $(3^6)^9$

   c. $(3^{10})(3^5)$

   d. $(3^3)(3^5)$

   e. $(3^{15})(3^1)$

   f. $(3^5)(3^5)(3^5)$

   g. $3^9 + 3^6$

   h. $(3^5)^3$

   i. $(3^3)^5$

   j. $9(3^{13})$

   k. $(3^5)^{10}$

   l. $(3^1)^{15}$

5. Suppose $M = c^4$ and $N = c^3$. Find at least two different ways to write c^{15} in terms of M and N.

6. **Write About It** Describe how you can use the Fundamental Law of Exponents (Theorem 1.3) to expand the product $(x^7 - 3x^2 + 6)(x^5 + 2x^3 + 3)$.

7. Write the following expression as a single power of 3.
$$3 \cdot 3^2 \cdot 3^4 \cdot 3^8 \cdot 3^{16}$$

8. Solve each equation.

   a. $2^x = 8$

   b. $2^{y-1} = 16$

   c. $2^{5z} = 64$

   d. $(2^w)(2^w) = 64$

9. Find a function that fits this table.

Input	Output
0	3
1	15
2	75
3	375
4	1875

10. Find the mean and the median of the following list of numbers.

$$5 \cdot 10^4 \qquad 5 \cdot 10^3 \qquad 5 \cdot 10^2 \qquad 5 \cdot 10^1 \qquad 5$$

11. Compute each quotient.

   a. $\dfrac{10^9}{10^8}$

   b. $\dfrac{3^2 y^8}{(2y)^3}$

   c. $\dfrac{6^3 x^9}{3^3 2^2 x^5}$

   d. $\dfrac{2^2}{2^5}$

12. Solve each equation for x.

   a. $(x - 1)(x + 1) = 15$

   b. $(2^x - 1)(2^x + 1) = 15$

On Your Own

13. Simplify each expression.

   a. $5^3 \cdot 2^3$

   b. $4^6 \cdot 25^6$

   c. $9^{10} \cdot \left(\dfrac{1}{9}\right)^{10}$

   d. $20^4 \cdot \left(\dfrac{1}{10}\right)^4$

   e. $20^4 \cdot 5^4$

   f. $\left(\dfrac{4}{3}\right)^4 \cdot \left(\dfrac{15}{2}\right)^4$

14. Use each method to prove the following statement.

   If $n > 1$ is a positive integer and $a \neq 0$, then $\dfrac{a^n}{a} = a^{n-1}$.

   a. The Fundamental Law of Exponents (Theorem 1.3)

   b. a product model

15. Find a function that fits this table.

Input	Output
0	5
1	15
2	45
3	135
4	405

16. Suppose $A = c^3$ and $B = c^2$. Find two different ways to write c^8 in terms of A and B.

17. The number 2^{10} is close to 1000. Use this fact to estimate the value of 2^{21}.

18. Decide whether each expression equals 2^3. Explain.

a. $\dfrac{2^6}{2^2}$ **b.** $\dfrac{2^6}{2^3}$ **c.** $(2^2)^1$ **d.** $\dfrac{(2^2)^5}{2^7}$

e. $\dfrac{2^9}{2^6}$ **f.** $\dfrac{2^9}{2^3}$ **g.** $\dfrac{2^7 2^8}{2^5}$

19. Use the fact $2^8 = 256$ to find the units digit of each number.

a. 2^9 **b.** 2^{10} **c.** 2^{16} **d.** 2^7

20. Find the units digit of $(2^5)^2 + (5^2)^2$.

21. Decide whether each expression equals 5^6. Explain.

a. $5 \cdot 5 \cdot 5 \cdot 5 \cdot 5 \cdot 5$ **b.** $5^4 5^2$

c. $(5^3)(3^5)$ **d.** $\dfrac{5^{15}}{5^9}$

e. $\dfrac{(5^2)(5^2)(5^3)}{5}$ **f.** $5^5 + 5$

g. $\dfrac{5^{18}}{5^{12}}$ **h.** $(5^2)^3$

i. $(5^6)^1$ **j.** $(5^3)^3$

k. $\dfrac{(5^3)^3}{5^3}$ **l.** $5 + 5 + 5 + 5 + 5 + 5$

22. Write each expression as a single power of x.

a. $(x^2)^6$ **b.** $(x^2)^5$ **c.** $(x^3)^9$ **d.** $(x^{10})^{10}$

e. $\dfrac{x^8}{x^2}$ **f.** $\dfrac{x^9}{x^7}$ **g.** $\dfrac{1}{x^6}(x^{14})$

23. Standardized Test Prep Which value of x satisfies the equation $6^{x-1} = \frac{3}{2} \cdot 12^2$?

A. 2   **B.** 3   **C.** 4   **D.** 5

Maintain Your Skills

24. Determine whether each relationship is an identity.

a. $(-x)^1 \stackrel{?}{=} -x^1$ **b.** $(-x)^2 \stackrel{?}{=} -x^2$

c. $(-x)^3 \stackrel{?}{=} -x^3$ **d.** $(-x)^4 \stackrel{?}{=} -x^4$

e. $(-x)^5 \stackrel{?}{=} -x^5$ **f.** $(-x)^{13} \stackrel{?}{=} -x^{13}$

Remember...

The units digit is the rightmost digit of an integer. For example, the units digit of 256 is 6.

Habits of Mind

Look for relationships. Try it without a calculator.

Remember...

An identity must be true for every possible choice of variable: positive, negative, zero, rational, irrational, etc.

1.09 Zero and Negative Exponents

In the last lesson, you studied the three basic rules for working with exponents.

Laws of Exponents

Let $a \neq 0$ and let b and c be positive integers.

The Fundamental Law of Exponents

- $a^b \cdot a^c = a^{b+c}$

Corollaries

- $\dfrac{a^b}{a^c} = a^{b-c}$, provided $b > c$
- $(a^b)^c = a^{bc}$

These rules apply when b and c are positive integers. However, you can extend the definition to allow for other numbers as exponents. Each equation below uses a law of exponents in a way that was not defined in the last lesson.

$$2^5 \cdot 2^0 = 2^5 \qquad \frac{3^5}{3^7} = 3^{-2} \qquad \left(7^{\frac{1}{3}}\right)^3 = 7^1$$

You must define symbols, such as 2^0, 3^{-2}, and $7^{\frac{1}{3}}$, in a way that is consistent with the rules. In this lesson, you will find that there is only one way to define zero and negative integral exponents that is consistent with these rules.

> You will explore rational exponents, such as $7^{\frac{1}{3}}$, later in this investigation.

For Discussion

1. Tony thinks that he should define 2^0 to equal 0. Use the laws of exponents to explain why this cannot work.

2. Explain why the equation $2^5 \cdot 2^0 = 2^5$ suggests that you should define 2^0 to equal 1.

Minds in Action

Tony wants to make up his own definition of negative exponents.

Tony   We're learning the definitions for zero and negative exponents, but why can't I make up my own definition?

Nina   Like what?

Tony   Well, the calculator says 10^{-2} is 0.01, which is $\frac{1}{100}$, but I think that's confusing. I think a negative exponent should give a negative answer, so 10^{-2} should be -100, the opposite of 10^2.

Nina	All right, but it better work.
Tony	What do you mean? I just defined it, so it must work.
Nina	I mean it has to be consistent with other exponents. All right, let's check it. What's 10^{-2} times 10^3?
Tony	I use the Fundamental Law of Exponents for that.

$$10^{-2} \cdot 10^3 = 10^{(-2+3)} = 10^1$$

The answer is 10.

Nina	Wait a second! What number did you define 10^{-2} to be?
Tony	-100.
Nina	I'm going to fill in your number for 10^{-2} and see what happens. If I use your number for 10^{-2}, I get $10^{-2} \cdot 10^3 = (-100) \cdot (1000) = -100{,}000$.

If I use your definition, the product is $-100{,}000$! You said it should be 10.

Tony	It should be 10. That's what the Fundamental Law of Exponents gives. Fine, I guess 10^{-2} can't be -100.

For You to Do

3. Use the example $10^{-2} \cdot 10^3 = 10^1$ to explain why 10^{-2} should equal $\frac{1}{100}$.

The following definitions allow the laws of exponents to work for any integer exponents, positive, negative, or zero.

Definitions

Zero exponent: If $a \neq 0$, then $a^0 = 1$.

Negative exponent: If $a \neq 0$ and m is a positive integer, then $a^{-m} = \frac{1}{a^m}$.

For Discussion

4. Here is a statement that uses both negative and zero exponents. Is it true? Explain.

$$a^b \cdot a^{-b} = a^0$$

With the proper definitions of zero and negative exponents, you can extend the laws of exponents to include all integer exponents.

Laws of Exponents

Let $a \neq 0$ and let b and c be integers.

The Fundamental Law of Exponents

- $a^b \cdot a^c = a^{b+c}$

Corollaries

- $\dfrac{a^b}{a^c} = a^{b-c}$
- $(a^b)^c = a^{bc}$

> Some of the exercises that follow ask you to justify extending the laws in this fashion.

There are still other exponents unaccounted for. Why is $9^{\frac{1}{2}}$ equal to 3, for example? The next two lessons look at how you can make the extension to include these exponents.

Exercises *Practicing Habits of Mind*

Check Your Understanding

1. Decide whether each expression equals 7^{-10}. Explain.

   a. $\left(\frac{1}{7}\right)^{10}$ **b.** $7^{-4} \cdot 7^{-3}$ **c.** $(7^{13})(7^{-6})$ **d.** $\dfrac{7^3}{7^{13}}$

   e. $\dfrac{7^2}{7^3 7^4 7^4}$ **f.** $\left(\dfrac{1}{7^{-10}}\right)$ **g.** $7^5 \cdot 7^{-2}$ **h.** $\left(\dfrac{1}{7^2}\right)^5$

   i. $\left(7^5\right)^{-15}$ **j.** $\left(7^5\right)^{-2}$ **k.** $(7^{-2})^5$ **l.** $\left(\dfrac{1}{7^{10}}\right)$

2. Use the definition of a negative exponent to show that $10^{-2} \cdot 10^3 = 10^1$.

3. **Write About It** Show that each of the three laws of exponents continues to work when one of the exponents is zero.

4. Suppose a is a number that satisfies the equation $3^a = 2$. Use the laws of exponents to simplify each expression.

   a. 3^{a+1} **b.** 3^{a-1} **c.** 3^{2a} **d.** 3^{3a} **e.** 3^{0a}

   f. Take It Further $3^{\frac{a}{2}}$

5. Find the units digit of $13^9 10^3 + (117 + 921)^0$.

6. The table below gives the minimum distance from the Earth to some astronomical objects.

Object	Distance From Earth (miles)
Moon	2.25×10^5
Mars	3.46×10^7
Pluto	2.66×10^9

A garden snail can move at the rate of 3×10^{-2} miles per hour. If a garden snail could fly through space at that rate, how many hours would it take to reach the Moon? To reach Mars? To reach Pluto?

7. Find the missing terms in each geometric sequence.

a. 16, 8, 4, ▦, ▦, ▦, . . .

b. 2, ▦, 18, ▦, ▦, ▦, . . .

c. 1, a, a^2, ▦, ▦, ▦, . . .

d. b^6, b^3, 1, ▦, ▦, ▦, . . .

e. c^{10}, ▦, ▦, c^4, ▦, ▦, . . .

8. Here is a table for a function $h(x)$.

x	$h(x)$
-3	▦
-2	▦
-1	▦
0	2
1	10
2	50
3	250
4	1250

a. Find a rule $h(x)$ in the form $h(x) = c \cdot a^x$ that matches the table.

b. Copy and complete the table using this rule.

9. Explain why $(2^3)(2^{-3}) = 1$.

On Your Own

10. Find each variable.

a. $2^5 \cdot 2^{-3} = 2^a$

b. $2^5 \cdot 2^{-7} = 2^b$

c. $\frac{2^5}{2^7} = 2^c$

d. $\frac{2^5}{2^{-7}} = 2^d$

e. $\frac{2^5}{2^f} = 2^8$

11. Decide whether each expression is equal to 5^3. Explain.

a. $\left(\frac{1}{5}\right)^{-3}$

b. $5^{-3} \cdot 5^3$

c. $\left(5^8\right)\left(5^{-2}\right)$

d. $\frac{5^6}{5^9}$

e. $\frac{5^{10}}{5^2 5^3 5^2}$

f. $\left(\frac{1}{5^3}\right)$

g. $5^5 \cdot 5^{-2}$

h. $\left(\frac{1}{5^3}\right)^{-1}$

i. $\left(5^{15}\right)^{\frac{1}{5}}$

j. $\left(5^2\right)^1$

k. $\left(5^4\right)^{-1}$

l. $\left(\frac{1}{5^{-3}}\right)$

Go Online
www.successnetplus.com

12. Write About It This lesson lists the laws of exponents twice, at the beginning and at the end of the lesson. Describe the differences between the first list and the second list.

13. Find the normal form of this polynomial.

$$(4x + 5y - 6z)^0 + (3xy^2 - 5z)^1$$

14. Expand each expression.

a. $(3^x + 3^{-x})^2$ **b.** $(3^x - 3^{-x})^2$ **c.** $(3^x + 3^{-x})^2 - (3^x - 3^{-x})^2$

15. Write each expression as a single power of z.

a. $(z^{-2})(z^4)$ **b.** $((z^3)^3)^{-3}$ **c.** $\dfrac{(z^2)(z^{-4})}{z^2}$

d. $\dfrac{(z^0)^4}{z^{10}}$ **e.** $\dfrac{(z^7)^0}{(z^0)(z^{11})}$

16. Suppose $f(x) = 3^x$ and $g(x) = x^2$. Find each value.

a. $g(f(1))$ **b.** $g(f(-1))$ **c.** $g(f(2))$

d. $g(f(x))$ **e.** $f(g(1))$ **f.** $f(g(-1))$

g. $f(g(2))$ **h.** $f(g(x))$

17. Copy and complete this table for $f(x) = 2^x$.

Input	Output
−3	■
−2	■
−1	■
0	■
1	■
2	4
3	■

18. Copy and complete this table for $g(x) = \left(\frac{1}{2}\right)^x$.

Input	Output
−3	■
−2	4
−1	■
0	■
1	■
2	■
3	■

19. Describe a relationship between the two tables in Exercises 17 and 18. Explain why the relationship holds.

20. Standardized Test Prep Simplify $\dfrac{5^2 \cdot (5^{-3})^0}{5^{-6}}$.

A. 5^{-4} **B.** 5^5 **C.** 5^6 **D.** 5^8

Maintain Your Skills

21. Find the missing values in each geometric sequence.

   a. 1, ▓ , ▓ ,125, . . .   **b.** 1, ▓ , ▓ ,27, ▓ , . . .

   c. 1, ▓ ,64, . . .   **d.** 1, ▓ , ▓ ,64, . . .

   e. 1, ▓ , ▓ , ▓ , ▓ , ▓ , 64, . . .

22. Solve each equation.

   a. $x^3 = 125$ **b.** $x^3 = 27$

   c. $x^2 = 64$ **d.** $x^3 = 64$

   e. $x^6 = 64$

23. Calculate each sum. Express each result as a mixed number, such as $1\frac{2}{3}$.

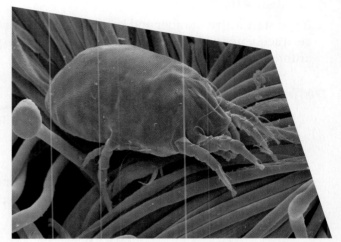

A dust mite is about 4.5×10^{-2} cm long.

   a. 2^0

   b. $2^0 + 2^{-1}$

   c. $2^0 + 2^{-1} + 2^{-2}$

   d. $2^0 + 2^{-1} + 2^{-2} + 2^{-3}$

   e. $2^0 + 2^{-1} + 2^{-2} + 2^{-3} + 2^{-4}$

   f. What is the sum if this pattern continues forever? Explain.

1.10 Sequences and Operations

So far, the laws and definitions about exponents apply only to integer exponents—expressions like 5^{-2} or $(-3)^0$. An expression like $8^{\frac{2}{3}}$ is still undefined. This lesson seeks to build a conceptual understanding of how you can define expressions like $8^{\frac{2}{3}}$. One way to approach this is to look at the connections between repeated addition and repeated multiplication.

$$3 + 3 + 3 + 3 + 3 = 3 \cdot 5 \qquad\qquad 3 \cdot 3 \cdot 3 \cdot 3 \cdot 3 = 3^5$$

You can apply these types of calculations to fractions.

Repeated Addition

If you start with a number and keep adding the same quantity, you get a sequence with constant differences. Such a sequence is an arithmetic sequence.

Definition

A list of numbers is an **arithmetic sequence** if the difference d between any two consecutive terms is constant.

You can use an arithmetic sequence to list the integer multiples of any number by starting with 0 and repeatedly adding that number. Here are the multiples of 27.

$$0, 27, 54, 81, 108, 135, \ldots$$

If you add 27 five times, you get 135, so $27 \cdot 5 = 135$. But what is $27 \cdot \frac{2}{3}$? The result is 18, but how can you add something $\frac{2}{3}$ of one time?

One way is to insert extra terms in the arithmetic sequence between 0 and 27.

$$0, \blacksquare, \blacksquare, 27, \blacksquare, \blacksquare, 54, \blacksquare, \ldots$$

Since it remains an arithmetic sequence, you can replace the first blank with d. Then you can find the others in terms of d.

$$0, d, 2d, 3d, 4d, 5d, 6d, 7d, \ldots$$

Find d by setting up the equation $3d = 27$. So, d must be 9. Then you know that the sequence is

$$0, 9, 18, 27, 36, 45, 54, 63, \ldots$$

You get the result $27 \cdot \frac{2}{3} = 18$, since 18 is two thirds of the way from 0 to 27 in an arithmetic sequence.

> The following lists are examples of arithmetic sequences.
>
> $$1, 4, 7, 10, \ldots$$
> $$5, 1, -3, -7, \ldots$$
> $$3, 3 + 2i, 3 + 4i, \ldots$$
> $$a, a + d, a + 2d, a + 3d, \ldots$$
>
> Chapter 2 will deal with these sequences in depth.

> Start with 0, the identity for addition.

For You to Do

1. Build an arithmetic sequence that shows that $16 \cdot \frac{3}{4} = 12$.

Repeated Multiplication

When you start with a number and keep multiplying by the same quantity, you get a sequence with constant ratios. This sequence is a *geometric sequence*.

Definition

A list of numbers is a **geometric sequence** if the ratio r between any two consecutive terms is constant.

The following lists are examples of geometric sequences.

$$1, 4, 16, 64, \ldots$$
$$2, 1, \frac{1}{2}, \frac{1}{4}, \ldots$$
$$-3, -6, -12, \ldots$$
$$a, ar, ar^2, ar^3, \ldots$$

You can use a geometric sequence to list the integer powers of any number by starting with 1 and repeatedly multiplying by that number. Here are the powers of 27.

$$1; 27; 729; 19{,}683; 531{,}441; \ldots$$

If you multiply 1 by 27 four times, or multiply 4 factors of 27, you get 531,441. So, $27^4 = 531{,}441$. But what is $27^{\frac{2}{3}}$? How can you multiply 1 by something $\frac{2}{3}$ of one time?

One way is to insert extra terms in the geometric sequence between 1 and 27.

$$1, \blacksquare, \blacksquare, 27, \blacksquare, \blacksquare, 729, \blacksquare, \ldots$$

Assume it remains a geometric sequence. If you replace the first blank with r, you can find the other numbers in the sequence in terms of r.

$$1, r, r^2, r^3, r^4, r^5, r^6, r^7, \ldots$$

Find r by setting up the equation $r^3 = 27$. So, one possible value of r is 3. Then the sequence is

$$1, 3, 9, 27, 81, 243, 729, 2187, \ldots$$

Look at the sequence. The number 9 is two thirds of the way from 1 to 27. Then it makes sense to say that $27^{\frac{2}{3}} = 9$.

For You to Do

2. What is $27^{\frac{1}{3}}$? $27^{\frac{4}{3}}$? $27^{\frac{3}{3}}$?

3. Build a geometric sequence that shows that $16^{\frac{3}{4}} = 8$.

The concept set forth here is an informal way of working with rational exponents. You will find a more formal definition in the next lesson. For the exercises that follow, use the laws of exponents or a geometric sequence model to work with expressions like $8^{\frac{2}{3}}$.

Habits of Mind

Check your method. You need to make sure that this way of thinking about fractional exponents is consistent with the laws of exponents.

Example 1

Problem Between what two integers is $17^{\frac{1}{3}}$?

Solution Build a geometric sequence starting with 1 and with the fourth term equal to 17.

$$1, \blacksquare, \blacksquare, 17, \blacksquare, \blacksquare, 289, \blacksquare, \ldots$$

The number for the first blank is $17^{\frac{1}{3}}$, the next is $17^{\frac{2}{3}}$, and so on.

If the ratio from one term to the next is r, the terms are

$$1, r, r^2, r^3, \ldots$$

If you match the two sequences, you can see that r equals $17^{\frac{1}{3}}$.

Since $2^3 = 8$ and $3^3 = 27$, the value of r is between 2 and 3. You can find a more accurate answer by solving $r^3 = 17$. Take the cube root:

$$r = \sqrt[3]{17} \approx 2.5713$$

For You to Do

4. Use the value of $17^{\frac{1}{3}}$ to find $17^{\frac{2}{3}}$ to three decimal places.

5. Between what two integers is $39^{\frac{1}{2}}$?

Example 2

Problem Solve $16^x = 32$ for x.

Solution Note that 16 and 32 are both powers of 2.

$$16^x = 32$$
$$(2^4)^x = 2^5$$
$$2^{4x} = 2^5$$
$$4x = 5$$
$$x = \frac{5}{4}$$

Another method is to write the geometric sequence of powers of 2, starting with $2^0 = 1$.

$$1, 2, 4, 8, 16, 32, 64, 128, \ldots$$

16 is 2^4. Counting by one-fourth powers, $16^{\frac{1}{4}} = 2$ and $16^{\frac{5}{4}} = 32$.

Habits of Mind

Use a key characteristic. To deduce $4x = 5$ from $2^{4x} = 2^5$, you can use the fact that the function $f(x) = 2^x$ is one-to-one. You will prove this later.

6. Solve $32^y = 16$ for y.

This lesson gives some ideas about the meaning of symbols like $27^{\frac{1}{3}}$. A big question remains: Does this method of extending the use of exponents still preserve the important laws of exponents? That question, along with the formal definition of rational exponents, is the subject of the next lesson.

Exercises *Practicing Habits of Mind*

Check Your Understanding

1. Find the missing terms in each arithmetic sequence.

   a. $0, 3, 6, \blacksquare, \blacksquare, \blacksquare, \ldots$

   b. $0, \blacksquare, \blacksquare, \blacksquare, \blacksquare, 30, \ldots$

   c. $1, \blacksquare, \blacksquare, \blacksquare, 81, \blacksquare, \ldots$

   d. $5, \blacksquare, \blacksquare, -7, \blacksquare, \blacksquare, \blacksquare, \ldots$

2. **Write About It** Describe how you can use the arithmetic sequence in Exercise 1b to show that $30 \cdot \frac{3}{5} = 18$.

3. Find the missing terms in each geometric sequence.

   a. $2, -6, 18, \blacksquare, \blacksquare, \blacksquare, \ldots$

   b. $1, \blacksquare, 5, \blacksquare, \blacksquare, \blacksquare, \ldots$

   c. $1, \blacksquare, \blacksquare, 125, \blacksquare, \ldots$

   d. $1, \blacksquare, \blacksquare, \blacksquare, 9, \blacksquare, \blacksquare, \ldots$

4. **Write About It** Describe how you can use the geometric sequence in Exercise 3d to show that $125^{\frac{2}{3}} = 25$.

5. Let $a, b > 0$. For each type of sequence, find an expression in terms of a and b for the missing number in the sequence below.

$$a, \blacksquare, b$$

   a. arithmetic sequence

   b. geometric sequence

6. a. Copy and complete the following table.

(a, b)	$\frac{a+b}{2}$	$\sqrt{ab}$
(1, 2)	1.5	1.4142
(2, 5)	■	■
(4, 1)	■	■
(3, 3)	■	■
(6, 9)	■	■
(8, 10)	■	■
(7, 7)	■	■

Approximate the square roots to 4 decimal places.

b. Take It Further Let $a > 0$ and $b > 0$. Which is greater, $\frac{a+b}{2}$ or $\sqrt{ab}$? Explain your reasoning.

7. Here is a geometric sequence with three missing terms.

$$1, \blacksquare, \blacksquare, \blacksquare, 16, \ldots$$

Alan says that there is more than one possible way to fill in the missing terms. Is he right? Find as many ways as you can to fill in the missing terms.

8. Suzanne has another method for calculating expressions like $81^{\frac{3}{4}}$. She says, "The Fundamental Law of Exponents says that I add exponents when I multiply, so I write down as many $81^{\frac{3}{4}}$ terms as I need to get rid of the denominator. The number of terms is always whatever the denominator is. So here it's 4 of them.

$$81^{\frac{3}{4}} \cdot 81^{\frac{3}{4}} \cdot 81^{\frac{3}{4}} \cdot 81^{\frac{3}{4}}$$

"The result is 81^3. So I have to multiply it four times. If we let x denote $81^{\frac{3}{4}}$, then $x^4 = 81^3$.

"Then I find the root on the calculator, if it's too big for me to figure out in my head: $x = \sqrt[4]{81^3} = 27$."

Use Suzanne's method to calculate $64^{\frac{2}{3}}$ and $625^{\frac{1}{4}}$.

9. Find each value to the nearest integer. Do not use a calculator.

a. $17^{\frac{1}{2}}$ **b.** $25^{\frac{1}{3}}$ **c.** $84^{\frac{1}{4}}$ **d.** $32^{\frac{4}{5}}$

On Your Own

10. Simplify each expression.

a. $81^{\frac{1}{2}} \cdot 81^{\frac{1}{2}}$ **b.** $(27^{\frac{1}{3}})^3$ **c.** $16^{\frac{3}{4}} \cdot 16^{\frac{1}{4}}$ **d.** $(9^{\frac{1}{2}})^3$

11. Find each value to the nearest integer. Do not use a calculator.

a. $27^{\frac{1}{2}}$ **b.** $7^{\frac{1}{3}}$ **c.** $64^{\frac{5}{6}}$ **d.** $117^{\frac{1}{3}}$

12. Sarah invests $500 in a savings account that grows by 3% per year.

    a. Copy and complete the table. Round to the nearest cent.

    b. Does the balance follow an arithmetic or a geometric sequence? Explain.

Years	Balance (dollars)
0	500.00
1	515.00
2	530.45
3	▩
4	▩
5	▩
6	▩

Go Online
www.successnetplus.com

13. Suppose $f(x) = x^{\frac{1}{2}}$. Calculate each value.

    a. $f(25)$ **b.** $f(100)$ **c.** $f(49)$ **d.** $f(1)$ **e.** $f(f(256))$

14. **a.** Based on your work in Exercise 13, write another function rule that could be equivalent to $f(x) = x^{\frac{1}{2}}$.

    b. **Take It Further** Write a function rule that could be equivalent to $f(f(x))$.

15. **Standardized Test Prep** What is the next term in the geometric sequence 4, 6, 9, . . . ?

    A. $\frac{3}{2}$ **B.** 12   **C.** $\frac{27}{2}$ **D.** 15

16. Are there any sequences that are both arithmetic and geometric? Explain.

17. Solve each equation.

    a. $8^x = 4$ **b.** $5^x = 25^{x-3}$ **c.** $3^{2x-1} = 9^{x+1}$

    d. $8^{2x} = 4^{x-1}$ **e.** $8^x = 3^x$

18. **Take It Further** Find all solutions to each equation.

    a. $4^x + 2^x - 6 = 0$ **b.** $9^x - 12 \cdot 3^x + 27 = 0$

    c. $16^x - 6 \cdot 4^x + 8 = 0$

Maintain Your Skills

19. Simplify each expression.

    a. $\dfrac{8^{\frac{4}{3}}}{8^{\frac{1}{3}}}$ **b.** $\dfrac{27^{\frac{1}{3}}}{27^{\frac{2}{3}}}$ **c.** $\dfrac{125^{\frac{1}{3}}}{125^{\frac{2}{3}}}$ **d.** $\dfrac{49^{\frac{1}{2}}}{49^{\frac{3}{2}}}$ **e.** $\dfrac{17^{\frac{7}{5}}}{17^{\frac{2}{5}}}$

Go Online
Video Tutor
www.successnetplus.com

20. Find the number of real solutions to each equation.

    a. $x^3 = 8$ **b.** $x^4 = 16$ **c.** $x^3 = 7$

    d. $x^5 = -32$ **e.** $x^4 = -4$ **f.** $x^3 = -27$

21. Given a real number $a \neq 0$ and a positive integer n, how many real solutions does $x^n = a$ have? Explain.

Defining Rational Exponents

The previous lesson introduced a way of thinking about rational exponents. This lesson focuses on rational exponents from an algebraic perspective. It also covers how you should define rational exponents for the laws of exponents to apply. This idea of extension is extremely important in algebra. You will extend the set of possible exponents from integers to rational numbers in a way that ensures the laws of exponents and the related formulas still hold.

Consider the expression $8^{\frac{1}{3}}$. Corollary 1.3.2 says,

$$(a^b)^c = a^{bc}$$

Suppose you apply this rule to $8^{\frac{1}{3}}$. Try cubing it.

$$\left(8^{\frac{1}{3}}\right)^3 = 8^{\left(\frac{1}{3} \cdot 3\right)} = 8^1 = 8$$

So, if $8^{\frac{1}{3}}$ means anything at all, it has to be a number with a cube that is 8. There is only one real number with a cube that is 8. Therefore, it makes sense to define

$$8^{\frac{1}{3}} = 2$$

For You to Do

1. Use Corollary 1.3.2 to determine what $8^{\frac{2}{3}}$ should mean.

2. What should $8^{-\frac{2}{3}}$ mean? Explain.

What is $7^{\frac{1}{3}}$? The same reasoning tells you that it should mean a number with a cube that is 7. The only real number with a cube that is 7 is $\sqrt[3]{7}$, so it makes sense to define

$$7^{\frac{1}{3}} = \sqrt[3]{7}$$

In general, if a is any real number, then $a^{\frac{1}{3}}$ is equal to $\sqrt[3]{a}$.

Minds in Action

Tony wonders what to do when there is more than one real-number choice for a root.

Tony So I realize I should pick the real number when I can. What can I do about $16^{\frac{1}{4}}$? It's a number with fourth power 16. But there's more than one choice.

$$2^4 = 16 \qquad (-2)^4 = 16$$

There are two numbers with a fourth power of 16. So now I have to pick one. I'll just pick 2. It's the positive one. Besides, it's the one I get when I type $16^{\frac{1}{4}}$ into a calculator.

Developing Habits of Mind

Establish a process. Consider the expression $a^{\frac{1}{n}}$. If $a^{\frac{1}{n}}$ equals a number x, then you can use Corollary 1.3.2 to remove the fraction.

$$x = a^{\frac{1}{n}}$$
$$x^n = \left(a^{\frac{1}{n}}\right)^n$$
$$x^n = a$$

The value of x comes from the equation $x^n = a$. This equation has either 0, 1, or 2 real solutions, and either 0, 1, or 2 of these solutions are real numbers.

Tony had to make a choice when there were two real solutions. He picked the one that is commonly used. The choice is arbitrary. It makes just as much sense to let $16^{\frac{1}{4}}$ equal -2. In general, you use the positive solution.

Overall, to find the value of an expression like $a^{\frac{1}{n}}$, look at the real solutions to $x^n = a$.

- If there is one real solution to the equation $x^n = a$, use it. For example, $(-8)^{\frac{1}{3}} = -2$.
- If there are two real solutions to the equation $x^n = a$, use the positive solution. For example, $9^{\frac{1}{2}}$ is 3 and not -3.
- If there are no real solutions to the equation $x^n = a$, then $a^{\frac{1}{n}}$ is left undefined in this course. For example, $(-4)^{\frac{1}{4}}$ is undefined.

There is more to this story. Later, you will learn about complex numbers. The equation $x^n = a$ has n solutions when complex numbers are used.

Definitions

Unit fraction exponent: The expression $a^{\frac{1}{n}}$ is defined, when possible, as the real **nth root** of a.

$$a^{\frac{1}{n}} = \sqrt[n]{a}$$

If there is no real nth root of a, then $a^{\frac{1}{n}}$ is undefined in this course.

Most scientific calculators have a square root key. Some have a cube root key. A few have keys for fourth roots or larger roots. This definition of rational exponents explains why: you can always evaluate $\sqrt[6]{5}$ on a calculator as $5^{\frac{1}{6}}$.

What is $8^{\frac{2}{3}}$? Use the laws of exponents. The rule $a^b \cdot a^c = a^{b+c}$ gives

$$8^{\frac{2}{3}} = 8^{\frac{1}{3}} \cdot 8^{\frac{1}{3}} = \sqrt[3]{8} \cdot \sqrt[3]{8} = \left(\sqrt[3]{8}\right)^2$$

You can also use the rule $(a^b)^c = a^{bc}$.

$$8^{\frac{2}{3}} = \left(8^{\frac{1}{3}}\right)^2 = \left(\sqrt[3]{8}\right)^2$$

Applying this logic to the general case gives the following definition.

Definition

Rational exponent: For integers p and q with $q > 0$, if $a^{\frac{1}{q}}$ is a real number, then

$$a^{\frac{p}{q}} = \left(a^{\frac{1}{q}}\right)^p = \left(\sqrt[q]{a}\right)^p$$

So, $a^{\frac{1}{2}} = \sqrt{a}$,

$a^{\frac{2}{3}} = (a^{\frac{1}{3}})^2 = (\sqrt[3]{a})^2$,

and $a^{\frac{3}{3}} = \sqrt[3]{a^3} = a$.

For You to Do

Simplify each expression in two different ways. Evaluate the rational exponents and use the laws of exponents.

3. $27^{\frac{2}{3}} \cdot 27^{\frac{1}{3}}$

4. $\dfrac{64^{\frac{1}{2}}}{64^{\frac{1}{3}}}$

5. $\left(16^{\frac{3}{4}}\right)^2$

The laws of exponents leave little choice for these definitions. If $9^{\frac{1}{2}}$ means anything at all, it must satisfy the equation

$$\left(9^{\frac{1}{2}}\right)^2 = 9$$

The only decision left is whether to let this expression equal 3 or -3. You learned to use the positive value when there is an option.

In the next investigation, you will see a few examples that the rules still do not cover. For example, how should you define $3^{\sqrt{2}}$?

Exercises Practicing Habits of Mind

Check Your Understanding

1. a. Give an approximation for $37^{\frac{1}{2}}$.

  b. Give an approximation for $37^{\frac{3}{2}}$.

2. Simplify each expression.

  a. $3^{\frac{1}{3}} \cdot 9^{\frac{1}{3}}$ **b.** $64^{\frac{5}{6}}$ **c.** $\left(7^{\frac{1}{3}}\right)^6$ **d.** $81^{\frac{1}{3}} \cdot 81^{\frac{1}{6}}$

3. Suppose two numbers a and b satisfy this relationship.

$$a^{\frac{2}{5}} = b$$

  a. Find possible values for a and b, not including $a = b = 1$ or $a = b = 0$.

  b. Is the equation $a^2 = b^5$ true for all numbers a and b that satisfy the equation $a^{\frac{2}{5}} = b$? Explain.

4. Use the definition of a rational exponent to prove that $1^{\frac{p}{q}} = 1$ for any integers p and q, with $q > 0$.

5. **Take It Further** The graph of $f(x) = 1^x$ is a horizontal line. Describe the graph of $g(x) = (-1)^x$.

6. Consider the functions $a(x) = x^2$ and $b(x) = x^{\frac{1}{2}}$.

   a. Calculate $a(b(9))$ and $b(a(7))$.

7. Prove this statement.

   If $a, b, c, d, \ldots$ is an arithmetic sequence, then $10^a, 10^b, 10^c, 10^d, \ldots$ is a geometric sequence.

On Your Own

8. **Write About It** Explain why $(-25)^{\frac{1}{2}}$ is undefined in this course.

9. Simplify each expression.

   a. $7^{\frac{1}{3}} \cdot 7^{-\frac{1}{3}}$ **b.** $27^{-\frac{2}{3}}$

   c. $\left(9^{\frac{2}{3}}\right)^{\frac{3}{4}}$ **d.** $\left(62^{\frac{a}{3}}\right)^{\frac{3}{a}}$

10. Find both real solutions to the equation $x^4 = 81$.

11. **a.** What number is defined to be $81^{\frac{1}{4}}$?

    b. What is $81^{-\frac{1}{4}}$? Use a law of exponents.

12. **Take It Further** Suppose a function $E(x)$ is defined for all real numbers x. Let $E(1) = 3$. The function follows the rule below for any numbers a and b.

    $$E(a + b) = E(a) \cdot E(b)$$

    a. Show that $E(0) = 1$.

    b. Find $E(4)$.

    c. Show that $E(n) = 3 \cdot E(n - 1)$ for any n.

    d. Write a function rule for $E(x)$.

13. Show that $8^{\frac{1}{6}} = \sqrt{2}$.

14. Here is a geometric sequence.

    $$1, \blacksquare, \blacksquare, a^2, \blacksquare, \blacksquare, \blacksquare, \blacksquare, \ldots$$

    Write the missing terms as expressions of a.

Go Online
www.successnetplus.com

15. Consider the functions $f(x) = x^3$ and $g(x) = x^{\frac{1}{3}}$.

  a. Copy and complete this table. Round to three decimal places.

x	$f(x) = x^3$	$g(x) = x^{\frac{1}{3}}$
-8	▨	▨
-2	▨	▨
-1	▨	▨
$-\frac{1}{2}$	▨	▨
$-\frac{1}{8}$	▨	▨
0	▨	▨
$\frac{1}{8}$	▨	▨
$\frac{1}{2}$	▨	▨
1	▨	▨
2	▨	▨
8	▨	▨

  b. Using the table, sketch the graphs of $f(x) = x^3$ and $g(x) = x^{\frac{1}{3}}$ on the same axes.

  Use the same scale on both axes.

  c. How are the two graphs related to each other?

  d. How many solutions are there to the equation $f(x) = g(x)$?

16. Standardized Test Prep Which expression is equal to $x^{\frac{2}{3}}$?

  A. $\frac{2}{3}x^{-1}$ **B.** $\frac{1}{x^{\frac{1}{3}}}$ **C.** $\sqrt{x^3}$ **D.** $\sqrt[3]{x^2}$

Maintain Your Skills

For Exercises 17 and 18, use a calculator to find each solution. Round to three decimal places.

17. a. $10^a = 2$ **b.** $10^b = 4$ **c.** $10^c = 8$ **d.** $10^d = 16$

18. a. $10^a = 2$ **b.** $10^b = 3$ **c.** $10^c = 6$ **d.** $10^d = 12$ **e.** $10^f = 36$

Mathematical 1B Reflections

In this investigation, you evaluated and simplified exponents. You developed the laws of exponents by extending exponents from positive integers to include zero, negative, and rational numbers. You also used sequences to explore exponents. These exercises will help you summarize what you have learned.

1. Use a product model to show why $\dfrac{b^6}{b^2} = b^{6-2}$.

2. Simplify each expression given $p, q, r, s, t, u \neq 0$.

   a. $p^6 \cdot p^{-6}$ b. $q^8 \cdot q^{\frac{1}{8}}$ c. $\left(r^2\right)^{-2}$

   d. $\left(s^4\right)^{\frac{1}{4}}$ e. $\dfrac{t^5}{t^{-2}}$ f. $\dfrac{u^6}{u^{\frac{1}{3}}}$

3. Suppose m is a number that satisfies the equation $2^m = 3$. Use the laws of exponents to find each value.

   a. 2^{m+1} b. 2^{3m}

   c. 2^{m-1} d. $\left(2^2\right)^m$

4. a. Build a geometric sequence that shows that $64^{\frac{2}{3}} = 16$. Show at least six terms of the sequence.

   b. What is the ratio between successive terms in your sequence? Why did you choose that ratio?

   c. Find $64^{\frac{4}{3}}$. Explain your method.

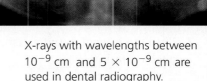

X-rays with wavelengths between 10^{-9} cm and 5×10^{-9} cm are used in dental radiography.

5. Simplify each expression.

   a. $81^{\frac{3}{4}}$ b. $32^{\frac{4}{5}}$

   c. $\left(11^4\right)^{\frac{1}{2}}$ d. $\left(\sqrt[3]{64}\right)^2$

6. What is the Fundamental Law of Exponents? What are some of its corollaries?

7. How do you extend the laws of exponents to define zero, negative, and rational exponents?

8. Simplify the expressions 4^0, 7^{-2}, and $5^{\frac{2}{3}}$.

Vocabulary and Notation

In this investigation, you learned these terms and symbols. Make sure you understand what each one means and how to use it.

- arithmetic sequence
- geometric sequence
- negative exponent, a^{-m}
- nth root, $\sqrt[n]{r}$
- rational exponent, $a^{\frac{p}{q}}$
- unit fraction exponent, $a^{\frac{1}{n}}$
- zero exponent, a^0

In **Investigation 1A,** you learned how to

- distinguish between rational and irrational numbers

- understand the meaning of other radicals, such as square roots, cube roots, and fourth roots

- calculate using square roots, cube roots, and other radicals

- express irrational expressions in simplified form

The following questions will help you check your understanding.

1. For each number, state whether it belongs to the set of real numbers ($\mathbb{R}$), rational numbers ($\mathbb{Q}$), or integers ($\mathbb{Z}$). Name all sets that apply.

   a. $\sqrt{2}$ **b.** 32

   c. $-\frac{1}{2}$ **d.** 3π

   e. $\sqrt{9}$ **f.** 4.831

2. Find the integer k that satisfies each equation.

   a. $\sqrt{24} = k\sqrt{6}$

   b. $\sqrt{200} = k\sqrt{2}$

   c. $\sqrt{3} + \sqrt{27} = k\sqrt{3}$

   d. $\sqrt{5} \cdot \sqrt{10} = 5\sqrt{k}$

   e. $\sqrt{2} \cdot \sqrt{k} = 2$

   f. $\sqrt{\dfrac{2}{3}} = \dfrac{\sqrt{k}}{3}$

3. Use the duck principle to show that each equation is true.

   a. $\sqrt{3} \cdot \sqrt{3} = 3$

   b. $\sqrt[3]{3} \cdot \sqrt[3]{9} = 3$

   c. $\sqrt[3]{4} \cdot \sqrt[3]{4} = 2\sqrt[3]{2}$

   d. $\sqrt{2} \cdot \sqrt[3]{3} = \sqrt[6]{72}$

   e. $\sqrt[3]{\dfrac{1}{4}} = \dfrac{\sqrt[3]{2}}{2}$

In **Investigation 1B,** you learned how to

- evaluate expressions involving exponents, including zero, negative, and rational exponents

- find the missing terms in a geometric sequence and make a geometric sequence to interpret expressions involving rational exponents

- convert between exponential and radical forms for rational exponents

The following questions will help you check your understanding.

4. Write each expression as a single power of x. Assume $x \neq 0$.

   a. $x^{-2} \cdot x^{-1}$ **b.** $\left(\frac{1}{x}\right)^{-2}$

   c. $\left((x^3)^{-2}\right)^{-5}$ **d.** $\dfrac{x^4}{x^{-4}}$

   e. $\left(x^6\right)^0 \cdot x^3$ **f.** $\dfrac{(x^5)(x^{-2})}{x^{10}}$

5. Find the missing terms in each geometric sequence.

   a. 5, 20, ■, ■, ■

   b. 6, ■, 24, ■, ■

   c. 1, ■, 6, ■

   d. 1, ■, ■, 125

   e. Use the sequence in part (d) to find $125^{\frac{2}{3}}$.

6. Simplify each expression.

   a. $49^{\frac{1}{2}}$ **b.** $81^{\frac{3}{4}}$

   c. $8^{-\frac{4}{3}}$ **d.** $\left(\sqrt[4]{16}\right)^5$

Test

Multiple Choice

1. Which of the following expressions is NOT equal to 1?

A. $3^2 \cdot 3^{-2}$

B. $\dfrac{5^2 \cdot 5^4}{(5^2)^3}$

C. $(2^3)^{\frac{1}{3}}$

D. $\left(\frac{1}{2}\right)^{-1} \cdot 2^{-1}$

2. Let $3^m = 2$. Find 3^{m+1}.

A. 3

B. 4

C. 5

D. 6

3. How many times greater than $\sqrt{3}$ is $\sqrt{75}$?

A. between 2 and 3

B. 5

C. 25

D. 625

4. Which of the following numbers is irrational?

A. $\sqrt{3} \cdot \sqrt{3}$

B. $\sqrt{3} \div \sqrt{3}$

C. $\sqrt{3} - \sqrt{3}$

D. $\sqrt{3} + \sqrt{3}$

5. Which of these statements is true?

A. All rational numbers are integers.

B. You can write all real numbers in the form $\frac{p}{q}$ where p and q are integers.

C. Some irrational numbers are integers.

D. All integers are rational numbers.

6. Which of these is equal to $\dfrac{\sqrt{28}}{\sqrt{63}}$?

A. $\frac{4}{9}$

B. $\frac{2}{3}$

C. $\frac{2\sqrt{7}}{3}$

D. $\sqrt{7}$

7. Which of the following points is closest to $2\sqrt{11}$ on a number line?

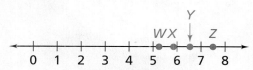

A. W

B. X

C. Y

D. Z

Open Response

8. Solve each equation with an exact answer.

a. $x \cdot 16^{\frac{1}{2}} = 64^{\frac{4}{3}}$

b. $45 = 5 \cdot 27^x$

9. Write 3 geometric sequences that start with 1 and include 16 as a term.

10. Explain why $\sqrt[4]{16^3} = 8$.

Polynomials

You can use algebraic expressions, or polynomials, to model smooth, unbroken curves of the natural world. As you model different curves in this chapter, you will extend your basic understanding of expressions.

You can write numbers using place-value parts. For instance, you can write 352 as $3 \times 100 + 5 \times 10 + 2$. Since you know that the places are powers of ten, you can rewrite the above expression as $3 \times 10^2 + 5 \times 10 + 2$. If you replace each 10 with a variable, the result is a polynomial expression, $3x^2 + 5x + 2$.

You can evaluate this polynomial expression for any value of x. In the original expression, if $x = 10$, the expression equals 352. If you substitute -2 for x, the expression equals 4.

In this chapter, you will look closely at the structure of polynomials. You will determine what types of expressions are polynomials and what properties of polynomials they have. You will also explore writing polynomials in different forms. For instance, you can use the fact that $3x^2 + 5x + 2 = (3x + 2)(x + 1)$ to solve the equation $3x^2 + 5x + 2 = 0$.

Vocabulary

- annulus
- binomial
- coefficient
- cubic polynomial
- degree of a monomial
- degree of a polynomial
- expand an expression
- factor an expression
- greatest common factor
- identity
- linear polynomial
- monic
- monomial
- normal form
- parameter
- perfect square trinomial
- polynomial
- polynomial equation
- quadratic polynomial
- quartic polynomial
- quintic polynomial
- trinomial

Investigation 2A

The Need for Identities— Equivalent Expressions

In *The Need for Identities*, you will use the basic rules of algebra to transform expressions. Sometimes when you transform an expression into another form, you will notice something about the expression that was not clear in the original form. You can also transform expressions to make your calculations easier.

By the end of this investigation, you will be able to answer questions like these.

1. How do you determine whether two different expressions define the same function?

2. When is it useful to write an expression as a product of expressions?

3. How do you write $3ab - 15a + b - 5$ as a product of two expressions?

You will learn how to

- use basic rules and moves to transform expressions to determine whether different expressions define the same function

- factor expressions by identifying a common factor

- apply the Zero-Product Property to factored expressions

- use algebra to simplify long computations such as computing large sums of consecutive numbers

You will develop these habits and skills:

- Expand powers and products of expressions.

- Identify factors and common factors.

- Divide common factors from an expression.

- Justify arguments using algebraic proof.

You can use either polynomial, $\pi R^2 - \pi r^2$ or $\pi(R - r)(R + r)$, to find the areas of the rings around the bull's-eye.

Activating Prior Knowledge
Exploring New Ideas

You can write algebraic expressions in many different ways. Using the basic rules of algebra, you can represent a function in another form.

For You to Explore

1. Expand each expression.

   a. $3(x + 4)$

   b. $2x(x - 1)$

   c. $-3x^2(x^2 - 2x + 1)$

   d. $(x - 4)(x + 3)$

   e. $(2x^2 - 1)(3x + 4)$

   f. $(3x - 5)(x^2 - 5x + 6)$

2. Tony and Sasha plan a student advisory board meeting. They use cafeteria tables that are shaped like hexagons. Each table seats six people.

They decide to form a row of three tables that will seat 14 people.

   a. Write at least two formulas for the number of people that you can seat at n tables.

   b. How many tables will be necessary to seat 18 people? To seat 19 people? To seat 67 people?

You **expand an expression** by multiplying it out. The result will be an expression without parentheses. You can use an expansion box to multiply expressions. Here, the expansion box illustrates the expansion for Exercise 1e.

	$3x$	4
$2x^2$	$6x^3$	$8x^2$
-1	$-3x$	-4

3. Use this input-output table.

Input	Output
0	0
1	4
2	10
3	18
4	28

a. Write at least two different functions to describe this table.

b. Do your functions from part (a) always result in the same output for any input? Explain.

4. Consider the function $f(x) = 3x + 7 + 5x(x - 1)(x - 2)$. Write a simpler function that has the same values when x equals 0, 1, and 2.

A class wrote 5 different rules that match the table. Can you write more rules than that?

Exercises *Practicing Habits of Mind*

On Your Own

5. Luca has a new method for multiplying numbers.

Find the sum and difference of the two numbers that you want to multiply. Square each result. Subtract the smaller result from the larger result. Divide the difference by 4. This solution is the product of the numbers. For instance, to multiply 12 times 8, you can follow these steps.

Is Luca's method easier than the methods you have used in the past to multiply? Explain.

- The sum is $12 + 8 = 20$. The difference is $12 - 8 = 4$.

- The square of 20 is $20^2 = 400$. The square of 4 is $4^2 = 16$.

- Subtract 16 from 400, or $400 - 16 = 384$.

- Divide the difference by 4, or $384 \div 4 = 96$.

Use Luca's method to find each product.

a. $21 \cdot 19$ b. $52 \cdot 48$ c. $107 \cdot 59$

d. **Take It Further** Prove that Luca's method works for any two numbers a and b.

6. Expand each side to prove that the equation $(a^2 + b^2)(c^2 + d^2) = (ac - bd)^2 + (bc + ad)^2$ is true.

7. a. Find integers a, b, c, and d such that $a^2 + b^2 = 34$ and $c^2 + d^2 = 13$.

b. Use the equation from Exercise 6. Show that you can write 34×13 as the sum of the squares of two integers.

c. Find three numbers that you cannot write as the sum of squares of two integers.

8. The factored expression $(m + 7)(m - 11)$ is equivalent to the expanded form $m^2 - 4m - 77$.

a. When $m = 6$, the value of $m^2 - 4m - 77$ is a multiple of 13. Explain why.

b. Name two other positive integers m that make $m^2 - 4m - 77$ a multiple of 13.

c. Explain why the following is true. If $(m + 7)$ or $(m - 11)$ is a multiple of 13, then $m^2 - 4m - 77$ is a multiple of 13.

d. Find two values of m that make $m^2 - 4m - 77$ equal to zero.

e. Explain why the following is true. If $(m + 7)$ or $(m - 11)$ is zero, then $m^2 - 4m - 77$ is zero.

> **Remember...**
>
> Two expressions are equivalent if you can get from one expression to the other using the basic rules of algebra.

9. Find four pairs of numbers x and y that make the value of the expression $xy^2 + x^2 + y - x - x^2y - y^2$ equal to 0.

10. Prove that $xy^2 + x^2 + y - x - x^2y - y^2 = (x - 1)(y - 1)(y - x)$.

11. If x and y are numbers and $xy^2 + x^2 + y - x - x^2y - y^2 = 0$, explain why either $x = 1$ or $y = 1$, or $x = y$ must be true.

12. Take It Further Consider the function below. Write a simpler function that has the same output values for x-values 0, 1, 2, 3, and 4. Does your function always agree with f? Explain.

$$f(x) = \frac{19}{24}x(x - 1)(x - 2)(x - 3) - \frac{8}{3}x(x - 1)(x - 2)(x - 4) +$$
$$\frac{13}{4}x(x - 1)(x - 3)(x - 4) - \frac{5}{3}x(x - 2)(x - 3)(x - 4) +$$
$$\frac{7}{24}(x - 1)(x - 2)(x - 3)(x - 4)$$

Maintain Your Skills

13. Expand each expression. Describe a pattern in the results.

a. $(x + 1)^2$ **b.** $(x + 1)^3$ **c.** $(x + 1)^4$

14. a. Expand $(x - 1)(1 + x + x^2 + x^3 + x^4 + x^5 + x^6 + x^7)$.

b. What is the value of $1 + 2 + 2^2 + 2^3 + 2^4 + 2^5 + 2^6 + 2^7$? Do not use a calculator.

15. Expand each expression. Describe a pattern in the results.

a. $(x + y)^2$ **b.** $(x + y)^3$ **c.** $(x + y)^4$

Form and Function—Showing Expressions are Equivalent

You may recall finding fitting lines for noncollinear data points. Sometimes, you can generate the data exactly with a polynomial function. In this lesson, you will learn how to find quadratic functions that fit a table of data exactly.

Minds in Action

Sasha, Tony, and Derman want to find a function that describes this table. The domain is all real numbers.

Input, n	Output, $f(n)$
0	0
1	3
2	8
3	15
4	24
5	35

Sasha   I have an idea. Let's factor each output. Look, 15 is 3 times 5. 24 is 4 times 6. 35 is 5 times 7. Each output is the input times two more than the input. It even works for the first one. 3 is 1 times 3. So the next number will be 6 times 8. That's 48. In general, if the input is n, the rule is to multiply n and $(n + 2)$.

Sasha writes an equation.

$$f(n) = n(n+2)$$

Input, n	Output, $f(n)$	n^2	$f(n) - n^2$
0	0	0	0
1	3	1	2
2	8	4	4
3	15	9	6
4	24	16	8
5	35	25	10

Tony	I actually got something different. The pattern reminded me of n^2, so I made a column for n^2 in the table. Then for each input, I subtracted n^2 from the output. That column showed a simple pattern: 2 times the input. So the rule I got is $f(n) = n^2 + 2n$.
Derman	I got something completely different! I noticed that the outputs are 1 less than a perfect square. For example, 35 is 1 less than 6^2, or 36, and 24 is 1 less than 5^2, or 25. The number that you square in each case is 1 more than the input. The next input is 6. If you add 1 to 6, the result is 7. Then find $7^2 - 1$. The result is 48.
Sasha	I already said that 48 is the next output!
Derman	True, but my rule is different. If the input is n, you square $(n + 1)$ and subtract 1.

Derman writes the following equation.

$$f(n) = (n + 1)^2 - 1$$

Tony	If you input 6 in my rule, you get $6^2 + 2(6) = 36 + 12 = 48$. They all seem to work. How did we all get different rules for the same table?
Sasha	Tony, I actually think our rules are the same. Even though we came up with the rules differently, I can prove they are identical.
Tony	Really? How can you do that?
Sasha	Your rule is $f(n) = n^2 + 2n$. If I expand my expression using the Distributive Property, the result is exactly the same. Likewise, if you factor your rule, the result is the same as mine.
Tony	That's neat! The equation $n^2 + 2n = n(n + 2)$ is an identity. It remains true if I replace n by any number. Since the expressions are equivalent, the functions are also the same.
Derman	Okay, I get it now. I wonder if that's true for my rule.

> An **identity** is a statement that two expressions are equivalent under the basic rules of algebra.

For Discussion

1. Is Derman's rule equivalent to both Sasha's rule and Tony's rule? If so, prove it.

Sasha's argument proves that the two expressions define the same function. You can use tables to provide evidence that two expressions are equivalent. However, tables are not sufficient for proving anything. You can always use the basic rules of algebra to prove that expressions are equivalent. The following principle summarizes these facts.

Principle *Form Implies Function*

If two expressions are equivalent under the basic rules of algebra,
they define functions that produce the same output for any
given input.

For Discussion

2. Give an example of the principle above. Two different rules define two
functions. Now, prove that the functions are the same.

In this chapter, you will build identities, or pairs of equivalent expressions.
Identities are extensions of the basic rules. You can use them in a variety of
places. For example, you can use identities to show that two functions are
the same.

Example

Problem Prove that $(3x + 1)^2 + (x + 2)^2 - 5$ is a multiple of $10x$, for any
integer x.

Solution First, consider a few examples. The table below shows some inputs
and outputs for the function $f(x) = (3x + 1)^2 + (x + 2)^2 - 5$.

Input, x	Output, $f(x)$
0	0
1	20
2	60
3	120
4	200
5	300

You may notice that $f(3)$ is a multiple of 30 and $f(4)$ is a multiple of 40.
A similar pattern works no matter what input you use.

As stated earlier in this lesson, you cannot prove that a statement is true
using a table. A table only provides evidence that a statement is true. You

can start a proof by finding an equivalent expression using the basic rules to expand each part of the expression.

$$(3x + 1)^2 = (3x + 1)(3x + 1)$$
$$= 9x^2 + 3x + 3x + 1$$
$$= 9x^2 + 6x + 1$$
$$(x + 2)^2 = (x + 2)(x + 2)$$
$$= x^2 + 2x + 2x + 4$$
$$= x^2 + 4x + 4$$

So, the expression $(3x + 1)^2 + (x + 2)^2 - 5$ is equivalent to $9x^2 + 6x + 1 + x^2 + 4x + 4 - 5$. Now you can combine like terms to establish the identity.

$$(3x + 1)^2 + (x + 2)^2 - 5 = 10x^2 + 10x$$

The expanded expression is easier to work with because the common factor, $10x$, is in both terms. By the Distributive Property, $10x^2 + 10x = 10x(x + 1)$.

The factored form provides the proof. Since $10x$ is one of the factors, the original expression must be a multiple of $10x$.

> The variable x represents an integer in this case.

Developing Habits of Mind

Experiment. Recall that $(3x + 1)^2$ is not equivalent to $(3x)^2 + 1^2$. Try replacing x with numbers! For example, if $x = 2$, $(3 \cdot 2 + 1)^2 = 49$ and $(3 \cdot 2)^2 + 1^2 = 37$. The expressions are not the same. Note that if $x = 0$, $(3x + 1)^2$ is the same as $(3x)^2 + 1^2$. Experimenting with just one number is not enough.

Are there any other values of x for which $(3x + 1)^2 = (3x)^2 + 1^2$?

> Be careful! You can distribute exponents over multiplication, $(ab)^2 = a^2b^2$. You cannot distribute exponents over addition, $(a + b)^2 \neq a^2 + b^2$.

For You to Do

3. Use the Distributive Property. Factor $8x^2 + 4x$ as completely as possible.

For Discussion

4. One expression below is a multiple of $10x$. How can you identify the expression and prove that it is a multiple of $10x$?

   A. $(3x + 1)^2 + (x + 5)^2$ **B.** $(6x + 1)^2 - (4x - 1)^2$

   C. $(3x - 1)^2 - (2x + 1)^2$

Exercises *Practicing Habits of Mind*

Check Your Understanding

1. In a list of consecutive integers, each integer is one greater than the preceding integer. For example, 8, 9, and 10 are three consecutive integers. Also, -7, -6, -5, and -4 are four consecutive integers.

   a. Start with -2. Write a list of four consecutive integers.

   b. Start with n. Write expressions for four consecutive integers.

   c. Write expressions for three consecutive integers if the middle integer is n.

   d. Write and simplify an expression for the sum of two consecutive integers.

   > The second expression is one more than n. The third expression is one more than the second expression.

2. a. Use your expression from Exercise 1d. Show that the sum of two consecutive integers is always odd.

   b. Show that the sum of three consecutive integers is always divisible by 3.

   c. Is the sum of four consecutive integers divisible by 4? Explain.

   d. Is the sum of five consecutive integers divisible by 5? Explain.

   e. **Take It Further** For what whole numbers k is the sum of k consecutive integers always divisible by k?

3. If n is an integer, then the expression $n(n + 1)$ represents the product of two consecutive integers.

   a. Explain how you know that the product of two consecutive integers is an even number.

   b. Is the product of three consecutive integers divisible by 3? Explain.

   c. Is the product of four consecutive integers divisible by 4? Explain.

   d. Is the product of five consecutive integers divisible by 5? Explain.

   e. **Take It Further** Is the product of k consecutive integers divisible by k? Explain.

4. There are two numbers n that make $n(n + 1) = 210$. Find both numbers.

5. Consider the following function.

   $$g(n) = \left(\frac{n(n + 1)}{2} + \frac{n(n - 1)}{2} \right) \left(\frac{n(n + 1)}{2} - \frac{n(n - 1)}{2} \right)$$

   Write a simpler expression that can define g.

On Your Own

6. Is the sum of seven consecutive integers always a multiple of 7? Explain.

7. The following function is defined by the messy rule below. Find each value.

$$s(x) = (x - 3)(x^2 - 3x + 2) - x(x^2 - 6x + 11)$$

   a. $s(0)$ **b.** $s(3)$ **c.** $s(11)$

   d. Expand the expressions in this function to find a simpler rule for $s(x)$.

8. **Write About It** Explain how you know the identity $n^2 + kn = n(n + k)$ is true for any numbers n and k.

> This identity is an extension of the identity Sasha found for $k = 2$ in Lesson 2.02.

9. A square is 23 inches on each side. You cut a 6-inch square from one corner.

   a. Find the area, in square inches, of the leftover shape. Explain your method.

   b. **Take It Further** Find the prime factors of the area. Relate them to the dimensions of the figure.

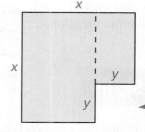

10. A square is x inches on each side. You cut a square, y inches on each side, from one corner. In terms of x and y, find the area, in square inches, of the leftover shape. Explain your method.

11. Tony discusses Exercise 10. "Okay, I can cut up the shape I have into two rectangles. One is larger than the other. Then I can measure the area of each rectangle separately. Last, I add them up." He draws this picture.

   a. Find the area of each rectangle.

   b. Find the total area of the paper.

   c. If $x = 23$ and $y = 6$, what is the total area according to Tony's formula?

   d. Does Tony's formula disagree with the formula you found in Exercise 10?

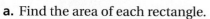
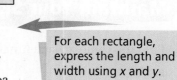

> For each rectangle, express the length and width using x and y.

12. Sasha discusses Exercise 10. "You can cut this shape into two matching shapes if you cut along the diagonal. Then you can flip one of them to make a large rectangle."

   a. Use your own paper to draw the picture above. Then make the cut. Show how the shape can become one rectangle.

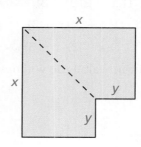

b. What are the length and width of the large rectangle?

c. What is the area of the rectangle if $x = 23$ and $y = 6$?

d. Does Sasha's formula disagree with the formula you found in Exercise 10?

e. Take It Further Explain how you know that this cut-and-paste method works to form a rectangle.

13. Derman discusses Exercise 10. "I can cut a strip off the bottom. I'll move it to the right side to make one large rectangle." He draws this picture to show where to make and move the cut.

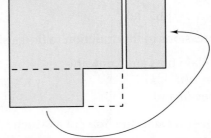

   a. Use your own paper to draw Derman's picture. Then make the cut. Show how the shape can become one rectangle.

   b. What are the length and width of the large rectangle?

   c. What is the area of the rectangle if $x = 23$ and $y = 6$?

   d. Does Derman's formula disagree with your formula in Exercise 10?

   e. Take It Further Explain how you know that Derman's cut-and-paste method works to form a rectangle.

14. **Standardized Test Prep** What is the expanded form of the product $(x + 1)(x^3 - x^2 + x - 1)$?

   A. $x^4 + 1$

   B. $x^4 - 1$

   C. $x^4 - 2x^3 + 2x^2 - 2x + 1$

   D. $x^4 + 2x^3 + 2x^2 + 2x + 1$

15. Suppose $g(x) = x^4 + x^2 + 1$ and $f(x) = (x^2 + x + 1)(x^2 - x + 1)$. Prove that g and f are the same function.

Maintain Your Skills

16. Find the value of each function for x values 1, 2, 3, and 4.

   a. $f(x) = 2x + 1$

   b. $g(x) = 2x + 1 + (x - 1)(x - 2)(x - 3)$

   c. $h(x) = 2x + 1 - 5(x - 1)(x - 2)(x - 3)$

   d. $j(x) = 2x + 1 - x^2(x - 1)(x - 2)(x - 3)$

   e. What pattern in the output values do you notice?

2.03 The Zero-Product Property

Look at the row and column at 0 on part of the multiplication table. Notice that all of the products are 0. If either number is zero when you multiply two numbers, the product is zero.

Also, notice that there is never a zero in a multiplication table that is not on the axes. If the product of two numbers is zero, then one or both of the numbers must be zero.

The Zero-Product Property summarizes this result.

Multiplication Table

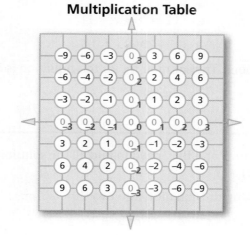

Theorem 2.1 *The Zero-Product Property*

The product of two numbers is zero if and only if one or both of the numbers is zero.

In symbols, if *a* and *b* are numbers, then $ab = 0 \Leftrightarrow a = 0$ or $b = 0$.

For Discussion

The reasons why the Zero-Product Property holds depend on some basic facts about numbers.

1. Why is a product 0 when one of the factors is 0?

2. Use what you know about the multiplication table. Argue that if *a* and *b* are both nonzero integers, $ab \neq 0$.

> What about numbers that are not integers? If *a* and *b* are any real numbers, and $ab = 0$, does either *a* or *b* have to be 0? Explain.

Theorem 2.1 is useful in situations if a product is 0. Here are some examples.

- If $(x - 11)(x + 7) = 0$, then $x - 11 = 0$ or $x + 7 = 0$.

- If $(2x - 7)(y - 12) = 0$, then $2x - 7 = 0$ or $y - 12 = 0$.

- If $5(z + 36) = 0$, then $5 = 0$ (which is impossible) or $z + 36 = 0$ (this must be true).

You can use the Zero-Product Property to solve complex equations. For the equation $(x - 11)(x + 7) = 0$, ZPP splits the larger equation into two smaller equations. Use the symbol $\Rightarrow$ for implies.

Use the abbreviation *ZPP* for the Zero-Product Property.

$$(x - 11)(x + 7) = 0 \Rightarrow x - 11 = 0 \text{ or } x + 7 = 0$$

$$x - 11 = 0 \Rightarrow x = 11$$

$$x + 7 = 0 \Rightarrow x = -7$$

There are no other solutions. The solution set for this equation is $x = -7$ or $x = 11$.

For Discussion

3. **What's Wrong Here?** Mandy and Billy need to find all the solutions to the equation $(x + 7)(x + 11) = 77$.

Mandy says, "I can break up the equation into two simpler ones.

$$(x + 7)(x + 11) = 77 \Rightarrow x + 7 = 77 \text{ or } x + 11 = 77.$$

So, there are two answers, $x = 70$ or $x = 66$."

Billy replies, "Those answers don't work! Try them in the original equation. I think the solution is $x = 0$. Check it. You'll see it works."

Mandy answers, "Okay, $x = 0$ works. I'm not convinced it's the only solution. How did I mess up?"

What is wrong with Mandy's solution? Is it possible to use ZPP to solve this equation? If so, how? Try to find a second solution to the equation.

ZPP works well if an expression is the product of two or more simple expressions. How do you use ZPP if you have an equation such as $2x^3 - 9x^2 - 38x + 21 = 0$?

When you factor an integer, you write it as a product of two or more integers. It is the same for expressions. To **factor an expression** means to write it as the product of two or more expressions. You can factor the expression on the left side of the equation above into three simpler expressions.

For example, 4×3, 2×6, and $2 \times 3 \times 2$ are all factored forms of the number 12.

$$2x^3 - 9x^2 - 38x + 21 = (x - 7)(x + 3)(2x - 1)$$

Now you can use ZPP to find solutions for x.

When using ZPP, remember the following.

- The expression must be in factored form, since ZPP only applies to products. For instance, you need to find the factored form of $x^3 - 9x$ to solve $x^3 - 9x = 0$.
- The product must be equal to zero.

Problem Find all the values of x that make $x^3 = 25x$ true.

Solution To solve using the ZPP, change the equation. Use a basic move to make one side equal to zero.

$$x^3 = 25x$$
$$x^3 - 25x = 25x - 25x$$
$$x^3 - 25x = 0$$

The ZPP works with products. Factor $x^3 - 25x$ into a product of simpler expressions. Start by finding the factors of each term.

$$x^3 = x \cdot x \cdot x$$
$$25x = 5 \cdot 5 \cdot x$$

The terms have a common factor of x. Use the Distributive Property to "pull out" this factor from each term.

$$x^3 - 25x = x(x^2 - 25)$$

Now the equation is ready for ZPP. Split the equation into simpler equations.

$$x^3 = 25x$$
$$x^3 - 25x = 0$$
$$x(x^2 - 25) = 0$$
$$x = 0, \text{ or } x^2 - 25 = 0$$

So either $x = 0$ or $x^2 - 25 = 0$. If $x^2 - 25 = 0$, then $x^2 = 25$. Therefore, x is either 5 or -5. There are three possible values for x in the solution set.

$$x \in \{-5, 0, 5\}$$

Check these answers.

> The expressions x^3 and $25x$ are different. They cannot be combined into one large term, just as a and b cannot be combined in $3a + 4b$.

> To find $x^3 - 25x$, you multiply x by an expression. Notice that the expression is inside the parentheses.

For You to Do

4. Sketch the graph of $f(x) = x^3 - 25x$. Where does the graph cross the x-axis?

5. Factor $2x^3 + 16xy$. What is a common factor of both terms? What is left when you pull out the common factor?

For Discussion

6. José thinks about the Example. He wonders if he can just divide by x in the beginning. He says, "Well, there's an x on each side, so I can just divide and then solve it from there.

$$x^3 = 25x$$

$$\frac{x^3}{x} = \frac{25x}{x}$$

$$x^2 = 25$$

Why doesn't this give me all the answers? It seems legal. I'm just dividing by x."

How can you help José? Is dividing by x a legal move? Explain.

Developing Habits of Mind

Work backward. What can you do if you do not know how to factor $x^3 - 25x$? You might think about it as follows.

$$x^3 - 25x = x\,(\text{an expression})$$

What goes inside the parentheses? One way to figure it out involves expansion boxes. Write the known factor x in the left column of the expansion box. In each box, write the product. Then find the missing terms in the first row.

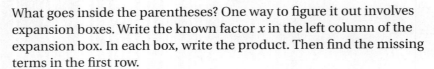

The terms x^2 and -25 are the missing terms, since $x \cdot x^2 = x^3$ and $x \cdot (-25) = -25x$. Now, change the equation.

$$x^3 - 25x = 0$$

$$x(x^2 - 25) = 0$$

For Discussion

Is each statement true or false? Explain.

7. $abc = 0 \Leftrightarrow a = 0$ or $b = 0$ or $c = 0$

8. $abcd = 0 \Leftrightarrow a = 0$ or $b = 0$ or $c = 0$ or $d = 0$

As you learn more factoring techniques in this chapter, do not forget ZPP! It is the key to solving many equations.

Exercises *Practicing Habits of Mind*

Check Your Understanding

1. Solve each equation for x.

   a. $x - 8 = 0$ **b.** $x + 17 = 0$ **c.** $x + b = 0$

   d. $27x + 13 = 0$ **e.** $cx - d = 0$ **f.** $5x = 0$

2. Find all of the solutions to each equation. Check your answers!

   a. $(x - 7)(x + 5) = 0$ **b.** $(x - 3)(y + 7) = 0$

   c. $5x(x + 2) = 0$ **d.** $(x + 3)(x + 4)(x + 5) = 0$

3. The equation $6x^2 + 11x - 35 = 0$ has two solutions.

   a. Make a table for $f(x) = 6x^2 + 11x - 35$. Use integer x-values from -5 to 5. Use this table to estimate the two solutions to the equation.

   b. Use an expansion box. Show that $6x^2 + 11x - 35$ is the same as the factored expression $(2x + 7)(3x - 5)$.

   c. What are the two solutions to $6x^2 + 11x - 35 = 0$?

4. **a.** Find the two numbers x that make $(x + 7)(x + 11) = 0$.

   b. Find the two numbers x that make $(x + 7)(x + 11) = 1$. Approximate your result.

5. Ling says, "Factoring is easy. Look at this.

   $$x^2 - 4 = 1 \cdot (x^2 - 4) = \tfrac{1}{2}(2x^2 - 8) = 3 \cdot \left(\tfrac{1}{3}x^2 - \tfrac{4}{3}\right) = \ldots$$

   I can go on like this all day."

   What would you say to Ling to explain why it is not helpful to factor this way?

   Consider another problem. Ling says, "Look, 5 is not a prime number because $5 = \tfrac{1}{2} \times 10$. So 5 factors into two other numbers, neither of which is 1." Is she right? Explain.

6. What are all the solutions to the equation $x^3 = x$?

7. A projectile travels straight up from the ground. Its height from the ground t seconds after it leaves the ground is given by $s(t) = 100t - 16t^2$.

   a. Explain how you could show that the expanded expression $100t - 16t^2$ is equivalent to $t(100 - 16t)$.

   b. Find all solutions to $t(100 - 16t) = 0$. What does each solution represent in the situation?

   c. Use a graphing calculator. Draw a graph to represent $s(t) = 100t - 16t^2$. What two values of t make $s(t)$ zero?

   d. At about what time is the projectile at its highest point? Can you predict this time if you know when $s(t) = 0$?

   e. Draw a picture of the actual path of the projectile.

8. Solve each equation for x.

   a. $x - 23 = 0$ **b.** $x - a = 0$ **c.** $3x - 7 = 0$

   d. $30x - 120 = 0$ **e.** $mx + b = 0$

9. Use ZPP. Find all of the solutions to each equation.

   a. $(x - 8)(x - 23) = 0$ **b.** $(x + 17)(x + 11) = 0$

   c. $(2x + 5)(x - 10) = 0$ **d.** $x(7x - 13) = 0$

10. Is each statement true or false? Explain.

    a. If the product of two integers is divisible by 5, one of the integers is also divisible by 5.

    b. If the product of two integers is divisible by 6, one of the integers is also divisible by 6.

    c. If the product of two real numbers is 5, one of the numbers is 5.

    d. If the product of two expressions is $x^2 - 4$, one of the expressions is $x^2 - 4$.

    e. If the product of two expressions is $x^2 + 4$, one of the expressions is $x^2 + 4$.

11. Consider these two identities. Are they different? Explain.

    A. $(x + a)(x + b) = x^2 + (a + b)x + ab$

    B. $(x - a)(x - b) = x^2 - (a + b)x + ab$

12. Use Exercise 11. Factor $x^2 + 5x + 6$.

13. **Standardized Test Prep** Austin factored the polynomial $15x^2 + x - 28$ into the product $(3x - 4)(5x + 7)$. What are the solutions to the equation $15x^2 + x - 28 = 0$?

    A. $\left\{\frac{4}{3}, -\frac{4}{3}\right\}$ **B.** $\left\{-\frac{5}{7}, \frac{4}{3}\right\}$ **C.** $\left\{-\frac{4}{3}, \frac{7}{5}\right\}$ **D.** $\left\{\frac{4}{3}, -\frac{7}{5}\right\}$

14. **Write About It** Which equation is more difficult to solve? Explain.

    $(2x + 7)(5x - 4) = 0$ $(x - 3)(x - 4) = 20$

Go **Online**
www.successnetplus.com

15. Find an equation with only the solutions listed.

    a. 3 and 5 **b.** −3 and 5 **c.** −3 and −5 **d.** −3, −5, and 0

16. Find two numbers with a sum that is the first number and a product that is the second number.

    a. 3, 2 **b.** 7, 10 **c.** 100, 196 **d.** 3, $\frac{5}{4}$

Go **Online**
Video Tutor
www.successnetplus.com

Transforming Expressions

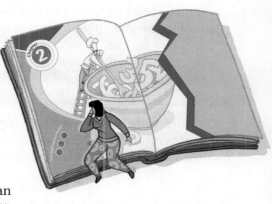

You can use transformations to simplify calculations and show that two expressions are equivalent. For reference, here is a list of some basic rules.

The Commutative Property for Addition The order in which you add expressions in a sum does not affect the result.

In symbols, for any two expressions a and b,

$$a + b = b + a.$$

The Associative Property for Addition If you are adding more than two expressions, the order in which you group them does not matter.

For any three expressions a, b, and c,

$$(a + b) + c = a + (b + c).$$

The Commutative Property for Multiplication The order in which you multiply expressions in a product does not affect the result.

For any two expressions a and b,

$$a \cdot b = b \cdot a, \text{ or } ab = ba.$$

The Associative Property for Multiplication If you are multiplying more than two expressions, the order in which you group them does not matter.

For any three expressions a, b, and c,

$$(a \cdot b) \cdot c = a \cdot (b \cdot c), \text{ or } (ab)c = a(bc).$$

The Distributive Property Multiplying an expression by a sum is the same as multiplying the expression by each term in the sum and adding the results.

For any three expressions a, b, and c,

$$a(b + c) = ab + ac.$$

In this chapter, you will often use the Distributive Property "backward." For instance, if you see something that looks like $ab + ac$, you can undistribute the a and write it as $a(b + c)$. Remember, to factor a polynomial means to pull out, or undistribute, a common factor of the terms.

> The expressions ab and ac have a common factor of a.

For example, the terms in the expression $6x^2 + 4ax^2 - 2bx^3$ have a common factor of $2x^2$. By the Distributive Property, this identity is true.

$$6x^2 + 4ax^2 - 2bx^3 = 2x^2(3 + 2a - bx)$$

> They also have a common factor of 2, x, $2x$, or x^2. However, $2x^2$ is the most you can pull out, so $2x^2$ is the **greatest common factor**.

As you learned in Lesson 2.03, it is easier to use the factored form of an expression to solve equations. You can use ZPP after you transform the original expression to the product $2x^2 (3 + 2a - bx)$.

You can use an expansion box to factor $6x^2 + 4ax^2 - 2bx^3$. Using the greatest common factor $2x^2$, you can find the other part of the product by working backward.

	■	■	■
$2x^2$	$6x^2$	$4ax^2$	$-2bx^3$

Check your work by expanding the result. The expanded expression matches the original expression.

Developing Habits of Mind

Consider more than one strategy. You have used the Distributive Property to make arithmetic calculations easier. Each step is easier because you break one multiplication into two multiplications and an addition.

$$65 \times 103 = 65(100 + 3)$$
$$= 65 \times 100 + 65 \times 3$$
$$= 6500 + 195$$
$$= 6695$$

Similarly, sometimes it is easier to break up a sum of products into one product using the Distributive Property. Multiplication is usually more difficult than addition, unless you multiply by a number such as 10 or 100. You can reduce the number of multiplications in a product to reduce the difficulty of the computations. Which of the following do you prefer to do?

$$57 \times 64 + 57 \times 16 \circ \circ \circ \circ \circ 57(64 + 16)$$

You can also use the Distributive Property on expressions. One reason to write an expression as a product instead of a sum of products is so you can use ZPP. This allows you to find out when the expression equals 0.

Example

Problem What values of a and b make $6ab^2 = 24a$ true?

Solution To solve, subtract $24a$ from each side. Pull out the common factor $6a$.

$$6ab^2 = 24a$$
$$6ab^2 - 24a = 0$$
$$6a(b^2 - 4) = 0$$
$$6a = 0 \text{ or } b^2 - 4 = 0$$

If $6a = 0$, then $a = 0$. What property makes this statement true?
If $b^2 - 4 = 0$, b must be either 2 or -2. Why is this statement true?

You cannot divide by a, because it might be zero! What values of b make $b^2 - 4 = 0$?

Go Online
www.successnetplus.com

For You to Do

1. For what values of x and y does $3xy = y^2$?

Exercises *Practicing Habits of Mind*

Check Your Understanding

1. Find the greatest common factor.

Sample $9x^3$ and $6x^2$

Solution $9x^3 = 3 \cdot 3 \cdot x \cdot x \cdot x$

$6x^2 = 2 \cdot 3 \cdot x \cdot x$

The expressions $9x^3$ and $6x^2$ have one 3 and two x's in common. The greatest common factor is $3x^2$.

a. $9x^3$ and $15x^2$

b. $9x^3$ and $36x$

c. $15a^2$ and $21b^2$

d. x^2 and y^2

e. ab and ac

f. ab, ac, and bc

g. p^3q^4 and p^2q^5

h. p^2q^4 and p^7q

i. p^3q^4, p^2q^5, and p^7q

j. $9(x+3)^3$ and $6(x+3)^2$

2. Write each expression as a product of two expressions. One expression is the greatest common factor of the terms. If there is no common factor, then the answer is the original expression.

Sample $9x^3 + 6x^2 = 3x^2(3x + 2)$

a. $9x^3 - 15x^2$

b. $9x^3 - 36x$

c. $15a^2 + 21b^2$

d. $x^2 + y^2$

e. $ab - ac$

f. $ab + ac + bc$

g. $p^3q^4 + p^2q^5 - p^7q$

> Do the terms look familiar? Recall Exercise 1.

3. Find all solutions to each equation. Use factoring and ZPP.

a. $9x^3 + 6x^2 = 0$

b. $9x^3 = 15x^2$

c. $9x^3 - 36x = 0$

d. $ab = ac$

e. $x^2 = 100x$

f. $x^2 + y^2 = 0$

4. Write the expression $2x(3x + 7) - 3(3x + 7)$ as a product.

> Why is the expression $2x(3x + 7) - 3(3x + 7)$ not a product?

5. Write each expression as a product of expressions.

   a. $3ax + 5bx$

   b. $3ax^2 + 5bx^2$

   c. $3a(x + 7) + 5b(x + 7)$

   d. $3ax + 21a + 5bx + 35b$

   e. $a(x + 1) + b(x + 1)$

   f. $x(a + b) + (a + b)$

6. **a.** Without using parentheses, write an expression equivalent to $x^2(x + 1) + x + 1$.

   b. Factor $x^3 + x^2 + x + 1$ into a product of two expressions.

7. The region between two circles with the same center is an **annulus**. Use the formula $A = \pi r^2$ for the area of a circle. Show that the area of the annulus is $\pi(R - r)(R + r)$.

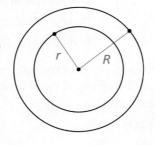

8. You can make a cylinder with a rectangle and two congruent circles. The rectangle's length is the circumference of the end circles. The width of the rectangle is the height of the cylinder.

The formula for the circumference of a circle is $C = 2\pi r$. The formula for the area of a circle is $A = \pi r^2$.

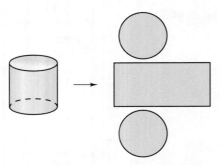

   a. Explain how you can calculate the total surface area of the cylinder.

   b. The total surface area is given by the formula below. Use common factors to find another expression for the total surface area.

   $$SA = 2\pi rh + 2\pi r^2$$

   c. **Take It Further** You can describe the total surface area of a cylindrical can as a product. Describe the factors in terms of measurements you can make.

Go **Online**
www.successnetplus.com

9. Standardized Test Prep Factor the expression $3x^3 - 5x^2 + 6x - 10$ into a product of two expressions.

Go Online
www.successnetplus.com

A. $(x^2 + 2)(3x - 5)$

B. $(x + 2)(3x^2 - 5)$

C. $(x^2 - 2)(3x + 5)$

D. $(x - 2)(3x - 5)$

Historical Perspective
Fermat Primes

In 1650, Pierre de Fermat conjectured that any number in the form $F(n) = 2^{2^n} + 1$ is prime, where n is a whole number $\{0, 1, 2, 3, \ldots\}$. He proved that the formula always produces primes if n has a value of 0, 1, 2, 3, or 4.

It also seemed to Fermat that the next number in the sequence (5) would produce a prime. Fermat therefore conjectured that all the numbers in the sequence are prime, but he never wrote a complete proof. Today, we call any number in the form $2^{2^n} + 1$ a Fermat number. A Fermat prime is a Fermat number that is prime.

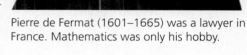

Pierre de Fermat (1601–1665) was a lawyer in France. Mathematics was only his hobby.

Mathematicians did not disprove his conjecture for many years. In 1732, Leonhard Euler found that

$$F(5) = 2^{32} + 1 = 4{,}294{,}967{,}297 = 641 \cdot 6{,}700{,}417$$

This calculation is easy today using a calculator, but Euler had to make hundreds of calculations without a calculator.

Euler narrowed the possibilities by finding the numbers that are most likely to be factors of $2^{32} + 1$. He discovered that only primes of the form $p = 32k + 1$ divided evenly into $2^{32} + 1$. Using this smaller set of possibilities, Euler used the guess-and-check method until he found the factors $k = 20$ and $p = 641$.

After the inventions of the calculator and the computer, mathematicians found the complete prime factorizations for the Fermat numbers up to $n = 11$. Mathematicians now believe that the only Fermat primes are $F(0)$ to $F(4)$. However, no one has proved this conjecture.

For Exercises 10 and 11, expand each expression.

10. a. $(x - 1)(x^5 + x^4 + x^3 + x^2 + x + 1)$

   b. $(x - 1)(x^7 + x^6 + x^5 + x^4 + x^3 + x^2 + x + 1)$

   c. $(x - 1)(x^9 + x^8 + x^7 + x^6 + x^5 + x^4 + x^3 + x^2 + x + 1)$

   d. $(x - 1)(x^4 + x^3 + x^2 + x + 1)$

11. a. $(x - 1)(x^4 + x^2 + 1)(x + 1)$

   b. $(x - 1)(x^6 + x^4 + x^2 + 1)(x + 1)$

   c. $(x - 1)(x^8 + x^6 + x^4 + x^2 + 1)(x + 1)$

12. Take It Further Consider the following.

$$x^3 + x^2 + x + 1 = x^2(x + 1) + (x + 1)$$
$$= (x + 1)(x^2 + 1)$$

Factor each expression if possible.

   a. $x^5 + x^4 + x^3 + x^2 + x + 1$

   b. $x^7 + x^6 + x^5 + x^4 + x^3 + x^2 + x + 1$

   c. $x^9 + x^8 + x^7 + x^6 + x^5 + x^4 + x^3 + x^2 + x + 1$

   d. $x^4 + x^3 + x^2 + x + 1$

13. Show that each statement is true.

   a. $x^3 + 1 = (x + 1)(x^2 - x + 1)$

   b. $x^5 + 1 = (x + 1)(x^4 - x^3 + x^2 - x + 1)$

   c. $x^7 + 1 = (x + 1)(x^6 - x^5 + x^4 - x^3 + x^2 - x + 1)$

   d. $x^9 + 1 = (x + 1)(x^8 - x^7 + x^6 - x^5 + x^4 - x^3 + x^2 - x + 1)$

14. Suppose that k is an odd integer greater than 1. Prove that $2^k + 1$ is divisible by 3 and is not a prime number.

15. A source for large primes are the so-called "Mersenne Primes." These prime numbers are in the form $2^n - 1$. For example, $2^3 - 1 = 7$, so 7 is a Mersenne prime. Not all numbers of this form are prime. For example, $2^4 - 1 = 15$, but 15 is not prime.

Make a table of output values for $2^n - 1$. Is there any pattern to the values of n that produce prime numbers and those that do not? Explain.

Mathematical 2A Reflections

In this investigation, you learned to use basic rules and moves to transform expressions. You also factored expressions and applied the Zero-Product Property to factored expressions. These questions will help you summarize what you have learned.

1. Use the polynomial $x^2 + xy - 6y^2$.
   a. Show that $(x - 2y)(x + 3y) = x^2 + xy - 6y^2$.
   b. If $x = 6$, find a value of y that makes $x^2 + xy - 6y^2 = 0$.
   c. If $y = 3$, find a value of x that makes $x^2 + xy - 6y^2$ a multiple of 11.

2. The following function $t(x)$ is defined by a messy rule. Find each value.
$$t(x) = (x + 1)(x^2 - 2x + 3) + 2x(x^2 + 5x - 1)$$
   a. $t(0)$ **b.** $t(1)$ **c.** $t(-2)$
   d. Expand the expressions in this function. Write a simpler rule for $t(x)$.

3. Use ZPP. Find all the solutions to each equation.
   a. $(x - 2)(x + 1) = 0$ **b.** $(2x - 3)(x + 5) = 0$
   c. $3x(x + 8) = 0$ **d.** $x^2 - 4x = 0$

4. What is the greatest common factor of each set of expressions?
   a. $8x^3$ and $12x$ **b.** $24x^2$ and $16x^3$
   c. a^3b^2, a^8b, and a^4b^5c **d.** $10(x + 2)^3$ and $15(x + 2)^4$

5. Solve for x in each equation. Use factoring and ZPP.
   a. $3x^3 + 9x^2 = 0$ **b.** $4x^3 = 8x^2$
   c. $x^2 = 49x$ **d.** $x^3 = 49x$
   e. $a(x - 2) + b(x - 2) = 0$ **f.** $x(a + 2b) + a + 2b = 0$

6. How do you determine whether two different expressions define the same function?

7. When is it useful to write an expression as a product of expressions?

8. How do you write $3ab - 15a + b - 5$ as a product of two expressions?

About how much closer to the target is the skydiver in this photo than the sky diver in the photo on page 64?

Vocabulary

In this investigation, you learned these terms. Make sure you understand what each one means and how to use it.

- annulus
- expand an expression
- factor an expression
- greatest common factor
- identity

Investigation 2B

Polynomials and Their Arithmetic

In *Polynomials and Their Arithmetic*, you will study some details of polynomials. You will be able to define polynomials. You will also add and multiply polynomials, and learn some conventions for writing them.

By the end of this investigation, you will be able to answer questions like these.

1. How can you decide whether two polynomials are equivalent?

2. How is a polynomial useful for describing a rule?

3. Suppose you roll three number cubes numbered 1–6. What is the probability of rolling a total of 12?

You will learn how to

- recognize and provide examples of polynomials

- understand the definitions and importance of the terms *coefficient* and *degree*

- expand polynomials and express them in normal form

- determine whether polynomials in different forms are equivalent

- add, subtract, and multiply polynomials

You will develop these habits and skills:

- Use substitution to make new identities.

- Use the language of polynomials to understand their properties.

- Use the basic rules of algebra to calculate with polynomial expressions.

- Use the Distributive Property to expand polynomials.

If track lanes are 4 ft wide, the polynomial $2\pi(R + 4) - 2\pi R$ tells you the difference in lengths between two lanes that are next to each other.

2.05 Getting Started

You can describe many situations using polynomials. For example, there is a relationship between the probability of rolling a certain sum with number cubes and a polynomial with corresponding exponents. After you learn the properties of polynomials, you can use polynomials to solve problems.

For You to Explore

1. Each face on a standard six-sided number cube has a number from 1 to 6. Suppose you roll two number cubes and want to find the probability of getting a certain sum. You can use a table to determine the number of outcomes. Copy and complete the table.

	1	2	3	4	5	6
1	■	■	■	■	■	■
2	■	■	■	6	■	■
3	■	■	■	■	■	■
4	5	■	■	■	■	■
5	■	■	■	■	■	■
6	■	■	■	■	■	■

> In this table, the row and column headers indicate the number rolled on each number cube. The numbers in the table are the sums of the numbers rolled.

2. Refer to the table in Problem 1.

   a. What is the most likely sum when rolling two number cubes? How many ways can you roll this sum?

   b. What is the probability of rolling a sum of 8?

   c. What is the probability of rolling a sum of at least 11?

3. Use an expansion box to expand $(x + x^2 + x^3 + x^4 + x^5 + x^6)^2$.

> Find the product of $(x + x^2 + x^3 + x^4 + x^5 + x^6)$ and $(x + x^2 + x^3 + x^4 + x^5 + x^6)$.

4. Refer to the expansion box in Problem 3.

   a. Which power of x occurs most often?

   b. How many x^8 terms are there?

   c. How many terms have exponents of 11 or higher?

5. **Write About It** Describe the relationship between the table in Problem 1 and the expansion box in Problem 3. How is the expression $(x + x^2 + x^3 + x^4 + x^5 + x^6)$ related to rolling a number cube? Why is the expression squared?

6. **Write About It** Describe how you can use expansion boxes to answer the following question. How many different ways are there to throw three number cubes and roll a total of 10?

Exercises Practicing Habits of Mind

7. George shows you an unusual pair of number cubes. The first cube has faces 1, 3, 4, 5, 6, and 8. The second cube has faces 1, 2, 2, 3, 3, and 4. George says something interesting happens if you look at the sum of two cubes.

Copy and complete the table. What might George have found surprising?

	1	3	4	5	6	8
1	▪	▪	▪	▪	▪	▪
2	▪	▪	▪	7	▪	▪
2	▪	▪	▪	▪	▪	▪
3	▪	6	▪	▪	▪	▪
3	▪	▪	▪	▪	▪	▪
4	▪	▪	▪	▪	▪	▪

8. Find the product using any method.

$$(x + x^3 + x^4 + x^5 + x^6 + x^8)(x + 2x^2 + 2x^3 + x^4)$$

9. State whether each equation is an identity.

a. $16a^2 - 9b^2 \stackrel{?}{=} (4a + 3b)(4a - 3b)$

b. $8n^2 - 4 \stackrel{?}{=} (4n + 2)(4n - 2)$

c. $25 - t^6 \stackrel{?}{=} (5 + t^3)(5 - t^3)$

d. $m^4n^2 - m^2n^4 \stackrel{?}{=} (m^2n + mn^2)(m^2n - mn^2)$

e. $n^3 - 100 \stackrel{?}{=} (n^2 + 10)(n - 10)$

f. $a^2 + 2ab + b^2 - 1 \stackrel{?}{=} (a + b - 1)(a + b + 1)$

10. **Take It Further** Show that this statement is true for any choice of a, b, and c.

$$2a^2c^2 + 2a^2b^2 + 2b^2c^2 - (a^4 + b^4 + c^4) =$$
$$(a + b - c)(a + b + c)(a + c - b)(b + c - a)$$

For Exercises 11 and 12, decide whether the conjecture must be true. If you think it must be true, prove it using the basic rules. If you think it may not be true, explain why.

11. Here are examples of odd numbers added together.

$$1 + 3 = 4 \qquad\qquad 5 + 7 = 12$$

$$3 + 11 = 14 \qquad\qquad 101 + 83 = 184$$

Conjecture: The sum of two odd numbers must be an even number.

12. Here are examples of odd numbers that are the sums of two consecutive integers.

$$3 = 1 + 2 \qquad\qquad 11 = 5 + 6$$

$$23 = 11 + 12 \qquad\qquad 831 = 415 + 416$$

Conjecture: It is always possible to express an odd number as the sum of two consecutive integers.

Remember...

You can write every even number as $2n$ for some integer n. You can write every odd number as $2n + 1$ for some integer n.

Maintain Your Skills

For Exercises 13 and 14, expand each product.

13. **a.** $(1 + x)(1 - x)$ **b.** $(1 + x)(1 - x + x^2)$
    c. $(1 + x)(1 - x + x^2 - x^3)$

14. **a.** $(a - b)(a + b)$ **b.** $(a - b)(a^2 + ab + b^2)$
    c. $(a - b)(a^3 + a^2b + ab^2 + b^3)$

These exercises are similar to those in Lesson 2.01.

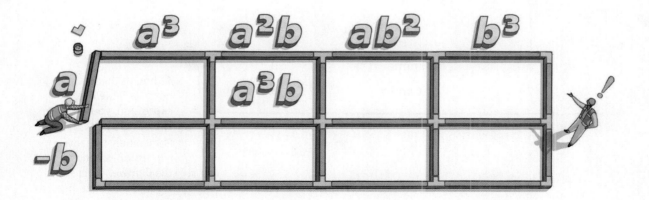

2.06 Anatomy of a Polynomial

It can be difficult to understand the definition of a polynomial without first seeing some examples. The following are all polynomials.

$$x^2 - 1 \qquad\qquad 3x + 5y + 1 \qquad\qquad 2x^3 - 9x^4 - 3x + 2$$

$$\frac{6}{7}x^3 - 8x^2 + 1 \qquad\qquad \frac{3}{7}x + \frac{1}{2} \qquad\qquad y^2 - x^3 - xy$$

$$x \qquad\qquad x^3 - 8x^2 + 1 \qquad\qquad 3$$

As you can see from the examples, a polynomial is a sum of one or more terms. Each term is called a monomial.

Definitions

A **monomial** is the product of a number, the **coefficient,** and one or more variables raised to nonnegative integer powers.

> The coefficient can be any real number. Most of the polynomials you will work with in this chapter will have integer or rational coefficients.

The **degree of a monomial** with only one variable is the exponent of the variable. If a monomial has more than one variable, the degree is the sum of the exponents of each variable.

Example 1

Problem Name the coefficient, variable, and degree of each monomial.

  a. $3x^2$ **b.** $-4a^5$ **c.** b^3

  d. $-\frac{1}{2}$ **e.** $7x^3y^5$

Solution

		Coefficient	Variable	Degree
a.	$3x^2$	3	x	2
b.	$-4a^5$	-4	a	5
c.	b^3	1	b	3
d.	$-\frac{1}{2}$	$-\frac{1}{2}$	none	0
e.	$7x^3y^5$	7	x and y	$3 + 5 = 8$

> Although there is not a variable in the expression, you can write $-\frac{1}{2}$ as $-\frac{1}{2}x^0$. Remember that any expression raised to the 0 power equals 1. Also, you can use any variable in this expression since there is not any context given.

You can define a polynomial as the sum of any number of monomials like these. Sometimes, a polynomial is made up of only one monomial.

	Coefficient	**Variables**	**Degree**
$7x^3y^5$	7	x, y	3 in x 5 in y

Definition

A **polynomial** is a monomial or a sum of two or more monomials.

Facts and Notation

There are many conventions for polynomials—conventions that have to do with the way people prefer to do things rather than with the algebra. You will use the following conventions in this book.

- Coefficients can be any real number. However, most of the polynomials in this book will have integer coefficients. Unless explicitly stated otherwise, assume that all coefficients are integers.

- Polynomials can have any number of variables. However, most polynomials in this book are of one variable. Unless explicitly stated otherwise, assume that *polynomial* means a polynomial of a single variable.

You can think of a polynomial such as $ax^2 + bx + c$ as a polynomial in 4 variables: *a*, *b*, *c*, and *x*. However, in most cases in this book, the polynomial is in *x*, with the other letters being unknown coefficients. The text is explicit about which letters are variables and which letters are unknown coefficients.

An unknown coefficient is also known as a **parameter**.

Definition

The **degree of a polynomial** is the greatest degree among all the monomials in the polynomial.

Here are some examples.

- $13x^5 - 9x^3 + \frac{2}{5}x^2 + \frac{1}{7}x - 13$ has degree 5.
- $\frac{13}{2}y - 4y^2 + 9$ has degree 2.
- $2s$ has degree 1.
- 17 has degree 0 $\left(\text{think of } 17x^0\right)$.

There are special names for some polynomials in one variable.

Degree	Type of Polynomial
1	linear
2	quadratic
3	cubic
4	quartic
5	quintic

For Discussion

Find polynomials that satisfy each condition. If it is impossible to satisfy the condition, explain why.

1. a cubic polynomial with three terms, all of different degrees

2. a linear polynomial with two terms, both of different degrees

3. a linear polynomial with three terms, all of different degrees

Polynomials have an arithmetic that is very similar to the arithmetic of numbers. In fact, since each variable is just a placeholder for a number, you might expect that all of the operations of number arithmetic would apply to polynomials. You may also think the basic rules apply the same way.

For You to Do

For Problems 4–7, is each result always a polynomial? Explain.

4. sum of two polynomials

5. product of two polynomials

6. difference of two polynomials

7. quotient of two polynomials

Adding polynomials is like adding any expressions. You combine the like terms to make a simplified expression. Two terms in a polynomial are like terms when they meet the following conditions.

- All variables are the same.
- The exponents of the variables are the same.

Terms	Variable	Exponent	Like Terms
$7x^3$	x	3	
$3x^3$	x	3	yes
$2x^5$	x	5	
$11x$	x	1	no
x^2	x	2	
$3y^2$	y	2	no

The expressions $3x^3$ and $3x^4$ are not like terms even though they have the same coefficient. Explain.

Example 2

Problem Calculate the sum and product of $x^2 - 6x + 5$ and $3x + 7$.

Solution Calculate the sum by combining like terms.

$$
\begin{aligned}
(x^2 - 6x + 5) + (3x + 7) &= (x^2 - 6x + 5) + (3x + 7) \\
&= x^2 - 6x + 3x + 5 + 7 \\
&= x^2 + (-6 + 3)x + (5 + 7) \\
&= x^2 - 3x + 12
\end{aligned}
$$

Calculate the product by expanding. Then collect like terms.

$$
\begin{aligned}
(x^2 - 6x + 5)(3x + 7) &= 3x(x^2 - 6x + 5) + 7(x^2 - 6x + 5) \\
&= 3x^3 - 18x^2 + 15x + 7x^2 - 42x + 35 \\
&= 3x^3 + ((-18) + 7)x^2 + (15 - 42)x + 35 \\
&= 3x^3 - 11x^2 - 27x + 35
\end{aligned}
$$

> Expand by multiplying everything in the first polynomial by $3x$. Then multiply by 7 and combine. What is another way to expand?

For Discussion

8. Which basic rules of algebra do you use to combine like terms?

For You to Do

9. What's Wrong Here? Jacob and Anna subtracted these polynomials. They got different answers.

$$3x^2 - 7x + 1 \text{ and } 10x^3 - x^2 + 3x$$

Jacob

$$
\begin{aligned}
(3x^2 - 7x + 1) - (10x^3 - x^2 + 3x) &= 3x^2 - 7x + 1 - 10x^3 - x^2 + 3x \\
&= -10x^3 + 2x^2 - 4x + 1
\end{aligned}
$$

Anna

$$
\begin{aligned}
(3x^2 - 7x + 1) - (10x^3 - x^2 + 3x) &= 3x^2 - 7x + 1 - 10x^3 + x^2 - 3x \\
&= -10x^3 + 4x^2 - 10x + 1
\end{aligned}
$$

Who is correct? What mistake did the other person make?

> **Habits of Mind**
>
> **Check your work.** Plug any number into the two expressions and subtract the results. Then plug the same number into each of the answers that Jacob and Anna found. If the results are different, you know that the answer is incorrect. If they are the same, you have evidence that they might be correct.

For You to Do

Expand each expression. Combine like terms to get a polynomial answer. Be careful of negative signs!

10. $3x^2 - 7x + 1 - 2(10x^3 - x^2 + 3x)$

11. $(3x - 1)(x^2 + 2x + 5)$

In-Class Experiment

Develop two theorems that answer the following questions.

12. How is the degree of the product of two nonzero polynomials related to the degrees of the polynomials that you are multiplying?

13. How is the degree of the sum of two nonzero polynomials related to the degrees of the polynomials that you are adding?

Here are some polynomials that you can use to develop your theorems.

- $x^2 + 4x + 5$
- $-2x^5 + 7x - 1$
- $3x + 7$
- $7x^3 - 2x^2 + 1$
- $2x^5 + 5$
- $14x$
- 9
- $x^9 + x^3 + 1$
- $4x^3 + 2x + 1$

> Why is it important that the polynomials be nonzero?

Exercises *Practicing Habits of Mind*

Check Your Understanding

1. Find two polynomials with a sum and product that have the following degrees. If you cannot find the polynomials, explain why.

a. The sum has degree 3 and the product has degree 6.

b. The sum has degree 4 and the product has degree 2.

c. The sum has degree 4 and the product has degree 4.

d. The sum has degree 2 and the product has degree 1.

2. Take It Further Find two polynomials with a sum that has degree 1 and a product that has degree 4. If you cannot find the two polynomials, explain why.

3. a. Find two polynomials with the same degree that have a sum of $3x^2 + 7x + 4$.

b. Find two polynomials with different degrees that have a sum of $3x^2 + 7x + 4$.

c. Find two polynomials that have a sum of 4.

d. Find two polynomials that have a product of $x^2 - 1$.

4. Write About It How does the degree of a polynomial compare to the degree of that polynomial squared? Support your conjecture with at least three examples.

On Your Own

5. Find two polynomials that meet each condition.

a. The product has degree 6.

b. The product has degree 1.

c. The sum has degree 4 and the product has degree 6.

6. a. Use $p(x) = x^2 + 4x + 9$. Find a polynomial $r(x)$ such that $p(x) + r(x) = 2x^2 - 6x + 14$.

b. Find a polynomial $s(x)$ such that $p(x) + s(x) = 2x^2 + 14$.

c. Find a polynomial $t(x)$ such that $p(x) + t(x)$ has degree 2 and $p(x) \cdot t(x)$ has degree 3.

7. Find the value of a such that $(x + a)(x + 3) = x^2 + 5x + 6$ is an identity. Copying and completing the expansion box at the right may be helpful.

	x	$+3$
x		
a		

8. Standardized Test Prep Use $q(x) = 2x - 3$ and $r(x) = 2x^2 + 3x - 5$. Find $s(x) = q(x) + r(x)$ and $p(x) = q(x) \cdot r(x)$.

A. $s(x) = 2x^2 + 5x + 8$ and $p(x) = 4x^3 + 12x^2 - 19x + 15$

B. $s(x) = 2x^2 + 5x + 8$ and $p(x) = 4x^3 - x + 15$

C. $s(x) = 2x^2 + 5x - 8$ and $p(x) = 4x^3 - 19x + 15$

D. $s(x) = 2x^2 + 5x - 8$ and $p(x) = 4x^3 - 19x - 15$

Go Online
www.successnetplus.com

9. Write About It Suppose you need to explain the phrase *like terms* to a student who has never heard it before. Write a definition of like terms. Explain how you add and subtract them. Be as precise as possible.

10. Suppose you make a frame for a square photo. The frame is 2 inches wide. Find the area of the frame if the photo has the following dimensions.

The area of the border does not include the area of the picture.

a. 3 in. by 3 in.

b. 9 in. by 9 in.

c. x in. by x in.

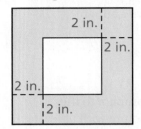

If each side of the photo is 6 inches, the area of the border is $(6 + 4)^2 - 6^2$ square inches.

Maintain Your Skills

For Exercises 11–13, expand and combine like terms.

11. a. $(x + 1)^2 - x^2$ **b.** $(x + 1)^3 - x^3$

     c. $(x + 1)^4 - x^4$ **d.** $(x + 1)^5 - x^5$

12. a. $(x + y)^2 - y^2$ **b.** $(x + y)^3 - y^3$

     c. $(x + y)^4 - y^4$

13. a. $x(x - 1) + x$ **b.** $x(x - 1)(x - 2) + x(x - 1)$

     c. $x(x - 1)(x - 2)(x - 3) + x(x - 1)(x - 2)$

2.07 Normal Form

Since polynomials are expressions, you can transform them with the basic rules. The reason for transforming polynomials is to find equivalent expressions. For example, if you expand $(x - 1)(x + 1)$, you get $x^2 - 1$. You have derived an identity. Therefore, the expressions are equal for any substitution.

$$(x - 1)(x + 1) = x^2 - 1$$

If you replace x with any number or expression, the resulting statement is true.

Remember...

Sometimes you can transform two expressions into each other using the basic rules of algebra. A statement where the two expressions are equivalent is an identity.

For You to Do

Explain how each fact follows from the above identity.

1. $3 \cdot 5 = 4^2 - 1$

2. Choose a number. Add 1 to it. Subtract 1 from the original number. Multiply your results. The result is one less than the square of the original number.

3. $a(a + 2) = (a + 1)^2 - 1$

4. The only values of x that make $x^2 - 1 = 0$ are 1 and -1.

How can you determine if an equation is an identity? In previous chapters, you transformed one side of an equation to match the other side. When you work with polynomials, it is sometimes easier to expand and collect like terms on each side of the equation. Then you order the terms of each polynomial in the same way. If polynomials are in the same form, or normal form, it is easy to see whether they are equivalent.

Minds in Action

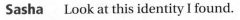

Sasha thinks she has found a new identity. She explains it to Tony.

Sasha Look at this identity I found.

$$(x + 1)(x^2 + 2x + 1) = x(3 + 3x + x^2) + 1$$

Tony That can't be true in all cases! What if x is 4?

Sasha The left side equals this.

$$(4 + 1)(4^2 + 2(4) + 1) = (5)(16 + 8 + 1)$$
$$= (5)(25)$$
$$= 125$$

Tony The right side equals this.

$$4(3 + 3(4) + 4^2) + 1 = 4(3 + 12 + 16) + 1$$
$$= 4(31) + 1$$
$$= 124 + 1$$
$$= 125$$

Sasha Both sides are equal. The identity is true.

Tony It might have been a coincidence. How are you sure the two sides will be equal for every number?

Sasha Let's expand and simplify each side. Expand the left side.

$$(x + 1)(x^2 + 2x + 1) = x(x^2 + 2x + 1) + 1(x^2 + 2x + 1)$$
$$= x(x^2) + x(2x) + x(1) + 1(x^2) + 1(2x) + 1(1)$$
$$= x^3 + 2x^2 + x + x^2 + 2x + 1$$
$$= x^3 + 3x^2 + 3x + 1$$

Tony When I expand the right side, I get this.

$$x(3 + 3x + x^2) + 1 = (x(3) + x(3x) + x(x^2)) + 1$$
$$= (3x + 3x^2 + x^3) + 1$$
$$= x^3 + 3x^2 + 3x + 1$$

The two polynomials expand to the same thing. It's an identity!

Sasha Didn't I tell you?

For Discussion

5. Suppose Sasha says "The right side is the same as the left side. They're just in a different order." Can you think of a method for organizing polynomials to make them easier to compare?

6. Show that $(x + 1)^3$ is equivalent to both of Sasha's polynomials.

For You to Do

7. Are the following polynomial expressions equivalent?

$$3x + 7x^4 - 2x^2 - 6 + 3x^2 - x^4 + 2$$
$$\overset{?}{=} -10 + 2(3x^4 + 2x^2 + x) - (3x^2 - x) + 6$$

You may have noticed that polynomials often appear with the monomial with the greatest degree at the beginning. For instance, you generally see $7x^3 - 3x^2 + \frac{1}{2}x + 5$ instead of $5 - 3x^2 + \frac{1}{2}x + 7x^3$.

In the first expression, $7x^3 - 3x^2 + \frac{1}{2}x + 5$, the term with the greatest exponent comes first. The term with the second-greatest exponent follows, and so on.

> Although $7x^3$ has a greater degree than $\frac{1}{2}x$, $7x^3$ might not have a greater value for every value of x. It depends on what value you substitute for x.

Definition

To write a polynomial in one variable in normal form, expand it completely and arrange the monomials by degree from greatest to least.

> There are different, acceptable definitions of normal form. Some mathematicians prefer to write the degrees from least to greatest.

Here are a few examples.

- $7x^3 - 3x^2 + \frac{1}{2}x + 5$ normal form
- $5 - 3x^2 + \frac{1}{2}x - 7x^3$ not normal form
- $(y^2 + 1)(y - 1)$ not normal form
- $x^2 - 3x + 9$ normal form

For You to Do

8. Explain why each polynomial in the above list is or is not in normal form. If the polynomial is not in normal form, rewrite it in normal form.

Developing Habits of Mind

Look for a relationship between numbers and polynomials. The normal form of a polynomial is similar to the standard way you write numbers. For instance, it is confusing to say 9378 as three hundred, nine thousand, eight, and seventy. Instead, you say nine thousand, three hundred, seventy-eight.

The same is true of polynomials. You can write 9378 as $9x^3 + 3x^2 + 7x + 8$, where $x = 10$.

Exercises *Practicing Habits of Mind*

Check Your Understanding

1. Use the polynomial $3 + 4x^2 - 5x + \frac{3}{4}x^5 - 17x^2 + x^4$.

   a. Write the polynomial in normal form.

   b. What is the degree of the polynomial?

   c. What is the coefficient of x?

   d. What is the coefficient of x^2?

   e. What is the coefficient of x^3?

   f. Find a polynomial that when added to this one gives a sum of degree 3.

2. Describe how each polynomial identity is related to the corresponding number fact.

   a. $(x + 5) + (x^2 + 2x + 4) = x^2 + 3x + 9$

   $15 + 124 = 139$

   b. $(x + 1)(x^2 + 2x + 4) = x^3 + 3x^2 + 6x + 4$

   $11 \cdot 124 = 1364$

   c. $(x + 1)^2 = x^2 + 2x + 1$

   $11^2 = 121$

   d. $(x + 1)^3 = x^3 + 3x^2 + 3x + 1$

   $11^3 = 1331$

3. **a.** What is the prime factorization of 120? Of 168?

   b. How can you use the prime factorizations to find the greatest common factor of 120 and 168?

   c. What is the greatest common factor of $273{,}375 = 3^7 \cdot 5^3$ and $140{,}625 = 3^2 \cdot 5^6$?

   d. Suppose x and y are prime numbers. What is the greatest common factor of $x^7 y^3$ and $x^2 y^6$?

   e. What is the greatest common factor of $120x^7 y^3$ and $168x^2 y^6$?

   > How do you find the greatest common factor for monomials?

4. Transform the expression below into normal form. For what values of a is the coefficient of x equal to 0?

   $$(x^2 + 3x + a)(x^2 + 3x - 7)$$

For Exercises 5–10, complete each of the following.

- Calculate three numeric examples that follow from each identity by substituting a number for each variable.

- Prove each identity is true. Use the basic rules of algebra.

5. $x^6 - 1 = (x^3 - 1)(x^3 + 1)$

6. $x^6 - 1 = (x - 1)(x + 1)(x^2 + x + 1)(x^2 - x + 1)$

7. $x^6 - 1 = (x^2 - 1)(x^4 + x^2 + 1)$

8. $x^3 - 1 = (x - 1)(x^2 + x + 1)$

9. $(s + t)^2 - (s - t)^2 = 4st$

10. $(n + 1)^2 - n^2 = 2n + 1$

11. Take It Further Show that this equation is an identity.

$$(x^3 - 1)(x^3 + 1) = (x^2 - 1)(x^4 + x^2 + 1)$$

On Your Own

12. Use the identity below. Calculate three numeric examples that follow by substituting for x. Then prove that the identity is true, using the basic rules of algebra.

$$(x^2 - x)(x + 1) = (x^2 + x)(x - 1)$$

13. Here are five equations of polynomials. All the expressions are in normal form. A few of the terms are hidden in each expression.

Three of these cannot be identities. Which three are they? Explain.

A. $3x^3 + \blacksquare + 2x + 1 \stackrel{?}{=} \blacksquare + 2x + 4$

B. $\blacksquare + x^2 - 9 \stackrel{?}{=} x^3 + \blacksquare - 9$

C. $\blacksquare + 3x^2 + \blacksquare + 6 \stackrel{?}{=} x^3 + 3x^2 + \blacksquare$

D. $x^7 + 7x + \blacksquare \stackrel{?}{=} 3x^7 + \blacksquare + 11$

E. $x^2 + \blacksquare + 4 \stackrel{?}{=} \blacksquare + x^2 + \blacksquare$

14. Show that each equation is an identity.

a. $m^2 - n^2 = m(m - n) + n(m - n)$

b. $m(m - n) + n(m - n) = (m + n)(m - n)$

c. $(m + 1)(m - n) + (n - 1)(m - n) = (m + n)(m - n)$

Go Online
www.successnetplus.com

15. **Standardized Test Prep** Which polynomial is NOT equivalent to the other three polynomials?

 A. $(3x^3 + 3x^2 + 6x - 1) - 7(x^2 - 1)$

 B. $(x^2 + 2)(3x - 4)$

 C. $(4x^3 - 4x^2 + 6x - 9) - (x^3 - 1)$

 D. $(x - 1)(3x^2 + 5) + (-x^2 + x - 3)$

16. What is the coefficient of the given term in the normal form of $(x + x^2 + x^3 + x^4 + x^5 + x^6)^2$?

 a. x^8 　　　　　　　　　　　　 **b.** x^{10}

 What is the coefficient of the given term in the normal form of $(x + x^2 + x^3 + x^4 + x^5 + x^6)^3$?

 c. x^{10} 　　　　　　　　　　　 **d.** x^{20}

Maintain Your Skills

17. Find the normal form of each polynomial.

 a. $(1 + x + x^2)(1 + x^3)$

 b. $(1 + x + x^2 + x^3)(1 + x^4)$

 c. $(1 + x + x^2 + x^3 + x^4)(1 + x^5)$

 d. Describe a pattern.

18. Expand each power. Replace x with 1. What is your result?

 a. $(x - 1)^2$ 　　　　 **b.** $(x - 1)^3$ 　　　　 **c.** $(x - 1)^4$

 d. Describe a pattern. Explain why this pattern exists.

19. Write each polynomial in normal form. What is the degree?

 a. $x(x + 1)$ 　　　　　　　　　 **b.** $x(x + 1)(x + 2)$

 c. $x(x + 1)(x + 2)(x + 3)$ 　　　 **d.** $x(x + 1)(x + 2)(x + 3)(x + 4)$

 e. Describe a pattern. Explain why this pattern exists.

20. Write each polynomial in normal form. What is the sum of the coefficients of each polynomial?

 a. $x(x + 1)$ 　　　　　　　　　 **b.** $x(x + 1)(x + 2)$

 c. $x(x + 1)(x + 2)(x + 3)$ 　　　 **d.** $x(x + 1)(x + 2)(x + 3)(x + 4)$

 e. Describe a pattern.

Go Online
Video Tutor
www.successnetplus.com

Arithmetic With Polynomials

Polynomials are a useful language for describing rules or defining functions. Instead of saying "the function that squares its input and adds 1," you can let the polynomial $x^2 + 1$ describe the rule.

In algebra, it is important to consider polynomials as unique mathematical concepts and to learn to calculate with them. You can transform polynomial expressions using the basic rules. Eventually, you will be able to visualize polynomial calculations. You might even be able to predict results without actually completing the computations.

Just as you calculate with numbers to do arithmetic, you calculate with polynomials to do algebra.

When you perform repeated calculations, you train your eye to notice patterns. This practice often leads to very useful theorems.

Minds in Action

Derman shows Tony and Sasha this problem from his algebra book.

Find the coefficient of x^6 in the normal form of
$(3x^2 + 2x + 7)(x^5 + 4x^4 - 2x^3 + 3x + 2)$.

Derman What am I supposed to do with this?

Tony Just multiply everything out. Then look at the coefficient of x^6.

Derman That's a lot of work for such a small question.

Sasha Wait a minute . . . you don't need to multiply it all out. Think about what you'd have to do. Multiply every term in the first polynomial by every term in the second one. Then collect like terms.

Tony Yes, that's exactly what we do with expansion boxes.

Sasha And where would x^6 come from?

Derman If I take $3x^2$ from the first parentheses, I'd have to take $4x^4$ from the second. There's no other way to get a monomial of degree 6.

Sasha So that gives us $(3x^2)(4x^4)$ or $12x^6$. Are there any more combinations?

Derman No, there aren't, if I stick to $3x^2$ from the first polynomial.

Tony We could pick a $2x$ from the first polynomial and match it with x^5 from the second. That would produce another x^6 since $(2x)(x^5) = 2x^6$.

When you perform repeated steps, you train your eye to notice patterns.

Sasha Good work. Any more?

Derman You won't get any more out of $2x$. How about using the 7 from the first polynomial?

Tony You can't get x^6. It doesn't matter what you pick from the second polynomial.

Sasha So, we'll only get two products in the expansion that have degree 6, $12x^6$ from $(3x^2)(4x^4)$, and $2x^6$ from $(2x)(x^5)$. How much do we have in total?

Tony We'll have $12x^6 + 2x^6 = 14x^6$.

Sasha So the coefficient of x^6 in the expansion is 14.

For You to Do

1. Find the coefficient of x^5 in the normal form of
$(3x^2 + 2x + 7)(x^5 + 4x^4 - 2x^3 + 3x + 2)$.

For Discussion

2. Find the values of a and b that make the polynomial $(x - a)(x - b)$ equal to $x^2 - 3x + 2$.

Think of *equal* as "the same."

Exercises *Practicing Habits of Mind*

Check Your Understanding

1. For each equation, find the value of k that makes it true.
   a. $(7x^2 + 2x + k) + (3x + 9) = 7x^2 + 5x + 13$
   b. $(x - 2)(x + k) = x^2 - 4$
   c. $(x^4 - 5x^2 + kx + 2) + (x^2 + 4x - 10) = x^4 - 4x^2 - 6x - 8$
   d. $(x + 2)(x + k) = x^2 + 7x + 10$
   e. $(3x^4 - \frac{1}{3}x^3 + 7x + 5) - (x^4 + kx^3 + 10) = 2x^4 + \frac{1}{6}x^3 + 7x - 5$
   f. $(2x + 1)(kx - 1) = 4x^2 - 1$

2. Without expanding, find the coefficient of x^4 in the normal form of each polynomial.

   a. $(2x^2 + 3x + 5)(x^3 - 1)$ **b.** $(x + 1)^5$

   c. $(x - 1)(x^4 + x^3 + x^2 + x + 1)$

3. **Write About It** Explain how you can find the coefficient of x^3 in $(x + 1)^4$ without expanding.

4. Without expanding the left side, explain why the following equation is definitely not an identity.

   $$(x^3 - 4x^2 + 5x - 7)(x^2 + 4x + 6) = x^6 - 7x^5 + 5x^3 - 4x^2 - 4x - 42$$

5. What is the coefficient of x^3y in $(x + y)^4$?

6. A quadratic polynomial is a polynomial of degree 2. It looks like $ax^2 + bx + c$, where $a \neq 0$. If $a = 1$, $b = 1$, and $c = -6$, the value of this polynomial is 0 when $x = 2$. Find three other possible choices for the numbers a, b, and c that also make the value of the polynomial 0 when $x = 2$.

7. Tony and Derman play a game in the cafeteria. They toss four pennies. If three heads come up, Derman wins. If two heads come up, Tony wins. Otherwise, it is a draw.

   Tony says, "Derman, I think you've got the advantage in this game. You've won 6 times. I've only won twice. There have been 5 draws."

   Derman argues, "You can't tell on the basis of 13 throws. You need about a million throws."

   Tony replies, "Neither of us has time for that. Besides, this is getting tedious."

   Sasha joins them. Tony and Derman fill her in.

   Sasha exclaims, "Algebra to the rescue! Multiply out $(h + t)^4$. You can determine the most likely toss from that."

   Derman agrees, "I guess we could expand $(h + t)^4$ quicker than we could toss a million times."

   Tony asks, "But how does the expansion help us? Why do you want us to use h and t, Sasha?"

   Explain Sasha's method to Tony and Derman.

   Try playing the game. However, experiments are not proof.

8. **Take It Further** Find a quadratic polynomial that defines the function represented in this table.

Input	Output
0	2
1	6
2	12

9. Suppose the sides of a triangle have lengths a, b, and c. A famous formula, proved by Heron of Alexandria in about A.D. 60, states that you can calculate the area of the triangle by this rule.

$$A = \tfrac{1}{4}\sqrt{(a + b + c)(a + b - c)(a + c - b)(b + c - a)}$$

a. Find the area of a triangle with side lengths 13, 14, and 15.

b. **Take It Further** Expand this product.

$$(a + b + c)(a + b - c)(c + a - b)(c - a + b)$$

c. Use Heron's formula to derive a formula for the area of a triangle with sides all the same length.

d. **What's Wrong Here?** What does the formula give for the area of a triangle with side lengths 6, 4, and 10? Explain.

10. **Take It Further** Many geometry books state Heron's formula as follows.

$$A = \sqrt{s(s - a)(s - b)(s - c)}, \text{ where } s = \tfrac{1}{2}(a + b + c)$$

Show that this expression is equivalent to the expression in Exercise 9.

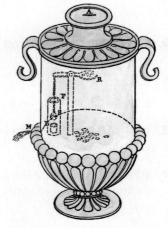

Heron invented the first vending machine. Can you see how inserting a coin would cause the machine to dispense a small amount of water?

On Your Own

11. Without expanding, what is the coefficient of x^4 in the normal form of $(x^2 + 3x^2 + 1)(2x^4 - x^3 + 5x + 2) + (2x^4 - x^3 + 5x + 2)$?

12. The coefficient of x^3 in the normal form of the polynomial below is 18.

$$(x^2 + 3x^2 + 1)(2x^4 - x^3 + 5x + 2) + (2x^4 - x^3 + 5x + 2)$$

What is the coefficient of x^3 in the normal form of $(x^2 + 3x^2 + 1)(2x^4 - x^3 + 5x + 2) - (2x^4 - x^3 + 5x + 2)$?

13. What is the coefficient of x^5 in the normal form of $(x + 1)^5$?

14. **Write About It** Revisit what you explored in Lesson 2.05.

a. Explain why the coefficient of x^8 in the normal form of this polynomial is 5.

$$(x + x^2 + x^3 + x^4 + x^5 + x^6)^2$$

b. Explain why the coefficient of x^{10} in the normal form of $(x + x^2 + x^3 + x^4 + x^5 + x^6)^2$ is the number of ways you can roll a sum of 10 if you throw two number cubes.

c. Explain why the coefficient of x^{14} in the normal form of $(x + x^2 + x^3 + x^4 + x^5 + x^6)^3$ is the number of ways you can roll a sum of 14 if you throw three number cubes.

Go **O**nline
www.successnetplus.com

15. Find the coefficient of xyz in the expanded form of
$(x + y + z)(x^2 - xy + y^2 - xz - yz + z^2)$.

16. **Standardized Test Prep** The coefficient of x^5 in the normal form of
$(x + x^2 + x^3 + x^4 + x^5 + x^6)^2$ is the number of ways you can roll a sum of
5 with two number cubes. What is the coefficient of x^5 in the normal form?

   A. 4   **B.** 5   **C.** 6   **D.** 7

17. Ed Barbeau, a mathematician from Toronto, writes the following
three equations.

$$1 + 2 = 3$$
$$4 + 5 + 6 = 7 + 8$$
$$9 + 10 + 11 + 12 = 13 + 14 + 15$$

Describe the pattern. What do you notice? What is the next equation in the
series? Make some conjectures. What can you prove?

Maintain Your Skills

18. Expand each product.

   a. $(1 - x)(1 + x)$

   b. $(1 - x)(1 + x + x^2)$

   c. $(1 - x)(1 + x + x^2 + x^3)$

19. Find the normal form of each polynomial.

   a. $(1 + x + x^2)(1 + x^3 + x^6)$

   b. $(1 + x + x^2 + x^3)(1 + x^4 + x^8)$

   c. $(1 + x + x^2 + x^3 + x^4)(1 + x^5 + x^{10})$

20. Expand each product.

   a. $(1 + x)(1 + x^2)(1 + x^4)$

   b. $(1 + x)(1 + x^2)(1 + x^4)(1 + x^8)$

   c. $(1 + x)(1 + x^2)(1 + x^4)(1 + x^8)(1 + x^{16})$

21. Expand and simplify each expression.

   a. $(a + b)(a^2 + b^2) - ab(a + b)$

   b. $(a + b)(a^3 + b^3) - ab(a^2 + b^2)$

   c. $(a + b)(a^4 + b^4) - ab(a^3 + b^3)$

In this investigation, you learned about certain types of polynomials. You also wrote polynomials in normal form and learned methods for adding, subtracting, and multiplying polynomials. These questions will help you summarize what you have learned.

1. Find the product of $(x + x^2 + x^3)$ and $(x^2 + x^3 + x^4 + x^5)$.

2. Let $p(x) = x^2 + 3x + 4$. Find polynomials $r(x)$, and $s(x)$, and $t(x)$ as described.

  a. $r(x)$ such that $p(x) + r(x) = 3x^2 - 8x + 1$

  b. $s(x)$ such that $p(x) - s(x) = 2x - 1$

  c. $t(x)$ such that $p(x) \cdot t(x)$ has degree 4 and $p(x) + t(x)$ has degree 1

3. For each identity, complete the following.

  • Calculate three numeric examples that follow from each identity by substituting a number for x.

  • Prove each identity is true. Use the basic rules.

  a. $x^3 + 1 = (x + 1)(x^2 - x + 1)$

  b. $x^8 - 1 = (x^4 + 1)(x^2 + 1)(x + 1)(x - 1)$

  c. $(x + 1)(x^2 - 5x + 3) = (x^3 + 3) - 2x(2x + 1)$

4. a. Write $p(x) = 3x^7 - 8x + x^6 - 5 + 4x^5 - 2x^4 + x^2 - 8x^3$ in normal form.

  b. What is the degree of the polynomial?

  c. What is the coefficient of x^3?

  d. What is the coefficient of x^2?

  e. Find a polynomial that you can add to $p(x)$ to get a polynomial of degree 5.

5. How can you decide whether two polynomials are equivalent?

6. How is a polynomial useful for describing a rule?

7. Suppose you roll three number cubes numbered 1–6.
What is the probability of rolling a total of 12?

Vocabulary

In this investigation, you learned these terms. Make sure you understand what each one means and how to use it.

- **coefficient**
- **cubic polynomial**
- **degree of a monomial**
- **degree of a polynomial**
- **linear polynomial**
- **monomial**
- **normal form**
- **parameter**
- **polynomial**
- **quadratic polynomial**
- **quartic polynomial**
- **quintic polynomial**

If track lanes are 4 ft wide and a race includes a semicircle, the starting blocks are staggered 4π ft apart.

Factoring to Solve: Quadratics

In *Factoring to Solve: Quadratics*, you will learn several techniques for factoring quadratic expressions. You will use factoring and the Zero-Product Property to find all the roots of a quadratic polynomial equation.

By the end of this investigation, you will be able to answer questions like these.

1. Suppose you know the sum and product of two numbers. How can you find the two numbers?

2. How do you determine quickly whether you can factor a monic quadratic expression over $\mathbb{Z}$?

3. How do you solve equations such as $x^2 = 15x + 250$?

You will learn how to

- apply the Difference of Squares Theorem to polynomial expressions and numerical examples

- use difference of squares factoring to solve equations

- factor monic quadratic polynomials

- factor general quadratic polynomials

- use factoring to solve equations

You will develop these habits and skills:

- Find patterns in repeated calculations and make conjectures based on these patterns.

- Use algebraic computation to prove theorems.

- Use geometric diagrams to understand theorems.

- Understand the relationship between the factorization of a quadratic expression and the solutions of a quadratic equation.

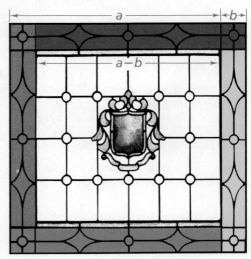

$$(a + b)^2 = (a - b)^2 + 4ab$$

112 **Chapter 2** Polynomials

In this investigation, you will learn to factor many different types of polynomials, especially quadratic polynomials.

For You to Explore

1. **Write About It** What is the Zero-Product Property (ZPP)? How can you use it?

2. A version of the multiplication table is below. Along the red diagonal, all the numbers are perfect squares.

> Why are the numbers on the diagonal perfect squares?

Multiplication Table

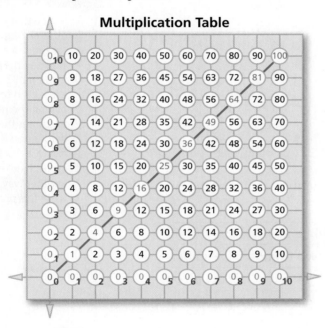

Start at any number on the perfect-square diagonal. There are eight different directions you can move.

a. Describe the numerical effect of moving in each direction.

b. Develop eight rules that explain how to get from any perfect square to its eight neighbors.

c. Try your rules on one of the perfect squares.

3. Choose a perfect square in the multiplication table in Problem 2. Move up any number of rows. Use that same number and move left that number of columns. How is the number that you land on related to the perfect square that you chose?

Use the pattern that you notice to find the missing expressions represented by gray boxes in a part of the multiplication table. First, write the missing expressions on the axes. Next, multiply an expression on the x-axis times an expression on the y-axis. Finally, write the product in the table. Write each product in terms of x as a difference of two numbers. The expression $x^2 - 4$ appears in the table as an example.

> **Habits of Mind**
>
> **Represent a rule.** You can find more than one way to describe each of the eight rules. Write each rule as many ways as possible.

Multiplication Table

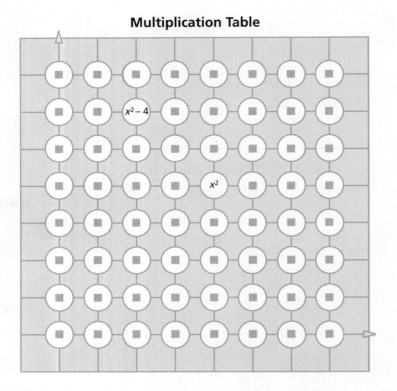

$x^2 - 4$

x^2

Notice that you can write different expressions for the same missing expression. For example, if you multiply the expression to the right of x on the horizontal axis times the expression below x on the vertical axis, the result is $(x + 1)(x - 1)$. What is another way that you can write this product?

4. Copy and complete this table. Find two numbers that have the given sum and product.

Numbers With a Given Sum and Product		
Sum of Two Numbers	Product of Two Numbers	Numbers
20	99	11 and 9
20	96	▪
20	75	▪
20	36	▪
20	-125	▪
20	47	▪
20	n	▪

The last two are much harder! Try to find a pattern in the other results.

Exercises *Practicing Habits of Mind*

On Your Own

5. This is a portion of a multiplication table surrounding 15^2, or 225.

   a. Copy and complete the table.

   b. Write each number as $15^2 \pm \blacksquare$.

   c. Write each number as $(15 \pm \blacksquare)(15 \pm \blacksquare)$.

Multiplication Table

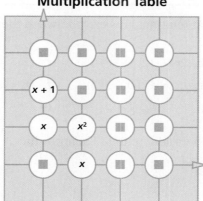

$15^2 = 225$

> For Exercises 5b and 5c, use your results from Problem 2.

6. Copy and complete the multiplication table.

Multiplication Table

7. Find two factors of each number.

   a. $23^2 - 6^2$

   b. $51^2 - 8^2$

   c. $99^2 - 10^2$

   d. $1,000,000^2 - 13^2$

   e. $a^2 - b^2$

8. a. Sketch the graph of $f(x) = x(100 - x)$. Make sure the graph includes any points where the graph changes direction. Also include any point where the graph crosses an axis.

   b. What are the exact coordinates of the graph's turning point?

> *Turning point* means maximum or minimum.

9. If two numbers add up to 100, can their product ever be the following?

   a. less than 2500   **b.** negative

   c. zero   **d.** more than 2500

   e. 2436   **f.** 1234

> Use the graph from Exercise 8. You can also use the TRACE function on a calculator to find the value of $x(100 - x)$ at different points.

10. Copy and complete this table. Find two numbers that have the given sum and product.

Numbers With a Given Sum and Product		
Sum of Two Numbers	Product of Two Numbers	Numbers
100	2500	50 and 50
100	2491	53 and 47
100	2484	■ and ■
100	2451	■ and ■
100	2379	■ and ■
100	2211	■ and ■
100	−309	■ and ■
100	1234	■ and ■
100	n	■ and ■

> In the last row, try to find a formula, in terms of n, for the numbers.

11. Expand each product. What relationships exist between the factored form and expanded form?

a. $(x + 11)(x + 8)$ **b.** $(x - 12)(x - 10)$ **c.** $(x + 9)(x - 7)$

d. $\left(x - \frac{2}{3}\right)\left(x - \frac{1}{3}\right)$ **e.** $(x - 12)(x - 13)$ **f.** $(x + 53)(x + 47)$

g. $(x + 21)(x - 21)$ **h.** $\left(x + \frac{7}{2}\right)\left(x - \frac{7}{2}\right)$

12. **Take It Further** Two numbers add up to b. Their product is c. Find the two numbers, in terms of b and c.

Maintain Your Skills

13. Show that each number fact is true.

a. $45^2 = 40 \cdot 50 + 5^2$ **b.** $35^2 = 30 \cdot 40 + 5^2$

c. $25^2 = 20 \cdot 30 + 5^2$ **d.** Describe the pattern.

For Exercises 14 and 15, prove each identity.

14. a. $x^2 - y^2 = (x + y)(x - y)$ **b.** $x^2 - 9 = (x + 3)(x - 3)$

c. $(x - 3)^2 - 16 = (x + 1)(x - 7)$ **d.** $\left(x - \frac{3}{2}\right)^2 - \frac{1}{4} = (x - 2)(x - 1)$

e. $(x - a)^2 - b^2 = (x - a + b)(x - a - b)$

15. a. $(a + b)^2 - (a - b)^2 = 4ab$ **b.** $\left(\frac{a + b}{2}\right)^2 - \left(\frac{a - b}{2}\right)^2 = ab$

c. $30^2 - 10^2 = 20 \cdot 40$ **d.** $18^2 - 7^2 = 25 \cdot 11$

2.10 Factoring a Difference of Squares

You have seen the identity $a^2 - b^2 = (a + b)(a - b)$ several times. Since this result is so important, you can state it as a theorem.

Theorem 2.2 The Difference of Squares

For any numbers a and b, the following is an identity.

$$a^2 - b^2 = (a + b)(a - b)$$

Note that you can replace a and b by any number, variable, or expression.

Proof Like all identities, you can establish this by showing that both sides are equivalent under the basic rules. Expand the right side of the equation and compare to the left side.

$$
\begin{aligned}
(a + b)(a - b) &= a(a - b) + b(a - b) &&\text{Distributive Property} \\
&= a^2 - ab + ba - b^2 &&\text{Distributive Property} \\
&= a^2 - b^2 &&-ab + ba = 0
\end{aligned}
$$

Using the basic rules, $(a + b)(a - b)$ became $a^2 - b^2$. This proves the identity.

> Why is $-ab + ba$ equal to 0?

Developing Habits of Mind

Visualize. You can also use a visual explanation to prove Theorem 2.2 above.

Calculate the area of a figure like this figure in two ways.

Let a be the length of the top side. Let b be the length of a side in the missing corner. First, notice that the area of the shaded region is the area of the larger square minus the area of the smaller square.

> In this argument, assume that a and b are positive and that $a > b$.

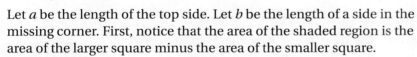
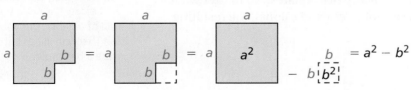

Therefore, the area of the shaded region is $a^2 - b^2$.

Now calculate the area another way. Cut up the shaded region and make another rectangle.

$$= (a + b)(a - b)$$

The area of the shaded region is $(a + b)(a - b)$.

Since $a^2 - b^2$ and $(a + b)(a - b)$ both represent the area of the shaded region, they are equal. Therefore, $a^2 - b^2 = (a + b)(a - b)$.

This is the result of Theorem 2.2.

For Discussion

1. In the first set of diagrams, why is the area of the shaded region $a^2 - b^2$?

2. Look at the final rectangle in the second set of diagrams. Why is the length of the bottom $(a - b)$? Why is the length of the side $(a + b)$?

3. The visual proof assumes that a and b are positive and that $a > b$. Why are these assumptions necessary for this argument?

Why is Theorem 2.2 important? You can use $a^2 - b^2 = (a + b)(a - b)$ to factor a quadratic that is the difference of any two squares. No matter what you substitute for a or b (numbers, variables, or expressions), the resulting statement is always true.

You have seen Theorem 2.2 before. It is not a basic rule of algebra, but you use Theorem 2.2 as if it were a basic rule.

Consider these examples.

If $a = 93$ and $b = 7$, then $93^2 - 7^2 = (93 + 7)(93 - 7)$.

If $a = 5x$ and $b = y^3$, then $25x^2 - y^6 = (5x + y^3)(5x - y^3)$.

This theorem also gives you a basis for factoring any quadratic polynomial.

 On the left side, why do you find $-y^6$? $25x^2$?

For You to Do

Each equation below is in the form $a^2 - b^2 = (a + b)(a - b)$. What represents a and b in each equation?

4. $9x^2 - 16 = (3x + 4)(3x - 4)$

5. $10,000 - 4 = (100 + 2)(100 - 2)$

6. $16x^6 - 4x^2 = (4x^3 + 2x)(4x^3 - 2x)$

Minds in Action

Sasha thinks she has invented a number trick. She tests it on Tony.

Sasha   Tony, give me any two numbers with an average of 100. I'll multiply them quickly in my head.

Tony   All right, 103 and 97.

Sasha   Easy! That's 9991.

Tony scribbles the calculation on paper.

Tony   Wow! That was fast.

Sasha   Give me another.

Tony   Okay, 109 and 91.

Sasha   9919.

Tony   112 and 88.

Sasha   9856.

Tony checks the answers on paper.

Tony   You're right! How can you do that so quickly?

Sasha   You think of a difference of squares. Instead of multiplying 91 by 109, I think of $(100 + 9)(100 - 9)$. That is the same as $100^2 - 9^2$.

Tony   Okay. So, it's $10,000 - 81 = 9919$.

Sasha   Exactly. Here's the first one.

Sasha scribbles on her piece of paper.

$$103 \cdot 97 = (100 + 3)(100 - 3) = 100^2 - 3^2$$

Tony   So, 100^2 is 10,000 and 3^2 is 9. I take 9 from 10,000 and get 9991.

Sasha   Exactly!

Tony   So, $105 \cdot 95$ is 10,000 minus 5 squared, which is 25. That makes it 9975.

Sasha   You got it.

Tony   Why do the numbers have to average 100?

Sasha   They don't really. It's just that 100^2 is easy to remember. If the two numbers averaged something else, that would just change things a little bit.

Tony   How about -9 times 209?

Sasha   Well, it's not always easier to do it my way.

For Discussion

7. How would you change Sasha's method if the two numbers average 80?

8. Find two numbers with an average of 100, such that it is easier to multiply them by using Sasha's method than it is to use paper and pencil.

9. Find two numbers with an average of 100, such that it is easier to multiply them by using paper and pencil than it is to use Sasha's method.

For You to Do

Find each product without using a calculator.

10. $89 \cdot 71$

11. $52 \cdot 48$

12. $1007 \cdot 993$

13. $(1000 + x)(1000 - x)$

Exercises Practicing Habits of Mind

Check Your Understanding

1. Theorem 2.2 states that $a^2 - b^2 = (a + b)(a - b)$. Some of the following equations are related identities that result from substituting for a and b.

   Determine whether each equation is an identity. If an equation is an identity, state the substitution that you made for a and b.

   a. $16x^2 - 9y^2 = (4x + 3y)(4x - 3y)$

   b. $8n^2 - 4 = (4n + 2)(4n - 2)$

   c. $25 - t^6 = (5 + t^3)(5 - t^3)$

   d. $(x + 3)^2 - 1 = (x + 4)(x + 2)$

   e. $9 - x^2 = (x + 3)(x - 3)$

   f. $n^3 - 100 = (n^2 + 10)(n - 10)$

2. **a.** What value of x makes the greatest possible product of $(50 + x)$ and $(50 - x)$? Explain.

   b. Consider all pairs of numbers x and y such that $x + y = 100$. Which pair has the greatest possible product?

3. Find all pairs of nonnegative integers x and y that satisfy each equation.

   a. $x^2 - y^2 = 7$

   b. $x^2 - y^2 = 13$

   c. $x^2 - y^2 = 9$

> **Habits of Mind**
>
> **Visualize.** Sketch the graph of each equation. Where do the graphs intersect the corners of a square on the graph paper?

4. Find each difference without using pencil and paper or a calculator.

   a. $80^2 - 20^2$

   b. $75^2 - 25^2$

   c. $87^2 - 13^2$

5. Hideki wants to find an identity for $a^2 + b^2$. He thinks that if you substitute $(-b)$ for b in Theorem 2.2, you get the following.

$$a^2 + b^2 = a^2 - (-b)^2$$
$$= (a + (-b))(a - (-b))$$
$$= (a - b)(a + b)$$

   Is Hideki right? Does $a^2 + b^2 = (a - b)(a + b)$? Explain.

6. Describe a pattern in this portion of the multiplication table. Explain why the pattern continues.

Multiplication Table

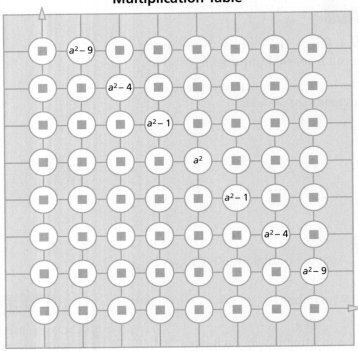

7. What values of k make each equation an identity?

a. $x^2 - 9 = (x + 3)(x + k)$

b. $y^2 - k = (y + 10)(y - 10)$

c. $a^4 - 16 = (a - 2)(a + 2)(a^2 + k)$

8. Use the diagram. Give another visual proof of Theorem 2.2.

9. **Write About It** If a is an integer, can $(a + 1)^2 - a^2$ be even? Explain.

10. Show that each equation is an identity.

a. $(x + 11)(x + 8) = (x + 9.5)^2 - (1.5)^2$

b. $(x + 12)(x + 8) = (x + 10)^2 - (2)^2$

c. $(x + 13)(x + 14) = \left(x + \frac{27}{2}\right)^2 - \left(\frac{1}{2}\right)^2$

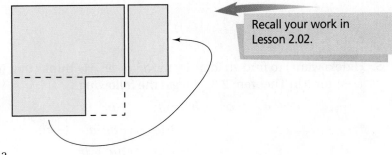

Recall your work in Lesson 2.02.

11. **Take It Further** For the following equation, find r and s in terms of a and b.

$$(x + a)(x + b) = (x + r)^2 - s^2$$

12. A straight metal rail is 2400 cm long. It is firmly fixed at each end. On a warm day, its length increases to 2402 cm. This causes it to buckle. Assume its final shape is closely approximated by an isosceles triangle. Determine how far from the ground its midpoint rises.

Habits of Mind

Experiment. Before you solve this exercise, guess an answer. Then determine how close your guess is.

2402 cm ⟋ h

2400 cm

13. Solve each equation.

a. $x^2 - 9 = 0$

b. $(x - 3)^2 - 16 = 0$

c. $\left(x - \dfrac{3}{2}\right)^2 - \dfrac{1}{4} = 0$

d. Express x in terms of a and b if $(x - a)^2 - b^2 = 0$.

On Your Own

14. Find each quotient. Do not use a calculator.

a. $\dfrac{13^2 - 4^2}{13 + 4}$

b. $\dfrac{9^2 - 4^2}{9 + 4}$

c. $\dfrac{27^2 - 4^2}{27 + 4}$

d. $\dfrac{x^2 - 4^2}{x + 4}$

Tree roots can cause a sidewalk to buckle.

15. a. Determine whether
$y^6 - 25 = (y^3 + 5)(y^3 - 5)$ is true.

b. What is the degree of $y^6 - 25$?

c. What is the degree of $(y^3 + 5)$? Of $(y^3 - 5)$? What is the degree of their product?

16. At the right is a diagram of a 7×7 square with a corner missing.

a. How many small squares are left in this shape? Explain how you calculated your answer without counting every square.

b. Suppose you cut off the bottom row of this shape and paste it on the right side. The result is a rectangle. What are the side lengths of this rectangle? Explain.

c. How is this related to the number fact $7^2 - 1 = (7 + 1)(7 - 1)$?

17. Solve the equation $10{,}000 - k^2 = 9879$. (*Hint:* 9879 is divisible by 89.)

18. Find the value of x that results in the least value of each polynomial.

　a. $(x + 3)(x - 3)$　　　　　**b.** $x^2 + 4$

　c. $(x - 7)^2 - 4$　　　　　**d.** $x^4 - 16$

19. Determine whether you can express each polynomial as a difference of squares in x with integer coefficients. Explain.

　a. $x^1 - 1$　　　**b.** $x^2 - 1$　　　**c.** $x^3 - 1$

　d. $x^4 - 1$　　　**e.** $x^5 - 1$　　　**f.** $x^6 - 1$

　g. $x^7 - 1$　　　**h.** $x^8 - 1$　　　**i.** $x^9 - 1$

For Exercises 20 and 21, factor each expression.

20. a. $36x^2 - 64$　　　　　**b.** $0.36x^2 - 0.64$

21. a. $y^3 - 9y$　　　　　**b.** $y^4 - 9y^2$

> If the exercise contains decimal coefficients, your solution can, too.

22. Standardized Test Prep Without using a calculator, find the product $593 \cdot 607$.

　A. 360,049　　**B.** 359,991　　**C.** 359,979　　**D.** 359,951

> Go Online
> www.successnetplus.com

23. Find all the real numbers that make each equation true.

　a. $x^2 - 4 = 0$　　　**b.** $x^2 - 9 = 0$　　　**c.** $x^2 + 4 = 0$

　d. $x^2 - 5 = 0$　　　**e.** $x^2 - 12 = 0$　　　**f.** $x^4 - 16 = 0$

Maintain Your Skills

24. Expand each product.

　a. $(a - b)(a + b)(a^2 + b^2)$

　b. $(a - b)(a + b)(a^2 + b^2)(a^4 + b^4)$

　c. $(a - b)(a + b)(a^2 + b^2)(a^4 + b^4)(a^8 + b^8)$

　d. What is the pattern? Explain.

25. Factor each polynomial.

　a. $x^2 - z^2$　　　**b.** $x^2 - 25$　　　**c.** $(x - 3)^2 - 36$

　d. $\left(x - \frac{3}{4}\right)^2 - \frac{1}{16}$　　**e.** $(x - p)^2 - b^2$

> If the exercise contains fractions for coefficients, your solution can, too.

26. Find the greatest prime factor of each number.

　a. $16^2 - 1$　　　**b.** $15^2 - 4$　　　**c.** $14^2 - 9$

　d. $13^2 - 16$　　　**e.** $12^2 - 25$

　f. What is the pattern? Explain.

2.11 Factoring Sums and Products

You have used expansion boxes to expand products of binomials such as the following.

> A **binomial** is a polynomial with two terms.

$$(x + 11)(x + 8) = x^2 + 19x + 88$$

$$(x - 12)(x - 10) = x^2 - 22x + 120$$

$$(x + 9)(x - 7) = x^2 + 2x - 63$$

You can also expand a more general case such as $(x + a)(x + b)$, where a and b are unknown numbers.

$$(x + a)(x + b) = x^2 + ax + xb + ab$$

$$= x^2 + ax + bx + ab$$

$$= x^2 + (a + b)x + ab$$

Look back at the examples above. The coefficient of x is the sum of the numbers a and b in the factorization. The constant term is the product of the numbers a and b. Note that both a and b can be either positive or negative. This result is important enough to state as a theorem.

Theorem 2.3 The Sum and Product Identity

For any numbers a and b, the following is an identity.

$$x^2 + (a + b)x + ab = (x + a)(x + b)$$

> The expansion above proves this theorem.

Notice that the coefficient of x is 1 in both factors. The coefficient of the x^2 term in the expanded quadratic is also 1. Any polynomial with lead coefficient 1 is **monic.** The lead coefficient is the coefficient of the term with the greatest degree. Two examples follow.

- $x^2 + 5x - 1$ is monic.
- $3x^2 + 5x - 1$ is not monic.

Theorem 2.3 gives you a way to factor monic quadratics.

Facts and Notation

If you can factor a polynomial into a product of polynomials with integer coefficients, you can say that the polynomial factors over $\mathbb{Z}$.

For example, you can factor the polynomial $x^2 + 5x + 6$ over $\mathbb{Z}$ since it factors into $(x + 2)(x + 3)$. However, $x^2 + 5x + 3$ does not factor over $\mathbb{Z}$.

> **Remember...**
>
> In Chapter 1, you identified these number systems.
> - integers ($\mathbb{Z}$)
> - rational numbers ($\mathbb{Q}$)
> - real numbers ($\mathbb{R}$)

Factoring an expression such as $x^2 + 6x - 7$ amounts to answering the following question. What two numbers have a sum 6 and a product -7? The numbers are -1 and 7. You use them in the factorization $(x - 1)(x + 7)$.

Example 1

Problem Factor $x^2 + 12x + 27$.

Solution Find two numbers that add to 12 and multiply to 27. You can make a table of all the possible combinations of numbers that add to 12. Then multiply them and look for a match.

From the table, notice that the two numbers that work are 3 and 9. You use those numbers to write the factored form.

$$(x + 3)(x + 9)$$

Be careful when you make a table of products. This table does not include all possible pairs of integers that add to 12. It does not include pairs with a negative integer, such as -5 and 17.

Sum 12	
Numbers	**Product**
6 and 6	36
5 and 7	35
4 and 8	32
3 and 9	27
2 and 10	20
1 and 11	11

This table starts with the number that is half of the sum. Why is this a reasonable approach?

For Discussion

1. Refer to the example. Why is it sufficient to look only at positive integers to factor $x^2 + 12x + 27$?

Minds in Action

Tony and Sasha discuss their homework.

Tony   So what's the problem?

Sasha reads this problem.

Sasha   Find all values of x that make $x^2 - 21x = 72$.

         The first thing we need to do is move the 72.

Tony   Why's that?

Sasha   Factoring doesn't help unless you set the equation equal to zero. So move the 72 by adding −72 to each side.

$$x^2 - 21x - 72 = 0$$

Now we have an equation that we're ready to factor.

> The left side must be equal to zero for you to apply the Zero-Product Property.

Tony   Okay, so we want to find two numbers that add to −21 and multiply to −72. That's a tough one.

Sasha   Usually, we start the table with two numbers that are equal or close to equal. In this case, we need a positive number and a negative number to get a negative product, −72. Let's start with −21 and 0 and go from there.

Bingo! The factors are $(x + 3)$ and $(x − 24)$.

Sum −21	
Numbers	Product
−21 and 0	0
−22 and 1	−22
−23 and 2	−46
−24 and 3	−72

Tony   Great! I wonder if we could start by looking at numbers that multiply to −72.

Habits of Mind

Look for a pattern. Notice the pattern in the sums.

Sasha   Good idea! Let's make a table. One number has to be positive and one has to be negative, since the product is −72.

Tony   Oh, no, that doubles our work!

Sasha   Not really. We know the sum is negative. We only have to look at pairs where the larger factor is negative.

Tony   Okay, how about this?

I can stop there, since I found the numbers. They're 3 and −24. So we're almost done.

$$x^2 - 21x - 72 = 0$$

$$(x + 3)(x - 24) = 0$$

Product −72	
Numbers	Sum
1 and −72	−71
2 and −36	−34
3 and −24	−21

Sasha   I can take it from here. We can use ZPP to break it up into two smaller equations. So, $x + 3 = 0$ or $x − 24 = 0$.

Tony   That means $x = −3$ and $x = 24$ are the two solutions.

Sasha   Nice! Okay, I checked the answers and they work. What's the next one?

For You to Do

2. Use Sasha and Tony's method. Factor $x^2 - 14x + 40$ and $x^2 + 14x - 120$.

Not all quadratic expressions factor so easily. Actually, it is pretty rare that you can break a monic quadratic polynomial into two factors using only integers. Take a look at the following example.

Example 2

Problem Factor $x^2 + 18x + 63$.

Solution Look for two numbers that add to 18 and multiply to 63. Since both the sum and the product are positive, both numbers have to be positive. The table to the right shows positive integers that add to 18.

The table could stop at 4 and 14, since the numbers just keep decreasing and you have already passed 63. There are no integers that add to 18 and multiply to 63.

The results are the same if you try the product method. No factors of 63 add to 18.

Can you factor this polynomial? Consider the tables that include the possible integer pairs for factoring this polynomial. You cannot factor the polynomial over $\mathbb{Z}$ using any of these pairs. You may be able to factor the polynomial with rational or irrational numbers.

Sum 18	
Numbers	**Product**
9 and 9	81
8 and 10	80
7 and 11	77
6 and 12	72
5 and 13	65
4 and 14	56
3 and 15	45
2 and 16	32
1 and 17	17

Product 63	
Numbers	**Sum**
1 and 63	64
3 and 21	24
7 and 9	16

For Discussion

3. Write down five quadratics that factor over $\mathbb{Z}$ and that start with the following expression.

$$x^2 + 15x + \blacksquare$$

Write five more quadratics that start this way and do not factor over $\mathbb{Z}$.

Can you write a rule to find the missing term? Start by finding pairs of numbers with a sum 15.

If b and c are integers, there are two reasons why you cannot factor the monic quadratic $x^2 + bx + c$ over $\mathbb{Z}$.

- The numbers in the factorization are not integers. A polynomial that does not factor over $\mathbb{Z}$ might factor over $\mathbb{R}$. For example, the table in the example gives factors for $x^2 + 18x + 77$, $x^2 + 18x + 72$, $x^2 + 18x + 32$, and others. The table does not work for $x^2 + 18x + 63$.

  There are two numbers that add to 18 and multiply to 63, but they are not integers. In fact, the two numbers are not even rational. They are $9 + 3\sqrt{2}$ and $9 - 3\sqrt{2}$. As decimals, these numbers are about 13.243 and 4.757.

For You to Do

4. Show that $3 + \sqrt{2}$ and $3 - \sqrt{2}$ add to 6 and multiply to 7.

5. Show that $(x + 3)^2 - 2 = x^2 + 6x + 7$.

- The product is too great for the sum. Recall working with the multiplication tables in Chapter 4. The maximum product for a given sum results when the numbers are equal. You can formalize this idea in a theorem.

Theorem 2.4

For a given number s, if $a + b = s$, the maximum value of the product ab occurs when $a = b$.

> The value s is constant. The variables a and b can change in value, but they must have a sum s.

If the sum of two numbers is 18, their maximum possible product is $9 \times 9 = 81$. This means that you cannot factor the expression $x^2 + 18x + 100$, since two real numbers that have a sum of 18 cannot also have a product of 100.

For Discussion

6. Use the following identity that you proved in Lesson 2.09. Prove Theorem 2.4.
$$\left(\frac{a + b}{2} \right)^2 - \left(\frac{a - b}{2} \right)^2 = ab$$

Exercises Practicing Habits of Mind

Check Your Understanding

1. Determine which equation has integer solutions. Explain.

   A. $x^2 + 14x + 46 = 0$ **B.** $x^2 + 14x - 46 = 0$

   C. $x^2 - 14x - 13 = 0$ **D.** $x^2 - 14x + 13 = 0$

2. Find integer solutions for each polynomial equation. If the equation does not have integer solutions, explain why.

   a. $x^2 + 13x + 36 = 0$ **b.** $x^2 + 13x + 42 = 0$

   c. $x^2 + 13x + 224 = 0$ **d.** $x^2 + 13x - 48 = 0$

   e. $x^2 + 13x + 22 = 0$ **f.** $x^2 + 13x - 114 = 0$

   g. $x^2 + 13x + 54 = 0$ **h.** $x^2 + 13x - 20 = 0$

   i. $x^2 + 13x + 17 = 0$ **j.** $x^2 + 13x - 14 = 0$

   > A **polynomial equation** is an equation with a polynomial equal to 0.

3. Use the Zero-Product Property and what you know about factoring. Find all integer solutions. To solve some equations, expand the product before using the Zero-Product Property. Equations may have zero, one, or two solutions.

   a. $x^2 = 16x - 60$ **b.** $x^2 = 16x - 70$

   c. $x^2 = 16x$ **d.** $x^2 - 6x + 9 = 0$

   e. $x^2 = 16$ **f.** $x^2 + 8x + 16 = 0$

   g. $(x + 1)(x + 2) = 12$ **h.** $x(x + 17) = -70$

   i. $(x + 2)(x + 4) = -4$ **j.** $x^2 - 10x = -25$

4. A *perfect square trinomial* is a trinomial with identical factors. For example, $x^2 + 6x + 9$ is a perfect square trinomial. Its factors are $(x + 3)(x + 3)$. The trinomial $x^2 + 6x + 8$ is not a perfect square trinomial. Which of the following are perfect square trinomials?

   > A **trinomial** is a polynomial expression with exactly three terms.

   A. $x^2 + 10x + 25$

   B. $x^2 + 10x + 26$

   C. $x^2 - 14x + 49$

   D. $x^2 + 12x - 36$

   E. $x^2 + 26x + 169$

   F. $x^2 + 54x + 728$

5. **a. Write About It** Explain why the expression $x^2 - 6x + 9$ is not negative if x is a real number.

   b. Take It Further Show that the expression $x^2 + y^2 + 10x - 8y + 42$ is a positive number, for all values of x and y.

6. Tony factors the quadratic $x^2 - 7x + 12$ by listing all the numbers that add to -7. Then he finds a pair that multiplies to 12. Sasha has another way. She looks at all the numbers that multiply to 12. Then she finds a pair that adds to -7. Which quadratic expressions are easier to factor with Sasha's method? With Tony's method? Explain.

   a. $x^2 - 2x - 35$ **b.** $x^2 - 13x + 36$

   c. $x^2 + 13x - 36$ **d.** $x^2 + 32x - 185$

   e. $x^2 + 30x + 189$ **f.** $x^2 + 19x - 34$

7. Factor each quadratic expression over $\mathbb{Z}$. If an expression is not factorable, explain why.

   a. $x^2 + 6x + 5$ **b.** $x^2 + 12x + 20$

   c. $x^2 + 18x + 45$ **d.** $x^2 + 6ax + 5a^2$

   e. $x^2 - 121$ **f.** $x^2 + 10x + 25$

   g. $x^2 + 10x + 24$ **h.** $x^2 + 10x + 23$

   i. $x^2 + 10x + 21$ **j.** $x^2 + 10x + 26$

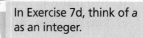

In Exercise 7d, think of a as an integer.

8. **a.** Two numbers add to -16. What is the maximum possible value of their product?

   b. Factor the perfect square trinomial $x^2 - 16x + 64$.

   c. The expression $x^2 + 22x + T$ is a perfect square trinomial. What number is T?

   d. A rectangle has a perimeter of 44 meters. What is the maximum possible area?

   e. Suppose $x^2 + Bx + C$ is a perfect square trinomial and you know B. How can you find C?

Go Online
www.successnetplus.com

44 m fencing

9. **Write About It** Suppose that you know the factorization of $x^2 + 30x + 216$. Does knowing the factorization help you find the factorization of each expression given? Explain.

   a. $x^2 - 30x + 216$

   b. $x^2 + 30x - 216$

10. **Standardized Test Prep** What are the integer solutions of $x^2 - 7x = 120$?

    A. $-15, -8$ **B.** $-15, 8$ **C.** $-8, 15$ **D.** $8, 15$

11. Use a multiplication table. Draw the line of factors that add to each given number. What is the greatest product on that line?

    a. 10   **b.** 16   **c.** even number, n

12. **a.** Use a multiplication table. Draw the line of factors that add to 9. Are there two numbers that add up to 9 with a product that is *more* than 20? Explain.

    Look at Lesson 2.10, Exercise 6.

    b. Two numbers add to 13. What is their greatest possible product?

    c. Two numbers add to n. What is their greatest possible product?

Maintain Your Skills

13. Solve each equation for integer solutions. If no solutions exist, explain why.

    a. $x^2 + 20x + 99 = 0$

    b. $x^2 - 20x + 51 = 0$

    c. $x^2 + 20x = -224$

    d. $x^2 + 20x = 69$

    e. $x^2 + 20x = -104$

    f. $x^2 + 20x - 48 = 0$

    g. $x^2 + 20x + 54 = 0$

    h. $x^2 - 20x = 96$

    i. $x^2 + 20x + 36 = 0$

Go Online
Video Tutor
www.successnetplus.com

2.12 Factoring by Completing the Square

To solve quadratic equations, you need to factor all kinds of quadratic polynomials. A polynomial that is the difference of squares is the easiest kind of polynomial to factor. You only need to use Theorem 2.2.

$$a^2 - b^2 = (a + b)(a - b)$$

Not every polynomial is as simple as the one above. However, you can write any quadratic polynomial as a difference of squares by completing the square.

Example 1

Problem Solve the equation $x^2 - 9 = 0$. Then solve $(x + 4)^2 - 9 = 0$.

Solution The left side of the first equation is a difference of squares. Factor this equation using Theorem 2.2. Then set each factor equal to 0 using ZPP.

$$x^2 - 9 = 0$$

$$(x + 3)(x - 3) = 0$$

$$x + 3 = 0 \quad \text{or } x - 3 = 0$$

$$x = -3 \text{ or} \qquad x = 3$$

To solve $(x + 4)^2 - 9 = 0$, you could expand the left side and put it in normal form to factor it. However, the form of the expression $(x + 4)^2 - 9$ looks just like the expression $x^2 - 9$. The only difference is that $x + 4$ is squared instead of x. Think of this expression as another difference of squares. Factor it accordingly.

$$(x + 4)^2 - 9 = ((x + 4) + 3)((x + 4) - 3) = (x + 7)(x + 1)$$

From here, you get the two solutions, $x = -7$ and $x = -1$.

Go Online
www.successnetplus.com

Habits of Mind

Visualize. You can cover $x + 4$ with one hand so you can think of it as one thing.

For You to Do

1. Use the method in Example 1 to solve the equation $(x - 4)^2 - 36 = 0$. Try expanding the left side. Factor by the usual method.

For Discussion

2. How does this method work for $(x - 5)^2 - 7 = 0$?

Completing the square is a part of a process that transforms a quadratic polynomial into a difference of squares. To complete the square, you need to build a perfect square trinomial. A **perfect square trinomial** is a trinomial with identical factors. Use this identity to build these trinomials.

Completing the square always works! If there is a factorization, this method finds it. If there is not a factorization, this method tells you why. Some quadratics only factor if you allow noninteger coefficients. This method will even help you find these.

Corollary 2.3.1 The Perfect Square Trinomial

For any x and a, the following equation is an identity.

$$(x + a)^2 = x^2 + (2a)x + a^2$$

For You to Do

3. Prove Corollary 2.3.1. Use the basic rules.

You can use Corollary 2.3.1 in reverse. Suppose a perfect square trinomial starts with the terms $x^2 + 6x +$ ■. You can find the missing term by recognizing that if $2a = 6$, then $a = 3$. Therefore, the missing term, a^2, is 9. Another way to describe this process is to take half of the coefficient of x and square it. This process completes the perfect square.

Example 2

Problem Factor $x^2 - 66x + 945$.

Solution One way to factor the expression is to find the factors of 945. Another way is to find integers with a sum of -66. Either method can take a long time, especially for a larger number such as 945.

To complete the square on $x^2 - 66x$, add 1089, which is 33^2.

$$x^2 - 66x + 1089 = (x - 33)^2$$

However, you are not trying to factor $x^2 - 66x + 1089$. You have $x^2 - 66x + 945$. So, write what you have in terms of the perfect square, fixing the constant term.

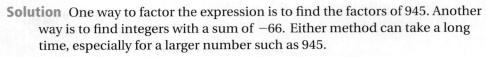

$$\underbrace{x^2 - 66x + 945}_{\text{your polynomial}} = \underbrace{x^2 - 66x + 1089}_{\text{perfect square}} - 144$$
$$= (x - 33)^2 - 144$$

Now it is the difference of two squares. In this form, you can factor $x^2 - 66x + 945$ and solve the equation $x^2 - 66x + 945 = 0$.

For You to Do

4. Factor $x^2 - 66x + 945$. Remember, it is equivalent to $(x - 33)^2 - 144$.

5. Find the two solutions to $x^2 - 66x + 945 = 0$.

For Discussion

For what values of c does $x^2 - 66x + c = 0$ have the following results?

6. two distinct integer solutions

7. only one integer solution

8. no solutions in $\mathbb{Z}$

Minds in Action

Tony and Derman try to solve the polynomial equation
$x^2 + 120 = 23x.$

Derman First, we subtract $23x$ from each side to get $x^2 - 23x + 120 = 0$.
The number 23 is an odd number. That's no fun! That means that
the perfect square trinomial will include a fraction.

Tony So what if it's a fraction? They're not that hard.

Derman Okay. To get the perfect square, I divide 23 by 2 and then square it.

$$x^2 - 23x + \left(\frac{23}{2}\right)^2 = x^2 - 23x + \frac{529}{4}$$

Tony Sounds good to me. Let's find the difference between $\frac{529}{4}$ and
120. I can write 120 as $\frac{480}{4}$.

$$
\begin{array}{r}
x^2 - 23x + \dfrac{529}{4} \\
(-)\quad x^2 - 23x + \dfrac{480}{4} \\
\hline
\dfrac{49}{4}
\end{array}
$$

Derman If you factor $x^2 - 23x + \frac{529}{4}$, you get this.

$$\left(x - \frac{23}{2}\right)\left(x - \frac{23}{2}\right) = \left(x - \frac{23}{2}\right)^2$$

So, $x^2 - 23x + 120$ is $\frac{49}{4}$ less than this.

> Do not forget the Zero-Product Property.

> How did Derman calculate $\frac{529}{4}$?

Derman writes on his paper.

$$x^2 - 23x + 120 = \left(x - \frac{23}{2}\right)^2 - \frac{49}{4}$$

Derman It's the difference of squares.

Tony So, this is what I get.

$$\left(x - \frac{23}{2}\right)^2 - \frac{49}{4} = \left(x - \frac{23}{2} + \frac{7}{2}\right)\left(x - \frac{23}{2} - \frac{7}{2}\right)$$

$$= (x - 8)(x - 15)$$

For You to Do

9. Use completing the square. Solve $x^2 + 19x + 84 = 0$.

For Discussion

10. What happens if you try to complete the square to solve $x^2 - 24x = -200$?

11. For what values of c can you find solutions for $x^2 - 24x = c$?

Minds in Action

Shannon and Sasha are sitting at a table next to Tony and Derman.
They try to solve the equation $x^2 - 24x + 42 = 0$.

Shannon It looks bad. There are no numbers that add to -24 and multiply to 42.

Sasha Right. So let's start with one that factors. We can see how far off we are. The perfect square trinomial in this case is $x^2 - 24x + 144 = (x - 12)(x - 12) = (x - 12)^2$.

Shannon What we've got is 102 less.

$$\begin{array}{r} x^2 - 24x + 144 \\ (-) \quad x^2 - 24x + 42 \\ \hline 102 \end{array}$$

Sasha If you factor $x^2 - 24x + 144$ you get $(x - 12)^2$. But $x^2 - 24x + 42$ is 102 less than this perfect square. That gives us this.

Sasha writes on her paper.

$$x^2 - 24x + 42 = (x - 12)^2 - 102$$

We made it a difference of squares. We know how to do those.

Shannon Difference of squares? But, Sasha, 102 isn't a square.

Sasha	Sure, 102 can be a square. It's just the square of an irrational number.

$$102 = \left(\sqrt{102}\right)^2$$

Shannon	So, $(x - 12)^2 - 102$ factors. It doesn't use integers, but it factors.

$$\left(x - 12 + \sqrt{102}\right)\left(x - 12 - \sqrt{102}\right)$$

Sasha	And the solutions are $x = 12 - \sqrt{102}$ and $x = 12 + \sqrt{102}$.

Sasha leans towards Tony and Derman's table.

	Tony, the one that you and Derman were working on would have factored in the first place.
Tony	Sure, but we used a way that always works, whether it factors or not. That makes the process mechanical. I like that.
Sasha	I'm impressed. What will you do if there's a number in front of the x^2?
Tony	I'm not sure. I'm sure we'll figure it out when we need it.

> How did Sasha get these numbers?

> Tony and Derman's equation was $x^2 - 23x + 120 = 0$.

For You to Do

12. What is the sum of $12 + \sqrt{102}$ and $12 - \sqrt{102}$?

13. What is the product of $12 + \sqrt{102}$ and $12 - \sqrt{102}$? Explain why both the sum and the product of these two irrational numbers are integers.

Developing Habits of Mind

Use a consistent process. In Lesson 2.11, you learned the sums and products method for finding integer solutions to monic quadratic equations. However, if a quadratic equation has an irrational solution, this method does not work. The sums and products method only works when you can factor a quadratic over $\mathbb{Z}$.

You can complete the square to find any real solution for a quadratic equation. In this lesson, you used this method to find the integer solutions for $x^2 - 66x + 945 = 0$. Also, Shannon and Sasha used this method in Minds in Action to find irrational solutions to $x^2 - 24x + 42 = 0$.

Completing the square can also help you determine whether a quadratic equation has no real solutions.

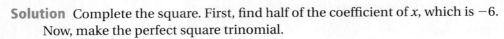

Example 3

Problem Find all real solutions to $x^2 - 12x + 45 = 0$.

Solution Complete the square. First, find half of the coefficient of x, which is -6. Now, make the perfect square trinomial.

$$(x - 6)^2 = x^2 - 12x + 36$$

Rewrite the original equation.

$$x^2 - 12x + 45 = 0$$
$$(x^2 - 12x + 36) + 9 = 0$$
$$(x - 6)^2 + 9 = 0$$

Look at the last equation. The minimum value for $(x - 6)^2$ is 0. So there is no way using real numbers to make the left side equal to 0. The expression $(x - 6)^2 + 9$ is a sum of squares. There is no factoring rule for the sum of squares. The equation $x^2 - 12x + 45 = 0$ has no real solutions.

For Discussion

For what values of c does $x^2 - 35x + c = 0$ have the following results?

14. two distinct solutions   **15.** only one solution

16. no solutions in $\mathbb{R}$

Exercises *Practicing Habits of Mind*

Check Your Understanding

1. Solve each equation.

   a. $(x - 3)^2 - 16 = 0$ **b.** $(2y + 1)^2 - 100 = 0$

   c. $(n + 5)^2 - 5 = 0$

2. What value of k makes each equation an identity?

   a. $x^2 + 2x = (x + k)^2 - 1$

   b. $x^2 + 4x + 2 = (x + k)^2 - 2$

> Sometimes, there are multiple methods you can use to solve an exercise. Use any factoring method you prefer.

c. $x^2 - 4x + 2 = (x + k)^2 - 2$

d. $x^2 + 12x + 40 = (x + k)^2 + 4$

e. $x^2 + 9x + 10 = (x + k)^2 - 10.25$

f. $x^2 - 25x + 125 = (x + k)^2 - 31.25$

g. $x^2 + 2kx + 72 = (x + k)^2 + k$

3. You can generate this identity by completing the square.

$$x^2 + 8x + 11 = (x + 4)^2 - 5$$

a. The graph of $y = x^2 + 8x + 11$ is symmetric with respect to a vertical line. What is the equation of the vertical line?

b. What is the least possible y-value in the graph of $y = x^2 + 8x + 11$?

4. Sasha has a quick way to estimate the square of numbers that are close to 1. Sasha says, "To square 1.01, I add 1 to $2 \times 0.01 = 0.02$ to get 1.02. The right answer is 1.0201. That's pretty close. The closer I am to 1, the better my estimate will be."

a. Try Sasha's method for 1.03^2.

b. Try Sasha's method for 1.005^2.

c. **Take It Further** Find a rule for how close Sasha's method gets you to the exact answer.

5. Solve each polynomial equation. Use completing the square or any other method. Check your answers.

a. $x^2 - 6x + 10 = 5$

b. $x^2 + 8x + 2 = 11$

c. $x^2 + 7 = 6x$

d. $(2x + 1)(2x - 3) = 5$

e. $(x + 2) = \dfrac{3}{x + 4}$

6. Expressions for the side lengths of a rectangle and its area are given. Find the value of x and the side lengths of the rectangle.

a. side lengths: $x + 2$ and $x + 10$

area: 105

b. side lengths: $x - 6$ and $x - 10$

area: 5

c. side lengths: $x + 3$ and $x + 5$

area: 30

7. The expression $9a^2 - 24a + 16$ is a perfect square trinomial. It is equivalent to $(3a - 4)^2$.

a. If $36z^2 + kz + 25$ is a perfect square trinomial, what number is k?

b. If $49p^2 + 28p + j$ is a perfect square trinomial, what number is j?

8. Derman wants to solve the equation $2x^2 + 4x = 9$. He asks, "How do I solve a nonmonic?" Sasha replies, "Make it a monic by dividing both sides by 2." Tony complains, "That will introduce fractions." Sasha says, "Come on, deal with it!"

Sasha writes the following.

$$2x^2 + 4x = 9$$
$$2x^2 + 4x - 9 = 0$$
$$x^2 + 2x - \frac{9}{2} = 0$$
$$x^2 + 2x + 1 - 1 - \frac{9}{2} = 0$$
$$x^2 + 2x + 1 - \frac{11}{2} = 0$$
$$(x + 1)^2 - \frac{11}{2} = 0$$
$$\left(x + 1 + \sqrt{\frac{11}{2}}\right)\left(x + 1 - \sqrt{\frac{11}{2}}\right) = 0$$

Where did $\frac{11}{2}$ come from?

Tony says, "I like the way you added and subtracted the thing that completes the square. I can finish it from here."

a. When Tony says to Sasha, "I like the way you added and subtracted the thing that completes the square," what does he mean?

b. Finish Derman's problem. Solve $2x^2 + 4x = 9$.

9. Build a polynomial equation of the form $x^2 + bx + c = d$.

Choose values for b, c, and d (positive or negative). The equation should be different than any of the other equations in this lesson. Solve the equation by completing the square.

Be careful. Some equations will have no solutions. Also, some values of b can make this exercise easier than others. Which ones are they?

10. Use the equation you built in Exercise 9. Change the value of d so the new equation has no solutions.

On Your Own

11. **Write About It** Suppose you need to teach a robot how to complete the square for any polynomial of the form $x^2 + bx + c$. Write a set of very precise instructions.

12. Solve the equation $x^2 - 6x + 8 = 3$. Use completing the square or any other factoring method. Explain why you chose your method.

13. For each equation, find the value of k that makes it an identity.

  a. $x^2 + 6x = (x + 3)^2 + k$ **b.** $x^2 + 4x + 3 = (x + 2)^2 + k$

  c. $x^2 - 6x = (x - 3)^2 + k$ **d.** $25x^2 - 30x + 15 = (5x - 3)^2 + k$

  e. $16x^2 + 16x + 72 = (4x + 2)^2 + k$

14. Solve each polynomial equation. Use completing the square or any other method. Check your answers.

  a. $x^2 + 8x = 33$ **b.** $x(x + 6) = 160$

  c. $x^2 - 16x + 83 = 20$ **d.** $(x + 2)(x - 6) = 240$

15. A number plus 12 times its reciprocal equals 8. What is the number? Is there more than one answer?

16. A number plus 12 times its reciprocal equals 10. What is the number? Is there more than one answer?

17. You can use perfect square trinomials to square some numbers quickly. For example, $1007^2 = 1,014,049$.

  a. **Write About It** Explain how knowing $(x + 7)^2 = x^2 + 14x + 49$ helps you calculate 1007^2 quickly.

  b. Calculate 1009^2, 1013^2, and 997^2 without a calculator.

18. **Standardized Test Prep** You cut a square from each corner of a rectangular piece of sheet metal 10 inches by 6 inches. This forms an open-top rectangular box with a bottom area of 32 square inches. What size squares should you cut from the corners?

  A. $\frac{1}{2}$ in.

  B. 1 in.

  C. $1\frac{1}{2}$ in.

  D. 2 in.

Go Online
www.successnetplus.com

19. Solve each equation. Use any method.

  a. $x^2 + 20 = -12x$ **b.** $x(x - 21) = 22$ **c.** $x^2 + 8x - 105 = 0$

Maintain Your Skills

20. Complete the square for each polynomial.

  a. $x^2 + 8x$ **b.** $x^2 - 8x$ **c.** $x^2 + 16x$

  d. $x^2 - 16x$ **e.** $x^2 + 5x$ **f.** $x^2 - 5x$

  g. $x^2 - bx$ **h.** $x^2 + bx$ **i.** $x^2 - x$

21. Solve each equation. If no solutions exist, explain why.

    a. $x^2 + 8x - 10 = 0$ **b.** $x^2 - 8x - 10 = 0$ **c.** $x^2 + 16x = 17$

    d. $x^2 - 16x = 17$ **e.** $x^2 + 5x + 10 = 0$ **f.** $x^2 - 5x + 10 = 0$

    g. $x^2 - x = 0$

22. Solve the equation $10x + x^2 = 39$ by completing the square.

Go Online
www.successnetplus.com

For Exercises 23 and 24, read the Historical Perspective below.

23. Solve the equation $10x + x^2 = 39$ by following al-Khwarizmi's instructions. (Note that al-Khwarizmi uses "root" to mean x.)

24. You found two solutions to Exercise 23. However, al-Khwarizmi only described one solution. Why do you think he missed the other solution?

Historical Perspective
The Word *Algebra*

The word *algebra* comes from the Arabic language. Abu Ja'far Muhammed ibn Musa al-Khwarizmi was an Arab mathematician and astronomer. In the 800s, he wrote the mathematics book *Al-jabr W'al Muqabala*.

    In this book, the phrase *al-jabr* refers to one of the two operations used to solve equations. The usual meaning is to add equal terms to both sides of an equation to eliminate negative terms. The less frequent meaning is to multiply both sides of an equation by one and the same number to eliminate fractions. The word *algebra* became the shorthand way of referring to the techniques in this book.

    Al-Khwarizmi's method for completing the square was one of his most powerful techniques. He wrote his problems and solutions using sentences instead of math symbols. One of his most famous problems is this: Add ten roots to one square, and the sum is equal to nine and thirty. You can rewrite this problem as $10x + x^2 = 39$. Here is al-Khwarizmi's solution.

    Take half the number of roots, that is, in this case five, and then multiply this by itself and the result is five and twenty. Add this to the nine and thirty, which gives sixty-four; take the square root, or eight, and subtract from it half the number of roots, namely five, and there remains three. This is the root.

This 1983 Union of Soviet Socialist Republics postage stamp with al-Khwarizmi's picture commemorates his birth about 1200 years ago.

In this investigation, you factored quadratics, using the difference of squares or the sums and products methods. These questions will help you summarize what you have learned.

1. Copy and complete this table. Find two numbers that have the given sum and product.

Sum of Two Numbers	Product of Two Numbers	Numbers
10	25	■, ■
10	24	■, ■
10	21	■, ■
10	16	■, ■
10	9	■, ■

2. Factor each of the following.

   a. $x^2 - 25$ **b.** $a^2 - 144$ **c.** $49 - y^2$ **d.** $4x^2 - 1$

3. Factor each quadratic expression over $\mathbb{Z}$. If you cannot factor an expression, explain why.

   a. $x^2 + 13x + 40$ **b.** $x^2 + 14x + 40$ **c.** $x^2 - 13x + 40$

   d. $x^2 + 10x + 40$ **e.** $x^2 + 3x - 40$ **f.** $x^2 - 3x - 40$

4. Factor each quadratic expression over $\mathbb{Z}$ by completing the square.

   a. $x^2 + 32x + 255$ **b.** $x^2 - 40x + 396$ **c.** $x^2 + 2x - 168$

5. Solve each equation. Use any method.

   a. $x^2 + 5x - 24 = 0$ **b.** $x^2 + 2x = 99$ **c.** $x(x + 8) = 209$

6. Suppose you know the sum and product of two numbers. How can you find the two numbers?

7. How do you determine quickly whether you can factor a monic quadratic expression over $\mathbb{Z}$?

8. How do you solve equations such as $x^2 = 15x + 250$?

Vocabulary

In this investigation, you learned these terms. Make sure you understand what each one means and how to use it.

- **binomial**
- **monic**
- **perfect square trinomial**
- **polynomial equation**
- **trinomial**

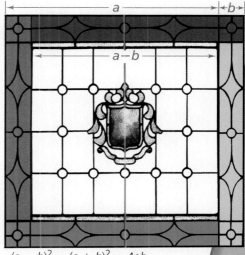

$(a - b)^2 = (a + b)^2 - 4ab$

Project: Using Mathematical Habits

Differences of Squares

In number theory, the analysis of what numbers are sums or differences of squares leads to some surprising results. In this chapter, you investigated the question, "Can you write every positive integer as a difference of two squares?" Here are some examples.

$$5 = 9 - 4 = 3^2 - 2^2$$
$$24 = 25 - 1 = 5^2 - 1^2$$
$$28 = 64 - 36 = 8^2 - 6^2$$
$$17 = 81 - 64 = 9^2 - 8^2$$

This project continues the investigation by developing a rule. The rule gives the number of ways you can write a positive integer as a difference of two squares.

For example, you can write 5 as a difference of squares one way, $5 = 9 - 4$. However, you can write 24 as a difference of squares in two ways. Check that there are no other ways.

$$24 = 5^2 - 1^2$$
$$24 = 7^2 - 5^2$$

Finding a Rule

Here are some suggested steps for finding the rule.

Step 1 Make a table. Copy and complete the table in Figure 1. In each cell, write the difference of the squares of the numbers in that row and column.

Difference of Squares

	0^2	1^2	2^2	3^2	4^2	5^2	6^2	7^2	8^2	9^2	10^2
10^2	100	■	96	■	■	■	■	■	■	■	■
9^2	81	■	■	■	■	■	■	■	17	■	
8^2	64	■	■	■	■	■	■	■	■		
7^2	49	■	■	■	33	■	■	■			
6^2	36	■	■	■	■	■	■				
5^2	25	■	■	■	■	■					
4^2	16	■	■	■	■						
3^2	9	■	■	■							
2^2	4	3	0								
1^2	1	0									
0^2	0										

Figure 1

Step 2 Gather data. Use the table below to organize your work. For each integer from 1 to 50, determine all the ways that number can be written as a difference of the squares of two nonnegative integers. The first integer must be positive. For example, the number 49 can be written as $7^2 - 0^2$, which fits the description.

Look for patterns in the data. Make some conjectures.

Number of Ways

Integer	Number of Ways	Difference
1	1	$1 - 0$
2	0	none
$\vdots$	$\vdots$	$\vdots$

Step 3 Analyze special cases. For example, show that 173 can be written as a difference of squares in only one way. Likewise, show that 519 can be written as a difference of squares in two ways.

Analyze the cases without listing every possible case. For example, connect the solution of this system of equations with the analysis of the 173 case.

$$\begin{cases} x + y = 173 \\ x - y = 1 \end{cases}$$

Step 4 Make and test conjectures. If you think something is true, write it down as a conjecture. Then experiment using numbers.

If you find an example for which your conjecture does not work, try to refine your conjecture to plug the hole. If you gain some confidence that your conjecture will always work, try to prove it by replacing the numbers with variables.

Step 5 Write about your work. Explaining a concept in words is the best way to understand it. Let someone read your description for clarity and accuracy.

Review

In **Investigation 2A,** you learned how to

- use basic rules and moves to transform expressions and determine whether different expressions define the same function

- factor expressions by identifying a common factor

- apply the Zero-Product Property to factored expressions

- use algebra to simplify long computations, such as computing large sums of consecutive numbers

The following questions will help you check your understanding.

1. Consider the following functions.

$$g(x) = (x + 3)(x^2 - 5x + 4)$$
$$h(x) = x^3 - 2x^2 - 11x + 12$$

   a. Find the values of each function if x equals 1, 2, or 3.

   b. Show that g and h are the same function.

2. Prove that the following equation is true.
$$2m^2n - m^3 - mn^2 - 2mn + m^2 + n^2$$
$$= (m - 1)(m - n)(n - m)$$

3. Find the sum of the odd numbers from 19 to 101.

4. A square has side length $(k - x)$. A smaller square with side length x is cut from a corner.

   a. In terms of k and x, find the area of the leftover shape.

   b. If k is 12 and x is 5, find the area of the leftover shape by using the formula you found in part (a).

5. Find all solutions to each equation. Use factoring and ZPP.

   a. $(x - 7)(2x + 1) = 0$

   b. $x^3 - 4x^2 = 0$

   c. $x^3 - 4x = 0$

   d. $3a^2 = 12ab$

   e. $a(x + 1) + 3(x + 1) = 0$

6. Write each expression as a product of expressions.

   a. $abc + acx$

   b. $4p(d - 3) + 5q(d - 3)$

   c. $(2 - x)(7) - (2 - x)(y)$

   d. $(a - b)(x) + (a - b)$

In **Investigation 2B,** you learned how to

- recognize and provide examples of polynomials

- understand the definitions and importance of the terms *coefficient* and *degree*

- expand polynomials and express them in normal form

- determine whether polynomials in different forms are equivalent

- add, subtract, and multiply polynomials

The following questions will help you check your understanding.

7. Use the equation $f(x) = x^2 - 4x + 4$.

   a. Find a polynomial $s(x)$ such that $f(x) + s(x) = x^2 - 3x - 6$.

   b. Find the difference $f(x) - s(x)$.

   c. Find the product $f(x) \cdot s(x)$.

8. Consider the following polynomials.

$$2x^3 - 3x^2 + x$$

$$2x^3 + 8x^2 - 1$$

a. Find their sum. What is the degree of the sum?

b. Find their difference if $2x^3 + 8x^2 - 1$ is subtracted from $2x^3 - 3x^2 + x$. What is the degree of the difference?

c. Find their product. What is the degree of the product?

9. Use the polynomial below.
$$2 - 3x^2 + 2x^5 - 4x - x^2 + x^4$$

a. Write the polynomial in normal form.

b. What is the degree of the polynomial?

c. Write the coefficients of each term.

d. Find a polynomial that, when added to this one, gives a sum of degree 3.

10. Show that each equation is an identity by writing it in normal form.

a. $a^3 + 8 =$
   $a(a^2 - 2a + 4) + 2(a^2 - 2a + 4)$

b. $(b - 1)^2 + 3(b - 1) = (b + 2)(b - 1)$

11. Without expanding, find the coefficient of x^5 in the normal form of the polynomial below.

$$(x^2 - 8x + 3)(x^4 - 2x^3 + x^2)$$
$$- (3x^6 + 2x^5 - x^4)$$

12. Find the value of m that makes each equality true.

a. $(x + 1)(x + m) = x^2 + 5x + 4$

b. $(2x - 1)(mx + 1) = 6x^2 - x - 1$

c. $x^4 - x^3 - 6 - (mx^3 - x^2 - 4)$
   $= x^4 - 5x^3 + x^2 - 2$

In **Investigation 2C,** you learned how to

- apply the Difference of Squares Theorem to polynomial expressions and numerical examples
- use difference of squares factoring to solve equations
- factor monic quadratic polynomials
- factor general quadratic polynomials
- use factoring to solve equations

The following questions will help you check your understanding.

13. Two numbers add to 16. Their product is as given. Give an example of the numbers. If it is not possible, explain.

a. less than 64 b. more than 64   c. 0

d. positive   e. negative   f. 39

g. −36

14. Factor each pair of expressions.

a. $49c^2 - 16$ and $0.49c^2 - 0.16$

b. $121p^3 - 81p$ and $121p^4 - 81p^2$

c. $9x^2 - 16$ and $\frac{4}{9}x^2 - \frac{9}{16}$

15. Factor each expression.

a. $x^2 + 12x + 27$

b. $x^2 - x - 12$

c. $x^2 - 12x + 27$

16. Factor using the given method.

a. $4x^2 - 9$ as a difference of two squares

b. $x^2 + 13x + 42$ using sums and products

c. $x^2 - 6x - 720$ by completing the square

17. What value of m makes each trinomial a perfect square?

a. $9x^4 + mx^2 + 16$

b. $36x^2 - 60x + m$

18. Use ZPP and what you know about factoring. Find the solutions to each equation.

a. $x^2 - 5x = 14$ b. $x(x + 3) = 40$

c. $x^2 - 10x + 2 = 0$ d. $x^2 + 4x = 165$

Multiple Choice

1. If you expand the expression

$$(x^2 + x - 2)(2x - 1)$$

what is the coefficient of x?

A. -3 **B.** 3

C. 1   **D.** -5

2. How many solutions are there to the equation $x(x^2 - 4) = 0$?

A. 0   **B.** 1

C. 2   **D.** 3

3. What is the greatest common factor of $12x^2y^3$ and $30xy^5z$?

A. $3xy^3z$ **B.** $6xy^3$

C. $6x^2y^5$ **D.** $360x^3y^8z$

4. Consider the two functions, p and q.

$$p(x) = 2x^4 - 3x^2 + x - 1$$

$$q(x) = kx^4 + x^3 - x^2 + 4x + 5$$

If $p(x) + q(x)$ has degree 3, what is the value of k?

A. 0   **B.** 2

C. -2 **D.** -1

5. If the following equation is true

$$x^2 + 5x - 8 = (x + m)(x + n)$$

what is $m + n$?

A. 5   **B.** -5

C. 8   **D.** -8

6. If the following equation is true

$$x^2 + 10x + 8 = (x + k)^2 - 17$$

what is the value of k?

A. 5   **B.** 9

C. 25   **D.** 64

7. Which value of k makes the equation $x^2 + 10x = (x + 5)^2 + k$ an identity?

A. -25 **B.** 0

C. 5   **D.** 25

8. For what value of c does the equation $x^2 - 10x + c = 0$ have only one solution?

A. 0   **B.** 4

C. 10   **D.** 25

9. What number must you add to $x^2 + \frac{3}{2}x$ to complete the square in $x^2 + \frac{3}{2}x + 2$?

A. $\frac{3}{16}$ **B.** $\frac{9}{16}$

C. $\frac{3}{4}$ **D.** $\frac{23}{16}$

Open Response

10. Find all the solutions to the equation $x^3 = 9x$.

11. Find two factors of each number.

  a. $25^2 - 2^2$

  b. $1000^2 - 89^2$

  c. $m^2 - n^2$

12. Find each product. Do not use a calculator.

  a. 39×81 **b.** 61×42

  c. 105×93 **d.** $(200 + x)(200 - x)$

13. Find each quotient. Do not use a calculator.

  a. $\dfrac{11^2 - 9^2}{11 + 9}$

  b. $\dfrac{15^2 - 4^2}{15 + 4}$

  c. $\dfrac{x^2 - 25^2}{x + 25}$

14. Consider these functions.

$$g(x) = x^2 - x + (x + 2)(x + 4)$$

$$h(x) = 2x^2 + 5x + 8$$

Show that g and h are the same function.

15. Suppose $f(x) = (x^2 + 4x - 2)(x^2 - 3x + 1)$.

    a. Write $f(x)$ in normal form.

    b. What is the degree of $f(x)$?

    c. Find a polynomial $g(x)$ so that $f(x) + g(x)$ will have degree 3 and the coefficient of x^2 will be 6.

16. a. Factor $9x^2 - 25y^2$ as the difference of two squares.

    b. Factor $x^2 + 10x + 16$ using sums and products.

    c. Factor $x^2 - 24x + 119$ by completing the square.

17. The sum of a number plus 12 times its reciprocal equals 7. What is the number? Is there more than one answer? Explain.

18. The area of a rectangle is 120. The length of the rectangle is $x - 5$. Its width is $x - 12$.

    Find x and the side lengths of the rectangle.

19. Two numbers add to -30. What is the greatest possible value of their product?

20. What value of m makes each trinomial a perfect square?

    a. $x^2 - 10x + m$ **b.** $4x^2 + mx + 9$

    c. $mx^2 - 16x + 1$ **d.** $81x^4 - mx^2 + 49$

21. Solve the equation $x^2 - 2x - 10 = 0$.

22. Solve the equation $(x - 2)(x + 3) = 36$.

23. A rectangle of width x is 4 times as long as it is wide. A square y units on a side is cut from one corner of the rectangle. In terms of x and y, find the area of the leftover shape.

24. State the Zero-Product Property. Explain how ZPP can help you solve certain equations. Give an example.

25. The equation $(x + 2)(x - 3) = 0$ has two solutions. Find a number that you can add to the left side of the equation that will give a new equation with integer solutions.

26. Suppose $p(x)$ and $q(x)$ are degree 2 polynomials that are impossible to factor over $\mathbb{Z}$. Decide whether each statement is true or false. Explain each answer.

    a. $p(x) + q(x)$ can be a degree 2 polynomial that you can factor over $\mathbb{Z}$.

    b. $p(x) - q(x)$ can be a degree 2 polynomial that you cannot factor over $\mathbb{Z}$.

Challenge Problem

27. For what value(s) of c does $x^2 + 6x + c = 0$ have no real solutions?

Chapter 3

Quadratics and Complex Numbers

Mathematicians invented much of algebra to find mechanical methods for working with general problems. Some of these problems relate to the motion of free-falling bodies that are affected solely by the force of gravity. Other problems relate to land and sea populations, environmental issues, and numerous other situations.

One of the most famous mechanical methods is the quadratic formula. It allows you to solve any quadratic equation. In this chapter, you will only solve quadratic equations that have real roots.

You also will look closely at the graphs of quadratic equations. Their shape, a parabola, has some special properties.

You have developed many tools for working with linear equations and functions. Now you will find that many of these tools apply to quadratic equations and functions.

Vocabulary

- complex numbers, $\mathbb{C}$
- conjugate, $\bar{z}$
- Fundamental Theorem of Algebra
- irrational numbers
- line of symmetry
- maximum
- minimum
- monic equation
- natural numbers, $\mathbb{N}$
- nonmonic quadratic
- parabola
- vertex
- vertex form
- $i\ (\sqrt{-1})$
- $a + bi$ (complex number)

Investigation 3A

The Quadratic Formula

In *The Quadratic Formula*, you will model functions using different forms of quadratic equations. You also will expand upon your work factoring quadratic equations, and you will factor nonmonic equations. Using the quadratic formula, you will find solutions to specific equations.

By the end of this investigation, you will be able to answer questions like these.

1. How can you solve any quadratic equation?

2. How can you factor any quadratic polynomial?

3. How are the roots of a quadratic equation related to its coefficients?

You will learn how to
- use the quadratic formula to solve equations or determine whether an equation has no real solutions

- construct a quadratic equation given the equation's two roots

- factor nonmonic quadratics

You will develop these habits and skills:
- Understand the connection between the quadratic formula and the process of completing the square.

- Calculate comfortably using radicals.

- Successfully apply the quadratic formula to specific examples.

- See the connection between the roots of a quadratic equation and the coefficients of a quadratic equation.

Quadratic functions $f(x) = ax^2 + bx + c$ model the parabolic paths of water spray.

Activating Prior Knowledge
Exploring New Ideas

A quadratic function is similar to a linear function. There is a pattern that relates the input of the function to its output. You will use a function table and the quadratic formula to analyze a quadratic function.

For You to Explore

1. Suppose $\alpha = 3 + \sqrt{2}$ and $\beta = 3 - \sqrt{2}$. Find the value of each expression.

a. $\alpha + \beta$ **b.** $\alpha\beta$ **c.** $\alpha^2 - 6\alpha + 7$

> In this exercise, the Greek letter α (AL fuh) stands for the quantity $3 + \sqrt{2}$. The Greek letter β (BAYT uh) stands for $3 - \sqrt{2}$.

For Problems 2–11, solve each equation.

2. $(x - 3)^2 - 2 = 0$ **3.** $x^2 - 6x + 7 = 0$

4. $x^2 - 8x + 11 = 0$ **5.** $x^2 - 7x + 7 = 0$

6. $2x^2 - 14x + 14 = 0$ **7.** $2x^2 - 7x + 4 = 0$

8. $2x^2 + 7x + 4 = 0$ **9.** $3x^2 - 28x + 9 = 0$

10. $4x^2 - 28x + 49 = 0$ **11.** $4x^2 - 28x + 50 = 0$

Exercises *Practicing Habits of Mind*

On Your Own

12. Solve each quadratic equation.

a. $x^2 - 6x + 4 = 0$

b. $x^2 + 6x + 4 = 0$

c. $x^2 - 6x + 2 = 0$

d. $x^2 + 6x + 2 = 0$

e. $2x^2 - 12x + 11 = 0$

f. $2x^2 + 12x + 25 = 0$

13. Complete the following for each equation.

   - Make a table of inputs and outputs. Use at least five different inputs.
   - Sketch each graph on a separate grid using the table.
   - Find the points where each graph crosses the x-axis.

   a. $(x - 3)^2 - 2 = y$ **b.** $x^2 - 6x + 7 = y$

   c. $x^2 - 7x + 7 = y$ **d.** $2x^2 - 7x + 4 = y$

   e. $2x^2 + 7x + 4 = y$ **f.** $4x^2 - 28x + 49 = y$

   g. $3x^2 - 28x + 9 = y$ **h.** $4x^2 - 28x + 50 = y$

Go Online
www.successnetplus.com

14. **Write About It** Why does the equation $(x - 4)^2 + 9 = 0$ have no solutions?

15. The graph of an equation can have a *line of symmetry*. Such a line divides a graph into two halves that are mirror images of each other. For example, the y-axis is the line of symmetry for the graph of $y = x^2$.

   Find equations for any lines of symmetry for each graph. Relate the lines of symmetry to the points where the graphs cross the x-axis.

   a. $(x - 3)^2 - 2 = y$ **b.** $x^2 - 6x + 7 = y$

   c. $x^2 - 7x + 7 = y$ **d.** $2x^2 - 7x + 4 = y$

   e. $2x^2 + 7x + 4 = y$ **f.** $4x^2 - 28x + 49 = y$

   g. $3x^2 - 28x + 9 = y$ **h.** $4x^2 - 28x + 50 = y$

Maintain Your Skills

16. Find the points of intersection for each pair of graphs.

   a. $(x - 3)^2 - 1 = y$ and $y = 1$ **b.** $x^2 - 6x + 10 = y$ and $y = 3$

   c. $x^2 - 7x + 7 = y$ and $y = 0$ **d.** $2x^2 - 7x + 6 = y$ and $y = 2$

   e. $2x^2 + 7x + 6 = y$ and $y = 2$ **f.** $4x^2 - 28x + 50 = y$ and $y = 1$

   g. $3x^2 - 28x + 12 = y$ and $y = 3$ **h.** $4x^2 - 28x + 49 = y$ and $y = -1$

   Review Exercise 13 in this lesson. For help finding the intersection points of two graphs, see the TI-Nspire™ Handbook, p. 990.

17. Find a quadratic equation with integer coefficients that has each of the following solutions.

   a. $x = 3$, $x = 2$ **b.** $x = -3$, $x = -2$

   c. $x = 6$, $x = 4$ **d.** $x = 3 + \sqrt{2}$, $x = 3 - \sqrt{2}$

   e. $x = -3 - \sqrt{2}$, $x = -3 + \sqrt{2}$ **f.** $x = 6 + 2\sqrt{2}$, $x = 6 - 2\sqrt{2}$

   g. $x = 1 + \sqrt{3}$, $x = 1 - \sqrt{3}$ **h.** $x = \dfrac{1 + \sqrt{3}}{2}$, $x = \dfrac{1 - \sqrt{3}}{2}$

   i. $x = \dfrac{-1 + \sqrt{3}}{2}$, $x = \dfrac{-1 - \sqrt{3}}{2}$

3.02 Making It Formal—Deriving the Quadratic Formula

Mathematicians look for patterns that may help them solve more complex problems. As you solve each equation in the experiment, keep track of the steps that you use to find the solution.

After working through the exercises in Lesson 3.02, you can probably solve any quadratic equation in the world.

In-Class Experiment

Solve $x^2 + rx + s = 0$ given the following conditions. Give precise results that may include radicals.

1. $r = -2$ and $s = -8$

2. $r = -4$ and $s = -1$

3. $r = \frac{5}{2}$ and $s = -\frac{3}{2}$

4. $r = -7$ and $s = 7$

5. in terms of s, $r = -6$

6. in terms of r and s

You have developed a mechanical process that always works. As long as the equation has real-number solutions, the process tells you what they are. The steps in the process are as follows.

> You call this mechanical set of steps an algorithm.

Step 1 Divide through by the coefficient of x^2 so that the equation becomes monic.

> A **monic equation** has a leading coefficient of 1.

Step 2 Complete the square.

Step 3 Factor the result as a difference of squares.

Step 4 Set each factor equal to 0. Solve for x.

For Discussion

7. Explain how this process shows when a quadratic equation has no real roots.

When a process becomes mechanical, you can use algebra to carry it out on a general example. A general example is an example in which you replace the numbers with letters. The result of this process is a formula, or an identity. You can use this formula to handle all of the specific cases by replacing the letters with numbers.

Instead of solving a specific equation in Problem 6, you solved a general equation $x^2 + rx + s = 0$. This result is very important, so it is stated as a theorem.

The equation $x^2 + rx + s = 0$ is a general monic quadratic.

Theorem 3.1

If the equation $x^2 + rx + s = 0$ has real-number solutions, they are

$$x = \frac{-r + \sqrt{r^2 - 4s}}{2} \text{ and } x = \frac{-r - \sqrt{r^2 - 4s}}{2}$$

Equivalently, you could use the $\pm$ sign to express both solutions in one statement.

$$x = \frac{-r \pm \sqrt{r^2 - 4s}}{2}$$

Proof The proof will be familiar if you did Problem 6 of the previous experiment.

Step 1 The equation is already monic. So you do not have to divide by the coefficient of x^2.

Step 2 Complete the square.

$$x^2 + rx + s = x^2 + rx + \frac{r^2}{4} - \frac{r^2}{4} + s$$
$$= \left(x + \frac{r}{2}\right)^2 - \frac{r^2 - 4s}{4}$$

Notice that $-\frac{r^2}{4} + s = -\frac{r^2 - 4s}{4}$. Make sure you understand why the equation is true.

Step 3 Factor the result as a difference of squares.

$$\Rightarrow \left(x + \frac{r}{2} + \sqrt{\frac{r^2 - 4s}{4}}\right)\left(x + \frac{r}{2} - \sqrt{\frac{r^2 - 4s}{4}}\right) = 0$$

Step 4 Set each factor equal to 0 and solve for x.

$$\Rightarrow x + \frac{r}{2} + \sqrt{\frac{r^2 - 4s}{4}} = 0 \text{ or } x + \frac{r}{2} - \sqrt{\frac{r^2 - 4s}{4}} = 0$$
$$\Rightarrow x = -\frac{r}{2} - \frac{\sqrt{r^2 - 4s}}{2} \text{ or } x = -\frac{r}{2} + \frac{\sqrt{r^2 - 4s}}{2}$$
$$\Rightarrow x = \frac{-r - \sqrt{r^2 - 4s}}{2} \text{ or } x = \frac{-r + \sqrt{r^2 - 4s}}{2}$$

Developing Habits of Mind

Simplify complicated problems. As equations get more complicated, you will need to do more work to find the solutions. Theorem 3.1 takes all the guesswork out of solving monic quadratic equations. You only need to replace r and s with the correct numbers and simplify.

For example, to solve $x^2 - 6x + 7 = 0$, compare it with the general example.

$$\begin{array}{ccccccc} x^2 & + & r & x & + & s & = 0 \\ & & \downarrow & & & \downarrow & \\ x^2 & + & (-6) & x & + & 7 & = 0 \end{array}$$

Replace r with -6 and s with 7 in the general solutions. Then simplify.

156 **Chapter 3** Quadratics and Complex Numbers

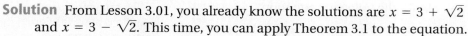

Example 1

Problem Solve the equation $x^2 - 6x + 7 = 0$.

Solution From Lesson 3.01, you already know the solutions are $x = 3 + \sqrt{2}$ and $x = 3 - \sqrt{2}$. This time, you can apply Theorem 3.1 to the equation.

The theorem states that the solutions of the equation $x^2 + rx + s = 0$, in terms of r and s, are as follows.

$$x = \frac{-r + \sqrt{r^2 - 4s}}{2} \text{ or } x = \frac{-r - \sqrt{r^2 - 4s}}{2}$$

Replace r with -6 and s with 7.

$$x = \frac{-(-6) + \sqrt{(-6)^2 - 4(7)}}{2} \text{ or } x = \frac{-(-6) - \sqrt{(-6)^2 - 4(7)}}{2}$$

Simplify the first solution.

$$x = \frac{-(-6) + \sqrt{(-6)^2 - 4(7)}}{2}$$

$$= \frac{6 + \sqrt{36 - 28}}{2}$$

$$= \frac{6 + \sqrt{8}}{2}$$

$$= \frac{6 + 2\sqrt{2}}{2}$$

$$= 3 + \sqrt{2}$$

For You to Do

8. Simplify the second solution from Example 1.

$$\frac{-(-6) - \sqrt{(-6)^2 - 4(7)}}{2}$$

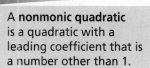

For Discussion

9. The equation $x^2 - 3x + 5 = 0$ has no real roots. What happens if you use the formula in Theorem 3.1 to solve the equation?

Theorem 3.1 only works if the equation is monic. To solve a nonmonic quadratic, divide through by the coefficient of x^2. Then replace r and s with the resulting fractions.

A **nonmonic quadratic** is a quadratic with a leading coefficient that is a number other than 1.

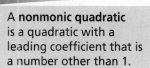

You could work out an example. However, all you will end up doing is running fractions through the formula. Instead, work it through generally. You will find a formula that works for any quadratic.

A general nonmonic equation is $ax^2 + bx + c = 0$. Suppose a is a positive number. Divide both sides by a to obtain the following equation.

$$x^2 + \frac{b}{a}x + \frac{c}{a} = 0$$

Why can you suppose that a is positive? Can you write any quadratic in this form such that a is positive? Explain.

Now match this equation with the quadratic from Theorem 3.1.

$$
\begin{array}{ccccc}
x^2 & + & r & x & + & s & = 0 \\
& & \downarrow & & & \downarrow & \\
x^2 & + & \dfrac{b}{a} & x & + & \dfrac{c}{a} & = 0
\end{array}
$$

Replace r with $\frac{b}{a}$ and s with $\frac{c}{a}$ in the general solutions.

$$x = \frac{-\frac{b}{a} + \sqrt{\left(\frac{b}{a}\right)^2 - 4\left(\frac{c}{a}\right)}}{2} \quad \text{and} \quad x = \frac{-\frac{b}{a} - \sqrt{\left(\frac{b}{a}\right)^2 - 4\left(\frac{c}{a}\right)}}{2}$$

Simplify the first solution.

$$\frac{-\frac{b}{a} + \sqrt{\left(\frac{b}{a}\right)^2 - 4\left(\frac{c}{a}\right)}}{2} = \frac{-\frac{b}{a} + \sqrt{\frac{b^2}{a^2} - 4\left(\frac{c}{a}\right)}}{2} \qquad \text{since } \left(\frac{b}{a}\right)^2 = \frac{b^2}{a^2}$$

$$= \frac{-\frac{b}{a} + \sqrt{\frac{b^2}{a^2} - 4\left(\frac{ac}{a^2}\right)}}{2} \qquad \text{since } \frac{c}{a} = \frac{ac}{a^2}$$

$$= \frac{-\frac{b}{a} + \sqrt{\frac{1}{a^2}\left(b^2 - 4ac\right)}}{2} \qquad \text{by the Distributive Property}$$

$$= \frac{-\frac{b}{a} + \frac{1}{a}\sqrt{b^2 - 4ac}}{2} \qquad \text{Because } a > 0, \text{ you can say that } \sqrt{\frac{1}{a^2}} = \frac{1}{a}.$$

$$= \frac{\frac{1}{a}\left(-b + \sqrt{b^2 - 4ac}\right)}{2} \qquad \text{by the Distributive Property}$$

$$= \frac{-b + \sqrt{b^2 - 4ac}}{2a} \qquad \text{since } \frac{\frac{1}{a}}{2} = \frac{1}{2a}$$

For You to Do

10. Show that the other root is $\dfrac{-b - \sqrt{b^2 - 4ac}}{2a}$.

The work you have just done results in one of the most famous theorems in algebra.

Theorem 3.2 The Quadratic Formula

If the equation $ax^2 + bx + c = 0$ has real-number solutions, they are given by the quadratic formula.

$$x = \frac{-b + \sqrt{b^2 - 4ac}}{2a} \text{ and } \frac{-b - \sqrt{b^2 - 4ac}}{2a}$$

Equivalently, you could use the ± sign to express both solutions in one statement.

$$x = \frac{-b \pm \sqrt{b^2 - 4ac}}{2a}$$

Example 2

Problem Solve the equation $2x^2 + 7x - 15 = 0$.

Solution First match a, b, and c with the appropriate coefficients.

$$ax^2 + bx + c = 0$$
$$\downarrow \qquad \downarrow \qquad \downarrow$$
$$2x^2 + 7x + (-15) = 0$$

So, $a = 2$, $b = 7$, and $c = -15$. Substitute these values into the quadratic formula.

$$\frac{-b \pm \sqrt{b^2 - 4ac}}{2a} = \frac{-(7) \pm \sqrt{(7)^2 - 4(2)(-15)}}{2(2)}$$

Simplify.

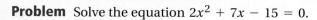
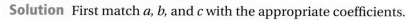

$$\frac{-7 \pm \sqrt{49 - (-120)}}{4} = \frac{-7 \pm \sqrt{169}}{4}$$

$$= \frac{-7 \pm 13}{4}$$

$$= \frac{-7 + 13}{4} \text{ and } \frac{-7 - 13}{4}$$

$$= \frac{6}{4} \text{ and } \frac{-20}{4}$$

$$= \frac{3}{2} \text{ and } -5$$

The two roots of $2x^2 + 7x - 15 = 0$ are $x = \frac{3}{2}$ and $x = -5$.

For Discussion

11. The equation $3x^2 - 5x + 7 = 0$ has no real roots. What happens when you try to solve it using the quadratic formula?

Exercises Practicing Habits of Mind

Check Your Understanding

For Exercises 1–8, solve the equations using any method. If there are no real number solutions, explain why.

1. $3x^2 + 7x + 1 = 0$

2. $3x^2 + 7x = 8$

3. $3x^2 - 7x = 8$

4. $3x^2 - 7x + 8 = 0$

5. $3x^2 - 7x + 2 = 0$

6. $w^2 - \sqrt{5}w = 5$

7. $z^2 - 1 = 2\sqrt{2}z$

8. $x^2 - 6x = k^2 - 9$ (in terms of k)

9. Find all numbers that are 930 less than their squares.

10. Derman poses a problem for Tony: "The square of a number is 29 more than 12 times the number." Help Tony solve Derman's puzzle.

11. a. Sasha's father hosts a dinner party. He proposes a toast, and everyone clinks glasses with everyone else, exactly once. There are four couples in all at the dinner party. How many clinks are there?

b. Derman's mother hosts a dinner party. Derman has no idea how many people are there. He hears 66 clinks for one toast. How many people are at the party?

On Your Own

For Exercises 12–16, solve each equation. If there are no real-number solutions, explain why.

12. $4x^2 - 6x + 1 = 0$

13. $9y^2 - 6y + 1 = 0$

14. $9y^2 + 6y + 1 = 0$

15. $9y^2 + 6y + 2 = 0$

16. $9z^2 + 6z - 2 = 0$

17. If possible, find two numbers with a sum that is 8 and a product that is $\frac{15}{4}$.

18. Standardized Test Prep Which quadratic equation has no real solutions?

   A. $-4x^2 - 12x = 0$

   B. $-4x^2 - 12x + 5 = 0$

   C. $-4x^2 - 12x - 9 = 0$

   D. $-4x^2 - 12x - 12 = 0$

Go Online
www.successnetplus.com

19. Find a value of k such that $3x^2 - 12x + k$ has the following solutions.

    a. two real-number solutions   **b.** exactly one real-number solution

    c. no real-number solutions

20. **Write About It** Consider the general quadratic equation $ax^2 + bx + c = 0$.
Give some conditions of a, b, and c if the equation has the following.

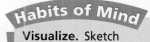

Assume a, b, and c are integers.

    a. two real roots   **b.** two rational roots

    c. exactly one rational root   **d.** no real roots

21. For what values of x is $6x^2 - 5x - 4$ negative?

For Exercises 22 and 23, find the intersection points for the graphs of each pair of equations.

Habits of Mind

Visualize. Sketch the graphs.

22. **a.** $4x - y = 2$ and $y = 3x^2 - 6x - 10$

    b. $4x - y = 13$ and $y = 3x^2 - 6x - 10$

23. **Take It Further**

    a. $3x - y = 1$ and $x^2 + y^2 = 1$

    b. $17x + 11y = 19$ and $x^2 + y^2 = 1$

24. For what values of x is each equation true?

    a. $\left(\frac{x+3}{2}\right)^2 - \left(\frac{x-3}{2}\right)^2 = 3x$

    b. $\left(\frac{x+3}{2}\right)^2 + \left(\frac{x-3}{2}\right)^2 = 3x$

25. **a.** Find a quadratic equation with roots 5 and 7.

    b. Can you find a second quadratic equation with roots 5 and 7?
A third quadratic equation with roots 5 and 7?

26. **Take It Further** Suppose you can take square roots of negative numbers.
Find two numbers with a sum of 4 and a product of 7.

Maintain Your Skills

27. Solve each quadratic equation. Find the sum and the product of the roots.

    a. $x^2 - 5x + 3 = 0$ **b.** $x^2 - 15x + 3 = 0$

    c. $x^2 + 15x + 56 = 0$ **d.** $2x^2 - 15x + 3 = 0$

    e. $x^2 + rx + s = 0$ **f.** $x^2 + 15x + 66 = 0$

    g. How do the sum and product of the roots relate to the numbers in
each equation?

Go Online
Video Tutor
www.successnetplus.com

Building the Quadratic Formula from Its Roots

A quadratic equation is like a puzzle. There are numbers that you know, the coefficients, and there are numbers that you do not know, the roots. The object of the puzzle is to find the numbers you do not know in terms of the numbers that you do.

In Lesson 3.02, you found the complete solution to the quadratic puzzle, the quadratic formula. Suppose you know the roots of a quadratic equation. Can you reconstruct the equation?

> Solving quadratic equations is like playing a game such as tic-tac-toe, where you know a foolproof strategy for winning. However, you can still enjoy the game.

Minds in Action

Tony and Sasha are having lunch after algebra class.

Tony Here's one for you. I had a quadratic equation, solved it, and got roots of 5 and 7. What was my equation?

Sasha thinks for a bit.

Sasha There's no one answer. I can give you a dozen equations that have 5 and 7 as roots.

Tony Give me one.

Sasha $x^2 - 12x + 35 = 0$.

Tony How'd you get that?

Sasha Well, I imagined I was solving it. Since the solutions are integers, it must have factored. Since the roots are 5 and 7, it must have factored like this.

Sasha writes on her napkin.

$$(x - 5)(x - 7) = 0$$

> *It must have factored* means *it must have factored over $\mathbb{Z}$*, the set of integers.

Sasha So, I multiplied this out and got $x^2 - 12x + 35 = 0$.

Tony Do you say that there are others?

Sasha Sure. Multiply both sides of my equation by 2, 3, π, or anything.

For You to Do

1. Find a quadratic equation with roots that are 9 and -5.

Tony and Sasha are still talking about equations.

Tony   Okay. Suppose I solved an equation and got roots of $3 + 2\sqrt{7}$ and $3 - 2\sqrt{7}$. Would you multiply this mess?

Tony writes on his napkin.

$$(x - (3 + 2\sqrt{7}))(x - (3 - 2\sqrt{7})) = 0$$

Sasha   Well, I could. But, there must be a better way.

Silence.

Sasha   I know. Let's do it generally, once and for all. Then we'll get a formula where we can plug in numbers.

Tony   You've lost me. What do you mean by generally?

Sasha   Well, suppose my roots are some numbers m and n. Then my equation must have factored like this.

Sasha pulls out a piece of paper and writes.

$$(x - m)(x - n) = 0$$

Sasha   Now multiply it out. See.

$$(x - m)(x - n) = x^2 - mx - nx + mn$$
$$= x^2 - (m + n)x + mn$$

So, I can get the coefficient of x by taking the opposite of the sum of the roots. I can get the constant term by taking the product of the roots.

Tony   So, in my example, if the roots are $3 + 2\sqrt{7}$ and $3 - 2\sqrt{7}$, I'd do something like this.

$$3 + 2\sqrt{7} + 3 - 2\sqrt{7} = 6 \text{ and}$$
$$(3 + 2\sqrt{7})(3 - 2\sqrt{7}) = 9 - (2\sqrt{7})^2$$
$$= 9 - 2^2(\sqrt{7})^2$$
$$= 9 - 4 \cdot 7 = -19$$

So, my equation is $x^2 - 6x - 19 = 0$.

Sasha   How could you check this?

Tony   I can use the quadratic formula, of course.

Tony and Sasha finish lunch and go back to class.

Any multiple of this equation has the same roots.

For You to Do

2. Solve the equation $x^2 - 6x - 19 = 0$.

The basic result that Sasha and Tony found may seem very different from the Sum and Product Identity in Lesson 2.11. Their work is really just a small step beyond Theorem 2.3. The key is realizing that the solution to the equation $(x + a)(x + b) = 0$ is $x = -a$ or $x = -b$.

Usually, the roots are the key part of the quadratic, so you want to write them without negative signs. You can make a small switch, as Theorem 3.3 shows.

Theorem 3.3 The Sum and Product Theorem

If m and n are real numbers, the quadratic equation $x^2 - (m + n)x + mn = 0$ has m and n as roots.

Some people remember the theorem using this sentence.

$$x^2 - \text{(the sum of the roots)} \cdot x + \text{(the product of the roots)} = 0$$

Proof

$$x^2 - (m + n)x + mn = 0 \Rightarrow (x - m)(x - n) = 0 \qquad \text{from Theorem 2.3}$$
$$\Rightarrow x - m = 0 \text{ or } x - n = 0 \quad \text{by ZPP}$$
$$\Rightarrow x = m \text{ or } x = n$$

By definition, if m and n are solutions to the quadratic equation, they are the roots of the equation.

Be careful. If a quadratic equation has roots m and n, then it has factors $(x - m)$ and $(x - n)$. The sign change can sometimes be tricky.

For You to Do

Find the roots of each equation. Then calculate the sum of the roots.

3. $x^2 - 10x + 21 = 0$

4. $x^2 + 10x + 24 = 0$

5. $x^2 - 5x - 1 = 0$

6. $x^2 + rx + s = 0$

7. $11x^2 - 71x + 30 = 0$

8. $15x^2 - 43x + 8 = 0$

9. $ax^2 + bx + c = 0$

In Lesson 3.02, you found a general formula for solving any quadratic equation with real roots. There is also a general solution to a basic linear equation of the form $ax + b = 0$. You can find it by following the basic moves for solving equations.

$$ax + b = 0$$
$$ax = -b$$
$$x = \frac{-b}{a}$$

The basic rules and moves are almost always easier than trying to apply the quadratic formula, but notice the result. How does it compare to your result in Problem 9 on the previous page? Are you surprised that the two results are the same?

This finding becomes very useful when graphing quadratic functions. It is stated here as Theorem 3.4.

Theorem 3.4 The Sum of the Roots Theorem

In a quadratic equation of the form $ax^2 + bx + c = 0$, the sum of the roots of the equation is $\frac{-b}{a}$.

Proof Your work from Problem 9 in For You to Do is the proof to this theorem.

Exercises *Practicing Habits of Mind*

Check Your Understanding

1. Find a quadratic equation for the given roots.

   a. 3 and 17

   b. -3 and -17

   c. 6 and 34

   d. $2 + \sqrt{3}$ and $2 - \sqrt{3}$

   e. $-2 - \sqrt{3}$ and $-2 + \sqrt{3}$

   f. $10 + 5\sqrt{3}$ and $10 - 5\sqrt{3}$

2. **Take It Further** Suppose the quadratic equation $x^2 - 17x - 78 = 0$ has roots α and β. Without solving the equation, find an equation with the following roots.

   a. $-\alpha$ and $-\beta$

   b. 3α and 3β

   c. $\frac{1}{\alpha}$ and $\frac{1}{\beta}$

   d. α^2 and β^2

3. Suppose a, b, and c are real numbers, and $a \neq 0$. Suppose also that the following equations are true.

$$\alpha = \frac{-b + \sqrt{b^2 - 4ac}}{2a} \text{ and } \beta = \frac{-b - \sqrt{b^2 - 4ac}}{2a}$$

   Write an expression, in terms of a, b, and c, that is equal to each of the following expressions.

   a. $\alpha + \beta$

   b. $\alpha\beta$

   c. the average of α and β

On Your Own

4. Find a quadratic equation with roots $\sqrt{5} + 3$ and $\sqrt{5} - 3$.

5. **a.** Solve the equation $40x^2 - 131x + 105 = 0$.

   b. Factor over $\mathbb{Z}$ the polynomial $40x^2 - 131x + 105$.

6. **Standardized Test Prep** Which of the following quadratic equations has $4 - \sqrt{3}$ and $4 + \sqrt{3}$ as solutions?

   I. $x^2 - 13x + 8 = 0$ **II.** $x^2 - 8x + 13 = 0$ **III.** $2x^2 - 16x + 26 = 0$

   A. I only   **B.** II only   **C.** I and II   **D.** II and III

7. **Write About It** Explain how to use the quadratic formula to factor quadratic polynomials over $\mathbb{Z}$.

8. Find two numbers with a sum of 1 and a product of -1.

9. Suppose α is one of the numbers you found in Exercise 8. Show each of the following.

   a. $\alpha^2 = \alpha + 1$ **b.** $\alpha^3 = 2\alpha + 1$ **c.** $\alpha^4 = 3\alpha + 2$

   d. **Take It Further** Express each of the first 10 powers of α in the form $a\alpha + b$ for integers a and b. Describe and explain some patterns.

You can choose which number to call α.

10. **Take It Further** Suppose you can take square roots of negative numbers. Find an equation with roots that are $1 + \sqrt{-3}$ and $1 - \sqrt{-3}$.

11. **Take It Further** Suppose you have a quadratic equation with rational-number coefficients. The root $1 + \sqrt{5}$ is one root of the equation. What is the other root? Explain.

Go Online
www.successnetplus.com

Maintain Your Skills

12. Suppose α and β are roots of the equation $40x^2 - 81x + 35 = 0$. Find an equation with the following roots.

   a. 2α and 2β **b.** 3α and 3β

   c. 4α and 4β **d.** $-\alpha$ and $-\beta$

   e. What patterns do you find?

13. **Take It Further** Find an equation with roots that are the reciprocals of the roots of each equation.

   a. $x^2 - 5x + 6 = 0$ **b.** $x^2 + 5x + 6 = 0$

   c. $40x^2 - 81x + 35 = 0$ **d.** What patterns do you find?

3.04 Factoring Nonmonic Quadratics

The quadratic formula gives you the solutions to any quadratic equation. With a little work, you can use these solutions to factor any quadratic polynomial.

What can you do if the quadratic is not monic? A good mathematical habit is to make use of something you already know how to do to solve problems you are unsure about.

Minds in Action

Tony and Sasha are trying to factor the quadratic $4x^2 + 36x + 45$.

Tony   It's not monic. Do we have to play with all the combinations?

Sasha   We could. Wait, I see something. $4x^2$ is the same as $(2x)^2$. So we could write the equation using $2x$ chunks.

$$(2x)^2 + 18(2x) + 45$$

Tony   Sure, you can do that, but it's still not monic.

Sasha   Well, no. But suppose I think of the $2x$ as one thing.

Sasha covers the first $2x$ with her left hand and the second $2x$ with her right hand.

$$(\text{✋})^2 + 18(\text{✋}) + 45$$

Sasha   Do you see? It's something squared plus 18 times that something plus 45. Here, I'll change what's under my hand, the $2x$, to z. Now it looks better.

$$z^2 + 18z + 45$$

Tony   Cool! I can factor that by finding numbers that add to 18 and multiply to 45. So, 15 and 3 will work. Look at what I get.

$$z^2 + 18z + 45 = (z + 15)(z + 3)$$

Sasha   Remember, we used z as a placeholder for $2x$, so now put the $2x$ back.

$$(z + 15)(z + 3) = (2x + 15)(2x + 3)$$

Tony   We should check by multiplying it out, just to be sure.

You can use what you know about riding a bicycle to help you ride a unicycle.

For You to Do

1. Expand $(2x + 15)(2x + 3)$ and make sure you get the original quadratic from Minds in Action.

Developing Habits of Mind

Simplify complicated problems. Sasha's idea of lumping a part of an expression into one unit is very useful in mathematics. People often say that $(2x)^2 + 18(2x) + 45$ is a monic quadratic in $2x$. This means that if you think of the variable as $2x$ instead of x, the quadratic looks monic.

Minds in Action

Sasha and Tony want to try their method on other quadratics.

Tony Here's one.

$$6x^2 + 11x - 10$$

I know the answer, because I got it by multiplying out two binomials. But I don't think our method will work here.

Sasha We were lucky with $4x^2 + 36x + 45$ because of the leading 4. It's a perfect square. So I could write the first term as $(2x)^2$. And I could write the second term as a multiple of $2x$ to the first power. So it all worked out.

Tony If it were an equation, we could multiply both sides by a number and maybe fix things up. But it's a polynomial, not an equation.

Sasha and Tony sit silently for a while.

Sasha Well, we can still multiply by 6. Just remember that we did it so we can undo it later.

Tony Okay, but let's not forget. It doesn't sound legal.

Sasha Well, like I said, as long as we undo it in end, it should be fine. So, take the quadratic $6x^2 + 11x - 10$ and multiply it by 6.

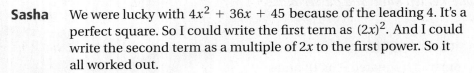

$$6(6x^2 + 11x - 10) = 36x^2 + 66x - 60 \text{ (6 times)}$$

Tony I see what you're doing. That "6 times" reminds us that we multiplied by 6. Now we can write the polynomial just like we did the last one.

$$(6x)^2 + 11(6x) - 60$$

Now it is monic in $6x$. Let $z = 6x$ and we get this.

$$z^2 + 11z - 60$$

I know how to factor that.

$$(z + 15)(z - 4)$$

Sasha   Now unreplace z with $6x$.

$$(6x + 15)(6x - 4)$$

Oh, wait. There are common factors in each binomial, a 3 in the first one and a 2 in the second one. That's the 6 that I multiplied by in the first place! I'll pull the 3 and the 2 out.

$$3(2x + 5) \cdot 2(3x - 2) = 6(2x + 5)(3x - 2)$$

Tony   So now I can divide by 6 to undo your multiplying by 6.

$$(2x + 5)(3x - 2)$$

So $6x^2 + 11x - 10 = (2x + 5)(3x - 2)$, and we are done.

Sasha   This method will always work, so things just got a lot simpler. All we need to worry about now is factoring monics. We can do that by sums and products.

> Make sure you know how to factor the quadratic.

> Check by multiplying out the right side.

For You to Do

2. Factor $6x^2 - 31x + 35$ using Sasha's method.

3. Factor $6x^2 - 31x + 35$ using the quadratic formula.

4. Which method is easier? Explain.

For Discussion

5. State Sasha and Tony's method as an algorithm, a sequence of steps that describes exactly what to do.

Exercises Practicing Habits of Mind

Check Your Understanding

For Exercises 1 and 2, factor each polynomial.

1. **a.** $9x^2 + 18x - 7$ **b.** $6x^2 - 31x + 35$

     c. $15x^2 + 16x - 7$ **d.** $9x^2 + 62x - 7$

     e. $9x^4 + 62x^2 - 7$

2. **a.** $9x^2 + 18xy - 7y^2$ **b.** $6x^2 - 31xy + 35y^2$

     c. $15x^2 + 16xa - 7a^2$ **d.** $9x^2 + 62xb - 7b^2$

3. When applying the scaling method to $6x^2 - 31x + 35$, you follow these steps.

   • Look at the quadratic expression $6x^2 - 31x + 35$.

   • Multiply by 6.

   • Get a monic quadratic in $6x$.

   • Let $z = 6x$ and work with the resulting quadratic in z.

Describe how you could get the monic quadratic without the middle steps.

On Your Own

For Exercises 4–6, factor each polynomial.

4. **a.** $-18x^2 - 65x - 7$ **b.** $-18x^2 + 61x + 7$

     c. $25 - 4x^2$ **d.** $18x^3 - 61x^2 - 7x$

5. **a.** $-18x^2 - 65xa - 7a^2$ **b.** $-18x^2 + 61xy + 7y^2$

     c. $25y^2 - 4x^2$ **d.** $18x^3 - 61x^2y - 7xy^2$

6. **a.** $4x^2 - 13x + 3$ **b.** $4x^2 - 8x + 3$

     c. $4x^2 + 4x - 3$ **d.** $4(x + 1)^2 + 4(x + 1) - 3$

     e. $4x^4 - 13x^2 + 3$ **f.** $4(x - 1)^4 - 13(x - 1)^2 + 3$

     g. $4(x - 1)^{12} - 13(x - 1)^6 + 3$ **h.** $(x^2 + 1)^2 - x^2$

7. **Standardized Test Prep** For what values of x is the equation $2x - \frac{15}{x} = 1$ true?

   A. 3 **B.** $-3, \frac{5}{2}$ **C.** $\frac{5}{2}, 3$ **D.** $-\frac{5}{2}, 3$

8. Solve the equation $2x - \frac{3}{x} = 5$ for x.

9. For the equation $x^2 - 6x + 7 = 0$, let $z = x - 3$.

   a. Express the equation in terms of z.

   b. Solve the equation in z.

   c. Use your result from part (b) to solve the original equation.

   > If $z = x - 3$, $x = z + 3$.

10. For parts (a) and (b), solve the quadratic equation.

    a. $3x^2 + 8x - 35 = 0$

    b. $x^2 + 8x - 105 = 0$

    c. Find a relationship between the solutions to these two equations.

Maintain Your Skills

11. Solve each pair of equations and compare the roots.

    a. $x^2 - 8x + 7 = 0$ and $x^2 - 24x + 63 = 0$

    b. $2x^2 + 11x - 21 = 0$ and $2x^2 + 22x - 84 = 0$

    c. $2x^2 + 11x - 21 = 0$ and $2x^2 + 33x - 189 = 0$

    d. $2x^2 + 11x - 21 = 0$ and $2x^2 + 55x - 525 = 0$

    e. $2x^2 + 11x - 21 = 0$ and $x^2 + 11x - 42 = 0$

    f. $3x^2 + 16x - 35 = 0$ and $x^2 + 16x - 105 = 0$

    g. $3x^2 + 16x - 32 = 0$ and $x^2 + 16x - 96 = 0$

    > How are the equations in each pair related?

12. Find an equation with roots that are as follows.

    a. 7 times the roots of $x^2 - 8x + 7 = 0$

    b. 7 times the roots of $2x^2 + 11x - 21 = 0$

    c. 2 times the roots of $2x^2 + 11x - 21 = 0$

    d. 3 times the roots of $3x^2 + 11x - 21 = 0$

    e. 5 times the roots of $5x^2 + 11x - 21 = 0$

In this investigation, you learned how to solve quadratic equations using the quadratic formula and to build a quadratic given its roots. These questions will help you summarize what you have learned.

1. Complete the following for each equation.

   • Make a table of inputs and outputs. Use at least five different inputs.

   • Sketch each graph on a separate grid using the table.

   • Find the points where each graph crosses the x-axis.

   a. $x^2 - 2x - 4 = y$

   b. $3x^2 - 2x - 5 = y$

   c. $x^2 - 6x + 9 = y$

   d. $2x^2 + 4x + 3 = y$

2. Find a value of k such that $2x^2 - 3x + k$ has each solution set.

   a. two real-number solutions

   b. one real-number solution

   c. no real-number solutions

3. Find a quadratic equation with the following roots.

   a. 4 and -5

   b. $3 + \sqrt{2}$ and $3 - \sqrt{2}$

4. Factor the following nonmonic polynomials by writing them as monic polynomials in $\mathbb{Z}$.

   a. $2x^2 - 5x - 12$

   b. $6x^2 + 25x + 25$

   c. $4x^2 + 8x - 5$

   d. $9x^2 + 12x + 4$

5. Factor the following quadratic expressions using the quadratic formula.

   a. $4x^2 + 12x + 5$

   b. $6x^2 - 5x - 4$

6. How can you solve any quadratic equation?

7. How can you factor any quadratic polynomial?

8. How are the roots of a quadratic equation related to its coefficients?

Vocabulary

In this investigation, you learned these terms. Make sure you understand what each one means and how to use it.

- **monic equation**
- **nonmonic quadratic**

Quadratic functions of the form $f(x) = ax^2 + bx + c$ use various a, b, and c values to model different parabolic paths.

Quadratic Graphs and Applications

In *Quadratic Graphs and Applications,* you will optimize quadratic functions. Graphs of quadratic functions have either a maximum or a minimum point. Locating these points helps you graph quadratics.

By the end of this investigation, you will be able to answer questions like these.

1. How can you quickly identify the vertex of the graph of a quadratic equation?

2. How does the symmetry of a parabola help you solve problems that use quadratic functions?

3. Using two different methods, how can you find the vertex of the parabola with the equation $y = x^2 - 4x + 9$?

You will learn how to

- use your knowledge of quadratics to optimize some quadratic functions

- graph quadratic functions and examine the graph to find the vertex

- explore word problems involving quadratic functions

You will develop these habits and skills:

- Use the arithmetic fact that a square is always nonnegative in order to optimize quadratic functions.

- See the connections between the geometry of quadratic graphs and the algebra of quadratic functions.

- Use the graph of a function to find numerical information.

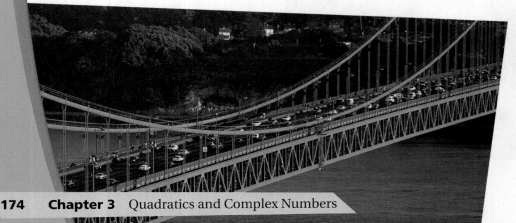

The vertex of a parabola that opens upward is the lowest point on the parabola.

You can use quadratic functions to model real-world situations. Optimization problems use quadratic functions to determine the greatest area for a rectangular region.

For You to Explore

1. You have 200 feet of fencing to use for building a rectangular dog pen. Find the dimensions of the pen having the greatest possible area.

2. Suppose you build the pen such that it borders an apartment building. You will only need to build three walls. Find the dimensions of the pen having the greatest possible area.

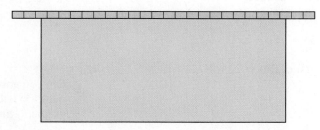

3. Suppose that you have three pets, a dog, a cat, and a monkey. You want to divide the pen into three smaller rectangular sections. There will be one pen for each animal. The pens will be side by side as shown below.

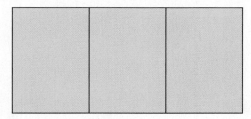

You still only have 200 feet of fencing. You will have to use some of the fencing to build the dividers between the pens. You want to maximize the area of the entire pen. What should the dimensions be?

The dimensions are the length and width of the pen.

4. Suppose you build a pen to separate five goats. You have 600 feet of fencing. What dimensions give the maximum area for the entire pen?

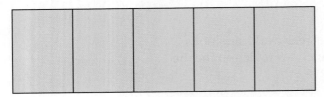

5. Take It Further Explain the pattern to the solutions of Problems 1–4 in as much detail as possible.

On Your Own

6. What is the least possible value of the function $f(x) = x^2 - 6x + 8$?

7. Suppose $f(x) = 3 - (x - 2)^2$. Find the value of each expression.

    a. $f(5) - f(-1)$ **b.** $f(8) - f(-4)$

    c. $f(3) - f(1)$ **d.** $f(2 + \sqrt{17}) - f(2 - \sqrt{17})$

8. Solve these equations using any method. Check each result.

    a. $x^2 + 14x + 40 = 0$ **b.** $x^2 - 5x = 24$

    c. $9x^2 = 49$ **d.** $x^3 - 4x = 0$

9. Does the graph of $y = (3x + 5)^2 + \frac{1}{3}$ intersect the x-axis? If so, where is the intersection? If not, explain.

> Can you answer this question without graphing the equation?

Maintain Your Skills

For Exercises 10–12, find the least possible value of each function. Find the value of x for which the least value occurs.

10. a. $a(x) = x^2$ **b.** $b(x) = (x - 1)^2$

    c. $c(x) = (x + 5)^2$ **d.** $d(x) = (x - \sqrt{13})^2$

    e. $e(x) = (x - k)^2$, where k is a constant

11. a. $f(x) = x^2$ **b.** $g(x) = x^2 + 5$

    c. $h(x) = x^2 - 17$ **d.** $j(x) = x^2 - \sqrt{13}$

    e. $k(x) = x^2 + r$, where r is a constant

12. a. $l(x) = (x - 5)^2$ **b.** $m(x) = (x - 3)^2 + 2$

    c. $n(x) = (x + 17)^2 - 11$ **d.** $p(x) = \left(x - \frac{5}{3}\right)^2 - \sqrt{13}$

    e. $q(x) = (x - h)^2 + k$, where h and k are constants

Finding a maximum or minimum of a function is a common use of quadratic functions. Linear functions do not have a maximum or a minimum value.

Higher-degree polynomial functions, however, have places on their graphs where the graph "turns around" and heads in the opposite direction, either up or down. These changes occur at the **maximum** or **minimum** of the function.

Businesses try to determine the price to charge for products to maximize their profit. Car designers try to minimize the air resistance of cars. Architects try to maximize the strength of buildings and bridges. Mathematicians try to optimize functions by finding the greatest or least outputs.

Many of these problems result in optimizing a function.

In Lesson 3.05, you optimized some quadratics. For instance, in Exercise 12 you found that the minimum value of $n(x) = (x + 17)^2 - 11$ is -11. It occurs at $x = -17$, but the minimum value is the least possible output.

Minds in Action

Sasha and Tony are working through a similar problem.

Consider the function $f(x) = x^2 - 6x + 8$. What is the least possible value of $f(x)$?

Tony   To solve this problem, I started making a table of values. I plugged in the values $x = -2$, $x = -1$, $x = 0$, and so on, up to $x = 6$. I collected all of the values in a table.

Sasha   What answer did you find?

Tony   Well, look. The values get smaller and smaller until $x = 3$. Then they start getting larger again. So it seems as if the minimum is $f(x) = -1$.

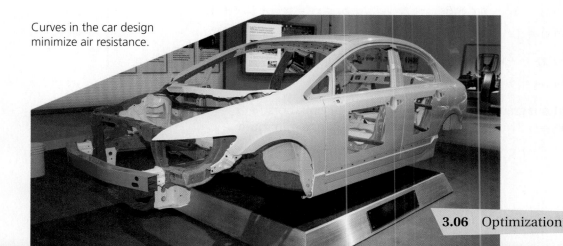

Curves in the car design minimize air resistance.

x	$f(x) = x^2 - 6x + 8$
-2	24
-1	15
0	8
1	3
2	0
3	-1
4	0
5	3
6	8

Sasha I got the same answer. I graphed the function $f(x) = x^2 - 6x + 8$ on a graphing calculator. Here's what it looks like.

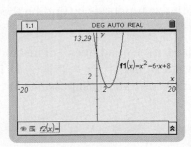

Tony Oh, you can see the minimum right there. $f(x)$ gets smaller and smaller, and then the graph turns around. I think it turns around at $(3, -1)$.

Sasha Yes, it does. This calculator can find the minimum if I command it. I can also trace the graph or zoom in. Here, I'll zoom in around the minimum point.

Looks to me like the minimum is where $x = 3$ and $f(x) = -1$.

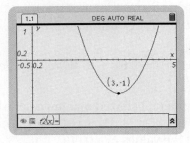

> For help finding the minimum point of the graph, see the TI-Nspire Handbook, p. 990.

For You to Do

By building a table or investigating a graph, find the maximum or minimum of each of the functions in Problems 1 and 2.

1. a. $r(x) = x^2 - 4x + 5$ **b.** $s(x) = x^2 - 10x + 15$

 c. $t(x) = (x - 3)^2 - 1$

2. a. $u(x) = -x^2 + 4x - 5$ **b.** $v(x) = -x^2 + 100x$

 c. $w(x) = 1 - (x - 3)^2$

3. Without graphing, determine whether the equation $z(x) = -2x^2 + 10x + 45$ has a maximum or a minimum.

Developing Habits of Mind

Prove the conjecture. Sasha and Tony look at a table and graph to determine the minimum of $f(x) = x^2 - 6x + 8$. They find evidence that $f(x) = -1$ is the minimum, but they do not prove that this is true.

You can use completing the square to prove that $f(x) = -1$ is the minimum.

First, complete the square.

$$f(x) = x^2 - 6x + 8$$
$$= (x - 3)^2 - 1$$

Next, look at this form of the function.

$$f(x) = (\text{something})^2 - 1$$

When you square any real number, the result is always positive or zero. So the least value that $(x - 3)^2$ equals is 0. If $(x - 3)^2$ is 0, then the minimum value of $f(x)$ is $f(x) = 0 - 1 = -1$.

The minimum value occurs when $(x - 3)^2$ is zero. So $x = 3$ is the input that gives the minimum, because $3 - 3 = 0$.

For Discussion

Use completing the square to find the minimum or maximum of each function. Then find the value of x that gives the minimum or maximum.

4. $f(x) = x^2 - 8x + 9$ **5.** $g(x) = x^2 - 11x - 2$ **6.** $h(x) = -x^2 - 4x - 1$

Minds in Action

Derman makes a discovery.

Derman Look, I can find the maximum or minimum much more quickly by calculating the average of the roots of each function.

Sasha What do you mean?

Derman Well, look at the example we already did, $f(x) = x^2 - 6x + 8$. This function has a minimum.

Sasha Yes, the minimum is $f(x) = -1$.

Derman Check this out. If $f(x) = x^2 - 6x + 8$, the sum of the roots is 6 from Theorem 3.4. Since there are two roots, their average is $\frac{6}{2} = 3$. If you plug $x = 3$ into $f(x)$, you get -1, the minimum.

Sasha That might just be a coincidence.

Derman We'll have to try some others to be sure, but I think I'm right.

For Discussion

7. Look at the optimization examples. Try to optimize these functions by using Derman's method of averaging the roots. Does it always work?

If Derman's method always works, you have a quick method for finding the maximum or minimum of a quadratic function. It is useful to state Derman's idea formally.

Conjecture *The Average of the Roots*

For any quadratic equation, the average of the roots is the *x*-coordinate of the maximum or minimum of the function.

Example

Problem You have 200 feet of fencing to build a rectangular dog pen. If you want the pen to have the maximum possible area, what should the dimensions of the pen be?

Solution Use the guess-check-generalize method to find the expression that you want to optimize. The perimeter of the rectangle is 200 feet. Suppose one side and its opposite side are both 30 feet. The other two sides equal 140 feet, since $200 - 2(30)$ is 140. Each of these two sides is half of 140 feet, or 70 feet. Multiply 30 by 70. The area of this pen is 2100 square feet.

Try another guess. Suppose one side is 40 feet. Then the opposite side is also 40 feet. The other two sides must total 120 feet, since $200 - 2(40)$ is 120. Each of these two sides is half of 120 feet, or 60 feet. Multiply 40 by 60. The area of this pen is 2400 square feet.

Suppose one side is w feet. The opposite side must also be w feet. The other two sides must total $200 - 2w$. Since the other two sides have equal length, the length of each side is $\frac{200 - 2w}{2}$, or $100 - w$.

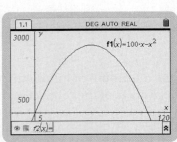

The area of that pen would be $w(100 - w)$. The equation for the area is $A = w(100 - w)$.

Expand the right side of the equation to get $A = 100w - w^2$. Graph the equation for w from 0 to 100.

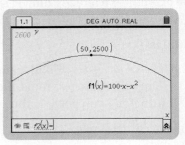

Zoom in to find a good estimate for the maximum. The maximum occurs when $w = 50$ and $A = 2500$, so the maximum area occurs when the pen is a 50-by-50 square.

> You can use the perimeter formula to find your equation. The typical area formula is $A = \ell w$. Since the perimeter is 200, you know that $2\ell + 2w = 200$. Solve for either variable. For example, solve for ℓ and find the equation $\ell = 100 - w$. Substitute the expression $100 - w$ into the original area formula to find $A = (100 - w)w$.

Habits of Mind

Find relationships. This function equals 0 if $w = 0$ or $w = 100$. Why does this make sense, given that you have 200 feet of fencing?

In Developing Habits of Mind, you used the method of completing the square to minimize $f(x) = x^2 - 6x + 8$. Maximizing $A = 100w - w^2$ will be trickier, since in this case there is a $-w^2$ term.

You can factor out a -1 first to make the quadratic easier to work with.

$$100w - w^2 = -w^2 + 100w$$
$$= -(w^2 - 100w)$$
$$= -(w^2 - 100w + 2500 - 2500)$$
$$= -((w - 50)^2 - 2500)$$
$$= -(w - 50)^2 + 2500$$
$$= 2500 - (w - 50)^2$$

The area of the pen with side w is $2500 - (w - 50)^2$. Since $(w - 50)^2$ is never negative, its minimum value is 0. So the expression will be maximized when $(w - 50)^2 = 0$. In this case, $w = 50$ and the maximum area is $2500 - (0) = 2500$.

For Discussion

8. Maximize the function $f(x) = 100x - x^2$ by following Derman's method of averaging the roots.

You need to be careful when choosing to apply Derman's method of averaging the roots. Derman's method only works for quadratic functions. It will not work for polynomial functions of degree 3 or more, such as $f(x) = x^3 + 4x^2 + x - 6$.

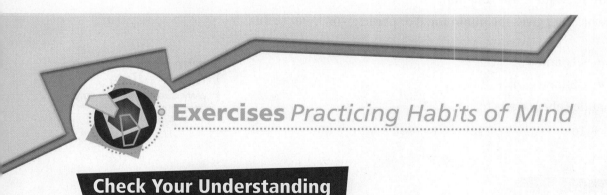

Exercises Practicing Habits of Mind

Check Your Understanding

1. Find the minimum value of each function.

a. $f(x) = (x - 3)^2 - 16$ **b.** $g(x) = (x - 3)(x - 7)$

c. $h(x) = x^2 - 8x - 9$

2. Find a quadratic function that has a minimum value of -12.

3. Of all the pairs of real numbers that sum to 20, which pair has the greatest product?

4. Of all the pairs of real numbers that have a sum 251, which pair has the greatest product?

5. Of all pairs of numbers that add to a constant c, which pair has the maximum product?

On Your Own

6. **Standardized Test Prep** What is the minimum value of the function $g(x) = x^2 + 24x - 18$?

A. -162 **B.** -126 **C.** -18 **D.** 414

7. What is the minimum value of the function $f(x) = 3x(x - 4)$?

8. You have 180 feet of fence to make a rectangular pen. What are the dimensions of the rectangle with the maximum area?

9. Of all the pairs of real numbers that have sum 90, which pair has the greatest product?

10. You have 180 feet of fence to make a rectangular pen. One side of the pen will be against a 200 foot wall, so it requires no fence. What are the dimensions of the rectangle with the maximum area?

For Exercises 11 and 12, do the following parts.

a. Find the minimum value of the function.

b. Find the value of x that gives the minimum. For parts (c)–(e), refer to this number as m.

c. Calculate $f(m + 1)$ and $f(m - 1)$.

d. Calculate $f(m + 2)$ and $f(m - 2)$.

e. What do you notice about parts (c) and (d)?

11. $f(x) = x^2 + 4x + 10$ **12.** $f(x) = 9x^2 - 60x + 80$

> For help finding the maximum of the function, see the TI-Nspire Handbook, p. 990.

Go Online
www.successnetplus.com

Maintain Your Skills

13. Sketch the graph of each equation.

a. $y = x^2$ **b.** $y = 2x^2$ **c.** $y = \frac{1}{2}x^2$

d. $y = -x^2$ **e.** $y = -4x^2$

Go Online
Video Tutor
www.successnetplus.com

One of the basic graphs is the graph of $y = x^2$, the most simple quadratic equation. The graph of every quadratic equation is a **parabola.** All parabolas have the same basic shape and properties as the graph of $y = x^2$.

Here are the graphs of $y = ax^2$ for various values of a.

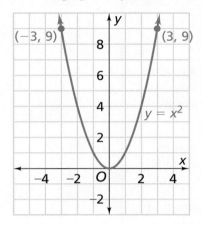

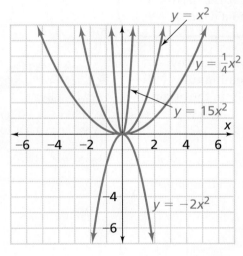

Quadratic functions of the form $f(x) = ax^2 + bx + c$ that model paths of lava ejected from a volcano have negative values of a.

For You to Do

For the values of a, describe how the parabola with equation $y = ax^2$ compares to the graph of $y = x^2$.

1. $a > 1$ **2.** $a = 1$ **3.** $0 < a < 1$

4. $-1 < a < 0$ **5.** $a = -1$ **6.** $a < -1$

How does the parabola compare to the graph of $y = x^2$ when $a = 0$?

Find relationships. How do different values of a affect the graphs of quadratic equations?

7. Sketch the horizontal line and the three parabolas below on the same coordinate plane.

- $y = x^2$
- $y = 4x^2$
- $y = \frac{1}{4}x^2$
- $y = 9$

Look at the basic graph of $y = x^2$. The x values 3 and -3 result in a y-value of 9. On the graph of $y = 4x^2$, a y-value of 9 results from x-values less than 3, specifically 1.5 and -1.5. So the graph of $y = 4x^2$ is narrower than the graph of $y = x^2$.

Look at the graph of $y = \frac{1}{4}x^2$. In this equation, a is less than 1. Therefore, you need a greater x-value to get a y-value of 9. So the graph of $y = \frac{1}{4}x^2$ is wider than the graph of $y = x^2$.

If you examine other equations with different a values, you will notice that these two observations are true. The greater the value of a is, the narrower the parabola is. Also, as the value of a decreases, the parabola widens.

You may recall how to translate a parabola on the coordinate plane by applying simple transformations. Recall that the transformation rule $(x, y) \mapsto (x + 1, y)$ means that you replace each instance of x in the original equation with $(x - 1)$.

Remember...

You read
$(x, y) \mapsto (x + 1, y)$
as "(x, y) maps to $(x + 1, y)$."

For You to Do

Apply each transformation rule to the graph of $y = x^2$. Write an equation for the parabola. Sketch a graph.

8. $(x, y) \mapsto (x, y + 3)$ 9. $(x, y) \mapsto (x, y - 3)$

10. $(x, y) \mapsto (x + 3, y)$ 11. $(x, y) \mapsto (x - 3, y)$

12. $(x, y) \mapsto (x + 3, y + 3)$

In For You to Do, you graphed several transformations of $y = x^2$. Notice that the size of the parabola stayed the same, but the parabola moved up, down, left, or right. In fact, the graph of any quadratic function is a translation of the graph of $y = ax^2$.

In Lesson 3.06, every parabola seemed to have exactly one point that was a minimum. The **vertex** is the maximum or minimum point of the parabola. The vertex for the basic parabola with equation $y = x^2$ is $(0, 0)$.

For You to Do

13. Find the vertex for each of the transformed parabolas that you sketched in For You to Do Problems 8–12.

You can summarize the transformation rules described above in a single theorem. Theorem 3.5 will help you relate quadratic equations and their graphs.

Theorem 3.5

The graph of the equation $y - k = a(x - h)^2$ is a parabola with vertex (h, k). It has the same shape as the graph of the equation $y = ax^2$.

You can use the basic rules and moves and the completing-the-square method to transform any quadratic equation from normal form $y = ax^2 + bx + c$ to vertex form.

Developing Habits of Mind

Represent an equation differently. By a simple basic move, you can rewrite the equation in Theorem 3.5 in vertex form. The **vertex form** of a quadratic function is $y = a(x - h)^2 + k$.

Why does it matter which form of an equation you use? Suppose $a > 0$. You know that the square of any number must be nonnegative. So $a(x - h)^2 \geq 0$ no matter what the value of x is. This also means that 0 is the least value of $a(x - h)^2$.

What value of x makes $a(x - h)^2$ equal 0? If you can find the x-value, the equation reduces to $y = k$. Then you know the minimum of the function.

If $x = h$, you can reduce the equation $y = a(x - h)^2 + k$ in the following way.

$$y = a(x - h)^2 + k$$
$$= a(h - h)^2 + k$$
$$= a(0)^2 + k$$
$$= 0 + k$$
$$= k$$

So h is the value of x that gives the minimum y-value, and (h, k) is the minimum point of the function's graph.

By the same argument, if $a < 0$, you can show that k is the greatest value of $a(x - h)^2 + k$. Following the same steps, you can find the maximum of the graph of a quadratic function.

Go Online
www.successnetplus.com

In Lesson 3.06, Tony and Sasha looked for the least possible value of a quadratic function. For the function $f(x) = x^2 - 6x + 8$, they made a table of values similar to this one.

x	$f(x) = x^2 - 6x + 8$
−2	24
−1	15
0	8
1	3
2	0
3	−1
4	0
5	3
6	8
7	15
8	24

Tony and Sasha saw that the outputs decreased in value until $x = 3$. After that, the outputs increased. What they did not mention was that the values repeated in reverse order.

Notice that $f(2) = f(4)$, $f(1) = f(5)$, and so on. Look at the graph. The left side of the parabola is the mirror image of the right side.

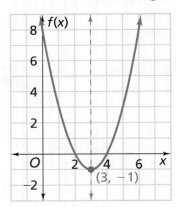

The **line of symmetry** acts as the mirror for the parabola. It will always pass through the vertex of the parabola. Finding the line of symmetry can help you make accurate sketches of the graph of a parabola.

Prove the conjecture. How can you be sure that a parabola actually has a line of symmetry? If you fold the graph along the line, both sides match at every point.

Look at the line of symmetry, which has equation $x = 1$. What is the mirror image of $(4, 5)$? Since the line is vertical, the point is at the same height. So its y-coordinate is 5.

For the x-coordinate, $(4, 5)$ is 3 units to the right of the graph of $x = 1$. The reflected point is 3 units to the left. So its x-coordinate is -2. The reflected point is $(-2, 5)$.

Look at the graph of $y = (x - 1)^2 - 4$. The parabola has a line of symmetry at $x = 1$. The points $(4, 5)$ and $(-2, 5)$ are both on the graph. You can see that they are mirror images of each other over the graph of $x = 1$.

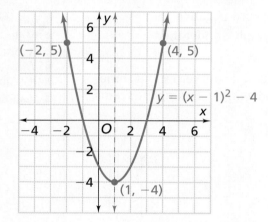

To prove that the line of symmetry reflects the entire parabola, choose a general point on the parabola. The x-coordinate of a point on the right side of the parabola is d units to the right of the line of symmetry. So you can name the point $1 + d$. The x-coordinate of the reflected point is d units to the left of the line of symmetry. So you can name the point $1 - d$.

Use the equation of the parabola to find the y-coordinates of these two points. You can substitute the x-coordinate, $d + 1$, to find the y-coordinate of the general point.

You can substitute the x-coordinate, $1 - d$, to find the y-coordinate of the reflected point.

$$
\begin{aligned}
y &= (x - 1)^2 - 4 \\
  &= ((1 + d) - 1)^2 - 4 \\
  &= (d)^2 - 4 \\
  &= d^2 - 4
\end{aligned}
\qquad\qquad
\begin{aligned}
y &= (x - 1)^2 - 4 \\
  &= ((1 - d) - 1)^2 - 4 \\
  &= (-d)^2 - 4 \\
  &= d^2 - 4
\end{aligned}
$$

Since both $1 + d$ and $1 - d$ have the same y-coordinate, the parabola is symmetric. This argument works in general. The graph of every equation of the form $y = ax^2 + bx + c$ has a line of symmetry.

> **Remember...**
>
> The line of symmetry has equation $x = 1$.

Problem A parabola has vertex $(-3, 10)$ and includes the point $(2, 0)$. Find an equation for the parabola. Sketch its graph.

Solution You can use Theorem 3.5 to find the equation. Since the vertex is $(-3, 10)$, the equation is $y - 10 = a(x + 3)^2$. You know the point $(2, 0)$ is on the graph, so it must satisfy the equation. To find a, substitute 2 for x and 0 for y. The result is an equation in one variable. Now you can solve for a.

$$0 - 10 = a(2 + 3)^2$$
$$-10 = a(25)$$
$$\frac{-10}{25} = a$$
$$-\frac{2}{5} = a$$

So the equation is $y - 10 = -\frac{2}{5}(x + 3)^2$. Since a is negative, the graph opens downward. Since $|a| < 1$, the graph is wider than the standard parabola.

To make an accurate graph, it helps to find not only the vertex, but some other points as well. When the vertex is near the origin, finding intercepts is often helpful.

You are already given the point $(2, 0)$, which is an x-intercept. The line of symmetry is $x = -3$. So the other intercept is at $(-8, 0)$. Using these points and the line of symmetry, you can sketch an accurate graph.

Another way to find the graph is to solve the equation for y and enter it into a graphing calculator.

$$y = -\frac{2}{5}(x + 3)^2 + 10$$

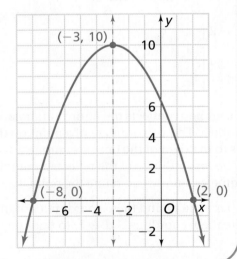

Habits of Mind

Make a connection.
A root of the equation $f(x) = 0$ is a zero of the function $f(x)$.

For Discussion

Refer to the Example.

14. Explain why the other x-intercept must be at $(-8, 0)$.

15. Explain why another way to write the equation is $y = -\frac{2}{5}(x - 2)(x + 8)$.

Exercises Practicing Habits of Mind

Check Your Understanding

1. For each of the equations below, sketch a graph. Find each vertex and line of symmetry.

   a. $y - 1 = 4(x - 2)^2$

   b. $y - 3 = -2(x + 1)^2$

   c. $y + 7 = (x - 4)^2$

   d. $y - 5 = -\frac{1}{2}(x + 6)^2$

2. The graph of a quadratic function passes through the origin and has vertex (3, 18).

   a. Use symmetry to identify one other point that must be on the graph of this function.

   b. Find an equation for this function. (*Hint:* There is more than one way to do this.)

3. Here are two quadratic functions.

$$f(x) = x^2 - 3x + 4$$

$$g(x) = 3x^2 + 5x - 8$$

   a. Graph both functions on a calculator. Sketch the graphs of f and g.

   b. Using the calculator, graph both $h(x) = f(x) + g(x)$ and $j(x) = f(x) - g(x)$. Sketch the graphs of h and j. What kind of graphs do the functions h and j produce?

   c. **Write About It** $f(x)$ and $g(x)$ are any two quadratic functions. Will $f(x) + g(x)$ and $f(x) - g(x)$ always be quadratic functions? If so, explain. If not, give some examples and find out what the other possibilities are.

4. If you throw a ball straight up in the air, a quadratic function describes its height in terms of time. Suppose you throw the ball straight up at 96 feet per second. The height of the ball after t seconds is given by the formula below.

$$h(t) = 96t - 16t^2$$

   What is the maximum height the ball will reach?

> **Remember...**
>
> The origin is the point (0, 0), the intersection of the axes in the coordinate plane.

If you throw a ball in the air at 50 ft/s, what quadratic function models the height of the ball?

5. If you throw the ball at a different speed, then you will use a different polynomial to calculate the maximum height. Find the maximum for each function.

  a. You throw a ball at 32 feet per second. The height function is $h(t) = 32t - 16t^2$.

  b. You throw a ball at 64 feet per second. The height function is $h(t) = 64t - 16t^2$.

  c. You throw a ball at 128 feet per second. The height function is $h(t) = 128t - 16t^2$.

6. Curt can throw a ball straight up in the air twice as fast as Ryan can. Ryan can throw a ball straight up in the air three times as fast Taylor can. You may find your work from Exercise 5 useful here.

  a. Curt's throw is how many times as high as Ryan's?

  b. Ryan's throw is how many times as high as Taylor's?

  c. Curt can throw a ball with a speed of 144 feet per second. Curt, Ryan, and Taylor all throw balls straight into the air. Find the maximum height of each throw.

The fastest pitch ever reliably measured was a fastball at 100.9 miles per hour by Nolan Ryan.

7. Take It Further The Empire State Building is approximately 1250 feet tall. About how fast, in feet per second, do you need to throw a ball for it to reach the top of the Empire State Building? How fast is that in miles per hour?

An approximate way to convert from feet per second to miles per hour is to multiply by $\frac{2}{3}$.

On Your Own

8. Standardized Test Prep What is the vertex form of the equation $y = -x^2 + 8x + 9$? (*Hint:* $y - k = a(x - h)^2$, where (h, k) is the vertex.)

  A. $y - 25 = -1(x - 4)^2$ **B.** $y + 25 = (x + 4)^2$

  C. $y - 7 = (x + 4)^2$ **D.** $y - 7 = (x + 4)^2$

9. Sketch the graph of each equation below. Find the vertex and line of symmetry.

  a. $(y + 8) = -3(x - 5)^2$ **b.** $y = -4(x - 7)^2 - 11$

  c. $(y - 9) = -\frac{3}{4}(x + 1)^2$ **d.** $y = 2(x + 6)^2 + 6$

10. Standardized Test Prep What are the roots of the quadratic equation $y = 2(x - 5)^2 - 8$?

  A. $x = 0$ and $x = 10$ **B.** $x = 1$ and $x = 9$

  C. $x = 2$ and $x = 8$ **D.** $x = 3$ and $x = 7$

Go Online
www.successnetplus.com

11. In the equation $x = y^2$, y is not a function of x. You cannot graph the function on a calculator.

  a. Find at least seven points on the graph of $x = y^2$.

  b. Sketch the graph of $x = y^2$. The graph extends into at least one other quadrant in addition to Quadrant I.

  c. **Write About It** How are the graphs of $y = x^2$ and $x = y^2$ related?

> A point is on the graph of an equation if and only if it makes the equation true under substitution. For example, (4, 2) is a point on the graph of $x = y^2$.

12. Sketch the graph of $(x - 3) = (y + 5)^2$. What is the line of symmetry for this graph? What is the vertex?

13. Two numbers have a sum of 20.

  a. Write an equation for the product of the two numbers.

  b. Use roots to explain why the maximum product must occur when the two numbers are both 10.

  c. Rewrite the equation you wrote in part (a) in vertex form.

14. Consider the quadratic function $y = 4x^2 + 24x - 28$.

  a. Find the vertex of the function's graph.

  b. Write the equation in vertex form.

  c. Find the y-intercept using either form.

15. A quadratic function has zeros -1 and 7. It passes through point (3, 8). What is the vertex of the graph?

> This means it passes through the points $(-1, 0)$ and $(7, 0)$. The zeros of the function $f(x)$ are the roots of the equation $f(x) = 0$.

Maintain Your Skills

16. What can you say about the vertex of the graph of each function?

  a. a quadratic function with zeros 0 and 1

  b. a quadratic function in the form $f(x) = kx(1 - x)$, where k is a nonzero real number

  c. a quadratic function in the form $f(x) = kx(c - x)$, where k and c are nonzero real numbers

3.08 Jiffy Graphs: Parabolas

In Lesson 3.07, you learned to graph a parabola with an equation in vertex form, $y = a(x - h)^2 + k$. However, as you discovered with lines, you can write the equations of parabolas in many different forms.

You already know that the graph of any quadratic is a parabola. How do you quickly make a sketch of a parabola when you are given its equation in normal form, such as $y = x^2 - 6x + 8$?

Minds in Action

Sasha and Tony talk about strategies for sketching parabolas quickly.

Sasha   All right, we need to sketch the graph of $y = x^2 - 6x + 8$.

Tony   Well, it factors nicely into $y = (x - 4)(x - 2)$.

Sasha   Oh, hey! You know, I think we can use the roots to find the line of symmetry.

Tony   Okay. Well, the roots are $x = 2$ and $x = 4$.

Sasha   Right, so the parabola goes through the points $(2, 0)$ and $(4, 0)$.

Tony   Fine. How will you use that to sketch the rest of the graph?

Sasha   Here's the thing. Points $(2, 0)$ and $(4, 0)$ have to be symmetric with respect to each other. Here's a picture.

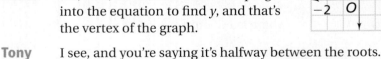

Whatever is halfway between the points is the x-value of the line of symmetry. The graph of the parabola starts from there.

Tony   Where does it start? That's an entire line.

Sasha   Oh, well, take that x-value and plug it into the equation to find y, and that's the vertex of the graph.

Tony   I see, and you're saying it's halfway between the roots.

Sasha   Right, as long as I can factor and find the roots, I can do it.

Tony   Wait, it might be even easier. You said halfway between the roots. That's the average! There's already a rule for that.

Sasha   What is the rule?

Tony   You need to pay more attention. We learned that the sum of the roots for $ax^2 + bx + c = 0$ is $-\frac{b}{a}$. So the average of the roots is $\frac{-b}{2a}$.

Since the starting equation is $y = x^2 - 6x + 8$, the average of the roots is $\frac{-(-6)}{2(1)}$. That's 3. It's a good thing, because that's what you got. So the line of symmetry is $x = 3$.

Sasha   Oh, I like that.

> Why is it true that the average of the roots equals the x-coordinate of the line of symmetry?

For You to Do

Find the line of symmetry for the graph of each equation. Draw each graph.

1. $y = (x + 7)(x - 3)$

2. $y = -3x^2 - 8x + 4$

3. $y = x(100 - x)$

Sasha and Tony decided that the average of the roots helps find the line of symmetry. In fact, you can use any pair of points on the graph that have the same y-value. You find the average of the x-coordinates of the points. The average gives you the x-coordinate of the vertex. It also gives the axis of symmetry.

In Investigation 3A, you found two points in particular, the roots of the equation, which are also the x-intercepts of the graph.

> What is the result when there are no real roots?

Facts and Notation

The following are true for the graph of $y = ax^2 + bx + c$.

- The vertex of the parabola has x-coordinate $-\frac{b}{2a}$. You can find its y-coordinate by substitution.

- The line of symmetry of the parabola has the equation $x = -\frac{b}{2a}$. The vertex is the only point that lies on both the parabola and its line of symmetry.

- The graph crosses the y-axis at the point (0, c). You call this point the y-intercept.

- The graph may cross the x-axis zero, one, or two times. When r is a solution to the quadratic equation $ax^2 + bx + c = 0$, (r, 0) is a point on the graph. You can find this point, called an x-intercept, by factoring, completing the square, or using the quadratic formula. You call the values of x at these points the roots or zeros.

Tony takes his concerns to Sasha.

Tony   Okay, now I'm worried about something.

Sasha   What are you worried about?

Tony   We just talked about the average of the roots, but there may not even be roots. The equation $y = x^2 - 6x + 8$ had two roots. We could move its graph up 4 units. Then the equation of the new graph doesn't have any roots.

Sasha   Oh, do you mean $y = x^2 - 6x + 12$?

Tony   Right, that equation has the same graph moved up 4 units. Here, I'll draw it.

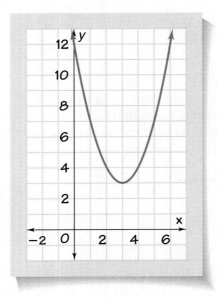

            If there aren't any roots, then how can we take their average?

Sasha   That's a stumper. Well, normally, I'd get roots from the quadratic formula. Let's see, $a = 1$, $b = -6$, and $c = 12$. The roots are $\frac{6 \pm \sqrt{36 - 48}}{2}$.

            If I simplify that, I get $3 + \frac{\sqrt{-12}}{2}$ and $3 - \frac{\sqrt{-12}}{2}$.

Tony   Yes, those numbers don't exist. There's no such number as $\sqrt{-12}$.

Sasha   Hold on a second. I can still find the average of the roots.

Tony   How can you find the average of things that don't exist?

Sasha   To take the average of two numbers, I add the numbers and divide by 2. I agree with you that $\sqrt{-12}$ doesn't exist, but I'm going to pretend it does exist for a little while.

Tony   Okay. I'm not convinced, but sure.

Sasha   So the roots are $3 + \dfrac{\sqrt{-12}}{2}$ and $3 - \dfrac{\sqrt{-12}}{2}$. If I add those up, I get $3 + \dfrac{\sqrt{-12}}{2} + 3 - \dfrac{\sqrt{-12}}{2}$.

Tony   Then you're adding and subtracting that *thing*! So it doesn't matter what it is, since it gets cancelled out. We can still use $-\dfrac{b}{2a}$.

Sasha   I was going to say that. Even when there aren't real-number roots, we can pretend there are. They're just not numbers we can plot on the number line, or on the graph.

Tony   Wait a second. So the line of symmetry is still $x = 3$. Of course it is, right? We only moved the parabola *up*, not left or right. So the x-coordinate of the vertex didn't change. Neither did the line of symmetry.

Sasha   You're right! And look, the a and b are the same in both equations. Only the c has changed. Of course the average of the roots wouldn't change either. All that work for nothing.

Tony   It's not for nothing, Sasha. At least we made sure it always works, whether there are real roots or not.

For You to Do

4. Find the two roots of the quadratic equation $2x^2 - 7x + 8 = 0$. What is the line of symmetry of the graph?

Now you have two ways to graph a parabola. The method you choose depends on the form of the equation you are given. How can you be sure that you can write every quadratic equation in the form $y - k = a(x - h)^2$? Look at an actual example.

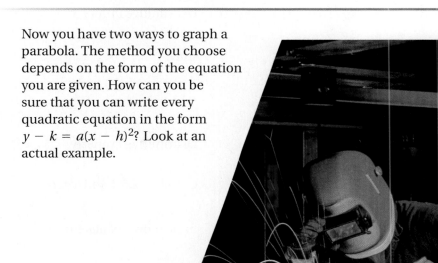

The molten-metal sparks follow parabolic paths with different maximum points.

Example

Problem Write $y = x^2 - 6x + 8$ in the form $y - k = a(x - h)^2$.

Solution The key is recognizing that the right side of the equation
$y - k = a(x - h)^2$ includes a perfect square trinomial. In order to find a
perfect square trinomial, you need to complete the square. What you use to
complete the square on the right side leads you to the value of k on the left side.

$$y = x^2 - 6x + 8$$
$$= (x^2 - 6x) + 8$$
$$= (x^2 - 6x + 9) - 9 + 8$$
$$= (x - 3)^2 - 1$$
$$y + 1 = (x - 3)^2$$

So $y = x^2 - 6x + 8$ is the same as $y + 1 = (x - 3)^2$.

This equation matches the results that Tony and Sasha found on page 194.
They found that the line of symmetry is at $x = 3$, and you just found that
the x-coordinate of the vertex is 3.

The evidence suggests that you can write every quadratic equation in the
form $y - k = a(x - h)^2$. You can prove your conclusion for the general
form of a quadratic equation by using the same manipulations that you
used to derive the quadratic formula.

Proof The normal form of a quadratic equation is $y = ax^2 + bx + c$.

$$y = ax^2 + bx + c$$

$$y = a\left(x^2 + \frac{b}{a}x\right) + c \qquad\qquad \text{Distributive Property}$$

$$y = a\left(x^2 + 2\left(\frac{b}{2a}\right)x\right) + c \qquad\qquad \text{since } 2\left(\frac{b}{2a}\right) = \frac{b}{a}$$

$$y = a\left(\left(x^2 + 2\left(\frac{b}{2a}\right)x + \left(\frac{b}{2a}\right)^2\right) - \left(\frac{b}{2a}\right)^2\right) + c \qquad\qquad \text{Add and subtract } \left(\frac{b}{2a}\right)^2.$$

$$y = a\left(x^2 + 2\left(\frac{b}{2a}\right)x + \left(\frac{b}{2a}\right)^2\right) - a\left(\frac{b^2}{4a^2}\right) + c \qquad\qquad \text{Distributive Property}$$

$$y = a\left(x + \frac{b}{2a}\right)^2 + \left(c - \frac{b^2}{4a}\right) \qquad\qquad \text{Corollary 2.3.1 and algebra}$$

$$y - \left(c - \frac{b^2}{4a}\right) = a\left(x + \frac{b}{2a}\right)^2 + \left(c - \frac{b^2}{4a}\right) - \left(c - \frac{b^2}{4a}\right) \qquad\qquad \text{basic moves of algebra}$$

$$y - \left(c - \frac{b^2}{4a}\right) = a\left(x + \frac{b}{2a}\right)^2$$

So the vertex of the graph of $y = ax^2 + bx + c$ is the point $\left(-\frac{b}{2a}, c - \frac{b^2}{4a}\right)$.

The result itself is not especially useful. The formula for the y-coordinate of the vertex is difficult to remember. Most people usually find the y-coordinate by substitution once they know the x-coordinate.

You have proven that you can write any quadratic in the form $y - k = a(x - h)^2$. You have also shown two other interesting facts.

- As expected, the x-coordinate of the vertex is $-\dfrac{b}{2a}$. So, once again, the line of symmetry is at $x = -\dfrac{b}{2a}$.

- The value of a in the normal form of the quadratic, $y = ax^2 + bx + c$, is also the value of a in the vertex form of the quadratic $y - k = a(x - h)^2$. So it is no coincidence that both forms use the letter a.

Exercises Practicing Habits of Mind

Check Your Understanding

1. **a.** Use factoring to find the two roots of the quadratic function $y = x^2 + 10x + 24$.

   b. Describe two ways you can show that the vertex of the graph of $y = x^2 + 10x + 24$ is $(-5, -1)$.

2. The quadratic function $y = x^2 + 9x + 30$ does not have real-number roots.

   a. Find the two roots by solving the equation. Express the results as radicals. Do not worry about a negative.

   b. What is the average of the roots?

3. Write the equations of three different quadratics that have $x = 4$ as their line of symmetry. Make sure that each equation has different coefficients of x^2.

4. A quadratic function has zeros at $x = 3$ and at $x = 8$. Its minimum y-value is -25. For parts (a) and (b), explain how you can use this information to find each of the following for the graph of the function.

   a. the line of symmetry **b.** the vertex

   c. An equation for this function is $f(x) = a(x - 3)(x - 8)$. Find the value of a.

> This means it passes through the points (3, 0) and (8, 0). The zeros are another name for roots or x-intercepts.

5. For each function, make a difference table for integers $0 \le x \le 6$.

a. $f(x) = x^2$

b. $g(x) = 2x^2$

c. $h(x) = 3x^2 - 6x - 1$

d. $j(x) = 9 - x^2$

Input, x	Output, x^2	Δ
0	0	■
1	1	■
2	4	5
3	9	7
4	16	■
5	■	11
6	36	

Some of the entries in the table for part (a) are complete.

6. Linda says that she graphs parabolas in the same way that she graphs lines.

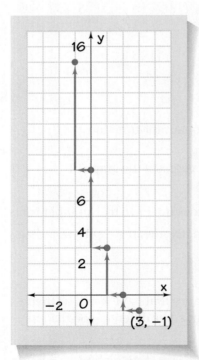

(3, −1)

Linda explains, "For $y = x^2 - 6x + 8$, I start from the vertex. Once I find that, I go left 1 and up 1, and that's another point. Then I go left 1 and up 3, and that's another point. Then left 1 and up 5, left 1 and up 7, and so on.

It looks a little like I'm finding the slope of a line, but it's different.

You have to move in both directions to find enough points to make the parabola look good. Oh, and it only works if there's no a number. I'm not sure what to do when there is one."

Using Linda's method, sketch a graph of each of the following quadratics.

a. $y = x^2 + 4x - 5$. Start by finding the vertex.

b. $y = 2x^2$. Is there any relationship similar to Linda's "left 1 and up 1, then left 1 and up 3, and then left 1 and up 5" for the points on this graph?

c. $y = 3x^2 - 6x - 1$

d. $y = 9 - x^2$

7. **Write About It** Describe the connections between Linda's method in Exercise 6 and the difference tables in Exercise 5.

> In part (c), you will need to find how many units to move from one point to the next. Left 1 and up 1 does not work here.

On Your Own

8. **Write About It** Consider the function $y = x^2 - 9$.

a. Sketch a graph of this function.

b. Explain why $x = 0$ is the equation of the line of symmetry.

c. Use the average-of-the-roots concept to explain why $x = 0$ is the equation of the line of symmetry.

d. What is the value of $-\frac{b}{2a}$ for this quadratic?

9. A quadratic function has roots at $x = 3$ and at $x = 8$. Its maximum y-value is 100. Find the vertex and an equation for the function.

10. Consider the quadratic function $y = -2x^2 - 10x - 12$.

a. Find the vertex of the graph.

b. Find all three intercepts for the graph.

c. Sketch a graph of the function.

> You find an intercept by setting variables equal to zero. There are two x-intercepts and one y-intercept.

11. A quadratic function in the form $y = x^2 - 6x + c$ has the line of symmetry $x = 3$. The location of the vertex depends on the value of c.

a. If $c = 0$, where is the vertex?

b. Find a value of c that makes the vertex $(3, 0)$.

c. If $c = 91$, where is the vertex?

d. Find the coordinates of the vertex in terms of c.

12. In Exercise 11b, you found the value of c that makes $y = x^2 - 6x + c$ have vertex $(3, 0)$. For parts (a)–(c), find the value of c such that the graph of each function has the given vertex.

a. $y = x^2 - 10x + c$, vertex $(5, 0)$ **b.** $y = x^2 - 14x + c$, vertex $(7, 0)$

c. $y = x^2 + 8x + c$, vertex $(-4, 0)$ **d.** Find the vertex of $y = (x - 9)^2$.

e. Find the vertex of $y = x^2 - 18x + 82$.

> **Go Online**
> www.successnetplus.com

13. Here is a table for a quadratic function with only the difference column completed.

Input	Output	Δ
0	■	−3
1	■	−1
2	■	1
3	■	3
4	■	5
5	■	7
6	■	

a. Find one way to complete the output column.

b. Find the vertex of the graph of the quadratic you used in part (a).

c. Is there more than one possible way to complete the table? Explain.

14. Standardized Test Prep Which of the following statements about the graph of $y = ax^2 + bx + c$ is NOT true?

A. The line of symmetry of the graph has the equation $x = -\frac{b}{2a}$.

B. The graph has a maximum if $a < 0$.

C. The graph has no x-intercepts if $b^2 - 4ac > 0$.

D. The y-intercept is equal to c.

Go Online
www.successnetplus.com

15. Take It Further $f(x) = ax^2 + bx + c$ is a quadratic function, and $f(m) = f(n)$ for two numbers m and n. Prove the following using algebra.

If $f(m) = f(n)$, then either $m = n$ or $\frac{m + n}{2} = -\frac{b}{2a}$.

Maintain Your Skills

16. For parts (a)–(d), find the vertex of the graph of each equation. Sketch a graph.

a. $y = 2x^2$

b. $y = 2(x - 5)^2$

c. $(y - 4) = 2(x + 3)^2$

d. $(y + 3) = 2(x - 1)^2$

e. What is the vertex of the graph of $(y + 11) = 2(x - 7)^2$?

17. Sketch the graph of each equation.

a. $y = x^2$

b. $y = (x - 2)^2$

c. $y - 3 = x^2$

d. $y = (2 - x)^2$

In this investigation, you explored optimization problems using quadratics. You also learned how to identify key components of the graphs of quadratic functions. These questions will help you summarize what you have learned.

1. Consider the function $f(x) = x^2 - 2x - 8$.

   a. Does the graph of $f(x)$ intersect the x-axis? If so, where does it intersect? If not, explain.

   b. What is the least possible value of $f(x)$? What value of x gives the least possible value of $f(x)$?

2. A farmer has 100 feet of fencing to build a corral in the shape of a rectangle. One side of the corral borders a river, so the farmer will only need to fence three sides. The farmer wants the corral to have the largest possible area. What should be the dimensions of the corral? What is the maximum area?

3. Sketch the graph for each of the equations below. Then find the vertex and line of symmetry.

   a. $(y - 3) = 2(x + 1)^2$ **b.** $(y + 4) = -(x - 2)^2$

   c. $y = \frac{1}{4}(x - 5)^2 + 1$ **d.** $y = x^2 - 4x + 3$

4. Consider the function $y = x^2 + 2x - 15$.

   a. Use factoring to find the roots of the function.

   b. Use the two roots to find the vertex.

   c. Find the point where the graph intersects the y-axis.

   d. Use the y-intercept and the line of symmetry to find another point.

5. How can you quickly identify the vertex of the graph of a quadratic equation?

6. How does the symmetry of a parabola help you solve problems that use quadratic functions?

7. Using two different methods, how can you find the vertex of the parabola with the equation $y = x^2 - 4x + 9$?

The suspension cables sag in a curve called a catenary until the added weight of the roadway reshapes them into a parabola.

Vocabulary

In this investigation, you learned these terms. Make sure you understand what each one means and how to use it.

- **line of symmetry**
- **maximum**
- **minimum**
- **parabola**
- **vertex**
- **vertex form**

Investigation 3C

Introduction to the Complex Plane

In *Introduction to the Complex Plane*, you will begin your exploration of complex numbers. When you solve a quadratic equation, you sometimes end up with the square root of a negative number in your solution. In the past, you have interpreted this to mean that there are no real-number solutions to the equation. That is true. However, if you expand your set of allowable solutions beyond the real numbers to the complex numbers, you can find solutions to all quadratic equations.

By the end of this investigation, you will be able to answer questions like these.

1. What are complex numbers?

2. What two numbers have a sum of 20 and a product of 109?

3. How can you use complex numbers to solve any quadratic equation?

You will learn how to

- understand the set of complex numbers as an extension of the real numbers

- use complex numbers as tools for solving equations

- be fluent in complex number arithmetic

You will develop these habits and skills:

- Think like an algebraist by examining extensions of number systems.

- Work with properties of complex numbers.

- Prove facts about operations on complex numbers and their conjugates.

In the Flammarion woodcut, a man peers beyond the familiar world. In this chapter, you will explore beyond $\mathbb{R}$.

You can construct a quadratic equation by using the sum and product of its roots.

For You to Explore

1. **a.** Is there a real number with a square -16? Explain.

   b. Is there a real number with a square -1? Explain.

2. The quadratic equation $x^2 - 12x + 27 = 0$ has two roots.

   a. What is the sum of the roots?   **b.** What is the product of the roots?

   c. What is the sum of the squares of the roots?

3. The quadratic equation $x^2 - 12x + 34 = 0$ has two roots.

   a. What is the sum of the roots?   **b.** What is the product of the roots?

   c. What is the sum of the squares of the roots?

4. **a.** Show that the identity $x^2 + y^2 = (x + y)^2 - 2xy$ is true.

   b. **Take It Further** Write $x^3 + y^3$ in terms of the expressions $(x + y)$ and xy.

5. For each quadratic equation, find the sum of the roots, the product of the roots, and the sum of the squares of the roots.

   a. $x^2 - 12x + 35 = 0$ **b.** $x^2 - 12x + 32 = 0$

   c. $x^2 - 12x + 33 = 0$ **d.** $x^2 + 12x + 32 = 0$

   e. $x^2 - 25 = 0$ **f.** $x^2 - 10 = 0$

   g. $x^2 + 8x - 33 = 0$

6. For the general monic quadratic $x^2 + bx + c$, find each quantity in terms of the coefficients b and c.

   a. the sum of the roots   **b.** the product of the roots

   c. the sum of the squares of the roots

> **Habits of Mind**
>
> **Establish a process.**
> Can you find the sum of the cubes of the roots without finding the roots?

7. **Take It Further** For each quadratic equation, find the sum of the cubes of the roots.

   a. $x^2 - 12x + 35 = 0$ **b.** $x^2 - 12x + 32 = 0$

   c. $x^2 - 12x + 33 = 0$

8. Consider the quadratic $x^2 - 14x + 50$.

   a. If two real numbers sum to 14, what is their largest possible product?

   b. What happens if you use the quadratic formula to solve $x^2 - 14x + 50 = 0$?

 **Exercises** *Practicing Habits of Mind*

On Your Own

9. Suppose $a + b = 14$ and $ab = 47$. Find the value of $a^2 + b^2$ in two ways.

   a. Use the identity from Problem 4.   **b.** Find a and b first.

10. **Write About It** Decide whether each statement is true or false. Explain.

    a. If $r + s$ is an integer, and rs is an integer, then $r^2 + s^2$ is an integer.

    b. If $r + s$ and rs are integers, then r and s are integers.

11. Explain why the graph of $y = x^2 - 10x + 29$ cannot cross the x-axis.

> What happens if you use the quadratic formula to find the roots of $x^2 - 10x + 29 = 0$?

12. Suppose $a + b = 10$ and $ab = 29$.

    a. Find the value of $a^2 + b^2$. Use the identity from Problem 4.

    b. What happens if you try to find $a^2 + b^2$ by finding a and b first?

13. **Take It Further** The quadratic $x^2 - 10x + 22$ has two roots. Find a quadratic with roots that are the *squares* of the roots of $x^2 - 10x + 22$.

14. Find two numbers with sum p and product q.

    a. $p = 7, q = 10$ **b.** $p = 2, q = -15$ **c.** $p = 2, q = \frac{3}{4}$ **d.** $p = 2, q = -1$

    e. Take It Further Express the two numbers in terms of p and q.

> These problems are all sum-and-product problems. However, you need different types of numbers for each one. Can you determine which type of numbers you need in each case?

Maintain Your Skills

15. Expand each expression.

    a. $(\sqrt{7} + \sqrt{3})(\sqrt{7} - \sqrt{3})$ **b.** $(\sqrt{5} + \sqrt{2})(\sqrt{5} - \sqrt{2})$

    c. $(3 + \sqrt{7})(3 - \sqrt{7})$ **d.** $(2\sqrt{3} + \sqrt{5})(2\sqrt{3} - \sqrt{5})$

    e. $(\sqrt{m} + \sqrt{n})(\sqrt{m} - \sqrt{n})$ **f.** $(a + \sqrt{b})(a - \sqrt{b})$

> Give exact answers, not decimal approximations.

16. Rewrite each fraction so that it has an integer denominator.

    a. $\dfrac{1}{\sqrt{7} + \sqrt{3}}$ **b.** $\dfrac{1}{\sqrt{5} + \sqrt{2}}$

17. Simplify each expression without using a calculator.

    a. $(\sqrt{2})^2 + (-\sqrt{2})^2$ **b.** $(1 + \sqrt{2})^2 + (1 - \sqrt{2})^2$

    c. $\sqrt{2} \cdot \sqrt{5}$ **d.** $\sqrt{3} \cdot \sqrt{5}$ **e.** $\sqrt{7} \cdot \sqrt{7}$

    f. $(b\sqrt{2}) \cdot (b\sqrt{2})$ **g.** $\sqrt{a} \cdot \sqrt{b}$ **h.** $\sqrt{k} \cdot \sqrt{k}$

3.10 Extending the Number System

The set of complex numbers is a number system that is an extension of the real numbers. In this lesson, you will examine why and how such extensions come about.

The earliest records of mathematics point to the system of counting numbers (1, 2, 3, . . .) and the operations of addition and multiplication. This system of counting numbers is referred to as the **natural numbers,** $\mathbb{N}$.

This system is closed under addition and multiplication. If you add or multiply two counting numbers, the result is a counting number. The counting numbers are not closed under other operations, but the results may still have meaning. This leads to extensions of $\mathbb{N}$.

- Consider $3 - 5 + 8$. The result is 6, but $3 - 5$ is not a counting number. So, you must "dip into" negative numbers in the middle of this calculation. However, the original expression and its result are both in $\mathbb{N}$. This type of calculation leads to the system of integers, $\mathbb{Z}$.

- Consider $28 \div 5 \times 10$. The result is 56, but $28 \div 5$, or $\frac{28}{5}$, is not an integer. This leads to the system of rational numbers, $\mathbb{Q}$. The rational numbers are closed under addition, subtraction, multiplication, and division (except division by 0).

> $\mathbb{Q}$ stands for "quotient." $\mathbb{Q}$ consists of all numbers $\frac{p}{q}$ where p and q are integers and $q \neq 0$.

Developing Habits of Mind

Experiment. You can define new numbers and incorporate them into an existing number system by extending the rules of calculation.

For example, start with $\mathbb{N}$ and extend to include 0, the identity for addition. Now you can define other numbers by how they operate under addition and multiplication.

- -5 is a new number defined by the fact that when you add it to 5, you get 0.
- $\frac{1}{5}$ is a new number defined by the fact that when you multiply it by 5, you get 1.

A number is something you can point to on the number line. The number line is a representation of all real numbers. Real numbers contain the rational numbers $\mathbb{Q}$ and **irrational numbers** that you cannot express as a quotient of integers. Irrational numbers include numbers such as $\sqrt{2}$ and π.

You have already seen problems where even real numbers are not enough. Take a closer look at Exercise 12 in Lesson 3.09.

> **Remember...**
> Use $\mathbb{R}$ to represent the real numbers. So, you have $\mathbb{N}$, $\mathbb{Z}$, $\mathbb{Q}$, and $\mathbb{R}$.

Example

Problem Suppose $a + b = 10$ and $ab = 29$. Find the value of $a^2 + b^2$.

Solution 1 Use the identity $x^2 + y^2 = (x + y)^2 - 2xy$.

If $a + b = 10$ and $ab = 29$, then

$$a^2 + b^2 = (a + b)^2 - 2ab$$
$$= 10^2 - 2 \cdot 29$$
$$= 100 - 58$$
$$= 42$$

The value of $a^2 + b^2$ is 42.

Solution 2 Another idea is to find a and b first. Think of it as a sum-and-product problem. If $a + b = 10$ and $ab = 29$, then a and b are the two roots of the equation $x^2 - 10x + 29 = 0$.

To find a and b, use the quadratic formula. This results in two strange-looking roots.

$$\frac{10 \pm \sqrt{100 - 4 \cdot 29}}{2} = \frac{10 \pm \sqrt{100 - 116}}{2} = \frac{10 \pm \sqrt{-16}}{2}$$

The expression $\sqrt{-16}$ seems to make no sense because there is no real number with square -16. But suppose that the roots are numbers. So, there are two numbers a and b.

$$a = \frac{10 + \sqrt{-16}}{2} \quad \text{and} \quad b = \frac{10 - \sqrt{-16}}{2}$$

There are still several steps to do to show that $a^2 + b^2 = 42$. Consider this method a work in progress.

> **Remember...**
> An *identity* is an equation that is true for any substitution for its variables.

> In algebra, you sometimes make believe certain numbers exist to help you solve problems.

For Discussion

1. What steps might you try next to show that $a^2 + b^2 = 42$? Do you have to make any assumptions about how $\sqrt{-16}$ behaves?

Often a problem and its solution are in the same number system, but the process of solving the problem requires you to leave the system. Sometimes you must invent new objects that cancel out at the end of the process.

Gradually, mathematicians regarded numbers such as $\sqrt{-16}$ as more than just convenient devices that might cancel out in a calculation. Mathematicians found more and more uses for such numbers. These types of numbers fill in many of the algebraic holes in $\mathbb{R}$, in a way similar to how the numbers in $\mathbb{R}$ fill in the geometric holes in $\mathbb{Q}$.

In this chapter you will work with square roots of negative numbers until you begin to feel comfortable working with them. Then you can use them to solve problems in algebra and geometry.

> **Habits of Mind**
> **Look for relationships.** Sometimes, you get answers that are familiar, but the computations go through unfamiliar territory. Other times, you get answers that come from unfamiliar territory.

 **Exercises** *Practicing Habits of Mind*

Check Your Understanding

1. For each equation, find the solutions, if any, that are in $\mathbb{N}$ (the natural numbers).

   a. $x^2 + 24 = 10x$
   b. $x^2 = 10x$
   c. $x^2 + 10x + 24 = 0$
   d. $24x^2 + 1 = 10x$
   e. $x^2 = 10$
   f. $x^2 + 10 = 0$
   g. $x^2 + x + 1 = 0$
   h. $x^3 = 1$

2. For each equation in Exercise 1, find the solutions, if any, that are in $\mathbb{Z}$ (the integers) but not in $\mathbb{N}$.

3. For each equation in Exercise 1, find the solutions, if any, that are in $\mathbb{Q}$ (the rational numbers) but not in $\mathbb{Z}$.

4. For each equation in Exercise 1, find the solutions, if any, that are in $\mathbb{R}$ (the real numbers) but not in $\mathbb{Q}$.

5. For each equation in Exercise 1, find the solutions, if any, that are not in $\mathbb{R}$.

6. For each equation, determine the number of real solutions.

   a. $x^2 + 4x + 3 = 0$
   b. $x^2 + 4x + 4 = 0$
   c. $x^2 + 4x + 5 = 0$
   d. $3x^2 - 10x + 8 = 0$

> **Remember...**
> An intercept is a point where a graph crosses either the *x*- or *y*-axis.

7. Graph each equation. Find the coordinates of all intercepts.

   a. $y = x^2 + 4x + 3$
   b. $y = x^2 + 4x + 4$
   c. $y = x^2 + 4x + 5$
   d. $y = 3x^2 - 10x + 8$

8. Suppose there is a number i with square –1.

   a. Simplify $(1 + i)^2 - 2(1 + i) + 2$.

   b. Explain why the number $1 + i$ is a solution of the equation $x^2 - 2x + 2 = 0$.

> Every time you see an i^2, replace it with -1.

9. Use the function $a(n)$. The domain is the whole numbers $\{0, 1, 2, 3, \ldots\}$.

$$a(n) = (\sqrt{3})^n + (-\sqrt{3})^n$$

   a. Find $a(n)$ for $n = 0$ through $n = 6$.

   b. Find $a(10)$ and $a(101)$.

   c. Is there a polynomial that agrees with this function a on all of $\mathbb{N}$? Explain.

10. Use the function $f(n)$. The domain is the whole numbers $\{0, 1, 2, 3, \ldots\}$.

$$f(n) = (1 + \sqrt{2})^n + (1 - \sqrt{2})^n$$

Determine whether each number is rational or irrational.

a. $(1 + \sqrt{2})^0$ **b.** $(1 + \sqrt{2})^1$ **c.** $(1 + \sqrt{2})^2$

d. Find $f(n)$ for $n = 0$ through $n = 6$.

e. Find an equation with integer coefficients that has $1 + \sqrt{2}$ as a solution.

f. **Take It Further** Show that $f(n) = 2f(n - 1) + f(n - 2)$ for any positive integer $n > 2$.

11. Suppose there is a number $\sqrt{-1}$, with square -1, that obeys the basic rules of arithmetic. The domain of the function $g(n)$ below is the whole numbers.

$$g(n) = (2 + \sqrt{-1})^n + (2 - \sqrt{-1})^n$$

> For convenience, you might use some letter instead of $\sqrt{-1}$. Many people use i.

a. Find $g(n)$ for $n = 0$ through $n = 6$.

b. Show that $(2 + \sqrt{-1})^2 = 3 + 4\sqrt{-1}$.

c. Find an equation with integer coefficients that has $2 + \sqrt{-1}$ as a root.

d. **Take It Further** Show that $g(n) = 4g(n - 1) - 5g(n - 2)$ for any positive integer $n > 2$.

On Your Own

12. For each case, give two examples of a calculation with two numbers.

a. The inputs are not positive integers, but the result is a positive integer.

b. The inputs are not integers, but the result is an integer.

c. The inputs are not rational numbers, but the result is a rational number.

d. The inputs are not real numbers, but the result is a real number.

e. The inputs are positive integers, but the result is not a positive integer.

f. The inputs are integers, but the result is not an integer.

g. The inputs are rational numbers, but the result is not a rational number.

h. The inputs are real numbers, but the result is not a real number.

13. For each equation, find the solutions, if any, that are in $\mathbb{N}$.

a. $x^2 + 5 = 6x$ **b.** $x^2 + 6x + 5 = 0$ **c.** $x^2 + 4x = -2$

d. $5x^2 + x = 6$ **e.** $x^2 = 5$ **f.** $x^2 + 11 = 6x$

14. For each equation in Exercise 13, find the solutions, if any, that meet the given condition.

a. in $\mathbb{Z}$ but not in $\mathbb{N}$ **b.** in $\mathbb{Q}$ but not in $\mathbb{Z}$

c. in $\mathbb{R}$ but not in $\mathbb{Q}$ **d.** not in $\mathbb{R}$

Go Online
www.successnetplus.com

15. Calculate the sum and product of each pair of numbers.

a. 13 and -23

b. $1 + 3$ and $1 - 3$

c. $1 + \sqrt{3}$ and $1 - \sqrt{3}$

d. $1 + \sqrt{n}$ and $1 - \sqrt{n}$

e. $1 + \sqrt{-3}$ and $1 - \sqrt{-3}$

You should give the answers for Exercise 15d in terms of n.

16. Standardized Test Prep What is the product of $3 + \sqrt{-2}$ and $3 - \sqrt{-2}$?

A. 1   **B.** 7   **C.** 9   **D.** 11

Maintain Your Skills

17. Decide whether each calculation results in a real number. Explain.

a. $(2 + \sqrt{-1}) + (2 - \sqrt{-1})$

b. $(2 + \sqrt{-1}) - (2 - \sqrt{-1})$

c. $(2 + \sqrt{-1})(2 + \sqrt{-1})$

d. $(2 + \sqrt{-1})(2 - \sqrt{-1})$

e. $\dfrac{2 + \sqrt{-1}}{2 + \sqrt{-1}}$

Again, assume you have a number $\sqrt{-1}$ that obeys the basic rules of arithmetic.

18. Suppose $x^2 = -1$. Write each expression in the form $A + Bx$, for real numbers A and B.

a. $(2 + 3x) + (5 + 6x)$ **b.** $(2 + 3x) + (2 - 3x)$ **c.** $(2 + 3x) - (2 - 3x)$

d. $(2 + 3x)(5 + 6x)$ **e.** $(2 + 3x)^2$ **f.** $(2 + 3x)(2 - 3x)$

Go Online
www.successnetplus.com

Historical Perspective

Square roots of negative numbers were first studied in the early 1500s. Mathematicians wanted to find a formula, similar to the quadratic formula, to solve cubic equations. Girolamo Cardano (1501–1576), Nicolo Tartaglia (1500–1557), and others developed and refined such a formula.

When they applied the formula to cubic functions with real roots, such as $x^3 - 15x - 4$, they ended up with expressions involving square roots of negative numbers.

The mathematicians did not let this strange result stop them. They imagined that they could calculate with these expressions, using the basic rules and the theorems of algebra.

Girolamo Cardano   Nicolo Tartaglia

3.11 Making the Extension: $\sqrt{-1}$

To find two numbers with a sum of 4 and a product of 16, you can solve the quadratic equation $x^2 - 4x + 16 = 0$. Use the quadratic formula to find the two solutions.

$$x = \frac{4 \pm \sqrt{4^2 - 4 \cdot 16}}{2} = \frac{4 \pm \sqrt{-48}}{2}$$

Because you cannot take the square root of a negative number in the real number system, no real solutions exist for the equation. So you cannot find two real numbers with a sum of 4 and a product of 16. However, if you allow for square roots of negatives, the two roots you found with the quadratic formula may solve the problem.

For You to Do

Evaluate each expression.

1. $\dfrac{4 + \sqrt{-48}}{2} + \dfrac{4 - \sqrt{-48}}{2}$

2. $\dfrac{4 + \sqrt{-48}}{2} \cdot \dfrac{4 - \sqrt{-48}}{2}$

> Assume that the basic rules for calculating with numbers still work, and that $(\sqrt{-48})^2 = -48$.

Example

Problem Rewrite $\dfrac{4 + \sqrt{-48}}{2}$ as an expression without a denominator.

Solution Note that $-48 = 16 \cdot -3$.

$$\sqrt{-48} = \sqrt{16 \cdot -3} = \sqrt{16} \cdot \sqrt{-3} = 4\sqrt{-3}$$

Rewrite $\sqrt{-48}$ to simplify the expression.

$$\begin{aligned}
\frac{4 + \sqrt{-48}}{2} &= \frac{4 + 4\sqrt{-3}}{2} \\
&= \frac{2(2 + 2\sqrt{-3})}{2} \\
&= 2 + 2\sqrt{-3}
\end{aligned}$$

Developing Habits of Mind

Check your work. Look more carefully at the calculation below.

$$\sqrt{-48} \overset{(1)}{=} \sqrt{16 \cdot -3} \overset{(2)}{=} \sqrt{16} \cdot \sqrt{-3} \overset{(3)}{=} 4\sqrt{-3}$$

Step (1) and Step (3) seem fine. But is Step (2) legitimate? Is the square root of a product always equal to the product of the square roots? It is true when the numbers are positive, but that is because of a convention. There are two numbers with a square 9, but we defined the symbol $\sqrt{9}$ to mean the positive number with a square 9.

You can use the "duck principle" to see if the ends of the calculation agree. Do you get -48 when you square $4\sqrt{-3}$?

$$(4\sqrt{-3})^2 = 4\sqrt{-3} \cdot 4\sqrt{-3} = 16 \cdot \sqrt{-3} \cdot \sqrt{-3} = 16 \cdot (-3) = -48$$

Since $\sqrt{-3} \cdot \sqrt{-3} = -3$, it seems reasonable for you to say that $\sqrt{-48} = 4\sqrt{-3}$. But what happens when both square roots are of negative numbers?

> The duck principle: If it walks like a duck and quacks like a duck, then it probably is a duck.

For Discussion

3. Find the value of $\sqrt{-12} \cdot \sqrt{-3}$.

4. Find the value of $\sqrt{-12} \cdot \sqrt{-12}$.

Minds in Action

Tony and Sasha debate their answers to the For Discussion problems.

Tony   I solved the first one. It's 6.

Sasha   I solved it too. It's -6.

Tony   Well, then you're wrong. It can't be both 6 *and* -6.

Sasha   No, you're wrong. I replaced $\sqrt{-12}$ with $2\sqrt{-3}$ and calculated.

$$\sqrt{-12}\sqrt{-3} = \sqrt{4 \cdot -3}\sqrt{-3} = \sqrt{4}\sqrt{-3}\sqrt{-3} = 2\sqrt{-3} \cdot \sqrt{-3}$$

The square roots $\sqrt{-3}$ and $\sqrt{-3}$ multiply to make -3. Then 2 times -3 is -6, and that's the answer.

Tony   Hmm. That looks pretty solid, actually.

Sasha   As I said, I'm right and you're wrong. What did you do?

Tony   I used the fact that $\sqrt{a}$ times $\sqrt{b}$ is $\sqrt{ab}$. So, $\sqrt{-12} \cdot \sqrt{-3}$ is the same as $\sqrt{-12 \cdot -3}$. I multiplied and got $\sqrt{36}$. Then $\sqrt{36}$ is 6, and that's my answer.

Sasha   Hmm. That looks pretty solid too. That's trouble. Did you get -12 for the second one?

Tony   Sure. That one was easier, $\sqrt{x} \cdot \sqrt{x}$ is just x, no matter what x is.

Sasha   Why didn't you use the rule you used for the first one?

Tony   I don't know, I guess I could have. Then $\sqrt{-12} \cdot \sqrt{-12}$ is the same as $\sqrt{-12 \cdot -12}$. That's . . . uh oh, that's $\sqrt{144}$ which is 12, not -12.

Sasha   Maybe you can't trust that $\sqrt{ab}$ rule after all . . .

Sasha and Tony's discussion leads to an important consequence. Known rules for calculation may no longer work in an extended system. The rule $\sqrt{a} \cdot \sqrt{b} = \sqrt{ab}$ works for nonnegative real numbers, but leads to a contradiction when both a and b are negative. Sasha and Tony discovered this contradiction when they compared their answers to Problem 3. Both 6 and -6 seem to make sense as values of $\sqrt{-12} \cdot \sqrt{-3}$. You need a more precise rule for handling square roots of negative numbers.

Think about the square roots of positive numbers. What does $\sqrt{49}$ mean? Your answer may be "a number with a square of 49," but there are two of these, 7 and -7. By convention, people decided that $\sqrt{49}$ represents the positive square root. Once you accept this convention, you can use it to prove theorems such as $\sqrt{a} \cdot \sqrt{b} = \sqrt{ab}$ (when a and b are nonnegative).

> What does this use of *convention* mean?

You need a similar convention for negative numbers in order to avoid Tony and Sasha's contradiction. The following definition does the trick.

- Start with the real numbers, $\mathbb{R}$. $\mathbb{R}$ already contains the square roots of positive numbers.
- Introduce one new number, $\sqrt{-1}$. This is just a symbol. The only property of $\sqrt{-1}$ is that its square is -1.
- If n is positive, define $\sqrt{-n}$ as $\sqrt{-n} = \sqrt{n} \cdot \sqrt{-1}$.

> **Remember...**
>
> You can use the letter i to represent $\sqrt{-1}$.

The following are some examples of numbers using this definition of $\sqrt{-n}$.

$$\sqrt{-4} = \sqrt{4} \cdot \sqrt{-1} = 2\sqrt{-1}$$
$$\sqrt{-6} = \sqrt{6} \cdot \sqrt{-1}$$
$$\sqrt{-100} = 10 \cdot \sqrt{-1}$$

This convention takes care of Tony and Sasha's contradiction. There is only one value for $\sqrt{-12} \cdot \sqrt{-3}$.

$$
\begin{aligned}
\sqrt{-12} \cdot \sqrt{-3} &= (\sqrt{12} \cdot \sqrt{-1}) \cdot (\sqrt{3} \cdot \sqrt{-1}) \\
&= (\sqrt{12} \cdot \sqrt{3}) \cdot (\sqrt{-1} \cdot \sqrt{-1}) \\
&= (\sqrt{12 \cdot 3}) \cdot (-1) \\
&= 6 \cdot -1 \\
&= -6
\end{aligned}
$$

For You to Do

Simplify. Each product is an integer.

5. $\sqrt{-2} \cdot \sqrt{-8}$

6. $\sqrt{-9} \cdot \sqrt{-1}$

7. $\sqrt{-18} \cdot \sqrt{-8}$

The convention eliminates the ambiguity in multiplying square roots of negative numbers. Clearly the theorem $\sqrt{ab} = \sqrt{a} \cdot \sqrt{b}$ stops working in this new system. Moving forward, you will work with *complex numbers*. Complex numbers are expressions of the form

$$a + b\sqrt{-1}$$

where a and b are real numbers.

In some of the exercises that follow, you will test whether other basic results extend to complex numbers. In others, you will investigate the nature of this new arithmetic.

You will explore a more formal definition of the complex numbers in the next lesson.

Exercises Practicing Habits of Mind

Check Your Understanding

1. Expand each expression.

a. $(a + b)(a - b)$

b. $(a + b\sqrt{2})(a - b\sqrt{2})$

c. $(a + b\sqrt{3})(a - b\sqrt{3})$

d. $(a + b\sqrt{c})(a - b\sqrt{c})$

e. $(a + b\sqrt{-1})(a - b\sqrt{-1})$

2. Sketch the graphs of $y = x^2$ and $y = 6x - 11$. How many times do the graphs intersect?

3. When you include square roots of negative numbers, the equation $x^2 = 6x - 11$ has two solutions.

a. Find the solutions. Express the solutions without denominators.

b. Find the sum and the product of the solutions.

4. Does every quadratic equation with real coefficients have a solution if you include square roots of negative numbers? Explain.

5. What two numbers have squares of 34? Provide approximations rounded to the nearest hundredth for these two numbers.

6. Decide whether the following statement is true. Explain.

For every nonnegative real number a, there are two numbers with squares equal to a.

7. Show that the equation $x^3 - 5x^2 + 8x - 6 = 0$ has the following solutions.
$$x = 3, x = 1 + \sqrt{-1}, x = 1 - \sqrt{-1}$$

8. Simplify each expression.
  a. $3 + (1 + \sqrt{-1}) + (1 - \sqrt{-1})$
  b. $3(1 + \sqrt{-1}) + 3(1 - \sqrt{-1}) + (1 + \sqrt{-1})(1 - \sqrt{-1})$
  c. $3(1 + \sqrt{-1})(1 - \sqrt{-1})$

On Your Own

9. Simplify each product.
  a. $\sqrt{-4} \cdot \sqrt{-9}$
  b. $\sqrt{-9} \cdot \sqrt{-4}$
  c. $\sqrt{-3} \cdot \sqrt{-27}$
  d. $\sqrt{-27} \cdot \sqrt{-3}$
  e. $(2 + \sqrt{-3}) \cdot \sqrt{-3}$
  f. $\sqrt{-3} \cdot (2 + \sqrt{-3})$

10. **Write About It** Does the Commutative Property of Multiplication apply to this new arithmetic? Explain. Use examples or proof.

11. Write each expression in the form $a + b\sqrt{-1}$, where a and b are real numbers.
  a. $(3 + 4\sqrt{-1}) + (4 + 5\sqrt{-1})$
  b. $(3 + \sqrt{-16}) + (4 + \sqrt{-25})$
  c. $(5 + \sqrt{-1})(5 + 2\sqrt{-1})$
  d. $(3 + \sqrt{-2}) + (3 - \sqrt{-2})$
  e. $(3 + \sqrt{-2})(3 - \sqrt{-2})$

12. **Standardized Test Prep** What are the solutions to $x^2 - 10x + 26 = 0$?
  A. $x = 5$ and $x = -5$
  B. $x = 5 + \sqrt{2}$ and $x = 5 - \sqrt{2}$
  C. $x = 5 + \sqrt{-1}$ and $x = 5 - \sqrt{-1}$
  D. $x = 5 + \sqrt{-2}$ and $x = 5 - \sqrt{-2}$

Go Online
www.successnetplus.com

13. The equation $x^3 - 8 = 0$ has one solution in $\mathbb{R}$, $x = 2$.

When you include square roots of negative numbers, the equation has three solutions.

a. Factor $x^3 - 8$.

b. Use the factored form to find all three solutions to the equation $x^3 - 8 = 0$.

c. Find the three solutions to $x^3 - 1 = 0$.

14. a. Use factoring to find the solutions to the equation $x^3 - 64 = 0$.

b. Compare the solutions with the solutions to $x^3 - 8 = 0$ and $x^3 - 1 = 0$.

15. Take It Further Find all six solutions to the equation $x^6 - 64 = 0$.

> You can start by factoring the left side as a difference of squares.

Maintain Your Skills

16. Simplify each expression.

a. $(3 + 4\sqrt{-1})(3 - 4\sqrt{-1})$ **b.** $(12 + 5\sqrt{-1})(12 - 5\sqrt{-1})$

c. $(7 + \sqrt{-1})(7 - \sqrt{-1})$ **d.** $(x + y\sqrt{-1})(x - y\sqrt{-1})$

17. Simplify each expression.

a. $\sqrt{-1} \cdot \sqrt{-1}$ **b.** $\sqrt{-1} \cdot \sqrt{-1} \cdot \sqrt{-1} \cdot \sqrt{-1}$

c. $(\sqrt{-1})^6$ **d.** $(\sqrt{-1})^8$

e. $(\sqrt{-1})^9$

Go **Online**
Video Tutor
www.successnetplus.com

3.12 Extension to Complex Numbers

Lesson 3.11 introduced the number $\sqrt{-1}$ to allow you to work with square roots of negative numbers. This number is just a symbol defined by its behavior.

$$(\sqrt{-1})^2 = -1$$

Rather than writing $\sqrt{-1}$, you can use the letter i. Again, this is just a symbol defined by its behavior.

If a and b are real numbers, a number written in the form $a + bi$ is a *complex number*. Here is the formal definition.

Definition

The system of **complex numbers** $\mathbb{C}$ consists of all expressions in the form $a + bi$ with the following properties.

- a and b are real numbers.
- $i^2 = -1$
- You can use addition and multiplication as if $a + bi$ were a polynomial.

> A real number is also a complex number. For example, $3 = 3 + 0i$.

For Discussion

1. Explain how you know that i is not a real number.

2. Is $(2 + 3i)(5 - 4i)$ a complex number? Explain.

The following examples show that calculating with complex numbers is very similar to calculating with polynomials.

Example 1

Problem Write each expression as a complex number in the form $a + bi$.

a. $(3 + 2i) + (2 - 5i)$ b. $(3 + 2i) - (2 - 5i)$ c. $(3 + 2i)(2 - 5i)$

Solution

a. Use the associative and commutative properties of addition. Then combine like terms.

$$(3 + 2i) + (2 - 5i) = 3 + 2 + 2i - 5i$$
$$= 5 + (2 - 5)i$$
$$= 5 - 3i$$

b. Distribute the negative. Then combine like terms.

$$(3 + 2i) - (2 - 5i) = 3 + 2i - 2 + 5i$$
$$= 1 + 2i + 5i$$
$$= 1 + 7i$$

c. Multiply. Then combine like terms.

$$(3 + 2i)(2 - 5i) = 6 - 15i + 4i - 10i^2$$
$$= 6 - 11i - 10i^2$$
$$= 6 - 11i - 10(-1)$$
$$= 6 - 11i + 10$$
$$= 16 - 11i$$

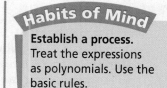

Establish a process. Treat the expressions as polynomials. Use the basic rules.

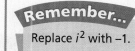

Replace i^2 with -1.

For You to Do

Write each expression as a complex number in the form $a + bi$.

3. $(10 - 11i) + (3 - 2i)$ **4.** $(5 + 7i) - (5 - 3i)$ **5.** $(3 - 2i)(2 + 5i)$

You can represent a generic complex number with a single letter. So, if $z = 3 + 2i$ and $w = -1 + i$, you can think about the expressions $z + w$, which equals $(2 + 3i)$, and zw, which equals $(-5 + i)$.

But, how do you know that there is only one way you can write a complex number in the form $a + bi$ with a and b real? Maybe you can find other real numbers x and y such that $x + yi$ is equal to $3 + 2i$. The following theorem and proof show that you cannot find such numbers.

Theorem 3.6

If a, b, c, and d are real numbers, then $a + bi = c + di$ only when $a = c$ and $b = d$.

Proof Suppose $a + bi = c + di$. Prove that $a = c$ and $b = d$. You can prove this with indirect reasoning. Suppose $b \neq d$. Then solve the equation for i.

$$a + bi = c + di$$
$$bi - di = c - a$$
$$i = \frac{c - a}{b - d}$$

The expression $\frac{c - a}{b - d}$ represents a real number. This is a contradiction because i is not a real number. Therefore, b must equal d.

Since $b = d$, then $bi = di$. You can subtract terms bi and di from each side of the original equation. This leaves $a = c$. So, if $a + bi = c + di$, then $a = c$ and $b = d$.

Because of Theorem 3.6, there is only one way you can write a complex number as $a + bi$, where a and b are real. So, every complex number is determined by two numbers—its real part and its imaginary part. Using this language, you can state Theorem 3.6 as follows.

Two complex numbers are equal if and only if their real parts are equal and their imaginary parts are equal.

> When you write a complex number in the form $a + bi$, you are expressing the number in standard form.

Example 2

Problem Find the complex number z that satisfies the equation below.

$$z \cdot (2 - i) = 21 + i$$

Solution Write $z = a + bi$ and multiply.

$$(a + bi)(2 - i) = 2a - ai + 2bi - bi^2$$
$$= 2a - ai + 2bi + b$$
$$= (2a + b) + (-a + 2b)i$$

So, $2a + b = 21$, and $-a + 2b = 1$. Now you have a system of two equations and two unknowns.

$$2a + \ b = 21$$
$$-a + 2b = \ 1$$

You can solve this system of equations in several ways. One way is to multiply each side of the second equation by 2 and then add.

$$
\begin{aligned}
2a + \ b &= 21 \\
+ \ -2a + 4b &= \ 2 \\
\hline
5b &= 23 \\
b &= \tfrac{23}{5}
\end{aligned}
$$

You can substitute to find the value $a = \frac{41}{5}$. The complex number z is $\frac{41}{5} + \frac{23}{5}i$.

> Complex numbers have two parts, the real part and the imaginary part. So, equationsv with complex numbers may result in two equations and two unknowns.

For You to Do

6. Find the complex number w that satisfies the equation $w + (3 - i) = 4i$.

You have extended $\mathbb{R}$ to include the square roots of all real numbers, keeping the basic rules intact. But you discovered that not all familiar properties hold true in this new number system. For example, you gave up $a^2 \geq 0$. This is similar to giving up the idea that multiplication makes things bigger in passing from $\mathbb{N}$ to $\mathbb{Z}$.

By extending $\mathbb{R}$ to $\mathbb{C}$, you now have a system in which all quadratic equations with real coefficients have roots. Over the centuries, mathematicians discovered that even more is true. $\mathbb{C}$ not only contains all roots of any quadratic equation, it also contains all roots of any polynomial equation with real coefficients. This was a big discovery, and it took mathematicians generations to fully understand its meaning. It is now called the **Fundamental Theorem of Algebra**. It was first proved by Carl Friedrich Gauss in the 1800s.

Go Online
www.successnetplus.com

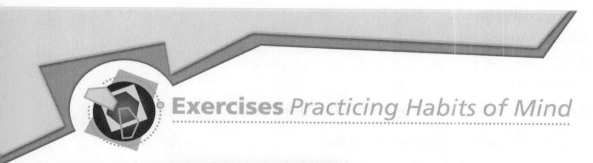

Exercises Practicing Habits of Mind

Check Your Understanding

1. Simplify each expression. Write your answer in the form $a + bi$, where a and b are real numbers.

   a. $(3 + 2i) + (9 - i)$
   b. $(3 + 2i)(9 + i)$

   c. $(5 + 2i) + (5 - 2i)$
   d. $(5 + 2i)(5 - 2i)$

   e. $(4 + 2i) + (2 + 4i)$
   f. $(4 + 2i)(2 + 4i)$

2. The complex number $3 - 5i$ is the *conjugate* of $3 + 5i$. Simplify each expression involving conjugates.

   a. $(3 + 5i) + (3 - 5i)$
   b. $(3 + 5i)(3 - 5i)$

   c. $(-7 + 2i) + (-7 - 2i)$
   d. $(-7 + 2i)(-7 - 2i)$

   e. $(12 + 5i) + (12 - 5i)$
   f. $(12 + 5i)(12 - 5i)$

3. **a.** What is the conjugate of $(a + bi)$?

   b. Show that when you add a complex number and its conjugate, the result is a real number.

   c. Show that when you multiply a complex number by its conjugate, the result is a real number.

   d. When is the sum of a number and its conjugate 0?

   e. When is the product of a number and its conjugate 0?

4. **What's Wrong Here?** Derman does not think that if two complex numbers are equal, their parts must be equal.

   Derman says, "I've got a really simple counterexample. If $a = i$ and $b = i$, it's the same as having $c = -1$ and $d = 1$. Try it, and you'll see. If $a + bi = c + di$, it doesn't mean $a = c$ and $b = d$."

   What happened? Is Derman correct? Explain.

5. Find the complex number $a + bi$ that satisfies the following equation.

$$(a + bi)(1 + i) = 11 - 3i$$

6. Every real number x has an opposite, a number that when added to x results in a sum of 0.

    a. Does $2 + 3i$ have an opposite? Explain.

    b. What complex numbers have opposites?

7. The conjugate of z is represented by $\bar{z}$. Show that if z and $\bar{z}$ are conjugates, then $z^2 + (\bar{z})^2$ is a real number.

8. **Take It Further** For each part, find an equation with real coefficients that has the listed numbers among its roots. Remember that when you add or multiply a complex number and its conjugate, the result is real.

    a. $3 + 2i$ **b.** $3 - 2i$

    c. $1 + 5i$ and $3 + 2i$ **d.** $1 + 5i$ and $-1 + 5i$

    e. $1 + i\sqrt{3}$ **f.** $\sqrt{2} + \sqrt{3}$

    g. $\sqrt{2} + i\sqrt{3}$

On Your Own

9. **Standardized Test Prep** If a and b are real numbers, what is the product $(a + bi)(b - ai)$?

    A. $(b^2 - a^2)i$ **B.** 0

    C. $2ab$ **D.** $2ab + (b^2 - a^2)i$

10. You can use the rule $i^2 = -1$ to simplify other powers of i.

    a. Express i^3 in simplest form without using an exponent.

    b. Express i^4 in simplest form without using an exponent.

    c. Simplify i^5, i^6, i^7, and i^8.

    d. What is i^{210}?

    e. **Take It Further** Express $\frac{1}{i}$ without a denominator.

11. Solve each equation. The solutions are complex numbers.

    a. $z + (3 - i) = 6 + 2i$ **b.** $w - 3 = 6 + i$

    c. $x^2 = -9$ **d.** $z^2 = 6z - 34$

Go Online
www.successnetplus.com

12. Find a complex number z such that the product $z \cdot (3 + 2i)$ is a real number.

13. Find a number that meets each set of given conditions. If no such number exists, explain why.

a. a complex number that is not real

b. a rational number that is also real

c. a real number that is not rational

d. a rational number that is not complex

e. a real number that is also complex

14. a. Show that $x^2 + 1 = (x + i)(x - i)$.

b. Write About It You may have learned in a previous course that $x^2 + 1$ does not factor. Does this statement contradict part (a)? Explain.

15. a. Use the quadratic formula to find the two solutions to the equation $x^2 - 10x + 34 = 0$.

b. Find the sum and product of the solutions.

c. Find the sum of the squares of the solutions.

16. Take It Further Find all complex numbers $a + bi$ that satisfy this equation.

$$(a + bi)^2 = -11 + 60i$$

Maintain Your Skills

17. Find each sum or difference.

a. $(2 + i) + (3 + i)$

b. $(3 + i) + (2 + i)$

c. $(5 + i) - (4 + 3i)$

d. $(4 + 3i) - (5 + i)$

e. $(5 + 3i) + (8 - 3i)$

f. $\left(3 + i\sqrt{2}\right) + \left(3 - i\sqrt{2}\right)$

18. Find each product.

a. $(2 + i)(3 + i)$

b. $(3 + i)(2 + i)$

c. $(5 + i)(5 - i)$

d. $(2 + i)^2$

e. $(3 + 2i)^2$

f. $(4 + i)^2$

19. Find the complex number z that satisfies each equation.

a. $z \cdot (2 - i) = 3 + i$

b. $z \cdot (2 - i) = 6 + 2i$

c. $z \cdot (2 - i) = 9 + 3i$

d. $z \cdot (2 - i) = 5$

e. $z \cdot (2 - i) = 10$

f. $z \cdot (2 - i) = 15$

Reciprocals and Division

Addition and multiplication of complex numbers share the following important properties with addition and multiplication of polynomials. Let z, w, and u be complex numbers.

Distributive Property: $z(w + u) = zw + zu$

Properties of Addition and Multiplication

Addition	Property	Multiplication
$z + w = w + z$	Commutative	$zw = wz$
$z + (w + u) = (z + w) + u$	Associative	$z(wu) = (zw)u$
$z + 0 = z$	Identity	$z \cdot 1 = z$
z has an opposite in $\mathbb{C}$.	Inverse	You will explore this now.

Developing Habits of Mind

Look for relationships. The fact that these properties hold for complex numbers is not anything magical. Remember the following from the definition of complex numbers in Lesson 3.12.

> You can use addition and multiplication as if $a + bi$ were a polynomial.

This more or less forces complex numbers to obey the rules for calculating that hold for polynomials.

Complex numbers have the structure of polynomials and the extra rule $i^2 = -1$. This is enough extra structure to guarantee that every nonzero complex number has a reciprocal. The following definition explains why.

Every complex number $a + bi$ has a **conjugate** $a - bi$. The product of a complex number and its conjugate is a real number. "Taking the conjugate" is the key operation that will allow you to divide complex numbers and to find their reciprocals.

When you extend the playing field, you have to adjust the rules to cover new situations.

Example 1

Problem Find the complex number z that satisfies $z \cdot (2 - i) = 21 + i$.

Solution In Lesson 3.12, you solved the same problem using a system of equations. It is simpler to solve using conjugates. Multiply the left and right sides of the equation by the conjugate of $(2 - i)$, which is $(2 + i)$.

$$z \cdot (2 - i) = 21 + i$$

$$z \cdot (2 - i)(2 + i) = (21 + i)(2 + i)$$

$$z \cdot 5 = 41 + 23i$$

The reason you want to multiply by $2 + i$ is that the product $(2 - i)(2 + i)$ is the real number 5. To solve the new equation $5z = 41 + 23i$, you just divide each side by 5.

$$z = \frac{41 + 23i}{5}$$

> You can also express this number as $\frac{41}{5} + \frac{23}{5}i$.

Multiplying a complex number by its conjugate always results in a real number. This property is the key to simplifying fractions involving complex numbers.

Example 2

Problem Express $\frac{18 + i}{3 - 4i}$ in the form $a + bi$.

Solution The denominator is a complex number. If you multiply the denominator by its conjugate, $3 + 4i$, the result is a real number. Since you do not want to affect the value of the original fraction, multiply both the numerator and the denominator by $3 + 4i$.

$$\frac{18 + i}{3 - 4i} \cdot \frac{3 + 4i}{3 + 4i} = \frac{50 + 75i}{25} = 2 + 3i$$

The fraction simplifies to $2 + 3i$. You can multiply to check the result.

$$(2 + 3i)(3 - 4i) = 6 - 8i + 9i - 12i^2 = 18 + i$$

Since $(2 + 3i)(3 - 4i) = 18 + i$, it is also true that $\frac{18 + i}{3 - 4i} = 2 + 3i$.

> **Remember...**
>
> When you multiply the numerator and denominator of a fraction by the same number, you are multiplying the fraction by 1.

For You to Do

1. Find the reciprocal of $2 + 3i$.

Represent conjugates. The symbol $\bar{z}$ represents the conjugate of z. This notation helps you to describe more simply the relationships between complex numbers and their conjugates. For example, you can state the multiplication property from this lesson in an abbreviated manner.

$$z\bar{z} \text{ is a real number.}$$

Conjugation is a function in which the input is a complex number and the output is a complex number. Here is a statement you will prove in the exercises.

$$\overline{z + w} = \bar{z} + \bar{w}$$

This statement illustrates the order of operations. The left side is the result of adding two complex numbers and then taking the conjugate. The right side is the result of taking both conjugates and adding them together.

Some of the exercises ask you to find or prove other statements about conjugation.

> $z\bar{z}$ is the product of a complex number and its conjugate.

For Discussion

2. Suppose z is some nonzero complex number. Show that z has a reciprocal in $\mathbb{C}$. Does 0 have a reciprocal? Explain.

You can now complete the Properties of Addition and Multiplication table from the beginning of the lesson. For the Inverse Property under multiplication, you can include the following statement.

$$\text{If } z \neq 0 \text{, then } z \text{ has a reciprocal in } \mathbb{C}.$$

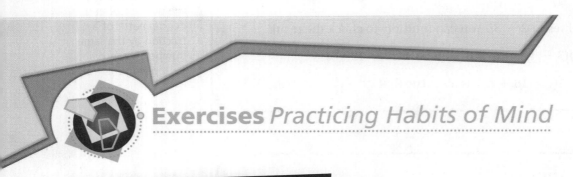

Exercises *Practicing Habits of Mind*

Check Your Understanding

1. Rewrite the following statement using z and $\bar{z}$.

The sum of a complex number and its conjugate is a real number.

2. a. What is the conjugate of $2i$?　　**b.** What is the conjugate of 7?

c. Show that the statement $\overline{z + w} = \bar{z} + \bar{w}$ is true when $z = 2i$ and $w = 7$.

3. Suppose $z = a + bi$ and $w = c + di$.

a. Write expressions for $\bar{z}$ and $\bar{w}$.

b. Prove that $\overline{z + w} = \bar{z} + \bar{w}$ is true for any complex numbers z and w.

Remember...

A real number is also a complex number.

4. Suppose $z = 3 + 2i$ and $w = 4 - 5i$. Write each of the following as $r + si$, where r and s are real numbers.

a. $\bar{z}$　　　**b.** $\overline{(\bar{z})}$　　　**c.** $\overline{z + w}$　　　**d.** $\bar{z} + \bar{w}$

e. $\overline{zw}$　　　**f.** $(\bar{z})(\bar{w})$　　　**g.** $z + \bar{z}$　　　**h.** $w\bar{w}$

5. Express each fraction in the form $a + bi$.

a. $\dfrac{11 - 3i}{1 + i}$

b. $\dfrac{4 + i}{2 - i}$

c. $\dfrac{8 + 4i}{2 + i}$

d. $\dfrac{3 + i}{3 - i}$

e. $\dfrac{3 - i}{3 + i}$

f. Take It Further $\dfrac{c + di}{a + bi}$

6. Find each product.

a. $(3 + 4i)(5 + 6i)$

b. $(3 - 4i)(5 - 6i)$

c. $(2 + 7i)(8 - 3i)$

d. $(2 - 7i)(8 + 3i)$

e. $(-10 + 3i)(2 - 7i)$

f. $(-10 - 3i)(2 + 7i)$

7. The results in Exercise 6 suggest the following relationship for conjugates.

$$\overline{zw} = (\bar{z})(\bar{w})$$

Prove that this statement is true for any complex numbers z and w.

8. Let $z = a + bi$. Show that each statement is true.

a. $z + \bar{z} = 2a$

b. $z\bar{z} = a^2 + b^2$

9. a. Find two real numbers a and b such that $2a = 14$ and $a^2 + b^2 = 74$.

b. Find two complex numbers with a sum of 14 and a product of 74.

These results prove that the sum and the product of conjugates are always real numbers.

On Your Own

10. Express each quotient in the form $a + bi$.

a. $\dfrac{1}{1 + i}$　　　**b.** $\dfrac{1}{1 - i}$　　　**c.** $\dfrac{1}{2 + 3i}$　　　**d.** $\dfrac{1}{5 + 6i}$

11. Suppose $z = a + bi$, where a and b are real numbers, and $z \neq 0$. Write $\frac{1}{z}$ in the form $c + di$ for real numbers c and d.

12. Consider the function $f(x) = x^2$, where the domain is $\mathbb{C}$. Write each output in the form $a + bi$.

a. $f(i)$ **b.** $f(-i)$ **c.** $f(2 + i)$

d. $f(2 - i)$ **e.** $f(3 + i)$ **f.** $f(3 - i)$

g. $f(-5 + 4i)$ **h.** $f(-5 - 4i)$

13. The results in Exercise 12 suggest the relationship $\overline{z^2} = (\overline{z})^2$.

a. Prove that this statement is true for any complex number z.

b. **Take It Further** Explain how this relationship is a consequence of the result in Exercise 7.

14. Write each complex number in the form $r + si$.

a. $\dfrac{4 + i}{4 - i}$ **b.** $\dfrac{2 + 3i}{2 - 3i}$ **c.** $\dfrac{a + bi}{a - bi}$

15. **Standardized Test Prep** Complex number w is the reciprocal of complex number z. If $z = x + yi$ and $w = u + vi$, what are the values of u and v in terms of x and y?

A. $u = x$ and $v = y$ **B.** $u = \dfrac{x}{x^2 + y^2}$ and $v = \dfrac{-y}{x^2 + y^2}$

C. $u = \dfrac{x}{x^2 - y^2}$ and $v = \dfrac{-y}{x^2 - y^2}$ **D.** $u = \dfrac{x}{x^2 + y^2}$ and $v = \dfrac{y}{x^2 + y^2}$

16. **a.** Show that $(a + bi)^2 = (a^2 - b^2) + (2ab)i$.

b. Show that $(a^2 + b^2)^2 = (a^2 - b^2)^2 + (2ab)^2$.

c. Let $a = 3$ and $b = 2$ in the equation from part (b). What are the values of $a^2 + b^2$, $a^2 - b^2$, and $2ab$?

17. List three quadratic equations with real coefficients and roots that are nonreal complex numbers. Then find the roots for each equation.

18. Prove that if z is a root of a quadratic polynomial with real coefficients, then $\overline{z}$ is also a root.

Maintain Your Skills

19. Express each quotient in the form $a + bi$.

a. $\dfrac{8 + i}{2 + i}$ **b.** $\dfrac{8 - i}{2 - i}$ **c.** $\dfrac{3 + 5i}{2 - 3i}$

d. $\dfrac{3 - 5i}{2 + 3i}$ **e.** $\dfrac{17 - 4i}{6 - 5i}$ **f.** $\dfrac{17 + 4i}{6 + 5i}$

20. Simplify each expression.

a. $\dfrac{1}{1 + i} + \dfrac{1}{1 - i}$ **b.** $\dfrac{1}{2 + 3i} + \dfrac{1}{2 - 3i}$ **c.** $\dfrac{1}{5 + i} + \dfrac{1}{5 - i}$

d. **Take It Further** Prove that if z is a nonzero complex number, then $\dfrac{1}{z} + \dfrac{1}{\overline{z}}$ is a real number.

In this investigation, you explored the set of complex numbers. You learned to calculate with complex numbers and you used complex numbers as tools to solve equations. These exercises will help you summarize what you have learned.

1. Find the solutions, if they exist, to $x^4 - 121 = 0$ that meet each of the following conditions.

   a. The solution is in $\mathbb{N}$.

   b. The solution is in $\mathbb{Z}$ but not in $\mathbb{N}$.

   c. The solution is in $\mathbb{Q}$ but not in $\mathbb{Z}$.

   d. The solution is in $\mathbb{R}$ but not in $\mathbb{Q}$.

   e. The solution is not in $\mathbb{R}$.

2. Use the quadratic polynomial $x^2 - 4x + 13$.

   a. Find its roots.

   b. Find the sum of its roots.

   c. Find the product of its roots.

   d. Find the sum of the squares of its roots.

3. Find all roots of the polynomial $x^3 - 64$.

4. Find a complex number $z = a + bi$, with a and b real numbers, that satisfies each equation.

   a. $z + (4 - 3i) = 6 + 8i$

   b. $z \cdot (4 - 3i) = 6 + 8i$

5. Given two complex numbers, $z = 2 - 5i$ and $w = -3 + 7i$, show that $\overline{zw} = (\overline{z})(\overline{w})$.

6. What are complex numbers?

7. What two numbers have a sum of 20 and a product of 109?

8. How can you use complex numbers to solve any quadratic equation?

Vocabulary and Notation

In this investigation, you learned these terms and symbols. Make sure you understand what each one means and how to use it.

- complex numbers, $\mathbb{C}$
- conjugate, $\overline{z}$
- Fundamental Theorem of Algebra
- irrational numbers
- natural numbers, $\mathbb{N}$
- i $\left(\sqrt{-1}\right)$
- $a + bi$ (complex number)

In **Investigation 3A,** you learned how to

- use the quadratic formula to solve equations or determine whether an equation has no real solutions

- construct a quadratic equation given the equation's two roots

- factor nonmonic quadratics

The following questions will help you check your understanding.

1. **a.** Solve the equation
   $84x^2 - 407x + 155 = 0$.

   b. Factor over $\mathbb{Z}$ the polynomial
   $84x^2 - 407x + 155$.

2. Solve the following equations. If there are no real-number solutions, explain.

   a. $x^2 - 5x - 14 = 0$

   b. $2x^2 + 5x + 3 = 0$

   c. $2x^2 + 5x = 4$

   d. $x^2 = x - 1$

   e. $(x + 3)(x - 4) = 8$

3. Find a quadratic equation for each of the following pairs of roots.

   a. 3 and -1

   b. $\frac{1}{2}$ and 5

   c. $\sqrt{3}$ and $-\sqrt{3}$

   d. 0 and -5

   e. $1 + \sqrt{2}$ and $1 - \sqrt{2}$

   f. $\sqrt{2} + 1$ and $\sqrt{2} - 1$

4. Factor each quadratic polynomial twice. First, write the quadratic as a monic polynomial. Then use the quadratic formula.

   a. $3x^2 + 11x + 10$

   b. $4x^2 + 4x - 15$

In **Investigation 3B,** you learned how to

- use your knowledge of quadratics to optimize some quadratic functions

- graph quadratic functions and examine the graph to find the vertex

- explore word problems involving quadratic functions

The following questions will help you check your understanding.

5. Each of the following describes a quadratic function. Find the vertex of the graph of each function.

   a. $y + 3 = 2(x - 5)^2$

   b. $y = (x + 1)(x - 3)$

   c. $y = 3x^2 + 18x + 8$

   d.

x	y
-2	9
0	-15
1	-21
2	-23
4	-15
6	9

6. There are many pairs of numbers that sum to 50.

   a. Which pair has the greatest product?

   b. What is that product?

7. A parabola has vertex $(4, -2)$ and includes the point $(3, -5)$.

  a. Use symmetry to identify one other point that must be on the graph of this function.

  b. Find an equation of the parabola.

  c. Sketch the graph of the equation.

  d. How does this graph compare to the graph of $y = x^2$?

8. Consider the quadratic function $y = -2x^2 + 4x - 3$.

  a. Find the vertex and line of symmetry of the graph of this equation.

  b. Find all three intercepts for the graph of this equation, if they exist.

  c. Sketch the graph of this equation.

  d. How does the graph of this equation compare to the graph of $y = x^2$?

In **Investigation 3C,** you learned how to

- understand complex numbers as an extension of the real numbers
- use complex numbers as tools for solving equations
- be fluent in complex-number arithmetic

The following questions will help you check your understanding.

9. Use the equation $x^5 - 36x = 0$. Find the solutions, if they exist, that meet each of the following conditions.

  a. The solution is in $\mathbb{N}$.

  b. The solution is in $\mathbb{Z}$ but not in $\mathbb{N}$.

  c. The solution is in $\mathbb{Q}$ but not in $\mathbb{Z}$.

  d. The solution is in $\mathbb{R}$ but not in $\mathbb{Q}$.

  e. The solution is not in $\mathbb{R}$.

10. a. Solve $2x^2 - x + 5 = 0$ over $\mathbb{C}$.

  b. Find a complex number $z = a + bi$, where a and b are real numbers, that satisfies $z + (3 - 7i) = -2 - 11i$.

  c. Find a complex number $z = a + bi$, where a and b are real numbers, that satisfies $(1 - i) \cdot z = 3$.

11. Given two complex numbers $z = -1 + 3i$ and $w = 4 + 2i$, find each of the following.

  a. $z + w$ **b.** $\overline{w}$

  c. $z \cdot w$ **d.** $2z \cdot \overline{w}$

  e. z^2 **f.** $\frac{1}{z}$

Multiple Choice

1. How many solutions does the quadratic equation $0 = 3x^2 - 7x - 13$ have?

   A. 0

   B. 1

   C. 2

   D. 3

2. In which quadrant is the vertex of the graph of $y = 3x^2 - 7x - 13$?

   A. I

   B. II

   C. III

   D. IV

3. Which of these points is NOT on the graph of the quadratic function $y = (x - 5)^2 + 10$?

   A. $(0, -15)$

   B. $(5, 10)$

   C. $(10, 35)$

   D. $(15, 110)$

4. For which value of k does the quadratic equation $3x^2 - 24x + k = 0$ have exactly one real-number solution?

   A. -48

   B. -16

   C. 16

   D. 48

5. Two real numbers add up to 50. Which of the following numbers could be their product?

   A. -1000

   B. 1000

   C. 2000

   D. 3000

6. If $z = 4 + 6i$, what is $z - \bar{z}$?

   A. 0

   B. 8

   C. $12i$

   D. $8 + 12i$

7. What is the value of $|5 - 12i|$?

   A. $\sqrt{119}$

   B. 7

   C. 13

   D. 17

8. One solution of $ax^2 + bx + c = 0$, where a, b, and c are real numbers, is $4 - 6i$. Which of the following is another solution?

   A. $-4 + 6i$

   B. $\sqrt{52}$

   C. $-4 - 6i$

   D. $4 + 6i$

9. Which equation has solutions $2 + \sqrt{5}$ and $2 - \sqrt{5}$?

   A. $x^2 - 20 = 0$

   B. $x^2 - 4x - 1 = 0$

   C. $x^2 + 4x - 1 = 0$

   D. $x^2 - 4x - 21 = 0$

10. Which is the minimum value of the function $f(x) = x^2 - 12x + 33$?

    A. -12

    B. -3

    C. 3

    D. 33

Open Response

11. You can model the stopping distance of a car with a quadratic function. The stopping distance d, in feet, is related to the speed m, in miles per hour. The equation is $d = \frac{1}{20}m^2 + m$.

   a. According to this rule, what is the stopping distance for a car traveling 30 miles per hour?

   b. If the speed of the car doubles, does the stopping distance double? Give an example.

   c. Use the quadratic formula and the following equation to find the speed m if a car's stopping distance is 300 feet.

$$300 = \frac{1}{20}m^2 + m$$

12. A parabola has vertex $(2, 27)$ and an x-intercept of -1.

   a. Use the symmetry of the parabola to find the other x-intercept.

   b. Find an equation for this parabola.

   c. Sketch the parabola.

13. Factor $6x^2 + 7x - 20$.

14. Find all the solutions to the equation $(2h + 3)(h - 4) = 13$.

15. How are the roots of a quadratic equation related to its coefficients?

16. Consider the graph of the function $f(x) = x^2 - 8x + c$.

   a. If $c = 0$, find the vertex.

   b. Find a value of c that makes the vertex $(4, 0)$.

   c. If $c = 24$, find the vertex.

   d. Find the coordinates of the vertex in terms of c.

17. Find the solutions of $x^2 - 2x + 10 = 0$ that are in each number system.

   a. $\mathbb{R}$ **b.** $\mathbb{C}$

18. Solve each equation over $\mathbb{C}$. Express your answer in the form $a + bi$, where a and b are real numbers.

   a. $z + 4i = 2(3 - i)$

   b. $z \cdot (5 + i) = 11 - 3i$

19. A complex number z has magnitude 4 and direction $30°$. Find the magnitude and direction of each power of z.

   a. z^2 **b.** z^3 **c.** z^4

Challenge Problem

20. Use the equation below.

$$w(x) = (x + 3)(x + 1)(x - 2)(x - 4)$$

What is the degree of $w(x)$?

Functions

Mathematics has a remarkable relationship with the natural world. Often a table of observations of two related quantities matches a mathematical function. Examination of this function can reveal the relationship between the two quantities.

Suppose you throw a ball up into the air and measure its height at different times. Suppose further that you make a table with columns for the time elapsed since the throw and the height observed at that time. There is a quadratic function that matches this table.

If you measure the velocity of the ball at several times and make a table of time and the ball's velocity, a linear function matches the table. The linear function shows that the upward velocity of the ball decreases at a constant rate, eventually becoming negative as the ball stops rising and begins to fall back down.

The functions tell you what is happening to the ball. A scientific explanation tells why the function has the structure it does and what the coefficients and roots of the polynomial mean.

Vocabulary and Notation

- base
- closed-form definition
- composite function, $g \circ f$
- cubic function
- degree of a monomial
- difference table
- domain
- equal functions
- even function
- exponential decay
- exponential function
- exponential growth
- function
- hockey stick property
- identity function
- inverse function, f^{-1}
- odd function
- one-to-one
- piecewise-defined function
- quadratic function
- range
- recursive definition
- slope
- strictly decreasing
- strictly increasing
- target
- unit circle
- up-and-over property
- $x \mapsto y$ (x maps to y)
- $\mathbb{R}$ (the real numbers)

Tables

In *Tables*, you will use algebra to describe patterns that you see in tables of numbers. You can describe mathematics as the "science of patterns." That is a big oversimplification, but it is true that the ability to find patterns in data is an important skill for mathematicians and people who use mathematical thinking in their work and in their lives.

By the end of this investigation, you will be able to answer questions like these.

1. How can you tell whether there is a linear function that fits a table?

2. How can you use differences to decide what type of function fits a table?

3. What polynomial function agrees with this table?

Input	Output
0	1
1	5
2	11
3	19
4	29
5	41

You will learn how to

- identify and describe specific patterns in input-output tables

- determine whether a linear function matches a table

- use differences to decide what type of function can fit a table

- compare recursive and closed-form rules for functions

You will develop these habits and skills:

- Look for patterns and describe them with algebra.

- "Work like a mathematician"—search for hidden regularities, describe the patterns explicitly, and explain inconsistencies.

- Generalize methods so that they work in a greater number of situations.

- Find laws and principles based on patterns in tables.

- Make conjectures using the guess and check method.

You can record a jumping frog's height in a table. Then you can fit a polynomial function to the table.

Getting Started

You can write a rule for a function based on the input and output values in a table.

For You to Explore

The object of the game is to find a simple function that agrees with each table.

> Some examples of simple functions are linear, quadratic, reciprocal, and square-root functions. You can also describe a simple function with words, such as "each output is 2 more than the previous output."

Table A

Input, n	Output, $A(n)$
0	0
1	2
2	4
3	6
4	8

Table B

Input, n	Output, $B(n)$
0	0
1	2
2	6
3	12
4	20

Table C

Input, n	Output, $C(n)$
0	2
1	1
2	0
3	−1
4	−2

Table D

Input, n	Output, $D(n)$
0	0
1	3
2	8
3	15
4	24

1. For each table above, find a rule that produces these outputs. Do not worry about the notation or vocabulary you use to describe the rule. You can use an equation such as

   $$\text{output} = 3 \times \text{input}$$

   or a sentence such as "each output is the output above it plus 4."

2. Richard notices there is more than one rule for Table A. He says, "Sure, I can find a rule that works: Double the input. But there are other functions that make that same table from 0 to 4 and produce different outputs for inputs greater than 4."

   a. Draw a graph with the 5 points of Table A. Then draw the graph of the function $n \mapsto 2n$.

   b. **Write About It** Do you agree or disagree with Richard? Explain your answer using additional graphs or tables as needed.

   c. **Take It Further** Find a function that supports Richard's claim. If no such function exists, explain why.

   > Richard claims that there are many functions that agree with Table A.

Exercises Practicing Habits of Mind

Habits of Mind

Think about it another way. There are many ways to think about these exercises. For example, you can suppose there is a mystery function generating each table. You want to find it.

On Your Own

For Exercises 3–20, find a function that agrees with each table. Keep track of the functions you find, because the solution for one exercise may be useful in a later exercise.

3. Table E

Input	Output
0	3
1	5
2	7
3	9
4	11

4. Table F

Input	Output
0	-2
1	$-1\frac{1}{2}$
2	-1
3	$-\frac{1}{2}$
4	0

5. Table G

Input	Output
0	-7
1	-4
2	-1
3	2
4	5

6. Table H

Input	Output
0	3
1	8
2	13
3	18
4	23

7. Table I

Input	Output
0	0
1	1
2	4
3	9
4	16

8. Table J

Input	Output
0	0
1	2
2	8
3	18
4	32

9. Table K

Input	Output
0	1
1	2
2	5
3	10
4	17

10. Table L

Input	Output
0	-25
1	-24
2	-21
3	-16
4	-9

11. Table M

Input	Output
0	9
1	15
2	21
3	27
4	33

Go Online
Video Tutor
www.successnetplus.com

12.

Table N

Input	Output
0	9
1	16
2	25
3	36
4	49

13.

Table O

Input	Output
0	0
1	5
2	20
3	45
4	80

14.

Table P

Input	Output
0	1
1	5
2	9
3	13
4	17

15.

Table Q

Input	Output
0	1
1	10
2	29
3	58
4	97

16.

Table R

Input	Output
0	0
1	1
2	8
3	27
4	64

17.

Table S

Input	Output
0	3
1	4
2	11
3	30
4	67
5	128

18.

Table T

Input	Output
0	1
1	3
2	9
3	27
4	81
5	243

19.

Table U

Input	Output
0	1
1	2
2	4
3	8
4	16
5	32

20.

Table V

Input	Output
0	0
1	1
2	3
3	7
4	15
5	31

Maintain Your Skills

21. Make a table for the inputs 0 through 5 for each of the following functions.

    a. $a(x) = x^2$ **b.** $b(x) = x^2 - 1$ **c.** $c(x) = x^2 - 4$ **d.** $d(x) = x^2 - 9$

22. Find a number c that makes $f(x) = x^2 - c$ equal to zero when $x = 5$.

23. Show that the following identity is true.

$$(x + 1)^2 - x^2 = 2x + 1$$

Two Types of Definitions—Closed Form and Recursive

The table below is from Exercise 6 of Lesson 4.01.

Table H

Input	Output
0	3
1	8
2	13
3	18
4	23

You can describe a function that agrees with this table in more than one way. For example,

- If the input n is zero, the output is 3. To get the next output, add 5 to the previous output.

- $g(n) = 5n + 3$

Developing Habits of Mind

Look for patterns. You will learn later on that Table H itself is a function. The set of possible inputs is $\{0, 1, 2, 3, 4\}$ and nothing else. When you think of the table as a function, you can write $H(2) = 13$, but $H(6)$ is not defined.

In this lesson, you are looking for something different—a way to express some regularity in the table. Finding and describing a pattern can allow you to extend the domain from $\{0, 1, 2, 3, 4\}$ to a larger set of numbers. Both bulleted descriptions above do this. When you match a table with a polynomial or another simple rule, you are uncovering a hidden relationship in the numbers. This is something that mathematicians really prize.

> You learned that the domain of a function is *the set of allowable inputs.*

For You to Do

1. When the input is 9, what is the output of each of the two functions described above?

2. Can you use each function to find the output when the input is −2? Explain.

Facts and Notation

A function definition such as "$g(n) = 5n + 3$" is a **closed-form definition**. A closed-form definition lets you find any output $g(n)$ for any input n by direct calculation.

A function definition such as "$f(0) = 3$ and any output is 5 more than the previous output" is a **recursive definition**. Recursive definitions are useful for expressing patterns in the outputs of a function. The notation below is a useful way to write a recursive definition.

$$f(n) = \begin{cases} 3 & \text{if } n = 0 \\ f(n-1) + 5 & \text{if } n > 0 \end{cases}$$

Notice that f is a recursive function and g is a closed-form function. Do the two definitions give the same function?

Developing Habits of Mind

Use a model. The closed-form definition below matches Table H from Exercise 6 of the Getting Started lesson.

$$g(n) = 5n + 3$$

You can build a computer or calculator model for function g in your function-modeling language. Then you can experiment with the model. You can do the following:

- Evaluate the function.
- Graph the function.
- Make a table of the function in a spreadsheet window.

It is a good habit to build models like these for the functions you use, especially when you want to get a feel for how the functions behave.

How you build a model depends on your computer or calculator. See the TI-Nspire™ Handbook, p. 990.

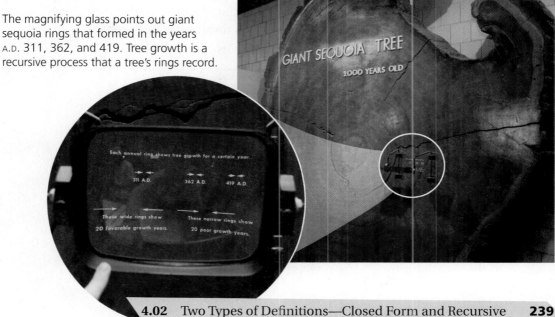

The magnifying glass points out giant sequoia rings that formed in the years A.D. 311, 362, and 419. Tree growth is a recursive process that a tree's rings record.

For You to Do

3. Build a model for g in your function-modeling language.

4. Make a table of your model for inputs between 0 and 10.

5. Graph your model in your graphing environment.

A recursive definition lets you calculate any output in terms of previous outputs. The simplest kind of recursive definition for a function f tells you how to compute $f(n)$ for an integer n in terms of $f(n - 1)$. You need a place to start. The definition below tells you to start at 3 (when $n = 0$) and to add 5 to get from one output to the next.

$$f(n) = \begin{cases} 3 & \text{if } n = 0 \\ f(n - 1) + 5 & \text{if } n > 0 \end{cases}$$

- $f(0) = 3$, because $n = 0$
- $f(1) = f(1 - 1) + 5 = f(0) + 5 = 3 + 5 = 8$
- $f(2) = f(2 - 1) + 5 = f(1) + 5 = 8 + 5 = 13$

Read the second line as "the current output is the previous output plus five." This recursively defined function fits all the entries in Table H.

For You to Do

You can use function-modeling language to model a recursive definition. Your technology may even provide a template like the one below. For help, see the TI-Nspire™ Handbook, p. 990.

$$\text{define } f(n) = \begin{cases} \blacksquare, \blacksquare \\ \blacksquare, \blacksquare \end{cases}$$

You just fill in the boxes.

$$\text{define } f(n) = \begin{cases} 3, & \text{if } n = 0 \\ f(n - 1) + 5, & \text{if } n > 0 \end{cases}$$

Recursive definitions tell you how the outputs are related. Closed-form definitions tell you how inputs are related to outputs. Each tells you something interesting. In some cases, you can convert one to the other. Later in this investigation you will see how.

6. Build a model for f and experiment with it. What numbers will f accept as inputs? Explain. How does g compare to f?

Difference Tables

A **difference table** can help you see patterns that lead to recursive definitions. Use Table H from Exercise 6 of Lesson 4.01.

Table H

Input	Output
0	3
1	8
2	13
3	18
4	23

To make a difference table, add a third column marked with the Δ symbol. Write the difference between one output and the next in the third column.

The Δ symbol is the capital Greek letter delta. It represents change or difference.

Input	Output	Δ
0	3	8 − 3 = **5**
1	8	13 − 8 = **5**
2	13	18 − 13 = **5**
3	18	23 − 18 = **5**
4	23	

The differences are exactly what you need to write a recursively defined function that matches Table H. In this case, all the differences are the same number, 5. The following recursive definition fits Table H.

$$f(n) = \begin{cases} 3 & \text{if } n = 0 \\ f(n-1) + 5 & \text{if } n > 0 \end{cases}$$

In some tables the differences are not constant, as in the table below.

Table D

Input, n	Output, $d(n)$	Δ
0	0	3
1	3	5
2	8	7
3	15	9
4	24	11
5	35	13
6	48	

In Lesson 4.05, you will see that you can still use the Δ column to find a recursive function that matches the table. Here is a recursive definition for d.

What function matches the Δ column?

$$d(n) = \begin{cases} 0 & \text{if } n = 0 \\ d(n-1) + 2n + 1 & \text{if } n > 0 \end{cases}$$

For You to Do

7. Show that the function d fits Table D.

Check Your Understanding

For Exercises 1–3, use Table B from Lesson 4.01.

Table B

Input, n	Output, $B(n)$
0	0
1	2
2	6
3	12
4	20

1. Make a difference table for Table B.

2. Decide whether each recursive definition fits Table B.

   a. $b(n) = \begin{cases} 0 & \text{if } n = 0 \\ b(n-1) + 2 & \text{if } n > 0 \end{cases}$

   b. $b(n) = \begin{cases} 0 & \text{if } n = 0 \\ b(n-1) + 2(n-1) & \text{if } n > 0 \end{cases}$

   c. $b(n) = \begin{cases} 0 & \text{if } n = 0 \\ b(n-1) + 2n & \text{if } n > 0 \end{cases}$

   d. $b(n) = \begin{cases} 2 & \text{if } n = 0 \\ b(n-1) + 2n & \text{if } n > 0 \end{cases}$

3. Decide whether each closed-form definition fits Table B.

   a. $b(n) = 2n$

   b. $b(n) = n^2 + n$

   c. To find each output, take the input and multiply by one more than the input.

   d. $b(n) = 2^{n+1} - 2$

For Exercises 4–6, copy and complete each difference table.

4.

Input	Output	Δ
0	5	6
1	11	▧
2	19	10
3	▧	15
4	▧	

5.

Input	Output	Δ
0	▧	3
1	▧	3
2	▧	3
3	▧	3
4	18	

6.

Input	Output	Δ
0	5	−3
1	▧	▧
2	17	▧
3	▧	−5
4	−1	

7. Use the recursive definition below.

$$f(n) = \begin{cases} 1 & \text{if } n = 0 \\ n \cdot f(n - 1) & \text{if } n > 0 \end{cases}$$

   a. Find the values of $f(1)$ through $f(6)$ for this function.

   b. What preprogrammed function on your calculator agrees with f?

8. The table at the right is an incomplete input-output table for a function.

You can use each rule to complete the table. Make a completed table for each rule.

Input	Output
0	2
1	6
2	▧
3	▧
4	▧

   a. To get each output, take the previous output and add four.

   b. To get each output, take the previous output and multiply by three.

   c. $n \mapsto 2(3^n)$

   d. To get each output, take the input, multiply by four, and then add two.

9. Write About It Consider the tables in Lesson 4.01. Find three tables that are related. Describe how they are related. You may find it helpful to make difference tables.

> **Remember...**
> $a^0 = 1$ for any nonzero number a, so $3^0 = 1$.

On Your Own

The *triangular numbers* are numbers determined by the pattern shown below. The number of dots in a triangular pattern with n dots on a side is the nth triangular number.

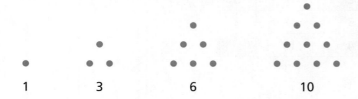

| 1 | 3 | 6 | 10 |

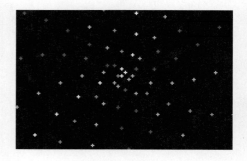

This pattern results when you arrange the counting numbers in a spiral and color the triangular numbers.

Here is a table for the triangular numbers.

Side Length	Number of Dots
0	0
1	1
2	3
3	6
4	10
5	15

10. Make a difference table for the triangular numbers.

11. a. Write a recursive function definition that fits the table of triangular numbers.

   b. Take It Further Find a closed-form definition for a function that generates the triangular numbers.

12. a. Copy and complete the difference table below.

Input, *x*	Output, *ax* + *b*	Δ
0	b	■
1	$a + b$	■
2	$2a + b$	■
3	$3a + b$	■
4	$4a + b$	■
5	$5a + b$	

   b. Find a formula for $f(x + 1) - f(x)$ when $f(x) = ax + b$.

You can define $f(x) = ax + b$ in your computer algebra system (CAS) and ask for $f(x + 1) - f(x)$. Make sure you have not assigned any values to a, b, or x.

13. a. Copy and complete the difference table below.

Input, x	Output, $ax^2 + bx + c$	Δ
0	c	▨
1	$a + b + c$	▨
2	$4a + 2b + c$	▨
3	$9a + 3b + c$	▨
4	$16a + 4b + c$	▨
5	$25a + 5b + c$	

b. Find a formula for $f(x + 1) - f(x)$ when $f(x) = ax^2 + bx + c$.

14. Standardized Test Prep Find the output of the function $g(n)$ below for the input $n = 4$.

$$g(n) = \begin{cases} 1 & \text{if } n = 1 \\ g(n - 1) + 2n - 1 & \text{if } n > 1 \end{cases}$$

A. 1   **B.** 4

C. 10   **D.** 16

Go Online
www.successnetplus.com

Maintain Your Skills

15. In each table below, the input-output pairs represent points on the graph of a linear function. Find the slope of each graph.

a.

Input	Output
0	-7
1	-4
2	-1
3	2
4	5
5	8

b.

Input	Output
0	-7
1	-11
2	-15
3	-19
4	-23
5	-27

c.

Input	Output
0	2
1	$1\frac{1}{2}$
2	1
3	$\frac{1}{2}$
4	0
5	$-\frac{1}{2}$

Remember...

Slope is the ratio of the change in the y-coordinates to the change in the x-coordinates.

d. Describe how you can find the slope of a linear function when you have a table for the function in which the inputs are consecutive integers.

Habits of Mind

Look for relationships. What is the connection between the two parts of this exercise?

4.03 Constant Differences

In this lesson, you will explore a specific type of difference table. The inputs are consecutive integers and all the differences between the outputs are constant. Here is Table H from Lesson 4.01.

Below is a difference table for Table H.

Table H

Input	Output
0	3
1	8
2	13
3	18
4	23

Input	Output	Δ
0	3	5
1	8	5
2	13	5
3	18	5
4	23	

In Lesson 4.02, you saw that the recursively defined function below fits the table.

$$f(n) = \begin{cases} 3 & \text{if } n = 0 \\ f(n-1) + 5 & \text{if } n > 0 \end{cases}$$

You can use a recursive definition that has constant differences to find a closed form that also fits the table.

Minds in Action

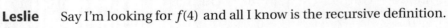

Leslie explains how she finds a closed-form definition that fits the table.

Leslie Say I'm looking for $f(4)$ and all I know is the recursive definition.

$$f(4) = f(3) + 5$$

So if I want to know $f(4)$, I just need to know what $f(3)$ was. But $f(3)$ depends on $f(2)$. Oh, I have to use the recursive definition *again*.

$$f(3) = f(2) + 5$$

And I can combine those two: $f(4) = f(2) + 5 + 5$. Two steps, two fives. Every step I take is another five. So if I go all the way back, that's four steps.

$$f(4) = f(0) + 4 \cdot 5$$

The definition tells me $f(0) = 3$, so $f(4)$ is 3 plus 4 fives. What's great about this is there isn't anything special about finding $f(4)$. If I want to find $f(17)$, I add 3 plus 17 fives. If I want to find $f(n)$, I add 3 plus n fives.

$$f(n) = 3 + n \cdot 5$$

I think I'd rather write that as $f(n) = 5n + 3$.

Input	Output	Δ
0	3	5
1	8	5
2	13	5
3	18	5
4	23	

Leslie used the numbers highlighted in this difference table to find $f(4) = f(0) + 4 \cdot 5$.

Developing Habits of Mind

Visualize. The two properties below apply to any difference table, whether or not it has constant differences.

- **Up-and-over property.** An output is the sum of two numbers above it: the output directly above and the difference above and to the right.

- **Hockey stick property.** An output is the sum of all the differences above it to the right and the single output at the top of the table.

The properties are easier to see than to describe. Here is an example of the up-and-over property for Table Q from Lesson 4.01.

Input	Output	Δ
0	1	9
1	10	19
2	29	29
3	58	39
4	97	

$10 + 19 = 29$

When you highlight all the numbers you add up, it looks like a hockey stick. Otherwise, this property has nothing to do with hockey!

The output for an input of 2 is the sum of the output for 1 and the difference next to the output for 1.

Here is an example of the hockey stick property for Table Q.

Input	Output	Δ
0	1	9
1	10	19
2	29	29
3	58	39
4	97	

$1 + (9 + 19 + 29) = 58$

The output for an input of 3 is the sum of all the differences in the column leading up to $Q(3)$ and the output for 0.

The hockey stick property leads to Theorem 4.1.

Theorem 4.1

You can match an input-output table with constant differences with a linear function. The slope of the graph of the function is the constant difference in the table.

In this chapter, assume that the inputs in the table are $\{0, 1, 2, 3, \ldots\}$ unless stated otherwise.

For Discussion

1. Show that the up-and-over property is a result of the way you construct difference tables.

2. Show that the hockey stick property is a result of the way you construct difference tables.

3. Use the hockey stick property to prove Theorem 4.1.

Theorem 4.2 is the converse of Theorem 4.1.

Theorem 4.2

If $f(x) = ax + b$ is a linear function, its differences are constant.

Habits of Mind

Detect the key characteristics. What is the value of the constant difference?

For You to Do

4. Prove Theorem 4.2.

You can use the hockey stick property to quickly find a closed-form definition for a function that fits a table with constant differences. Here is Table H again with a hockey stick illustrated.

Input	Output	Δ
0	3	5
1	8	5
2	13	5
3	18	5
4	23	

The output is the number at the tip of the hockey stick plus the sum of the numbers on the handle.

For You to Do

5. Describe how you can find the number 23 using the hockey stick property.

6. How can you use the hockey stick property to find a closed form that agrees with the table?

Exercises *Practicing Habits of Mind*

Check Your Understanding

For Exercises 1–4, use Table G from this investigation's Getting Started lesson.

1. Make a difference table for Table G.

2. Write a recursive definition for a function that fits Table G.

3. Write a closed-form definition for a function that fits Table G.

4. Use the functions from Exercises 2 and 3. What does each function give as output for each input below?

    a. 10

    b. 10.1

Table G

Input	Output
0	−7
1	−4
2	−1
3	2
4	5

> **Habits of Mind**
>
> **Look for relationships.**
> Model your recursive and closed-form rules in your function modeling language. Do they agree for all inputs?

5. **What's Wrong Here?** Leslie built a difference table for the input-output table at the right.

    Leslie says, "All the differences are 6. So, this table has constant differences. Then the rule for the table is $f(n) = 6n + 11$. Hmm, that doesn't seem right. That rule says $f(4)$ is 35, but it's not."

    Find the flaw in Leslie's logic.

n	f(n)
0	11
1	5
2	11
3	5
4	11

6. The table at the right has constant differences. Copy and complete the table.

7. Suppose the table from Exercise 6 continues with constant differences. Find the values of $p(10)$, $p(100)$, and $p(263)$.

8. **Standardized Test Prep** Suppose you have a table with constant differences. The input 2 gives the output 11. The input 3 gives the output 14. What is the output for the input 7?

    A. 10   **B.** 17

    C. 21   **D.** 26

n	p(n)	Δ
0	3	■
1	■	■
2	■	■
3	■	■
4	−4	

9. Use the function table for $F(n)$.

   a. Build a difference table for $F(n)$.

   b. How are the differences related to the outputs?

   c. Predict the value of $F(10)$ by extending the pattern in the table.

n	F(n)
0	1
1	1
2	2
3	3
4	5
5	8
6	13

Can you model this function in your function-modeling language?

On Your Own

For Exercises 10–12, use Table M from Lesson 4.01.

10. Make a difference table for Table M.

11. Write a recursive definition for a function that fits Table M.

12. Write a closed-form definition for a function that fits Table M.

13. Model your recursive and closed-form definitions from Exercises 10 and 11 in your function-modeling language. Do they agree for all inputs?

14. Use the function table for $D(n)$.

   a. Build a difference table for $D(n)$.

   b. How are the differences related to the outputs?

   c. Predict the value of $D(10)$ by extending the pattern.

Table M

Input	Output
0	9
1	15
2	21
3	27
4	33

n	D(n)
0	1
1	2
2	4
3	8
4	16
5	32
6	64

Habits of Mind

Experiment. In Exercise 13, what does each model give as an output when you input 7? What does each model give as an output when you input −7?

You can use a keyboard or voice-recognition software. If the words you input are the same, then the outputs will be the same.

Go Online
www.successnetplus.com

15. **Write About It** Describe how to find a closed-form definition for a function that fits a table with constant differences. Include an example.

16. Which of the Tables A–V in Lesson 4.01 have constant differences?

17. A table with integer inputs has constant differences. When the input is 3, the output is 9. When the input is 11, the output is −3. Calculate the constant difference.

18. **Take It Further** Suppose you reverse the inputs and outputs of Table M. You get the input-output table at the right.

    a. Find a function that fits the table.

    b. Using your function, copy and complete the difference table below that has integer inputs from 0 to 4.

Inverse of Table M

Input	Output
9	0
15	1
21	2
27	3
33	4

Habits of Mind

Organize what you know. It may help to make the table, even if you cannot fill in very much of it at first.

Input	Output	Δ
0	▦	▦
1	▦	▦
2	▦	▦
3	▦	▦
4	▦	

c. How is the constant difference in the table from part (b) related to the constant difference in the original Table M?

Maintain Your Skills

19. The table at the right has constant differences. Copy and complete the table.

20. Find the slope between each pair of points.

    a. $A(2, -5)$ and $B(5, 22)$

    b. $C(7, -5)$ and $D(10, 22)$

    c. $E(-5, 2)$ and $F(22, 5)$

Input	Output	Δ
0	▦	▦
1	▦	▦
2	−5	▦
3	▦	▦
4	▦	▦
5	22	▦
6	▦	

4.04 Tables and Slope

In the last lesson, you saw that you can fit a linear function to a table with constant differences. In this lesson, you will learn the relationship between difference tables and slope.

Example

Problem An input-output table has constant differences. When the input is 2, the output is 9. When the input is 7, the output is −6. Find the constant difference.

Solution Suppose the constant difference is k. You can make this difference table.

Input	Output	Δ
0	?	k
1	?	k
2	9	k
3	?	k
4	?	k
5	?	k
6	?	k
7	−6	

Now that you have labeled the difference column, you can write other outputs as expressions in terms of k. For example, you can use the up-and-over property of difference tables to find the output when the input is 3.

Input	Output	Δ
0	?	k
1	?	k
2	**9**	k
3	**9 + k**	k
4	?	k
5	?	k
6	?	k
7	−6	

> Assume that the inputs are consecutive integers.

> Since the table has a constant difference, you can label every entry in the Δ column k.

You can calculate the other outputs in the same way. When the input is 4, the output is $9 + 2k$. The completed table at the right shows the outputs written in terms of k.

Input	Output	Δ
0	$9 - 2k$	k
1	$9 - k$	k
2	9	k
3	$9 + k$	k
4	$9 + 2k$	k
5	$9 + 3k$	k
6	$9 + 4k$	k
7	$\mathbf{9 + 5k}$	

Now you know two expressions for the output when the input is 7. The up-and-over property gives $9 + 5k$, but the output is supposed to be -6. These must be equal.

$$9 + 5k = -6$$

Solve for k to find the constant difference.

$$9 + 5k = -6$$
$$5k = -15$$
$$k = -3$$

For Discussion

1. Can you use the hockey stick property, instead, to find the constant difference? Explain.

2. Find a linear function that fits the table.

Developing Habits of Mind

Consider more than one strategy. There is another way to find the constant difference.

Theorem 4.1 says that you can match a table with constant differences with a *linear* function. The graph of the function is a line with slope equal to the constant difference in the table.

You can calculate the slope of that line by finding the slope between any two points on the line. Any input-output pair from the table gives the coordinates of a point on that line.

Therefore, you can calculate the constant difference as $\dfrac{\text{change in output}}{\text{change in input}}$.

For You to Do

3. A table has constant differences. When the input is 6, the output is 10. When the input is 15, the output is also 15. Find the constant difference.

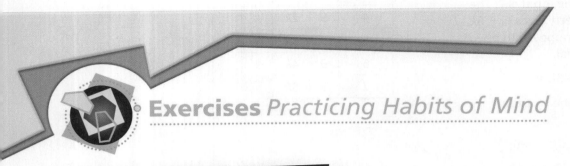

Exercises *Practicing Habits of Mind*

Check Your Understanding

1. An input-output table has constant differences. When the input is 3, the output is 10. When the input is 7, the output is 24.

a. Find the constant difference.

b. Find the output when the input is 0.

c. Find the linear function that fits the table.

2. A line passes through the points (3, 10) and (7, 24).

a. Find the slope of the line.

b. Find an equation for the line.

3. **Write About It** Is there a line that contains the points (0, −12), (3, 5), and (4, 10)? Explain.

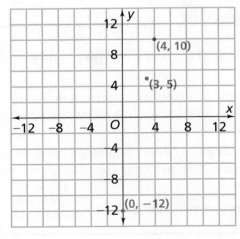

4. Some entries are missing from the table below. Can a linear function generate the table? Explain.

Input	Output
0	−12
1	?
2	?
3	5
4	10

5. A linear function generated the table below left. Find the values of a and b.

Input	Output
0	?
1	4
2	a
3	?
4	?
5	?
6	−21
7	b

Input	Output
0	−4
1	$-3\frac{1}{2}$
2	−3
3	$-2\frac{1}{2}$
4	−2

6. Find a linear function that agrees with the table above right.

7. An input-output table has constant difference 5. When the input is 6, the output is −3.

   a. Find the output when the input is 7.

   b. Find the output when the input is 3.

   c. Find a linear function that fits the input-output table.

8. Use differences to prove that you cannot find a linear function that matches Table K from Lesson 4.01.

Table K

Input	Output
0	1
1	2
2	5
3	10
4	17

9. Copy and complete the difference table from Table K. Complete the last column by finding the differences of the numbers in the Δ column.

x	K(x)	Δ	Δ²
0	1	1	2
1	2	3	■
2	5	■	■
3	10	7	
4	17		

> The symbol Δ² means "Δ of the Δ." Find the differences of the difference column.

On Your Own

10. A line contains the points $(1, 4)$ and $(6, -21)$.

   a. Find the slope of the line.

   b. Find the value of a such that the point $(2, a)$ lies on the line.

   c. Find the value of b such that the point $(7, b)$ lies on the line.

11. **Write About It** Does the table below have constant differences? Explain.

Input, x	Output, y
0	11
1	11
2	11
3	11
4	11

> **Habits of Mind**
>
> **Look for patterns.** What is the value of c such that $(6, c)$ lies on the line?

12. A line connects the points $(3, 7)$ and $(-2, 7)$.

   a. Draw the line on a coordinate plane.

   b. Find the slope of the line.

   c. Write an equation for the line.

13. A line connects the points $(7, 3)$ and $(7, -2)$.

   a. Draw the line on a coordinate plane.

   b. Explain why the slope of this line is undefined.

   c. Write an equation for the line.

14. Make a difference table for Table O from Lesson 4.01. Explain why Table O *cannot* come from a linear function.

Table O

Input	Output
0	0
1	5
2	20
3	45
4	80

Go Online
www.successnetplus.com

15. Use differences to find a linear rule that agrees with Table P from Lesson 4.01.

Table P

Input	Output
0	1
1	5
2	9
3	13
4	17

16. Take It Further Here is a difference table for Table Q from Lesson 4.01.

a. Describe the relationship between Tables O, P, and Q.

b. Describe the relationship between the difference tables that come from Tables O, P, and Q.

n	$Q(n)$	Δ
0	1	9
1	10	19
2	29	29
3	58	39
4	97	

17. The table below comes from the function $R(w) = w^3$. You can find the entries in the Δ, Δ^2, and Δ^3 difference columns by finding the differences of the numbers in the respective previous columns.

Copy and complete the table.

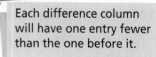

Each difference column will have one entry fewer than the one before it.

w	$R(w)$	Δ	Δ^2	Δ^3
0	0	1	6	▨
1	1	▨	▨	▨
2	8	19	▨	▨
3	27	▨	24	6
4	64	61	30	▨
5	125	91	▨	
6	216	▨		
7	343			

The Sudbury Neutrino Observatory is enclosed in this sphere with a 9-m radius. You can use the cubic function $V = \frac{4}{3}\pi r^3$ to find the volume of the sphere.

18. Derman is making a table for the function below.

$$d(x) = x^4 - 6x^3 + 11x^2 - 4x + 3$$

x	d(x)	Δ
0	■	■
1	■	■
2	■	■
3	■	

a. Copy and complete Derman's table for him.

b. Derman says, "What? Do I have a linear function?" How can you help Derman figure this out?

19. **Standardized Test Prep** Ramon accidentally shredded his physics homework. He knows the relationship he was graphing is linear. He is able to reconstruct two table values. For the input of 2, the output is 17. For the input of 11, the output is 38. What is the slope of the relationship Ramon was graphing?

A. $\frac{39}{17}$ **B.** $\frac{3}{7}$ **C.** $\frac{7}{3}$ **D.** $\frac{9}{5}$

Maintain Your Skills

20. Make a difference table for each function. Include inputs 0 through 4.

a. $a(x) = x^2$

b. $b(x) = 2x^2$

c. $c(x) = 5x^2$

d. $d(x) = -10x^2$

e. Find an integer k such that the function $e(x) = kx^2$ has the number 50 in its difference column.

f. **Take It Further** Find all integers k such that the function $e(x) = kx^2$ has the number 50 in its difference column.

21. Make a difference table for each function. Use inputs 0, 1, 2, 3, and 4.

a. $f(x) = 3x + 2$

b. $g(x) = f(x + 1) - f(x)$

c. $h(x) = x^2 + 3x$

d. $k(x) = h(x + 1) - h(x)$

e. $r(x) = x^3$

f. $s(x) = r(x + 1) - r(x)$

Habits of Mind

Organize what you know. How can you use your CAS for this exercise?

4.05 Difference Tables for Polynomial Functions

Here is a difference table for the function $D(n) = n^2 + 2n$.

You can look at the first and third columns at the right as a new table. You can match this new table with $n \mapsto 2n + 3$. Then you can make another difference column showing the differences of the new outputs. These "differences of the differences" are second differences.

Input, n	Output, D(n)	Δ
0	0	3
1	3	5
2	8	7
3	15	9
4	24	11
5	35	13
6	48	

So far in this chapter, you have found functions that match a table. In this lesson, you will also start with a function and use it to generate a table.

Here is the table with a second differences column.

You can continue this process to find third differences and even more differences. For the table that comes from $D(n)$, all the third differences are equal to zero. So are any fourth differences, fifth differences, and so on.

Input, n	Output, D(n)	Δ	Δ²
0	0	3	2
1	3	5	2
2	8	7	2
3	15	9	2
4	24	11	2
5	35	13	
6	48		

Habits of Mind

Understand the notation. The second differences are in the column labeled Δ^2. This notation means you perform the Δ operation twice. It does not mean to square the differences.

Example

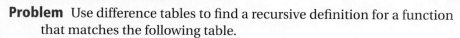

Problem Use difference tables to find a recursive definition for a function that matches the following table.

Input	Output
0	−2
1	0
2	16
3	46
4	90

Solution A recursive definition for a function that fits this table might look something like the one below.

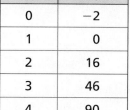

$$f(x) = \begin{cases} -2 & \text{if } x = 0 \\ f(x-1) + (\blacksquare) & \text{if } x > 0 \end{cases}$$

Here is the difference table. The Δ column tells you what to add to move from one output to the next. So finding a rule for the Δ column gives the missing information for the recursive definition.

Input	Output	Δ
0	−2	2
1	0	16
2	16	30
3	46	44
4	90	

Now you need to find a function that fits the Δ column. Try finding the second differences.

Input	Output	Δ	Δ²
0	−2	2	14
1	0	16	14
2	16	30	14
3	46	44	
4	90		

The second differences are constant. Therefore, you can find a linear function that gives the first differences in the Δ column as outputs. In this case, a linear function that matches the input column with the Δ column is $x \mapsto 14x + 2$.

New "Output"

Input	Δ	Δ²
0	2	14
1	16	14
2	30	14
3	44	
4		

Ignore the output column. Think of the Δ column as a new output column.

Before you write down the recursive definition, you may find it helpful to write out a few specific examples with numbers. This can give you the rhythm of how to produce the outputs.

$$f(1) = f(0) + 14 \cdot 0 + 2$$
$$f(2) = f(1) + 14 \cdot 1 + 2$$
$$f(3) = f(2) + 14 \cdot 2 + 2$$
$$f(4) = f(3) + 14 \cdot 3 + 2$$
$$f(5) = f(4) + 14 \cdot 4 + 2$$
$$\vdots \qquad \vdots$$
$$f(175) = f(174) + 14 \cdot 174 + 2$$

The rhythm of the outputs suggests this general definition.

$$f(x) = \begin{cases} -2 & \text{if } x = 0 \\ f(x - 1) + 14(x - 1) + 2 & \text{if } x > 0 \end{cases}$$

or

$$f(x) = \begin{cases} -2 & \text{if } x = 0 \\ f(x - 1) + 14x - 12 & \text{if } x > 0 \end{cases}$$

Where did the expression $14x - 12$ come from?

For You to Do

Derman looks at all this and says, "I have a closed-form definition for a function that matches the table." Here is Derman's definition:

$$f(x) = 7x^2 - 5x - 2$$

1. Does Derman's function match the table?
2. How do you think he found his definition?

"He guessed" is not the best answer to Problem 2.

A **quadratic function** is a function defined by a polynomial of degree 2. For example, $f(x) = 3x^2 + 5x - 7$ is quadratic. But $g(x) = 3x^2 + 5x - 7x^3$ is not quadratic—it has degree 3.

So far, you have seen two quadratic functions in this lesson. The first, $D(n) = n^2 + 2n$, has constant second differences equal to 2. The second, $f(x) = 7x^2 - 5x - 2$, has constant second differences equal to 14. Notice that 14 is twice 7, and 7 is the coefficient of x^2.

Look at another example. Here is a difference table for $s(t) = -16t^2 + 150t$.

Input, t	Output, $s(t)$	Δ	Δ^2
0	0	134	-32
1	134	102	-32
2	236	70	-32
3	306	38	
4	344		

The function $s(t)$ gives the height of an object thrown up in the air at 150 feet per second. Here, t is the number of seconds since the throw, and $s(t)$ is the height of the object.

The leading coefficient is the coefficient of the highest-degree term. For $s(t) = -16t^2 + 150t$, the leading coefficient is -16. The second differences in the table are constant and twice the leading coefficient.

You can use the general quadratic $p(x) = ax^2 + bx + c$ to show that this happens in general. In the table below, note that the second differences are constant and twice the leading coefficient.

Input, x	Output, $ax^2 + bx + c$	Δ	Δ^2
0	c	$a + b$	$2a$
1	$a + b + c$	$3a + b$	$2a$
2	$4a + 2b + c$	$5a + b$	$2a$
3	$9a + 3b + c$	$7a + b$	$2a$
4	$16a + 4b + c$	$9a + b$	
5	$25a + 5b + c$		

This table suggests that the second differences for any quadratic function are constant.

Theorem 4.3

For any quadratic function $p(x) = ax^2 + bx + c$, the second differences are constant. The constant second difference is $2a$, twice the coefficient of the squared term.

Proof Basically, you want to show that the pattern in the above table continues. First, compute the entry in the Δ column for any input n.

Input	Output	Δ
$\vdots$	$\vdots$	$\vdots$
n	$p(n) = an^2 + bn + c$	?
$n + 1$	$p(n + 1) = a(n + 1)^2 + b(n + 1) + c$	$\vdots$
$\vdots$	$\vdots$	$\vdots$

Use the up-and-over property.

$$p(n + 1) - p(n) = (a(n + 1)^2 + b(n + 1) + c) - (an^2 + bn + c)$$
$$= a((n + 1)^2 - n^2) + b((n + 1) - n) + (c - c)$$
$$= a(2n + 1) + b = 2an + a + b$$

This gives you a formula for the Δ column. It agrees with the table above for the general quadratic. Also, as predicted, the formula for the Δ column defines a linear function.

$$n \mapsto 2an + (a + b)$$

Here, a and b are constants. By Theorem 4.2, the first differences of this linear function—that is, the second differences of the original function p—are constant. Below, you will finish the proof by finding the value of the constant difference.

> Use the identity from Exercise 23 in Lesson 4.01. You can also define $p(x) = ax^2 + bx + c$ in your CAS and ask for $p(n + 1) - p(n)$. Make sure you have not assigned any values to a, b, c, or d.

For You to Do

3. Finish the proof by showing that the value of the constant second difference is twice the coefficient of x^2.

Minds in Action

Tony is trying to figure out how Derman got that function in the For You to Do section on the previous page.

Tony   Derman's definition is $f(x) = 7x^2 - 5x - 2$. I think I can figure it out for myself. The second differences are constant, so I bet there's a quadratic function that fits the table. And since the second difference is 14, the coefficient of x^2 would be 7.

So now I'm going to make a table with the inputs and outputs for $f(x)$, and an extra column with just the values of $7x^2$.

Input, x	Output, $f(x)$	Output, $7x^2$
0	−2	0
1	0	7
2	16	28
3	46	63
4	90	112

The real rule is $f(x)$ equals $7x^2$ plus something. I can figure out that something by subtracting $7x^2$ from all the outputs of $f(x)$. I'll make a new column for that.

Input, x	Output, $f(x)$	Output, $7x^2$	$f(x) - 7x^2$
0	−2	0	−2
1	0	7	−7
2	16	28	−12
3	46	63	−17
4	90	112	−22

Check it out: −2, −7, −12, −17, and −22. Those numbers can be matched with a linear function, and I know how to find one. The linear function is $x \mapsto -5x - 2$. So the whole thing must be

$$f(x) = 7x^2 + (-5x - 2)$$

And this works! It's like breaking down the problem into a simpler one. Once you subtract $7x^2$, the rest of it has to be linear.

Try using your function-modeling language to do this experiment.

For Discussion

4. Use Tony's ideas to find a closed-form definition for a function that fits Table R from Lesson 4.01.

Table R

Input	Output
0	0
1	1
2	8
3	27
4	64

Tony suspects that if the second differences are constant, a quadratic function will fit the table.

Theorem 4.4

If a table has constant second differences, there is some quadratic function that agrees with the table.

This is the converse of Theorem 4.3. It is true, and you can use Tony's method to prove it.

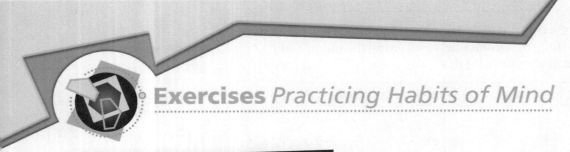

Exercises *Practicing Habits of Mind*

Check Your Understanding

1. Is there a quadratic function that fits the table below? If so, find one. If not, explain why.

n	y(n)
0	−2
1	6
2	24
3	52
4	90

2. Find a quadratic function that fits the table below.

n	y(n)
0	10
1	22
2	28
3	28
4	22

Copy and complete the difference table for each function.

3. $R(w) = w^3$

w	R(w)	Δ	Δ²	Δ³
0	0	1	6	■
1	1	■	■	■
2	8	19	■	■
3	27	■	24	6
4	64	61	30	■
5	125	91	■	
6	216	■		
7	343			

4. $m(x) = 5x^3 + 2x^2 - 10x + 4$

x	m(x)	Δ	Δ²	Δ³
0	4	■	■	■
1	1	■	■	■
2	32	■	■	■
3	127	■	■	■
4	316	■	■	■
5	629	■	■	
6	1096	■		
7	1747			

Can you use your spreadsheet tool to create the difference table for you?

5. Write About It Make a difference table for a cubic function of your choice. Answer the following questions based on your tables from Exercises 3 and 4.

a. When does a cubic function yield constant differences?

b. What is the relationship between the constant difference and the leading coefficient?

A **cubic function** is a polynomial in which the highest-degree term is cubed.
$f(x) = 3x^3 + 5x - 7$ is cubic, while $g(x) = 3x^2 + 5x - 7$ is quadratic.

6. Take It Further Sasha thinks she has an efficient way to do Exercise 4. She says, "I make a record of the formulas for the Δs of the basic powers like x^3, x^2, and so on.

- The Δ for $x \mapsto x^3$ is $x \mapsto 3x^2 + 3x + 1$.
- The Δ for $x \mapsto x^2$ is $x \mapsto 2x + 1$.
- The Δ for $x \mapsto x$ is $x \mapsto 1$.
- The Δ for $x \mapsto 1$ is $x \mapsto 0$.

So, the Δ for $x \mapsto 5x^3 + 2x^2 - 10x + 4$ is

$x \mapsto 5(3x^2 + 3x + 1) + 2(2x + 1) - 10(1) + 4(0)$."

Does Sasha's method work for all cubic functions? Justify your answer with a proof or a counterexample.

7. Take It Further Make a difference table for the general cubic function $f(x) = ax^3 + bx^2 + cx + d$. Include enough inputs and difference columns to show the constant difference.

8. **a.** Find three values of x that make the following equation true.

$$(x - 3)(x - 5)(x - 6) = 0$$

   b. Expand the expression $(x - 3)(x - 5)(x - 6)$ so that it has no parentheses.

9. Copy and complete the difference table for the following function.

$$v(x) = (x - 3)(x - 5)(x - 6)$$

x	v(x)	Δ	Δ²	Δ³
0	−90	■	■	■
1	−40	■	■	■
2	−12	■	■	■
3	0	■	■	■
4	2	■	■	■
5	0	■	■	
6	0	■		
7	8			

Habits of Mind

Look for patterns.
What is the degree of $(x - 3)(x - 5)(x - 6)$? What is the constant term? Can you answer these questions without expanding or using a CAS?

You can define $v(x)$ in your CAS and ask for $v(x + 1) - v(x)$. Make sure you have not assigned any value to x.

10. Find a quadratic function that fits the table below.

Input	Output
0	7
1	−6
2	1
3	28
4	75

11. Use this table for $F(n)$ from Lesson 4.03. Use difference tables to answer the following questions.

   a. Could the table have come from a cubic function?

   b. Describe any patterns you find in the repeated difference that comes from the function.

n	F(n)
0	1
1	1
2	2
3	3
4	5
5	8
6	13

12. Take It Further Find a function that fits the table at the right.

Input	Output
0	−3
1	−5
2	−5
3	9
4	49
5	127

On Your Own

13. Could the table at the right have come from a quadratic function? Explain.

n	y(n)
0	−7
1	−5
2	3
3	23
4	61

For Exercises 14 and 15, find a function that agrees with each table.

14.

Input, a	Output, b
0	25
1	11
2	−3
3	−17
4	−31

15.

n	c(n)
0	−8
1	0
2	4
3	4
4	0

16. Use the table at the right for $D(n)$ from Lesson 4.03.

Use difference tables to answer these questions.

a. Could the table have come from a cubic function?

b. Describe any patterns you find in the difference table.

n	D(n)
0	1
1	2
2	4
3	8
4	16
5	32
6	64

For Exercises 17–19, use the input-output table below.

Input, x	Output, y
0	1
1	1
2	4
3	7
4	12

17. Show that the table could not have come from a linear, quadratic, or cubic function.

18. None of the rules below exactly matches the input-output table, but which rule is the closest fit? Explain.

   Rule 1: $y = 2x - 5$ **Rule 2:** $y = 2.8x - 0.6$

   Rule 3: $y = x^2 - x + 1$ **Rule 4:** $y = x^3 - 3x^2 - 2x + 1$

19. **Take It Further** Find a polynomial function that fits the table exactly.

20. **Standardized Test Prep** What is the value of the constant third differences of the cubic function $f(x) = x^3 + 2x^2 + 7$?

   A. 0   **B.** 3

   C. 6   **D.** 7

Maintain Your Skills

21. Make an input-output table for each function. Use the inputs 0 through 5.

   a. $f(x) = (x - 7)(x - 2)$ **b.** $g(x) = (x - 6)(x - 13)$

   c. $h(x) = x(x - 9)$ **d.** $j(x) = 3(x - 1)(x - 3)$

   e. a function $k(x)$ for which $k(5)$ and $k(6)$ both equal zero

   f. **Take It Further** a function $m(x)$ for which
   $m(0) = 0, m(1) = 0, m(2) = 0,$ and $m(3) = 24$

22. Make an input-output table for each function. Use the inputs 0 through 4.

   a. $f(x) = 3x$ **b.** $g(x) = 3x + x$

   c. $h(x) = 3x + x(x - 1)$ **d.** $j(x) = 3x + x(x - 1)(x - 2)$

   e. a function $k(x)$ that is different from $f(x)$, but has the same outputs for the inputs 0 through 4 (For example, the two functions might have different outputs for an input of 5.)

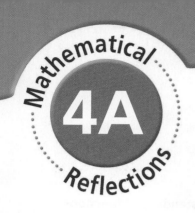

Mathematical 4A Reflections

In this investigation, you learned how to find closed-form and recursive function definitions that fit tables and how to use difference tables to decide whether a linear or quadratic function fits a given table. These questions will help you summarize what you have learned.

Use Table B for Exercises 1 and 2.

1. Find a recursively defined function g that agrees with Table B.

2. Find a closed-form definition for a function f that agrees with Table B.

3. Find an equation for the line that contains $(2, 5)$ and $(-4, 8)$.

4. How can you tell whether there is a linear function that fits a table?

5. How can you use differences to decide what type of function fits a table?

6. What polynomial function agrees with this table?

Table B

Input, n	Output, $B(n)$
0	1
1	3
2	7
3	13
4	21

Input	Output
0	1
1	5
2	11
3	19
4	29
5	41

You can use the polynomial function that describes the frog's motion to predict the time the frog will land.

Vocabulary

In this investigation, you learned these terms.
Make sure you understand what each one means and how to use it.

- **closed-form definition**
- **cubic function**
- **degree of monomial**
- **difference table**
- **hockey stick property**

- **quadratic function**
- **recursive definition**
- **slope**
- **up-and-over property**

About Functions

In *About Functions*, you will build on your understanding of functions as machines that accept inputs and produce outputs. You will also see that the definition of a function is not complete unless you specify the set of allowable inputs.

By the end of this investigation, you will be able to answer questions like these.

1. What is a function?

2. How do you compose two functions to make a new function?

3. What function undoes $x \mapsto 3x + 7$?

You will learn how to

- decide whether a table, graph, or closed-form rule is a function
- use function notation
- decide whether two rules define the same function
- determine the domain, target, and range of a function
- compose functions
- decide whether a given function has an inverse
- find the inverse of a one-to-one function

You will develop these habits and skills:

- Write, compose, and invert functions.
- Model functions in a function-modeling language.
- Develop an algebraic perspective on functions.
- "Work like a mathematician"—search for hidden regularities, describe the patterns explicitly, and explain inconsistencies.
- Establish properties of functions.

A function machine can double the size of the input.

By now, you have some idea of what a function is. Here are a few functions.

SQRT(x) = the square root of a real number x
SQR(x) = the square of a real number x
REC(n) = the reciprocal of a real number n
BD(p) = the birthday of a person p
SUM(a, b) = the sum of two numbers a and b
PR(a, b) = the product of two numbers a and b
QUO(a, b) = the quotient of two numbers a and b

> Here is a formula for QUO.
> $$QUO(a, b) = \frac{a}{b}$$
> Not all functions have formulas. For example, BD does not have one.

For You to Explore

1. If possible, find the value of each expression. If an expression cannot be evaluated, explain why not.

   a. PR(3, 4)

   b. QUO(3, 4)

   c. QUO(6, 8)

   d. QUO(0, 23)

   e. QUO(23, 0)

   f. SQR(SQRT(5))

   g. SQRT(SQR(5))

   h. SQR(SQRT(−5))

   i. SQRT(SQR(−5))

   j. QUO(PR(3, 4), PR(2, 6))

   k. BD(Pierre de Fermat)

   l. BD(3)

   m. SQRT(SUM(9, 16))

   n. SUM(SQRT(9), SQRT(16))

   o. SQRT(BD(Isaac Newton))

   p. SQRT(PR$\left(-2, \frac{1}{3}\right)$)

   q. REC(2)

   r. REC(REC(2))

   s. REC(REC(REC(2)))

   t. REC(0)

2. A mystery function $m(x)$ has the inputs and outputs below. How can you define the function?

   $m(\pi) = 3°$ $m(2.9) = 2°$ $m(5) = 5°$ $m(11.6) = 11°$ $m(-1.3) = -2$

3. Consider the function SQRT.

   a. Is the following equation true?

   $$SQRT(a + b) = SUM(SQRT(a), SQRT(b))$$

   b. **Take It Further** If the equation above is true for all numbers, prove it. If it is not, find the conditions on a and b that make it true.

SQRT(Joseph-Louis Lagrange) does not make sense. The largest set of inputs for which a function produces an output is the function's natural domain.

4. Find the natural domain of each function. Describe the domain in detail.

   a. BD

   b. SQRT

   c. QUO

   d. REC

   e. $f(x) = \dfrac{\sqrt{x}}{x - 2}$

> You can restrict the domain even further. For example, the function $A(r) = \pi r^2$ gives the area of a circle with radius r. You want to restrict the domain to positive numbers.

The key property of a function is that it turns each input into a well-defined output. The inputs are members of the domain. The set of all outputs is the *range* of the function.

5. For each function in Problem 4, you defined a domain. Using that domain, describe each function's range.

Exercises Practicing Habits of Mind

On Your Own

6. Suppose each function gives an output of 9. Do you have enough information to determine the input? Explain.

   a. PR   **b.** SQRT   **c.** SQR

7. If possible, find two different inputs for each function that give the same output.

   a. SQR   **b.** BD   **c.** QUO

   d. SQRT   **e.** REC

8. Use the definition of function D below.

$$D(x, y) = \sqrt{x^2 + y^2}$$

   Find each value.

   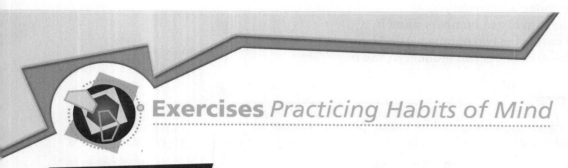

   What is the natural domain of D?

   a. $D(0, 0)$ **b.** $D(3, 4)$ **c.** $D(-3, 4)$ **d.** $D(4, 3)$

   e. Find another input that makes $D(x, y) = 5$.

   f. **Take It Further** Draw a graph of all the coordinate pairs (x, y) that make $D(x, y) = 5$.

   Can you find a pair of irrational numbers (x, y) that makes $D(x, y) = 5$?

9. Suppose you define the function $B(x, y, z)$ in terms of $D(x, y)$ from Exercise 8 as follows.

$$B(x, y, z) = D(x, y) + z$$

   For example, $B(3, 4, 10) = 15$, since $D(3, 4) = 5$.

   Find each value.

   a. $B(0, 0, 0)$ **b.** $B(3, 4, 5)$ **c.** $B(4, 3, 5)$ **d.** $B(-3, 4, -5)$

   e. Find the value of z such that $B(5, 12, z) = 7$.

   f. Find all triples (x, y, z) such that $B(x, y, z) = 0$.

10. a. Is it possible for the output of $D(x, y)$ to be negative? Explain.

b. Is it possible for the output of $B(x, y, z)$ to be negative? Explain.

Maintain Your Skills

11. Use the definitions of functions f and g below.

$$f(x) = 3x - 7$$

$$g(x) = \frac{x + 7}{3}$$

Find each value.

a. $f(10)$ **b.** $g(23)$

c. $f(f(0))$ **d.** $g(g(-28))$

e. $f(g(172))$ **f.** $g(f(0.27))$

g. $f(g(f(g(1000))))$

12. Use the definitions of functions h and j below.

$$h(x) = (x - 1)^2$$

$$j(x) = \sqrt{x} + 1$$

Find each value.

a. $h(4)$ **b.** $j(9)$

c. $h(h(3))$ **d.** $j(j(16))$

e. $j(h(5))$ **f.** $j(h(-5))$

g. $h(j(-3))$

> What are the natural domains of h and j?

13. Suppose $f(x) = x + 4$. Find each value.

a. $f(3)$ **b.** $f(f(3))$

c. $f(f(f(3)))$ **d.** $f(f(f(f(3))))$

e. $\dfrac{f(f(\ldots(f(3)))))))))))))}{12\ f\text{'s}}$

14. Suppose $g(x) = \frac{x + 1}{x}$. Find each value.

a. $g(1)$ **b.** $g(g(1))$

c. $g(g(g(1)))$ **d.** $g(g(g(g(1))))$

e. $g(g(g(g(g(1)))))$ **f.** $\dfrac{g(g(\ldots(g(1)))))))))))}{10\ g\text{'s}}$

Getting Precise About Functions

Mathematics I

You may think of functions as machines that take inputs and produce outputs.

The function is the machine. An input is anything you pass into a function, and the corresponding output is whatever the machine produces. You can define many functions with rules or algorithms, sets of instructions about what to do to an input to produce an output.

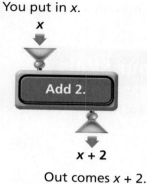

You put in x.

x

Add 2.

x + 2

Out comes x + 2.

Input

Rule

Output

The function is the machine.

The rule is what the machine does to the input to get the output.

> **Remember...**
>
> An algorithm or rule is a recipe. Two kinds of rules are especially useful in algebra: polynomial rules and recursive rules.

You can use arrow notation to write a function.

$$x \mapsto \frac{1}{x}$$

For this function, the input is a nonzero number x and the output at x is the reciprocal of x.

> You say "x maps to 1 over x."

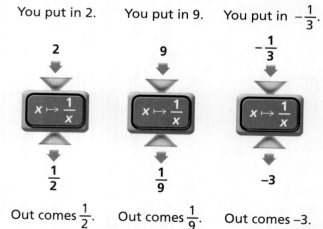

You put in 2.   You put in 9.   You put in $-\frac{1}{3}$.

2   9 $-\frac{1}{3}$

$x \mapsto \frac{1}{x}$ $x \mapsto \frac{1}{x}$ $x \mapsto \frac{1}{x}$

$\frac{1}{2}$ $\frac{1}{9}$ -3

Out comes $\frac{1}{2}$.   Out comes $\frac{1}{9}$.   Out comes -3.

> **Habits of Mind**
>
> **Detect the key characteristics.** Why does the input have to be a nonzero number?

Another way to describe functions is to name the machine, usually with a letter, such as *f*, or a shorthand, such as ABS. Then you can use the name of the function to describe the output. If you call a function *f* and you give it an input of 3, the output is *f*(3).

If the input is *x* and the function is *f*, then the output is *f*(*x*).

Not every rule gives a function. The rule "to find *f*(*x*), flip a coin; if it comes up heads, output *x* + 2; otherwise output *x* + 3" does not define a function.

You put in 3.

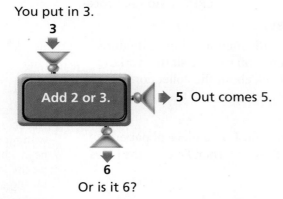

Or is it 6?

A good example of a function on your calculator is the square root function. You give it an input, and it gives you exactly one output.

For You to Do

1. Experiment with the square root function on your calculator. Find the outputs for the inputs 4, 8, and −4. What numbers are their own square roots?

2. Pick a positive number. Take its square root. Take the square root of the result. Keep going. What happens?

You can also define your own function in a function-modeling language. You give the function a name and a rule for finding outputs.

$$\text{define } g(x) = \tfrac{1}{x} + 1$$

You can then use this model just like a built-in function—give it inputs, tabulate it, graph it, and experiment with it.

Try evaluating
5 + 2*g(6).

For You to Do

3. Pick a positive number. Take *g* of it. Take *g* of the result. Keep going. What happens?

In your first-year algebra course, you may have learned that the set of all possible inputs that cause a function to produce an output is the domain of the function.

The calculator model of $g(x) = \frac{1}{x} + 1$ can take any input except 0. Asking for $g(0)$ generates an error. This means that 0 is not in the domain of g.

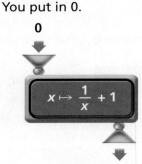

You put in 0.

0

$x \longmapsto \frac{1}{x} + 1$

ERROR: no reciprocal.

Building on *Mathematics I's* point of view

In this book, it is essential to make some finer distinctions about functions and to state things in a more precise way. Here, you will revisit the working definitions of *function* and *domain*. You will talk about the collection of outputs for a function. This discussion focuses on two of the finer distinctions about functions.

> In the next lesson, you will do a kind of algebra with functions. You will need a better and more precise language for talking about functions.

The domain of a function is part of its definition. Take a piece of paper, say 5 inches × 8 inches. Cut a little square out of each corner. Fold up the sides to make a box.

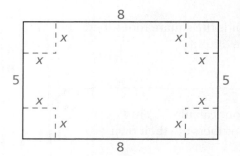

If the side length of the cutout is x, the volume V of the box is a function of x.

For You to Do

4. Let $V(x)$ be the volume of the box when a square of side length x is cut from each corner. Show that $V(x) = x(5 - 2x)(8 - 2x)$.

There is a problem here. The natural domain for V is all real numbers, $\mathbb{R}$. But, in terms of the box, an input of -2 makes no sense. You cannot cut -2 inches from the corners of the rectangle. In fact, the only numbers that make sense for the size of a cutout are $0 \leq x \leq \frac{5}{2}$. So, a complete definition of V is

> Besides, $V(-2) = -216$.

> V is the function defined on the domain $0 \leq x \leq \frac{5}{2}$ such that $V(x) = x(5 - 2x)(8 - 2x)$.

Functions on different domains are different functions, even if they share the same formula. The function defined on all of $\mathbb{R}$ by

$$f(x) = x(5 - 2x)(8 - 2x)$$

is different from V. In fact, since the domain for f contains the domain for V, you call V a restriction of f and you call f an extension of V.

Functions are determined by their behavior. Look at these machine models for two functions.

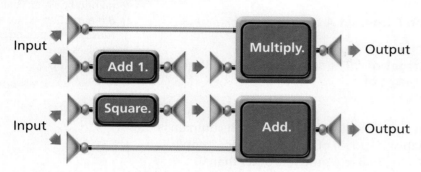

The domain for both functions is all of $\mathbb{R}$. These networks look as if they do very different things to their inputs. But if you build models for the functions in a function-modeling language and display tables of them side by side, you cannot tell them apart.

For advice on modeling, graphing, and making tables of functions, see the TI-Nspire™ Handbook, p. 990.

For You to Do

5. Try it. Build a model for each network above. Call the models f and g. Make a table for f and g. Then graph them. Do you see any difference? Can you prove that the two functions act the same for all inputs?

For all practical purposes, these two functions are the same. This point of view—two functions are the same if they give the same outputs for all inputs is—is the one that people use in most parts of mathematics and science today. As long as two functions refer to the same input-output pairings, it does not matter how the rule works on the inside.

For You to Do

6. Suppose f has domain $\mathbb{R}^+$ and the rule $f(x) = 3x + 7$. Show that the two functions below agree with f on its domain.

- $x \mapsto 3|x| + 7$
- $x \mapsto |3x + 7|$

Does either of them agree with f on all of $\mathbb{R}$?

In this course, $\mathbb{R}^+$ stands for the nonnegative real numbers.

Habits of Mind

Consider the context. Sometimes you use the same expression to define a function on different domains. The appropriate domain depends on the context.

To define a function, you must first specify two sets: a *domain A* and a *target B*. Then a function from *A* to *B* is a recipe that produces, for each member of *A*, a unique member of *B*.

Definitions

Suppose *A* and *B* are two sets of objects. A **function** from *A* to *B* is a pairing between *A* and *B* such that each element in *A* pairs with exactly one element of *B*.

This notation denotes a function *f* from set *A* to set *B*:

$$f : A \rightarrow B$$

A is the **domain** of *f*. *B* is the **target** of *f*. The set of objects in *B* that are paired with objects in *A* is the **range** of *f*.

If the domain of a function is not stated explicitly, assume that its domain is as large as possible. This is the natural domain of a function. For example, the natural domain of $f(x) = \frac{1}{x} + 1$ is all real numbers other than 0.

Developing Habits of Mind

Visualize. The key idea here is that a function assigns each object in *A* to exactly one object in *B*. Here is a picture of a function from *A* to *B*.

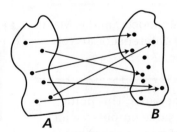

This is a "potato-and-arrow" diagram.

Each element of *A* is paired with exactly one element of *B*. Note the following:

- Not every element of *B* is an output. The range (things that are outputs) does not have to match the entire target (things that might be outputs).

- Two elements of *A* can be paired with the same element of B. The definition of a function only prohibits one element of A from being paired with more than one element of *B*.

Think about the birthday function from Lesson 4.06. One possible domain (Set *A*) might be the students in your class. The target (Set *B*) is the days of the year. The range is not all days in the year, however. It is only those days that actually get paired. The range for that domain is the days of the year that are birthdays for at least one person in your class.

Note that it is still a function if two students in the same class have the same birthday. It would not be a function if one student had two birthdays!

Example

Problem Find the domain, target, and range for the function $f : \mathbb{R} \to \mathbb{R}$, where $f(x) = x^2$.

Solution The domain and target are given by the function statement. The domain is $\mathbb{R}$, and so is the target.

The rule $f(x) = x^2$ determines the range. This function produces squares. No squares are negative. So the range is the set of all nonnegative real numbers, $\mathbb{R}^+$.

> **Remember...**
>
> The domain is the first set, and the target is the second.

So, when are two functions the same? You now have the language to talk about this.

Definition

Two functions f and g are **equal functions** if both these conditions are satisfied.

- f and g have the same domain.
- $f(a) = g(a)$ for every a in the common domain.

> If f and g are equal functions, you write $f = g$. This means the functions satisfy the conditions in this definition.

Developing Habits of Mind

Look for relationships. Two functions may be different (not equal) on their natural domains and yet be equal if you restrict their domains to some smaller set. For example, the two functions below are not equal.

$$f : \mathbb{R} \to \mathbb{R}, \text{ where } f = 2x + 1$$

$$g : \mathbb{R} \to \mathbb{R}, \text{ where } g(x) = 2x + 1 + (x - 1)(x - 2)(x - 3)$$

For example, $f(5) = 11$ and $g(5) = 35$. But f and g are equal if you restrict the domain to the numbers 1, 2, and 3. So you can say $f = g$ on the domain $\{1, 2, 3\}$.

For You to Do

7. Suppose you have the following function.

$$f(x) = \begin{cases} 3 & \text{if } x = 0 \\ f(x - 1) + 5 & \text{if } x > 0 \end{cases}$$

What is the natural domain of f? Find a function $g : \mathbb{R} \to \mathbb{R}$ that is equal to f on the natural domain of f.

Exercises Practicing Habits of Mind

Check Your Understanding

1. Let $f : \mathbb{R} \to \mathbb{R}$ and $f(x) = 72x - x^2$.

   a. What is the range of f?

   b. Graph f over its domain.

2. There are many rectangles with perimeter 144. Let x be the length of such a rectangle and let $A(x)$ be the area of the rectangle in terms of x.

   a. Express $A(x)$ as a function of x.

   b. What is the domain of A?

   c. What is the range of A?

   d. Graph A over its domain.

3. **Write About It** Are the functions in Exercises 1 and 2 equal? Explain.

4. Here are two functions.

   $$H(n) = 3 + 5n$$

   $$K(n) = \begin{cases} 3 & \text{if } n = 0 \\ K(n-1) + 5 & \text{if } n > 0 \end{cases}$$

   a. Make a table of values for H and K that includes inputs from 0 to 5.

   b. What is the natural domain of H? What is the natural domain of K?

   c. Are H and K equal functions? Explain.

> Use the definition of equal functions from this lesson.

5. Consider the function $h(x) = \sqrt{x^3}$.

   a. What is the natural domain of h?

   b. Find the range of h using the natural domain.

6. Let $f : \mathbb{R}^2 \to \mathbb{R}$ and $f(a, b) = 2a + 3b$.

   a. Find the domain and target of f.

   b. Find some pairs (x, y) that make $f(x, y) = 12$.

   c. Graph the set of all points (x, y) for which $f(x, y) = 12$.

> $\mathbb{R}^2$ means that the function takes two real numbers as inputs. The SUM, PR, and QUO functions from the Getting Started lesson have $\mathbb{R}^2$ as their domains.

7. Let $f : \mathbb{R} \to \mathbb{R}$ and $f(x) = 3x^2$.

   a. Calculate $f(3)$ and $f(-3)$.

   b. Find all values of x for which $f(x) = 12$.

   c. Calculate $f(11) - f(10)$.

   d. Show that you can write $f(x + 1)$ as $f(x + 1) = 3x^2 + 6x + 3$.

   e. Write a simplified expression for $f(x + 1) - f(x)$.

   f. If $g(x) = f(x + 1) - f(x)$, what is $g(10)$?

8. Suppose $g(x) = f(x + 1) - f(x)$, where f is another function. For each $f(x)$, find a polynomial formula in normal form for $g(x)$.

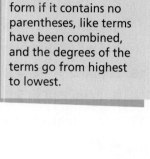
Remember...

A polynomial is in normal form if it contains no parentheses, like terms have been combined, and the degrees of the terms go from highest to lowest.

a. $f(x) = 5x$

b. $f(x) = 5x + 7$

c. $f(x) = 10x - 12$

d. $f(x) = Ax + B$

e. $f(x) = x^2$

f. $f(x) = 3x^2$

g. $f(x) = 10x^2$

h. $f(x) = x^2 + 10x - 12$

i. $f(x) = 3x^2 + 10x - 12$

9. Suppose you define function f in two pieces.

$$f(x) = \begin{cases} x & \text{if } x < 0 \\ 2x & \text{if } 0 \le x \le 6 \end{cases}$$

a. What is the natural domain of f?   **b.** Sketch the graph of f.

On Your Own

10. Consider the function $j(x) = \left(\sqrt{x}\right)^3$.

a. What is the natural domain of j?

b. Find the range of j using the natural domain.

11. A recipe takes a date as input, such as May 12. The output is the day of the week (Sunday, Monday, and so on) on which that date next occurs.

a. Find the output for your birthday.

b. Find the output for the day after your birthday.

c. Does this recipe define a function? Explain.

12. Suppose $N : \mathbb{R}^2 \to \mathbb{R}$ and $N(a, b) = a^2 + b^2$.

a. Find the domain and target of N.

b. Find some pairs (x, y) that make $N(x, y) = 25$.

c. Find all pairs (x, y) that make $N(x, y) = 0$.

d. Graph the set of all points (x, y) that make $N(x, y) = 25$.

e. **Take It Further** What is the range of N? Explain.

13. **What's Wrong Here?** While using a calculator, Derman noticed that $\left(\sqrt{3}\right)^2 = 3$ and $\left(\sqrt{9}\right)^2 = 9$ and $\left(\sqrt{10}\right)^2 = 10$. He says that the function $t(x) = \left(\sqrt{x}\right)^2$ is the same function as $f(x) = x$. Why is this incorrect?

14. For each function, find the natural domain, target, and range.

a. $f(x) = 6x^2 - x - 2$ **b.** $f(x) = \sqrt{x - 3}$ **c.** $f(x) = \dfrac{1}{\sqrt{x - 3}}$

d. $f(x) = \frac{1}{x} + 1$ **e.** $f(x, y) = x + 3y$ **f.** $f(x) = \left(x, x^3\right)$

g. $f(x, y) = (y, x)$

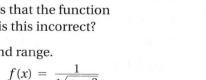

15. Suppose $f(x) = x^2 - 4x$ and $g(x) = x - 6$. Find each value.

  a. $f(g(2))$ **b.** $g(f(2))$ **c.** $f(g(z))$

  d. $g(f(z))$ **e.** $f(f(z))$ **f.** $g(g(z))$

  g. Find all numbers a such that $f(a) = g(a)$.

  h. Find all numbers b such that $f(g(b)) = g(f(b))$.

16. Suppose $f : \mathbb{R} \to \mathbb{R}$ and $f(x) = 3x + 2$. Find the value of a in each case.

  a. $2f(a) + 3 = 5$ **b.** $f(2a + 3) = 5$ **c.** $f(2a + 3) = a + 3$

17. For each function, find all values of x such that $f(x) = 12{,}290$.

  a. $f(x) = 3x + 2$ **b.** $f(x) = 3x^2 + 2$

  c. $f(x) = 3x^3 + 2$ **d.** $f(x) = 3x^6 + 2$

18. Derman says that for any function $f : \mathbb{R} \to \mathbb{R}$, if $f(r) = f(s)$, then $r = s$. Check Derman's conjecture for each function.

  a. $f(x) = 3x + 2$ **b.** $f(x) = 3x^2 + 2$

  c. $f(x) = 3x^3 + 2$ **d.** $f(x) = 3x^6 + 2$

19. Standardized Test Prep What is the natural domain of the function $f(x) = \dfrac{1}{x^2 - 5x + 4}$?

  A. $x \geq -3$ **B.** $x > 5$

  C. $x > 4$ **D.** $x \neq 1$ and $x \neq 4$

20. Spiro the Spectacular has a number trick: A player picks a number, adds 3, divides by 2, subtracts 3, and multiplies by 4. Find the inverse of Spiro's trick.

The inverse of Spiro's trick lets you figure out what number the player picked.

21. Suppose $f : \mathbb{R} \to \mathbb{R}$ and $f(3a + 1) = a - 2$. Find each value.

  a. $f(7)$ **b.** $f(14)$ **c.** $f(16)$ **d.** $f(z)$ (in terms of z)

22. Find two different functions f and g such that $f(g(x)) = g(f(x))$ for every number x.

Maintain Your Skills

23. Each of these functions has a domain of $\mathbb{R}$. Which functions have a range of $\mathbb{R}$?

  a. $f(x) = x^2$ **b.** $g(x) = x^3$ **c.** $h(x) = x^4$ **d.** $j(x) = x^5$

  e. Take It Further $k(x) = x^3 - 4x$

24. Take It Further Suppose $g : \mathbb{R}^2 \to \mathbb{R}$ and $g(x, y) = \dfrac{f(x) - f(y)}{x - y}$.

  For each function f, find $g(x, y)$.

  a. $f(x) = 3x + 5$ **b.** $f(x) = 5x + 5$ **c.** $f(x) = 12x + 5$

  d. $f(x) = x^2$ **e.** $f(x) = x^2 + x$ **f.** $f(x) = 3x^2 + 2x - 1$

Go Online
www.successnetplus.com

282 Chapter 4 Functions

The basic rules of algebra tell you how the operations of addition and multiplication behave. Addition and multiplication are operations that combine numbers. In this lesson, you will learn about an operation that combines functions. Here are two functions.

- $B(p)$ is the birthday of person p. The domain is all people, and the target is the days of the year.

- $W(d)$ is the day of the week on which a date d will occur next year. The domain is the days of the year, and the target is the seven days of the week.

You can compose these two functions to form a third function.

- $C(p)$ is the day of the week of person p's birthday next year. The domain is all people, and the target is the seven days of the week.

So B(Carl Gauss) = April 30.

C is a composition of functions W and B. To find $C(p)$, you start with the person, find that person's birthday, and then find the day of the week of that date next year. In other words, C is the result of running an input through B, taking the output, and running that output through W.

For You to Do

Find each value.

1. B(you) **2.** W(you) **3.** C(you)

You can express the relationship between these functions with the equation

$$C(p) = W(B(p))$$

This tells you how to compute the output of C for any input. If you just want to say that C is the composition of W and B, you write it as $C = W \circ B$.

Composing functions together by using the output of one as the input of the next is very common. You can do this with any two functions for which the domain of one function contains the target of another. If $f : A \to B$ and $g : B \to C$, you can define a new function that maps inputs in A to outputs in C with the following rule.

$$x \mapsto g(f(x))$$

This new function has domain A and target C. Instead of using a new letter to name it, you can just call the composition $g \circ f$. You read $g \circ f$ as "g circle f" or "g composed with f."

Remember...

When you evaluate $g(f(x))$, first you do f and then you do g.

Look for relationships. You can think of functions as objects on which you can perform operations, just as you do with numbers.

- $g \circ f$ is a function.
- $g(f(x))$ is the output of that function for input x.

Composition takes two functions and produces a third function. The concept of an operation with two inputs and one output is very common in algebra. Composition of functions is another example.

The addition and the multiplication of two numbers are two more examples of a binary operation. Some of the concepts that apply to addition and multiplication may carry over to composition. Here are some questions to consider.

- Addition and multiplication have identity elements. You can add 0 to a number and it does not change. You can multiply a number by 1 and it does not change. Is there an identity function for composition?

- Addition and multiplication have inverses (with one exception). All numbers have opposites that sum to 0, the identity. All numbers other than 0 have reciprocals. Do compositions of functions have inverses?

- Addition and multiplication are commutative. You can add or multiply in either order: $3 + 5 = 5 + 3$ and $3 \cdot 5 = 5 \cdot 3$. Is composition commutative?

When you work on these questions, you are thinking about functions as objects rather than machines. Composition is an operation on these objects, just as addition and multiplication are operations on numbers.

> Operations that take two inputs and produce one output are binary operations. They are functions, too, as long as they always produce the same output given the same two inputs.

> Artist's rendition of $f \circ g$

Here is the formal definition of composition.

Definition

For two functions $f : A \rightarrow B$ and $g : B \rightarrow C$, the **composite function** $g \circ f$ meets the following conditions.

- $g \circ f : A \rightarrow C$
- $g \circ f(x) = g(f(x))$

For You to Do

Suppose $f, g, h : \mathbb{R} \to \mathbb{R}$ and

$$f(x) = 2x^2 - 1$$

$$g(x) = x + 1$$

$$h(x) = 4x^3 - 3x$$

4. Build models for the three functions in your function-modeling language.
5. Show that $f \circ g(5) = 71$.
6. Find $g \circ f(5)$, $f \circ h(5)$, and $h \circ f(5)$.
7. Find formulas for $f \circ g$ and $g \circ f$. Are these functions the same?

> The notation $f, g, h : \mathbb{R} \to \mathbb{R}$ means that f, g, and h all have domain $\mathbb{R}$ and target $\mathbb{R}$.

Historical Perspective

Algebra began as a collection of methods for finding unknown numbers—for solving equations. The object was to find general formulas, like the quadratic formula, that provided recipes for solving a class of equations. Mathematicians stated the recipes in terms of the operations of arithmetic. (Take the *negative* of the coefficient of x, *add* it to the *square root* of the *square* of that coefficient *minus* . . .) The goal was to make the recipe independent of the actual numbers in the equations. Over time, mathematicians began to look for similar formulas in systems other than numbers that had different operations. Gradually, the focus shifted from the formulas to the operations themselves. This systems approach to algebra led people to investigate properties of operations and to make lists of the properties that are useful in calculating—properties that are very similar to the basic rules of arithmetic.

Algebra today deals with all kinds of systems—numbers, polynomials, matrices, functions, and more exotic objects. Each system has one or more operations that allow for calculations. One such system is the set of functions, all with the same domain and target, in which the operation is composition.

The output is dependent on the input, but the recipe itself is independent of both.

Exercises Practicing Habits of Mind

Check Your Understanding

1. Consider the functions $f(x) = 2x + 3$ and $g(x) = 5x + 1$. Find each value.

   a. $f(3)$ **b.** $g(3)$ **c.** $f(g(3))$

   d. $f \circ g(3)$ **e.** $g \circ f(3)$ **f.** $f(3) \cdot g(3)$

> Unless otherwise stated, all functions in these exercises have domain $\mathbb{R}$ and target $\mathbb{R}$.

2. Let $f(x) = 2x + 3$ and $g(x) = 5x + 1$.

   a. Find a formula for $g \circ f(x)$.

   b. Find a formula for $f \circ g(x)$.

3. Suppose you drop a stone into a pond. It makes concentric circular ripples. The radius of a ripple as a function of time is $r = 4t$, where r is the radius in inches and t is the time in seconds.

   a. Express the area of a ripple as a function of its radius.

   b. Express the area of a ripple as a function of time.

4. Suppose $f : \mathbb{R} \to \mathbb{R}$ and $f(x) = x$. For each definition of g, find formulas for $f \circ g(x)$ and $g \circ f(x)$.

   a. $g(x) = x^2 + 3$

   b. $g(x) = 2x - 7$

   c. $g(x) = (x - 4)^3$

   d. **Write About It** Explain what it might mean to say that the function f is the identity function on $\mathbb{R}$.

5. Suppose $f(x) = 3x - 1$. If possible, find a function g such that $f \circ g(x) = x$.

6. Suppose $f(x) = 2x + 3$. If possible, find a function g such that $g \circ f(x) = x$.

7. Suppose $f(x) = 2x + 5$. If possible, find a function g that makes each equation true.

   a. $f \circ g(x) = 4x^2 + 1$

   b. $g \circ f(x) = 4x^2 + 1$

8. **Take It Further** Let $f(x) = ax + b$ and $g(x) = cx + d$.

   a. Find formulas for $f \circ g(x)$ and $g \circ f(x)$.

   b. Find conditions on a, b, c, and d that make $f \circ g = g \circ f$.

9. **Take It Further** Find a linear function $f(x) = ax + b$ such that $f \circ f(x) = 4x + 9$.

> **Go Online**
> www.successnetplus.com

10. Consider the functions $f(x) = x^2 - 1$ and $g(x) = 3x + 1$. Find each value.

    a. $f(4)$ **b.** $g(4)$

    c. $f(4) \cdot g(4)$ **d.** $f(g(4))$

    e. $f \circ g(4)$ **f.** $g \circ f(4)$

11. Suppose $h : \mathbb{R} \to \mathbb{R}$ and $h(x) = \sqrt{x^2}$. Show that $h = a$, where $a(x) = |x|$.

12. Suppose $f(x) = x^2 - 5x + 6$ and $g(x) = x - 2$. Find each value.

    a. $f \circ g(3)$ **b.** $g \circ f(3)$

    c. $f \circ g(a)$ **d.** $g \circ f(a)$

    e. $(f \circ g) \circ f(a)$ **f.** $f \circ (g \circ f)(a)$

    g. Find all numbers a such that $f \circ g(a) = 0$.

    h. Find all numbers a such that $g \circ f(a) = 0$.

13. Use the functions below.

$$f(x) = x^2 - 6x + 8$$
$$g(x) = x + 3$$
$$h(x) = x + 1$$

Find a formula for each composition.

    a. $h \circ (f \circ g)(x)$ **b.** $(h \circ f) \circ g(x)$

14. Suppose $f(x) = x^2 - 10x + 21$. If possible, find linear functions g and h that make each equation true.

    a. $f \circ g(x) = x^2 - 4$ **b.** $h \circ (f \circ g)(x) = x^2$

15. If $f(x) = x^2$, find a function g, that is not equal to f, such that $f \circ g = g \circ f$.

16. **Standardized Test Prep** Suppose $f(x) = x - 5$. Find a function g such that $g \circ f(x) = 3x^2 - 11x - 20$.

    A. $g(x) = 3x^2 + 19x$

    B. $g(x) = 3x^2 + 4$

    C. $g(x) = (3x - 4)$

    D. $g(x) = (3x + 4)$

Go Online
www.successnetplus.com

Remember...

A linear function is a function in the form $x \mapsto ax + b$ for some numbers a and b. Why do you call it linear?

17. Consider these three functions.

$$a(x) = 3x + 1$$
$$b(x) = x^2 - 7$$
$$c(x) = x - 5$$

Find a formula for each composition.

a. $a \circ b$

b. $b \circ c$

c. $(a \circ b) \circ c$

d. $a \circ (b \circ c)$

18. Suppose $a, b, c : \mathbb{R} \to \mathbb{R}$. Show that $(a \circ b) \circ c = a \circ (b \circ c)$.

19. **Take It Further** Suppose $f(x) = 2x + 3$ and $g(x) = x^2$. Find a way to construct the graph of $f \circ g$ from the graphs of f and g.

In arithmetic, addition is associative. For any numbers a, b, and c,
$(a + b) + c = a + (b + c)$.

Maintain Your Skills

20. For each function f, find a function g such that $f \circ g(x) = x$.

a. $f(x) = x + 3$

b. $f(x) = x - 3$

c. $f(x) = 3x + 5$

d. $f(x) = 3x - 5$

e. $f(x) = 2x + 5$

f. $f(x) = Ax + B$, where $A \neq 0$

21. For each function f, find a function g such that $g \circ f(x) = x$.

a. $f(x) = x + 3$

b. $f(x) = x - 3$

c. $f(x) = 3x + 5$

d. $f(x) = 3x - 5$

e. $f(x) = 2x + 5$

f. $f(x) = Ax + B$, where $A \neq 0$

Go Online
Video Tutor
www.successnetplus.com

4.09 Inverses: Doing and Undoing

Suppose you have an output and you want to find the input that generated it. Can you always find it?

In-Class Experiment

Have everyone think of an integer from 1 to 20. Then, follow these steps:

- Subtract 10 from your number.
- Square the result.
- Add 7 to the squared result to get an ending number.

List everyone's starting and ending numbers.

1. Did any students get the same ending number? More important, did any two students who got the same ending number start with different numbers?

2. If a student gives you an ending number, can you always find the starting number? Explain.

   Try the experiment again. This time, cube the number in the second step.

3. Did any students get the same ending number this time? Did any two students who got the same ending number start with different numbers?

4. If a student gives you an ending number, can you always find the starting number? Explain.

Minds in Action

Sasha and Derman are looking at the results from the In-Class Experiment.

Derman Tony and Michelle got the same number at the end, and they started with different numbers: Tony had 13 and Michelle had 7.

Sasha Maybe we should look at what they did with their numbers.

	Tony	Michelle
Starting number	13	7
After subtracting 10	3	−3
After squaring	9	9
After adding 7	16	16

Derman Either way, they end up with 16. I wonder if we can retrace the steps from the output 16.

	Tony	Michelle
Ending number	16	16
After undoing addition by 7	9	9
After undoing squaring	???	???

Derman Hmm. We can't undo the squaring. If $x^2 = 9$, then x could be 3 or -3.

Sasha It looks like there's no way to decide. If you only told me Tony and Michelle ended up with 16, I couldn't figure out what their original numbers were.

Derman It's weird. That didn't happen the second time we ran the experiment. If two people started with different numbers, they always got different results. That time, Tony started with 5 and Michelle started with 12.

	Tony	Michelle
Starting number	5	12
After subtracting 10	−5	2
After cubing	−125	8
After adding 7	−118	15

Sasha What happens if we try to undo the operations?

	Tony	Michelle
Ending number	−118	15
After undoing addition by 7	−125	8
After undoing cubing	−5	2
After undoing subtraction by 10	5	12

Derman No problems this time. We found their starting numbers. I think you could do this with any ending number.

Sasha To go from the ending number back to the starting number, we should start with the last operation. So we have these steps:

- Subtract seven from the ending number.
- Take the cube root of that.
- Add ten to *that*.

We *will* be able to get back the starting number!

Derman As long as all the steps can be undone. I wonder how we can decide whether or not a step can be undone.

Why can Sasha and Derman undo cubing but not squaring?

For Discussion

5. In the second experiment, why can Sasha and Derman always derive the starting number from the ending number?

6. Change the first experiment in some way to make its process reversible.

The second In-Class Experiment amounted to evaluating the function $f(x) = (x - 10)^3 + 7$ for different starting values of x. When your class evaluated this function in the In-Class Experiment, you found that, if two students got the same output, they must have started with the same input. When a function has this behavior, it is *one-to-one*.

Definition

A function is **one-to-one** if its ouputs are unique. That is, a function f is one-to-one if $f(r) = f(s)$ only when $r = s$.

Habits of Mind

Establish a process. To check if a function f is one-to-one, assume that $f(r) = f(s)$ and try to show that $r = s$.

The function from the first In-Class Experiment is not one-to-one, since the different inputs 13 and 7 both give the same output, 16. That is, $f(13) = f(7)$. But $13 \neq 7$.

For You to Do

7. Which of these functions are one-to-one?

$$P(x) = x^2 \qquad Q(x) = x^3 \qquad R(x) = |x - 10| \qquad S(x) = \sqrt{x + 15}$$

Is P one-to-one? That is, if $P(r) = P(s)$, does r have to equal s? If $r^2 = s^2$, does $r = s$? No, not necessarily!

You can sometimes tell that a function from $\mathbb{R}$ to $\mathbb{R}$ is not one-to-one from its graph. Here is the graph of a function $g: \mathbb{R} \to \mathbb{R}$.

From the graph, you can see that there are different inputs that give the same output. If two points on the graph have the same y-height, they correspond to different inputs that produce the same output. This graph shows two different inputs a and b with $g(a) = g(b)$.

If a horizontal line crosses the graph of a function in more than one place, the function cannot be one-to-one.

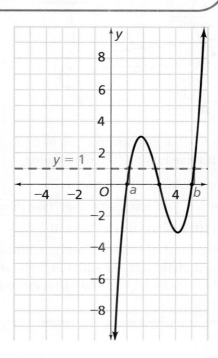

Habits of Mind

Be careful. The graph of an $\mathbb{R}$-to-$\mathbb{R}$ function cannot tell you with certainty that a function *is* one-to-one, because you can never see the complete graph. For example, suppose $f(x) = x^3 - x$ and $g(x) = f(x - 20)$. Graph g over the interval $-10 \leq x \leq 10$. No horizontal line cuts the graph twice. But is g one-to-one? Check out the graph over the interval $-10 \leq x \leq 30$.

For You to Do

Use graphs to determine which functions are not one-to-one. Which functions are one-to-one? Explain.

8. $A(x) = x$

9. $B(x) = x^2$

10. $C(x) = x^3$

11. $D(x) = \frac{1}{x}$

12. $E(x) = |x|$

13. $F(x) = \sqrt{x}$

14. $G(x) = x^3 - x$

15. $H(x) = x^3 + x$

Developing Habits of Mind

Visualize. Here is a potato-and-arrow diagram for a one-to-one function.

One important fact about one-to-one functions is that they are reversible, as Derman and Sasha noticed. In the diagram, if you pick any output in Set *B*, it is always possible to determine where it came from.

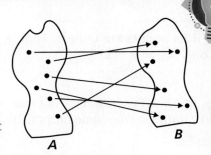

Any two arrows from *A* end at different objects in *B*. Only a one-to-one function has this property.

This means there is another function, an *inverse function*, from Set *B* to Set *A*. In a potato-and-arrow diagram, the inverse function looks similar, but all the arrows reverse direction.

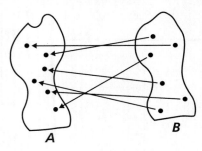

The domain and range switch. If you follow an arrow in the original function and then the corresponding arrow of the inverse function, you are back where you started.

You will see the formal definition of an inverse function in a moment. Derman and Sasha used inverse functions in their dialog.

• The function "add 7" has an inverse: "subtract 7."

• The function "cube the number" has an inverse: "take the cube root."

• The function "subtract 10" has an inverse: "add 10."

It might appear that the squaring and square root functions are inverses, but they are not. When the domain is $\mathbb{R}$, the squaring function is not one-to-one, so the squaring step cannot be inverted. What do you find if the domain is different?

See Exercise 4.

You can write the inverse of f as f^{-1}. Here is the formal definition.

Definition

Suppose f is a one-to-one function with domain A and range B. The <mark>**inverse function**</mark> f^{-1} **is a function with these properties:**

- f^{-1} **has domain B and range A.**
- **For all x in B, $f(f^{-1}(x)) = x$.**

There is another way to state this definition that puts the emphasis on the function rather than on its output. The <mark>**identity function**</mark> on a set is the function id that simply returns its input.

$$\mathrm{id}(x) = x$$

> There is an identity function for each domain, but they all behave the same way: They do nothing to an input. What is the graph of id : $\mathbb{R} \to \mathbb{R}$?

Definition

(Alternate Version) Suppose f is a one-to-one function with domain A and range B. The <mark>**inverse function**</mark> f^{-1} **is a function with these properties:**

- f^{-1} **has domain B and range A.**
- **For all x in B, $f \circ f^{-1} = \mathrm{id}$.**

Derman's description of the function $f(x) = (x - 10)^3 + 7$ refers to f as a composition of three simpler functions, in this order.

- Subtract 10.
- Cube.
- Add 7.

Sasha and Derman then describe how to recover the original input from the output.

- Subtract 7.
- Take the cube root.
- Add 10.

This process describes the inverse function of $f(x) = (x - 10)^3 + 7$. You can build the inverse function by starting with x and applying the three reversing rules in the order above.

$$f^{-1}(x) = \sqrt[3]{x - 7} + 10$$

When an inverse function exists, you can often find it by describing the steps to reverse the process.

> The original function f is the composition $f = c \circ b \circ a$ of the steps listed. Then the inverse f^{-1} is $f^{-1} = a^{-1} \circ b^{-1} \circ c^{-1}$. You invert each function and reverse their order.

Example

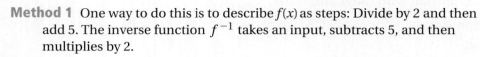

Problem Find the inverse function of $f(x) = \frac{x}{2} + 5$.

Solution

Method 1 One way to do this is to describe $f(x)$ as steps: Divide by 2 and then add 5. The inverse function f^{-1} takes an input, subtracts 5, and then multiplies by 2.

$$f^{-1}(x) = 2(x - 5)$$

Method 2 The other way to find an inverse function is to use the definition.

$$f(f^{-1}(x)) = x$$

If $f(x) = \frac{x}{2} + 5$, then

$$f(f^{-1}(x)) = \frac{f^{-1}(x)}{2} + 5$$

Since $x = f(f^{-1}(x))$, you have

$$x = \frac{f^{-1}(x)}{2} + 5$$

Solve for $f^{-1}(x)$ as you would for any variable. You can subtract 5 from each side and then multiply by 2.

$$x = \frac{f^{-1}(x)}{2} + 5$$

$$x - 5 = \frac{f^{-1}(x)}{2}$$

$$2(x - 5) = f^{-1}(x)$$

Habits of Mind

Represent a function.
You can think of this equation as
$f(\text{anything}) = \frac{\text{anything}}{2} + 5$.

For You to Do

16. Find the inverse of $g(x) = 2(x - 5)$.

For Discussion

17. What happens when you try to find the inverse of $h(x) = (x - 10)^2 + 7$?

Developing Habits of Mind

Look for relationships. In arithmetic, numbers have additive inverses. When you add a number to its additive inverse, you get 0, the identity for addition. The additive inverse of a number is its opposite.

Nonzero numbers have multiplicative inverses. When you multiply a number by its multiplicative inverse, you get 1, the identity for multiplication. The multiplicative inverse of a number is its reciprocal.

One-to-one functions have inverses with respect to composition. When you compose a function with its inverse, you get id, the identity for composition. There is one hitch: composition, unlike addition and multiplication, is not commutative. $f \circ g \neq g \circ f$ unless f and g are special functions. For a function and its inverse, though, the story is much simpler, thanks to the following theorem.

Remember...

The functions $f \circ g$ and $g \circ f$ do not necessarily have the same domain.

Theorem 4.5

Suppose $f : A \rightarrow B$ is one-to-one. Then

- **$f^{-1} : B \rightarrow A$ is one-to-one**
- **$(f^{-1})^{-1} = f$**

Proof

- Suppose $f^{-1}(r) = f^{-1}(s)$. Take f of each side to conclude that $r = s$.
- For f to be the inverse of f^{-1} (that is, $f = (f^{-1})^{-1}$), f must have a domain A and range B (which it does).

  Also, $f^{-1}(f(a))$ must equal a for all a in A.

  You know $f \circ f^{-1}$ is the identity, so

  $$f(f^{-1}(f(a)) = f \circ f^{-1}(f(a)) = \mathrm{id}(f(a) = f(a).$$

  The fact that f is one-to-one and $f(f^{-1}(f(a)) = f(a)$ means that

  $$f^{-1}(f(a)) = a.$$

  Thus f fits the definition of the inverse of f^{-1}. So, $f = (f^{-1})^{-1}$).

Habits of Mind

Detect the key characteristics. Study the two characteristics of f proved in the second part. They meet the requirements for f to be the inverse of f^{-1}. That is why you can conclude $f = (f^{-1})^{-1}$.

Exercises Practicing Habits of Mind

Check Your Understanding

1. The basic functions below are all from $\mathbb{R}$ to $\mathbb{R}$. For each function, determine whether the function has an inverse. If it does, find the inverse function. If it does not, explain why not.

   a. $f(x) = x$ **b.** $g(x) = \frac{1}{x}$ **c.** $h(x) = x^2$

   d. $k(x) = x^3$ **e.** $\ell(x) = x^3 - x$ **f.** $m(x) = \sqrt{x}$

   g. $n(x) = |x|$

2. Use the graph of a function and its inverse at the right.

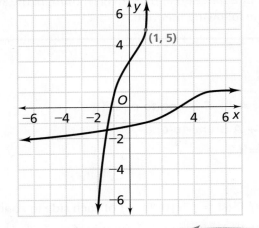

  a. The point $(1, 5)$ is on the graph of the function. What point must be on the graph of the inverse function?

  b. If $f : \mathbb{R} \to \mathbb{R}$, describe how you get the graph of f^{-1} from the graph of f.

  c. How does this graph connect to the statement of Theorem 4.5?

3. Use the definition of f below.

$$f(x) = \begin{cases} x & \text{if } x < 0 \\ 2x & \text{if } 0 \le x \le 6 \end{cases}$$

> This is the function from Exercise 9 in Lesson 4.07.

  a. What is the natural domain of f?

  b. Sketch the graph of f.

  c. Extend the definition of f so that its domain is all of $\mathbb{R}$ and f is one-to-one.

  d. Extend the definition of f so that its domain is all of $\mathbb{R}$ and f is not one-to-one.

4. The function $x \mapsto x^2$ is not one-to-one on its natural domain.

  a. Restrict its domain to a set on which the function is one-to-one.

  b. On this restricted domain, what is the inverse of $x \mapsto x^2$?

5. The table at the right defines the function t.

  a. What is the domain of t?

  b. Draw a potato-and-arrow diagram that illustrates $t(x)$.

  c. Why is t a function?

  d. Does t have an inverse? If so, give the table for t^{-1}. If not, change the table to make a new function that is one-to-one.

x	t(x)
1	3
5	7
9	11
13	11

> **Remember...**
> In exercises like this, the table is the entire function. If an input is not in the table, then it is not in the domain of t.

6. Find the inverse of $f(x) = \dfrac{x}{x-1}$, where $x \ne 1$.

7. Functions h and j are defined on $\mathbb{R}^+$.

$$h(x) = x^2$$

$$j(x) = \sqrt{x}$$

Graph $h(x)$ and $j(x)$. Is h equal to j^{-1}?

8. Suppose $f, g : \mathbb{R} \to \mathbb{R}$, with $f(x) = 5x^2 - 17x + 6$ and $g(x) = 5x$.

   a. Find a formula for $g \circ f(x)$.

   b. Find a formula for $h(x) = g \circ f \circ g^{-1}(x)$.

   c. Draw the graphs of f and h on the same axes.

   d. Find the zeros of h and the zeros of f.

9. Take It Further Prove or disprove the following statement.

   If $f(x) = f^{-1}(x)$ for an input x, then $f(x) = x$.

Remember...

The zeros of a function j are the numbers a that make $j(a) = 0$.

On Your Own

10. Here are the graphs of four functions. Which functions are definitely not one-to-one?

Habits of Mind

Visualize. Some of these functions may be one-to-one. Think about how the graph may extend for $x > 4$ if the function really is one-to-one. How might it look if the function is not one-to-one?

a.

b.

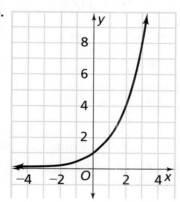

c.

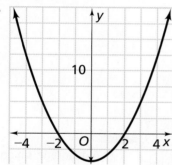

d.

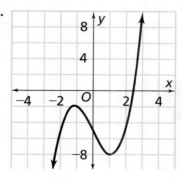

11. Standardized Test Prep Function $f(x)$ is one-to-one, with $f(3) = 7$ and $f(7) = 5$. Which equation must be true?

   A. $f^{-1}(3) = \frac{1}{7}$ **B.** $f^{-1}(3) = 7$

   C. $f^{-1}(7) = 5$ **D.** $f^{-1}(7) = 3$

12. Prove that, if functions $f, g : \mathbb{R} \to \mathbb{R}$ are one-to-one, then $f \circ g$ is one-to-one.

Go Online
www.successnetplus.com

13. Functions f and g are one-to-one. Which function is the inverse function of $f \circ g$?

A. $f^{-1} \circ g^{-1}$ **B.** $g^{-1} \circ f^{-1}$

C. $f^{-1} \circ g$ **D.** $g^{-1} \circ f$

14. Find the inverse of each function.

a. $m(x) = 5x + 3$ **b.** $n(x) = 2x - 11$

c. $p(x) = -3x + 4$ **d.** $q(x) = \frac{x}{5} - 0.6$

> The domain of each function is $\mathbb{R}$.

15. The graph of the function $f(x) = ax + b$ is a line with slope a.

a. If $a \neq 0$, show that f is one-to-one.

b. Find a formula for $f^{-1}(x)$.

c. Find the slope of the graph of the inverse function f^{-1}.

d. Find three linear functions g, h, and j such that each is its own inverse.

16. Suppose $f, g, k : \mathbb{R} \to \mathbb{R}$, $f(x) = 5x^3 - 12x^2 - 11x + 6$, $g(x) = 25x$, and $k(x) = 5x$.

a. Find a formula for $g \circ f(x)$.

b. Find a formula for $h(x) = g \circ f \circ k^{-1}(x)$.

c. Draw the graphs of f and h on the same axes.

d. Find the zeros of f and the zeros of h.

17. **Take It Further** Suppose $f : \mathbb{R} \to \mathbb{R}$ and $f(x) = 7x^2 - 15x + 2$. Find a linear function g such that $g \circ f \circ g^{-1}$ is a monic quadratic polynomial.

> A quadratic is monic if the coefficient of x^2 is 1.

18. **Write About It** The graph of function $f : \mathbb{R} \to \mathbb{R}$ is increasing, which means that as x increases, $f(x)$ also increases.

a. Draw a possible graph of function f.

b. Roy says that any increasing function, no matter what its graph looks like, must be one-to-one. Do you agree? Explain.

Maintain Your Skills

19. Let $f(x) = 4x + 3$. Find each value.

a. $f(10)$ **b.** $f^{-1}(43)$ **c.** $f(f(0))$

d. $f^{-1}(f^{-1}(15))$ **e.** $f(f^{-1}(289))$ **f.** $f^{-1}(f(-162.3))$

g. $f(f^{-1}(f(10)))$

20. Let $f(x) = 4x + 3$. Find each value in terms of r.

a. $f(r)$ **b.** $f(f(r))$ **c.** $f(f(f(r)))$

d. $f(f(f(f(r))))$ **e.** $f(f(f(f(f(r)))))$ **f.** $f^{12}(r)$

> The notation $f^{12}(r)$ means "compose 12 copies of f and apply the composition to r."

Graphing Functions

There is a relationship between the graphs of a function and its inverse.

Minds in Action

Tony and Sasha are discussing Exercise 2 from Lesson 4.09.

Sasha   Tony, how did you answer part (b)?

Tony   Well, when you look at the two graphs, they're mirror images of each other.

Tony copies the graphs onto his graph paper.

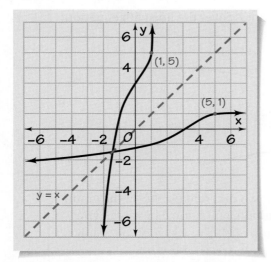

Tony   See, if you fold the paper on the diagonal, the graphs line up.

Sasha   What you're really doing is folding it so that the *x*-axis and the *y*-axis line up, right?

Tony   Um, yeah, that's right. Hey, that's what part (a) is getting at . . . if (1, 5) is on the graph of *f*, then (5, 1) is on the graph of f^{-1}.

Sasha   Right, because *f* maps 1 to 5, so f^{-1} maps 5 back to 1.

Tony   Good. Okay, so now when you fold it along that diagonal . . .

Sasha   Which is the graph of $y = x$, by the way . . .

Tony   Right, when you fold it along $y = x$, (1, 5) and (5, 1) will line up since the *x* from the first point is equal to the *y* of the second, and vice versa.

Sasha   Cool. So we're reflecting over the line $y = x$. We can reflect anything over that line, can't we?

Tony   I don't see why not. How does that help us figure out if a function has an inverse?

For Discussion

1. Reflect the graph on page 291 over the line with equation $y = x$. Is the reflection the graph of a function? Why or why not?

Example 1

Problem

a. Draw the graph of $f(x) = x^2$. Sketch the reflection of the graph of f over the line $y = x$. Is the reflection the graph of a function? Why or why not?

b. Draw the graph of $g(x) = x^3$. Sketch the reflection of the graph of g over the line $y = x$. Is the reflection the graph of a function? Why or why not?

Solution

a. Here is a sketch of the reflection of the graph of f over the line with equation $y = x$.

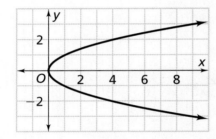

From the graph, you can see that there are two different points on the graph for every positive value of x. Since by definition a function can only have a single output for a given input, the reflection of $f(x) = x^2$ is not the graph of a function.

If you draw just the top part of the reflection (the part where $y \geq 0$), you get the graph of the equation $y = \sqrt{x}$.

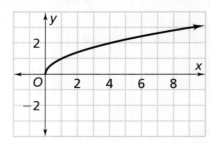

The square root function is a function from $\mathbb{R}^+ \to \mathbb{R}^+$.

What do you get if you reflect the graph of the square root function over the line with equation $y = x$?

b. Here is a sketch of the reflection of the graph of g over the line with equation $y = x$.

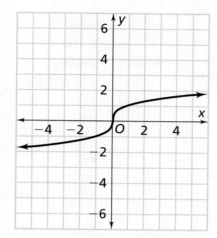

The reflection does appear to be the graph of a function. And, in fact, since $g(x) = x^3$ is one-to-one, its inverse is a function. The graph above is the graph of the function $h(x) = \sqrt[3]{x}$.

You showed this fact in Lesson 4.09 Exercise 1.

For You to Do

2. Find the inverse of $r(x) = 2x^3 - 5$. Draw a graph of both r and r^{-1}.

Previously, you looked at a number of functions that were defined recursively. Consider $f(n)$ below, for whole number values of n.

$$f(n) = \begin{cases} 3, & \text{if } n = 0 \\ f(n-1) + 5, & \text{if } n > 0 \end{cases}$$

A graph of the function $f(n)$ is shown below.

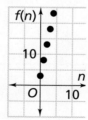

The graph of any function with a recursive definition will simply be a set of discrete points. In this case, since the natural domain of the function is $\mathbb{Z}^+$, the x-coordinate of each point will be a whole number.

Compare the definitions of the functions below.

$$f(n) = \begin{cases} 3, & \text{if } n = 0 \\ f(n-1) + 5, & \text{if } n > 0 \end{cases} \qquad g(x) = \begin{cases} 3, & \text{if } x < 0 \\ 5x + 3, & \text{if } x \geq 0 \end{cases}$$

They are similar in structure, but the definition of g is not recursive. The function g is called a **piecewise-defined function**. It is defined in pieces. The domain of g is the union of each domain in the definition, which in this case is all real numbers. Here is a graph of g.

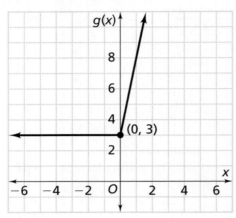

You have to make sure the domains for each piece do not overlap; otherwise you might not be defining a function. Why?

You may be familiar with this function:

$$a(x) = \begin{cases} -x, & \text{if } x < 0 \\ x, & \text{if } x \geq 0 \end{cases}$$

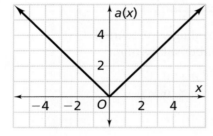

Function f from Lesson 4.09 Exercise 3 is also a piecewise function. You know the function a by its more familiar notation, $a(x) = |x|$.

Example 2

Problem Sketch the graph of the function k shown below.

$$k(x) = \begin{cases} 2 - x, & \text{if } x \leq 1 \\ \frac{1}{2}x - 1, & \text{if } 1 < x \leq 4 \\ -3x + 11, & \text{if } x > 4 \end{cases}$$

Solution This graph has three pieces, and each piece is linear. The key part of graphing piecewise-defined functions is to be attentive to the end points of each domain interval. For instance, the first part of the definition is for $x \leq 1$. The graph will include the point $(1, 1)$, which is the rightmost point on the section of the graph that includes the line with the equation $y = 2 - x$. Indicate this by drawing a solid circle at $(1, 1)$, the endpoint of that piece of the graph.

The second domain interval is $1 < x \leq 4$, so the second piece will not include the leftmost endpoint, but will include the rightmost. Draw an open circle at the point $\left(1, -\frac{1}{2}\right)$ and a solid circle at (4, 1).

The last domain interval is $x > 4$. For the third piece, use an open circle at the point (4, −1).

Now, when you look at the graph, it satisfies the conditions for being a function. No vertical line passes through more than one point on the graph.

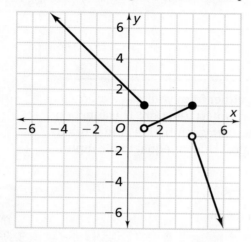

For Discussion

3. What are the domain and range of k? Does k have an inverse function? Explain your reasoning. If not, how can you change the definition of k so that it does have an inverse function?

Each piece of a piecewise-defined function can be any kind of function, not just lines. For instance, the graph below represents a piecewise-defined function.

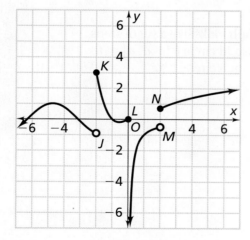

For You to Do

4. Sketch a graph of each of the following functions. Indicate whether the function is one-to-one.

   a. $f(x) = \begin{cases} 3, & \text{if } x \le -1 \\ -2, & \text{if } x > -1 \end{cases}$

   b. $g(x) = \begin{cases} 2x - 4, & \text{if } x < 0 \\ 2x + 4, & \text{if } x \ge 0 \end{cases}$

   c. $k(x) = \begin{cases} x^2, & \text{if } x \le -1 \\ |x|, & \text{if } -1 < x \le 1 \\ x^2, & \text{if } x > 1 \end{cases}$

Another function you may be familiar with, either from your calculator or from a computer programming class, is the int(x) function. This function is also called the *floor* function, or the *greatest integer* function, and is often written as $\lfloor x \rfloor$. It returns the greatest integer less than or equal to the input. For instance:

$$\lfloor 2.5 \rfloor = 2, \lfloor \pi \rfloor = 3, \text{ and } \lfloor -4.08 \rfloor = -5$$

The graph of the equation $y = \lfloor x \rfloor$ is shown below.

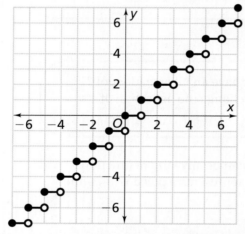

> You might see the greatest integer function represented as [x] or as $\llbracket x \rrbracket$.

This is called a step function because its graph looks like a set of steps. Notice that for each step, the left side has a solid circle (since $\lfloor n \rfloor = n$ if n is an integer), and the right side has an open circle.

> Be careful! Some people think of the floor function as "stripping off the fractional part," but that isn't true when the input is negative.

Look for relationships. One way to think of the floor function is that it is a piecewise-defined function with infinitely many pieces.

$$\lfloor x \rfloor = \begin{cases} \vdots \\ -1, & \text{if } -1 \le x < 0 \\ 0, & \text{if } 0 \le x < 1 \\ 1, & \text{if } 1 \le x < 2 \\ 2, & \text{if } 2 \le x < 3 \\ \vdots \end{cases}$$

For You to Do

5. Evaluate each of the following.

a. $\lfloor 2.17 \rfloor$ **b.** $\lfloor -6.85 \rfloor$ **c.** $\lfloor 2\pi \rfloor$ **d.** $\lfloor -\frac{\pi}{2} \rfloor$

e. $\lfloor \frac{112}{2} \rfloor$ **f.** $\lfloor 14\frac{1}{2} \rfloor$ **g.** $\lfloor -8\frac{2}{3} \rfloor$

For Discussion

6. Suppose $\lfloor x \rfloor = 17$. What are possible values for x?

Exercises Practicing Habits of Mind

Check Your Understanding

1. Use the floor function to write the following functions.

a. a function that rounds a number to the nearest integer

b. a function that rounds to the nearest $\frac{1}{100}$

c. a function that rounds to the nearest multiple of 5

There are several different conventions for rounding halfway numbers like 4.5 or −7.5. Use the rounding rule that halfway numbers always round up, so 4.5 rounds to 5 and −7.5 rounds to −7.

2. What are the domain and range of $f(x) = \lfloor x \rfloor$? Does the floor function have an inverse?

3. Here is the graph of a piecewise-defined function.

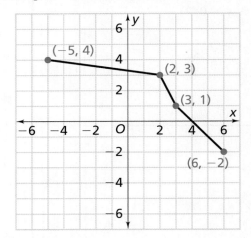

a. Write a function for this graph.

b. Explain why the function has an inverse function.

c. Write the piecewise definition for the inverse of this function.

d. Carefully sketch the graph of the inverse of this function.

e. **Write About It** Compare the rule for the function with the rule for the inverse. How are they similar?

4. Sketch a graph for each function and its inverse.

a. $f(x) = \sqrt{x + 3}$

b. $f(x) = \sqrt{x} + 3$

c. $f(x) = \sqrt{2x}$

d. $f(x) = 2\sqrt{x}$

e. $f(x) = \sqrt[3]{x - 5}$

f. $f(x) = \sqrt[3]{8x}$

g. $f(x) = 2\sqrt[3]{x}$

h. $f(x) = \sqrt{x^2}$

i. $f(x) = \sqrt[3]{x^3}$

5. Consider the following story.

> Colleen is going on a field trip at school today. She rode her bike to school at 10 mi/h for 15 minutes. She waited 7 minutes for the bus. She then rode in the bus for 35 minutes at a speed of 35 mi/h.

Write a piecewise-defined function s that represents Colleen's speed t minutes after she left her house. Sketch a graph of s.

6. Compare the following two functions. Are they equivalent? Explain your reasoning.

$$f(x) = \lfloor x + 4 \rfloor \text{ and } g(x) = \lfloor x \rfloor + 4$$

7. What's Wrong Here? Derman wrote the following piecewise definition:

$$f(x) = \begin{cases} -2x & \text{if } x < 1 \\ 2x & \text{if } x \geq -1 \end{cases}$$

Is f a function? Explain your reasoning.

8. Determine whether each function is one-to-one. Explain your reasoning.

a. $f(x) = x - \lfloor x \rfloor$

b. $f(x) = x - 2\lfloor x \rfloor$

c. $f(x) = x - \lfloor 2x \rfloor$

d. $f(x) = x + \lfloor x \rfloor$

e. $f(x) = x + 2\lfloor x \rfloor$

f. $f(x) = 2x - \lfloor x \rfloor$

> Sketching a graph of the function may help you decide.

On Your Own

9. The "ceiling" function, written $\lceil x \rceil$, is similar to the floor function. Given an input of a real number, it returns the smallest integer greater than or equal to the given number. So, $\lceil 2 \rceil = 2$, $\lceil 3.53 \rceil = 4$, $\lceil 1.00001 \rceil = 2$, and $\lceil -5.39 \rceil = -5$.

a. Sketch a graph of the equation $y = \lceil x \rceil$.

b. Write the ceiling function in terms of the floor function.

10. Here is the graph of a piecewise-defined function.

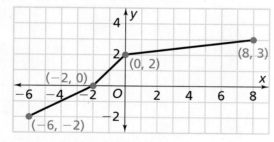

a. Write a function f that represents this graph.

b. Translate the graph of f to the right 5 units. Write a function to represent this new graph.

c. Translate the graph of f up 3 units. Write a function to represent this new graph.

11. Joe was looking at the data plan for his smartphone.

> **Joe** I pay $60 a month, and with that I get 5 gigabytes of data that I can download. If I go past that, I pay $5 per gigabyte. But that means that if I go over even by a little bit, I pay the extra charge. So if I download 6.02 gigabytes, I have to pay for 7 gigabytes.

Write a piecewise-defined function c that returns Joe's bill for d gigabytes of data downloaded in one month. Sketch a graph of c.

Hint: One of the pieces is a step function. You can use any of the step functions from this lesson.

12. Compare the two functions below. Are they equivalent? Explain your reasoning.

$$f(x) = \lfloor 2x \rfloor \text{ and } g(x) = 2\lfloor x \rfloor$$

13. Compare the functions below. Are they equivalent? If not, for what values (if any) are they equal? Explain your reasoning.

$$f(x) = \lfloor x^2 \rfloor \text{ and } g(x) = \lfloor x \rfloor^2$$

Try sketching the graph of each function. Some graphing calculators have a *floor* function.

Another way to describe a piecewise-defined function is to use the *Heaviside step function* $h_a(x) = \begin{cases} 0, & \text{if } x < a \\ 1, & \text{if } x \geq a \end{cases}$. You can use a Heaviside step function to write piecewise-defined functions on a single line. For example, $f(x) = \begin{cases} 2, & \text{if } x < 1 \\ 5x + 2, & \text{if } x \geq 1 \end{cases}$ can be written as $f(x) = 2 + h_1(x) \cdot 5x$. When $x < 1$, $h_1(x) = 0$, so $f(x) = 2$. When $x \geq 1$, $h_1(x) = 1$, so $f(x) = 2 + 5x$, as desired.

14. Write the following piecewise-defined functions on a single line using one or more Heaviside step functions.

a. $f(x) = \begin{cases} 4, & \text{if } x < -2 \\ 4 - 3x, & \text{if } x \geq -2 \end{cases}$

b. $f(x) = \begin{cases} -6, & \text{if } x < 3 \\ 7x + 1, & \text{if } x \geq 3 \end{cases}$

c. $f(x) = \begin{cases} 2x + 4, & \text{if } x < -1 \\ 3, & \text{if } x \geq -1 \end{cases}$

d. $f(x) = \begin{cases} 2, & \text{if } x < -3 \\ x + 1, & \text{if } -3 \leq x < 4 \\ 6, & \text{if } x \geq 4 \end{cases}$

e. $f(x) = \begin{cases} 1 - x^2, & \text{if } x \leq 1 \\ 1, & \text{if } 1 < x < 5 \\ 1 + x^2, & \text{if } x \geq 5 \end{cases}$

15. Write the function $a(x) = |x|$ using one or more Heaviside step functions. ←

16. Write the floor function on the domain $-3 \leq x < 3$ using a Heaviside step function.

There are at least two ways of writing this function. One way has only one term.

Maintain Your Skills

17. Evaluate the expression $(x - 4)(x - 1)(x + 3)(x + 5)(x + 9)$ for each x-value.

   a. 1

   b. -5

   c. 4

   d. -9

   e. -3

   f. What is similar about these five cases? Is there a sixth similar case? Explain.

18. Evaluate the expressions

$$2x^2 - 3x + 4$$
$$2x^2 - 3x + 4 + (x - 4)(x - 1)(x + 3)(x + 5)(x + 9)$$

for each x-value below.

   a. 1

   b. -5

   c. 0

   d. 4

   e. What are the x-values that produce the same result in both expressions?

Mathematical 4B Reflections

In this investigation, you learned how to determine whether a table, graph, or closed-form rule is a function; compose functions; and find the inverse of a function if it exists. These exercises will help you summarize what you have learned.

1. Suppose $f : \mathbb{R} \to \mathbb{R}$ and $f(x) = 3x^2 - 6x + 1$.

   a. Calculate $f(3)$ and $f(-3)$.

   b. Find all values of x for which $f(x) = 12$.

   c. Calculate $f(11) - f(10)$.

   d. Show that you can write $f(x + 1)$ as $f(x + 1) = 3x^2 - 2$.

   e. Write a simplified expression for $f(x + 1) - f(x)$.

   f. If $g(x) = f(x + 1) - f(x)$, what is $g(10)$?

2. Consider the functions $f(x) = 3x + 2$ and $g(x) = x + 5$. Calculate each value.

   a. $f(3)$

   b. $g(3)$

   c. $f(g(3))$

   d. $f \circ g(3)$

   e. $g \circ f(3)$

   f. $f(3) \cdot g(3)$

3. Consider the function $f(x) = 3x + 2$. Find a function g that makes each equation true.

   a. $f \circ g(x) = x$

   b. $g \circ f(x) = x$

   c. $f \circ g(x) = x^2$

   d. $g \circ f(x) = x^2$

   e. $g \circ f(x) = f(x)$

   f. $f \circ g(x) = f(x)$

4. Suppose $f, g, k : \mathbb{R} \to \mathbb{R}$, $f(x) = -3 + x + 8x^2 + 4x^3$, $g(x) = 16x$, and $k(x) = 4x$.

   a. Find a formula for $g \circ f(x)$.

   b. Find a formula for $h(x) = g \circ f \circ k^{-1}(x)$.

   c. Draw the graphs of f and h on the same axes.

   d. Find the zeros of h and the zeros of f.

5. What is a function?

6. How do you compose two functions to make a new function?

7. What function undoes $x \mapsto 3x + 7$?

Vocabulary and Notation

In this investigation you learned these terms and symbols. Make sure you understand what each one means and how to use it.

- composite function, $g \circ f$
- domain
- equal functions
- function
- identity function
- inverse function, f^{-1}

- one-to-one
- piecewise-defined function
- range
- target
- $x \mapsto y$ (x maps to y)
- $\mathbb{R}$ (the real numbers)

Investigation 4C

Exponential Functions

In *Exponential Functions,* you will use the laws of exponents to explore exponential functions. You will sketch the graphs of exponential functions and write exponential function rules from tables and points on graphs. You will also explore the properties of the inverse of the function $y = b^x$.

By the end of this investigation, you will be able to answer questions like these.

1. For $f(x) = b^x$, why is it true that $f(m) \cdot f(n) = f(m + n)$?

2. Why must an exponential function have an inverse function?

3. If you invest $1000 in an account at 6% interest, compounded annually, how much money will you have after 30 years?

You will learn how to

- graph an exponential function and determine the equation of an exponential function given two points on its graph

- identify an exponential function from the table it generates and use the table to create a closed-form or recursive definition of the function

- evaluate the inverse of the function $y = b^x$ either exactly or by approximation

You will develop these habits and skills:

- Reason by continuity to extend the definition of exponent to include all real numbers.

- Visualize exponential growth by examining graphs and tables of exponential functions.

- Draw logical conclusions from the laws of exponents and properties of exponential functions to solve problems and prove conjectures.

Archaeologists use exponential functions that model radioactive decay to determine the age of objects.

4.11 Getting Started

Activating Prior Knowledge
Exploring New Ideas

A difference table can help you find a function rule that fits a table. For some tables, a ratio table will help you find a rule that fits the table.

For You to Explore

For each function in Problems 1–5, make a difference table. Show the outputs for the inputs 0 through 5 and the differences between terms.

Input	Output	Δ
0	■	■
1	■	■
2	■	■
3	■	■
4	■	■
5	■	

1. $a(x) = 3x + 1$

2. $b(x) = x^2 - x + 1$

3. $c(x) = 3^x$

4. $d(x) = 3 \cdot 5^x$

5. $f(x) = \left(\frac{1}{2}\right)^x$

Note that $d(x)$ is not equal to 15^x, since only the 5 is raised to the xth power.

6. Find a function $g(x)$ for which the difference column is equal to the output column.

Instead of calculating the difference between one term and the next, it sometimes makes sense to calculate the ratio of one term to the next.

7. a. Copy and complete this ratio table for $a(x) = 3x + 1$. Round to the nearest hundredth.

b. What happens to the numbers in the ratio column if you continue the table for larger inputs? Explain.

Input	Output	÷
0	1	4
1	4	■
2	7	■
3	10	1.3
4	13	■
5	16	

8. For each function from Problems 2–5, build a ratio table with the inputs from 0 to 5.

9. Write About It Suppose you have an input-output function table with integer inputs from 0 to 5.

a. Describe how to find a rule that fits the table if the table has constant differences.

b. Describe how to find a rule that fits the table if the table has constant ratios.

10. Take It Further Find a function $h(x)$ for which the ratio column is equal to the output column.

On Your Own

11. Solve each equation any way you choose. Then, decide which equation was the most difficult for you to solve. Explain.

 a. $5 = x^2$

 b. $5 = 2^x$

 c. $x = 5^2$

 d. $8 = 2^x$

12. Sketch the graph of $c(x) = 3^x$.

> You will need more input-output pairs than the ones you found in Problem 3.

 The expression $3^{\sqrt{2}}$ is undefined so far, since you cannot write $\sqrt{2}$ as a rational number.

13. Use your graph of $c(x) = 3^x$ to explain why $3^{\sqrt{2}}$ should be between 3 and 9.

14. **Write About It** Describe how you can make a more accurate estimate of $3^{\sqrt{2}}$.

15. Copy and complete the table of values for each exponential function.

 a. $f(a) = 3 \cdot 2^a$

Input, a	Output, f(a)
−2	■
−1	■
0	■
1	■
2	■

 b. $g(a) = 30 \cdot 2^a$

Input, a	Output, g(a)
−2	■
−1	■
0	■
1	■
2	■

 c. $h(a) = \frac{1}{5} \cdot 5^a$

Input, a	Output, h(a)
0	■
1	■
2	■
3	■
4	■

 d. $j(a) = 27 \cdot \left(\frac{1}{3}\right)^a$

Input, a	Output, j(a)
−1	■
0	■
1	■
2	■
3	■

16. Find an exponential function that agrees with each table.

a.

Input, a	Output, $k(a)$
0	4
1	12
2	36
3	108
4	324

b.

Input, h	Output, $L(h)$
0	100
1	50
2	25
3	12.5
4	6.25

> An *exponential function* is a function that you can write in the form $f(x) = a \cdot b^x$.

c.

Input, x	Output, $p(x)$
0	2
1	$\frac{1}{2}$
2	$\frac{1}{8}$
3	$\frac{1}{32}$
4	$\frac{1}{128}$

d.

Input, n	Output, $Q(n)$
0	8
1	12
2	18
3	27
4	40.5

17. Copy and complete this input-output table for $f(x) = 2^x$. Round to three decimal places.

x	$f(x) = 2^x$
0	1
1	▧
1.4	▧
1.41	▧
1.414	▧
1.4142	▧
1.41421	▧
1.414213	▧

18. a. Explain why there are no integers a and b other than $a = b = 0$ that satisfy the equation $2^a = 5^b$.

b. Determine whether there are integers c and d other than $c = d = 0$ that satisfy the equation $4^c = 8^d$. If so, what are c and d?

Maintain Your Skills

19. Consider the function $f(x) = 2^x$. State whether you believe each value is a rational number. Find each rational value exactly, without using a calculator.

a. $f(0)$ **b.** $f\left(\frac{1}{2}\right)$ **c.** $f(\pi)$ **d.** $f(f(2))$

e. all values of a such that $f(a) = \frac{1}{8}$

f. all values of a such that $f(a) = 7$

g. all values of a such that $f(a) = -1$

Graphs of Exponential Functions

Several of the functions in the Getting Started lesson of this investigation
are *exponential functions*.

Definitions

An **exponential function** is a function *f* that you can write in the
form $f(x) = a \cdot b^x$, where $a \neq 0$, $b > 0$, and $b \neq 1$. The number *b* is
the **base**.

> The function
> $d(x) = 3 \cdot 5^x$ is
> exponential. What is
> its domain?

For Discussion

1. What happens if $a = 0$? What happens if $b = 1$?

Here are the graphs of
$f(x) = 2^x$ and $g(x) = 5^x$.

Both graphs have their *y*-intercept
at (0, 1). Both graphs pass through
Quadrants I and II. Both functions
are increasing. The greater *x* is, the
greater the corresponding *y* is.

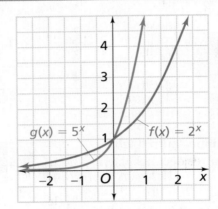

Habits of Mind

Establish a process.
How can you decide
whether the point
$(-3.5, 0.1)$ is on the
graph of $f(x)$?

For You to Do

2. According to the graphs, for what values of *x* is $2^x > 5^x$?

Here are the graphs of $h(x) = \left(\frac{1}{2}\right)^x$ and
$j(x) = \left(\frac{1}{5}\right)^x$.

Both graphs have their *y*-intercept
at (0, 1). Both graphs pass through
Quadrants I and II. Both functions are
decreasing. The greater *x* is, the less the
corresponding *y* is.

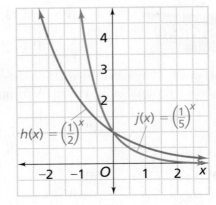

Habits of Mind

Establish a process.
How can you decide
whether the point
(3.5, 0.1) is on the graph
of $h(x)$?

3. Graph $f(x) = 2^x$ and $k(x) = 3 \cdot 2^x$. How are the graphs related?
4. Graph $k(x) = 3 \cdot 2^x$ and $m(x) = -3 \cdot 2^x$. How are the graphs related?
5. Graph $f(x) = 2^x$ and $h(x) = \left(\frac{1}{2}\right)^x$. How are the graphs related?

Monotonic Functions

As you have seen, the graph of $f(x) = 2^x$ seems to indicate that this function is **strictly increasing.** In other words, if $s > t$, then $f(s) > f(t)$. You will now verify this observation.

Lemma 4.1

Let $b > 1$ and let x be a positive rational number. Then $b^x > 1$.

Proof Since x is positive and rational, you can write $x = \frac{p}{q}$ for some positive integers p and q. First, use the following fact about power functions.

Let $g(x) = x^n$, where n is a positive integer. Then $g(x)$ is strictly increasing on nonnegative inputs. In other words, if s and t are nonnegative, then $s^n > t^n$ if and only if $s > t$.

Now, let $s = b^{\frac{1}{q}}$, $t = 1$, and $n = q$. By the above fact,

$$\left(b^{\frac{1}{q}}\right)^q > 1^q \Leftrightarrow b^{\frac{1}{q}} > 1$$

But $\left(b^{\frac{1}{q}}\right)^q = b$, so

$$b > 1 \Leftrightarrow b^{\frac{1}{q}} > 1$$

Since $b > 1$ is given, then $b^{\frac{1}{q}} > 1$.

Now use the above fact again, with $n = p$.

$$\left(b^{\frac{1}{q}}\right)^p > 1^p \Leftrightarrow (b)^{\frac{1}{q}} > 1$$

Therefore $b^{\frac{p}{q}} > 1$ for any positive integers p and q.

So $b^x > 1$, as desired.

> **Remember...**
>
> A function of the form $y = x^n$ is a polynomial function and not an exponential function.

Theorem 4.6

If $b > 1$, then the function $f(x) = b^x$ is strictly increasing on rational-number inputs. In other words, if s and t are rational numbers such that $s > t$, then $f(s) > f(t)$.

Proof Suppose s and t are rational numbers such that $s > t$. Then $s - t > 0$, so Lemma 4.1 gives

$$b^{s-t} > 1$$

You know b^t is positive. You can multiply each side of the inequality by b^t.

$$b^{s-t} \cdot b^t > 1 \cdot b^t$$

$$b^{s-t+t} > b^t \quad \text{using Theorem 1.3}$$

$$b^s > b^t$$

$$f(s) > f(t)$$

This is the desired result.

Similarly, you have observed from its graph that the function $h(x) = \left(\frac{1}{2}\right)^x$ is **strictly decreasing**. In general, if $0 < b < 1$, the function $g(x) = b^x$ is strictly decreasing on rational number inputs. See Exercise 4 for the proof.

Domain and Range

You can draw the graph of $f(x) = 2^x$ without any gaps. This suggests that its domain should be the set of all real numbers, $\mathbb{R}$, but the work in Investigation 1B only defines exponents for integers and rational numbers. The real numbers include irrational numbers such as $\sqrt{2}$ and π. How should you define $2^{\sqrt{2}}$?

You want to define $2^{\sqrt{2}}$ in such a way that the function $f(x) = 2^x$ is increasing on all real-number inputs. For example, since

$$1 < \sqrt{2} < 2$$

you must have

$$2^1 < 2^{\sqrt{2}} < 2^2$$

Thus, you must define $2^{\sqrt{2}}$ to be a number between 2 and 4. In fact, the graph suggests $2^{\sqrt{2}}$ should be between 2 and 3.

The key to defining irrational exponents is that, even though $\sqrt{2}$ is irrational, you can pick rational numbers that are as close to $\sqrt{2}$ as desired. As the rational numbers on either side get closer to $\sqrt{2}$, the outputs of $f(x) = 2^x$ get closer to a specific real number. You use this number for $2^{\sqrt{2}}$.

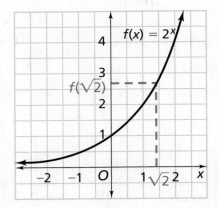

Habits of Mind

Extend what you know. This type of reasoning is *extension by continuity*. You can often use it to take things that work for integers or rational numbers and apply them to real numbers.

Establish a process. Evaluate $2^{\sqrt{2}}$ by approximating it with nearby rational exponents. Terminating decimals work well, since they are all rational numbers. Since $\sqrt{2} \approx 1.41421356$, you can get a good estimate for $2^{\sqrt{2}}$ by finding $2^{1.41}$ and $2^{1.42}$.

$$2^{1.41} < 2^{\sqrt{2}} < 2^{1.42}$$

You can do even better using better approximations.

$$2^{1.414} < 2^{\sqrt{2}} < 2^{2.415}$$

This table shows how you can approximate $2^{\sqrt{2}}$ by using decimals close to $\sqrt{2}$ as inputs to the function $f(x) = 2^x$, with outputs rounded to five decimal places.

Input, x	Output, $f(x) = 2^x$
1.41	2.65737
1.414	2.66475
1.4142	2.66512
1.41421	2.66514
1.414213	2.66514
1.4142135	2.66514

The value of $2^{\sqrt{2}}$ to five decimal places is 2.66514. As the inputs get closer to $\sqrt{2}$, the outputs get closer to a number, and you take that number as the value of $2^{\sqrt{2}}$. It is possible to approximate any irrational number with rational numbers. Therefore, it is possible to define $f(x) = 2^x$ for any real number x. So, the domain of f is the set of all real numbers.

This limiting process only works for positive bases. Therefore, you cannot define expressions like $(-2)^{\sqrt{2}}$ in a reasonable way.

Based on this extension, the domain of an exponential function is the set of all real numbers. The range of $f(x) = b^x$ is restricted to positive numbers as long as $b > 0$ (see Exercise 20). Then the value of a determines whether the range of $f(x) = a \cdot b^x$ is all positive numbers or all negative numbers.

As the input x becomes more negative, the corresponding output y approaches but never reaches 0. This behavior—approaching but not reaching $f(x) = 0$—is very different from the behavior of any polynomial function.

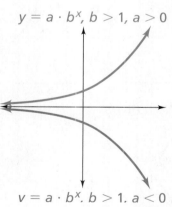

$y = a \cdot b^x, b > 1, a > 0$

$y = a \cdot b^x, b > 1, a < 0$

Summary Properties of Exponential Functions

An exponential function $f : \mathbb{R} \mapsto \mathbb{R}$ is defined as $f(x) = a \cdot b^x$.

- The value of a cannot be zero, and b must be positive and not 1.

- The domain of f is $\mathbb{R}$.

- The range of f is all positive real numbers if $a > 0$, and all negative real numbers if $a < 0$.

- The graph of $y = f(x)$ has one y-intercept at $(0, a)$ and no x-intercepts.

- If $a > 0$, the graph of $y = f(x)$ is strictly increasing when $b > 1$ and strictly decreasing when $0 < b < 1$.

Exercises *Practicing Habits of Mind*

Check Your Understanding

1. Match each graph with its equation.

$$f(x) = 3 \cdot 2^x \qquad f(x) = 3 \cdot \left(\tfrac{1}{2}\right)^x \qquad f(x) = 3 \cdot 5^x \qquad f(x) = -3 \cdot 2^x$$

a.
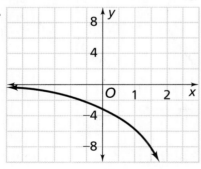

b.
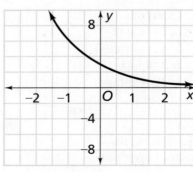

c.
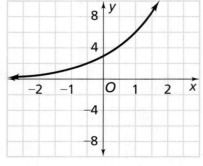

d.
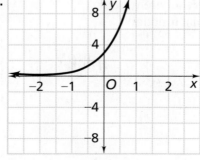

2. a. The graph of an exponential function contains the points $(0, 12)$ and $(2, 3)$. Find its equation.

b. The graph of an exponential function contains the points $(2, 12)$ and $(4, 3)$. Find its equation.

3. a. Write the equations for at least two exponential functions with graphs that contain the point $(2, 72)$.

b. Take It Further Write the general form for any exponential function with a graph that contains the point $(2, 72)$.

4. Prove the following lemma and theorem.

Lemma 4.2

Let $0 < b < 1$ and let x be a positive rational number. Then $b^x < 1$.

Theorem 4.7

Let $0 < b < 1$. Then the function $f(x) = b^x$ is strictly decreasing on rational-number inputs.

5. The graphs of $f(x) = 2^x$ and $g(x) = \left(\frac{1}{2}\right)^x$ are reflections of each other in the y-axis.

Explain why this reflection property makes sense, using the definition of a negative exponent.

$$b^{-x} = \frac{1}{b^x}$$

> If $f(x) = 2^x$ is increasing and $g(x) = \left(\frac{1}{2}\right)^x$ is its reflection over the y-axis, what can you say about $g(x)$?

For Exercises 6 and 7, estimate the solution to each equation.

6. $2^x = 7$

7. $2^x = \frac{1}{7} \cdot 4^x$

8. a. Sketch the graph of each function for $-10 \le x \le 10$ and $-10 \le y \le 10$.

$$f(x) = 5 \cdot (1.07)^x$$
$$g(x) = (1.12)^x$$

Do the graphs intersect in this window?

b. Determine the total number of intersections of the two graphs.

9. In the lesson, you learned that $2^{\sqrt{2}}$ is a number $a \approx 2.66514$.

a. Calculate $a^{\sqrt{2}}$.

b. Is there a way to directly calculate $\left(2^{\sqrt{2}}\right)^{\sqrt{2}}$? Explain.

> For advice on how to find an intersection point, see the TI-Nspire™ Handbook, p. 990.

10. Try to use the method in the Developing Habits of Mind section to define $(-2)^{\sqrt{2}}$. What happens?

11. Explain why the y-intercept of the graph of $f(x) = a \cdot b^x$ is $(0, a)$.

Go Online
www.successnetplus.com

12. **Standardized Test Prep** Which of these points is on the graph of $f(x) = -3 \cdot 2^x$?

    A. $(0, 1)$ **B.** $(-1, 6)$

    C. $(-2, -0.75)$ **D.** $(2, 36)$

13. Due to inflation, the cost of a Big Burger grows by 3% every year. This year a Big Burger costs $3.99.

    a. How much will a Big Burger cost next year and the year after that?

    b. How can you find the cost of a Big Burger ten years from now?

    c. Will a Big Burger ever cost more than $20? Explain.

    d. Find a rule for the function $C(n)$, with an output that is the cost of a Big Burger n years from now.

14. **What's Wrong Here?** Cody says, "The graph of $y = 2^x$ can't get to *every* positive number if it doesn't make it to zero. It has to stop somewhere. I'll bet it never gets below one millionth."

    Show that Cody is mistaken by finding a number x such that 2^x is positive but less than $\frac{1}{1,000,000}$.

15. Explain why $3^{\sqrt{6}}$ must be greater than 9 and less than 27.

16. Dorris claims the solution x in Exercise 6 must be an irrational number. She says, "If $2^x = 7$ is solved by a fraction, then it looks like $2^{\frac{p}{q}} = 7$. Then I raise both sides to a power of q.

$$2^{\frac{p}{q}} = 7$$
$$\left(2^{\frac{p}{q}}\right)^q = 7^q$$
$$2^p = 7^q$$

"And p and q have to be integers. I'm pretty sure that can't happen unless p and q are both zero."

Is it possible for $2^p = 7^q$ if p and q are nonzero integers? Explain.

17. Dorris's explanation above shows that the solution to $2^x = 7$ must be irrational. How does her argument break down if you try to apply it to the equation $2^x = 8$?

18. a. Copy and complete this table for $f(x) = (-2)^x$.

b. What happens if you try to make a smooth graph for $f(x) = (-2)^x$?

Input	Output
−2	■
−1	■
0	■
1	■
2	■
3	■

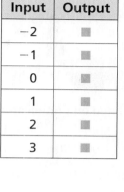

19. Take It Further The equation

$$a \cdot b^x = c \cdot d^x$$

may have a different number of solutions, depending on the values of a, b, c, and d. Describe the conditions on these parameters that make the equation have each number of solutions.

- exactly one
- none
- more than one

20. a. If $b > 0$ and x is an integer, explain why b^x must be positive.

b. If $b > 0$ and x is rational, use the definition of rational exponent to explain why b^x must be positive.

Maintain Your Skills

21. Simplify each expression.

a. $\left(3^{\sqrt{2}}\right)^{\sqrt{2}}$ **b.** $\left(3^{\sqrt{2}}\right)^2$ **c.** $\left(3^{-\sqrt{2}}\right)^{-1}$

d. $\left(3^{\sqrt{8}}\right)^{\sqrt{2}}$ **e.** $3^{\sqrt{2}} \cdot 3^{-\sqrt{2}}$ **f.** $\left(3^{-\sqrt{2}}\right)^{-\sqrt{2}}$

g. $3^{\sqrt{2}} \cdot 5^{\sqrt{2}}$ **h.** $\left(3^{\sqrt[3]{2}}\right)^{\sqrt[3]{2}}$ **i.** $\left(3^{\sqrt[3]{2}}\right)^{\sqrt[3]{4}}$

> Decide for yourself what *simplify* means, but your answer cannot be identical to the given expression.

22. Graph each function on the same set of axes.
Let $-10 \leq x \leq 10$ and let $0 \leq y \leq 10$.

- $a(x) = 3^x$
- $b(x) = 3 \cdot 3^x$
- $c(x) = 9 \cdot 3^x$
- $d(x) = 27 \cdot 3^x$
- $f(x) = 81 \cdot 3^x$

How are these graphs related?

The logarithmic spiral is the graph of $r = ae^{b\theta}$ in polar coordinates. The arrangement of seeds in a sunflower approximates the logarithmic spiral.

4.13 Tables of Exponential Functions

This lesson focuses on exponential functions from a tabular perspective. It also focuses on how recursive rules can generate exponential functions.

In-Class Experiment

Consider this function defined on nonnegative integers.

$$B(n) = \begin{cases} 500 & \text{if } n = 0 \\ 1.06 \cdot B(n-1) & \text{if } n > 0 \end{cases}$$

1. Use the definition to calculate $B(10)$. Then figure out a more direct way to get $B(10)$.

2. Calculate $B(50)$.

3. Find the smallest integer n such that $B(n) > 4000$.

> This recursive function can be modeled. See the TI-Nspire Handbook, p. 990.

The exponential function $L(h) = 100 \cdot \left(\frac{1}{2}\right)^h$ is decreasing. If $h = 0$, $L = 100$.

> If the base b is between 0 and 1, it is an **exponential decay** function. If the base is greater than 1, it is an **exponential growth** function.

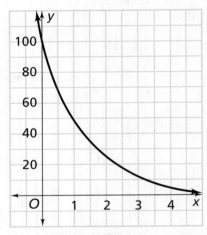

Here is a table for $L(h)$ for integer values of h from 0 to 4.

h	L(h)
0	100
1	50
2	25
3	12.5
4	6.25

Tony thinks he can start with the table and find an exponential function rule.

Tony If you just gave me that table, I could find an exponential function that matches it. There's an exponential that matches the table, since it has a constant ratio between any pair of successive terms. Here's a ratio table.

h	L(h)	÷
0	100	$\frac{1}{2}$
1	50	$\frac{1}{2}$
2	25	$\frac{1}{2}$
3	12.5	$\frac{1}{2}$
4	6.25	

You calculate the ÷ column by computing ratios of successive terms.
$$\frac{50}{100} = \frac{1}{2}$$

And I know $L(0) = 100$, so $L(h)$ is 100 times one half to the h. Now, that's not the only function that matches the table, but it's probably the simplest one. And I can describe $L(h)$ term by term. Start with 100 and divide by 2 each time the input increases by 1.

For You to Do

4. Find a rule that fits this table.

x	f(x)
0	12
1	18
2	27

Make strategic choices. Tony describes $L(h)$ using a recursive rule: Start with $L(0) = 100$ and divide by 2 each time. You can describe any exponential function $f(x) = a \cdot b^x$ in this way. In this case, the value of a is 100 and the base b is $\frac{1}{2}$, since dividing by 2 is the same as multiplying by one half.

Exponential functions arise naturally in situations like the following.

- the number of teams in an elimination tournament (Half of the teams move on to the next round.)

- the growth of money in a bank account (with 6% interest compounded annually)

- the growth of a population over time (The population doubles every 50 years.)

The function L is connected to the concept of a half-life in biology. Specifically, $L(h)$ outputs the percentage remaining of an element after h half-lives.

The recursive definition for $L(h)$ looks like this.

$$L(h) = \begin{cases} 100 & \text{if } h = 0 \\ 0.5 \cdot L(h-1) & \text{if } h > 0 \end{cases}$$

There is an important concern about domain here. The recursive rule for $L(h)$ limits its domain to nonnegative integers, since it fails to give a value for something like $L(1.5)$ or $L(-2)$. In some situations, it may make sense to use only nonnegative integers as inputs. However, remember that there is a difference between this version of $L(h)$ and the closed-form definition $L(h) = 100 \cdot \left(\frac{1}{2}\right)^h$, which has all real numbers as its domain.

Habits of Mind

Experiment. Build a model for L in your function-modeling language.

If you have a table for an exponential function, but the inputs do not start at 0 or they have gaps, you can still find the function using algebra if you know at least two input-output pairs.

Example

Problem An exponential function P defined as $P(x) = a \cdot b^x$ has this table of inputs and outputs. Find the values of a and b.

x	P(x)
−2	108
−1	36
2	$\frac{4}{3}$

The outputs are positive and decreasing, so it must be exponential decay. The base b must be between 0 and 1.

Solution

Method 1 When two terms have inputs that differ by 1, you can calculate the base b directly as the ratio between these successive terms.

$$b = \frac{36}{108} = \frac{1}{3}$$

Then $P(x) = a \cdot \left(\frac{1}{3}\right)^x$. You can find a using any of the input-output pairs. Use $(-1, 36)$.

$$P(x) = a \cdot \left(\frac{1}{3}\right)^x$$
$$36 = a \cdot \left(\frac{1}{3}\right)^{-1}$$
$$36 = a \cdot 3$$
$$12 = a$$

The function is $P(x) = 12 \cdot \left(\frac{1}{3}\right)^x$.

Method 2 Pick any two points and set up the equation $P(x) = a \cdot b^x$ for each. For example, take $(-1, 36)$ and $\left(2, \frac{4}{3}\right)$.

$$36 = a \cdot b^{-1}$$
$$\frac{4}{3} = a \cdot b^2$$

Then divide to build an equation for b.

$$\frac{36}{\frac{4}{3}} = \frac{a \cdot b^{-1}}{a \cdot b^2}$$
$$27 = b^{-3}$$

Solve for b. If $b^{-3} = 27$, then $b^3 = \frac{1}{27}$ and $b = \frac{1}{3}$. Then find a.

For You to Do

5. Find the exponential function with a graph that contains the points $(1, 36)$ and $(2, 108)$.

Minds in Action

Tony has another way to think about finding an exponential function from two points on its graph.

Tony   I guess the example does the same thing, but I like to think of it as how far apart the points are in a geometric sequence. Say the points are $(-3, 10)$ and $(2, 20)$. The x-values have a difference of 5, so it's a geometric sequences with five steps from 10 to 20.

$$10, \blacksquare, \blacksquare, \blacksquare, \blacksquare, 20$$

So whatever the base is, the output doubles from 10 to 20 in five terms. That means the base has to solve the equation $b^5 = 2$. And once you find b, you can use either point to find a.

Exercises Practicing Habits of Mind

Check Your Understanding

1. For each table, find the exponential function that matches the table or explain how you know that an exponential function cannot fit the table.

a.

n	A(n)
0	18
1	6
2	2
3	$\frac{2}{3}$

b.

x	B(x)
0	−2
1	−8
2	−32
3	−128

c.

t	C(t)
0	4
1	6
2	9
3	12

d.

z	D(z)
1	2
2	12
3	72
4	432

2. For each exponential function in Exercise 1, build a recursive model in your function-modeling language.

3. Suppose q is an exponential function with $q(3) = 100$ and $q(5) = 4$. Find $q(x)$.

4. **What's Wrong Here?** George says there are two possible values of the base b for the exponential function in Exercise 3.

   George says, "The function goes from 100 to 4 in two steps, which means dividing by 25. So $b^2 = \frac{1}{25}$. But then there are two possible values of b. It could be either $\frac{1}{5}$ or $\frac{-1}{5}$. Either could be right."

   Do you agree or disagree with George's statement? Explain.

5. Find two functions for which $f(-3) = 10$ and $f(2) = 20$.

> The function $f(x)$ does not need to be an exponential function.

6. *T* is an exponential function with this table.

  a. If $T(x) = a \cdot b^x$, find a and b.

  b. Copy and complete the table.

x	T(x)	÷
0	100	▦
1	▦	▦
2	▦	▦
3	▦	▦
4	▦	▦
5	300	

7. Suppose a new car that costs $20,000 depreciates in value about 20% each year.

  a. How much will the car be worth after 1 year? After 2 years? After 3 years?

  b. Find a rule for $V(n)$, the value of the car after n years of driving.

  c. Will the car ever be worth less than $1000? Explain.

> Most cars actually depreciate more than 20% the first year.

8. Take It Further The graph of an exponential function passes through the points (x_1, y_1) and (x_2, y_2). Find the function in terms of these coordinates.

> **Habits of Mind**
>
> **Generalize.** Exercise 8 is a generalization of the type of problem found in Exercises 3 and 12.

On Your Own

9. Standardized Test Prep Suppose f is an exponential function $f(x) = a \cdot b^x$ with $f(0) = 4$ and $f(2) = 25$. What are the values of a and b?

  A. $a = 1, b = 5$ **B.** $a = 1, b = 10$

  C. $a = 4, b = 2.5$ **D.** $a = 4, b = 5$

10. The ratio column of this table is filled in.

n	M(n)	÷
0	16	1.5
1	▦	1.5
2	▦	1.5
3	▦	1.5
4	▦	

Copy and complete the table. Define $M(n)$ with both a closed-form rule and a recursive rule.

11. This table has the first output and the ratio column filled in.

n	F(n)	÷
0	1	1
1	■	2
2	■	3
3	■	4
4	■	5
5	■	6
6	■	

a. Copy and complete the table.

b. Is F an exponential function? Explain.

c. Describe how to calculate $F(10)$ if the pattern in the ratio column continues.

12. Here are the graphs of three exponential functions. Find a closed-form rule that defines each function.

a.

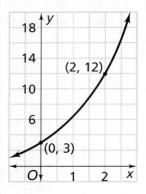

b.

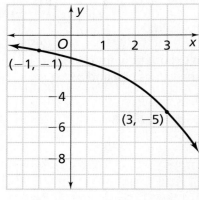

c.

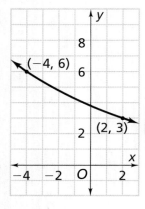

13. Money in a savings account typically grows by about 3% per year. Kara's savings account has $1000 in it.

    a. Find the amount of money in Kara's account after 1 year, 2 years, and 3 years.

    b. Find the amount of money in Kara's account after 20 years.

So, Kara will earn $30 (3% of $1000) interest during the first year. Why will she earn more than $30 interest during the second year?

14. Some credit cards offer 0% interest on their balance for 12 months, as long as you make a required monthly payment of at least 2% of the balance. Suppose you owe $2000 on one of these cards and make only the minimum payment each month.

    a. Find the balance after 1 month, 2 months, and 3 months.

    b. Find a rule for $B(n)$, the balance after n months.

    c. What is the domain of $B(n)$? Explain.

15. Suppose you have the credit card in Exercise 14, but want to be sure to pay off half the total balance by the end of the first year. If you plan to pay the same percentage of the remaining balance each month, about what percent of the balance do you need to pay?

16. **Write About It** Use the two function definitions below.

$$f(x) = 5 \cdot 2^x$$

$$g(x) = \begin{cases} 5 & \text{if } x = 0 \\ 2 \cdot g(x - 1) & \text{if } x > 0 \end{cases}$$

Explain why the graphs of these functions do not look the same.

Maintain Your Skills

17. Suppose $b(x) = 3^x$. Calculate each value.

    a. $b(5)$ **b.** $b(3) \cdot b(2)$ **c.** $b(1)$

    d. $\dfrac{b(3)}{b(2)}$ **e.** $b(6)$ **f.** $(b(2))^3$

18. Suppose $f(x) = b^x$ for $b > 0$ with $f(3) = p$ and $f(5) = q$. Find each value in terms of p and q.

    a. $f(0)$ **b.** $f(-3)$ **c.** $f(8)$

    d. $f(6)$ **e.** $f(15)$

Habits of Mind

Look for relationships. How is $f(8)$ related to $f(3)$ and $f(5)$? Use the fact that $f(x) = b^x$.

In this investigation, you graphed exponential functions. You wrote rules for exponential functions, given a table of inputs and outputs or two points on the graph of the function. These exercises will help you summarize what you have learned.

1. Give the definition of *exponential function*. Pay special attention to any restrictions on the variables in your definition. Give an example of an exponential function and describe its domain and range. Describe where your function is increasing and where it is decreasing.

2. Use this table for the exponential function $g(x)$.

x	g(x)
0	−5
1	−10
2	−20
3	−40
4	−80

   a. Write a recursive definition for $g(x)$.

   b. Write a closed-form definition for $g(x)$.

   c. Do your answers for parts (a) and (b) define the same function? Explain.

3. a. Copy and complete this ratio table for $h(x)$.

x	h(x)	÷
0	■	$\frac{2}{3}$
1	6	$\frac{2}{3}$
2	■	$\frac{2}{3}$
3	■	$\frac{2}{3}$
4	■	

   b. Find $h(23)$ to four decimal places.

   c. Could $h(x)$ be an exponential function? Explain.

4. Find the exact values of x that solve each equation.

   a. $12 = 3x^2$

   b. $x = 5 \cdot 4^{-\frac{1}{2}}$

   c. $16 = 4 \cdot 32^x$

   d. $-5 = x \cdot 27^{\frac{2}{3}}$

5. For $f(x) = b^x$, why is it true that $f(m) \cdot f(n) = f(m + n)$?

6. Why must an exponential function have an inverse function?

7. If you invest $1000 in an account at 6% interest, compounded annually, how much money will you have in 30 years?

Vocabulary

In this investigation, you learned these terms. Make sure you understand what each one means and how to use it.

- **base**
- **exponential decay**
- **exponential function**
- **exponential growth**
- **strictly decreasing**
- **strictly increasing**

Investigation 4D

Transforming Basic Graphs

In *Transforming Basic Graphs*, you will sketch basic graphs. You will explore the effects, on both the graphs and on their equations, of translating, stretching, shrinking, and reflecting the basic graphs.

By the end of this investigation, you will be able to answer questions like these.

1. How are the graphs of $y = x^2$ and $y = (x - 3)^2$ related?

2. What does the graph of $(x + 1)^2 + (y - 4)^2 = 36$ look like?

3. What does the graph of $-2y = x^3 - x$ look like?

You will learn how to

- sketch basic graphs

- describe the effect of a translation of one of the basic graphs on both the graph and the equation of the graph

- describe the effect of scaling an axis or reflection on both the graph and the equation of the graph

- compose transformations and sketch the effect of such a composition

You will develop these habits and skills:

- Visualize variations of the basic graphs under translations, reflections, scaling, and compositions of those transformations.

- Match a transformation of a graph to a corresponding transformation of its equation.

- Analyze the operation of function compositions on transformations.

One image is a stretch of the original figure. The other is a reflection. Can you tell which is which?

Getting Started

As you graph equations, you may notice that related equations have similar graphs.

For You to Explore

1. Sketch the graph of $y = x^2$.

2. Here are four equations related to $y = x^2$. Sketch the graph of each equation. Describe how the graph is related to the graph of $y = x^2$.

    a. $y + 5 = x^2$ **b.** $y = (x + 5)^2$

    c. $y = x^2 + 5$ **d.** $y - 3 = (x + 2)^2$

3. Sketch the graph of $y = x^3$.

4. Here are four equations related to $y = x^3$. Sketch the graph of each equation. Describe how the graph is related to the graph of $y = x^3$.

    a. $y + 5 = x^3$ **b.** $y = (x + 5)^3$

    c. $y = x^3 + 5$ **d.** $y - 3 = (x + 2)^3$

5. **Write About It** Compare the graphs of $y = x^2$ and $y = x^3$. In particular, address the following questions.

- What type of symmetry does each graph have?
- Through which quadrants does each graph pass?
- How do the graphs compare near the origin? Away from the origin?

6. Sketch the graph of $y = \sqrt{x}$.

7. Here are four equations related to $y = \sqrt{x}$. Sketch the graph of each equation. Describe how the graph is related to the graph of $y = \sqrt{x}$.

    a. $y + 5 = \sqrt{x}$ **b.** $y = \sqrt{x + 5}$

    c. $y = \sqrt{x} + 5$ **d.** $y - 3 = \sqrt{x + 2}$

8. Sketch the graph of $y = |x|$, the absolute value function.

9. Here are four equations related to $y = |x|$. Sketch the graph of each equation. Describe how the graph is related to the graph of $y = |x|$.

    a. $y + 5 = |x|$ **b.** $y = |x + 5|$

    c. $y = |x| + 5$ **d.** $y - 3 = |x + 2|$

> For help defining the absolute value function, see the TI-Nspire™ Handbook, p. 990.

10. a. Sketch the graph of $y = 3^x$ and $y = \log_3 x$ on the same axes.

    b. How are the two graphs related?

11. **Take It Further** Find three different equations with graphs that pass through the points $(6, 0)$ and $(-3, 0)$.

Exercises *Practicing Habits of Mind*

For Exercises 12–15, use this list of instructions.

- Connect endpoints (0, 0) and (3, 3).
- Connect endpoints (2, 2) and (3, 1).
- Connect endpoints (3, 3) and (5, 1).

12. a. Follow the instructions to plot figure *F*.

   b. Make a new list of instructions by replacing each point (*x*, *y*) in the list above with the point (−*x*, −*y*).

   c. Follow your new instructions to plot figure *G* on the same set of axes.

   d. Describe how figures *F* and *G* are related to each other.

13. Think of figures *F* and *G* from Exercise 12 together as a single figure *O*. What kind of symmetry does figure *O* have?

14. a. Follow the instructions to plot figure *F* again on a new set of axes.

   b. Make a new list of instructions by replacing each point (*x*, *y*) in the list with the point (−*x*, *y*).

   c. Follow your new instructions to plot figure *H* on the same set of axes.

   d. Describe how figures *F* and *H* are related to each other.

15. Think of figures *F* and *H* from Exercise 14 together as a single figure *E*. What kind of symmetry does figure *E* have?

16. Sketch each graph.

   a. $y = x^2$ **b.** $y = x^2 + 7$

   c. $y = x^2 - 3$ **d.** $y = x^2 - 10$

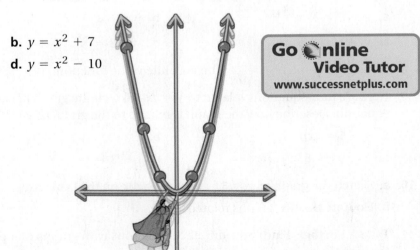

Go Online
Video Tutor
www.successnetplus.com

17. Write About It Describe the relationship between the graphs of $y = x^2$ and $y = x^2 + C$ for any number C.

18. Sketch each graph.

a. $y = |x|$

b. $y = |x| + 7$

c. $y = |x| - 3$

d. $y = |x| - 10$

19. Write About It Describe the relationship between the graphs of $y = |x|$ and $y = |x| + C$ for any number C.

20. Here are four equations related to $y = 3^x$. Sketch the graph of each equation. Describe how the graph is related to the graph of $y = 3^x$.

a. $y + 5 = 3^x$

b. $y = 3^{x+5}$

c. $y = 3^x + 5$

d. $y - 3 = 3^{x+2}$

21. a. Sketch the graph of $y = \frac{1}{x}$.

b. Explain why the graph never intersects the x-axis or the y-axis.

22. Here are four equations related to $y = \frac{1}{x}$. Sketch the graph of each equation. Describe how the graph is related to the graph of $y = \frac{1}{x}$.

a. $y + 5 = \frac{1}{x}$

b. $y = \frac{1}{x + 5}$

c. $y = \frac{1}{x} + 5$

d. $y - 3 = \frac{1}{x + 2}$

23. Plot all the points on the xy-plane that are exactly 1 unit from the origin.

> You use the capital letter C here to show that C is a parameter rather than one of the variables you are graphing with. It is a value that you can change to produce different graphs. The idea is to see how different values of C change the graph.

Maintain Your Skills

24. Find the solutions to each equation.

a. $5x - 7 = 2x + 5$

b. $5 \cdot \frac{x}{3} - 7 = 2 \cdot \frac{x}{3} + 5$

c. $5 \cdot \frac{x}{10} - 7 = 2 \cdot \frac{x}{10} + 5$

d. $5 \cdot \frac{x}{100} - 7 = 2 \cdot \frac{x}{100} + 5$

25. Describe what happens to the solutions of an equation when you replace the variable x with $\frac{x}{C}$.

4.15 More Basic Graphs

You have worked with the graphs of the following equations before, in this course or in your first-year algebra course.

- $y = x$

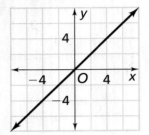

- $y = \frac{1}{x}$

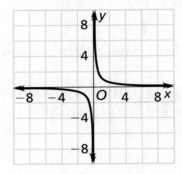

- $y = x^2$

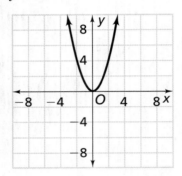

- $y = x^3$

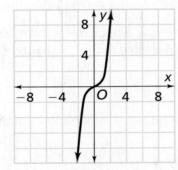

- $y = \sqrt{x}$

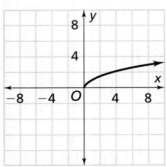

- $y = |x|$

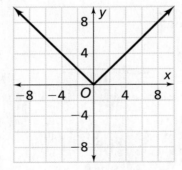

- $y = 3^x$

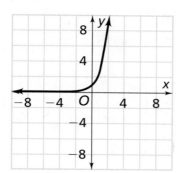

- $y = \log_3 x$

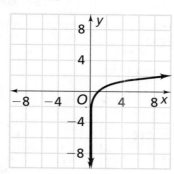

Any graph of $y = b^x$ with $b > 1$ looks similar to the graph of $y = 3^x$. Any graph of $y = \log_b x$ with $b > 1$ looks similar to the graph of $y = \log_3 x$.

You saw in the Getting Started lesson how, by changing these equations slightly, you can translate—move up, down, left, or right—the corresponding graphs without changing their shapes. In this lesson, you will learn three new basic graphs, namely the graphs of the equations $x^2 + y^2 = 1$ and $y = x^3 \pm x$.

Graphing $x^2 + y^2 = 1$

The graph of the equation $x^2 + y^2 = 1$ is a shape you are familiar with.

The notation $y = x^3 \pm x$ really refers to two different equations: $y = x^3 + x$ and $y = x^3 - x$.

Minds in Action

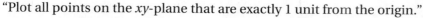

Tony and Sasha are working on Exercise 23 from Lesson 4.14.

"Plot all points on the xy-plane that are exactly 1 unit from the origin."

Tony   Well, there are four obvious ones: $(1, 0)$, $(-1, 0)$, $(0, 1)$, and $(0, -1)$.

Sasha   Is there a point that has x-coordinate $\frac{1}{2}$?

Tony   Well, we would write it $\left(\frac{1}{2}, b \right)$. Then we need to find b. And we want its distance to $(0, 0)$ to be 1. What was the distance formula again?

Sasha   The distance between the points (x_1, y_1) and (x_2, y_2) is
$$d = \sqrt{(x_1 - x_2)^2 + (y_1 - y_2)^2}$$

Tony   Right. So we want
$$\sqrt{\left(\frac{1}{2} - 0 \right)^2 + (b - 0)^2} = 1$$

We can get rid of the square root by squaring both sides. So we get
$$\frac{1}{4} + b^2 = 1$$

If we solve for b, we get
$$b^2 = \frac{3}{4}$$
$$b = \frac{\sqrt{3}}{2}$$

Sasha   Don't forget the negative root.

Tony   Oh, right. Thanks. So b is either $\frac{\sqrt{3}}{2}$ or $-\frac{\sqrt{3}}{2}$. Let's see, my calculator says $\frac{\sqrt{3}}{2}$ is about 0.866. So we get two points, $(0.5, 0.866)$ and $(0.5, -0.866)$.

Tony plots the six points they have found so far.

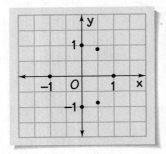

Sasha   Hey, shouldn't we also have $(-0.5, 0.866)$ and $(-0.5, -0.866)$ in there?

Tony   That makes sense. This picture should be symmetric. So we can also plot $(0.866, 0.5)$, $(0.866, -0.5)$, $(-0.866, 0.5)$, and $(-0.866, -0.5)$, right?

Sasha   Yeah, that sounds good.

Sasha plots the six new points.

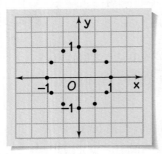

Sasha   Hey, it looks like a circle!

Suppose (a, b) is a point on the xy-plane that is exactly 1 unit from the origin. You can write this statement in symbols, using the distance formula.

$$\sqrt{(a - 0)^2 + (b - 0)^2} = 1$$

Square both sides and simplify.

$$a^2 + b^2 = 1$$

In other words, the point (a, b) satisfies the equation $x^2 + y^2 = 1$. Conversely, any point (a, b) that satisfies the equation $x^2 + y^2 = 1$ must be exactly 1 unit away from the origin. Therefore, you have just shown that the graph of the equation below is the unit circle.

$$x^2 + y^2 = 1$$

One such point is $\left(\frac{1}{2}, \frac{\sqrt{3}}{2}\right)$.

The **unit circle** is a circle of radius 1, centered at the origin.

For You to Do

1. Verify that $\left(\frac{3}{5}, \frac{4}{5}\right)$ is a point on the unit circle.

2. Using the point $\left(\frac{3}{5}, \frac{4}{5}\right)$, find as many other points on the unit circle as you can.

Using the distance formula, you can find an equation of a circle with any center and radius.

Example

Problem

a. Write an equation that describes the set of points that are exactly 1 unit away from $(3, -4)$, and sketch its graph.

b. Write an equation of the circle centered at the origin with radius r.

Solution

a. Using the distance formula as before, you know a point (a, b) is 1 unit away from $(3, -4)$ when

$$\sqrt{(a - 3)^2 + (b - (-4))^2} = 1$$

Square both sides and simplify.

$$(a - 3)^2 + (b + 4)^2 = 1$$

In other words, the desired equation is

$$(x - 3)^2 + (y + 4)^2 = 1$$

The graph is a circle of radius 1, centered at $(3, -4)$.

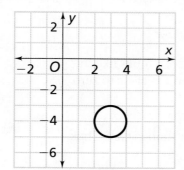

b. A point (a, b) is on a circle centered at the origin when it is r units away from the origin. In symbols,

$$\sqrt{(a - 0)^2 + (b - 0)^2} = r$$

Square both sides and simplify.

$$a^2 + b^2 = r^2$$

In other words, the desired equation is

$$x^2 + y^2 = r^2$$

For Discussion

3. If you square both sides of the equation $x = 3$, you introduce solutions that do not satisfy $x = 3$. So, $x^2 = 9$ and $x = 3$ are not equivalent equations.

   Explain why the following two equations are equivalent.
   $$\sqrt{(a-3)^2 + (b+4)^2} = 1 \text{ and } (a-3)^2 + (b+4)^2 = 1$$

The Equation $y = x^3 + x$

Here is the graph of the equation $y = x^3 + x$.

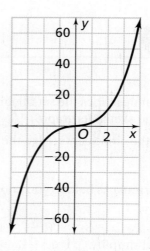

Zoom in on this graph near the origin.

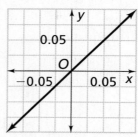

It looks like a straight line with slope 1. In other words, it looks like the graph of $y = x$. Why does it look that way? Well, when x is close to zero, say $x = 0.1$, you have

$$x^3 = (0.1)^3 = 0.001$$

This is very small. Most important, it is much smaller than x itself. Thus, you get

$$\begin{aligned} x^3 + x &= 0.001 + 0.1 \\ &= 0.101 \\ &\approx 0.1 \\ &\approx x \end{aligned}$$

In other words, when x is close to zero, you have

$$x^3 + x \approx x$$

And so the graph of $y = x^3 + x$ looks like the graph of $y = x$ near the origin.

> You could also say that when x is small, the term x^3 becomes *negligible* in the expression $x^3 + x$.

For Discussion

4. Explain why the graph of $y = x^3 + x$ starts to look like the graph of $y = x^3$ far away from the origin, as shown below.

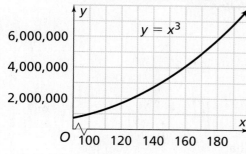

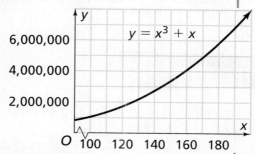

Here is a graph of $y = x^3 - x$.

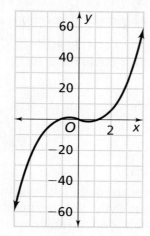

Again, zoom in near the origin.

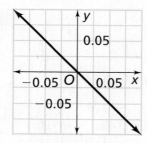

It looks like the graph of $y = -x$. And far away from the origin, the graph of $y = x^3 - x$ starts to resemble the graph of $y = x^3$, as shown below.

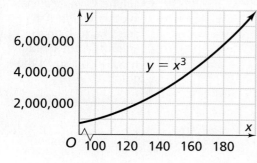

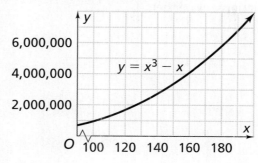

Exercises *Practicing Habits of Mind*

Check Your Understanding

1. **a.** Find all points on the graph of $x^2 + y^2 = 1$ with x-coordinates equal to $\frac{4}{5}$.

   b. Using the point or points you found in part (a), find as many other points on the unit circle as you can.

2. **a.** Find all points on the graph of $x^2 + y^2 = 1$ with y-coordinates equal to $\frac{5}{13}$.

   b. Find all points on the graph of $x^2 + y^2 = 1$ with x-coordinates equal to $\frac{8}{17}$.

3. Mariko writes down some points on the unit circle with rational coordinates.

   Mariko says, "Let's see, so far I've found

   $$\left(\tfrac{3}{5}, \tfrac{4}{5}\right), \left(\tfrac{12}{13}, \tfrac{5}{13}\right), \left(\tfrac{8}{17}, \tfrac{15}{17}\right)$$

   I've also found all the points I could get from these using the symmetry of the circle. Wait, I recognize those numbers. They're Pythagorean triples! So we can use Pythagorean triples to find rational points on the unit circle."

   What does Mariko mean? Explain.

   > Here are some other Pythagorean triples.
   > - 7, 24, and 25
   > - 9, 40, and 41
   > - 20, 21, and 29

4. Let $f(x) = x^2$.

   a. Show that f is an **even function** by showing that $f(-x) = f(x)$.

   b. Show that f is an even function using the graph of $y = x^2$.

5. Let $f(x) = x^3 + x$.

   a. Show that f is an odd function by showing that $f(-x) = -f(x)$.

   b. Show that f is an odd function by using the graph of $y = x^3 + x$.

   > A function f is an **odd function** if it satisfies $f(-x) = -f(x)$ for all numbers x in its domain. In other words, if a point (x, y) is on the graph of f, the point $(-x, -y)$ is also on the graph.

6. Classify all of the basic graphs shown in this lesson as graphs of odd functions, even functions, or neither.

7. Explain why the graph of $y = x^3 + x$ has no x-intercept other than the origin.

Remember...

An intercept is a point where a graph intersects one of the axes.

8. **a.** Copy and complete the following table.

x	$x - 3$	$(x - 3)^2$
−1	■	■
0	■	■
1	■	■
2	■	■
3	■	■
4	■	■
5	■	■
6	■	■
7	■	■

   b. Using the table from part (a), sketch the graph of $y = (x - 3)^2$.

   c. How are the graphs of $y = x^2$ and $y = (x - 3)^2$ related?

On Your Own

9. Let $g(x) = x^3 - x$.

   a. Show that g is an odd function by showing that $g(-x) = -g(x)$.

   b. Show that g is an odd function by using the graph of $y = x^3 - x$.

10. **a.** Explain why the graph of $y = x^3 - x$ resembles the graph of $y = -x$ near the origin.

   b. Explain why the graph of $y = x^3 - x$ resembles the graph of $y = x^3$ far away from the origin.

11. Find the x-intercepts of the graph of $y = x^3 - x$.

12. **a.** Sketch the graph of $y = (x - 3)^3 - (x - 3)$.

   b. Find the x-intercepts of the graph of $y = (x - 3)^3 - (x - 3)$.

   c. How are the graphs of $y = x^3 - x$ and $y = (x - 3)^3 - (x - 3)$ related?

13. Write an equation for a circle with radius 5, centered at the origin.

14. Write an equation of a circle with radius 5, centered at the point (3, 0).

Go Online
www.successnetplus.com

15. Serge takes the following approach to Exercise 14.

Serge says, "Let's see, in Exercise 13, I found an equation of a circle with radius 5, centered at the origin. It was $x^2 + y^2 = 25$.

"Now they're asking for the same circle translated three units to the right. Wait, this is just like the way the graphs of $y = x^2$ and $y = (x - 3)^2$ in Exercise 8 are related! So the equation of the new circle must be $(x - 3)^2 + y^2 = 25$."

Use Serge's method to find an equation of each circle.

a. radius 5, center at $(6, 0)$　　　　**b.** radius 4, center at $(-3, 0)$

c. radius 1, center at $(0, -4)$　　　　**d.** radius 1, center at $(3, -4)$

e. radius 3, center at $(-2, 3)$　　　　**f.** radius r, center at (a, b)

16. Take It Further Sketch the graph of $(3x)^2 + y^2 = 1$. How is this graph related to the graph of $x^2 + y^2 = 1$?

17. Standardized Test Prep Which translation transforms the graph of $y = x^3 + x$ into the graph of $y = (x - 2)^3 + (x - 2)$?

A. 2 units up　　　**B.** 2 units down　　　**C.** 2 units left　　　**D.** 2 units right

Maintain Your Skills

18. Find the solutions to each equation.

a. $x^2 + 5x - 14 = 0$

b. $(x - 3)^2 + 5(x - 3) - 14 = 0$

c. $(x - 5)^2 + 5(x - 5) - 14 = 0$

d. $(x + 2)^2 + 5(x + 2) - 14 = 0$

19. Describe what happens to the solutions of an equation when the variable x is replaced by $x - C$.

Which of the equations $y = \pm x^3$ and $y = x^3 \pm x$ has a graph that resembles this water slide near the origin?

4.16 Translating Graphs

Recall the lumping method of factoring. You can also use the lumping technique to help you graph equations.

Minds in Action

Sasha and Derman are trying to graph the equation $y = (x - 3)^2$.

Derman The equation $y = (x - 3)^2$ looks a lot like $y = x^2$. If I just cover the $x - 3$ part with my hand, it's easier, it is

$$y = M^2$$

Sasha That's pretty neat! And $y = M^2$ is one of the basic graphs we've already seen. Let me start with a table first.

M	y
−3	9
−2	4
−1	1
0	0
1	1
2	4
3	9

Derman Oh, I can graph that . . .

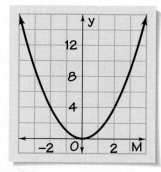

Are we done? I just graphed $y = M^2$, and since $M = x - 3$, is this the graph of $y = (x - 3)^2$?

Sasha Not quite. This is the graph of y against M. For example, the point $(2, 4)$ is on this graph, because when $M = 2$, we have $y = 4$. But what we need is a graph of y against x.

Derman Oh . . . When $x = 2$, we have $y = (2 - 3)^2 = 1$, but the point $(2, 1)$ is not on this graph. So what can we do?

Sasha Well, since $M = x - 3$, we can solve for x and get

$$x = M + 3$$

Let me write this in our table.

Sasha includes a new column of x-values in the table.

$x = M + 3$	M	y
0	−3	9
1	−2	4
2	−1	1
3	0	0
4	1	1
5	2	4
6	3	9

Derman The table has $(2, 1)$ in it! Cool.

Sasha Now we can just ignore the middle column and plot the points (x, y).

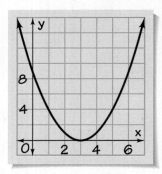

Derman It's the same graph as the graph of $y = M^2$, shifted three units to the right!

Sasha It makes sense, doesn't it? Since $x = M + 3$, the x-values just get shifted to the right by three. For example, the point $(-3, 9)$ on the graph of $y = M^2$ matches up with the point $(0, 9)$ on the graph of $y = (x - 3)^2$.

For Discussion

1. How are the graphs of $y = x^2$ and $y = (x + 5)^2$ related? Explain.

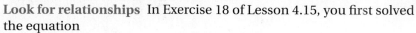

Developing Habits of Mind

Look for relationships In Exercise 18 of Lesson 4.15, you first solved the equation

$$x^2 + 5x - 14 = 0$$

The solutions are $x = -7$ and $x = 2$.

Next, you had to solve

$$(x - 3)^2 + 5(x - 3) - 14 = 0$$

An efficient way of solving this equation is to make the substitution $M = x - 3$. Then you get

$$M^2 + 5M - 14 = 0$$

Its solutions are $M = -7$ and $M = 2$. And since $x = M + 3$, you add three to each solution to get

> Why does $x = M + 3$?

$$x = -4 \text{ and } x = 5$$

You can use the same idea to graph the equation $y = (x - 3)^2$. First make the substitution $M = x - 3$ so that $y = M^2$. Any point (M, y) that satisfies $y = M^2$ corresponds to a point (x, y) that satisfies $y = (x - 3)^2$. You can find the corresponding point by sending M to $x = M + 3$. For example, you translate the point $(-3, 9)$ on the graph of $y = M^2$ three units to the right to the point $(0, 9)$ on the graph of $y = (x - 3)^2$.

Similarly, you can translate graphs vertically (up or down) by making substitutions such as $N = y + 4$. Here are two examples.

Example

Problem Sketch the graph of each equation.

a. $x^2 + (y + 4)^2 = 1$

b. $y = (x - 3)^2 - 4$

Solution

a. With the substitution $N = y + 4$, this equation becomes

$$x^2 + N^2 = 1$$

The graph of this equation is the unit circle, which is a circle of radius 1 centered at the origin. The table at the right shows some points on the unit circle.

x	N
1	0
−1	0
0	1
0	−1

Since $N = y + 4$, solving for y gives

$$y = N - 4$$

Now, include a column of y-values in the table.

x	N	y = N − 4
1	0	−4
−1	0	−4
0	1	−3
0	−1	−5

Ignore the middle column and plot the points (x, y).

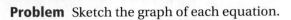

Use these points as the "corner points" of the new circle.

This is the unit circle, translated four units down. The key here is that since $y = N - 4$, you shift the y-values down by four.

b. You can rewrite this equation as

$$(y + 4) = (x - 3)^2$$

With the substitution $N = y + 4$, the equation becomes

$$N = (x - 3)^2$$

The graph of this equation is the same as the graph of $N = x^2$, just translated three units to the right.

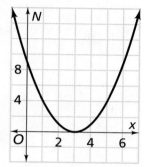

Since $N = y + 4$, solving for y gives $y = N - 4$. Therefore, the graph of $(y + 4) = (x - 3)^2$ is the same as the graph of $N = (x - 3)^2$, shifted down by four units.

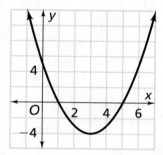

Or, you can compare these two expressions.

$$(x - 3)^2 \text{ and } (x - 3)^2 - 4$$

For each input x, the output $y = (x - 3)^2 - 4$ is four less than the output $y = (x - 3)^2$. So you can get the graph of the equation $y = (x - 3)^2 - 4$ by shifting the graph of $y = (x - 3)^2$ down by four units.

You can roll coins together in order to exchange them for bills.

Exercises Practicing Habits of Mind

Check Your Understanding

1. Consider the equation $y = \sqrt{x + 5}$. Let $M = x + 5$.

   a. Copy and complete the following table.

$x = M - 5$	M	$y = \sqrt{M}$
▨	0	▨
▨	1	▨
▨	4	▨
▨	9	▨
▨	16	▨
▨	25	▨

   b. Using the table from part (a), explain how the graphs of $y = \sqrt{x}$ and $y = \sqrt{x + 5}$ are related.

   c. Sketch the graph of $y = \sqrt{x + 5}$. According to the graph, what are the domain and the range of the function defined by $f(x) = \sqrt{x + 5}$?

2. Sketch the graph of each equation.

   a. $y = |x + 2|$

   b. $(x + 2)^2 + y^2 = 25$

   c. $(y - 3) = \log x$

   d. $y = \frac{1}{x} + 3$

3. Sketch the graph of each equation.

   a. $(y + 1) = |x + 2|$

   b. $(x + 2)^2 + (y - 4)^2 = 25$

   c. $y = \log(x - 5) + 3$

   d. $(x - 2)(y - 3) = 1$

4. **What's Wrong Here?** Walter is working on the following problem. The graph below is a graph of $y = x^3 - x$ translated two units to the right. Find its equation.

   Walter says, "Since it's two units to the right, I should replace x^3 with $(x - 2)^3$. So the equation I want is $y = (x - 2)^3 - x$."

   Do you agree or disagree with Walter? Explain.

   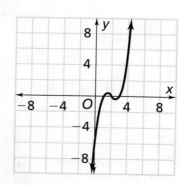

5. a. Explain how the graphs of the following equations are related.

- $y = x^3 + 6x^2 + 11x + 7$
- $y = (x - 2)^3 + 6(x - 2)^2 + 11(x - 2) + 7$

b. Expand $(x - 2)^3 + 6(x - 2)^2 + 11(x - 2) + 7$.

c. Using parts (a) and (b), sketch the graph of $y = x^3 + 6x^2 + 11x + 7$.

6. a. Find the coordinates of the vertex of the parabola with equation $y = (x + 3)^2$.

b. Find the coordinates of the vertex of the parabola with equation $y - 2 = (x + 3)^2$.

c. In terms of h and k, find the coordinates of the vertex of the parabola with equation $y = (x + h)^2 + k$.

7. Sketch the graph of each equation.

a. $y = x^2 + 6x + 9$ **b.** $y = x^2 + 6x + 7$

On Your Own

8. Sketch the graph of each equation.

a. $y = (x - 2)^3 + (x - 2)$

b. $y + 1 = (x - 2)^3 + (x - 2)$

c. $y = (x - 2)^3 + x - 3$

d. Take It Further $y = x^3 - 6x^2 + 13x - 11$

9. Sketch the graph of each equation. Then find the slope of the graph.

a. $y = 3x$

b. $y = 3(x - 2)$

c. $y - 5 = 3(x - 2)$

d. How are the graphs in parts (a), (b), and (c) related? Explain.

10. a. Sketch the graph of $y = \frac{1}{2}x$.

b. Translate the graph of $y = \frac{1}{2}x$ three units to the right so that the origin $(0, 0)$ maps to the point $(3, 0)$ in the translated image. Find the equation of this new line.

c. Translate the graph of $y = \frac{1}{2}x$ three units to the right and one unit up so that the origin $(0, 0)$ maps to the point $(3, 1)$ in the translated image. Find the equation of this new line.

Go Online
www.successnetplus.com

11. **a.** Find an equation of the line with slope 4 that passes through the point $(3, 1)$.

    b. Find an equation of the line with slope $\frac{2}{3}$ that passes through the point $(-2, -1)$.

    c. Find an equation of the line with slope m that passes through the point (h, k).

12. The graph of the equation $y = x^2 + 6x + 7$ is a parabola with vertex at $(-3, -2)$.

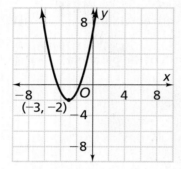

    a. How are the graphs of $y = x^2 + 6x + 7$ and $y = (x - 3)^2 + 6(x - 3) + 7$ related? Explain.

    b. How are the graphs of $y = (x - 3)^2 + 6(x - 3) + 7$ and $y - 2 = (x - 3)^2 + 6(x - 3) + 7$ related? Explain.

    c. Simplify the expression below as much as possible.

$$y - 2 = (x - 3)^2 + 6(x - 3) + 7$$

13. **What's Wrong Here?** Susan is working on Exercise 11.

Susan says, "Let's see, I need a line with slope 4 that passes through the point $(3, 1)$. I can certainly start with $y = 4x$ and translate it to the right three and up one, so that the origin goes to $(3, 1)$. That gives me

$$y - 1 = 4(x - 3)$$

"But I can also take the point $(1, 4)$ on the graph of $y = 4x$ and move that to the point $(3, 1)$. That would mean translating the graph of $y = 4x$ to the right two and down 3, which gives me

$$y + 3 = 4(x - 2)$$

"I get two different answers. So this must mean there are at least two different lines with slope 4 that pass through the point $(3, 1)$."

Do you agree or disagree with Susan? Explain.

14. Take It Further Derman is thinking about the graph of $y = (x - 3)^2$ again.

Derman thinks, "Instead of translating the graph of $y = x^2$ three units to the right, I can just keep it where it is and shift the coordinate axes three units to the left."

This figure shows the original axes in green and Derman's new axes in purple.

Use the substitution $M = x - 3$ to explain why Derman's method is valid.

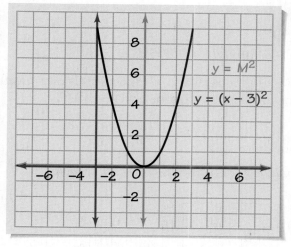

15. Standardized Test Prep Which equation has a graph that is a parabola with vertex at $(-1, -2)$?

A. $(y - 2) = (x - 1)^2$

B. $(y + 1) = (x - 2)^2$

C. $y = (x - 2)^2 + 1$

D. $y = (x + 1)^2 - 2$

Maintain Your Skills

16. a. Sketch the graphs of $y = 3^x$ and $y = \log_3 x$. How are the graphs related? Explain why they are related in this way.

Sketch the graphs of each equation. Explain how the graphs for each pair of equations are related to the graphs of $y = 3^x$ and $y = \log_3 x$, respectively. Then explain how the graphs of the two equations are related to each other.

b. $y = 3 \cdot 3^x$ and $y = \log_3 \frac{x}{3}$

c. $y = 9 \cdot 3^x$ and $y = \log_3 \frac{x}{9}$

d. $y = 27 \cdot 3^x$ and $y = \log_3 \frac{x}{27}$

e. $y = 3^n \cdot 3^x$ and $y = \log_3 \frac{x}{3^n}$, for a fixed positive integer n

Habits of Mind

Experiment. What do you find if n is negative?

4.17 Scaling and Reflecting Graphs

This lesson explores how to change an equation to resize its graph along either axis or reflect its graph over an axis.

Minds in Action

Sasha and Derman are trying to graph the equation $y = \left(\frac{x}{3}\right)^2$.

Sasha The equation $y = \left(\frac{x}{3}\right)^2$ looks like $y = x^2$ to me. If I cover $\frac{x}{3}$ with my hand like you did last time, this looks like $y = M^2 \ldots$

This time $M = \frac{x}{3}$.

Derman We know this one pretty well.

Derman finds the table and the graph of $y = M^2$ *in his notebook.*

M	y
−3	9
−2	4
−1	1
0	0
1	1
2	4
3	9

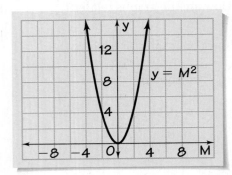

Sasha   Great. Now, since $M = \frac{x}{3}$, solving for x gives us

$$x = 3M$$

Can you include this in your table?

Derman adds a column of x-values to his table.

x = 3M	M	y
−9	−3	9
−6	−2	4
−3	−1	1
0	0	0
3	1	1
6	2	4
9	3	9

Derman Oh, I can ignore the middle column and plot the points (x, y).

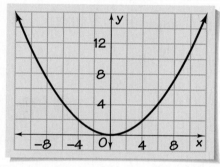

Sasha   It looks just like the graph of $y = M^2$, stretched horizontally by a factor of 3.

Derman It makes sense to me. The x-values got tripled. $(2, 4)$ on the graph of $y = M^2$ became $(6, 4)$ on the new graph.

For You to Do

1. How are the graphs of $y = x^2$ and $y = \left(\frac{x}{5}\right)^2$ related?

2. How are the graphs of $y = x^2$ and $y = (5x)^2$ related?

Habits of Mind

Visualize. If $x = 3M$, each jump of one space in M corresponds to a jump of three spaces in x. If you look at a set of points on a graph that are all one unit apart in M, they are three units apart in x.

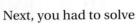
Look for relationships. In Exercise 24 of Lesson 4.14, you solved the equation $5x - 7 = 2x + 5$. The solution is $x = 4$.

Next, you had to solve

$$5 \cdot \frac{x}{3} - 7 = 2 \cdot \frac{x}{3} + 5$$

You can solve this equation by making the substitution $M = \frac{x}{3}$.

$$5M - 7 = 2M + 5$$

The solution to this equation must be $M = 4$. But, since $x = 3M$,

$$x = 3(4) = 12$$

You can also use this idea to graph the equation $y = \left(\frac{x}{3}\right)^2$. Make the substitution $M = \frac{x}{3}$ to get the equation $y = M^2$. And by sending M to $x = 3M$, we find any point (M, y) on the graph of $y = M^2$ corresponds to a point (x, y) on the graph of $y = \left(\frac{x}{3}\right)^2$. For example, the point $(-1, 1)$ that is on the graph of $y = M^2$ gets scaled horizontally by the factor of 3 to the point $(-3, 1)$ on the graph of $y = \left(\frac{x}{3}\right)^2$.

You can use the same substitution technique when dealing with a reflection.

Example 1

Problem Sketch the graph of $y = 2^{-x}$.

Solution With the substitution $M = -x$, this equation becomes

$$y = 2^M$$

Here are the table and graph of this exponential function.

M	y
−3	$\frac{1}{8}$
−2	$\frac{1}{4}$
−1	$\frac{1}{2}$
0	1
1	2
2	4
3	8

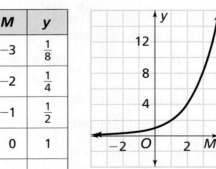

Since $M = -x$, solving for x gives

$$x = -M$$

Now, include a column of x-values in the table.

$x = -M$	M	y
3	−3	$\frac{1}{8}$
2	−2	$\frac{1}{4}$
1	−1	$\frac{1}{2}$
0	0	1
−1	1	2
−2	2	4
−3	3	8

Ignore the middle column and plot the points (x, y).

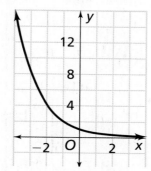

This graph is the same as the graph of $y = 2^M$ reflected over the y-axis. In other words, a point (M, y) on the graph of $y = 2^M$ corresponds to a point (x, y) on the graph of $y = 2^{-x}$, where $x = -M$.

You could also rewrite the equation.

$$y = 2^{-x} = \left(\frac{1}{2}\right)^x$$

Then you could use a relationship that you discovered previously: the graph of $y = \left(\frac{1}{n}\right)^x$ is the reflection over the y-axis of the graph of $y = n^x$.

Similarly, you can scale graphs vertically, or reflect them over the *x*-axis, by making substitutions such as $N = -2y$.

Example 2

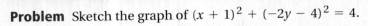

Problem Sketch the graph of $(x + 1)^2 + (-2y - 4)^2 = 4$.

Solution With the substitution $N = -2y$, this equation becomes

$$(x + 1)^2 + (N - 4)^2 = 4$$

This is a circle of radius 2 with the center at the point $(-1, 4)$. Here is its graph and a table showing some of its points.

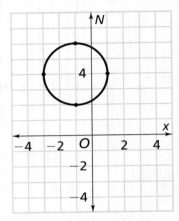

x	N
1	4
−3	4
−1	6
−1	2

Since $N = -2y$, solving for *y* gives

$$y = -\frac{N}{2}$$

Now, include a column of *y*-values in the table.

x	N	$y = -\dfrac{N}{2}$
1	4	−2
−3	4	−2
−1	6	−3
−1	2	−1

Ignore the middle column and plot the points (x, y).

To get this new graph, reflect the original circle over the *x*-axis and then scale it vertically by a factor of $\frac{1}{2}$. Algebraically, this corresponds to the fact that $y = -\frac{N}{2}$.

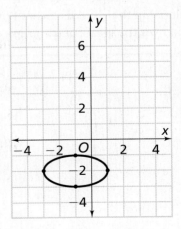

Habits of Mind

Experiment. Could you scale first and then reflect? Does it matter? Explain why or why not.

Check Your Understanding

1. Consider the equation $5y = x^2 + 1$.
   Let $N = 5y$.

   a. Copy and complete the
   following table.

   b. Using the table from part (a),
   explain how the graphs of
   $y = x^2 + 1$ and $5y = x^2 + 1$
   are related.

   c. Sketch the graph of $5y = x^2 + 1$.

x	$N = x^2 + 1$	$y = \dfrac{N}{5}$
-2	▦	▦
-1	▦	▦
0	▦	▦
1	▦	▦
2	▦	▦
3	▦	▦

2. Sketch the graph of each equation.

   a. $x^2 + y^2 = 36$
   b. $(2x)^2 + y^2 = 36$
   c. $x^2 + (3y)^2 = 36$
   d. $(2x)^2 + (3y)^2 = 36$
   e. $\left(\dfrac{x}{2}\right)^2 + \left(\dfrac{y}{3}\right)^2 = 36$

3. For each function f, sketch the graph of $y = f(x)$. Find the domain
   and range.

   a. $f(x) = -\sqrt{x}$
   b. $f(x) = -3\sqrt{x}$
   c. $f(x) = \sqrt{-3x}$
   d. $f(x) = \sqrt{1 - x}$

4. This figure shows the basic
   graph of $y = x^2$ and the graph of
   another parabola.

   The second parabola is the image of the
   basic graph after a horizontal scaling by
   a factor of 2 and a translation of 3 units
   up and 4 units to the right. What is an
   equation for the second parabola?

> For help graphing
> an equation in two
> variables, see the
> TI-Nspire Handbook,
> p. 990.

> *Hint:*
> $1 - x = -(x - 1)$.

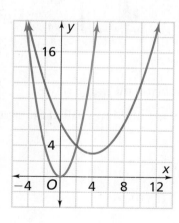

5. Sketch the graph of each equation.

   a. $y = (-x)^2$ **b.** $y = |-x|$ **c.** $(-x)^2 + y^2 = 1$

6. Tony and Sasha are arguing about the definition of an even function.

   Tony says, "A function f is even if it has the property that $f(-x) = f(x)$ for all x in its domain."

   Sasha says, "No, no. A function f is even if it looks the same when you reflect it over the y-axis."

   Do you agree with Sasha or with Tony? Explain.

7. Explain how you can tell *without graphing* that the graph of $y = x^8 + 37x^6 - 71x^2 + 4$ looks the same when you reflect it over the y-axis.

8. **Take It Further** Given any function $f(x)$, explain why the function defined by $g(x) = f(x) + f(-x)$ looks the same when you reflect it over the y-axis.

9. Copy this graph of $x + y = 1$.

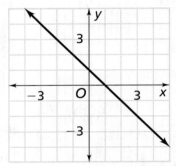

   a. Sketch the graph of $\frac{x}{5} + \frac{y}{3} = 1$.

   b. Sketch the graph of $\frac{x}{3} + \frac{y}{7} = 1$.

   c. Find two points that must be on the graph of $\frac{x}{-17} + \frac{y}{12} = 1$.

   d. The equation $\frac{x}{a} + \frac{y}{b} = 1$ is sometimes called the two-intercept form of a line. Explain.

Habits of Mind

Detect the key characteristics. Does every line have an equation of this form?

On Your Own

10. Sketch the graph of each equation.

    a. $y = (-x)^3 + (-x)$ **b.** $y = (-x)^3 - (-x)$ **c.** $y = -x^3 - x$

    d. $y = -x^3 + x$ **e.** $-y = (-x)^3 + (-x)$ **f.** $-y = (-x)^3 - (-x)$

11. Describe how the graph of each equation is related to the graph of $y = \frac{1}{x}$.

 a. $y = \frac{1}{-x}$ b. $y = \frac{1}{-4x}$ c. $y = \frac{4}{-x}$ d. $-y = \frac{1}{x}$

 e. $-4y = \frac{1}{x}$ f. $-\frac{y}{4} = \frac{1}{x}$ g. $-y = \frac{1}{-x}$ h. $-\frac{y}{4} = \frac{1}{-4x}$

12. This time, Tony, Sasha, and Derman are all arguing about odd functions.

   Tony says, "A function f is odd if it has the property that $f(-x) = -f(x)$ for all x in its domain."

   Sasha says, "No, no. A function f is odd if its reflection over the y-axis and its reflection over the x-axis look the same."

   Derman says, "I always thought that f was odd if rotating its graph $180°$ around the origin gave you a graph that looked the same as the original."

   Do you agree with Tony, Sasha, or Derman? Explain.

13. Explain how the graphs of the following equations are related.

   • $(x + 3)^2 + (y - 4)^2 = 1$
   • $(-x + 3)^2 + (-y - 4)^2 = 1$

14. Sketch the graph of each equation.

   a. $(3x)^2 + (2y)^2 = 36$
   b. $(3(x + 1))^2 + (2(y - 4))^2 = 36$
   c. $\dfrac{(x + 1)^2}{4} + \dfrac{(y - 4)^2}{9} = 1$

15. **Standardized Test Prep** Which equation can you use to graph the reflection of the graph of $y = \sqrt{x - 2} + 3$ over the y-axis?

   A. $y = \sqrt{x + 2} - 3$ B. $y = \sqrt{x - 2} - 3$

   C. $y = \sqrt{-x - 2} + 3$ D. $y = \sqrt{-x + 2} + 3$

16. **Write About It** Consider the equation $y = mx$. Its graph is a straight line through the origin. As the slope m increases, the line becomes more steep. On the other hand, you can rewrite the equation as

   $$\frac{y}{m} = x$$

   Looking at it this way, you can say that as m increases, the line gets scaled vertically.

   Are these two ways of visualizing this situation geometrically consistent with each other? Explain.

Go Online
www.successnetplus.com

17. Take It Further

    a. Explain how the graphs of the following equations are related.

       • $y = x^3 + 3x^2 + 7x + 13$

       • $y = (x - 1)^3 + 3(x - 1)^2 + 7(x - 1) + 13$

    b. Expand $(x - 1)^3 + 3(x - 1)^2 + 7(x - 1) + 13$.

    c. If you divide the equation $y = x^3 + 4x + 8$ by 8, you get

$$\tfrac{1}{8}y = \left(\tfrac{1}{2}x\right)^3 + \left(\tfrac{1}{2}x\right) + 1$$

    Use the second equation to explain how the graph of $y = x^3 + 4x + 8$ is related to the graph of $y = x^3 + x + 1$.

    d. Sketch the graph of $y = x^3 + x + 1$.

    e. Use parts (a)–(d) to sketch the graph of $y = x^3 + 3x^2 + 7x + 13$.

18. Take It Further At home, Derman is thinking about the graph of $y = \left(\tfrac{x}{3}\right)^2$ again.

Derman thinks, "Instead of scaling the graph of $y = x^2$ horizontally by the factor of 3, I can just keep it where it is and scale the x-axis instead by the factor of $\tfrac{1}{3}$."

This figure shows the original axes in green and Derman's new axes in purple.

> If the scale factor is greater than 1, the object stretches. If the scale factor is less than 1, the object shrinks.

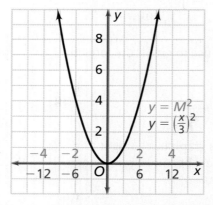

Use the substitution $M = \tfrac{x}{3}$ to explain why Derman's method is valid.

Maintain Your Skills

19. Determine whether each function is even, odd, or neither.

    a. $f(x) = x^2$ **b.** $f(x) = x^3$ **c.** $f(x) = x^4$ **d.** $f(x) = x^5$

    e. $f(x) = x^{10}$ **f.** $f(x) = x^{-1}$ **g.** $f(x) = x^n$, where n is an integer

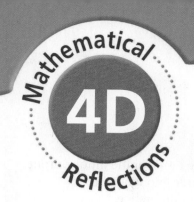

In this investigation, you sketched basic graphs. You learned to relate the effects on a basic graph and on the equation of the graph of a translation, a scaling, or a reflection of the graph. These exercises will help you summarize what you have learned.

1. **a.** Explain what it means for a function to be even, both algebraically and graphically, and give an example of an even function.

   b. Explain what it means for a function to be odd, both algebraically and graphically, and give an example of an odd function.

2. Sketch the graph of $y = |x - 2| + 3$. How is your graph related to the graph of $y = |x|$?

3. Write an equation for a function with a graph that is the graph of $y = x^3$ after a translation 3 units to the left and 1 unit up.

4. Sketch the graph of $\left(\frac{x}{2}\right)^2 + (3y)^2 = 25$. How is your graph related to the graph of $x^2 + y^2 = 25$?

5. Write an equation for a function with a graph that is the graph of $y = \frac{1}{x}$ scaled horizontally by the factor 6.

6. How are the graphs of $y = x^2$ and $y = (x - 3)^2$ related?

7. What does the graph of $(x + 1)^2 + (y - 4)^2 = 36$ look like?

8. What does the graph of $-2y = x^3 - x$ look like?

Vocabulary

In this investigation, you learned these terms. Make sure you understand what each one means and how to use it.

- **even function**
- **odd function**
- **unit circle**

One image is a stretch. The other image is a reflection. $100 question: What does the original figure look like?

In **Investigation 4A,** you learned how to

- find closed-form and recursive functions to fit input-output tables

- use difference tables to determine whether a linear or a quadratic function will fit a given table

- use the up-and-over and hockey stick properties of difference tables

The following questions will help you check your understanding.

1. Write a closed-form and a recursive rule to match the table below. Use either rule to find $a(15)$.

n	a(n)
0	1
1	5
2	25
3	125
4	625
5	3125

2. Copy and complete the difference table below.

x	b(x)	Δ	Δ²
0	1	2	3
1	▪	▪	3
2	▪	8	3
3	▪	▪	3
4	▪	▪	
5	41		

What kind of function agrees with the inputs and outputs in the table?

3. Make a difference table for the input-output table below. Include enough columns to show a constant difference. Use your difference table to find a closed-form function that matches the table. Explain how you used the information in the table to find the function.

x	c(x)
0	−3
1	4
2	15
3	30
4	49

In **Investigation 4B,** you learned how to

- determine whether a table, graph, or closed-form rule is a function

- compose functions

- find the inverse of a function, if it exists

The following questions will help you check your understanding.

4. Consider the functions f and g.

$$f(x) = 3x + 7$$
$$g(x) = \frac{x + 1}{3}$$

Calculate each value.

a. $f(2)$ b. $g(2)$

c. $f(g(2))$ d. $g(f(2))$

e. $f \circ g(2)$ f. $f(2) \cdot g(2)$

5. Use the definitions of functions f and g below.

$$f(x) = x - 2$$
$$g(x) = x^2 + 4x + 1$$

a. Find a formula for $f \circ g(x)$.

b. Find a formula for $g \circ f(x)$.

6. Use the definitions of functions f, g, and h below.

$$f(x) = \frac{x}{2} + 3$$

$$g(x) = x^2$$

$$h(x) = -3x$$

   a. Sketch the graph of each function.

   b. Determine whether each function is one-to-one.

   c. For each function that is one-to-one, find the inverse function.

In **Investigation 4C,** you learned how to

- graph an exponential function and determine the equation of an exponential function given two points on its graph

- identify an exponential function from the table it generates and use the table to write a closed-form or recursive definition of the function

- evaluate the inverse of the function $y = b^x$, either exactly or by approximation

The following questions will help you check your understanding.

7. a. Suppose f is an exponential function with $f(2) = \frac{9}{2}$ and $f(3) = \frac{27}{2}$. Find $f(x)$.

   b. Sketch the graph of $y = f(x)$.

8. Copy this table for the exponential function $g(x)$.

x	g(x)	÷
0	−2	■
1	−20	■
2	−200	■
3	−2000	

   a. Complete the ratio column and write a recursive definition for $g(x)$.

   b. Write a closed-form definition for $g(x)$.

   c. Find $g(4)$ and $g(6)$.

In **Investigation 4D** you learned how to

- sketch the basic graphs

- relate the effect of a translation of a basic graph on both the graph and the equation of the graph

- relate the effect of a scale or reflection of a basic graph on both the graph and the equation of the graph

- compose transformations and sketch the effect of a composition on one of the basic graphs

The following questions will help you check your understanding.

9. a. Sketch the graph of $y - 2 = |x + 1|$. How is your graph related to the graph of $y = |x|$?

   b. Sketch the graph of $(x - 4)^2 + (y + 6)^2 = 4$. How is your graph related to the graph of $x^2 + y^2 = 4$?

10. a. Sketch the graph of $\frac{y}{2} = (x - 4)^2$. How is your graph related to the graph of $y = x^2$?

   b. Sketch the graph of $\left(\frac{x}{3}\right)^2 + (2y)^2 = 4$. How is your graph related to the graph of $x^2 + y^2 = 4$?

   c. Sketch the graph of $y = (-x)^3 - (-x)$. How is your graph related to the graph of $y = x^3 - x$?

11. Suppose you scale the graph of $y = |x|$ horizontally by the factor 2 and then translate the graph 3 units left and 7 units down. Write an equation to describe the resulting graph and sketch the graph of the equation.

Multiple Choice

1. Which equation describes the graph of $x^2 + y^2 = 4$ after a translation 2 units to the right and 7 units down?

   A. $(x - 2)^2 + (y - 7)^2 = 4$

   B. $(x + 2)^2 + (y - 7)^2 = 4$

   C. $(x - 2)^2 + (y + 7)^2 = 4$

   D. $(x + 7)^2 + (y - 2)^2 = 4$

2. Which equation describes the graph of $y = \frac{1}{x}$ after a horizontal scale by the factor 4?

   A. $y = \frac{4}{x}$

   B. $y = \frac{x}{4}$

   C. $y = 4x$

   D. $y = x + 4$

3. Which of the following recursive functions best fits the table below?

Input, n	Output, a(n)
0	2
1	-1
2	-7
3	-19
4	-43

   A. $a(n) = \begin{cases} 2 & \text{if } n = 0 \\ a(n-1) - 3 & \text{if } n > 0 \end{cases}$

   B. $a(n) = \begin{cases} 2 & \text{if } n = 0 \\ 2 \cdot a(n-1) - 5 & \text{if } n > 0 \end{cases}$

   C. $a(n) = \begin{cases} 2 & \text{if } n = 0 \\ a(n-1) + 2n - 5 & \text{if } n > 0 \end{cases}$

   D. $a(n) = \begin{cases} 2 & \text{if } n = 0 \\ a(n-1) - 2n - 2 & \text{if } n > 0 \end{cases}$

4. The table below is part of a difference table for a function $b(n)$. The table has constant first differences. Find $b(20)$.

Input, n	Output, b(n)
0	■
1	-3
2	■
3	■
4	24

   A. 168

   B. 177

   C. 180

   D. You cannot determine the value of $b(20)$ from the information given.

5. Use functions f and g below.
   $$f(x) = 2x - 3$$
   $$g(x) = 4x + 1$$
   Which value is equal to $f \circ g(3)$?

   A. 3

   B. 13

   C. 23

   D. 39

6. Suppose $f(x) = \sqrt[3]{x} + 1$. Which expression is equal to $f^{-1}(x)$?

   A. $x^3 - 1$

   B. $(x - 1)^3$

   C. $-\sqrt[3]{x} - 1$

   D. $(x + 1)^3$

Open Response

7. Sketch the graph of each equation. How is each graph related to the corresponding basic graph?

   a. $y - 1 = (2x)^2$

   b. $y = \left(\frac{x}{2}\right)^3 - \frac{x}{2}$

   c. $2y = |x - 5|$

   d. $y = 2^{x+1}$

8. What does the graph of $(x + 1)^2 + (y - 4)^2 = 36$ look like?

9. Make a table of the following recursive function with inputs from 0 to 10.

$$m(n) = \begin{cases} 4 & \text{if } n = 0 \\ 2 \cdot m(n - 1) + 3n - 10 & \text{if } n > 0 \end{cases}$$

   Find a closed-form function that agrees with your table. Use it to find $m(80)$.

10. Find a recursive function definition and a closed-form function definition that agree with the table below.

n	p(n)
0	−8
1	−5
2	−2
3	1
4	4

11. Copy and complete the difference table below.

x	g(x)	Δ	Δ²
0	4	■	■
1	7	■	■
2	8	■	■
3	7	■	
4	4		

Find a closed-form function definition that agrees with the table. Explain how you can find the coefficients of the function from the difference table.

12. Copy this table for the exponential function $h(x)$.

   a. Complete the ratio column.

   b. Find a recursive definition for $h(x)$.

   c. Find a closed-form definition for $h(x)$.

   d. Find the exact value of $h(8)$.

x	h(x)	÷
0	6	■
1	3	■
2	$\frac{3}{2}$	■
3	$\frac{3}{4}$	■
4	$\frac{3}{8}$	

Investigations at a Glance

5A Probability and
Polynomials

Applications of Probability

Although there is much variation between individuals, populations are often quite consistent. Probability and statistics allow you to quantify a population and make predictions about it.

In this picture of a school of fish, you see that this fish can be yellow or red but the yellow occurs more frequently. Is that true of this type of fish in general or just this school of fish? You can use probability and statistics to quantify this information accurately.

Vocabulary and Notation

- conditional probability
- event
- expected value, $E(X)$
- frequency, $|A|$
- independent
- mutually exclusive
- outcome
- Pascal's Triangle
- probability of an event
- random variable
- sample space

5.0 Binomials and Pascal's Triangle

For You to Do

For each name, find the number of different arrangements of its letters.

1. PAT   2. ANN   3. TONY

4. DERMAN   5. SASHA   6. DEEDEE

Minds in Action

Tony and Sasha discuss the names from For You To Do above.

Sasha: It's pretty awesome that our names are in the book!

Tony: I know! My name was pretty simple to deal with, too. Any of the four letters in TONY could come first, then any of the three remaining letters, then two, then one. Then I multiply that:

$$4 \times 3 \times 2 \times 1 = 24 \text{ ways}$$

Sasha: That's the factorial function. 24 is 4 factorial, and you write it as 4!

Tony: Right, 4 factorial.

Sasha: My name was much harder to deal with. Yours has no repeated letters. If my name had no repeated letters there would be 5 factorial ways. That's 120. But I'm pretty sure I found all the ways and there were only 30.

Tony: There must be a way to figure out that there should be 30 without writing them all down.

They think about this for a little while.

Tony: What if you wrote five letters down all 120 ways? The spellings would repeat. But how many times?

Sasha: That's a good idea. The double A means every spelling would happen twice.

Tony: Your name also has a double S, so that's twice again.

Sasha: Every spelling would happen four times! And that's right on: 120 divided by 4 is 30.

Tony: Let me try DEEDEE the same way. Normally six letters would have 6! ways, which is 720. The double D means you have to divide by 2. But four Es... does that mean divide by 4?

Sasha: No. Any of the four Es could come first, then any of the three remaining Es, then two, then one.

Tony: Just like my name! I get it. If there are 4 repeated letters we have to divide by 4 *factorial*, not by 4.

Sasha: And 2 factorial is 2, so you can do it with any number of repeated letters. For my name you could divide 5! by the factorial for how many times each letter repeats.

$$\frac{5!}{2! \cdot 2! \cdot 1!} = 30$$

Sasha: I guess I don't really need the 1!, but it looks more elegant. I'll bet we could do this with any word.

Tony: For DEEDEE it would be

$$\frac{6!}{2! \cdot 4!} = 15$$

Sasha: Exactly right.

Remember...

1! = 1 and 2! = 2. Also, 0! = 1.

For You to Do

For each set of letters, determine the number of different arrangements of the set.

7. GREG

8. ABBA

9. BENBEN

10. HHHTT

The method Sasha and Tony used can calculate the number of possible ways a group of *n* things can be divided into two smaller groups.

Definition (n choose k)

The number of ways that *n* things can be divided into a group of *k* things and a second group of (*n-k*) things is given by

$$\binom{n}{k} = \frac{n!}{k! \cdot (n-k)}$$

The notation $\binom{n}{k}$ is read as "*n* choose *k*."

Habits of Mind

Use precise language. The name should remind you of the purpose: n choose k is the number of ways to choose k things from among n options. The alternate name *combination* and the alternate notation nCk are sometimes used instead.

For Discussion

Picking only the letters X and Y, it is possible to make many four-letter arrangements.

Two arrangements are XXYX and YYXY.

11. How many arrangements use four X's and no Y's? Three X's and one Y? Two X's and two Y's? One X and three Y's? No X's and four Y's?

12. How many total arrangements of four X's and Y's are there?

The values of $\binom{n}{k}$ form **Pascal's Triangle.** The nth row of Pascal's Triangle contains all values from $\binom{n}{0}$ to $\binom{n}{n}$, arranged like this:

$$\binom{0}{0}=1$$

$$\binom{1}{0}=1 \qquad \binom{1}{1}=1$$

$$\binom{2}{0}=1 \qquad \binom{2}{1}=2 \qquad \binom{2}{2}=1$$

$$\binom{3}{0}=1 \qquad \binom{3}{1}=3 \qquad \binom{3}{2}=3 \qquad \binom{3}{3}=1$$

$$\binom{4}{0}=1 \qquad \binom{4}{1}=4 \qquad \binom{4}{2}=6 \qquad \binom{4}{3}=4 \qquad \binom{4}{4}=1$$

$$\binom{5}{0}=1 \quad \binom{5}{1}=5 \quad \binom{5}{2}=10 \quad \binom{5}{3}=10 \quad \binom{5}{4}=5 \quad \binom{5}{5}=1$$

The numbers in each row of Pascal's Triangle can be generated from the previous row by adding. For example, $\binom{5}{2}=10$ is the sum of $\binom{4}{1}=4$ and $\binom{4}{2}=6$.

Example

Problem Expand $(x+y)^4$.

Solution First, examine $(x+y)^2 = (x+y)(x+y)$. The expansion includes all possible pairs of choices among x and y:

$$(x+y)(x+y) = xx + xy + yx + yy$$
$$= x^2 + 2xy + y^2$$

There are four possible pairs, 1 pair with no y's, 2 pairs with one y, and 1 pair with two y's.

The expansion of $(x+y)^3 = (x+y)(x+y)(x+y)$ includes all possible triples of choices among x and y:

$$(x+y)(x+y)(x+y) = xxx + xxy + xyx + yxx + xyy + yxy + yyx + yyy$$
$$= x^3 + 3x^2y + 3xy^2 + y^3$$

There are eight possible triples, **1** with no y's, **3** with one y, **3** with two y's, and **1** with three y's.

The expansion of $(x+y)^4 = (x+y)(x+y)(x+y)(x+y)$ includes all possible four-letter arrangements of the letters x and y. *This is precisely given by the 4th row of Pascal's Triangle!* The expansion is

$$(x+y)^4 = \binom{4}{0}x^4 + \binom{4}{1}x^3y + \binom{4}{2}x^2y^2 + \binom{4}{3}xy^3 + \binom{4}{4}y^4$$
$$= x^4 + 4x^3y + 6x^2y^2 + 4xy^3 + y^4$$

There are 16 possible arrangements, **1** with no y's, **4** with one y, **6** with two y's, **4** with three y's, and **1** with four y's.

Habits of Mind

Look for structure. xy and yx are equal, but think of them as different arrangements

The arrangement $xx\ yx$ is one of the four ways with three x's and one y, giving $4x^3y$.

The coefficients for any binomial expansion $(a+b)^n$ are found in Pascal's Triangle. The Binomial Theorem states this relationship.

Theorem 5.1 The Binomial Theorem

For $n \geq 0$,

$$(a + b)^n = \binom{n}{0}a^nb^0 + \binom{n}{1}a^{n-1}b^1 + \binom{n}{2}a^{n-2}b^2 + \cdots + \binom{n}{k}a^{n-k}b^k$$

$$+ \cdots + \binom{n}{n-1}a^1b^{n-1} + \binom{n}{n}a^0b^n$$

The variables a and b can be replaced by any expression, including other variables and numbers.

Exercises Practicing Habits of Mind

Check Your Understanding

Here are rows 0 through 5 of Pascal's Triangle:

```
              1
            1   1
          1   2   1
        1   3   3   1
      1   4   6   4   1
    1   5   10  10   5   1
```

The inclusion of Row 0 makes it more difficult to remember which row is which. This may help. Row 3 starts with 1, then 3. Row 5 starts with 1, then 5. Row n starts with 1, then n.

1. Use the given rows to determine all the numbers in Rows 6-8 of Pascal's Triangle.

2. Find the values of $\binom{6}{2}$ and $\binom{6}{4}$.

3. Write the expansion of $(x+y)^6$.

4. For each set of letters, determine the number of different arrangements of the set.

    a. DADDAD

    b. GOGOGO

    c. OHHHHH

    d. AAAAAA

5. **Write About It** Explain why, for any n, it makes sense that $\binom{n}{0} = 1$ and $\binom{n}{1} = n$.

6. 42 people have applied for a job. The company must select 6 people to interview. Write an expression for the number of different possible groups of people the company may select.

7. Dr. Brown places two E's, two M's, and two T's in a bag. He will pull all six letters from the bag, one by one. What is the probability that he draws the letters in the exact order EMMETT?

Habits of Mind

Solve a similar problem. Try finding a set of 42 letters where the number of different arrangements gives the answer.

On Your Own

Picking only the letters H and T, it is possible to make many five-letter arrangements.

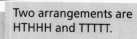
Two arrangements are HTHHH and TTTTT.

8. How many arrangements use

a. five H's and no T's?

b. four H's and one T?

c. three H's and two T's?

d. two H's and three T's?

e. one H and four T's?

f. no H's and five T's?

9. How many total arrangements of five H's and T's are there?

10. Write the expansion of $(H+T)^5$.

11. For each set of letters, determine the number of different arrangements of the set.

a. DOOD   **b.** MUUMUU   **c.** ACCIARI   **d.** FRANK

12. Explain why $\binom{6}{2}$ and $\binom{6}{4}$ are equal.

13. Find another pair of n and k so that $\binom{n}{k} = \binom{8}{3}$.

14. Write out the powers of 11 starting with $11^0 = 1$ up to 11^5. What do you notice? Can you explain why this might happen, and what was different for 11^5?

15. **Take It Further** Without using a calculator, write out the powers of 101 starting with $101^0 = 1$ up to 101^6.

Maintain Your Skills

16. Compute each sum.

a. $\binom{2}{0} + \binom{2}{1} + \binom{2}{2}$

b. $\binom{3}{0} + \binom{3}{1} + \binom{3}{2} + \binom{3}{3}$

c. $\binom{4}{0} + \binom{4}{1} + \binom{4}{2} + \binom{4}{3} + \binom{4}{4}$

d. $\binom{5}{0} + \binom{5}{1} + \binom{5}{2} + \binom{5}{3} + \binom{5}{4} + \binom{5}{5}$

e. What is the sum of the numbers in the 8th row of Pascal's Triangle?

Probability and Polynomials

In *Probability and Polynomials,* you will learn basic probability definitions and rules. You will discover connections between probability and Pascal's Triangle. You will model a variety of experiments with polynomials. You will calculate the likelihood of each outcome in an experiment, and also predict the average outcome of an experiment.

By the end of this investigation, you will be able to answer questions like these.

1. If you are to roll four number cubes, what is the probability they sum to 12?

2. What is expected value?

3. How can you use polynomials to solve probability problems?

You will learn how to

• calculate probabilities of simple random events

• build a set of equally likely outcomes for a probability experiment

• find a polynomial to model a probability experiment and interpret expansions of its powers

• calculate the expected value of a random variable

You will develop these habits and skills:

• Visualize the process of a probability experiment in order to count its outcomes.

• Reason from definitions, such as for *mutually exclusive* and *independent,* and apply them to probability situations.

• Understand the domains and ranges of various functions related to probability, including random variables, frequency, expected value, and probability functions.

Considering all possible outcomes is a good habit when calculating probabilities. If you know all possible outcomes in an experiment, you can find the likelihood of any particular outcome occurring.

For You to Explore

1. When you flip a coin three times, there are eight possible outcomes. For example, one outcome is heads-tails-heads. Write out the eight outcomes. Determine how many outcomes are in each category.

   a. no heads   **b.** one head   **c.** two heads   **d.** three heads

2. There are 16 possible outcomes when you flip a coin four times. For example, one outcome is heads-tails-heads-heads. Write out the 16 outcomes. Determine how many outcomes are in each category.

   a. no heads   **b.** one head   **c.** two heads

   d. three heads   **e.** four heads

3. You are to flip a coin five times.

   a. Write down the ten different ways you could flip two heads and three tails.

   b. What is the probability that you flip two heads and three tails?

4. Expand each of these expressions.

   a. $(t + h)^2$ **b.** $(t + h)^3$ **c.** $(t + h)^4$ **d.** $(t + h)^5$

One of the outcomes is "heads, tails, tails, heads, tails" but you might prefer to write it as HTTHT.

See the TI-Nspire™ Handbook on p. 990, for instructions on how to expand these expressions with a CAS.

If the survival rate for turtle eggs is 38%, how many are expected to hatch from a nest of 120 eggs?

Exercises *Practicing Habits of Mind*

On Your Own

5. Write out the first eight rows of Pascal's Triangle. Count your rows so that the third row is

$$1 \quad 3 \quad 3 \quad 1$$

6. Determine the probability that if you flip a coin eight times, you will flip exactly four heads and four tails. Explain in detail how you arrived at your answer.

7. a. Picture two spinners that are equally likely to land on any integer between 1 and 5, inclusive. List all 25 ways the spinners could land if you spin them both.

    b. Find the probability that the two numbers spun do not share a common factor greater than 1.

    c. Repeat parts (a) and (b) for two spinners that are equally likely to land on any integer between 1 and 6, inclusive. For this, there are 36 outcomes.

    d. Repeat parts (a) and (b) for two spinners that are equally likely to land on any integer between 1 and 7, inclusive.

> Here is one way: first spinner 3, second spinner 4. And here is another, different way: first spinner 4, second spinner 3.

8. a. If you flip a fair coin 240 times, how many heads would you expect?

    b. Guess the probability of getting exactly this many heads.

9. a. If you roll a fair number cube 240 times, how many ones would you expect?

    b. Guess the probability of getting exactly this many ones.

> You may assume that a number cube has the numbers 1 through 6 on its faces, unless stated otherwise.

Maintain Your Skills

10. For each value of n, you are to pick an integer at random from 1 to n. What is the probability it will be a perfect square?

    a. $n = 10$ **b.** $n = 100$ **c.** $n = 1000$ **d.** $n = 10{,}000$

    e. What is happening "in the long run" (as n grows larger without bound)?

5.02 Probability and Pascal's Triangle

In this section you will learn some basic definitions and rules of probability. If you have not done so already, start to think about how you can count the possible outcomes of experiments more efficiently.

In-Class Experiment

Here are four similar games.

Game 1: Flip two coins. If you get exactly two heads, you win.

Game 2: Flip three coins. If you get exactly two heads, you win.

Game 3: Flip four coins. If you get exactly two heads, you win.

Game 4: Flip five coins. If you get exactly two heads, you win.

1. Which game gives you the greatest probability of winning?

You can use probability theory to determine how likely it is that an event will occur. Consider a multiple-choice question with five options. Only one is right. If you guess randomly, the probability of getting the correct answer is $\frac{1}{5}$. The probability of getting an incorrect answer is $\frac{4}{5}$.

Example

Problem Roll two different-colored number cubes. Find the probability of each event.

a. At least one number cube shows a 5.

b. The sum of the numbers is exactly 5.

Solution One way to proceed is to write out the *sample space*, the entire list of possible outcomes. Since each number cube has 6 possible outcomes, there are 36 total outcomes for this experiment.

	1	2	3	4	5	6
1	(1,1)	(1,2)	(1,3)	(1,4)	**(1,5)**	(1,6)
2	(2,1)	(2,2)	(2,3)	(2,4)	**(2,5)**	(2,6)
3	(3,1)	(3,2)	(3,3)	(3,4)	**(3,5)**	(3,6)
4	(4,1)	(4,2)	(4,3)	(4,4)	**(4,5)**	(4,6)
5	**(5,1)**	**(5,2)**	**(5,3)**	**(5,4)**	**(5,5)**	**(5,6)**
6	(6,1)	(6,2)	(6,3)	(6,4)	**(6,5)**	(6,6)

a. The 11 highlighted outcomes have at least one 5. So, the probability of rolling at least one 5 is

$$P \text{ (at least one 5)} = \frac{\text{number of successful outcomes}}{\text{total number of outcomes}} = \frac{11}{36}$$

b. Make a second table showing the sums of the numbers on the two number cubes.

+	1	2	3	4	5	6
1	2	3	4	5	6	7
2	3	4	5	6	7	8
3	4	5	6	7	8	9
4	5	6	7	8	9	10
5	6	7	8	9	10	11
6	7	8	9	10	11	12

The 4 highlighted outcomes each show a sum of 5. So, the probability of rolling a sum of exactly 5 is $\frac{4}{36}$ or $\frac{1}{9}$.

For You to Do

2. Find the probability that when rolling two number cubes, the sum is less than or equal to 5.

Several definitions come in handy when talking about probability problems.

Definitions

The **sample space** is a set. Its elements are **outcomes.**

An **event** is a subset of the sample space, a set of outcomes. $|A|$ denotes the number of outcomes in event A.

$P(A)$, the **probability of an event** A, is the number of outcomes in A, divided by the number of outcomes in the sample space S.

$$P(A) = \frac{\text{number of outcomes in } A}{\text{total number of outcomes}} = \frac{|A|}{|S|}$$

> An *outcome* could be anything, such as "rolling a 3" or "heads, heads, tails." The situation determines the appropriate outcomes.

When rolling a number cube, there are six outcomes in the sample space, all equally likely. One outcome is "roll the number 5." An event might be "roll a prime number." There are three outcomes in this event, so $P(\text{roll a prime number}) = \frac{3}{6}$ or $\frac{1}{2}$.

> This definition of probability depends on the assumption that all outcomes in the sample space are equally likely. You cannot use this definition when the outcomes are not equally likely.

Often, there are shortcuts to counting either the number of outcomes in an event, or the number of outcomes in the sample space. The sample space for rolling two number cubes has $6 \times 6 = 36$ outcomes since there are six ways each number cube can land.

Derman and Sasha are working on Game 4 from the In-Class Experiment.

Derman We want to find the probability of getting exactly two heads when you flip five coins.

Sasha All right, so we need to know the number of outcomes with exactly two heads, and the total number of outcomes in the sample space.

Derman I think the probability should be 1 out of 6.

Sasha Oh?

Derman Well, you could get 0 heads, 1 head, 2, 3, 4, or 5 heads. Six ways it could happen. It's 1 out of 6.

Sasha Wait, wait, wait. That's not going to work, those things would have to be equally likely. But I'm not convinced that they are.

Derman Well, flipping a coin is equally likely: heads or tails.

Sasha Right. So start from there. Five coin flips.

Derman The total number of outcomes is . . . I think it's 32, 2 to the fifth.

Sasha That's a much better sample space. The probability's got to be something out of 32, then. Now we just have to figure out how many of those 32 outcomes have exactly two heads.

Derman I'll make a list . . .

HHTTT	TTTHH	THTHT
HTHTT	HTTTH	HTTHT
THHTT	THTTH	TTHHT

Derman Nine! It's nine out of 32.

Sasha You missed one: TTHTH. It's ten.

Derman It's hard to know the list is complete. There must be a better way to count these.

Sasha It's two H's out of a total of five spots.

Derman Ohh . . . just like in Pascal's Triangle! From Lesson 5.0, I know that 10 is in Pascal's Triangle.

Sasha Hey, nice. Five flips and two H's. So the number of ways should be 5 choose 2, which is 10.

Derman So the probability is 10 out of 32. Guess it wasn't 1 out of 6 after all.

Remember...

The notation for "five choose 2" is $\binom{5}{2}$ or $_5C_2$. You can calculate it as $\dfrac{5!}{2! \cdot 3!}$.

Look for relationships. The connection to probability can also explain a property about the sum of the numbers in a row of Pascal's Triangle. Consider row 5:

$$1 \quad 5 \quad 10 \quad 10 \quad 5 \quad 1$$

When you toss five coins, these numbers show up as the number of ways to get 0 heads, 1 head, 2 heads, and so on. For example, the probability of getting no heads when you flip five coins is $\frac{1}{32}$, since there is 1 successful outcome out of 32 total. Now look at the sum of all the probabilities.

$$\frac{1}{32} + \frac{5}{32} + \frac{10}{32} + \frac{10}{32} + \frac{5}{32} + \frac{1}{32}$$

If you toss five coins, you have to get *some* number of heads from 0 to 5. If you add up the probability of getting 0 heads, 1 head, 2 heads, 3 heads, 4 heads, and 5 heads, you have covered all the possibilities. Also, there is no overlap between these events. When you count the number of heads, the answer cannot be 2 *and* 4. So, the sum of these probabilities must be 1.

$$\frac{1}{32} + \frac{5}{32} + \frac{10}{32} + \frac{10}{32} + \frac{5}{32} + \frac{1}{32} = 1$$

This happens with any row of Pascal's Triangle. The sum of the numbers in the nth row of Pascal's Triangle is 2^n, which equals the total number of outcomes when tossing n coins.

For You to Do

3. Which is more likely, flipping exactly 3 heads in 10 coin flips, or flipping exactly 4 heads in 5 coin flips?

Here are two additional terms that apply to events.

Definitions

Two events A and B are **mutually exclusive** if they do not share any outcomes in the same sample space: whenever $P(A \text{ and } B) = 0$. If A and B are mutually exclusive, then $P(A \text{ or } B) = P(A) + P(B)$.

Two events A and B are **independent** if the result from one event has no effect on the other. If A and B are independent, then $P(A \text{ and } B) = P(A) \cdot P(B)$.

Consider rolling a single number cube. Rolling a 5 and rolling a 6 are mutually exclusive: you cannot do both at once. To find the probability of rolling a 5 or 6, add the probabilities of rolling each.

$P(5 \text{ and } 6) = 0$
$P(5 \text{ or } 6) = P(5) + P(6)$

Consider rolling two number cubes. The probability of rolling a 5 on the first number cube is $\frac{1}{6}$. The probability of rolling a 6 on the second number cube is also $\frac{1}{6}$. These events are independent: the result for the second number cube does not rely in any way on the result for the first number cube. So, the probability of rolling a 5 on the first number cube and a 6 on the second number cube is $\frac{1}{6} \cdot \frac{1}{6} = \frac{1}{36}$.

Developing Habits of Mind

Extend the process. The rule for $P(A \text{ or } B)$ is slightly different when A and B share outcomes. For any events A and B,

$$P(A \text{ or } B) = P(A) + P(B) - P(A \text{ and } B)$$

One way to look at this is with a Venn diagram.

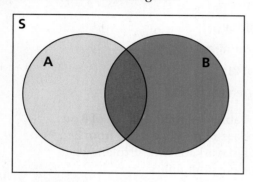

Let S be the sample space. In the diagram, the entire yellow circle represents event A. The entire blue circle represents event B. The green intersection of the two circles (where the yellow and blue overlap) represents the event $(A \text{ and } B)$. The union of the two circles represents the event $(A \text{ or } B)$.

In the diagram, this union is the part that is either yellow or blue, or is both yellow and blue. How could you compute the area of this colored region? You cannot just add the area of the entire yellow circle and the area of the entire blue circle. If you were to do this, you would double-count the middle green area, where the two circles intersect. So, subtract that green area from the sum and you will get the correct area.

Note that if A and B are mutually exclusive, $P(A \text{ and } B) = 0$. Then you do not have to take the intersection into account. This makes sense, since for mutually exclusive events $P(A \text{ or } B) = P(A) + P(B)$.

You can find probabilities for more than two overlapping events by using the inclusion-exclusion principle. For three events A, B, and C, first add the probabilities of the events. Next subtract all the intersections of pairs of events. Then add back in the intersection of *triples* of events.

$$
\begin{aligned}
P(A \text{ or } B \text{ or } C) = {} & P(A) + P(B) + P(C) \\
& - P(A \text{ and } B) - P(A \text{ and } C) - P(B \text{ and } C) \\
& + P(A \text{ and } B \text{ and } C)
\end{aligned}
$$

> What happens if A, B, and C are mutually exclusive?

You can extend this principle to find probabilities for any number of overlapping events.

Exercises *Practicing Habits of Mind*

Check Your Understanding

1. Determine each probability.

   a. P(flip 1 coin, heads)

   b. P(flip 2 coins, both heads)

   c. P(roll a number cube and get an odd number)

   d. P(roll a number cube and get an even number)

   e. P(roll a number cube and get a negative number)

   f. P(roll two number cubes and get a sum of 2)

   g. P(roll two number cubes and get a sum greater than 2)

2. **What's Wrong Here?** Russ says that the probability of rolling a sum of 8 on two number cubes should be $\frac{1}{11}$, since there are 11 possible sums from 2 to 12. "It works for one number cube, so it should work for two." Explain what is wrong with his reasoning, and find the correct probability.

3. If you flip a coin six times, how many different ways are there for the result to be 2 heads and 4 tails? Write them out.

4. Calculate the value of $\binom{6}{2}$. Explain how your result relates to the work in Exercise 3.

5. Use the expansion of $(t + h)^6$ to find the total number of ways you could flip 3 heads and 3 tails in a sequence of six coin tosses.

6. **Take It Further** Suppose you are to roll a number cube three times. Find the probability that the sum of the numbers will be 8.

On Your Own

7. Make a game where the probability of winning is about $\frac{1}{3}$. Explain clearly how the game is played, and what the winning condition is. The best games are simple to play but complex in their potential outcomes.

   > So, one game would be "Roll a number cube. If it comes up 1 or 2, you win." But you can make something more interesting!

8. You flip a coin eight times.

   a. Explain why there are 256 outcomes in the sample space.

   b. What is the most likely number of heads? How likely is it to occur?

9. In a carnival game, you roll a standard number cube and flip a coin. The coin has a 0 on one side, and a 5 on the other side. Your score is the sum of the values that appear on the number cube and the coin.

   a. You win the game if you score 10 points or more. Find the probability that you win the game.

   b. The man running the carnival says that every score from 1 to 11 is equally likely. Is he right? Explain.

10. Consider the set S of ordered pairs (x, y) such that x and y are both integers between 1 and 8, inclusive, and $x \geq y$.

   a. How many such ordered pairs are there?

   b. If you are to pick an ordered pair (x, y) at random, what is the probability that x and y do not have any common factor greater than 1?

   c. In the coordinate plane, plot all the ordered pairs (x, y) in S that do not have any common factor greater than 1.

   (7, 3) is in this set, but (3, 7) is not, since $x \geq y$ is required.

11. Repeat Exercise 11 with the integer pairs satisfying $1 \leq y \leq x \leq 9$.

12. **Take It Further** Flip a coin 10 times, keeping score as follows. If you flip heads, you get one point. If you flip tails, you are in "danger." If you flip tails twice in a row, you "bust," lose all your points, and the game ends.

   a. What is the probability you survive all ten flips without busting?

   b. What is the average score players achieve in this game?

13. **Standardized Test Prep** In the sample space for rolling two number cubes, how many outcomes will have neither a one nor a two on either cube?

   A. 16   **B.** 18   **C.** 20   **D.** 24

Go Online
www.successnetplus.com

Maintain Your Skills

14. This is F_5, the *Farey sequence* of order 5:

$$\frac{0}{1}, \frac{1}{5}, \frac{1}{4}, \frac{1}{3}, \frac{2}{5}, \frac{1}{2}, \frac{3}{5}, \frac{2}{3}, \frac{3}{4}, \frac{4}{5}, \frac{1}{1}$$

   F_5 is all fractions from 0 to 1, inclusive, with denominators less than or equal to 5. It is written in increasing order with fractions in lowest terms.

   Find the number of elements in F_n. Copy and complete the table for n from 1 to 10, inclusive. Describe any patterns you find.

n	Number of elements in F_n
1	2
2	3
3	▇
4	▇
5	11

Conditional Probability

What is the probability that a randomly-picked high school student has his or her driver's license? Perhaps the best answer is "it depends." The probability might be different if you only picked among students from a certain school or from a certain state. It would definitely be different if you only picked among students from a certain grade!

Sometimes the probability of an event can be influenced by other events. How do you calculate probabilities in these cases?

Minds in Action

Tony, Derman, and Sasha are playing a game to divide up some spare change.

Sasha We have 30 coins between us: 15 quarters, 5 dimes, 2 nickels, and 8 pennies.

Tony I numbered the coins, and we'll use this calculator to pick random numbers from 1 to 30. If it's your turn you get the coin with that number.

Sasha Great. But don't count any repeats, since you can't pick the same coin twice. Derman, you go first.

Tony, Derman, and Sasha complete three turns each.

Derman What bad luck! I've got 3 pennies. I want a quarter. The probability of getting a quarter is $\frac{15}{30}$, the same as one half. Right?

Tony That can't be right, Derman. We've each taken 3 turns. There are only 21 coins left.

Derman So then it's $\frac{15}{21}$, that's even better.

Sasha Not all the quarters are left. Tony and I each have two quarters.

Derman Oh, I get it now: it's $\frac{11}{21}$. That's still better than one half, since there are 11 quarters and 10 other coins.

Sasha The probability of getting a quarter changes each time based on what happened before.

Derman picks a random number.

Derman Sweet, a quarter!

For You to Do

1. Find the probability that the next two coins picked are both quarters.

The probability that an event occurs can be influenced by other events. In the Minds in Action dialogue, the probability of Derman drawing a quarter on his fourth turn is influenced by what was picked in previous turns. The notation $P(B|A)$ denotes the **conditional probability** that event B occurs given that event A has occurred.

For Discussion

Suppose you choose a high school student at random. Let A, B, and C be the following events.

A = the student has his or her driver's license
B = the student is a senior
C = the student is a freshman

For each expression, describe what it means and estimate its probability.

2. $P(A)$

3. $P(B)$

4. $P(C)$

5. $P(A|B)$

6. $P(C|A)$

7. $P(A$ and $B)$

Calculating $P(A$ and $B)$ can be challenging when events A and B are not independent. The notation of conditional probability is very helpful here.

Remember...

In Lesson 5.02 you learned that events are independent if the result from one event has no effect on the other.

Example 1

Problem When drawing two cards from a deck of playing cards without replacement, what is the probability that both are face cards?

Solution Define event X as "drawing a face card on the first draw" and event Y as "drawing a face card on the second draw." In a standard deck of playing cards, there are 12 face cards among 52 total cards. The probability of event X is $P(X) = \frac{12}{52}$.

The first card is not replaced. The probability of drawing a second face card, given that you drew a face card first, is $P(Y|X) = \frac{11}{51}$.

The probability of drawing two face cards is $P(X$ and $Y) = \left(\frac{12}{52}\right)\left(\frac{11}{51}\right) = \frac{11}{221}$, or just under 5%.

After the first draw, how many face cards are left? How many total cards?

Using the notation of conditional probability, you can generalize the result in Example 1 to any two events:

$$P(A \text{ and } B) = P(A) \cdot P(B|A)$$

If you want to know the probability that two events both occur, you can compute the probability for one of the two events, then multiply by the conditional probability that the second event occurs *given that the first event has occurred.*

This also leads to the formal definition of conditional probability.

Definition

Let A and B be two events such that $P(A) > 0$. The conditional probability of B given A is:

$$P(B|A) = \frac{P(A \text{ and } B)}{P(A)}$$

If $P(A) = 0$, then event A is impossible, and $P(B|A)$ does not make sense.

For Discussion

Explain in words what each statement means. Then either explain why it is always true, or give a counterexample to show that it is not always true.

8. $P(A|B) = P(B|A)$

9. $P(A) \cdot P(B|A) = P(B) \cdot P(A|B)$

Example 2

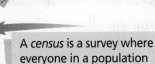

A 9th grade class has 210 students: 120 boys and 90 girls. A census asks the students if they play a popular mobile phone game every day. Here are the results:

A *census* is a survey where everyone in a population responds.

	Boys	Girls	Total
Plays Every Day	80	15	95
Does Not Play Every Day	40	75	115
Total	120	90	210

Problem

a. Find the probability that a student who plays the game every day is a girl.

b. Given that a student is a boy, find the probability that he does not play every day.

c. Find the probability that a student picked at random is a boy who does not play the game every day.

d. Find $P(\text{Boy}) \cdot P(\text{Does Not Play Every Day} \mid \text{Boy})$

Solution

a. There are 95 students who play the game every day. The fraction of those who are girls is $\frac{15}{95}$, or $\frac{3}{19}$. This is the probability that a student who plays the game every day is a girl.

b. There are 120 boys and 40 do not play every day. The probability is $\frac{40}{120}$, or $\frac{1}{3}$.

c. There are 210 students. Of these, 40 are boys who do not play every day. The probability is $\frac{40}{210}$, or $\frac{4}{21}$.

d. There are 120 boys out of 210 total students. From part (b), the probability that a boy does not play every day is $\frac{1}{3}$. The product is $\frac{120}{210} \cdot \frac{1}{3} = \frac{4}{21}$.

For You to Do

Use the table in Example 2 to calculate each of the following.

10. P(Does Not Play Every Day | Girl)

11. P(Girl)

12. P(Girl and Does Not Play Every Day)

In Lesson 5.02 you learned the definition of independence: two events are independent if the occurrence of one has no effect on the other. If A and B are independent events, then:

$$P(A \text{ and } B) = P(A) \cdot P(B)$$

Conditional probability gives us two additional ways of determining $P(A \text{ and } B)$ that work even when the events are not independent:

$$P(A \text{ and } B) = P(A) \cdot P(B|A)$$

$$P(A \text{ and } B) = P(B) \cdot P(A|B)$$

By combining these formulas, the following theorem can be proved.

Theorem 5.2

Let A and B be events with $P(A) > 0$ and $P(B) > 0$.

- Events A and B are independent if and only if $P(A|B) = P(A)$.
- Events A and B are independent if and only if $P(B|A) = P(B)$.

Remember...

$P(A|B)$ is meaningless if $P(B) = 0$, and $P(B|A)$ is meaningless if $P(A) = 0$.

For You to Do

Use the scenario in Example 2 to define the following events.

$B =$ a student chosen at random is a boy
$C =$ a student chosen at random plays the game every day

13. Are B and C independent? Explain how you know.

Interpret formulas The previous theorem states that events A and B are independent if you know the following:

$$P(A \mid B) = P(A)$$

What does this statement mean? It says that the probability that event A occurs given that event B occurs equals the probability that event A occurs. This is consistent with the definition of independence: that B occurs has no effect on the probability that A will occur. For example, getting heads on a coin flip will not change the probability of drawing a face card from a standard deck of playing cards.

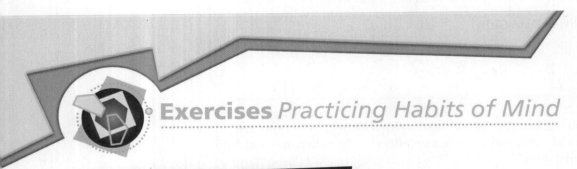

Exercises *Practicing Habits of Mind*

Check Your Understanding

1. When drawing two cards from a standard deck *without replacement*, what is the probability that the first card is a king and the second is a face card? Are the events "drawing a king first" and "drawing a face card second" independent?

2. When drawing two cards from a standard deck *with replacement*, what is the probability that the first card is a king and the second is a face card? Are the events "drawing a king first" and "drawing a face card second" independent?

3. **a.** Describe a pair of events X and Y that are independent. Approximate $P(X)$, $P(Y)$, and $P(X \text{ and } Y)$.

   b. Describe a pair of events A and B that are not independent. Approximate $P(A)$, $P(B)$, and $P(A \text{ and } B)$.

4. A bag contains 5 green chips, 2 red chips, and 3 blue chips. If you draw two chips, what is the probability that both chips are the same color? Clearly describe any assumptions you make while answering this question.

5. Another school has the same number of students as the school from Example 2. In this school, event *C* (a student chosen at random plays the game every day) is independent of event *B* (a student chosen at random is a boy). Copy and complete the two-way table below.

	Boys	Girls	Total
Plays Every Day	80	▦	▦
Does Not Play Every Day	▦	▦	▦
Total	120	90	210

On Your Own

6. What other pairs of events are independent in the table from Exercise 5?

7. An insurance company has done a long-term study of cars from three different manufacturers (*A*, *B*, and *C*). Some have had a serious accident (*S*) while others have not (Not *S*). The data have been organized in the two-way table below.

	A	*B*	*C*	Total
S	275	120	105	▦
Not S	▦	▦	▦	▦
Total	4500	3000	2500	10,000

a. Copy and complete the table.

In parts (b) through (i), find the probabilities.

b. $P(A|S)$

c. $P(A)$

d. $P(B|S)$

e. $P(B)$

f. $P(C|S)$

g. $P(C)$

h. $P(B \text{ and } S)$

i. $P(C \text{ and Not } S)$

j. Are *A* and *S* independent? Are *B* and *S* independent? Are *C* and *S* independent? Explain how you know.

> Here, event *A* is "a car picked randomly from these 10,000 cars is from manufacturer *A*," and so on. Event *S* is "a car picked randomly from these 10,000 cars has had a serious accident."

8. The following year a different sample of cars from the same three manufacturers was studied. Here are the new results:

	A	B	C	Total
S	225	120	155	■
Not S	■	■	■	■
Total	4500	3000	2500	10,000

For each pair of events, decide whether or not they are independent. Explain how you know.

a. A and S

b. B and S

c. C and S

9. a. Copy and complete the table so that each of the events A, B, and C are independent from event S.

	A	B	C	Total
S	■	■	■	500
Not S	■	■	■	■
Total	4500	3000	2500	10,000

b. Are each of the events A, B, and C independent from the event Not S?

10. A bag contains 5 green chips, 2 red chips, and 3 blue chips. Chips are drawn without replacement. Compute each probability.

a. P(first chip is red)

b. P(second chip is blue | first chip is red)

c. P(first chip is red and second chip is blue)

d. P(second chip is blue | first chip is blue)

e. P(second chip is blue | first chip is green)

f. P(second chip is blue)

g. P(first five chips are green)

h. **Take It Further** P(last chip is green)

Maintain Your Skills

11. Two events A and B are independent. Could they also be mutually exclusive? Explain why or why not.

Probabilities of Compound Events

Every year, a large company surveys a representative sample of its employees. Among the survey questions are, "Do you exercise regularly?" and "Do you usually feel alert or tired at work?" The company wants to conduct an analysis of the data to see if encouraging employees to exercise may increase their alertness on the job.

Of the employees surveyed this year, 65% exercise regularly. Of those who exercise regularly, 81% feel alert during the workday. Of those who do not exercise regularly, 69% feel alert during the workday.

Data like these need to be organized. There are two categorical variables here: whether the employee feels alert or tired, and whether the employee exercises regularly or not. A two-way table is useful as an organizational tool for these data.

Minds in Action

Tony and Derman try to make a two-way table to organize the employee survey data.

Tony   This seems hard. Are you sure we have all the necessary information?

Derman   Let's just begin by making a table like the ones in the last lesson. We can put the possibilities for one variable as the rows, and the possibilities for the other variable as the columns. I'll label each category with a letter, too.

	Exercise (*E*)	No Exercise (*N*)	Total
Alert (*A*)	■	■	■
Tired (*T*)	■	■	■
Total	■	■	■

> An employee selected at random is either alert or tired, and either exercises regularly or does not exercise regularly.

Tony   Great, but now what?

Derman   65% of all the employees surveyed exercise regularly. That's a percentage of the total, right? But we don't know how many total employees were surveyed. I'm lost. How can we put this information in the table?

Tony   We don't know the number of employees surveyed, but maybe we can make a table using the percentages. Actually, let's use decimals, like this:

	Exercise (E)	No Exercise (N)	Total
Alert (A)	■	■	■
Tired (T)	■	■	■
Total	0.65	■	■

Derman   I like it. And we know the other 35% do not exercise regularly. That's 0.35.

Tony   Oh, and we know the row adds up to the total! The total is 1, or 100%.

	Exercise (E)	No Exercise (N)	Total
Alert (A)	■	■	■
Tired (T)	■	■	■
Total	0.65	0.35	1.00

Derman   What's next? 81% of employees who exercise regularly feel alert. So in the top-left cell I'm going to write 0.81.

Tony   Wait. The numbers in the first column should add up to 0.65. If you write 0.81 there it means 81% of *everyone*, but that can't be right.

Derman   So how do I do it? What is it 81% of?

Tony   I think it's 81% of the employees who exercise. So 81% of 65%.

Derman   Sounds good. My calculator says that $(0.81)(0.65) = 0.5265$. Let's put that in the table.

Tony   We should round off. The data were given to the nearest percent, so any calculation we do can only be accurate to the nearest percent.

Derman   Okay, let's round it to 53%, or 0.53. That makes sense. 53% is about four fifths of 65%.

	Exercise (E)	No Exercise (N)	Total
Alert (A)	0.53	■	■
Tired (T)	■	■	■
Total	0.65	0.35	1.00

Tony   We got this. Let's fill in the rest.

For You to Do

1. Copy and complete the table from the dialogue. Round to the nearest hundredth.

2. What percentage of all employees feel alert? What percentage of employees who exercise regularly feel alert?

3. You select an employee from the survey at random. Is selecting an employee who feels alert during the workday independent of selecting an employee who exercises regularly? Explain.

The survey also asked the employees who exercise regularly how long they have been doing so, in years. The two-way table below shows the number of employees that feel alert and tired according to the number of years they have been exercising regularly. (Employees who do not exercise regularly are included among those who have exercised for less than 1 year.)

	< 1 y	1 y	2–4 y	5–9 y	≥ 10 y	Total
Alert	284	93	88	75	55	595
Tired	108	23	18	16	11	176
Total	392	116	106	91	66	771

For Discussion

4. Describe some general observations about the table.

5. Does the number of years of regular exercise appear to affect whether an employee feels alert or tired? Explain.

6. Estimate the probability that an employee who feels alert has been exercising regularly for at least 5 years.

7. Estimate the probability that an employee who feels tired has been exercising regularly for at least 5 years.

Exercises Practicing Habits of Mind

Check Your Understanding

Exercises 1–4 use the data from the employee survey.

Remember...

In the notation for conditional probability, $P(A|N)$ is the probability that an employee feels alert, given that he or she does not exercise regularly.

1. Find each probability among employees in the survey. Round to the nearest hundredth.

   a. $P(N)$ **b.** $P(A|N)$ **c.** $P(N|A)$

2. Find each probability among employees in the survey. Round to the nearest hundredth.

   a. $P(E)$ **b.** $P(A|E)$ **c.** $P(A)$ **d.** $P(E|A)$

   e. $P(E) \cdot P(A|E)$ **f.** $P(A) \cdot P(E|A)$ **g.** $P(A \text{ and } E)$

3. Compute each probability. Round to the nearest hundredth.

   a. that an employee feels alert, given that they have at least 10 years of regular exercise

   b. that an employee has exercised regularly for at least 10 years, given that they feel alert

   c. that an employee feels tired, given that they have less than 1 year of regular exercise

   d. that an employee has less than 1 year of regular exercise, given that they feel tired

4. The employee survey also grouped data by employee age. Of the employees surveyed who feel alert during the workday, 36% were over 50 years old. Of the employees surveyed who feel tired, 21% were over 50 years old.

   a. Construct a two-way table of the data. Round to the nearest hundredth.

   b. Are selecting an employee who is at most 50 years old and selecting an employee who feels alert independent events? Explain.

5. Suppose that in a high school, 450 juniors and 550 seniors were asked how long they have been regularly using a cell phone. The two possible responses in the survey are "less than 5 years" and "5 years or more."

   a. **Reflect and Write** Describe how you could use the survey's results to decide if selecting a senior at random and selecting someone who has used a cell phone for less than 5 years at random are independent events.

   b. Build a possible two-way frequency table in which juniors and seniors are equally likely to have used a cell phone for 5 years or more.

   c. Use your two-way table to build a second table giving the percentage of the population for all categories instead of frequencies.

Remember...

A *frequency table* shows the number of students in each category.

6. In a student survey, students were asked two questions:

   • What school do you attend?

   • Describe your level of agreement with the following statement: "School should start and end one hour later."

   Here is partial information from the survey, displayed in a two-way table.

	Countryside HS	Cityside HS	Total
Strongly Agree	▣	▣	20
Agree	▣	▣	38
Disagree	▣	▣	46
Strongly Disagree	▣	▣	18
Total	41	81	122

   a. Suppose that the school students attended did not affect their responses to the second question. Copy and complete the table with a plausible set of results for the sample survey.

   b. Suppose, instead, that Cityside students were more likely to agree with the statement. Copy and complete the table a second time with a plausible set of results for this situation.

7. A survey was conducted in a large Statistics class. Students were asked the following questions:

   • What is your gender?

   • Are you wearing a watch right now?

   One way to use this survey is to decide whether randomly selecting a watch-wearer and randomly selecting a male student are independent events. Parts (a) through (e) show several different interpretations of the sentence "Being male and wearing a watch are independent." Which interpretations are accurate? Explain how you know.

   a. Knowing the gender of a person in the survey sheds no light on the probability that he or she is wearing a watch.

   b. The probability of being male is the same as the probability of wearing a watch.

   c. The number of males wearing a watch is the same as the number of females wearing a watch.

   d. Watch-wearers are just as likely as non-watch wearers to be male.

   e. Watch-wearers are just as likely to be male as they are to be female.

> **Habits of Mind**
>
> **Attend to precision**
> You might say the students' responses were *independent* of their school, but be careful: independence refers to events, not variables. To say two variables are independent implies that all possible events associated with those variables are independent.

8. Here is a partial two-way table of the survey from Exercise 7:

	Male	Female	Total
Wearing Watch	◼	◼	30
Not Wearing Watch	◼	◼	◼
Total	72	◼	120

    a. Copy and complete the table if the number of males wearing a watch is the same as the number of females wearing a watch.

    b. In this situation, is the statement "Being male and wearing a watch are independent" true or false? Explain how you know.

9. Use the table from Exercise 8 to compute each of the following.

    a. $P(\text{male})$

    b. $P(\text{watch-wearing} \mid \text{male})$

    c. $P(\text{watch-wearing} \mid \text{female})$

    d. $P(\text{watch-wearing})$

10. a. Complete the table from Exercise 8 again so that being male and wearing a watch *are* independent.

    b. Compute the probabilities from Exercise 9 using the new data. What do you notice?

Maintain Your Skills

11. Using the table of 771 employees from page 10, copy and complete the table below with relative frequency rounded to the nearest thousandth.

	< 1 y	1 y	2−4 y	5−9 y	≥ 10 y	Total
Alert	◼	0.121	◼	◼	◼	◼
Tired	◼	◼	◼	◼	◼	0.228
Total	◼	◼	◼	◼	◼	◼

Polynomial Powers and Counting

You can use Pascal's Triangle to quickly count the number of each type of outcome for coin-flip experiments. But what about other experiments, like rolling a number cube or answering multiple-choice questions? This lesson explores the use of polynomials to solve probability problems.

For You to Do

1. Copy and complete the expansion box below to find the expanded form of $(x + x^2 + x^3 + x^4 + x^5 + x^6)^2$.

   Write the result in ascending powers of x.

$\cdot$	x	x^2	x^3	x^4	x^5	x^6
x	■	■	■	■	■	■
x^2	■	■	x^5	■	■	■
x^3	■	■	■	■	■	■
x^4	■	■	■	■	■	■
x^5	■	x^7	■	■	■	■
x^6	■	■	■	■	■	x^{12}

2. When you roll two number cubes, what is the probability that the sum of the numbers will be exactly 5?

> **Remember...**
>
> You first used expansion boxes in CME Project *Algebra 1* as a way to keep track of all the terms when you were multiplying two expressions.

Developing Habits of Mind

Recognize a similar process. Consider the table from Lesson 5.02, with the 36 possible outcomes for the sum when rolling two number cubes.

+	1	2	3	4	5	6
1	2	3	4	5	6	7
2	3	4	5	6	7	8
3	4	5	6	7	8	9
4	5	6	7	8	9	10
5	6	7	8	9	10	11
6	7	8	9	10	11	12

This table and the one from For You To Do are nearly identical, and they should be! Think about how you might get an x^5 in the expansion: multiply two terms like x^2 and x^3, or x^4 and x^1. In all, there are four ways to do this. Now think about how you get a 5 from the sum of the numbers on two cubes: roll a 2 and a 3, or a 4 and a 1. There are four ways to do this, too. It works because when you multiply polynomials, you are adding exponents.

So, you can use the polynomial $(x + x^2 + x^3 + x^4 + x^5 + x^6)$ to model the results when rolling a number cube with the numbers 1 through 6 on it.

Consider this frequency chart, listing the number of ways to get each sum when rolling two number cubes:

Roll	2	3	4	5	6	7	8	9	10	11	12
Frequency	1	2	3	4	5	6	5	4	3	2	1

Compare it to the result when squaring the polynomial that models a number cube roll:

$$(x + x^2 + x^3 + x^4 + x^5 + x^6)^2 =$$

$$1x^2 + 2x^3 + 3x^4 + 4x^5 + 5x^6 + 6x^7 + 5x^8 + 4x^9 + 3x^{10} + 2x^{11} + 1x^{12}$$

The expansion gives the same frequency information. There is one way to make x^2, two ways to make x^3, and so on. The table analyzing the sample space is really the same as the expansion box multiplying the polynomials.

The **frequency** of an event A is the number of outcomes in A. The frequency of the event "roll a sum of 10 on two number cubes" is 3, since there are 3 different outcomes with sum 10. In shorthand, $|A| = 3$.

Polynomials come in handy when exploring sample spaces that are too complex to list by hand. The sample space for rolling two number cubes has 36 outcomes, but the sample space for rolling four number cubes has $6^4 = 1296$ outcomes. This is tough to build by hand, but a CAS can quickly perform the corresponding polynomial expansion.

$$(x + x^2 + x^3 + x^4 + x^5 + x^6)^4 =$$
$$x^{24} + 4x^{23} + 10x^{22} + 20x^{21} + 35x^{20} + 56x^{19}$$
$$+ 80x^{18} + 104x^{17} + 125x^{16} + 140x^{15} + 146x^{14} + 140x^{13}$$
$$+ 125x^{12} + 104x^{11} + 80x^{10} + 56x^9 + 35x^8 + 20x^7 + 10x^6 + 4x^5 + x^4$$

See the TI-Nspire Handbook on p. 990, for details on how to expand polynomials.

This expansion gives a lot of information. For example, there are exactly 80 ways to roll a sum of 18 on four number cubes. Since there are $6^4 = 1296$ outcomes, $P(\text{rolling a sum of 18}) = \frac{80}{1296}$.

A spinner has five wedges of equal area. The wedges are labeled with the numbers 1, 2, 3, 3, and 8.

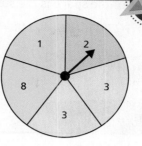

Problem What is the most likely sum of the numbers from four spins. How likely is it?

Solution First, model the spinner using the polynomial $(x + x^2 + x^3 + x^3 + x^8)$, matching the five possible outcomes from one spin. With five outcomes on each spin, there will be a total of $5^4 = 625$ outcomes from four spins.

Expand the polynomial to the fourth power.

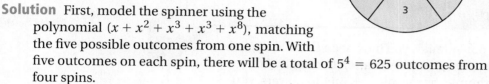

$(x + x^2 + x^3 + x^3 + x^8)^4 =$

$x^{32} + 8x^{27} + 4x^{26} + 4x^{25} + 24x^{22} + 24x^{21} + 30x^{20}$
$+ 12x^{19} + 6x^{18} + 32x^{17} + 48x^{16} + 72x^{15} + 52x^{14} + 36x^{13}$
$+ 28x^{12} + 36x^{11} + 56x^{10} + 56x^9 + 49x^8 + 28x^7 + 14x^6 + 4x^5 + x^4$

Each coefficient is the frequency for a specific sum, indicated by the exponent. The greatest coefficient is 72. There are 72 ways to make a sum of 15. The probability of this sum occuring is $\frac{72}{625}$, since there are $5^4 = 625$ total outcomes.

> **Habits of Mind**
>
> **Look for a relationship.** You could also write the polynomial as $(x + x^2 + 2x^3 + x^8)$. What does the coefficient 2 mean here?

For You to Do

3. A second similar spinner has the numbers 2, 4, 6, 6, 16. What is the most likely sum from four spins?

4. Let $f(x) = (x + x^2 + x^3 + x^3 + x^8)^4$. What is the value of $f(1)$?

You can model other situations using polynomials as well. To model a coin flip, use the polynomial $(t + h)$ as seen in Lesson 5.01. Look at this expansion:

$$(t + h)^5 = t^5 + 5t^4h + 10t^3h^2 + 10t^2h^3 + 5th^4 + h^5$$

You can interpret this as, "There is one way to get five tails, then five ways to get four tails and one head, then ten ways to get three tails and two heads . . ."

To model a multiple-choice question with one right answer and three wrong answers use the polynomial $(r + w + w + w)$, or $(r + 3w)$. Here is another expansion:

$$(r + 3w)^5 = r^5 + 15r^4w + 90r^3w^2 + 270r^2w^3 + 405rw^4 + 243w^5$$

> **Habits of Mind**
>
> **Represent the situation.** An appropriate choice of letters can be helpful. Here, you use t and h for tails and heads. You use r and w for right and wrong answers.

You can use the expression to show that on five questions, there are 270 different ways to get exactly two right and three wrong answers. The total number of outcomes in the sample space is the sum of the coefficients.

$$1 + 15 + 90 + 270 + 405 + 243 = 1024 = 4^5$$

So, $P(2 \text{ right and } 3 \text{ wrong}) = \frac{270}{1024} \approx 0.2637$.

Developing Habits of Mind

Extend the process. The polynomials you have seen so far are helpful in counting outcomes, but you can use a variation to calculate the probability directly. For example, by raising $(r + 3w)$ to powers, you can see how many ways there are to get right and wrong answers to a multiple-choice test. But the probability of getting a question right is $\frac{1}{4} = 0.25$ and the probability of getting it wrong is $\frac{3}{4} = 0.75$.

By raising $(0.25r + 0.75w)$ to the nth power, you can see the probabilities of the different events when guessing at n questions.

Consider the expansion of $(0.25r + 0.75w)^5$.

$$0.000977r^5 + 0.014648r^4w + 0.087891r^3w^2 + 0.263672r^2w^3$$
$$+ 0.395508rw^4 + 0.237305w^5$$

Expand using the Binomial Theorem or a CAS.

Now each coefficient gives the probability of each event occurring, rather than its frequency. The probability of getting 2 right and 3 wrong is the coefficient of the r^2w^3 term.

You can also obtain more information by evaluating the polynomial. For example, take the polynomial for rolling a number cube, $p(x) = x + x^2 + x^3 + x^4 + x^5 + x^6$. The output $p(1) = 6$ gives the total number of outcomes. Also, $(p(1))^3$ equals $6^3 = 216$. This is the total number of outcomes when rolling three number cubes.

But consider $p(-1) = 0$ and how it is built term by term. Let $x = -1$. Then $x^k = 1$ if k is even and $x^k = -1$ if k is odd. So, $p(-1) = 0$ means there are just as many even numbers on a number cube as odd numbers.

Now look at $(p(-1))^4$. It also equals zero, but models the sum of four number cubes. So, there are just as many ways to roll an odd sum from four number cubes as an even sum. This is pretty surprising, but you can verify it using the expansion on page 402. In fact, it must be true no matter how many number cubes are thrown.

One important thing to remember is that the method of polynomial powers is useful when performing the same experiment several times. Experiments involving coins, number cubes, and spinners are good examples. Picking a committee or drawing balls out of a bingo machine are not good examples, since the experiment changes over time. To see this, think about drawing a bingo number. When you draw that number, you remove it from the machine. You have fewer numbers for the next draw.

Exercises Practicing Habits of Mind

Check Your Understanding

1. The polynomial on page 402 gives the distribution of possible sums for rolling four number cubes.

   a. Build a histogram showing the frequency for each outcome, from 4 to 24.

   b. Explain why there are exactly as many ways to roll a sum of 5 as there are ways to roll a sum of 23.

2. Suppose you roll three number cubes. Calculate the probability that the sum of the numbers will be greater than 10.

3. On an unusual number cube the "1" face has a 10 instead.

   a. Find a polynomial that models one roll of this number cube.

   b. In four rolls, what is the most likely sum? How likely is it?

   > The six faces on this number cube have the numbers 2, 3, 4, 5, 6, and 10.

4. On another number cube the "6" face has a 5 instead.

   a. Explain why the polynomial $p(x) = x + x^2 + x^3 + x^4 + 2x^5$ models one roll of this number cube.

   b. In four rolls, what is the most likely sum? How likely is it?

   > The six faces on this number cube have the numbers 1, 2, 3, 4, 5, and 5.

5. Consider the number cube from Exercise 4 and its corresponding polynomial p.

   a. Expand $q(x) = (p(x))^2$. What does q represent?

   b. Find the value of $q(1)$.

   c. There are 36 outcomes when rolling this number cube twice. How many more ways are there to roll an even sum than an odd sum?

   d. Find the value of $q(-1)$.

6. A board game has a spinner with the numbers 1 through 10 on it. All numbers are equally likely. As you near the end of the game, you have 18 spaces left to move.

   a. Find the probability that you spin a total of *at least* 18 on just two spins.

   b. Find the probability that you spin a total of *at least* 18 on three spins.

   c. Find the probability that you spin a total of *at least* 18 on four spins.

On Your Own

7. A spinner has the five numbers 0, 1, 2, 2, and 7.

    a. Find a polynomial to model one spin.

    b. What is the most likely sum of the numbers from four spins. How likely is it?

8. Avery takes a multiple-choice test with six questions. There are five choices per question. He guesses at each question.

    a. What is the probability that Avery guesses correctly on the first question? on the second question?

    b. What is the probability that Avery guesses correctly on all six questions?

    c. Write a polynomial expansion to model this situation.

    d. Find the probability that Avery guesses correctly on exactly two of the six questions.

9. A local market has a prize wheel. Lucky customers can spin the wheel to win free fish. On one spin, it is possible to win 1 fish, 2 fish, 3 fish, or 10 fish.

    a. What is the average number of fish the market can expect to give away, per spin?

    b. Three customers spin the wheel. What is the most likely total number of fish that they win? How likely is this?

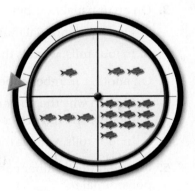

10. **Take It Further** Ten customers spin the Wheel of Fish from Exercise 9. Find the probability that the total number of fish they win is even.

11. Use a coordinate grid with $1 \le x \le 10$, $1 \le y \le 10$. Plot all 55 points with integer coordinates (x, y) in this range with $x \ge y$. Use one color if the two numbers share a common factor greater than 1. Use a second color if they do not.

12. You are to choose two integers x and y between 1 and 10, inclusive, with $x \ge y$. Use your plot from Exercise 11. Determine the probability that the pair of integers will have no common factor greater than 1.

Maintain Your Skills

13. Write out F_{10}, the Farey sequence of order 10.

14. Take a coordinate grid with $0 \le x \le 10$, $0 \le y \le 10$. Plot all points (x, y) in this range where the fraction $\frac{y}{x}$ is in F_{10}, the Farey sequence of order 10. Compare the results to Exercise 11.

> **Remember...**
>
> The *Farey sequence* of order *n* is all fractions between 0 and 1 in lowest terms with denominators less than or equal to *n*, written from least to greatest.

5.06 Expected Value

The expected value for a game is how much you could expect to win per game, on average. It is not necessarily the most likely amount you would win in any one game. Instead, if you played many times over, your average score would approach this expected value in the long run.

In-Class Experiment

On a popular game show, the game of Plinko is a favorite. All the player has to do is drop a chip, and they can win up to $10,000. Here is a simplified version of the Plinko board:

Whenever the chip hits a peg, it has a 50-50 chance of going left or right as it falls. After the chip has hit eight pegs and gone left or right eight times, it falls into one of nine slots with dollar amounts on them, from $0 to $10,000.

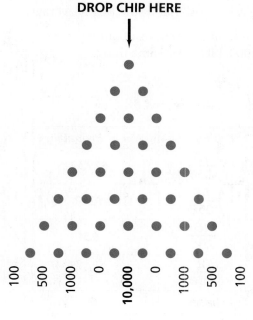

DROP CHIP HERE

100 500 1000 0 10,000 0 1000 500 100

1. Describe the relationship between the falling chip and coin flipping.

2. Write a polynomial, raised to a power, to model this game.

3. Find the probability that the chip falls into the center slot for a $10,000 win.

4. Find the probability that the chip falls into a $0 slot. Note there are two such slots.

5. What is the probability of winning $1000? $500? $100?

6. How much, on average, would you win per chip if you were to keep playing this game for a long, long time?

The sample space here has 256 outcomes. Why?

A student is thinking about the last problem from the In-Class Experiment.

Wendy Let me answer a simpler question first: let's say you paid me $10,000 if I flip a coin heads, and $0 if it's tails. I've got a $\frac{1}{2}$ chance to make heads, so it should be $5000 per flip, on average.

So now let me look at this bigger problem. I'll focus on the $10,000 first. Every time I drop a chip, there's a $\frac{70}{256}$ chance of getting the 10 grand. If you sat me there all day dropping chips, I can find the average by multiplying.

$$\$10,000 \cdot \frac{70}{256} \approx \$2734$$

So if everything else was zeros, that would be my average.

But I could win some smaller amounts of money. There's a $\frac{56}{256}$ chance of hitting $1000. I'll do the same thing:

$$\$1000 \cdot \frac{56}{256} \approx \$219$$

So, I'll build a table for all the options.

Win	Probability	Win × Probability
$10,000	$\frac{70}{256}$	$2734
$1000	$\frac{56}{256}$	$219
$500	$\frac{16}{256}$	$31
$100	$\frac{2}{256}$	$1
$0	whatever	$0

I'm not sure what to do now, I think I'll just add the dollar values. On average, I'd expect to win around $2985 per chip, if you let me sit there all day and drop chips. Not a bad day's work.

Often, it makes sense to assign a number to each outcome of an experiment, such as "3" instead of "rolling a 3 on the number cube," or "2" instead of "heads, tails, heads, tails, tails" or "10,000" instead of "the chip falls in the middle slot." Each set of these numerical assignments is a random variable, and typically uses a capital letter like X or Y.

Wendy's method calculates the *expected value* of a random variable.

> A **random variable** is a function whose inputs are outcomes, and whose outputs are numbers.

Definition

The **expected value** of a random variable X is the sum when each value of X is multiplied by its probability. The typical notation is $E(X)$.

$$E(X) = x_1 \cdot p_1 + x_2 \cdot p_2 + \ldots + x_n \cdot p_n$$

where the x_i are the values of the random variable, and the p_i are the probabilities of the values, respectively.

The definition is a mouthful, but the Plinko game is a good example. For the Plinko board, each x_n is a dollar value. Each p_n is the probability of hitting that value.

Example

Problem Toss five coins. What is the expected value for the number of heads?

Solution Define a random variable H as the number of heads in 5 coin tosses. This experiment has 32 outcomes. List the possible values of H, along with the probability for each.

Number of Heads	Probability
0	$\frac{1}{32}$
1	$\frac{5}{32}$
2	$\frac{10}{32}$
3	$\frac{10}{32}$
4	$\frac{5}{32}$
5	$\frac{1}{32}$

> **Remember...**
>
> A random variable takes in outcomes and returns numbers. For example, one outcome is $a =$ "heads, tails, heads, tails, tails." The random variable H takes in that outcome and returns the number 2, $H(a) = 2$.

Calculate expected value. Multiply each value of H by its probability. Then add the results.

Number of Heads	Probability	Product
0	$\frac{1}{32}$	0/32
1	$\frac{5}{32}$	5/32
2	$\frac{10}{32}$	20/32
3	$\frac{10}{32}$	30/32
4	$\frac{5}{32}$	20/32
5	$\frac{1}{32}$	5/32
Total		80/32

The expected value is $\frac{80}{32}$, which simplifies to $\frac{5}{2}$.

Habits of Mind

Check the result. Does $\frac{5}{2}$ make sense as the average number of heads when flipping five coins?

Developing Habits of Mind

Use a different process. You might have thought about the Plinko game in a different way. You could add up all the money you would win from each path. There are 2 ways to win $100, 16 ways to win $500, 56 ways to win $1000, and 70 ways to win $10,000. The total winnings from all the different paths is

$$2 \cdot \$100 + 16 \cdot \$500 + 56 \cdot \$1000 + 70 \cdot \$10,000 = \$764,200$$

This is the total value for all 256 paths, so the average would have to be

$$\frac{\$764,200}{256} \approx \$2985.16$$

This gives the correct result! Both methods are valid. It comes down to whether you prefer to count probabilities or frequencies. The result Wendy comes up with is

$$\frac{2}{256} \cdot \$100 + \frac{16}{256} \cdot \$500 + \frac{56}{256} \cdot \$1000 + \frac{70}{256} \cdot \$10,000$$

The distributive law shows that both these results must be identical. So, you can also calculate the expected value by taking the sum of all the outputs from the random variable, then dividing by the total number of outcomes. The expected value is the mean result from the random variable.

For example, the expected value of the numeric result when rolling one number cube is the mean of the numbers on the six faces.

$$\frac{1 + 2 + 3 + 4 + 5 + 6}{6} = 3.5$$

Minds in Action

Tony and Derman look at Exercise 9 from Lesson 5.05.

Tony   So, it's a wheel with 1, 2, 3, and 10 fish on it. And we want to know the average from one spin.

Derman I'll just add and divide. The sum is . . . 16. So the average is 4.

Tony   Sounds good. Now what about two spins?

Derman I think it's going to be 8. Two times four. Two spins, 4 fish each?

Tony   I'm not sure it works that way. Let's just write out the sample space. There are only 16 ways it can go.

Derman A table it is.

+	1	2	3	10
1	2	3	4	11
2	3	4	5	12
3	4	5	6	13
10	11	12	13	20

Tony   Cool. I'm going to add all these numbers then divide by 16. Since the sample space is small, I won't bother making a frequency table.

The sum is 128. So, the expected value for two spins is 128 over 16 . . . hey, you were right! It is 8.

Derman It was bound to happen sometime. If I'm right, for three spins the expected value should be 12. The table's going to be a mess!

Tony   Well, we should use a polynomial power instead. The outcomes are 1, 2, 3, and 10, so the polynomial for one spin should be

$$(x^1 + x^2 + x^3 + x^{10})$$

Derman Isn't x^1 just x?

Tony   I like writing x^1, it makes it more clear where it came from. I'd do that for x^0 instead of writing 1.

Derman Fair enough. And we raise that to the third power, since it's three spins. Expand that and . . .

Tony   Let's write that out.

For You to Do

7. Complete the work from the dialog. Write out the expansion of $(x^1 + x^2 + x^3 + x^{10})^3$, then use it to show that the expected value for three spins is 12.

Exercises *Practicing Habits of Mind*

Check Your Understanding

Alice, Bev, Craig, and Dawn sit at a table for four in no particular order. Rey, the host of the party, tells them their seats are assigned at the table and shows them the chart.

1. a. What is the probability that all four of them are already in the right seat?

   b. What is the probability that all four of them are in the *wrong* seat?

2. On average, how many of the four will be sitting in the right seat?

3. Suppose a Plinko board has a center hole worth \$20,000.

Find the average amount a player will win, per chip, in the long run.

4. What's Wrong Here? Daisuke had trouble calculating the expected number of heads when tossing three coins.

Daisuke: I built the table with each outcome and its probability, then added it up. I got the probabilities from the Getting Started lesson. I could use Pascal's Triangle to get them, too.

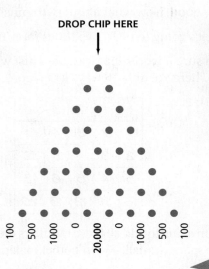

DROP CHIP HERE

100 500 1000 0 20,000 0 1000 500 100

Habits of Mind

Make a list. There are 24 possible ways for the four guests to sit down. Do you see why there are 24 possible outcomes? Try listing them.

This is another way to say, "Calculate the expected value" for this new version of the game.

Number of Heads	Probability	Product
0	$\frac{1}{8}$	$\frac{0}{8}$
1	$\frac{3}{8}$	$\frac{3}{8}$
2	$\frac{3}{8}$	$\frac{6}{8}$
3	$\frac{1}{8}$	$\frac{3}{8}$
Total		$\frac{12}{8}$

Daisuke: But it doesn't make sense to me to get $\frac{12}{8}$ as the answer: that's one and a half, and I thought probability was never supposed to be more than one.

What would you say to Daisuke? Has he made a mistake in the calculation?

5. Avery is taking a six-question multiple choice test, with five choices for each question. He guesses at each question.

   a. Expand the polynomial $(0.2r + 0.8w)^6$. What do the results represent?

   b. Find the expected value for the number of questions Avery gets right when taking the test.

6. Three customers spin the Wheel of Fish as seen in Exercise 9 on page 406.

   a. Use a polynomial expansion to find the frequency of each outcome.

   b. Find the probability that the market will give away fewer than 10 total fish to these three customers.

On one spin, the possible outcomes are 1, 2, 3, and 10 fish.

7. Find the expected value for the total number of fish the market gives away when four customers spin the Wheel of Fish.

On Your Own

8. In this lesson's In-Class Experiment, you calculated the expected value for dropping one Plinko chip. Now suppose you drop five chips.

   a. What is the expected value, in dollars, for the first chip? the second chip? the third chip?

   b. What is the expected value for the total earned from all five chips?

Go Online
www.successnetplus.com

9. Find the expected value for the number of heads when tossing six coins.

10. a. Find the expected value for the sum when rolling two number cubes.

    b. Find the expected value for the sum when rolling three number cubes.

11. **Take It Further**

    a. Find the expected value for the *product* when rolling two number cubes.

    b. Find the expected value for the product when rolling three number cubes. How could you use a polynomial here?

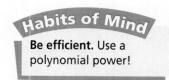

Habits of Mind

Be efficient. Use a polynomial power!

Suppose a friend gives you five envelopes, each with a different address on it. You are to put one of five different letters in each envelope. But you have no idea which letter is for which person, so you stuff them in at random.

12. What is the probability that all five envelopes contain the right letter?

13. What is the probability that exactly four envelopes contain the right letter?

14. What is the probability that all five envelopes contain the wrong letter?

15. Find the expected value for the number of letters correctly addressed.

16. **Standardized Test Prep** A student randomly guesses on a true-false test with five questions. Which of the following is the probability that the student will score at least 80%?

> This exercise is in the same style as Exercises 1 and 2. You might want to think of this as five people and five seats.

A. $\frac{5}{32}$ **B.** $\frac{3}{16}$ **C.** $\frac{1}{4}$ **D.** $\frac{1}{2}$

Maintain Your Skills

17. Copy and complete this table using your work from previous lessons.

n	Number of Elements in F_n	Relatively Prime Pairs
1	2	▪
2	▪	▪
3	▪	4
4	▪	▪
5	11	▪
6	▪	▪
7	▪	18
8	▪	▪
9	▪	▪
10	33	▪

Here, F_n is the Farey sequence of order n. *Relatively prime pairs* refers to the number of pairs that have no common factors greater than 1 as plotted in Exercise 11 on page 406.

18. **Take It Further** Find the number of elements in F_{30}, the Farey sequence of order 30. Your goal is only to find the number of elements, not list them all.

> **Habits of Mind**
>
> **Look for relationships.** Look for a simpler method than writing out the entire sequence F_{30}.

5.07 Lotteries

One application of expected value is a lottery. There are several different kinds of lotteries. In some lotteries, expected value can be directly calculated, while others require an approach based on combinations.

Scratch Tickets

State lotteries print batches of tickets, some of which are prize winners. Players pay to get a ticket. Most tickets lose, but some tickets are worth hundreds or thousands of dollars.

Here is the distribution from a scratch ticket game where each ticket costs $1.

Payout	Frequency
$1	163,500
$2	62,800
$4	20,945
$8	4,189
$12	4,189
$50	5,621
$100	128
$1,000	4
$0 (lose)	995,324
Total	**1,256,700**

Most of the tickets lose. Only a small percentage give the player more money than the price of the ticket.

How much is the average ticket worth in this game? To find this, calculate the expected value.

Payout	Frequency	Product
1	163,500	163,500
2	62,800	125,600
4	20,945	83,780
8	4,189	33,512
12	4,189	50,268
50	5,621	281,050
100	128	12,800
1,000	4	4,000
0 (lose)	995,324	0
Total	**1,256,700**	**754,510**

The random variable is the dollar value (payout) of the ticket, from 0 to 1000. The sample space is all 1,256,700 tickets. The expected value is the sum of each payout, multiplied by its probability.

The expected value is $\frac{754,510}{1,256,700}$, very close to 60 cents. This lottery ticket actually costs $1, so roughly 60% of the money paid for tickets is returned to players as prizes, while 40% is kept by the state that runs this lottery.

Example

In a 6-ball lottery a player picks six numbers, from 1 to 42. Then a machine draws six balls at random from a set of 42 numbered balls. The order of the drawing does not matter. The amount the player wins depends on how many of the numbers match numbers on their ticket.

The sample space has $\binom{42}{6} = 5,245,786$ elements.

This table shows the possible outcomes and their frequencies.

Matches	Frequency	Payout
0 correct	1,947,792	$0 (loss)
1 correct	2,261,952	$0 (loss)
2 correct	883,575	$0 (loss)
3 correct	142,800	$1
4 correct	9,450	$75
5 correct	216	$1,500
6 correct	1	$2,000,000 jackpot
Total	5,245,786	

Problem A ticket in this lottery costs $1. Find the expected value for one ticket.

Solution Multiply the frequencies by the payouts.

Matches	Frequency	Payout	Product
0 correct	1,947,792	0	0
1 correct	2,261,952	0	0
2 correct	883,575	0	0
3 correct	142,800	1	142,800
4 correct	9,450	75	708,750
5 correct	216	1,500	324,000
6 correct	1	2,000,000	2,000,000
Total	5,245,786		3,175,550

Note that the majority of the payouts go to the single jackpot winner (if there is one). Overall the expected value is

$$\frac{3,175,550}{5,245,786} \approx 0.6054$$

The $1 ticket is worth just over 60 cents, so the lottery earns an average profit of nearly 40 cents per dollar played.

For You to Do

1. Suppose the lottery is considering changing the rules to give a $5 prize for 3 numbers correct. What would happen to the expected value of a ticket? Would the lottery still be profitable for whoever is running it?

Combinatorics and Lotteries

You can determine the frequencies in the previous example by counting combinations. Picture the 42 balls in the lottery drawing. The player picks 6 numbers, dividing the 42 balls into two categories: 6 that they want to see, and 36 others that they do not want to see.

Suppose you want to know how many different ways there are to get exactly four balls correct in the lottery drawing. Well, out of the 6 balls the player wants to see, the machine draws 4. That can happen $\binom{6}{4}$ ways. But the machine also draws 2 of the "other" balls. That can happen $\binom{36}{2}$ ways. So, the number of ways to get exactly four balls correct is

$$\binom{6}{4} \cdot \binom{36}{2} = 15 \cdot 630 = 9450$$

You can use this approach for any count between 0 and 6.

Matches	Frequency
0 correct	$\binom{6}{0} \cdot \binom{36}{6} = 1{,}947{,}792$
1 correct	$\binom{6}{1} \cdot \binom{36}{5} = 2{,}261{,}952$
2 correct	$\binom{6}{2} \cdot \binom{36}{4} = 883{,}575$
3 correct	$\binom{6}{3} \cdot \binom{36}{3} = 142{,}800$
4 correct	$\binom{6}{4} \cdot \binom{36}{2} = 9{,}450$
5 correct	$\binom{6}{5} \cdot \binom{36}{1} = 216$
6 correct	$\binom{6}{6} \cdot \binom{36}{0} = 1$

Note that the total number of outcomes is $\binom{42}{6}$ since there are 42 balls and 6 are picked. This leads to a theorem about combinations.

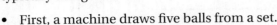

Study the difference. Larger multi-state lotteries now exist, typically using these rules:

- First, a machine draws five balls from a set.

- Second, another machine draws the sixth ball (the "bonus ball") from a second set of balls, a completely different group.

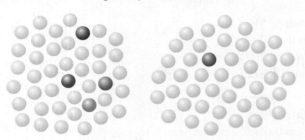

In order to win the jackpot, the player must get all five regular balls correct, plus the bonus ball. What effect does the existence of the bonus ball have on the sample space? Consider a game with 42 balls for the regular drawing, and a new set of 42 balls for the "bonus."

The size of the sample space becomes

$$\binom{42}{5} \cdot \binom{42}{1}$$

since 5 balls are chosen from the first set of 42, then 1 ball is chosen from the second set. While it may not seem like much of a difference, this has a huge effect on the size of the sample space.

$$\text{sample space for 6-ball lottery} = \binom{42}{6} = 5{,}245{,}786$$

$$\text{sample space with bonus ball} = \binom{42}{5} \cdot \binom{42}{1} = 35{,}728{,}056$$

The sample space is roughly 7 times bigger. It is much less likely a player will win. As of April 2008, one multi-state lottery had a sample space of over 146 million, while another had a sample space of over 175 million!

Think about flipping a coin 27 times in a row, and having all 27 coin flips come up heads. This would happen once every 134 million tries. In other words, flipping 27 heads in a row is *more* likely to happen than buying a winning ticket in either of these multi-state lotteries.

For Discussion

2. A multi-state lottery could increase its sample space by adding more balls to either the regular pool or the "bonus" pool. How many more regular-pool balls would be needed to double the sample space? How many more "bonus" balls would be needed to double the sample space?

Exercises *Practicing Habits of Mind*

Check Your Understanding

1. A 5-ball lottery has 55 numbered balls. A player selects five numbers. Then, five of the balls are drawn by a machine.

   Copy and complete this frequency table.

Matches	Frequency
0 correct	▣
1 correct	1,151,500
2 correct	▣
3 correct	▣
4 correct	▣
5 correct	1

2. Find the expected value for the number of balls a player will correctly match in the 5-ball lottery presented in Exercise 1.

3. Suppose an interstate lottery has a 5-ball component with 55 balls, and then a bonus ball from a separate set of 42 balls. This table lists the payouts for this lottery.

Ticket Type	Frequency	Payout
5 balls + bonus	1	Jackpot
5 balls + no bonus	41	$200,000
4 balls + bonus	250	$10,000
4 balls + no bonus	10,250	$100
3 balls + bonus	12,250	$100
3 balls + no bonus	502,250	$7
2 balls + bonus	196,000	$7
1 ball + bonus	1,151,500	$4
Bonus only	2,118,760	$3
Losing ticket	142,116,660	$0
Total outcomes	**146,107,962**	

   The base jackpot for this lottery is $16,000,000. Find the expected value of a $1 ticket in this lottery.

4. The jackpot in the game from Exercise 3 may grow as high as $100 million!

   a. Suppose the jackpot is worth m million dollars. Find the expected value of a ticket, in terms of m.

   b. If the jackpot is $100 million, what is the expected value of a ticket?

   c. How high must the jackpot be for the expected value to be greater than $1 per ticket?

5. **Take It Further** A second multistate lottery has a 5-ball component with 56 balls, and then a bonus ball from a separate set of 46 balls.

Copy and complete this table for the frequency of each payout.

Ticket Type	Frequency	Payout
5 balls + bonus	1	Jackpot
5 balls + no bonus	■	$250,000
4 balls + bonus	■	$10,000
4 balls + no bonus	11,475	$150
3 balls + bonus	■	$150
3 balls + no bonus	■	$7
2 balls + bonus	■	$10
1 ball + bonus	■	$3
Bonus only	■	$2
Losing ticket	171,306,450	$0
Total outcomes	**175,711,536**	

Then, find the expected value of a $1 ticket at the base jackpot of $12 million.

6. A state-run raffle offers a number of prizes. A total of 500,000 tickets are available. Each ticket costs $20. These prizes are available:

Payout	Frequency
$1,000,000	4
$100,000	5
$10,000	8
$5,000	8
$1,000	500
$100	2000
$0 (lose)	497,475

Find the expected value of a $20 raffle ticket.

The jackpots that lotteries report are actually much more than the money that they pay out or that a player would get. A player has to pay taxes on winnings. Also, the lottery pays the jackpot over many years, not all up front. In fact, it is rare for the jackpot to grow above $100 million in most lotteries.

On Your Own

Go Online
www.successnetplus.com

7. Consider the 6-ball lottery with 42 balls from this lesson. Find the expected value for the number of balls that a player will correctly match.

8. Consider the following prize distribution from a large scratch ticket game.

Payout	Frequency
$10,000,000	10
$1,000,000	130
$25,000	130
$10,000	1,820
$1,000	33,670
$500	109,200
$200	336,700
$100	1,791,335
$50	1,310,400
$40	2,620,800
$25	7,862,400
$20	7,862,400
$0 (lose)	43,585,545
Total tickets	**65,520,000**

   a. Find the expected value of one ticket.

   b. Each ticket costs $20. If all tickets are sold, how much profit will be made by the state running this lottery?

9. A 6-ball lottery in Italy is the largest of its kind with 90 balls to pick from. A player wins a prize in this lottery if they get at least 3 of the 6 numbers right. What is the probability of winning a prize in this lottery?

10. Use the Internet to find information on a lottery or scratch ticket game. Determine the expected value on a ticket in that game.

11. Suppose a friend gives you six envelopes, each with a different address on it. You are to put one of six different letters in each envelope. But you have no idea which letter is for which person, so you stuff them in at random. You hope at least some of the envelopes contain the correct letter.

This frequency table lists the number of different permutations with 0 correct envelopes, 1 correct, and so on.

Number Correct	Frequency
0	265
1	264
2	135
3	40
4	15
5	0
6	1

a. What is the total number of outcomes in this sample space?

b. Find the expected value for the number of correct envelopes.

12. **Standardized Test Prep** A bag contains 16 red chips and 4 blue chips. Amy picks one chip. After returning the chip to the bag and remixing the chips, she reaches in a second time and picks one chip. If Amy is paid as shown in the table, what is the expected value of the amount she will win?

Outcome	Payout
Two blue	wins $10
One blue, one red	wins $1
Two red	loses $1

A. loses at least $1   **B.** loses less than $1   **C.** Breaks even

D. wins less than $1   **E.** wins at least $1

Maintain Your Skills

13. The numbers 7, 21, and 35 appear in the 7th row of Pascal's Triangle. These numbers are unusual in that they form an arithmetic sequence: add 14 to 7 to get 21, then add another 14 to get 35. Or, put another way, 21 is the mean of 7 and 35.

a. Find the next time this occurs in Pascal's Triangle.

b. **Take It Further** If $\binom{n}{k}$ is the mean of $\binom{n}{k-1}$ and $\binom{n}{k+1}$, find a relationship between n and k.

5A

Mathematical Reflections

In this investigation, you calculated probabilities using Pascal's Triangle and polynomial powers. You also learned about expected value and its uses. The following questions will help you summarize what you have learned.

1. How can you use the expansion of $(t + h)^5$ to find the probability of getting exactly two heads on five coin tosses?

2. **a.** Al wins a game if he flips a coin heads, and rolls less than a six on a number cube. What is the probability that Al wins the game?

   b. Beth wins a game if she flips a coin tails, or (after flipping heads) if she rolls a six on a number cube. What is the probability that Beth wins the game?

3. A wheel has the numbers 5 through 100 on it, in multiples of 5. What is the expected value of one spin of this wheel?

4. A 5-ball state lottery uses 49 balls. What is the probability of getting exactly four of the five balls correct?

5. A wheel has the numbers 1, 2, 3, and 6 on it. After spinning the wheel four times, what is the most likely total?

6. If you are to roll four number cubes, what is the probability they sum to 12?

7. What is expected value?

8. How can you use polynomials to solve probability problems?

Vocabulary and Notation

In this investigation, you learned these terms and symbols. Make sure you understand what each one means and how to use it.

- **conditional probability**
- **event**
- **expected value, $E(X)$**
- **frequency, $|A|$**
- **independent**
- **mutually exclusive**

- **outcome**
- **Pascal's Triangle**
- **probability of an event**
- **random variable**
- **sample space**

If the survival rate for a hatchling to make it to the sea is 32%, how many in a group of 46 are expected to reach the sea?

Review

In **Investigation 5A,** you learned to

- calculate probabilities of simple random events.
- determine a set of equally likely outcomes for a probability experiment.
- find a polynomial to model a probability experiment and interpret expansions of its powers.
- calculate the expected value of a random variable.

The following questions will help you check your understanding.

1. In a game you are to roll a pair of regular octahedrons each with eight faces numbered 1–8.

   a. Write out the sample space for this experiment.

   b. What is the probability of rolling two 5's?

   c. What is the probability of rolling exactly one 5?

   d. What is the probability that the sum of the numbers on the faces is 9?

2. A game spinner has three colors, red, green, and blue. Each is equally likely. Expand $(r + b + g)^3$ to find the probability of getting two reds and one green when you spin three times.

3. A local high school is holding a raffle to raise money for extracurricular activities at the school. They plan to sell 1000 tickets. There will be one prize of $500, 2 prizes of $200, and 5 prizes of $100. What is the expected value of one ticket?

4. A bag contains 5 orange chips, 2 purple chips, and 3 yellow chips. Chips are drawn without replacement. Compute each probability.

   a. P (first chip is purple)

   b. P (second chip is yellow | first chip is purple)

   c. P (second chip is yellow | first chip is yellow)

   d. P (second chip is yellow | first chip is orange)

Multiple Choice

1. If you are to toss a coin five times, what is the expected value for the number of tails flipped?

  A. 2   **B.** 2.5

  C. 3   **D.** 3.5

2. Consider the following two spinners with five equal spaces.

Spinner A: 1, 3, 5, 6, 7
Spinner B: 2, 4, 5, 7, 8

What is the expected value for the sum when you spin the two spinners?

  A. 10.2   **B.** 8

  C. 5   **D.** 9.6

3. The probability a batter gets a hit is $p = 0.3$. What is the probability that in eight at-bats the batter will get exactly four hits? Round to two decimal places.

  A. 0.14   **B.** 0.31

  C. 0.01   **D.** 0.25

4. A spinner contains the numbers 1, 1, 2, 2, 4, and 6 in equal wedges. Which polynomial models the sum of three spins?

  A. $(x^1 + x^2 + x^4 + x^6)^3$

  B. $(2x^1 + 2x^2 + x^4 + x^6)^3$

  C. $(x^1 + x^2 + 2x^4 + 2x^6)^3$

  D. $(3x^1 + 3x^2 + 3x^4 + 3x^6)^3$

Open Response

5. You play a game where you roll a standard number cube 10 times. Each time you roll a six you win. Round answers to two decimal places.

  a. What is the probability that you never win?

  b. What is the probability that you win exactly twice?

  c. What is the average number of wins in ten rolls?

6. A game involves rolling a standard number cube and spinning a spinner with the numbers 2, 3, and 5 in equal wedges. Then find the sum of the two results.

  a. How many equally-likely outcomes are in this sample space?

  b. What is the probability of getting a sum of 7?

  c. What is the probability of getting a sum of 12?

7. A bag contains 2 green marbles, 4 red marbles, and 4 blue marbles. Marbles are drawn without replacement. Compute each probability.

  a. P (first marble is red)

  b. P (second marble is blue | first marble is red)

  c. P (second marble is blue | first marble is green)

  d. P (second marble is blue | first marble is blue)

8. A lottery is played by choosing six numbers from the set 1–42, with payouts as shown.

Matches	Frequency	Prize
0 correct	▪	$0
1 correct	▪	$0
2 correct	▪	$2
3 correct	▪	$10
4 correct	▪	$50
5 correct	▪	$20,000
6 correct	▪	$1,000,000

  a. Copy and complete the table.

  b. What is the probability of matching exactly four numbers?

  c. What is the probability of winning the million dollar prize?

  d. Find the expected value of one ticket.

Chapter 6

Congruence and Proof

You may have heard the saying, "Red sky at night, sailor's delight. Red sky at morning, sailors take warning." Through years of experience, sailors learned that they can use this saying, within limits, to predict the weather. You can use your own experiences, as well, to make predictions or conjectures. After you complete the following activity, you will be able to make a conjecture about the sum of the measures of the angles of a triangle.

Draw a large triangle on paper and cut it out. Tear off the angles. Place the vertices of the three angles together. Arrange the sides of the angles edge to edge, so there are no gaps. One edge of your new figure should appear to form a straight angle, which measures 180°. But how can you be sure? You can measure the three angles with a protractor, but measurement is not exact.

For problems like this, you can use mathematical proof to verify your results. Mathematical proof is a method that relies on certain assumptions, precise definitions, and logical deductions to prove new facts. In this chapter, you will prove, among many other results, that the sum of the measures of the angles of a triangle is 180°.

Vocabulary and Notation

- alternative exterior angles
- alternate interior angles
- base angle
- base of a trapezoid
- base of an isosceles triangle
- concave
- conclusion
- collinear points
- consecutive angles
- concurrent lines
- constant
- converse
- corollary
- corresponding angles
- disc
- equiangular
- exterior angle
- hypothesis
- invariant
- isosceles trapezoid
- isosceles triangle
- kite
- leg
- parallel lines
- parallelogram
- proof
- quadrilateral
- rectangle
- rhombus
- scalene triangle
- side
- skew quadrilateral
- square
- supplementary angles
- transversal
- trapezoid
- trisected
- vertex (vertices)
- vertex angle
- vertical angles
- ≇ (is not congruent to)
- ‖ (is parallel to)

Triangle Congruence

You know that corresponding parts of congruent figures are congruent. For triangles, you say that corresponding parts of congruent triangles are congruent. In other words, if two triangles are congruent, then their corresponding sides and corresponding angles are also congruent.

The converse of this statement is also true. If the corresponding sides and corresponding angles of two triangles are congruent, then the triangles are congruent. This gives an exact method for proving triangles are congruent, but checking the six pairs of corresponding parts is a great deal of work.

> You can abbreviate *corresponding parts of congruent triangles are congruent* as CPCTC.

For Discussion

1. Can you check fewer than six pairs of corresponding parts to determine whether two triangles are congruent? For instance, if the three angles in one triangle are congruent to the three angles in another triangle, are the two triangles congruent? Or if the three sides in one triangle are congruent to the three sides of another triangle, are the two triangles congruent?

2. Discuss the meaning of the following statement. *Information that is enough to specify one triangle is also enough to ensure that two triangles are congruent.* Is the statement true? Explain.

Classifying Your Information

You can *sometimes* determine whether two triangles are congruent when three parts of one triangle are congruent to three parts of another triangle. But not any three pairs of congruent parts guarantee that two triangles are congruent. For example, two triangles that have congruent corresponding angles are not necessarily congruent.

Which sets of three pairs of congruent parts guarantee that two triangles are congruent? To answer that question, first make a list of the possible combinations of three parts in one triangle. For example, $\triangle ABC$ has six parts: three sides and three angles.

three sides: $\overline{AB}$, $\overline{BC}$, and $\overline{AC}$
three angles: $\angle A$, $\angle B$, and $\angle C$

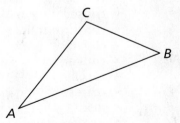

For You to Do

3. List the possible combinations of three parts of $\triangle ABC$. Here are two examples.

- $\angle A$, $\angle B$, $\angle C$
- $\overline{AB}$, $\angle A$, $\angle B$

You can classify your combinations in many ways. Here is a scheme that people have found useful. Note that this is *not* a list of ways to show two triangles are congruent.

Three Parts	Abbreviation Triplet	Meaning for a Triangle	Example for △*ABC*
Three angles	AAA	Three angles of the triangle	∠A, ∠B, ∠C
Two angles, one side	ASA	Two angles and the side between them	∠A, $\overline{AB}$, ∠B
	AAS	Two angles and a side not between the angles	∠A, ∠B, $\overline{BC}$
Two sides, one angle	SAS	Two sides and the angle between them	$\overline{AC}$, ∠A, $\overline{AB}$
	SSA	Two sides and an angle not between the sides	$\overline{AC}$, $\overline{AB}$, ∠B
Three sides	SSS	Three sides of the triangle	$\overline{AC}$, $\overline{AB}$, $\overline{BC}$

You read *ASA* as "angle-side-angle."

Order is important. SAS is not the same as SSA.

Which of these triplets can you use to prove that two triangles are congruent? You can investigate this question. Try to build two noncongruent triangles that share a given triplet. If you can, then the triplet does not guarantee triangle congruence. If you cannot, then there is a good chance that the triplet does guarantee congruence.

In-Class Experiment

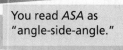

Work with a partner or in a small group to determine which of the triplets below guarantee triangle congruence. For each triplet, try to build two noncongruent triangles with the given angle measures and side lengths.

4. **ASA** $m\angle A = 40°$, $AB = 2$ in., $m\angle B = 70°$

5. **AAS** $m\angle A = 40°$, $m\angle B = 70°$, $BC = 2$ in.

6. **SAS** $AC = 2$ in., $m\angle A = 60°$, $AB = 3$ in.

7. **SSA** $AC = 2$ in., $AB = 4$ in., $m\angle B = 20°$

8. **SSS** $AC = 2$ in., $AB = 3$ in., $BC = 4$ in.

The results of the In-Class Experiment suggest the following assumption.

Postulate 6.1 The Triangle Congruence Postulates

If two triangles share the following triplets of congruent corresponding parts, then the triangles are congruent.

- **ASA**
- **SAS**
- **SSS**

Remember...

Another word for assumption is *postulate*. A **postulate** is a statement that is accepted without proof.

What can you do with the AAS triplet? You can prove that this triplet guarantees triangle congruence if you assume that the other triangle congruence postulates are true. You also have to assume that the sum of the measures of the angles of a triangle is 180°.

And what can you do with the SSA triplet? In Exercise 7, you will show why this triplet does not guarantee triangle congruence.

Mathematicians like to make as few assumptions and to prove as many theorems as possible.

Exercises *Practicing Habits of Mind*

Check Your Understanding

For Exercises 1 and 2, do each of the following:

a. Construct △*ABC* with the given angle measures and given side lengths.

b. Compare results with a classmate. Are your triangles congruent?

c. If your triangles are not congruent, what additional information will guarantee that the triangles are congruent?

1. $m\angle A = 36°$, $m\angle B = 72°$, $m\angle C = 72°$

2. $m\angle A = 60°$, $AB = 8$ cm, $BC = 7$ cm

In Exercises 3 and 4, is △*ABC* ≅ △*ADC*? If the two triangles are congruent, state which triangle congruence postulate helped you decide.

3.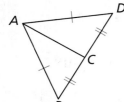

4.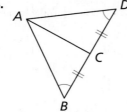

5. Show in two different ways that a diagonal of a square divides the square into two congruent triangles. Use a different triangle congruence postulate each time.

6. You and a friend are making triangular pennants. Your friend says that each pennant should have a 30° angle, a 14-inch side, and an 8-inch side. Explain why this information does not guarantee that all the pennants will be congruent.

7. The diagram at the right proves, without words, that the SSA triplet does not guarantee triangle congruence. Explain the proof.

Remember...

A *square* is a quadrilateral with four congruent sides and four right angles.

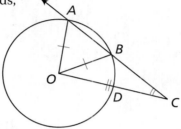

Note that point *O* is the center of the circle. Why use a circle in this proof without words?

On Your Own

For Exercises 8–12, do each of the following:

a. Tell whether the given information is enough to show that the triangles are congruent. The triangles are not necessarily drawn to scale.

b. If the given information is enough, list the pairs of corresponding vertices of the two triangles. Then state which triangle congruence postulate guarantees that the triangles are congruent.

8.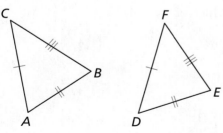

9.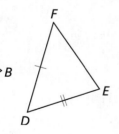

10.

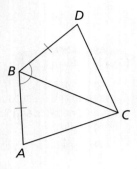

11.

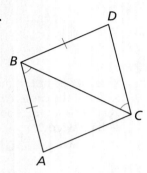

12.

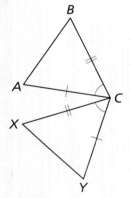

13. **Standardized Test Prep** In $\triangle ABC$, $\overline{CD}$ is the bisector of $\angle ACB$. Which of the following conjectures is true?

A. There is not sufficient evidence to prove that $\triangle ACD \cong \triangle BCD$.

B. $\triangle ACD \cong \triangle BCD$ is true by the Angle-Side-Angle postulate. In each triangle, the side between the two angles is $\overline{CD}$.

C. $\triangle ACD \cong \triangle BCD$ is true by the Side-Angle-Side postulate. Angle ACD and $\angle BCD$ are the congruent angles that are between the two pairs of congruent sides.

D. $\triangle ACD \cong \triangle BCD$ is true by the Side-Side-Side postulate.

14. In the figure at the right, $\overline{BD}$ is the perpendicular bisector of $\overline{AC}$. Based on this statement, which two triangles are congruent? Prove that they are congruent.

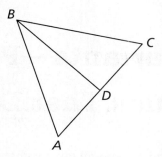

15. Take It Further In the figure at the right, $\overline{AD}$ is the perpendicular bisector of $\overline{BC}$. Based on this information, two triangles in the figure are congruent.

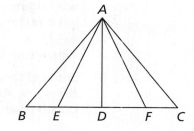

For each part, does the given piece of information help you determine that any additional triangles are congruent? If so, state the triangles and the congruence postulate that guarantees their congruence.

a. $AB = AC$

b. $\overline{AD}$ is the perpendicular bisector of $\overline{EF}$.

c. $\angle EAD \cong \angle FAD$

16. Assume you know that the sum of the measures of the angles in a triangle is 180°.

a. In $\triangle ABC$ and $\triangle DEF$, $m\angle A = m\angle D = 72°$, $m\angle B = m\angle E = 47°$, and $AC = DF = 10$ in. Is $\triangle ABC \cong \triangle DEF$? Explain.

b. Explain why the AAS triplet guarantees triangle congruence.

Maintain Your Skills

17. Does a diagonal of a rectangle divide the rectangle into two congruent triangles? Can you say the same for the diagonals of a parallelogram? For the diagonals of a trapezoid? For the diagonals of a kite? Explain.

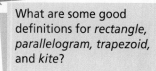

What are some good definitions for *rectangle, parallelogram, trapezoid,* and *kite*?

Invariants—Properties and Values That Don't Change

In *Invariants*, you will use geometry software to experiment with figures. You will stretch and squash parts of a figure to get a feel for how the parts work together, which patterns exist, and which values or relationships stay the same, even when others change.

Some of the invariants that you discover will lead to useful theorems. As you proceed, visualize, draw pictures, and make calculations. Do whatever helps you make an educated guess.

By the end of this investigation, you will be able to answer questions like these.

1. What is an invariant? What kinds of invariants should you look for in geometry?

2. What invariant relationship exists when a line parallel to the base of a triangle intersects the other sides of that triangle?

3. What shape do you form when you connect the consecutive midpoints of a quadrilateral?

You will learn how to

- describe various types of invariants in geometry

- identify the invariant relationships for the sums of the measures of the angles of polygons

- identify the invariant relationship that exists when a line parallel to one side of a triangle cuts the other two sides of the triangle proportionally

- search for geometric invariants, such as points of concurrency and collinearity of points

You will develop these habits and skills:

- Search for numerical invariants.

- Search for spatial invariants.

- Make conjectures.

- Use software to tinker with geometric models.

Pop-up book artists are experts on how parts of a figure work together.

6.01 Getting Started

Activating Prior Knowledge
Exploring New Ideas

Something that is true for each member of a collection is an **invariant** for the collection.

For You to Explore

1. Study the three different collections below.

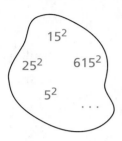 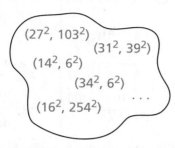 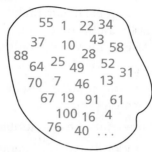

a. In the first set, each number before squaring ends in 5. Evaluate the squares. What invariants do you find?

b. The second set contains pairs of square numbers. In each pair, the two numbers before squaring end in digits that add to 10. Evaluate all the squares. What invariants do you find?

c. The third set contains 1, 4, 7, 10, 13, and so on. Decide whether 301 is in the set. Choose pairs of numbers from the set and find their products. What seems to be true about their products? What seems to be true about the sums of four numbers chosen from the set? What seems to be true about the differences of any two numbers chosen from the set?

2. Draw two polygons like quadrilateral *ABCD* and △*EFG* below. On each side, draw two points that roughly divide the sides into thirds. Connect each vertex to two points on different sides to form the largest angle possible. The connecting segments surround a region. The two diagrams here suggest

- the region has eight sides when the original shape has four sides
- the region has six sides when the original shape has three sides

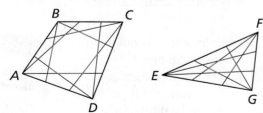

Is this a reliable pattern? In other words, does the inside region always have twice the number of sides as the original shape when you connect vertices to "third points" in this way? Explain.

> **Remember...**
> An invariant over a set is something that is the same for every member of the set.

> To make the angle with vertex at *B*, connect *B* to the point on $\overline{AD}$ that is closer to *A*, and to the point on $\overline{CD}$ that is closer to *C*.

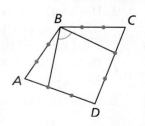

Exercises Practicing Habits of Mind

On Your Own

3. The table at the right shows pairs of numbers. An invariant for the table is 4 because $\frac{r}{q} = 4$ for each pair. Make three different tables like the one at the right so that the invariant for each table is 8. Use a different operation to build each table.

q	r
$\frac{1}{8}$	$\frac{1}{2}$
4	16
8	32
100	400

4. Draw a quadrilateral. Construct the midpoints of its sides. Then connect the consecutive midpoints.

    a. Explain why the figure formed must be a quadrilateral.

    b. Can the figure formed be *any* kind of quadrilateral, or are certain kinds of quadrilaterals not possible? Explain.

> In other words, besides the number of sides, what other invariants, if any, exist?

Maintain Your Skills

5. a. Use geometry software to construct a figure like the one at the right, in which lines ℓ and m are parallel. Then drag a point or one of the lines to change the appearance of the figure. Lines ℓ and m should remain parallel.

    b. List some invariants that you find.

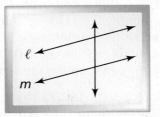

6. a. Use geometry software to construct a square like the one at the right.

    b. Drag some points. List some invariants that you find.

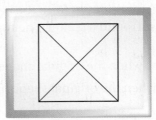

> A square is a regular polygon. For help, see the TI-Nspire Handbook, p. 990.

7. a. Use geometry software. Construct a line ℓ and a point P that is not on ℓ. (Do not place P too far away from ℓ.) Choose a point Q on line ℓ. Draw $\overline{PQ}$. Construct the circle with $\overline{PQ}$ as a diameter. Keep P and ℓ fixed. Place three or four more points on ℓ. Connect each of these new points to P with a line segment. Draw a circle with this segment as its diameter.

    b. List some invariants that you find.

> **Habits of Mind**
>
> **Visualize.** If $\overline{PQ}$ is a diameter, where is the center of the circle?

6.02 Numerical Invariants in Geometry

Positions of points, intersections of lines, lengths of segments, measures of angles, and even sums or ratios of these measurements may be invariant.

A numerical invariant is called a **constant.** In this section, *invariant* and *constant* mean the same thing.

For the problems in the following In-Class Experiments, do each of the following tasks.

- Draw and measure the objects with geometry software.
- Drag parts of the figure. Watch what changes and what remains the same.
- Make conjectures that seem likely. Then find a way to test them.
- Organize and record your results.

In-Class Experiment

Geometric Objects

1. Use geometry software to construct a circle and one of its diameters. Find the circumference, the length of the diameter, and the area of the circle. Also calculate the ratio of each pair of these measurements. Which ratios, if any, seem invariant as you change the size of the circle?

2. Construct two parallel lines that are a fixed distance apart. Construct △*DEF* such that points *D*, *E*, and *F* are on the lines, as shown.

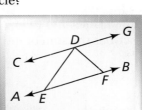

In parts (a)–(e), which measures seem invariant in △*DEF* as *D* moves along $\overleftrightarrow{CD}$?

   a. the measure of ∠*EDF*
   b. the sum of the lengths of $\overline{DE}$ and $\overline{DF}$
   c. the perimeter of △*DEF*
   d. the area of △*DEF*
   e. the sum of the measures of ∠*D*, ∠*E*, and ∠*F*
   f. Can you find any other invariants?

3. Study your construction from Problem 2 as *D* moves along $\overleftrightarrow{CD}$.

   a. Find two angles that have equal measure, no matter where *D* is located on $\overleftrightarrow{CD}$.
   b. Find pairs or groups of angles that have an invariant sum of 180°.
   c. Can you find two angles such that the measure of one is always greater than the measure of the other? Explain.

For help finding the area of the triangle, see the TI-Nspire Handbook, p. 990.

4. Draw △ABC. Construct the midpoint D of $\overline{BC}$. Construct median $\overline{AD}$. As you stretch and distort △ABC, what is invariant? (Be sure that D remains the midpoint of $\overline{BC}$!)

a. Find two segments such that their lengths are a constant ratio.

b. Are there any invariant areas? Invariant ratios of areas?

c. Find at least one other invariant. Provide a chart or table of measurements and some sketches to show the measures or ratios that do not change.

Remember...

A median of a triangle is a line segment that connects one of the triangle's vertices to the midpoint of the opposite side.

In-Class Experiment

Constant Sum and Difference

You may be convinced that the sum of the angle measures of a triangle is invariably 180°. What do you think about the sums of the angle measures of other kinds of polygons? Are they also 180°? Or do different kinds of polygons—quadrilaterals, pentagons, hexagons, and so on—have their own special fixed numbers? If so, is it possible to predict the sum of the angle measures of a given polygon?

5. Experiment with the sums of the angle measures of quadrilaterals, pentagons, hexagons, and so on. Be sure to test both regular and irregular shapes. Which types of polygons, if any, have constant sums of angle measures?

6. You can divide a polygon with n sides into $(n - 2)$ triangles. How might this help you find a rule that describes the sum of the measures of the angles of a polygon?

Habits of Mind

Generalize. Trying this for a few simple polygons may suggest what you can do for any polygon. Once you get the general idea, try to make a convincing argument that applies to every polygon.

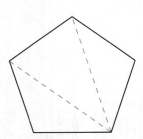

Three triangles form a pentagon.

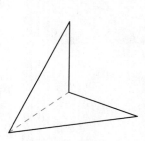

Two triangles form a quadrilateral.

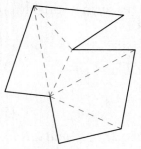

Six triangles form an octagon.

7. Assume that the sum of the angle measures of a triangle is invariant. Write an argument that shows that the sum of the angle measures of an n-sided polygon is also invariant. Find a rule that will tell you the angle sum if you know n, the number of sides.

Constant Product and Ratio

Use geometry software to draw a triangle. Construct and connect the midpoints of two sides. Your construction will look something like the construction below. Point D is the midpoint of $\overline{AC}$, and E is the midpoint of $\overline{AB}$.

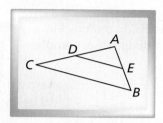

8. Move one of the triangle's vertices. As you distort the triangle, look for invariants.

9. Measure the lengths of $\overline{DE}$ and $\overline{BC}$. Compare these lengths as you drag one of the vertices.

You know about the following invariants because you deliberately built them into your triangle.

- $CD = DA$ (because D is the midpoint of $\overline{AC}$)
- $AE = EB$ (because E is the midpoint of $\overline{AB}$)
- $\dfrac{AD}{AC} = \dfrac{1}{2}$
- $\dfrac{AE}{AB} = \dfrac{1}{2}$

You may not have listed this next invariant because it is almost too obvious. It is built into the software, and it is important.

- As you drag one vertex of the triangle, the other two vertices do not move. Therefore, the length of the side opposite the vertex you move does not change.

The remaining invariants were not built in by anyone. They are natural consequences of the invariants listed above.

- As $\overline{CB}$ gets longer, so does $\overline{DE}$. In fact, $\dfrac{DE}{CB} = \dfrac{1}{2}$.
- $\dfrac{\text{area}(\triangle ABC)}{\text{area}(\triangle AED)} = 4$
- $\overline{DE}$ is parallel to $\overline{CB}$.

> **Go Online**
> www.successnetplus.com

> CD, without the overbar, represents the length of segment $\overline{CD}$.

The results of the In-Class Experiment suggest the following conjecture.

Conjecture 6.1 Midline Conjecture

A segment connecting the midpoints of two sides of a triangle is parallel to the third side and is half its length.

Exercises Practicing Habits of Mind

Check Your Understanding

1. Use geometry software to construct a circle and one of its diameters. Place a point on the circle away from an endpoint of the diameter. Then complete the triangle as shown in the third figure below.

For help placing a point on the circle, see the TI-Nspire Handbook, p. 990.

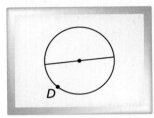
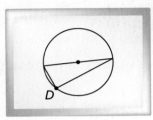

   a. Move *D* around the circle. What measures or relationships are invariant as *D* moves? Look at angles, lengths, sums, and ratios.

   b. Leave *D* in one place and stretch the circle. What measures or relationships are invariant as the size of the circle changes?

2. Construct a rectangle *ABCD* so that you can stretch its length and width. Which of the following are invariants?

   a. the length-to-width ratio: $\frac{AB}{AD}$

   b. the ratio of the lengths of the opposite sides: $\frac{AB}{DC}$

   c. the perimeter of rectangle *ABCD*

   d. the ratio of the lengths of the diagonals: $\frac{AC}{BD}$

   e. the ratio of the perimeter of rectangle *ABCD* to its area

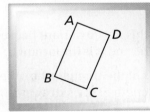

3. In the figure below, *C* is fixed on $\overline{AB}$, but *D* is not fixed. Move *D*. Find two sums related to the figure that are constant.

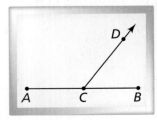

4. Use geometry software to draw two parallel lines *m* and *n*. Fix points *A* and *B* on line *m*. Place point *C* on line *n*. Draw △*ABC*. Now move point *C* along *n*. Look at the area and perimeter of the triangle. What invariants do you notice?

Use geometry software to construct a circle. Place a point C anywhere inside the circle. Place point D on the circle. Construct the line through D and C to meet the circle a second time at point E. Then hide $\overleftrightarrow{DC}$. Construct $\overline{DC}$, $\overline{EC}$, and $\overline{DE}$. As you move D along the circle, $\overline{DE}$ will pivot about C.

5. Measure $\overline{CE}$ and $\overline{CD}$. When the chord pivots about C, do CE and CD change in opposite ways (one increases while the other decreases) or in the same way? Use that information to help you find a numerical invariant.

6. The number you found does not depend on the location of D. You can move D, and the number remains fixed. But the number does *not* remain fixed when C is moved. For which location of C inside the circle is the number greatest? Explain.

7. Draw $\triangle ABC$. Place a point D arbitrarily on $\overline{AC}$. Through D, construct the line that is parallel to $\overline{CB}$. Use that line to construct $\overline{DE}$. Then hide $\overleftrightarrow{DE}$, leaving just $\overline{DE}$ showing. Your construction should resemble your construction from the Constant Product and Ratio In-Class Experiment earlier in the lesson. This time, D and E are movable points rather than midpoints.

A *chord* of a circle is a segment with endpoints that are on the circle.

$\overline{AB}$ is a chord of the circle.

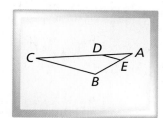

As D moves along $\overline{AC}$, $\overline{DE}$ moves with it. Look at different lengths and areas. Try to find some invariants. Record your conjectures and appropriate supporting evidence.

Developing Habits of Mind

Experiment. Exercise 7 is a good example of how you get different results when you slightly change a problem. You know from earlier work that certain ratios are invariant when D is the midpoint of $\overline{AC}$. When D is fixed on $\overline{AC}$ but is *not* its midpoint, are those ratios still invariant? Or does their invariance depend on D being the midpoint?

When you move D, are the ratios constant? If so, the ratios are again invariant. If not, perhaps a relationship exists between two or more of the ratios.

8. Tennis balls are sold in cans of three stacked balls. Which is greater—the height of the can or the circumference of the can?

9. In the figure below, $\overleftrightarrow{CD} \parallel \overrightarrow{AB}$. How can you construct a right triangle that has the same area as $\triangle EFG$?

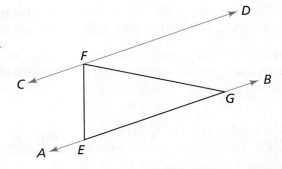

10. **Take It Further**

   a. Use geometry software to construct a rectangle. Then divide the rectangle into a square and a smaller rectangle.

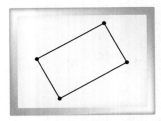 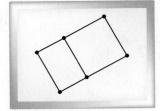

   a rectangle   the rectangle divided
                        into a square and a
                        smaller rectangle

   Find the length-to-width ratio in each nonsquare rectangle. Are the two ratios equal?

   b. The figure at the right illustrates a special ratio for a particular type of rectangle. If you divide this type of rectangle into a square and a smaller rectangle, as shown, the length-to-width ratios of the large and small nonsquare rectangles are equal. In fact, you can divide the smaller rectangle into a square and an even smaller rectangle. The length-to-width ratio of the smaller rectangle is the same as the length-to-width ratio of the first two rectangles. What is the numerical value of this length-to-width ratio?

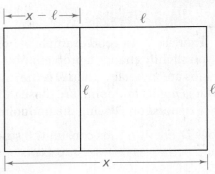

11. Decide whether each ratio in parts (a)–(c) is constant, even if you stretch the given figure with the given restrictions. Justify each answer.

a. The square remains square. Is the ratio $\dfrac{\text{area of triangle}}{\text{area of square}}$ invariant? If so, what is the ratio?

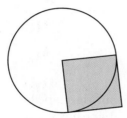

b. The circle remains a circle. The square remains a square. Is the ratio $\dfrac{\text{area of circle}}{\text{area of square}}$ invariant? If so, what is the ratio?

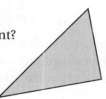

c. The triangle remains a triangle. You can reshape it in any way. Is the ratio $\dfrac{\text{perimeter of triangle}}{\text{area of triangle}}$ invariant? If so, what is the ratio?

12. Standardized Test Prep Maya constructed a regular hexagon inside a circle. The hexagon consists of six equilateral triangles. To compute the sum of the measures of the angles of the regular hexagon, she found the sum of the measures of the angles of the six triangles. From that sum, she subtracted the measure of each angle with a vertex at the center of the circle.

What is the sum of the measures of the angles of Maya's regular hexagon?

A. 360°   **B.** 540°   **C.** 720°   **D.** 1080°

Go Online
www.successnetplus.com

Maintain Your Skills

Go Online
Video Tutor
www.successnetplus.com

13. Find five cylindrical objects. Measure the diameter and the circumference of each. What is the $\dfrac{\text{circumference}}{\text{diameter}}$ ratio for each object?

Spatial Invariants—Shape, Concurrence, and Collinearity

Shape: A Geometric Invariant

Invariants do not have to be numbers or relationships between numbers. Invariants can be shapes or relationships between shapes, as well. In Lesson 6.01, you searched for shape invariants in the figures below.

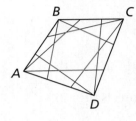

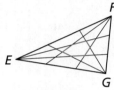

It appears that when the outside shape has four sides, the inside shape has eight. When the outside shape has three sides, the inside shape has six. It turns out that, in the case of a triangle, the figure formed on the inside is always a hexagon. Otherwise, the strict doubling pattern is not reliable.

Investigate these figures further. Learn or invent a way to divide a segment accurately into thirds. For this investigation, however, it is acceptable to divide the segment by estimating or by measuring.

Geometry software preserves proportions along a segment when you stretch or shrink the segment. So, your estimated thirds will stay fixed throughout the experiment, unless you deliberately change them.

For Discussion

What *can* happen is often as useful as what *must* happen.

1. If the outside polygon has *n* sides, can the inside polygon ever have more than 2*n* sides? If so, what is the greatest number of sides the inside polygon can have?

2. Can the inside polygon ever have fewer than 2*n* sides? If so, what is the fewest number of sides the inside polygon can have?

3. Can the inside polygon ever be regular? Explain.

Concurrence: A Geometric Invariant

You may recognize the picture below from one of the experiments you performed earlier.

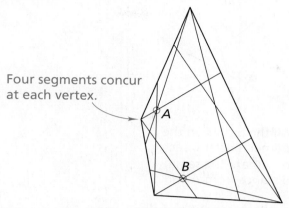

Four segments concur at each vertex.

At each vertex of the outside quadrilateral, four segments intersect or concur. That is no surprise. It was intentional.

Definition

Three or more lines that meet or intersect at one point are concurrent lines.

Lines ℓ, m, and n are concurrent lines.

In the first figure above, three *inside* segments are also concurrent. Two such concurrences are at points A and B. These concurrences were not deliberately built in. They are something of a surprise. If you move the vertices of the quadrilateral, you will see that these concurrences are not invariant.

When concurrence is an invariant for a given figure, a special relationship exists.

For You to Do

4. Use geometry software to draw a triangle. Construct the perpendicular bisector of each side. Can you adjust the triangle so that the three perpendicular bisectors are concurrent?

For help constructing the perpendicular bisectors, see the TI-Nspire Handbook, p. 990.

5. Hide the perpendicular bisectors. Construct the angle bisectors of your triangle. Can you adjust the triangle so that the three angle bisectors are concurrent?

6. Under which circumstances, if any, are the three perpendicular bisectors and the three angle bisectors of a triangle all concurrent?

It may surprise you that the perpendicular bisectors in a triangle are concurrent. If you analyze the situation, though, it becomes less surprising.

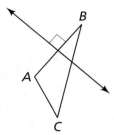

All the points on the perpendicular bisector of $\overline{AB}$ are the same distance from A and B.

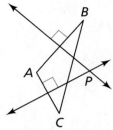

All the points on the perpendicular bisector of $\overline{AC}$ are the same distance from A and C.

Point P is constructed so that it is equidistant from A and B and equidistant from A and C. So P is also equidistant from B and C. P must lie on the perpendicular bisector of $\overline{BC}$.

Theorem 6.1 Concurrence of Perpendicular Bisectors

In any triangle, the perpendicular bisectors of the sides are concurrent.

In $\triangle ABC$, the perpendicular bisectors of $\overline{AB}$, $\overline{BC}$, and $\overline{AC}$ are concurrent at G.

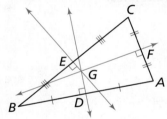

You can make a similar argument for the angle bisectors of a triangle. Any point on the bisector of $\angle ABC$ is the same distance from $\overline{AB}$ and $\overline{BC}$. Any point on the bisector of $\angle CAB$ is the same distance from $\overline{AC}$ and $\overline{AB}$. The point of intersection of the two angle bisectors is the same distance from $\overline{AC}$ and $\overline{BC}$. That puts it on the bisector of $\angle ACB$ as well.

Theorem 6.2 Concurrence of Angle Bisectors

In any triangle, the angle bisectors are concurrent.

In $\triangle XYZ$, the angle bisectors of $\angle X$, $\angle Y$, and $\angle Z$ are concurrent at K.

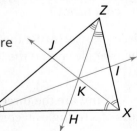

Collinearity

It is noteworthy when three lines intersect at the same point. It is also noteworthy when three apparently unrelated points lie on the same line.

Definition

Three or more points that are on the same line are **collinear points.**

For You to Do

Step 1 Trace a circle onto a sheet of paper.

Step 2 Poke a small hole through the paper at the center of the circle.

Step 3 Carefully cut out your **disc** (the circle and its interior).

Step 4 Work with three or four classmates who made discs of different sizes. Draw two points on a large sheet of paper. Place them close enough together that the smallest disc can touch both.

Step 5 Place one of your discs on the large sheet. Move it so that the edge of the disc touches both points.

Step 6 Mark the center of the circle on the large sheet.

Step 7 Remove the disc. Repeat Steps 5 and 6 with the other discs.

Step 8 After using all your discs, look at the circles' center marks. What is invariant about their positions?

Step 9 Draw two new points. Without using your discs, draw the figure that would be formed by a large number of circle center marks.

Exercises *Practicing Habits of Mind*

Check Your Understanding

1. Use geometry software. Place five points on your screen. Connect them with segments so that you have an arbitrary convex pentagon. Construct the perpendicular bisector of each side of your pentagon. See the diagrams and answer the questions on the next page.

a. In the diagram at the left below, is there a point at which three or more perpendicular bisectors are concurrent?

b. If not, is it possible to adjust the vertices of the pentagon so that at least three bisectors are concurrent?

c. Is it possible to adjust the vertices of the pentagon so that all five bisectors are concurrent?

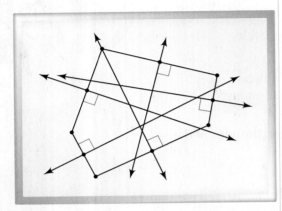
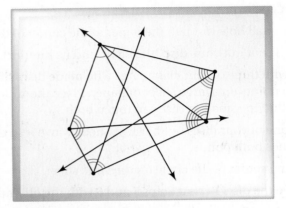

2. Try the same kind of experiment with the angle bisectors of a pentagon. See the diagram at the right above. Start with an arbitrary pentagon. Construct the angle bisector of each angle. Is it possible to adjust the vertices of the pentagon so that all five angle bisectors are concurrent?

It is a good habit to start an investigation with a special case. It simplifies what you have to look at. It can also suggest what to look for in other cases. Among polygons, the triangle is special because it is the simplest. Exercises 3–6 suggest other special cases.

3. Regular polygons are a very special case. Is concurrence of perpendicular bisectors an invariant for regular polygons? Experiment. Be sure to experiment with regular quadrilaterals (squares), regular pentagons, and regular hexagons. What do your experiments suggest? Explain.

4. Is concurrence of angle bisectors an invariant for regular polygons? Experiment, describe a conjecture, and explain the result.

5. Use geometry software to construct a circle. Place five points on the circle. Connect the points to form an irregular pentagon. Check the angle bisectors and perpendicular bisectors of the pentagon for concurrence. Do you observe any invariants? Explain.

6. Draw a circle. Construct an irregular polygon outside the circle so that all the sides of the polygon are tangent to the circle. Perform the two concurrence experiments. Do you observe any invariants? Explain.

On Your Own

7. Construct several different triangles. Then construct their medians. Describe any concurrence or collinearity you find.

8. Standardized Test Prep Triangle ABC is an isosceles triangle. $\overline{AD}$, $\overline{BE}$, and $\overline{CF}$ are altitudes. $\overline{AD}$, $\overline{BG}$, and $\overline{CH}$ are angle bisectors. Points D, I, and J are the midpoints of $\overline{BC}$, $\overline{AC}$, and $\overline{AB}$, respectively.

Which of the following statements may NOT be true?

A. The concurrences of the altitudes, angle bisectors, and medians are collinear.

B. $\overline{CI} \cong \overline{CD}$

C. $\overline{AD}$ is a median.

D. $\angle BCH \cong \angle HCA$

9. Use a piece of paper or geometry software to build an arbitrary quadrilateral. On one side, place an arbitrary point. Connect the point to the two opposite vertices of the quadrilateral. Do the same on the opposite side.

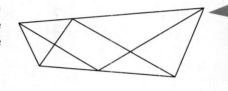

For help constructing an irregular polygon, see the TI-Nspire Handbook, p. 990.

Finally, draw the diagonals of the quadrilateral. Find two obvious collinearities. Find one surprising collinearity.

10. Take It Further Consider this statement: In any hexagon, there can be at most one concurrence of three diagonals. Is this statement true or false? Explain your reasoning.

Maintain Your Skills

11. Construct trapezoid $ABCD$ such that you can drag its vertices and sides.

a. Construct the diagonals and their point of intersection. Then construct the midpoints of the two parallel sides.

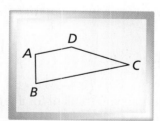

b. Find two collinearities that are intentionally built in. Find one collinearity that is not intentionally built in. Experiment to determine whether that collinearity is invariant.

Go Online
www.successnetplus.com

In this investigation you studied invariants—things that are the same for every member of a collection. You explored numerical invariants and spatial invariants, including concurrence and collinearity. The following questions will help you summarize what you have learned.

1. What is the sum of the measures of the angles of a pentagon? Of a hexagon?

2. In $\triangle ABC$, D and E are the midpoints of $\overline{BC}$ and $\overline{AC}$, respectively. The lengths of some segments are marked. Find $\frac{CD}{CB}$ and $\frac{CF}{CH}$. Explain your reasoning.

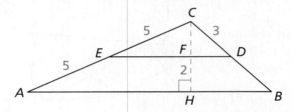

3. Draw a circle. Place and label two fixed points on the circle. Then place and label a third point on the circle that is not fixed. Build segments from it to each of the two fixed points. What invariant(s) do you notice in your construction?

4. Are the medians of an equilateral triangle concurrent? Explain.

5. What invariants can you think of for a regular hexagon? List as many as you can.

6. What is an invariant? What kinds of invariants should you look for in geometry?

7. What invariant relationship exists when a line parallel to the base of a triangle intersects the other sides of that triangle?

8. What shape do you form when you connect the consecutive midpoints of a quadrilateral?

Vocabulary

In this investigation, you learned these terms.
Make sure you understand what each one means
and how to use it.

- **collinear points**
- **concurrent lines**
- **constant**
- **disc**
- **invariant**

What remains invariant
when you open the
pop-up book?

Investigation 6B

Proof and Parallel Lines

In *Proof and Parallel Lines,* you will study one of the basic objects in geometry, the line. Some distinct lines in a plane intersect, while others do not. When lines intersect, they form angles. These angles have special relationships. You will prove some of these relationships in this investigation. When lines do not intersect, there are also provable consequences. As you investigate parallel lines and angle measures, you will gather what you need to prove that the sum of the angle measures in a triangle is 180 degrees.

By the end of this investigation, you will be able to answer questions like these.

1. Why is proof so important in mathematics?

2. What are some invariant angle relationships when parallel lines are cut by a transversal?

3. What is the sum of the measures of the interior angles of any triangle?

You will learn how to

- identify pairs of congruent angles when parallel lines are cut by a transversal

- make assumptions and write proofs in order to understand the need for proof in mathematics

- prove that the sum of the angle measures in any triangle is $180°$

You will develop these habits and skills:

- Develop and present a deductive proof.

- Search for invariants.

- Visualize key elements of a problem situation.

As parallel lines, the E, F, G, R, and V routes form congruent alternate exterior angles with the Shea Stadium route.

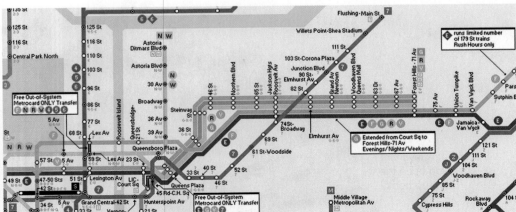

You can use geometry software to discover important relationships between angles.

For You to Explore

Use geometry software to complete Problems 1 and 2.

1. Construct two parallel lines cut by a transversal. Measure the angles.

   a. Move the transversal while the parallel lines remain fixed. Which angles remain congruent? Move one of the parallel lines while keeping remain parallel. Which angles remain congruent?

   b. Which sums of angle measures are invariant?

2. Construct a pair of intersecting lines cut by a transversal. Measure the angles.

   a. Move the transversal while the intersecting lines remain fixed. What invariants can you find? Move one of the intersecting lines while the transversal remains fixed. What invariants can you find?

   b. How do the angle measures compare to the angle measures in Problem 1? How do the sums of angle measures compare to the sums of angle measures in Problem 1?

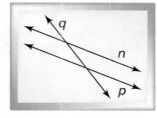

> **A transversal** is a line that intersects two or more lines.

> **Remember...**
> Congruent angles have the same measure and vice versa.

> Find the measure of each angle in degrees. See the TI–Nspire™ Handbook, p. 990.

Exercises *Practicing Habits of Mind*

On Your Own

3. Construct a triangle. Draw its three midlines. Consider the side lengths, angle measures, and areas of the figures formed. If you know each of the following, what else can you determine about the triangle?

   a. the length of one midline   b. the area of the original triangle

> **Remember...**
> A midline (or midsegment) connects the midpoints of two sides of a triangle.

4. In this figure, M is the midpoint of $\overline{BC}$, and $AM = MR$. Prove that $m\angle C = m\angle CBR$.

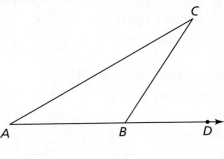

5. A common problem in geometry involves a triangle with one side extended. In the figure below, $\angle CBD$ is an **exterior angle** of $\triangle ABC$.

One form of the Exterior Angle Theorem states that the measure of a triangle's exterior angle is greater than the measures of either of the triangle's two remote interior angles. The remote interior angles are nonadjacent to the exterior angle. In this case, $m\angle CBD$ is greater than either $m\angle A$ or $m\angle C$. How can you prove the Exterior Angle Theorem?

> In order to actually *prove* the Exterior Angle Theorem, you must show that the measure of any exterior angle is greater than the measures of either remote interior angle in any triangle.

6. Use the figure at the right. Find the measures of $\angle BDA$, $\angle ADQ$, and $\angle CDQ$ for the following conditions.

a. $m\angle BDC = 62°$

b. $m\angle BDC = 72°$

c. $m\angle BDC = 55°$

d. $m\angle BDC = x°$

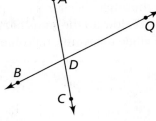

Maintain Your Skills

Use geometry software. Draw a line ℓ. Draw a point P not on line ℓ.

7. How many lines will the software allow you to construct parallel to ℓ through P? How many lines exist that are parallel to ℓ through P?

8. How many lines will the software allow you to construct perpendicular to ℓ through P? How many lines exist that are perpendicular to ℓ through P?

> For help constructing the parallel and perpendicular lines, see the TI-Nspire Handbook, p. 990.

9. a. Construct a line through P that is perpendicular to ℓ. Label it n.

b. Construct a line through P that is perpendicular to n. Label it m.

c. What happens when you use the software to determine the intersection of ℓ and m?

6.05 Deduction and Proof

How do you know the length of a segment or the measure of an angle? One way is to measure using a ruler or protractor, respectively. But measurement has some drawbacks.

- Measurement is not exact. No matter how precise your ruler or protractor is, neither will provide an exact measurement.

- Certain measurements are difficult or impossible to determine. For instance, the distance between two cities is difficult to find directly. The distance between Earth and the moon is impossible to measure directly.

- A measurement is only reliable if it holds true for an infinite number of cases.

The Developing Habits of Mind section below illustrates the third point.

In many real-life cases, estimation is sufficient. In mathematics, however, exactness is necessary to eliminate error.

Developing Habits of Mind

Use a Deductive Process. In Lesson 6.02, you explored the angle measures in a figure similar to the one below.

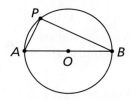

You may have noticed that, no matter where P is on the circle, the measure of $\angle P$ seems to be 90°. How can you prove that this is true? You can measure $\angle P$ when P is at various points until you grow tired of it. Suppose you do this 100 times. Will you know for sure that $m\angle P$ is always 90°? You may be very convinced, but you cannot be certain. Mathematicians establish certainty by proving a statement is true using the deductive method.

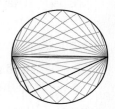

You could check all these angles.

You can prove statements using the deductive method by showing that a simple statement leads to a desired conclusion based on logical reasoning. Important conclusions are called theorems. Conclusions that are accepted without proof are called postulates, axioms, or assumptions. Once you prove a theorem, you can use it as an assumption to prove other theorems.

You may wonder where ideas for new theorems come from or who gets to decide what statements are assumed without proof. Ideas from theorems often come from experiments. The postulates that are assumed depend on what information is necessary and what is already known.

One reason to prove results in geometry is to check measurements. For example, if you know from a theorem that two segments should be equal, then the measurements of those segments should be the same. Measurements are subject to error in a way that logical deduction is not.

Minds in Action

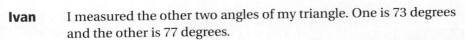

Sasha and Ivan are making triangular pennants for the school's sports teams. Ivan made a pennant with two 14-in. sides and a 30° angle between those two sides.

Ivan   I measured the other two angles of my triangle. One is 73 degrees and the other is 77 degrees.

Sasha   But they should both be the same. Measure more carefully.

So Ivan did.

Ivan   This time, I got 74 degrees and 76 degrees.

Sasha   Close. But they have to be the same.

Ivan   What do you mean? How do you know they have to be the same? My protractor says they are a little off. The bottom one is always a little bigger than the top one.

Sasha   They have to be the same. Draw a median. The two triangles are congruent.

Ivan   Okay, I see.

Sasha   And the two angles you are measuring are corresponding angles in the congruent triangles. So they have to be congruent.

Ivan   I guess I'll get a better protractor.

Remember...

A *median* of a triangle is a line segment drawn from one of the triangle's vertices to the midpoint of the opposite side.

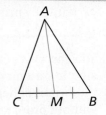

$\overline{AM}$ is a median of △*ABC*.

For Discussion

1. Ivan agrees that the two triangles formed by Sasha's median are congruent. Do you? Explain.

2. How do you know that the two angles that Ivan measured are corresponding parts of the two triangles formed by the median?

For You to Do

The result of the experiment below may lead to a theorem.

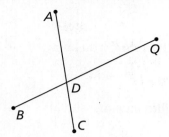

two intersecting segments

Suppose that $\overline{AC}$ and $\overline{BQ}$ intersect so that $m\angle BDC = 72°$. What is the measure of each angle below?

3. $m\angle BDA$ **4.** $m\angle ADQ$ **5.** $m\angle QDC$

> Angles such as $\angle ADB$ and $\angle CDQ$ are called *vertical angles*.

> You may find it helpful to look back at Exercise 6 in Lesson 6.04.

You should notice that some of the angle measures are the same. Now suppose that $m\angle ADB = 125°$. What are the measures of the other angles?

Each time you repeat this experiment, you should find that two pairs of angles have the same measure. Your measurements may lead you to believe that the statement below is true.

Theorem 6.3   The Vertical Angles Theorem

In the figure below, $m\angle ADB = m\angle CDQ$ and $m\angle BDC = m\angle ADQ$.

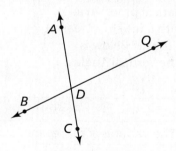

How can you prove this theorem true without using measurement? Since angle measures are numbers, you can use algebra. Use guess-check-generalize to show that the theorem is true for certain angle measures. Do not forget to keep track of your steps. For instance, the steps shown on the following page are for the case in which $m\angle ADB = 125°$.

Step 1 Suppose that $m\angle ADB = 125°$.

Step 2 You know that $m\angle ADB + m\angle ADQ = 180°$. Therefore, you know that $125° + m\angle ADQ = 180°$.

Step 3 So, $m\angle ADQ = 180° - 125° = 55°$.

Step 4 You also know that $m\angle ADQ + m\angle CDQ = 180°$. Therefore, you know that $55° + m\angle CDQ = 180°$.

Step 5 Then, $m\angle CDQ = 180° - 55° = 125°$.

Step 6 So, $m\angle ADB = m\angle CDQ$ because they both have the same measure, 125°.

If you repeat this process with several different angle measures, you may convince yourself that the steps will always work. To present a more convincing argument, repeat this process with a generic value for the measure of $\angle ADB$. Simply use a variable to represent $m\angle ADB$.

> **Habits of Mind**
>
> **Generalize.** The idea is to get into the rhythm of the steps.

Step 1 Suppose that $m\angle ADB = x°$.

Step 2 You know that $m\angle ADB + m\angle ADQ = 180°$. Therefore, $x° + m\angle ADQ = 180°$.

Step 3 So, $m\angle ADQ = 180° - x°$.

Step 4 You also know that $m\angle ADQ + m\angle CDQ = 180°$. Therefore, $(180° - x°) + m\angle CDQ = 180°$.

Step 5 So $m\angle CDQ = 180° - (180° - x°) = 180° - 180° + x° = x°$.

Step 6 Then $m\angle ADB = m\angle CDQ$ because they both measure $x°$.

This argument is convincing, but it is not a mathematical proof. In a mathematical proof, each statement is supported with a reason. A reason is an assumption or theorem that you already know is true. Below is an incomplete two-column mathematical proof of the Vertical Angles Theorem.

Statement	Reason
1. Let $m\angle ADB = x°$.	The variable x represents any number.
2. $m\angle ADB + m\angle ADQ = 180°$, so $x° + m\angle ADQ = 180°$.	
3. $m\angle ADQ = 180° - x°$	basic rules of algebra
4. $m\angle ADQ + m\angle CDQ = 180°$, so $(180° - x°) + m\angle CDQ = 180°$.	
5. $m\angle CDQ = 180° - (180° - x°) = 180° - 180° + x° = x°$	basic moves and rules of algebra
6. $m\angle ADB = m\angle CDQ$	If the measures of two angles are equal to the same value, then the measures of the two angles are equal to each other.

For Discussion

6. As a class, choose a reason to support statements 2 and 4 in the proof. Your reason should be an assumption or theorem that you can accept without proof.

7. The reasons for statements 3 and 5 in the proof on the previous page come from algebraic reasoning. What basic rules of algebra are used in these steps?

Exercises Practicing Habits of Mind

Check Your Understanding

1. Use the figure below. $\angle COA$ and $\angle DOB$ are right angles.

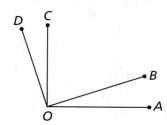

   a. If $m\angle BOA = 25°$, find $m\angle COB$ and $m\angle COD$.
   b. If $m\angle COB = 63°$, find $m\angle BOA$ and $m\angle COD$.
   c. If $m\angle DOC = 31°$, find $m\angle COB$ and $m\angle BOA$.
   d. If $m\angle DOC = 31°$, find $m\angle DOA$.
   e. If $m\angle AOB = x°$, find $m\angle COB$ and $m\angle COD$.

2. Use the figure below. $\angle COA$ and $\angle DOB$ are right angles. Prove that $m\angle BOA = m\angle COD$.

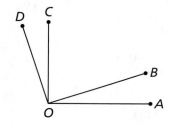

> When you write a proof, be sure to state explicitly any assumptions you make.

3. **Standardized Test Prep** $\overline{BE}$ bisects $\overline{AD}$ at C. Point C is the midpoint of $\overline{BE}$. Choose the correct reason for step 4 in the following proof.

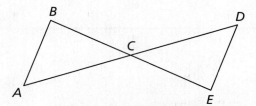

Statements	Reasons
1. $\overline{BE}$ bisects $\overline{AD}$ at C. Point C is the midpoint of $\overline{BE}$.	1. Given
2. $\overline{AC} \cong \overline{DC}$	2. Definition of bisects
3. $\overline{BC} \cong \overline{EC}$	3. Definition of midpoint
4. $\angle BCA \cong \angle ECD$	4. ___?___
5. $\triangle ABC \cong \triangle DEC$	5. SAS triangle congruence postulate

A. Straight angles are congruent.

B. Corresponding angles are congruent.

C. Opposite angles are congruent.

D. Vertical angles are congruent.

4. Use the figure below. $\overline{AB} \cong \overline{DB}$ and $m\angle ABC = m\angle DBC$.

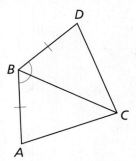

Provide the missing reasons in the proof to show that $\overline{AC} \cong \overline{DC}$.

Statements	Reasons
a. $\overline{AB} \cong \overline{BD}$	Given
b. $m\angle ABC = m\angle DBC$	___?___
c. $\overline{BC} \cong \overline{BC}$	___?___
d. $\triangle ABC \cong \triangle DBC$	___?___
e. $\overline{AC} \cong \overline{DC}$	___?___

5. In this figure, $\overline{PL} \cong \overline{RQ}$ and $\overline{PQ} \cong \overline{RL}$.
Prove each of the following.

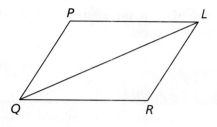

   a. $\triangle QPL \cong \triangle LRQ$

   b. $\angle P \cong \angle R$

6. Use the figure below.
$m\angle DCB = m\angle ECA.$ Points E, C, and D
are collinear. $\overline{FC} \perp \overline{ED}$.

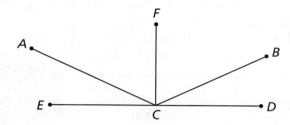

   a. Based on the given information, what can you prove?

   b. Prove your conjecture from part (a).

Maintain Your Skills

7. Use the figure below. Suppose that $m\angle 1 + m\angle 6 = 90°$ and $m\angle 7 = 140°$.

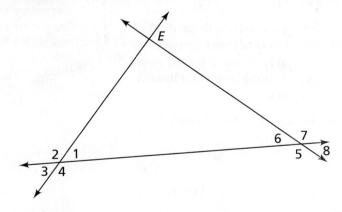

   a. Find the measure of each numbered angle.

   b. Assume you know that the sum of the measures of the angles in a
   triangle is $180°$. Find the measure of each angle around point E.

> **Go Online**
> www.successnetplus.com

> In Lesson 6.07, you will
> prove that the sum of
> the measures of the
> angles in a triangle
> is $180°$.

6.06　Parallel Lines

This lesson is different from many of the others in this book. You will need to read and comprehend a set of ideas.

Developing Habits of Mind

Read to understand. The mathematical principles in this lesson have been studied for centuries. Some of them took generations to solve or prove. An important part of mathematics is the ability to read and understand the mathematical writing of others. To understand a new idea, sometimes you may need to read it more than once. You will practice these skills in this lesson.

You see parallel lines in your everyday life. You have probably studied them in previous mathematics courses. Parallel lines will be the focus of this lesson and the following lesson. You will address these questions.

1. How can you determine whether two lines are parallel?

2. What information can you draw from parallel lines?

Here is the definition of parallel lines given from the previous course.

Definition

Parallel lines are lines in the same plane that do not intersect.

This seems like a simple definition. However, if you need to determine whether two given lines are parallel, the definition is not very helpful. You cannot graph both lines forever in each direction to check that they never intersect. In this lesson, you will develop several simple tests that involve measuring angles to determine if lines are parallel.

First, you need to be familiar with the vocabulary on the next page.

Remember...
You have studied the equations of parallel lines. How can you determine whether two lines are parallel from their equations?

Remember...
You can also say that parallel lines are everywhere equidistant. *Everywhere equidistant* means "the same distance apart at every point."

The Blue Angels of the U.S. Navy fly parallel paths.

Facts and Notation

The pairs of angles that are formed when a transversal intersects two lines have special names based on their positions.

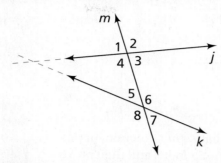

- Pairs of angles such as ∠3 and ∠5, or ∠4 and ∠6, are **alternate interior angles.**

- Pairs of angles such as ∠1 and ∠5, or ∠4 and ∠8, are **corresponding angles.**

- Pairs of angles such as ∠2 and ∠4, or ∠5 and ∠7, are **vertical angles.**

- Angles on the same side of the transversal and between the lines (for example, ∠3 and ∠6) are **consecutive angles.**

Pairs of angles such as ∠1 and ∠7, or ∠2 and ∠8, are **alternate exterior angles.**

For You to Do

1. Use the figure at the right. Suppose you have three sticks. The sticks represent lines ℓ, m, and n. The sticks ℓ and n are fixed together to form a 62° angle at point A. The sticks representing m and n intersect at P. You can pivot the stick representing m about point P.

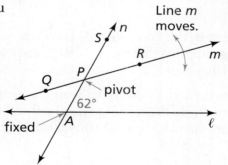

How can you adjust the angles at P to ensure that line ℓ is parallel to line m (ℓ ∥ m)? Explain.

Habits of Mind

Experiment. This is a thought experiment. You can turn it into a physical experiment by building a model with sticks.

The result of the experiment above suggests several theorems that allow you to say that two lines are parallel.

Theorem 6.4   The AIP Theorem

If two lines form congruent alternate interior angles with a transversal, then the two lines are parallel.

AIP stands for "alternate interiors parallel." You can think of the *AI* as the hypothesis of the theorem, and the *P* as the conclusion.

The AIP Theorem on the previous page is illustrated in the figure below.

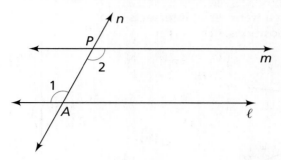

Remember...

Congruent angles have the same measure and vice versa.

Proof Assume that $m\angle 1 = m\angle 2$. You need to show that $\ell \parallel m$. The proof of this fact is indirect. Begin by supposing the lines are not parallel and then prove the theorem by contradiction.

Suppose lines ℓ and m are not parallel. Then they must intersect somewhere. Suppose they intersect at a point R like this.

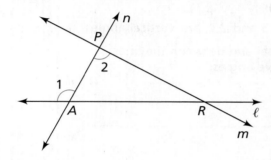

A triangle, $\triangle ARP$, is formed. By the Exterior Angle Theorem, $m\angle 1 > m\angle 2$. But this contradicts our assumption that $m\angle 1 = m\angle 2$. Therefore, point R cannot exist. This implies that lines ℓ and m do not intersect. So, $\ell \parallel m$.

The AIP Theorem and the corollaries that you will soon investigate allow you to use certain angle measures to determine whether two lines are parallel. This is much easier than checking whether two lines intersect.

A **corollary** is a consequence that logically follows from a theorem.

For Discussion

2. The proof of the AIP Theorem depends on the Exterior Angle Theorem shown here.

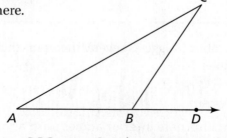

$m\angle DBC > m\angle C$ and $m\angle DBC > m\angle A$

The Exterior Angle Theorem also depends on some basic assumptions. Discuss these assumptions.

Exercises Practicing Habits of Mind

1. Give a precise definition for each term listed below. Illustrate each with a diagram.

   a. alternate interior angles   **b.** alternate exterior angles

   c. corresponding angles   **d.** consecutive angles

> These types of angles are formed when two lines are cut by a transversal. The two lines may or may not be parallel.

2. Use the figure below. The tick marks indicate congruent segments.

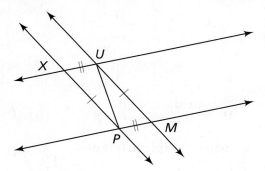

   a. Which triangles, if any, are congruent? Explain.

   b. Which angles, if any, are congruent? Explain.

   c. Which lines, if any, are parallel? Explain.

3. Use the figure below. The tick marks indicate congruent segments.

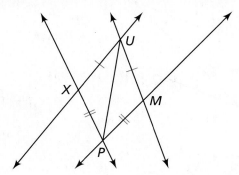

   a. Which triangles, if any, are congruent? Explain.

   b. Which angles, if any, are congruent? Explain.

   c. Which lines, if any, are parallel? Explain.

4. Decide whether each statement below is true. Prove why or why not.

   a. If two lines form congruent corresponding angles with a transversal, then the two lines are parallel.

   b. If two lines form congruent alternate exterior angles with a transversal, then the two lines are parallel.

   c. If two lines form congruent consecutive angles with a transversal, then the two lines are parallel.

   d. If two lines form supplementary alternate exterior angles with a transversal, then the two lines are parallel.

   e. If two lines form supplementary consecutive angles with a transversal, then the two lines are parallel.

Each statement that is true is a corollary of the AIP Theorem.

Remember...

Two angles are **supplementary angles** if the sum of their measures is 180°.

On Your Own

5. Suppose two lines are perpendicular to the same line. Are the two lines parallel? Explain.

6. Two lines in the same plane either intersect or are parallel. Explain. Is the statement true of two lines in space? Explain.

   In Exercises 7 and 8, use the given information to determine which segments in each figure must be parallel. For each exercise, provide a proof to support your answer.

7. Point O is the midpoint of both $\overline{NP}$ and $\overline{MQ}$.

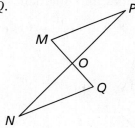

8. The diagonals of quadrilateral $MPQN$ intersect at point O. $MO = PO$ and $NO = QO$.

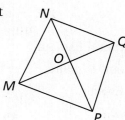

9. Standardized Test Prep In the figure at the right, $\overrightarrow{BG}$ intersects $\overline{AC}$ at point B. $\overrightarrow{BG}$ intersects $\overline{DF}$ at point E. Angle ABG and $\angle GEF$ are supplementary.

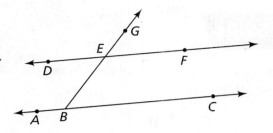

Choose the correct reason for step number 8 in the following proof that $\overleftrightarrow{AC} \parallel \overleftrightarrow{DF}$.

Statements	Reasons
1. $\overline{BG}$ intersects $\overline{AC}$ and $\overline{DF}$ at points B and E, respectively.	**1.** Given
2. $\angle ABG$ and $\angle GEF$ are supplementary.	**2.** Given
3. $m\angle ABG + m\angle GEF = 180°$	**3.** definition of supplementary angles
4. $\angle GEF \cong \angle DEB$	**4.** Vertical angles are congruent.
5. $m\angle GEF = m\angle DEB$	**5.** definition of congruent angles
6. $m\angle ABG + m\angle DEB = 180°$	**6.** substitution property of equality
7. $\angle ABG$ and $\angle DEB$ are supplementary angles.	**7.** definition of supplementary angles
8. $\overleftrightarrow{AC} \parallel \overleftrightarrow{DF}$	**8.** __?__

A. If corresponding angles are congruent, then the lines are parallel.

B. If consecutive angles are supplementary, then the lines are parallel.

C. If alternate interior angles are congruent, then the lines are parallel.

D. If alternate exterior angles are supplementary, then the lines are parallel.

10. In the figure below, $m\angle DEG + m\angle HFI = 180°$, and $m\angle FGE = m\angle HFI$.

Find the lines in the figure that must be parallel, if there are any. Prove what you find.

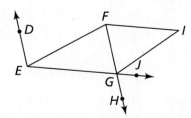

11. Use the figure below. For each statement, find all the missing angle measures.

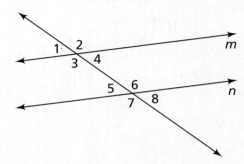

 a. $m\angle 1 = 58°$ and $m\angle 5 = 58°$ **b.** $m\angle 1 = 58°$ and $m\angle 6 = 125°$

 c. $m\angle 4 = 55°$ and $m\angle 6 = 125°$ **d.** $m\angle 7 = 125°$ and $m\angle 3 = 125°$

 e. $m\angle 7 = 125°$ and $m\angle 1 = 55°$

12. Decide whether each statement below guarantees that $m \parallel n$. If so, explain.

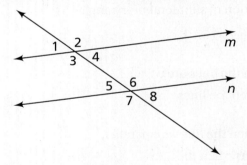

 a. $m\angle 1 = 58°$ and $m\angle 5 = 58°$ **b.** $m\angle 1 = 58°$ and $m\angle 6 = 125°$

 c. $m\angle 4 = 55°$ and $m\angle 6 = 125°$ **d.** $m\angle 7 = 125°$ and $m\angle 3 = 125°$

 e. $m\angle 7 = 125°$ and $m\angle 1 = 55°$ **f.** $m\angle 7 = m\angle 6$

 g. $m\angle 7 = m\angle 2$ **h.** $m\angle 7 + m\angle 3 = 180°$

 i. $m\angle 4 + m\angle 6 = 180°$

6.07 The Parallel Postulate

Suppose you have a line ℓ and a point P that is not on ℓ. How many lines through P can you draw that are parallel to ℓ? The experiments in this book and your common sense suggest that there is only one. People tried for centuries to prove this from simpler statements, and they had no success. The concept that there exists only one line parallel to a given line through a point not on the given line cannot be proved. In this course, it is accepted that no proof exists, and it is assumed true.

Postulate 6.2 The Parallel Postulate

If a point P is not on a line ℓ, exactly one line through P exists that is parallel to ℓ.

> In this case, the word *exists* means that there is a parallel line.

Now that you have assumed that a parallel to a given line through a point exists and is unique, you can answer the second question from the beginning of Lesson 6.06: What information can you draw from parallel lines? In Lesson 6.06, you used certain angle measures to determine whether lines were parallel. Now you can work in the other direction and determine the measures of certain angles when two parallel lines are cut by a transversal.

For You to Do

1. Use geometry software to construct two parallel lines and a moveable transversal. Measure all the angles and note any two angles that have the same measure and any two angles with measures that add to $180°$.

   Move the transversal. Check which of the equalities found above is invariant. Is there a state of the sketch in which all the angles have the same measure?

This activity leads to the converse of the AIP Theorem.

Theorem 6.5 The PAI Theorem

If two parallel lines are cut by a transversal, then the alternate interior angles are congruent.

> To form the **converse** of an *if-then* statement, interchange the *if* and *then* clauses. So the PAI Theorem is the converse of the AIP Theorem.

You can prove the PAI Theorem with an indirect proof.

Proof Suppose parallel lines n and ℓ are cut by a transversal t, as shown in the figure below.

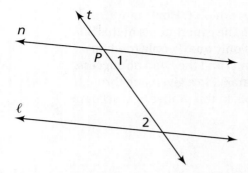

You want to prove that $\angle 1 \cong \angle 2$. Since this is an indirect proof, suppose that $\angle 1 \not\cong \angle 2$ and show that this leads to something that is impossible. Construct a line m through P so that the intersection of m and t form an $\angle 3$ that is congruent to $\angle 2$.

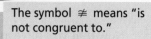

The symbol $\not\cong$ means "is not congruent to."

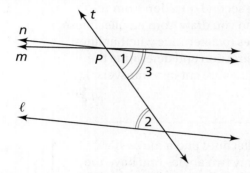

By the AIP Theorem, you can conclude that $m \parallel \ell$. However, you originally assumed that $n \parallel \ell$. So there are two distinct lines through P that are parallel to ℓ. This contradicts the Parallel Postulate. So you can conclude that $\angle 1 \cong \angle 2$. Therefore, if two parallel lines are cut by a transversal, then the alternate interior angles are congruent.

Developing Habits of Mind

Use a different process to get the same result. You can prove the PAI Theorem in a more direct way. Without assuming that $\angle 1 \not\cong \angle 2$, construct line m as you did above so that $\angle 3 \cong \angle 2$. By the AIP Theorem, $m \parallel \ell$. Since there is only one line parallel to ℓ through P, m and n must be the same line. Therefore, $\angle 1$ and $\angle 3$ must be the same angle, so $\angle 1 \cong \angle 2$.

For Discussion

2. What assumptions do you need to make in this argument?

For You to Do

3. Use the figure below. Lines *n* and *m* are parallel, as indicated by the red arrowhead on each line. Find the measures of all the numbered angles.

4. Explain how you found each angle measure.

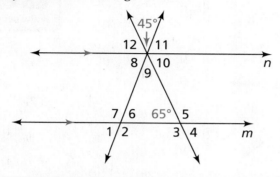

For Discussion

5. You already have overwhelming evidence that the sum of the angle measures in a triangle is 180°. You have used this idea to support other arguments. You may even know several different ways to explain why it is true. Use the diagram below to write an argument that proves that the sum of the angle measures in any triangle is 180°.

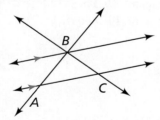

You can state the result of this discussion as a theorem.

Theorem 6.6   *The Triangle Angle-Sum Theorem*

The sum of the measures of the angles of a triangle is 180°.

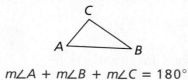

$$m\angle A + m\angle B + m\angle C = 180°$$

Check Your Understanding

1. Use the figure below. Assume $m \parallel n$.

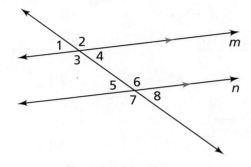

Go Online
www.successnetplus.com

Find the measure of each numbered angle for each of the following conditions.

a. $m\angle 6 = 108°$

b. $m\angle 8 = 46°$

c. $m\angle 4 = x°$

d. $2m\angle 4 = m\angle 7$

e. $m\angle 7 = 2x°$ and $m\angle 4 = x°$

2. Use geometry software to construct two parallel lines a and b. Then construct two transversals c and d that each intersect a and b. See the figure below.

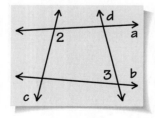

In this figure, lines a and b were drawn carelessly. They are clearly *not* parallel.

a. Move the lines so that $\angle 2 \cong \angle 3$. Do lines c and d have any special relationship? Is this relationship invariant or is it dependent on the congruence of $\angle 2$ and $\angle 3$?

b. Move the lines so that $c \parallel d$. What is the relationship between $\angle 2$ and $\angle 3$?

c. How would your answers to parts (a) and (b) differ if lines a and b were not parallel?

3. Use geometry software to construct a pair of parallel lines so that point *A* is on one line and point *B* is on the other. Place a moveable point *P* between the parallel lines. Construct $\overline{PA}$ and $\overline{PB}$, as shown in the figure below. What invariants can you find?

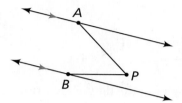

How does the angle formed by the two bungee cords compare to the angles they form with the poles?

4. The following theorem is an important consequence of the Triangle Angle-Sum Theorem.

Theorem 6.7   *The Unique Perpendicular Theorem*

If a point *P* is not on line ℓ, there is exactly one line through *P* that is perpendicular to ℓ.

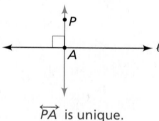

$\overleftrightarrow{PA}$ is unique.

Prove this theorem. (*Hint:* You may want to prove the theorem by contradiction. What would happen if there were more than one line through *P* that was perpendicular to ℓ?)

5. Is the sum of the measures of the angles of a quadrilateral invariant? Explain.

6. **Write About It** Explain the difference between the AIP and PAI Theorems.

7. Use geometry software to construct $\overrightarrow{AD}$ and $\overrightarrow{AE}$. Place point B on $\overrightarrow{AD}$ and point C on $\overrightarrow{AE}$. Then construct $\overline{BC}$, $\overline{CD}$, and $\overline{DE}$, as shown in the figure below. Move the parts so that $\overline{BC} \cong \overline{CD} \cong \overline{DE}$.

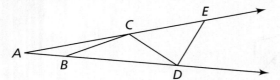

   a. What conjectures can you make about the angles in the figure? Describe any invariant relationships you find.

   b. Is it possible to make $\overline{BC}$ and $\overline{DE}$ parallel *and* congruent? Explain.

On Your Own

8. **Standardized Test Prep** In the figure, $\overleftrightarrow{AB} \parallel \overleftrightarrow{EF}$.
   The measure of $\angle BCD$ is 25°. The measure of $\angle ABD$ is 125°.
   What is the measure of $\angle BDC$?

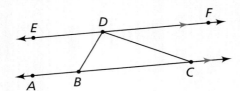

   A. 55°

   B. 80°

   C. 100°

   D. 125°

9. In the figure, lines p and t are parallel.

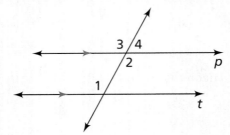

   a. Why is $\angle 1 \cong \angle 2$?

   b. Why is $\angle 2 \cong \angle 3$?

   c. Why is $\angle 1 \cong \angle 3$?

10. **Take It Further** Prove that, in a plane, two lines that are both parallel to a third line are parallel to each other.

11. Prove that the AAS triplet guarantees triangle congruence. Use the triangle congruence postulates and the Triangle Angle-Sum Theorem in your proof.

12. The Exterior Angle Theorem says that the measure of an exterior angle of a triangle is greater than the measure of either of the two remote interior angles. You can take this one step further. Prove that the measure of an exterior angle of a triangle is equal to the sum of the measures of the two remote interior angles.

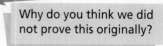

Why do you think we did not prove this originally?

13. For each polygon listed below, prove that the sum of the measures of its angles is invariant. Then find the sum of the measures of the angles for each polygon. Justify your answers.

   a. pentagon (five-sided polygon)

   b. hexagon (six-sided polygon)

14. **Take It Further** Use your knowledge of parallel lines. Decide whether each of the constructions (a)–(d) is possible. Explain.

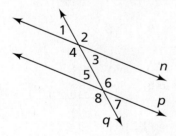   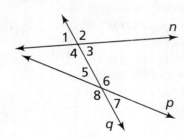

   a. Lines n and p are not parallel and $m\angle 3 + m\angle 6 = 180°$.

   b. Line n is parallel to line p and $m\angle 4 = m\angle 6$.

   c. Line n is parallel to line p and $m\angle 2 = m\angle 5$.

   d. $m\angle 4 + m\angle 5 > m\angle 2 + m\angle 7$

Maintain Your Skills

15. In the figure at the right, lines m and n are parallel. $\overline{PR}$ bisects $\angle WPQ$. $\overline{QR}$ bisects $\angle XQP$.

In parts (a)–(f), use each angle measure given to find the measure of the remaining numbered angles.

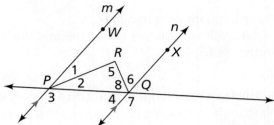

a. $m\angle 1 = 64°$ **b.** $m\angle 1 = 68°$

c. $m\angle 3 = 130°$ **d.** $m\angle 8 = 60°$

e. $m\angle 7 = 140°$ **f.** $m\angle 2 = x°$

Habits of Mind

Look for invariants. Which angle measures are invariant? What conjecture, if any, can you make?

Historical Perspective

Around 300 B.C., Euclid and other Greek mathematicians tried to formalize the system of mathematical proof. They wanted to start with a few basic facts that everyone agreed were true. These facts allowed them to derive statements that were not as obvious and that could not be checked by physical experiment. These mathematicians wrote a series of books called *Elements*.

Much of *Elements* is about numbers, arithmetic, and what we now call algebra. There is also a detailed treatment of geometry. *Elements* formed the basis of how geometry has been taught and learned for centuries.

The Euclidean tradition of deducing new results from simple assumptions and other established results is the "gold standard" in mathematics. Mathematicians discover results, solve problems, and get insights in a variety of ways. Many of these methods are very complex. But when mathematicians present their results to others, their claims are accepted only when they can justify them with a logical deductive proof.

Mathematical 6B Reflections

In this investigation, you studied lines and angles. You learned about the types of angles formed when two lines intersect and the types of angles formed when two parallel lines are intersected by a transversal. You also learned about mathematical proof—a logical way to move from a simple statement to a desired conclusion.

1. Use the figure at the right. Find the measure of each numbered angle. Lines *m* and *n* are parallel.

2. Two lines are intersected by a transversal. The measures of the consecutive angles that are formed are 103° and 75°. Are the two lines parallel? Explain.

3. Draw two segments $\overline{AB}$ and $\overline{CD}$ that intersect at point *O* so that $\overline{AO} \cong \overline{OB}$ and $\overline{CO} \cong \overline{OD}$. Prove that $\overline{AC} \cong \overline{BD}$.

4. Use the figure at the right. Explain how to construct a line through *P* that is parallel to ℓ.

5. Why is proof so important in mathematics?

6. What are some invariant angle relationships when parallel lines are cut by a transversal?

7. What is the sum of the measures of the interior angles of any triangle?

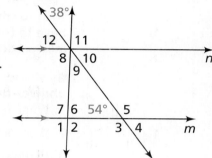

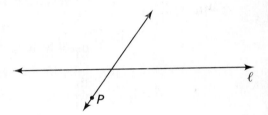

Vocabulary and Notation

In this investigation, you learned these terms and symbols. Make sure you understand what each one means and how to use it.

- **alternate exterior angles**
- **alternate interior angles**
- **consecutive angles**
- **converse**
- **corollary**
- **corresponding angles**
- **exterior angle**
- **parallel lines**
- **supplementary angles**
- **transversal**
- **vertical angles**
- **≇ (is not congruent to)**
- **∥ (is parallel to)**

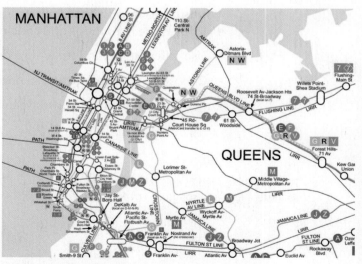

As one line, the E, F, G, R, and V trains form congruent vertical angles with the Shea Stadium train.

Writing Proofs

In *Writing Proofs,* you will study mathematical proof. A proof is a logical argument that explains a new observation using facts you already know. You start with statements that everyone agrees with. Then you use logic that everyone agrees with to convince yourself and others that other statements have to follow. Your proof must be clear, so that alternate interpretations or counterexamples are not possible.

By the end of this investigation, you will be able to answer questions like these.

1. What are the different ways to organize and analyze a proof?

2. What is the Perpendicular Bisector Theorem?

3. In the statement "All trees are green," what is the hypothesis and what is the conclusion?

You will learn how to

- use a variety of ways to write and present proofs

- identify the hypothesis and conclusion of a given statement

- write simple triangle congruence proofs

- use the Perpendicular Bisector Theorem and the Isosceles Triangle Theorem to prove that two parts of a figure are congruent

You will develop these habits and skills:
- Identify the hypothesis and conclusion of a statement.

- Use different methods to write a proof.

- Choose an appropriate way to present a proof.

- Recognize the difference between experimentation and deduction.

The triangle formed by this ski bridge has congruent legs and congruent base angles.

Activating Prior Knowledge
Exploring New Ideas

In previous lessons, you used assumptions and theorems to informally prove that triangles are congruent and lines are parallel. In this lesson, you will write more informal **proofs,** or convincing arguments, in preparation for writing formal mathematical proofs.

How is the term *argument* used differently in mathematics than in everyday language?

For You to Explore

1. Draw a square and divide it into four equal parts. Write an argument that convinces a classmate that each part has the same area. Share your argument with a classmate. Is your argument convincing?

2. Draw a square and divide it into five equal parts. Write an argument that shows that each of the five parts has the same area. Make sure that your argument is convincing.

3. If you find the sum of an odd number and an even number, is the result an odd number or an even number? Write a convincing argument to prove that your result is correct for each of the following audiences.

   a. fourth graders

   b. algebra students

4. You know that the sum of the measures of the angles in a triangle is 180°. Use this fact to show that the sum of the measures of the angles in a quadrilateral is 360°.

Exercises *Practicing Habits of Mind*

On Your Own

5. Use the figure at the right. Ruth claims that $\triangle ABC \cong \triangle DBC$.

   Her argument states the following.
   - The triangles share side $\overline{BC}$.
   - $\angle ACB \cong \angle DCB$ because they are both right angles.
   - The diagram tells us that $\overline{AC} \cong \overline{DC}$.

   Does Ruth's argument support her claim? What triangle congruence postulate should she use to conclude that $\triangle ABC \cong \triangle DBC$? Explain.

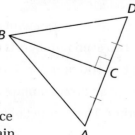

6. What's Wrong Here? Ruth was asked to make a conjecture about the figure below and then prove it. The given information is $\angle ABC \cong \angle ACB$ and $\overline{BE} \cong \overline{CD}$.

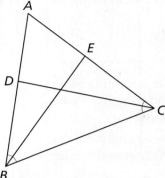

Ruth decided that $\triangle BDC \cong \triangle CEB$. She used the following argument.

- The triangles share side $\overline{BC}$.
- This, with the given information, shows that $\triangle BDC \cong \triangle CEB$ by SAS.

Explain what is wrong with Ruth's argument.

7. Write an argument to show that the measure of one of a triangle's exterior angles is equal to the sum of the measures of the two remote interior angles. Use the figure below to show that $m\angle DAB = m\angle B + m\angle C$.

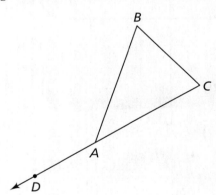

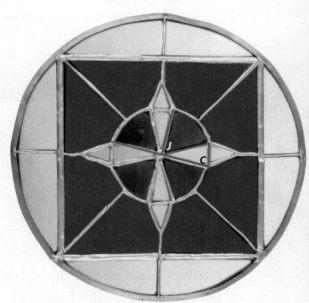

Maintain Your Skills

8. Prove each of the following statements using algebra.

a. The sum of two even numbers is even.

b. The sum of two odd numbers is even.

c. The product of an even number and another integer is even.

d. Take It Further The product of two odd numbers is odd.

In this stained glass suncatcher, which is greater, $m\angle C$ or $m\angle J$? Give a convincing argument.

What Does a Proof Look Like?

As you might imagine, the way that you make your argument in a proof can vary. The rules of reasoning govern the logic of the proof, no matter who writes it. However, the way the proof looks depends on the customs and culture of the country where you study. Schools in China, Israel, France, or Russia sometimes teach ways to present proofs that are quite different from the methods taught in most American schools.

Following the diagram below are four different proofs that $\triangle ABE \cong \triangle DCE$. The given information is $\overline{AB} \parallel \overline{CD}$, and E is the midpoint of $\overline{AD}$.

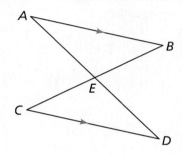

Two-Column Statement-Reason Proof

In the two-column statement-reason proof below, a set of true statements, logically ordered, appears in the left column. The given information usually appears first in the left column. The last statement shows what you are trying to prove.

The right column explains why each statement in the left column is true. You usually state the reasons as assumptions, theorems, or definitions, or as "givens." Givens are statements that one assumes are true for the proof.

Statements	Reasons
1. $\overline{AB} \parallel \overline{CD}$	1. given
2. $\angle ABE \cong \angle DCE$	2. Parallel lines form congruent alternate interior angles with a transversal.
3. $\angle BAE \cong \angle CDE$	3. Parallel lines form congruent alternate interior angles with a transversal.
4. E is the midpoint of $\overline{AD}$.	4. given
5. $\overline{AE} \cong \overline{DE}$	5. The midpoint is defined as the point that divides a segment into two congruent parts.
6. $\triangle ABE \cong \triangle DCE$	6. AAS

Paragraph Proof

In the paragraph proof below, a series of sentences fit together logically to establish that the two triangles are congruent. The sentences are written in paragraph form.

> Because $\overline{AB} \parallel \overline{CD}$, the alternate interior angles are congruent. So $\angle ABE \cong \angle DCE$ and $\angle BAE \cong \angle CDE$. Also, because E is the midpoint of $\overline{AD}$, $\overline{AE} \cong \overline{DE}$. Therefore, $\triangle ABE \cong \triangle DCE$ by AAS.

Notice that a paragraph proof consists of several sentences that contain both words and mathematical symbols.

Outline-Style Proof

Students who study in China may use an outline-style proof. You can use the symbol $\because$ meaning *because* to indicate the given information. The symbol $\therefore$ means *therefore*. It indicates that the information follows from the given information. You write the important reasons inside the parentheses.

$\because$ $\overline{AB}$ is parallel to $\overline{CD}$.

$\therefore$ $\angle ABE \cong \angle DCE$ (alternate interior angles)

$\therefore$ $\angle BAE \cong \angle CDE$ (alternate interior angles)

$\because$ E is the midpoint of $\overline{AD}$.

$\therefore$ $\overline{AE} \cong \overline{ED}$ (definition of midpoint)

$\therefore$ $\triangle ABE \cong \triangle DCE$ (AAS)

Students who study in Russia may use another type of outline-style proof. The proof below illustrates this type of proof. You make an outline of the written statements and justify each statement.

Given that $\overline{AB}$ is parallel to $\overline{CD}$ and E is the midpoint of $\overline{AD}$, $\triangle ABE \cong \triangle DCE$ by AAS because

1. $\angle ABE \cong \angle DCE$ (PAI Theorem)
2. $\angle BAE \cong \angle CDE$ (PAI Theorem)
3. $\overline{AE} \cong \overline{DE}$ (definition of midpoint)

For Discussion

1. Each of the four proofs above uses the AAS triangle congruence postulate to show that $\triangle ABE \cong \triangle DCE$. What else do the four proofs have in common?

2. What are the advantages and disadvantages of each type of proof?

You have just learned several different ways to present a mathematical proof. However, you may still be wondering, "Why bother doing a proof at all?" This is a surprisingly complex question. The need for proof is a result of tradition, necessity, and culture.

Mathematicians are experimenters performing thought experiments. They build models, gather data, and use data to make conjectures. To reach a valid conclusion, mathematicians rely on deduction and proof. New insights, or results, come from reasoning about things that must follow logically from what they already know or assume.

The combination of deduction and experimentation is one of the distinguishing characteristics of mathematical research. The results of mathematical research do not hold true because they are *observed* to hold true. Instead, mathematicians derive results logically from some very simple assumptions.

Early in your geometry course, you prove that two triangles are congruent for two reasons. Triangle concepts are important, and the structure of these proofs is relatively simple. In most of the proofs that follow, you can follow a straightforward plan.

- Determine which parts of the two triangles are congruent.
- Determine whether you have enough information to prove that the triangles are congruent. Which set of congruent parts (SSS, SAS, ASA, or AAS) can you use to prove that they are congruent?
- Organize the information. Then write the proof.

Exercises *Practicing Habits of Mind*

Check Your Understanding

1. Use the following conjecture to answer parts (a) and (b). The sum of the measures of the interior angles of an n-gon is $(n - 2)180°$.

   a. Describe an experiment you can perform to test this conjecture.

   b. Write a deductive proof to prove the conjecture.

An n-gon is a polygon with n sides, where n is a whole number greater than or equal to 3.

For Exercises 2–4, use each figure and the given information to write a proof. Use a proof style described in this lesson.

2. **Given** $\overline{AB} \cong \overline{CB}$ and $\overline{BD} \cong \overline{BE}$

   Prove $\triangle ABD \cong \triangle CBE$

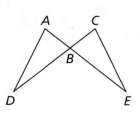

3. Given $\overline{SV} \cong \overline{UT}$ and $\overline{ST} \cong \overline{UV}$

Prove $\triangle STV \cong \triangle UVT$

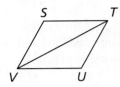

4. Given $SEBW$ is a square.

Prove $\triangle SWB \cong \triangle EBW$

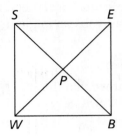

On Your Own

5. Standardized Test Prep In the figure below, $\triangle ABC$ is an isosceles triangle with $\overline{AC} \cong \overline{BC}$. $\overline{CD}$ is a median of $\triangle ABC$. $\overline{CE}$ bisects $\angle ACD$. $\overline{CF}$ bisects $\angle BCD$. Which of the following is a correct way to prove that $\triangle ACE \cong \triangle BCF$?

> **Remember...**
>
> An **isosceles triangle** is a triangle with at least two congruent sides. You call the congruent sides **legs**. The **vertex angle** is the angle formed by the two legs. You call the third side the **base**. The angles on either side of the base are the **base angles**.

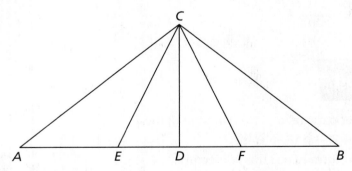

A. It is *not* possible to prove that $\triangle ACE \cong \triangle BCF$ based on the information given.

B. $\overline{AD} \cong \overline{BD}$, since D is the midpoint of $\overline{AB}$. So $\triangle ACD \cong \triangle BCD$ by SSS. This implies $\angle A \cong \angle B$ and $\angle ACD \cong \angle BCD$ by CPCTC. So $m\angle ACD = m\angle BCD$. Because $\overline{CE}$ and $\overline{CF}$ are angle bisectors, $m\angle BCF = \frac{1}{2}m\angle BCD = \frac{1}{2}m\angle ACD = m\angle ACE$. So $\angle BCF \cong \angle ACE$. Then $\triangle ACE \cong \triangle BCF$ by ASA.

C. Point D is the midpoint of $\overline{AB}$, so $\overline{AD} \cong \overline{BD}$. Then $\triangle ACD \cong \triangle BCD$ by SSS and $\overline{AE} \cong \overline{FB}$ by CPCTC. This implies $\triangle ACE \cong \triangle BCF$ by SAS.

D. Since $\overline{CD}$ is a median of $\triangle ABC$, D is the midpoint of $\overline{AB}$. So $\overline{AD} \cong \overline{BD}$. Because $\overline{CE}$ and $\overline{CF}$ are angle bisectors, they divide $\overline{AD}$ and $\overline{BD}$, respectively, into two congruent segments. So $\overline{AE} \cong \overline{ED}$ and $\overline{BF} \cong \overline{FD}$. Because $\triangle ABC$ is an isosceles triangle with $\angle A \cong \angle B$, the sides opposite those angles are congruent. So $\overline{AC} \cong \overline{BC}$. Since $\overline{AE} \cong \overline{BF}$, $\triangle ACE \cong \triangle BCF$ by SAS.

6. Draw an isosceles triangle and the bisector of its vertex angle. Prove that the two smaller triangles formed are congruent.

7. In $\triangle XMY$, $\overline{XE}$ is a median, and $\overline{XY} \cong \overline{XM}$. The bulleted list below is a sketch of a proof that $\triangle XEM \cong \triangle XEY$. Study the list. Then write the proof in either two-column, paragraph, or outline style.

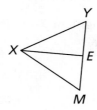

- $\overline{XE}$ is a median, so E is the midpoint of $\overline{MY}$. Then $\overline{ME} \cong \overline{EY}$.
- $\overline{XY} \cong \overline{XM}$ is given.
- The two triangles share $\overline{XE}$.
- The triangles have three pairs of congruent sides.

8. **What's Wrong Here?** Below is a proof that shows that any two lines are parallel. Explain what is wrong with the proof.

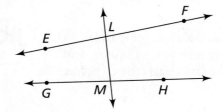

Suppose $\overleftrightarrow{EF}$ and $\overleftrightarrow{GH}$ are lines. Draw transversal $\overleftrightarrow{LM}$.

$\because \angle ELM$ and $\angle HML$ are alternate interior angles.

$\therefore \angle ELM \cong \angle HML$

$\therefore \overleftrightarrow{EF} \parallel \overleftrightarrow{GH}$ (AIP Theorem)

9. In the figure at the right, $\overleftrightarrow{AB} \parallel \overleftrightarrow{ED}$ and $\overline{AB} \cong \overline{ED}$.

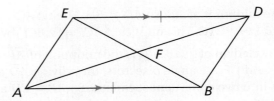

a. Timothy uses this information to prove that $\triangle ABF \cong \triangle DEF$. Explain why his paragraph proof is incorrect.

It is given that $\overleftrightarrow{AB} \parallel \overleftrightarrow{ED}$, so $\angle DEB \cong \angle ABE$ because parallel lines form congruent alternate interior angles with a transversal. And $\angle AFB \cong \angle DFE$ because they are vertical angles, and vertical angles are congruent. It is also given that $\overline{AB} \cong \overline{ED}$, so $\triangle ABF \cong \triangle DEF$ by ASA.

b. Is it possible to prove that $\triangle ABF \cong \triangle DEF$? If so, write a correct proof.

10. To show that a statement is true, mathematicians require deductive proof. Explain how you can convince someone that the statement "All horses are the same color" is *not* true.

11. Use circle P below to prove that the three triangles are congruent. Point P is the center of the circle.

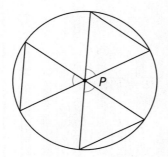

Maintain Your Skills

12. Use this conjecture about prime numbers. "Choose an integer n and square it. Then find the sum of the original whole number, its square, and 41. The sum is a prime number." For each value of n in parts (b)–(i) below, determine whether the sum is a prime number.

Go Online
www.successnetplus.com

a. What is a prime number?

b. $n = 1$ **c.** $n = 2$ **d.** $n = 3$ **e.** $n = -1$

f. $n = -2$ **g.** $n = -10$ **h.** $n = 15$ **i.** $n = 100$

j. Determine whether the conjecture is true. If it is true, prove it. If it is not true, find a counterexample.

Remember...

A counterexample is an example that makes the statement false.

Analyzing the Statement to Prove

Usually, statements that you prove are not expressed in the following Given-Prove form.

Given isosceles triangle ABC with $AB = BC$
Prove $\angle A \cong \angle C$

Instead, you may make statements about things that you suspect are true, such as the results of an experiment. Most likely, you use English sentences to make these statements. For instance, you might say, "Vertical angles are congruent," or "Base angles of an isosceles triangle are congruent," or "If it rains this afternoon, then practice will be canceled."

In the above statements, how do you know what to prove? You can break each sentence into two parts, a hypothesis and a conclusion. In the sentence "Vertical angles are congruent," the hypothesis is "The angles are vertical angles." The conclusion is "The angles are congruent." Then you can rewrite the sentence "Vertical angles are congruent." You can write, "If two angles are vertical angles, then they are congruent."

Here are two rules of thumb that may help you recognize each part of a sentence.

- If a sentence appears in *if-then* form, the clause beginning with *if* is the hypothesis. The clause beginning with *then* is the conclusion.

- If a sentence does not appear in *if-then* form, the subject of the sentence is the hypothesis. The predicate of the sentence is the conclusion.

The fact that a sentence states a conclusion does not necessarily mean that the conclusion is true. Carefully read the table below before beginning the exercises.

> **Remember...**
> The **hypothesis** is what you are assuming is true. The **conclusion** states what you need to prove.

> Sometimes the word *then* is not stated. For example, "If it is raining this afternoon, practice will be canceled."

Sentence	Hypothesis	Conclusion
If two parallel lines are cut by a transversal, the alternate interior angles are congruent.	Two parallel lines are cut by a transversal.	The alternate interior angles are congruent.
The base angles of an isosceles triangle are congruent.	Two angles are base angles of an isosceles triangle.	These two angles are congruent.
Two triangles with the same area are congruent.	Two triangles have the same area.	The two triangles are congruent.
Congruent triangles have the same area.	Two triangles are congruent.	They have the same area.
People with large hands have large feet.	Certain people have large hands.	These people have large feet.
Out of sight, out of mind.	Something is out of sight.	It is also out of mind.

Exercises *Practicing Habits of Mind*

Check Your Understanding

1. Which of the statements in the table on the previous page are not necessarily true? Explain.

2. In each sentence below, identify the hypothesis and conclusion.

   a. If two lines form congruent alternate interior angles with a transversal, then the lines are parallel.

   b. If n is any whole number, $n^2 + n + 41$ is prime.

   c. Two triangles are congruent if three sides of one triangle are congruent to three sides of the other triangle.

   d. Two lines that are parallel to a third line are also parallel to each other.

Go Online
Video Tutor
www.successnetplus.com

On Your Own

3. **Standardized Test Prep** Which is the hypothesis of the following statement? If two angles are congruent, then they have the same measure.

   A. Two angles are congruent.   **B.** They have the same measure.

   C. Two angles are not congruent.   **D.** They do not have the same measure.

For Exercises 4–9, draw a picture that illustrates the hypothesis. Then determine whether the statement is true. If a statement is true, give a proof. If a statement is not true, give a counterexample.

4. In a plane, two lines that are perpendicular to the same line are parallel to each other.

5. A line that bisects an angle of a triangle also bisects the side that is opposite the angle.

6. Equilateral quadrilaterals are **equiangular** (all angles congruent).

7. If a triangle has two congruent angles, it is isosceles.

8. Equiangular triangles are equilateral.

9. Equiangular quadrilaterals are equilateral.

> The prefix *equi-* means "equal." *Lateral* means "side." **Equilateral** means "sides with equal length."

Maintain Your Skills

Go Online
www.successnetplus.com

10. In a right $\triangle ABC$ with hypotenuse $\overline{CB}$, $AB = \frac{1}{2}AC$. Prove that $(CB)^2 = 5(AB)^2$. Then write this result as a statement in if-then form.

6.11 Analysis of a Proof

You have had some practice writing proofs. However, the real question is, how do you come up with a proof in the first place? Coming up with a proof is sometimes called the "analysis of the proof."

Analysis is always necessary before writing a proof. Sometimes analysis is very brief and occurs almost without you noticing it. If you readily find the logic underlying the proof, then writing the proof is just a matter of expressing the logic clearly.

How can you begin a proof if you do not yet understand the logic? Suppose that you have many facts and clues, but none of them points to a solution. In this chapter, you will learn three techniques for analyzing proofs.

- visual scan
- flowchart
- reverse list

You may find that a single method makes the most sense to you and becomes your main tool for analysis. However, to be skilled at analysis, you will need to use all three techniques. In fact, if you are having trouble understanding a proof using one method, it can be quite helpful to switch from one technique to another.

The Visual Scan

A visual scan is a strategy that involves careful examination of the figures in the proof. First, you can mark a sketch of the figure to show all of the known congruent parts. Next, you can mark additional parts that you can conclude are congruent. Finally, study the figure and a strategy for writing the proof may become clear.

The visual-scan strategy may be the simplest way to analyze a proof. The strategy is similar to doing mental math. You simply see what you have to do.

A basketball player visually scans the court before passing the ball.

Example 1

Given E is the midpoint of $\overline{HF}$. $\overline{EG} \perp \overline{HF}$.

Prove $\overline{HG} \cong \overline{FG}$

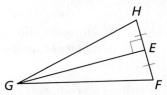

First, sketch $\triangle FGH$. Then mark the triangle showing the given information. The marked triangle may suggest the following proof.

- Show that $\triangle HEG \cong \triangle FEG$ by SAS.

- Then conclude that $\overline{HG} \cong \overline{FG}$ because they are corresponding parts of congruent triangles.

You can use this strategy to write the proof below.

Proof Point E is the midpoint of $\overline{HF}$. So $\overline{HE} \cong \overline{FE}$. $\overline{EG} \perp \overline{HF}$. So $m\angle GEF = m\angle GEH = 90°$. It follows that $\angle GEF \cong \angle GEH$. Triangle HEG and $\triangle FEG$ share $\overline{EG}$. So $\triangle HEG \cong \triangle FEG$ by SAS. Since corresponding parts of congruent triangles are congruent, $\overline{HG} \cong \overline{FG}$.

For You to Do

1. Use the visual-scan strategy. Prove that the base angles of an isosceles triangle are congruent. Below is an outline for your proof.

   - First sketch an isosceles triangle. Label its vertices.

   - Construct the bisector of the vertex angle. Label the point where the bisector intersects the base of the triangle.

   - Show that the two triangles formed by the bisector are congruent.

   - Conclude that the base angles of the isosceles triangle are congruent.

For Discussion

2. How can you use a proof like the one above to prove that an equilateral triangle is equiangular?

In the proofs above, you used the CPCTC strategy to prove that corresponding sides or corresponding angles of two triangles are congruent. To show that two segments or angles are congruent, you can use this strategy:

> This strategy is simple and direct. Can you only use it with triangles, though?

- First, find two triangles that contain the segments or the angles that you are trying to prove congruent. Prove that the triangles are congruent.

- Then, conclude that the segments or the angles are congruent, because they are corresponding parts of congruent triangles.

Keep the CPCTC strategy in mind as you work on this lesson. Notice how often you use it.

The Flowchart

The flowchart strategy is a "top-down" analysis technique. For instance, at the top of the flowchart you write statements about what you know is true. Below each statement you write conclusions based on the statement. You continue to write statements, moving down in the flowchart, until you reach the desired conclusion. An example of a flowchart is shown in Example 2.

Example 2

Make a flowchart for the following proof.

Given isosceles $\triangle ABC$ with $\overline{AB} \cong \overline{CB}$ and $\overline{AE} \cong \overline{CD}$

Prove $\angle BDE \cong \angle BED$

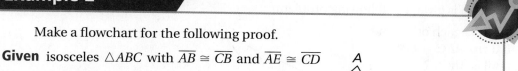

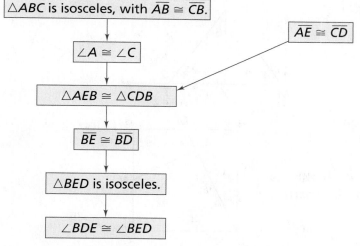

For You to Do

3. Write the proof that is outlined in the flowchart above.

A flowchart strategy has several advantages. When a flowchart is complete, it forms an outline for writing the actual proof. A flowchart also gives you a way to investigate and organize what you know, even if the entire proof is still unclear. You may also write any extra information in the flowchart. This information may help you generate alternate ways to write the proof.

Habits of Mind

Be concise. When you write a proof, leave out any unnecessary information. A well-written proof takes the most direct route through the flowchart.

Exercises *Practicing Habits of Mind*

Check Your Understanding

1. **What's Wrong Here?** Kenneth is given the following problem.

   Given that $\overline{AC}$ and $\overline{BH}$ bisect each other and that $\overline{AB} \cong \overline{CH}$, show that $m\angle ABC = m\angle AHC$. What type of quadrilateral is *ABCH*?

   Kenneth uses the visual-scan strategy and marks the figure at the right.

   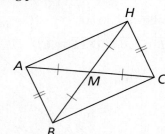

   a. What marking error did Kenneth make?

   b. What incorrect conclusion in a proof might result from his marking error?

2. Use the figure and the given information. Make a flowchart for the proof without writing the actual proof.

   Given $\angle 1 \cong \angle 2$. $\overline{XY}$ bisects $\angle MXT$.

   Prove $\overline{MY} \cong \overline{YT}$

   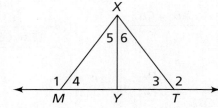

3. In the figure at the right, *ABCD* is a square. Points *M* and *N* are the midpoints of $\overline{AB}$ and $\overline{BC}$, respectively.

   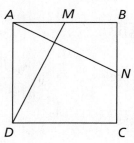

   a. The flowchart below outlines a proof that shows $\overline{AN} \cong \overline{DM}$. Copy and complete the flowchart.

   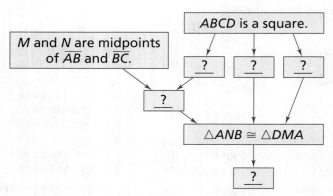

   b. Use the completed flowchart to write the proof.

4. Standardized Test Prep $\triangle ABC$ is an isosceles triangle with $\overline{AB} \cong \overline{AC}$. $\overline{AE}, \overline{BF},$ and $\overline{CD}$ are medians.

The flowchart below outlines a proof that shows that $\overline{FB} \cong \overline{DC}$. Which of the statements below best completes the flowchart?

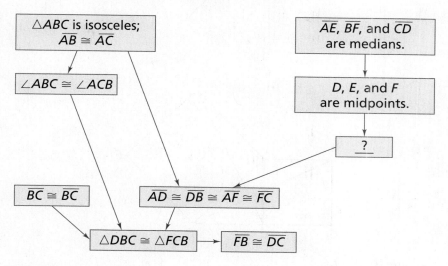

A. $\angle ABF \cong \angle FBC$

B. $\overline{AD} \cong \overline{DB};\ \overline{AF} \cong \overline{FC};\ \overline{BE} \cong \overline{EC}$

C. $\overline{AE} \cong \overline{AE}$

D. $\triangle ABE \cong \triangle ACE$

For Exercise 5, use the visual scan strategy to analyze the proof. Copy the figure onto a separate piece of paper, and mark the given information. Then write an outline for the proof.

5. Given $\overline{HJ} \cong \overline{HL}$ and $\overline{JK} \cong \overline{LK}$
  Prove $\triangle HJM \cong \triangle HLM$

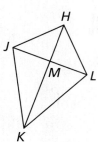

6. Given $\overleftrightarrow{GF} \perp \overleftrightarrow{GH}$ and $\overleftrightarrow{GJ} \perp \overleftrightarrow{GK}$
   Prove $\angle JGF \cong \angle KGH$

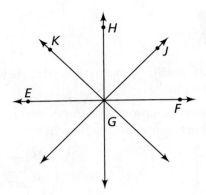

7. Given *FACG* and *DABE* are squares.
   Prove $\triangle FAB \cong \triangle CAD$

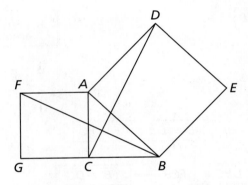

8. Given $\triangle LJM$ and $\triangle LKN$ are equilateral.
   Prove $\overline{MK} \cong \overline{NJ}$

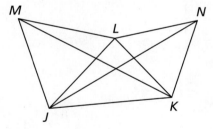

9. Given $\triangle QRT$ is an isosceles triangle. $\overline{QT} \cong \overline{TR}$. $\overline{VR}$ and $\overline{UQ}$ are medians.
   Prove $VR = UQ$

Go **Online**
www.successnetplus.com

10. Given Point *P* is on the perpendicular bisector of $\overline{LM}$.
   Prove $PL = PM$

Maintain Your Skills

11. Draw a coordinate plane. Plot points $O(0, 0)$ and $A(6, 0)$. Choose
   and label point *B* on the line $x = 3$ such that *B* is *not* on the *x*-axis.
   Prove that $\triangle AOB$ is an isosceles triangle.

Habits of Mind

Visualize. Before you
write the proof, sketch a
coordinate plane. Draw
$\triangle AOB$ and the line
$x = 3$. Then use the
visual-scan strategy.

6.12 The Reverse List

When you use the visual-scan strategy or the flowchart strategy, you start with what you know and work toward the final conclusion that you want to prove. The reverse-list strategy works in the opposite direction. You start with the information that you want to prove and work backward. You repeatedly ask yourself, "What information do I need?" and "What strategy can I use to prove that?"

Habits of Mind

Different Approaches
The reverse-list strategy is a bottom-up strategy rather than a top-down strategy.

Make a reverse list.

Below is an analysis of a proof that uses the reverse-list strategy.

Given $TUVW$ is a rectangle. X is the midpoint of $\overline{TU}$.

Prove $\triangle XWV$ is isosceles.

You need to prove that $\triangle XWV$ is an isosceles triangle.

Need $\triangle XWV$ is an isosceles triangle.
Use A triangle is isosceles if two of its sides are congruent.

Need $\overline{VX} \cong \overline{WX}$
Use CPCTC

Need congruent triangles: $\triangle WXT \cong \triangle VXU$
Use SAS

Need two congruent sides: $\overline{TW} \cong \overline{UV}$
Use Opposite sides of a rectangle are congruent.

Need $TUVW$ is a rectangle.
Use given information

Need two congruent angles: $\angle T \cong \angle U$
Use Each angle in a rectangle is a right angle. So the four angles in a rectangle are congruent.

Need $TUVW$ is a rectangle.
Use given information

Need two congruent sides: $\overline{TX} \cong \overline{UX}$
Use The midpoint of a segment divides the segment into two congruent segments.

Need X is the midpoint of $\overline{TU}$.
Use given information

Habits of Mind

Draw a diagram.
When you use the reverse-list strategy, how do you know which sides, angles, or triangles to try to prove congruent? A careful sketch often helps.

A complete reverse-list analysis outlines the proof in reverse order. Below is the proof that is outlined in the reverse list above.

Proof Point X is the midpoint of $\overline{TU}$. So $\overline{TX} \cong \overline{UX}$. $TUVW$ is a rectangle. So its opposite sides are congruent, and its four right angles are congruent. So $\overline{TW} \cong \overline{UV}$ and $\angle T \cong \angle U$. Therefore $\triangle WXT \cong \triangle VXU$ by SAS. So $\overline{VX} \cong \overline{WX}$ by CPCTC. This tells us that $\triangle XWV$ is an isosceles triangle.

How do you decide which strategies to use when you write a reverse list? There is no foolproof method. However, there is a straightforward way to narrow down the number of strategies.

What results prove the needed conclusion?

Look back through your notes or back in your book. Find all the previously established results that you have used to prove a needed conclusion. For example, in the reverse list above, you needed to show that $\overline{TX} \cong \overline{UX}$. This is your needed conclusion. So you should look for previously established results with the conclusion "congruent segments." At this point, you have only used a few.

- The legs of an isosceles triangle are congruent.

- The corresponding sides of congruent triangles are congruent.

- The two segments formed by the midpoint of a segment are congruent.

Which results relate to what I know?

Once you narrow down your list, you go through the results one by one. Decide which result you can really use to prove your conclusion. How do you choose? You decide whether a relationship exists between the conclusion you need and each result. In this case, you can go down the list of results and ask a question for each one.

- Are $\overline{TX}$ and $\overline{UX}$ the sides of an isosceles triangle?
  No; $\overline{TX}$ and $\overline{UX}$ are not sides of the same triangle.

- Are $\overline{TX}$ and $\overline{UX}$ the corresponding sides of two congruent triangles? $\overline{TX}$ and $\overline{UX}$ are the corresponding sides of $\triangle WXT$ and $\triangle VXU$. The reason you want to prove that $\overline{TX} \cong \overline{UX}$ in the first place is so you can prove that $\triangle WXT \cong \triangle VXU$.

- Are $\overline{TX}$ and $\overline{UX}$ two segments that are formed by the midpoint of a segment? Yes; you know from the given information that X is the midpoint of $\overline{TU}$.

When you use the reverse-list strategy to analyze a proof, here are some points to remember:

- Use the given information to prove a needed result when possible.

- Use CPCTC to prove that corresponding sides or corresponding angles of congruent triangles are congruent.

- Right now, you have four ways to prove that two triangles are congruent: SSS, SAS, ASA, and AAS.

- The reverse-list strategy almost always works.

You may go down some dead ends before you hit the right path.

Check Your Understanding

1. In the figure at the right, P is a point on the perpendicular bisector of $\overline{AB}$.

   a. Make a reverse list that you can use to prove that $\triangle APB$ is an isosceles triangle.

   b. Write a proof that shows $\triangle APB$ is an isosceles triangle. Use your reverse list from part (a).

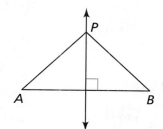

2. In the figure at the right, $\overline{AD}$ is the perpendicular bisector of $\overline{BC}$.

   a. Which triangles must be congruent?

   b. Write a proof that shows that the two triangles in part (a) are congruent.

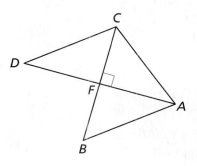

On Your Own

In Exercises 3–8, prove each statement. Use a reverse list to write each proof.

3. If a triangle is isosceles, then the medians from its legs to the vertices of its base angles are congruent.

4. If a triangle is isosceles, then the bisectors of its base angles are congruent.

5. If two altitudes of a triangle are congruent, then the triangle is isosceles.

6. If a triangle is isosceles, then the altitudes drawn to its legs are congruent.

7. In isosceles triangle ABC, $\overline{AC} \cong \overline{BC}$. Point M is the midpoint of $\overline{AC}$. Point N is the midpoint of $\overline{CB}$. Prove that $\triangle CMN$ is an isosceles triangle.

8. **Take It Further** In the two triangles below, $\overline{AC} \cong \overline{DF}$ and $\overline{CB} \cong \overline{FE}$. $\overline{AM}$ and $\overline{DN}$ are congruent medians. Show that $\triangle ABC \cong \triangle DEF$.

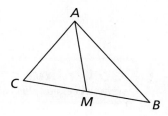
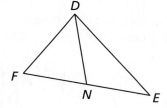

9. Standardized Test Prep Triangle *ABC* at the right is an isosceles triangle with $\overline{AB} \cong \overline{AC}$ and $\angle ABC \cong \angle ACB$. $\overline{CD}$ is the bisector of $\angle ACB$. $\overline{BE}$ is the bisector of $\angle ABC$. Suppose you want to prove that $\overline{EF} \cong \overline{DF}$.

Which of the statements and reasons below complete the following reverse list?

Need $\overline{EF} \cong \overline{DF}$
Use CPCTC

Need I
Use I

Need II
Use II

Need III
Use III

Need $\triangle BCE \cong \triangle CBD$
Use ASA

Need $\overline{BC} \cong \overline{BC}$
Use The two triangles share the side.

Need $\angle ACD \cong \angle DCB \cong \angle ABE \cong \angle EBC$
Use definition of congruent angles

Need $m\angle ACD = m\angle DCB = m\angle ABE = m\angle EBC$
Use definition of angle bisector

Need $\overline{CD}$ is the bisector of $\angle ACB$. $\overline{BE}$ is the bisector of $\angle ABC$.
Use given

Need $\frac{1}{2}m\angle ABC = \frac{1}{2}m\angle ACB$
Use multiplication property of equality

Need $m\angle ABC = m\angle ACB$
Use definition of congruent angles

Need $\angle ABC \cong \angle ACB$
Use given

A. I. $\triangle BDF \cong \triangle CEF$; AAS

II. $\angle CFE \cong \angle BFD$; the Vertical Angles Theorem

III. $\overline{CE} \cong \overline{BD}$; CPCTC

B. I. $\triangle ADC \cong \triangle AEB$; SAS

II. $\overline{AB} \cong \overline{AC}$; given

III. $\overline{BE} \cong \overline{CD}$; CPCTC

C. I. $\triangle ADC \cong \triangle AEB$; AAS

II. $\overline{AB} \cong \overline{AC}$; given

III. $\angle A \cong \angle A$; the two triangles share this angle.

D. I. $\triangle BDF \cong \triangle CEF$; ASA

II. $\angle BDF \cong \angle CEF$; CPCTC

III. $\overline{BE} \cong \overline{CD}$; CPCTC

Maintain Your Skills

10. In $\triangle ABC$, $m\angle CAB = 90°$. To conclude that each statement listed below is true, what additional information do you need about the *angles* of $\triangle ABC$? About the *sides*?

a. $\triangle ABC$ is half of an equilateral triangle.

b. $\triangle ABC$ is half of a square.

c. $\triangle ABC$ is half of an isosceles triangle.

Go Online
www.successnetplus.com

6.13 Practicing Your Proof-Writing Skills

Below are some general guidelines for you to follow as you work on a mathematical investigation.

- *Explore* the problem. Use hand or computer drawings to help you understand the statement of the problem.

- *Explain* what you observe. If you can, justify your observations with a proof. If you cannot write a complete proof, describe the information you have. Then say what information is missing from your proof.

- *Summarize* your work. Include drawings, conjectures that you made, a list of important vocabulary words, theorems, rules or ideas that you discovered, and questions that require further exploration.

Below is the Perpendicular Bisector Theorem again, along with its proof.

Theorem 6.8 *Perpendicular Bisector Theorem*

Each point on the perpendicular bisector of a segment is equidistant from the two endpoints of the segment.

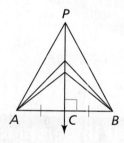

Proof Suppose $\overline{PC}$ is the perpendicular bisector of $\overline{AB}$. Then C is the midpoint of $\overline{AB}$. So $\overline{AC} \cong \overline{BC}$.

Also, because $\overline{PC}$ is the perpendicular bisector of $\overline{AB}$, $m\angle PCA = m\angle PCB = 90°$.

Triangle PCA and $\triangle PCB$ share $\overline{PC}$, so $\triangle PCA \cong \triangle PCB$ by SAS.

Since $\triangle PCA \cong \triangle PCB$, $\overline{AP} \cong \overline{BP}$ by CPCTC.

A similar argument proves that $\overline{AP} \cong \overline{BP}$ for any point P on $\overleftrightarrow{PC}$.

Therefore, any point on the perpendicular bisector of a line segment is equidistant from the endpoints of the line segment.

For You to Do

1. State and prove the converse of the Perpendicular Bisector Theorem.

Remember...

Where have you seen this proof before?

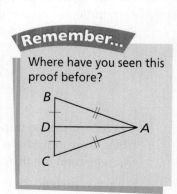

The measures of the angles in a triangle are related to the lengths of the triangle's sides. For example, suppose a triangle has two congruent sides. Then it must also have two congruent angles.

Proof Suppose $\triangle ABC$ is an isosceles triangle, with $\overline{AB} \cong \overline{AC}$. Construct the median from A. Call the point where the median intersects $\overline{BC}$ point D. Point D is the midpoint of $\overline{BC}$. So $\overline{BD} \cong \overline{CD}$.

Triangle ADB and $\triangle ADC$ share side $\overline{AD}$. So $\triangle ADB \cong \triangle ADC$ by SSS. Then, by CPCTC, $\angle B \cong \angle C$.

You proved the following theorem in Lesson 6.11.

Theorem 6.9 *Isosceles Triangle Theorem*

The base angles of an isosceles triangle are congruent.

If $\overline{AB} \cong \overline{BC}$, then $\angle A \cong \angle C$.

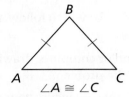

$\angle A \cong \angle C$

For You to Do

2. State and prove the converse of the Isosceles Triangle Theorem.

3. Can a scalene triangle have two angles the same size? Develop a conjecture that you can use to identify the largest, smallest, and middle-sized angles in a triangle. How can you prove your conjecture?

> **Remember...**
> A **scalene triangle** has no sides that are the same length.

Exercises *Practicing Habits of Mind*

Check Your Understanding

1. Use the figure at the right. $\overleftrightarrow{ST}$ is the perpendicular bisector of $\overline{RQ}$. Prove that $\angle SRT \cong \angle SQT$.

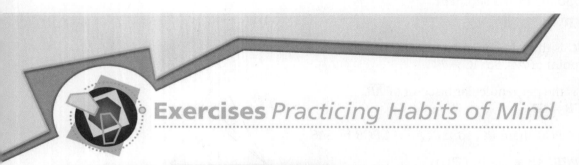

2. The SAS postulate implies that if two sides and the included angle of one triangle are congruent to two sides and the included angle of another triangle, then the third sides of the two triangles are also congruent.

Suppose, instead, that two sides of one triangle are congruent to two sides of another, but that the included angle in the first triangle is larger than the included angle in the second triangle. What can you conclude about the third sides of the two triangles?

> This result is sometimes called the Hinge Theorem. Can you think of a reason why?

For Exercises 3–5, do each of the following.

- Draw the figure described.
- Use your drawing. Explain what the statement says about the figure.
- Write what you know about the figure. Then make and explain conjectures about what you think might be true.
- Try to prove the last sentence. Use any method.

3. Draw square $ABCD$. Construct rays $\overrightarrow{AB}$, $\overrightarrow{BC}$, $\overrightarrow{CD}$, and $\overrightarrow{DA}$. Choose point E on $\overrightarrow{AB}$, point F on $\overrightarrow{BC}$, point G on $\overrightarrow{CD}$, and point H on $\overrightarrow{DA}$ such that the points are not on the sides of square $ABCD$ and $\overline{BE} \cong \overline{CF} \cong \overline{DG} \cong \overline{AH}$. Quadrilateral $EFGH$ is a square.

4. Draw a quadrilateral with congruent diagonals and one pair of opposite sides that are congruent. At least one of the four triangles into which the quadrilateral is divided is isosceles.

5. Draw an isosceles triangle. Pick any point along the base. From this point, draw lines parallel to the congruent sides, forming a parallelogram. The perimeter of the parallelogram is fixed, regardless of which point you pick along the base.

> **Remember...**
>
> In order to *prove* that a quadrilateral is a square, you need to show that its sides are all congruent and its angles are all congruent.

> You can do this exercise with geometry software.

6. The four statements below describe this figure.

- $\triangle ABC$ is isosceles with base $\overline{AB}$.
- $\overline{CD}$ is a median.
- $\overline{CD}$ is an altitude.
- $\overline{CD}$ is the angle bisector of $\angle ACB$.

Show that if any two of the statements are given, you can prove the other two statements. For example,

Given   statements 1 and 2
Prove   statements 3 and 4

Continue writing proofs until you have used two of the statements to prove the remaining two for all but one case. How many theorems do you have?

Write up your work for this exercise. Organize your sketches, notes, questions, ideas, and proofs. Prepare a page on which you will write the proof for the one remaining case. Write and hand in that proof when you know you have the information needed.

On Your Own

7. Refer to the diagram for Exercise 6. Write one new statement, either about $\triangle ABC$ or about $\triangle ADC$ and $\triangle BDC$, that guarantees that all four of the statements in Exercise 6 are true.

8. Describe the set of triangles that meets each of the following conditions.

   a. The perpendicular bisector of exactly one side passes through the opposite vertex.

   b. The perpendicular bisector of each of exactly two of the sides passes through the opposite vertex.

   c. The perpendicular bisector of each of the sides passes through the opposite vertex.

   You may find it helpful to construct some triangles that meet each condition and some triangles that do not. Explain what you find.

9. Use a cup or glass to trace a circle on a sheet of paper. Explain how to find the center of the circle.

10. **Standardized Test Prep** Brittany found a piece of broken pottery that looks like part of a circular dinner plate. She wants to determine the radius of the plate, but she has less than half of the plate. First, she traces the outline of the outer edge of the pottery on a sheet of paper. Then she draws two line segments with endpoints that are on different parts of the curve. Next, she constructs the perpendicular bisector of each line segment. She extends the perpendicular bisectors until they intersect. Finally, she measures the distance from the point of intersection of the perpendicular bisectors to a point on the curve. Why does this procedure guarantee that she has found the radius of the plate?

    A. A line that is perpendicular to a tangent of a circle will always go through the center of the circle. Each bisected line segment is tangent to the circle.

    B. The perpendicular bisector of a chord divides the arc associated with the chord into two congruent arcs. The length of each arc is equal to the radius of the circle.

    C. A point on the perpendicular bisector of a segment is equidistant from the endpoints of the segment. The distance from the intersection of the perpendicular bisectors to a point on a circle is the radius of the circle.

    D. The point of intersection of the perpendicular bisectors, along with the midpoints of the bisected segments, determine an isosceles triangle. The segment that connects the midpoints of bisected segments is the base of the isosceles triangle. The radius of the circle is the length of one of the legs of the isosceles triangle.

11. Describe an algorithm that you can use to construct a circle that passes through the vertices of a given triangle.

12. A circular saw blade shattered. All you can find is a piece that looks like the figure at the right. Explain how to find the diameter of the blade so you can buy a new one.

How can you make a model of the original plate if you find only this piece?

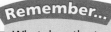

Remember...

What does the term *algorithm* mean?

13. Show that if the hypotenuse and a leg of one right triangle are congruent to the hypotenuse and a leg of another right triangle, then the triangles are congruent.

This test for right-triangle congruence is sometimes called "hypotenuse-leg" and is abbreviated HL.

14. Draw several triangles. In each triangle, construct the perpendicular bisector of each side. Notice that the perpendicular bisectors in each triangle intersect in one point. Is this true for all triangles? Provide a proof or a counterexample.

15. Perform the paper-folding construction shown at the right. Start with a rectangular sheet of paper.

Fold *A* onto *B* and crease along the dotted line.

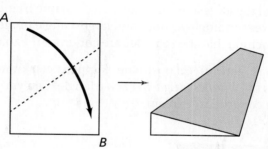

Then fold *C* onto *D*, and crease along the dotted line.

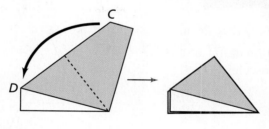

Unfold the paper. The creases should look like this.

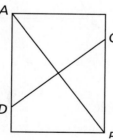

Prove that any point on $\overline{CD}$ is the same distance from *A* as from *B*.

There is no SSA triangle postulate. Two sides and a nonincluded angle of one triangle can be congruent to two sides and the corresponding nonincluded angle of another triangle without the two triangles being congruent.

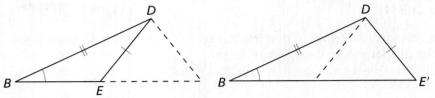

16. **Take It Further** Could there be an SS**A** postulate? Suppose you know that the nonincluded angle is the *largest* angle in each triangle. That is, suppose that the two sides and the largest nonincluded angle of one triangle are congruent to the corresponding two sides and largest angle of the other triangle. Can you conclude that the triangles are congruent? Explain.

If SS**A** does guarantee triangle congruence, it is a generalization of HL. Explain.

17. **Take It Further** And is there an SS**a** postulate? Suppose you know that the nonincluded angle is the *smallest* angle in each triangle. Can you conclude that the triangles are congruent? Explain.

Maintain Your Skills

18. In the figure at the right, $\overline{AD} \cong \overline{BC}$ and $\overline{AB} \parallel \overline{DC}$.

    Point E is the intersection of $\overleftrightarrow{AD}$ and $\overleftrightarrow{BC}$.
    Prove that $\triangle ABE$ is isosceles.

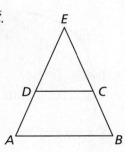

19. Here are two quite plausible statements.

    In a triangle,

    • the longest side is opposite the largest angle
    • the shortest side is opposite the smallest angle

    You may assume that both statements are theorems. Use one or both of the statements to help you prove the Triangle Inequality Theorem:

    In a triangle, the length of one side is less than the sum of the lengths of the other two sides.

    In other words, in $\triangle ABC$, prove that $AB < AC + CB$. (*Hint:* Use the figure at the right to write a reverse list.)

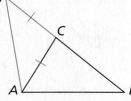

Mathematical 6C Reflections

In this investigation, you studied mathematical proof. You learned different ways to think about and analyze the proof-writing process. You also learned several ways to write and organize a mathematical proof. You used these skills to practice and improve your own proof-writing techniques.

1. In the figure at the right, $\triangle ABC$ is isosceles with $\overline{AC} \cong \overline{BC}$. $\overleftrightarrow{CP}$ is the bisector of $\angle ACB$. Point P is on this angle bisector. Prove that $\triangle APB$ is isosceles.

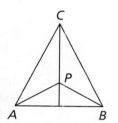

2. The hypotenuse and one of the acute angles of a right triangle are congruent to the hypotenuse and one of the acute angles of another right triangle. Prove that the two triangles are congruent or give a counterexample.

3. In the figure at the right, $\triangle ABC$ is isosceles with $\overline{AC} \cong \overline{BC}$. $\overline{EA} \cong \overline{FB}$ and $\overline{AS} \cong \overline{BT}$. Prove that $\triangle AES \cong \triangle BFT$.

4. The base and the angle opposite the base in one isosceles triangle are congruent to the base and the angle opposite the base in another isosceles triangle. Prove that the two triangles are congruent or provide a counterexample.

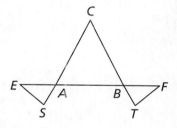

5. Write a reverse list for this statement about the figure at the right.

   If $\overline{TA} \cong \overline{TC} \cong \overline{TB}$, then $\triangle ABC$ is a right triangle.

   Then use the list to prove the statement.

6. What are the different ways to organize and analyze a proof?

7. What is the Perpendicular Bisector Theorem?

8. In the statement "All trees are green," what is the hypothesis and what is the conclusion?

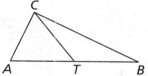

The steel cables form congruent angles with the roadway, so the triangle is isosceles.

Vocabulary

In this investigation, you learned these terms. Make sure you understand what each one means and how to use it.

- base angle
- base of an isosceles triangle
- conclusion
- equiangular
- hypothesis

- isosceles triangle
- leg
- proof
- scalene triangle
- vertex angle

Investigation 6D

Quadrilaterals and Their Properties

In *Quadrilaterals and Their Properties*, you will explore four-sided figures. Chances are you already know a great deal about quadrilaterals. From the earliest elementary grades, you have constructed, measured, cut, and folded squares and rectangles. Now you will use this practical experience as you begin a more formal study of quadrilaterals. All of the properties of these shapes are important in understanding what makes each one unique.

By the end of this investigation, you will be able to answer questions like these.

1. What are some special properties of parallelograms? Of kites? Of trapezoids?

2. Are all squares also considered parallelograms? Are all parallelograms also considered squares? Explain.

3. If a statement is true, must its converse also be true?

You will learn how to
- define and classify quadrilaterals
- write the converse of a conditional statement
- understand the meaning of *always, never,* and *sometimes* in mathematics

You will develop these habits and skills:
- Characterize sets in a given class.
- Understand that the converse of a statement is not automatically true when the initial statement is true.
- Reason by continuity.

A nonconformist use of quadrilaterals

6.14 Getting Started

You will use your basic knowledge of squares and rectangles to discover additional properties and characteristics of quadrilaterals.

For You to Explore

1. Use any method you choose to construct a square and a rectangle.

2. List as many properties as you can of the sides, angles, and diagonals of the square and of the rectangle.

3. Can you find a property of the rectangle that is not a property of the square?

> **Remember...**
> A diagonal is a segment that connects two non-consecutive vertices of a polygon.

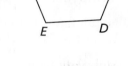

Exercises *Practicing Habits of Mind*

On Your Own

4. Draw a quadrilateral with four congruent sides that is not a square. What do you call this type of quadrilateral?

5. Draw a quadrilateral with two congruent diagonals that is not a rectangle.

6. Draw a quadrilateral with four congruent angles. Must it be a rectangle?

7. Construct a rectangle with perpendicular diagonals that are 4 cm.

8. Write another description for the figure you constructed in Exercise 7. Use a different name for the quadrilateral.

9. **Take It Further** Without using a ruler to measure, fold a nonsquare sheet of paper into a square. How do you know that the figure you folded is a square?

> **Remember...**
> A polygon with exactly four sides is called a *quadrilateral*.

Maintain Your Skills

Find the area of each figure.

10.
$\frac{1}{2}$ in.
8 in.
not to scale

11. 4 cm

12. 10 ft
2 ft

> **Go Online**
> **Video Tutor**
> www.successnetplus.com

6.15 General Quadrilaterals

You have already explored some properties and characteristics of familiar quadrilaterals, such as squares and rectangles. Now, you are going to take a look at some less-common quadrilaterals.

In-Class Experiment

On a separate sheet of paper, sketch several figures that each have the following properties.

- The figure is made of four segments.
- The segments intersect at their endpoints.
- Each endpoint is shared by exactly two segments.

Answer the following questions about each of your figures.

1. Is your figure closed? Can you draw a figure with the three properties listed above that is not closed?

2. Must your figure lie on a plane? Can you show a figure with the three properties listed above that does not lie on a plane?

3. Does your figure intersect itself? Explain.

> A figure is **closed** if you can "walk" its outer edges and get back to where you started.

The following definition is not new to you, but here it is stated formally.

Definition

A **quadrilateral** is a figure that consists of four segments called its **sides**. The sides intersect at their endpoints, called the quadrilateral's **vertices**, so that each vertex is the endpoint of exactly two sides.

> *Vertices* is the plural of *vertex*.

Are these figures quadrilaterals?

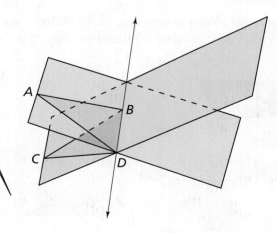

The definition of quadrilateral does not say that the sides of a quadrilateral are only connected to each other at their endpoints. The first two figures on the previous page have points in common in addition to their endpoints. You call such figures self-intersecting quadrilaterals.

The definition of a quadrilateral also does not say that the quadrilateral must lie in one plane. The last figure on the previous page does not. You call it a **skew quadrilateral.**

The two figures below are also quadrilaterals, but it is often inconvenient to include them in a discussion. You call them **concave** (or nonconvex) quadrilaterals. A concave quadrilateral has at least one diagonal outside the quadrilateral.

> A figure is **self-intersecting** if you "walk" its outer edges and go through the same point more than once before you get back to where you started.

diagonal outside the quadrilateral

diagonal outside the quadrilateral

In this book, the term *quadrilateral* does not include self-intersecting, skew, or concave quadrilaterals, unless mentioned specifically.

Exercises *Practicing Habits of Mind*

Check Your Understanding

1. A figure is closed if you can walk its outer edges and get back to where you started. The definition of *quadrilateral* does not say that a quadrilateral must be closed. Can you draw a quadrilateral that satisfies the definition, but is not closed?

2. A figure is *planar* if all its points lie in the same plane. The definition of *quadrilateral* does not say that a quadrilateral must be planar. Can you draw a quadrilateral that satisfies the definition but is not planar?

3. Explain why each figure below is not a quadrilateral.

a. 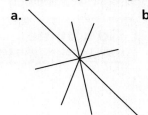   b. 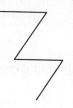   c.   d.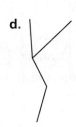

On Your Own

4. **Standardized Test Prep** Which of the following statements is NOT true about a quadrilateral in a plane?

   A. Except for its endpoints, all the points on at least one of a quadrilateral's diagonals lie in the interior of the quadrilateral.

   B. At least one diagonal of a quadrilateral divides the quadrilateral into two triangles.

   C. The sum of the measures of the interior angles of a quadrilateral is 360°.

   D. The four vertices of every quadrilateral lie on a unique circle.

   Review the following triangle theorems. Then complete Exercises 5–8.

   - The sum of the measures of the angles of a triangle is 180°.
   - The sum of the lengths of any two sides of a triangle is greater than the length of the third side.

5. The sum of the measures of the angles of a quadrilateral is always 360°. Explain why this is true.

6. Is the sum of the measures of the angles of a self-intersecting quadrilateral always 360°? Explain.

7. Is the sum of the measures of the angles of a skew quadrilateral always 360°? Explain.

8. **Take It Further** Prove that the sum of the lengths of any three sides of a quadrilateral is greater than the length of the fourth side. Determine whether your proof works for each type of quadrilateral listed below.

   - concave
   - self-intersecting
   - skew

   If your proof does not work for one or more types of the quadrilaterals listed above, can you write a different proof that will hold? Or does the proof fail because the property is not a characteristic of that type of quadrilateral?

> How would you define the angles of a self-intersecting quadrilateral?

Maintain Your Skills

9. Two angles of a quadrilateral both measure $x°$. The other two angles both measure $2x°$.

   a. Find the value of x.

   b. Find the measure of each angle.

   c. Can you determine the shape of the quadrilateral? Is more than one type of quadrilateral possible?

Properties of Quadrilaterals

Certain quadrilaterals have properties and characteristics that distinguish them from other quadrilaterals. For example, a square is the only quadrilateral that has four congruent sides and four congruent angles.

You can use the special properties of certain quadrilaterals to prove additional properties. You will do this in the exercises.

Below are the definitions of two special types of quadrilaterals.

Definition

A **trapezoid** is a quadrilateral with **exactly one pair** of parallel sides. The two parallel sides are called the **bases** of the trapezoid.

Definition

A **kite** is a quadrilateral in which two adjacent sides are congruent, and the other two adjacent sides are congruent as well.

> **Habits of Mind**
>
> **Understand more than one meaning.**
> A trapezoid is sometimes defined as a quadrilateral with *at least* one pair of parallel sides. According to this definition, a parallelogram is a special type of trapezoid.

Example

Prove that one of the diagonals of a kite divides it into two congruent triangles.

First you must determine which diagonal appears to divide the kite into two congruent triangles. Unless your kite is a square, only one of its diagonals will divide the kite into two congruent triangles. This diagonal is sometimes called the *symmetry diagonal*.

> What is so special about the diagonals of a square?

Given   kite *ABCD* with diagonal $\overline{BD}$
Prove $\triangle DAB \cong \triangle DCB$

Proof   Because *ABCD* is a kite,
$\overline{AB} \cong \overline{CB}$ and $\overline{AD} \cong \overline{CD}$.
$\triangle DAB$ and $\triangle DCB$ share $\overline{BD}$.
So $\triangle DAB \cong \triangle DCB$ by SSS.

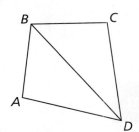

Minds in Action

Sasha and Tony are working on Exercises 2–8 in the
Check Your Understanding section of this lesson.

Tony   Here are the directions: Complete each sentence with *always,*
            sometimes, or *never* to make the statement true.

Sasha   *Always* means you can prove it. So if we choose *always,* we have to
            be ready to write a proof.

Tony   Proofs mean work. Let's try to answer *never.*

Sasha   But for *never* we have to give a proof also—a proof that shows that
            the statement cannot be true.

Tony   Well, maybe we can answer *sometimes.*

Sasha   *Sometimes* means we have to show an example when the
            statement is true, and another example when the statement is
            false. We need two different examples!

Tony   So these kinds of questions are like true-or-false questions. *Always*
            is the same as *true.*

Sasha   Yeah, but *false* is divided into *sometimes* statements, which are
            sometimes true (and sometimes false), and *never* statements,
            which are never true.

Tony   That's terrible—whatever we answer, we have to prove something!

Sasha   Come on—proofs are fun!

Exercises Practicing Habits of Mind

Check Your Understanding

1. Which of the figures A–L, here and on the next page, appear to be
   trapezoids? Explain.

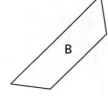

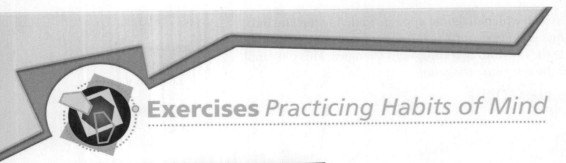

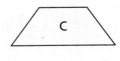

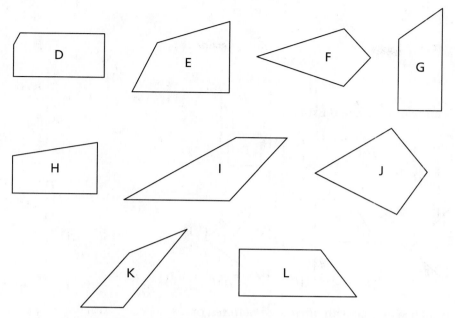

For Exercises 2–8, complete each sentence with *always*, *sometimes*, or *never* to make the statement true. Justify your answer with a proof or some examples.

Go Online
www.successnetplus.com

2. The sum of the measures of the angles of a trapezoid is __?__ 360°.

3. The diagonals of a trapezoid are __?__ congruent.

4. Two sides of a trapezoid are __?__ congruent.

5. Three sides of a trapezoid are __?__ congruent.

6. One diagonal of a trapezoid __?__ bisects one of the trapezoid's angles.

7. Two angles of a trapezoid are __?__ right angles.

8. A trapezoid __?__ has exactly one right angle.

9. Two parallel lines can be close to each other or far apart. So it is natural to refer to the distance between two parallel lines. Write a definition that describes the distance between parallel lines.

10. Read the following definition. Then prove that the base angles of an isosceles trapezoid are congruent.

Definition

An **isosceles trapezoid** is a trapezoid with opposite nonparallel sides that are congruent. Each pair of angles with vertices that are the endpoints of the same base are called **base angles**.

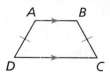

∠A and ∠B are base angles.
∠D and ∠C are base angles.

11. Prove that the diagonals of an isosceles trapezoid are congruent.

On Your Own

12. Which of the following figures appear to be kites? Explain.

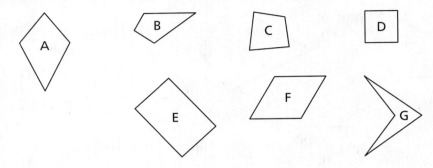

For Exercises 13–17, complete each sentence with *always*, *sometimes*, or *never* to make the statement true.

13. The sum of the measures of the angles of a kite is __?__ 360°.

14. The diagonals of a kite are __?__ perpendicular.

15. A kite __?__ has two congruent angles.   16. A kite __?__ has a right angle.

17. One diagonal of a kite __?__ bisects one of its angles.

18. **Standardized Test Prep** Which of the following statements is always true?

   I. A kite has at least one pair of congruent adjacent sides.

   II. A kite has at least one pair of congruent opposite angles.

   III. The diagonals of an isosceles trapezoid are congruent.

   A. I only   **B.** I and II only   **C.** I and III only   **D.** I, II, and III

19. Prove that the symmetry diagonal of a kite bisects two angles of the kite.

20. Prove that the diagonals of a kite are perpendicular.

Maintain Your Skills

Determine whether each statement is true or false. Provide a counterexample if the statement is false.

21. If you live in Canada, then you live in Montreal.

22. If you live in Montreal, then you live in Canada.

23. If a figure has an area of 16 square units, then it is a square.

24. All telephone numbers in Vermont have an area code of 802.

25. If your home telephone number area code is 802, then you live in Vermont.

6.17 Parallelograms

You define special quadrilaterals, such as parallelograms, by their characteristics. You can probably guess the defining characteristic of a parallelogram, just from its name.

Definition

A **parallelogram** is a quadrilateral with two pairs of opposite parallel sides.

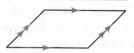

For You to Do

1. Which of the figures below appear to be parallelograms? Explain.

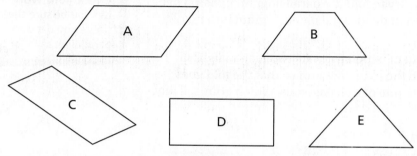

2. Notice that a rectangle is a parallelogram, according to the definition of *parallelogram* above. Which other common quadrilaterals fit the definition of *parallelogram*?

When you study any kind of quadrilateral, it is often useful to draw its diagonals. The following is an important theorem about the diagonals of a parallelogram.

Theorem 6.10

Each diagonal of a parallelogram divides the parallelogram into two congruent triangles.

Given   Parallelogram *ABCD* with diagonal $\overline{AC}$

Prove $\triangle ABC \cong \triangle CDA$

Proof   *ABCD* is a parallelogram. By definition, $\overline{BC} \parallel \overline{AD}$ and $\overline{BA} \parallel \overline{CD}$. From the PAI Theorem, it follows that $\angle BCA \cong \angle DAC$ and $\angle BAC \cong \angle DCA$. Triangle *ABC* and $\triangle CDA$ share $\overline{AC}$. So $\triangle ABC \cong \triangle CDA$ by ASA.

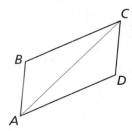

For Discussion

3. Prove that $\overline{BD}$ also divides parallelogram $ABCD$ into two congruent triangles.

In-Class Experiment

4. Use geometry software. Construct several different parallelograms. Then construct the diagonals of each parallelogram. Compare the lengths of the two diagonals of each parallelogram.

5. The diagonals of a parallelogram divide each of the parallelogram's four angles into a pair of smaller angles. Find the measure of each angle in each pair. What invariant relationship, if any, exists between the measures of the two angles in each pair?

6. Cut a parallelogram out of paper. Try to fold the parallelogram in half. That is, try to find a line of symmetry that divides the parallelogram into two congruent pieces.

7. Use the parallelogram you cut out of paper. Draw its two diagonals. Call their point of intersection P. Fold the parallelogram so that the fold goes through P and is perpendicular to one of the diagonals. Which points, if any, coincide after you make the fold?

Discuss your results with the rest of the class.

Habits of Mind

Check your work. How can you be sure that the figure you cut out is a parallelogram?

For Discussion

8. Do you think the statement below is true or false?

The intersection point of the diagonals of a parallelogram is the midpoint of each diagonal.

Give a proof or find a counterexample.

You can prove that the statement is true. This important fact leads to the theorem below.

Theorem 6.11

The diagonals of a parallelogram bisect each other.

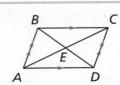

$AE = EC$ and $BE = ED$

You now know several things about parallelograms. If you know that a figure is a parallelogram, then all of the following statements are true:

1. Its opposite sides are parallel. (definition of *parallelogram*)

2. Its opposite sides are congruent. (See Exercise 7 part (a).)

3. Its opposite angles are congruent. (See Exercise 7 part (b).)

4. Its consecutive angles are supplementary. (See Exercise 6.)

5. Either diagonal divides the figure into two congruent triangles. (Theorem 6.10.)

6. Its diagonals bisect each other. (Theorem 6.11.)

Converses

Later you will investigate the converses of the statements listed above. What will the converses tell you? Well, for example, here is the converse of statement 6:

> If the diagonals of a quadrilateral bisect each other, then the quadrilateral is a parallelogram.

You can use converse statements that are true to classify quadrilaterals as parallelograms.

Developing Habits of Mind

Communicate a conditional situation. Statements of the form "if A, then B" are sometimes called conditional statements. One or more conditions are implied by the *if* part.

Some *if-then* statements are descriptions of elements of sets. You may see a statement like this one: "If an object belongs to set A, then it also belongs to set B."

For example, you can restate one of the corollaries to Theorem 6.10 this way:

> If a quadrilateral belongs to the set of parallelograms, then it also belongs to the set of quadrilaterals with opposite sides congruent.

The converse of this statement, also a conditional statement, is the following:

> If a quadrilateral belongs to the set of quadrilaterals with opposite sides congruent, then it also belongs to the set of parallelograms.

You can prove that the converse of the statement is also true. Start with a quadrilateral with opposite sides that are congruent. Draw the diagonals of the quadrilateral. By SSS, there is a pair of congruent triangles. Then by CPCTC, the alternate interior angles are congruent. By AIP, the sides of the figure are parallel.

In this example, the statement and its converse are both true, but this is not always the case. Sometimes the converse of a true conditional statement is false. For example, consider this statement: "If a person lives in Dallas, then that person lives in Texas." The converse of this statement is "If a person lives in Texas, then that person lives in Dallas." You can easily find a counterexample to the converse, such as "the person lives in Austin."

> **Remember...**
> A corollary is a consequence of a main theorem.

Exercises Practicing Habits of Mind

Check Your Understanding

For Exercises 1–5, do the following.

- Write the converse of the statement.
- Decide whether the converse is true or false.
- If the converse is true, provide a proof.
- If the converse is false, give a counterexample.

1. If a quadrilateral is a parallelogram, then its opposite sides are congruent.

2. If a quadrilateral is a parallelogram, then its consecutive angles are supplementary.

3. If a quadrilateral is a parallelogram, then its opposite angles are congruent.

4. If a quadrilateral is a parallelogram, then each diagonal divides the parallelogram into two congruent triangles.

5. If a quadrilateral is a parallelogram, then its diagonals bisect each other.

6. The two angles at either end of a side in a parallelogram are called *consecutive angles*. State and prove a theorem about the consecutive angles of a parallelogram.

7. Prove the following corollaries of Theorem 6.10.
   a. Both pairs of opposite sides of a parallelogram are congruent.
   b. Both pairs of opposite angles of a parallelogram are congruent.

8. **Take It Further** A line that passes through the intersection point of a parallelogram's diagonals intersects the parallelogram in two points. Prove that the intersection point of the parallelogram's diagonals is the midpoint of the line segment that connects these points.

On Your Own

For Exercises 9–28, complete each sentence with *always*, *sometimes*, or *never* to make the statement true.

9. A parallelogram __?__ has two congruent sides.

10. A parallelogram __?__ has three congruent sides.

11. A parallelogram __?__ has exactly three congruent sides.

12. A parallelogram __?__ has four congruent sides.

13. A parallelogram __?__ has congruent diagonals.

14. A quadrilateral with congruent diagonals is __?__ a parallelogram.

15. If one diagonal of a quadrilateral divides it into two congruent triangles, then the quadrilateral is __?__ a parallelogram.

16. If two consecutive angles of a quadrilateral are supplementary, then the quadrilateral is __?__ a parallelogram.

17. A quadrilateral with one right angle is __?__ a parallelogram.

18. A quadrilateral with exactly one right angle is __?__ a parallelogram.

19. A quadrilateral with two right angles is __?__ a parallelogram.

20. A quadrilateral with exactly two right angles is __?__ a parallelogram.

21. A quadrilateral with exactly two right angles opposite each other is __?__ a parallelogram.

22. A quadrilateral with three right angles is __?__ a parallelogram.

> *Hint:* Can a quadrilateral have exactly three right angles?

23. A quadrilateral with diagonals that bisect each other is __?__ a parallelogram.

24. If the longer diagonal of a quadrilateral bisects the shorter diagonal, then the quadrilateral is __?__ a parallelogram.

25. A quadrilateral with two congruent sides is __?__ a parallelogram.

26. A quadrilateral with three congruent sides is __?__ a parallelogram.

27. A quadrilateral with exactly three congruent sides is __?__ a parallelogram.

28. A quadrilateral with four congruent sides is __?__ a parallelogram.

29. **Standardized Test Prep** Which of the following statements is NOT true?

   A. Every parallelogram has at least one line of symmetry.

   B. The diagonals of a parallelogram always bisect each other.

   C. Opposite angles of a parallelogram are congruent.

   D. Consecutive angles of a parallelogram are supplementary.

30. **Take It Further** In the figure at the right, the sides of parallelogram *MNPQ* are trisected. Four of the trisection points form quadrilateral *STWX*.

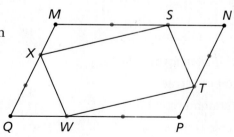

> A segment is **trisected** if it is divided into three congruent parts.

   a. List some facts that you can prove about quadrilateral *STWX*.

   b. What type of quadrilateral is *STWX*? Prove your conjecture.

   c. Suppose you draw $\overline{SW}$ and $\overline{TX}$. What can you say about these two segments?

31. Prove the theorem below.

Theorem 6.12

If two opposite sides of a quadrilateral are congruent and parallel, then the figure is a parallelogram.

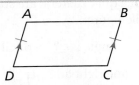

ABCD is a parallelogram.

32. In the figure at the right, M and N are midpoints of $\overline{AB}$ and $\overline{AC}$, respectively. Point P lies on the same line as M and N, and $\overline{MN} \cong \overline{NP}$.

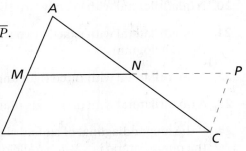

  a. Prove that $\triangle AMN \cong \triangle CPN$.

  b. What can you conclude about quadrilateral $MPCB$? Explain.

  c. Show that $MN = \frac{1}{2}BC$.

  d. What else can you conclude about the relationship between $\overline{MN}$ and $\overline{BC}$? Explain.

You can state the results of Exercise 32 as a theorem.

Theorem 6.13 Midline Theorem

The segment that joins the midpoints of two sides of a triangle is parallel to the third side and half the length of the third side.

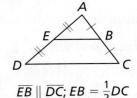

$\overline{EB} \parallel \overline{DC}; EB = \frac{1}{2}DC$

Maintain Your Skills

For Exercises 33–37, do each of the following.

  a. Rewrite each statement in *if-then* form.

  b. Decide whether the statement is true.

  c. Write the converse of the statement.

  d. Decide whether the converse is true.

33. People who live in New York City also live in New York State.

34. Every lizard is a reptile.

35. A bird is an animal with feathers.

36. All cowboys are from Texas.

37. Every piece of fruit is an apple.

6.18 Classifying Quadrilaterals

The different types of parallelograms are ordinary parallelograms, rectangles, rhombuses, and squares. Rectangles and rhombuses are special types of parallelograms. Squares are a special type of rectangle and a special type of rhombus.

You may be surprised that an ordinary rectangle is a type of parallelogram. This is probably because you more often think of a rectangle's four right angles than of its parallel sides.

Definitions

A **rectangle** is a parallelogram with four right angles.

A **rhombus** is a parallelogram with four congruent sides.
A common term for a rhombus is *diamond.*

A square is a special kind of rectangle with four congruent sides. A square is also a special kind of rhombus, with four congruent angles.

The definition for a square is given below.

A **square** is a rectangle with four congruent sides.

A square has all the properties of both a rectangle and a rhombus. Of course, a square also has the properties of a parallelogram and of a quadrilateral.

- The diagonals of a square are congruent because a square is a rectangle. (See Exercise 1.)

- The diagonals of a square are perpendicular because a square is a rhombus. (See Exercise 21.)

- The diagonals of a square bisect each other because a square is a parallelogram.

- The sum of the measures of the angles of a square is 360° because a square is a quadrilateral.

For You to Do

Decide whether each statement is true.

1. All rectangles are parallelograms.

2. Some parallelograms are rhombuses.

3. All rectangles are squares.

4. Some squares are rectangles.

The word *some* means "at least one."

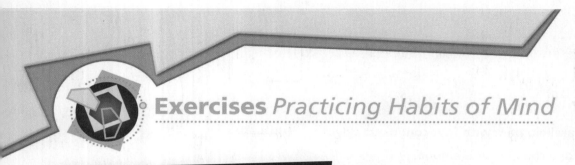

Exercises *Practicing Habits of Mind*

Check Your Understanding

1. Prove that the diagonals of a rectangle are congruent.

2. Prove that a parallelogram with two congruent adjacent sides is a rhombus.

For Exercises 3–13, complete each sentence with *always*, *sometimes*, or *never* to make the statement true.

3. A rhombus is _?_ a rectangle.

4. A square is _?_ a parallelogram.

5. A rectangle is _?_ a rhombus.

6. A square is _?_ a rectangle.

7. The opposite sides of a rectangle are _?_ congruent.

8. The diagonals of a rectangle are _?_ congruent.

9. If the diagonals of a quadrilateral are congruent, then the quadrilateral is _?_ a rectangle.

10. Two adjacent sides of a rectangle are _?_ congruent.

11. The diagonals of a rectangle _?_ bisect its angles.

12. A rhombus _?_ has a right angle.

13. Opposite sides of a rhombus are _?_ congruent.

14. Standardized Test Prep Which of the following statements is NOT true?

A. A square is different from a rhombus because a square has four congruent sides.

B. A rectangle is a parallelogram with four congruent angles.

C. A square is a rectangle with four congruent sides.

D. A rhombus is a parallelogram with four congruent sides.

15. Prove that a parallelogram with one right angle is a rectangle.

16. Prove that if the diagonals of a parallelogram are congruent, then the parallelogram is a rectangle.

17. What type of quadrilateral do you form when you connect the midpoints of a rectangle's sides? Prove your conjecture.

> In Exercises 17 and 18, make sure you do not assume that the quadrilateral is a parallelogram.

For Exercises 18–23, prove each statement.

18. If a quadrilateral has four congruent sides, then it is a rhombus.

19. Either diagonal of a rhombus divides the rhombus into two isosceles triangles.

20. The diagonals of a rhombus bisect the vertex angles of the rhombus.

21. The diagonals of a rhombus are perpendicular.

22. If the diagonals of a parallelogram are perpendicular, then the parallelogram is a rhombus.

23. If one diagonal of a parallelogram bisects two opposite angles of the parallelogram, then the parallelogram is a rhombus.

24. Draw a square and connect the midpoints of its sides. Prove that the figure formed is also a square.

Habits of Mind

Think it through. To prove that a quadrilateral is a square, can you just prove that its four sides are congruent?

Maintain Your Skills

Rectangles, rhombuses, and squares are special types of quadrilaterals. You can show the relationships among these quadrilaterals with a Venn diagram. In a Venn diagram, a circle represents a set.

25. Copy and complete each Venn diagram with the correct type of quadrilateral.

a.

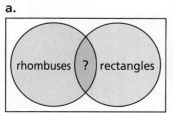

b.

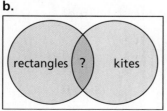

c.

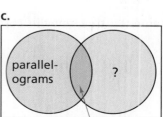

In this investigation, you studied different types of quadrilaterals, such as kites and trapezoids. You also studied the characteristics of the special types of parallelograms—rectangles, rhombuses, and squares.

1. Is a quadrilateral with perpendicular diagonals always a kite? Explain.

2. In the figure below, $\overline{ST} \cong \overline{RT}$, but the segments are not congruent to $\overline{TQ}$. All angles of $\triangle PTS$ and $\angle RTQ$ measure 60°. Prove that *PQRS* is a trapezoid.

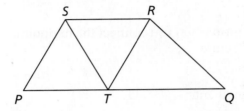

3. Describe the difference between a parallelogram and a rectangle.

4. Can a kite ever be a parallelogram? Explain.

5. Prove that a kite can be divided into two isosceles triangles by a single segment. Can this be done in more than one way? Explain.

6. List some special properties of each quadrilateral below.

   • parallelogram

   • kite

   • trapezoid

7. Are all squares also parallelograms? Are all parallelograms also squares? Explain.

8. If a statement is true, must its converse also be true?

Vocabulary

In this investigation, you learned these terms. Make sure you understand what each one means and how to use it.

- **base angle**
- **base of a trapezoid**
- **concave**
- **isosceles trapezoid**
- **kite**
- **parallelogram**
- **quadrilateral**
- **rectangle**
- **rhombus**
- **side**
- **skew quadrilateral**
- **square**
- **trapezoid**
- **trisected**
- **vertex (vertices)**

Nonconformity stands out.

Chapter Review

In **Investigation 6A** you learned how to

- apply the Midline Conjecture
- search for numerical and spatial invariants
- make conjectures and use software to experiment with geometric models

The following questions will help you check your understanding.

1. What is the definition of a perpendicular bisector? Explain why the three perpendicular bisectors of the sides of a triangle are concurrent.

2. Decide whether each ratio below is constant, even if the given figure is stretched, with the given restrictions. Justify each answer.

   a. The rectangle remains a rectangle. Points E and F remain the midpoints of $\overline{AB}$ and $\overline{DC}$, respectively. Is the ratio

   $$\frac{\text{area of } AEFD}{\text{area of } ABCD}$$

   invariant? If so, what is the ratio?

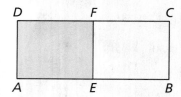

   b. You can stretch the sides of the regular hexagon below. Is the ratio

   $$\frac{\text{area of hexagon}}{\text{perimeter of hexagon}}$$

   invariant? If so, what is the ratio?

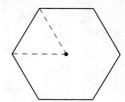

In **Investigation 6B** you learned how to

- identify parallel lines by looking at pairs of angles that are formed when the lines are cut by transversals
- identify pairs of congruent angles when parallel lines are cut by transversals
- write and present a deductive proof
- prove that the sum of the angle measures of a triangle is 180°

The following questions will help you check your understanding.

3. Draw $\overline{AB}$. Draw two parallel lines—one through A and one through B. Choose a point C on the line through A. Choose a point D on the line through B. Choose C and D so that they are on opposite sides of $\overline{AB}$ and $\overline{AC} \cong \overline{BD}$. Draw $\overline{CD}$. Let E name the point where $\overline{AB}$ and $\overline{CD}$ intersect. Prove that E is the midpoint of $\overline{AB}$.

4. What is the sum of the measures of the angles of a quadrilateral?

5. Use the figure below. Suppose $\angle 1 \cong \angle 5$. What can you conclude about lines ℓ and m? Explain.

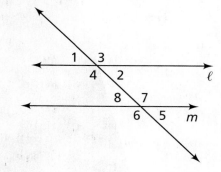

In **Investigation 6C** you learned how to

- recognize the difference between experimentation and deduction
- write and present triangle congruence proofs
- use the Perpendicular Bisector Theorem
- apply the Isosceles Triangle Theorem to prove parts of a figure are congruent

The following questions will help you check your understanding.

6. Draw $\overline{AB}$ that is less than 4 cm long. Find a point R that is 2 cm from both A and B. Find a point S that is 3 cm from both A and B. Draw $\overleftrightarrow{RS}$. Prove that $\overleftrightarrow{RS} \perp \overline{AB}$.

7. Describe the type of triangle that has the given property.

   a. The bisector of exactly one angle of the triangle contains the midpoint of the opposite side.

   b. Each altitude of the triangle coincides with a perpendicular bisector of a side.

8. Use the figure below. $\triangle ABC \cong \triangle DCB$. Prove that $\triangle CTB$ is isosceles.

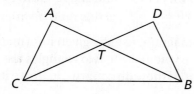

In **Investigation 6D** you learned how to

- classify quadrilaterals
- understand the meaning of *converse*
- reason by continuity
- understand the meaning of *always, never,* and *sometimes* in mathematics

The following questions will help you check your understanding.

9. Write the converse of the following statement.

   If a quadrilateral is a kite, then the diagonals of the quadrilateral intersect to form right angles.

   Determine whether the converse is true. If it is true, provide a written proof. If it is not, provide a counterexample.

10. Write *always, sometimes,* or *never* to best complete each sentence.

    a. A kite __?__ has four congruent sides.

    b. The diagonals of a parallelogram __?__ bisect each other.

    c. The diagonals of a rectangle are __?__ perpendicular.

    d. A kite __?__ has exactly one pair of parallel sides.

Multiple Choice

1. Lines *a* and *b* are parallel. Which statement can you deduce from this information?

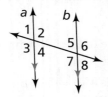

A. $\angle 3 \cong \angle 8$ **B.** $\angle 3 \cong \angle 4$

C. $\angle 3 \cong \angle 7$ **D.** $\angle 3 \cong \angle 5$

2. The diagonals of a certain quadrilateral bisect each other and are perpendicular. What kind of quadrilateral must the figure be?

A. parallelogram   **B.** rhombus

C. rectangle   **D.** square

3. Which method describes how to divide a segment into four congruent segments?

A. Construct the midpoint of the segment.

B. Construct the perpendicular bisector of the segment.

C. Construct a square with each side congruent to the original segment.

D. Construct the perpendicular bisector of the segment. Then construct the perpendicular bisector of each of the new segments.

4. Which word or phrase best completes the following sentence?

The point of concurrency of the medians of a triangle is always __?__ the triangle.

A. inside   **B.** on a vertex of

C. on a side of   **D.** outside

Open Response

5. Make a table that shows the following invariant relationship: *m* and *n* are numbers such that their product *mn* is invariant. (Choose a specific value of *mn*.)

6. Imagine that you construct $\triangle ABC$ using geometry software so that *A* and *B* are fixed. You can move *C*, but $\overline{AC}$ remains congruent to $\overline{BC}$. (*Hint:* Along what path can you move *C*?)

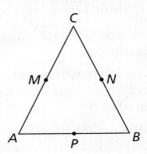

The midpoints of the sides of $\triangle ABC$ are *M*, *N*, and *P*. Connect them and shade $\triangle MNP$. Find the ratio $\frac{\text{area } \triangle MNP}{\text{area } \triangle ABC}$. Is this ratio invariant?

7. For each diagram, use the given information. Determine whether the two triangles are congruent. If they are congruent, prove it.

a. *ABCD* is a parallelogram. Is $\triangle ABC \cong \triangle CDA$?

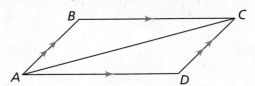

b. $\angle ADE \cong \angle B$ and $\angle AED \cong \angle C$. Is $\triangle ABC \cong \triangle ADE$?

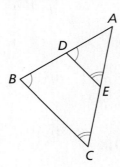

c. △*ABC* is an equilateral triangle. Points *E* and *F* are the midpoints of $\overline{AB}$ and $\overline{CB}$, respectively. Is △*EAC* ≅ △*FCA*?

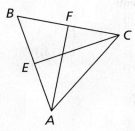

8. Recall the definition of an equilateral triangle.

   a. Describe an experiment that would lead you to conjecture that the altitudes of an equilateral triangle are congruent.

   b. Prove that the altitudes of an equilateral triangle are congruent.

9. Use the figure below. Lines *m* and *n* are parallel. Prove that *m*∠1 = *m*∠2.

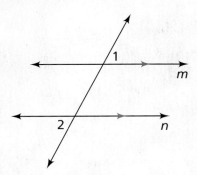

10. Decide whether each statement is true. If a statement is not true, provide a counterexample.

   a. All rectangles are squares.

   b. All trapezoids are parallelograms.

   c. All rectangles are parallelograms.

   d. All rhombuses are squares.

   e. All squares are rhombuses.

   f. All squares are kites.

   g. All parallelograms are kites.

11. Write *always*, *sometimes*, or *never* to best complete each sentence.

   a. The diagonals of a kite __?__ bisect each other.

   b. The diagonals of a parallelogram __?__ bisect each other.

   c. A median of a triangle is __?__ an altitude of the triangle.

   d. The diagonals of a rhombus are __?__ perpendicular.

12. Write the converse of the following statement.

   If an altitude of a triangle is the perpendicular bisector of one side of the triangle, then the triangle is equilateral.

   If the statement is true, provide a written proof.

   If the converse is true, provide a written proof.

Chapter 7

Similarity

Scaled images are an important application of mathematical similarity. A liquid crystal display (LCD) monitor on the back of a digital camera lets you see a scaled-down picture of what you are about to photograph.

A map is one kind of scale drawing. Its outline is the same as the region it represents, but it is obviously much smaller. By making a map to scale, you guarantee that distances you measure on the map are proportional to actual instances in the real world.

Architects also use scale drawings to plan buildings. The drawings ensure that the required features of a building fit together, illustrate traffic flow through the building, and allow the customer to visualize the design.

A microscope is a tool that changes the scale of what you view. It allows you to see objects on a large-enough scale to be able to distinguish critical features.

In art, the use of different scales for figures in a painting gives the illusion of depth. Smaller figures are perceived as being farther away from the viewer. Larger figures seem closer. In animation, a figure that becomes smaller appears to move away from the viewer.

Vocabulary and Notation

- center of dilation
- common ratio
- dilation
- nested triangles
- parallel method
- ratio
- ratio method
- scale a figure
- scaled figure
- scale factor
- similar figures
- splits two sides proportionally
- ~ (is similar to)

Scaled Copies

In *Scaled Copies*, you will learn how you can model a very large or very small figure with a figure that is a manageable size. For example, you could sketch a rough map of your school on paper. You could show some important locations, such as drinking fountains and the cafeteria. You might, however, need the map for something more precise, such as a science project on air quality and ventilation. Then you would want to show more detail, such as the dimensions of rooms and hallways.

You could draw your map *to scale.* Then the dimensions of any room on your map would be proportional to the actual dimensions by the *scale factor* of your map.

By the end of this investigation, you will be able to answer questions like these.

1. Why is it important to know the scale factor when reading a map?

2. What is a well-scaled drawing?

3. How can you decide whether two rectangles are scaled copies of each other?

You will learn how to
- approximate the scale factor relating two pictures by measuring
- use a given scale factor to interpret a map or blueprint
- decide whether two figures are well-scaled copies of each other

You will develop these habits and skills:
- Identify scaled copies of figures.
- Use a scale factor to approximate distances on blueprints and maps.
- Apply a scale factor to make similar figures.

How can a grid help you draw a scaled copy?

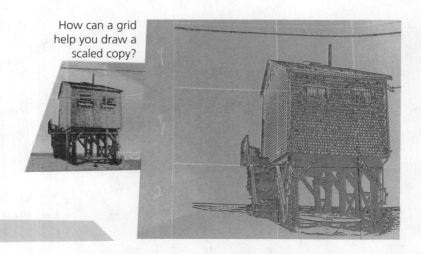

7.01 Getting Started

Activating Prior Knowledge
Exploring New Ideas

You can draw a whole city, a state, or an even larger region with a given scale so that it can fit on a piece of paper. In reading a map, it is important to keep the scale in mind.

For You to Explore

Here is a map of Sasha's neighborhood.

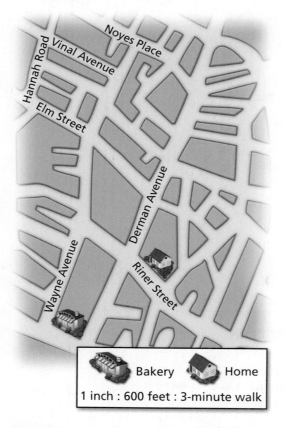

Bakery   Home
1 inch : 600 feet : 3-minute walk

1. The scale shows that 1 inch on the map represents 600 feet of actual distance. It also says that an inch on the map represents about a three-minute walk. What distance does it suggest you can walk in one minute? Is this reasonable?

2. In Sasha's neighborhood, find the actual distance between the following locations. (Travel only on streets.)

   a. the Bakery and the intersection of Wayne Avenue and Noyes Place

   b. Sasha's house and the Bakery

3. Sasha is at the Bakery. She will walk to meet a friend at the intersection of Vinal Avenue and Hannah Road. About how much time will her walk take?

4. Recalculate your answers to Problem 2 using the scale 1 inch : 450 feet.

An architect's plans for an apartment building, a house, a school, an office, a park, or a sports complex can include many different sketches. Each sketch serves a different purpose. This blueprint drawing shows the floor plan of the second story of a house.

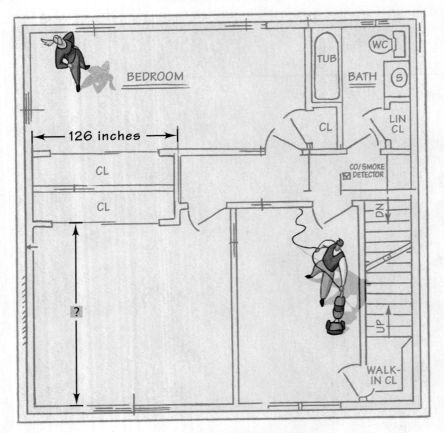

SECOND FLOOR PLAN

5. In this floor plan, someone erased a measurement and replaced it with a question mark. Calculate the missing value.

6. Find the actual dimensions of the entire second story.

Exercises Practicing Habits of Mind

Go Online
Video Tutor
www.successnetplus.com

On Your Own

7. Drivers sometimes estimate the driving time between two points based on their average driving speed and a map's scale. They are often surprised by how much longer the trip actually takes. What are some reasons that a trip can take longer than the length of the route suggests?

8. For traveling in Wisconsin, Sydney and Mark used a map that has a scale of 1 inch: 15 miles. Sydney's index finger is 3 inches long. On the trip from Madison to Greenlake, Sydney announced the following distances in "fingers." Convert Sydney's estimates to miles.

   a. At the beginning of the trip, Sydney said, "We're one finger away!"

   b. After a stop for ice cream, Sydney announced, "We've got only half a finger to go!"

   c. When they got back into the car after taking a picture of some cows, Sydney said, "Only one fingernail left in the trip!" (Her fingernail is about an eighth of her finger.)

9. The owners of the house with the floor plan shown in Problem 5 want to carpet the bedroom floor. They can use the floor plan to estimate how much carpet they need.

   a. What are the dimensions of the bedroom? (Do not include the closet.)

   b. How much carpet do the owners need to cover the bedroom floor? Give your answer in square inches.

   c. If carpet sells by the square yard, how many square yards of carpet do they need?

Maintain Your Skills

10. Find the perimeter and area of a rectangle with the given dimensions.

    a. 1 in. by 3 in.

    b. 2 in. by 6 in.

    c. 3 in. by 9 in.

    d. 4 in. by 12 in.

    e. n in. by $3n$ in.

7.02 Scale Factors

Maps and blueprints provide scales that allow you to calculate actual distances and lengths. Depending on the map, 1 inch might represent 1 mile, or 1 inch might represent 100 miles. The **scale factor** is a number that describes how much you reduce or enlarge a map, blueprint, or picture. In this lesson, you will develop a more precise definition of scale factor and learn how to calculate it.

For Discussion

Each side of this square has length 2 inches.

1. What do you think it means to "scale the square by the factor $\frac{1}{2}$"? Draw a figure to show what you think it means. Can you think of more than one way to interpret the statement? If so, draw a separate figure for each meaning.

Minds in Action

Tony and Amy have different meanings for scaling the square by the factor $\frac{1}{2}$. See if you agree with either of their explanations.

Tony To scale by $\frac{1}{2}$, I drew a square that is half the size of the first one. You know, half the area. The area of the original square is 2×2 or 4 square inches. I made a square with an area of 2 square inches. A neat way to do this is to fold all four corners of the square to the center.

Habits of Mind

Visualize. Why does Tony's folding method work? How long are the sides of his new square?

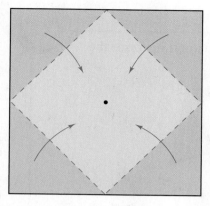

Amy I think that scaling by half means we are supposed to draw the sides half as long. The first square has sides that are 2 inches long, so the scaled square should have sides that are 1 inch long. I drew a horizontal line and a vertical line on the square to divide the length and width in half. This gives me four squares, each scaled by the factor $\frac{1}{2}$.

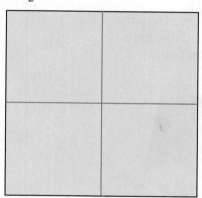

In fact, there is more than one correct way to interpret the phrase *scale by $\frac{1}{2}$*. Words can mean different things to different people. But Amy's meaning is the one that most people use.

Definition

When you **scale a figure** by the factor *r*, you draw a new figure, called a **scaled figure**, that is the same shape as the given figure. In the scaled figure, each length is *r* times the corresponding length of the original figure. The scale factor *r* can be any positive number, including a fraction.

Sometimes a scale factor is not given. You may, however, be able to compare parts of figures to calculate the scale factor.

Problem For each pair of pictures below, what scale factor transforms the
larger picture into the smaller scaled picture?

a.

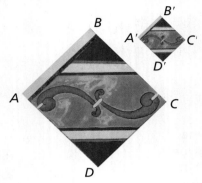

b.

Solutions

a. Measure each side of the first figure. Compare the lengths to the
lengths of the sides in the second figure. You will find that each
length in the second figure is $\frac{1}{3}$ the length in the first figure.
The scale factor is $r = \frac{1}{3}$.

b. Rotate the kite on the right clockwise
to match the orientation of the kite
on the left. Once you have done this,
measure the distances between
corresponding points. For example,
the distance from L to M is 1.5 cm.
The distance from L' to M' is 1.2 cm.
This gives a scale factor of $\frac{1.2}{1.5}$, or $\frac{4}{5}$.

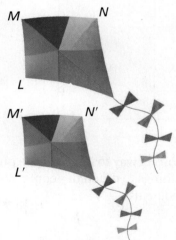

For You to Do

2. For each part of the Example, by what factor should you scale the smaller
figure on the right to get the figure on the left?

In-Class Experiment

3. Draw a square with 1-inch sides. Scale the square by the factor 2. How many copies of the 1-inch square fit inside the scaled square?

4. Start with a 1-inch square again. Scale the square by the factor 3. How many copies of the 1-inch square fit inside the scaled square?

For Discussion

5. If you scale a 1-inch square by a positive integer *r*, how many copies of the 1-inch square fit inside the scaled square?

Minds in Action

Derman and Tony have just finished the In-Class Experiment and are trying to apply what they learned to the following problem.

A cube has edges of length 1 inch. You scale the cube by the factor 2. How long are the sides of the new cube? How many copies of the original cube fit inside the scaled cube?

Tony Well, if you scale the cube by the factor 2, then the new cube must be twice as big. Two cubes fit inside the scaled cube!

Derman That sounds right. The original cube has edges that are 1 inch long. The scaled cube must have edges that are 2 inches long.

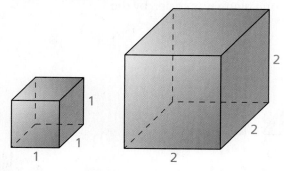

Derman Wait! Look at the picture, Tony. Your answer can't be right! More than two of the original cubes are going to fit into the big cube.

Tony Nothing is ever that easy. So, how many 1-inch cubes fit into the scaled cube?

Derman The volume of the original cube is $1 \times 1 \times 1$, or 1 cubic inch. The volume of the scaled cube is $2 \times 2 \times 2$, or 8 cubic inches. Think of the larger cube as a box. You pack in four small cubes to fill the bottom. Then pack in one more layer of four small cubes to fill the box.

For Discussion

6. If you scale the original cube by the factor 3, how long are the sides of the new cube? How many copies of the original cube fit inside the scaled cube?

7. If you scale the original cube by a positive integer r, how many copies of the original cube fit inside the scaled cube?

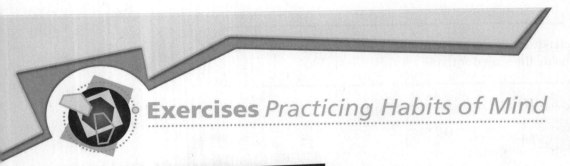

Exercises *Practicing Habits of Mind*

Check Your Understanding

1. What features of a square are invariant when you scale the square by the factor $\frac{1}{2}$?

2. You scale a figure by each given value of r. Will the new figure be smaller, larger, or the same size as the original figure?

a. $r = \frac{3}{5}$

b. $r = 1$

c. $r = 3$

d. $r = 0.77$

3. For each pair of figures, determine whether one figure was scaled by the factor $\frac{1}{2}$ to obtain the other figure. Explain.

a.

b.

c.

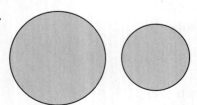

4. For each pair of figures, what scale factor transforms the picture on the left into the scaled picture on the right?

a.

b.

5. For each pair of figures in Exercise 4, what scale factor transforms the picture on the right into the scaled picture on the left?

6. Compare the scale factors you found for Exercises 4 and 5. How are they related?

7. This equilateral triangle has 2-inch sides.

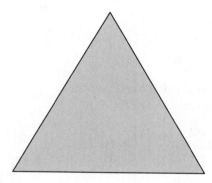

a. Draw a scaled version of the triangle. Use the factor $\frac{1}{2}$. How many of the scaled triangles fit inside the original triangle?

b. Draw a scaled version of the triangle using the factor $\frac{1}{3}$. How many of the scaled triangles fit inside the original triangle?

8. Suppose you scale a 6 in.-by-6 in. square by each factor. How many 1-in. squares will fit inside each scaled square?

a. $\frac{1}{3}$ **b.** 3 **c.** $\frac{2}{3}$

Scale the house at the far left by the factor $\frac{1}{42}$. You get a 4-ft-wide model.

9. Many photocopy machines allow you to scale (reduce or enlarge) a picture. You enter the desired percent and press Copy.

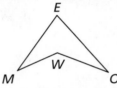

   a. If you enter 80%, by what factor do you scale the picture?

   b. To scale a picture by the factor $\frac{3}{4}$, what percent should you enter?

10. Label the two scalings as *same* or *different*.

   a. scaling by 2 and scaling by $\frac{1}{2}$

   b. scaling by $\frac{1}{3}$ and scaling by 30%

   c. scaling by $\frac{3}{5}$ and scaling by 0.6

   d. scaling by 1 and scaling by 100%

11. Give a scale factor that changes the quadrilateral *MEOW* as indicated.

   a. shrinks it

   b. enlarges it

   c. shrinks it very slightly

   d. keeps it the same size

12. A rectangle has width 12 inches and length 24 inches. You scale it using the following factors. In each case, what are the dimensions of the scaled rectangle?

   a. $\frac{1}{3}$ **b.** $\frac{1}{4}$ **c.** 0.3   **d.** 2.5   **e.** 0.25

13. Examine each pair of figures below.

- What scale factor can you apply to figure X to get figure Y?
- What scale factor can you apply to figure Y to get figure X?
- How are the two scale factors you found related?

a.

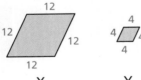

b.

c.

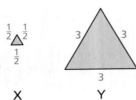

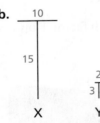

14. Standardized Test Prep Jamal scales a triangle by the factor 4. How many copies of the original triangle can he use to fill the scaled copy?

A. 4   **B.** 8   **C.** 12   **D.** 16

15. Take It Further Suppose you scale a picture by the factor $\frac{1}{2}$. Then you scale your scaled picture by the factor $\frac{1}{4}$. By what overall factor have you scaled the original picture?

Maintain Your Skills

16. Scale each figure below by the factor 4.

- What are the dimensions of the scaled figure?
- How many of the original figures fit into the scaled figure?

a.
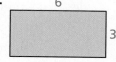

b.
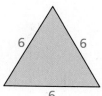

c.

17. Apply the scale factor $\frac{1}{3}$ to each figure in Exercise 16.

- What are the dimensions of the scaled figure?
- How many of the original figure fit into the scaled figure?

18. Take It Further Apply a scale factor n to each figure in Exercise 16.

- What are the dimensions of the scaled figure?
- How many of the original figure fit into the scaled figure?

What Is a Well-Scaled Drawing?

The map and blueprint in Lesson 7.01 are both well-scaled drawings. Sometimes, though, a reduction or enlargement is not a good copy of the original. When you look at yourself in a funhouse mirror, you see that your body is scaled in a very unusual way indeed. The mirror might stretch your image so that you appear as skinny as a matchstick. It might shrink your image so that you appear one foot tall!

Here is a picture of a dog.

Here are four other images of the dog.

I.

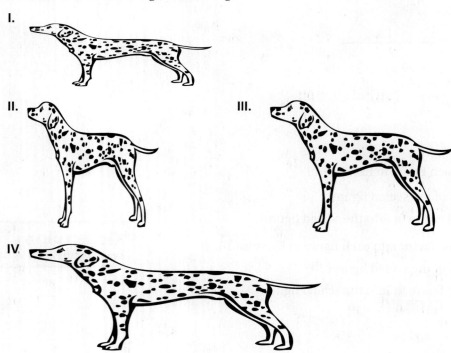

II.

III.

IV.

Tony and Sasha try to decide which images could be accurate reductions or enlargements of the dog picture.

Tony   If one of these pictures is an accurate copy of the original dog picture, it's got to look exactly like the original, right?

Sasha   Well, we're not necessarily looking for an exact copy of the original. We're just looking for a picture that keeps the same shape, but not necessarily the same size. The original picture may have been enlarged or shrunk down—like on a copy machine.

Tony   The first copy is shorter than the original, but it's not smaller all around. It just looks like someone stepped on it. If we're looking for an accurate smaller copy of the original picture, the copy needs to be smaller all around.

Sasha   I know what you mean. The fourth copy is bigger than the original, but it's not bigger all around. It got bigger, but it's too long.

For Discussion

1. Decide which of the four images are accurate enlargements or reductions of the original dog picture.

2. What characteristics of the dog images helped you make your decisions?

Exercises *Practicing Habits of Mind*

Check Your Understanding

Exercises 1–3 on the next page will help you make decisions about whether you are looking at a good copy or a bad copy. You will use measurements rather than just judging by eye.

1. Here are drawings of two baby chicks with points labeled *A* through *H*.

   Here are the distances between some of the points.

   $AB = 4$ cm $CD = 2$ cm $EF = 2.5$ cm $GH = 1.25$ cm

   How can you use these measurements to help convince someone that the two chicks are well-scaled copies of each other? Are there other measurements that could be important to compare?

2. The labels *A*, *B*, *C*, and *D* name four points on this fish. The fish is not drawn to scale.

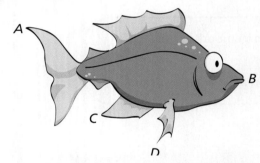

   Jo measures the distance *AB*, as well as the distance *CD*. She calculates that $\frac{AB}{CD} = 2.6$. Michael sees her answer and asks, "But what's your unit? Is the answer 2.6 centimeters, 2.6 inches, 2.6 feet, or something else?"

   How would you respond to Michael's question?

3. Name at least four different pairs of measurements you could take on these two figures to convince someone that the two figures are well-scaled copies of each other.

For Exercises 4–6, use graph paper to scale the pictures by the given scale factor.

4.

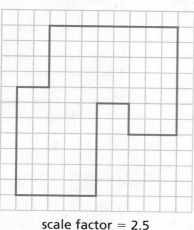

scale factor = 2.5

5.

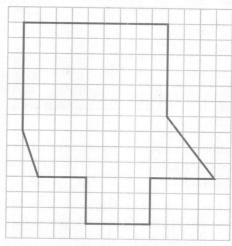

scale factor = 0.5

6.

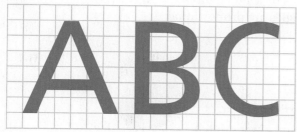

scale factor = 2

7. Standardized Test Prep A rectangle has dimensions 25 cm by 10 cm. It is scaled by the factor $\frac{3}{5}$. What is the perimeter of the scaled rectangle?

A. 35 cm   **B.** 42 cm   **C.** 70 cm   **D.** 90 cm

Maintain Your Skills

8. A rectangle has dimensions 3 cm by 4 cm. You scale it using the following factors. Find the area of each scaled rectangle.

a. 2   **b.** 3   **c.** 0.5

d. $\frac{5}{12}$ **e.** n

Go Online
www.successnetplus.com

7.04 Testing for Scale

In Lesson 7.03, you thought about the characteristics that did or did not make pictures of a dog well-scaled copies of each other. Now you will do the same for pairs of simple geometric figures such as rectangles, triangles, and other polygons.

Here are two rectangles.

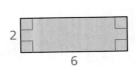
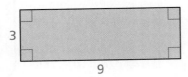

> Mathematicians usually use *scaled,* rather than *well-scaled,* to refer to proportional figures. From here on, you will use *scaled* rather than *well-scaled.* Both terms have the same meaning.

To tell whether one rectangle is a scaled copy of the other, you could look for a scale factor that would work. In this case, scale the left rectangle by the factor $\frac{3}{2}$ to get the right rectangle.

Some people use the phrase *corresponding sides,* or "sides that match up," when talking about scaled copies. If you scale one side, you get the corresponding side of the other figure. For the two rectangles above, the 2-unit side and the 3-unit side are corresponding. Also, the 6-unit side and the 9-unit side are corresponding. Corresponding sides of scaled figures are proportional. Corresponding sides in these rectangles are proportional because $\frac{2}{3} = \frac{6}{9}$.

> **Remember...**
>
> You use *corresponding sides* here the same way you used it for congruent figures.

Example

Problem The lengths and widths of seven rectangles A–G are given. Match the rectangles that are scaled copies of each other.

A: 4 in. by 1 in.

B: 3 in. by 2 in.

C: 10 in. by 5 in.

D: 4 in. by 6 in.

E: 5 in. by 3 in.

F: 16 in. by 4 in.

G: 8 in. by 4 in.

Solutions There are three pairs of scaled copies. Rectangles C and G are scaled copies $\left(\text{since } \frac{10}{8} = \frac{5}{4}\right)$, as are A and F $\left(\text{since } \frac{4}{16} = \frac{1}{4}\right)$.

Rectangles B and D are also scaled copies. Notice, however, that $\frac{3}{4} \neq \frac{2}{6}$. To see that the rectangles have equal side-length ratios, you need to make your ratios in a consistent way. If one ratio is in the form of $\frac{\text{shorter side}}{\text{shorter side}}$, then the other must be $\frac{\text{longer side}}{\text{longer side}}$. Thus, you have $\frac{2}{4} = \frac{3}{6}$.

Exercises Practicing Habits of Mind

Check Your Understanding

1. The ratio of length to width for a particular rectangle is 1.5. A scaled copy has width 6. What is the length of the scaled copy?

2. Two rectangles are scaled copies of each other. The ratio of their lengths is 0.6. The smaller rectangle has width 3. What is the width of the larger rectangle?

3. Are the two triangles below scaled copies of each other? Take measurements and do calculations as necessary. Explain what you find.

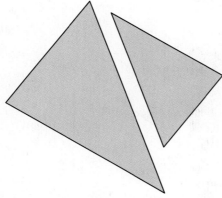

A **ratio** is the quotient of two numbers. If only one number is given, the second number is understood to be 1. *A ratio of 1.5 really means "1.5 to 1."*

4. Kaori has two triangles that have all corresponding angles congruent. The sides of one triangle are 4, 6, and 8. The sides of the other are 9, 6, and 12. She says that because

$$\frac{4}{9} = 0.44\ldots,$$

$$\frac{6}{6} = 1,$$

and

$$\frac{8}{12} = 0.66\ldots,$$

the triangles are not scaled copies. Do you agree?

On Your Own

5. Can a 3 foot-by-9 foot rectangle be a scaled copy of a 3 foot-by-1 foot rectangle? Explain.

6. You scale a square by the factor 2.5. The resulting square has a side length of 8 inches. What is the length of a side of the original square?

7. One triangle has side lengths of 21, 15, and 18. Another triangle has side lengths of 12, 14, and 16. Are these triangles scaled copies? How can you tell?

8. Carefully trace the triangles below. Cut out the traced triangles. Decide whether any two of the triangles are scaled copies of each other. Use any of the methods discussed in class.

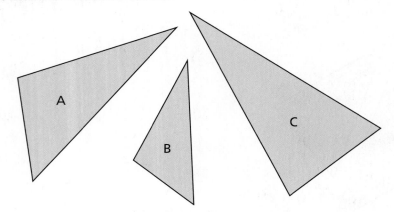

9. **Standardized Test Prep** Elisha has two triangles. One triangle has side lengths of 3 cm, 5 cm, and 7 cm. The other triangle has side lengths of 40 cm, 24 cm, and 56 cm. Are the two triangles scaled copies of each other? If so, what scale factor transforms the first triangle into the second triangle?

   A. No, the two triangles are not scaled copies of each other.

   B. yes; 8   **C.** yes; $\frac{40}{3}$ **D.** yes; $\frac{24}{5}$

Maintain Your Skills

10. Suppose $f(x, y) = xy$. Evaluate each of the following.

   a. $f(2, 3)$ **b.** $f(4, 6)$ **c.** $f(6, 9)$

   d. $f(a, b)$ **e.** $f(2a, 2b)$ **f.** $f(ka, kb)$

11. Write an algebraic equation to define a function that has a rectangle's length and width as input and the area of the rectangle as output.

Checking for Scaled Copies

Think for a moment about congruent triangles. Recall how you determine whether two triangles are congruent without taking measurements or performing calculations.

One way is to cut out the triangles and lay one on top of the other. If you can arrange the triangles so that they perfectly coincide, then they are congruent.

Perhaps there is also a visual way to test whether two shapes are scaled copies of each other without having to take measurements.

Minds in Action

Hannah and Derman are trying to determine whether the pairs of rectangles in each figure below are scaled copies.

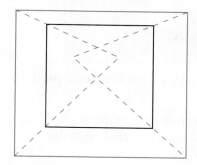

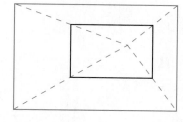
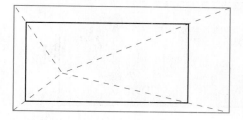

Hannah Why are there dashed lines in these figures? They're just confusing me!

Derman I don't know—let's just try to ignore them for now. How are we going to decide whether the rectangles are scaled copies?

Hannah Well, we've been taking measurements and comparing corresponding sides. Let's do that here.

Derman Do that with the first pair of rectangles. I'm going to try to decide this without measuring.

Moments later . . .

Hannah I measured the sides of the first pair of rectangles in centimeters. I made ratios of the sides for each rectangle. I got $\frac{2.8}{4.5}$ and $\frac{2.8}{4.0}$. The ratios aren't equal, so they're not scaled copies of each other.

Derman I thought the second pair might be scaled copies. I wanted to be sure, so I measured them, too. They are. So I decided to trace them, cut them out, and fool around with them. I wanted to see whether there is another way to show they're scaled copies.

I noticed a couple of things with the second pair of rectangles.

First, I can fit four copies of the small rectangle perfectly inside the big rectangle.

And, I can draw one diagonal in both rectangles. Then, when I slide the small rectangle down to one corner, the diagonals match up perfectly.

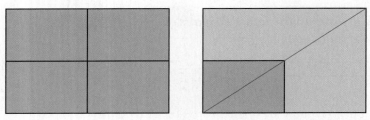

Hannah That's cool. Did your cutting and moving tests work with the third pair of rectangles?

Derman Well, the first test didn't work. I couldn't fit copies of the small rectangle perfectly inside the big one. But I *could* show that the diagonals match up.

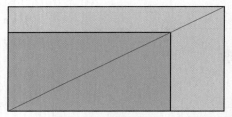

Hannah So, does that mean that the two rectangles in the third pair are scaled copies of each other?

For Discussion

1. What do you think? Are the rectangles in the second pair scaled copies? Are the rectangles in the third pair scaled copies? Can you figure out what the dashed lines in the original figures might be for? Explain.

The triangles in each pair below are scaled copies of each other. Trace and cut out the triangles in each pair. Then move the triangles around. Look for some visual clues that suggest good tests for recognizing scaled triangles. For instance, if you place one angle on top of another and find they match, what do you notice about the triangles' corresponding sides?

2.

3.

For Discussion

4. Share your findings with your class. Did placing one angle on top of a matching angle help you decide whether the triangles are scaled copies? What other tests did you use?

In the figure below, $\overline{DE} \parallel \overline{BC}$. Prove that all pairs of corresponding angles for $\triangle ADE$ and $\triangle ABC$ are congruent.

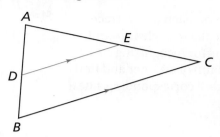

Habits of Mind

Understand context.
Corresponding angles can have two different meanings in this discussion. Think about the context to understand the meaning.

Proof

Because $\overline{DE}$ is parallel to $\overline{BC}$, it follows that $\angle ADE \cong \angle ABC$ and $\angle AED \cong \angle ACB$. Since $\angle A \cong \angle A$, you know that $\triangle ADE$ and $\triangle ABC$ have congruent corresponding angles.

If two triangles have congruent corresponding angles, does that mean that the triangles are scaled copies of each other? It seems like a reasonable conjecture, and it is, in fact, true. You will prove it in Investigation 4D.

Remember...

When parallel lines are cut by a transversal, the corresponding angles formed are congruent.

Exercises *Practicing Habits of Mind*

Check Your Understanding

1. Martin thinks that the angle test for triangles might also be a good way to check whether other polygons (such as rectangles) are scaled copies. If the angles of quadrilateral $ABCD$ are congruent to the corresponding angles of quadrilateral $A'B'C'D'$, are the quadrilaterals scaled copies? Explain.

2. Sheena has an idea for making a scaled copy of a triangle.

   Measure the sides of the triangle. Then add the same constant value (such as 1, 2, or 3) to each side length. Draw a triangle with these new side lengths.

   Will this new triangle be a scaled copy of the original? Try it.

You now have tests for scaled rectangles and triangles. How can you test other polygons?

3. For each figure, decide whether the two polygons are scaled copies. Explain your decision.

a.

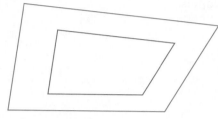

b.

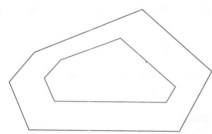

4. Trace trapezoid *ABCD*. Inside the traced trapezoid, draw another trapezoid that is a scaled copy. (You choose the scale factor.) Explain how you made the scaled copy.

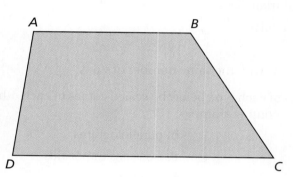

5. You scale a polygon by the factor $\frac{3}{4}$. You then compare the original polygon to the scaled one. Find each ratio.

a. the lengths of any two corresponding sides

b. the measures of any two corresponding angles

6. Is either statement below a valid test for whether two polygons are scaled copies? Explain. If the test is not valid, what additional requirement(s) would make each test work?

- Two polygons are scaled copies if you can show that their corresponding angles all have equal measures.

- Two polygons are scaled copies if you can show that the lengths of their corresponding sides are all in the same ratio.

On Your Own

7. Two angles of one triangle measure 28° and 31°. Another triangle has two angles that measure 117° and 31°. Are the triangles scaled copies? How can you tell?

8. How can you tell whether two squares are scaled copies of each other?

9. Draw two quadrilaterals that are not scaled copies but in which the sides of one quadrilateral are twice as long as the corresponding sides of the other quadrilateral.

Go Online
www.successnetplus.com

10. Explain why the figures in each pair below are scaled copies of each other, or give a counterexample to show that they need not be scaled copies.

    a. two quadrilaterals

    b. two squares

    c. two quadrilaterals with equal corresponding angle measures

    d. two triangles

    e. two isosceles triangles

    f. two isosceles right triangles

    g. two equilateral triangles

    h. two rhombuses

    i. two regular polygons with the same number of sides

11. Must any two figures of each type below be scaled copies of each other? Explain why or give a counterexample.

    a. rectangles
    b. parallelograms
    c. trapezoids
    d. isosceles trapezoids
    e. regular hexagons
    f. octagons
    g. circles
    h. cubes
    i. spheres
    j. cylinders
    k. boxes
    l. cones

12. **Standardized Test Prep** Which two figures are not necessarily scaled copies of each other?

    A. two rhombuses
    B. two squares
    C. two circles
    D. two isosceles right triangles

Maintain Your Skills

13. Scale this circle by the given scale factors.

    a. 2   b. 2.5

    c. 0.5   d. 1

Habits of Mind

Simplify. When you must show an example, keep it simple. For Exercise 13a, which length related to a circle is easy to double?

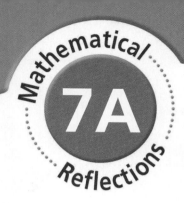

In this investigation, you studied scaled copies—accurate reductions or enlargements of given figures. You used scale factors to draw similar figures and to approximate distances on blueprints and maps. You also studied ways to decide whether two shapes were well-scaled copies of each other. These questions will help you summarize what you have learned.

1. Give an approximate scale factor for the following pairs of figures. If you think that the figures are not scaled copies of each other, explain why.

   a.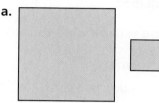

   b.

   c.

2. Scale the triangle at the right by the factor $\frac{1}{4}$.

3. Check, without measuring, whether the two rectangles below are scaled copies of each other. Explain.

   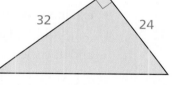

4. Why is it important to know the scale factor when reading a map?

5. What is a well-scaled drawing?

6. How can you decide whether two rectangles are scaled copies of each other?

Copy a gridded figure frame by frame into a larger grid to get a scaled copy of the original.

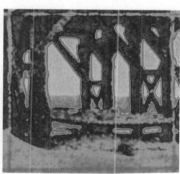

Vocabulary

In this investigation, you learned these terms. Make sure you understand what each one means and how to use it.

- ratio
- scale a figure
- scaled figure
- scale factor

Curved or Straight?

Just Dilate!

In *Curved or Straight? Just Dilate!*, you will learn two techniques for making scaled copies. The process of making a scaled copy is called *dilation*. The copy you make may sometimes be larger or smaller than the original figure, depending on the scale factor of the dilation.

By the end of this investigation, you will be able to answer questions like these.

1. What is the mathematical meaning of *dilation*?

2. How do you use the parallel method to scale a polygon?

3. What is the result of applying scale factor 3 to a polygon? The result of applying scale factor $\frac{1}{3}$?

You will learn how to

- describe and use methods for constructing enlargements or reductions of shapes

- explain and contrast the ratio method and parallel method for dilation

- identify parallel segments and corresponding segments in a drawing and its scaled copy

You will develop these habits and skills:

- Identify a dilation as an enlargement or reduction by looking at the scale factor.

- Dilate figures using the ratio method and the parallel method.

- Describe the effects of the choice for center of dilation on the resulting dilation.

Why is it important that Russian nesting dolls be scaled copies of one another?

Activating Prior Knowledge
Exploring New Ideas

You have thought about what a scaled copy is. You have learned to recognize a well-scaled copy. Now you may be wondering how to make scaled copies.

For You to Explore

1. Use only a ruler and pencil. Try to scale figures like these by the factor 2.

a.    b.    c.

2. Share your drawings with classmates. Decide which drawings are well scaled. Discuss why.

3. Of the scaling processes that seem to work, describe the two that you think work best.

Exercises *Practicing Habits of Mind*

On Your Own

4. Find several meanings of the word *dilation*.

5. Trace this hexagon onto a sheet of paper. Then use a ruler to scale the traced figure by the given scale factors.

   a. 0.5   b. 1

   c. $\frac{3}{2}$ d. $\frac{3}{4}$

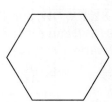

6. Describe the effect of each scale factor in Exercise 5.

7. Use geometry software. Construct a rectangle. Find its area and perimeter. Then scale your rectangle by each scale factor given below. Record the area and perimeter of the scaled copy.

a. 2   **b.** 3   **c.** $\frac{1}{2}$ **d.** $\frac{1}{3}$

See the TI-Nspire™ Handbook, p. 990, for help with finding the area of a polygon and scaling a figure.

8. For a given rectangle, describe the effects of a scale factor on the area and perimeter. Can you predict the area and perimeter of a scaled copy without first scaling the original rectangle? Without finding the dimensions of the scaled copy?

9. Use geometry software. Construct a triangle. Find its area and perimeter. Scale your triangle by each scale factor given below. Record the area and perimeter of each scaled copy.

a. 4   **b.** 0.1   **c.** $\frac{3}{5}$ **d.** $\frac{1}{7}$

Go Online
Video Tutor
www.successnetplus.com

10. For a given triangle, describe the effects of a scale factor on the area and perimeter. Can you predict the area and perimeter of a scaled copy without first scaling the original triangle? Without finding the dimensions of the scaled copy?

Maintain Your Skills

11. Use the figure below to find each length.

a. *AZ*
b. *BY*
c. *CX*
d. *DW*
e. *EV*

See the Tables section at the back of the book for a reminder of the Pythagorean Theorem formula.

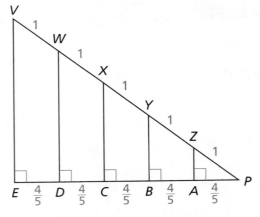

12. $\overline{AZ}$, $\overline{BY}$, $\overline{CX}$, $\overline{DW}$, and $\overline{EV}$ are corresponding sides in triangles *AZP, BYP, CXP, DWP,* and *EVP,* respectively. Use your results from Exercise 11. Find each ratio.

a. $\frac{AZ}{AZ}$ **b.** $\frac{BY}{AZ}$ **c.** $\frac{CX}{AZ}$ **d.** $\frac{DW}{AZ}$ **e.** $\frac{EV}{AZ}$

13. How do the ratios you found in Exercise 12 compare to the ratios of other pairs of corresponding sides in triangles *AZP, BYP, CXP, DWP,* and *EVP?*

Making Scaled Copies

To scale an image on film, a light source sends beams of light through the film. A screen that is parallel to the film catches the beams. This is a "point-by-point" process.

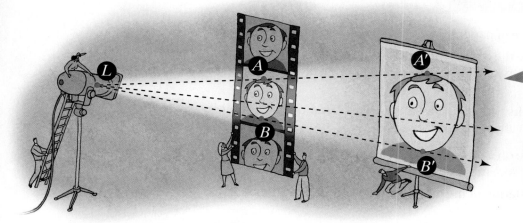

Here the enlargement is by the factor 2. Point A' is twice as far from the center of dilation as point A. Concisely put, $LA' = 2LA$. Likewise, $LB' = 2LB$.

In mathematics, the procedure of scaling a figure is called **dilation**. In the figure above, the point that corresponds to the light source is the **center of dilation**. The rays coming from it represent the beams of light. The points farther out along the rays (like A' and B') represent the screen images of points on the film (A and B, respectively). To get more image points, draw more rays.

You can think of dilation as a particular way of scaling a figure. If you are asked to "dilate a figure by 2," this means to use dilation to scale it by 2.

Habits of Mind

Communicate context.
You can use *dilation* to refer to the dilation copy when this meaning is clear in context.

Developing Habits of Mind

Make strategic choices. Representing a scaled figure on paper is sometimes easy but can also be challenging. To dilate a line segment, you need to dilate only two points. Which two are they?

To dilate the film image above and get a reasonably good copy, you must dilate many points. The more points you choose to dilate and the more strategically you choose them, the more accurate your dilation.

How many points would you have to dilate to make a good sketch of each of the following?

- a triangle
- a square
- a circle with a given center
- a circle with its center not given

The number needed is not necessarily obvious. For a square, three points are enough. On the other hand, even four points (as suggested in the diagram) might not be enough if the points are not well chosen.

Exercises *Practicing Habits of Mind*

1. Draw a circle on a piece of paper.

   a. Use dilation to scale the circle by the factor 2. Choose enough points on the circle that you can judge whether your dilation really does produce a scaled copy.

> Pick any center of dilation that you want.

   b. Compare your results with your classmates' work. How does the choice of center of dilation affect the result?

2. a. Draw a tilted square on a piece of paper. Dilate it by the factor 2. Dilate at least eight points before drawing the entire dilation image.

   b. How does the orientation of the dilated square compare with that of the original tilted square?

   c. Is orientation affected by your choice for the center of dilation?

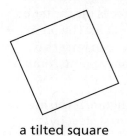

a tilted square

3. Explain how to dilate a circle or square by the factor $\frac{1}{2}$. Explain how to dilate it by the factor 3.

4. The ornamental pattern on the left below was dilated by the factor 2. The dilation copy is on the right. Trace the figures and locate the center of dilation.

On Your Own

5. Choose a favorite picture. It might be like Trig, the horse shown here. Dilate the picture by the factor 2 to make a scaled sketch. You do not need to scale all the details from your picture. A rough outline is fine, but be sure to include at least the important ones.

In Exercises 6–9, you can investigate a dilation that has surprising results. Stand in front of a mirror (perhaps a bathroom mirror at home). Trace your image with a bar of soap. Include important features like your eyes, nose, mouth, and chin.

6. Use a ruler. Measure a few of the distances on your mirror picture. How far apart are your eyes? How wide is your mouth? How far is it from your chin to the top of your head?

7. Compare the distances you've measured on the mirror to the actual measurements of your face. Are they the same?

8. How can the concept of dilation help explain your results?

9. Stand in front of the mirror again. Have a friend trace the image of your face. Is the picture the same as the one you traced? Explain.

10. Standardized Test Prep Suppose you dilate a square by the factor 2. How does the area of the dilated square compare to the area of the original square?

A. It is the same.   **B.** It is 2 times greater.

C. It is 4 times greater.   **D.** It is 8 times greater.

11. Take It Further Dilating a figure with a pencil and ruler takes plenty of patience. You need to dilate many points to get a good outline of the scaled copy. Geometry software lets you speed up the process.

With geometry software, draw $\overline{AB}$. Construct its midpoint, M. Select points B and M. Use the Trace feature to indicate that you want the software to keep track of the paths of B and M.

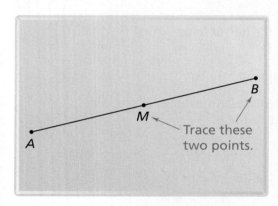

a. Move point B around the screen to draw a picture or perhaps sign your name. Compare point B's path to the path traced by point M. Are they the same? How are they related?

> Point A should stay fixed as you move point B.

b. Use the software's segment tool. Draw a polygon on your screen. Move point B along the sides of the polygon. Describe the path traced by point M.

c. As you move point B, trace $\overline{AB}$ as well as points B and M. How does your final picture illustrate the concept of dilation?

> Move point B fairly quickly. If you move it slowly, the screen fills up with traced segments and the picture is hard to see.

Maintain Your Skills

12. Trace this figure. Scale it using the given scale factors. You can choose your own center of dilation.

a. 2   **b.** 0.5

c. 1   **d.** 0.1

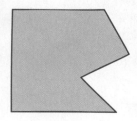

Go Online
www.successnetplus.com

7.08 Ratio and Parallel Methods

When you use dilation to scale a figure such as a horse's head, you need to dilate a fair number of points before the scaled copy is recognizable. For figures made of line segments, such as polygons, you need to keep track of only a few critical points.

In this lesson, you will learn two shortcuts, the **ratio method** and the **parallel method**. You can use each method with those critical points to make the dilation process much faster.

Habits of Mind

Make strategic choices. For dilating a segment, you choose the endpoints of the segment. Are they strategically good choices? Explain.

Example 1

The Ratio Method

Problem Use point *L* as the center of dilation. Dilate polygon *ABCDE* by $\frac{1}{2}$.

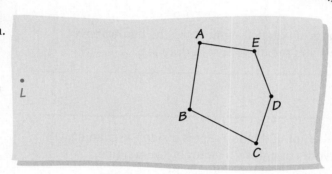

See the TI-Nspire Handbook, p. 990, to learn how to use the ratio method with geometry software.

Solution

Step 1 Draw a ray from point *L* through each vertex of the polygon.

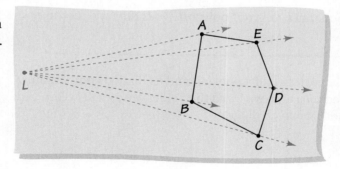

Step 2 Find the midpoint of each of the segments $\overline{LA}$ through $\overline{LE}$.

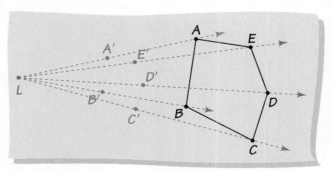

Step 3 Connect the midpoints to form a new polygon, $A'B'C'D'E'$.

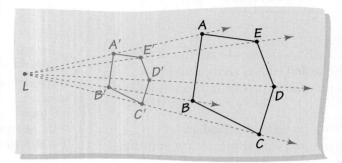

For Discussion

1. Is your new polygon a scaled $\left(\text{by } \frac{1}{2}\right)$ copy of the original? How can you tell?

2. There seem to be many pairs of parallel segments in the figure above. Label the parallel segments you see on your own drawing.

Habits of Mind

Check your results. You can take measurements to check your work. How many measurements would you take to convince yourself that the polygon is a scaled copy of the original? Explain.

For You to Do

3. Draw a triangle. Choose a center of dilation that is inside the triangle. Use the ratio method to scale your triangle by a factor of your choice.

   Does the ratio method work if the center of dilation is inside the polygon?

4. Choose a center of dilation that is on your polygon. Does the ratio method still work?

Look at each figure you have drawn of a polygon and its dilated companion. The polygons are oriented the same way, and their sides are parallel. This observation suggests another way to dilate.

Example 2

The Parallel Method

Problem Use point *E* as the center of dilation. Dilate polygon *ABCD* by 2.

Solution

Step 1 Draw a ray from *E* through each vertex.

Step 2 Along one ray ($\overrightarrow{EA}$ below), find a point that is twice as far from *E* as the vertex *A*. Mark this location *A'*.

Step 3 Start at point *A'*. Draw segments parallel to $\overline{AB}$, $\overline{BC}$, $\overline{CD}$, and finally $\overline{DA}$.

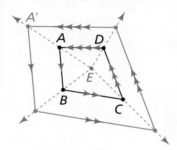

> Estimate the slope of the parallel segments as best you can.

For Discussion

Draw a polygon. Follow the steps in Example 2 to dilate your polygon by 2.

5. Is your new polygon a scaled (by the factor 2) copy of the original? How can you tell?

6. Label the pairs of parallel segments on your drawing.

For You to Do

7. Draw a triangle. Choose a center of dilation that is on the triangle. Use the parallel method to scale your triangle by a factor of your choice. Does the parallel method work if the center of dilation is on the polygon?

8. Try the parallel method again. This time choose a center of dilation that is outside your polygon. Does the parallel method still work?

Exercises Practicing Habits of Mind

Check Your Understanding

As well as making half-size reductions, the ratio method demonstrated in this lesson can dilate a figure by any scale factor you choose.

1. Start with a polygon. Use the ratio method to dilate it by the factor $\frac{1}{3}$.

2. Use the ratio method to enlarge a polygon by the factor 2.

3. Rosie wants to make two scale drawings of $\triangle ABC$. One is to be dilated by the factor 2. The other is to be dilated by the factor 3. She decides to make the triangle vertex A her center of dilation. Draw a picture like the one below. Then finish her construction.

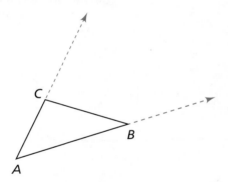

> **Habits of Mind**
>
> **Visualize.** When you have to draw a picture carefully, such as in a construction, it can be very helpful to first sketch what the final picture should look like.

4. **What's Wrong Here?** Steve uses the ratio method to enlarge $\triangle ABC$ below by the factor 2.

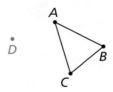

He follows this procedure. (See diagram at the top of the next page.)

- He measures the distance DA to be 1. He moves out along $\overrightarrow{DA}$ until he finds a point A' such that $AA' = 2$ (twice as much as DA).

- He measures the distance DB to be 2. He moves out along $\overrightarrow{DB}$ until he finds a point B' such that $BB' = 4$ (twice as much as DB).

- He measures the distance DC to be 1.5. He moves out along $\overrightarrow{DC}$ until he finds a point C' such that $CC' = 3$ (twice as much as DC).

- He draws $\triangle A'B'C'$.

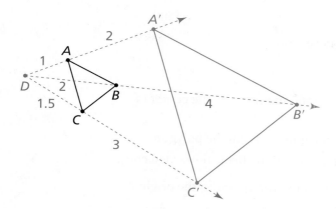

To Steve's surprise, △A′B′C′ has sides that are proportional to the sides of △ABC, but they are not twice as long. How many times as long are they? What is the matter here?

5. Oh no! There is a problem at the print shop. The picture below was supposed to show △ABC and its dilated companion, △A′B′C′, but an ink spill spoiled the page. Can you salvage something from this disaster by calculating how much △ABC has been scaled?

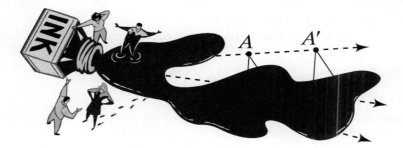

6. Trace the figure below onto a sheet of paper, including the center of dilation, D. Use the ratio method to scale the figure by the given factor.

a. $\frac{3}{4}$ **b.** 1.5

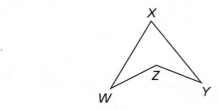

7. Draw a polygon. Use the parallel method to reduce the polygon by the factor $\frac{1}{2}$.

8. Draw a polygon. Use the parallel method to enlarge the polygon by the factor 3. Make three enlargements. Locate the centers of dilation inside the polygon, on the polygon, and outside the polygon.

9. Draw any polygon. Scale it by 2 using the ratio method. Let the center of dilation be as given.

   a. outside the polygon   **b.** inside the polygon   **c.** on the polygon

   d. Explain how the location of the center of dilation affects the scaled copy.

10. Draw a polygon. Make a scaled copy that shares a vertex with the original. Use any scale factor you like (other than 1).

11. Draw a polygon. Make a scaled copy that has one side containing the corresponding side of the original.

    > One side of the copy contains the corresponding side of the original. From this, what can you conclude about the dilation?

12. Julia scaled a polygon three times.

    a. The first scaled copy was closer to the center of dilation than the original polygon. What can you say about the scale factor?

    b. The second scaled copy was farther from the center of dilation than the original polygon. What can you say about the scale factor?

    c. The third scaled copy was the same distance from the center of dilation as the original polygon. What can you say about the scale factor? Be careful!

If you use the parallel method with geometry software, you can make a whole series of different-sized scaled polygons. And you do not have to start from scratch each time. The next exercise describes how to do it.

13. Use geometry software. Construct a polygon and a center of dilation. Construct rays from this center through the polygon's vertices. Then place a point anywhere along one of the rays. This will be a "slider point." It will control the amount of dilation.

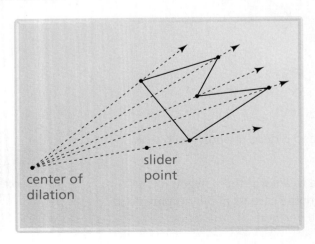

center of dilation   slider point

Use the slider point as the starting point for the dilated image. With the parallel method, complete a dilated copy of the polygon. When your dilated copy is complete, move the slider point back and forth along its ray. Describe what happens.

14. **Take It Further** With your polygon and its scaled copy from Exercise 13, use the software to calculate the scale factor. This scale factor should update itself automatically as you move the slider point. For what location(s) of the slider point is the scale factor as follows?

   a. less than one **b.** greater than one **c.** equal to one

15. **Standardized Test Prep** One figure is made of segments. A second figure is made of segments *and* curved parts. Why is the first figure easier to dilate?

   A. You can easily move the center of dilation of the first figure.

   B. You only have to dilate the endpoints of the first figure's segments and then connect those points.

   C. It is easier to place the center of the dilation inside the first figure.

   D. You cannot dilate the curved parts.

16. **Take It Further** Draw △ABC with pencil and paper or geometry software. Your challenge is to construct a square with one side lying on $\overline{BC}$ and the other two vertices on sides $\overline{AB}$ and $\overline{AC}$.

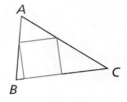

Habits of Mind

Visualize. You can shrink the square, keeping three vertices on the triangle. This should suggest an enlargement dilation that will reveal the construction steps.

Maintain Your Skills

17. Use both the ratio method and the parallel method to scale the figure below by the given scale factors.

   a. 2.5
   b. $\frac{1}{2}$
   c. $\frac{5}{2}$
   d. $\frac{1}{4}$

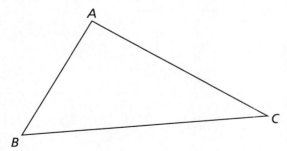

Go Online
www.successnetplus.com

In this investigation, you explored dilations. You applied scale factors to construct enlargements and reductions. You explored choices for the center of dilation. Also, you learned the ratio and parallel methods. These questions will help you summarize what you have learned.

1. You scale a figure by the factor $\frac{3}{5}$. How do the areas of the original figure and the scaled copy compare?

2. Draw $\triangle ABC$ and a point X outside of $\triangle ABC$. Use the ratio method or parallel method. Scale $\triangle ABC$ by $\frac{3}{2}$. Use X as the center of dilation.

3. Trace polygon $ABCD$ and point X.
   Use the parallel method. Dilate $ABCD$
   by the factor $\frac{1}{5}$. Use X as the center of dilation.

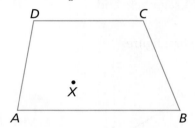

4. Explain how to find the center of dilation that maps $\triangle ABC$ to $\triangle DEF$.

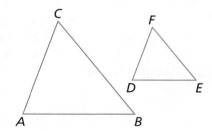

5. If you scale a cube by the factor 2, how do the surface areas of the original figure and the scaled copy compare?

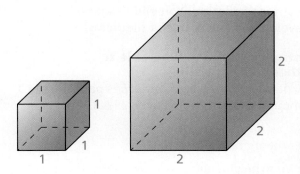

6. What is the mathematical meaning of *dilation*?

7. How do you use the parallel method to scale a polygon?

8. What is the result of applying scale factor 3 to a polygon? The result of applying scale factor $\frac{1}{3}$?

If nesting dolls are dilation images of one another, where is the center of dilation?

Vocabulary

In this investigation, you learned these terms. Make sure
you understand what each one means and how to use it.

- **center of dilation**
- **dilation**
- **parallel method**
- **ratio method**

The Side-Splitter Theorems

In *The Side-Splitter Theorems,* you will dilate a triangle using one of its vertices as the center of dilation. You will examine the result in detail and develop some very useful theorems.

By the end of this investigation, you will be able to answer questions like these.

1. If a point D is on side $\overline{AB}$ of $\triangle ABC$, E is on $\overline{AC}$, and $\overline{DE}$ is parallel to $\overline{BC}$, then what can you say about the relationship between $\triangle ABC$ and $\triangle ADE$?

2. What are the side-splitter theorems?

3. If two triangles have the same height, and you know the ratio of their areas, what is the ratio of the lengths of their bases?

You will learn how to

- investigate proportional relationships in nested triangles

- investigate how lines parallel to a side of a triangle cut the other two sides

- prove the side-splitter theorems

You will develop these habits and skills:

- Use ratios and proportions.

- Prove conjectures using scaled figures.

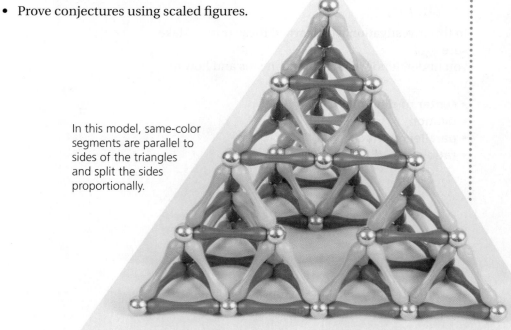

In this model, same-color segments are parallel to sides of the triangles and split the sides proportionally.

Activating Prior Knowledge
Exploring New Ideas

In this investigation, you will construct proofs for most parts of the side-splitter theorems. At the core of these proofs is an ingenious area argument devised by Euclid. To prepare for the proofs, you have several questions about area to work on first.

For You to Explore

1. Points A and B of $\triangle ABC$ are fixed on line ℓ. Line m is parallel to line ℓ. Point C, which is not shown, is free to wander anywhere along line m. For what location of point C is the area of $\triangle ABC$ the greatest? Explain.

Geometry software makes it easy for you to experiment with different locations of point C.

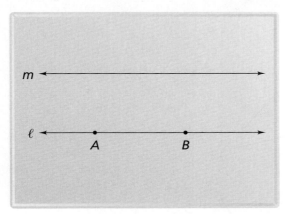

In Exercises 2 and 3, you prove that if two triangles have the same height, the ratio of their areas is the same as the ratio of their bases.

2. Both $\triangle ABC$ and $\triangle DEF$ have height h. Write an expression for the area of each triangle. Then show that the ratio of their areas is $\frac{AC}{DF}$.

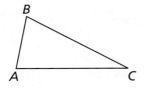

Remember...

The area formula of a triangle is $A = \frac{1}{2}bh$.

3. The area of $\triangle GEM$ is 3 square inches. The area of $\triangle MEO$ is 2 square inches. What is the value of $\frac{GE}{EO}$? Explain. What is value of $\frac{GE}{GO}$?

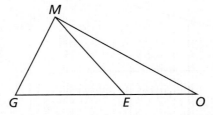

Remember...

Use the result from Problem 2 to help you.

On Your Own

4. In this figure, $\dfrac{\text{area of } \triangle PQS}{\text{area of } \triangle RPS} = \dfrac{1}{2}$. If $SQ = 4$ and $PS = 6$, find the lengths PQ, SR, QR, and PR.

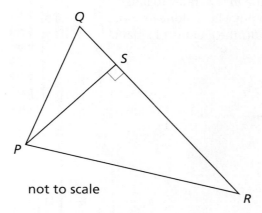

not to scale

5. $ABCD$ is a trapezoid with $\overline{AB} \parallel \overline{DC}$.

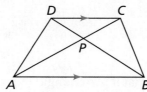

  a. Explain why the area of $\triangle ACB$ is equal to the area of $\triangle ADB$.

  b. Name one other pair of triangles in the figure that have equal areas. Explain how you know.

6. $GRAM$ is a parallelogram. Which of $\triangle GAM$, $\triangle ARM$, $\triangle MRG$, and $\triangle RAG$ has the greatest area? Explain.

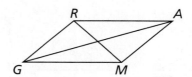

Maintain Your Skills

7. This figure is a scaled copy. Draw an original figure that would result in this copy for each of the following scale factors.

  a. 2   **b.** 3

  c. 0.5   **d.** 0.1

Nested Triangles—One Triangle Inside Another

Here are a polygon (black) and a scaled copy (blue). The copy was made using the parallel method.

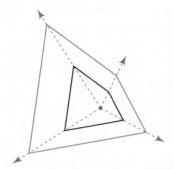

a polygon and a scaled copy

The four pictures below show the same polygons. Each picture highlights a pair of **nested triangles**—one triangle inside another. Notice that each pair of nested triangles contains a side from the original polygon and a parallel side from the scaled polygon.

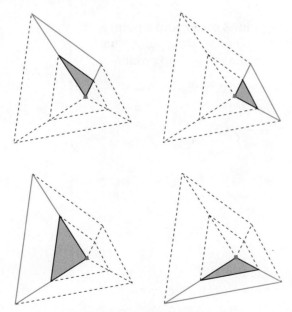

four pairs of nested triangles

In the In-Class Experiment that follows, you should discover some important relationships between parallel lines and the sides of the triangles that they intersect.

In-Class Experiment

Part 1A Parallel Lines and Midpoints

Draw a picture like the one below. Show two parallel lines and a point. Make the distance between the point and the closer line equal to the distance between the two lines.

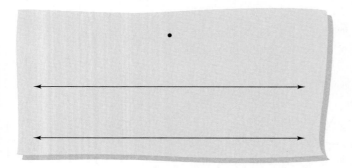

1. Use your picture. Find a quick way to draw ten segments so that each will have its midpoint automatically marked.

2. Find a way to position two parallel lines and a point that gives a quick way to draw ten segments with each segment divided into two smaller segments with lengths in the ratio 1 to 3.

Part 1B Midpoints and Parallel Lines

Use geometry software. Draw $\overline{XY}$. Construct a point A on $\overline{XY}$ and a point B that is not on $\overline{XY}$. Draw $\overline{AB}$ and construct its midpoint M. Drag point A back and forth along the entire length of $\overline{XY}$ while tracing the path of point M.

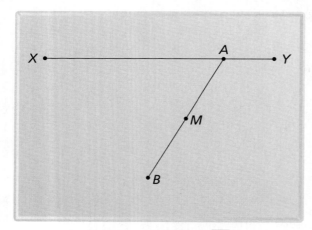

Drag point A along $\overline{XY}$.

3. **a.** Describe the path traced by M.

   b. How does the path traced by point M compare to $\overline{XY}$?

4. Repeat the construction above. This time, instead of constructing the midpoint of $\overline{AB}$, place the point M somewhere else on $\overline{AB}$. How does the position of M affect the path traced by M?

5. Use geometry software. Draw $\overline{XY}$. Locate a point A on $\overline{XY}$. Then construct three segments, each with A as an endpoint. Construct the midpoints M_1, M_2, and M_3 of the three segments. Move point A back and forth along $\overline{XY}$ while tracing the paths of these midpoints. Describe the paths of the midpoints, including what you know about their locations and lengths.

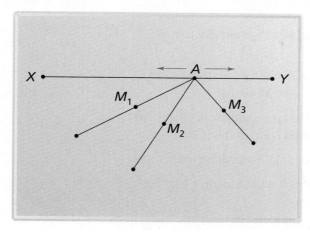

Part 2 Splitting Two Sides of a Triangle

Use geometry software. Draw $\triangle ABC$. Place a point D anywhere on side $\overline{AB}$. Then construct a segment $\overline{DE}$ that is parallel to $\overline{BC}$.

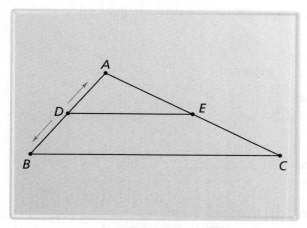

$\triangle ADE$ and $\triangle ABC$ are a pair of nested triangles.

Drag point D along $\overline{AB}$.

6. Use the software to find the ratio $\dfrac{AD}{AB}$.

7. Find two other length ratios with the same value. Do all three ratios remain equal to each other when you drag point D along $\overline{AB}$?

8. As you drag D along $\overline{AB}$, describe what happens to the figure. Make a conjecture about the effect of $\overline{DE}$ being parallel to $\overline{BC}$.

Tony and Sasha are finishing the In-Class Experiment.

Tony   I like dragging points on the computer screen and watching what happens.

Sasha   Me too. Triangle *ADE* and the ratios all got small when we dragged *D* close to *A*.

Tony   And when we dragged *D* close to *B*, the two triangles were almost the same, and the ratios were almost 1!

Sasha   The two triangles always had the same shape too. I think that happened because we constructed $\overline{DE}$ parallel to $\overline{BC}$.

Tony   The parallel segment seemed to make everything work nicely.

Sasha   So, can we make a conjecture about what having a parallel segment like $\overline{DE}$ does for the figure?

Tony   Can we say something like "A parallel-to-one-side segment inside a triangle makes two proportional triangles"?

Sasha   Hmm. I get the idea. I think we have to work on the wording.

Sasha and Tony need a definition of what it means for a segment to divide two sides of a triangle proportionally.

Definitions

In $\triangle ABC$ with *D* on $\overline{AB}$ and *E* on $\overline{AC}$, $\overline{DE}$ **splits two sides proportionally** ($\overline{AB}$ and $\overline{AC}$) if and only if $\frac{AB}{AD} = \frac{AC}{AE}$.

You call the ratio $\frac{AB}{AD}$ the **common ratio.**

The In-Class Experiment may have suggested statements like the two theorems that follow. You will prove these theorems in the next two lessons.

Theorem 7.1   *The Parallel Side-Splitter Theorem*

If a segment with endpoints on two sides of a triangle is parallel to the third side of the triangle, then

- the segment splits the sides it intersects proportionally

- the ratio of the length of the third side of the triangle to the length of the parallel segment is the common ratio

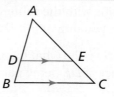

Theorem 7.2   The Proportional Side-Splitter Theorem

If a segment with endpoints on two sides
of a triangle splits those sides proportionally,
then the segment is parallel to the third side.

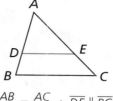

$$\frac{AB}{AD} = \frac{AC}{AE} \Rightarrow \overline{DE} \parallel \overline{BC}$$

Exercises *Practicing Habits of Mind*

Check Your Understanding

In Exercises 1–5, $\overline{DE} \parallel \overline{BC}$.

1. If $AD = 1$, $AB = 3$, and $AE = 2$, what is AC?

2. If $AE = 4$, $AC = 5$, and $AB = 20$, what is AD?

3. If $AD = 3$, $DB = 2$, and $AE = 12$, what is EC?

4. If $AE = 1$, $AC = 4$, and $DE = 3$, what is BC?

5. If $AD = 2$ and $DB = 6$, what is the value of $\frac{DE}{BC}$?

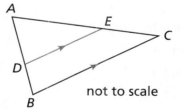

not to scale

On Your Own

6. Understanding Theorems 7.1 and 7.2 by reading
   through their words can be difficult. It may help to
   replace some of the words with actual segment
   names. Rewrite each theorem using the nested
   triangles shown here as a reference. Make each
   theorem as specific as possible. If a theorem
   mentions a segment length or a proportion,
   substitute the name of that segment or
   proportion in place of the words.

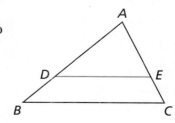

7. Standardized Test Prep In $\triangle ABC$, D lies on $\overline{AB}$ and E lies on $\overline{AC}$. Suppose $\overleftrightarrow{DE} \parallel \overleftrightarrow{BC}$. Which proportion is NOT correct?

A. $\dfrac{AD}{AB} = \dfrac{AE}{AC}$ **B.** $\dfrac{AD}{DB} = \dfrac{AE}{EC}$

C. $\dfrac{AD}{DB} = \dfrac{DE}{BC}$ **D.** $\dfrac{AD}{AB} = \dfrac{DE}{BC}$

8. Write About It The Parallel Side-Splitter Theorem says that a segment parallel to a side of a triangle with endpoints on the other two sides "splits the other two sides proportionally."

Tammy Jo has three sayings that help her remember this:

    Whole is to part as whole is to part.

    Part is to part as part is to part.

    Part is to whole as part is to whole.

What do these sayings mean?

Maintain Your Skills

For Exercises 9 and 10, use the figure at the right. $\overline{DE} \parallel \overline{BC}$.

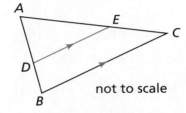

not to scale

9. Find EC given the following conditions.

    a. $AD = 1$, $DB = 4$, and $AE = 3$

    b. $AD = 1$, $DB = 4$, and $AE = 7$

    c. $AD = 1$, $DB = 7$, and $AE = 4$

    d. $AD = 1$, $DB = 10$, and $AE = 10$

    e. $AD = 1$, $DB = \frac{1}{2}$, and $AE = 3$

    f. $AD = 1$, $DB = x$, and $AE = y$

10. Find EC given the following conditions.

    a. $AE = 1$, $AD = 4$, and $DB = 8$

    b. $AE = 1$, $AD = 8$, and $DB = 4$

    c. $AE = 1$, $AD = 2$, and $DB = 10$

    d. $AE = 1$, $AD = 2$, and $DB = \frac{1}{2}$

    e. $AE = 1$, $AD = \frac{1}{2}$, and $DB = 2$

    f. $AE = 1$, $AD = x$, and $DB = y$

Go Online
www.successnetplus.com

Recall what the first part of the Parallel Side-Splitter Theorem says:

> If a segment with endpoints on two sides of a triangle is parallel to the third side of the triangle, then it splits the sides it intersects proportionally.

To begin the proof of this theorem, you can show that, in the figure below, if $\overline{VW} \parallel \overline{RT}$, then $\frac{SV}{VR} = \frac{SW}{WT}$.

In the figures below, triangles SVW and RVW have the same height. This means that the ratio of their areas is equal to the ratio of their base lengths, SV and VR.

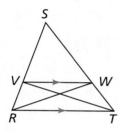

$$\frac{\text{area}(\triangle SVW)}{\text{area}(\triangle RVW)} = \frac{SV}{VR}$$

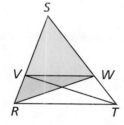

> This fact comes from Lesson 7.09.

In the figures below, triangles SVW and TVW have the same height. Thus, the ratio of their areas is equal to the ratio of their base lengths, SW and WT.

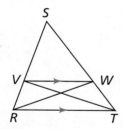

$$\frac{\text{area}(\triangle SVW)}{\text{area}(\triangle TVW)} = \frac{SW}{WT}$$

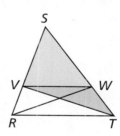

Habits of Mind

Understand the process. A "tidy" proof like this may not necessarily be easy to write. You build it from many notes, sketches, erasures, more sketches, more notes, and plenty of talking to yourself!

You have two fractions with the same numerator,

$$\frac{\text{area}(\triangle SVW)}{\text{area}(\triangle RVW)} \text{ and } \frac{\text{area}(\triangle SVW)}{\text{area}(\triangle TVW)}.$$

The denominators are not the same, but are they equal? Recall Problem 1 from Lesson 7.9. Triangles RVW and TVW share the same base $\overline{VW}$. They have the same height, since $\overline{VW}$ is parallel to $\overline{RT}$. So they have the same area.

You can combine all of these results to draw a conclusion about SV, VR, SW, and WT.

$$\frac{SV}{VR} = \frac{\text{area}(\triangle SVW)}{\text{area}(\triangle RVW)} = \frac{\text{area}(\triangle SVW)}{\text{area}(\triangle TVW)} = \frac{SW}{WT}$$

For You to Do

1. Using what has been outlined in this lesson, write a complete proof of the first part of the Parallel Side-Splitter Theorem.

Exercises *Practicing Habits of Mind*

Check Your Understanding

1. Recall the Proportional Side-Splitter Theorem:

   If a segment with endpoints on two sides of a triangle splits those sides proportionally, then the segment is parallel to the third side.

   This time, the proof is up to you. Use the same setup that you used to prove the Parallel Side-Splitter Theorem. Write your proof so that someone else can follow it.

2. In the diagrams below, $\overline{AB}$ is parallel to $\overline{DE}$. Find as many lengths as you can.

   a.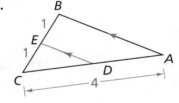

   b.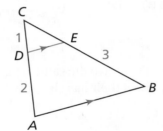

   c.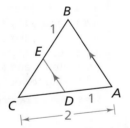

The main entrance to the Rock and Roll Hall of Fame is at the base of this glass-and-steel triangle. Can you find horizontal steel ribbing in the triangle that is half the length of the base? Three fourths the length of the base?

3. Use the lengths given in each figure below to decide whether $\overline{AB}$ is parallel to $\overline{DE}$. Explain.

a.

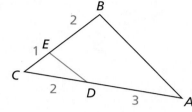

b.

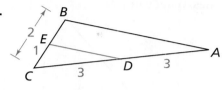

c.

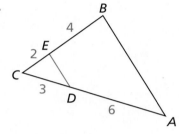

On Your Own

4. Standardized Test Prep In $\triangle STR$, U lies on $\overline{SR}$, V lies on $\overline{RT}$, and $\overline{VU} \parallel \overline{TS}$. Suppose that $TS = 540$, $VU = 180$, $US = 667$, and $RT = 600$. What is RV?

A. 200   **B.** 240   **C.** 270   **D.** 333

5. The dashed lines in the figure are all parallel to $\overline{AC}$ and equally spaced. What can you conclude about how they intersect $\overline{AB}$ and $\overline{BC}$?

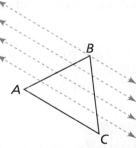

6. Make two copies of the diagram below. Use the fact that the points shown in red trisect $\overline{BC}$ to do the following.

a. Trisect $\overline{AB}$.

b. Trisect $\overline{AC}$.

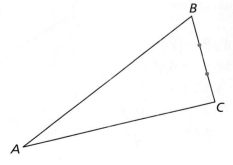

Habits of Mind

Make connections.
How does the definition of *bisect* help you define *trisect*?

7. Both $\overline{AB}$ and $\overline{BC}$ are cut into five equal-length segments by the dashed lines. What can you conclude?

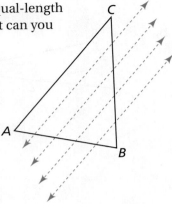

The first part of the Parallel Side-Splitter Theorem tells you that two sides of a triangle are split proportionally. By now, you should suspect that there are several proportions possible, such as $\frac{AB}{AD} = \frac{AC}{AE}$ and $\frac{DB}{AD} = \frac{EC}{AE}$ in the triangle at the right.

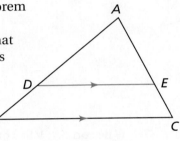

Exercises 8 and 9 show how to prove that these proportions are two different ways of writing the same information.

8. Take It Further First, you can prove a related fact using algebra. Suppose that r, s, t, and u are any four nonzero numbers. If $\frac{r}{s} = \frac{t}{u}$, explain why it is also true that $\frac{r-s}{s} = \frac{t-u}{u}$.

Hint: $\frac{r-s}{s} = \frac{r}{s} - \frac{s}{s}$

9. Take It Further Use Exercise 8 as a guide. Explain how the proportion $\frac{AB}{AD} = \frac{AC}{AE}$ leads directly to $\frac{DB}{AD} = \frac{EC}{AE}$.

Maintain Your Skills

10. Does the given information guarantee that $\overline{BC} \parallel \overline{DE}$?

a. $AB = 1$, $BD = 4$, $AC = 3$, $CE = 12$

b. $AB = 8$, $BD = 4$, $AC = 16$, $CE = 8$

c. $AB = 3$, $BD = 12$, $AC = 4$, $CE = 1$

d. $AB = 7$, $BD = 3$, $AC = 7$, $CE = 8$

e. $AB = 0.5$, $BD = 7$, $AC = 28$, $CE = 2$

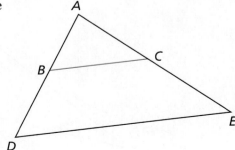

Go Online
www.successnetplus.com

Now you will finish proving the Parallel Side-Splitter Theorem. Recall that the theorem says

If $\overline{VW}$ is parallel to $\overline{RT}$, then $\frac{SR}{SV} = \frac{ST}{SW} = \frac{RT}{VW}$.

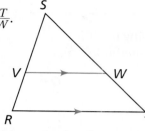

In Lesson 7.11, you proved that $\frac{SV}{VR} = \frac{SW}{WT}$. You can use this to show that $\frac{SR}{SV} = \frac{ST}{SW}$.

$$\frac{SV}{VR} = \frac{SW}{WT}$$

$$\frac{VR}{SV} = \frac{WT}{SW}$$

$$1 + \frac{VR}{SV} = 1 + \frac{WT}{SW}$$

$$\frac{SV}{SV} + \frac{VR}{SV} = \frac{SW}{SW} + \frac{WT}{SW}$$

$$\frac{SV + VR}{SV} = \frac{SW + WT}{SW}$$

$$\frac{SR}{SV} = \frac{ST}{SW}$$

In-Class Experiment

Trace and make paper cutouts of $\triangle SVW$ and $\triangle SRT$. Place them on top of each other. Slide $\triangle SVW$ along $\overline{SR}$ until vertices V and R coincide.

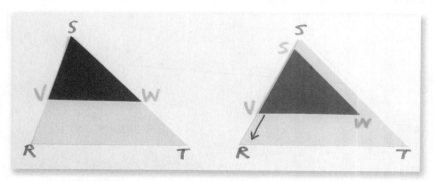

1. Why does $\angle SVW$ fall precisely on top of $\angle SRT$?

2. Draw a picture of how the triangles look after you slide $\triangle SVW$ to $\overline{RT}$.

3. Which two segments are now parallel? Explain.

For You to Do

4. Use the setup from the In-Class Experiment to prove the last part of the Parallel Side-Splitter Theorem—namely, that $\frac{RT}{VW}$ equals both $\frac{SR}{SV}$ and $\frac{ST}{SW}$.

For Discussion

5. Show that if $\overline{AB}$ is dilated from O using first the ratio method and then the parallel method, you get the same result.

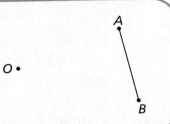

Exercises *Practicing Habits of Mind*

Check Your Understanding

In Exercises 1–3, $\overline{AC} \parallel \overline{DE}$. Copy the diagrams. Find as many lengths as you can.

1.

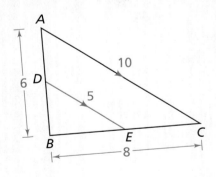

2.

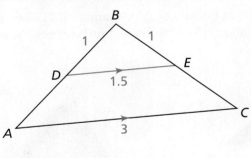

3.

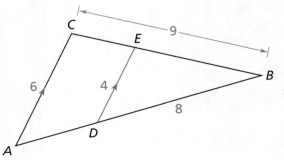

4. Use the side-splitter theorems. Explain why the two rectangles in each figure below are scaled copies of each other.

a.

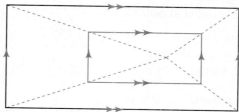

b.

5. In the triangle shown here, $\overline{DE} \parallel \overline{BC}$. Explain why $\triangle ABC$ is a scaled copy of $\triangle ADE$.

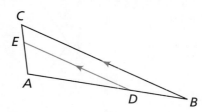

6. You draw the sides of the outer polygon parallel to the sides of the inner polygon as shown at the right. Explain why the polygons are scaled copies.

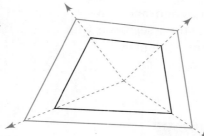

7. Standardized Test Prep Suppose $\triangle ABC$ is a scaled copy of $\triangle BED$. Which of the following lists the congruent corresponding angles of these two triangles?

A. $\angle A \cong \angle DBE$, $\angle ABC \cong \angle BDE$, $\angle C \cong \angle DEB$

B. $\angle A \cong \angle DBE$, $\angle ABC \cong \angle BED$, $\angle C \cong \angle BDE$

C. $\angle A \cong \angle DBE$, $\angle ABC \cong \angle BED$, $\angle B \cong \angle BDE$

D. $\angle A \cong \angle DBE$, $\angle ABC \cong \angle BDE$, $\angle C \cong \angle DEB$

How might you extend the idea of nested triangles to nested circles? What proportional relationships do nested circles suggest? Find out in Lesson 8.10.

8. **Take It Further** Here is a way to construct △*ABE* to have the same area as quadrilateral *ABCD*, without taking any measurements.

First, draw diagonal $\overline{AC}$. Then draw a line through point *D* parallel to $\overline{AC}$. Extend $\overline{BC}$ to meet the parallel at point *E*.

This completes the construction. The area of △*ABE* is equal to the area of quadrilateral *ABCD*. Explain why.

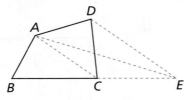

9. **Take It Further** Extend the method used in Exercise 8. Construct a triangle with area equal to that of pentagon *ABCDE* shown here.

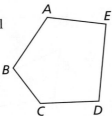

10. **Take It Further** $\overline{AB}$ and $\overline{BC}$ represent the border between land owned by Wendy and land owned by Juan. How can you replace these segments with a single segment such that the amount of land owned by each person does not change? Justify your answer.

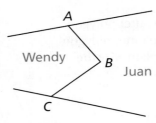

Maintain Your Skills

11. Decide whether $\overline{AB}$ is parallel to $\overline{DE}$. In each case, give a reason for your decision. The triangles are not necessarily drawn to scale.

a.

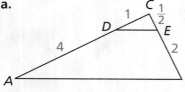

b.

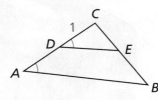

c.

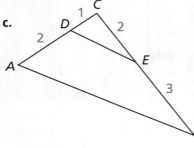

d.

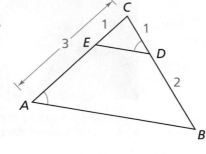

Go Online
www.successnetplus.com

In this investigation, you explored parallels and proportions in nested triangles. You proved the side-splitter theorems. These questions will help you summarize what you have learned.

1. In △ABC, $\overline{DE} \parallel \overline{AC}$, $DB = \frac{1}{3}AB$, $AB = 6$, $BE = 3$, and $AC = 12$. What are BC, DE, and DB?

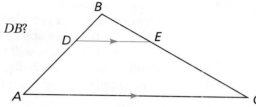

2. $EFGH$ is a quadrilateral. $CH = \frac{1}{3}HE$, $HD = \frac{1}{3}HG$, $AF = \frac{1}{4}EF$, and $BF = \frac{1}{4}FG$. Prove that $\overline{AB} \parallel \overline{CD}$.

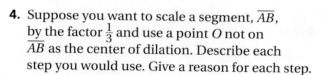

3. Use the side-splitter theorems to prove the Midline Theorem. See Lesson 6.17 for a reminder of the Midline Theorem.

4. Suppose you want to scale a segment, $\overline{AB}$, by the factor $\frac{1}{3}$ and use a point O not on $\overline{AB}$ as the center of dilation. Describe each step you would use. Give a reason for each step.

5. In the diagram at the right, $AD = 24$, $ED = 8$, $DC = 21$, and $DF = 7$. △HBG is a scaled copy of △ABC with a scale factor of $\frac{1}{3}$. Prove that $EFGH$ is a parallelogram.

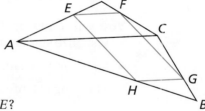

6. If a point D is on side $\overline{AB}$ of △ABC, E is on $\overline{AC}$, and $\overline{DE}$ is parallel to $\overline{BC}$, then what can you say about the relationship between △ABC and △ADE?

7. What are the side-splitter theorems?

8. If two triangles have the same height, and you know the ratio of their areas, what is the ratio of the lengths of their bases?

Vocabulary

In this investigation, you learned these terms. Make sure you understand what each one means and how to use it.

- **common ratio**
- **nested triangles**
- **splits two sides proportionally**

The Midline Theorem is a special case of the side-splitter theorems.

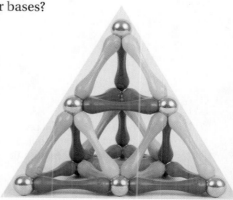

Defining Similarity

In *Defining Similarity,* you formally define the mathematical term *similar.* You will closely tie its definition to all the work you have done on scaled copies. Your ability to recognize and create scaled copies will be very useful. You will learn the implications of similarity. You will also learn how to test for similarity in triangles and other figures.

By the end of this investigation, you will be able to answer questions like these.

1. What does it mean for two figures to be similar?

2. What are some tests for triangle similarity?

3. If the common ratio of two similar figures is r, what is the ratio of their areas?

You will learn how to

- identify corresponding parts of similar triangles

- develop and use the AA, SAS, and SSS tests for similarity in triangles

- understand that the ratio between the area of a polygon and the area of a copy of that polygon scaled by the factor r will be r^2

You will develop these habits and skills:

- Visualize similar triangles.

- Look for invariant ratios.

- Make logical inferences to prove similarity.

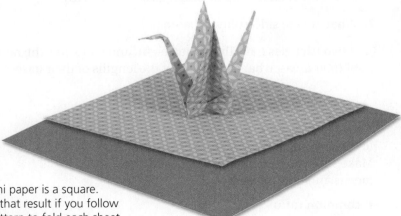

Each sheet of origami paper is a square.
Describe the figures that result if you follow
the same origami pattern to fold each sheet.

Words such as *enlargements, reductions, scale factors,* and *dilations* are some of the terms you have met again and again in this chapter.

The common theme uniting them is called *similarity.* By enlarging or reducing a picture, you make another picture that is similar to the first. One way to define *similar figures* in geometry is as follows.

- Two figures are similar if one is a scaled copy of the other.

The ratio method suggests another possible definition.

- Two figures are similar if one is a dilation of the other.

To test this definition, look at the picture of the head of Trig the horse. Trig is accompanied here by his little sister, Girt. Girt is smaller than Trig but her head shares all of his features.

> **Remember...**
>
> You can use dilation to refer to the dilation image when this meaning is clear in context.

For You to Explore

1. Is Girt a dilated copy of Trig? If so, find the center of dilation.

2. Is the picture of Girt similar to the picture of Trig?

Here is another family portrait of Trig and Girt, this time in a different pose.

3. Is the picture of Girt still similar to the picture of Trig?

4. Can you still dilate one picture onto the other? Explain.

5. Expand the dilation definition of similar so you can say that even these two pictures are similar.

Exercises Practicing Habits of Mind

On Your Own

6. Look at your notes for Investigation 7A. Write your test for telling whether two figures are scaled copies of each other.

7. These two triangles are scaled copies of each other.

List the angle measurements that are equal and the side lengths that are proportional.

8. If two polygons are dilations of each other, describe how to find the center of dilation. Is that center unique?

9. Will you always be able to find a center of dilation for two similar polygons? If so, describe how to do it. If not, sketch a counterexample.

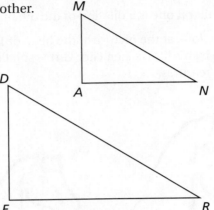

Maintain Your Skills

10. Use a standard rectangular sheet of paper that measures $8\frac{1}{2}$ in. by 11 in. For parts (a)–(d) below, fold the paper in half the given number of times by matching the two shorter sides. When done folding, do the following.

- Unfold the paper.

- Count the number of rectangles that are formed.

- Find the dimensions of each rectangle.

- Decide whether each rectangle is similar to the shape of the original sheet of paper.

  a. Make one fold.   **b.** Make two folds.

  c. Make three folds.   **d.** Make four folds.

  e. Some numbers of folds produce rectangles that are similar to the shape of the original sheet of paper. What do these numbers have in common?

7.14 Similar Figures

Here are some suggestions for ways to define similar figures using dilation terminology.

Definitions

- Two figures are **similar** if you can rotate and/or flip one of them so that you can dilate it onto the other.

- Two figures are **similar** if one is congruent to a dilation of the other.

For Discussion

In Lesson 7.13, you tried to extend a dilation definition of similarity so that it would work with the second family portrait of Trig and Girt.

1. Do the two definitions above solve any problems you may have had?

2. Are the two definitions above equivalent?

Developing Habits of Mind

Consider the converse. If two figures are congruent, are they similar? If two figures are similar, are they congruent?

If the two congruent figures below are similar, then you must be able to apply a scale factor to one of them and produce the other.

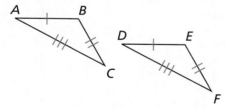

In this case, a scale factor of 1 applied to $\triangle ABC$ will produce $\triangle DEF$. But here are two similar figures that are obviously not congruent.

The symbol for similarity, ~, is the upper part of the symbol ≅ for congruence. Thus, you read the statement *ABCD ~EFGH* as "*ABCD* is similar to *EFGH*." It means that the two polygons are scaled copies of each other.

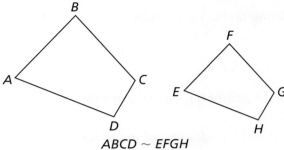

ABCD ~ EFGH

The similarity symbol, ~, means "has the same shape as," and the congruence symbol, ≅, means "has the same shape *and* the same size as."

For congruent triangles, the statement △*ABC* ≅ △*XYZ* conveys specific information about their corresponding parts. For figures that are similar, the order of their vertex letters also specifies which parts correspond, but the conclusions you draw will be different.

For You to Do

△*ABC ~* △*XYZ* and *ABCDE ~PQRST*. Copy the figures. Label the vertices of △*XYZ* and *PQRST* correctly.

3.

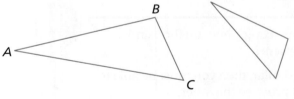

4.

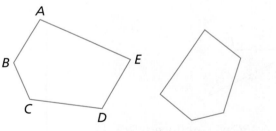

In Investigation 7A, you devised several ways to test whether two triangles are similar. (Only then, you used the phrase *scaled copies*.) One test was probably the following.

> Two triangles are similar (scaled copies) if their corresponding angles are congruent and their corresponding sides are proportional.

For future reference, you can call this the Congruent Angles, Proportional Sides test.

Using the word *dilation,* here is another test for similar triangles.

Two triangles are similar if one is congruent to a dilation of the other.

You can refer to this as the Congruent to a Dilation test.

For You to Do

5. Suppose that $\triangle NEW \sim \triangle OLD$. If $m\angle N = 19°$ and $m\angle L = 67°$, find the measures of the other angles.

Exercises *Practicing Habits of Mind*

Check Your Understanding

1. Is each given similarity statement true or false? Take measurements to decide. Explain your answer.

a. $ABCD \sim EFGH$

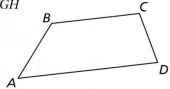

b. $ABCD \sim EFGH$

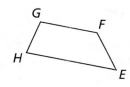
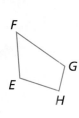
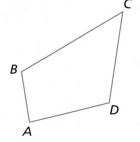

c. $\triangle ABC \sim \triangle DEF$

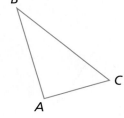
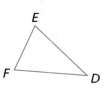

2. Suppose $\triangle ABC \sim \triangle DEF$. Must each statement be true?

a. $\dfrac{AB}{DE} = \dfrac{BC}{EF}$

b. $\dfrac{AC}{BC} = \dfrac{DF}{EF}$

c. $\dfrac{BC}{AB} = \dfrac{DF}{DE}$

d. $AC \cdot DE = AB \cdot DF$

3. In the figure below, $\triangle ABC \sim \triangle BDA$. Explain why $\triangle ABC$ is isosceles.

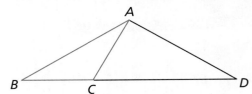

Habits of Mind

Think it through.
Recall some conditions
for a triangle to be
isosceles.

4. In the figure at the right, F, G, and H are midpoints of the sides of $\triangle ABC$. Show that $\triangle ABC \sim \triangle GHF$.

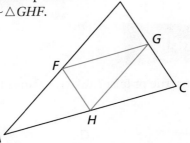

5. Make a large copy of the figure from Exercise 3. On your copy, mark the measurements shown at the right. Then fill in the rest of the angle measures and side lengths.

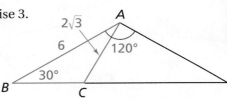

Go Online
Video Tutor
www.successnetplus.com

On Your Own

6. In the figure, $\triangle ABC \sim \triangle CDE$.

Decide whether each statement is correct or incorrect.

a. $\triangle ABC \sim \triangle DEC$

b. $\triangle BCA \sim \triangle DEC$

c. $\triangle BAC \sim \triangle DEC$

d. $\triangle CAB \sim \triangle ECD$

e. $\triangle CBA \sim \triangle ECD$

f. $\triangle CBA \sim \triangle CDE$

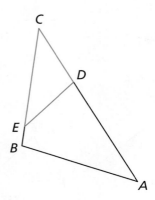

7. $\triangle QRS \sim \triangle VUT$.

Decide whether each statement is correct or incorrect.

a. $\dfrac{QR}{TU} = \dfrac{SR}{TV}$ **b.** $\dfrac{QR}{SR} = \dfrac{TU}{TV}$

c. $\dfrac{QR}{QS} = \dfrac{UV}{TV}$ **d.** $\dfrac{QT}{QV} = \dfrac{RT}{TU}$

e. $\dfrac{QR}{TV} = \dfrac{SR}{TU}$ **f.** $\dfrac{QS}{VT} = \dfrac{RS}{UT}$

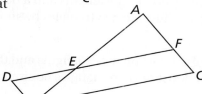

8. $\triangle CAT \sim \triangle DOT$.

Complete each statement.

a. $\angle C \cong \underline{\ \ ?\ \ }$ **b.** $\angle CTA \cong \underline{\ \ ?\ \ }$

c. $\angle DTO \cong \underline{\ \ ?\ \ }$ **d.** $\angle A \cong \underline{\ \ ?\ \ }$

e. $\angle D \cong \underline{\ \ ?\ \ }$ **f.** $\angle O \cong \underline{\ \ ?\ \ }$

9. Standardized Test Prep In the figure at the right, $\triangle ABC \sim \triangle BED$. Which length correctly completes the following proportion?

$$\dfrac{AB}{BE} = \dfrac{AC}{\blacksquare}$$

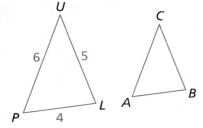

A. BD **B.** ED **C.** BC **D.** EB

Maintain Your Skills

10. $\triangle PLU \sim \triangle ABC$. Find AC and BC for each of the given lengths of AB.

a. $AB = 1$ **b.** $AB = 2$

c. $AB = 3$ **d.** $AB = 4$

e. $AB = x$

not to scale

7.15 Tests for Similar Triangles

You know several tests to decide whether triangles are congruent, for example SSS. It would be useful to have comparable tests for similar triangles.

In-Class Experiment

The main tests for congruent triangles are SAS, ASA, AAS, and SSS. Are there similar tests for similar triangles? Below are some possibilities. For each proposed test, draw a pair of triangles that share the attributes listed. Then check to see whether they must be similar. See if you can find a counterexample.

1. Three angles of one triangle are congruent to three angles of the other. Must the two triangles be similar? (AAA similarity)

2. Two triangles have a pair of proportional side lengths and a pair of congruent corresponding angles. Must the two triangles be similar? (SA similarity)

3. Two triangles have two pairs of proportional side lengths and the included angles are congruent. Must the two triangles be similar? (SAS similarity)

4. Two triangles have three pairs of proportional side lengths. Must the two triangles be similar? (SSS similarity)

AAA Similarity

Suppose △ABC and △PQR have congruent corresponding angles. Can you prove that the triangles are similar?

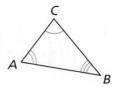
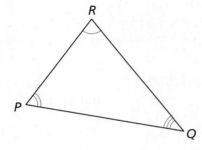

In previous lessons, you checked whether triangles were scaled copies (similar to each other) by placing one triangle inside the other triangle to form a pair of nested triangles.

So try placing △*ABC* inside △*PQR* so that congruent angles *C* and *R* coincide. The triangles line up because ∠*C* and ∠*R* are congruent. The rays that form the angles lie on top of each other.

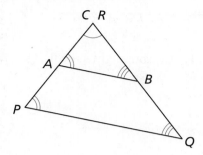

For You to Do

5. Use the figure above to prove that $\overline{AB}$ is parallel to $\overline{PQ}$. Then apply the Parallel Side-Splitter Theorem to write several proportions using the side lengths of the two triangles. Which definition of similarity allows you to conclude that △*ABC* ~ △*PQR*?

Theorem 7.3 AAA Similarity Theorem

If three angles of one triangle are congruent to three angles of another triangle, the triangles are similar.

△*ABC* ~ △*DEF*

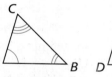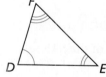

For Discussion

6. Use the information from Problem 5 to prove the AAA Similarity Theorem.

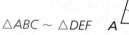 **Developing Habits of Mind**

Simplify. In a sense, the requirement that the three angles of one triangle be congruent to the three angles of the other triangle is too much.

The AAA test can actually be replaced by an AA test. Once you know the measures of two angles of a triangle, the measure of the third angle is completely determined, since the sum of the measures of the three angles of a triangle is 180°. Thus, you can rewrite the theorem as follows.

If two angles of one triangle are congruent to two angles of another triangle, then the triangles are similar.

> When you write proofs, you may use the AA Similarity Theorem, instead of the AAA Similarity Theorem.

For Discussion

7. Does it make sense to have an ASA test for triangle similarity? Explain.

SAS Similarity

Is there an SAS similarity test? If such a theorem did exist, you might state it as follows.

Theorem 7.4 SAS Similarity Theorem

If two triangles have two pairs of proportional side lengths and the included angles are congruent, the triangles are similar.

$$\frac{AC}{DF} = \frac{AB}{DE}; \ \angle A \cong \angle D \Rightarrow \triangle ABC \sim \triangle DEF$$

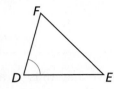

Developing Habits of Mind

Think it through. Suppose you have two triangles, $\triangle ABC$ and $\triangle DEF$, such that the following statements are true:

$$\frac{AC}{DF} = \frac{AB}{DE} \text{ and } \angle A \cong \angle D$$

These are the hypotheses of the SAS test. Now you need to show that the triangles are similar.

The key is to arrange the triangles, one inside the other, so that the congruent angles at A and D line up:

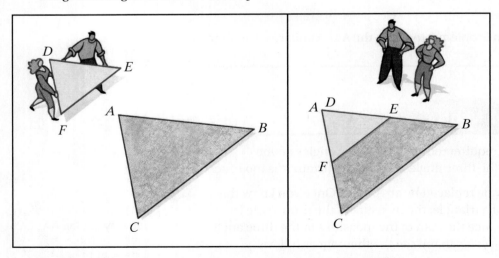

Because of the equal ratios given above, the Proportional Side-Splitter Theorem implies that $\overline{FE}$ is parallel to $\overline{CB}$. So you know that $\angle DFE \cong \angle ACB$ and $\angle DEF \cong \angle ABC$.

Moreover, the Parallel Side-Splitter Theorem tells you that

$$\frac{AC}{DF} = \frac{AB}{DE} = \frac{CB}{FE}$$

Thus, the angles of the two triangles are congruent and corresponding sides are proportional, so

$$\triangle ABC \sim \triangle DEF$$

This proves the SAS similarity theorem.

For Discussion

8. The AAA condition was too strong. Is SAS too strong as well?

SSS Similarity

Is there an SSS similarity test? If such a theorem did exist, you might state it as follows.

Theorem 7.5 SSS Similarity Theorem

If two triangles have all three pairs of side lengths proportional, the triangles are similar.

$$\frac{AC}{DF} = \frac{AB}{DE} = \frac{CB}{FE} \Rightarrow \triangle ABC \sim \triangle DEF$$

 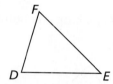

If you try to prove this theorem with the method used in the AAA and SAS proofs, something does not work.

In the AAA and SAS proofs, you had at least one pair of corresponding angles that you knew were congruent. This meant you could fit one triangle inside the other so that the congruent angles aligned perfectly. In the case of SSS, however, you have no congruent angles to use.

Since the Congruent Angles, Proportional Sides method does not seem well suited to prove SSS, try using the Congruent to a Dilation definition of similar triangles instead.

Habits of Mind

Make a choice. When you know equivalent definitions, use the one that best suits your needs.

For You to Do

9. Suppose the corresponding side lengths of $\triangle ABC$ and $\triangle PQR$ are proportional.

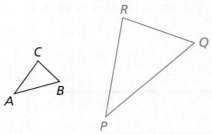

  a. Write the proportionality statement for the side lengths of these two triangles.

  b. If $\frac{PQ}{AB} = k$, where k is some positive number, complete each of the following statements.

    • ▨ $= k(AB)$

    • ▨ $= k(BC)$

    • ▨ $= k(CA)$

  Next, dilate $\triangle ABC$ by k, picking any point as the center of dilation.

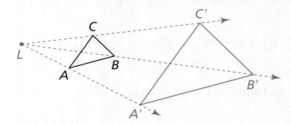

  c. How do the sides of the dilated triangle $\triangle A'B'C'$ compare with the sides of $\triangle PQR$? Justify your answer.

  d. Is it true that $\triangle A'B'C' \cong \triangle PQR$? Which congruence postulate can you use?

  e. Is $\triangle PQR$ congruent to a dilation of $\triangle ABC$? Explain your answer.

For Discussion

10. Using your results from Problem 9, prove the SSS Similarity Theorem.

Exercises *Practicing Habits of Mind*

Check Your Understanding

1. $\triangle JKL$ has $JK = 8$, $KL = 12$, and $LJ = 16$. Points M and N are on $\overline{JK}$ and $\overline{KL}$ respectively, with $JM = 6$ and $LN = 9$.

   a. Explain why $\overline{MN} \parallel \overline{JL}$.

   b. Prove $\triangle MKN \sim \triangle JKL$ in three ways. Use each of the following similarity theorems.

   - AA
   - SAS
   - SSS

2. $\triangle DEF$ is similar to $\triangle ABC$ and has sides that are three times as long. Find the ratios of the lengths of the segments listed below. Name the triangle similarity theorem that allows you to draw your conclusion.

   a. two corresponding altitudes

   b. two corresponding angle bisectors that terminate on the opposite side

   c. two corresponding medians

   Remember that a *median* is a segment that connects a vertex of a triangle to the midpoint of the opposite side. The height of a triangle is the length of the *altitude* drawn from a vertex to a line containing the base.

   For Exercises 3 and 4, decide whether quadrilaterals $ABCD$ and $EFGH$ are similar for the given conditions. Prove what you decide either as a theorem or by finding a counterexample.

3. The angles of one are congruent to the corresponding angles of the other.

4. Three corresponding sides are proportional and two corresponding included angles are congruent.

5. In the figure below, $\overline{DG} \parallel \overline{BC}$ and $\overline{EF} \parallel \overline{BA}$. Prove that $\triangle ABC \sim \triangle FHG$.

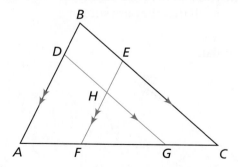

6. **Standardized Test Prep** Suppose $\triangle ABC \sim \triangle FHG$, $AB = 10$ ft, $AC = 20$ ft, $BC = 25$ ft, and $\frac{AB}{FH} = 2.5$. What is FG?

   A. 4 ft **B.** 8 ft **C.** 10 ft **D.** 50 ft

7. The sides of a triangle have lengths 4, 5, and 8. Another triangle similar to it has one side of length 3. What are the lengths of its other two sides? Is more than one answer possible?

8. A triangle has sides of lengths 2, 3, and 4 inches. Another triangle similar to it has a perimeter of 6 inches. What are the side lengths of this triangle?

9. In the figure at the right, $\angle ADE \cong \angle ACB$. Explain why $\triangle ADE \sim \triangle ACB$.

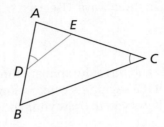

10. In the figure at the right, $AB = 2$ and $BC = 1$. Without making any measurements, find the values of $\frac{AD}{DE}$ and $\frac{AF}{FG}$. Explain how you got your answers.

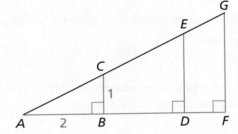

11. Draw a scalene right triangle ABC. Draw the altitude from the right angle to the hypotenuse. The altitude divides $\triangle ABC$ into two smaller right triangles.

a. There are two pairs of congruent angles (other than the right angles) in your picture. Find and label them.

b. Make a copy of your triangle. Then cut out the two smaller right triangles. Position them in such a way as to convince yourself that they are similar to each other and to $\triangle ABC$.

c. Explain why all three of these triangles are similar.

12. In the figure at the right, $AB = 4$, $BC = 5$, $AC = 6$, $DC = 2.5$, and $EC = 3$. Prove that $\triangle ABC \sim \triangle EDC$. Find the length of $\overline{DE}$.

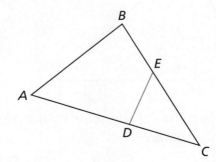

13. Quadrilateral *RATS* is a trapezoid with $\overline{RA} \parallel \overline{ST}$. Diagonals $\overline{RT}$ and $\overline{AS}$ meet at O.

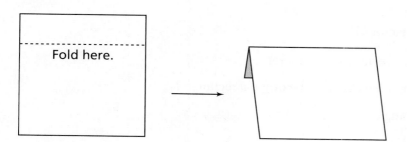

a. Explain why $\triangle ROA \sim \triangle TOS$.

b. From part (a) you can say that $\frac{RO}{TO} = \frac{OA}{OS}$. Explain.

c. Mary Elizabeth knows that $\frac{RO}{TO} = \frac{OA}{OS}$ and $\angle ROS \cong \angle TOA$. She claims that $\triangle ROS \sim \triangle TOA$ by the SAS similarity test. Is this true? Explain.

14. Take It Further Take a square sheet of paper. Fold back one fourth of it. You are left with a rectangle. The challenge is to fold the sheet of paper to form a rectangle that is similar to this one, but has half its area. You may not use a ruler.

Even though you have folded part of the square, you can still unfold it and work with the entire square.

Fold here.

Maintain Your Skills

15. Although similarity for three-dimensional shapes has not been defined here, you can think about what it means to scale a three-dimensional figure. You would make a new figure with sides proportional to the sides of the original figure. For example, scale a rectangular prism 1 cm by 2 cm by 3 cm by the factor 2. You get a new rectangular prism measuring 2 cm by 4 cm by 6 cm.

a. The surface area of the original 1 cm-by-2 cm-by-3 cm rectangular prism is $2 \cdot 1(2) + 2 \cdot 3(2) + 2 \cdot 1(3) = 22$ cm^2. What is its volume?

b. What are the surface area and volume of the scaled copy?

In Exercises 16–18, scale a 1 cm-by-2 cm-by-3 cm rectangular prism by the given factor. What are the dimensions, the surface area, and the volume of the scaled copy?

16. scale factor 3

17. scale factor 4

18. scale factor k

Go Online
www.successnetplus.com

7.16 Areas of Similar Triangles

How do the areas of similar polygons compare? Checking simple polygons, such as rectangles, is a good place to start.

In-Class Experiment

Draw a rectangle. Scale it by the factor 2.

1. How do the dimensions of the original rectangle compare with the dimensions of the scaled rectangle?

2. How many copies of the original rectangle fit into the scaled rectangle?

3. How does the area of the scaled rectangle compare to the area of the original rectangle?

Draw a rectangle. Scale it by the factor $\frac{1}{3}$.

4. How do the dimensions of the two rectangles compare?

5. How many copies of the scaled rectangle fit into the original rectangle?

6. How do the areas of the two rectangles compare?

If two triangles are similar and the scale factor is r, you know that the ratio of the lengths of two corresponding sides is r. Show that the following statements are true.

7. The ratio of their perimeters is r.

8. The ratio of the lengths of two corresponding altitudes is also r.

9. The ratio of their areas is r^2.

Minds in Action

Hannah and Derman complete the In-Class Experiment.

Hannah According to the In-Class Experiment, if you scale a triangle by 4, then 16 copies of the original triangle should fit inside the scaled copy.

Derman That sounds like a lot of triangles. Let's try to draw it out.

Hannah I've got it. Look, here's a small triangle. And here's a picture showing 16 copies of the small triangle inside the triangle that has been scaled by 4.

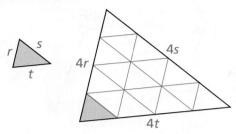

Now that you have calculated the areas of similar rectangles and triangles, take a look at similar polygons with any number of sides.

For You to Do

In the figures below, you scale polygon 1 by the factor r to obtain polygon 2. You divide polygon 1 into four triangles with areas a, b, c, and d.

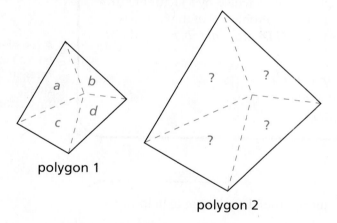

polygon 1

polygon 2

11. What are the areas of the corresponding triangles in polygon 2?

12. What is the total area of polygon 2?

13. What is the total area of polygon 1?

The results of your work lead to the following theorem.

Theorem 7.6

If you scale a polygon by some positive number r, then the ratio of the area of the scaled copy to the area of the original polygon is r^2.

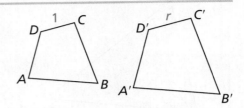

Developing Habits of Mind

Prove a special case. An argument for a special case can suggest how an argument could be made in general. Here's a proof of Theorem 7.6 for a quadrilateral. It suggests how a proof might proceed for any polygon.

Suppose you scale $ABCD$ by r to get $A'B'C'D'$. Pick a point O inside $ABCD$. Connect it to each of the vertices, dividing $ABCD$ into triangles. (There would be four in this case, but in general there would be as many as there are sides.) Let the areas of these triangles be a, b, c, and d. Then

$$\text{area}(ABCD) = a + b + c + d$$

If the image of O is O', then the triangle AOB gets scaled by a factor of r to triangle $A'O'B'$, and so on. So, by the results of Problem 9 of the In-Class Experiment, the area of the triangles in $A'B'C'D'$ are r^2a, r^2b, r^2c, and r^2d. Then

$$\begin{aligned} \text{area}(A'B'C'D') &= r^2a + r^2b + r^2c + r^2d \\ &= r^2(a + b + c + d) \\ &= r^2 \cdot \text{area}(ABCD) \end{aligned}$$

There are some quadrilaterals for which picking an inside point would not necessarily work. For example:

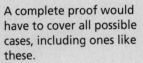

A complete proof would have to cover all possible cases, including ones like these.

For You to Do

14. Draw diagrams to go along with the above proof. Label them to help you understand this proof.

Check Your Understanding

1. One side of a triangle has length 10. The altitude to that side has length 12. If you make a new triangle for which all the sides of the original triangle are tripled, what is the area of the new triangle?

2. Jerry wants to plant two cornfields. One measures 400 ft by 600 ft. The other measures 200 ft by 300 ft. Becky, the owner of the seed-and-grain store, says, "The big field will take eight bags of seed. The small field has sides half as big, so you'll need four more bags for that. Will that be cash or charge?" A few days later, Jerry returns to the store very upset. Explain.

3. **a.** Trace this polygon onto a sheet of paper. Estimate its area in square centimeters.

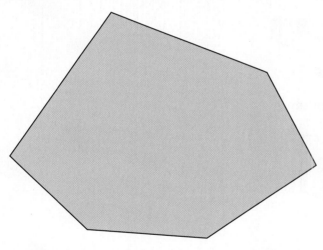

> **Habits of Mind**
>
> **Recall what you know.** Think about figures for which a ruler can help you find area. Can you see such figures in this polygon?

b. If you scale the polygon by the factor 1.5, what will be the area of the scaled copy?

On Your Own

4. The area of one square is 12 times the area of another square. Find the ratio of the lengths of the following.

   a. their sides

   b. their diagonals

5. You scale a rectangle by the factor $\frac{1}{4}$. Compare the area of the scaled rectangle to the area of the original rectangle.

6. You scale a triangle by the factor 5. Compare the area of the scaled triangle to the area of the original triangle.

7. The area of a polygon is 17 square inches. You scale the polygon by the factor 2. What is the area of the new polygon?

8. **Standardized Test Prep** The area of a regular hexagon with 10-cm sides is about 259.8 cm^2. To the nearest square centimeter, what is the area of a regular hexagon with 5-cm sides?

A. 130 cm^2 **B.** 100 cm^2 **C.** 65 cm^2 **D.** 52 cm^2

Maintain Your Skills

In Exercises 9–12, find the volume of each figure. Then apply the given scale factor and find the volume of the new figure.

9. scale factor = 3

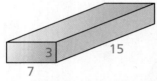

3   15

7

rectangular prism

10. scale factor = 2

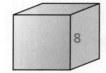

8

11. scale factor = 5

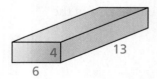

4   13

6

12. scale factor = r

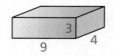

3

9   4

rectangular prism

Go **O**nline
www.successnetplus.com

Mathematical

7D

Reflections

In this investigation, you studied similar figures—figures with congruent corresponding angles and proportional corresponding sides. You used the AA, SAS, and SSS tests to determine whether two triangles are similar. You also used scale factors to find the areas of two similar figures. These questions will help you summarize what you have learned.

1. In the figure at the right, suppose $\overline{CD} \perp \overline{AB}$. How many similar triangles can you find? Prove that all the ones you find are similar. Use the triangle similarity tests.

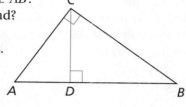

2. In the figure at the right, $\triangle ABC \sim \triangle EDC$. Prove that $\triangle FDA \sim \triangle FBE$.

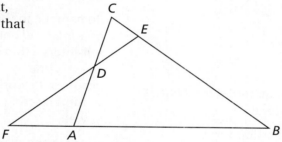

3. In quadrilateral $EFGH$, $\overline{EF} \parallel \overline{HG}$, $\overline{EH} \perp \overline{EF}$, $EF = 6$, $FG = 5$, $GH = 10$, and $EH = 3$.

   a. Find the area of $EFGH$.

   b. Scale $EFGH$ by 3. Call the scaled copy $IJKL$, so that $EFGH \sim IJKL$. Find the area of $IJKL$.

   The two different-sized squares have similar fold patterns. Fold them and you get two origami figures that are similar.

   c. What is the ratio of the areas of $EFGH$ and $IJKL$?

4. What does it mean for two figures to be similar?

5. What are some tests for triangle similarity?

6. If the common ratio of two similar figures is r, what is the ratio of their areas?

Vocabulary and Notation

In this investigation, you learned this term and this symbol. Make sure you understand what each one means and how to use it.

- similar figures
- ~ (is similar to)

Project Using Mathematical Habits

Midpoint Quadrilaterals

Use either pencil and straightedge or geometry software. Draw quadrilateral *ABCD*. Construct the midpoint of each side. Label the midpoints of $\overline{AB}$, $\overline{BC}$, $\overline{CD}$, and $\overline{DA}$ as *E*, *F*, *G*, and *H*, respectively.

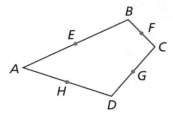

Connect the midpoints to form quadrilateral *EFGH*. Call this the midpoint quadrilateral.

1. Describe the features of your midpoint quadrilateral *EFGH*.

2. Try to classify it as a particular kind of quadrilateral.

- If you are using geometry software, experiment by moving the vertices and sides of *ABCD*.

- If you are working on paper, repeat the experiment with a significantly different starting quadrilateral.

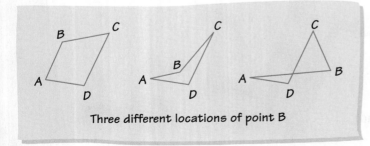

Three different locations of point B

3. Does the midpoint quadrilateral retain its special features?

4. Use the Proportional Side-Splitter Theorem. Prove that each conjecture you have made about a midpoint quadrilateral is correct. Make sure that your proof is valid for each of the three locations of *B* shown in the preceding diagram. It may help to draw the diagonals of each quadrilateral.

Remember, in this book, the term *quadrilateral* does not include self-intersecting quadrilaterals like this one. However, your proof could work for self-intersecting quadrilaterals, as well.

5. Suppose the diagonals of quadrilateral *ABCD* measure 8 inches and 12 inches. What is the perimeter of the midpoint quadrilateral?

Using the Midline Theorem

Juan said that he did not use a side-splitter theorem in his proof for his conjecture about midpoint quadrilaterals. Here is an outline of his proof.

- In quadrilateral *ABCD*, find the midpoints and connect them in order to make the midpoint quadrilateral.

- Draw the diagonal $\overline{AC}$. Two opposite sides of the midpoint quadrilateral are parallel to and half as long as $\overline{AC}$ because of the Midline Theorem. To see this, you just have to look at *ABCD* as two triangles that share a base $\overline{AC}$.

6. Write out Juan's proof. Include a statement of his conjecture, any helpful diagram(s), and a conclusion about the midpoint quadrilateral.

Special Quadrilaterals

Special types of quadrilaterals include

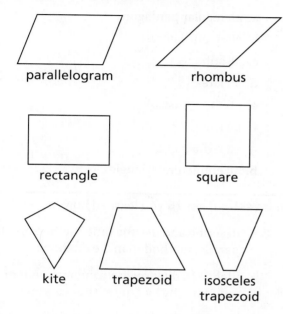

parallelogram   rhombus

rectangle   square

kite   trapezoid   isosceles trapezoid

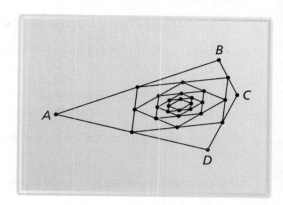

Jessica extended her investigation. She used a diagram like the one below to make a conjecture. She claimed that she could prove her conjecture using the Proportional Side-Splitter Theorem.

7. Does any special type of quadrilateral have a special midpoint quadrilateral (different from what you found in the preceding exercises)? Prove each conjecture you make.

8. If quadrilateral *ABCD* has a square (or rhombus or rectangle) as a midpoint quadrilateral, make a conjecture about *ABCD*. Prove your conjecture. How can you support your conjecture using software?

Extending the Idea

9. Describe a connection between midpoint quadrilaterals and dilations. (*Hint:* A midpoint quadrilateral has, of course, its own midpoint quadrilateral. Think about the sequence of midpoint quadrilaterals for a given figure. One such sequence is shown on the diagram that follows.)

10. a. Describe the points that Jessica connected in her diagram. It may help to redraw the diagram and label some points.

   b. Use the Proportional Side-Splitter Theorem to prove that the inner quadrilateral is a parallelogram.

11. Here is another "inside quadrilateral" that Jessica's diagram suggests. Make a thoughtful conjecture about this quadrilateral. Prove, or at least give some support for, your conjecture.

Review

In **Investigation 7A** you learned how to

- apply a scale factor to make similar figures

- decide whether two figures are well-scaled copies of each other

- use a scale factor to approximate distances in blueprints and maps

The following questions will help you check your understanding.

1. Scale this parallelogram by the factor $\frac{1}{3}$.

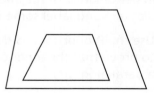

12

45°

6

2. Without measuring, check whether the figures below are scaled copies of each other.

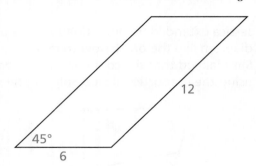

3. Decide whether all members of each collection below must be scaled copies of each other. Explain why they are, or find a counterexample.

   a. all regular pentagons

   b. all quadrilaterals

   c. all spheres

   d. all kites

   e. all rhombuses

   f. all triangles

   g. all right triangles

   h. all equilateral triangles

In **Investigation 7B** you learned how to

- describe and use the ratio method and the parallel method to make dilations

- identify a dilation as an enlargement or reduction by looking at the scale factor

- describe the effect of the choice for center of dilation on the resulting dilation

The following questions will help you check your understanding.

4. Trace the pentagon and point T onto a sheet of paper. Use the ratio method to scale the pentagon by the factor 1.5. Use T as the center of dilation.

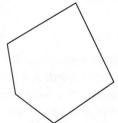

.T

5. Trace *ABCDEF* and point *O* onto a sheet of paper. Use the parallel method to scale the hexagon by the factor $\frac{1}{3}$. Use *O* as the center of dilation.

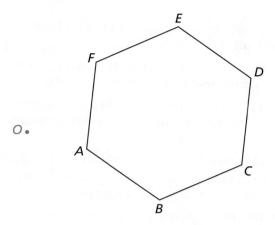

In **Investigation 7C** you learned how to

- decide how lines parallel to a side of a triangle split the other two sides

- understand and prove the side-splitter theorems

- use ratios and proportions.

The following questions will help you check your understanding.

6. In the diagram below, $EB = \frac{1}{3}AB$, $BC = 3BF$, $DA = 2AH$, and $DG = \frac{1}{2}DC$. Prove that *EFGH* is a trapezoid.

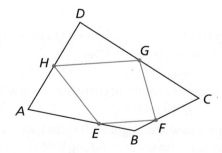

7. $\triangle ABC$ is a right triangle. $AC = 10$, $AD = 4$, $CB = 15$, and $EB = 6$. Prove that $\triangle DEC$ is a scaled copy of $\triangle ABC$.

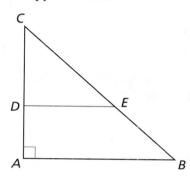

8. Draw a triangle. Label its vertices *A*, *B*, and *C*. Choose point *P* on $\overline{AC}$ such that $\frac{PA}{AC} = \frac{2}{9}$. Then choose point *Q* on $\overline{BC}$ such that $\frac{BQ}{CB} = \frac{6}{27}$. If $AB = 27$, what is *PQ*?

In **Investigation 7D** you learned how to

- identify corresponding parts of similar triangles

- use the AA, SAS, and SSS tests for similarity in triangles

- understand that the ratio between the area of a polygon and the area of a copy of that polygon scaled by the factor *r* must be r^2

The following questions will help you check your understanding.

9. Draw a square and its diagonals. How many similar triangles can you find? Prove that they are similar. Use the triangle similarity tests.

10. You scale an *n*-gon by the factor 7. What is the ratio of the areas of the scaled *n*-gon and the original *n*-gon?

Multiple Choice

1. In this triangle, $\overline{BC} \parallel \overline{DE}$. Also, $AB = DE = 5$, and $BC = 7$. What is DB?

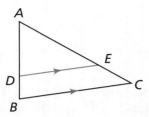

A. $\frac{7}{25}$ B. $\frac{25}{7}$ C. $\frac{10}{7}$ D. 7

2. In the triangle below, $\overline{DE} \parallel \overline{AB}$. Which of the following is true?

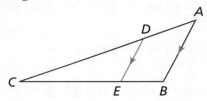

A. $\frac{AD}{BE} = \frac{CE}{AD}$ B. $\frac{AB}{DE} = \frac{BC}{BE}$

C. $\frac{DE}{AB} = \frac{CE}{BC}$ D. $\frac{DE}{CE} = \frac{AC}{BC}$

3. In the figure below, $\angle B \cong \angle E$. Which of the following does NOT allow you to conclude that $\triangle ABC \sim \triangle DEF$?

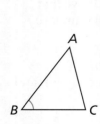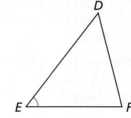

A. $\frac{AB}{DE} = \frac{BC}{EF}$ B. $\angle C \cong \angle F$

C. $\frac{AB}{DE} = \frac{AC}{DF}$ D. $\angle A \cong \angle D$

4. Why can you say that an AAA test for triangle similarity is "too strong?"

A. Only two pairs of congruent angles are needed to prove that two triangles are similar.

B. An AAA test determines whether two triangles are congruent, and congruence is stronger than similarity.

C. Three angles of one triangle can be congruent to three angles of another triangle, but the triangles need not be congruent.

D. You only need one pair of congruent angles to prove that two triangles are similar.

Open Response

5. Copy the figure below onto a sheet of paper. Use the ratio method or the parallel method to scale $\triangle ABC$ by $\frac{1}{4}$.

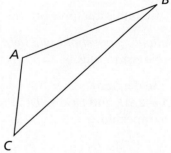

6. Draw a rectangle with sides of 6 cm and 4 cm. This is your original rectangle.

   a. Draw a new rectangle with sides that are 2 cm shorter than the corresponding sides of your original rectangle.

   b. Draw a new rectangle with sides that are $\frac{1}{2}$ as long as the corresponding sides of your original rectangle.

   c. Is either of the rectangles you drew in parts (a) or (b) a scaled copy of the original rectangle? Are they both scaled copies? Explain.

   d. What kind of rectangle must you start with to have the directions in both parts (a) and (b) produce scaled copies of the original rectangle?

7. Given: $SUZI \sim CUHE$. Determine whether each of the following statements is *true* or *not necessarily true*.

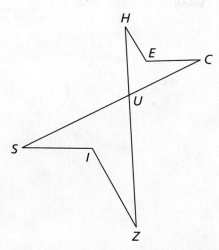

a. $\angle S \cong \angle C$

b. $\dfrac{CU}{SU} = \dfrac{ZU}{HU}$

c. $\angle E \cong \angle C$

d. $\angle CUH \cong \angle SUZ$

e. $\dfrac{HU}{ZU} = \dfrac{CU}{SU}$

f. $\dfrac{CH}{SZ} = \dfrac{CE}{IZ}$

8. Are the triangles in each pair scaled copies of each other? Explain.

a.

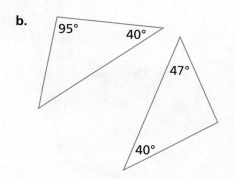

b.

9. Explain how you know that any two squares are similar.

10. Consider the following figure.

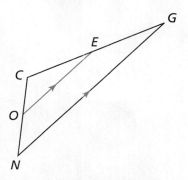

$\overline{OE}$ is parallel to $\overline{NG}$.

a. If $CN = 5$, $CO = 1$, and $CE = 2$, what is CG?

b. If $CG = 7.5$, $CO = 3$, and $CN = 6$, what is CE?

c. If $CE = 3$, and $CG = 12$, what is the value of $\dfrac{CO}{CN}$?

d. If $CO = 1$, and $ON = 4$, what is the value of $\dfrac{OE}{NG}$?

11. Given: $BC = 3 \cdot EC$, and $AC = 3 \cdot CD$

Prove: $\triangle BAC \sim \triangle EDC$

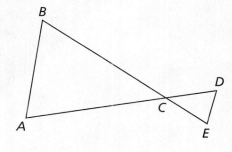

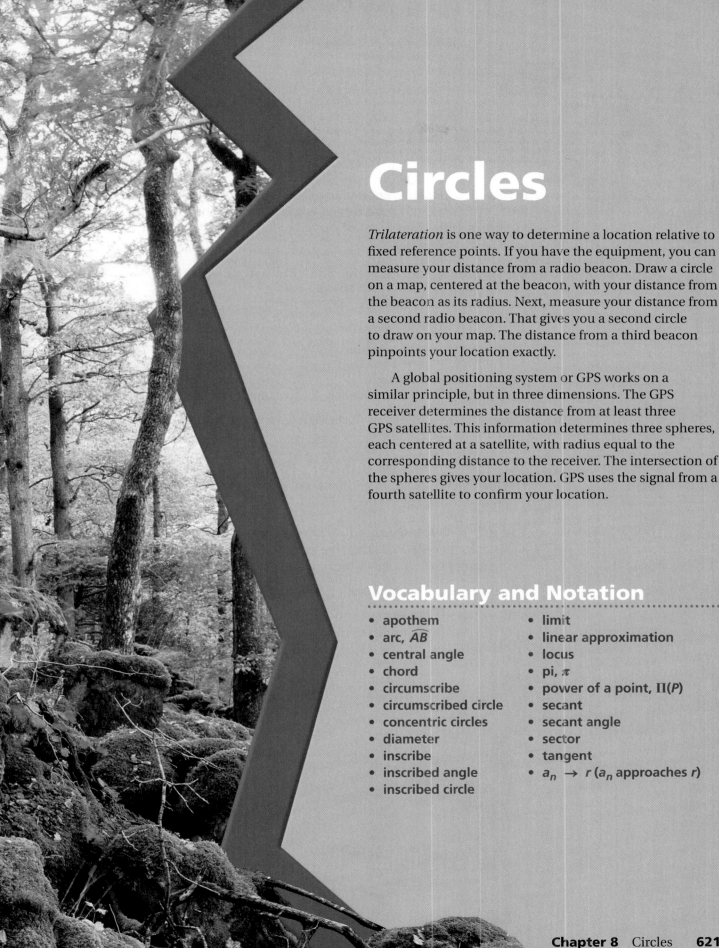

Circles

Trilateration is one way to determine a location relative to fixed reference points. If you have the equipment, you can measure your distance from a radio beacon. Draw a circle on a map, centered at the beacon, with your distance from the beacon as its radius. Next, measure your distance from a second radio beacon. That gives you a second circle to draw on your map. The distance from a third beacon pinpoints your location exactly.

A global positioning system or GPS works on a similar principle, but in three dimensions. The GPS receiver determines the distance from at least three GPS satellites. This information determines three spheres, each centered at a satellite, with radius equal to the corresponding distance to the receiver. The intersection of the spheres gives your location. GPS uses the signal from a fourth satellite to confirm your location.

Vocabulary and Notation

- apothem
- arc, $\overset{\frown}{AB}$
- central angle
- chord
- circumscribe
- circumscribed circle
- concentric circles
- diameter
- inscribe
- inscribed angle
- inscribed circle
- limit
- linear approximation
- locus
- pi, π
- power of a point, $\Pi(P)$
- secant
- secant angle
- sector
- tangent
- $a_n \rightarrow r$ (a_n approaches r)

Area and Circumference

In *Area and Circumference*, you will learn ways to find the areas of figures that have curved edges. You will find areas of figures with other types of curved edges, such as figures formed by spilled paint.

By the end of this investigation, you will be able to answer questions like these.

1. How can you calculate the area of a blob?

2. What is the circumference of a circle?

3. What formula relates the area of a circle to its circumference?

You will learn how to

- approximate areas of closed curves with inner and outer sums

- approximate perimeters of closed curves with linear approximation

- establish that the area of a regular polygon is $\frac{1}{2}$ the perimeter times the apothem

- approximate areas and perimeters of circles with inscribed and circumscribed regular polygons

You will develop these habits and skills:

- Visualize the effect of a finer mesh on area approximation or smaller segments on perimeter approximation.

- Determine the effect of scaling on the area of a figure.

- Relate areas and perimeters of regular polygons with increasing numbers of sides to the area and circumference of a circle.

How would you measure the size of an oil spill?

Triangles and other polygons are convenient geometric shapes to study, but many objects in our world are not composed of line segments. Circles, egg shapes, and curves of all types are as common as polygons. How can you find the area of a shape that has curves?

For You to Explore

One way to find the area of a polygon is to divide it into triangles and then find the area of each triangle. What can you do for a figure that is not a polygon? For example, how can you estimate the area of this blob? Can you find it exactly?

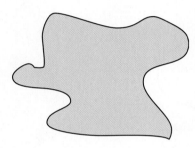

For shapes such as this, the best you can do is estimate the area.

1. List several ways that you can estimate the area of an irregular shape such as the blob above.

2. List several ways that you can estimate the perimeter of an irregular shape such as the blob above.

3. Try each of your methods with the blob or some other shape.

On Your Own

One mathematical habit for estimating a value is to find upper and lower bounds for the value. Then you squeeze those bounds together. Follow the steps in Exercises 4 and 5 to find bounds for the area of the blob.

4. Begin by placing the blob on a piece of graph paper that has $\frac{1}{2}$ in.-by-$\frac{1}{2}$ in. squares.

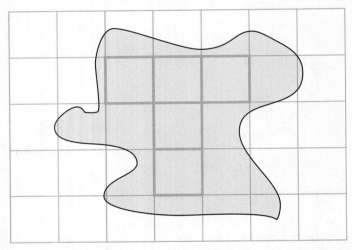

   a. Count the number of squares that are completely inside the figure.

   b. Add the areas of those inner squares to find an area that is definitely less than the area of the blob.

5. Now count all the squares that are either inside the blob or touching it.

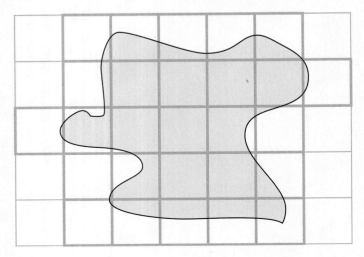

a. How many of these squares are there?

b. Add the areas of these squares to find an area that is definitely greater than the area of the blob.

Maintain Your Skills

6. Trace this square and scale it by a factor of $\frac{1}{2}$.

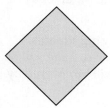

What is the area of the initial square? What is the area of the scaled square?

7. Trace this octagon and scale it by a factor of 2.

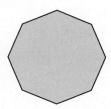

What is the approximate area of the initial octagon? What is the approximate area of the scaled octagon?

8. Trace this parallelogram and scale it by a factor of $\frac{1}{3}$.

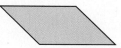

What is the approximate area of the initial parallelogram? What is the approximate area of the scaled parallelogram?

In order to scale these polygons, you should measure their sides. To calculate their areas, either use a formula or think of a way to estimate each area.

Go Online
Video Tutor
www.successnetplus.com

Area and Perimeter

Now you can refine your approach to find the area of an irregular shape, such as the area of the blob in Lesson 8.01.

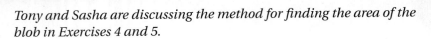

Minds in Action

Tony and Sasha are discussing the method for finding the area of the blob in Exercises 4 and 5.

Tony There's a pretty wide range between the inner and outer areas we found for the blob in these two exercises.

Sasha Well, the grid that the blob is on is made of really big squares. I bet if we put the blob on a grid with smaller squares, there will be less of a range. By doing that, more of the blob will be covered by whole squares.

Tony Let's try this grid. Each square is $\frac{1}{4}$ in. by $\frac{1}{4}$ in. So each square has an area of $\frac{1}{16}$ square inch.

> Mathematicians say that you are making a "finer mesh."

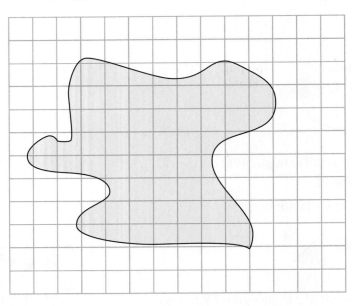

Sasha I'll take it from here. There are 32 squares completely inside the blob. So that's $32 \times \frac{1}{16}$ square inch, or $\frac{32}{16}$ square inches. There are 47 border squares. So that's $(32 + 47) \times \frac{1}{16}$ square inch, or $\frac{79}{16}$ square inches.

Tony Hmm, the area of the blob must be somewhere in between those two numbers.

Sasha That's still not very accurate. We'd better use smaller squares!

For You to Do

In this picture, the squares on the graph paper are $\frac{1}{8}$ in. by $\frac{1}{8}$ in.

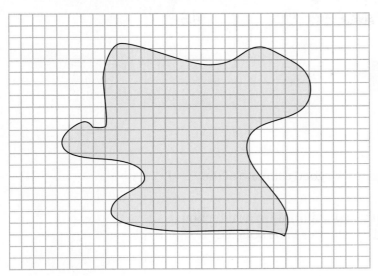

1. **a.** What is the area of each small square?

   b. Calculate the inner sum and the outer sum to place the area of the blob between two numbers.

   c. Are these numbers closer to each other than the numbers Sasha found?

2. Give an argument to support the claim that as the number of squares per inch increases (that is, as the mesh of the graph paper gets finer), the difference between the outer sum and the inner sum decreases.

You now have the basic idea behind how the area of a closed curve (like the blob) is defined. In summary:

- You cover the region with graph paper and compute the inner and outer sums. You make the mesh finer and repeat the process.

- This produces a sequence of inner and outer sums. The difference between these inner and outer sums can be made as small as you want by making the mesh even finer.

- This means the inner and outer sums get closer and closer to a single number. This is the **limit** of the whole process.

- This single number is the area of the region.

You already know a way to compare the areas of two polygons when one is a scaled copy of the other. If a polygon is scaled by some positive number r, then the ratio of the area of the scaled copy to the original is r^2. Is this true for blobs, too?

Imagine that a blob and a grid of squares are drawn onto a big rubber sheet.

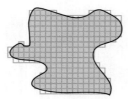

The area of these 228 squares gives a reasonably good estimate of the blob's area.

Now imagine that the rubber sheet is stretched uniformly in all directions by a factor of 2. This causes the blob and the squares to be scaled by 2 as well.

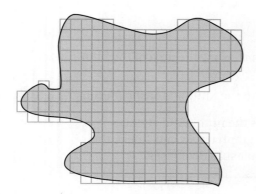

Estimate the area of the blob, now that the squares have been stretched by a factor of 2.

3. By what factor did the area of each square increase?

4. What is a good estimate for the blob's area in terms of the number of squares?

5. If the area of one square before was S, what is it now? What is the area of the 228 stretched squares?

For You to Do

6. What would have happened if you had stretched the rubber sheet uniformly in all directions by a factor of r? Answer the questions from the In-Class Experiment for a rubber sheet stretched by a factor of r.

Archimedes used a **linear approximation** method for estimating the length of a curved path that is easy to apply. Just approximate the curve with line segments and add the lengths of the segments.

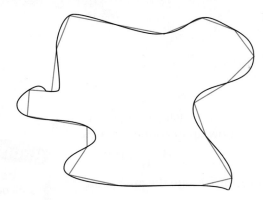

Archimedes was born around 287 B.C. in Syracuse, Sicily, which was a Greek city-state.

For You to Do

7. Approximate the perimeter of the blob above using this linear approximation technique.

For Discussion

8. How can you improve your estimate?

Perimeters of Circles

Of all curves, perhaps the most recognizable is the circle. The name given to the perimeter of a circle is one you already know—the circumference. Circumference is reserved for circles and the round cross sections of three-dimensional shapes such as spheres and cylinders.

The perimeter of a circle can be found through the following process.

- Inscribe a regular polygon in the circle. Circumscribe a regular polygon with the same number of sides around the circle.

- Calculate the perimeter of each polygon.

- Make another pair of inscribed and circumscribed polygons with double the number of sides. Then calculate the perimeters of the new polygons.

- Continue this process. The inner and outer perimeters will approach a common value. That number is the circle's circumference.

To **inscribe** a polygon in a circle means to draw it so that all of its vertices are on the circle. To **circumscribe** a polygon around a circle means to draw it so that all of its sides are touching the circle.

Exercises *Practicing Habits of Mind*

Check Your Understanding

1. Draw a circle of radius one inch and approximate its area using each of the following mesh sizes. Describe any patterns that show up in your estimates.

   a. $\frac{1}{2}$ in. **b.** $\frac{1}{4}$ in. **c.** $\frac{1}{8}$ in. **d.** $\frac{1}{16}$ in.

2. **a.** Explain in words a method you have used to approximate the area of an irregular shape.

   b. Find the area of a right triangle with sides 3 in., 4 in., and 5 in.

   c. Suppose you did not know the area formula for a triangle. Go through the inner and outer sums process for a 3-4-5 triangle to approximate its area. See how close you can get to the actual area.

3. The two crescent moons are scaled copies of each other. What is the ratio of their areas?

├──── 4.5 cm ────┤   ├── 3.5 cm ──┤

4. How do the areas of the two circles compare?

   a. A circle of radius 2 is scaled to a circle of radius 6.

   b. A circle of radius 2 is scaled to a circle of radius 1.

> **Habits of Mind**
>
> **Strategize.** Sometimes a shape has symmetry that allows you to make counting easier with shortcuts. Use shortcuts wherever possible.

In Exercises 5–10, you will practice the process of drawing inscribed and circumscribed polygons for a circle. If you are not able to make the drawings yourself, just copy and complete the table in Exercise 8 by taking measurements directly from the drawings provided.

5. Draw a circle. Inscribe a square in the circle and circumscribe a square around the circle. Calculate the perimeters of the two squares and thus place the circumference of the circle between two numbers.

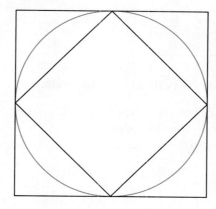

Remember...

Draw means to use either pencil-and-paper drawing tools or geometry software.

6. Using a circle of the same size, inscribe a regular octagon in the circle and circumscribe a regular octagon around the circle. Calculate the perimeter of the two octagons and thus place the circumference of the circle between two numbers.

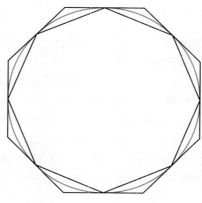

Go Online
www.successnetplus.com

7. Carry this process one step further with inscribed and circumscribed 16-gons.

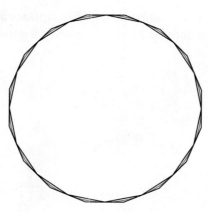

8. Copy the table. Use the data from Exercises 5–7 to complete it.

Number of Sides	Outer Perimeter	Inner Perimeter	Difference
4	▪	▪	▪
8	▪	▪	▪
16	▪	▪	▪

9. Give an approximation for the perimeter of the circle.

10. Explain why the difference between the outer and inner perimeters decreases as the number of sides increases.

On Your Own

11. **a.** Draw a blob.

- Estimate its area using a mesh of $\frac{1}{2}$ in.
- Estimate the same blob's area using a mesh of $\frac{1}{4}$ in.

b. Now draw the blob again, scaled by a factor of 2. Estimate the new blob's area three times. Use a mesh of $\frac{1}{2}$ in., $\frac{1}{4}$ in., and 1 in.

c. Which estimates from part (a) and part (b) are approximately the same?

d. Explain the following claim. You have a good estimate for a blob's area in terms of a number of squares on graph paper. That same number of squares is a good estimate if the graph paper and the blob get stretched by a factor of r.

12. **Take It Further** Imagine that a blob and a grid of squares are drawn onto a big rubber sheet. The area of these 228 squares gives a good estimate of the blob's area.

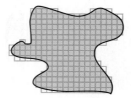

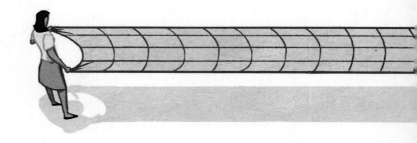

Imagine that the rubber sheet is stretched in just one direction. Now all of the squares have one side length doubled and one unchanged.

a. What shape do the squares become?

b. What is the area of the new shapes compared to the area of the squares?

c. What happens to the area of the blob?

d. Is the blob a scaled copy of the original? If your answer is yes, what is the scale factor? If your answer is no, explain why not.

Sasha has a way to make the linear approximation technique easier. She uses what she calls a regular approximation for a curve. She picks some length, say $\frac{1}{4}$ in., and marks it off around the curve until she gets too close to the starting point to mark another segment. Then she just multiplies the number of segments by $\frac{1}{4}$ and adds on the last little gap.

13. Use Sasha's regular approximation method to estimate the length of the curve below.

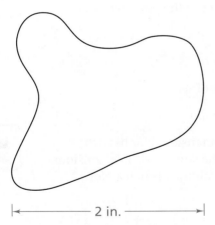

|←———— 2 in. ————→|

14. Many people use Sasha's regular approximation to estimate distance on road maps.

a. Explain how this works.

b. Use a road map and regular approximation to estimate the distance between your hometown and a city many states away.

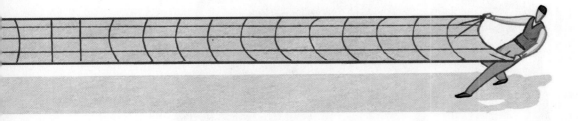

15. Standardized Test Prep The circle has a square circumscribed around it. It has another square inscribed inside it. What is the ratio of the perimeter of the circumscribed square to the perimeter of the inscribed square?

A. $\sqrt{2}$ **B.** 2

C. $2\sqrt{2}$ **D.** 4

Maintain Your Skills

For Exercises 16–19, answer parts (a), (b), and (c).

a. What is the new side length of the cube?

b. What was the area of a face on the original cube? What is the new area of a face?

c. What was the volume of the original cube? What is the new volume?

16. A cube with side length 1 cm is scaled by a factor of 2.

17. A cube with side length 1 cm is scaled by a factor of 3.

18. A cube with side length 1 cm is scaled by a factor of $\frac{1}{2}$.

19. A cube with side length 1 cm is scaled by a factor of r.

20. You learned how to approximate the area of 2-dimensional blobs with squares. In a similar way, you can approximate the volume of 3-dimensional blobs with cubes. Write a rule that tells how the volume of such a blob changes when it is scaled by a factor of r.

Go Online
www.successnetplus.com

How can volume help you guess the number of pennies that would fill the jar?

8.03 Connecting Area, Circumference

In Lesson 8.02, you approximated the circumference of a circle with inscribed and circumscribed polygons. Now the idea is to find a formula that connects the area of a circle to its circumference. First you must learn about the *apothem* of a regular polygon.

Definition

The **apothem** *a* of a regular polygon is the length of the perpendicular segment from the center point of the polygon to one of its sides.

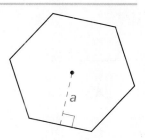

In-Class Experiment

In this experiment, you will find a formula for the areas of regular polygons.

1. Look at the regular pentagon and divide it into five congruent triangles meeting at the center. What role does the apothem *a* of the pentagon play for each of these triangles?

2. If *s* is the length of each side of the pentagon, what is the area of each congruent triangle? What is the area of the whole pentagon?

3. What would change if the regular polygon had four sides, six sides, or *n* sides? Can you find the polygon's perimeter somewhere in the formula for its area?

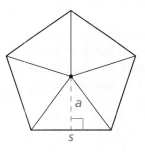

8.03   Connecting Area, Circumference   **635**

The result of the In-Class Experiment is important enough to record as a theorem.

Theorem 8.1

The area A of a regular polygon is equal to half of the product of its perimeter P and its apothem a.

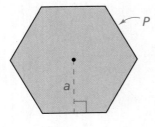

$$A = \tfrac{1}{2} Pa$$

For You to Do

4. Use the area formula $A = \frac{1}{2}Pa$ to calculate the area of a square with side length 12. Check your result by calculating the area of the square another way.

For Discussion

5. Below are three regular polygons, each inscribed in a circle with radius r. The number of sides in each polygon increases from 4 to 8 to 16. Imagine that these pictures continue for a sequence of regular polygons with more and more sides inscribed in this same circle.

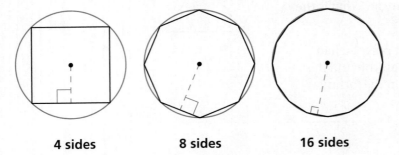

| 4 sides | 8 sides | 16 sides |

Think about how the length of each polygon's apothem changes as you draw polygons with more and more sides. Compare each polygon's perimeter and area with the circumference and area of the circle each is inscribed in.

Habits of Mind

Detect the key characteristics. As the number of sides in each polygon increases, it becomes very difficult to distinguish the polygon from the circle and an apothem from a radius.

Minds in Action

Tony and Sasha look at Theorem 8.1.

Sasha   Tony, do you think we could find a similar formula relating the area of a circle to its perimeter?

Tony   Well, I know that circumference is a circle's perimeter. How does the apothem *a* for different shapes compare to the radius *r*?

Sasha   The apothem is the distance from the center of a regular polygon to any of its sides. And as the number of sides increases, a regular polygon starts to look like a circle. The equivalent of the apothem in a circle has to be the radius.

Tony   Ah . . . now I get it! So the formula for the area of a circle should be something like one half the circumference times the radius.

Sasha   I think we can basically prove that by approximating circles with polygons. We could inscribe a sequence of regular polygons in a circle and study their areas. Let's try . . .

Facts and Notation

To make this more precise, use the following notation.

- **Let *A*, *C*, and *r* be the area, circumference, and radius of the circle.**

- **Number the polygons in the sequence 1, 2, 3, ...**

- **Let the areas of the polygons be A_1, A_2, A_3, . . . ; let their perimeters be P_1, P_2, P_3, . . . ; and let their apothems be a_1, a_2, a_3, ...**

Instead of saying that the length of the apothem approaches the radius as *n* gets larger and larger, write $a_n \to r$. Using this shorthand notation, rewrite the assumptions as follows.

1. $a_n \to r$ **2.** $P_n \to C$ **3.** $A_n \to A$

Here is the formula for the area of the *n*th regular polygon in the sequence.

$$A_n = \tfrac{1}{2} P_n a_n$$

Now, because of the three assumptions, as *n* gets larger and larger, you can rewrite the formula.

$$\tfrac{1}{2} P_n a_n \to \tfrac{1}{2} Cr$$

You can conclude the following.

$$A_n \to A$$

This arrow notation means something quite precise in calculus. It means that you can make the difference between the length of the apothem and the radius as small as you want by increasing the number of polygon sides enough.

You can think of it this way.

$$A_n = \tfrac{1}{2} P_n \, a_n$$
$$\downarrow \qquad \downarrow \ \downarrow$$
$$A = \tfrac{1}{2} C \quad r$$

This argument leads to the following theorem.

Theorem 8.2

The area of a circle is one half its
circumference times its radius.

$$A = \tfrac{1}{2} Cr$$

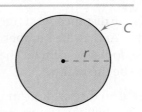

To make this proof completely rigorous, you would need to fill in several
gaps about limits and be more precise about the definitions of area and
circumference. For now, an intuitive understanding is sufficient.

For a precise proof of
this theorem, you will
have to wait until you
study calculus.

For You to Do

6. A flying disc has an approximate area of 154 in.^{2} and a diameter of 14 in.
Find its circumference to the nearest inch.

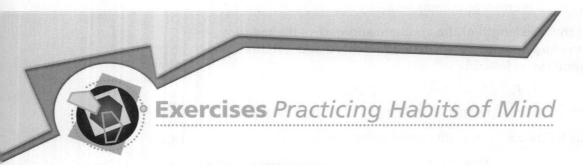

Exercises Practicing Habits of Mind

Check Your Understanding

1. A circular garden has a radius of 1 meter and a circumference of about
6.25 meters. What is the area of the garden?

2. A square with side 2 cm is inscribed in a circle.

   a. Find the radius of this circle.

   b. The circumference of the circle is about
   8.9 cm. What is its area?

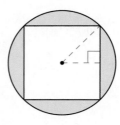

3. Why is a regular hexagon's side the same length as the radius of its circumscribed circle? Explain your answer with a proof.

On Your Own

4. Find the area of each figure.

a. A stop sign has sides that are 6 inches long and an apothem that is 7.2 inches.

b. In the figure, an equilateral triangle is inscribed in a circle of radius 2 cm. The center of the circle that circumscribes a triangle is the triangle's circumcenter. The circumcenter of an equilateral triangle divides each of the triangle's medians into two segments. One is twice as long as the other. This should give you enough information to find the side length of the equilateral triangle using the shaded triangle in the figure.

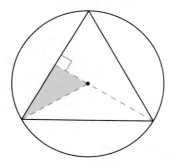

5. Can you use the formula $A = \frac{1}{2}Pa$ for irregular polygons? Explain.

6. A wheel of a toy car has an area of 5 cm^2 and a radius of about 1.26 cm. There is a mark on the point of the wheel that touches the floor. You start pushing the car forward and the marked point does not touch the floor any more. What is the shortest distance you have to push the car for the mark to touch the floor again?

7. **Standardized Test Prep** Beth wants to find the area she can enclose with 264 mm of string. She makes a circle so that the ends of the string touch. The circle has a radius of about 42 mm. What is its approximate area?

A. 1764 mm^2 **B.** 3353 mm^2 **C.** 5544 mm^2 **D.** 11,088 mm^2

8. **Take It Further** The Moriarity sisters have to move the shed in their backyard. They jack up the shed and slip two pipes under it, each with a circumference of 8 inches. The sisters get the pipes to roll three revolutions. How far do the sisters move the shed?

9. **Take It Further** A regular polygon with n sides and side length s is inscribed in a circle of radius 1. Show that a regular polygon with $2n$ sides inscribed in the same circle has side length $\sqrt{2 - \sqrt{4 - s^2}}$.

Maintain Your Skills

10. J is the midpoint of side $\overline{NM}$ of an equilateral triangle inscribed in a circle. A regular hexagon is also inscribed in the circle. $\overline{OH}$ is an apothem of the triangle, and $\overline{OK}$ is an apothem of the hexagon.

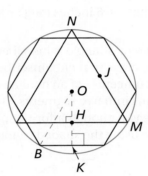

   a. Trace the figure onto a sheet of paper. Draw the radius $\overline{NO}$ and the segment $\overline{OJ}$.

   b. Find the degree measure for each of the following angles.

   - $\angle BKO$
   - $\angle JON$
   - $\angle KOB$
   - $\angle ONJ$
   - $\angle OBK$
   - $\angle NJO$

   c. Now consider $\triangle BKO$ and $\triangle OJN$. Prove that they are congruent.

   d. Now show that $\overline{OK}$ and $\overline{NJ}$ are congruent.

   e. Compare the hexagon's apothem with the triangle's side. Explain your conclusion.

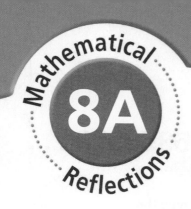

In this investigation, you explored ways to find the perimeters and areas of shapes with curved edges. These questions will help you summarize what you have learned.

1. Describe a technique you learned in this investigation for approximating the perimeter of a curve. Use the method you described to approximate the perimeter of the curve at the right.

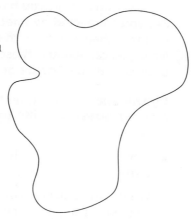

2. Bill spilled paint and left the blob at the right. Describe how you would use the grid method to estimate the area of Bill's mess.

3. What is the area of a regular octagon with apothem 15 in. and side length 12.4 in.?

4. What is the area of a regular hexagon with side length 3 cm?

5. What is the approximate area of a circular pool with an approximate circumference of 12.6 ft and radius 2 ft?

Is there a relationship between the length of the boom surrounding the oil and the area of the oil spill?

6. How can you calculate the area of a blob?

7. What is the circumference of a circle?

8. What formula relates the area of a circle to its circumference?

Vocabulary and Notation

In this investigation, you learned these terms and this symbol. Make sure you understand what each one means and how to use it.

- **apothem**
- **circumscribe**
- **inscribe**
- **limit**
- **linear approximation**
- $a_n \rightarrow r$ (**a_n approaches r**)

Circles and 3.14159265358979 . . .

In *Circles and 3.14159265358979 . . .* , you will examine the circle formulas that you have known for years. In Investigation 8A, you connected perimeter and area for inscribed and circumscribed polygons to circumference and area for circles. Now you can expand these concepts and develop a deeper understanding of circles and the role of π.

By the end of this investigation, you will be able to answer questions like these.

1. What is π?

2. How can you express the area and the circumference of a circle in terms of π?

3. What is the exact area of the shaded portion of the circle with center O?

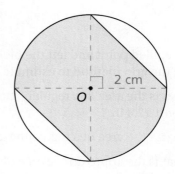

2 cm

O

You will learn how to

- use the definition of π as the area of the unit circle

- develop and use the formula $A = \pi r^2$

- develop and use the formula $C = 2\pi r$

You will develop these habits and skills:

- Realize that any decimal or fractional representation of π is only an approximation.

- Apply the area formula for circles to find areas of composite shapes.

- Relate and use different definitions of π.

What questions could you ask about these crop circles?

You have already learned quite a bit about circles in this chapter. It is time to pull together some ideas.

For You to Explore

All circles are similar. This means that all circles have the same shape, but not necessarily the same size.

1. Two circles have radii 12 cm and 30 cm. Can one of them be scaled to give a congruent copy of the other? Explain.

2. Two circles have radii r and R. Can one of them be scaled to give a congruent copy of the other? Explain.

3. a. Use a ruler and compass or geometry software to copy and complete this table. All the polygons are regular.

Number of Sides	$\dfrac{\text{Perimeter}}{\text{Apothem}}$
4	▦
6	▦
8	▦
16	▦

b. Continue the table for larger numbers of sides.

c. Do the ratios seem to approach any particular number?

> **Habits of Mind**
>
> **Visualize.** Why do you think all circles are similar?

Exercises Practicing Habits of Mind

On Your Own

4. This figure is made up of a quarter circle with radius 1 cm and two equilateral triangles. If the circumference of the whole circle is 6.28 cm, what is the perimeter of the whole shape?

5. A circle's area is about 25.1 square centimeters. A square is inscribed in the circle. Its apothem is 2 cm. What is the total area of the shaded region shown in the figure?

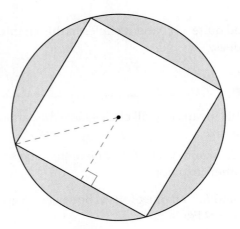

Maintain Your Skills

6. Look at the circles below.

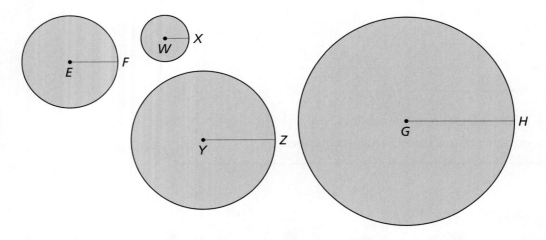

a. Estimate the area A of each circle using any method.

b. Use a ruler to measure each circle's radius r. Then copy and complete the following table.

Circle With Radius	A	$\frac{A}{r^2}$	C	$2r$	$\frac{C}{2r}$
$\overline{EF}$	■	■	■	■	■
$\overline{WX}$	■	■	■	■	■
$\overline{YZ}$	■	■	■	■	■
$\overline{GH}$	■	■	■	■	■

Habits of Mind

Look for relationships. You might want to look at your answer to Problem 3 in this lesson and see if there are any similarities.

c. Compare the data in the columns of the table and look for invariants.

8.05 An Area Formula for Circles

How does the area of a circle change when the circle is scaled? Since you know you can approximate a circle's area with a sequence of regular *n*-gons, you can scale all of the polygons by *s* to approximate the area of the scaled circle. The polygons' areas would all change by a factor of s^2, so it seems plausible that the circle's area would, too.

Below is a theorem that summarizes this.

Theorem 8.3

If a circle is scaled by a positive number *s*, then its area is scaled by s^2.

For You to Do

In Exercise 1 in Lesson 8.02, you approximated the area of a circle with radius one inch to be a bit more than three square inches. Use that result and the theorem above to find a good approximation for the area of a circle with each radius.

1. 2 inches

2. 5 inches

3. 6 inches

4. $\sqrt{3}$ inches

5. $7\frac{1}{2}$ inches

Theorem 8.4

If the area of a circle with radius 1 is *k*, then the area of a circle with radius *r* is kr^2.

This theorem says that you can find the area of any circle once you know the area of a circle with radius 1. As you have calculated, the value of that area is a bit more than 3. Rather than call it *k*, most people call it *pi* and represent it with the Greek letter π.

Definition

Pi (π) is the numerical value of the area of a circle with radius 1.

Therefore, thanks to Theorem 8.4, there is a formula you can use for calculating the area of a circle when you know only its radius.

Theorem 8.5

The area of a circle of radius *r* is π times the radius squared.

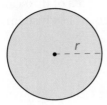

$$A = \pi r^2$$

If you ask a person to tell you the value of π, you might hear 3.14 or $\frac{22}{7}$. While these are indeed approximations of π, neither is equal to π. In fact, π cannot be represented as a ratio of two whole numbers because π is not a rational number. Since π is irrational, its decimal representation is infinite and nonrepeating.

> π is usually defined as the ratio of the circumference of a circle to its diameter.

Often, people leave the result of calculations about circles in terms of π. That way, if you want a numerical approximation of the result, you can use whatever approximation for π you prefer.

For Discussion

6. Tony is puzzled. He asks himself, "What do they mean π is the area of a circle of radius 1? One what? If you have a circle of radius 1 foot, it can't have the same area as a circle whose radius is 1 inch. This is all nonsense." Suggest an answer to Tony's question.

Exercises Practicing Habits of Mind

Check Your Understanding

1. Find the area of a circle with the given dimension.

    a. a radius of 10 in.   **b.** a radius of 5 cm   **c.** a diameter of 3 ft

    d. the circle obtained by scaling a circle of radius 2 in. by a factor of 5

2. The angle of the wedge in the circle is 45°. The radius of the circle is 1.

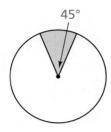

45°

This wedge is really called a **sector** of the circle, which is a region bound by two radii and the circle.

   a. What fraction of the circle's area is the wedge?

   b. What is the exact area of the circle?

   c. What is the exact area of the wedge?

   d. Use two common approximations for π to find the area of the wedge.

3. Find the area of each shaded region.

a.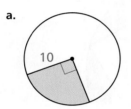

10

b.

12

On Your Own

4. Find the area of each shaded region.

a.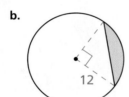

60°   5

b.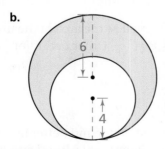

6

4

5. An equilateral triangle with sides of length 6.9 cm is inscribed in a circle.

   a. Find the length of the apothem and draw a sketch.

   b. Find the area of the circle.

   c. Shade the part of the circle that is outside the triangle. Find that area.

Go **nline**
Video Tutor
www.successnetplus.com

6. Suppose the side length of each square is 6 cm. Find the area of each shaded region and each white region.

a.
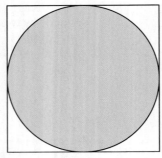

b.
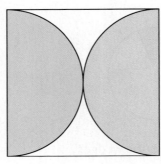

c. Compare your answers for parts (a) and (b) above. What do you notice? Explain.

7. The square at the right is inscribed in a circle. The square's apothem is 2 cm. What is the total area of the shaded region?

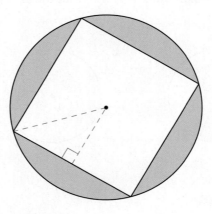

8. Standardized Test Prep For Zach's birthday, his grandmother makes an extra large cheesecake. She usually uses a pan that has a 7-inch diameter. This time she uses a pan with a 14-inch diameter. She usually serves wedges that are $\frac{1}{12}$ of the cake. This time Zach asks for a wedge with an angle twice the usual size. How many times greater than normal is the area of Zach's birthday serving?

A. 2 times   **B.** 4 times   **C.** 6 times   **D.** 8 times

9. Take It Further In this lesson, π is defined as the area of the unit circle. In a note, another definition given is $\pi = \frac{C}{d}$. Other definitions of π could be as follows.

a. $\pi = \dfrac{A}{r^2}$

b. $\pi = \dfrac{C}{2r}$

c. π is the number you can approximate better and better by calculating the ratio $\frac{P}{2a}$ for regular polygons with perimeter P and apothem a that have more and more sides.

d. π is half the circumference of the unit circle.

e. π is the circumference of the circle with a unit diameter.

Choose at least two of these definitions of π and prove that they are equivalent to one of the two definitions given in this lesson.

Maintain Your Skills

10. The following figures are unit circles with a shaded sector. Find the area of each sector.

a.

10°

b.

20°

c.

30°

d.

40°

e.

50°

f.

60°

Go Online
www.successnetplus.com

g. When the angle grows by 10°, how does the area of the sector change?

Historical Perspective
Representations of π

The number π has intrigued people for centuries. The number π is not the ratio of two integers, but there are many ways to represent it. Here are a few. The numbers given in parentheses represent the years in which the equations were discovered.

(1655, Wallis) $\quad \dfrac{\pi}{2} = \dfrac{2 \cdot 2}{1 \cdot 3} \cdot \dfrac{4 \cdot 4}{3 \cdot 5} \cdot \dfrac{6 \cdot 6}{5 \cdot 7} \cdots$

(1593, Viète) $\quad \dfrac{2}{\pi} = \sqrt{\dfrac{1}{2}} \cdot \sqrt{\dfrac{1}{2} + \dfrac{1}{2}\sqrt{\dfrac{1}{2}}} \cdot \sqrt{\dfrac{1}{2} + \dfrac{1}{2}\sqrt{\dfrac{1}{2} + \dfrac{1}{2}\sqrt{\dfrac{1}{2}}}} \cdots$

(1748, Euler) $\quad \dfrac{\pi^2}{6} = 1 + \dfrac{1}{4} + \dfrac{1}{9} + \dfrac{1}{16} + \dfrac{1}{25} + \cdots$

(1914, Ramanujan)

$\dfrac{1}{\pi} = \dfrac{5}{2^4} + \dfrac{47}{2^{13}} + \dfrac{3^3 \cdot 89}{2^{25}} + \dfrac{5^3 \cdot 131}{2^{34}} + \cdots + \left(\dbinom{2n}{n}\right)^3 \dfrac{42n + 5}{2^{12n+4}} + \cdots$

The notation $\dbinom{n}{k}$ stands for the kth entry in the nth row of Pascal's Triangle. For example, $\dbinom{4}{3} = \dfrac{4!}{(4-3)! \cdot 3!} = \dfrac{4 \cdot 3 \cdot 2 \cdot 1}{1 \cdot 3 \cdot 2 \cdot 1} = 4$.

8.06 Circumference

You can use Theorem 8.2 to express the circumference of a circle in terms of its radius. Suppose a circle has radius r, circumference C, and area A. You know the following two formulas, so you just need to do some algebra.

$$A = \tfrac{1}{2}\,Cr \qquad A = \pi r^2$$

For Discussion

1. Combine the two equations above and write a formula for C (the circumference) in terms of r (the radius).

Your answer is very important and you should remember it as a theorem.

Theorem 8.6

The circumference of a circle of radius r is 2π times the radius.

$$C = 2\pi r$$

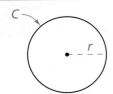

For You to Do

2. The circumference of a circle is approximately how many times its radius?

   A. five   **B.** six   **C.** seven

3. The circumference of a circle is approximately how many times its diameter?

   A. three   **B.** four   **C.** five

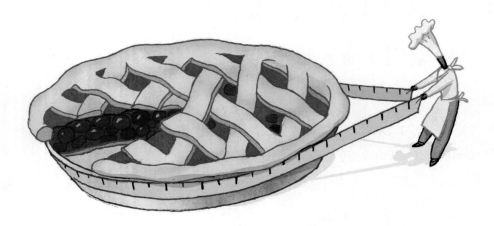

Exercises Practicing Habits of Mind

Check Your Understanding

For Exercises 1–3, you are given a circle of radius 2 cm. Draw a sector of the given size. The sector determines two arcs on the circle. How long is each arc in centimeters?

> An *arc* is the set of points on a circle that lie on the round edge of a sector.

1. 60°

2. 30°

3. 45°

4. True or false: The ratio of a circle's circumference to its diameter is the same for all circles. Explain your answer.

On Your Own

5. The table gives one piece of information about four different circles. Copy the table and find the missing parts for each circle.

Radius	Diameter	Area	Circumference
3	▪	▪	▪
▪	3	▪	▪
▪	▪	3	▪
▪	▪	▪	3

6. A canister contains three tennis balls each with a diameter of 2.5 in. Which distance do you think is greater, the height of the canister or the circumference of the canister? Guess the answer and then do the calculations to see if your guess is correct.

> **Habits of Mind**
>
> **Experiment.** Find a tennis ball canister and check this out!

7. Good'n Yummy Spaghetti Company makes canned spaghetti. The cans measure 5 in. high and 3 in. in diameter. What size piece of paper does the company need to make a label for the outside of its can?

8. **Standardized Test Prep** The rotating globe Eartha in Yarmouth, Maine, is 12.535 meters in diameter. Imagine there is a satellite orbiting one meter above Eartha's equator. How much longer than Eartha's circumference would the path of this satellite be?

A. 1 meter

B. 3.142 meters

C. 6.283 meters

D. 12.535 meters

9. **Take It Further** A speedometer company makes electronic speedometers for bicycles. The device consists of a small magnet on a spoke and a sensor on the fork of the same wheel. The magnet sends a signal every time the wheel makes one revolution. When you install one on your bike, you need to know how far the wheel travels in one revolution. The instructions say to use the rollout method: Put a chalk mark on the tire where it touches the ground (and mark the ground, too). Then roll the bike until the mark comes back to the ground and measure the distance between the chalk marks. What is an easier way to find the distance for one revolution? Try both methods with a bike.

Maintain Your Skills

10. The Bernoulli sisters claim to have a way to calculate π. They calculate two sequences of numbers, n and s_n, and then find $\frac{ns_n}{2}$.

n	s_n	$\frac{ns_n}{2}$
6	1	3
12	0.51763809	3.105828541
24	■	■
48	■	■

Each n is twice the one above it. Each s_n is computed from the previous one with the following steps.

a. Square the previous s_n.   b. Subtract the result from 4.

c. Take the square root of the result from part (b).

d. Subtract the result from part (c) from 2.

e. Take the square root of the result from part (d).

You can represent steps (a)–(e) with this formula.

$$s_n = \sqrt{2 - \sqrt{4 - \left(s_{\frac{n}{2}}\right)^2}}$$

Copy the Bernoulli table. Use a calculator to complete it. See whether $\frac{ns_n}{2}$ gets close to π as n increases. The formula below is from Exercise 9 in Lesson 8.03. How is it related to the formula for s_n above?

$$\sqrt{2 - \sqrt{4 - s^2}}$$

11. **Take It Further** Explain why the steps described in the previous exercise work. Why does $\frac{ns_n}{2}$ get closer to π as n increases?

Marc Umile set an American record in 2007 by listing 12,887 digits of pi from memory.

Historical Perspective
Pieces of π

The number π has intrigued people for centuries. Below are a few interesting facts and an experiment you can try.

- Around 2000 B.C., the Egyptians knew π to nearly 2 decimal places and used the number $3\frac{13}{81}$.

- Around 200 B.C., Archimedes found π to be between $3\frac{10}{71}$ and $3\frac{1}{7}$ (about 3.14). To obtain these values, Archimedes calculated the perimeters of polygons with $6\cdot2^n$ sides inscribed and circumscribed about a circle of diameter 1. This is known as the method of exhaustion.

- In the 1500s, Ludolph van Ceulen calculated π to 35 decimal places and had the result carved on his tombstone. To this day, Germans still refer to π as *die Ludolphsche Zahl* (the Ludolphine number).

- In 1991, David and Gregory Chudnovsky calculated π to more than 2,260,821,336 decimal places. To perform the calculation, the brothers built a supercomputer assembled from mail-order parts and placed it in what used to be the living room of Gregory's apartment.

- Ten decimal places of π would be enough to calculate the circumference of Earth to within a fraction of an inch if Earth were a smooth sphere.

- Do an experiment, either with a computer or by polling people in the halls of your school or at lunch. Get many pairs of whole numbers, chosen at random. If you can, get 1000 such pairs. Count the number of pairs that have no common factor (such as (5, 8) or (9, 16)). Then take this number and divide it by the total number of pairs. Your answer should be close to $\frac{6}{\pi^2} \approx 0.6079$.

Arc Length

Earlier in this investigation, you learned that all circles are similar. Here is a quick proof. If a circle is dilated with center of dilation at the center of the circle, the new shape is still a circle. Two figures are similar if one is congruent to a dilation of the other. So, any two circles are similar because you can dilate the first circle so the radius of the image equals the radius of the second circle.

When two shapes are similar, any lengths in one shape have the same ratio as corresponding lengths in the other shape. In this lesson, you will focus on the lengths of *arcs* in circles and the relationship to their circles' radii. This relationship also leads to a new way to measure angles called *radian measure*.

For You to Do

For each circle O, do the following:

- Find L, the length of $\overarc{AB}$.
- Calculate the exact value of $\frac{L}{r}$, where r is the radius of the circle.

1.

2.

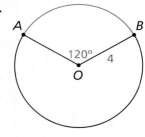

3.

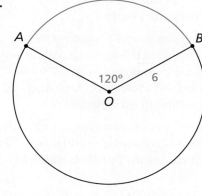

> Unless otherwise stated, *arc AB* refers to the shorter of the two possible arcs from *A* to *B*. The two arcs are called the *minor arc* and *major arc*, and the shorter arc is the minor arc. Arc *AB* can also be written as $\overarc{AB}$.

For Discussion

4. What do you notice about the value of $\frac{L}{r}$?

5. What is the value of $\frac{L}{r}$ when the arc is the entire 360° of the circle?

Developing Habits of Mind

Look for invariants. The ratio $\frac{L}{r}$ seems to be invariant for circles of any radius, as long as the central angle is 120°. Any lengths in one shape have the same ratio as the same lengths in another similar shape.

You can show that the ratio $\frac{L}{r}$ depends only on the central angle θ. First write an expression for the arc length L. Notice that L is some fraction of the circle's circumference C. That fraction is equal to the fraction of the entire circle's angle measure, 360°, that is taken up by the central angle θ. You can express this relationship using the equation below.

$$L = C \cdot \frac{\theta}{360}$$

Because $C = 2\pi r$, this equation can be rewritten as follows.

$$L = 2\pi r \cdot \frac{\theta}{360}$$

If you divide each side of the equation above by r, you obtain an equation for $\frac{L}{r}$.

$$\frac{L}{r} = 2\pi \cdot \frac{\theta}{360}$$

The only variable on the right side of the last equation is θ. This shows that the ratio $\frac{L}{r}$ depends only on the central angle, and not on the circle's radius or circumference. For example, when $\theta = 120°$ (as in the *For You to Do* on page 654), you get the following value for $\frac{L}{r}$.

$$\frac{L}{r} = 2\pi \cdot \frac{120}{360} = 2\pi \cdot \frac{1}{3} = \frac{2\pi}{3}$$

> A *central angle* is an angle whose vertex is the center of the circle.

Example 1

Problem For each circle M, the radius and arc length are given. Find the
measure of each central angle in degrees.

a.

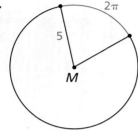

b.

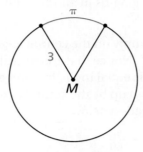

Solution Here are two different ways to solve these types of problems.

a. A circle of radius 5 has circumference 10π. The given arc length is 2π,
which is one fifth of the circumference. The measure on the central angle
is one fifth of 360°, which is **72°**.

b. Use the relationship $\frac{L}{r} = 2\pi \cdot \frac{\theta}{360}$. The values of L and r are known.

$$\frac{\pi}{3} = 2\pi \cdot \frac{\theta}{360}$$

$$\frac{1}{3} = 2 \cdot \frac{\theta}{360}$$

$$\frac{1}{6} = \frac{\theta}{360}$$

By solving the proportion, the measure of the central angle is **60°**.

> What number is one sixth of 360?

It is possible to determine any central angle using the ratio of arc length
to radius. For example, when the ratio is $\frac{2\pi}{3}$, the measure of the central
angle is one third of the circle, and when the ratio is $\frac{2\pi}{5}$, the measure of the
central angle is one fifth of the circle.

Angles are usually measured in degrees, where 360° is the measure of a full circle. There are other ways to measure angles. The ratio of arc length to radius defines a measure of angle called the **radian**.

Definition (radian)

The measure in *radians* of a central angle of a circle is the ratio $\frac{L}{r}$ of the intercepted arc length L to the circle's radius r.

Alternately, the angle in radians is the arc length in a circle of radius 1, using the special case $r = 1$.

> Why are there 360 degrees in a circle? The degree is defined this way. No one knows the exact origin, but the Babylonians used a base-60 number system that could have led to 60 degrees in each angle of an equilateral triangle.

Example 2

Problem The circles and central angles from Example 1 are shown below. Find the measure of each central angle in radians.

a.

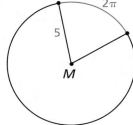

b.

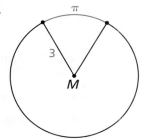

Solution

a. The angle measure in radians is given by the ratio $\frac{L}{r}$. Here, $L = 2\pi$ and $r = 5$, so the angle measure in radians is $\frac{2\pi}{5}$. The angle has not changed: it still measures one fifth of the entire circle.

b. The formula for the angle changes to the much simpler $\frac{L}{r} = \theta$.

Since $L = \pi$ and $r = 3$, the angle in radians is $\frac{\pi}{3}$. This angle is still one sixth of the circle.

As you can tell from the example, radian measure can make some calculations much easier. An angle's radian measure will not increase or decrease when the circle's radius changes, since arc length and radius both change in such a way that their ratio remains constant.

For Discussion

6. About how big is one radian? How many degrees are in one radian?

Exercises Practicing Habits of Mind

Check Your Understanding

1. How many radians are in a full circle? How many degrees?

2. Calculate, in radians and degrees, the measure of each central angle shown.

   a.
   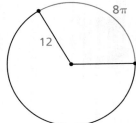

   b.
   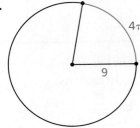

   c.
   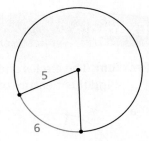

3. **a.** Draw a circle with a radius of 5 centimeters and a central angle of 2 radians.

   b. Find the length of the arc intercepted by this central angle.

   c. A similar figure is drawn with a radius of 10 centimeters. What happens to the radian measure of the central angle?

4. Triangle *RLO* is equilateral, and *R* is the center of the circle.

   a. Explain why the length of minor arc $\overset{\frown}{OL}$ *must* be more than 5 cm.

   b. Find the exact length of minor arc $\overset{\frown}{OL}$ and compare it to the length of chord $\overline{OL}$.

   c. Find the measure of angle *R* in radians.

   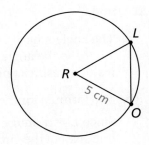

5. Ryan's tricycle tire has a radius of 6 inches. He rode through some wet paint and kept going as the tricycle left a trail of paint behind him. How many revolutions would his tire need to make in order to leave a trail of paint at least 20 feet long?

6. **Take It Further** Determine a formula relating the area of a sector to the radius and arc length of the sector.

7. What is the radian measure of a central angle that is a straight angle? What is the degree measure?

8. Determine the measure of the central angle, in radians and degrees, for each portion of a circle.

    a. $\frac{1}{3}$ of a circle   **b.** $\frac{1}{5}$ of a circle

    c. $\frac{1}{9}$ of a circle   **d.** $\frac{1}{4}$ of a circle

    e. $\frac{1}{360}$ of a circle

9. A circle has a circumference of 360 centimeters. Find the length of an arc with the given central angle measure.

    a. 120°   **b.** 72°   **c.** 40°   **d.** 90°   **e.** 1°

10. A circle has a radius of 1 centimeter. Find the length of an arc whose central angle is:

    a. 120°   **b.** 72°   **c.** 40°   **d.** 90°   **e.** 1°

11. Matt, Liz, and Benny were asked to find the measure of central angle P given the information at the right. Who is right? Explain.

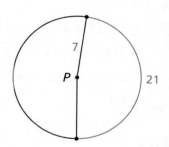

    Matt: I divide the radius by the arc length. The angle in radians is $\frac{7}{21}$, or $\frac{1}{3}$.

    Liz: I divide the arc length by the radius. The angle in radians is $\frac{21}{7}$, which equals 3.

    Benny: You're both wrong. The whole circumference is 14π because the radius is 7. Then the angle is the solution to the proportion $\frac{21}{14\pi} = \frac{x}{360}$, which is $x \approx 172$.

12. Given that major arc $\overset{\frown}{AB}$ has length 24, and central angle AOB measures 120°, find the length of minor arc $\overset{\frown}{AB}$.

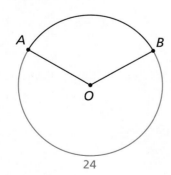

13. Two circles are centered at X.

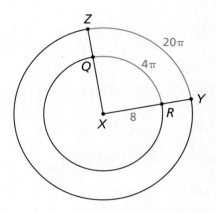

Is this figure drawn to scale?

  a. Find the measure of central angle X in radians and in degrees.

  b. Find the length of $\overline{QZ}$.

14. Find the area of a sector of a circle with radius 10 for each given arc length.

  a. 5π **b.** 4π **c.** π **d.** 10

Mathematical 8B Reflections

In this investigation, you explored relationships between π and measurements of circles. These questions will help you summarize what you have learned.

1. Why is it possible to calculate the circumference of a circle when you know only the length of its radius? Explain in detail.

2. What is the perimeter of a circle with diameter 2.5 in.?

3. What is the area of the shape at the right, composed of a square and a semicircle of radius 4 cm?

4. Find the radius of a circle with area π

5. What is the area of the blue sector?

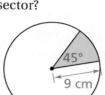

6. What is π?

7. How can you express the area and the circumference of a circle in terms of π?

8. What is the exact area of the shaded portion of the circle with center O?

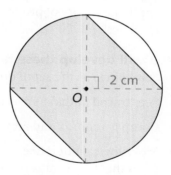

Vocabulary and Notation

In this investigation, you learned these terms and this symbol. Make sure you understand what each one means and how to use it.

- pi, π
- sector

The technology behind crop circles is the compass.

Investigation 8C

Classical Results About Circles

In *Classical Results About Circles*, you will study lines passing through circles and the angles formed by these lines. Studying their many relationships will improve your inductive reasoning, proof-writing skills, and understanding of circles.

By the end of this investigation, you will be able to answer questions like these.

1. What are arcs and chords in circles?

2. How much smaller is the measure of an inscribed angle than the measure of its corresponding central angle?

3. What is the power of a point? What are the maximum and minimum values of the power of a point in a circle with radius *r*?

You will learn how to

- recognize the relationship between inscribed angles and their corresponding central angles

- prove and use general theorems on chords and inscribed angles

- identify properties of tangents

- apply the theory of proportion to chords, secants, and tangents of circles

You will develop these habits and skills:

- See a circle as the set of points with a given distance from one point.

- See "traced paths" as sets of points with a common property.

- Compare chords and arcs of a circle.

- Make logical inferences to prove results about similar triangles with sides that are secants or tangents with respect to a circle.

In a windmill pitch, the hand sweeps out a circle centered on the pitcher's shoulder.

To understand relationships between circles and lines, it is helpful to see figures in motion. It is good practice to try visualizing such motion in your mind's eye. It is also helpful to see the motion on a computer screen.

For You to Explore

1. Draw a circle and a line. Depending on where you draw your line, you will notice a different number of intersection points. List all the possibilities.

2. Draw two circles. How many intersections can two circles have? List all the possibilities.

3. Use the figure to answer the following questions.

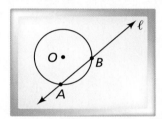

For help finding intersection points, see the TI-Nspire™ Handbook, p. 990.

   a. If you move ℓ around and leave A fixed, what happens to $\overline{AB}$? Under which conditions does $\overline{AB}$ disappear?

   b. In what position does $\overline{AB}$ have the greatest possible length? What does this length represent?

   c. Draw a segment that you could measure to find the distance of $\overline{AB}$ from the center of the circle. When is this distance at a maximum? When is it at a minimum?

4. The circles with centers A and B are congruent. For which points P on either of the two circles does $PA = PB$? Explain.

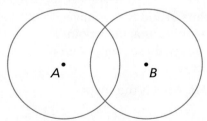

5. The two circles below have radii r_A and r_B respectively.

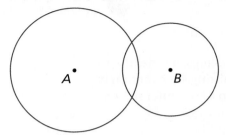

a. For which points P on either of the two circles is the sum of the distances from the two centers equal to the sum of the lengths of the two radii ($PA + PB = r_A + r_B$)?

b. Are there any other points P (not on either circle) for which $PA + PB = r_A + r_B$? Describe the locus of points.

> A **locus** is a set of points that all have a given property. For example, the locus of points in a plane r units from a given point P is the circle with center P and radius r.

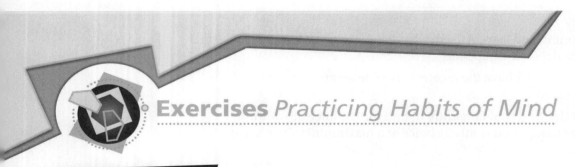

Exercises *Practicing Habits of Mind*

On Your Own

6. On paper or with geometry software, draw two points, A and B, that never move. Make the distance between them less than 6 units. Imagine a point P that can move along various paths described in terms of these points. Draw and describe what the path of P looks like in each case.

a. P moves along a path so that PA always equals PB. What is the shape of the path?

b. This time the path of P keeps $PA = 5$.

c. P moves along a path where $PA + PB = 6$.

d. $m\angle APB = 90°$, no matter where P is along this path.

e. $m\angle APB = 60°$, no matter where P is along this path.

f. $m\angle APB = 30°$, no matter where P is along this path.

7. Draw a circle with a diameter having endpoints *A* and *B*. Now choose a point *P* on the circle that is not *A* or *B* and answer the following questions.

a. What kind of triangle is $\triangle APB$?

b. On which side of $\triangle APB$ does the center of the circle lie, and what is its position on that side?

c. Where would a point *Q* be if $m\angle AQB < 90°$? Where would *Q* be if $m\angle AQB > 90°$?

8. How could you draw a circle if you were given tacks, a length of string, and a pencil? Explain why your method works.

Maintain Your Skills

Use this construction for Exercises 9 and 10. A triangle inscribed in a semicircle has one side that is a diameter of the semicircle. All three of its vertices lie on the circle. Assume that the following statement is true: Any triangle inscribed in a semicircle is a right triangle. Draw a semicircle and inscribe a triangle in it. Then reflect your drawing about the diameter of the semicircle. Now you have a circle with a quadrilateral inscribed in it, as shown in this figure.

Habits of Mind

Look for relationships. Look for similar triangles in the semicircle that contains $\triangle ABC$. How many can you find? How can you compare the lengths of their sides?

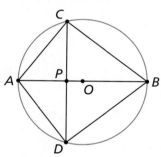

9. Suppose $AP = 3\,\text{cm}$ and $PB = 5\,\text{cm}$. Find *CD*.

10. Use the construction above. Suppose $AP = a$ and $PB = b$. Find $CP = c$ as a function of *a* and *b*.

Circles are a compulsory element in the ribbon component of rhythmic gymnastics. What length ribbon would you use?

Here are some definitions you need for this lesson.

Definitions

A **central angle** for a circle is an angle that has its vertex at the center of the circle.

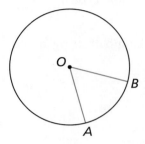

The set of points on a circle that lie on or in the interior of a particular central angle is called the **arc** intercepted by the angle. If the central angle is ∠*AOB,* then you refer to the arc as "the arc *AB* intercepted by angle *AOB.*" You can write the arc *AB* as $\overarc{AB}$.

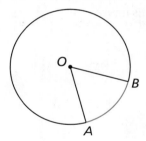

A **chord** is a segment that connects two points on a circle. Any chord through the center of the circle is a **diameter.**

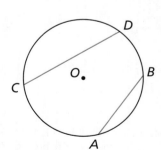 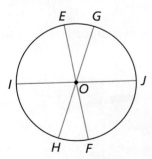

Looking at the definition of diameter, *Tony wonders about chords.*

Tony   I once heard that the diameter is the longest chord you can draw for a given circle. Did you know that, Sasha?

Sasha   As a matter of fact, I did! I think I can prove it. Let's see.

Tony   Well, make life simple and start with the first circle at the bottom of the last page. You already have a chord, $\overline{CD}$.

Sasha   Right! All we have to do is look for triangles, and I love triangles! Connect C, D, and O. Now I remember that in a triangle the sum of two sides is always greater than the third one. So $CD < CO + OD$.

Tony   You're brilliant! I know what to do now. I just noticed that $\overline{CO}$ and $\overline{OD}$ are two radii, so their sum is equal to the diameter. So we've proven that any chord $\overline{CD}$ is shorter than a diameter.

For Discussion

1. How does Sasha and Tony's discussion prove that the diameter is the longest chord of a circle?

2. Use tracing paper.

a. Draw a black circle with center O. Choose points A and B on the circle.

b. Choose two more points C and D such that $\overset{\frown}{AB} \cong \overset{\frown}{CD}$. You can do this by tracing your circle in blue on tracing paper and marking A and B on it. Then choose C on the black circle and pin the centers together with the blue circle on top. Rotate the blue circle until A is on top of C. Now mark the point on the black circle that corresponds to the position of B. This is point D.

You have two arcs $\overset{\frown}{AB}$ and $\overset{\frown}{CD}$. Compare $\angle AOB$ and $\angle COD$.

For You to Do

3. Use a technique similar to the one above to prove the following statement.

If two central angles are congruent, then their intercepted arcs are congruent.

Remember...

This is the converse of what you proved in the In-Class Experiment above.

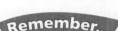

For Discussion

4. Tony is a bit confused by the definition of arc. He thinks, "How can a single arc be intercepted by a central angle? I see two arcs intercepted by ∠AOB because the circle is divided into a big part and a little part. Which part is the intercepted arc?" How could you answer Tony's questions?

The confusion arises from the uncertainty about the central angle. If it is not specified, the interior of ∠AOB refers to the convex region enclosed by the angle. A good way to avoid confusion is to define a **major arc** and a **minor arc** for each central angle. The major arc is the larger part of the circle, and the minor arc is the smaller part of the circle. In this book, you may assume that an arc is a minor arc unless stated otherwise.

Arcs, as well as angles, can be measured in degrees. The **measure of an arc** is the measure of the central angle that intercepts it. If the measure of a minor arc is $x°$, then the measure of the corresponding major arc is $360° - x°$. You write the measure of an arc $\overarc{AB}$ as $m\overarc{AB}$.

The degree measure of an arc divided by 360 tells you how much of the circle is contained by the arc.

The chord of a minor arc is the segment with ends that are the intersections of the central angle with the circle. Now you can prove a theorem on minor arcs and chords.

Theorem 8.7

Two chords are congruent if and only if their corresponding arcs are congruent.

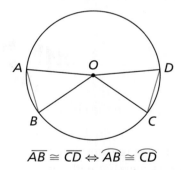

$$\overline{AB} \cong \overline{CD} \Leftrightarrow \overarc{AB} \cong \overarc{CD}$$

Proof If you start with two congruent chords, then △COD and △AOB are congruent by SSS. Therefore, all of their corresponding elements are congruent. In particular ∠AOB ≅ ∠COD. So the corresponding arcs are congruent.

If you start with two congruent arcs $\overarc{AB}$ and $\overarc{CD}$, the two central angles that intercept them on the circle are congruent (as you saw in the In-Class Experiment on the previous page). Therefore, △AOB and △COD are congruent by SAS, because $\overline{OA}$, $\overline{OD}$, $\overline{OB}$, and $\overline{OC}$ are all radii of the same circle. All their corresponding elements are congruent, so sides $\overline{AB}$ and $\overline{CD}$ are congruent.

Exercises Practicing Habits of Mind

Check Your Understanding

1. What parts of the circle are the following elements?

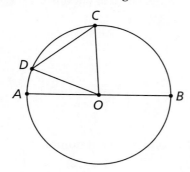

   a. $\overline{AB}$ **b.** $\overline{OB}$ **c.** $\overline{OD}$

   d. $\overline{CD}$ **e.** $\angle COD$ **f.** $\angle AOC$

   g. $\overparen{CD}$ **h.** $\overparen{AB}$

2. In a circle with center O and radius 1 inch, $\overparen{MN}$ is an arc that measures $60°$. What are $m\angle MON$, MN, and OH, where H is the base of the height through O of $\triangle MON$?

3. Look at this picture, where $m\overparen{AB} = 60°$, $m\overparen{CD} = 30°$, and $m\angle AOC = 45°$.

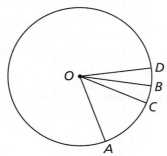

   Find the measures of the following elements. (The arcs are all minor arcs.)

   a. $\angle AOB$ **b.** $\angle COD$ **c.** $\overparen{AC}$

   d. $\overparen{CB}$ **e.** $\angle COB$ **f.** $\angle BOD$

   g. $\overparen{AD}$

4. Is it true that if point C is on minor arc $\overparen{AB}$ of a circle with center O, then $m\overparen{AC} + m\overparen{CB} = m\overparen{AB}$? Explain.

> This is known as the Arc Addition Postulate.

5. $\overline{OZ}$ is the bisector of $\angle QOR$. Prove that $\overline{QP}$ is congruent to $\overline{PR}$.

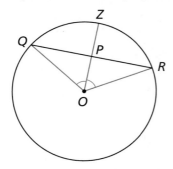

6. Draw a circle and two congruent chords $\overline{FH}$ and $\overline{JI}$ that intersect at point E (not the center O). Draw radii $\overline{OF}$, $\overline{OH}$, $\overline{OI}$, and $\overline{OJ}$.

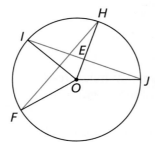

   Prove that $\angle OFH$, $\angle FHO$, $\angle OJI$, and $\angle JIO$ are congruent.

7. Prove that chords of equal lengths are equally distant from the center of the circle.

How do you measure the distance from a chord to the center?

8. Construct two congruent circles. Draw two noncongruent chords—one in each circle. Which chord is closer to the center of its circle? Explain.

9. Standardized Test Prep In the diagram, O is the center of the circle and $\overline{AB} \cong \overline{CD}$. Which statement is NOT necessarily true?

A. $\triangle ABO \cong \triangle DCO$

B. $\triangle ABO$ is isosceles.

C. $\overarc{AC} \cong \overarc{DB}$

D. $\triangle DCO$ is equilateral.

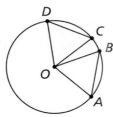

10. Take It Further Two lines r and r' cut a circle in four points as shown. If $\overarc{AB} \cong \overarc{CD}$, prove that $\angle APO$ and $\angle OPD$ are congruent.

> Lines that cut a circle in two points are called *secants*.

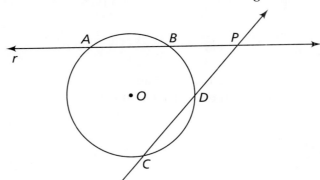

11. Look at the following figure.

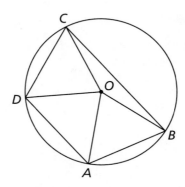

a. Knowing only that $\overarc{AB} \cong \overarc{CD}$, give a reason for each of the following statements.

- $\angle AOB \cong \angle COD$

- $\triangle AOB \cong \triangle COD$

- $\overline{AB} \cong \overline{CD}$

b. Copy the figure and draw the heights through O for the two triangles, $\triangle AOD$ and $\triangle BOC$. Prove that these heights lie on the same line and therefore $\overline{AD} \parallel \overline{BC}$.

12. $\overline{BA}$ is the perpendicular bisector of $\overline{DC}$. Assume that the center of the circle O is on $\overline{BA}$, as it appears to be in the figure. Then, given $BA = 5$ in. and $BE = 2$ in., find DC. Justify your answer.

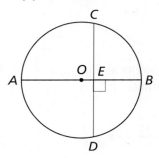

13. $\overline{CD}$ is the perpendicular bisector of $\overline{AB}$. Assume that $\overline{CD}$ is also a diameter of the circle, as it appears to be in the figure. Then, given $CK = 1.5$ cm and $OK = 2$ cm, find DC, AO, and AK. Justify your answers.

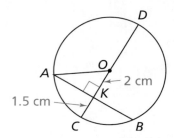

14. $\overline{AB}$ is the diameter perpendicular to $\overline{DC}$. Assume that $\overline{BA}$ bisects $\overline{DC}$. Then, given $BA = 12$ in. and $BE = 3$ in., find DC. Justify your answer.

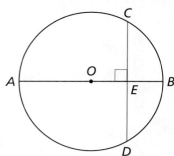

15. $\overline{DC}$ is the diameter perpendicular to $\overline{AB}$. Assume $\overline{DC}$ bisects $\overline{AB}$. Suppose $AK = 1.2$ cm and $KO = 3$ cm. Find DC and AB. Justify your answer.

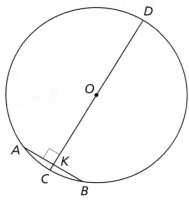

16. Diameter $\overline{JL}$ bisects $\overline{NK}$. Assume that $\overline{JL}$ is also perpendicular to $\overline{NK}$. Suppose $NA = 14$ cm and $OJ = 16$ cm. Find OA. Justify your answer.

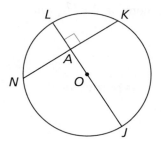

Go Online
www.successnetplus.com

As the moon rises, the horizon forms a chord that gets longer and then shorter. When is the chord the longest?

8.10 Chords and Inscribed Angles

In Lesson 8.09, you studied angles that have a vertex at the center of a circle. In this lesson, angles of interest have their vertices elsewhere inside the circle, or on the circle itself.

In-Class Experiment

1. Draw a circle and a chord, $\overline{AB}$, that is not a diameter. Use a straightedge to draw various lines that are perpendicular to $\overline{AB}$. How many of these perpendicular lines can you draw through the center of the circle?

2. Using the figure from Problem 1, find a proof for the following statement. There is one and only one line perpendicular to $\overline{AB}$ through the center of the circle.

Now you can prove a theorem about chords and lines through the center of a circle. Learn the technique and use it to solve the problems in the For You to Do that follows.

Theorem 8.8

A line through the center of a circle bisects a chord if it is perpendicular to the chord.

> The result of this theorem was assumed in Exercises 14 and 15 of Lesson 8.09.

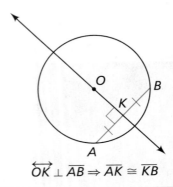

$$\overleftrightarrow{OK} \perp \overline{AB} \Rightarrow \overline{AK} \cong \overline{KB}$$

Proof Consider the line that contains $\overline{OK}$ through the center O of the circle above. Suppose it is perpendicular to $\overline{AB}$. You have to prove that it also bisects $\overline{AB}$. $\triangle AOB$ is isosceles because $AO = r = OB$, where r is the length of the radius of the circle. In any isosceles triangle, the height with respect to the base is also the bisector of the angle and the perpendicular bisector of the side it cuts. Therefore $\overline{AK}$ and $\overline{KB}$ are congruent, which is what you wanted to prove.

For Discussion

3. Prove the following theorems. Refer to the figure from Theorem 8.8.

Theorem 8.9

If a line through the center of a circle bisects a chord, then it is perpendicular to the chord.

> The result of this theorem was assumed in Exercise 16 of Lesson 8.09.

Theorem 8.10

The center of a circle lies on the line perpendicular to a chord if and only if the line bisects the chord.

> The result of this theorem was assumed in Exercises 12 and 13 of Lesson 8.09.

Definition

An **inscribed angle** is an angle that has its vertex on the circle and has sides that are chords of the circle. You say that $\angle ABC$ intercepts $\overset{\frown}{AC}$ and that it is inscribed in $\overset{\frown}{ABC}$.

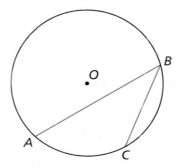

In-Class Experiment

4. Draw a circle and a central angle, $\angle AOC$. How many inscribed angles can you draw that intercept $\overset{\frown}{AC}$? Draw a few of these inscribed angles.

5. Measure $\angle AOC$ and then measure all the inscribed angles you drew. Can you find a relationship between them?

Theorem 8.11

The measure of an inscribed angle is equal to half the measure of its intercepted arc.

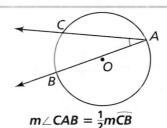

$$m\angle CAB = \tfrac{1}{2}m\overset{\frown}{CB}$$

For Discussion

6. Prove Theorem 8.11 for $\angle ACB$.

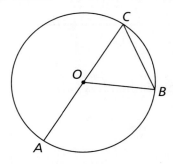

Habits of Mind

Prove. Can you use the Arc Addition Postulate to prove Theorem 8.11 in general? See Exercise 4 in Lesson 8.09 for a reminder.

Theorem 8.11 has two important corollaries.

Corollary 8.11.1

Inscribed angles are congruent if and only if they intercept the same arc or congruent arcs.

Corollary 8.11.2

Any triangle inscribed in a semicircle is a right triangle.

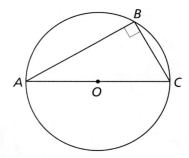

Remember...

One side of a triangle inscribed in a semicircle is a diameter of the circle. So $\angle ABC$ intercepts an arc of 180° and therefore measures 90°.

For You to Do

7. In a circle, two parallel chords contain opposite endpoints of a diameter. Prove that the chords are congruent.

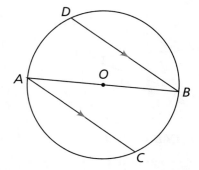

Check Your Understanding

1. What is the measure of any angle inscribed in a semicircle?

2. Choose a point *A* inside a circle. Describe the shortest chord that you can draw through *A*. Justify your answer.

3. Draw a circle and two congruent chords and letter the endpoints *A*, *B*, *C*, and *D* as you go counterclockwise around the circle. Connect *A* with *C* and *B* with *D*. Prove that $\overline{AC}$ and $\overline{BD}$ are congruent.

4. Prove that in a circle two adjacent chords that form equal angles with a radius are congruent.

> Adjacent chords share an endpoint.

5. In the figure, $m\widehat{ABC} = 46°$ and $\widehat{AB} \cong \widehat{BC}$. Find the measures of the inscribed angles.

   a. $\angle CFB$

   b. $\angle CFA$

   c. $\angle CEA$

   d. $\angle FAC$

   e. $\angle FCA$

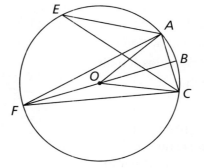

On Your Own

6. The midpoints of two chords of a circle are the same distance from the center *O*. Prove that these chords are congruent.

7. Draw a circle with a 3-cm radius. Consider a chord that is 2 cm long and draw at least ten other chords 2 cm long on the circle. What is the locus of the midpoints of these chords?

> **Remember...**
>
> A locus is a set of points with a given property. In this case, the points are all midpoints of equal-length segments.

8. $\overline{AB}$ is a diameter of a circle. $AB = 2$ in. Draw this circle and diameter and then select a point C on the circle such that $m\angle BAC = 30°$. In how many ways can you choose C? Shade the part of the circle that lies in the interior of $\angle BAC$. What is its area?

9. The line through the center of the circle below is the bisector of $\angle AOB$. Prove that $\overline{AE}$ is congruent to $\overline{BF}$.

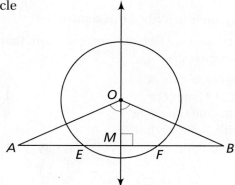

10. In the figure at the right, $m\angle CAD = 20°$ and $DP = PB$. What is the measure of each angle?

    a. $\angle DPA$, $\angle DPC$, $\angle CPB$, $\angle BPA$ b. $\angle ADB$

    c. $\angle AOB$ d. $\angle ACB$

    e. $\angle COB$

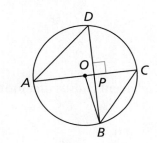

11. Two concentric circles are cut by line ℓ. (Two circles are **concentric circles** if their centers coincide.) Prove that $\overline{AC}$ is congruent to $\overline{DB}$.

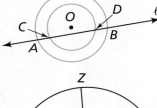

12. In the figure below, $FZ = 10$ cm, $PQ = 5$ cm, and the distance from the center of the circle O to $\overline{MN}$ is 2.5 cm. $\overline{FZ}$ is perpendicular to $\overline{MN}$, which is parallel to $\overline{PQ}$. Answer the following questions.

    a. Why is $\overline{FZ}$ the perpendicular bisector of $\overline{PQ}$ and $\overline{MN}$?

    b. What is the radius of the circle?

    c. How long is $\overline{MN}$?

    d. How far is $\overline{PQ}$ from O?

    e. What is $m\angle NOQ$?

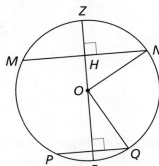

13. Given $m\widehat{AB} = 30°$ and $m\widehat{CD} = 60°$, find $m\angle APB$.

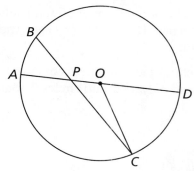

14. The diagram shows a pair of nested circles. One circle is inside the other, and the two circles have point A in common.

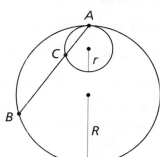

a. Why are the circles similar?

b. Let the ratio of corresponding lengths be the common ratio for the two circles. In terms of the radii r and R, what is the common ratio?

c. Any chord $\overline{AB}$ of the larger circle determines a chord $\overline{AC}$ of the smaller circle. Explain why the ratio of AB to AC equals the common ratio.

15. **Standardized Test Prep** What is $m\angle EFH$ if $m\angle EOF = 30°$ and $m\angle FGH = 40°$?

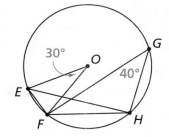

A. 80°   **B.** 110°   **C.** 125°

D. not enough information to answer

Maintain Your Skills

16. Draw a unit circle with center O and a radius $\overline{OA}$. Label the midpoint of the radius M_1.

a. Draw a chord with midpoint M_1. How many can you draw? Explain.

b. Label one of the chords you drew $\overline{C_1D_1}$. How long is it?

c. Label the midpoint of $\overline{M_1A}$ M_2. Draw a chord $\overline{C_2D_2}$ with midpoint M_2. How long is $\overline{C_2D_2}$?

d. Label the midpoint of $\overline{M_2A}$ M_3. Draw a chord $\overline{C_3D_3}$ with midpoint M_3. How long is $\overline{C_3D_3}$?

e. As you continue this process, what happens to $\overline{OM_n}$? To $\overline{C_nD_n}$?

f. Draw a series of lines ℓ_n through C_n and D_n. What happens to the lines ℓ_n as the value of n increases?

8.11 Circumscribed and Inscribed Circles

In Lesson 6.03, you constructed the perpendicular bisectors of the sides of a triangle and the angle bisectors of a triangle. In each case, the three lines you constructed were concurrent.

This lesson explores the connections between these concurrencies and ways to draw circles that surround polygons, and circles that are contained within polygons.

In-Class Experiment

1. Use dynamic geometry software to construct $\triangle ABC$.

2. Construct the perpendicular bisectors of the three sides of the triangle.

3. Label point X, the intersection point of the perpendicular bisectors.

4. Construct a circle centered at X with an adjustable radius. Adjust the radius until the circle passes through all three of the triangle's vertices.

> **Remember...**
> The name *perpendicular bisector* should remind you of its properties.

For Discussion

5. Use properties of perpendicular bisectors to prove that $\overline{AX}$, $\overline{BX}$, and $\overline{CX}$ are all the same length. How can you use this to prove that if point A is on circle X, then points B and C must also be on circle X?

6. Is it possible for point X to lie outside $\triangle ABC$? On $\triangle ABC$? If so, how?

Definitions

A **circumscribed circle** of a polygon is a circle that passes through all of the polygon's vertices. The center of a circumscribed circle is the *circumcenter*, equidistant from the polygon's vertices.

An **inscribed circle** of a polygon is a circle that is tangent to all of the polygon's sides. The center of an inscribed circle is the *incenter*, equidistant from the polygon's sides.

> **Habits of Mind**
> **Use precise language.**
> The word *circumscribed* means *drawn around*, and is closely related to *circumference*.

The In-Class Experiment shows how to construct a circumscribed circle for any triangle. If point X is the intersection of any two perpendicular bisectors of the sides of a triangle, then the circle with center X that passes through any vertex must pass through them all.

Every triangle has a circumscribed circle. In Exercises 3 and 4, you'll learn how to construct the inscribed circle for any triangle.

For You to Do

7. In the following diagram, quadrilateral *ABCD* has a circumscribed circle. Angle *D* measures 50°. Determine any other angle measures, arc measures, or lengths that are possible to find.

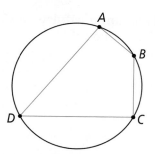

Minds in Action

Derman and Sasha are working on the For You to Do problem above.

Derman I don't think we can measure anything else. We don't even know how big the circle is.

Sasha Good point. We definitely can't measure any *lengths* without knowing the size of the circle. But angles, maybe.

Derman Could we use the fact that there are 360 degrees in a quadrilateral?

Sasha We only know that angles *A*, *B*, and *C* add up to 310 degrees, but we don't know the exact measure of any of them.

Derman Fine! No lengths, no angles. That leaves arcs. Isn't angle *D* a circumscribed angle or something?

Sasha It's an *inscribed* angle. Oh cool, we can measure something. It's arc *AC*.

Derman Huh? Which one?

Sasha Arc *AC*. It measures 100 degrees. Angle *D* has half the measure of arc *AC*, because of the inscribed angle theorem.

Derman But which one? There are two arcs we could call *AC*. What about the big *AC*?

Sasha Oh, the major arc. Could we figure that out? Oh wow, we can. And we can use that to find the measure of angle *B*! That's really clever, Derman.

Derman Ummm… sure, thanks!

Habits of Mind

Use precise language.
The angle is *inscribed* in the circle, and the circle is *circumscribed* around the quadrilateral.

To clarify this confusion about arcs, a third point is sometimes used. Saying *arc ABC* or *arc ADC* would also answer Derman's question.

For You to Do

8. Find the measure of major arc $\overset{\frown}{AC}$ and the measure of $\angle B$. Explain your reasoning.

The argument used above is general in nature; it works for any quadrilateral with a circumscribed circle. A quadrilateral with a circumscribed circle is called a *cyclic quadrilateral* and has the following property.

Theorem 8.12

In a cyclic quadrilateral, opposite angles are supplementary.

Proof Suppose $\angle D$ measures x degrees. It is an inscribed angle, so its intercepted arc $\overset{\frown}{ABC}$ measures $2x$ degrees.

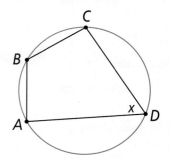

$\overset{\frown}{ADC}$ is the rest of the circle, so it measures $(360 - 2x)$ degrees.

Inscribed angle B intercepts $\overset{\frown}{ADC}$, so it measures half of $(360 - 2x)$ degrees, or $(180 - x)$ degrees. It is supplementary to angle D, which measures x degrees.

The measures of the four angles in a quadrilateral add up to 360 degrees. If angles B and D measure 180 degrees together, the remaining 180 degrees must come from angles A and C. They also must be supplementary.

For Discussion

9. Do *all* quadrilaterals have circumscribed circles? Explain.

10. Do *some* quadrilaterals have inscribed circles?

11. Do *all* quadrilaterals have inscribed circles?

Exercises Practicing Habits of Mind

Check Your Understanding

1. If possible, determine the values of x and y. If it is not possible to determine the values of x and y, explain why.

a.

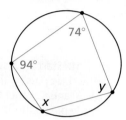

74°
94°
y
x

b.

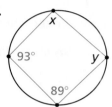

x
93°
y
89°

c.

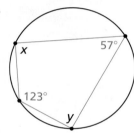

x
57°
123°
y

d.

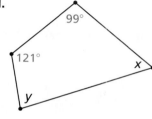

99°
121°
x
y

2. In the diagram below, O is the center of the circle, and $AB = BC = 10$.

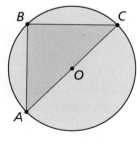

> Is $\triangle ABC$ acute, right, or obtuse? How do you know?

   a. Find the area of the triangle.

   b. Find the area of the circle.

3. Complete this experiment to construct the *inscribed circle* for any triangle.

   a. Use dynamic geometry software to construct $\triangle ABC$.

   b. Construct the angle bisector of two angles of the triangle.

   c. Label point X, the intersection point of the two angle bisectors.

   d. Construct the angle bisector of the third angle.

   e. Construct a circle centered at X with a movable radius. Adjust the radius until the circle just touches all three sides of the triangle.

> **Remember...**
> The points on an angle bisector are equidistant from the two rays that form the angle.

4. a. Explain why point *X* in the construction from Exercise 3 must be equidistant from all three sides of the triangle.

  b. How could you *construct* the inscribed circle, instead of adjusting the radius of the circle centered at *X*?

5. Trapezoid *TRAP* is cyclic and has a 50° angle.

  a. Draw a sketch of what *TRAP* might look like.

  b. Find the other angle measures of trapezoid *TRAP*.

  c. Use this example to find and prove a theorem about cyclic trapezoids.

6. Prove that if the opposite angles of quadrilateral *ABCD* are supplementary, then the quadrilateral is cyclic.

> **Hint:** Start by drawing the circle passing through *A, B,* and *C*. Either this circle passes through *D*, or it does not.

On Your Own

7. Calculate all missing angle measures and arc measures in the diagram below.

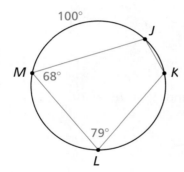

8. What's Wrong Here? James was asked to determine the measures of the angles in cyclic quadrilateral *ABCD*. Explain how you know his answers cannot be correct, and find the correct measures.

> *James:* It's a cyclic quadrilateral, so that means $x + 95 = 180$. Then x is 85 degrees. Angle *D* is $x - 25$, so it's 60 degrees. I can use the fact that there are 360 degrees in a quadrilateral to find the measure of angle *C*. It's 120 degrees.

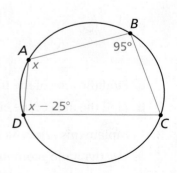

9. Cyclic quadrilateral *ECTR* is also a parallelogram. Find its angle measures, and determine whether there is a more accurate classification of cyclic parallelogram *ECTR*.

10. Find the area of a cyclic quadrilateral with side lengths 1, 8, 4, and 7. The angle between the sides of length 1 and 8 is 90 degrees.

11. Draw or construct $\triangle ABC$ and its inscribed circle with center X.

    a. Find the area of $\triangle AXC$ in terms of other measurements in your diagram.

    b. Similarly, find the area of $\triangle AXB$ and $\triangle BXC$ in terms of other measurements in your diagram.

    c. Show that the area of $\triangle ABC$ is given by $A = \frac{1}{2}Pr$, where P is the perimeter of the triangle and r is the radius of its inscribed circle.

12. Do all regular polygons have inscribed circles? For regular polygons that do have inscribed circles, what is the radius of the inscribed circle?

13. **Take It Further** Some, but not all, quadrilaterals can have an *inscribed circle*, a circle tangent to all four sides. Find a property for a quadrilateral that determines whether or not it can have an inscribed circle.

Maintain Your Skills

14. Given circle A and cyclic quadrilateral $BDCE$, find the values of x and y.

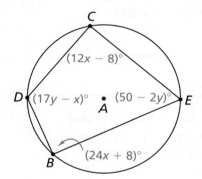

15. Use circle A below to determine all missing angle measures and arc measures.

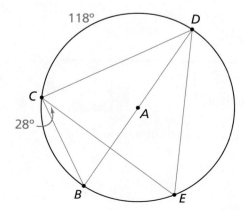

Just as chords have special relationships with circles, so do lines that contain the chords.

In-Class Experiment

Use geometry software or a compass and straightedge for the following experiment.

1. Draw a circle of radius 1 and a diameter $\overline{AB}$.

2. Select a point C on the circle and draw $\triangle ABC$. What kind of triangle is it?

3. Move C along the circle. What kind of triangle do you have when C is on the diameter perpendicular to $\overline{AB}$?

4. Is it always true that $m\angle ACB = 90°$? Explain. What is the measure of $\angle ACB$ if C is very close to A or B?

5. If ℓ is the line that coincides with $\overline{CA}$, what happens to ℓ as you move C around? How many intersections does ℓ have with the circle in every position, including when C and A coincide?

6. What is the maximum distance you can find from ℓ to the center of the circle?

In general, if a line has two intersections with a circle it is called a **secant.** When a line has only one intersection point with a circle, it is said to be a **tangent** of the circle or tangent to the circle at the point of contact.

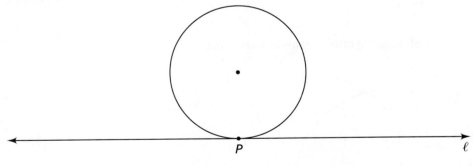

Line ℓ is tangent to the circle at P.

Now you can prove a theorem about your answers to questions 4, 5, and 6 of the In-Class Experiment.

Theorem 8.13

If a line intersects a circle in one point (that is, the line is tangent to the circle), it is perpendicular to the radius drawn to the point of contact.

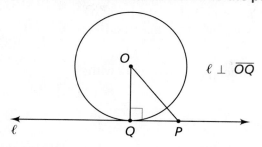

$\ell \perp \overline{OQ}$

Proof Suppose ℓ is tangent to the circle with center O at point Q. Then $\overline{OQ}$ is a radius and $OQ = r$. If you choose a point P on ℓ, other than Q, $OP > r$, because P is outside the circle. So the shortest way to get from O to ℓ is along $\overline{OQ}$. The shortest way to get from O to ℓ is measured along the perpendicular to ℓ, so $\overline{OQ}$ is perpendicular to ℓ.

For You to Do

7. Draw a circle and a point outside of it. Think of all the tangent lines to the circle through that point. How many are there?

8. Draw two circles that intersect. How many lines are tangent to both circles?

9. Draw two circles that do not intersect and neither of which contains the other. How many lines are tangent to both circles?

Definition

A **secant angle** is an angle with sides that are two secants of a circle. A secant angle's vertex can be inside or outside the circle.

Remember...

What do you call a secant angle with its vertex on the circle?

Minds in Action

Tony and Sasha were told to find m∠APD (and therefore m∠APC). They know that mÂD = 122° and mB̂C = 140°.

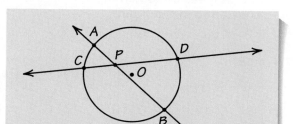

Tony	I don't know how to relate the measures of the minor arcs to the angle we are looking for. What can we do?
Sasha	Well, we have to work from the information we have. The measures of the arcs give us the measures of their corresponding central angles and therefore the measures of all the inscribed angles that intercept them.
Tony	Let's try to use triangles. I know how much you like to work with them. You find triangles everywhere!

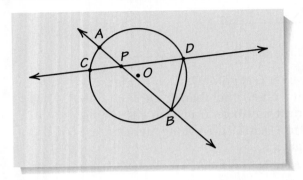

Sasha	Good idea! I see $\triangle PBD$, for example. From the theorem on the exterior angles of a triangle, we know that $m\angle APD = m\angle PDB + m\angle PBD.$
Tony	I know that $$m\widehat{AD} = m\angle AOD = 2m\angle ABD = 2m\angle PBD$$
Sasha	Right! And the same is true for $\angle CDB$, so $$m\widehat{CB} = m\angle COB = 2m\angle CDB = 2m\angle PDB$$
Tony	So $m\widehat{AD} + m\widehat{CB} = 2m\angle PBD + 2m\angle PDB = 2m\angle APD.$
Sasha	Therefore, $m\angle APD = \frac{1}{2}(m\widehat{AD} + m\widehat{CB}).$ That's pretty neat, isn't it?

You can express the theorem Tony and Sasha found this way.

Theorem 8.14

A secant angle with vertex inside a circle is equal in measure to half of the sum of the arcs it intercepts. If you use the lettering in the figure from Minds in Action, the result is below.

$$m\angle APD = \frac{1}{2}(m\widehat{AD} + m\widehat{CB})$$

For You to Do

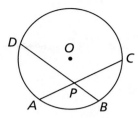

10. If $m\widehat{AB} = 69°$ and $m\widehat{DC} = 163°$, what is $m\angle APB$?

Theorem 8.15

A secant angle with vertex outside a circle is equal in measure to half of the difference of the measures of the arcs it intercepts. If you use the lettering in the figure below, the result is as follows.

$$m\angle APD = \tfrac{1}{2}(m\widehat{AD} - m\widehat{CB})$$

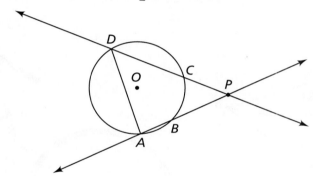

For Discussion

11. Use the figure above to prove Theorem 8.14.

For You to Do

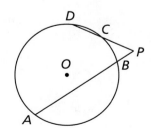

12. If $m\widehat{AD} = 133°$ and $m\widehat{BC} = 48°$, what is $m\angle APD$?

Check Your Understanding

1. $\overline{PA}$ and $\overline{PB}$ are the tangents to a circle through *P*. Prove that $\overline{PA} \cong \overline{PB}$.

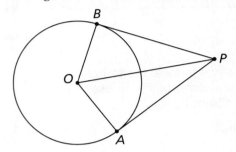

$\overline{PA}$ and $\overline{PB}$ are called *tangent segments*.

2. $\overline{PA}$ and $\overline{PB}$ are the tangents to a circle through *P*.

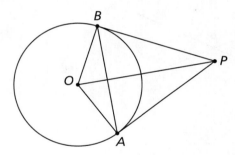

Prove that $\overline{PO}$ is the perpendicular bisector of $\overline{AB}$.

3. Construct a circle, an external point, and the tangents from the external point to the circle. Describe the steps you take and why your construction works.

4. In the figure, $m\widehat{CB} = 45°$, $m\widehat{AD} = 69°$, $m\angle DCE = 13°$, and $m\angle CPF = 68°$. Find the measures of the following angle and arcs.

   a. $\angle CQB$ **b.** $\widehat{ED}$ **c.** $\widehat{FB}$

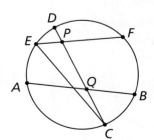

5. In this figure, $m\widehat{CE} = 69°$ and $m\widehat{EF} = 97°$

   a. What is $m\widehat{FB}$?

   b. What is $m\angle CAD$?

   c. Suppose you do not know that a
tangent is perpendicular to the radius
through its point of tangency. Use the
formula from Theorem 8.14 or Theorem 8.15
to prove that $\overline{DC}$ is perpendicular to $\overline{AC}$.

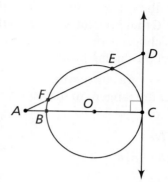

On Your Own

6. In the circle with center O, $OP = 1$ in.,
$m\angle POQ = 30°$, and $\overline{PQ}$ is tangent to the circle.
Find OQ and PQ. Then calculate OQ and PQ
for $m\angle POQ = 45°$ and for $m\angle POQ = 60°$.

7. Draw two parallel lines and inscribe a circle
between them. What can you say about the
segment that connects the intersections of the
circle with the parallel lines? Explain.

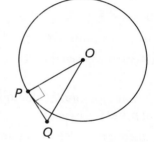

8. **Standardized Test Prep** Given $m\angle AQF = 22°$
and $m\widehat{QHP} = 110°$, what is $m\angle QRP$?

   A. 67°

   B. 77°

   C. 82°

   D. 88°

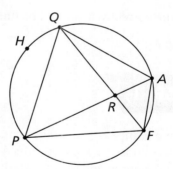

9. Draw a circle and two different-length adjacent chords $\overline{AB}$ and $\overline{AC}$. Mark
the midpoints P and Q of the minor arcs $\widehat{AB}$ and $\widehat{AC}$ and connect them.
M and N are the points in which this segment intersects $\overline{AB}$ and $\overline{AC}$. Prove
that $\overline{AM} \cong \overline{AN}$.

10. Take It Further Draw a circle and inscribe a right triangle so that $m\angle ABC = 90°$. Through the center of the circle O, draw a line ℓ parallel to $\overline{AB}$. Draw a line through C that intersects ℓ at P so that $\angle CPO \cong \angle ACB$. In how many ways can you choose P on ℓ? In how many points does the line through C and P intersect the circle?

11. In this figure, the two circles are concentric and $\overline{PA}$, $\overline{PB}$, $\overline{PC}$, and $\overline{PD}$ are tangent to the circle their endpoints lie on.

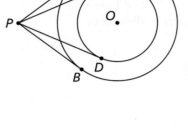

a. Prove $\angle APC \cong \angle DPB$.

b. Prove that quadrilateral $ABDC$ is an isosceles trapezoid.

12. Take It Further Follow these steps to draw a figure.

a. Draw a circle and call it γ.

b. Draw a diameter $\overline{AB}$ of γ.

c. Choose a point D on $\overline{AB}$ and a point C on γ.

d. Draw the line through A and C. Label it m. Draw the line through C and B. Label it n.

e. Draw the line through D that is perpendicular to $\overline{AB}$. Label it p. Use E to name the intersection of p and n. Use F to name the intersection of p and m.

f. Draw the tangent to γ through C. Use M to name its intersection with p.

If you have drawn the figure correctly, M should be the midpoint of $\overline{EF}$. Prove it.

Maintain Your Skills

13. Use geometry software or a compass and straightedge for the following exercise. Draw a circle and choose two fixed points A and C on it. Now choose a third point B on the circle and move it gradually toward A.

a. What is the measure of $\angle ABC$ as you move B along the circle?

b. Draw the line ℓ that contains $\overline{BA}$ and move B until it coincides with A. What does ℓ become? Explain.

c. When B coincides with A, what arc does the angle that ℓ forms with $\overline{AC}$ intercept?

d. Think about the angle that ℓ forms with $\overline{AC}$ when B coincides with A. Can you prove that its measure is the same as the measure of $\angle ABC$ that is formed when B does not coincide with A? Explain.

14. Can Theorem 8.11 be considered a special case of Theorem 8.14 or of Theorem 8.15?

Power of a Point, Part 1

Every point in the plane of a circle has a number associated with it. That number is called the power of the point.

In-Class Experiment

The Power of a Point

1. Draw a circle and pick a point P anywhere inside it. Then draw a chord of the circle that passes through P. Point P divides the chord into two segments $\overline{PA}$ and $\overline{PB}$.

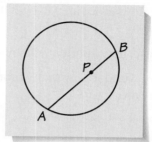

   a. Measure the lengths of these segments and calculate the product $(PA) \cdot (PB)$.

   b. Draw another chord through P and calculate the same product of the lengths of its two segments. Record your observations and repeat the process for several more chords.

   The product is called the *power of point P with respect to the circle*. You write $\Pi(P)$.

2. The circle at the right has two chords $\overline{AB}$ and $\overline{CD}$ that intersect at point P.

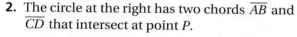

   a. What can you predict about the lengths PA, PB, PC, and PD?

   b. Copy the figure and add segments $\overline{AC}$ and $\overline{BD}$ to the illustration. The first step in proving your conjecture from part (a) is to show that $\triangle APC \sim \triangle DPB$. Explain why these two triangles must be similar.

   c. Use the fact that $\triangle APC \sim \triangle DPB$ to write a proportion that includes PA, PB, PC, and PD. Rearrange the proportion to prove your conjecture from part (a).

   d. How does this result prove that the product of the chord lengths is the same for any chord through P?

> If you see $\Pi(P) = \ldots$ in reference to a circle and a point P, you say "the power of P with respect to the circle is . . . ."

> Hint: $\angle ACD$ and $\angle ABD$ intercept the same arc.

One of the pleasures of mathematics comes from finding an unexpected connection between two topics that seem to have nothing in common. For example, you can use your findings about the power of a point to answer the following question.

Is there a way to construct a rectangle with geometry software so that when you drag a vertex the perimeter changes but the area remains the same?

If you could build such a rectangle, you could call it a *constant-area rectangle*.

Derman and Tony are discussing the possible dimensions of different rectangles with an area of 24 square feet.

Derman Tony, I found two rectangles that have an area of 24 square feet—a 24 ft-by-1 ft and a 12 ft-by-2 ft.

Tony I think there are more than two rectangles that have an area of 24 square feet! How about an 8 ft-by-3 ft rectangle, or a 6 ft-by-4 ft rectangle?

Derman Okay, in that case, how about a $\frac{1}{2}$ ft-by-48 ft rectangle?

Tony Wow, Derman, I wonder how many more 24-square-foot rectangles there are.

For Discussion

3. If ℓ represents the lengths of the rectangles in the above dialog and w represents their widths, what is the relationship between ℓ and w?

4. How many rectangles are there with an area of 24 square feet?

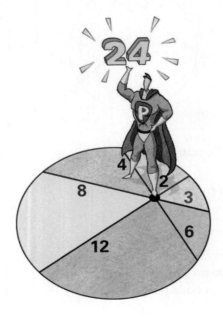

Using what you found out about the power of a point, you can construct constant-area rectangles. To begin, the computer screen shows a rectangle on one side and the power-of-a-point construction on the other. The length *PA* and the width *PB* of the rectangle are linked to the corresponding chord segments and are equal to them. So when the chord segment lengths change, the rectangle's dimensions will, too.

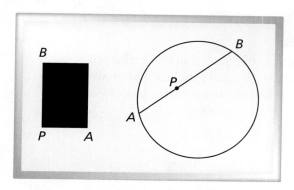

As you move point *A* around the circle, the chord $\overline{AB}$ spins, always passing through the stationary point *P*.

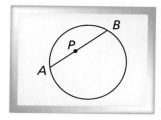 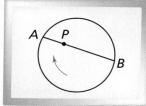 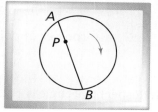

For You to Do

Use geometry software to build a construction like the one described above. Your construction might include an animation button that allows point *A* to travel automatically around the circle.

5. As chord $\overline{AB}$ spins, describe what happens to the rectangle.

6. The purpose of this geometry construction is to create a rectangle of constant area. Explain why you think this construction does or does not satisfy this goal.

7. Does your construction show all possible rectangles that share the same area? Explain.

Exercises Practicing Habits of Mind

Check Your Understanding

1. Suppose that you decide to build a collection of equal-area rectangles out of pencils. Each rectangle is to have an area of 6 square inches, and no two rectangles can have the same dimensions. You can measure the pencils and then cut them at appropriate places, but that becomes tedious.

   How can the setup below help you make your rectangles?

a few pencils

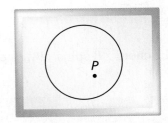

power of point $P = 6$

The actual circle and pencils would be larger.

2. The power of point P with respect to a circle is 112. A chord $\overline{ST}$ contains P. If $PT = 32$ in., how long is $\overline{ST}$?

3. Draw a circle with center O, radius r, and a diameter $\overline{AE}$. Find and label the midpoint of $\overline{OE}$ B, the midpoint of $\overline{BE}$ C, and the midpoint of $\overline{CE}$ D. Find $\Pi(B)$, $\Pi(C)$, $\Pi(D)$, and $\Pi(O)$. How would you define $\Pi(E)$?

On Your Own

4. **Write About It** Suppose you want to make a constant-area triangle instead of a rectangle. Describe at least one way to alter the methods in this lesson to make a triangle instead. Include pictures.

5. Parts (a)–(d) give an outline for a proof that the power of a point is invariant. Justify each step and then write the proof.

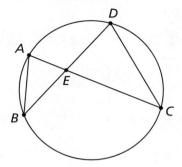

a. $\angle ABE \cong \angle DCE$

b. $\angle AEB \cong \angle DEC$

c. $\triangle ABE \sim \triangle DCE$

d. $\dfrac{AE}{DE} = \dfrac{BE}{CE}$

e. Write the complete proof showing that $(AE)(CE) = (BE)(DE)$.

Hint: Look for inscribed angles.

6. The power of a point P with respect to a circle is 126. Draw two chords $\overline{AB}$ and $\overline{CD}$ through P, such that $AP = 21$ cm and $CD = 25$ cm. Find PB, CP, and DP.

7. Two chords $\overline{AB}$ and $\overline{CD}$ through a point P inside a circle measure 7 cm and 13 cm respectively. If $AP = 3$ cm, find PB, CP, and PD.

8. **Standardized Test Prep** In the figure, $CD = 7$ cm, $CP = 3$ cm, and $PG = 5$ cm. What is FP?

A. 2.0 cm

B. 2.4 cm

C. 2.5 cm

D. 4.2 cm

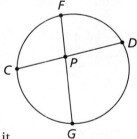

9. **Take It Further** Draw a circle and a point P within it. Measure to calculate the power of P.

a. Are there other locations for P within the same circle that have the same power? Find a few and explain your reasoning.

b. Find the locations of all points within your circle that have the same power as P. What does this collection of points look like?

10. Take It Further If P is a point outside the circle, as in the figure below left, you can still prove that the product $(PA)(PB)$ is invariant. Copy the figure below right and connect B to C and A to D.

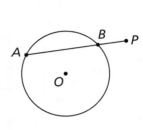

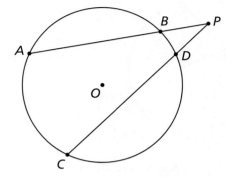

a. Prove that $\triangle PAD \sim \triangle PCB$.

b. Write proportions for the sides of the triangles and deduce that $(PA)(PB)$ is invariant.

You can, therefore, generalize the definition of $\Pi(P)$ this way.

Definition

The **power of a point** P with respect to a circle is the product (PA) (PB), where A and B are the points of intersection of a line through P and the circle.

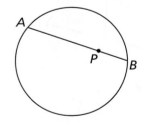

Habits of Mind

Explore. What is the power of P if P lies *on* the circle?

Maintain Your Skills

For Exercises 11–14, draw a circle and a chord $\overline{AB}$ through a point P inside the circle.

11. For $\Pi(P) = 6$ and $PA = 3$ cm, find PB and AB.

12. For $\Pi(P) = 9$ and $AB = 10$ in., find PA and PB.

13. For $\Pi(P) = 28$ and $AB = 16$ cm, find PA and PB.

14. For $\Pi(P) = k$ and $AB = a$ cm, find PA and PB as functions of k and a.

Go Online
www.successnetplus.com

In this investigation, you examined chords, secants, and tangents of circles and proved many relationships involving these figures. These questions will help you summarize what you have learned.

1. In the circle at the right with center O, M is the midpoint of $\overline{AB}$. Prove that $\triangle AOM$ is a right triangle.

2. Draw any right triangle ABC and let $m\angle ABC = 90°$. Why is the median from B to the midpoint of $\overline{AC}$ always half as long as $\overline{AC}$?

3. In the figure at the right below, $m\angle ABC = 31°$ and O is the center of the circle. What is the measure of each angle?

   a. $\angle AOC$

   b. $\angle AEC$

   c. $\angle CDA$

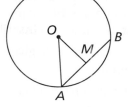

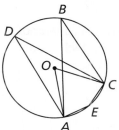

4. Draw a circle with center O and radius 35 mm, choose a point P on the circle, and draw the line ℓ through P tangent to the circle. What is the distance from O to ℓ?

5. What are arcs and chords in circles?

6. How much smaller is the measure of an inscribed angle than the measure of its corresponding central angle?

7. What is the power of a point? What are the maximum and minimum values of the power of a point in a circle with radius r?

Vocabulary and Notation

In this investigation, you learned these terms and symbols. Make sure you understand what each one means and how to use it.

- arc, $\widehat{AB}$
- central angle
- chord
- circumscribed circle
- concentric circles
- diameter
- inscribed angle
- inscribed circle
- locus
- major arc
- measure of an arc, $m\widehat{AB}$
- minor arc
- power of a point, $\Pi(P)$
- secant
- secant angle
- tangent

The ball flies off on a tangent.

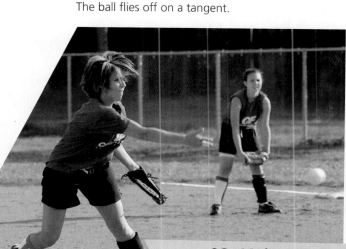

Review

In **Investigation 8A** you learned how to

- approximate the area and perimeter of blobs
- find the area of regular polygons
- solve problems using the relationship between a regular hexagon's side and the radius of the circle it is inscribed in
- find the area of a circle given its circumference

The following questions will help you check your understanding.

1. Estimate the perimeter of the blob and describe your technique.

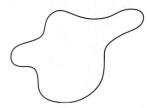

2. Will the formula $A = \frac{1}{2}Pa$ work on the following pentagon with perimeter 45 units? If it will, find the area of the pentagon; otherwise, explain why it will not work.

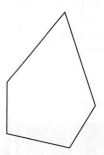

In **Investigation 8B** you learned how to

- calculate the area of a circle, given its radius
- find the perimeter of a circle, given its radius

The following questions will help you check your understanding.

3. If you scale a circle by 6, how does the radius of the scaled circle compare to the radius of the original circle? How does the area of the scaled circle compare to the area of the original circle?

4. What is the perimeter of a circle of radius 216 cm? What is its area?

In **Investigation 8C** you learned how to

- prove and apply theorems about arcs, chords, and inscribed angles of a circle

- prove and apply theorems about secants and tangents of a circle

- look for invariants in circles

- define the power of a point with respect to a circle

The following questions will help you check your understanding.

5. The circle has center P, and $\overline{CB}$ and $\overline{CA}$ are tangent to the circle. Prove that $\overline{PC} \perp \overline{AB}$.

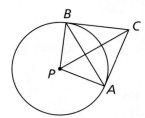

6. If $m\widehat{AB} = 62°$ and $m\widehat{DQC} = 170°$, what is $m\angle APB$?

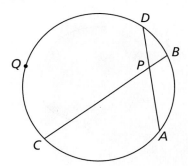

7. What is $\Pi(P)$ in the figure below?

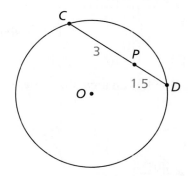

8. Without using a ruler, explain why the measures of the segments in this diagram must be incorrect.

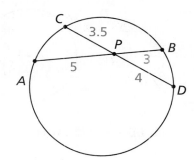

Multiple Choice

1. Which pink region has an area of π square inches?

A.
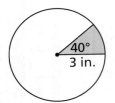
40°
3 in.

B.
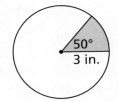
50°
3 in.

C.
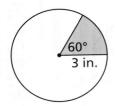
60°
3 in.

D.
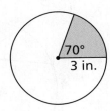
70°
3 in.

2. If $m\angle ZPY = 83°$ and $m\widehat{ZY} = 112°$, what is $m\widehat{WX}$?

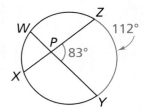

W
Z
112°
P
83°
X
Y

A. 29°   B. 54°   C. 56°   D. 165°

3. The two circles are concentric. The radius of the smaller circle is $\frac{2}{3}$ the radius of the larger circle. If the larger circle has a circumference of 30π feet, what is the approximate area of the shaded region?

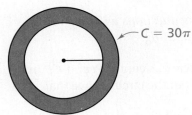

$C = 30\pi$

A. 63 ft^2 B. 314 ft^2

C. 393 ft^2 D. 471 ft^2

Open Response

4. Describe a technique you learned in this chapter for approximating the area of a blob. Use the method you describe to approximate the area of this blob.

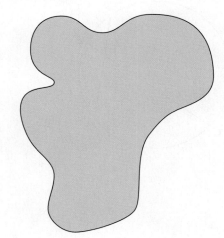

5. Find the areas of the following blue circle sectors.

a.

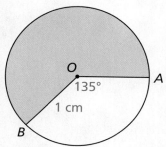

b.

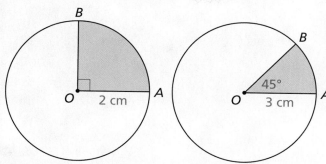

c.

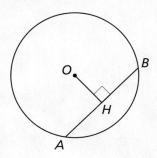

d.

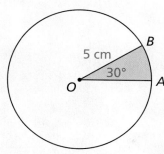

6. Give a definition for the diameter of a circle and prove that a diameter is the longest of all chords of a circle.

7. In the following circle with center O, $\overline{OH}$ is perpendicular to the chord $\overline{AB}$. Find the length of $\overline{AB}$ if the radius of the circle is 5 and $OH = 3$. Justify each step of your answer.

8. In the figure, $m\widehat{ABC} = 52°$. Find the measure of each angle.

    a. $\angle ADC$ **b.** $\angle AOC$

    c. $\angle CEA$ **d.** $\angle ACF$

    e. $\angle AFC$ **f.** $\angle OCF$

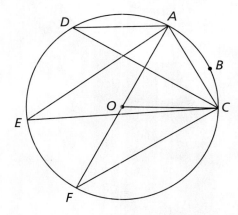

9. What is the power of P in the following figure?

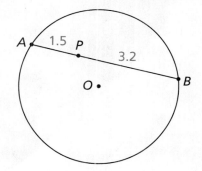

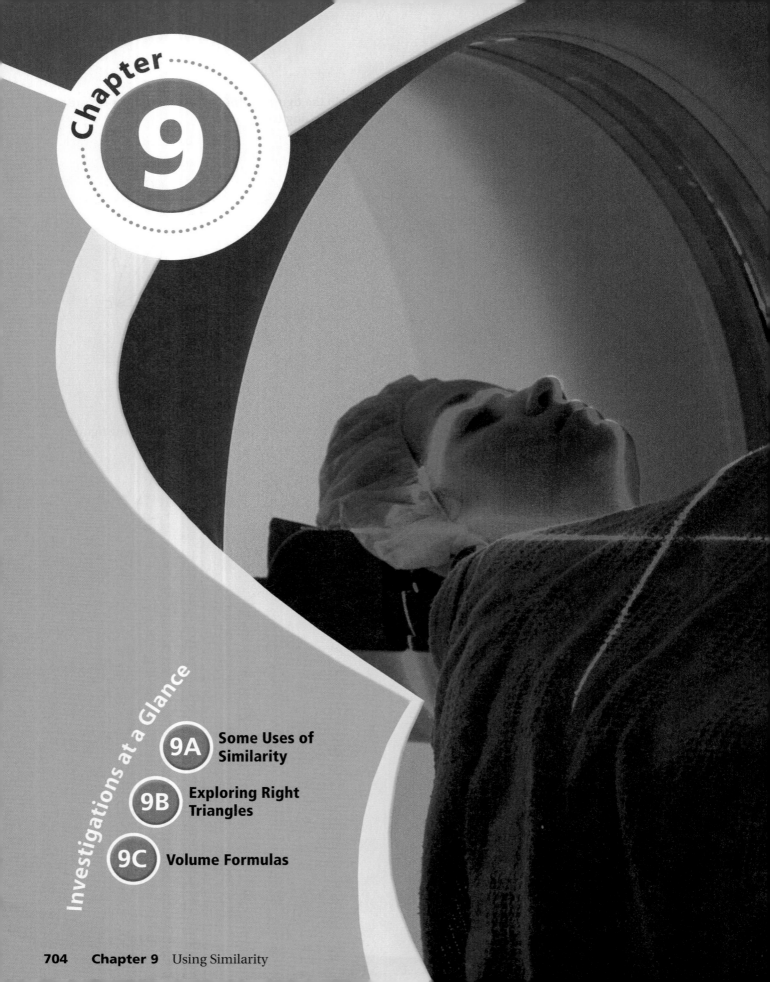

Using Similarity

One application of *trigonometry* (a topic introduced in this chapter) is in *tomographic reconstruction*. This is the process by which three-dimensional images are created in diagnostic medical tests such as CT scans.

In a CT scan, an X-ray machine moves around above the patient as a sensor moves around below. The area to be scanned is between them. The X-ray emission is absorbed in differing amounts by materials of differing density within the patient's body. The intensity of the X-rays coming through the patient is recorded from moment to moment as the scanner moves around. The X-ray sensor data are converted into density readings through a complicated formula involving trigonometric functions and some operations of calculus.

These readings are used to create a two-dimensional scan of a horizontal "slice" of the patient. Many horizontal slices, or cross sections, are "stacked" to create a three-dimensional image. You can picture a three-dimensional object as a stack of two-dimensional cross sections. You can think of this as a CT scan of a geometric solid!

Vocabulary and Notation

- arithmetic mean
- geometric mean
- projection
- trigonometry
- sine, sin θ

- cosine, cos θ
- tangent, tan θ
- $\sin^{-1} x$
- $\cos^{-1} x$
- $\tan^{-1} x$

Investigation 9A

Some Uses of Similarity

In *Some Uses of Similarity,* you will explore applications of similarity, including its use in some classical Greek proofs. Similarity and proportionality are important ideas in mathematics. They allow you to calculate and prove many things.

By the end of this investigation, you will be able to answer questions like these.

1. What is the Arithmetic-Geometric Mean Inequality?

2. Why does the altitude to the hypotenuse of a right triangle form three similar triangles?

3. In $\triangle ABC$, suppose that $AH = 12$ cm and $BA = 15$ cm. What is HC?

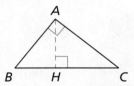

You will learn how to

- state and use the Arithmetic-Geometric Mean Inequality

- use similar triangles to find unknown lengths

- prove theorems using similarity

You will develop these habits and skills:

- Find invariants in triangles.

- Visualize similar triangles to solve problems.

- Choose and draw strategic circles, segments, and points to solve problems.

Drawing details square by square can help you capture a similar image.

You can use similar triangles to measure inaccessible distances by comparing them to distances between objects close at hand. You have likely seen (or even used) this technique before.

For You to Explore

1. Choose an object and measure the length of the shadow the object casts in sunlight. Also measure the shadow cast by a yardstick (or some other object of known height) standing straight up on the ground at the same time of day.

   Use the fact that the sun's rays are approximately parallel to set a proportion using similar triangles. Find the height of your object.

2. From their boat off the coast, two sailors can see the faraway top of Mount Pythagoras, towering 6600 feet above sea level. One of the two sailors holds her left arm straight out in front of her in a "thumbs up" gesture to get an idea of their distance from the base of the mountain.

   She positions herself so that she can see how much of her thumb covers the mountain. She covers the mountain completely—the whole 6600 feet behind her thumb!

   Her companion measures the distance from her eye to the place on her thumb that lines up with the edge of the shore. Then they measure the length of the thumb that covers Mount Pythagoras. Using similar triangles, they calculate their distance to the base of the mountain.

   Here is a rough sketch of the situation.

   a. What assumption is built into the sketch?

   b. Name a pair of similar triangles in the sketch.

   c. The length of your thumb covering the mountain is 1 inch. The distance from your eye to the bottom of your thumb is 14 inches. Calculate your distance from the mountain.

   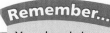

   d. Measure the length of your thumb. Also measure the distance from the base of your thumb to your eye when your arm is fully extended. If you know the height of an object that is covered by your thumb, you can then determine your distance from that object. Pick an object you know the height of. Use the sailors' technique to figure out how far away it is. Check your results by measuring the actual distance.

> **Remember...**
> You already know that the height of the mountain is 6600 feet.

> **Habits of Mind**
> **Estimate.** You can estimate what your thumb covers. If your thumb covers about one third of a 60-meter building, then about 20 meters are covered.

3. You look out a window and see a person standing far away. The person's image fills just part of the window. If you could trace the image on the window, you could measure the height of the image. You could also find the height of the image if you knew the following.

- the person's height
- your distance from the window
- your distance from the person

Here is a sketch of that situation. Carefully describe how you could use similar triangles to determine how tall the image on the window would be.

4. A tree's shadow is 20 feet long, and a yardstick's shadow is 17 inches long.

a. Draw a diagram that shows the tree, the yardstick, the sun's rays, and the shadows.

b. Find a pair of similar triangles and explain why they are similar.

c. How tall is the tree?

Exercises *Practicing Habits of Mind*

On Your Own

5. On a sunny day, Melanie and Nancy noticed that their shadows were different lengths. Nancy measured Melanie's shadow and found that it was 96 inches long. Melanie found that Nancy's was 102 inches long.

a. Who do you think is taller, Nancy or Melanie? Explain.

b. If Melanie is 5 feet 4 inches tall, how tall is Nancy?

c. If Nancy is 5 feet 4 inches tall, about how tall is Melanie?

Habits of Mind

Represent the situation. Drawing a picture might help you answer these questions.

6. Use the shadow method to find the height of some tall object for which you can obtain the actual height. Record the details of your measurements and prepare a presentation for your class. By how much did the result of your calculations differ from the actual height? What might cause these differences?

7. Apply your theory from Problem 3. You see a person 5 feet tall standing outside your window about 30 feet away from you. You are about 2 feet from the window. About how tall will the image be?

8. A light-year is a unit of distance—the distance that light travels in 1 year. The star nearest to us (other than our own sun) is about 4 light-years away. Light travels at 186,000 miles per second. How far does light travel in one year? How far away is the nearest star?

9. A planet is the same distance away as the star in Exercise 8 and has the same diameter as Earth. How large will the planet's image appear on a window that is 2 feet away from you?

10. About how much must that image be magnified to be as big as the letter o on this page? Use $\frac{1}{20}$ inch for the width of the letter o.

11. A child $3\frac{1}{2}$ feet tall is standing next to a very tall basketball player. The child's sister notices that the player's shadow is about twice as long as the child's. She quickly estimates the player's height. What value does she get?

Maintain Your Skills

12. Find all the similar triangles in each diagram. Explain your answers.

a. △*ABC* is isosceles. *D*, *E*, and *F* are midpoints.

b. △*ACB* is equilateral.

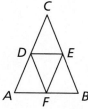

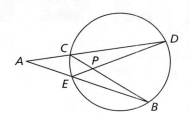

c. ∠*ACB* is a right angle.

d.

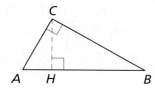

An Inequality of Means

The figure below shows a complete rectangle on the left and only the length of another rectangle on the right.

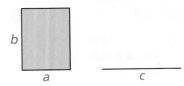

b

a

c

For Discussion

1. How can you construct the missing width of a rectangle with length *c*, so that both rectangles have the same area? Look at the following pictures and think about how they might be useful to solve your problem.

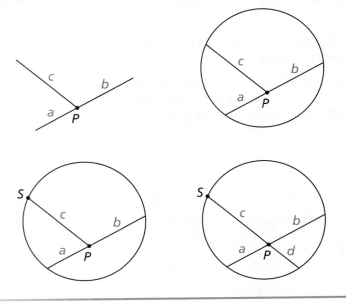

Remember...

The power of a point with respect to a circle is the product *PA* · *PB*.

A

P

B

You can construct these equal-area rectangles based on the circle and point *P* given in the For Discussion section. How are the two rectangles at the ends related? (*Hint:* The rectangle at the right is square.)

Tony wants to take the For Discussion idea further.

Tony   It's cool how we can use the power-of-a-point construction to construct the missing width of the rectangle, so that both rectangles have the same area. But I was thinking that it would be even cooler to use the construction to find a square with the same area as this rectangle.

Tony points to a rectangle like the one below.

Tony   But I'm stuck.

Sasha   Well, it's an interesting idea. Let me think about it.

After a while Sasha draws the following diagrams, in which $\overline{AB}$ is a diameter.

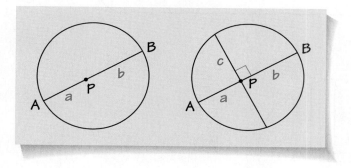

Tony   So you're saying that c is the length of the side of the square we're looking for? How do you know?

For You to Do

2. Explain why Sasha's construction method works.

3. Write a formula that relates a, b, and c. What is the algebraic relationship between a, b, and c?

Definition

The **geometric mean** of a and b is c if $c > 0$ and $c^2 = ab$. Equivalently, $c = \sqrt{ab}$.

Explore Relationships. The **arithmetic mean,** or average, of two numbers a and b is $\frac{a + b}{2}$.

So the arithmetic mean of 10 and 40 is $\frac{10 + 40}{2} = 25$. The mean 25 is midway between 10 and 40. Examine the following pairs of equations to see how the arithmetic mean 25 relates to the two numbers 10 and 40.

$$25 - 10 = 15 \qquad\qquad 10 + 15 = 25$$
$$40 - 25 = 15 \qquad\qquad 25 + 15 = 40$$

The geometric mean of two numbers defines a different kind of midway point. The geometric mean is "midway with respect to multiplication." To get from 10 to 40, you can multiply by 2 ($10 \times 2 = 20$) and then by 2 again ($20 \times 2 = 40$). Thus 20, the midway point in your journey, is the geometric mean of 10 and 40. Another way to say that 20 is midway with respect to multiplication between 10 and 40 is to write the proportion $\frac{10}{20} = \frac{20}{40}$.

$$10 \xrightarrow{+\,15} 25 \xrightarrow{+\,15} 40 \qquad\qquad 10 \xrightarrow{\times\,2} 20 \xrightarrow{\times\,2} 40$$

arithmetic mean geometric mean

The Arithmetic-Geometric Inequality

Look at the figure below.

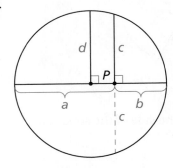

The following relationships hold. If you calculate the power of point P, you get

$$c^2 = a \cdot b$$
$$c = \sqrt{ab}$$

Since d is a radius of the circle, it is half the diameter $a + b$.

$$d = \frac{a + b}{2}$$

You can see from your work that $d \geq c$.

Therefore, you get the Arithmetic-Geometric Mean Inequality.

arithmetic mean $\geq$ geometric mean

$$\frac{a + b}{2} \geq \sqrt{ab}$$

> Can you explain why these relationships are true?

Exercises Practicing Habits of Mind

Check Your Understanding

1. Compute the geometric mean and the arithmetic mean of the following pairs of numbers.

   a. 2 and 8

   b. 3 and 12

   c. 4 and 6

   d. 5 and 5

2. If you add two extra segments to the geometric mean, as shown below, three right triangles are formed in the semicircle. Explain.

 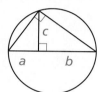

   Usually, just the right triangles are shown and not the circle that is used to construct them. In the next exercise, the circles were erased after the right triangles were constructed.

3. Find all of the unknown segment lengths in these two figures.

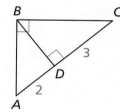 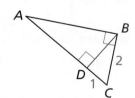

4. Construct a segment with length that is the geometric mean of a 1-inch segment and a 3-inch segment.

5. **Standardized Test Prep** Three of the following pairs of numbers have the same geometric mean. Which pair has a geometric mean that is different?

   A. 2 and 72   **B.** 3 and 48

   C. 4 and 36   **D.** 6 and 30

6. The illustration below shows four frames from a geometric mean construction as point D moves to the left and point A remains stationary.

1

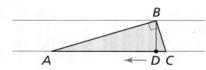

2

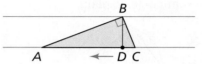

3

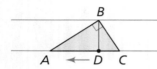

4

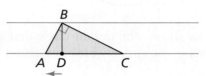

Make a sketch like this using geometry software.

   a. The product of two lengths remains the same throughout each of these four frames. Which lengths are they?

   b. Use this setup to build a rectangle of constant area sketch.

   c. Does your construction show *all* possible rectangles that share the same area? Explain.

7. **Write About It** Your constant-area-rectangle sketches show rectangles that range from narrow and tall to wide and short. Which of the two constructions—the power of a point or the geometric mean—seems to generate a larger range of constant-area rectangles? Explain.

8. Here is a diagram of a square and a rectangle.

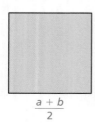

$$\frac{a + b}{2}$$

   a. Which has the greater perimeter?   **b.** Which has the greater area?

   Try it with numbers.

9. Begin with an $a \times b$ rectangle. Explain how to construct a rectangle with length c that has the same area as the $a \times b$ rectangle.

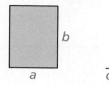

a. Can you use the same circle as in the Minds in Action dialog to complete this construction? Explain.

b. What difficulties do you encounter?

c. Explain how to redraw the circle so that the construction works.

Maintain Your Skills

10. The segments below have lengths a and b. For each value in parts (a)—(d), construct either a segment with that length or a rectangle with that area. Your constructions should lead towards a geometric proof that

$$\left(\frac{a+b}{2}\right)^2 - \left(\frac{a-b}{2}\right)^2 = ab$$

Go Online
www.successnetplus.com

---
a

---
b

All of the constructions can be done with just an unmarked straightedge, a compass, and some lined notebook paper. Resist the urge to measure with a ruler—you will not need to!

a. $a + b$ and $\left(\frac{a+b}{2}\right)^2$

b. $a - b$ and $\left(\frac{a-b}{2}\right)^2$

c. $\left(\frac{a+b}{2}\right)^2 - \left(\frac{a-b}{2}\right)^2$

d. ab

In which cases will you construct a segment? In which cases will you construct a rectangle?

e. Use algebra to prove $\left(\frac{a+b}{2}\right)^2 - \left(\frac{a-b}{2}\right)^2 = ab$. Use the equation to prove the Arithmetic-Geometric Mean Inequality.

9.03 Similarity in Ancient Greece

As you have seen in these lessons and in Chapter 7, similarity is very useful and has a wide variety of applications. In this lesson you will use similarity to prove the Pythagorean Theorem and other theorems of ancient Greece.

For You to Do

In $\triangle ABC$, $\angle ACB$ is a right angle.

1. Why are $\triangle CAH$, $\triangle ABC$, and $\triangle CHB$ right triangles?

2. Why are the two sums $m\angle ACH + m\angle HCB$ and $m\angle ABC + m\angle HCB$ both equal to 90°?

3. Why are the three triangles, $\triangle CAH$, $\triangle ABC$, and $\triangle CHB$, similar?

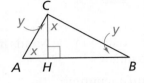

Example

Problem $\triangle ABC$ is a right triangle with $m\angle ACB = 90°$. Prove the Pythagorean Theorem using similar triangles.

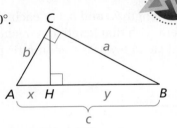

Solution You need to prove that $c^2 = a^2 + b^2$. Consider $\triangle CAH$, $\triangle ABC$, and $\triangle CHB$. They are all right triangles.

Also, $m\angle ACH + m\angle HCB = 90°$ and $m\angle ABC + m\angle HCB = 90°$, so $m\angle ACH \cong \angle ABC$.

By the AA Similarity Theorem, the three triangles are similar. Therefore, the ratios of corresponding sides are the same.

$$\frac{b}{c} = \frac{x}{b} \text{ and } \frac{a}{c} = \frac{y}{a}$$

So $b^2 = cx$ and $a^2 = cy$. Add these two equations and remember that $x + y = c$.

$$b^2 + a^2 = cx + cy$$
$$= c(x + y)$$
$$= c^2$$

There are many other proofs of the Pythagorean Theorem. You saw some of the proofs by dissection in Chapter 6. The following is another proof that goes back to Euclid.

In this figure, *ACRS*, *BCPQ*, and *ABNM* are squares constructed on the sides of right triangle *ABC*.

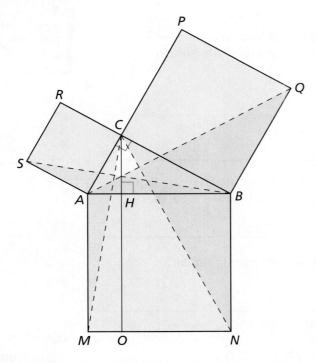

$\triangle ACM$ and $\triangle ASB$ are congruent and $\triangle ABQ$ and $\triangle CBN$ are congruent. Also, remember that the area of a triangle is equal to half the area of a parallelogram with a congruent base and height. So, the area of $\triangle ACM$ is equal to half the area of *AMOH*. The area of $\triangle ASB$ is equal to half the area of *ACRS*.

Why are these two pairs of triangles congruent?

$$A_{ACRS} = 2A_{ASB} = 2A_{CAM} = A_{AMOH}$$

What are the common bases and heights of *ACRS* and *ASB*? Of *AMOH* and *CAM*?

For You to Do

4. Finish proving the Pythagorean Theorem using the method above. Prove that $A_{CBQP} = A_{HONB}$ and that therefore $A_{ABNM} = A_{ACRS} + A_{CBQP}$.

Minds in Action

Derman and Sasha are thinking about the following question.

If a triangle has side lengths a, b, and c, such that $c^2 = a^2 + b^2$, is the triangle a right triangle?

Derman It has to be a right triangle with legs of lengths a and b and hypotenuse c, because if it weren't, then the Pythagorean Theorem wouldn't be true.

Sasha What do you mean?

Habits of Mind

Explore. a, b, c are not zero . . . what would happen if one of them was zero?

For Discussion

5. What do you think Derman means? Pretend that you are Derman. Explain to Sasha why you think that a triangle with sides a, b, and c, such that $c^2 = a^2 + b^2$, must be a right triangle.

There are many more theorems that you can prove using similarity.

Theorem 9.1

In a right triangle, the length of either leg is the geometric mean of the length of its projection on the hypotenuse and the length of the whole hypotenuse.

$$CA^2 = AH \cdot AB$$

$$CB^2 = HB \cdot AB$$

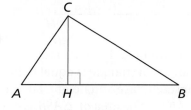

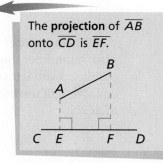

The **projection** of $\overline{AB}$ onto $\overline{CD}$ is $\overline{EF}$.

Theorem 9.2

In a right triangle, the length of the altitude relative to the hypotenuse is the geometric mean of the lengths of the two segments of the hypotenuse.

$$CH^2 = AH \cdot HB$$

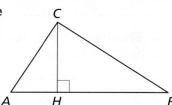

Exercises *Practicing Habits of Mind*

Check Your Understanding

1. Prove Theorem 9.2.

2. In $\triangle ABC$, $\frac{AH}{CH} = \frac{CH}{HB}$. Prove that $\triangle ABC$ is a right triangle.

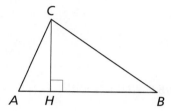

3. Copy the figure onto a separate sheet of paper. Then draw a diameter of the circle below, so that A or B lies on the diameter.

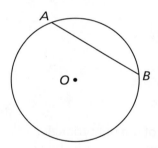

Prove that AB^2 is equal to the product of the diameter and the chord's projection on the diameter.

4. If $AH = r$ and $HB = s$ in the right triangle below, what is CH?

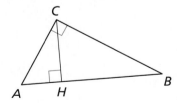

5. In the right triangle below, $AH = r$ and $AB = c$. Using similarity, find AC and CB.

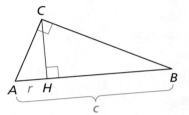

6. **Standardized Test Prep** $\overline{RT}$ is the hypotenuse of $\triangle RST$. $RU = 2$ and $UT = 6$. What are the values of x and y?

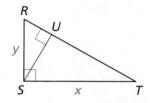

A. $x = 2\sqrt{3}$, $y = 3$ **B.** $x = 4\sqrt{3}$, $y = 4$

C. $x = 4$, $y = 2\sqrt{3}$ **D.** $x = 8$, $y = 6$

7. Draw a right triangle. Draw a semicircle on each side of the right triangle, such that each side of the right triangle is a diameter of a semicircle. Prove that the area of the semicircle on the hypotenuse is equal to the sum of the areas of the semicircles on the legs of the triangle.

8. In $\triangle ABC$, $AC = BC$. Prove that $\dfrac{AC}{AB} = \dfrac{AB}{2HB}$.

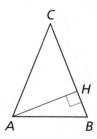

Use △*POD* for Exercises 9 and 10.

9. *PI* = 4 and *DI* = 9. What is *OI*?

10. *PI* = 7.2 and *DI* = 12.8. What is *PO*?

11. In a right triangle *ABC* with hypotenuse $\overline{BC}$, the altitude from vertex *A* reaches side $\overline{BC}$ at *H*. *BH* = 3.6 and the length of the hypotenuse is 10. What are the lengths of the legs of △*ABC* ?

> *H* is also called the projection of vertex *A* onto the hypotenuse $\overline{BC}$.

12. Take It Further The mathematicians of ancient Greece proved Theorem 9.1 using a technique like the one in Euclid's proof of the Pythagorean Theorem. At the right is a diagram of the proof. Think about the diagram and write a proof.

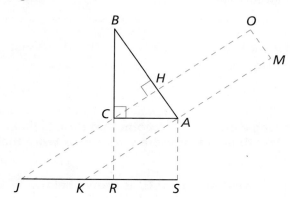

Go Online
www.successnetplus.com

Maintain Your Skills

13. a. The height from the hypotenuse of a right triangle is 6 cm. A projection of a leg onto the hypotenuse is 4 cm. What is the length of the hypotenuse of the triangle?

b. The two projections of the legs of a right triangle onto its hypotenuse are 5 in. and 45 in. What is the area of the right triangle?

c. In a right triangle the hypotenuse measures 24 cm. The projection of a leg onto the hypotenuse measures 6 cm. What is the triangle's perimeter?

9.04 Concurrence of Medians

A median of a triangle is a segment with endpoints that are a vertex of the triangle and the midpoint of the opposite side. Every triangle has three medians.

In-Class Experiment

1. Using geometry software, draw $\triangle ABC$. Construct the medians from A and B.

2. Drag the vertices of your triangle and describe all the invariants that you can find.

3. Construct the median from C.

4. Drag the vertices of your triangle again. Do the invariants you found in Problem 2 still hold for the new median?

During the experiment, you made some conjectures about invariants that may have included the following.

Conjecture 9.1

1. Any two medians of a triangle intersect in a point that divides them into two segments. The length of one of these segments is twice the length of the other.

2. The three medians are concurrent at a point G, as shown below.

> G is the *centroid* of the triangle.

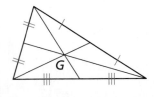

Tony and Sasha are trying to prove both parts of Conjecture 9.1.

Habits of Mind

Explore. Think about why this lesson is in an investigation on similarity.

Sasha   I have an idea. In △*ABC*, *M* and *N* are the midpoints of the sides $\overline{AC}$ and $\overline{CB}$. The medians $\overline{AN}$ and $\overline{BM}$ intersect at *G*. *P* and *Q* are the midpoints of $\overline{AG}$ and $\overline{GB}$.

Look at triangles *PQG* and *NMG*.

Tony   I wouldn't be surprised if those were congruent triangles.

Sasha   They are, and here's why. Apply the Midline Theorem to △*ABC*. You get $\overline{MN} \parallel \overline{AB}$ and $MN = \frac{1}{2}AB$. Apply the Midline Theorem to △*ABG*. You get $\overline{PQ} \parallel \overline{AB}$ and $PQ = \frac{1}{2}AB$. So $\overline{MN} \parallel \overline{PQ}$ and $MN = PQ$. This means that $\angle QPN \cong \angle PNM$ and $\angle PQG \cong \angle QMN$. Finally, △*PQG* ≅ △*NMG* by ASA. Neat, huh?

Tony   That means we've proven the first conjecture. After all, $\overline{GM} \cong \overline{GQ} \cong \overline{QB}$. That tells us that *G* divides $\overline{BM}$ into two pieces, one of which is twice as long as the other.

Sasha   Right, and $\overline{GN} \cong \overline{GP} \cong \overline{PA}$, so *G* also divides $\overline{AN}$ the same way.

Tony   Wait! There wasn't anything special about *G*. The result must be the same for any two medians. The point of intersection must divide the medians into two segments with one segment twice the length of the other. That means if the third median $\overline{CK}$ intersects $\overline{BM}$ in point *G'*, *G'* has to have the same property. So $CG' = 2G'K$ and $BG' = 2G'M$.

Remember...

You proved the Midline Theorem in Chapter 7.

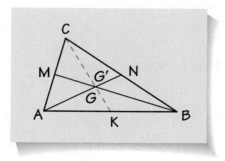

Sasha   But you already know that *G* is the point that divides $\overline{BM}$ into two segments and that one segment is twice the length of the other.

Tony   Right! So *G* = *G'* and therefore, *G* lies on $\overline{CK}$, too.

For You to Do

5. Explain why knowing that $\triangle PQG \cong \triangle NMG$ is enough to conclude that $AG = 2GN$ and $BG = 2GM$.

Exercises Practicing Habits of Mind

Check Your Understanding

1. **Write About It** Use Sasha's triangle. In your own words, prove Conjecture 9.1, namely that $AG = 2GN$ and $BG = 2GM$.

2. Think about how Sasha proved that $AG = 2GN$ and $BG = 2GM$ in her figure. Can you think of another way of proving the same thing that does not use the congruence of $\triangle PQG$ and $\triangle NMG$? Explain.

   Hint: Think about parallelograms.

3. Do you know other special three-segment sets that are concurrent in triangles? List each set of three segments you know. Draw a diagram for each set.

On Your Own

4. **Standardized Test Prep** Which of the following statements does the diagram below illustrate?

   A. The altitudes of a triangle are concurrent.

   B. The medians of a triangle are perpendicular to the sides of the triangle.

   C. The medians of a triangle are concurrent.

   D. The altitudes of a triangle are parallel.

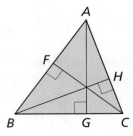

5. For this exercise, you need a piece of cardboard or thick paper and a piece of string knotted at one end.

   • Cut a triangle from the cardboard or paper.

   • Construct the medians of the triangle. Mark the point of concurrence.

   • Poke a tiny hole through the centroid you found. Thread the string through the hole.

   • Hold the end of the string. Let the triangle hang down on the knot.

   • Describe the triangle's position when it stabilizes.

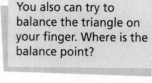

You also can try to balance the triangle on your finger. Where is the balance point?

6. Copy the figure below onto a separate sheet of paper. Then choose a point P on the median $\overline{CM}$ of $\triangle ABC$.

   a. Draw the altitudes from P for $\triangle APM$ and $\triangle BPM$.

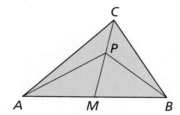

   b. Complete the following statements and justify your answers.

   $$A_{\triangle APC} = A_{\triangle ACM} - A_{\triangle\_?}$$

   $$A_{\triangle BPC} = A_{\triangle\_?} - A_{\triangle\_?}$$

   c. Prove that if P is not on the median $\overline{CM}$, then $A_{\triangle APC} \neq A_{\triangle BPC}$.

   d. Now describe the median $\overline{CM}$ as the set of points with a given property.

Remember...

A *locus* is a set of points with a given property.

7. Use $\triangle ABC$ from Exercise 6. Consider the medians of a triangle as the set of points P with the following property: $A_{\triangle APC} = A_{\triangle BPC}$, (in the case of median $\overline{CM}$). Use an argument similar to Tony's to prove that the three medians of a triangle are concurrent.

8. In this exercise, you will prove that the three altitudes of a triangle are concurrent.

   a. Draw $\triangle ABC$ and its three altitudes.

   b. Through vertex A draw the perpendicular to the altitude through A. Repeat this for the other two vertices.

   c. Mark the three points of intersection of the lines you drew in part (b) and label them D, E, and F.

   d. What are the altitudes of $\triangle ABC$ with respect to $\triangle DEF$?

   e. Explain why the three altitudes of $\triangle ABC$ are concurrent.

9. You can use the following formula to find the area *A* of a triangle if you know the lengths, *a*, *b*, and *c*, of its sides.

$$A = \sqrt{\left(\frac{a+b+c}{2}\right)\left(\frac{b+c-a}{2}\right)\left(\frac{a-b+c}{2}\right)\left(\frac{a+b-c}{2}\right)}$$

The formula above is called *Heron's formula*. Use Heron's formula to find the areas of the triangles below.

   a. a triangle with sides 6 in., 12 in., and 13 in.

   b. $\triangle ABC$

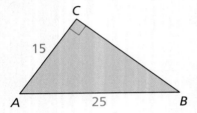

   c. an equilateral triangle with sides 3 cm

   d. an isosceles triangle with base 43 cm and perimeter 89 cm

   e. a triangle with sides 6 cm, 8 cm, and 10 cm

   f. a triangle with sides 4, 6, and 10

Does Heron's formula make sense? Find the areas of the triangles above in a different way and check the answers you found with Heron's formula.

10. Take It Further Brahmagupta's formula is similar to Heron's formula from Exercise 9. Suppose a quadrilateral with side lengths a, b, c, and d is inscribed in a circle. Brahmagupta's formula finds the area A of the quadrilateral.

$$A = \sqrt{\left(\frac{a + b + c - d}{2}\right)\left(\frac{a + b - c + d}{2}\right)\left(\frac{a - b + c + d}{2}\right)\left(\frac{-a + b + c + d}{2}\right)}$$

a. Use Brahmagupta's formula to find the area of the cyclic quadrilateral below.

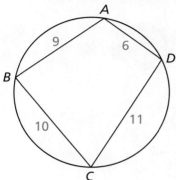

Cyclic quadrilaterals are quadrilaterals inscribed in a circle.

b. Write About It Compare Heron's formula with Brahmagupta's formula. If $d = 0$, what does Brahmagupta's formula become?

c. Is Brahmagupta's formula a generalization of Heron's formula? Explain.

Midpoint and Distance Formulas

Here is some very convenient notation.

When only a few points need names, you can call them A, B, C, and so on, and name their coordinates (a, b), (c, d), (e, f), and so on. If you have too many points, however, you can run out of letters. Since you can never run out of numbers, the convention is to use numbers as subscripts. For example, you could name the vertices of a decagon A_1, A_2, A_3, ..., A_{10}. You could name the vertices of an n-gon B_1, B_2, B_3, ..., B_n.

In-Class Experiment

Copy and complete the table below. Then answer the questions that follow.

Assume that point V_1 has coordinates (x_1, y_1), point V_2 has coordinates (x_2, y_2), and so on.

i	Coordinates of V_i	x_i	y_i
1	(■, ■)	■	■
2	(■, ■)	-2	■
3	$(-4, -2)$	-4	-2
4	(■, ■)	2	■

1. Here is a claim about the coordinates of the vertices of square $V_1 V_2 V_3 V_4$.

   $$x_i = y_{i+1}$$

   Is the claim true when $i = 1$? That is, is it true that $x_1 = y_2$? Is the claim true when $i = 2$? When $i = 3$? When $i = 4$?

2. Here is another claim about the vertices of square $V_1 V_2 V_3 V_4$.

   If V_i has coordinates (x_i, y_i), then V_{i+1} has coordinates $(-y_i, x_i)$.

   a. When $i = 2$, the claim says, "If V_2 has coordinates (x_2, y_2), then V_3 has coordinates $(-y_2, x_2)$." Look at the table and decide whether this is true.

   b. Find a value of i for which the statement does not make sense.

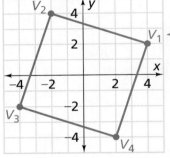

square $V_1 V_2 V_3 V_4$

For example, is it true that $x_1 = y_{1+1} = y_2$?

3. Name the vertices of the square for which it is true that $y_i = \frac{1}{2}x_i$.

4. Here is a rule for deriving a new set of points Q_i from the points V_1, V_2, V_3, and V_4.

   If $V_i = (x_i, y_i)$, then $Q_i = (x_i - 3, y_i + 4)$.

   a. The rule is written in algebraic symbols. Explain the rule in words.

   b. Find the new points Q_1, Q_2, Q_3, and Q_4 and plot them.

5. If $P_1 = (x_1, y_1)$, and you know that P_2 is a second point on the same horizontal line, how can you write its coordinates?

6. Let $P_i = (x_i, y_i)$, $x_i = i + 3$, and $y_i = x_i - 4$. Plot P_i as i goes from 1 to 8. Describe the result.

Minds in Action

Sasha and Derman are trying to write a formula for finding the distance between two points. They are given

$$G = (x_1, y_1), \quad H = (x_2, y_2)$$

Sasha   Well, the distance between two points on a vertical or horizontal line is easy to find. Just subtract the unlike coordinates. If G is (3, 4) and H is (3, 90), then the distance between G and H is $90 - 4 = 86$.

Derman   But we don't know that G and H are on a horizontal or vertical line. They're just *any* two points.

We used the Pythagorean Theorem to help us find the distance between two points that weren't on the same horizontal or vertical line before. Let's try that here.

Sasha   Don't we need three points to make a triangle so we can use the Pythagorean Theorem?

Derman   Watch! I'll make a third point:

Before you ask, I know that the third point is (x_1, y_2). In my picture I had to go over as far as the (x_1, y_1) point—that's where I got the x_1—and up as far as the (x_2, y_2) point—that's where I got the y_2.

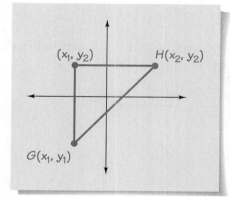

What are the lengths of the legs of this right triangle?

Sasha   Great! Now let's use the Pythagorean Theorem to find the length of the hypotenuse of that triangle.

$$(x_2 - x_1)^2 + (y_2 - y_1)^2 = GH^2$$

So,

$$GH = \sqrt{(x_2 - x_1)^2 + (y_2 - y_1)^2}$$

Derman and Sasha's explanation is a proof of the following theorem.

Theorem 9.3 Distance Formula

The distance between two points (x_1, y_1) and (x_2, y_2) can be found using the Pythagorean Theorem. It is the square root of the sum of the square of the difference in the *x*-coordinates and the square of the difference in the *y*-coordinates.

Habits of Mind

Use facts you know. If you remember how you found it, you do not have to remember the Distance Formula. You can figure it out just by remembering the Pythagorean Theorem.

For You to Do

Find the distance between each pair of points.

7. $(1, 1)$ and $(-1, -1)$

8. $(1, 1)$ and $(4, 5)$

9. $(2, 4)$ and $(-4, -2)$

When you found the midpoint of a segment previously, you may have used a method like this:

The *x*-coordinate is equal to the average of the *x*-coordinates of the endpoints. The *y*-coordinate is equal to the average of the *y*-coordinates of the endpoints.

Or, you can write it algebraically.

$$\left(\frac{x_1 + x_2}{2}, \frac{y_1 + y_2}{2}\right)$$

You can use Derman's diagram from Minds in Action to help justify this method for finding the midpoint.

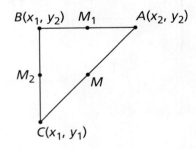

Theorem 9.4 Midpoint Formula

Each coordinate of the midpoint of a line segment is equal to the average of the corresponding coordinates of the endpoints of the line segment.

Proof First, find the midpoint M_1 of $\overline{AB}$. This segment is horizontal, so every point on it has the same y-coordinate. You also know that $\frac{x_1 + x_2}{2}$ is the number halfway between x_1 and x_2. This means that the coordinates of M_1 are $\left(\frac{x_1 + x_2}{2}, y_2\right)$.

You can show that the distance from M_1 to A is the same as the distance from B to M_1 by looking at the difference in the x-coordinates of these points, since they are all on the same horizontal line.

$$M_1 \text{ to } A: x_2 - \left(\frac{x_1 + x_2}{2}\right) = \frac{x_2 - x_1}{2}$$

$$B \text{ to } M_1: \frac{x_1 + x_2}{2} - x_1 = \frac{x_1 + x_2}{2} - \frac{2x_1}{2} = \frac{x_2 - x_1}{2}$$

The same reasoning shows that the midpoint M_2 of the segment with coordinates (x_1, y_1) and (x_1, y_2) has coordinates $\left(x_1, \frac{y_1 + y_2}{2}\right)$. In this case, the three points are on a vertical line, so they must all have the same x-coordinate.

Now you need to find the coordinates of M, the midpoint of $\overline{AC}$. The Midline Theorem (Theorem 6.13) says that the segment joining the midpoints of two sides of a triangle is parallel to the third side. Also, its measure is equal to half the measure of the third side.

This means that if you draw a line through M_1 and M (wherever it is), that line must be parallel to $\overline{BC}$. And that means that the line through M_1 and M is vertical. Because you know that on a vertical line all points have the same x-coordinate, you know that the x-coordinate of M is $\frac{x_1 + x_2}{2}$.

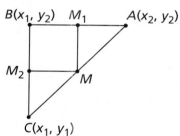

Similarly, if you draw a line through M_2 and M, that line will be parallel to $\overline{AB}$. It will be horizontal and will have the same y-coordinate as M_2, namely $\frac{y_1 + y_2}{2}$.

So the coordinates of M are $\left(\frac{x_1 + x_2}{2}, \frac{y_1 + y_2}{2}\right)$.

About halfway between Penzance and Land's End is the hamlet of Crows-an-wra. About how far, and in what direction, is the hamlet from this marker?

For You to Do

10. Find the midpoint of the segment with endpoints $(1327, 94)$ and $(-668, 17)$.

11. Find the midpoint of the segment with endpoints $(1776, 13)$ and $(2000, 50)$.

Check Your Understanding

1. Points A and B are endpoints of a diameter of a circle. Point C is the center of the circle. Find the coordinates of C given the following coordinates for A and B.

   a. $(-79, 687)$, $(13, 435)$

   b. $(x, 0)$, $(5x, y)$

2. Points A through G lie on a circle of radius 10, as shown in the figure. Find their missing coordinates.

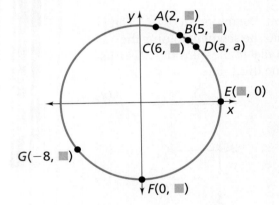

3. The vertices of $\triangle ABC$ are $A(2, 1)$, $B(4, 8)$, and $C(6, -2)$.

   a. Find the lengths of the three sides of the triangle.

   b. Find the lengths of the three medians of the triangle.

4. Consider the six points $A(5, 1)$, $B(10, -2)$, $C(8, 3)$, $A'(2, 3)$, $B'(7, 0)$, and $C'(5, 5)$. Show that $\triangle ABC \cong \triangle A'B'C'$.

5. Consider the six points $A(-800, -500)$, $B(160, 12)$, $C(-737, -484)$, $A'(0, 0)$, $B'(3840, 2048)$, and $C'(252, 64)$. Show that $\triangle ABC \sim \triangle A'B'C'$.

6. **Write About It** Explain how to tell whether two triangles are congruent by doing calculations on the coordinates of their vertices.

7. **Write About It** Explain how to tell whether two triangles are similar by doing calculations on the coordinates of their vertices.

8. Quadrilateral *STAR* has vertices $S(-2, 8)$, $T(8, 2)$, $A(0, -4)$, and $R(-2, 0)$. Find the coordinates of the midpoints of the four sides of quadrilateral *STAR*. These points determine a new quadrilateral. Show that this new quadrilateral is a parallelogram.

9. Pick any four points that form a quadrilateral in the coordinate plane. Find the midpoints of all four sides. Show that if you connect the midpoints in order, you get a parallelogram.

> One way to show that a quadrilateral is a parallelogram is to show that opposite sides are parallel. What is another way?

On Your Own

10. Three vertices of a square are $(-1, 5)$, $(5, 3)$, and $(3, -3)$.
    a. Find the center of the square.
    b. Find the fourth vertex.

11. Three vertices of a square are $(-114, 214)$, $(186, 114)$, and $(-214, -86)$.
    a. Find the center of the square.
    b. Find the fourth vertex.

12. $\overline{DE}$ has midpoint $F(4.5, 17)$ and one endpoint $D(2, 16)$. What are the coordinates of the other endpoint, E?

13. $\overline{AB}$ and $\overline{CD}$ bisect each other. Given the points $A(110, 15)$, $B(116, 23)$, and $C(110, 23)$, find E, the point of bisection. Also, find the coordinates of D.

> **Remember...**
>
> Two segments bisect each other if they intersect at each other's midpoint.

14. A segment has length 25. Give possible coordinates for the endpoints of this segment in each case below.
    a. The segment is on a horizontal line.
    b. The segment is on a vertical line.
    c. The segment is neither horizontal nor vertical.

15. A segment has its midpoint at $(8, 10)$. List four possibilities for the coordinates of its endpoints.

16. A segment has one endpoint at $(-7, -2)$ and its midpoint at $(-2, 1.5)$. What are the coordinates of the other endpoint?

17. **Standardized Test Prep** Julio is planning to swim across the lake at his summer camp. On a map, the coordinates of his starting point are $(-2 \text{ cm}, 3.5 \text{ cm})$. The dock to which he will swim has coordinates $(14 \text{ cm}, -8.5 \text{ cm})$. The scale on the map is 1 cm : 100 m. What distance will Julio have to swim?

A. 1200 meters

B. 1300 meters

C. 1600 meters

D. 2000 meters

18. Suppose you have points $P(5, 0)$ and $Q(15, 0)$.

a. Find six points that are just as far from P as they are from Q.

b. Find six points that are closer to P than they are to Q.

c. How can you tell if a point is equidistant from P and Q just by looking at its coordinates?

19. The endpoints of a line segment are the midpoints of two sides of a triangle. Show that the length of this segment is one half the length of the third side of that triangle. Show that this is true for any triangle. (Use subscript notation.)

Habits of Mind

Use a symbol. You could use d_s for the length of a side of the triangle. You must show that d_m, the distance between the midpoints, is $\frac{1}{2}d_s$. But think ahead. Would it be helpful to use $2d_s$ for the length of a side?

Maintain Your Skills

Find the slope between each pair of points.

20. $(3, 85)$ and $(0, 124)$

21. $(0, 124)$ and $(4, 72)$

22. $(4, 72)$ and $(-111, 1567)$

23. $(-111, 1567)$ and $(2, 98)$

24. $(2, 98)$ and $(3, 85)$

Remember...

You find slope by calculating the ratio between the change in y-coordinates and the change in x-coordinates.

Go Online
www.successnetplus.com

Mathematical 9A Reflections

In this investigation, you learned how to apply properties of similarity, prove theorems using similarity, and draw strategic circles, segments, and points to solve problems. These questions will help you summarize what you have learned.

1. Sophie and Erin are measuring things for a school project. They accidentally drop their yardstick down a hole, where it lies flat along the bottom.

    Erin holds a 12-in. ruler out over the hole at ground level. Sophie looks straight down into the hole and notices that, from her perspective, the ruler *exactly* covers the yardstick.

    If Sophie's eyes are 5 feet above the ruler, how deep is the hole?

2. Find the arithmetic and geometric mean for the numbers 6 and 24. Explain how each of the means is halfway between the two numbers.

3. If the altitude to the hypotenuse of a right triangle is also a median, what can you conclude about the original right triangle? Explain.

4. Prove that if $\triangle ABC \sim \triangle AHB$, then $\triangle AHB \sim \triangle BHC$.

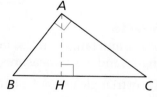

5. Describe how to locate the centroid of a triangle without constructing more than one of its medians.

6. What is the Arithmetic-Geometric Mean Inequality?

7. Why does the altitude to the hypotenuse of a right triangle form three similar triangles?

8. In $\triangle ABC$, suppose that $AH = 12$ cm and $BA = 15$ cm. What is HC?

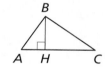

Vocabulary

In this investigation, you learned these terms. Make sure you understand what each one means and how to use it.

- **arithmetic mean**
- **geometric mean**
- **projection**

Use 1-inch grid paper to capture an image similar to this prince.

Exploring Right Triangles

In *Exploring Right Triangles*, you will learn a great deal about all triangles, and even all polygons. Every *n*-sided polygon can be subdivided into $n - 2$ triangles by connecting one vertex of the polygon to each nonadjacent vertex.

In this investigation, you will see how to use ratios of side lengths in right triangles to determine side lengths and angle measures in triangles and in other figures.

By the end of this investigation, you will be able to answer questions like these.

1. How can you use half of a square or half of an equilateral triangle to evaluate trigonometric functions for angles measuring 30°, 45°, and 60°?

2. Find the sine, cosine, and tangent of α and β in terms of the side lengths of $\triangle ABC$.

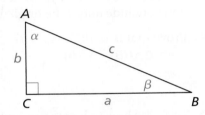

How far out and how high up can the ladder reach?

3. What is the area of $\triangle LMN$? What is the approximate length of $\overline{MN}$?

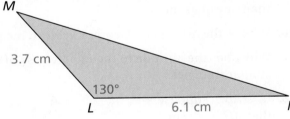

You will learn how to

• use the sine, cosine, and tangent ratios and their inverses to find missing side lengths and angle measures in triangles

• find the area of any triangle given the lengths of two sides and the measure of their included angle

• find the length of the third side of a triangle given the lengths of two sides and the measure of their included angle

You will develop these habits and skills:

• Find invariants in classes of right triangles.

• Visualize right triangles in different problem situations.

• Choose appropriate strategies to find missing angle measures and side lengths.

You have already investigated the Pythagorean Theorem, which explains how the lengths of the sides of right triangles are related to each other. But how can you use information about the lengths of the sides of a right triangle to tell you about the measures of its angles?

In the following In-Class Experiment, you will study a right triangle that is the side view of a ramp. You will vary the lengths of the sides of the triangle. You will develop some conjectures about how different side lengths relate to the ramp's angle of inclination.

In-Class Experiment

You can specify a ramp by giving any two of the measurements indicated in the figure below.

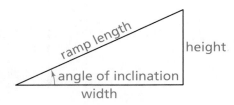

Habits of Mind

Visualize. Why are only two of these measurements enough? What else do you know about the ramp?

1. Decide which ramp is the steepest.

   Use any method you like, such as constructing physical scale models, making graphical models, or using calculations. Be prepared to explain why your method is valid as well as why your choice is the steepest ramp.

   Ramp A: width 9.2 feet, height 3.3 feet

   Ramp B: ramp length 10.2 m, height 3.8 m

   Ramp C: height 3.1 feet, width 8.5 feet

   Ramp D: width 9 m, ramp length 10.8 m

   Ramp E: ramp length 3 yards, angle of inclination 30°

   Ramp F: height 3 feet, width 7 feet

For You to Explore

2. Two ladders are leaned against a wall so that they make the same angle with the ground.

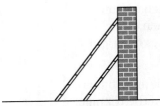

The 10-foot ladder reaches 8 feet up the wall. How much farther up the wall does the 18-foot ladder reach?

3. Workers accidentally drop a metal pipe that is 10 feet long. It falls into a cylindrical hole with a radius of 4 feet and a grate across the top. The pipe comes to rest leaning across the bottom of the hole. The workers are able to just reach the upper end of the pipe through the grate with a magnet at the end of a rope that is 7 feet long. About how deep is the hole?

4. **Write About It** Describe how to compare the steepness of two ramps given the following measurements for each ramp.

   • ramp length and width
   • ramp length and height
   • width and height

As you raise the truck bed, which measures change?

On Your Own

5. The width and height of four ramps are given. Which ramp is the steepest? Explain.

   Ramp A: width 10 feet, height 6 feet

   Ramp B: width 5 miles, height 3 miles

   Ramp C: width 15 inches, height 9 inches

   Ramp D: width 50 cm, height 30 cm

6. **What's Wrong Here?** Derman says that Exercise 5 proves that units are completely irrelevant when you compare the steepness of ramps. Explain how units *can* have an effect when you compare the steepness of two ramps.

7. Hannah's method for comparing the steepness of ramps is to construct a triangle that is similar to the triangle formed by the ramp, but with a width of 1. Then she compares the heights of the similar triangles in order to choose the steepest ramp. Try Hannah's method to determine which of the following ramps is the steepest.

   Ramp A: ramp length 18 cm, height 6 cm

   Ramp B: ramp length 43 inches, width 41 inches

   Ramp C: width 50.9 mm, height 18.5 mm

8. Ramp A has an angle of inclination of 30°. Ramp B has width 8.9 feet and height 5.3 feet. Which ramp is steeper? How did you decide?

9. When you are standing at point *A*, you have to tilt your head up 27° to see the very top of a tree. You are 40 feet from the tree. Approximately how tall is the tree?

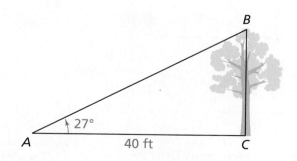

This picture is not exactly right. To simplify the problem, something was ignored. What is it?

10. When you are in a boat at point A, you have to tilt your head up 27° to see the very top of the Statue of Liberty. The statue (including its base) is about 300 feet tall. Approximately how far are you from the bottom of the base?

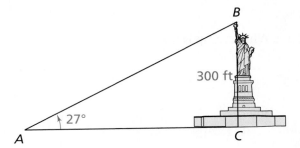

11. Refer to Exercises 9 and 10 to answer the following questions.

  a. List some things that these two exercises have in common.

  b. Explain why the value of $\frac{BC}{AC}$ is the same for both triangles.

  c. Measure one of the triangles and calculate this constant value. Did you use this relationship in your solutions to Exercises 9 and 10?

12. You have likely conjectured that there is a relationship between the height-to-width ratio of a ramp and its angle of inclination. The larger the height-to-width ratio, the larger the angle. Estimate the height-to-width ratio for each angle of inclination.

  a. 30°   **b.** 37°   **c.** 45°   **d.** 60°

Maintain Your Skills

13. In the following series of ramps, the height is always 1 foot, but the width of the ramp gets progressively wider.

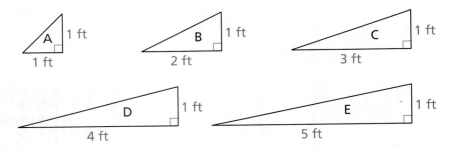

Compute or measure the following quantities for each ramp. Describe how the quantity changes from Ramp A to Ramp E.

  a. ramp length

  b. angle of inclination

  c. ratio of height to width

  d. ratio of height to ramp length

Some Special Triangles

Every triangle has three side lengths and three angle measures. In fact, you only need to know three of the measurements—all three side lengths (SSS), two sides and the included angle (SAS), or two angles and one side length (ASA and AAS). There must be some way to figure out what the other three measurements are from the ones you know.

Minds in Action

Tony and Sasha are talking about situations in which they could use three triangle facts to determine the others.

Tony   If you just know three sides of a triangle, how could you ever figure out what the angles are without constructing it?

Sasha   Well, I don't know how to do it for *every* triangle. I bet I can give you three facts that you could use to solve for the other three.

Here's one I *know* you know. What if △ABC has three sides that all measure 6.17 cm? What are its angle measures?

Tony   Okay. That one I get. So I agree that there are some special cases that are possible to do. How about a side-angle-side set?

Sasha   How about △DEF with DE = 4 in., EF = 4 in., and m∠E = 90°?

Tony   With two sides of a right triangle, I can always figure out the length of the third side, but how can I figure out the other two angle measures? Oh, it's an isosceles right triangle.

Now I've got an angle-side-angle set for you, Sasha: △GHI where m∠G = 30°, m∠H = 60°, and GH = 6 mm.

Sasha   That one's tricky, but at least it must be a right triangle. I'll draw a sketch.

Hey! This is just half of an equilateral triangle!

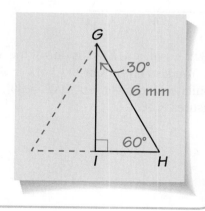

△ABC looks like this:

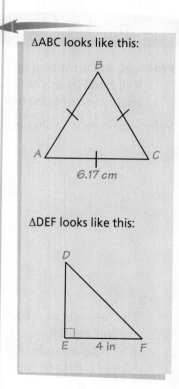

△DEF looks like this:

For You to Do

Answer these questions about the several triangles that were mentioned in the Minds in Action.

1. What are the measures of the angles of △*ABC*? Explain.

2. What are the missing measures of △*DEF*? Explain.

3. What are the missing measures of △*GHI*? Explain.

4. Create a new problem in which you specify only three measurements for a triangle. Make sure the other three measurements can be determined from the given information. Exchange problems with a classmate.

In the Minds in Action, Tony and Sasha discussed an isosceles right triangle and a triangle that is half of an equilateral triangle. You already know many properties of these two triangles. Now it is time to learn how the angle measures and the three side lengths in each are related.

> A 30-60-90 triangle is a right triangle that is half of an equilateral triangle.

Example

Problem An altitude of an equilateral triangle cuts it into two right triangles. If the side length of the original triangle is *a*, find all the side lengths and angle measures for one such right triangle.

Solution Here is a diagram of the situation.

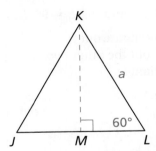

The measure of ∠*KLM* = 60°, because ∠*KLM* is one of the angles of the original equilateral triangle. You also know that $m\angle LMK = 90°$, because $\overline{KM}$ is an altitude of the equilateral triangle. $m\angle MKL = 30°$, because the sum of the three angle measures is 180°.

$KL = a$, because $\overline{KL}$ is one of the sides of the original equilateral triangle. $LM = \frac{a}{2}$, because the altitude of an isosceles triangle bisects the base. You can find KM by using the Pythagorean Theorem.

$$KM^2 + LM^2 = KL^2$$

$$KM^2 + \left(\frac{a}{2} \right)^2 = a^2$$

$$KM^2 = \frac{3a^2}{4}$$

$$KM = \frac{\sqrt{3}a}{2}$$

Habits of Mind

Prove. If you did not remember that the altitude of an isosceles triangle must bisect its base, you could quickly prove it using AAS congruence of the two right triangles.

Here is the triangle with all of its angle measures and side lengths marked. Learn to look for and recognize triangles with these angles, or with side lengths that are proportional to those in this triangle.

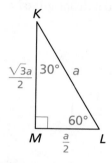

You can also call this triangle a 30-60-90 triangle. The ratio of side lengths in a 30-60-90 triangle is $1 : \sqrt{3} : 2$.

For You to Do

A diagonal of a square cuts it into two congruent right triangles.

5. If the side length of the square is a, find all the side lengths and angle measures for one such right triangle.

A right triangle that is half of a square is an isosceles right triangle. You can also call it a 45-45-90 triangle. Learn to look for and recognize triangles with these angles, or with side lengths that are proportional to those of an isosceles right triangle. The ratio of side lengths in a 45-45-90 triangle is $1 : 1 : \sqrt{2}$.

Exercises *Practicing Habits of Mind*

Check Your Understanding

1. When you are trying to recognize the special right triangles discussed in this lesson, it will be useful to remember the converse of the Pythagorean Theorem. If the three side lengths a, b, and c are such that $a^2 + b^2 = c^2$, then the triangle they form must be a right triangle. Prove this.

For Exercises 2 and 3, find the missing angle measures and side length of each triangle. Explain your answers.

2.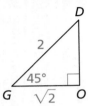

3.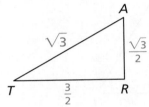

4. Suppose you know that two sides of a triangle measure 1 in. and 2 in. One of the angles of this triangle measures 60°. Is this triangle a 30-60-90 triangle? Sketch any possible triangles that meet these requirements.

On Your Own

For Exercises 5–8, find any missing angle measures or side lengths. Explain your answers.

5.

6.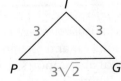

7.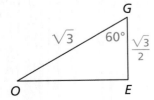

8.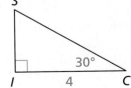

9. **Standardized Test Prep** The Garden Club is building a flower garden for Lincoln High School. The design is a square with diagonal walkways. The length of each walkway is 49.5 ft. Find the approximate area of the garden.

   A. $1225\,\text{ft}^2$ **B.** $1980\,\text{ft}^2$ **C.** $2450\,\text{ft}^2$ **D.** $4900\,\text{ft}^2$

10. **What's Wrong Here?** Derman and Sasha made up triangle problems so they could practice with the special right triangles from this lesson.

    Derman wrote this problem:

    In $\triangle DER$, $DE = 2$ cm, $DR = 1$ cm, and $m\angle EDR = 30°$. Find the missing side lengths and angle measures.

    Sasha said, "I don't think we can solve that one yet." Derman said, "Oh come on, it's easy. Here's a picture."

    Explain what is wrong with Derman's solution. Use paper and pencil or geometry software to construct the triangle with Derman's given information.

    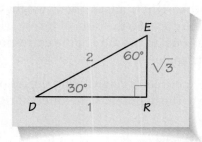

11. A right triangle with a 30° angle has one side that is 1 inch long. Show all possible triangles. Find and label the lengths of the other two sides in each case.

12. A right triangle with a 45° angle has one side that is 1 inch long. Show all possible triangles. Find and label the lengths of the other two sides in each case.

13. Given $AB = 4\sqrt{3}$ cm, find AE.

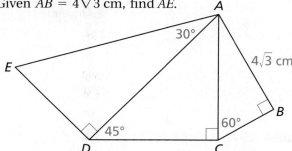

Maintain Your Skills

14. $\triangle ABC$ is a right triangle with $m\angle B = 90°$. Find $\dfrac{AB}{AC}$, $\dfrac{BC}{AC}$, and $\dfrac{AB}{BC}$ for each measure of $\angle C$ below.

    a. $m\angle C = 30°$ **b.** $m\angle C = 45°$ **c.** $m\angle C = 60°$

9.08 Some Special Ratios

If you have enough information to determine a triangle completely, then there ought to be a way to figure out all of the missing measurements. Right now, you can figure out the missing measurements for two special triangles: a 30-60-90 triangle and a 45-45-90 triangle.

For example, suppose you know that the hypotenuse of a 30-60-90 triangle is 4 feet long. From this information, you can conclude that the side opposite the 30° angle is 2 feet long. This is because you know that the ratio of the side opposite the 30° angle to the hypotenuse of a 30-60-90 triangle is always $\frac{1}{2}$.

The ratios of the side lengths of other right triangles are also constant ratios. For instance, suppose a nonright angle in one right triangle is congruent to a nonright angle in another right triangle. The two right triangles must be similar by the AA similarity test. So the ratio of two side lengths of the first right triangle must be equal to the ratio of the corresponding two side lengths of the other right triangle.

In the following In-Class Experiment, you will find the ratio of the side opposite a nonright angle to the hypotenuse in different right triangles.

> *To determine a triangle completely* means that you know enough measurements to guarantee that any other triangle with those measurements must be congruent to your triangle.

In-Class Experiment

Use geometry software to construct $\triangle ABC$ with $m\angle ABC = 90°$. Start with a small value for $m\angle C$ and gradually increase it. Make a table showing $m\angle C$ and the ratio $\frac{AB}{AC}$.

1. As $m\angle C$ increases, what happens to the value of $\frac{AB}{AC}$?

2. What is the value of $\frac{AB}{AC}$ when $m\angle C = 30°$? When $m\angle C = 45°$? When $m\angle C = 60°$?

3. What value does the ratio $\frac{AB}{AC}$ approach as $m\angle C$ approaches 0°? As $m\angle C$ approaches 90°?

4. If $\frac{AB}{AC} \approx 0.34$, what is an approximate measure for $\angle C$?

Discuss your results with your classmates.

> If you do not have access to geometry software, you can still make this table, but your measurements will be less accurate.

The problems you have been solving in this investigation are all examples of **trigonometry,** the study of triangles, in action. For easy reference, names are given to some of the constant ratios found in right triangles. In right triangle *ABC,* the names of these ratios are given and defined on the following page.

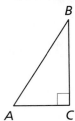

Trigonometric Ratios

The **sine** of $\angle A$ is defined as $\frac{BC}{AB}$, the ratio of the length of the side opposite $\angle A$ to the length of the hypotenuse.

Sine is often abbreviated as sin, so sin A is the same as sine A.

The **cosine** of $\angle A$ is defined as $\frac{AC}{AB}$, the ratio of the length of the side adjacent to $\angle A$ to the length of the hypotenuse.

Cosine is often abbreviated as cos, so cos A is the same as cosine A.

The **tangent** of $\angle A$ is defined as $\frac{BC}{AC}$, the ratio of the length of the side opposite $\angle A$ to the length of the side adjacent to $\angle A$.

Tangent is often abbreviated as tan, so tan A is the same as tangent A.

In this course, you define the sine, cosine, and tangent ratios of an acute angle of a right triangle as the ratios of the side lengths of the right triangle. So, you define the trigonometric ratios for angles with measures that are greater than 0° and less than 90°.

Facts and Notation

When you find the trigonometric ratio of an acute angle of a right triangle, you can identify the acute angle in three ways.

- by degree measure: sin 27°
- by vertex: sin A
- by Greek letter: sin θ

The notation you choose will depend on the figure you are considering. If more than one angle has the same vertex, you have to use a three-letter angle name, such as sin $\angle BAC$. The alternative is to name the interior of each angle with a Greek letter, such as θ.

In *Mathematics III,* you will extend the domain of the trigonometric ratios and be able to evaluate them for angles that cannot occur in right triangles.

You can find the values of sine, cosine, and tangent for any angle using the trigonometric functions on your calculator. For example, if you enter "tan 27°" into a calculator, it gives the value 0.51, to the nearest hundredth. Different calculators may evaluate trigonometric functions differently. Determine the keystrokes needed on your calculator to evaluate tan 27°.

Note that your calculator can give you the values of these ratios to many decimal places of accuracy. However, even when your calculator shows a full display of digits, it may still be expressing an approximation of the actual value.

Example

Problem In △*ABC*, *m*∠*B* = 90° and *BC* = 8. The area of △*ABC* is 24 cm². Find the rest of the side lengths and angle measures of the triangle. Indicate whether your measurements are *exact* or *approximate* in each case.

Solution The height of the triangle relative to $\overline{BC}$ is *AB*.

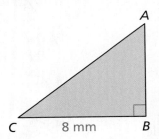

To find *AB*, use the area formula for a triangle.

$$A_{\triangle ABC} = \tfrac{1}{2}(BC)(AB)$$
$$24 = \tfrac{1}{2}(8)(AB)$$
$$AB = 6$$

$\overline{AB}$ is exactly 6 cm long.

Since △*ABC* is a right triangle, use the Pythagorean Theorem to find *AC*.

$$8^2 + 6^2 = (AC)^2$$

This gives *AC* = 10 cm, so $\overline{AC}$ is exactly 10 cm long.

To find the angle measures, use the inverse of a trigonometric function on your calculator. The notation $\sin^{-1} 0.6$ is used for the *inverse* of the sine function. It means, "Find the angle with a sine of 0.6."

$$\sin C = \tfrac{6}{10}, \text{ so } m\angle C = \sin^{-1} 0.6$$
$$m\angle C \approx 36.87°$$

Similarly,

$$\cos A = \tfrac{6}{10}, \text{ so } m\angle A = \cos^{-1} 0.6$$
$$m\angle A \approx 53.13°$$

These angle measures are approximate.

For You to Do

5. In △*MIN*, *m*∠*M* = 25°, *m*∠*N* = 90°, and *MI* = 5 inches. Find the rest of the side lengths and angle measures of the triangle. Indicate whether your measurements are *exact* or *approximate* in each case.

Exercises Practicing Habits of Mind

In the exercises for this lesson, be sure to indicate whether your solutions are *exact* or *approximate*. Find exact answers when possible.

Check Your Understanding

1. Rewrite these statements using the language of trigonometry:

a. In right triangle *ABC* with $m\angle A = 40°$, the ratio of the length of the side opposite $\angle A$ to the length of the hypotenuse is 0.64.

b. In right triangle *DEF* with $m\angle E = 70°$, the ratio of the length of the side adjacent to $\angle E$ to the length of the hypotenuse is 0.34.

c. In right triangle *GHI* with $m\angle H = 55°$, the ratio of the length of the side opposite $\angle H$ to the length of the side adjacent to $\angle H$ is 1.43.

> The ratios in parts (a)–(c) are accurate to two decimal places.

In Exercises 2 and 3,

a. Find $\sin A,\ \cos A,$ and $\tan A$ for each triangle.

b. Find $\sin B,\ \cos B,$ and $\tan B$ for each triangle.

c. Which of your answers from parts (a) and (b) are the same? Explain.

2.

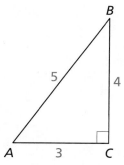

3.

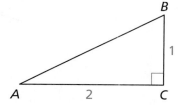

4. Find $\sin B$ and $\cos B$ for isosceles triangle *ABC* at the right.

5. An airplane takes off and flies 10,000 feet in a straight line, making a 25° angle with the ground. How high above the ground does the airplane rise?

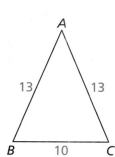

6. In $\triangle TUB$, $m\angle T = 90°$, $m\angle U = 70°$, and $TU = 8$ cm. Find the rest of the side lengths and angle measures.

7. **Standardized Test Prep** Find $\sin\theta$, $\cos\theta$, and $\tan\theta$ for the triangle below.

   A. $\sin\theta = \frac{1}{4}$, $\cos\theta = \frac{3}{4}$, $\tan\theta = 3$

   B. $\sin\theta = \frac{3}{\sqrt{10}}$, $\cos\theta = \frac{1}{\sqrt{10}}$, $\tan\theta = 3$

   C. $\sin\theta = 1$, $\cos\theta = 3$, $\tan\theta = \sqrt{10}$

   D. $\sin\theta = \frac{1}{\sqrt{10}}$, $\cos\theta = \frac{3}{\sqrt{10}}$, $\tan\theta = \frac{1}{3}$

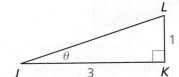

8. Triangle RST is a right triangle with right angle at S. If $\tan R = \frac{2}{3}$, find $\sin R$ and $\cos R$.

9. Triangle JKL is a right triangle with right angle at K. $\overline{JK}$ is three times the length of $\overline{KL}$. Find the sine, cosine, and tangent of $\angle J$ and of $\angle L$.

> Drawing a sketch will help.

10. For each right triangle below, find the exact values for the sine, cosine, and tangent of $\angle A$ and $\angle B$.

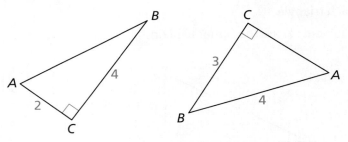

11. Use your calculator to evaluate the following expressions. Round your answers to the nearest hundredth.

   a. $\sin 33°$ **b.** $\cos 33°$ **c.** $\tan 33°$ **d.** $\frac{\sin 33°}{\cos 33°}$

   e. $\sin 57°$ **f.** $\cos 57°$ **g.** $\tan 57°$ **h.** $\frac{\sin 57°}{\cos 57°}$

12. In Exercise 11, there are several expressions that have the same value. Identify those expressions. In each case, explain why the two expressions are equal.

   Refer to $\triangle ABC$ for Exercises 13–16.

13. Find $\sin\theta$, $\cos\theta$, and $\tan\theta$.

14. How is $\tan\theta$ related to $\sin\theta$ and $\cos\theta$? Write an equation that represents this relationship.

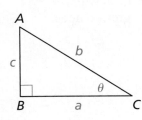

15. Sophia says the following equations are true for all values of θ.

$$\sin\theta = \cos(90° - \theta) \qquad \cos\theta = \sin(90° - \theta)$$

Is she right? Explain.

16. Joe says the following equation is true for all values of θ.

$$(\sin\theta)^2 + (\cos\theta)^2 = 1$$

Is he right? Try it out for a few numerical values of θ and then in a general triangle with sides a, b, and c.

> You will often see $(\sin\theta)^2$ written as $\sin^2\theta$. This is a common notation used to show a trigonometric ratio raised to a power.

17. To the nearest tenth, the value of $\tan 57°$ is 1.5. To the nearest thousandth, it is 1.540. Solve for the length of $\overline{BC}$ in $\triangle ABC$ using each of these values. By how much do your two answers differ?

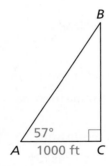

18. The piece of paper below originally showed a complete right triangle, $\triangle ABC$, with right angle at C. The paper was ripped, though, so that all you can see now is $\angle A$.

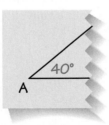

Find as many of these values as you can using a calculator. Some values might not be possible to find.

a. $\dfrac{BC}{AC}$ **b.** $AC + BC$ **c.** $\dfrac{BC}{AB}$ **d.** $AB \cdot AC$

e. $\dfrac{AC}{AB}$ **f.** $AB - BC$ **g.** $\dfrac{AC}{BC}$

19. Take It Further Follow the steps in parts (a)–(f) below to find the exact value of cos 72°. The isosceles triangle *ABC* at the left has base angles measuring 72°. *AB* = 1 and *AC* = 1. The same triangle is at the right with $\overline{BD}$ bisecting ∠*B*. *BD* = *x*.

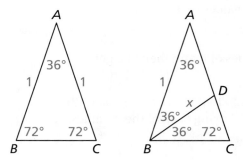

a. Find the lengths of $\overline{BC}$, $\overline{AD}$, and $\overline{DC}$ in terms of *x*.

b. Explain why △*ABC* ~ △*BCD*.

c. Write a proportion involving *AB*, *BC*, and *CD*.

d. Use your proportion from part (c) and the Quadratic Formula to solve for *x*.

e. Divide △*ABC* into two right triangles by drawing its altitude from *A*.

f. Use either of these right triangles and the value of *x* to find cos 72°.

Now find cos 72° on a calculator. Compare the value the calculator gives to the exact value you found.

20. Take It Further Find cos 36° by dividing △*ABD* in Exercise 19 into two right triangles. As in Exercise 19, compare this exact value to the value a calculator gives for cos 36°.

Maintain Your Skills

For each triangle, find the missing side lengths and angle measures.

21.

22.

23.

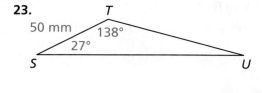

Go Online
www.successnetplus.com

Finding Triangle Areas

The trigonometric functions sine, cosine, and tangent have proven very valuable in determining missing side lengths and angle measures in right triangles. In this lesson, you will use trigonometric functions to determine areas and other measurements in nonright triangles.

 Go Online
www.successnetplus.com

Minds in Action

Derman has made a discovery!

Derman I can find the area of any triangle if you tell me two sides and the included angle!

Tony Any triangle? Really? Okay, in $\triangle ABC$, $AB = 6$ cm, $AC = 8$ cm, and $m\angle B = 20°$.

Derman Here's my sketch.

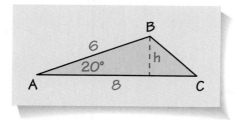

So $\frac{h}{6} = \sin 20°$ and $h = 6 \sin 20°$, which is about 2 cm. That means the area of $\triangle ABC$ is about $\frac{1}{2}(2)(8)$, or about 8 cm².

Tony Nice! Does it work if the angle is obtuse? After all, we've only defined the sine function for acute angles.

Derman I'm not sure. Let's try one.

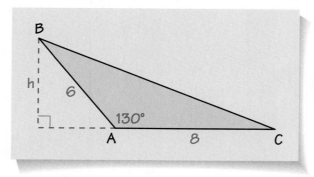

Tony   I see how to do it. You just use the little right triangle that has the height as one of its legs.

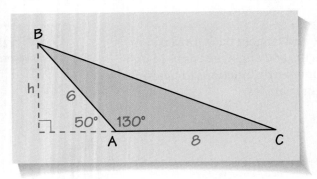

And we've got it. The area is approximately 18.4 cm².

Check Tony's calculations.

For You to Do

Find the area of each triangle.

1.

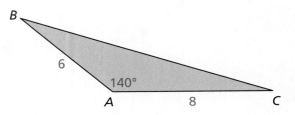

2.

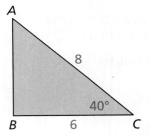

3.

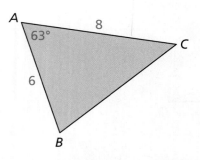

In this lesson, you have already seen that you can determine the area of any triangle given two sides and their included angle. There should be a way to find approximations for the other two angle measures, and the missing side length, as well. The following example shows one way to do this.

Example

Problem Find the missing side length and angle measures in $\triangle ABC$.

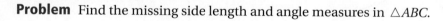

Solution Derman has already found that the height of this triangle is approximately 2 cm. You can use the same technique to find the length marked x, and then y.

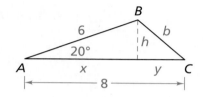

$$\frac{x}{6} = \cos 20° \qquad y = 8 - x$$

$$x = 6 \cos 20° \qquad y \approx 8 - 5.6$$

$$\approx 5.6 \text{ cm} \qquad \approx 2.4 \text{ cm}$$

Since $\tan C = \frac{h}{y}$, you can find $m\angle C$ and $m\angle B$.

$$\tan C = \frac{h}{y} \qquad\qquad m\angle B = 180° - m\angle A - m\angle C$$

$$m\angle C = \tan^{-1}\left(\frac{2}{2.4}\right) \qquad\qquad \approx 180° - 20° - 39.8°$$

$$\approx 39.8° \qquad\qquad \approx 120.2°$$

All that is left to find is b. One way to find it is to see that $\frac{h}{b} = \sin C$.

$$b = \frac{h}{\sin C}$$

$$\approx \frac{2}{0.64}$$

$$\approx 3.1 \text{ cm}$$

For You to Do

4. Find the missing side length and angle measures.

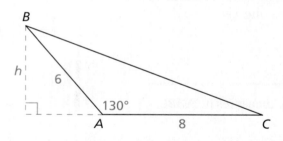

Remember...

Since you can find the sine ratio of an acute angle only, look in the diagram for an acute angle that will help you.

Exercises *Practicing Habits of Mind*

Check Your Understanding

In Exercises 1–3, find all the missing side lengths and angle measures of each triangle.

1.

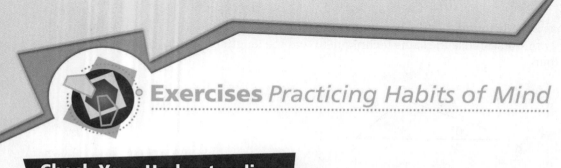

2.

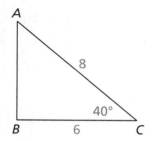

3.

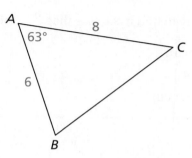

4. a. Find the area of the triangle in terms of a, b, and θ.

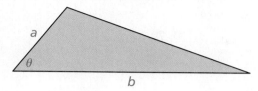

Remember...

θ (the Greek letter *theta*) is a variable that is often used to represent angle measures.

b. Use the area formula from part (a) to show that if you scale the triangle by the factor r, then you scale its area by r^2.

5. Find the area of parallelogram *ABCD*.

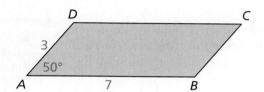

On Your Own

6. The altitude of $\triangle ABC$ from *B* intersects $\overline{AC}$ at *D*.

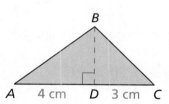

The area of $\triangle ABC$ is exactly 10.5 cm². $AD = 4$ cm and $DC = 3$ cm. Find the missing side lengths and angle measures.

Hint: Find the right triangles.

7. $\triangle DEW$ is isosceles. $DE = 65.3$ mm, $EW = 65.3$ mm, and $DW = 100$ mm. Find the angle measures and area of $\triangle DEW$.

8. In $\triangle RAT$, $m\angle A = 80°$, $RA = 1.74$ in., and $AT = 5$ in. Find TR, the other angle measures, and the area of the triangle.

9. The area of $\triangle ABC$ is 30 in.², $AC = 10$ in., and $m\angle A = 45°$. Find the rest of the side lengths and angle measures.

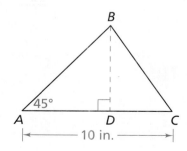

10. Standardized Test Prep You are given that $AB = 4$, $BC = 5$, $AC = 7$, and the area of $\triangle ABC$ is 9.798. Which value is closest to $m\angle A$?

A. $39.68°$ **B.** $44.48°$ **C.** $68.48°$ **D.** $70.8°$

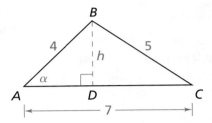

11. Find the area of a regular octagon that has a side length of 4 inches. You might also consider this picture that shows the octagon sitting in a square. If you can find the area of the square and the four triangles, how will this help?

Hint: Divide the octagon into triangles and find the area of each one.

In Exercises 12–15, find the missing side length and angle measures of each triangle.

12.

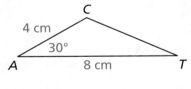

13.

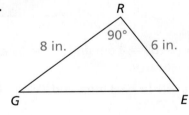

14.

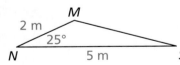

15.

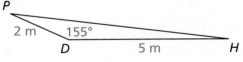

The Example earlier in this lesson demonstrated a technique you could use to find all the missing measurements for a triangle given the lengths of two sides and the measure of their included angle.

In Exercises 16–18, you will work through a technique that allows you to find all the missing measurements of a triangle given the measures of two angles and the length of their included side.

16. Explain why each equation is valid for $\triangle ABC$.

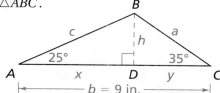

    a. $h = c \sin 25°$

    b. $h = a \sin 35°$

    c. $c = \dfrac{a \sin 35°}{\sin 25°}$

    d. $x = c \cos 25°$

    e. $y = a \cos 35°$

    f. $a \cos 35° + c \cos 25° = 9$

17. Find approximations for a and c in $\triangle ABC$ from Exercise 16.

18. Use the value you found for a and the given values for AC and $m\angle C$ to find c using the method from the Example. Did you get the same value for c as you did in Exercise 17?

19. Find the missing side lengths and angle measure of $\triangle REX$.

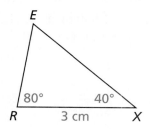

20. **Take It Further** Find the value of α in the triangle at the right.

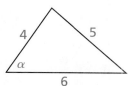

Maintain Your Skills

21. There are many triangles with two sides measuring 4 in. and 6 in. Among those triangles, which one has the maximum area? To investigate this question, use $\triangle ABC$ with $AB = 4$ in. and $BC = 6$ in. Using the different values for $m\angle B$ below, calculate the area. Which value of $m\angle B$ gives the greatest area for the triangle?

    a. $m\angle B = 10°$ **b.** $m\angle B = 30°$ **c.** $m\angle B = 50°$ **d.** $m\angle B = 70°$

    e. $m\angle B = 90°$ **f.** $m\angle B = 110°$ **g.** $m\angle B = 130°$

Mathematical 9B Reflections

In this investigation, you learned how to use trigonometric functions. You found areas, angle measures, and side lengths of triangles. You used right triangles to solve problems. These questions will help you summarize what you have learned.

1. A ramp to a loading dock must slope at a 10° angle.

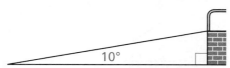

10°

   a. If the ramp meets the ground 25 feet from the base of the building, how long is the ramp?

   b. Construction workers are building a ramp up to a door that is 2 feet off the ground. Find the length of the ramp.

2. $\triangle JKL$ is a right triangle with right angle at K. If $\overline{JK}$ is four times the length of $\overline{KL}$, find the sine, cosine, and tangent of $\angle J$ and $\angle L$.

3. Given $\triangle ABC$ with $AB = 4$, $BC = 3$, and $AC = 6$, find the measure of angle C.

4. How can you use half of a square or half of an equilateral triangle to evaluate trigonometric functions for angles measuring 30°, 45°, and 60°?

5. Find the sine, cosine, and tangent of α and β in terms of the side lengths of $\triangle ABC$.

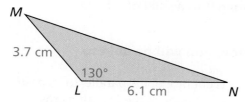

6. What is the area of $\triangle LMN$? What is the approximate length of $\overline{MN}$?

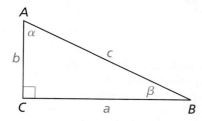

Vocabulary and Notation

In this investigation, you learned these terms and symbols. Make sure you understand what each one means and how to use it.

- **trigonometry**
- **sine, sin θ**
- **cosine, cos θ**
- **tangent, tan θ**
- **$\sin^{-1} x$**
- **$\cos^{-1} x$**
- **$\tan^{-1} x$**

The ladder can reach out $\ell \cos \theta$ and up a height of $t + \ell \sin \theta$. ℓ can extend as θ increases.

Investigation 9C

Volume Formulas

In *Volume Formulas,* you will learn a new technique for finding the volume of a solid. In Investigation 3D, you found the volumes and surface areas of some three-dimensional solids.

For many of the solids, you worked with formulas that were given to you. In this investigation, you will learn how to find the volume of a solid by comparing it to a solid of known volume.

By the end of this investigation, you will be able to answer questions like these.

1. A hexagonal pyramid of height h is cut by a plane parallel to its base at height r above the base. How is the shape of the resulting cross section related to the shape of the base of the pyramid? How are their areas related?

2. Explain Cavalieri's Principle.

3. A spherical melon has radius 3 inches. You cut a slice 2 inches from its center. What is the volume of the piece you cut from the melon?

You will learn how to
- find the areas of cross sections formed when planes intersect with solids under certain conditions

- understand and use Cavalieri's Principle

- prove basic volume formulas using Cavalieri's Principle

You will develop these habits and skills:
- Visualize cross sections of solids.

- Use similar triangles to find measurements of cross sections.

- Choose appropriate solids to compare using Cavalieri's Principle.

The two stacks have identical bases and the same height. How do the numbers of napkins in the stacks compare?

9.10 Volumes of Solids

Now you will explore the **volumes** of some special solids.

Prisms and Cylinders

The first volume you encountered was probably that of a box (a right rectangular prism). You likely think of volume as the following formula.

volume = length × width × height

This formula works well for a right rectangular prism. But will it work for other solids?

Volume is measured in cubic units, such as cubic meters (m^3), cubic centimeters (cm^3), cubic feet (ft^3), and cubic inches ($in.^3$). When you measure the volume of a solid, you are trying to determine how many cubes of a particular size would fit inside the solid.

Suppose you have a box that is 4 in. long, 3 in. wide, and 2 in. tall.

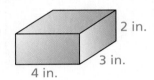

You can draw a number of cubes inside the box, each with a side length of 1 in. Then you can count how many cubes fill the box.

Each cube measures 1 in. by 1 in. by 1 in.

When you say the volume of the box is 24 cubic inches, you mean that you can fit 24 cubes, each with side length 1 inch, inside the box.

24 cubes fill the box.

> You sometimes see the abbreviation "cc" for cubic centimeter (cm^3), often for medicine and motorcycles.

Example

Problem Find the volume of this right triangular prism. The base is a
right triangle.

7 ft

4 ft   3 ft

Solution The base of the prism is a right triangle. So you can take a copy of the
prism and place it next to the original to make a box. And you know how to
find the volume of the box! So all you have to do is find the volume of the
box and divide by 2.

The volume of the box is length × width × height.

$$V_B = 3 \times 4 \times 7$$
$$= 84\,\text{ft}^3$$

The volume of the original triangular prism is half of that.

$$V_P = \frac{84}{2}$$
$$= 42\,\text{ft}^3$$

Is it possible that the rules and formulas you learned earlier in this chapter
will help you compute volume? Indeed, it is! Just as cutting a polygon and
rearranging it leaves area unchanged, so cutting and rearranging a solid
leaves volume unchanged. The diagrams show how to cut an oblique prism,
rearrange the pieces, and make a right prism with the same volume.

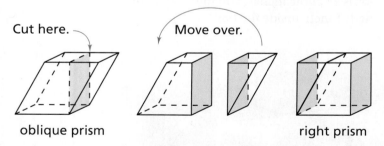

Cut here.   Move over.

oblique prism   right prism

When you find volume, you can use the same view of cylinders that helped
you find surface area. Visualize a cylinder as a prism with many, many sides.

Here is a general formula for volume of prisms and cylinders.

Facts and Notation *Volume of a Prism or Cylinder*

$$V = Bh$$

where *B* is the area of a base and *h* is the height.

For You to Do

Find the volume of each right prism.

1. a right square prism with base side length 4 cm and height 100 cm

2. a right octagonal prism with base area 145 cm^2 and height 2 cm

3. a cube with side length 3 ft

4. a cylinder with base radius 1 in. and height 1 ft

Facts and Notation

There are other units (besides cubic units) used to measure volume. These include fluid ounces, gallons, liters, and milliliters. You can define these units to be equal to specific cubic measurements. For example, a milliliter is the same amount as a cubic centimeter (1 mL = 1 cm^3). A gallon is exactly 231 cubic inches.

Pyramids and Cones

There is a relationship between the volumes of a pyramid and a prism when the two figures have the same height and base area.

In-Class Experiment

Estimating volume. In this experiment, you compare the volumes of a pyramid and a prism with the same base and height.

You will need rice or dry sand, 1 hollow square prism, and 1 hollow square pyramid. Both must have the same base area and height as well as an open base.

Fill the pyramid completely with the rice or sand. Then pour the contents of the pyramid into the prism. Continue to fill the pyramid and pour into the prism until the prism is full. Keep track of how many times you pour.

5. How many pyramids full of rice does the prism hold? How many times can you fill the pyramid from a full prism? Explain why your results suggest that a formula for the volume of a pyramid is

$$V = \frac{1}{3}Bh$$

Here is another way to make sense of the formula for the volume of a pyramid. Take a cube and dissect it along its diagonals. You get 6 identical square pyramids.

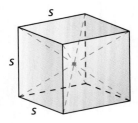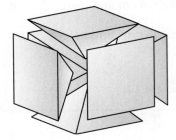

Since the pyramids are identical, they all have a volume that is $\frac{1}{6}$ that of the cube. The height of each pyramid is $h = \frac{1}{2}s$. The area of each base is $B = s^2$.

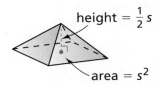

height $= \frac{1}{2}s$

area $= s^2$

The volume of the cube must be s^3, so the volume of each pyramid must be $\frac{1}{6}s^3$.

$$V = \frac{1}{6}s^3$$
$$= \frac{1}{3} \cdot \frac{1}{2} \cdot s \cdot s^2$$
$$= \frac{1}{3} \cdot s^2 \cdot \frac{1}{2}s$$
$$= \frac{1}{3}Bh$$

You can generalize this volume formula by visualizing a cone as a pyramid with a base of many, many sides.

Go Online
www.successnetplus.com

Facts and Notation

In the following formulas, *B* is base area, and *h* is height of the solid.

Volume of prism or cylinder   **Volume of pyramid or cone**

$$V = Bh$$ $$V = \frac{1}{3}Bh$$

By substituting the area formulas for the bases, you have these common volume formulas:

Cube	$V = s^3$
Rectangular prism (box)	$V = \ell wh$
Cylinder	$V = \pi r^2 h$
Square pyramid	$V = \frac{1}{3}s^2 h$
Cone	$V = \frac{1}{3}\pi r^2 h$

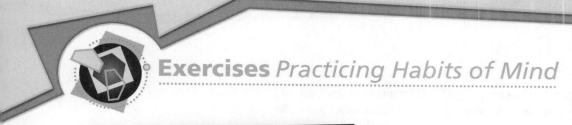

Exercises *Practicing Habits of Mind*

Check Your Understanding

1. Find the volume of each solid.
   a. a right triangular prism with a base that is an equilateral triangle of side length 4 inches, and with a height that is 10 inches
   b. a square pyramid with height 3 ft and base side length 2 ft
   c. a cylinder with radius 12 cm and height 13 cm
   d. a cone with radius 12 cm and slant height 13 cm

2. A pyramid and a prism have the same regular hexagonal base and the same volume. The pyramid has a base with side length 4 in. and height 13 in. Find the dimensions of the prism.

3. A cylinder and a cone have the same height and the same volume. The radius of the cylinder is 9 cm. What is the radius of the cone?

On Your Own

4. You have some apple cider in a cylindrical pot that has a radius of 4 in. You pour cider from the pot into a cylindrical cup that has a radius of $1\frac{1}{2}$ in. until the cider in the cup is 4 in. deep. How much did the level of cider in the pot go down?

5. A square prism and a cylinder have the same volume. The side length of the base of the prism is the same as the radius of the cylinder. The height of the prism is 7 cm. What is the height of the cylinder?

6. A factory has three cylindrical chimneys to release waste gases. Each chimney is 150 feet tall. The base of a chimney has a diameter of 15 feet. A can of paint can cover 100 square feet of surface. How many cans of paint are needed to paint the outsides of all three chimneys?

7. The factory in Exercise 6 needs to install filters inside the chimneys. The filter completely fills the interior of each chimney. The thickness of each chimney wall is $1\frac{1}{2}$ feet. How many cubic feet of filter are needed?

8. Sean is making a replica of the Washington Monument for history class. He decides to simplify the structure so that the replica resembles a square prism on the bottom and a square pyramid on the top. Sean's measurements are listed below. What is the volume of Sean's replica?

   • The total height of the replica is 24 inches.

   • The height of the pyramid at the top is 4 inches.

   • The length of one side of the square base of the replica is 3 inches.

9. **Standardized Test Prep** Chef Jasper's signature dessert is an individual carrot cake in the form of a right circular cone. The diameter of the cone is 3 in. and the height is 4 in. What is the approximate volume of carrot cake in each dessert?

   A. 9.425 in.^{3} **B.** 12 in.^{3} **C.** 28.27 in.^{3} **D.** 37.70 in.^{3}

10. **Take It Further** Margherite wants to make a more accurate replica of the Washington Monument. She determined the measurements as follows.

    - The height of her replica is 22 inches.
    - The length of one side of the square at the base of her replica is 2 inches.
    - The length of one side of the square at the base of the pyramid at the top is $1\frac{3}{8}$ inches.
    - The height of the pyramid is 2 inches.

    Margherite has one quart of plaster. Does she have enough to make the model? Explain.

Remember...

1 gal = 231 in.^{3}

1 gal = 128 fl oz

1 gal = 4 qt

11. Terry wants to find out how much liquid a paper cup will hold. He measures the cup to be 4 inches high. The diameter of the bottom of the cup is 2 inches. The diameter of the top is 3 inches. How many fluid ounces of liquid can the cup hold?

12. **Take It Further** A tall cone has radius 5 m and height 9 m. A short cone has radius 9 m and height 5 m.

    a. Find the volume of each cone. Which has a greater volume, the tall cone or the short cone?

    b. Cut another cone off of the tip of the cone that has the greater volume. Your goal is to leave a frustum that has the same volume as the smaller of the two original cones. What must be the height of the cone you cut off?

Maintain Your Skills

13. Find the volume and total surface area of a right rectangular prism that measures 1 cm by 2 cm by 4 cm.

14. Two other right rectangular prisms with whole number centimeter measurements have the same volume as the prism in Exercise 13. Find their dimensions and surface areas.

15. A right rectangular prism with whole-number centimeter dimensions has volume 7 cm^3. What are its dimensions and total surface area?

16. Is it true that solids with greater volume have greater total surface area? If so, explain why. If not, provide a counterexample.

Go Online
www.successnetplus.com

In *Mathematics I,* you did some preliminary work in visualizing the cross sections of different three-dimensional objects cut by planes. Now you can describe these cross sections more thoroughly. The Ratio and Parallel methods for dilation that you learned in Chapter 7 also work in three dimensions. Work in groups of at least three to complete the following experiment.

In-Class Experiment

You will need: cardboard, scissors, string, markers, tape, paper, and a ruler.

Step 1 Cut a triangle out of a piece of cardboard.

Step 2 Now punch three small holes near the vertices of your cardboard triangle.

Step 3 Pass the end of a piece of string through each hole.

Step 4 Have one student hold the cardboard triangle so that it is in a plane parallel to the plane of the desk.

Step 5 Have another student gather the three pieces of string together above the triangle.

Step 6 Have the third student stretch the other ends of the strings out and tape them to a piece of paper on the desk. Mark the three points where the strings touch the desk, and connect them to form a new triangle.

Step 7 Mark the strings where they touch the apex A, the cardboard triangle B, and the paper triangle C. Find the ratios $\frac{AB}{AC}$ for each string. How do they compare?

Step 8 Now compare the cardboard triangle to the triangle drawn on the paper.

> This is a very important job. You must hold the triangle in a plane parallel to the plane of the desk at all times.

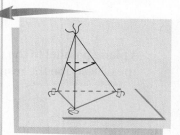

As you discuss your results with the whole class, relate the experience to dilation by the Ratio Method.

- Where is the center of dilation in this experiment?

- Why were the strings cut proportionally by the cardboard triangle?

- What is the relationship between the cardboard triangle and the paper triangle?

In the In-Class Experiment, you showed that the Ratio Method works in three dimensions. So when you cut a pyramid with a plane parallel to the base of the pyramid, the resulting cross section will be a polygon similar to the base of the pyramid.

For You to Explore

1. A right square pyramid has a base with side length 6 in. and height 9 in. A plane cuts the pyramid 3 inches above and parallel to the base.

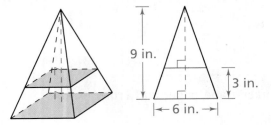

Describe the shape of the intersection of the pyramid with the cross-sectional plane. Calculate the area of the cross section.

2. The pyramid from Exercise 1 is cut by a plane that is parallel to its base and h inches above its base. Describe the resulting cross section. Calculate the area of the cross section in terms of h.

3. The square pyramid below has a base with side length 8 cm and height 5 cm.

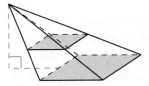

A plane parallel to the plane of its base cuts the pyramid 3 cm below its apex. Describe the resulting cross section. Calculate its area.

On Your Own

4. A line parallel to $\overline{BC}$ intersects $\triangle ABC$ in $\overline{DE}$ as shown.

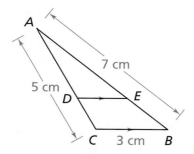

a. Find *DE* if the distance from *D* to $\overleftrightarrow{BC}$ is 1 cm.

b. What is the distance from *D* to $\overleftrightarrow{BC}$ when *DE* is 2 cm?

5. This triangular pyramid has a base with area $4\,cm^2$ and height 2 cm.

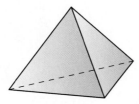

a. The pyramid is cut by a plane parallel to its base and 1 cm above it. Find the area of the cross section.

b. You want to make a parallel cross section of the pyramid with area $3\,cm^2$. How high above the base of the pyramid must you cut?

Go Online
Video Tutor
www.successnetplus.com

6. In the figure below, $\overline{VH}$ is the altitude of the pyramid $VABC$. $\overline{VH'}$ is an altitude of the smaller pyramid $VA'B'C'$. Determine the scale factor of $\triangle ABC$ and $\triangle A'B'C'$ in terms of VH and VH'.

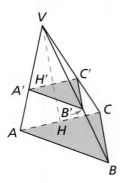

7. The rectangular prism and cone below both have height 8 in.

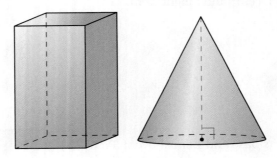

The prism has a square base. The radius of the base of the cone is 4 in. The cross section of the prism has the same area as the cross section of the cone at a height of 3 in. from their bases. What is the side length of the square base of the prism?

9.12 Cavalieri's Principle

Below are three diagrams of the same deck of cards in three different positions.

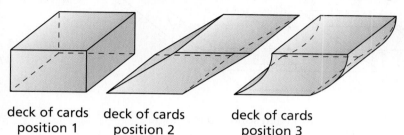

deck of cards
position 1

deck of cards
position 2

deck of cards
position 3

For Discussion

1. Compare the volumes of the deck of cards in positions 2 and 3 with the volume of the deck of cards in position 1. Does your result make sense? Explain and discuss your ideas with the class.

Minds in Action

Sasha, Tony, and Derman are thinking about the deck of cards in the pictures above.

Tony I think the volume of the deck in the first position is greatest.

Derman I think the volume is the same in all three positions. After all, it's the *same* deck of cards!

Tony But the deck in position 1 *looks* bigger.

Sasha Well, you know that looks can be deceiving. Think of the deck of cards as a building. Every "floor" of the building has the same area. Each floor is a single card and all the cards in the deck are the same size. Since the number of cards, or floors, is always the same, it would make sense that the three volumes are the same.

In the 1600s, an Italian mathematician named Bonaventura Cavalieri formalized Sasha's idea.

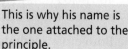

This is why his name is the one attached to the principle.

Postulate 9.1   *Cavalieri's Principle*

Two solids of the same height are cut by a plane so that the resulting cross sections have the same area. If the solids also have cross-sectional areas equal to each other when cut by any plane parallel to the first, then they have the same volume.

Picture how Cavalieri's Principle can be used to find the volume of the deck of cards in positions 2 and 3. The bottom card of the deck, in each position, lies in the same plane—the plane of the table. The plane in the figure below is parallel to this bottom plane.

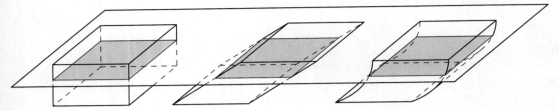

You can see that the intersection of this plane with each solid is a rectangle of equal area—the area of a single card. This means that each cross section has equal area. This is also true for *every* plane parallel to the bottom plane, all the way up to the plane that passes through the top card of each deck.

Cavalieri's Principle states that all three decks must have the same volume.

Example

Problem Show that all pyramids that have the same height and the same base area must have the same volume.

Solution Start with two pyramids with height h and bases with area A. The two bases can be any polygonal shape. Position the pyramids so that their bases both lie in the same plane. Then find any other plane parallel to the plane of the bases that intersects the two pyramids.

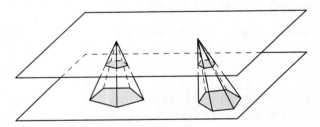

Call the distance of this cutting plane from the apexes of the pyramids b. Think of the apex of each pyramid as a center of dilation in the ratio method. You can conclude that the cross sections created by the cutting plane are similar to the bases of their corresponding pyramids.

You also know the scale factor of the dilation must be $\frac{b}{h}$. Since the area of each base is A, the areas of these cross sections must both be $A\left(\frac{b}{h}\right)^2$.

Both cross sections must have the same area for any height b. So you can conclude that these two pyramids must have the same volume.

Remember...

The area of a dilation is equal to the square of the scale factor multiplied by the area of the original figure.

For You to Do

2. A triangular pyramid and a square pyramid have equal volume and the same height, 3 in. The base of the triangular pyramid has side lengths 3 in., 4 in., and 5 in. Find the side length of the base of the square pyramid.

Exercises *Practicing Habits of Mind*

Check Your Understanding

1. The two shaded circles in the figure below have the same area. Must the two solids have the same volume? Explain.

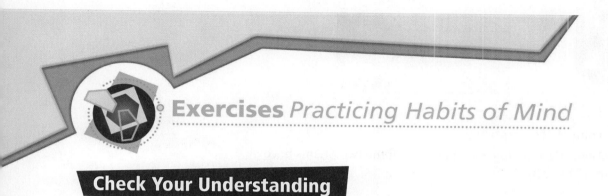

2. You can deform a right prism by pushing it sideways as shown below, to form a new solid. Do the two solids have the same volume? Explain.

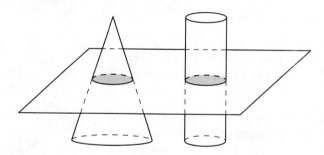

3. Here are two rectangular prisms.

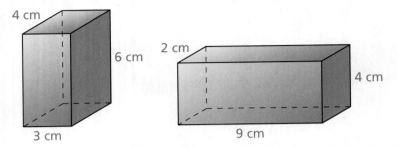

    a. Calculate the volume of each prism.

    b. Can you use Cavalieri's Principle to conclude that the two prisms have the same volume? Explain.

On Your Own

4. The converse of Cavalieri's Principle is not necessarily true.

You have two solids that have equal volumes. Suppose there is a plane that intersects those two solids in equal-area cross sections. This does *not* guarantee that every plane parallel to the first plane will also intersect the solids in equal-area cross sections.

Show an example that demonstrates this. Give enough measurements to define each of the solids. Locate a plane that produces equal-area cross sections and a parallel plane that produces unequal-area cross sections.

5. **Write About It** What happens to the assertion in Exercise 4 if you are comparing two prisms of equal height? Are there any other shapes that could be included in this exception? Explain.

6. A cylinder has height 6 inches and radius 3 inches. A prism with a square base has the same volume and height. What is the side length of the base of the prism?

7. A cylinder and a prism with a square base have the same volume V and height h. The cylinder has radius r. What is the side length of the square base of the prism?

8. Standardized Test Prep A right cylinder is cut in half vertically to form a semi-cylinder. It has the same height h and the same volume as a right cylinder with radius r. What is the diameter of the semi-cylinder?

A. $2r$ **B.** $r\sqrt{2}$ **C.** $2r\sqrt{2}$ **D.** $4r$

Exercises 9 and 10 ask you to think about Cavalieri's Principle in two dimensions.

You can divide the two quadrilaterals in the figure into an equal number of congruent rectangles with height that can be as small as you want. Because the corresponding rectangles in each quadrilateral are always congruent no matter how small they get, the two quadrilaterals must have the same area.

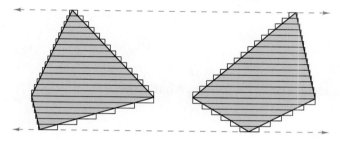

Habits of Mind

Reason. Reason by continuity, making the heights smaller and smaller. What happens as the height of the rectangles approaches zero?

In two dimensions, Cavalieri's Principle can be stated as follows.

Suppose you have two 2-dimensional figures. Draw a line that intersects both figures. In each figure, that intersection will be a segment. If both segments have equal length, and if every line parallel to your original line also intersects both figures in segments of equal length, then the two figures must have equal area.

Go Online
www.successnetplus.com

9. Use Cavalieri's Principle to show that any two triangles that have the same base and height must also have the same area.

10. Two polygons have the same area. Line ℓ intersects them both in segments of equal length. Does this guarantee that every line parallel to ℓ intersects both polygons in segments of equal length? If so, explain your reasoning. If not, give a counterexample.

11. A hollow square prism with height 1 foot, as pictured below, has the same volume as a solid square prism with the same height and a base with a 2-inch side length.

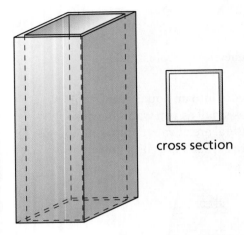

cross section

The thickness of the sides of the hollow square prism is $\frac{1}{4}$ inch. What is the side length of the outside square?

12. A hollow cylindrical pipe with height 1 foot has the same volume as a solid square prism with the same height and a base with a 2-inch side length.

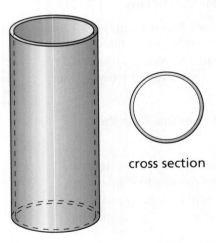

cross section

The thickness of the wall of the cylindrical pipe is $\frac{1}{4}$ inch. What is the radius of the outside circle?

13. Compare the volumes of each pair of solids. In each case, explain why their volumes are the same or different.

a.

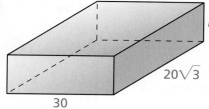

30    $20\sqrt{3}$ h

20   h

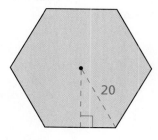

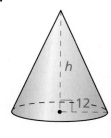

view of top
base of prism

20

b.

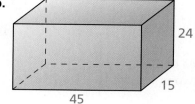

45   15   24

24

15

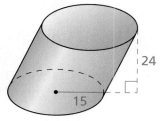

c.

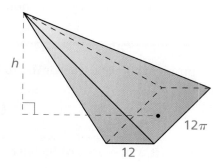

h   12

h

12   12π

Go Online
www.successnetplus.com

9.13 Proving Volume Formulas

Cavalieri's Principle is very useful when it comes to proving volume formulas. In this lesson, you will prove formulas for a general prism, a cylinder, a pyramid, and a cone. You will start with the formula for the volume of a right rectangular prism and use Cavalieri's Principle.

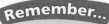

Remember...

Do you remember how to find the volume of a right rectangular prism with dimensions *a*, *b*, and *c*?

For You to Do

The picture below represents two prisms: the prism on the left is a right rectangular prism, and the prism on the right has a triangular base and is not right. Both prisms have the same height.

 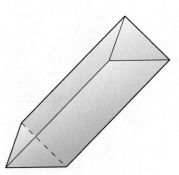

The area of the base of the rectangular prism is 24 cm². The area of the base of the triangular prism is also 24 cm². The heights of the two prisms are both 7 cm.

1. Determine the volume of the triangular prism, if possible. If you cannot, explain why.

You can generalize your solution for the problem above in the For You to Do with the following theorem.

Theorem 9.5

The volume of a prism is equal to the product of the area of its base and its height.

$$V_{prism} = A_{base} \cdot h$$

Suppose the base of the triangular prism in the For You to Do is a circle. You can generalize Theorem 9.5 as follows.

Theorem 9.6

The volume of a cylinder is equal to the product of the area of its base (a circle) and its height.

$$V_{cylinder} = A_{base} \cdot h$$

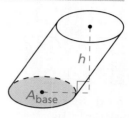

For Discussion

The area of the base of the cylinder is the same as the area of the base of the rectangular right prism. The height of the cylinder is the same as the height of the rectangular prism.

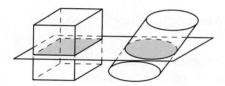

2. Explain how to apply Cavalieri's Principle to the two solids.

3. What can you prove about their volumes?

Minds in Action

Tony, Sasha, and Derman are trying to use Cavalieri's Principle to find the formula for the volume of the pyramid below.

10

$A_{base} = 32$

Sasha Let's think of some kind of pyramid we already know how to find the volume of.

Tony I know! Look at this. A cube contains exactly three congruent square pyramids.

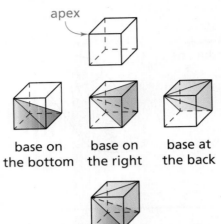

Sasha Great, that's really cool! So we know that the volume of a square pyramid with height equal to the side length of its base is $\frac{1}{3}$ the volume of the cube it's contained in.

Now what if we had a square pyramid with height different from its base?

Derman Oh, that's easy. If the cube's height is scaled by some factor, say, 3, then its volume is three times larger. So the volume of the pyramid must also be three times larger, too, because it was scaled in the same way.

Tony OK, so now if we construct a square pyramid with the same height as our pyramid with base area 32, we can use Cavalieri's Principle.

Each pair of cross sections is similar to the base. For any cutting plane, the scale factor for both cross sections is the same. That means each pair of cross sections will have the same area.

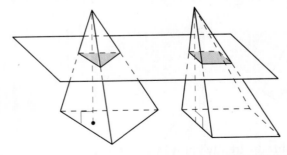

Remember...

Remember the In-Class Experiment in Lesson 9.11? The intersection of a plane parallel to the base of a pyramid with the pyramid is a polygon similar to the base of the pyramid.

Sasha Right! So the volume of our pyramid is $\frac{32 \cdot 10}{3}$. That's one third of the corresponding prism's volume.

For You to Do

4. Use Cavalieri's Principle to help you find the volume of a triangular pyramid by comparing it to a square pyramid. Could you find the volume of any pyramid in this way?

Theorem 9.7 summarizes your work.

Theorem 9.7

The volume of a pyramid is equal to one third of the product of the area of its base and its height.

$$V_{pyramid} = \frac{A_{base} \cdot h}{3}$$

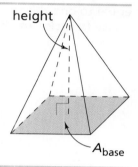

Example

Problem Find a square pyramid that has the same height and volume as a cone of radius r and height h. What is the volume of the square pyramid?

Solution To show that the pyramid and the cone have the same volume, consider the cross sections of the pyramid and the cone that are formed by a set of parallel planes. The corresponding cross sections must have equal areas. It makes the most sense to consider the cross sections that are formed by planes that are parallel to the base of each figure.

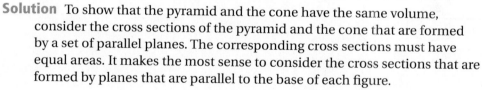

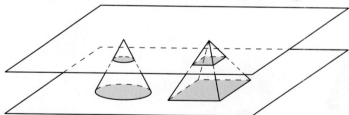

In particular, the area of the square base of the pyramid must be equal to the area of the circular base of the cone. The area of the cone's base is πr^2. For the square to have this area, its side length must be $\sqrt{\pi r^2}$, or $r\sqrt{\pi}$. To be certain that the areas of the corresponding cross sections of the pyramid and cone are the same, remember the ratio method. Suppose a plane intersects the pyramid and the cone at some distance d from the plane that contains the apexes of the pyramid and cone. This plane forms two corresponding cross sections. You can think of these cross sections as the bases of a dilated pyramid and cone. The scale factor is $\frac{d}{h}$. The areas of the dilated bases, or cross sections, will both be equal to $\left(\frac{d}{h}\right)^2$ times the areas of the bases of the original pyramid and cone.

Since the pyramid and the cone have the same height and the same cross-sectional area for any plane that is parallel to their bases, the pyramid and the cone have the same volume. The volume of the square pyramid is $\frac{1}{3}(r\sqrt{\pi})^2 \cdot h$, or $\frac{1}{3}(\pi r^2)(h)$.

Theorem 9.8 is a result of the example above.

Theorem 9.8

The volume of a cone is equal to one third of the product of the area of its base (a circle) and its height.

$$V_{cone} = \frac{A_{base} \cdot h}{3}$$

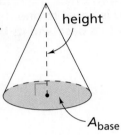

For Discussion

5. Explain why you cannot use the techniques from this lesson to find a volume formula for a figure like the one below.

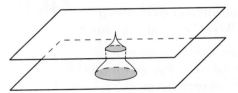

What angle cut at the center of a circle will give you a cone with the greatest volume?

Exercises Practicing Habits of Mind

Check Your Understanding

1. Use the cone at the right. A plane containing O' and parallel to the base of the cone intersects the cone in a circle. Prove the following.

$$\frac{A_{circle}}{A_{base}} = \frac{(VO')^2}{VO^2}$$

2. Use Cavalieri's Principle to find the volume of the pyramid below.

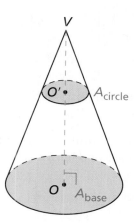

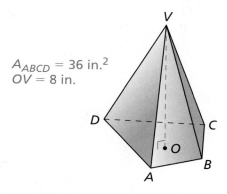

$A_{ABCD} = 36$ in.^{2}
$OV = 8$ in.

3. **a.** Find the volume of a triangular pyramid of height 5 cm that has a right triangle base with legs that measure 4 cm and 6 cm.

   b. Find the radius of the cone that has the same volume and height as the triangular pyramid.

4. A triangular pyramid and a cone are standing on the same plane. They have equal base areas and the same height h. The cone has base radius r.

   a. Give a possible set of dimensions for the base of the pyramid.

   b. A plane parallel to the bases intersects the two solids. What can you say about the resulting cross sections?

5. Use Cavalieri's Principle to conclude that the volume of the cone and the volume of the pyramid from Exercise 4 are the same.

On Your Own

6. The base of a cone has radius 2 ft. The height of the cone is 6 ft. What is the volume of the cone?

7. A prism has a square base of side 4 cm. Its lateral faces are two rectangles and two parallelograms like the ones below. Determine the volume of the prism.

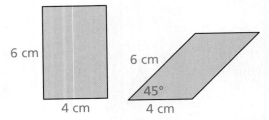

6 cm 4 cm

6 cm 45° 4 cm

8. The area of one face of a regular tetrahedron is $16\sqrt{3}$ cm^2. What is its volume?

Remember...

A tetrahedron is a pyramid that has congruent equilateral triangles for all faces.

9. Another way to see that the volume of a pyramid is one third the volume of the prism with the same base and height is to look at a triangular prism.

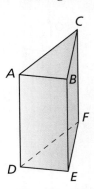

You can cut a triangular prism into three triangular pyramids. In the dissection of the cube in the lesson, the three pyramids were congruent. Here they are not, but you can show that they do have the same volume.

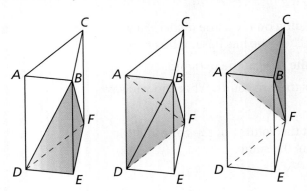

a. Consider the green and blue pyramids. The height of each pyramid is the length of a perpendicular from C to plane *ABED*. If the bases are congruent, then they have the same volume. Show that $\triangle BDE \cong \triangle DBA$.

b. Consider the green and purple pyramids. The green pyramid has base △*DEF* and height *BE*. What base and height for the purple pyramid would show that these two pyramids must have the same volume?

c. Complete the argument to show that the volume of a pyramid is one-third the area of the prism with the same base and height.

10. What is the volume of the solid below?

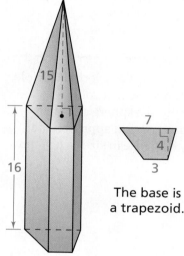

The base is a trapezoid.

11. Standardized Test Prep A square pyramid has height 10 cm and a base area of 36 cm². A second square pyramid has the same height but the side lengths of its base are double those of the side lengths of the first pyramid. What is the ratio of the volume of the second pyramid to the volume of the first pyramid?

A. 2 : 1   **B.** 4 : 1   **C.** 6 : 1   **D.** 8 : 1

Maintain Your Skills

12. Find the volume of a pyramid with height 12 inches and each base described below. Approximate if necessary.

a. an equilateral triangle with apothem 1 in.

b. a square with apothem 1 in.

c. a regular pentagon with apothem 1 in.

d. a regular hexagon with apothem 1 in.

e. a regular octagon with apothem 1 in.

13. Find the volume of a cone with height 12 in. and radius 1 in.

Remember...

The apothem *a* of a regular polygon is the length of a perpendicular segment from the center point of the polygon to one of its sides.

9.14 Volume of a Sphere

You can use Cavalieri's Principle to show that two different solids have the same volume. If you know how to find the volume of one of the solids, you can use that result as the volume of the other. You can even develop new volume formulas for new classes of solids. However, the tricky part of using Cavalieri's Principle is that you have to know which two solids to compare.

For Discussion

To find a solid to compare to a sphere of radius r using Cavalieri's Principle, it might be a good idea to use one of the round solids with a volume formula that you already know. The cross sections of a sphere are small circles at first. Then the circles get larger and larger as you approach the center of the sphere. The circles then gradually decrease in size as you move away from the center of the sphere.

1. Would a bicone work?

If so, describe the dimensions of the bicone as completely as possible. If not, describe the problems you encounter.

In fact, this is not a simple problem to solve. The Greek mathematician Archimedes was finally able to prove the volume formula for a sphere. It is said that he was so thrilled that he wanted his solution to the problem to be engraved on his tombstone.

You and your classmates may not have been able to think of a choice of what solid to compare to the sphere. But you can still demonstrate the comparison.

Sasha and Tony are comparing the cross sections of a sphere and a cylinder with a double cone removed from it. The sphere has radius r, and the cross section of the sphere is at a distance h from the center of the sphere. The cylinder with the double cone removed from it has radius r and height 2r.

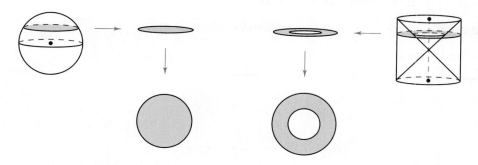

Sasha   The cross sections of the cylinder-minus-cones solid will be rings. The outside radius of the ring will always be the same, but the inside radius will get smaller and then larger as you move downward from the top.

Tony   We can say that the areas of three cross sections are the same right away. At the very top and bottom, the ring has zero area. At those same two heights, the plane that intersects the sphere will intersect it in a point, so that intersection will have zero area, too.

Sasha   Yes, and halfway up the cylinder, the radius of each cone is zero. The intersection with the plane is just a circle of radius *r*. That's exactly the same area and shape as the intersection of that plane with the sphere.

Tony   But now we have to prove it works for all the planes parallel to the base of the cylinder-minus-cones solid.

Sasha   I'm guessing similar triangles are going to help us.

We know $\triangle ABD$ is an isosceles right triangle, because the cones both have base radius *r* and height *r*. Since $\triangle ECD \sim \triangle ABD$, then it's an isosceles right triangle, too! So we know the inner radius and the outer radius. So we can find the area of the ring.

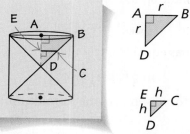

Tony   So now we have to find the area of the intersection of the plane at height *h* with the sphere. I'm going to label the sphere with everything I know.

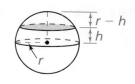

If the area of the cross section of the sphere is the same as the ring, we've done it!

> How does Sasha know that the two triangles are similar?

For You to Do

Use the figures and dimensions from the Minds in Action. Finish Tony and Sasha's work.

You may want to use the ratio method.

2. Find the area of the intersection of the plane and the cylinder-minus-cones solid using Sasha's similar triangles.

3. Find the area of the cross section of the sphere using Tony's sketch.

4. How can you be sure that these two solids have the same volume? Explain.

5. What is the volume of the cylinder-minus-cones solid?

Your work so far is proof of the following formula.

Theorem 9.9

The volume of a sphere with radius r is $\frac{4}{3}\pi r^3$.

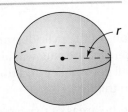

You also can confirm the formula for the surface area of a sphere now that you are sure about its volume. Think of the sphere as being made of some large number n of tiny congruent square pyramids that are all joined so that the apex of each pyramid is at the center of the sphere.

Each pyramid has height r and a square base that is on the sphere. Call the area of each square base b. The areas of all n bases, or nb, is the surface area of the sphere.

Each pyramid has volume $\frac{1}{3}br$. If you add the volumes of the n pyramids, you get the total volume of the sphere, so

$$V_{\text{sphere}} = n\left(\tfrac{1}{3}br\right)$$

Set the two volume formulas equal to each other.

$$n\left(\tfrac{1}{3}br\right) = \tfrac{4}{3}\pi r^3$$

If you solve this equation for nb, you get the formula for the surface area of the sphere.

Habits of Mind

Look for connections. The argument here is very similar to the argument in Chapter 8 relating the area and circumference of a circle.

Theorem 9.10

The surface area of a sphere with radius r is $4\pi r^2$.

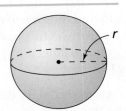

Exercises *Practicing Habits of Mind*

Check Your Understanding

1. Can two parallel planes intersect a sphere and result in cross sections with equal areas? If so, in how many ways can this happen?

   Can two nonparallel planes intersect a sphere and create cross sections with equal areas? If so, in how many ways can this happen? Explain.

2. The figure shows a cylinder with a cone cut out of it.

   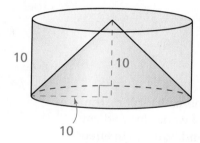

   Find the volume of the cylinder-minus-cone solid. Now, use Cavalieri's Principle to compare that solid to a part of a sphere. What is the radius of the sphere the piece comes from? What is the volume of the piece of the sphere?

   > What fraction of a sphere should you use?

3. You have a piece of cloth with area 45 cm². You can cut the cloth and arrange the pieces any way you like. What is the volume of the greatest sphere you can cover with it?

On Your Own

4. A sphere has radius 15 cm. If the shaded circle has area 25π cm², what is h?

   > Try using Cavalieri's Principle for this.

   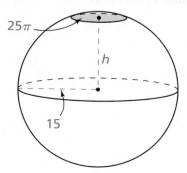

5. **Standardized Test Prep** Sasha peels an orange. The peel is 0.5 cm thick and each slice of orange is 5 cm long. What was the volume of the unpeeled orange?

   A. 65.4 cm^3 **B.** 113.1 cm^3 **C.** 523.5 cm^3 **D.** 904.8 cm^3

In Exercises 6–9, you will investigate the problem of drilling a cylindrical hole through the center of a sphere. You begin with a wooden sphere with a radius of 5 mm. You plan to drill a cylindrical hole of radius 3 mm through its center to make it into a bead.

The original sphere and the finished bead are shown below.

Notice that the bead is shorter than the original sphere. By drilling the cylinder, you have not precisely cut out a cylinder of wood. Instead you have cut out a sort of cylinder with a rounded top and bottom. In effect, a cap has been cut off of both the top and bottom of the sphere in addition to the cylindrical hole.

6. What is the height of the finished bead?

7. Find the volume of the finished bead. You will want to use the volume of the original wooden sphere, the volume of the cylindrical hole, and the volumes of the rounded caps that were cut off.

8. **a.** What is the radius of the sphere that has the same volume as the finished bead?

   b. Show that the bead and this same-volume sphere actually have the same area at every cross section for planes perpendicular to the bead's cylindrical hole.

9. Find the volume of a bead formed by drilling a cylindrical hole of radius 2 mm through a sphere of radius 6 mm.

10. You have a perfectly spherical onion with a diameter of 13 cm. You cut off a slice $\frac{1}{2}$ cm thick as shown below.

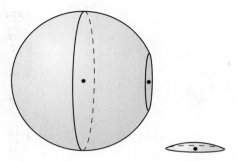

a. The slice created a circular cross section of the onion. What is the radius of that cross section?

b. You want to use Cavalieri's Principle to find the volume of your slice. As in the lesson, you will use the idea of subtracting a cone from a cylinder. What are the dimensions and the volume of the cylinder you should use?

c. You will need to subtract the volume of the frustum of a cone from that of your cylinder because you're not finding the volume of an entire sphere—just a piece. The frustum has two radii—a large radius on top and a smaller radius on the bottom. What are its radii and height?

d. What is the volume of the frustum?

e. What is the volume of your onion slice?

Remember...

Just think of a frustum as the difference of two cones. You start with a large cone and remove its tip by making a cut parallel to the base of the cone.

11. The volume of the hemisphere is 9216 in.³.

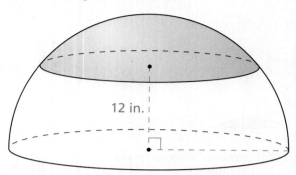

Remember...

A *hemisphere* is half of a sphere.

The vertical segment is 12 inches long. What is the volume of the shaded region?

Maintain Your Skills

12. Each figure below is rotated around line ℓ to make a solid. Find the surface area and volume of each solid.

a.

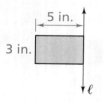

5 in.

3 in.

ℓ

b.

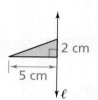

2 cm

5 cm

ℓ

c.

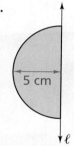

5 cm

ℓ

Habits of Mind

Visualize. If you have trouble visualizing this, tape a cutout of the shape to a pencil, and spin the pencil between your hands. This should help you see what the solid will look like.

d.

5 cm

2 cm

ℓ

e.

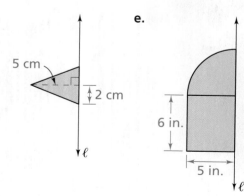

6 in.

5 in.

ℓ

Go Online
www.successnetplus.com

Mathematical 9C Reflections

In this investigation, you learned how to find areas of cross sections of solids, apply Cavalieri's Principle, and prove basic volume formulas using Cavalieri's Principle. These questions will help you summarize what you have learned.

1. A sphere with radius 5 cm is cut by a plane 3 cm from the top. Find the area of the resulting cross section.

2. An architect created a plan for a four-story building with a central courtyard.

   The building measures 96 feet on each side. The courtyard measures 40 feet on a side. His clients asked him to work out an alternative design with the same volume but without the courtyard. Find the side length of such a building if it is designed as a four-story square prism.

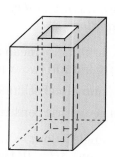

3. **a.** Kirima lives in a hemispherical dome with radius 12 feet. How many square feet should her air conditioner be rated for?

   Kirima discovers that the air conditioner ratings are really based on the cubic footage of air to be cooled, and that the square footage listed is assumed to be in a rectangular room with an 8 foot ceiling.

   b. If she decides to buy an air conditioner based on this discovery, how many square feet should her air conditioner be rated for?

4. A hexagonal pyramid of height h is cut by a plane parallel to its base at height r above the base. How is the shape of the resulting cross section related to the shape of the base of the pyramid? How are their areas related?

5. Explain Cavalieri's Principle.

6. A spherical melon has radius 3 inches. You cut a slice 2 inches from its center. What is the volume of the piece you cut from the melon?

Horizontal cross sections are congruent at every level. The two stacks have equal volumes.

In **Investigation 9A** you learned how to

- state and use the Arithmetic-Geometric Mean Inequality
- use similar triangles to find unknown lengths
- use similarity to prove theorems

The following questions will help you check your understanding.

1. Find the arithmetic mean and geometric mean of 4 and 7 in two ways.

   a. Use a numerical calculation.

   b. Use a geometric construction.

2. In the triangle below, $m\angle ACB = 90°$, $AC = 15$, and $AH = 9$. Find the following side lengths.

   a. AB

   b. BC

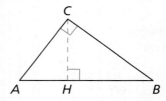

3. How can you use similarity to prove that the medians of a triangle are concurrent?

In **Investigation 9B** you learned how to

- use the sine, cosine, and tangent functions and their inverses to find missing sides and angles in triangles
- find the area of any triangle given two sides and the included angle
- find the length of the third side of a triangle given two sides and the included angle

The following questions will help you check your understanding.

4. A triangle has sides of length 52 meters and 16 meters. If the angle between these two sides is 38°, what is the triangle's area?

5. Find the missing side lengths and angles of the triangle below.

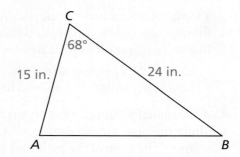

6. Find the perimeter of the triangle below.

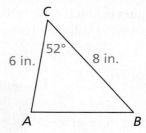

7. The lengths of two sides of a triangle are 11 m and 6 m. The measure of their included angle is 57°. What is the area of the triangle?

In **Investigation 9C** you learned how to

- find the areas of cross sections created when planes intersect solids
- understand and use Cavalieri's Principle
- prove basic volume formulas using Cavalieri's Principle

The following questions will help you check your understanding.

8. Can you use Cavalieri's Principle to determine the volume of the solid below? The solid is made from a deck of cards with volume 90 cm³.

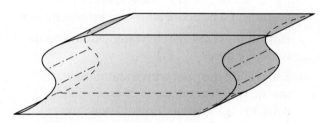

9. You have a piece of cloth with area 64 cm². You can cut and rearrange the cloth however you would like. What is the volume of the greatest cube that you can cover with the cloth?

10. Find the combined volume of the two right pyramids below.

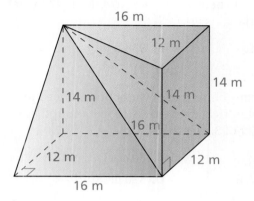

11. Explain how you can use Cavalieri's Principle to prove the volume formula for a sphere of radius *r*.

Multiple Choice

1. A triangle has sides of length 45 feet and 57 feet. If the angle between these two sides is 47°, what is the triangle's area?

   A. 682 ft^2 **B.** 938 ft^2

   C. 1876.5 ft^2 **D.** 2115 ft^2

2. How many cubic feet of water do you need to fill a cylindrical tank that is 10 feet tall and has a diameter of 3.2 feet?

   A. 32 ft^3 **B.** 80.4 ft^3

   C. 100.5 ft^3 **D.** 320 ft^3

3. The cone has radius 8 inches and height 12 inches. You place the cone in a cylindrical hole of radius 3 inches. How deep into the hole is the apex of the pyramid?

   A. 1 in.   **B.** 3 in.

   C. 4.5 in.   **D.** 5.5 in.

Open Response

4. State Cavalieri's Principle and show an example of when you can use it.

5. Calculate the arithmetic and geometric mean of the following pairs of numbers.

   a. 3, 16   **b.** 45, 56   **c.** 21, 7

6. Find the volume of the prism below.

   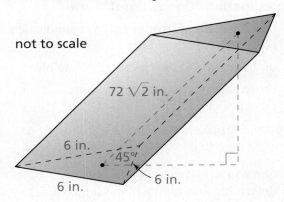

   not to scale

7. A swimming pool is 50 feet long and 23 feet wide. The pool is 2 feet deep at one end and 12 feet at the opposite end. The pool's bottom is a plane surface.

   a. How many cubic feet of water would you need to fill the pool?

   b. You will fill the pool with a standard water pump, which generates a flow of about 300 GPH (gallons per hour). There are approximately 0.134 cubic feet in a gallon. How long will it take you to fill the pool?

8. The area of the base of the cone below is 40 cm^2 and its height is 15 cm. The heights of the two solids are the same and the areas of the shaded regions are the same.

   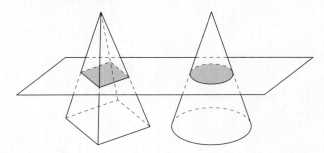

   Can you use Cavalieri's Principle to determine the volume of the pyramid? Explain.

9. For each of the right triangles below, find the exact values for sine, cosine, and tangent of $\angle A$ and $\angle B$.

a.

b.

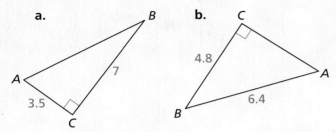

10. Find the missing angle and side lengths for $\triangle MNO$.

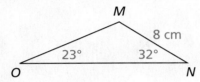

11. You are given a rectangle with the dimensions shown, as well as the length of another rectangle.

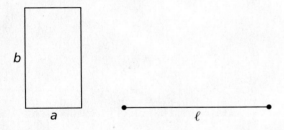

Explain how to construct the width of the second rectangle so that both rectangles have the same area.

12. Find the following measures for the cone.

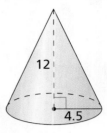

a. volume

b. lateral surface area

c. total surface area

13. What is the volume of the shaded region of the hemisphere?

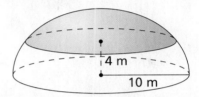

14. You have two beads, one shaped like a rectangular prism and one shaped like a cylinder.

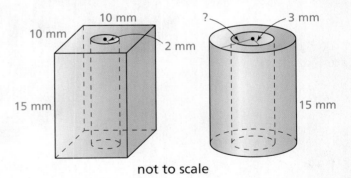

not to scale

The rectangular prism has height 15 mm and a square base with 10-mm side lengths. The hole drilled through the rectangular prism has radius 2 mm. The cylindrical bead has the same height as the rectangular bead, but the hole drilled through it has radius 3 mm. Find the outer radius of the cylindrical bead such that the two beads have equal volume.

10

Investigations at a Glance

10A **Coordinate Geometry**

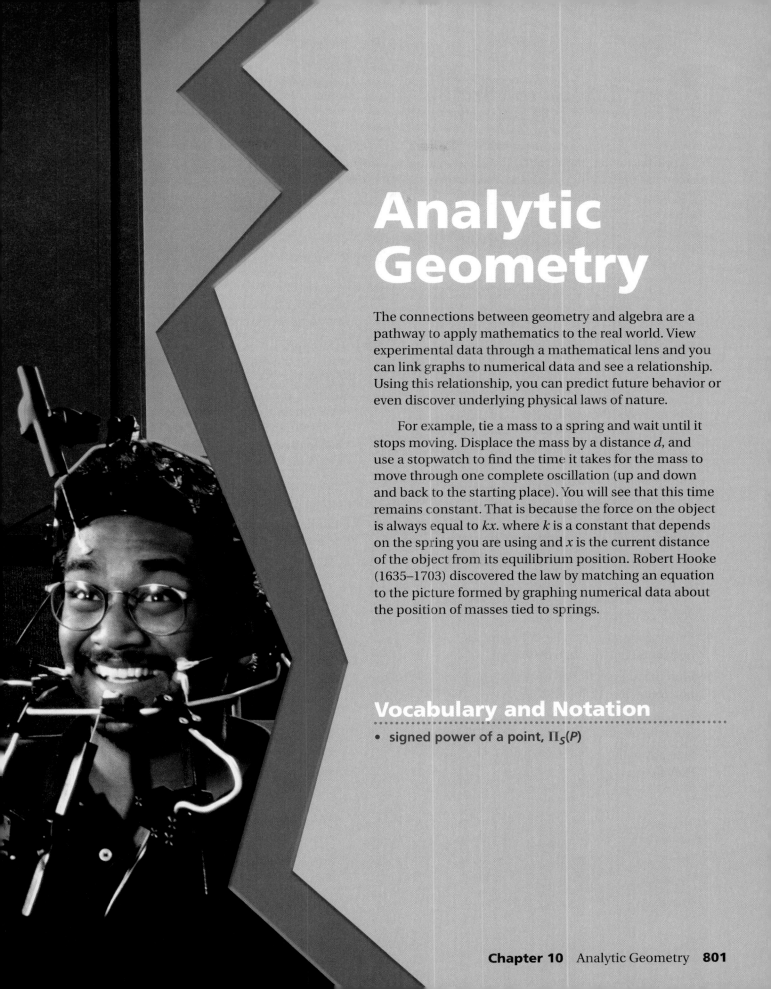

Analytic Geometry

The connections between geometry and algebra are a pathway to apply mathematics to the real world. View experimental data through a mathematical lens and you can link graphs to numerical data and see a relationship. Using this relationship, you can predict future behavior or even discover underlying physical laws of nature.

For example, tie a mass to a spring and wait until it stops moving. Displace the mass by a distance d, and use a stopwatch to find the time it takes for the mass to move through one complete oscillation (up and down and back to the starting place). You will see that this time remains constant. That is because the force on the object is always equal to kx. where k is a constant that depends on the spring you are using and x is the current distance of the object from its equilibrium position. Robert Hooke (1635–1703) discovered the law by matching an equation to the picture formed by graphing numerical data about the position of masses tied to springs.

Vocabulary and Notation

- signed power of a point, $\Pi_S(P)$

Equations of Circles

A circle is the set of points that are a fixed distance from one particular point, called the circle's center. You can use equations to represent circles in a coordinate plane, such as the circles below.

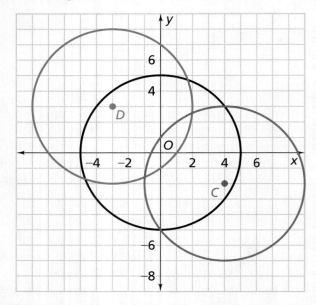

Let circle O be the circle with center $(0, 0)$.

1. How can you tell if a point is on the circle O?

2. Find any points on circle O that are also on the vertical line through $(4, -9)$.

3. Find the intersection(s) of circle O with the vertical line through $(3, 2)$.

4. Find any points on circle O that are also on the horizontal line through $(8, 0)$.

5. Find the intersection(s) of circle O with the horizontal line through $(8, 3)$.

6. Find any points on circle O that are 13 units from the origin.

7. Find any points on circle O that are 11 units from $(0, 16)$.

Circle O is the set of all points (x, y) that are 5 units from the center, the origin $(0, 0)$. You can use the distance formula to write an equation for the circle.

Step 1 Use the distance formula.

$$\sqrt{(x - 0)^2 + (y - 0)^2} = 5$$

Step 2 Square both sides to get rid of the radical.

$$(x - 0)^2 + (y - 0)^2 = 5^2$$

Remember that equations are point testers, so all the points on the circle should satisfy this equation.

Step 3 Simplify.

$$x^2 + y^2 = 5^2, \text{ or } 25$$

Suppose, though, that you want to write an equation for a circle with center somewhere other than the origin. To do that, you have to go back to the distance formula. Let circle C be the circle with center C.

8. Find any points on circle C that are also on the vertical line through $(4, -9)$.

9. Find the intersection(s) of circle C with the horizontal line through $(8, 3)$.

10. **a.** What point is the center of circle C?

b. What is the radius of the circle?

c. Copy and complete the distance formula below to write an equation for circle C. Use the steps above to simplify your equation.

$$\sqrt{(x - \blacksquare)^2 + (y - \blacksquare)^2} = \blacksquare$$

Another way to write an equation for circle C is to use a translation.

You can translate circle C left 4 and up 2—a translation of $(-4, 2)$—to move its center to the origin.

Point $P(p_1, p_2)$ on circle C translates to point $P'(p_1 - 4, p_2 + 2)$. This point is a solution to the equation for circle O, $x^2 + y^2 = 25$.

$$x^2 + y^2 = 25, \text{ so}$$

$$(p_1 - 4)^2 + (p_2 + 2)^2 = 25$$

11. Expand and simplify the following equation.

$$(p_1 - 4)^2 + (p_2 + 2)^2 = 25$$

Compare this equation to the equation you wrote for circle C in Problem 10c above.

12. Write an equation for the circle with center D above.

13. Write an equation for a circle with center $(0, 2)$ and radius 3 units.

14. **Take It Further** Consider the equation

$$\frac{x^2}{4} + \frac{y^2}{25} = 1$$

a. **Write About It** How is the equation similar to the equation of a circle? How is it different?

b. Graph the equation on a coordinate plane. What shape do you have?

If the center axle of this double Ferris wheel is at the origin, equations for the circles are $(x - a)^2 + (y - b)^2 = r^2$ and $(x + a)^2 + (y + b)^2 = r^2$.

Coordinate Geometry

In *Coordinate Geometry*, you will reap the benefits of the insight of Rene Descartes. His coordinate system lets you transform geometric problems into algebraic problems. Then you will use algebra to solve those problems.

By the end of this investigation, you will be able to answer questions like these.

1. What is the set of points equidistant from the *x*-axis and the point (0, 4)?

2. How can you use coordinates to show that the diagonals of a parallelogram bisect each other?

3. How can you find the center and radius of a circle with an equation written in normal form?

You will learn how to
- sketch the graphs of equations in two variables

- use distance and slope relationships to prove geometric results

- evaluate and use the signed power of a point with respect to a circle

You will develop these habits and skills:
- Use equations as point-testers for graphs.

- Visualize collections of points that meet particular conditions—points that satisfy a distance relationship, points with the same signed power with respect to a given circle, and so on.

- Choose coordinate systems strategically to facilitate calculation and proof.

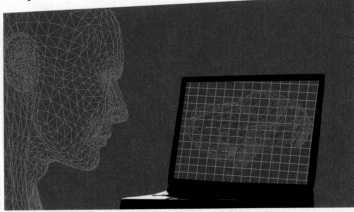

Artists and engineers employ digital wire frame models to represent three dimensional objects. The surface and underlying structure of the item is first coordinatized. Then the animator uses powerful computer software to study, manipulate, or bring the entity to virtual life.

10.01 Getting Started

Previously, you have explored versions of the addition and multiplication tables placed upon a coordinate grid. Here is the multiplication table.

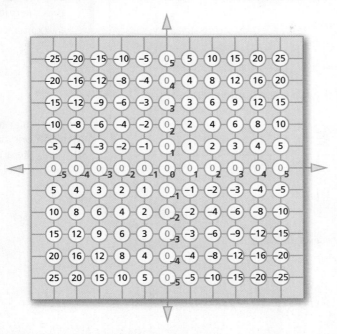

You can use the coordinate grid to visualize the outputs of any two-variable function, such as $f(x, y) = x^2 - y^2$.

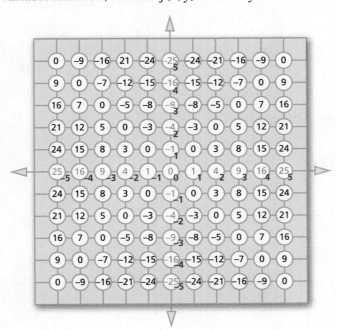

For You to Explore

1. Use the grid for f to find several solutions to the equation $x^2 - y^2 = 9$.

2. Use the grid to help draw an accurate graph of the equation $x^2 - y^2 = 9$.

3. Use the grid to help draw an accurate graph of the equation $y^2 - x^2 = 5$.

4. Find all solutions to this system of equations.
$$x^2 - y^2 = 9$$
$$x + y = 5$$

5. **Take It Further** Use the grid to help you draw a reasonable sketch of the graph of this equation.
$$z = x^2 - y^2$$

> You may need to find other points besides the ones in the grid.

> The z-axis is perpendicular to the xy-plane, and passes through the origin.

Exercises Practicing Habits of Mind

On Your Own

6. Build a grid similar to the one for $f(x, y) = x^2 - y^2$ for the function g defined as
$$g(x, y) = x^2 + y^2$$

7. Use the grid to help draw an accurate graph of the equation $x^2 + y^2 = 17$.

8. Solve this system of equations.
$$x^2 + y^2 = 17$$
$$x^2 - y^2 = 9$$

9. **Take It Further** Draw a rough three-dimensional sketch of the graph of this equation.
$$z = x^2 + y^2$$

10. The graph of the equation $x^2 + y^2 = 13$ is a circle. For each point listed below, determine whether or not it is on this circle.

    a. $(3, 2)$ **b.** $(2, -3)$ **c.** $(0, 4)$ **d.** $(2\sqrt{3}, -1)$

    e. Write About It Describe how you would determine if any point (x, y) is on this circle.

11. Here is the graph of two chords of the circle given by the graph of the equation $x^2 + y^2 = 13$.

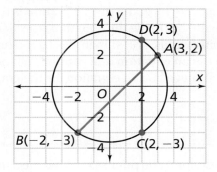

  a. Find an equation for the line containing $A(3, 2)$ and $B(-2, -3)$.

  b. Find an equation for the line containing $C(2, -3)$ and $D(2, 3)$.

  c. Find the coordinates of the point of intersection X of the two chords.

  d. Show that the following statement is true by calculating the length of each chord.

$$AX \cdot BX = CX \cdot DX$$

12. Here is the graph of two chords of the circle given by the graph of the equation $x^2 + y^2 = 25$.

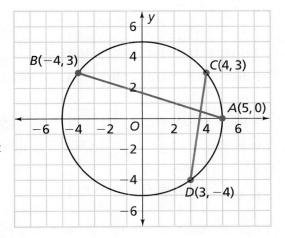

  a. Find an equation for the line containing $A(5, 0)$ and $B(-4, 3)$.

  b. Find an equation for the line containing $C(4, 3)$ and $D(3, -4)$.

  c. Find the coordinates of the point of intersection X of the two chords.

  d. Show that the following statement is true by calculating the length of each chord.

$$AX \cdot BX = CX \cdot DX$$

Maintain Your Skills

13. For each statement, write an expression that matches the description.

  a. the slope between $(2, 4)$ and (x, y)

  b. the distance from the origin $(0, 0)$ to (x, y)

  c. the distance from $(2, 4)$ to (x, y)

  d. the distance from $(3, 0)$ to (x, y), plus the distance from $(-3, 0)$ to (x, y)

  e. the distance from (x, y) to the line with equation $y = -3$

  f. **Take It Further** the distance from (x, y) to the line with equation $x + y = 10$

Equations as Point-Testers

Graphs are point-testers. The graph of an equation is the set of the points on the Cartesian plane that make the equation true. Sometimes you can describe a graph using words, and sometimes by its shape and some key points. If you can write an equation that captures all the characteristics of the graph, that equation will be an equation for the graph.

For You to Do

1. Find an equation describing the points (x, y) that are 5 units away from $(3, 4)$.
2. Sketch a graph of all points (x, y) in the plane satisfying the equation $|y - 2| = 3$.

Facts and Notation

Here are some useful formulas from previous courses.

- *Distance formula*: The distance between points $A(x_1, y_1)$ and $B(x_2, y_2)$ is

$$d(A, B) = \sqrt{(x_2 - x_1)^2 + (y_2 - y_1)^2}$$

- *Midpoint formula*: The midpoint of the segment between points $A(x_1, y_1)$ and $B(x_2, y_2)$ is

$$M(A, B) = \left(\frac{x_1 + x_2}{2}, \frac{y_1 + y_2}{2} \right)$$

- *Slope formula*: The slope between points $A(x_1, y_1)$ and $B(x_2, y_2)$ is

$$m(A, B) = \frac{y_2 - y_1}{x_2 - x_1}$$

This assumes that $x_1 \neq x_2$. What happens if $x_1 = x_2$?

- *Perpendicular slopes*: Two lines in the plane are perpendicular if the product of their slopes is -1, or if one line is vertical and the other is horizontal.

Remember...

In your geometry class, you proved that if the slope of a line ℓ is m (with $m \neq 0$), then the slope of any line perpendicular to ℓ is $-\frac{1}{m}$.

Example 1

Problem Find an equation for the set of points equidistant from (5, 2) and (11, 0).

Solution

Method 1 Use the distance formula. Consider any point (x, y) on the graph. Its distance from (5, 2) must equal its distance from (11, 0).

$$\text{distance from } (x, y) \text{ to } (5, 2) = \text{distance from } (x, y) \text{ to } (11, 0)$$

$$\sqrt{(x - 5)^2 + (y - 2)^2} = \sqrt{(x - 11)^2 + y^2}$$

This is a valid equation but you can simplify it. Since the expressions under the radicals are nonnegative (why?), squaring both sides will not introduce any new solutions.

$$(x - 5)^2 + (y - 2)^2 = (x - 11)^2 + y^2$$
$$x^2 - 10x + 25 + y^2 - 4y + 4 = x^2 - 22x + 121 + y^2$$
$$-10x - 4y + 29 = -22x + 121$$
$$-4y = -12x + 92$$
$$y = 3x - 23$$

Method 2 Use the geometric observation that the solution will be the equation of the perpendicular bisector of the segment connecting (5, 2) and (11, 0).

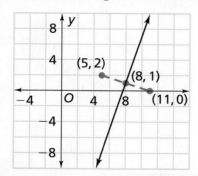

The perpendicular bisector must pass through the midpoint (8, 1) and be perpendicular to the segment. The slope between (5, 2) and (11, 0) is $-\frac{1}{3}$, so the slope of the perpendicular bisector is 3. One equation for the perpendicular bisector is $y - 1 = 3(x - 8)$. This equation is equivalent to $y = 3x - 23$ as found earlier.

> **Remember...**
> If you write the equation of a line in the form $y - k = m(x - h)$, the line passes through the point *(h, k)* and has slope *m*.

Example 2

Problem Find an equation for the set of points that are equidistant from the origin and the line with equation $y = 2$.

Solution Take an arbitrary point (x, y). Its distance to the origin is $\sqrt{x^2 + y^2}$. Its distance from the line with equation $y = 2$ is $|y - 2|$.

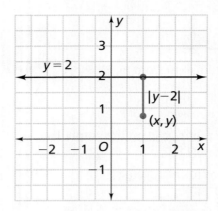

The set of points equidistant from both satisfies the equation
$\sqrt{x^2 + y^2} = |y - 2|$. Simplify and solve for y.

$$\sqrt{x^2 + y^2} = |y - 2|$$
$$x^2 + y^2 = (y - 2)^2$$
$$x^2 + y^2 = y^2 - 4y + 4$$
$$x^2 + 4y = 4$$
$$y = -\tfrac{1}{4}x^2 + 1$$

The graph of the equation is a downward opening parabola.

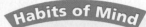

Habits of Mind

Understand the process. Why is it legal to square both sides?

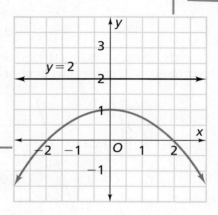

Developing Habits of Mind

Establish a process. The intersection of the graphs of two equations is the set of points that satisfies both of their equations. For example, the Getting Started lesson for this investigation asked you to find the intersection of the graphs of the equations $x^2 - y^2 = 9$ and $x + y = 5$. You can solve this algebraically. Note that you can factor $x^2 - y^2$.

$$(x + y)(x - y) = 9$$

But $x + y = 5$ is known, so $x - y$ must equal 1.8. Then a system of equations emerges.

$$x + y = 5$$
$$x - y = 1.8$$

You can solve this system of equations by many methods, including adding the two equations together. The solution $x = 3.4$, $y = 1.6$ is the only intersection of the two graphs.

Exercises Practicing Habits of Mind

Check Your Understanding

1. **a.** Write a point-tester that is true for any point (x, y) 3 units away from the line with equation $y = 2$.

   b. Sketch the graph of all points (x, y) that are 3 units away from the line with equation $y = 2$.

2. Consider the set of all points (x, y) that are the same distance away from $(4, 0)$ as they are from the y-axis.

   a. Determine whether $(3, 3)$ is in this set of points.

   b. Determine whether $(10, 8)$ is in the set.

   c. Explain why any point (a, b) with $a < 0$ cannot be in this set of points.

   d. Write a point-tester that is true for any point (x, y) equidistant from $(4, 0)$ and the y-axis.

3. You have learned that the set of points equidistant from two given points in the plane is a line. But now, consider the set of points that are twice as far away from $(15, 0)$ as they are from $(6, 0)$.

   a. Is $(5, 3)$ in this set? Justify your answer.

   b. Find the two points on the x-axis that are in this set.

   c. Write a point-tester equation that you can use to determine whether any point (x, y) is in this set.

   d. Sketch the graph of the point-tester equation.

4. A triangle has vertices $A(2, 0)$, $B(6, -2)$, and $C(8, 4)$.

   a. Find an equation for the perpendicular bisector of $\overline{AB}$.

   b. Find an equation for the perpendicular bisector of $\overline{AC}$.

   c. Find the intersection of the two perpendicular bisectors.

5. Point-testers can be useful to find equations in three-dimensional space. Consider the set of points exactly 5 units away from the point $(2, 3, 4)$.

   a. Find five points that are in this set.

   b. Find five points that are not in this set.

   c. Write a point-tester equation that you can use to determine whether any point (x, y, z) is in this set of points.

6. Consider the set of points in space that are the same distance from the origin $(0, 0, 0)$ as they are from the point $(2, 4, 6)$.

   a. In the plane, the set of points equidistant from two points would be a line. What kind of shape should it be in space?

   b. Determine whether or not $(3, 7, -1)$ is in this set of points.

   c. What equation would you use to check to see if (x, y, z) is in this set of points? Simplify the equation as much as possible.

   d. Use the point-tester from part (c) to determine whether or not the point $(15, 4, -3)$ is in this set of points.

   e. **Take It Further** Sketch the graph of all points in this set.

On Your Own

7. Exercise 4 looked at the perpendicular bisectors of $\triangle ABC$.

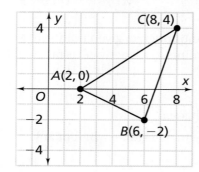

   a. Find an equation for the perpendicular bisector of $\overline{BC}$.

   b. Find an intersection for the perpendicular bisectors of $\overline{AB}$ and $\overline{BC}$.

8. Find equations for the three medians of $\triangle ABC$. Show that the three medians intersect in one point.

9. As in the Getting Started lesson, build a grid for the function h,

$$h(x, y) = x^2 + y^2 - 4x + 2y - 4$$

if $-5 \leq x \leq 5$, $-5 \leq y \leq 5$.

10. a. Use the grid from Exercise 9 to describe the graph of the equation

$$x^2 + y^2 - 4x + 2y - 4 = 0$$

   b. Prove that your description in part (a) is correct.

> **Remember...**
> A median of a triangle is a segment connecting a vertex to the midpoint of the opposite side.

> You may need to add or subtract terms from each side.

11. Consider the equation in three variables

$$z^2 = x^2 + y^2$$

a. Find several points (x, y, z) that are on the graph of this equation.

b. Suppose $z = 5$. Describe the set of x and y values that make the equation true.

c. Suppose $z = 11$. Describe the set of x and y values that make the equation true.

d. Suppose $z = -11$. Describe the set of x and y values that make the equation true.

e. Suppose $z = 0$. Describe the set of x and y values that make the equation true.

f. Sketch the graph of $z^2 = x^2 + y^2$ as accurately as you can.

12. Take It Further The graph of $z^2 = x^2 + y^2$ is sometimes called a *double cone.*

a. What kind of figure does slicing the double cone perpendicular to the z-axis (say, with the plane with equation $z = 5$) produce?

b. What is the graph that results when the plane with equation $x = 3$ slices the double cone?

c. Find what other shapes might be possible with other slices. Give some examples.

13. Standardized Test Prep Which of the following is an equation for the set of points equidistant from $(2, 3)$ and $(6, 1)$?

A. $\sqrt{(x - 2)^2 + (y - 3)^2} = \sqrt{(x - 6)^2 + (y - 1)^2}$

B. $\dfrac{y - 3}{x - 2} = \dfrac{y - 1}{x - 6}$

C. $y - 3 = -\dfrac{1}{2}(x - 2)$

D. $2x + 3y = 6x + y$

Go Online
www.successnetplus.com

An equation for the plane that contains the point $(0, 0, c)$ is $z = c$. Similarly, an equation for the plane that contains the point $(a, 0, 0)$ is $x = a$.

Maintain Your Skills

14. The *centroid* of a triangle is the intersection of its medians. Given the three vertices of $\triangle ABC$, find its centroid.

a. $A(0, 0)$, $B(10, 0)$, $C(2, 9)$

b. $A(0, 0)$, $B(10, 0)$, $C(2, -9)$

c. $A(0, 0)$, $B(100, 0)$, $C(20, 90)$

d. $A(1, 2)$, $B(10, 11)$, $C(19, 5)$

e. $A(0, 0)$, $B(3a, 0)$, $C(3b, 3c)$

f. $A(x_1, y_1)$, $B(x_2, y_2)$, $C(x_3, y_3)$

Coordinates and Proof

In this lesson, you will learn how to use coordinate methods to prove geometric facts. For example, consider quadrilateral *ABCD* in the plane.

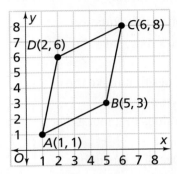

If you wanted to prove that it is a parallelogram you could use any of the following approaches.

- If a quadrilateral has pairs of opposite sides that are parallel, then it is a parallelogram.

- If a quadrilateral has pairs of opposite sides that are congruent, then it is a parallelogram.

- If a quadrilateral has one pair of opposite sides that are congruent and parallel, then it is a parallelogram.

For You to Do

1. Pick one of the three approaches above. Then use it to show that the quadrilateral *ABCD* is a parallelogram.

To prove something more generally, *coordinatize* a geometric shape by making a general version in the coordinate plane. For example, a general parallelogram might look like as follows.

If a general parallelogram lies in the plane, you can define the coordinates however you like. So, define the origin to be one of the vertices. Let one of the sides lie along the *x*-axis. But be careful not to overdefine the shape. For example, if you already defined $Q(0, a)$, point *S* in the parallelogram cannot be defined as (a, b). That assumes too much about where *S* is located. A good choice of coordinates is one that needs as few variables as possible, but does not assume any more about the shape than is necessary.

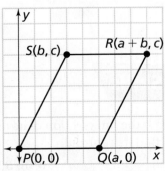

Derman and Sasha are coordinatizing △EON.

Derman What about a general triangle like this one?

Sasha So how do you want to label the points?

Derman Why not just use six letters? Make the vertices $O(a, b)$, $N(c, d)$, and $E(e, f)$.

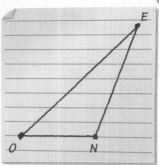

Sasha I think we can do it with fewer variables. We can put the axes wherever we want, so let's put point O at the origin. Then we can place $\overline{ON}$ on the x-axis. Point N would have y-coordinate 0, so say its coordinates are $(c, 0)$.

Derman I can do that with the y-axis, too. Line it up with $\overline{OE}$. Then E has x-coordinate 0!

Sasha Wait a minute! If you line up $\overline{ON}$ with the x-axis and $\overline{OE}$ with the y-axis, then something is wrong. Just draw it.

Derman Okay.

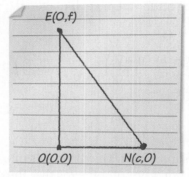

Derman Oh. I get it now. I forced $\angle EON$ to be a right angle. I'll bet these would be useful coordinates for a right triangle, though.

Sasha You're right. But this is the way our general triangle should look.

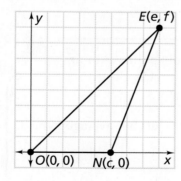

Coordinatizing lets you use formulas to obtain other information about the shape.

Example 1

Problem Show that the diagonals of a parallelogram bisect each other.

Solution Here is a diagram for a general parallelogram, with coordinates labeled.

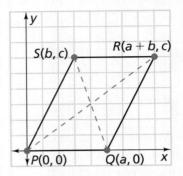

The diagonals bisect each other if their midpoints are the same. So, use the midpoint formula to find the midpoint of each diagonal.

The midpoint of diagonal $\overline{PR}$ is

$$\left(\frac{0 + (a + b)}{2}, \frac{0 + c}{2} \right) = \left(\frac{a + b}{2}, \frac{c}{2} \right)$$

The midpoint of diagonal $\overline{QS}$ is

$$\left(\frac{a + b}{2}, \frac{0 + c}{2} \right) = \left(\frac{a + b}{2}, \frac{c}{2} \right)$$

The two midpoints are the same point. The diagonals must intersect at the point $\left(\frac{a + b}{2}, \frac{c}{2} \right)$. This common midpoint means that the diagonals bisect one another.

Developing Habits of Mind

Make connections. Some people like to think about points as things they can add or subtract, just like numbers. They would write

$$(3, 7) + (11, 5) = (14, 12)$$

If you think of points this way, finding a midpoint is just like averaging the points. The average of $(3, 7)$ and $(11, 5)$ is

$$\frac{(3, 7) + (11, 5)}{2} = (7, 6)$$

And, as you saw, $(7, 6)$ is the midpoint of the segment from $(3, 7)$ to $(11, 5)$.

This algebra of points can come in handy, and matches up with the matrix concepts of addition and scalar multiplication.

For You to Do

2. Plot the points $A(3, 7)$ and $B(11, 5)$ on graph paper. Then calculate and plot $P = \frac{3}{4}(3, 7) + \frac{1}{4}(11, 5)$. How could you describe the location of P relative to points A and B?

Example 2

Problem Prove that the diagonals of a rhombus are perpendicular.

Solution A *rhombus* is a quadrilateral with four congruent sides. Start with a diagram for a general parallelogram.

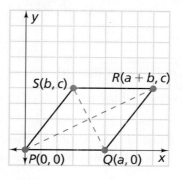

Since $PQRS$ is a rhombus, $PQ = PS$. So $a = \sqrt{b^2 + c^2}$. Or, $a^2 = b^2 + c^2$.

The slope of diagonal $\overline{PR}$ is $\frac{c}{a + b}$. The slope of diagonal $\overline{QS}$ is $\frac{-c}{a - b}$. These slopes are perpendicular if their product is -1.

$$\frac{c}{a + b} \cdot \frac{-c}{a - b} = \frac{-c^2}{a^2 - b^2}$$

Since $a^2 = b^2 + c^2$

$$\frac{-c^2}{a^2 - b^2} = \frac{-c^2}{(b^2 + c^2) - b^2} = \frac{-c^2}{c^2} = -1$$

The product of the slopes of the diagonals is -1, so they are perpendicular.

For You to Do

The proof above only holds if neither of the diagonals is vertical (has undefined slope). However, the way you set up the coordinates means that a vertical diagonal will have interesting consequences.

3. What would the coordinates of the vertices of rhombus $PQRS$ have to be if the diagonal $\overline{QS}$ were vertical? What do these coordinates imply about $PQRS$?

4. What would the coordinates of the vertices of rhombus $PQRS$ have to be if the diagonal $\overline{PR}$ were vertical? What do these coordinates imply about $PQRS$?

Make strategic choices. The choice of coordinates is often influenced by what you are trying to prove. If you are trying to prove a statement about medians, it may make more sense to label a triangle as follows.

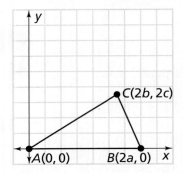

This makes working with medians a little easier, since the midpoints will not have fractional coordinates.

If your geometric shape has a line of symmetry, one choice is to place the line of symmetry on an axis. Here is one way to coordinatize an isosceles triangle.

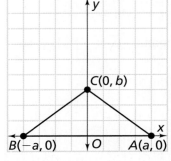

It takes some practice to develop the knack for choosing a convenient set of coordinates. You want your choice to make the calculations easier, but you do not want to introduce any extra assumptions, as Derman did in the Minds in Action box on page 815. Try to think about what you are trying to prove and how to get there. A good choice of coordinates can reduce the work of the proof.

The massive cables of the Golden Gate Bridge, as with most suspension bridges, form parabolic arcs.

Check Your Understanding

1. **a.** Find four coordinate pairs to represent the vertices of a rectangle.

   b. Prove that the diagonals of a rectangle are equal in length.

2. Use coordinates to prove the *Midline Theorem*:

   > The segment joining the midpoints of two sides of a triangle is parallel to the third side. Its measure is equal to half the measure of the third side.

> **Remember...**
> You first proved the Midline Theorem in Chapter 7.

3. Prove that if you connect the midpoints of the sides of any quadrilateral, the resulting quadrilateral is a parallelogram.

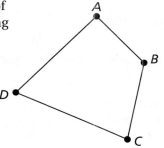

> **Go Online**
> www.successnetplus.com

4. Determine what type of quadrilateral results when you connect the midpoints of the sides of a rectangle. Prove your result.

5. **What's Wrong Here?** Joey says that he can quickly prove that the diagonals of a rhombus are perpendicular.

   Joey: I used the symmetry of the rhombus. The diagonals ended up being right on the axes. Then of course the diagonals are perpendicular. They're the axes.

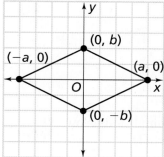

   What is wrong with Joey's reasoning?

6. **Take It Further** Prove that if the diagonals of a parallelogram are perpendicular, then the parallelogram is a rhombus.

Habits of Mind

Make strategic choices. You can do this with only one variable.

7. Coordinatize a general square.

8. In this figure, $\triangle ABC$ is a right triangle and point D is the midpoint of hypotenuse $\overline{BC}$. Set coordinates for points B and C, then prove that $AD = BD = CD$.

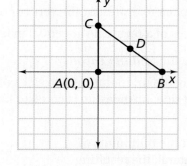

9. a. Coordinatize a general equilateral triangle.

   b. Prove that in an equilateral triangle, any median is also a perpendicular bisector.

10. a. Coordinatize an *isosceles trapezoid*, a trapezoid with congruent non-parallel sides.

   b. Prove that the diagonals of an isosceles trapezoid are equal in length, but do not bisect each other.

11. Use coordinates to prove that the length of the *midline of a trapezoid* is the average of the lengths of its two bases.

12. Take It Further Coordinatize a regular hexagon centered at the origin. Use only one variable.

13. Standardized Test Prep Given a parallelogram with three of its vertices at the points $(1, 5)$, $(5, -1)$, and $(2, 2)$, which of the following could not be the fourth vertex?

   A. $(6, -4)$ **B.** $(4, 2)$ **C.** $(3, 2)$ **D.** $(-2, 8)$

Remember...

The *midline* of a trapezoid is a segment connecting the midpoints of the two nonparallel sides. For the trapezoid given, the midline connects the midpoint of $\overline{AD}$ with the midpoint of $\overline{BC}$.

Maintain Your Skills

14. The graph of the equation

$$x^2 + y^2 - 8x + 10y + 24 = 0$$

is a circle centered at the point $(4, -5)$. For each point listed below, determine whether or not it is on the graph of the circle.

   a. $(4, -1)$ **b.** $(5, -1)$ **c.** $(8, -6)$

   d. $(8, 0)$ **e.** $(0, 0)$ **f.** $(3, -9)$

The Power of a Point, Part 2

Consider a circle with center (h, k) and radius r. If you picked any point (x, y), how would you decide whether it was on the circle? You can find a point-tester for a circle by calculating the distance from (x, y) to the center, which must equal r.

$$\sqrt{(x - h)^2 + (y - k)^2} = r$$
$$(x - h)^2 + (y - k)^2 = r^2$$

This second equation is the *center-radius form* for a circle. Equations for circles are not always in this form. You can use the method of *completing the square* to rewrite an equation of a circle in this form.

Example 1

Problem The graph of the equation

$$x^2 + y^2 - 10x + 14y - 26 = 0$$

is a circle. Find its center and radius.

Solution You can identify the center and radius if the equation is in the form

$$(x - h)^2 + (y - k)^2 = r^2$$

Start by moving terms to make the result appear as follows.

$$(x^2 - 10x \quad) + (y^2 + 14y \quad) = 26$$

Now find constants that produce perfect square trinomials. For the first term this constant is $\left(-\frac{10}{2}\right)^2 = 25$. For the second term this constant is $\left(\frac{14}{2}\right)^2 = 49$. Add these constants to each side of the equation.

$$(x^2 - 10x + \mathbf{25}) + (y^2 + 14y + \mathbf{49}) = 26 + \mathbf{25} + \mathbf{49}$$

Factor each expression in parentheses.

$$(x - 5)^2 + (y + 7)^2 = 100$$

The center is $(5, -7)$ and the radius is $\sqrt{100} = 10$.

> **Remember...**
>
> This technique is called completing the square because you add the number that produces a complete perfect square trinomial.

For You to Do

1. Find the center and radius for the circle with equation
   $x^2 + y^2 + 12x - 8y + 3 = 0$.

2. Find the center for the circle with equation
   $x^2 + y^2 + 50x - 18y + 100 = 0$.

   Can you do this without completing the square? Explain.

In Chapter 8, you discovered the *Power of a Point Theorem*.

Theorem 10.1 Power of a Point

Given a point P and a circle, take any line through P that intersects the circle in two points A and B. Then $PA \cdot PB$ is constant, no matter what line you choose through P. This constant is called the power of the point P. The power is a function of the point, so write the power of P as $\Pi(P)$.

Go Online
www.successnetplus.com

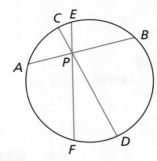

$$PA \cdot PB = PC \cdot PD = PE \cdot PF$$

Here are two corollaries.

Corollary 10.1.1

Inside a circle, the power of a point d units away from the center of a circle with radius r is $r^2 - d^2$.

Corollary 10.1.2

Outside a circle, the power of a point d units away from the center of a circle with radius r is $d^2 - r^2$.

For Discussion

3. Suppose point P is on the circle. What is its power?

Here is a proof of Corollary 10.1.1.

Proof The Power of a Point Theorem applies to any line through P that intersects the circle at two points. So, pick $\overleftrightarrow{OP}$, where O is the center of the circle.

This line intersects the circle at points A and B. Since $OP = d$, and $\overline{AB}$ is a diameter, you know the lengths PA and PB: $PA = r + d$ and $PB = r - d$. The power of point P with respect to the circle is

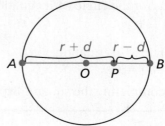

$$PA \cdot PB = (r + d)(r - d) = r^2 - d^2$$

You will prove Corollary 10.1.2 in Exercise 1 below. Note that the two rules are nearly identical. Also, the quantity $d^2 - r^2$ is invariant for any point P. This quantity is negative for points inside the circle and positive for points outside the circle. Now name this quantity.

Definition

Given point P, d units from the center of a circle of radius r. The **signed power of point** P with respect to the circle is given by

$$\Pi_S(P) = d^2 - r^2$$

Example 2

Problem Calculate the signed power of each point with respect to the circle with equation

$$x^2 + y^2 - 10x + 14y - 26 = 0$$

a. $(8, -3)$ **b.** $(-1, 1)$ **c.** $(5, -7)$

d. $(5, 18)$ **e.** (x, y)

Solution Earlier, you showed that the center of this circle is $(5, -7)$ and its radius is 10. For each point, calculate $d^2 - r^2$, where d is its distance from the center, and r is the radius (10).

a. The distance from $(8, -3)$ to $(5, -7)$ is $\sqrt{3^2 + 4^2} = 5$, so the signed power is $5^2 - 10^2 = -75$. If a chord $\overline{AB}$ of this circle passes through $P(8, -3)$, the product of PA and PB will be 75.

b. The distance from $(-1, 1)$ to $(5, -7)$ is $\sqrt{6^2 + 8^2} = 10$, so the signed power is $10^2 - 10^2 = 0$. This point is on the circle.

c. This point is the center, so its signed power is $0^2 - 10^2 = -100$.

d. The distance from $(5, 18)$ to $(5, -7)$ is 25, so the signed power is $25^2 - 10^2 = 525$.

e. The distance from (x, y) to $(5, -7)$ is

$$\sqrt{(x - 5)^2 + (y + 7)^2}$$

The signed power of point (x, y) is

$$(x - 5)^2 + (y + 7)^2 - 100$$

Expanding and collecting terms gives

$$(x^2 - 10x + 25) + (y^2 + 14y + 49) - 100$$
$$x^2 + y^2 - 10x + 14y - 26$$

Amazing! This is exactly the left side of the equation that defines the circle.

You generalize the process in Example 2.

Theorem 10.2

The signed power of point $P(x, y)$ with respect to the circle with equation $x^2 + y^2 + Cx + Dy + E = 0$ is

$$\Pi_S(P) = x^2 + y^2 + Cx + Dy + E$$

If you want to, you can write the equation that defines the circle as $\Pi_S(P) = 0$.

Developing Habits of Mind

Find another way. Given a specific circle, what is the minimum value that the signed power can have. And where does this value occur? The signed power is $d^2 - r^2$. Since r is fixed, the signed power is smallest when $d = 0$. This d is the distance to the center, so the signed power takes on its minimum value at the center of the circle. The minimum value is $-r^2$.

This gives an interesting way to find the center and radius of a circle based on its equation in normal form. For example, take the circle with equation

$$x^2 + y^2 - 16x + 22y - 344 = 0$$

If you were finding the center and radius by completing the square, you would look at the coefficients of the linear x and y terms and write an equation that looked like this:

$$(x - 8)^2 + (y + 11)^2 = \text{something}$$

The center of this circle is $(8, -11)$. You can quickly find the center for any circle this way. Then, use the signed power calculation to find the radius. The signed power of the center $(8, -11)$ is

$$\Pi_S(8, 11) = 8^2 + (-11)^2 - 16(8) + 22(-11) - 344 = -529$$

This value is equal to $-r^2$, so the radius is $\sqrt{529} = 23$. The signed power of a point allows you to find the center and radius for a circle with an equation in normal form without having to finish completing the square.

Let P be the point of intersection of the chopsticks. Can you find the power of a point P with respect to the rim of the plate?

Check Your Understanding

1. Prove Corollary 10.1.2.

   > Outside a circle, a point d units away from the center of a circle with radius r has power $d^2 - r^2$.

2. The graph of the equation $x^2 + y^2 + 6x - 8y - 24 = 0$ is a circle.

   a. Find the center and radius of the circle.

   b. Sketch the graph of the circle.

   c. Find the exact coordinates of all intercepts.

3. The point $P(0, 0)$ lies inside the circle from Exercise 2. Several chords of the circle defined by the graph of $x^2 + y^2 + 6x - 8y - 24 = 0$ pass through the origin.

   a. One such chord lies along the x-axis. Calculate the power of P with respect to this circle using this chord.

   b. Calculate the power of P using the chord that lies along the y-axis.

   c. Find the two intersection points of the circle with the line with equation $y = x$. Use these intersections to calculate the power of P.

4. **Write About It** The Power of a Point Theorem applies to any line drawn through a point P that intersects a circle twice. What happens when P is outside the circle and the intersection points get closer together? How could you rephrase the Power of a Point Theorem to address this situation?

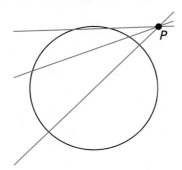

5. **Take It Further** Find the two intersection points of the circle from Exercise 3 with the line with equation $y = kx$. Then show that the power of $P(0, 0)$ with respect to this circle is independent of k.

6. Find the signed power of point $P(6, 5)$ with respect to the circle
$$(x - 3)^2 + (y + 1)^2 = 25$$

Go Online
www.successnetplus.com

7. Find some other points with the same signed power as $P(6, 5)$ with respect to the circle
$$(x - 3)^2 + (y + 1)^2 = 25$$

8. Calculate the value of $f(x, y) = (x - 3)^2 + (y + 1)^2 - 25$ for each set of inputs.

   a. $x = 6, y = 5$ **b.** $x = 9, y = -4$ **c.** $x = 0, y = -7$ **d.** $x = -3, y = 2$

9. If C is the center of a circle with radius r, explain why the signed power of C with respect to the circle is $-r^2$.

10. **Take It Further** Given two circles, describe the set of points that have the same signed power with respect to both circles. Does your answer change depending on how the circles are positioned?

11. **Take It Further** Prove Theorem 6.1 in general. In other words, show that the signed power of a point $P(a, b)$ with respect to the circle with equation $x^2 + y^2 + Cx + Dy + E = 0$ is
$$\Pi_S(P) = a^2 + b^2 + aC + bD + E$$

12. **Standardized Test Prep** Which of the following is the center of the circle with equation $x^2 + y^2 + 4x - 2y = 0$?

   A. $(4, -2)$ **B.** $(-4, 2)$ **C.** $(2, -1)$ **D.** $(-2, 1)$

Maintain Your Skills

13. Let the point X be the intersection of chords $\overline{AB}$ and $\overline{CD}$ inside a circle.

   a. If $AX = 4$, $BX = 6$, $CX = 9$, find DX.
   b. If $AX = 8$, $BX = 6$, $CX = 9$, find DX.
   c. If $AX = 4$, $BX = 6$, $CX = 18$, find DX.
   d. If $AX = 4$, $BX = 6$, $CX = c$, find DX.
   e. If $AX = 4$, $BX = 6$, find the smallest possible length of chord $\overline{CD}$.

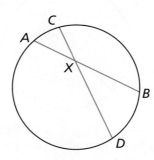

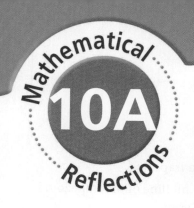

In this investigation, you found equations that characterized descriptions of various point sets. You used coordinate methods to prove geometric facts. You investigated the signed power of a point. The following questions will help you summarize what you have learned.

1. Which points with integer coordinates lie on the circle with equation $x^2 + y^2 = 25$?

2. Which of the following points lie on the ellipse with equation
$$\frac{(x - 3)^2}{16} + \frac{(y + 1)^2}{12} = 1?$$

   a. $(-1, -1)$ b. $(3, -1)$ c. $(1, 2)$

3. For which values of x can the equation $\dfrac{(x - h)^2}{a^2} - \dfrac{(y - k)^2}{b^2} = 1$ be true?

4. Prove the following consequence of the Pythagorean Theorem: *The sum of the squares of the lengths of the diagonals of a parallelogram is equal to the sum of the squares of the lengths of its four sides.*

5. Determine the power of the point $(16, 6)$ with respect to the circle $(x - 4)^2 + (y + 3)^2 = 25$.

6. What is the set of points equidistant from the x-axis and the point $(0, 4)$?

7. How can you use coordinates to show that the diagonals of a parallelogram bisect each another?

8. How can you find the center and radius of a circle with an equation written in normal form?

Vocabulary and Notation

In this investigation, you learned these terms and symbols. Make sure you understand what each one means and how to use it.

• signed power of a point, $\mathrm{II}_S(P)$

Chapter 10

Review

In **Investigation 10A,** you learned to

- sketch the graphs of equations in two variables
- use distance and slope relationships to prove geometric results
- evaluate and use the signed power of a point with respect to a circle

The following questions will help you check your understanding.

1. a. Find an equation for the set of points equidistant from the point $(0, 2)$ and the line with equation $y = -2$.

b. Sketch a graph of all points satisfying the equation.

2. a. Coordinatize a trapezoid.

b. Prove that the midline of the trapezoid is parallel to its bases.

3. The graph of $x^2 + y^2 + 4x - 12y + 31 = 0$ is a circle.

a. Find the center and the radius of the circle.

b. Sketch the graph of the circle.

c. Find the signed power of point $P(2, 3)$ with respect to the circle.

d. Find the signed power of point $Q(-1, 7)$ with respect to the circle.

Multiple Choice

1. Determine the equation in the form $y = a(x - h)^2 + k$ for the parabola having focus $(3, 4)$ and directrix the x-axis.

A. $y = 8(x - 4)^2 + 3$

B. $y = \frac{1}{4}(x - 3)^2 + 4$

C. $y = \frac{1}{8}(x - 3)^2 + 2$

D. $y = 3(x - 4)^2 + \frac{1}{2}$

2. Determine which of the following points is on the graph of $X = (-1, 4) + t(2, 6)$.

A. $(1, 8)$

B. $(5, 20)$

C. $(-1, -3)$

D. $(-5, -8)$

3. Determine which of the points would form a parallelogram with the three points on the graph.

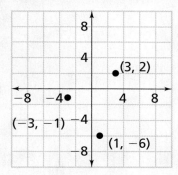

A. $(0, 2)$

B. $(-1, 6)$

C. $(-1, 7)$

D. $(-2, 4)$

4. Consider the line with parametric equation $X = (3, -1) + t(-1, 5)$. Which of the following is a Cartesian equation for the line?

A. $y = \frac{1}{5}x + 3$

B. $y = -\frac{1}{5}x + 1$

C. $y = 5x + 3$

D. $y = -5x + 14$

Open Response

5. The graph of the equation

$$x^2 + y^2 + 4x - 26y - 52 = 0$$

is a circle.

a. Find the radius and center of the circle.

b. Calculate the signed power of the point $(1, 17)$ and describe its location with respect to the circle.

c. Calculate the signed power of the point $(7, 25)$ and describe its location with respect to the circle.

6. Two cars drive along straight, flat lines. At time t, Car A is at $(80, 60) + t(10, 15)$ and Car B is at $(40, 15) + t(20, 25)$.

a. Determine if the cars collide. If they do, find at what time.

b. Determine if their paths intersect. If they do, find at what time each car passes the intersection point.

7. Let L be the line through $(4, 6)$ with direction vector $(2, -5)$. Find y so that $(-2, y)$ is on L.

8. Consider the lines given by the equations $X = (2, 5) + t(-1, -3)$ and $Y = (1, 4) + t(6, -2)$.

a. Graph both lines.

b. Determine if these lines are parallel, perpendicular, or neither.

Honors Appendix

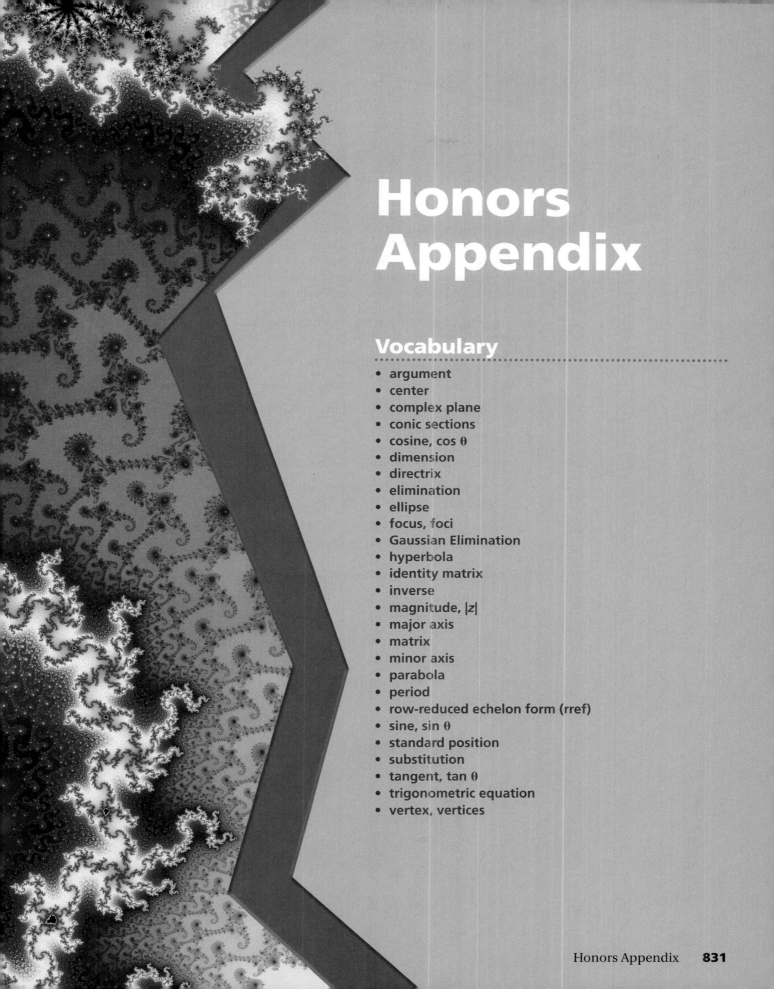

Honors Appendix

The Complex Plane

In *The Complex Plane*, you will visualize complex numbers as points or vectors on a coordinate plane. This visual representation of complex numbers will help you develop new insights into addition, multiplication, and conjugation of complex numbers. By translating algebraic calculations into geometric operations, you can form a new understanding of the algebraic calculations.

By the end of this investigation, you will be able to answer questions like these.

1. How do you represent a complex number graphically?

2. What is the graphical effect of adding two complex numbers?

3. What is the graphical effect of multiplying a complex number by i?

You will learn how to

- graph complex numbers on the complex plane

- visualize operations on complex numbers as transformations on the complex plane

- develop greater fluency with complex number calculations, which include finding magnitude and direction

You will develop these habits and skills:

- Extend the concept of absolute value in the real numbers to magnitude in the complex numbers.

- Visualize complex numbers and operations on them in the context of the complex plane.

- Represent complex numbers as points or as vectors, depending upon the context.

a Julia set fractal on the complex plane

Activating Prior Knowledge
Exploring New Ideas

You can use properties of geometry and trigonometry to find angle measures and segment lengths on the coordinate plane.

For You to Explore

1. A triangle on the coordinate plane has vertices $O(0, 0)$, $A(4, 0)$, and $B(4, 3)$.

a. Explain why this is a right triangle.

b. Find the length of the hypotenuse.

c. Angle B has a measure of approximately $53.13°$. Find the approximate measure of angle O.

d. Use a calculator in degree mode to find the value of $\tan^{-1}\left(\frac{3}{4}\right)$ to two decimal places.

> **Remember...**
> The hypotenuse of a right triangle is the side opposite the right angle.

2. A triangle has vertices $O(0, 0)$, $P(\sqrt{3}, 1)$, and $Q(\sqrt{3}, -1)$.

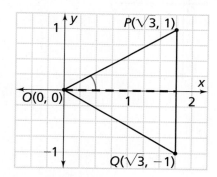

a. Show that all three sides have the same length.

b. Find the measure of the marked angle between $\overline{OP}$ and the x-axis.

3. A line segment on the coordinate plane has endpoints at $(0, 0)$ and $(7, 24)$.

a. Find the slope of the line segment.

b. Find the length of the line segment.

c. Estimate the measure of the marked angle.

d. Use a calculator in degree mode to find the value of $\tan^{-1}\left(\frac{24}{7}\right)$ to two decimal places.

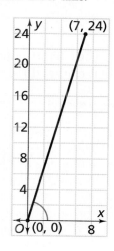

> **Habits of Mind**
> **Look for relationships.**
> What does part (d) have to do with the other parts of this problem?

4. A triangle has vertices $A(2, 0)$, $P(-1, \sqrt{3})$, and $Q(-1, -\sqrt{3})$. Its circumcenter is $O(0, 0)$.

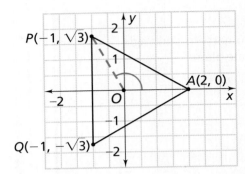

Remember...

The circumcenter of a polygon is the center of the circle that contains the vertices of the polygon.

a. Show that all three sides have the same length.

b. Find the measure of the marked angle between $\overline{OP}$ and the x-axis.

5. For each triangle, find the coordinates of points A and B.

a.

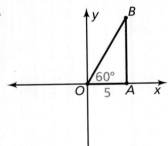

b.

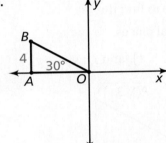

c.

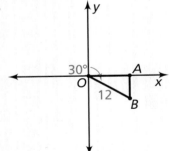

6. A square has a vertex at $(1, 0)$. The circumcenter of the square is at the origin. Find the coordinates of the other three vertices of the square.

Exercises Practicing Habits of Mind

On Your Own

Remember...

Exact means no approximations. For example, $\sqrt{13}$ is exact, but 3.60555 is an approximation to $\sqrt{13}$.

7. Graph each line segment. Then find the exact length of each segment.

a. endpoints at $(0, 0)$ and $(4, 1)$

b. endpoints at $(0, 0)$ and $(2, 1)$

c. endpoints at $(0, 0)$ and $(7, 6)$

d. endpoints at $(0, 0)$ and $(3, 4)$

e. endpoints at $(0, 0)$ and $(6, 8)$

f. endpoints at $(0, 0)$ and $(1, \sqrt{3})$

8. Find each product.

a. $(4 + i)(4 - i)$

b. $(2 + i)(2 - i)$

c. $(4 + i)(2 + i)$

d. $(7 + 6i)(7 - 6i)$

e. $(3 + 4i)(3 - 4i)$

f. $(1 + i\sqrt{3})(1 - i\sqrt{3})$

9. Use the inverse tangent function on a calculator. Find the measure of each marked angle to two decimal places.

a.

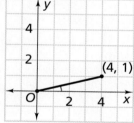

b.

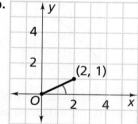

c.

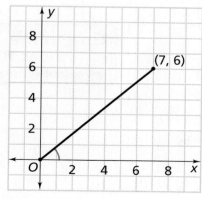

d.

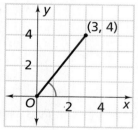

10. An isosceles right triangle has a right angle and two 45° angles.

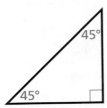

a. If one leg has length 4, find the length of the hypotenuse.

b. If one leg has length 10, find the length of the hypotenuse.

c. If one leg has length a, find the length of the hypotenuse.

d. If the hypotenuse has length 4, find the length of each leg.

e. If the hypotenuse has length 10, find the length of each leg.

f. If the hypotenuse has length b, find the length of each leg.

Remember...

The legs in a right triangle are the sides adjacent to the right angle.

11. For each triangle, find the coordinates of points A and B.

a.

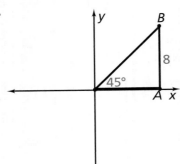

b.

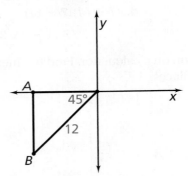

12. An equilateral triangle has a vertex at $(1, 0)$. The circumcenter of the triangle is at the origin. Find the exact coordinates of the other two vertices.

Maintain Your Skills

Go Online
Video Tutor
www.successnetplus.com

13. Evaluate each expression.

a. $(-1 + i\sqrt{3})^3$

b. $(-1 - i\sqrt{3})^3$

c. 2^3

d. $2(-1 + i\sqrt{3})(-1 - i\sqrt{3})$

e. $2 + (-1 + i\sqrt{3}) + (-1 - i\sqrt{3})$

14. For each point A, find the coordinates of point A', which you locate by rotating A 90° counterclockwise about the origin.

a. $A(1, 0)$

b. $A(0, -1)$

c. $A(3, 5)$

d. $A(6, -1)$

15. Write each complex number in the form $a + bi$, where a and b are real numbers.

a. $(3 + 4i)^2$

b. $(3 + 4i)^3$

c. $(3 + 4i)^4$

d. $(3 + 4i)^5$

H.02 Graphing Complex Numbers

Throughout the 1600s and 1700s, mathematicians used "imaginary" numbers as tools to solve problems involving real numbers. However, they did not feel that these numbers had any existence on their own.

Around 1800, mathematicians invented a geometric representation for numbers like $2 + i$. This graphic representation of complex numbers led to an explosion of activity in mathematics—many new fields were born.

The geometric representation, along with the use of i, was made popular by Gauss in the early 1800s.

On the number line, you represent real numbers as points. For example, here is how you represent 5 on the number line.

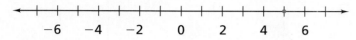

And here is -3.

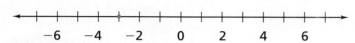

Developing Habits of Mind

Look for relationships. How do you represent a complex number geometrically? To know a complex number, you need to know two numbers—the real part and the imaginary part.

Two complex numbers are equal if and only if both their real and imaginary parts are equal by Theorem 3.6. So there is a one-to-one correspondence between complex numbers and pairs of real numbers. And how do you represent ordered pairs of real numbers? You represent ordered pairs as points on the coordinate plane.

So, take the number line and make a second axis, perpendicular to the first, to record multiples of i. This is the **complex plane**. Each complex number $a + bi$ is represented on the complex plane by a point at the coordinates (a, b).

The complex plane is sometimes called the *Argand plane* in honor of Jean Argand, the author of one of the first papers about it.

Problem Graph each complex number.

- $3i$
- $2 + i$
- $4 - 3i$
- -3

Solution The complex plane below shows the four points that correspond to the given numbers.

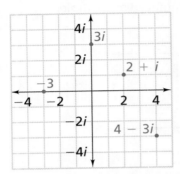

Note that you still represent a real number as a point on the real number line.

Remember...

Any real number is also a complex number.

For You to Do

1. Identify the complex number represented by each point.

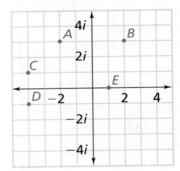

2. Which two points on the complex plane above are conjugates of each other?

3. If z is a complex number, compare the locations of z and $-z$ on the complex plane.

Exercises *Practicing Habits of Mind*

Check Your Understanding

1. Graph and label each complex number on the same complex plane.

   a. $4 + 3i$ **b.** $4 - 3i$

   c. $-4 + 3i$ **d.** $-4 - 3i$

2. You can write a complex number as $z = a + bi$. What can you say about a and b if z is located in the given quadrant?

   a. Quadrant I   **b.** Quadrant II

   c. Quadrant III   **d.** Quadrant IV

3. **a.** Graph both solutions to the equation $x^2 + 13 = 4x$ on the complex plane.

   b. Compute the sum and product of the two solutions.

4. **a.** Graph all three solutions to the equation $x^3 - 8 = 0$ on the complex plane.

   b. The roots lie on the vertices of a triangle. Is this triangle equilateral, isosceles, or scalene? Justify your answer.

   c. Compute the sum and product of the three solutions.

5. Find four complex numbers that lie on the vertices of a square on the complex plane.

6. Graph and label each complex number on the same complex plane.

   a. i^0 **b.** i^1 **c.** i^2

   d. i^3 **e.** i^4 **f.** i^5

Habits of Mind

Look for relationships. How are the graphs of the solutions related?

On Your Own

For Exercises 7 and 8, graph and label the four complex numbers on a single complex plane.

7. **a.** $3 + 2i$ **b.** $3 - 2i$

   c. $-3 - 2i$ **d.** $-3 + 2i$

8. **a.** $2 + i$ **b.** $(2 + i)^2$

   c. $(2 + i)^3$ **d.** $(2 + i)^4$

Go Online
www.successnetplus.com

9. Suppose a and b are positive real numbers.

   a. Graph what $a + bi$ and $a - bi$ might look like on the same complex plane.

   b. Graph the sum of $z = a + bi$ and $\bar{z} = a - bi$.

   c. Describe how the sum $z + \bar{z}$ is geometrically related to z and $\bar{z}$.

   d. Describe how the difference $z - \bar{z}$ is geometrically related to z and $\bar{z}$.

In Exercises 10 and 11, solve each equation. Then graph the solutions on the complex plane.

10. a. $x^2 + 6x + 5 = 0$

   b. $x^2 + 6x + 8 = 0$

   c. $x^2 + 6x + 10 = 0$

   d. $x^2 + 6x + 13 = 0$

   e. $x^2 + 6x + 18 = 0$

11. a. $x^4 - 1 = 0$

   b. $x^4 - 16 = 0$

   c. $x^4 - 81 = 0$

   d. $x^4 - 256 = 0$

12. Graph each complex number on the same complex plane.

   a. i^{10} **b.** i^{11} **c.** i^{243}

   d. i^{-1} **e.** i^{-11} **f.** i^{-243}

13. Suppose $z = 3 + i$ and $w = 2 - i$. Graph each group of numbers on the complex plane.

   a. $w, 2w, 3w$

   b. $z + w, z + 2w, z + 3w$

   c. $\overline{w}, \overline{2w}, \overline{3w}$

   d. $\overline{z + w}, \overline{z + 2w}, \overline{z + 3w}$

14. Standardized Test Prep Suppose $z = 5 + i$ and $w = 4 - i$. Which of the following numbers is NOT in Quadrant IV on the complex plane?

A. zw

B. w^2

C. $\bar{z}$

D. $3z + 2w$

15. Take It Further Suppose $z = \dfrac{\sqrt{2}}{2} + \dfrac{\sqrt{2}}{2}i$. Simplify each expression. Then graph all the numbers on the same complex plane.

a. z^0 b. z^1 c. z^2 d. z^3

e. z^4 f. z^8 g. z^{27} h. z^{275}

Maintain Your Skills

16. Graph and label each complex number on the same complex plane.

a. $-3 + i$

b. $2(-3 + i)$

c. $3(-3 + i)$

d. $4(-3 + i)$

e. $-1(-3 + i)$

17. Write each expression as a complex number $a + bi$. Then graph and label each complex number on the same complex plane.

a. $3 + 5i$

b. $(3 + 5i) \cdot i$

c. $(3 + 5i) \cdot i^2$

d. $(3 + 5i) \cdot i^3$

e. $(3 + 5i) \cdot i^4$

Arithmetic in the Complex Plane

Once mathematicians realized that there is a one-to-one correspondence between points on a plane and complex numbers, they started asking questions about visualizing operations on complex numbers.

Suppose z and w are complex numbers, represented as points on the complex plane. How can you locate the following numbers?

- $z + w$

- $3z$

- zw

- $\bar{z}$

- $-z$

You have already explored some of these questions. In this lesson, you will focus on addition, and you will begin to explore multiplication.

Addition

The graph below shows $z = 2 + 3i$, $w = 6 + i$, and the sum $z + w = 8 + 4i$ on the complex plane.

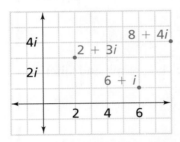

These may look like three random points, but if you draw vectors from the origin to z and w, you see more structure.

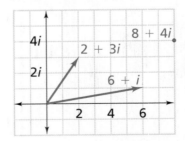

Tony draws the vector for the sum 8 + 4i.

Tony   Hey, look, Sasha. If I draw in the vector for the sum, I get this.

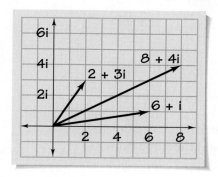

Sasha draws on Tony's graph.

Sasha   And if I connect the dots, it looks like a parallelogram.

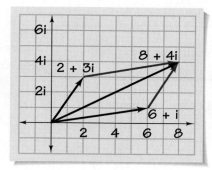

For You to Do

1. Prove Sasha correct. Show that if $z = 2 + 3i$ and $w = 6 + i$, then 0, z, w, and $z + w$ are the vertices of a parallelogram.

The following theorem shows that Sasha's parallelogram law always works. The proof is just a general version of what you did above with $2 + 3i$ and $6 + i$.

Theorem H.1

Suppose $z = a + bi$ and $w = c + di$ are complex numbers. Then, on the complex plane, the numbers 0, z, w, and $z + w$ form the vertices of a parallelogram.

Proof $z + w = (a + c) + (b + d)i$, so the coordinates of the point corresponding to $z + w$ are $(a + c, b + d)$.

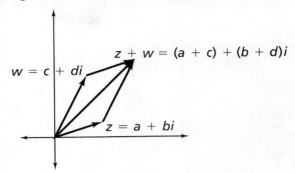

A figure is a parallelogram if its opposite sides are parallel. Parallel lines have the same slope. The slope from 0 to w is $\frac{d}{c}$, and the slope from z to $z + w$ is

$$\frac{(b + d) - b}{(a + c) - a} = \frac{d}{c}$$

So these two sides are parallel.

For You to Do

2. Complete the proof by showing that the other two sides are also parallel.

> Or you can show that the sides you proved parallel are also congruent.

You can also use the parallelogram law to subtract complex numbers by adding the opposite.

Multiplication: First Steps

How do you visualize multiplication? This is more difficult. Given z and w on the complex plane, can you locate zw? In this lesson, you will look at two special cases: when w is a real number, and when $w = i$.

You can visualize multiplication of a complex number z by a positive real number k as stretching or shrinking the vector by a factor of k. For example, for $z = -3 + i$, the graph below shows vectors for z and $4z$.

> Stretches and shrinks by a factor of k are dilations.

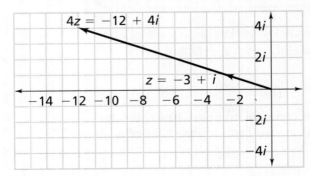

For Discussion

How do you prove that three points are collinear?

3. In the graph, $4z$, z, and 0 appear to be collinear. Prove that this is, in fact, true.

You can multiply z by a negative real number $-k$ by graphing $-z$ and then scaling that vector by k. For example, the graph below shows $-3 + i$ and $-2 \cdot (-3 + i)$ drawn as vectors.

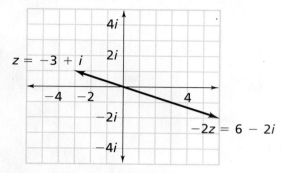

This works since $z \cdot (-k) = (-z) \cdot k$.

In-Class Experiment

For each z, graph z and iz as vectors on the same complex plane.

4. $z = 3 + 5i$

5. $z = -2 + i$

6. $z = -3 - 4i$

7. Describe how the graph of iz compares to the graph of z in the complex plane.

Habits of Mind

Experiment. Try more examples if you need to. Choose other complex numbers for z.

The In-Class Experiment above suggests the following relationship.

Theorem H.2 Multiplication by i

If z is a complex number, iz is obtained from z by rotating it $90°$ counterclockwise about the origin.

The fact that the rotation is counterclockwise instead of clockwise is surprisingly technical. Ask your teacher if you are curious about the details.

Proof Show that the vectors representing iz and z are perpendicular and are the same distance from the origin. Then you obtain iz from z by a 90° rotation.

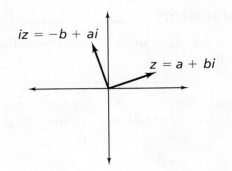

Start by writing $z = a + bi$. Then $iz = -b + ai$.

You can use slope to prove that the two vectors are perpendicular. The slope of the vector representing z is $\frac{b}{a}$. The slope of the vector representing iz is $\frac{a}{-b}$. These slopes are negative reciprocals.

$$\frac{b}{a} \cdot \frac{a}{-b} = -1$$

Therefore, the vectors are perpendicular, and the angle between z and iz is 90°.

In the exercises, you will prove that $z = a + bi$ and $iz = -b + ai$ are the same distance from the origin.

You can use vectors to describe the magnitude and direction of the wind, currents, and movement of the ship.

Developing Habits of Mind

Represent complex numbers graphically. You can think about a complex number graphically in two ways: as a point and as a vector. By thinking about complex numbers as points, you can apply all the machinery of geometry. This representation helps you perform algebraic tasks, such as solving equations.

By thinking about complex numbers as vectors, you can visualize operations, such as adding or multiplying by i. Vectors also help you compare the relative sizes of complex numbers.

It is important that you become comfortable with both representations and that you develop a sense of when it is appropriate to "think point" or to "think vector."

You use vectors extensively in navigation and physics. Complex numbers are also key in analyzing signals, such as radio waves or electric current.

For You to Do

8. Which of these four complex numbers has the longest vector?

$$-5 - 6i \quad ° \quad ° \quad 6 + i \quad ° \quad ° \quad 4 + 5i \quad ° \quad ° \quad 8$$

Exercises *Practicing Habits of Mind*

Check Your Understanding

1. Illustrate each addition equation on the complex plane.

   a. $(4 + i) + (2i) = 4 + 3i$

   b. $(2i) + (4 + i) = 4 + 3i$

   c. $(4 + i) + (4 - i) = 8$

   d. $(4 + i) + (-3 + i) = 1 + 2i$

   e. $-8 + 3 = -5$

2. The graph below shows two complex numbers z and w.

   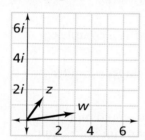

   Graph each expression.

   a. $z + w$ **b.** $2z$

   c. $-w$ **d.** $2z + 2w$

   e. $2z - w$ **f.** **Take It Further** $z + wi$

3. If $z = a + bi$ is a complex number, show that z and iz are the same distance from the origin.

4. For each complex number, find the distance to the origin on the complex plane.

   a. $4 + i$ **b.** $2 + i$

   c. $3 - 2i$ **d.** $6 + 5i$

5. Find each product.

   a. $(4 + i)(4 - i)$ **b.** $(2 + i)(2 - i)$

   c. $(3 - 2i)(3 + 2i)$ **d.** $(6 + 5i)(6 - 5i)$

Go Online
www.successnetplus.com

6. Consider the triangle with the following vertices.

$$-18 + 49i \qquad 15 - 7i \qquad 30 - 15i$$

   a. Find the lengths of the sides of the triangle.

   b. If you multiply each vertex by -1, what is the position of the resulting triangle compared to the original triangle in the complex plane? Draw a picture to support your answer.

   c. If you multiply each vertex by i, what is the position of the resulting triangle compared to the original triangle in the complex plane? Draw a picture to support your answer.

7. For each complex number z, graph z and iz as vectors on the same complex plane.

   a. $z = 3 + 2i$ **b.** $z = -1 + 4i$

   c. $z = -1 - 3i$ **d.** $z = 2 - 3i$

8. **a.** Describe the effect, in the complex plane, of multiplying a complex number by i^2.

   b. Describe the effect, in the complex plane, of multiplying a complex number by $-i$.

9. **Write About It** For each statement, decide whether you would represent the complex numbers as points or as vectors. Give reasons for your choice. Then draw a diagram.

   a. The numbers 1, i, -1, and $-i$ lie on the vertices of a square on the complex plane.

   b. You can use the parallelogram law to visualize the sum $(3 + 2i) + (7 - 6i)$.

   c. If you multiply the vertices of a triangle by i, the new triangle is congruent to the original.

   d. The distance from $5 + 12i$ to the origin is greater than the distance from $3 + 4i$ to the origin.

On Your Own

10. Illustrate the following equation graphically.

$$(3 - i) + (3 - i) + (3 - i) = 9 - 3i$$

11. For each complex number, find its distance from the origin on the complex plane.

   a. $3 + i$ **b.** $4 - i$ **c.** $(3 + i)(4 - i)$

   d. $(2 + i)^2$ **e.** $(2 + i)^3$

Go Online
www.successnetplus.com

12. Does Theorem H.2 work for two real numbers? Explain.

13. Order the following complex numbers from least to greatest, based on how far each number is from the origin.

$$5 + 3i \qquad 2 - 7i \qquad 8 \qquad -6 - 4i$$

14. Standardized Test Prep Here is a graph of $2iz$, for a complex number z, on the complex plane. Which of the following numbers is z?

A. $-3 + 2i$

B. $2 + 3i$

C. $3 - 2i$

D. $4 + 6i$

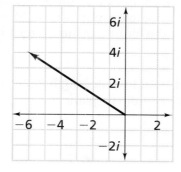

15. Suppose $z = \frac{\sqrt{2}}{2} + \frac{\sqrt{2}}{2}i$. Graph each pair of complex numbers.

a. $1 + i$ and $(1 + i) \cdot z$

b. $3 + 5i$ and $(3 + 5i) \cdot z$

c. $-2 + i$ and $(-2 + i) \cdot z$

d. $-3 - 4i$ and $(-3 - 4i) \cdot z$

16. a. Write About It Describe the effect, in the complex plane, of multiplying by $z = \frac{\sqrt{2}}{2} + \frac{\sqrt{2}}{2}i$ in Exercise 15.

b. Take It Further Describe the effect, in the complex plane, of multiplying by $z^2 = \left(\frac{\sqrt{2}}{2} + \frac{\sqrt{2}}{2}i\right)^2$.

Maintain Your Skills

17. Solve each equation.

a. $x^3 - 1 = 0$ **b.** $x^3 - 8 = 0$ **c.** $x^3 = 27$ **d.** $x^3 = 64$

e. Find an equation with integer coefficients having solutions that include 8 and $-4 + 4i\sqrt{3}$.

For Exercise 17 help, see the TI-Nspire™ Handbook, p. 990.

18. Suppose $z = 1 + i$. For each value of w, draw a diagram that shows z, w, and zw.

a. $w = 3 + 4i$

b. $w = -3 + 4i$

c. $w = -5 + 12i$

d. $w = 7$

e. $w = 3i$

Habits of Mind

Make strategic choices. You can represent complex numbers as vectors or as points. Decide which form is most helpful to you in each case.

Magnitude and Direction

In the last lesson, you represented complex numbers as vectors. Now you will focus on two properties of vectors, *magnitude* and *direction*.

Definition

> The **magnitude** of the complex number *z*, denoted by |*z*|, is the distance between the complex number and (0, 0) in the complex plane. In other words, |*z*| is the length of the vector that represents *z*.

If $z = a + bi$, the magnitude is the length of the line segment connecting (0, 0) and (*a*, *b*) in the coordinate plane.

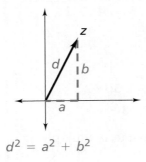

$$d^2 = a^2 + b^2$$

For You to Do

1. Find $|-3 + 5i|$.

2. Find a complex number in the fourth quadrant with magnitude 5.

3. Show that the magnitude of $z = a + bi$ is $|z| = \sqrt{a^2 + b^2}$.

To calculate magnitude, see the TI-Nspire Handbook, p. 990.

Theorem H.3 Magnitude and Conjugates

> The magnitude |*z*| of a complex number is given by
> $$|z| = \sqrt{z\bar{z}}$$

Proof Let $z = a + bi$. The conjugate is $\bar{z} = a - bi$. Find $\sqrt{z\bar{z}}$.
$$\sqrt{z\bar{z}} = \sqrt{(a + bi)(a - bi)} = \sqrt{a^2 + b^2}$$
This is the same as the expression for magnitude that you verified in Problem 3. So, $|z| = \sqrt{z\bar{z}}$.

Look for relationships. The symbol for magnitude is the same as the symbol for absolute value. There are at least two reasons that this makes sense.

- Find the magnitude of a real number $a + 0i$.

$$|a + 0i| = \sqrt{a^2 + 0^2} = \sqrt{a^2}$$

This satisfies one definition of absolute value: $|a| = \sqrt{a^2}$. For real numbers, magnitude and absolute value are equal.

> **Remember...**
>
> Real numbers are still complex numbers. They have imaginary parts equal to 0.

- The absolute value of a real number is its distance from $(0, 0)$ on a number line. Magnitude is also distance from $(0, 0)$, but on the complex plane.

By defining $|z|$ as the distance between z and $(0, 0)$, you extend the definition of absolute value from $\mathbb{R}$ to $\mathbb{C}$.

For You to Do

4. Find as many complex numbers as you can with magnitude 5. Are any of them also real numbers?

Example 1

Problem Graph each complex number as a vector and find its magnitude.

   a. $(2 + i)^0$

   b. $(2 + i)^1$

   c. $(2 + i)^2$

   d. $(2 + i)^3$

   e. $(2 + i)^4$

> For help with the calculations, see the TI-Nspire Handbook, p. 990.

Solution Evaluate each expression to find the real and imaginary parts of each number.

   a. A number raised to the zero power is 1, so $(2 + i)^0 = 1$.

   b. A number raised to the first power is itself, so $(2 + i)^1 = 2 + i$.

   c. $(2 + i)^2 = 3 + 4i$

   d. $(2 + i)^3 = (3 + 4i)(2 + i) = 2 + 11i$

   e. $(2 + i)^4 = (2 + 11i)(2 + i) = -7 + 24i$

This plot shows all five complex numbers drawn as vectors.

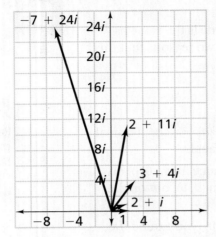

To find the magnitude of each number, use the expression $\sqrt{a^2 + b^2}$ or the Pythagorean Theorem.

a. $|1| = 1$

b. $|2 + i| = \sqrt{2^2 + 1^2} = \sqrt{5}$

c. $|3 + 4i| = \sqrt{3^2 + 4^2} = \sqrt{25} = 5$

d. $|2 + 11i| = \sqrt{2^2 + 11^2} = \sqrt{125} = 5\sqrt{5}$

e. $|-7 + 24i| = \sqrt{(-7)^2 + 24^2} = \sqrt{625} = 25$

For You to Do

5. Find the magnitude of $2 + 3i$ and $(2 + 3i)^2$.

For real numbers, the absolute value $|x - y|$ is defined as the distance between x and y on the number line. If magnitude is an extension of absolute value from $\mathbb{R}$ to $\mathbb{C}$, this should still apply in $\mathbb{C}$. The distance between two complex numbers z and w is $|z - w|$, the magnitude of the difference between the two numbers.

Example 2

Problem Find the distance between $3 + 2i$ and $4 - i$ on the complex plane.

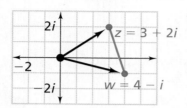

Solution Draw a right triangle with z and w as two vertices.

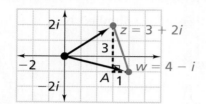

Using the Pythagorean theorem, the length of the segment joining z and w is $\sqrt{1^2 + 3^2} = \sqrt{10}$.

Alternately, you can calculate $|z - w|$ to find the distance between $3 + 2i$ and $4 - i$.

$$|(3 + 2i) - (4 - i)| = |-1 + 3i| = \sqrt{(-1)^2 + 3^2} = \sqrt{10}$$

Both methods give the same answer.

> A similar diagram can be used to find the distance between any two points in the plane: the distance between $A = (x_1, y_1)$ and $B = (x_2, y_2)$ is
> $$\sqrt{(x_2 - x_1)^2 + (y_2 - y_1)^2}$$

For You to Do

6. Find the distance between $-2 + 5i$ and $1 + i$.

> **Remember...**
> The magnitude of $a + bi$ is $\sqrt{a^2 + b^2}$.

Tony and Derman are working on some complex arithmetic problems.

Derman So this magnitude rule is like the distance formula. What's that other formula? It's got *x* over 2 and *y* over 2.

Tony The midpoint formula?

Derman Yeah! I wonder if the midpoint formula works for complex numbers. Here, I'll draw $6 + 5i$ and $10 + 3i$.

Derman draws a sketch of his two complex numbers.

Derman What complex number is halfway between those?

Tony On the number line, you can take the average of two numbers by adding them up and dividing by 2.

Derman Can you take averages of complex numbers?

Tony I don't see why not. Let's add them up and divide by 2. I get

$$\frac{(6 + 5i) + (10 + 3i)}{2} = \frac{16 + 8i}{2} = 8 + 4i.$$

Derman Here, let me graph it.

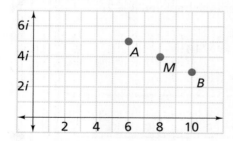

Tony That looks like it works to me.

Derman Me too, but how can we be sure?

For Discussion

7. Prove that $8 + 4i$ is the midpoint between $6 + 5i$ and $10 + 3i$.

> Use what you know about the coordinate plane to help.

A complex number has magnitude. But, if you think of a complex number as a vector, it also has a specific direction. How should you define direction? You can define direction by using the counterclockwise angle measured from the positive real axis.

Definition

The **direction** of the complex number z is the angle measured from the positive real axis in a counterclockwise direction.

Generally, you express direction with a measure at least 0° and less than 360°. What does a direction of 450° mean?

Example 3

Problem Find the magnitude and direction of each complex number.

    a. $-2i$

    b. $-1 + i$

    c. $1 + 3i$

    d. $(1 + 3i)^2 = -8 + 6i$

Habits of Mind

Visualize. Graphing a complex number as a vector helps to illustrate its magnitude and direction.

Solution

    a. The magnitude of $-2i$ is 2. Since $-2i$ lies directly along the negative imaginary axis, its direction angle is three-fourths of a full circle. The direction is 270°.

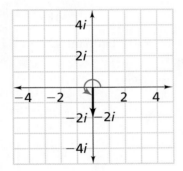

    b. $|-1 + i| = \sqrt{2}$ because

$$|-1 + i| = \sqrt{(-1 + i)(-1 - i)} = \sqrt{(-1)^2 + 1^2} = \sqrt{2}.$$

By dropping an altitude from the point $(-1, 1)$, you make an isosceles right triangle. The measures of the angles in this triangle are 45°, 45°, and 90°.

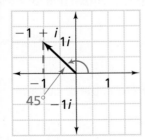

Where is $|-1 + i|$ in this picture?

The direction angle is supplementary to the 45° angle in the isosceles right triangle. Therefore, the direction is 135°.

c. The magnitude of $1 + 3i$ is $\sqrt{10}$ because $\sqrt{1^2 + 3^2} = \sqrt{10}$. By dropping an altitude from the point $(1, 3)$, you make a right triangle.

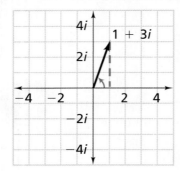

This triangle is not a special right triangle. So use trigonometry to approximate the measure of the marked angle. Since you know the lengths of all the sides, you can use any of the trigonometric ratios. For example, find the angle measure by using tangent.

$$\tan x = \frac{3}{1}$$

$$x = \tan^{-1}\left(\frac{3}{1}\right)$$

$$x \approx 71.565°$$

So, $71.565°$ is the approximate direction.

d. The magnitude of $-8 + 6i$ is 10 because $\sqrt{(-8)^2 + 6^2} = 10$. Drop an altitude from the point $(-8, 6)$ to make a right triangle.

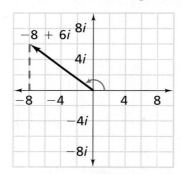

This triangle is not a special right triangle. So use trigonometry to approximate the angle formed by the hypotenuse and the negative real axis.

$$\tan x = \frac{6}{8}$$
$$x = \tan^{-1}\left(\frac{6}{8}\right)$$
$$x \approx 36.870°$$

The direction angle is supplementary to this angle. Therefore, the direction angle is approximately $180° - 36.870° = 143.130°$.

Facts and Notation

You will typically use the word *direction* when referring to vectors. However, when the vectors stand for complex numbers, it is more conventional to use the older term **argument** and the notation "arg." Below are some examples.

- $\arg(-2i) = 270°$
- $\arg(-1 + i) = 135°$
- $\arg(1 + 3i) \approx 71.565°$

For help calculating the argument of a complex number, see the TI-Nspire Handbook, p. 990.

For You to Do

Find $|z|$ and arg z for each complex number z.

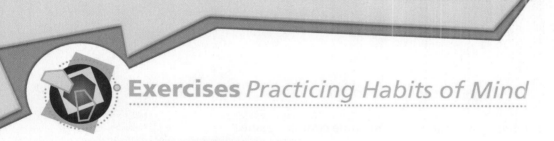

8. $z = 2 + 2i$

9. $z = (1 + 3i)^3$

10. $z = 3$

11. $z = 1 - i\sqrt{3}$

Exercises *Practicing Habits of Mind*

Check Your Understanding

1. Find the magnitude and direction of each complex number.

a. $4 + 3i$

b. $4 - 3i$

c. $-4 + 3i$

d. $-4 - 3i$

Throughout these exercises, calculate the direction to the nearest thousandth degree if you cannot find the exact angle.

2. Find $|w|$ and arg w for each complex number w.

a. $w = 2 + 2i$

b. $w = 2 - 2i$

c. $w = -2 + 2i$

d. $w = -2 - 2i$

3. Without using a calculator, estimate the direction of each complex number to within 10°.

a. $5 + 4i$

b. $-5 + 4i$

c. $5 - 4i$

d. $-5 - 4i$

4. Describe what happens to the magnitude and direction of a complex number when you double the complex number.

5. For real numbers x and y, absolute value is multiplicative.

$$|xy| = |x| \cdot |y|$$

With a partner, test two examples to see if $|zw| = |z| \cdot |w|$ is true when z and w are complex numbers.

6. Let $z = 1 + i$ and $w = -2 - 7i$. Calculate each value.

  a. $|z|$

  b. $|w|$

  c. $|z + w|$

  d. the distance from z to w

  e. the midpoint of the segment with endpoints at z and w

  f. the midpoint of the segment with endpoints at the origin and at $z + w$

7. For each complex number z, find the magnitude and direction of z and of z^2.

  a. $z = 2i$

  b. $z = -1 + i$

  c. $z = 4 + i$

  d. $z = -4 + i$

8. For each complex number z, plot z and $\frac{1}{z}$ on the same complex plane.

  a. $z = 1 + i$

  b. $z = 2 + i$

  c. $z = 1 + i\sqrt{3}$

  d. $z = -1 - i$

> **Remember...**
>
> The expression $\frac{1}{z}$ is the reciprocal of a complex number z. You worked with reciprocals in Lesson 3.13.

9. For each complex number z in Exercise 8, find the magnitude and direction of z and of $\frac{1}{z}$.

10. Write each complex number as a product of a positive real number and a complex number of magnitude 1.

  a. $4 + 3i$ **b.** $5 + 12i$ **c.** $1 + i$

  d. $1 - i$ **e.** $2 + 3i$ **f.** $-1 + i\sqrt{3}$

11. Show that you can write any nonzero complex number as the product of a positive real number and a complex number of magnitude 1.

12. Find the magnitude and direction of each complex number.

   a. $3 + 2i$ **b.** $3 - 2i$

   c. $-3 - 2i$ **d.** $-3 + 2i$

13. Find $|z|$ and arg z for each complex number z.

   a. $z = 1 + i\sqrt{3}$ **b.** $z = 1 - i\sqrt{3}$

   c. $-z = 1 + i\sqrt{3}$ **d.** $z = \left(1 + i\sqrt{3}\right)\left(1 - i\sqrt{3}\right)$

Go Online
www.successnetplus.com

14. Let $z = 1 + 2i$ and $w = -3 + 6i$. Calculate each value.

   a. $|z|$ **b.** $|w|$

   c. $|z + w|$ **d.** the distance from z to w

   e. the midpoint of the segment with endpoints at z and w

   f. the midpoint of the segment with endpoints at the origin and at $z + w$

   g. What kind of quadrilateral is formed by the origin, z, w, and $z + w$?

15. In Geometry, you learned that if the diagonals of a quadrilateral bisect each other, then the quadrilateral is a parallelogram. Prove Theorem H.3 using this property of quadrilaterals.

16. **Standardized Test Prep** To the nearest degree, arg $(-2 + 5i)$ is 112°. Which is the direction of $-2 - 5i$?

   A. 202°   **B.** 224°   **C.** 248°   **D.** 292°

17. A complex number z has magnitude 5 and direction 50°.

   a. Graph z as a vector on the complex plane.

   b. Graph the conjugate $\bar{z}$ on the same complex plane.

   c. Find the magnitude and direction of $\bar{z}$.

18. Describe what happens to the magnitude and direction of a complex number when you multiply the number by i.

19. Find the direction of each of these complex numbers from Example 1.

   a. $(2 + i)^0$ **b.** $(2 + i)^1$

   c. $(2 + i)^2$ **d.** $(2 + i)^3$

   e. $(2 + i)^4$

Use approximations if necessary.

20. Consider the complex numbers $a = 3 + i$, $b = 9 + i$, and $c = 5 + 7i$.

   a. Plot these three numbers as points in the complex plane.

   b. Determine d, the complex number halfway between a and b, and e, the complex number halfway between a and c. Plot d and e in the same complex plane.

   c. Calculate the distance between b and c.

   d. Calculate the distance between d and e.

   e. What do you notice about the distances you found in parts (c) and (d)?

21. Consider the complex numbers $a = 3 + i$ and $b = 2 - 6i$.

   a. Draw a diagram showing a, b, and $a - b$ in the complex plane.

   b. Show that, for these values of a and b, $|a|^2 + |b|^2 = |a - b|^2$.

   c. **Take It Further** Show that for any complex number a and real number k, if $b = (ki)a$, then $|a|^2 + |b|^2 = |a - b|^2$.

22. For each pair of complex numbers, calculate $|z|$, $|w|$, and $|zw|$.

   a. $z = 2 + i$ and $w = 3 + i$

   b. $z = 2 + i$ and $w = 3 + 2i$

   c. $z = 5i$ and $w = 3i$

   d. $z = 2 + i$ and $w = \dfrac{2 - i}{5}$

23. **a.** Based on your results from Exercise 22, make a conjecture about the relationship among $|z|$, $|w|$, and $|zw|$.

   b. **Take It Further** Prove your conjecture.

Maintain Your Skills

24. Find the magnitude of each complex number.

   a. $(1 + i)^2$ **b.** $(2 + i)^2$

   c. $(3 + i)^2$ **d.** $(7 + i)^2$

   e. $(2 + 3i)^2$

   f. Find a complex number $a + bi$, with nonzero a and b, that has magnitude 29.

25. For each equation, find the magnitude and direction of all the solutions.

   a. $x^2 - 1 = 0$ **b.** $x^3 - 1 = 0$ **c.** $x^4 - 1 = 0$

The equation $x^4 - 1 = 0$ has four solutions in $\mathbb{C}$.

In this investigation, you graphed complex numbers as points and as vectors on the complex plane. You also calculated magnitude and direction of complex numbers. These exercises will help you summarize what you have learned.

1. Graph and label each pair of numbers on the same complex plane.

   a. $u = 2 - 3i$ and $\bar{u}$
   b. $v = -2$ and $\bar{v}$
   c. $w = 4i$ and $\bar{w}$
   d. $z = -3 + i$ and $\bar{z}$

2. For $z = -1 + i$ and $w = 4 + 2i$, graph and label z, w, $z + w$, $-w$, iw, zw, and z^2 on the same complex plane.

3. Prove that, for any nonzero real number r and nonzero complex number z, the product rz is collinear with 0 and z on the complex plane.

4. Find the magnitude and direction of each complex number.

   a. $1 + 2i$
   b. $(1 + 2i)^2$
   c. $(1 + 2i)^3$

5. A complex number has magnitude 4 and direction $120°$. Write this complex number in the form $a + bi$, where a and b are exact real numbers.

6. How do you represent a complex number graphically?

7. What is the graphical effect of adding two complex numbers?

8. What is the graphical effect of multiplying a complex number by i?

Vocabulary and Notation

In this investigation, you learned these terms and symbols. Make sure you understand what each one means and how to use it.

- **argument, arg z**
- **direction**
- **complex plane**
- **magnitude, |z|**

another Julia set fractal

Complex Numbers, Geometry, and Algebra

In *Complex Numbers, Geometry, and Algebra,* you will connect many of the results you have proved about complex numbers and develop them further. You will also prove some conjectures you made in previous investigations.

By the end of this investigation, you will be able to answer questions like these.

1. How are the magnitude and argument of the product of two complex numbers related to the magnitude and argument of the original numbers?

2. If $-2 + i$ is a root of the polynomial $x^3 + 7x^2 + 17x + 15$, what is another root?

3. How can you graph the solutions to the equation $x^{10} - 1 = 0$ on the complex plane without doing many calculations?

You will learn how to

- describe relationships between magnitudes and arguments of factors and products

- prove the relationship between the function values of complex conjugates

You will develop these habits and skills:

- Visualize algebraic calculations as geometric transformations.

- Tinker with complex number calculations to find patterns and develop conjectures.

- Reason deductively to prove conjectures about the complex numbers.

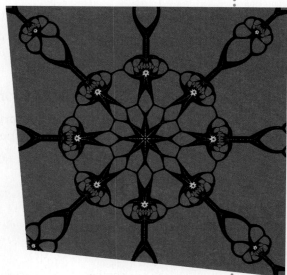

An artist used algorithms for approximating the roots of a complex polynomial to render this polynomiograph.

Activating Prior Knowledge
Exploring New Ideas

You can find relationships between the magnitudes and directions of two complex numbers and the magnitude and direction of their product.

For You to Explore

1. For each complex number, find the exact magnitude and the direction to the nearest tenth of a degree.

a. $3 + i$

b. $2 + i$

c. $(3 + i)(2 + i)$

d. $4 + 3i$

e. $1 + 2i$

f. $(4 + 3i)(1 + 2i)$

2. Complex number z has magnitude 5 and direction 60°.
Complex number w has magnitude 2 and direction 150°.

a. Graph z and w on the complex plane.

b. Estimate the magnitude and direction of the product zw.

c. **Take It Further** Determine zw and write it in the form $a + bi$.

3. Graph each complex number on the complex plane. Then find its direction.

a. $1 + i\sqrt{3}$ **b.** $-1 + i\sqrt{3}$ **c.** $-1 - i\sqrt{3}$ **d.** $1 - i\sqrt{3}$

> What is the magnitude of each number?

4. Establish the following identity.

$$(ac - bd)^2 + (bc + ad)^2 = \left(a^2 + b^2\right)\left(c^2 + d^2\right)$$

5. You can write a cubic with three roots in either expanded or factored form, where r, s, and t are the roots.

$$x^3 + ax^2 + bx + c = (x - r)(x - s)(x - t)$$

> **Remember...**
>
> What does the Factor Theorem say?

a. Expand the right side of the equation.

b. Write a in terms of r, s, and t.

c. Write b in terms of r, s, and t.

d. Write c in terms of r, s, and t.

6. For $f(x) = x^3 - 4x^2 - 2x + 20$, how are the following outputs related?

a. $f(2 + i)$ and $f(2 - i)$ **b.** $f(4 + i)$ and $f(4 - i)$

c. $f(-1 + 3i)$ and $f(-1 - 3i)$

d. Evaluate $f(3 + i)$ and use it to calculate $f(3 - i)$.

7. **Take It Further** Find two complex numbers with the indicated sum and product. Graph them on the coordinate plane.

a. sum $\dfrac{-1 + \sqrt{5}}{2}$, product 1   **b.** sum $\dfrac{-1 - \sqrt{5}}{2}$, product 1

c. Expand the following product.

$$\left(x - 1\right)\left(x^2 + \frac{1 + \sqrt{5}}{2}x + 1\right)\left(x^2 + \frac{1 - \sqrt{5}}{2}x + 1\right)$$

> For expansion help, see the TI-Nspire Handbook, p. 990.

Exercises Practicing Habits of Mind

On Your Own

8. Graph each complex number. Then calculate its direction to the nearest degree.

   a. $4 + i$

   b. $4 - i$

   c. $-4 + i$

   d. $-4 - i$

9. Find the direction of each complex number.

   a. $\sqrt{3} + i$

   b. $\sqrt{2} + i\sqrt{2}$

   c. $\left(\sqrt{3} + i\right)\left(\sqrt{2} + i\sqrt{2}\right)$

   d. Take It Further $\left(\sqrt{3} + i\right)^2\left(\sqrt{2} + i\sqrt{2}\right)^2$

10. Use the complex numbers $z = 2 + 3i$ and $w = 1 + i$. Find each of the following.

   a. $\overline{z}$

   b. $\overline{z} \cdot \overline{w}$

   c. $\overline{zw}$

   d. z^2

   e. $\overline{z^2}$

   f. $\left(\overline{z}\right)^2$

11. If w and z are any two complex numbers, then $\overline{z} \cdot \overline{w} = \overline{zw}$.

   a. Express the statement in words.

   b. Prove that the statement is true.

> **Remember...**
>
> $\overline{z}$ is the conjugate of the complex number z. The conjugate of $a + bi$ is $a - bi$.

Maintain Your Skills

12. Use the complex number $w = \dfrac{1 + i\sqrt{3}}{2}$. Graph each of the following on the same complex plane.

   a. w

   b. w^2

   c. w^3

   d. w^4

   e. w^5

   f. w^6

   g. w^7

   h. w^{12}

Multiplying Complex Numbers

In the last investigation, you learned that representing a complex number as a vector helps to show three operations.

- Add two numbers by completing the parallelogram.

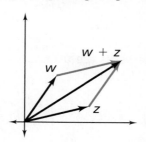

- Multiply a complex number by a real number *k* by dilating the vector for the complex number by a factor of *k*.

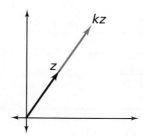

If $k > 0$, the head of the vector is *k* times as far from the origin in the same direction. If $k < 0$, the head of the vector is *k* times as far from the origin in the opposite direction.

- Multiply a complex number by *i* by rotating the complex number 90° counterclockwise.

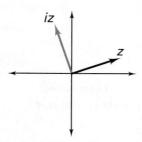

Some of the questions in Lesson H.01 asked you to look at the relationship between the magnitude and direction of complex numbers and their products. Here is an example, using the product of $1 + 2i$ and $1 + 3i$.

$$(1 + 2i)(1 + 3i) = -5 + 5i$$

Habits of Mind

Establish a process. To find the direction, first build a right triangle. Then use trigonometry, geometry, or the complex number functions on your calculator.

Number *z*	Magnitude |*z*|	Direction: arg *z* (within 0.001°)
$1 + 2i$	$\sqrt{5}$	63.435°
$1 + 3i$	$\sqrt{10}$	71.565°
$-5 + 5i$	$\sqrt{50}$	135.000°

The magnitude of the product is the product of the magnitudes.

$$\sqrt{5} \cdot \sqrt{10} = \sqrt{50}$$

The direction of the product is the sum of the directions.

$$63.435° + 71.565° = 135°$$

This suggests the following theorem about the magnitude and direction of products.

Theorem H.4

Given complex numbers z and w, the following statements are true.

- $|zw| = |z| \cdot |w|$

- $\arg zw = \arg z + \arg w$.

Habits of Mind

Experiment. If you are not convinced it works, try another example.

In other words, magnitudes multiply and directions add when you consider the product of two complex numbers.

Remember...

The terms *argument* and *direction* have the same meaning when you refer to a complex number vector.

For Discussion

1. The argument of the product is the sum of the arguments. If $\arg z = 150°$ and $\arg w = 310°$, $\arg zw = 460°$. What does it mean to have an argument of 460°? In what quadrant is zw?

You can prove Theorem H.4 using the properties of addition and multiplication you learned in the last lesson.

Minds in Action

Sasha helps Tony prove Theorem H.4.

Tony   Let's say I want to multiply $(4 + 3i)$ and $(1 + 2i)$. I can find the product $-2 + 11i$. Then I can graph the two numbers and their product. Now what do I do?

Sasha   We know how to add, so let's break it up.

$$(4 + 3i)(1 + 2i) = 4(1 + 2i) + 3i(1 + 2i)$$

That's four $(1 + 2i)$'s and $3i$ more $(1 + 2i)$'s. Well, I can make $4(1 + 2i)$ by extending $1 + 2i$ to four times its original size.

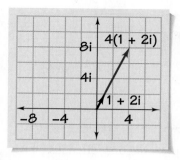

Now I need $3i(1 + 2i)$'s. I multiply by i by rotating 90° counterclockwise. So multiplying by $3i$ is rotating 90° and scaling by 3.

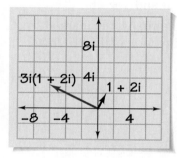

Then I can use the parallelogram law to add. I've got it.

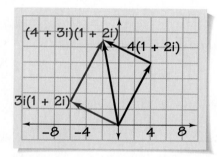

The parallelogram law is Theorem H.1 from Lesson H.3.

This dark triangle looks a lot like the triangle I drew in Lesson H.05 to measure $4 + 3i$. Here, I'll show you what I mean.

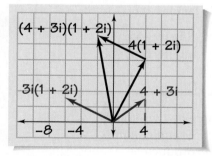

The big triangle for $(4 + 3i)(1 + 2i)$ looks just like the smaller triangle for $4 + 3i$. It's just larger and rotated a little. I'll bet I can prove those triangles are similar. Then I'll have enough evidence to prove Theorem H.4.

For You to Do

2. Explain why the two drawn triangles both have a 90° angle.

3. Explain why each leg in the larger triangle is $\sqrt{5}$ times as long as each leg in the smaller triangle.

4. Explain why the two right triangles are similar.

The triangle similarity in the dialog above has two important consequences.

- The sides in similar triangles are proportional. Each side in the larger triangle is $\sqrt{5}$ times as long as the corresponding side in the smaller triangle. The magnitude of the product is $5\sqrt{5}$. This is also the product of the magnitudes of the original numbers $4 + 3i$ and $1 + 2i$.

- Corresponding angles in similar triangles are congruent. The marked angles on the graph below are congruent. The direction of the product is the sum of the two original angles.

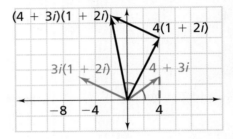

A formal proof of Theorem H.4 uses the generic complex numbers $(a + bi)$ and $(c + di)$, but the ideas are the same.

Developing Habits of Mind

Visualize. The magnitude of a product is the product of the magnitudes. The argument of a product is the sum of the arguments.

If z and w are complex numbers, you obtain zw from z by a rotation and a scaling. The angle of rotation is arg w and the scale factor is $|w|$.

For example, if you multiply by $(1 + i)$, you are rotating by 45° (the argument of $1 + i$) and scaling by $\sqrt{2}$. If you multiply by i, you are rotating by 90° and scaling by 1.

You can also use algebra to prove that the magnitude of a product is the product of the magnitudes. The product of $a + bi$ and $c + di$ is $(ac - bd) + (bc + ad)i$. Find the magnitude of the product.

$$\sqrt{(ac - bd)^2 + (bc + ad)^2}$$

Then find the product of the magnitudes.

$$\sqrt{a^2 + b^2} \cdot \sqrt{c^2 + d^2}$$

The numbers under the square roots are not negative. Rewrite the expression above as $\sqrt{(a^2 + b^2)(c^2 + d^2)}$.

The result follows from an identity you established in Lesson H.05.

Another algebraic method is to use the fact that the magnitude equals $\sqrt{z\bar{z}}$, where $\bar{z}$ is the conjugate.

$$
\begin{aligned}
|zw| &= \sqrt{zw\,\overline{zw}} \\
&= \sqrt{zw\,\bar{z}\,\bar{w}} \\
&= \sqrt{z\bar{z}\,w\bar{w}} \\
&= \sqrt{z\bar{z}}\sqrt{w\bar{w}} = |z||w|
\end{aligned}
$$

Remember...

$\sqrt{r}\sqrt{s} = \sqrt{rs}$ when r and s are nonnegative real numbers.

For Discussion

5. Give reasons for every step in the calculation above. At one point, a square root becomes the product of two square roots. Is that a legal step? Explain.

For You to Do

6. Describe multiplication by each number, in terms of rotation and scaling.

$$2 + i \qquad -i \qquad -1$$

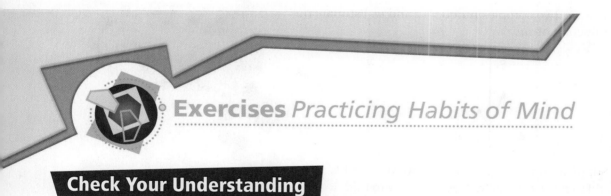

Exercises *Practicing Habits of Mind*

Check Your Understanding

1. Complex number z has magnitude 3 and direction $120°$.

  a. Find the magnitude and direction of z^2.

  b. Find the magnitude and direction of z^3.

  c. Find an equation with integer coefficients such that z is a solution of the equation.

2. Write About It Suppose you know the magnitude and direction of complex number z. Describe how to find the magnitude and direction of z^2, z^3, and the general number z^n.

3. A complex number z^3 has magnitude 27 and direction 180°. Which of the following statements could be true about z?

A. z has magnitude 9 and direction 60°.

B. z has magnitude 3 and direction 60°.

C. z has magnitude 3 and direction 180°.

D. z has magnitude 3 and direction 300°.

For Exercises 4 and 5, use the following complex numbers.

- w, with magnitude 5 and direction 40°
- $x = 1 - i$
- $y = -w$
- $z = -x$

4. Sketch w, $\overline{w}$, y, and $\overline{y}$ on the same complex plane. Label each vector with its magnitude and direction.

5. a. Find the exact magnitude and direction of wx.

b. Find the exact magnitude and direction of yz.

c. Use algebra to show that $wx = yz$.

6. The graph below shows two complex numbers z and w. Estimate the magnitude and direction of zw.

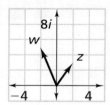

Electrical engineers use complex numbers to describe the voltage and current in a circuit.

7. Write About It Suppose you have two complex numbers with directions that add to more than 360°. Describe how to find the magnitude and direction of their product.

8. For each z, graph the first few powers of z (z^0, z^1, z^2, ...). Describe what happens if you graph higher powers of z. Explain why.

a. $z = i$

b. $z = -i$

c. $z = 1 + i$

d. $z = 1 - i$

e. $z = 2 + i$

f. $z = 2 - i$

9. Suppose z and w are complex numbers with magnitude 1. Determine whether each number must also have magnitude 1.

   a. zw **b.** $z + w$ **c.** $\overline{w}$

   d. $\frac{1}{z}$ **e.** z^2 **f.** $2z$

Go Online
www.successnetplus.com

10. **a.** Graph the triangle with vertices $2 + 3i$, $4 + 6i$, and $7 - i$.

    b. Graph the triangle that results if you multiply each vertex by i.

    c. Graph the triangle that results if you multiply each vertex by $1 + i$.

    d. Graph the triangle that results if you add $1 + i$ to each vertex.

11. Two complex numbers have product $10i$. Neither number is a real number.

    a. Find one possible pair of numbers that fits this description.

    b. **Take It Further** Given any nonzero complex number z, explain how to find w such that $zw = 10i$.

12. The graph below shows two complex numbers z and w. Estimate the magnitude and direction of zw.

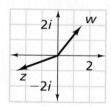

13. **a.** On the complex plane, graph, as points, four different numbers with direction $210°$.

    b. Graph the set of all points with direction $210°$.

    c. What complex number has magnitude 10 and direction $210°$?

14. **Standardized Test Prep** Which of the following describes multiplication by $4 + 4i$?

    A. Rotate by $90°$ and scale by $4\sqrt{2}$.

    B. Rotate by $45°$ and scale by $2\sqrt{2}$.

    C. Rotate by $45°$ and scale by $4\sqrt{2}$.

    D. Rotate by $90°$ and scale by 4.

15. Use the complex numbers $z = 3 - 2i$ and $w = 1 + 3i$.

    a. Graph z and w as vectors. Determine the magnitude and direction of each.

    b. Find the magnitude and direction of zw.

    c. Find the magnitude and direction of $\overline{zw}$ and $\frac{1}{zw}$.

16. You learned how to find the magnitude and direction of the product of two complex numbers, but how do you find the quotient? Use the complex numbers $z = 4 + 2i$ and $w = 3 + i$.

   a. Write $\frac{z}{w}$ in the form $a + bi$, where a and b are in $\mathbb{R}$.

   b. Find the magnitude and direction of $\frac{z}{w}$.

   c. Describe the relationship between the magnitude and direction of z, w, and $\frac{z}{w}$.

17. a. Find five complex numbers with magnitude 13.

   b. Take It Further Graph the set of all complex numbers z such that $|z| = 13$.

18. Take It Further For each equation or inequality, graph the set of all complex numbers that satisfy the equation or inequality.

   a. $|z| = 3$ **b.** $|z| = 1$ **c.** $|z| < 1$ **d.** $|z| > 1$

   e. $|z| = \left|\frac{1}{z}\right|$ **f.** $z^2 = z$ **g.** $\bar{z} = z$ **h.** $|z^2| = |z|$

Maintain Your Skills

19. For each polynomial $p(x)$, calculate $p(2 + i)$ and $p(2 - i)$.

   a. $p(x) = x^2$

   b. $p(x) = x^2 + 5x + 7$

   c. $p(x) = x^3$

   d. $p(x) = x^3 + x^2$

   e. $p(x) = x^3 + x^2 - 15x + 25$

   f. $p(x) = x^3 - 3x^2 + x + 5$

Is $x^2 - 4x + 5$ a factor of any these polynomials?

20. Write each sum in the form $a + bi$, where a and b are in $\mathbb{R}$.

   a. $1 + i + i^2$

   b. $1 + i + i^2 + i^3$

   c. $1 + i + i^2 + i^3 + i^4$

   d. $1 + i + i^2 + i^3 + i^4 + i^5$

   e. $1 + i + i^2 + i^3 + i^4 + i^5 + i^6$

   f. $1 + i + i^2 + i^3 + i^4 + i^5 + i^6 + i^7 + \cdots + i^{67}$

21. Take It Further Suppose that $w = -\frac{1}{2} + \frac{\sqrt{3}}{2}i$. Write each sum in the form $a + bi$, where a and b are in $\mathbb{R}$.

   a. $1 + w + w^2$

   b. $1 + w + w^2 + w^3$

   c. $1 + w + w^2 + w^3 + w^4$

   d. $1 + w + w^2 + w^3 + w^4 + w^5$

   e. $1 + w + w^2 + w^3 + w^4 + w^5 + w^6$

   f. $1 + w + w^2 + w^3 + w^4 + w^5 + w^6 + w^7 + \cdots + w^{67}$

H.07 Conjugates and Roots

One focus of this chapter is the properties of the conjugate of a complex number. This lesson explores an important property of conjugates that you can apply to find the roots of polynomials. In Exercise 18 of Lesson 3.13, you showed that if z is a root of a quadratic polynomial with real coefficients, so is $\bar{z}$. This result holds for higher-degree polynomials as well.

Theorem H.5 lists the main algebraic properties of conjugation.

One root of
$x^2 - 4x + 5$ is $2 + i$.
The other root is
$2 - i = \overline{2 + i}$.

Theorem H.5

Suppose that z and w are complex numbers. Then the following statements are true.

- $\bar{z} + \bar{w} = \overline{z + w}$

    When you add conjugates, the result is the conjugate of the sum of the original numbers.

- $\bar{z} \cdot \bar{w} = \overline{zw}$

    When you multiply conjugates, the result is the conjugate of the product of the original numbers.

- $(\bar{z})^2 = \overline{z^2}$

    When you square a conjugate, the result is the conjugate of the square of the original number.

- If z is a real number, then $\bar{z} = z$.

Remember...

The sum of the conjugates is the conjugate of the sum. And the product of the conjugates is the conjugate of the product.

For Discussion

1. Why does $(\bar{z})^2 = \overline{z^2}$ follow from $\bar{z} \cdot \bar{w} = \overline{zw}$?

2. Explain why $(\bar{z})^3 = \overline{z^3}$.

In the exercises, you will explain why $(\bar{z})^k = \overline{z^k}$ for any positive integer k. This fact leads to the following theorem about conjugates.

Theorem H.6 Polynomials and Conjugates

For any polynomial f with real coefficients and any complex number z,
$\overline{f(z)} = f(\overline{z})$.

Proof Consider the case in which f is a cubic polynomial.

$$f(x) = ax^3 + bx^2 + cx + d$$
$$\overline{f(z)} = \overline{az^3 + bz^2 + cz + d}$$
$$= \overline{az^3} + \overline{bz^2} + \overline{cz} + \overline{d}$$
$$= \overline{a} \cdot \overline{z^3} + \overline{b} \cdot \overline{z^2} + \overline{c} \cdot \overline{z} + \overline{d}$$
$$= a\overline{z^3} + b\overline{z^2} + c\overline{z} + d$$
$$= a(\overline{z})^3 + b(\overline{z})^2 + c\overline{z} + d$$
$$= f(\overline{z})$$

So $\overline{f(z)} = f(\overline{z})$. The proof of the general case involves the same ideas.

For Discussion

3. Theorem H.6 states that the polynomial has real coefficients. Which step of the proof uses this requirement?

Corollary H.6.1 Conjugate Pairs

If f is a polynomial with real coefficients, and f(z) = 0, then $f(\overline{z}) = 0$.

For Discussion

4. Prove Corollary H.6.1 using Theorem H.6.

Corollary H.6.1 says that complex roots come in conjugate pairs. If $2 + i$ is a root of a polynomial with real coefficients, then $2 - i$ must be another root.

Example 1

Problem Use the polynomial $f(x) = x^3 - 2x^2 - 14x + 40$.

  a. Show that $z = 3 + i$ is a root of f.   **b.** Find the other two roots.

Solution

  a. Let $x = 3 + i$ in $f(x)$.

$$f(3 + i) = (3 + i)^3 - 2(3 + i)^2 - 14(3 + i) + 40$$
$$= (18 + 26i) - 2(8 + 6i) - 14(3 + i) + 40$$
$$= (18 + 26i) + (-16 - 12i) + (-42 - 14i) + 40$$
$$= (18 - 16 - 42 + 40) + (26 - 12 - 14)i$$
$$= 0$$

    Since $f(3 + i) = 0$, then $3 + i$ is a root of f.

  b. Since f has real coefficients, the conjugate is also a root. So, $3 - i$ is a root.

> You can confirm this by showing that $f(3 - i) = 0$.

    There are a few ways to find the third root. One is to use the sum property. The sum of the three roots is 2. If the third root is r, then $(3 + i) + (3 - i) + r = 2$.

    Combine like terms and solve to get $r = -4$. So, -4 is the third root.

For You to Do

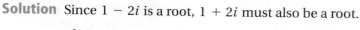

5. How do you solve the equation $x^3 - 5x^2 + 11x - 15 = 0$ if you do not know any of the roots of the polynomial $x^3 - 5x^2 + 11x - 15$?

> For this polynomial, the sum of the three roots is 5 and the product is 15.

Example 2

Problem Find a polynomial with real coefficients and $1 - 2i$ and -4 as roots.

Solution Since $1 - 2i$ is a root, $1 + 2i$ must also be a root.

$$f(x) = (x - (1 - 2i))(x - (1 + 2i))(x + 4)$$

Multiply the first two terms. The sum of $1 - 2i$ and $1 + 2i$ is 2, and the product is 5.

$$(x - (1 - 2i))(x - (1 + 2i)) = x^2 - 2x + 5$$

To find $f(x)$, expand the entire expression.

$$f(x) = (x^2 - 2x + 5)(x + 4)$$
$$= x^3 + 2x^2 - 3x + 20$$

Note that this is not the only possible polynomial with these roots, but it is the polynomial with the least possible degree.

Exercises Practicing Habits of Mind

Check Your Understanding

1. At the right is the graph of $f(x) = x^3 + 6x + 20$.

   a. Use the graph to find a root of $f(x)$.

   b. Find the other two roots.

2. Find a polynomial equation with real coefficients that has $4 - i$ as one of its solutions.

3. Find a polynomial equation with real coefficients that has $4 - i$ and 7 as solutions.

4. **a.** Show that $-1 + 2i$ is a root of $g(x) = x^3 - 4x^2 - 7x - 30$.

   b. Find the other two roots.

5. **a.** Show that $3 + i$ is a solution to the equation $x^2 - (8 + 6i) = 0$.

   b. **What's Wrong Here?** Gina says that because $3 + i$ is a solution, then $3 - i$ must also be a solution. Is Gina correct? Explain.

6. **Take It Further** Given p is a polynomial with real coefficients, prove the following statement.

   The product of all the roots of p is positive if and only if the product of all the real roots of p is positive.

On Your Own

7. Use the complex numbers $z = 5 + i$ and $w = 2 + 3i$.

   a. Find the magnitude and direction of z and w.

   b. Find the magnitude and direction of zw without finding zw.

   c. Find the magnitude and direction of z^2 and w^2.

   > Give the exact magnitude and approximate the direction to the nearest degree.

8. **a.** Show that $4 - i$ is a root of $x^3 - 5x^2 - 7x + 51 = 0$.

   b. Find the other two roots.

   c. Graph the three roots as points on the complex plane.

   > To find complex roots, see the TI-Nspire Handbook, p. 990.

9. Use the function $p(x) = (x - 3)^3 - 5(x - 3)^2 - 7(x - 3) + 51$.

   a. Show that $7 - i$ is a root of $p(x)$.

   b. Find the other two roots.

   c. Plot the three roots as points on the complex plane.

10. Suppose $f(x)$ is a polynomial with real coefficients and z is a complex number. Find $f(\bar{z})$ for each value of $f(z)$.

Go Online
www.successnetplus.com

   a. $f(z) = 0$ **b.** $f(z) = 7$

   c. $f(z) = 1 + 3i$ **d.** $f(z) = -5i$

11. Find a polynomial function with real coefficients that has $4 - i$ and -5 as roots.

Historical Perspective

Complex numbers first emerged in mathematics as algebraic objects, useful in solving cubic equations. Once mathematicians got used to them as numbers, they realized that they could solve every quadratic equation with real coefficients in the complex numbers.

Not only does every quadratic equation with real coefficients have all its roots in $\mathbb{C}$, every polynomial of any degree n with real coefficients has exactly n roots in $\mathbb{C}$. This fact is the Fundamental Theorem of Algebra. The first rigorous proof of the theorem was given by Gauss in his doctoral thesis in 1799.

This important development in mathematics history is still relevant today. Of course, if you need complex numbers to solve polynomial equations with real coefficients, you probably think you need some other kind of number to solve polynomial equations with complex coefficients. Amazingly, this is not the case. Even if you allow the coefficients of a polynomial to be complex numbers, you still have exactly n roots for a polynomial of degree n, and you can find all those roots in the complex number system.

This number system, in which any polynomial with coefficients from the system has all its roots in the system, is considered algebraically closed. So, the Fundamental Theorem of Algebra states that $\mathbb{C}$ is algebraically closed.

The Fundamental Theorem of Algebra is an existence theorem. It states that an nth-degree polynomial has all its roots in $\mathbb{C}$, but it does not tell you how to find them. In fact, for polynomials of degree five or more, there is no analog to the quadratic formula that allows you to solve all polynomials of a given degree.

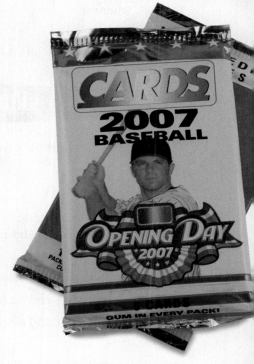

The packaging is like the Fundamental Theorem of Algebra. It tells you how many cards you get, but not what they are.

12. Standardized Test Prep If $3 + 4i$ is a root of $f(x) = x^3 - 2x^2 + x + 100$, which are the other two roots?

A. $3 - 4i$ and 4

B. $3 - 5i$ and -4

C. $-3 - 5i$ and 8

D. $3 - 4i$ and -4

13. a. Find a cubic function with real coefficients for which one root is $2 + 7i$ and the sum of the roots is 0.

   b. Find a cubic function with real coefficients for which one root is $2 + 7i$ and the product of the roots is 106.

14. Use the function $g(x) = x^6 - 1$. Calculate each value.

   a. $g(-1)$

   b. $g(w)$, where $w = \dfrac{1 + i\sqrt{3}}{2}$

   c. $g(w^2)$

   d. Take It Further Plot all six complex numbers that make $g(x) = 0$.

Maintain Your Skills

15. For each complex number z, calculate the magnitude and direction of z^4.

   a. $z = 1 + i$

   b. $z = 1 - i$

   c. $z = -1 + i$

   d. $z = -1 - i$

16. Suppose z^5 has magnitude 1 and direction $0°$. Determine whether each statement could be true about z.

   a. $z = 1$

   b. z has magnitude 1 and direction $72°$.

   c. z has magnitude 1 and direction $120°$.

   d. z has magnitude 1 and direction $144°$.

   e. $z = -1$

   f. z has magnitude 1 and direction $216°$.

This is a more complicated way to say $z^5 = 1$.

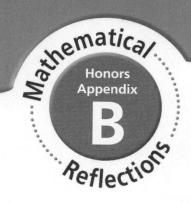
In this investigation, you found relationships between magnitudes and arguments of factors and products. You also graphed the solutions to equations in the form $x^n - 1 = 0$. These exercises will help you summarize what you have learned.

1. Use $z = 1 - \sqrt{3}i$. Find the magnitude and direction for each power of z.

   a. z **b.** z^2 **c.** z^3 **d.** z^4

   e. Which, if any, of the powers of z that you found is a real number? Explain.

2. A complex number z has magnitude 6 and direction $135°$. A complex number w has magnitude 2 and direction $240°$.

   a. Find the magnitude and direction of the product zw.

   b. Find the magnitude and direction of v such that zv has magnitude 3 and direction $30°$.

3. Find a polynomial with real coefficients that has $2 - i$ and 3 among its roots. Is your polynomial the only possible polynomial? If so, explain why. If not, find another polynomial.

4. Show that $6i$ is a root of the polynomial $x^3 + 2x^2 + 36x + 72$. Then find the other roots.

5. Find the magnitude and direction of all solutions to the equation $x^5 - 1 = 0$. If there are any solutions in Quadrant II, express them in the form $a + bi$, where a and b are real numbers. Approximate to the nearest hundredth if you cannot find an exact answer.

6. How are the magnitude and argument of the product of two complex numbers related to the magnitude and argument of the original numbers?

7. If $-2 + i$ is a root of the polynomial $x^3 + 7x^2 + 17x + 15$, what is another root?

This sculpture is based on the polynomiograph on p. 862.

Matrices

In *Matrices*, you will review several methods for solving systems of equations. You will also learn about matrices and how to use them to solve systems of equations.

By the end of this investigation, you will be able to answer questions like these.

1. Why is it possible to solve systems of linear equations in matrix form?

2. What is the process of Gaussian Elimination?

3. Find x, y, and z such that

$$4x - y + 4z = 1$$
$$2x - y + 8z = 11$$
$$2x - 2y + 4z = 0$$

You will learn how to

- solve a system of three equations in three unknowns

- write a system of linear equations in matrix form or translate a matrix into a system of equations

- describe and apply the process of Gaussian Elimination and apply it both by hand and with technology to solve a system

You will develop these habits and skills:

- Connect the results from substitution and elimination methods and show that the methods are equivalent.

- Strategize to solve a system of equations systematically.

- Reason about how to describe an algorithm generally as a series of steps that you can apply to any situation.

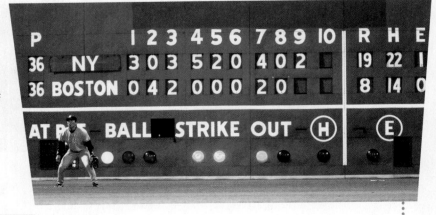

The scoreboard shows the score of the baseball game in matrix form.

Activating Prior Knowledge
Exploring New Ideas

You have learned several ways to solve a system of equations.

For You to Explore

1. Solve the following system in at least two ways.

$$x + y = 4$$
$$2x - y = -1$$

2. Solve the following system.

$$2x + y = 1$$
$$3x + 2y = 1$$

3. Find the point where the lines given by the following equations intersect.

$$y = 3x + 2$$
$$y = -2x + 1$$

4. Find an x-value for which these two functions have the same output.

$$f(x) = 3x + 2$$
$$g(x) = -2x + 1$$

5. Find a polynomial $p(x)$ with a graph that passes through the points $(0, 1)$, $(1, -1)$, and $(3, 1)$.

6. Another way to find a polynomial with a graph that passes through the points $(0, 1)$, $(1, -1)$, and $(3, 1)$ is to first realize that the highest-degree polynomial you need to fit these three points is a quadratic. Then you can begin with a general form of a quadratic function, $q(x) = ax^2 + bx + c$. Use the data points to write a system of equations for finding the coefficients a, b, and c.

a. Explain why $q(3) = 1$ implies that $9a + 3b + c = 1$.

b. Find two more equations involving a, b, and c using the other data points.

c. Find an equation for the polynomial.

Habits of Mind

Detect the key characterisitics. Why do three points determine a quadratic?

Exercises Practicing Habits of Mind

On Your Own

7. Solve the following system.

$$2x + 3y = 1$$
$$\tfrac{1}{2}x + \tfrac{1}{3}y = 1$$

8. Find the point of intersection of the line with equation $\frac{y-1}{x-1} = 2$ and the line with slope -1 and x-intercept 3.

Remember...

If a line has x-intercept a, that means that the graph of the line intersects the x-axis at the point $(a, 0)$.

9. The simplest graph that goes through two points is a line. You know many ways to find an equation for this line. Here is a technique that uses a system of equations. Suppose the two points are (1, 4) and (3, 2). The polynomial must be of the form $p(x) = ax + b$. Use the two points to find two equations in a and b. Then solve them to find the polynomial.

10. Solve the following system.

$$x + y + z = 2$$
$$2x - y + z = 5$$
$$x + 2y + 3z = 5$$

Habits of Mind

Use a consistent process.
Exercise 9 is like Problem 6. To understand a method, one good habit is to apply it in simpler situations.

11. **Take It Further** The system below has more unknowns than equations. However, you can still use the methods for solving two equations in two unknowns to find all the solutions.

$$x + 2y + 3z = 4$$
$$2x + y - z = -2$$

a. Solve the first equation for x and substitute into the second equation, eliminating x.

b. Eliminate x from the second equation another way: by subtracting a multiple of the first equation.

c. After using either method, solve the new second equation for y in terms of z.

d. Substitute your result from part (c) into the original first equation to eliminate y. Then express x in terms of z.

e. Explain why there is one solution (x, y, z) of the original system of equations for each value of z.

The solutions to part (e) form a *one-parameter family*. You can express all the solutions in terms of the single variable z. This gives you a way to manage an infinite set of solutions.

12. Solve each system. What new situations arise? How would you describe each solution?

a. $x + 2y = 3$
$2x + 4y = 6$

b. $x + 2y = 3$
$2x + 4y = 7$

Habits of Mind

Consider more than one strategy. Along with the algebraic solution methods you have been reviewing, you might want to solve these systems graphically, too.

Maintain Your Skills

Solve each system.

13. $x + 2y + 3z = 1$
$3y - z = 4$
$2z = -2$

14. $2x - 3y + 5z - 2t = 9$
$5y - z + 3t = 1$
$7z - t = 3$
$2t = 8$

15. 4×4 systems (four equations in four unknowns) are usually quite difficult to solve by hand, but the one in Exercise 14 is not. Explain.

Solve each system.

16. $2x = 4$
$x - y = 3$
$-x + 2y + z = 2$

17. $x + 2z = 4$
$3z = -3$
$x + 2y - z = 1$

18. Consider the following system.

$$x + 2y + 3z = 4$$
$$-3y - 7z = -10$$

You can rewrite it with z's on the right side.

$$x + 2y = 4 - 3z$$
$$-3y = -10 + 7z$$

a. What does this new system now have in common with other Maintain Your Skills exercises?

b. Use this similarity to solve for x and y in terms of z.

19. Solve the following system.

$$x - 2y + z = 7$$
$$2x - y + 4z = 17$$
$$3x - 2y + 2z = 14$$

Go Online
Video Tutor
www.successnetplus.com

Exercise 10 in Lesson H.08 asked you to solve the system

$$x + y + z = 2 \tag{1}$$

$$2x - y + z = 5 \tag{2}$$

$$x + 2y + 3z = 5 \tag{3}$$

The numbers in parentheses are equation labels. They are helpful when you want to discuss several equations at once, or describe operations involving two equations. Remember to distinguish the number 2 from the equation (2).

This is a 3 × 3 system—three linear equations in three unknowns. It is natural to try the methods you used on two equations in two unknowns. The two main methods were *substitution* and *elimination*. In **substitution,** you solve one equation for one variable and substitute that solution into the other equation. Then you have an equation in the other variable alone, which you can solve. In **elimination,** you add or subtract the two equations so that one variable cancels out, again resulting in an equation in the other variable alone.

In a 3 × 3 system, both methods allow many more choices. Say you solve Equation (1) for x and substitute the result into (2). That still gives an equation in two unknowns, y and z, so what do you do next? You can do another substitution, but if you are not careful you may go in circles. The way to succeed is to substitute the same expression for x into the third equation. That gives you two equations in the same two unknowns, which you know how to solve.

Specifically, solving (1) for x gives

$$x = 2 - y - z \tag{4}$$

Substituting into (2) gives

$$2(2 - y - z) - y + z = 5$$

$$4 - 2y - 2z - y + z = 5$$

$$-3y - z = 1$$

Substituting (4) into (3) gives

$$(2 - y - z) + 2y + 3z = 5$$

$$2 + y + 2z = 5$$

$$y + 2z = 3$$

Substitution has given you a 2 × 2 system.

$$-3y - z = 1$$

$$y + 2z = 3$$

Habits of Mind

Make strategic choices. Going from three equations in three unknowns to two equations in two unknowns is an instance of *reducing a problem to a simpler case.*

For You to Do

1. Solve the 2 × 2 system above.

Once you solve the 2 × 2 system, substitute the values of y and z into (4) to find x. In this problem, the final result is $x = 1$, $y = -1$, and $z = 2$.

> You can also write
> $(x, y, z) = (1, -1, 2)$.

Minds in Action

Sasha and Derman are trying to solve the same system (1)–(3) using the elimination method.

Sasha I think this will be easiest if we follow the method just shown as closely as possible.

Derman How can it be close? In elimination, you add and subtract equations, you don't substitute.

Sasha Right, but I mean let's use the same equations in the same order. I think that's our best chance to get down to two equations in y and z.

Derman I don't think it would have to be y and z, but yeah, let's do that. In the substitution method, we solved Equation (1) for x and substituted the result into Equations (2) and (3).

Sasha So let's try adding or subtracting (1) from (2) and (1) from (3) to eliminate x twice.

Derman But we've got to eliminate $2x$ from (2).

Sasha So let's multiply (1) by 2 and then subtract the result from (2).

$$
\begin{array}{r}
2x - y + z = 5 \\
(-)2x + 2y + 2z = 4 \\
\hline
-3y - z = 1
\end{array}
$$

Derman It's easier to eliminate x from (3)—just subtract (1) as it is.

$$
\begin{array}{r}
x + 2y + 3z = 5 \\
(-)x + y + z = 2 \\
\hline
y + 2z = 3
\end{array}
$$

Derman So the reduced system we get is

$$-3y - z = 1$$
$$y + 2z = 3$$

It's the same as before. Hmm.

Sasha That's good. We'll get the same solution as before, and we should.

Derman But lots of 2 × 2 systems have the same solution $y = -1$, $z = 2$. Do the two methods always give the same reduced system?

For Discussion

2. Think about Derman's question. Can you explain why the substitution and elimination methods ended up with the same 2×2 reduced system? Look carefully at the work shown in the text for solving the system (1)–(3).

This lesson has been about extending the methods you know for solving two equations in two unknowns to larger systems. It is time to put the pieces together and do one example from start to finish.

Example

Problem Solve the following system.

$$x - y + z = 0 \qquad (5)$$
$$x + y + 2z = 1 \qquad (6)$$
$$-x + 2y - 3z = 3 \qquad (7)$$

Solution This solution uses the elimination method. Subtract (5) from (6) and add (5) to (7). You get

$$2y + z = 1 \qquad (8)$$
$$y - 2z = 3 \qquad (9)$$

Now subtract (9) multiplied by 2 from (8).

$$5z = -5$$

So $z = -1$. Substitute this value into (9).

$$y + 2 = 3 \quad \text{so} \quad y = 1$$

Now substitute the y- and z-values into any one of the original equations, for example (5).

$$x - 1 - 1 = 0 \quad \text{so} \quad x = 2$$

Conclusion: $(x, y, z) = (2, 1, -1)$

> Substituting into (8) would also work.

> You can describe this process by saying that you solved the system by eliminating x first and then y.

Exercises Practicing Habits of Mind

Consider the system (5)–(7) from the Example.

1. Solve the system again, this time eliminating y first by adding or subtracting (5) from (6) and (5) from (7).

2. Solve the system again, this time eliminating z first.

3. Solve the system again, this time by the substitution method. Solve for x from (5) and substitute into the other equations. Do you get the same 2×2 reduced system as in the solution by elimination in the Example?

4. Solve the system again, this time by the substitution method. Solve for y from (5) and substitute into the other equations. Do you get the same 2×2 reduced system as in Exercise 1? Can you explain why?

5. A quadratic function $f(x) = ax^2 + bx + c$ passes through the points $(1, 1)$, $(2, 3)$, and $(3, 6)$. Find a, b, and c.

On Your Own

6. **Standardized Test Prep** Which is the solution to the system of equations at the right?

$$x - 3y + 6z = 2$$
$$-2x + 2y + z = 9$$
$$-x + 3y - 7z = -3$$

   A. $(-7, 1, 2)$ **B.** $(-7.75, -3.25, 0)$

   C. $(-4, 0, 1)$ **D.** $(5, 7.8, 3.4)$

7. Consider the 4×4 system at the right.

$$x + y + z - w = -1$$
$$x + y - z + w = 0$$
$$x - y + z + w = 1$$
$$-x + y + z + w = 2$$

   a. Reduce this system to a 3×3 system by elimination, eliminating x.

   b. Reduce this system to a 3×3 system by substitution, again eliminating x.

   c. Solve the 3×3 system you got in part (a).

   d. Solve the original 4×4 system.

   > You may have gotten different systems for parts (a) and (b). Do the two systems have the same solution?

8. Solve the 4×4 system at the right.

$$u + 2x - y + z = 1$$
$$x + y + z = 2$$
$$2x - y + z = 5$$
$$x + 2y + 3z = 5$$

9. Try using both substitution and elimination to solve the following system. What happens?

$$x + 2y = 3$$
$$2x + 4y = 4$$

Go Online
www.successnetplus.com

10. **Take It Further** Consider this system.

$$x + 2y + z = 2$$
$$2x + 4y + 3z = 5$$

The last time you had two equations in three unknowns (see Lesson H.08, Exercise 18), there was one solution for every value of z. What happens for this system?

11. **Take It Further** You write the equation for the graph of a circle in the form $(x - a)^2 + (y - b)^2 = r^2$, where (a, b) is the center and r is the radius.

   a. By solving a system of equations, find the center and radius of the circle that goes through the points $(-4, 0)$, $(0, 2)$, and $(4, 0)$.

   b. Find the center and radius using geometric methods.

These equations are not linear equations, but the method of adding and subtracting equations still works.

Maintain Your Skills

12. Solve this system.

$$x = y + z$$
$$y = x + z$$
$$z = x + y$$

13. Solve each system. Compare the solutions to the ones from the dialog.

   a. $x + y + z = 2$
   $2x - y + z = 5$
   $3x + y + 4z = 10$

   b. $x + y + z = 2$
   $2x - y + z = 5$
   $2x + 3y + 4z = 7$

14. In Exercise 13 from Lesson H.08, you solved the following system.

$$x + 2y + 3z = 1$$
$$3y - z = 4$$
$$2z = -2$$

The natural way to solve such a triangular system is to solve for z and then substitute. However, you have learned that adding and subtracting equations can accomplish the same thing as substitution. Solve this system again without any substitutions.

15. Solve this system using addition and subtraction.

$$2x - 3y + 5z - 2t = 9$$
$$5y - z + 3t = 1$$
$$7z - t = 3$$
$$2t = 8$$

It is more work to add and subtract equations, but there is a reason for doing it. Stay tuned for the next lesson.

H.10 Solving Again, in Matrix Form

Substitution and elimination are effectively the same—if you apply them to the equations in the same order, you get the same key equations along the way. So, is there any reason to recommend one method over the other?

For large systems, it is much easier to implement elimination. You can describe elimination as a consistent series of steps that you always apply in the same order.

In the elimination method, you can consistently put each variable in the same place. For instance, you can always make the x's be first and the y's second. Also, the variables play almost no role! Only the coefficients and the constants on the right side of the equations change. The only role the variables play is as labels for the coefficients. For instance, if you subtract $2x + 4y = 6$ from $2x + 5y = 2$, the y's tell you that the 4 and the 5 both belong to the same variable and you can subtract them from each other.

> You can more easily implement elimination methods with technology.

But if the variables are always in the same place, then the position alone determines which coefficient goes with which variable. You do not need to write the variables at all! For instance, consider again Sasha and Derman's old friend.

$$x + y + z = 2 \tag{1}$$
$$2x - y + z = 5 \tag{2}$$
$$x + 2y + 3z = 5 \tag{3}$$

You can instead write

$$A = \begin{pmatrix} 1 & 1 & 1 & \bigm| & 2 \\ 2 & -1 & 1 & \bigm| & 5 \\ 1 & 2 & 3 & \bigm| & 5 \end{pmatrix}$$

Now, instead of subtracting 2 times (1) from (2), multiply row 1 of A by 2 and subtract the result from row 2, entry by entry. Instead of writing a new system of equations with a new second equation, write a new matrix A' with a new second row.

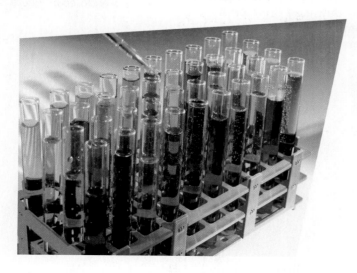

Sometimes it makes sense to record data from experiments in matrix form.

Look at the process up close.

$$\begin{pmatrix} 1 & 1 & 1 & \bigm| & 2 \\ 2 & -1 & 1 & \bigm| & 5 \\ 2 & 2 & 2 & \bigm| & 4 \\ 1 & 2 & 3 & \bigm| & 5 \end{pmatrix} \quad \longrightarrow \quad A' = \begin{pmatrix} 1 & 1 & 1 & \bigm| & 2 \\ 0 & -3 & -1 & \bigm| & 1 \\ 1 & 2 & 3 & \bigm| & 5 \end{pmatrix}$$

In the diagram, you see matrix A in black. Then, two times row 1 is shown in blue below row 2. Subtract term by term and replace row 2 with the result. The new resulting row is shown in blue in the second matrix.

To continue, instead of subtracting (1) from (3), subtract row 1 from row 3 to make a new row that replaces row 3.

$$A' = \begin{pmatrix} 1 & 1 & 1 & \bigm| & 2 \\ 0 & -3 & -1 & \bigm| & 1 \\ 1 & 2 & 3 & \bigm| & 5 \\ 1 & 1 & 1 & \bigm| & 2 \end{pmatrix} \quad \longrightarrow \quad A'' = \begin{pmatrix} 1 & 1 & 1 & \bigm| & 2 \\ 0 & -3 & -1 & \bigm| & 1 \\ 0 & 1 & 2 & \bigm| & 3 \end{pmatrix}$$

The bottom two rows now correspond to

$$-3y - z = 1$$
$$y + 2z = 3$$

These are the same equations as before.

Facts and Notation

A rectangular array like A is a **matrix**. This matrix has 3 rows (the horizontals) and 4 columns (the verticals). The vertical bar is an augmentation line. The whole matrix A is an augmented matrix. The thing that is augmented in A is the coefficient matrix of the linear system (1)–(3). The matrix below shows what that coefficient matrix looks like by itself.

The plural of *matrix* is *matrices*.

$$B = \begin{pmatrix} 1 & 1 & 1 \\ 2 & -1 & 1 \\ 1 & 2 & 3 \end{pmatrix}$$

Matrix B does not have an augmentation line. In fact, even in an augmented matrix, the augmentation line is just a convenient reminder. Some books do not use them. (You cannot usually use them on a calculator.) The augmented matrix A has **dimension** 3×4 (3 rows, 4 columns). The coefficient matrix B has dimension 3×3.

This book shows matrices enclosed by parentheses. In some books they are enclosed in square brackets, [ ].

For You to Do

1. Write down (but do not solve) the coefficient matrix and the augmented matrix for the linear system below.

$$x - 2y + z = 7$$
$$2x - y + 4z = 17$$
$$3x - 2y + 2z = 14$$

2. Write down (but do not solve) the system of equations corresponding to matrix M below. Let the variables be x, y, z in that order.

$$M = \begin{pmatrix} 1 & 2 & -3 & \bigm| & 2 \\ 2 & 0 & -1 & \bigm| & 4 \\ -3 & 1 & 2 & \bigm| & -5 \end{pmatrix}$$

3. Start with matrix M from Problem 2. Make a new matrix M' by subtracting 2 times row 1 from row 2. (The row you subtract from is always the one you change.) Then, from M', make M'' by adding 3 times row 1 to row 3.

Now you have reduced Sasha and Derman's problem to a 2×2 system. You can continue to solve it in matrix form starting from

$$C = \begin{pmatrix} -3 & -1 & \bigm| & 1 \\ 1 & 2 & \bigm| & 3 \end{pmatrix}$$

Remember, the variables here are y and z. Eliminate y by adding 3 times the second row of C to the first row. You get

$$D = \begin{pmatrix} 0 & 5 & \bigm| & 10 \\ 1 & 2 & \bigm| & 3 \end{pmatrix}$$

The first row of D says that $5z = 10$, so $z = 2$. You can now substitute in the equation for the second row to find y. Then you can substitute in the original equation (1) to find x.

There is just one problem with this method. You deal partly with matrices and partly with equations. You jump around picking information from different matrices and different equations. Also, you use matrices of different sizes. None of this is good for calculators or computers. For them, it is much easier and more efficient if all matrices for a given situation are the same size, operations are always done in the same order, and all the information ever needed is kept in the current matrix (so they can discard any earlier matrices).

You could also say that you subtracted -3 times the second row from the first row. Why be so complicated? Because in some contexts it is cleaner to always solve systems with the same operation.

You can solve Sasha and Derman's problem entirely in the matrix world. The expressions over the arrows summarize what steps you take. You will learn their meaning shortly. The first half goes like this.

$$A = \begin{pmatrix} 1 & 1 & 1 & | & 2 \\ 2 & -1 & 1 & | & 5 \\ 1 & 2 & 3 & | & 5 \end{pmatrix} \xrightarrow{(2)-2(1)} \begin{pmatrix} 1 & 1 & 1 & | & 2 \\ 0 & -3 & -1 & | & 1 \\ 1 & 2 & 3 & | & 5 \end{pmatrix}$$

$$\xrightarrow{(3)-(1)} \begin{pmatrix} 1 & 1 & 1 & | & 2 \\ 0 & -3 & -1 & | & 1 \\ 0 & 1 & 2 & | & 3 \end{pmatrix} \xrightarrow{\text{Switch (2), (3)}} \begin{pmatrix} 1 & 1 & 1 & | & 2 \\ 0 & 1 & 2 & | & 3 \\ 0 & -3 & -1 & | & 1 \end{pmatrix}$$

$$\xrightarrow{(3)+3(2)} \begin{pmatrix} 1 & 1 & 1 & | & 2 \\ 0 & 1 & 2 & | & 3 \\ 0 & 0 & 5 & | & 10 \end{pmatrix} \xrightarrow{(3)\div 5} \begin{pmatrix} 1 & 1 & 1 & | & 2 \\ 0 & 1 & 2 & | & 3 \\ 0 & 0 & 1 & | & 2 \end{pmatrix}$$

Now the third row says that $z = 2$. You can begin the process of substitution. Both the matrix and the corresponding equations are in triangular form, so you could easily solve for z, y, and x in that order by returning to equations and using substitution.

But you have already learned that you can accomplish substitution by elimination—adding and subtracting equations. So you can also carry out the substitution in matrix form. Machines do that easily. So continue.

$$\begin{pmatrix} 1 & 1 & 1 & | & 2 \\ 0 & 1 & 2 & | & 3 \\ 0 & 0 & 1 & | & 2 \end{pmatrix} \xrightarrow{(2)-2(3)} \begin{pmatrix} 1 & 1 & 1 & | & 2 \\ 0 & 1 & 0 & | & -1 \\ 0 & 0 & 1 & | & 2 \end{pmatrix} \xrightarrow[(1)-(3)]{(1)-(2)} \begin{pmatrix} 1 & 0 & 0 & | & 1 \\ 0 & 1 & 0 & | & -1 \\ 0 & 0 & 1 & | & 2 \end{pmatrix}$$

This final matrix corresponds to the three equations $x = 1$, $y = -1$, and $z = 2$, so you have solved the original problem by using only matrices.

Can you figure out the expressions over and under the arrows? For instance, between matrix A and the next one, you see the expression $(2) - 2(1)$. This means replace row 2 of A with row 2 minus two times row 1.

For Discussion

4. Figure out the meanings of all the other expressions over and under the arrows.

This solution method is called **Gaussian Elimination**. Gaussian Elimination is an algorithm that transforms the matrix of any given system of linear equations through a sequence of other matrices. It ends in a final matrix from which the solution to the corresponding system is obvious. You call it Gaussian Elimination because the first stage (the reduction to triangular form) corresponds on the equation level to eliminating the variables one at a time.

Experiment. Is this pure matrix approach an improvement? Some people like the time saving from not having to write variables and equations. However, they do not like the extra work of keeping all the rows and columns. But remember, this is not a method intended for humans, except for small examples. So why take you through it? Because, like most good algorithms, it can tell you a lot. For instance, thinking about the patterns that could appear in the final matrix can lead to insights about the theory of solutions to equations. But you cannot think about what the final form might look like without understanding the algorithm. So, the point of the following exercises is to help you develop a feel for the algorithm.

In Gaussian Elimination, the transformations from one system of equations (or one matrix) to another use only three kinds of steps:

- *Scaling.* Replace one equation (row) with a multiple of itself.

- *Switching.* Switch the order of two equations (rows).

- *Subtracting.* Subtract or add a multiple of one equation (row) from another and replace the other equation with the result.

Not only do these steps allow you to go forward, they allow you to go backward: You can reverse every step. For instance, if you subtract three times (1) from (2), you can reverse this by adding three times (1) to the new (2). This means that you can always get from the last system back to the first.

Facts and Notation

Since you can get from the first system of equations to the last, any solution to the first system is a solution to the last. Since you can get from the last system to the first, any solution to the last system is a solution to the first. This means that the first and last systems are equivalent. They have the same solutions. Usually the last system has exactly one solution—for instance, in Sasha and Derman's example $(x, y, z) = (1, -1, 2)$. In that case, Gaussian Elimination has revealed for us the one and only solution to the original system.

> Each step you take preserves the solution set.

This situation is like the situation with basic moves for equations in one variable: You can reverse a basic move, and a basic move preserves the solution set. Therefore, you might call scaling, switching, and subtracting the basic moves for linear systems. The formal name is *elementary row operations.*

The final matrix you get to in Gaussian Elimination is in **row-reduced echelon form**, abbreviated *rref*. For instance, the last matrix in Sasha and Derman's example is

> You can call row-reduced echelon form just "row-reduced form." You can describe a matrix as "row reduced."

$$\begin{pmatrix} 1 & 0 & 0 & | & 1 \\ 0 & 1 & 0 & | & -1 \\ 0 & 0 & 1 & | & 2 \end{pmatrix}$$

Most graphing calculators are also matrix calculators. They can store matrices and do many matrix computations, such as finding row-reduced echelon form. Look for an **rref** command in the matrix menus. Find out how to input matrices and how to get your calculator to display their row-reduced forms. You cannot input the augmentation line, but you know where it goes.

For instructions for using the rref command, see the TI-Nspire™ Handbook, p. 990.

In the example, the part of the row-reduced echelon form before the augmentation line is an **identity matrix**: a square matrix with all entries 0 except for 1's along the main diagonal from top left to lower right. This always happens when there is a unique solution. However, not every linear system has a unique solution, so the row-reduced form is not always so simple.

Some of the exercises will illustrate what happens when there is not a unique solution and begin to hint at the general pattern.

Exercises Practicing Habits of Mind

Check Your Understanding

1. Consider this augmented matrix.

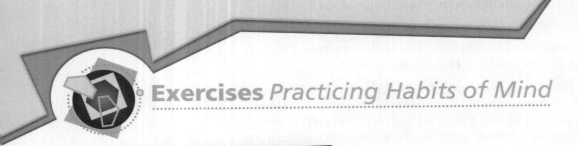

$$\begin{pmatrix} 1 & -1 & 2 & \bigm| & 5 \\ 2 & -3 & 1 & \bigm| & 3 \\ 1 & 0 & 7 & \bigm| & 16 \end{pmatrix}$$

   a. What system of equations does it correspond to?

   b. Solve this system in matrix form.

2. Solve the following system using Gaussian Elimination on matrices.

$$x + y + z = 1$$
$$2y + z = 2$$
$$3z = 3$$

3. Go back to the complete matrix solution of system (1)–(3) to the point where the system was

$$\begin{pmatrix} 1 & 1 & 1 & | & 2 \\ 0 & -3 & -1 & | & 1 \\ 0 & 1 & 2 & | & 3 \end{pmatrix}$$

Instead of then switching the last two rows, add or subtract a multiple of the second row from the third to eliminate y. Then continue with the type of steps shown in the lesson until you reach a matrix in the form below.

$$\begin{pmatrix} 1 & 0 & 0 & | & \blacksquare \\ 0 & 1 & 0 & | & \blacksquare \\ 0 & 0 & 1 & | & \blacksquare \end{pmatrix}$$

Do you get the same solution you got before?

4. Illustrate the claim that you can reverse every step in a matrix solution. Reverse every step in the complete matrix solution of Sasha and Derman's problem. That is, show that using just scaling, switching, and subtracting, you can get from the matrix form of the final system back to the matrix form of the original system.

$$\begin{array}{lll} x = 1 & & x + y + z = 2 \\ y = -1 & \longrightarrow & 2x - y + z = 5 \\ z = 2 & & x + 2y + 3z = 5 \end{array}$$

5. Write About It Subtracting a multiple of one equation from another is a basic move for systems. Yet sometimes it would be best to add a multiple of one equation to another. Explain why you do not have to list adding as a fourth basic move.

6. Solve this system by Gaussian Elimination in matrix form.

$$\begin{array}{l} x + 2y = -3 \\ 2x - y = 4 \end{array}$$

7. The function $f(n) = a2^n + b3^n$, where a and b are constants, satisfies the conditions $f(1) = 1$ and $f(2) = 10$. Find a and b.

8. If you think of equations representing lines in the plane, you have a geometric interpretation for 2×2 systems. This interpretation helps explain why the solution to most, but not all, 2×2 systems is a single pair (x, y).

a. How can you interpret the solution of a 2×2 system geometrically?

b. Use that interpretation to help you to conjecture what can happen with $m \times 2$ systems. Remember, an $m \times 2$ system has m equations and two unknowns.

c. Take It Further Make a conjecture about a geometric interpretation for $m \times 3$ systems.

> **Habits of Mind**
>
> **Check your method.**
> When mathematicians come up with a new approach, one of the things they do to test it out is to try it on a simpler system that they already know how to solve by other methods.

> You might want to make a table for f and apply the methods of Chapter 4. Can you find any patterns? Your main task here, however, is to determine the function by the methods of the current chapter.

On Your Own

9. **Standardized Test Prep** In Gaussian Elimination, which of the following transformations can you NOT use?

   A. scaling

   B. subtracting

   C. switching columns

   D. switching rows

10. Solve the following system.

$$x + y + z = 3$$
$$2x - y + z = 2$$
$$x + 2y + 3z = 6$$

> Notice that this system is the same as Sasha and Derman's problem (1)–(3) except that the constants on the right are different.

11. Solve each system.

    a.
    $$x + y + z = 1$$
    $$2x - y + z = -2$$
    $$x + 2y + 3z = 4$$

    b.
    $$x + y + z = 1$$
    $$2x - y + z = 3$$
    $$x + 2y + 3z = -1$$

12. Find the unique linear function that goes through the points (2, 2) and (5, 8). You know several ways to solve this type of problem. Use Gaussian Elimination in matrix form.

> **Go Online**
> www.successnetplus.com

13. Solve the following system by matrix methods.

$$x + y = 2$$
$$y + z = 4$$
$$z + x = 6$$

14. Derman is thinking of three numbers. He says, "The average of the first two numbers is 1. The average of the last two numbers is 2. The average of the first number and last number is 3." What are Derman's numbers?

15. Rewrite the following system in a form to which you can apply Gaussian Elimination. You do not need to solve the system.

$$x + y + 2(y + z) = 3$$
$$x = \frac{1}{2}(y + z + 2)$$
$$x + \frac{y + \frac{1}{2}z}{3} = 1$$

16. Solve the following system.

$$x + y + 2z = 2$$
$$x - y + z = 5$$
$$2x + 2y + 3z = 5$$

> Notice that this problem has the same constants on the right as Sasha and Derman's problem (1)–(3), but the rest is different.

17. Take It Further Solve the system represented by the following augmented matrix without using a calculator. Even though it is 4×4, you can solve it by hand with Gaussian Elimination.

$$\left(\begin{array}{cccc|c} 1 & -1 & -1 & 0 & 1 \\ 0 & 1 & -1 & -1 & 1 \\ -1 & 0 & 1 & -1 & 1 \\ -1 & -1 & 0 & 1 & 1 \end{array}\right)$$

18. Do Exercise 5 from Lesson H.09 in matrix form.

19. A rectangular box has six sides that come in three congruent pairs. Suppose the perimeters of the three different rectangular sides are 20 in., 24 in., and 28 in., respectively. What are the dimensions (length, width, and height) of the box?

20. Take It Further Consider another rectangular box. Suppose that the perimeters of all six sides of the box are the same. Does the box have to be a cube? Explain.

21. Find the unique polynomial of degree 3 or less that goes through the points $(1, 1)$, $(2, 3)$, $(3, 6)$, and $(4, 10)$.

> Solve this exercise using the rref command. See the TI-Nspire Handbook, p. 990.

22. Solve each system. If you use Gaussian Elimination, what situations arise?

a. $x + 2y = 3$

$2x + 4y = 6$

b. $x + 2y = 3$

$2x + 4y = 7$

Maintain Your Skills

23. What is the system of equations associated with the following augmented matrix? Assume the variables are x and y.

$$\left(\begin{array}{cc|c} 1 & 3 & 5 \\ 2 & 4 & 6 \end{array}\right)$$

24. Use Gaussian Elimination to solve the system from Exercise 23.

25. Do Exercise 12 from Lesson H.09 again, this time in matrix form.

26. Use your calculator to compute the rref of each matrix below. Divide up the work with your friends so that no one has many to do. Describe any patterns you discover about the form of rrefs. Randomly create some more matrices and find their rrefs with your calculator. Do the rrefs of these matrices confirm the patterns you have found?

a. $\begin{pmatrix} 1 & -2 & | & -8 \\ -3 & 5 & | & 21 \end{pmatrix}$

b. $\begin{pmatrix} 1 & -2 & | & -8 \\ -3 & 6 & | & 21 \end{pmatrix}$

c. $\begin{pmatrix} 1 & -2 & | & -2 \\ -3 & 6 & | & 6 \end{pmatrix}$

d. $\begin{pmatrix} 1 & 2 & 3 & | & 5 \\ 2 & 3 & 4 & | & 8 \\ 3 & 2 & 1 & | & 7 \end{pmatrix}$

e. $\begin{pmatrix} 3 & 1 & -1 & | & 5 \\ 1 & -4 & -9 & | & -7 \\ 4 & 0 & -4 & | & 4 \end{pmatrix}$

f. $\begin{pmatrix} 1 & 2 & 3 & | & 8 \\ 2 & 3 & 4 & | & 12 \\ 3 & 2 & 1 & | & 6 \end{pmatrix}$

g. $\begin{pmatrix} 3 & 1 & -1 & | & 4 \\ 1 & -4 & -9 & | & 2 \\ 4 & 0 & -4 & | & 3 \end{pmatrix}$

h. $\begin{pmatrix} 1 & -2 & 2 & | & 4 \\ 2 & -4 & 3 & | & 5 \\ 3 & -6 & 2 & | & 0 \end{pmatrix}$

i. $\begin{pmatrix} 3 & -6 & 1 & | & -3 \\ 1 & -2 & -4 & | & -14 \\ 4 & -8 & 0 & | & -8 \end{pmatrix}$

j. $\begin{pmatrix} 1 & 3 & 2 & | & 4 \\ 2 & 6 & 3 & | & 5 \\ 3 & 9 & 2 & | & 0 \end{pmatrix}$

k. $\begin{pmatrix} 3 & 9 & 1 & | & -3 \\ 1 & 3 & -4 & | & -14 \\ 4 & 12 & 0 & | & -8 \end{pmatrix}$

l. $\begin{pmatrix} 1 & 2 & -2 & | & 8 \\ 2 & 3 & -3 & | & 13 \\ 3 & 2 & -2 & | & 12 \end{pmatrix}$

m. $\begin{pmatrix} 3 & 1 & -1 & | & 9 \\ 1 & -4 & 4 & | & -10 \\ 4 & 0 & 0 & | & 8 \end{pmatrix}$

n. $\begin{pmatrix} 1 & 2 & 3 & | & 9 \\ 2 & 3 & 4 & | & 13 \\ 3 & 2 & -1 & | & 1 \end{pmatrix}$

o. $\begin{pmatrix} 3 & 1 & -1 & | & 2 \\ 1 & -4 & 9 & | & 33 \\ 4 & 0 & -1 & | & 5 \end{pmatrix}$

p. $\begin{pmatrix} 1 & 2 & 9 & 3 & | & 14 \\ 2 & 3 & 15 & 4 & | & 20 \\ 3 & 2 & 15 & -1 & | & 4 \\ 3 & 1 & 12 & 2 & | & 11 \end{pmatrix}$

q. $\begin{pmatrix} 1 & 2 & 3 & -5 & | & -6 \\ 2 & 3 & 4 & -5 & | & -8 \\ 3 & 2 & -1 & 9 & | & 0 \\ 3 & 1 & 2 & 4 & | & -1 \end{pmatrix}$

r. $\begin{pmatrix} 1 & -2 & 3 & 0 & 1 & | & 4 \\ 0 & 0 & 0 & 1 & 3 & | & 5 \end{pmatrix}$

27. For parts (d), (f), (h), and (j) of Exercise 26, write down the equations that the original matrix represents and the equations that the rref represents. In what sense do the equations represented by the rref solve the problem?

Matrix notation gives you another way to solve systems of equations.

Minds in Action

Sasha is doing her matrix homework in the cafeteria when Xavier wanders up and looks over her shoulder. Xavier is taking first-year algebra.

Xavier   Hey Sasha, that looks pretty hard.

Sasha   That's what I thought. We're solving several equations at the same time, with several variables. But at least now we've learned a shorthand for writing it. We can write a system of equations of any size as simple as this: $AX = B$.

Xavier   I don't know anything about that several-equations stuff, but come on, $AX = B$ is easy.

Sasha   What do you mean?

Xavier   Just divide by A. We learned that in first-year algebra. So $X = \frac{B}{A}$.

Sasha   Nice try, Xavier, but you don't understand. We're not talking about $ax = b$ where a, b, and x are numbers. Why do you think I wrote capital letters? A and B are matrices.

Xavier   So what? Just do a basic move and divide by A.

Sasha   You can't divide by matrices. It hasn't been defined.

Xavier   Well, can you multiply by matrices, whatever they are?

Sasha   Yes.

Xavier   You can undo multiplication by using the inverse. Multiplying by 5 is undone by multiplying by $\frac{1}{5}$. So find the inverse A^{-1}.

Sasha   Who says there's an inverse matrix?

Xavier   Well, every number a has an inverse a^{-1}, where $a^{-1}a = 1$. So if you multiply both sides of $ax = b$ by a^{-1}, you get $1x = x = a^{-1}b$. Just do the same with your matrices, whatever they are—you still haven't told me.

> Well, 0 does not have a multiplicative inverse.

Sasha   Look, they're these two-way tables on my paper. They're not numbers and you can't multiply them to get numbers, so there's no way there's going to be some A^{-1} that you can multiply by A to get 1. You've got to do a lot more, like row reduce or add and subtract equations.

Xavier   Sorry! But it looked so simple, written $AX = B$.

Using good notation has several advantages. Yes, it makes complicated things easier to write, but it also suggests a way to think about an idea. The matrix equation notation made Xavier think about solving equations as seen in Book I. As it turns out, he is right!

This was his argument: You solve $ax = b$ by multiplying both sides by a^{-1} to get $x = a^{-1}b$. Sasha objected because she thinks there is no matrix C such that $CA = 1$, so there cannot be a matrix that deserves to be called A^{-1}.

There is a matrix I such that $IX = X$. Such a matrix is an **identity matrix**, because multiplying by it gives you back what you start with identically.

What does I look like? Perhaps you know from earlier exercises. Consider the following equations.

$$\begin{pmatrix} 1 & 0 \\ 0 & 1 \end{pmatrix}\begin{pmatrix} x \\ y \end{pmatrix} = \begin{pmatrix} x \\ y \end{pmatrix} \qquad \begin{pmatrix} 1 & 0 & 0 \\ 0 & 1 & 0 \\ 0 & 0 & 1 \end{pmatrix}\begin{pmatrix} x \\ y \\ z \end{pmatrix} = \begin{pmatrix} x \\ y \\ z \end{pmatrix}$$

If X is $m \times 1$, then I is the $m \times m$ matrix with 0's everywhere except for 1's along the main diagonal. You denote all these matrices as I and call each one an identity matrix. If it is important to indicate the size, you can write I_2, I_3, etc.

So, Sasha was mistaken. You do not need the number 1. You need something that serves the same function as 1 in the matrix context. It exists: I.

If there is a matrix M such that $MA = I$, then M will serve the same role as a^{-1}, and Xavier's method for solving matrix equations will work. Starting with $AX = B$, multiply on the left by M, you get

$$X = IX = MAX = MB$$

Example

Problem See if Xavier's method works for the following system.

$$s + 2t = 5$$
$$3s + 4t = 6$$

Solution First, rewrite the system in matrix form.

$$\begin{pmatrix} 1 & 2 \\ 3 & 4 \end{pmatrix}\begin{pmatrix} s \\ t \end{pmatrix} = \begin{pmatrix} 5 \\ 6 \end{pmatrix} \tag{12}$$

Now you need a 2×2 matrix M such that

$$M\begin{pmatrix} 1 & 2 \\ 3 & 4 \end{pmatrix} = \begin{pmatrix} 1 & 0 \\ 0 & 1 \end{pmatrix}$$

In Exercise 12, you will show that there is such a matrix.

$$M = \begin{pmatrix} -2 & 1 \\ \frac{3}{2} & -\frac{1}{2} \end{pmatrix}$$

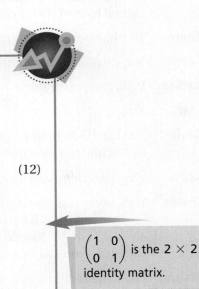

$\begin{pmatrix} 1 & 0 \\ 0 & 1 \end{pmatrix}$ is the 2×2 identity matrix.

Therefore, multiply both sides of (12) by M, just as you would to solve a real-number equation.

$$\begin{pmatrix} 1 & 2 \\ 3 & 4 \end{pmatrix} \begin{pmatrix} s \\ t \end{pmatrix} = \begin{pmatrix} 5 \\ 6 \end{pmatrix}$$

$$\begin{pmatrix} -2 & 1 \\ \frac{3}{2} & -\frac{1}{2} \end{pmatrix} \begin{pmatrix} 1 & 2 \\ 3 & 4 \end{pmatrix} \begin{pmatrix} s \\ t \end{pmatrix} = \begin{pmatrix} -2 & 1 \\ \frac{3}{2} & -\frac{1}{2} \end{pmatrix} \begin{pmatrix} 5 \\ 6 \end{pmatrix}$$

$$\begin{pmatrix} 1 & 0 \\ 0 & 1 \end{pmatrix} \begin{pmatrix} s \\ t \end{pmatrix} = \begin{pmatrix} -2 & 1 \\ \frac{3}{2} & -\frac{1}{2} \end{pmatrix} \begin{pmatrix} 5 \\ 6 \end{pmatrix} = \begin{pmatrix} -4 \\ \frac{9}{2} \end{pmatrix}$$

$$\begin{pmatrix} s \\ t \end{pmatrix} = \begin{pmatrix} -4 \\ \frac{9}{2} \end{pmatrix}$$

The solution is $s = -4$ and $t = 4\frac{1}{2}$.

For You to Do

1. It is often easier to check a possible solution than to find it. In the example above, check that M really is the inverse of $A = \begin{pmatrix} 1 & 2 \\ 3 & 4 \end{pmatrix}$ by computing MA.

   Then check that $\begin{pmatrix} s \\ t \end{pmatrix} = \begin{pmatrix} -4 \\ 4\frac{1}{2} \end{pmatrix}$ really does solve the original equations.

When a matrix A has a companion matrix M such that $MA = I$, this companion matrix is the **inverse**. You write it as A^{-1}.

Good news and bad news The good news is that your calculator knows how to find matrix inverses. Therefore, your calculator provides a quick way to solve the matrix system $AX = B$.

Step 1 Input A.

Step 2 Press one or more keys to get A^{-1}.

Step 3 Compute the product $A^{-1}B$.

The answer appears on your screen.

The bad news is that the inverse method does not always work, because A^{-1} does not always exist. The inverse never exists if A is not square, and it often does not exist even if A is square. This is quite different from the situation with real numbers, where only 0 has no multiplicative inverse. In contrast, Gaussian Elimination always works when solving the system $AX = B$ for any matrix A. It turns out A^{-1} exists precisely when the system $AX = B$ has a unique solution. Gaussian Elimination handles those systems, as well as systems with no solution or many solutions. On the other hand, in this course, you will mostly consider systems with unique solutions, so the inverse matrix method will generally work for you.

Habits of Mind

Check your definition. This is a working definition. As you will see in Exercise 5, you have to say a little more.

You can always press the exponent key ($\wedge$) followed by -1. On some calculators, there is an x^{-1} button that allows you to find inverses with a single keystroke. See the TI-Nspire Handbook, p. 990.

The 2 × 2 case In general, there is no simple formula for A^{-1} in terms of A, although there is a straightforward algorithm to determine whether A has an inverse and to find A^{-1} when it does—a variant of Gaussian Elimination! However, in the 2 × 2 case, there is a nice formula, which is worth knowing.

If $A = \begin{pmatrix} a & b \\ c & d \end{pmatrix}$ and $B = \begin{pmatrix} d & -b \\ -c & a \end{pmatrix}$, then $BA = AB = (ad - bc)I$.

Therefore, as long as $ad - bc \neq 0$,

$$A^{-1} = \frac{1}{ad - bc} \begin{pmatrix} d & -b \\ -c & a \end{pmatrix}$$

What can you do if $ad - bc = 0$? It turns out there is never an inverse when $ad - bc = 0$, so the 2 × 2 case is completely resolved: A^{-1} exists if and only if $ad - bc \neq 0$, in which case you use the formula above for A^{-1}. See Exercise 12.

Exercises *Practicing Habits of Mind*

Check Your Understanding

1. Return again to Sasha and Derman's favorite problem.

$$x + y + z = 2$$
$$2x - y + z = 5$$
$$x + 2y + 3z = 5$$

Solve this system using inverses.

2. Solve Exercise 21 from Lesson H.10 again, this time using the inverse.

3. Consider the system below.

$$\begin{pmatrix} 1 & 2 \\ 2 & 4 \end{pmatrix} \begin{pmatrix} x \\ y \end{pmatrix} = \begin{pmatrix} 1 \\ 1 \end{pmatrix}$$

a. Attempt to solve it geometrically, that is, by graphing the line corresponding to each equation. What happens?

b. Attempt to solve it by Gaussian Elimination. What happens?

c. Attempt to solve it by the inverse method. What happens?

> There is one matrix equation here, but there are two linear equations.

4. **Write About It** In proposing how to solve $AX = B$, Xavier initially wrote $\frac{1}{A}$ and put the A directly under the B, as in $\frac{B}{A}$. Why does the book only show the notation A^{-1}, and why always on the left, as in $A^{-1}B$, instead of BA^{-1} or $\frac{B}{A}$?

5. Let $A = \begin{pmatrix} 1 & 0 \\ 3 & 4 \\ 0 & 1 \end{pmatrix}$ and $M = \begin{pmatrix} 1 & 0 & 0 \\ 0 & 0 & 1 \end{pmatrix}$.

Check that $MA = I$ and $AM \neq I$. So M is only a one-sided inverse of A, something that does not happen with number multiplication.

6. In the example, you showed that $M = \begin{pmatrix} -2 & 1 \\ \frac{3}{2} & -\frac{1}{2} \end{pmatrix}$ is the inverse of

$A = \begin{pmatrix} 1 & 2 \\ 3 & 4 \end{pmatrix}$ in the sense that $MA = I$. Check whether $AM = I$.

7. Xavier said that every real number a has an inverse $\frac{1}{a}$. Is his statement true or false? Explain.

8. Consider the following equation: $\begin{pmatrix} 3 & -1 \\ -2 & 2 \end{pmatrix}\begin{pmatrix} 1 \\ 2 \end{pmatrix} = \begin{pmatrix} 1 \\ 2 \end{pmatrix}$

Does this mean that $\begin{pmatrix} 3 & -1 \\ -2 & 2 \end{pmatrix}$ is also an identity matrix? Explain.

Habits of Mind

Detect the key characteristics.
As it turns out, the correct definition of an inverse for matrices is that M is an inverse of A if $MA = AM = I$. The working definition in the lesson was incomplete. The complete definition implies that only square matrices can have inverses, but a matrix being square is not sufficient.

On Your Own

9. Show that the only matrix $\begin{pmatrix} a & b \\ c & d \end{pmatrix}$ that satisfies $\begin{pmatrix} a & b \\ c & d \end{pmatrix}\begin{pmatrix} x \\ y \end{pmatrix} = \begin{pmatrix} x \\ y \end{pmatrix}$ for all x and y is the 2×2 identity matrix $\begin{pmatrix} 1 & 0 \\ 0 & 1 \end{pmatrix}$.

Historical Perspective
Linear Equations and CAT Scans

When you get a CAT scan, the machine shoots X-rays through a slice of you from various angles. The strength of each beam when it comes out the other side reports the sum of the densities of matter along the ray. But your doctor is not interested in sums of densities. Your doctor wants to know the density at each point in the slice. The density indicates what sort of tissue, bone, or tumor is there. So, the software that creates the picture from the CAT scan essentially has to solve a system of summation equations similar to the one in Exercise 15, only much bigger.

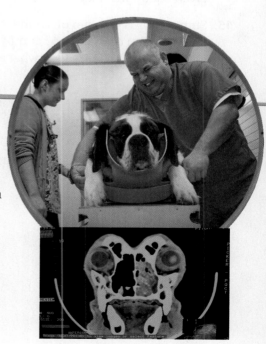

10. Is there a matrix $\begin{pmatrix} x & y \\ z & w \end{pmatrix}$ that solves the following equation?

$$\begin{pmatrix} x & y \\ z & w \end{pmatrix}\begin{pmatrix} 1 & 2 \\ 3 & 4 \end{pmatrix} = \begin{pmatrix} 1 & 0 \\ 0 & 1 \end{pmatrix}$$

Write this single matrix equation as four ordinary equations. This gives you four linear equations in four unknowns. However, if you look at it carefully, you will see that this particular system is not hard to solve even by hand. Do it.

11. Is there a matrix $\begin{pmatrix} x & y \\ z & w \end{pmatrix}$ that solves the following equation?

$$\begin{pmatrix} 1 & 2 \\ 3 & 4 \end{pmatrix}\begin{pmatrix} x & y \\ z & w \end{pmatrix} = \begin{pmatrix} 1 & 0 \\ 0 & 1 \end{pmatrix}$$

Find out by converting this single matrix equation into four ordinary equations.

12. You already know that if $ad - bc \neq 0$, then $M = \begin{pmatrix} a & b \\ c & d \end{pmatrix}$ has the inverse $\dfrac{1}{ad - bc}\begin{pmatrix} d & -b \\ -c & a \end{pmatrix}$. Now show that you have not missed any matrices. Prove that M has an inverse only if $ad - bc \neq 0$.

13. Standardized Test Prep Suppose a_1 is the sum of x_1 and x_2, a_2 is the sum of x_2 and x_3, and a_3 is the sum of x_3 and x_1. If $(a_1, a_2, a_3) = (1, 2, 3)$, what are x_1, x_2, and x_3?

A. $(1, 2, 2)$ **B.** $(1, 2, 3)$ **C.** $(1, 0, 2)$ **D.** $(0, 1, 2)$

14. Take It Further Continuing with Exercise 15, forget all the work to find the individual x values. Is it possible to find the sum $x_1 + x_2 + x_3$ by adding the given equations? Explain.

15. Suppose b_1 is the sum of x_1 and x_2, b_2 is the sum of x_2 and x_3, b_3 is the sum of x_3 and x_4, and b_4 is the sum of x_4 and x_1. If $(b_1, b_2, b_3, b_4) = (1, 2, 3, 4)$, what are x_1, x_2, x_3, and x_4?

Go Online www.successnetplus.com

Remember...

The system
$$ax + by = e$$
$$cx + dy = f$$
where a, b, c, d, e and f are known constants, has the unique solution $(x, y) =$
$$\left(\dfrac{de - bf}{ad - bc}, \dfrac{af - ce}{ad - bc}\right)$$

Maintain Your Skills

16. Compute the inverse of each matrix.

a. $\begin{pmatrix} 1 & 0 & 0 \\ 0 & 2 & 0 \\ 0 & 0 & \frac{1}{3} \end{pmatrix}$ **b.** $\begin{pmatrix} 1 & 1 \\ 0 & 1 \end{pmatrix}$ **c.** $\begin{pmatrix} 1 & 2 & 3 \\ 0 & 4 & 5 \\ 0 & 0 & 6 \end{pmatrix}$ **d.** $\begin{pmatrix} 1 & 0 & 0 \\ 2 & 1 & 0 \\ 2 & 1 & 2 \end{pmatrix}$

e. $\begin{pmatrix} 1 & 2 & 0 & 0 \\ 3 & 4 & 0 & 0 \\ 0 & 0 & 1 & 2 \\ 0 & 0 & 3 & 4 \end{pmatrix}$ **f.** $\begin{pmatrix} 1 & \frac{1}{2} \\ \frac{1}{2} & \frac{1}{3} \end{pmatrix}$ **g.** $\begin{pmatrix} 1 & \frac{1}{2} & \frac{1}{3} \\ \frac{1}{2} & \frac{1}{3} & \frac{1}{4} \\ \frac{1}{3} & \frac{1}{4} & \frac{1}{5} \end{pmatrix}$

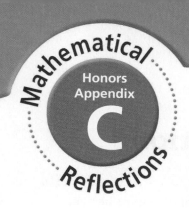

Mathematical
Honors
Appendix
C
Reflections

In this investigation, you learned how to solve a system of three equations in three unknowns. You also learned how to use matrices and Gaussian Elimination to solve systems. These questions will help you summarize what you have learned.

1. Show how to solve this system using each technique.

$$2x - y = 3$$
$$x + 3y = 5$$

   a. substitution
   b. elimination

2. Solve this system.

$$3x - y + 2z = 4$$
$$4y - 3z = 3$$
$$6z = -6$$

3. Write the following system of equations as an augmented matrix.

$$x - 3z = 5$$
$$6y = 7 - z$$
$$2y + 6 = x$$

4. Find the row-reduced echelon form for this matrix.
$$\begin{pmatrix} 1 & 1 & 1 & | & 1 \\ 0 & 1 & 2 & | & 4 \\ 3 & 0 & 2 & | & 6 \end{pmatrix}$$

You can use a matrix to organize a large amount of information, such as a bus schedule.

5. Sasha used Gaussian Elimination to solve a system of equations. She ended up with the following matrix. How should she interpret these results?
$$\begin{pmatrix} 1 & 0 & 0 & | & -2 \\ 0 & 1 & 0 & | & 4 \\ 0 & 0 & 0 & | & 3 \end{pmatrix}$$

6. Why is it possible to solve systems of linear equations in matrix form?

7. What is the process of Gaussian Elimination?

8. Find x, y, and z such that
$$4x - y + 4z = 1$$
$$2x - y + 8z = 11$$
$$2x - 2y + 4z = 0$$

Vocabulary

In this investigation, you learned these terms. Make sure you understand what each one means and how to use it.

- **dimension**
- **elimination**
- **Gaussian Elimination**
- **identity matrix**
- **inverse**
- **matrix**
- **row-reduced echelon form (rref)**
- **substitution**

Trigonometric Functions

In *Trigonometric Functions*, you will explore the relationships between points on a circle with radius 1 centered at the origin and angles with vertex at the origin. You will learn how to find the sine, cosine, and tangent of angles of any measure.

By the end of this investigation, you will be able to answer questions like these.

1. How can you extend the definitions of sine, cosine, and tangent to any angle, not just acute angles?

2. If an angle is in Quadrant IV, what can you say about the sign of its sine, cosine, and tangent?

3. What is the relationship between the equation of the unit circle and the Pythagorean Identity?

You will learn how to

- use right triangle trigonometry to find the coordinates of a person walking on the unit circle, given an angle through which an observer has turned

- evaluate the sine, cosine, and tangent functions for any angle

- solve equations involving trigonometric functions

You will develop these habits and skills:

- Visualize relationships between coordinates of a point on the unit circle and the angle that an observer at the origin must turn through to look at that point.

- Extend the sine, cosine, and tangent functions carefully, in order to preserve key properties.

- Use logical reasoning to find all possible solutions of a trigonometric equation.

As this drawbridge rises, the angle it forms with the river increases. The right end traces part of a circle.

Activating Prior Knowledge
Reviewing Key Ideas

In geometry, you learned about similarity and the AA Theorem: Two triangles are similar if two pairs of corresponding angles have the same measure.

If two right triangles have one pair of acute angles with the same measure, then they are similar. The ratio of any two side lengths in one of the triangles is the same as the ratio of the corresponding side lengths in the other triangle.

If two triangles have two pairs of corresponding angles with the same measure, the third pair of angles also has the same measure, because the sum of the measures of the angles in a triangle is 180°.

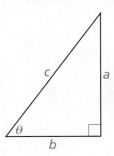

$$\frac{a}{c} = \frac{x}{z}$$

$$\frac{b}{c} = \frac{y}{z}$$

$$\frac{a}{b} = \frac{x}{y}$$

These ratios are determined by the marked angle in the triangle. In other words, each ratio is a function of the given angle. It helps to refer to the three sides of the triangle in terms of their position from the perspective of this angle. There are the leg opposite the angle, the leg adjacent to the angle, and the hypotenuse.

Which side is which depends on which angle you are talking about. The side opposite one acute angle is adjacent to the other. The hypotenuse does not change.

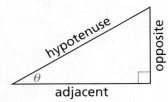

The three ratios are functions of the angle θ. Since they are helpful in many problems, they have standard names.

Definitions

The **sine** of an acute angle θ is the ratio of the opposite side to the hypotenuse in any right triangle that has θ as an acute angle. It is denoted by sin θ.

The **cosine** of an acute angle θ is the ratio of the adjacent side to the hypotenuse. It is denoted by cos θ.

The **tangent** of an acute angle θ is the ratio of the opposite side to the adjacent side. It is denoted by tan θ.

Here are those ratios again, written in the form of equations.

$$\sin \theta = \frac{\text{opposite}}{\text{hypotenuse}}$$

$$\cos \theta = \frac{\text{adjacent}}{\text{hypotenuse}}$$

$$\tan \theta = \frac{\text{opposite}}{\text{adjacent}}$$

Calculators have keys for all three of these functions. They also have keys for their inverse functions, which allow you to calculate an angle if you know its sine, cosine, or tangent.

Example 1

Problem A wheelchair ramp should not incline at an angle steeper than 5°. You are building a ramp next to a staircase that rises a total of 2 feet. How long will the ramp be if the angle is 5°?

Solution The picture below shows what the ramp would look like.

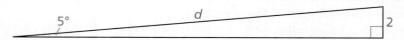

The hypotenuse and the side opposite the 5° angle are involved, so it is simplest to use the sine function. You know the angle measure, and that the length of the opposite side is 2. The hypotenuse is the unknown d.

$$\sin 5° = \frac{2}{d}$$

Solve for d: $d = \frac{2}{\sin 5°}$. You can use a calculator to find that $d \approx 23$ feet.

> A 5° angle is quite small. How does the length of the ramp compare with the horizontal distance from the end of the ramp to the building?

For You to Do

1. For safety, a ladder manufacturer recommends that you should place a ladder's base a minimum distance from the wall. This distance is at least one foot for every 6 feet of ladder length. How high on the wall can a 20-foot ladder reach if the base is at the minimum distance from the wall?

Example 2

Problem For some angle θ, $\cos\theta = \frac{3}{5}$. Find $\sin\theta$ and $\tan\theta$.

Solution

Method 1 You can use any right triangle with this angle θ, so pick one that has convenient side lengths. Since the ratio given is $\frac{3}{5}$, set up a right triangle with a side of length 3 adjacent to angle θ and a hypotenuse of length 5.

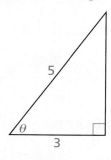

> Method 1 gives exact answers.

You can find the length of the remaining side with the Pythagorean Theorem or by recognizing the famous 3-4-5 right triangle. Since the third side's length is 4, you know the other ratios.

$$\sin\theta = \frac{\text{opposite}}{\text{hypotenuse}} = \frac{4}{5}$$

$$\tan\theta = \frac{\text{opposite}}{\text{adjacent}} = \frac{4}{3}$$

Method 2 Use the inverse function to find the angle θ.

$$\cos\theta = \frac{3}{5} \Rightarrow \theta = \cos^{-1}\left(\frac{3}{5}\right)$$

> Method 2 gives approximate answers.

The angle θ is approximately 53.130°. Once you know θ, you can find the other ratios with your calculator.

$$\sin 53.130° \approx 0.8000$$

$$\tan 53.130° \approx 1.3333$$

These values are very close to the exact fractions $\frac{4}{5}$ and $\frac{4}{3}$ you found using Method 1.

For Discussion

2. For this example, it seems that Method 1 gives more accurate answers, more quickly. Can you think of a situation in which Method 2 might be necessary?

Look for relationships. You can express the Pythagorean Theorem using sine and cosine. Consider the triangle drawn at the right. The Pythagorean Theorem tells you that for this triangle,

$$a^2 + b^2 = c^2$$

Divide each side by c^2.

$$\frac{a^2}{c^2} + \frac{b^2}{c^2} = 1$$

The trigonometric functions define $\cos \theta$ as $\frac{a}{c}$ and $\sin \theta$ as $\frac{b}{c}$. So,

$$(\cos \theta)^2 + (\sin \theta)^2 = 1$$

The parentheses can get in the way. The exponent is frequently moved to appear next to the function name.

$$\cos^2 \theta + \sin^2 \theta = 1$$

You read this equation as "cosine squared theta plus sine squared theta equals 1." It is one of the most fundamental relationships in trigonometry.

> How far is the point $(\cos \theta, \sin \theta)$ from the origin?

Exercises *Practicing Habits of Mind*

Check Your Understanding

1. A right triangle has a 40° angle and hypotenuse of length 10. Find the triangle's perimeter to two decimal places.

2. A right triangle has legs of lengths 20 and 21.

   a. What is the area of this triangle?

   b. How long is the hypotenuse?

   c. Draw an accurate picture of this triangle. Estimate the acute angle measures.

   d. Using a calculator, find the measure of each acute angle to the nearest degree.

3. In a right triangle, the value of $\cos \theta$ is $\frac{8}{17}$. Find the values of $\sin \theta$ and $\tan \theta$ exactly (without decimal approximations).

4. Show that for any angle measure θ such that $0° < \theta < 90°$,

$$\tan \theta = \frac{\sin \theta}{\cos \theta}$$

5. For some angle θ, $\sin \theta$ is exactly $\frac{1}{4}$. Find the exact value of $\cos \theta$ for this angle by drawing a right triangle.

6. Take It Further A right triangle has a 30° angle and one side length that is 12. Find all possible values for the area of the triangle.

On Your Own

7. A right triangle has an angle θ and a hypotenuse of length 1. Find the lengths of the other two sides in terms of θ.

8. Explain why it is true that for any angle θ, $0° < \theta < 90°$,

$$\sin \theta = \cos (90° - \theta)$$

Remember...

Angles with measure θ and $90° - \theta$ are complementary. Hence the name cosine.

9. Use this triangle to find the exact values of sine, cosine, and tangent for 30° and 60°.

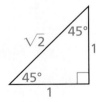

θ	sin θ	cos θ	tan θ
30°	■	■	■
60°	■	■	■

10. Use this triangle to find the exact values of sine, cosine, and tangent for 45°.

θ	sin θ	cos θ	tan θ
45°	■	■	■

11. Derman wants to extend the domain of sine and cosine so that he can give a value for sin 90° and cos 90°. What are good values for Derman to pick? Explain.

12. a. What are the largest and smallest possible values for sin θ? Explain.

　　b. What are the largest and smallest possible values for cos θ? Explain.

　　c. What are the largest and smallest possible values for tan θ? Explain.

For Exercise 12, assume $0° < \theta < 90°$.

13. For each triangle, find $\sin \theta$, $\cos \theta$, and $\tan \theta$.

a.

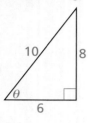

b.

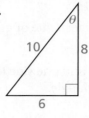

c.

d.

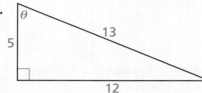

14. **What's Wrong Here?** Trent sees $\triangle TRI$.

Trent says, "So side TI is 10 and angle T is 70°, that means I can find side RI by using sine of 70°. So I know $\sin 70° = \frac{RI}{10}$."

What is wrong with Trent's reasoning?

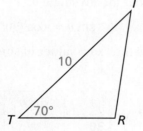

15. **Take It Further** Prove that for any angle θ such that $0° < \theta < 90°$, $\tan (90° - \theta) = \frac{1}{\tan \theta}$.

Maintain Your Skills

16. Copy the following table. Use a calculator to complete it for the sine, cosine, and tangent of angles in increments of 10°. Find each value to three decimal places.

θ	$\sin \theta$	$\cos \theta$	$\tan \theta$
10°	▪	▪	▪
20°	▪	▪	▪
30°	▪	▪	▪
40°	▪	▪	▪
50°	▪	▪	▪
60°	▪	▪	▪
70°	▪	▪	▪
80°	▪	▪	▪

Habits of Mind

Look for relationships.
Review Exercise 8.

17. Explain why $\sin 10°$ and $\cos 80°$ are equal.

Activating Prior Knowledge
Exploring New Ideas

The values of trigonometric functions are related to the coordinates of points on a circle with radius 1 centered at the origin.

For You to Explore

Olivia watches Paul walk around a circle. The circle's radius is 1 meter. Olivia stands at the center, and Paul begins walking counterclockwise. Consider a coordinate grid, with Olivia standing at the origin and Paul starting at the point (1, 0).

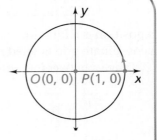

> **Remember...**
> This circle, with center (0, 0) and radius 1, is the unit circle.

As Paul walks, Olivia watches Paul and keeps track of the angle she has turned. For example, when Olivia has turned 70°, the situation looks like this.

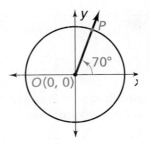

1. **a.** Explain why the distance between Olivia and Paul is always 1.

   b. Suppose Paul is at a point with coordinates (x, y). Write an equation in x and y to express the fact that Paul is 1 unit away from (0, 0).

2. Find the coordinates of Paul's location when Olivia has turned 70°. Round to three decimal places.

3. Find the lengths of the other two sides of this triangle.

4. Find the coordinates of Paul's location when Olivia has turned 45°.

   (*Hint:* Your work in Problem 3 should be helpful here.)

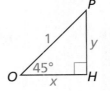

5. Find the coordinates of Paul's location when Olivia has turned 90°.

6. **a.** Explain why Paul will pass through the point $\left(\frac{3}{5}, \frac{4}{5}\right)$.

   b. When Paul is at $\left(\frac{3}{5}, \frac{4}{5}\right)$, find the angle Olivia has turned to the nearest degree.

> Draw a diagram. You do not need to use triangles this time.

7. **Write About It** Describe how the y-coordinate of Paul's location changes as Olivia's angle increases.

8. Copy and complete this table, giving the coordinates of Paul's location when Olivia has turned each angle.

Angle	Coordinates	Angle	Coordinates
0°	(1, 0)	270°	■
45°	■	315°	■
90°	■	360°	■
135°	■	405°	■
180°	(−1, 0)	450°	■
225°	■		

9. The *y*-coordinate of Paul's position is a function of the angle through which Olivia has turned. Make a coordinate grid labeled like the one below. Draw the graph of the function for angles between 0° and 360°.

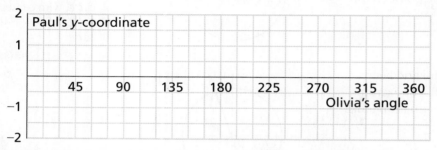

10. **Take It Further** Find the coordinates of Paul's location when Olivia has turned 10,000°. Calculate to three decimal places.

Exercises *Practicing Habits of Mind*

On Your Own

11. Copy and complete this table, giving the coordinates of Paul's location when Olivia has turned through each angle. Find each answer to three decimal places.

Angle	Coordinates	Angle	Coordinates
0°	(1, 0)	50°	■
10°	■	60°	■
20°	■	70°	■
30°	■	80°	■
40°	■	90°	(0, 1)

12. Find the magnitude and argument of each complex number.

   a. $3 + 4i$

   b. $\frac{3}{5} + \frac{4}{5}i$

   c. $-5 + 12i$

   d. $-\frac{5}{13} + \frac{12}{13}i$

Approximate the arguments to the nearest degree.

13. Which of these points is on the unit circle $x^2 + y^2 = 1$?

   A. $\left(\frac{1}{2}, -\frac{1}{2}\right)$

   B. $(1, -1)$

   C. $\left(-\frac{5}{13}, \frac{12}{13}\right)$

   D. $\left(\frac{2}{3}, -\frac{4}{5}\right)$

14. **a.** Find the coordinates of Paul's location to three decimal places when Olivia has turned $130°$.

   b. Find the coordinates of Paul's location to three decimal places when Olivia has turned $230°$.

15. Describe how the x-coordinate of Paul's location varies as Olivia's angle increases.

16. In Problem 9, you graphed Paul's y-coordinate as a function of the angle Olivia had turned. Now graph Paul's x-coordinate as a function of the angle Olivia has turned.

17. Find the coordinates of Paul's location to three decimal places when Olivia has turned $430°$.

Include the points $(0, 1)$ and $(180, -1)$.

18. Suppose a and b are real numbers and $z = a + bi$, a complex number. If $|z| = 2$ and $\arg z = 120°$, find a and b.

Maintain Your Skills

19. Draw the graphs of each pair of equations on the same axes. Find the number of intersections of the two graphs.

   a. $x^2 + y^2 = 1$
      $x = 0.5$

   b. $x^2 + y^2 = 1$
      $x = 0.9$

   c. $x^2 + y^2 = 1$
      $x = 1$

   d. $x^2 + y^2 = 1$
      $x = 1.3$

20. Draw the graphs of each pair of equations on the same axes. Find the number of intersections of the two graphs.

   a. $x^2 + y^2 = 1$
      $y = 0.5$

   b. $x^2 + y^2 = 1$
      $y = -0.5$

   c. $x^2 + y^2 = 1$
      $y = -0.9$

   d. $x^2 + y^2 = 1$
      $y = -1$

Go Online
Video Tutor
www.successnetplus.com

Extending the Domain, Part 1—0°–360°

Right now, you can only find the sine, cosine, or tangent of an angle if the angle has measure between 0° and 90°, since these functions have been defined as ratios of sides in a right triangle. By following Olivia and Paul around their circle, you can extend the domain of these trigonometric functions to include all angles from 0° to 360°. Here is how.

Consider the situation in Lesson H.13. Suppose Paul has moved along the circle, and Olivia has turned through an angle of 70°.

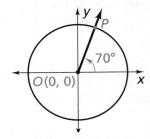

The 70° angle Olivia has turned is part of a right triangle with vertices at O and P. You complete the triangle by dropping an altitude from point P to the x-axis.

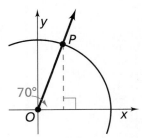

The position of the hammer at the moment of release is related to the angle the athlete has rotated.

The hypotenuse of this right triangle has length 1, so the horizontal leg has length cos 70° and the vertical leg has length sin 70°. The coordinates of point P are $(\cos 70°, \sin 70°)$.

In fact, this works for any angle in Quadrant I. Angles with measures between 0° and 90° are in Quadrant I. If the angle at the origin is θ, the coordinates of point P are $(\cos\theta, \sin\theta)$.

In the other quadrants, you can draw right triangles to find Paul's coordinates, but one or both of the coordinates will be negative.

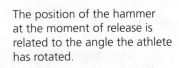

You can find the approximate values of cos 70° and sin 70° on a calculator. Note that calculators typically have more than one way to measure angles. Refer to the TI-Nspire™ Handbook on p. 990 to see how to check that your calculator is in degree mode.

Problem Find Paul's coordinates when Olivia has turned 210°.

Solution First, draw a diagram for the situation. The angle is in Quadrant III, so both coordinates will be negative. To find the exact coordinates, draw an altitude from *P* to the *x*-axis.

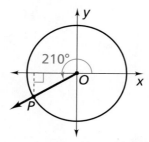

You can use sine and cosine to find the side lengths in this triangle. The triangle has a 30° angle at the origin, so it is a 30-60-90 triangle with hypotenuse length 1. Because this is a special right triangle, you can write exact expressions for its side lengths without using a calculator.

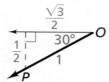

The side opposite the 30° angle has length $\frac{1}{2}$, and the side opposite the 60° angle has length $\frac{\sqrt{3}}{2}$.

To determine the coordinates of point *P*, use the side lengths of the triangle. Note that both coordinates are negative, since *P* is in Quadrant III. The coordinates of point *P* are $\left(-\frac{\sqrt{3}}{2}, -\frac{1}{2}\right)$.

Remember...

The values $\frac{1}{2}$ and $\frac{\sqrt{3}}{2}$ come up often in trigonometry.

For Discussion

1. Why does the hypotenuse of the triangle in the Example have length 1?
2. Find another angle in Quadrant III where you can find the coordinates of point *P* exactly without including a trigonometric function or using a calculator.

The unit circle gives you a way to extend the domain of sine and cosine.

Habits of Mind

Give an exact answer.
Finding coordinates exactly means to use a rational number written as a fraction or an expression involving rational numbers and square roots. For example, $\cos 45° = \frac{\sqrt{2}}{2}$ is exact. But 0.707107 is an approximation of $\frac{\sqrt{2}}{2}$.

Definitions

Let θ be an angle centered at the origin and measured counter-clockwise from the positive x-axis. The left side of θ intersects the graph of $x^2 + y^2 = 1$ (the unit circle) in exactly one point.

This is the same as the situation with Olivia and Paul. You measure angles in the same way you measured the direction (or argument) of complex numbers in Chapter 3.

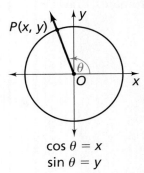

$$\cos \theta = x$$
$$\sin \theta = y$$

The **cosine** of angle θ is the x-coordinate of this intersection.

The **sine** of angle θ is the y-coordinate of this intersection.

Remember...

The coordinates of a point P on the unit circle are $(\cos \theta, \sin \theta)$.

This definition is the one calculators use. For example, a calculator gives $\cos 180° = -1$.

For You to Do

3. Is $\sin 280°$ positive or negative? Answer without using a calculator.

4. In which quadrants is cosine negative?

For acute angles θ, one of the properties of the tangent function is that

$$\tan \theta = \frac{\sin \theta}{\cos \theta}$$

Since you now have a definition for the sine and cosine of any angle, you can use the above formula to extend the domain of the tangent function to any angle, as well. For example, you can say that

$$\tan 120° = \frac{\sin 120°}{\cos 120°} = \frac{\dfrac{\sqrt{3}}{2}}{-\dfrac{1}{2}} = -\sqrt{3}$$

Now you have a tentative definition. If θ is any angle, define $\tan \theta$ by the rule

$$\tan \theta = \frac{\sin \theta}{\cos \theta}$$

Check your definition. Why is this definition only tentative? The formula $\tan \theta = \frac{\sin \theta}{\cos \theta}$ is valid only for $0 \le \theta < 90$, but is often used to define $\tan \theta$ for any angle.

In mathematics, it often happens that you can have a functional equation $\left(\text{in this case, } \tan \theta = \frac{\sin \theta}{\cos \theta}\right)$ that is valid for certain values (in this case, for $0 \le \theta < 90$). Sometimes the right side of the equation makes sense for many more values, so you define the left side for those additional values.

When you do this, you have to be careful. In the case of $\tan \theta = \frac{\sin \theta}{\cos \theta}$, you have to check two things:

- Does the right side make sense for all angles θ? Clearly, the numerator and denominator do, but does the fraction?

- You originally defined the left side of the equation to be "opposite over adjacent" for acute angles θ. Does this still make sense for angles with measure greater than $90°$?

For Discussion

5. As a class, discuss the two bullet points above and make a more precise definition of the tangent function.

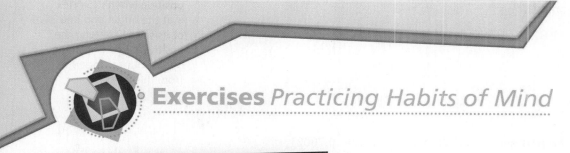

Habits of Mind

Represent a function.
To define a function, you have to give its domain.

Exercises *Practicing Habits of Mind*

Check Your Understanding

1. **What's Wrong Here?** Jo says that $\sin 45°$ should be $\frac{1}{2}$. Jo explains, "Well, $\sin 0° = 0$ and $\sin 90° = 1$. The same is true for cosine, except reversed. Halfway between, they should both be $\frac{1}{2}$." Use the unit circle to explain what is wrong with Jo's reasoning.

2. A complex number $w = a + bi$ has $|w| = 1$ and $\arg w = 70°$. Find a and b to three decimal places.

3. What complex number has magnitude 1 and direction 210°?

4. Write About It Write an identity that gives the relationship between the two expressions.

   a. $\cos\theta$ and $\cos(\theta + 180°)$

   b. $\sin\theta$ and $\sin(\theta + 180°)$

   c. $\tan\theta$ and $\tan(\theta + 180°)$

5. Find each value.

   a. $(\cos 150°)^2 + (\sin 150°)^2$

   b. $(\cos 52.696°)^2 + (\sin 52.696°)^2$

6. Write About It Suppose you know a complex number has magnitude 1, but you do not know its direction. Describe, with some examples, where that complex number can be located.

7. a. Find a formula for all values of θ such that $\sin\theta = 0$.

   b. Find a formula for all values of θ such that $\cos\theta = 0$.

   c. Find a formula for all values of θ such that $\tan\theta = 0$.

On Your Own

8. For each angle, draw the angle in standard position. Find the sine, cosine, and tangent of the angle.

   a. 210°

   b. 330°

   c. 40°

   d. 320°

   e. 360°

9. Standardized Test Prep If $\sin\theta = 0.57358$ and $\tan\theta = 0.70021$, what is $\cos\theta$?

   A. 0.40163   **B.** 0.81915   **C.** 1.22077   **D.** 1.27379

> **Remember...**
>
> An angle is in **standard position** when its vertex is at the origin and one of its sides lies along the positive x-axis. The angle opens counterclockwise from this fixed side.

10. For each angle in the table, find the cosine, sine, cosine squared, and sine squared. Look for rules and relationships that allow you to find the results more quickly.

11. Explain why sin 310° = −sin 50°.

12. Let $\theta = 150°$. Find each value.

   a. $\sin 2\theta$

   b. $2 \cdot \sin\theta \cdot \cos\theta$

13. Find a formula for all values of θ such that the given equation is true.

   a. $\sin\theta = 1$

   b. $\cos\theta = 1$

   c. $\tan\theta = 1$

θ	$\cos\theta$	$\sin\theta$	$\cos^2\theta$	$\sin^2\theta$
0°	▪	0	▪	0
30°	$\frac{\sqrt{3}}{2}$	▪	$\frac{3}{4}$	▪
45°	▪	$\frac{\sqrt{2}}{2}$	▪	$\frac{1}{2}$
60°	▪	▪	▪	▪
90°	0	1	0	1
120°	▪	▪	▪	▪
135°	▪	▪	▪	▪
150°	▪	$\frac{1}{2}$	▪	$\frac{1}{4}$
180°	▪	▪	▪	▪
210°	▪	▪	▪	▪
225°	$-\frac{\sqrt{2}}{2}$	▪	▪	$\frac{1}{2}$
240°	▪	▪	▪	▪
270°	0	▪	▪	▪
300°	▪	▪	▪	▪
315°	▪	▪	▪	▪
330°	▪	▪	▪	▪
360°	1	▪	▪	▪

Go Online
www.successnetplus.com

14. a. Find the magnitude and direction of $-6\sqrt{3} + 6i$.

   b. What complex number has magnitude 10 and direction 30°?

   c. What complex number has magnitude 1 and direction 60°?

Maintain Your Skills

15. Take It Further Find the value of θ in each equation.

   a. $\cos\theta + i\sin\theta = (\cos 40° + i\sin 40°)(\cos 50° + i\sin 50°)$

   b. $\cos\theta + i\sin\theta = (\cos 40° + i\sin 40°)(\cos 20° + i\sin 20°)$

   c. $\cos\theta + i\sin\theta = (\cos 40° + i\sin 40°)(\cos 80° + i\sin 80°)$

   d. $\cos\theta + i\sin\theta = (\cos 45° + i\sin 45°)^2$

Extending the Domain, Part 2—All Real Numbers

In the last lesson, you learned the meaning of cosine, sine, and tangent for values from 0° to 360°. This lesson extends the definitions to all real numbers.

For You to Do

1. Using a calculator, find cos 20°, cos 380°, and cos 1100°. Find another angle that produces the same value for the cosine.

The table in Exercise 10 from Lesson H.14 only goes from 0° to 360°. The reason is that turning through any angle larger than 360° returns you to an angle between 0° and 360°. The coordinates after turning through a 20° angle are the same as the coordinates after turning 360° + 20° = 380° or 720° + 20° = 740°. It makes sense, then, to define the cosine of 740° to be the same as the cosine of 20°.

> Two numbers that differ by a multiple of 360 are *congruent modulo 360*. *Modulo* means "except for." The numbers 20 and 380 are the same, except for 360.

The same goes for negative angle measures: An angle of −35° puts you at the same place on the unit circle as an angle of 325°. So it makes sense to say that sin (−35°) = sin 325°.

With this extension, you can find the sine or cosine for any angle measure from the set of real numbers. For an angle θ with measure outside of 0° < θ < 360°, simply find another angle that is between 0° and 360° but has the same coordinates on the unit circle. You can use almost exactly the same definition as the one in Lesson H.14 to extend the definition to any angle measure.

> **Habits of Mind**
>
> **Experiment.** Will the tangent of any angle be the same as the tangent of an angle between 0° and 360°?

Definitions

Let θ be an angle centered at the origin and measured from the positive *x*-axis. The terminal side of θ intersects the graph of $x^2 + y^2 = 1$ (the unit circle) in exactly one point.

The **cosine** of angle θ is the *x*-coordinate of this intersection.

The **sine** of angle θ is the *y*-coordinate of this intersection.

The **tangent** of angle θ is $\frac{\sin\theta}{\cos\theta}$, whenever cos $\theta \neq 0$.

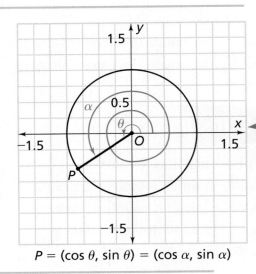

$P = (\cos\theta, \sin\theta) = (\cos\alpha, \sin\alpha)$

> One side of θ passes through (1, 0). This is its initial side. The other side is the terminal side. When are these two sides the same ray?

For You to Do

2. Using a calculator, find $\cos 20°$, $\cos 160°$, $\cos 200°$, and $\cos 340°$.

Theorem H.7

If *n* is an integer and *x* is an angle in degrees,

- $\cos (x + 360n) = \cos x$
- $\sin (x + 360n) = \sin x$

For Discussion

3. The functions sine and cosine are periodic with period 360°. What does this mean? Is the tangent function a **periodic function**?

Developing Habits of Mind

Visualize. In H.4, you learned how to calculate the direction of complex numbers. You noticed that the direction of $4 + 3i$ is related to the direction of $-4 + 3i$, $-4 - 3i$, and $4 - 3i$.

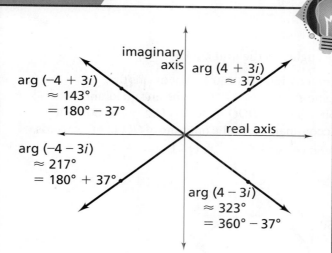

arg $(-4 + 3i)$
$\approx 143°$
$= 180° - 37°$

arg $(4 + 3i)$
$\approx 37°$

arg $(-4 - 3i)$
$\approx 217°$
$= 180° + 37°$

arg $(4 - 3i)$
$\approx 323°$
$= 360° - 37°$

imaginary axis

real axis

This is the same picture you see now in the unit circle. Each quadrant has a related angle with coordinates that are the same, except for a sign.

For example, if you know the cosine and sine of a 20° angle, you automatically know the cosine and sine of a 160° angle, as well as a 200° angle and a 340° angle, and many other angles.

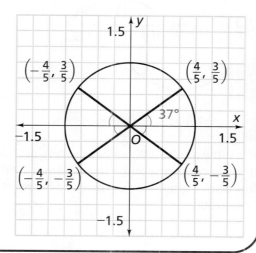

$\left(-\dfrac{4}{5}, \dfrac{3}{5}\right)$ $\left(\dfrac{4}{5}, \dfrac{3}{5}\right)$

$\left(-\dfrac{4}{5}, -\dfrac{3}{5}\right)$ $\left(\dfrac{4}{5}, -\dfrac{3}{5}\right)$

37°

Habits of Mind

Look for relationships. Equations like $\cos x = -\cos (180° - x)$ express a symmetry of the cosine function.

Knowing about the signs of the coordinates in each quadrant will help you decide quickly about whether the cosine, sine, or tangent of an angle is positive or negative. For example, in Quadrant I, cosine is positive and sine is positive. Therefore, tangent is positive.

Habits of Mind

Look for relationships. If you are familiar with angles in Quadrant I, then you can handle any other angle using these relationships.

For You to Do

Find the sign of the sine, cosine, and tangent for angles in each quadrant.

4. Quadrant II

5. Quadrant III

6. Quadrant IV

Example

Problem Express each value as the value of the sine or cosine of an acute angle.

   a. $\cos 150°$

   b. $\sin 460°$

   c. $\sin 290°$

Solution It helps to draw the angles on the unit circle:

a. The coordinates of P are $(\cos 150°, \sin 150°)$. That means that $m\angle POC = 30°$. Imagine $\triangle QOD \cong \triangle POC$ in the first quadrant, oriented as in the graph. Then $m\angle DOQ = 30°$, so $OD = \cos 30°$. But $OC = OD$, and the x-coordinate of P is the opposite of OD. In other words, $\cos 150° = -\cos 30°$. Since $\cos 30° = \frac{\sqrt{3}}{2}$, $\cos 150° = -\frac{\sqrt{3}}{2}$.

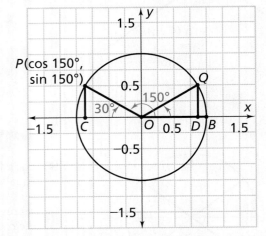

b. Note that $\sin 460°$ is the same as $\sin 100°$, since traveling around the circle $460°$ is the same as making one complete revolution ($360°$) with an additional $100°$. Now draw a graph like the one above and convince yourself that $\sin 100° = \sin 80°$.

c. The graph shows that $\sin 290° = -\sin 70°$.

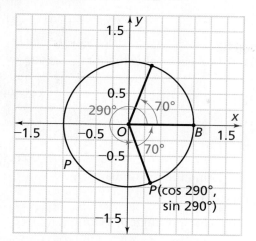

Habits of Mind

Generalize. Convince yourself that $\sin(-x) = -\sin x$ for any angle measure x.

Exercises Practicing Habits of Mind

Check Your Understanding

1. **Write About It** Explain why $\sin 160° = \sin 20°$ but $\cos 160° = -\cos 20°$.

2. Suppose $\sin \theta = \frac{20}{29}$ for some angle θ.

   a. In what quadrants can θ be located?

   b. Find both possible values for $\cos \theta$.

   c. Find both possible values for $\tan \theta$.

3. Find an angle θ for which $\tan \theta > 100$, or explain why no such angle exists.

4. **What's Wrong Here?** Herb wants to calculate $\cos(-60°)$. He says, "I know that $\cos 60°$ is $\frac{1}{2}$. So $\cos(-60°)$ should just be the negative. The answer is $-\frac{1}{2}$."

   What is wrong with Herb's reasoning? What is the correct value of $\cos(-60°)$?

5. List the following values in order from least to greatest.

   $$\tan 70° \quad \sin 120° \quad \cos 120° \quad \cos 720° \quad \tan 110° \quad \sin 210°$$

6. Find the two angles between $0°$ and $360°$ for which
   $\sin \theta + \sin(180° - \theta) = 1$.

7. Given that $\sin 50° \approx 0.7660$ and $\cos 50° \approx 0.6428$, find each value to four decimal places.

You do not need a calculator for any of the parts of this exercise.

    a. $\sin 130°$ **b.** $\cos 130°$

    c. $\cos 230°$ **d.** $\sin 310°$

    e. $\cos^2 230° + \sin^2 230°$ **f.** $\sin 40°$

8. **a.** There is a relationship between $\tan^2 \theta$ and $\frac{1}{\cos^2 \theta}$. Find the relationship by calculating each expression for several angles.

    b. Take It Further Prove that this relationship holds for any angle θ, as long as $\tan \theta$ is defined.

On Your Own

9. Find the values of $\cos(-30°)$, $\sin(-30°)$, and $\tan(-30°)$.

10. Express each value as a sine or cosine of an acute angle.

    a. $\sin 400°$ **b.** $\cos 400°$ **c.** $\cos 300°$

    d. $\sin 315°$ **e.** $\sin(-100°)$

11. Express each value as a sine or cosine of θ.

Habits of Mind

Use what you know. There is no need to memorize these identities. You can reconstruct them by looking at the unit circle.

    a. $\sin(180° - \theta)$ **b.** $\cos(180° - \theta)$ **c.** $\sin(180° + \theta)$

    d. $\cos(180° + \theta)$ **e.** $\sin(270° - \theta)$ **f.** $\cos(270° - \theta)$

    g. $\sin(270° + \theta)$ **h.** $\cos(270° + \theta)$

12. Is this statement true or false? Explain.

    For any two angles a and b, $\sin(a + b) = \sin a + \sin b$ and $\cos(a + b) = \cos a + \cos b$.

This statement says that addition is distributive over the sine and cosine functions. But maybe it is not!

13. Suppose an angle θ is unknown, but it is between $300°$ and $350°$. Determine whether each expression is positive or negative.

    a. $\cos \theta$ **b.** $\sin \theta$ **c.** $\tan \theta$

    d. $\cos^2 \theta + \sin^2 \theta$ **e.** $\tan^3 \theta$

14. What is the value of $\cos 120° + \sin 120°$?

    A. 0 **B.** $\frac{\sqrt{3} - 1}{2}$ **C.** 1 **D.** $\frac{\sqrt{3} + 1}{2}$

15. Find this sum: $\sin 60° + \sin 120° + \sin 180° + \cdots + \sin 360°$.

16. For which angles between 0° and 360° can you find the sine and cosine exactly without using a calculator or an approximation?

17. Suppose θ is an angle in Quadrant II with $\sin \theta = \frac{35}{37}$.

    a. Find the value of $\cos \theta$.

    b. Find the value of $\tan \theta$.

    c. Suppose θ is between 0° and 360°. Find θ to the nearest degree.

18. a. There is a relationship between $\frac{1}{\tan^2 \theta}$ and $\frac{1}{\sin^2 \theta}$. Find the relationship by calculating each expression for several angles.

    b. Take It Further Prove that this relationship holds for any angle θ, as long as $\tan \theta$ is defined and $\tan \theta$ and $\sin \theta$ are not equal to 0.

19. Standardized Test Prep Lindsay has a four-function calculator $(+, -, \times, \div)$. She also has a printed table showing values of $\sin \theta$ for values of θ from 0° to 90° in increments of 1°. Which formula will allow her to use this table and her calculator to compute the values of $\cos \theta$ for several different angles between 0° and 90°?

    A. $\cos \theta = 1 - \sin \theta$ **B.** $\cos \theta = \sin (90 - \theta)$ **C.** $\cos \theta = -\sin \theta$

    D. No relation exists between $\cos \theta$ and $\sin \theta$ for values of θ between 0° and 90°.

> The missing terms all follow the arithmetic sequence set up by 60, 120, and 180.

Go Online
www.successnetplus.com

Maintain Your Skills

20. Find an angle θ, not equal to 30°, that satisfies each equation.

    a. $\cos \theta = \cos 30°$ **b.** $\sin \theta = \sin 30°$ **c.** $\tan \theta = \tan 30°$

    d. Describe how you can find ten other angles θ such that $\cos \theta = \cos 30°$.

The Pythagorean Identity

While solving Exercise 10 in Lesson H.14, you may have noticed the following equation is true for all angles between 0° and 360°.

$$\cos^2 \theta + \sin^2 \theta = 1$$

Since then, you have extended the domain for sine and cosine to include all angles. Does the identity still hold? Happily, it does.

Theorem H.8 The Pythagorean Identity

If α is any angle, then

$$\cos^2 \alpha + \sin^2 \alpha = 1$$

The symbol α is the Greek letter alpha. You pronounce it AL fuh.

Proof For any angle α, $\cos \alpha$ and $\sin \alpha$ are the coordinates of the point P on the unit circle, where the left side of α intersects the unit circle.

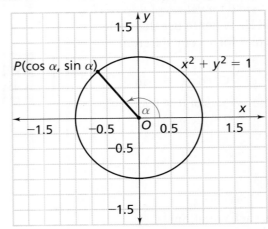

There are several ways to see that the sum of the squares of the coordinates of P is 1.

Method 1 The equation of the unit circle is $x^2 + y^2 = 1$, and the coordinates of P satisfy this equation.

Method 2 The distance from P to the origin is 1.

Method 3 Drop a perpendicular from P to the x-axis and use the Pythagorean Theorem.

For You to Do

1. Pick one of the methods above (or one of your own) and finish the proof of Theorem H.8.

Example

Problem If $\sin \gamma = \frac{1}{2}$, find $\cos \gamma$.

Solution Think of $(\cos \gamma, \sin \gamma)$ as a point P on the unit circle. Then $\sin \gamma$ is the y-coordinate of P. How many points have a y-coordinate of $\frac{1}{2}$ on the unit circle?

In Exercise 20a from Lesson 8.01, you saw that there are two points on the unit circle with y-coordinate $\frac{1}{2}$. The x-coordinates of these two points are precisely the values of $\cos \gamma$ for which $\sin \gamma = \frac{1}{2}$.

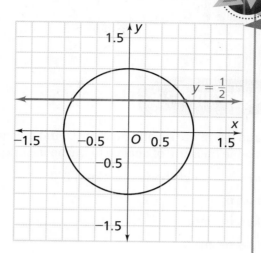

The symbol γ is the Greek letter gamma. You pronounce it GAM uh.

To find the two intersection points, you can do one of two equivalent things.

Method 1 In the equation $x^2 + y^2 = 1$, substitute $y = \frac{1}{2}$ and solve for x.

$$x^2 + \left(\tfrac{1}{2}\right)^2 = 1$$

$$x^2 + \tfrac{1}{4} = 1$$

$$x^2 = \tfrac{3}{4}$$

$$x = \pm\sqrt{\tfrac{3}{4}} = \pm\tfrac{\sqrt{3}}{2}$$

Methods 1 and 2 really are the same. On the unit circle, if (x, y) is the point where a radius that forms an angle γ with the x-axis intersects the circle, then $\cos \gamma = x$ and $\sin \gamma = y$.

Method 2 Use the Pythagorean Identity.

$$\cos^2 \gamma + \sin^2 \gamma = 1$$

Substitute $\sin \gamma = \frac{1}{2}$.

$$\cos^2 \gamma + \left(\tfrac{1}{2}\right)^2 = 1$$

$$\cos^2 \gamma + \tfrac{1}{4} = 1$$

$$\cos^2 \gamma = \tfrac{3}{4}$$

$$\cos \gamma = \pm\sqrt{\tfrac{3}{4}} = \pm\tfrac{\sqrt{3}}{2}$$

For You to Do

2. Solve $\sin \gamma = \frac{1}{2}$ for γ.

Habits of Mind

Consider more than one solution. If you ask your calculator for $\sin^{-1}(0.5)$, it will probably return $30°$. It is true that $\sin 30° = 0.5$, but is that the only solution for γ? The calculator picks its values for $\sin^{-1}$ from a restricted sine domain.

Exercises Practicing Habits of Mind

Check Your Understanding

1. Suppose $\sin q = 0.72$ and q is in the second quadrant. Find the approximate value of $\cos q$. Then find the measure of angle q to the nearest degree.

2. Suppose $\cos x = \frac{1}{2}$ and x is an angle between $0°$ and $360°$.

   a. Find all possible values of x.

   b. Find all possible values of $\sin x$.

   c. Find all possible values of $\sin^2 x$.

3. Graph both equations on the same axes.
   $$x^2 + y^2 = 1$$
   $$y = 0.6$$

4. Find all solutions to the system of equations in Exercise 3.

5. Suppose $\cos x = 0.6$ and x is an angle between $0°$ and $360°$.

   a. Find all possible values of x.

   b. Find all possible values of $\sin x$.

   c. Find all possible values of $\sin^2 x$.

6. Suppose that $z = \cos 30° + i \sin 30°$. Show that $\frac{1}{z} = \bar{z}$.

Approximate to one decimal place if necessary.

Remember...

The notation $\bar{z}$ means the complex conjugate of z.

On Your Own

7. Suppose that $z = \cos \theta + i \sin \theta$. Show that $\frac{1}{z} = \bar{z}$.

8. Solve each equation or system for $0 \leq x \leq 360°$.

   a. $\sin x = \frac{\sqrt{2}}{2}$

   b. $\begin{cases} \sin x = \frac{\sqrt{2}}{2} \\ \cos x > 0 \end{cases}$

   c. $\begin{cases} \sin x = \frac{\sqrt{2}}{2} \\ \cos x < 0 \end{cases}$

   d. $\begin{cases} \sin x = -\frac{\sqrt{2}}{2} \\ \cos x < 0 \end{cases}$

9. Find ten pairs of rational numbers (a, b) such that $a^2 + b^2 = 1$.

10. Write About It The Pythagorean Identity says that, if θ is any angle, $\cos^2 \theta + \sin^2 \theta = 1$.

Suppose you have numbers a and b such that $a^2 + b^2 = 1$. Is there an angle θ such that $\sin \theta = a$ and $\cos \theta = b$? Explain.

11. a. Show that
$$\tan^2 30° = \frac{1}{\cos^2 30°} - 1.$$

b. If α is any angle, is the equation below true? Explain.
$$\tan^2 \alpha = \frac{1}{\cos^2 \alpha} - 1$$

12. a. Calculate $\cos^2 30° - \sin^2 30°$.

b. Calculate $\cos^4 30° - \sin^4 30°$.

c. Verify that $\cos^2 \theta - \sin^2 \theta = \cos^4 \theta - \sin^4 \theta$ for a new choice of θ.

d. Prove that for any angle θ, it must be true that
$$\cos^2 \theta - \sin^2 \theta = \cos^4 \theta - \sin^4 \theta.$$

13. Standardized Test Prep If $\cos \theta = \frac{1}{3}$ and $0° < \theta < 90°$, what is the value of $\sin \theta$?

A. $\frac{2}{3}$ **B.** $\frac{4}{9}$

C. $\frac{2\sqrt{2}}{3}$ **D.** $\frac{8}{9}$

Alpha is the first letter of the Greek alphabet. The alpha wolf is the leader of the pack.

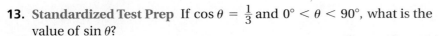

Pick a θ, any θ.

Go Online
www.successnetplus.com

14. Copy and complete the table without using a calculator.

θ	$\cos\theta$	$\sin\theta$	$\tan\theta$
0°	■	0	■
30°	$\dfrac{\sqrt{3}}{2}$	■	$\dfrac{1}{\sqrt{3}}$
45°	■	$\dfrac{\sqrt{2}}{2}$	1
60°	■	■	■
90°	0	1	■
120°	■	■	■
135°	■	■	■
150°	■	$-\dfrac{1}{2}$	■
180°	■	■	■
210°	■	■	■
225°	$-\dfrac{\sqrt{2}}{2}$	■	■
240°	■	■	■
270°	0	■	■
300°	■	■	■
315°	■	■	■
330°	■	■	■
360°	1	■	■

You have done much of the work for this table before.

H.17 Solving Trigonometric Equations

You solve equations with trigonometric functions in much the same way you solve other equations.

Minds in Action

Tony and Sasha are trying to solve the equation 5 cos x + 6 = 9 for x between 0° and 360°.

Tony   I'm not sure what to do with the cos x.

Sasha   It's like in Chapter 2, when we lumped things.

Sasha goes to the board and covers up the cos x with her hand.

$$5 \text{ co\kern-0.3em \raisebox{0.2em}{✋} x} + 6 = 9$$

Sasha   See? Now it looks like it's saying "5 times something plus 6 is 9."

So, let z stand for cos x, for the time being, and solve

$$5z + 6 = 9$$

Tony   I know how to do that. You get $z = \frac{3}{5} = 0.6$.

Sasha   But z is just an alias for cos x, so our equation is cos x = 0.6.

Tony   And I know how to do that, too. In fact, we have already done it in Exercise 5 in the last lesson. You just use the inverse cosine button and get 53.13°. That's an approximation, I know.

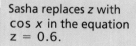

Sasha replaces z with cos x in the equation $z = 0.6$.

Sasha   Yes, but that's not the only answer. Look:

Sasha draws on the board.

Sasha   See? Cosine is the x-coordinate, and there are two points on the unit circle with x-coordinate 0.6. One has a central angle of about 53.13°.

Tony   And the other is −53.13°.

Sasha   Or, if you want your angles to measure between 0° and 360°, the second angle is about 306.87°.

Habits of Mind

Make strategic choices. What happens when you allow angles with measure greater than 360°?

For You to Do

1. Solve $5 \sin x + 3 = 7$ for x between $0°$ and $360°$.

Developing Habits of Mind

Look for patterns. The lumping idea is often used to solve trigonometric equations that look like ordinary algebraic equations.

For example, the trigonometric equation below is a quadratic equation in $\sin x$.

$$10 \sin^2 x - 3 \sin x = 4$$

That is, if you let $z = \sin x$, the equation becomes

$$10z^2 - 3z = 4$$

You can solve this with the methods of Chapter 2. When you find two values for z, replace z with $\sin x$. Then solve for x.

A **trigonometric equation** is an equation that involves trigonometric functions.

For You to Do

2. Solve the equation $10 \sin^2 x - 3 \sin x = 4$ for x, where $0° \leq x \leq 360°$.

Exercises Practicing Habits of Mind

Check Your Understanding

1. Suppose $\sin x = \sin 50°$. Find all possible values of x.

2. **a.** Find, to the nearest degree, the two angles between $0°$ and $360°$ that make $\sin x = 0.6$.

   b. Find, to the nearest degree, the two angles between $0°$ and $360°$ that make $\sin x = -0.6$.

3. **a.** Find, to the nearest degree, all angles between $0°$ and $360°$ that make $\cos x = 0.8$.

  b. Find, to the nearest degree, all angles between $0°$ and $360°$ that make $\cos x = -1.2$.

4. Find all solutions to each equation for $0° \leq x \leq 360°$.

  a. $3 \cos x + 4 = 0$ **b.** $6 \sin x - 1 = 3$

  c. $4 \sin^2 x = 1$ **d.** $4 \sin^2 x = 4 \sin x + 3$

5. **a.** Find, to the nearest degree, all angles between $0°$ and $360°$ that make $\sin x = \cos x$.

  b. Find, to the nearest degree, all angles between $0°$ and $360°$ that make $\sin x = -\cos x$.

  c. **Take It Further** Find, to the nearest degree, all angles between $0°$ and $360°$ that make $\sin x = \tan x$.

6. Solve the equation $6 \cos^2 x + \sin x - 5 = 0$ for x, where $0° \leq x \leq 360°$. (*Hint:* $\cos^2 x + \sin^2 x = 1$)

7. Suppose z is a complex number and arg $z = \theta$. Use geometry to show that $z + \bar{z} = 2|z| \cos \theta$.

8. In the isosceles triangle below, $OA = OB = 1$ and $m\angle O = 36°$.

  Show that $z = 2 \cos 72°$.

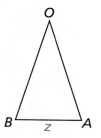

Habits of Mind

Detect the key characteristics. What is special about the parallelogram that has vertices $0, z, z + \bar{z}$, and $\bar{z}$?

On Your Own

9. Find all solutions to each equation for $0° \leq x \leq 360°$.

  a. $5 \cos x + 4 = 0$ **b.** $\sqrt{2} \sin x - 1 = 3$

  c. $4 \cos^2 x = 1$ **d.** $4 \cos^2 x = 4 \cos x + 3$

10. Find all solutions to each equation for $0° \leq x \leq 360°$.

  a. $2 \cos x + 1 = 0$ **b.** $\tan x - 1 = 0$

  c. $1 - 3 \sin x + 2 \sin^2 x = 0$ **d.** $2 \cos^2 x - 5 \cos x = 2$

11. For what values of α between $0°$ and $360°$ is the following equation true?

$$2 \sin^2 \alpha + 5 \cos \alpha = 2$$

www.successnetplus.com

12. Find or approximate the complex number on the unit circle that has each argument. Write your answers in $a + bi$ form.

   a. 20°   **b.** 330°   **c.** −30°   **d.** 100°   **e.** 227°   **f.** 75°

13. For each complex number z, find arg z.

   a. $z = \frac{4}{5} + \frac{3}{5}i$ **b.** $z = \frac{3}{5} + \frac{4}{5}i$ **c.** $z = -\frac{3}{5} - \frac{4}{5}i$ **d.** $z = -\frac{4}{5} + \frac{3}{5}i$

14. Solve the equation $2 \sin^3 x - \sin^2 x - 2 \sin x + 1 = 0$ for x, where $0° \le x \le 360°$.

15. In the isosceles triangle below, $OA = OB = 1$ and $m\angle O = 36°$. $\overline{BC}$ bisects $\angle OBA$.

See Exercise 8.

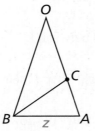

Habits of Mind

Look for relationships.
There are similar triangles in the figure.

   a. Show that $1 - z^2 = z$.

   b. Use the result of part (a) to find an exact value for z.

   c. Use parts (a) and (b) and the result of Exercise 8 to find an exact value for cos 72°.

   d. **Take It Further** Find an exact value for sin 72°.

16. **Take It Further** Solve the equation $5 \cos 2x + 6 = 9$, where $0° \le x \le 360°$.

17. **Standardized Test Prep** Solve, to the nearest hundredth of a degree, $\tan x - 10 = -\tan x$ for $-90° < x < 90°$.

   A. −80°   **B.** 1.37°   **C.** 78.69°   **D.** 84.29°

Maintain Your Skills

18. Here is a graph of the unit circle with a line ℓ that intersects the circle at the points $A(0, -1)$ and $P(a, b)$.

Find the coordinates of P for each slope of ℓ.

   a. 1   **b.** 2   **c.** $\frac{3}{2}$

   d. 4   **e.** $\frac{6}{5}$

   f. **Take It Further** $\frac{r}{s}$

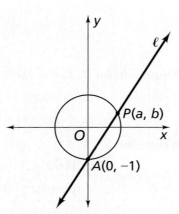

In this investigation, you learned how to evaluate the sine, cosine, and tangent functions for any angle and to solve equations involving trigonometric equations. These questions will help you summarize what you have learned.

1. A line through the origin forms a 30° angle with the x-axis. What are the coordinates of the points where this line intersects the graph of the unit circle?

2. Sketch each angle in standard position. Find its sine, cosine, and tangent.

   a. 150°   b. 315°   c. 240°

3. Find five solutions to the equation $\sin x = -1$.

4. For some angle θ, $\sin \theta = \frac{12}{13}$.

   a. Find all possible values for $\cos \theta$.

   b. Find all possible values for $\tan \theta$.

   c. Find a possible θ between 0° and 360° to the nearest tenth of a degree.

5. Solve the following equation for α between 0° and 360°.

$$10 \cos^2 \alpha + \cos \alpha - 3 = 0$$

6. How can you extend the definitions of sine, cosine, and tangent to any angle, not just acute angles?

7. If an angle is in Quadrant IV, what can you say about the sign of its sine, cosine, and tangent?

8. What is the relationship between the equation of the unit circle and the Pythagorean Identity?

Vocabulary and Notation

In this investigation, you learned these terms and symbols. Make sure you understand what each one means and how to use it.

- cosine, cos θ
- periodic function
- sine, sin θ
- standard position
- tangent, tan θ
- trigonometric equation

The tip of the wiper moves along a circle as the wiper rotates.

Graphs of Trigonometric Functions

In *Graphs of Trigonometric Functions*, you will sketch the graphs of the sine, cosine, and tangent functions. You can use these graphs to explore trigonometric identities.

By the end of this investigation, you will be able to answer questions like these.

1. What do the graphs of the sine and cosine functions look like?

2. Why does the tangent function have a period of 180°?

3. What is a simple rule for finding the value of cos $(90° + \theta)$?

You will learn how to

- sketch graphs of the sine, cosine, and tangent
- use the graphs of trigonometric functions to solve problems
- prove and use trigonometric identities

You will develop these habits and skills:

- Visualize relationships between graphs of trigonometric functions.
- Choose the appropriate representation—graph or unit circle—to understand and develop trigonometric identities.
- Reason logically to prove trigonometric identities.

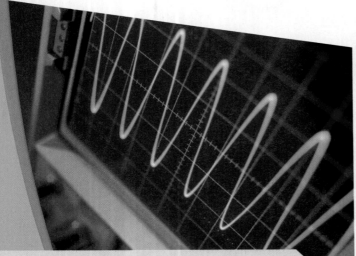

An oscilloscope displays voltage as a function of time. The graph is a sine wave.

The graphs of the sine, cosine, and tangent functions show the periodic nature of these functions.

For You to Explore

An exact value for a trigonometric function is an expression that may include square roots. If you use your calculator, it may return a decimal approximation and not an exact value.

1. Find the exact values of cos 30° and sin 30°.

2. Find the exact values of cos 45° and sin 45°.

3. Calculate each value.

   a. $\cos^2 30°$

   b. $\sin^2 30°$

   c. $\cos^2 45°$

   d. $\sin^2 45°$

   e. $\cos^2 30° + \sin^2 30°$

   f. $\cos^2 45° + \sin^2 45°$

4. Describe how the cosine and sine of 60° are related to the cosine and sine of 30°.

5. Describe how the cosine and sine of 150° are related to the cosine and sine of 30°.

Exercises Practicing Habits of Mind

On Your Own

6. Use the information from Exercise 14 in Lesson H.16 to draw a graph of $y = \cos x$ for $0° \leq x \leq 360°$.

7. Use the graph of $y = \cos x$ to answer this question: Is cos 230° greater or less than cos 190°?

8. Use the information from Exercise 14 in Lesson H.16 to draw a graph of the function $y = \sin x$ for $0° \leq x \leq 360°$.

9. Use the graph of $y = \sin x$ to answer this question: Is $\sin 230°$ greater or less than $\sin 190°$?

10. Find and describe a relationship between $\sin \theta$ and $\sin (180° + \theta)$.

11. **Take It Further** Which is greater, $\tan 190°$ or $\tan 230°$? Determine the answer without a calculator. Justify your answer.

Maintain Your Skills

12. For each complex number, calculate the magnitude and direction.

    a. $3 + 2i$ **b.** $(3 + 2i)^2$ **c.** $1 + 2i$

    d. $(1 + 2i)^2$ **e.** $-\frac{8}{17} + \frac{15}{17}i$ **f.** $\left(-\frac{8}{17} + \frac{15}{17}i\right)^2$

    g. z^2, where z has magnitude 5 and direction $100°$

Calculate the direction to the nearest tenth of a degree.

13. Here is the table you completed in Lesson H.16, Exercise 14. What patterns can you find in each column?

θ	$\cos \theta$	$\sin \theta$	$\tan \theta$
0°	1	0	0
30°	$\frac{\sqrt{3}}{2}$	$\frac{1}{2}$	$\frac{1}{\sqrt{3}}$
45°	$\frac{\sqrt{2}}{2}$	$\frac{\sqrt{2}}{2}$	1
60°	$\frac{1}{2}$	$\frac{\sqrt{3}}{2}$	$\sqrt{3}$
90°	0	1	undefined
120°	$-\frac{1}{2}$	$\frac{\sqrt{3}}{2}$	$-\sqrt{3}$
135°	$-\frac{\sqrt{2}}{2}$	$\frac{\sqrt{2}}{2}$	-1
150°	$-\frac{\sqrt{3}}{2}$	$\frac{1}{2}$	$-\frac{1}{\sqrt{3}}$
180°	-1	0	0
210°	$-\frac{\sqrt{3}}{2}$	$-\frac{1}{2}$	$\frac{1}{\sqrt{3}}$
225°	$-\frac{\sqrt{2}}{2}$	$-\frac{\sqrt{2}}{2}$	1
240°	$-\frac{1}{2}$	$-\frac{\sqrt{3}}{2}$	$\sqrt{3}$
270°	0	-1	undefined
300°	$\frac{1}{2}$	$-\frac{\sqrt{3}}{2}$	$-\sqrt{3}$
315°	$\frac{\sqrt{2}}{2}$	$-\frac{\sqrt{2}}{2}$	-1
330°	$\frac{\sqrt{3}}{2}$	$-\frac{1}{2}$	$-\frac{1}{\sqrt{3}}$
360°	1	0	0

Graphing Cosine and Sine

In Lesson H.15, you extended the domain of sine and cosine to all of $\mathbb{R}$. This means that you can graph $\sin x$ or $\cos x$ against x on a Cartesian graph. One way to do this is to use the completed table on the facing page.

Remember...

$\mathbb{R}$ is the set of real numbers.

Consider the sine function first. Notice that the second column in the table starts at 0, climbs to 1, then retreats backs to 0, plunges to −1, and then climbs back up to 0.

For You to Do

1. To get a feeling for the relative sizes, rewrite the sine values as decimal approximations.

Once you get the decimal approximations, you can plot points. If you use your calculator to get decimal approximations for even more sines, you will end up with a graph that looks like this.

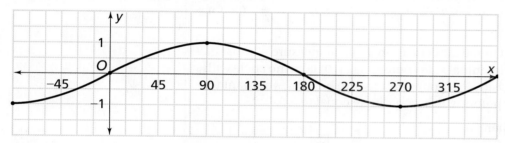

For Discussion

2. Use the fact that sine is periodic to extend the graph to $-360° \leq x \leq 720°$.

For You to Do

3. Sketch the graph of $y = \cos x$ for $-360° \leq x \leq 720°$. Describe how the graph of $y = \cos x$ is related to the graph of $y = \sin x$.

Along with the unit circle, the graphs of sine and cosine give you a toolkit that will help you think about the properties of the trigonometric functions.

Habits of Mind

Visualize. Because of the symmetry of the graphs, there are many ways to describe this relationship.

Example

Problem For how many values of α between $0°$ and $360°$ is $\cos \alpha = -0.4$? What are they, approximately?

Solution There are two ways to think about this.

Method 1 Use the graph of the function $\cos x = y$. Just as on the graph of any function, the output at x is the y-height above or below x on the graph. So, to find α such that $\cos \alpha = -0.4$, find the intersections of the graphs of $y = -0.4$ and $y = \cos x$.

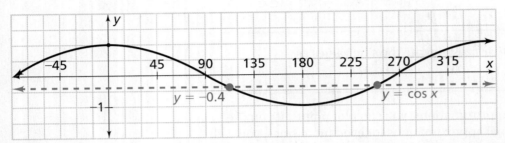

There are two such intersections in the interval $0° \leq x \leq 360°$. And it looks as if the intersections occur at $x \approx 110°$ and $x \approx 250°$. So, $\cos \alpha = -0.4$ for $\alpha \approx 110°$ and $\alpha \approx 250°$.

Method 2 Use the unit circle. On the unit circle, an angle of measure α with vertex at the origin and with initial side containing $(1, 0)$ cuts the circle with its terminal side at $(\cos \alpha, \sin \alpha)$. If you want $\cos \alpha$ to be -0.4, you want to look on the unit circle for points with x-coordinate equal to -0.4.

Once again, we see that there are two such angles between $0°$ and $360°$. They are approximately $110°$ and $250°$.

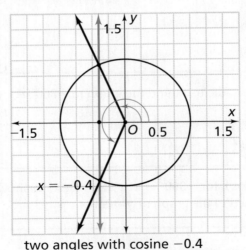

two angles with cosine -0.4

Go Online
www.successnetplus.com

For You to Do

4. Use your calculator's $\cos^{-1}$ key to get better approximations of the angles with cosine -0.4. Round to three decimal places.

Consider more than one strategy. These two ways of thinking—using the graphs and using the unit circle—complement each other in many ways. The graph, because of its symmetry, is useful for discovering interesting things like the fact that cos 20° = cos(−20°). But the proof of such a fact usually relies on the geometry of the unit circle.

The unit circle is ideal for figuring out exact values for things like sin 240°, because you can use what you know from geometry. The graph is ideal for finding qualitative facts, such as the number of solutions to sin x = 0.7.

For You to Do

5. Explain why cos 20° = cos (−20°). Is it always true that cos x = cos (−x)?

For Discussion

For each question, decide whether it is a good idea to use the unit circle, the graph, or both. Then answer each question.

6. How many solutions are there to $|\sin x| = 1$ for −360° ≤ x ≤ 360°?

7. Find the solutions to $|\sin x| = 1$ for −360° ≤ x ≤ 360°.

8. Find a formula for all solutions of $|\sin x| = 1$.

Exercises *Practicing Habits of Mind*

1. The values of sin 50° and sin (−50°) are related.

   a. Use the unit circle to describe and illustrate this relationship.

   b. Use the graph of $y = \sin x$ to describe and illustrate this relationship.

2. **What's Wrong Here?** Derman uses his graphing calculator to sketch the graph of $y = \sin x$. As is his custom, he sets the window so that x and y go from −10 to 10. He is surprised by what he sees. Describe what Derman sees. How can he fix the problem?

   > To help Derman, see the TI-Nspire Handbook, p. 990.

3. Sketch the graph of $f(x) = \cos(x + 360°)$. Describe why the graph looks the way it does.

4. **a.** How many x-intercepts does the graph of $y = \cos x$ have?

   b. Explain why the cosine function cannot be a polynomial function.

   > Consider the entire graph, not just a small section.

   c. Where is the tangent function undefined? Explain.

5. Sketch the graph of $f(x) = \sin(30° + x) + \sin(30° - x)$.

6. Sketch the graph of $g(x) = \cos(x - 90°)$.

7. Here are the graphs of $y = \sin x$ and $y = 0.6$ on the same axes.

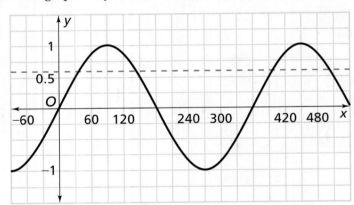

   The least positive value of x that solves $\sin x = 0.6$ is about 37°. Find the next two values of x, to the nearest degree, that solve the equation.

8. **Take It Further** Sketch the graph of $k(x) = \cos 2x$ without the aid of a graphing calculator. Then use a calculator to check your work.

9. **a.** Sketch the graphs of $f(x) = \cos x$ and $g(x) = \sin x$ on the same axes.

   b. Use the graphs to find two angles θ for which $\sin \theta = \cos \theta$.

10. **a.** For each angle θ you found in Exercise 9, find $\tan \theta$.

    b. If $\sin \theta = \cos \theta$, prove that $\tan \theta = 1$.

Habits of Mind

Make strategic choices. For Exercises 11 and 12, should you draw a unit circle or a graph? You decide.

11. Draw a picture to explain why $\cos(-\theta) = \cos\theta$.

12. Draw a picture to explain why $\sin(-\theta) = -\sin\theta$.

13. Sketch the graph of $s(x) = \cos^2 x + \sin^2 x$.

14. **Standardized Test Prep** Which function has the same graph as $y = \sin x$?

   A. $y = 180° + \cos x$ **B.** $y = -\sin x$

   C. $y = \sin(x + 360°)$ **D.** $y = 2\sin x$

15. Below are the graphs of $y = \cos x$ and $y = 0.8$ on the same axes. The least positive value of x that solves $\cos x = 0.8$ is about 37°. Find the next two values of x that solve the equation, to the nearest degree.

Go Online
www.successnetplus.com

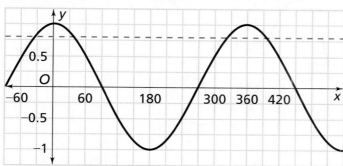

16. Use the unit circle or graphs to illustrate that each identity is true for all θ.

   a. $\sin(180° - \theta) = \sin\theta$ **b.** $\cos(180° - \theta) = -\cos\theta$

   c. $\sin(180° + \theta) = -\sin\theta$ **d.** $\cos(360° - \theta) = \cos\theta$

   e. $\sin\theta = \cos(\theta - 90°)$ **f.** $\cos\theta = -\sin(\theta - 90°)$

17. Sketch the graph of $h(x) = -\sin x$ for at least two periods.

A **period** is a full cycle of the wave: up, down, and back again. It is the smallest piece that you can repeat over and over to produce the entire graph.

18. Describe the graph of $h(x) = -\sin x$ as a translation of the graph of $g(x) = \sin x$.

19. Sketch an accurate graph of each function.

   a. $j(x) = \cos^2 x - \sin^2 x$ **b.** $r(x) = \cos 2x$

   c. $k(x) = \cos^4 x - \sin^4 x$

Maintain Your Skills

20. The graph below in black shows a portion of the graph of $y = \cos x$. Find the coordinates of each marked point.

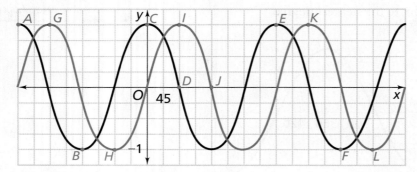

21. The graph above in red shows a portion of the graph of $y = \sin x$. Find the coordinates of each marked point.

Graphing the Tangent Function

You have extended the definition of tangent to $\tan x = \frac{\sin x}{\cos x}$, whenever $\cos x \neq 0$. In other words, tangent is defined for all real numbers except odd multiples of 90°. In this lesson, you will build the graph of $y = \tan x$. First, however, note this interesting way to picture the tangent.

Developing Habits of Mind

Visualize. Why do you call it *tangent*? The diagrams below show a tangent to the unit circle at (1, 0). The angle x is shown in each of the four quadrants.

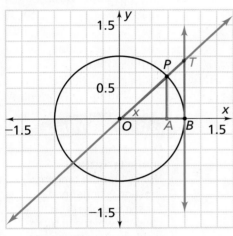
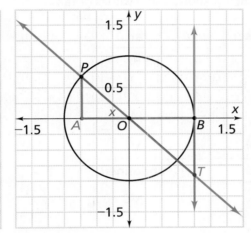

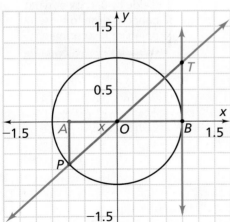
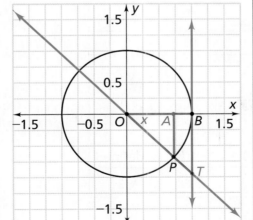

In each case, $\triangle POA \sim \triangle TOB$, so $\frac{TB}{OB} = \frac{PA}{OA}$.

But $OB = 1$, so $TB =$ the length of the tangent $= \frac{PA}{OA}$.

You can use this to show that the coordinates of T are $(1, \tan x)$. So you measure $\tan x$ along the tangent.

For Discussion

1. Finish the argument above by showing that the coordinates of T are $(1, \tan x)$.

2. What happens when the angle is $90°$ or $270°$?

Check the signs.

For You to Do

3. What happens to $\tan x$ for values of x close to, but slightly less than, $90°$?

4. What happens to $\tan x$ for values of x close to, but slightly greater than, $90°$?

Along with the definition of the tangent function, some other information may help you think about the shape of the graph of $y = \tan x$.

The familiar completed table below shows some values of $\tan \theta$.

θ	$\cos \theta$	$\sin \theta$	$\tan \theta$
$0°$	1	0	0
$30°$	$\frac{\sqrt{3}}{2}$	$\frac{1}{2}$	$\frac{1}{\sqrt{3}}$
$45°$	$\frac{\sqrt{2}}{2}$	$\frac{\sqrt{2}}{2}$	1
$60°$	$\frac{1}{2}$	$\frac{\sqrt{3}}{2}$	$\sqrt{3}$
$90°$	0	1	undefined
$120°$	$-\frac{1}{2}$	$\frac{\sqrt{3}}{2}$	$-\sqrt{3}$
$135°$	$-\frac{\sqrt{2}}{2}$	$\frac{\sqrt{2}}{2}$	-1
$150°$	$-\frac{\sqrt{3}}{2}$	$\frac{1}{2}$	$-\frac{1}{\sqrt{3}}$
$180°$	-1	0	0
$210°$	$-\frac{\sqrt{3}}{2}$	$-\frac{1}{2}$	$\frac{1}{\sqrt{3}}$
$225°$	$-\frac{\sqrt{2}}{2}$	$-\frac{\sqrt{2}}{2}$	1
$240°$	$-\frac{1}{2}$	$-\frac{\sqrt{3}}{2}$	$\sqrt{3}$
$270°$	0	-1	undefined
$300°$	$\frac{1}{2}$	$-\frac{\sqrt{3}}{2}$	$-\sqrt{3}$
$315°$	$\frac{\sqrt{2}}{2}$	$-\frac{\sqrt{2}}{2}$	-1
$330°$	$\frac{\sqrt{3}}{2}$	$-\frac{1}{2}$	$-\frac{1}{\sqrt{3}}$
$360°$	1	0	0

Habits of Mind

Detect the key characterisitics. Notice that the tangent function is undefined for some angles. This happens when you try to divide by 0. Look at what happens close to these points of **discontinuity**.

The discussion and graphs in Developing Habits of Mind show that $\tan x$ is the coordinate of a point related to x.

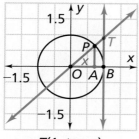

$T(1, \tan x)$

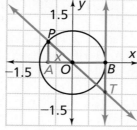

$T(1, \tan x)$

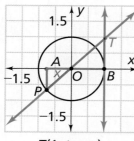

$T(1, \tan x)$

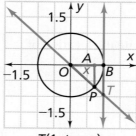

$T(1, \tan x)$

In-Class Experiment

5. Use these ideas or any other information you have to carefully draw the graph of $y = \tan x$. Label the coordinates of all points you plot.

For Discussion

6. Explain why the tangent function is periodic. What is its period?

The periods of the traffic lights are set to manage the flow of traffic.

Check Your Understanding

1. **a.** Explain why $\cos(180° + \theta) = -\cos\theta$.

   b. Explain why $\sin(180° + \theta) = -\sin\theta$.

2. Use the results from Exercise 1 to explain why $\tan(180° + \theta) = \tan\theta$.

3. Suppose θ is in Quadrant I and $\tan\theta = \frac{2}{3}$.

   a. Draw a right triangle in the unit circle to indicate the location of θ.

   b. Find the exact values of $\sin\theta$ and $\cos\theta$.

4. Suppose θ is in Quadrant I and $\tan\theta = \frac{2}{3}$.

   a. Find the value of $\tan(90° + \theta)$ in terms of $\tan\theta$.

   b. Suppose that ℓ is a line. Show that the slope of ℓ is the tangent of the angle ℓ makes with the positive x-axis.

   c. Show that two lines are perpendicular if and only if their slopes are negative reciprocals.

5. As stated at the beginning of this lesson, cosine is equal to 0 for odd multiples of 90°. Explain why this is true.

6. Find the argument of each complex number to the nearest degree.

   a. $4 + i$

   b. $(4 + i)^2$

   c. $-1 + 4i$

   d. $(-1 + 4i)^2$

7. Find each angle to the nearest degree.

   a. θ is in Quadrant I, and $\tan\theta = \frac{1}{4}$.

   b. θ is in Quadrant I, and $\tan\theta = \frac{8}{15}$.

   c. θ is in Quadrant II, and $\tan\theta = -4$.

   d. θ is in Quadrant III, and $\tan\theta = \frac{8}{15}$.

8. **a.** Calculate $(x + yi)^2$ and write the results in the form $\blacksquare + \blacksquare i$.

   b. Suppose $\tan\theta = \frac{y}{x}$. Find an expression for $\tan 2\theta$, the tangent of twice the given angle.

9. **Write About It** Give two different explanations for why $\tan \theta$ is positive when θ is in Quadrant III but negative when θ is in Quadrant II.

Go Online
www.successnetplus.com

10. **a.** What is the domain of the tangent function? Give a complete answer, not just one for angles from 0° to 360°.

   b. What is the range of the tangent function?

This graph of $y = \tan x$ may be helpful for Exercises 11–13.

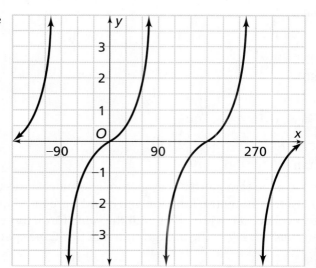

11. **a.** Approximate the solutions to the equation $\tan x = 2$.

   b. Approximate the solutions to the equation $\tan x = -2$.

12. Explain how the graph of the tangent function suggests that $\tan (180° + x) = \tan x$.

13. **Take It Further** Use the graph of $y = \tan x$ to sketch an accurate graph of the function $y = \frac{1}{\tan x}$.

Habits of Mind

Experiment. Where is tangent undefined?

14. **Standardized Test Prep** Use the equation $\tan (A + B) = \frac{\tan A + \tan B}{1 - (\tan A)(\tan B)}$. What is the value of $\tan 2\theta$ if $\tan \theta = \frac{1}{2}$?

   A. $\frac{3}{4}$ **B.** 1   **C.** $\frac{4}{3}$ **D.** 2

Maintain Your Skills

15. For each angle θ, calculate $\sin (120° + \theta)$.

   a. $\theta = 0°$ **b.** $\theta = 30°$ **c.** $\theta = 60°$ **d.** $\theta = 90°$

   e. Suppose $\sin (120° + \theta) = A \cos \theta + B \sin \theta$. Find the values of A and B.

H.21 The Angle-Sum Identities

If you look back at the results of some of the problems you have solved in this chapter, you can see a thread that has woven its way through many of them. For example, Exercise 16 from Lesson H.19 and Exercises 1 and 2 from Lesson 8.08 give some interesting identities.

For all x:

- $\sin(180° - x) = \sin x$
- $\cos(180° - x) = -\cos x$
- $\cos(360° - x) = \cos x$
- $\sin x = \cos(x - 90°)$
- $\cos x = -\sin(x - 90°)$
- $\cos(180° + x) = -\cos x$
- $\sin(180° + x) = -\sin x$
- $\tan(180° + x) = \tan x$

All of these identities have the same form. They give an alternate expression for $f(a + b)$, where f is a trigonometric function and a and b are numbers. Usually when you see a collection of identities with the same form, there are a few general identities lurking in the background that tie all the special identities together.

Habits of Mind

Look for relationships. For example, $25 - 9 = (5 + 3)(5 - 3)$, $49 - 25 = (7 + 5)(7 - 5)$, and $x^2 - 1 = (x - 1)(x + 1)$ are all special cases of the general identity $a^2 - b^2 = (a + b)(a - b)$. An important part of algebra is looking for general identities that yield many special ones.

For You to Do

Derman says, "I bet $\sin(\alpha + \beta) = \sin \alpha + \sin \beta$ for all numbers α and β."

1. Help Derman see that this is not an identity.

2. Do any values of α and β make Derman's equation work? If so, find them.

3. Is $\cos(\alpha + \beta) = \cos \alpha + \cos \beta$ an identity for all α and β? Explain.

Can you find a function f such that $f(a + b) = f(a) + f(b)$ for all numbers a and b?

So, Derman's try at a formula for $\sin(\alpha + \beta)$, while simple, is not correct. The purpose of this lesson is to come up with formulas for $\sin(\alpha + \beta)$ and $\cos(\alpha + \beta)$ that are true for all values of α and β. The main result is the following theorem.

Theorem H.9 Angle-Sum Identities

For all α and β,

- $\cos(\alpha + \beta) = \cos\alpha\cos\beta - \sin\alpha\sin\beta$
- $\sin(\alpha + \beta) = \sin\alpha\cos\beta + \cos\alpha\sin\beta$

Identities that involve functions, such as
$\cos(\alpha + \beta) = \cos\alpha\cos\beta - \sin\alpha\sin\beta$ or
$\log_2 ab = \log_2 a + \log_2 b$,
are functional equations.

Pick a Proof

This time, you will find the formula and build the proof. In this section, there are three sketches of a derivation for the formulas you want. Your job is to pick a method, study it, and write it up in your own words. You will fill in all the missing steps and explain all the statements.

Proof 1 (Rotated Triangles) This derivation uses the unit circle definitions of sine and cosine. Here you will look at sine. (You can look at cosine on your own.) In the graph below, $AD = \sin\alpha$ and $BK = \sin\beta$.

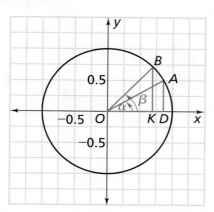

Habits of Mind

Work like a mathematician. An important part of learning mathematics is learning to read mathematics and to fill in the gaps for yourself.

You want a picture of $\sin(\alpha + \beta)$. To get an $\alpha + \beta$ in the picture, rotate $\triangle OBK$ upward through an angle of α.

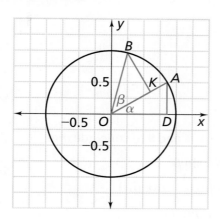

The sine of $\alpha + \beta$ is the y-height of B—the length of the perpendicular from B to the x-axis. Copy the diagram below. Make sure the segments are parallel and perpendicular to the appropriate axes.

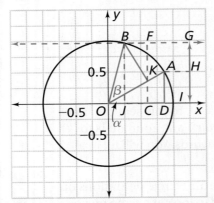

Here is where the work really starts. You need to justify these basic steps.

Step 1 $BJ = \sin(\alpha + \beta)$, $BK = \sin\beta$, and $AD = \sin\alpha$.

Step 2 Also, $KO = \cos\beta$ and $DO = \cos\alpha$.

Step 3 $\sin(\alpha + \beta) = IH + HG$

Step 4 $IH = KC$

Step 5 Now, to get KC, prove that $\triangle KCO \sim \triangle ADO$, so
$$\frac{KC}{KO} = \frac{AD}{AO}$$

Step 6 Use Steps 1 and 2 to conclude that
$$\frac{KC}{\cos\beta} = \frac{\sin\alpha}{1}$$

So, $KC = \sin\alpha \cos\beta$.

Step 7 Next, show $GH = FK$.

Step 8 To get FK, prove that $\triangle FKB \sim \triangle DOA$, so
$$\frac{FK}{BK} = \frac{DO}{AO}$$

Step 9 Use Steps 1 and 2 to conclude that
$$\frac{FK}{\sin\beta} = \frac{\cos\alpha}{1}$$

So $FK = \sin\beta \cos\alpha$.

Step 10 Now comes the grand finale. Combine Steps 3, 6, and 9 to conclude that
$$\sin(\alpha + \beta) = \sin\alpha \cos\beta + \cos\alpha \sin\beta$$

Step 11 To complete your proof, use the same diagram to prove that
$$\cos(\alpha + \beta) = \cos\alpha \cos\beta - \sin\alpha \sin\beta$$

In your description, you might want to explain why the same formulas work if α and β are in other quadrants. You can also show how some of the facts from the beginning of the lesson follow from your formulas.

Proof 2 (Coordinate Geometry) This derivation uses ideas from basic algebra (slope), geometry (coordinates and vectors), and Investigation HC of this book.

The setup is in the graph below. In this picture of the unit circle, $(r, s) = (\cos \alpha, \sin \alpha)$, and $(a, b) = (\cos \beta, \sin \beta)$.

The segment $\overline{HO}$ is perpendicular to $\overline{AO}$. The coordinates of H are $(-s, r)$.

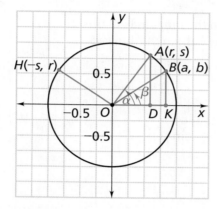

Step 1 Explain why the coordinates of H are $(-s, r)$.

Copy the graph. Now draw in some lines. Pick Q along $\overline{HO}$ such that $QO = BK$. Pick R along $\overline{AO}$ such that $RO = KO$. Then draw a line through Q parallel to $\overline{OA}$ and a line through R parallel to $\overline{OH}$. These segments intersect at S.

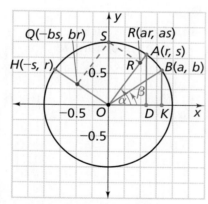

Step 2 Show that $Q = (-bs, br)$ and $R = (ar, as)$.

Step 3 Show that $S = (ar - bs, as + br)$.

Step 4 Show that S is on the circle by showing that it is 1 unit from O.

Step 5 Show that $\triangle OSR \cong \triangle OBK$. Then $m\angle SOR = \beta$ and $m\angle SOK = \alpha + \beta$.

Step 6 So, the coordinates of S are $(\cos (\alpha + b), \sin (\alpha + b))$.

Step 7 Combine steps 3 and 6 to get your formulas.

In your description, you might want to explain why the same formulas work if α and β are in other quadrants. You can also show how some of the facts from the beginning of the lesson follow from your formulas.

> **Remember...**
>
> You can use the distance formula.

Proof 3 (Complex Numbers) Previously, you saw a derivation of the fact that when you multiply two complex numbers, the length of the product is the product of the lengths of the factors. The argument (direction) of the product is the sum of the arguments of both factors.

Fact 1 $|zw| = |z| \cdot |w|$ **Fact 2** $\arg zw = \arg z + \arg w$

Step 1 Look back at this derivation and summarize it as part of your description.

The basic idea of this proof is to think of points on the unit circle in the complex plane. So, instead of $(\cos \alpha, \sin \alpha)$ and $(\cos \beta, \sin \beta)$, think of $z = \cos \alpha + i \sin \alpha$ and $w = \cos \beta + i \sin \beta$.

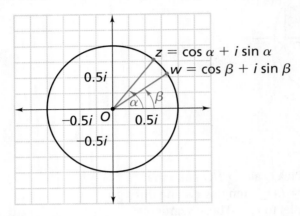

The idea is to write zw in two ways.

Step 2 Show that $|zw| = 1$. Then zw is on the unit circle.

If zw is on the unit circle, it is of the form $\cos x + i \sin x$ for some angle x. But what is the angle? By Fact 2 above, it is the sum of the angles of z and w.

$$zw = \cos(\alpha + \beta) + i \sin(\alpha + \beta)$$

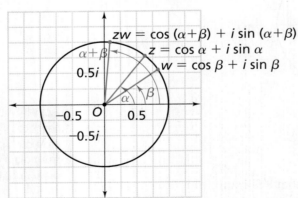

Step 3 Multiply $z = \cos \alpha + i \sin \alpha$ by $w = \cos \beta + i \sin \beta$, using the usual rules for multiplying complex numbers, to show that

$$zw = (\cos \alpha \cos \beta - \sin \alpha \sin \beta) + i (\sin \alpha \cos \beta + \cos \alpha \sin \beta)$$

Step 4 Combine the results from Steps 2 and 3 to get your formulas.

In your description, you might want to explain why the same formulas work if α and β are in other quadrants. You can also show how some of the facts from the beginning of the lesson follow from your formulas.

Exercises Practicing Habits of Mind

Check Your Understanding

1. One identity for cosine is
$$\cos(a - b) = \cos a \cos b + \sin a \sin b$$

   a. Use Exercises 11 and 12 from Lesson H.19 to derive this formula.

   b. What happens in this identity if $a = b$? Evaluate the left and right sides separately.

   c. Use this identity to find an exact value for $\cos 15°$.

2. Prove each identity by making appropriate substitutions into the angle-sum identities.

   a. $\cos 2x = \cos^2 x - \sin^2 x$

   b. $\sin 2x = 2 \sin x \cos x$

   c. $\cos 2x = 2 \cos^2 x - 1$

3. From the identity in Exercise 2c, you know $\cos 30° = 2 \cos^2 15° - 1$.
   Also, $\cos 30° = \frac{\sqrt{3}}{2}$. So if you let $z = \cos 15°$, this equation becomes
   $$\frac{\sqrt{3}}{2} = 2z^2 - 1$$

   a. Use this equation to find an exact value for $\cos 15°$.

   b. Compare your answer with the answer to Exercise 1c. Are they equal? Explain.

4. **Take It Further** Use the angle-sum identities to develop formulas for $\cos 3x$ and $\sin 3x$ in terms of $\cos x$ and $\sin x$.

5. Find a complex number z such that
   $$z^2 = \frac{1}{2} + i\frac{\sqrt{3}}{2}$$

6. Here is an interesting fact about the sine function.
   $$\sin 10° + \sin 50° = \sin 70°$$

   a. Find the values of $\sin 10°$, $\sin 50°$, and $\sin 70°$ to four decimal places. Then verify that the above equation is approximately true.

   b. For some acute angle x, $\sin 20° + \sin 40° = \sin x$. Find x.

   c. For some acute angle x, $\sin 5° + \sin 55° = \sin x$. Find x.

7. **Take It Further** Find a general result from the examples in Exercise 6. Prove it using angle-sum identities.

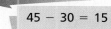

45 − 30 = 15

Habits of Mind

Visualize. Check your results from Exercise 18 in Lesson H.19.

8. Which expression is equal to $\cos(90° - \theta)$?

    A. $\cos\theta$ **B.** $-\cos\theta$ **C.** $\sin\theta$ **D.** $-\sin\theta$

9. Derive a formula for $\sin(\alpha - \beta)$ in terms of sine and cosine of α and β.

10. Use the angle-sum identities to prove the following identities.

$$\cos(180° + \theta) = -\cos\theta$$

$$\sin(180° + \theta) = -\sin\theta$$

11. Simplify each expression.

    a. $\sin(360° + x)$ **b.** $\sin(90° + x)$ **c.** $\cos(90° + x)$

    d. $\sin(90° - x)$ **e.** $\sin(180° - x)$

12. Match each function in List A with its functional equation in List B.

A	B
$x \mapsto 2^x$	$f(a + b) = f(a) + f(b)$
$z \mapsto \lvert z \rvert$	$f(a + b) = f(a)f(b)$
$z \mapsto \arg z$	$f(ab) = f(a)f(b)$
$x \mapsto 2x$	$f(ab) = f(a) + f(b)$
$x \mapsto \log_3 x$	

The matching is not one-to-one.

13. Use the angle-sum identities to find another expression for $\tan(45° + x)$.

14. Use the angle-sum identities to find a rule for $\tan(x + y)$ in terms of $\tan x$ and $\tan y$.

15. **Take It Further** Use your derivation of the formulas in Theorem H.9, adjusting the diagrams if necessary, to justify the formulas for $\cos(a - b)$ and $\sin(a - b)$.

16. **Standardized Test Prep** If $\cos 2A = \frac{5}{8}$, what is the value of $\dfrac{1}{(\cos^2 A) - (\sin^2 A)}$?

    A. -4.57 **B.** 0.31 **C.** 1.6 **D.** 4

Maintain Your Skills

17. Rewrite each expression in the form $A\cos\theta + B\sin\theta$.

    a. $\sin(30° + \theta)$ **b.** $\sin(45° + \theta)$ **c.** $\sin(60° + \theta)$

    d. $\sin(120° + \theta)$ **e.** $\sin(150° + \theta)$

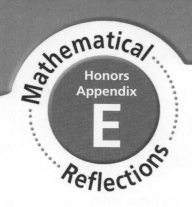

Mathematical

Honors Appendix

E

Reflections

In this investigation, you learned how to use the graphs of trigonometric functions to solve problems and to prove and use trigonometric identities. These questions will help you summarize what you have learned.

1. Sketch a graph of $y = \cos x$ for $90° \leq x \leq 180°$. Label five points on your graph with exact coordinates.

2. For each interval below, state whether $\sin x$ is *positive* or *negative* in the interval and whether its value is increasing or decreasing as x increases through the interval.

   a. $0° < x < 90°$

   b. $90° < x < 180°$

   c. $180° < x < 270°$

   d. $270° < x < 360°$

3. Sketch a picture of the unit circle. Use it to locate and label points with coordinates $(\cos 210°, \sin 210°)$ and $(1, \tan 210°)$.

4. Sketch a graph of $y = \tan x$ that shows two periods of the function.

5. Simplify each expression.

   a. $\sin(270° - x)$

   b. $\cos(180° - x)$

6. What do the graphs of the sine and cosine functions look like?

7. Why does the tangent function have a period of 180°?

8. What is a simple rule for finding the value of $\cos(90° + \theta)$?

Vocabulary

In this investigation, you learned these terms. Make sure you understand what each one means and how to use it.

• period

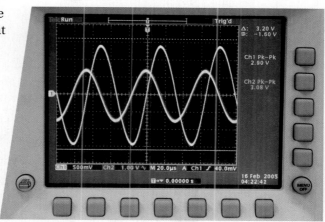

Investigation

Honors Appendix

F

Conics

In *Conics*, you will study circles, ellipses, parabolas, and hyperbolas from visual, verbal, geometrical, and analytical viewpoints.

By the end of this investigation, you will be able to answer questions like these.

1. How do you slice an infinite double cone with a plane to get a parabola?

2. What is the locus definition of a hyperbola?

3. What kind of conic section do you get when you graph $x^2 + 16y^2 - 8x + 64y + 64 = 0$? How can you identify the conic section from its equation?

You will learn how to
- visualize each of the conic sections as the intersection of a plane with an infinite double cone
- give a locus definition for each of the conic sections
- identify the equations for the graphs of the conic sections, and sketch their graphs

You will develop these habits and skills:
- Visualize the effect of different angles of intersection of a plane with an infinite double cone.
- Make connections between the different definitions of each type of conic section.
- Reason by continuity to make connections between the different types of conic section.

Parabolic curves form the surfaces of radio telescopes, freeway overpass arches, field microphones, solar ovens, and these reflectors of a solar electric generating system.

Activating Prior Knowledge
Exploring New Ideas

The intersection of a plane and a solid gives you a cross section of the solid. It is a challenging visualization habit to determine what cross section shapes are possible for different solids.

For You to Explore

1. Consider a cube.

When you take a planar slice through the cube (a smooth cut with a knife), what possible shapes could you make?

2. Consider a sphere.

> Consider the boundary of the cut as the shape of the slice. One possible shape for the slice is a square, but there are a lot more.

When you take a planar slice through the sphere, what possible shapes could you make?

3. Consider a cone that extends forever from its tip.

When you take a planar slice through the cone, what possible shapes could you make?

4. Sketch the graph of each equation.

   a. $x^2 + y^2 = 16$

   b. $x^2 - y^2 = 16$

   c. $4x^2 + y^2 = 16$

   d. $x^2 + y = 16$

5. **Take It Further** Find and graph an equation for the set of points $\frac{4}{5}$ times as far from $(5, 2)$ as they are from the line $x = 14$.

On Your Own

6. Find all solutions to the following equation.

$$\sqrt{x - 12} + \sqrt{x - 7} = 5$$

7. Sketch the graph of each equation.

a. $x^2 + y^2 = 25$

b. $(x - 3)^2 + y^2 = 25$

c. $(x + 3)^2 + y^2 = 25$

d. $(x - 1)^2 + (y + 4)^2 = 25$

e. $\dfrac{x^2}{5^2} + \dfrac{y^2}{5^2} = 1$

8. Sketch the graph of each equation.

a. $x^2 + y^2 = 1$

b. $\dfrac{x^2}{4^2} + \dfrac{y^2}{4^2} = 1$

c. $\dfrac{x^2}{3^2} + \dfrac{y^2}{5^2} = 1$

d. $\dfrac{x^2}{3^2} + \dfrac{y^2}{2^2} = 1$

e. $9x^2 + 25y^2 = 225$

Remember...

Equations are point-testers. Find some points that make the equations true.

This whispering gallery is in the Cincinnati Museum Center. To concentrate sound of one point in the hall, architects make use of the reflective properties of one of the conics. As you work through this investigation, can you guess which one?

9. You are on a camping trip. As you are returning from a hike in the woods, you see that your tent is on fire. Luckily, you are holding an empty bucket and you are near a river. You plan to run to the river to fill the bucket and then run to the tent.

Students of this text always carry a bucket when hiking.

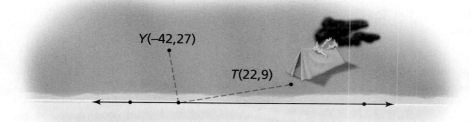

Y(–42,27)

T(22,9)

a. You found the shortest total path by reflecting your position Y over the line of the river's edge and connecting the reflected image Y' to T with a straight line. The intersection of that line and the river's edge is the point P that minimizes the path. Explain why this method produces the shortest path.

b. You also looked at contour lines for this situation. A contour line is the collection of all points P for which the path Y–P–T has the same length. What shapes are the contour lines for the burning tent problem? Why?

c. How is the contour line that contains the optimum point P that you found in part (a) positioned in relation to you, the river, and the tent? Why?

Maintain Your Skills

10. Find all solutions to the following equation.

$$\sqrt{x + 10} + \sqrt{x + 31} = 7$$

Slicing Cones

The theory of **conic sections** ties together algebra, geometry, and the analysis of functions. In this lesson, you start with the geometry and lay the foundations for the connections with other parts of mathematics.

Picture a line in space, fixed at one point, while another point on the line moves along a circle.

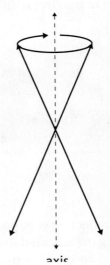

axis

The fixed point is the cone's *apex*. The rotating line is called the *generator* of the cone. The line through the apex perpendicular to the circle is the cone's *axis*.

The surface made by the moving line is an infinite double cone. Now picture a plane passing through the cone.

The plane slices the cone in a curve. That curve is a conic section. You get different kinds of curves depending on how the plane slices the cone.

In-Class Experiment

Draw sketches of the possible intersections of a plane with this infinite double cone. Classify and name your sketches. Discuss their features. Here are some questions you should answer about your intersections.

1. Is the intersection curve closed like a polygon or circle, or open like the graph of $y = x^2$?

2. Does the intersection curve have two branches like the graph of $xy = 1$ or is it a single connected curve?

3. Does the intersection curve have any symmetry?

The intersection curves look like curves you have encountered before in previous lessons. And it turns out that they are the same curves.

Facts and Notation

- The curve you get by slicing the cone with a plane that intersects only one branch of the cone is an **ellipse.**

- The curve you get by slicing the cone with a plane that is parallel to its generator is a **parabola.**

- The curve you get by slicing the cone with a plane that intersects both branches of the cone is a **hyperbola.**

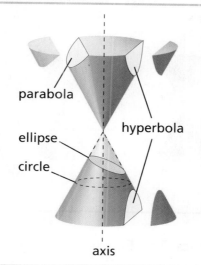

parabola

ellipse

hyperbola

circle

axis

A circle is a special kind of ellipse.

Because the plane is parallel to the generator, it only slices one branch of the cone but it does not produce an ellipse. (Why?)

It should not be obvious to you that the curve you get when you slice a cone parallel to its generator is exactly the same kind curve as the one you get when you graph $y = x^2$. Or that the oval conic section is the same kind of curve as the oval you get when you graph $4x^2 + 9y^2 - 36 = 0$. Or that the conic section called "hyperbola" has the same kind of shape as the graph of $xy = 1$. One purpose of the lessons in this investigation is to see why this is the case.

Developing Habits of Mind

Visualize. Here is an interesting thought experiment: Picture a fixed line ℓ in space, outside a cone and between the apex and the base. The line ℓ is parallel to the base of the cone. Next imagine a single plane that contains ℓ and rotates around ℓ. The plane starts out perpendicular to the axis of the cone, cutting the cone in a circle. Then it rotates down, creating a family of ellipses (increasing in size) until it is parallel to the generator, producing a parabola. It continues its rotation down, creating hyperbolas until it is parallel to the generator again (now on the opposite side of the cone).

In some sense, these conic sections are all the same.

Where did the names "ellipse," "parabola," and "hyperbola" come from? They bear a striking resemblance to the English language terms "ellipsis," "parable," and "hyperbole."

Locus Definitions for Conics: The Ellipse

Previously, you defined an ellipse with a pin and string construction. Suppose F_1 and F_2 are two fixed points—the **foci** of the ellipse—and you have a fixed length, say s. Then the ellipse with foci F_1 and F_2 and string length s is the set (locus) of all points P such that $PF_1 + PF_2 = s$.

The singular of *foci* is *focus*.

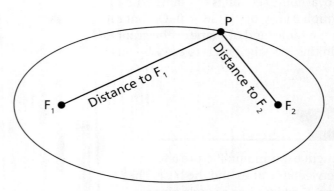

distance to F$_1$ + distance to F$_2$ = a constant

For You to Do

4. You can draw half of an ellipse by taking a string of length s and pinning its ends to F_1 and F_2. Then use a pencil to pull the string tight and trace the curve by moving the pencil, keeping tension on the string. Try it. How does the string length affect the size of the ellipse? How does the distance between the foci affect the size of the ellipse?

See the TI-Nspire™ Handbook on p. 990 for instructions about using the pin and string idea to make an ellipse with your geometry software.

You may also have a feeling that a section of a cone sliced by a plane that only cuts one branch of the cone and is not parallel to the generator is an ellipse.

A proof by the French mathematician Germinal Dandelin shows why this is so. Begin with a cone that a plane has passed through. Now imagine placing two spheres in this cone. Put the first one into the top of the cone, big enough so it just touches the sides of the cone and just touches the plane in only one spot—it is tangent to both the cone and the plane. Then put a larger sphere into the cone under the ellipse. Again make this sphere just the right size, so it is tangent to the cone and to the plane of the ellipse.

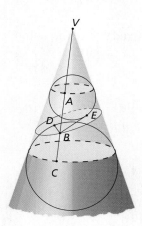

Pass a straight line down the surface of the cone, beginning at the apex V. Label the points of intersection with the smaller sphere, the plane, and the larger sphere A, B, and C in the figure above. Point D is the point where the larger sphere is tangent to the plane. Point E is the point where the smaller sphere is tangent to the plane. $BA = BE$ because $\overrightarrow{BA}$ and $\overrightarrow{BE}$ each emanates from B and are tangent to the smaller sphere.

For this same reason $BC = BD$, because both $\overrightarrow{BC}$ and $\overrightarrow{BD}$ are tangent to the larger sphere.

No matter what line you choose to draw from V, the lengths VA and VC are invariant. Note that since this is so, AC, the difference between VA and VC, is also invariant. Also note that $AC = BA + BC$. Since $BA = BE$ and $BC = BD$ then $BA + BC = BD + BE$. $BA + BC$ is constant so this means that $BD + BE$ must also be constant. So an ellipse must be a set of all points in the plane, such that the sum of the distances from two fixed points (E and D) remains constant.

Locus Definitions for Conics: The Parabola and the Hyperbola

There are similar ways to show that the other two conics have locus properties.

- A hyperbola is the set of points such that the absolute value of the difference of the distances from two fixed points is constant.

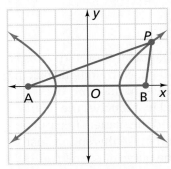

|PA − PB| = Constant

See the TI-Nspire Handbook on p. 990 for instructions to use the locus definition to draw a hyperbola and a parabola in your dynamic geometry environment.

Why did you not need the absolute value in the definition of the ellipse?

- A parabola is the set of points equidistant from a fixed point and a line.

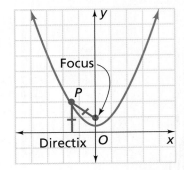

A hyperbola has two foci. A parabola has only one. The fixed line in the parabola definition is called its **directrix**.

Dandelin showed that the cone slices that you call parabola and hyperbola are the same ones that satisfy the locus descriptions above, using the same idea of putting spheres around the slicing planes. The spheres are now called Dandelin spheres. The arguments are the same in spirit, but they are considerably more complicated.

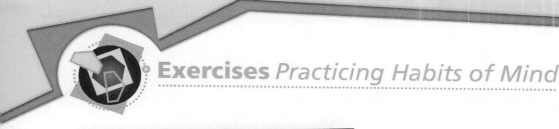

Exercises *Practicing Habits of Mind*

Check Your Understanding

1. **a.** Using the pin-and-string model, draw an ellipse that closely resembles a circle.

   b. Using the same string but different pin locations, draw an ellipse that does not resemble a circle.

   c. Where might you place the pins to draw a circle?

   The locus definition of an ellipse uses two points F_1 and F_2, the foci, and a distance s. The ellipse is the set of points P with $PF_1 + PF_2 = s$.

2. Consider foci $F_1(3, 0)$ and $F_2(-3, 0)$, and the distance $s = 10$.

   a. Find the two values of b so that $(0, b)$ is on the ellipse.

   b. Find the two values of a so that $(a, 0)$ is on the ellipse.

   c. Is the point $(2, 3)$ on the ellipse? Explain how you know.

   d. Write an equation that you could use to test whether or not any point (x, y) is on the ellipse.

3. The lesson shows what the two Dandelin spheres look like after slicing a double-cone to produce an ellipse. Suppose you slice a double cone to produce a circle. Describe what the two Dandelin spheres look like. Also, describe the points where the Dandelin spheres touch the sliced circle.

Go **Online**
www.successnetplus.com

4. By its locus definition, a hyperbola is the set of points such that the absolute value of the difference of the distances from two fixed points is constant. Suppose the two points are $F_1 = (3, 0)$ and $F_2 = (-3, 0)$, with the fixed difference $d = 4$.

   a. Find five points that are on this hyperbola.

   b. Sketch a graph of the hyperbola.

   c. **Take It Further** Find an equation for the graph of the hyperbola.

5. **What's Wrong Here?** Joachim decides to make a hyperbola with fixed points $A(3, 0)$ and $B(-3, 0)$, and the fixed difference $d = 10$. But he is having trouble finding points that work. Why?

On Your Own

6. On the coordinate plane, a parabola has focus $(1, 0)$ and directrix with equation $x = -1$. Which of these points is on the parabola?

   A. $(1, 1.5)$ **B.** $(1.5, 2.5)$ **C.** $(2.25, 3)$ **D.** $(9, 36)$

7. Find three points on the parabola with focus $(1, 0)$ and directrix with equation $x = -1$. Do not use points listed in Exercise 6.

8. Find a given each condition.

   a. $(1, a)$ is on the parabola with focus $(1, 0)$ and directrix with equation $x = -1$.

   b. $(a, 1)$ is on the parabola with focus $(1, 0)$ and directrix with equation $x = -1$.

9. Find an equation of the parabola with focus $(1, 0)$ and directrix with equation $x = -1$.

10. One equation for an ellipse with foci $(3, 0)$ and $(-3, 0)$ and string length $s = 10$ is

$$\sqrt{(x - 3)^2 + y^2} + \sqrt{(x + 3)^2 + y^2} = 10$$

   a. Write another equation that must also be true but only involves a single square root. Proceed as follows. Move one square root to the other side. Square both sides. Simplify the equation as much as possible.

   b. Show that you can simplify the equation above to

$$\frac{x^2}{25} + \frac{y^2}{16} = 1$$

11. **Take It Further** In Exercise 2 you found an equation for an ellipse with foci $(3, 0)$ and $(-3, 0)$ and string length $s = 10$.

   a. Find an equation for the ellipse with the same foci, but leave string length as a variable s.

   b. If $s = 20$, find several points on the ellipse.

   c. Sketch the graph of the ellipse when $s = 20$.

   d. Sketch the graph of the ellipse when $s = 8$.

   e. Sketch the graph when $s = 6$.

12. **Standardized Test Prep** Which of the following points is on the parabola with focus $(3, 4)$ and directrix $y = 5$?

   A. $(-3, 4)$ **B.** $(0, 0)$ **C.** $(3, 3)$ **D.** $(5, 4)$

Habits of Mind

Represent the situation. Equations are point testers.

Go Online
www.successnetplus.com

Maintain Your Skills

13. Sketch the graph of each equation.

   a. $x^2 + y^2 - 2x + 4y - 4 = 0$ b. $x^2 + y^2 - 2x + 4y = 0$

   c. $x^2 + y^2 - 2x + 4y + 4 = 0$ d. $x^2 + y^2 - 2x + 4y + 5 = 0$

   e. $x^2 + y^2 - 2x + 4y + 9 = 0$

H.24 Conics at the Origin

The words *ellipse, parabola,* and *hyperbola* showed up in your previous courses in another context. You gave these names to graphs of certain equations. In this lesson, you will find general forms for equations for each of the conics when you put them on the coordinate plane. These equations will connect to the curves you already know about.

Equations for Parabolas

You already found an equation for one parabola in Exercise 9 from the previous lesson. Suppose $c \neq 0$. Consider the parabola with focus $(0, c)$ and directrix with equation $y = -c$.

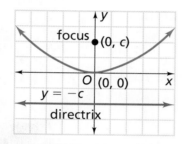

The origin is on this parabola because it is equidistant from the focus and the directrix. In fact, the parabola looks like the graph of a quadratic function with vertex $(0, 0)$.

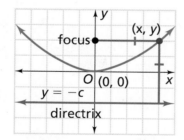

What is the point-tester for this graph? You want the distance from (x, y) to the point $(0, c)$ to be the same as the distance from (x, y) to the line $y = -c$. That gives you

$$\sqrt{x^2 + (y - c)^2} = |y + c|$$

This is fine as a point-tester. For example, $(2c, c)$ is on the graph because

$$\sqrt{(2c)^2 + (c - c)^2} = |c + c|$$

as you can check.

For You to Do

1. Find all values of x so that (x, c) is on the parabola.

> In the figures that accompany this derivation, $c > 0$. The same derivation works if $c < 0$. Try it.

You can simplify the equation in ways that will make it look familiar.

$$\sqrt{x^2 + (y - c)^2} = |y + c| \qquad \text{Square both sides.}$$
$$x^2 + (y - c)^2 = (y + c)^2 \qquad \text{Expand.}$$
$$x^2 + y^2 - 2cy + c^2 = y^2 + 2cy + c^{2°} \quad \text{Cancel and simplify.}$$
$$x^2 = 4cy$$

Theorem H.10

An equation for the parabola with focus (0, c) and directrix with equation $y = -c$ is

$$x^2 = 4cy$$

This should look familiar. In earlier courses, you wrote it as

$$y = \frac{1}{4c} x^2$$

So, your parabola is the graph of the quadratic function $f(x) = \frac{1}{4c} x^2$.

Example

Problem A favorite quadratic curve has equation $y = x^2$.

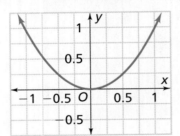

It has a focus and directrix. What are they?

Solution You can read the information from the general equation

$$x^2 = 4cy$$

In this equation, $4c = 1$ so $c = \frac{1}{4}$. Hence the focus of the standard parabola is $\left(0, \frac{1}{4}\right)$ and its directrix has equation $y = -\frac{1}{4}$.

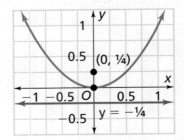

For Discussion

2. Find the equation of the parabola with focus $(c, 0)$ and directrix with equation $x = -c$.

Equations for Ellipses

Suppose an ellipse has foci $(c, 0)$ and $(-c, 0)$ and has string length is s.

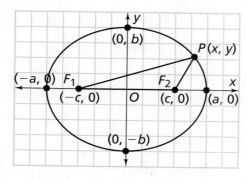

> **Remember...**
>
> An ellipse is the set of points such that the sum of the distances to two fixed foci is constant.

Facts and Notation

- The **center** of the ellipse is the origin.

- The ellipse has two lines of symmetry. They intersect the interior of the ellipse in two segments. The longer segment is called the **major axis** for the ellipse and the shorter segment is called the **minor axis.**

- The endpoints of the axes for the ellipse are sometimes called the **vertices** of the ellipse. Label the vertices $(a, 0)$, $(-a, 0)$, $(0, b)$ and $(0, -b)$.

- For any point P on the ellipse with foci F_1 and F_2 and string length s, $PF_1 + PF_2 = s$.

> **Habits of Mind**
>
> **Explore the possibilities.** Can an ellipse have major and minor axes of the same length?

What is the point-tester for this ellipse? The "sum of distances is constant" becomes, in this notation

$$\sqrt{(x - c)^2 + y^2} + \sqrt{(x + c)^2 + y^2} = 2a$$

This is a perfectly good point-tester, but you can simplify it. Isolate the radicals.

$$\sqrt{(x - c)^2 + y^2} = 2a - \sqrt{(x + c)^2 + y^2}$$

Square both sides.

$$(x - c)^2 + y^2 = 4a^2 - 4a\sqrt{(x + c)^2 + y^2} + (x + c)^2 + y^2$$

$s = 2a$

Expand a little and isolate again.

$$x^2 - 2cx + c^2 + y^2 = 4a^2 - 4a\sqrt{x^2 + 2cx + c^2 + y^2} + x^2 + 2cx + c^2 + y^2$$

so

$$-4cx - 4a^2 = -4a\sqrt{x^2 + 2cx + c^2 + y^2}$$

or

$$cx + a^2 = a\sqrt{x^2 + 2cx + c^2 + y^2}$$

Now square both sides once more.

$$c^2x^2 + 2a^2cx + a^4 = a^2x^2 + 2a^2cx + a^2c^2 + a^2y^2$$

The $2a^2cx$ cancels. You can rearrange terms to look like this.

$$a^4 - a^2c^2 = (a^2 - c^2)x^2 + a^2y^2$$

or

$$a^2(a^2 - c^2) = (a^2 - c^2)x^2 + a^2y^2$$

But $a^2 = b^2 + c^2$, so $a^2 - c^2 = b^2$. So the equation simplifies to

$$a^2b^2 = b^2x^2 + a^2y^2$$

It is often useful to divide both sides of this equation by a^2b^2 to get

$$1 = \frac{x^2}{a^2} + \frac{y^2}{b^2}$$

Theorem H.11

The ellipse with foci $(c, 0)$ and $(-c, 0)$ and string length $2a$ has equation

$$1 = \frac{x^2}{a^2} + \frac{y^2}{b^2} \quad \text{where} \quad b^2 = a^2 - c^2.$$

Developing Habits of Mind

Understand the process. A careful proof of this theorem would require you to show that you did not gain or lose any points when you went from the raw point-tester to the equation in the theorem. There is some work to do here, because you squared both sides of the equation twice, making it possible for extra solutions to creep in. Make sure every step is reversible.

For Discussion

3. Discuss what happens to the graph of the equation $1 = \dfrac{x^2}{a^2} + \dfrac{y^2}{b^2}$ as a gets closer and closer to b.

4. Find an equation for the ellipse with foci at $(0, c)$ and $(0, -c)$ and string length $2a$.

Equations for Hyperbolas

Consider a hyperbola with foci $F_1(c, 0)$ and $F_2(-c, 0)$ defined by the condition

$$|PF_1 - PF_2| = s$$

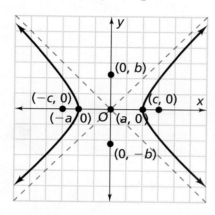

Facts and Notation

- The points **(a, 0)** and **(−a, 0)** are the *vertices* of the hyperbola. Therefore, **s = 2a**. The segment connecting the vertices is the hyperbola's *major axis*.

- The constant *b* is defined by the equation $a^2 + b^2 = c^2$.

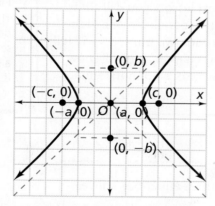

You can construct *b* by creating a rectangle around the origin with sides parallel to the axes, one side of length **2a**, and diagonals of length **2c**. The vertical side of the rectangle is **2b**. The segment connecting **(0, b)** to **(0, −b)** is the hyperbola's *minor axis*.

> The diagonals of this little rectangle have an interesting relationship to the hyperbola. You will explore that relationship in the exercises.

The point-tester for the hyperbola is $|PF_1 - PF_2| = 2a$. In terms of coordinates, this translates into

$$\left| \sqrt{(x + c)^2 + y^2} - \sqrt{(x - c)^2 + y^2} \right| = 2a$$

This is a perfectly good point-tester. But you can simplify it considerably using exactly the same algebraic technique that you used to derive the equation of the ellipse. You will take care of the details in Exercise 12.

Well, there is one complication that you did not have with the ellipse: the absolute value. But you can avoid this by treating one branch of the hyperbola at a time. In the end, both equations come out the same.

Theorem H.12

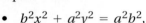

The hyperbola with foci $(c, 0)$ and $(-c, 0)$ and constant difference $2a$ has equation

$$1 = \frac{x^2}{a^2} - \frac{y^2}{b^2}$$

where $b^2 = c^2 - a^2$.

Developing Habits of Mind

Generalize. You now have equations for all three conics, at least when they are placed on the coordinate plane in certain positions. The three equations

- $b^2x^2 + a^2y^2 = a^2b^2$,
- $b^2x^2 - a^2y^2 = a^2b^2$, and
- $x^2 = 4cy$

are all special cases of the following general quadratic equation in two variables.

$$rx^2 + sxy + ty^2 + ux + vy + w = 0$$

where r, s, t, u, v, and w are real numbers. In the next lesson, you will show that if $s = 0$, the equation's graph is a conic with axis parallel to one of the coordinate axes. In fact, a very simple calculation with two numbers will tell you what kind of a conic it is. In the project for this chapter, you will show that even if $s \neq 0$, the graph is a conic, although its axis is not horizontal or vertical.

Habits of Mind

Find relationships. This predictive power—being able to tell the shape of a graph from a simple calculation— is something that mathematicians prize.

For You to Do

5. Find the values of r, s, t, u, v, and w in each of the three equations above.

Check Your Understanding

1. Many different ellipses have centers at the origin and pass through the point $(0, 5)$.

   a. Show that the ellipse with equation $25x^2 + 169y^2 = 4225$ passes through $(0, 5)$.

   b. Find four other points on the ellipse from part (a).

   c. Show that the length of the major axis is 26.

   d. The foci of this ellipse are $(c, 0)$ and $(-c, 0)$. Find the value of c.

   e. Sketch a graph of this ellipse.

2. The ellipse with equation $25x^2 + 9y^2 = 225$ also has its center at the origin and passes through $(0, 5)$.

   a. Find four other points on this ellipse.

   b. Show that the length of the major axis is 10.

   c. The foci of this ellipse are $(0, c)$ and $(0, -c)$. Find the value of c.

   d. Sketch a graph of this ellipse.

3. **Write About It** Describe, as completely as possible, how to find the foci and sketch the graph of
   $$1 = \frac{x^2}{a^2} + \frac{y^2}{b^2}$$

   Be careful to describe cases where $a > b$, $a = b$, and $a < b$.

4. The graph of the equation $y^2 - 9x^2 = 36$ is a hyperbola.

   a. Show that the points $(0, 6)$ and $(0, -6)$ are on the hyperbola.

   b. If $x = 1$, find approximate values of y to four decimal places.

   c. If $x = 5$, find approximate values of y to four decimal places.

   d. If $x = 100$, find approximate values of y to four decimal places.

   e. As x grows larger, what relationship is there between the x- and y-coordinates of points on the hyperbola?

5. In Exercise 4, you worked with the equation

$$y^2 - 9x^2 = 36$$

A slight change to this equation can produce very different results.

a. Sketch the graph of $y^2 - 9x^2 = 9$. How is the graph similar to the one from Exercise 4. How is it different?

b. Sketch the graph of $y^2 - 9x^2 = 1$.

c. Sketch the graph of $y^2 - 9x^2 = 0$.

6. Take It Further The following equation gives the distance from a point (x, y) to the line with equation $x + y = 10$.

$$D = \frac{|x + y - 10|}{\sqrt{2}}$$

a. Find an equation for the parabola with focus at the origin and with directrix with equation $x + y = 10$.

b. Find the two points on the graph with x-coordinate -5.

c. Sketch the graph of this parabola.

Habits of Mind

Recall what you know.
What techniques can you use when one side of an equation is set equal to zero?

Go Online
www.successnetplus.com

On Your Own

7. Find an equation for the parabola with focus $(-2, 0)$ and directrix with equation $x = 2$.

8. The graph of the following equation is a hyperbola.

$$\frac{x^2}{16} - \frac{y^2}{9} = 1$$

a. If (x, y) is on this hyperbola, then so are $(-x, y)$, $(-x, -y)$ and $(x, -y)$. Explain.

b. Copy and complete this table to find the nonnegative value of y for each value of x. Approximate your results to four decimal places.

x	y
3	undefined
4	0
5	■
6	■
8	■
10	■
20	■
40	■
100	■
1000	■

c. As x grows larger, what relationship is there between the x- and y-coordinates of points on the hyperbola?

9. Show that every point on the graph of $y = x^2$ is equidistant from the focus $\left(0, \frac{1}{4}\right)$ and the directrix with equation $y = -\frac{1}{4}$.

10. Consider the equation $1 = \frac{x^2}{9} + \frac{y^2}{4}$.

  a. Find all values of x if $(x, 0)$ is on the graph of the equation.

  b. Find all values of y if $(0, y)$ is on the graph of the equation.

  c. Sketch the graph of the equation.

  d. Find all values of x if (x, x) is on the graph of the equation.

  e. Find three points that are close to being on the graph but not actually on it.

11. **Take It Further** An ellipse has foci $(8, -6)$ and $(-6, 8)$ and string length 20.

  a. Show that this ellipse passes through the origin.

  b. Find the center of the ellipse.

  c. Find the endpoints of the major axis.

  d. Find an equation of the ellipse.

  e. Sketch the graph of the ellipse.

The major axis contains the foci. It has the same length as the string length.

12. Prove Theorem 6.5, which gives an equation for a hyperbola.

13. **Standardized Test Prep** Which of the following are the foci of the ellipse with equation $\frac{x^2}{25} + \frac{y^2}{9} = 1$?

  A. $(-1, 0), (1, 0)$ **B.** $(-2, 0), (2, 0)$

  C. $(-3, 0), (3, 0)$ **D.** $(-4, 0), (4, 0)$

Maintain Your Skills

14. Each of these is the equation of a parabola. For each, find the coordinates of the focus and an equation of the directrix.

  a. $y = \frac{1}{4}x^2$ **b.** $x = \frac{1}{4}y^2$ **c.** $y = -\frac{1}{4}x^2$

  d. $x = -\frac{1}{4}y^2$ **e.** $y = 2x^2$ **f.** $x = 2y^2$

In this lesson, you will look at equations for conics where the center (or vertex, for the parabola) is not at the origin.

You looked at various affine transformations of parabolas in earlier lessons. The ideas here are exactly the same. It is easiest to understand the general methods through examples.

Example 1

Problem Find equation of the ellipse $\mathcal{E}$ with foci at (3, 16) and (3, −8) and with string length 26.

Solution The situation looks like this.

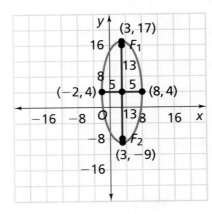

The center of an ellipse is the midpoint of the segment connecting its foci, so the center of this ellipse is (3, 4). The major axis is vertical and the distance from the center to each focus is $c = 12$. Since the string length is 26, $a = 13$ and the vertices are at (3, 4 + 13) = (3, 17) and (3, 4 − 13) = (3, −9).

Since $a^2 = b^2 + c^2$, $b = 5$. So the minor axis connects (−2, 4) to (8, 4).

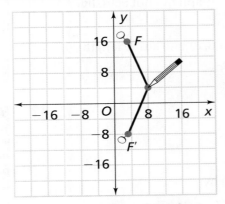

This ellipse $\mathcal{E}$ is a translation of an ellipse $\mathcal{E}'$, centered at the origin with foci located at $(0, 12)$ and $(0, -12)$ and string length 26.

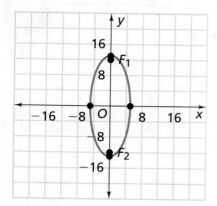

You already know how to find an equation of ellipse centered at the origin. An equation for $\mathcal{E}'$ is

$$\frac{x^2}{25} + \frac{y^2}{169} = 1$$

How can you use this equation to find an equation of the ellipse centered at $(3, 4)$? Notice that the distance from any point (x, y) to $(3, 16)$ is the same as the distance from $(x - 3, y - 4)$ to $(3 - 3, 16 - 4) = (0, 12)$. (Why?) Similarly, the distance from any point (x, y) to $(3, -8)$ is the same as the distance from $(x - 3, y - 4)$ to $(3 - 3, -8 - 4) = (0, -12)$. So, the sum of the distances from (x, y) to $(3, 16)$ and $(3, -8)$ is the same as the sum of the distances from $(x - 3, y - 4)$ to $(0, 12)$ and $(0, -12)$. In particular, it follows that (x, y) is on $\mathcal{E}$ if and only if $(x - 3, y - 4)$ is on $\mathcal{E}'$.

So, the point-tester for $\mathcal{E}$ is "See if $(x - 3, y - 4)$ is on $\mathcal{E}'$." That is the same as "See if $(x - 3, y - 4)$ satisfies the equation for $\mathcal{E}'$." In other words, check to see if

$$\frac{(x - 3)^2}{25} + \frac{(y - 4)^2}{169} = 1$$

So this is an equation for the ellipse $\mathcal{E}$.

Habits of Mind

Use what you know. You have done translations of basic graphs for quite a while now. Conic sections work the same way.

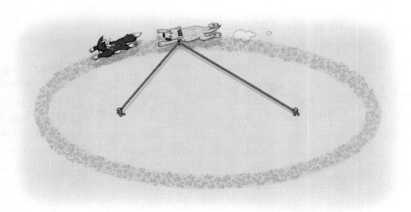

Developing Habits of Mind

Simplify complicated problems. In the above example, you could have gone right to the locus definition. The point $P = (x, y)$ is on $\mathcal{E}$ if and only if the sum of the distances from P to the foci is 26, so the point-tester is

$$\sqrt{(x-3)^2 + (y-16)^2} + \sqrt{(x-3)^2 + (y+8)^2} = 26$$

To simplify this, you would have to face some hefty algebra (similar to what you did in the proof of Theorem H.11). But using the translation idea reduces the problem to one you have already solved and eliminates the need for the complex calculations.

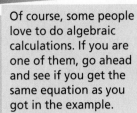

Of course, some people love to do algebraic calculations. If you are one of them, go ahead and see if you get the same equation as you got in the example.

For Discussion

1. Suppose $F_1 = (1, 1)$ and $F_2 = (11, 1)$. Find an equation of the hyperbola defined by

$$|PF_1 - PF_2| = 8$$

Minds in Action

Tony and Sasha are looking at the example above

Sasha   I'm one of those people who loves algebra. I think I'll see what our equation

$$\frac{(x-3)^2}{25} + \frac{(y-4)^2}{169} = 1$$

looks like if I expand everything and put it in normal form.

Tony   Be my guest.

Sasha pulls out some chalk and begins to write on the board. A few minutes later, she smiles at her work.

Sasha   I get

$$169x^2 - 1014x + 25y^2 - 200y - 2304 = 0$$

Tony   I wonder how we could have graphed the ellipse if we had been given this equation.

Habits of Mind

Find a process. How would you help Tony answer his question?

Example 2

Problem Is the graph of

$$9y^2 + 18y - 16x^2 + 64x - 199 = 0$$

a conic? If so, what kind is it?

See the TI-Nspire Handbook on p. 990 for ideas about how to use your calculator to graph the equation.

Solution Complete the square in x and y on the left side so that you can write the equation in terms of $x - r$ and $y - s$ for some constants r and s.

$$9y^2 + 18y - 16x^2 + 64x - 199 = 0$$
$$9y^2 + 18y - 16x^2 + 64x = 199$$
$$9(y^2 + 2y + ?) - 16(x^2 - 4x + ??) = 199 + 9 \cdot ? - 16 \cdot ??$$
$$9(y^2 + 2y + 1) - 16(x^2 - 4x + 4) = 199 + 9 \cdot 1 - 16 \cdot 4$$
$$9(y + 1)^2 - 16(x - 2)^2 = 199 + 9 - 64$$
$$9(y + 1)^2 - 16(x - 2)^2 = 144$$

So the equation is

$$9(y + 1)^2 - 16(x - 2)^2 = 144$$

Divide both sides by 144 to get

$$\frac{(y + 1)^2}{16} - \frac{(x - 2)^2}{9} = 1$$

The graph is a hyperbola with center $(2, -1)$.

Developing Habits of Mind

Generalize. This method will work on any equation of the form

$$rx^2 + ty^2 + ux + vy + w = 0$$

and the result will tell you what kind of a conic the graph is. When you complete the square on the left side and simplify, you will get an equation of the form

$$r(x - h)^2 + t(x - k)^2 = c$$

for constants h, k, and c.

The graph might be a degenerate conic—a point or a pair of lines, for example. See the Maintain Your Skills exercises from Lesson H.23.

For Discussion

Suppose the conic is not degenerate. Discuss each statement.

2. If either r or t is 0, the graph is a parabola.

3. If r and t have the same sign, the graph is an ellipse.

4. If r and t have opposite signs, the graph is a hyperbola.

A little more work produces the following classification theorem.

To a mathematician a classification theorem is truly a thing of beauty.

Theorem H.13

The graph of

$$rx^2 + ty^2 + ux + vy + w = 0$$

is a (possibly degenerate) conic. In fact, the nature of the conic is determined by the sign of rt:

- If $rt > 0$, the graph is an ellipse.
- If $rt = 0$, the graph is a parabola.
- If $rt < 0$, the graph is a hyperbola.

For You to Do

5. How can you tell from the equation if the graph is a circle?

6. How can you tell from the equation if the graph is a single point?

Educators and scientists use ripple tanks to discover and demonstrate the additive and subtractive properties of combinations of waves in a shallow basin of water. Here the spreading rings of drops of liquid produce interference patterns. Such patterns are the common conic sections you studied in this chapter.

Check Your Understanding

1. The graph of the following equation is a hyperbola.

$$\frac{(x-3)^2}{16} - \frac{(y-2)^2}{9} = 1$$

> The hyperbola is related to the one from Exercise 8 of Lesson H.24.

a. What is the center of the hyperbola?

b. Copy and complete this table to find the nonnegative value of *y* for each value of *x*. Approximate your results to four decimal places.

x	y
6	undefined
7	2
8	■
9	■
11	■
13	■
23	■
43	■
103	■
1003	■

c. As *x* grows larger, what relationship is there between the *x*- and *y*-coordinates of points on the hyperbola?

2. The graph of the equation

$$9(x-3)^2 + 16(y+2)^2 = N$$

depends on the value of *N*.

a. Sketch the graph when *N* = 144.

b. Does the ellipse you drew in part (a) pass through the origin?

c. Sketch the graph when *N* = 36.

d. Sketch the graph when *N* = 0.

e. Sketch the graph when *N* = −144.

f. Find all values of *N* such that the graph passes through the point (13, −1).

3. a. Is the graph of $25x^2 - 4y^2 + 150x + 32y + 61 = 0$ a conic? If so, what kind is it?

   b. Sketch the graph of the equation.

4. a. Is the graph of $4x^2 + 25y^2 - 16x + 250y + 641 = 0$ a conic? If so, what kind is it?

   b. Sketch the graph of the equation.

5. The graph of $\dfrac{(x+3)^2}{4} - \dfrac{(y-2)^2}{16} = 1$ is not the graph of a function, but it can be the union of two function graphs.

   a. Solve the equation above for $(y-2)^2$.

   b. Why is it not possible to uniquely solve for y?

   c. Write y as two functions. Plot each function. Then combine them to sketch the entire hyperbola.

6. Sketch an accurate graph of these two equations on the same axes.

$$\frac{(x-3)^2}{16} - \frac{(y-2)^2}{9} = 1$$

$$\frac{(x-3)^2}{16} - \frac{(y-2)^2}{9} = 0$$

7. Take It Further Find an equation of a hyperbola that is the graph of all points P with

$$|PF_1 - PF_2| = 2\sqrt{2}$$

with foci $F_1 = (\sqrt{2}, \sqrt{2})$ and $F_2 = (-\sqrt{2}, -\sqrt{2})$.

On Your Own

8. Explain why the equation $\dfrac{(x+5)^2}{16} + \dfrac{(y-3)^2}{9} = -1$ has no graph, but the equation $\dfrac{(x+5)^2}{16} - \dfrac{(y-3)^2}{9} = -1$ does.

9. Consider the equation

$$\dfrac{(x-11)^2}{36} + \dfrac{(y+14)^2}{25} = 1$$

    a. What possible values of x could make the equation true? Explain.

    b. What possible values of y could make the equation true?

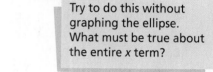

Try to do this without graphing the ellipse. What must be true about the entire x term?

10. Consider the equation $\dfrac{(x+9)^2}{49} - \dfrac{(y-5)^2}{16} = 1$.

    a. What possible values of x could make the equation true? Explain.

    b. What possible values of y could make the equation true?

11. Find the coordinates of the foci of the ellipse with equation
$$36x^2 + 11y^2 - 288x - 110y + 455 = 0$$

12. **What's Wrong Here?** Pam thought about stretching an ellipse.

    Pam: You can stretch these ellipses in any direction, and everything moves along. If you double the length of an axis, I think you'll double the distance between the foci, too.

    a. Give an example that shows Pam's conjecture is not correct.

    b. Can you stretch an ellipse to double the distance? Explain.

13. An ellipse is centered at (3, 5) and (10, 5) is one of its foci.

    a. Find the coordinates of the other focus.

    b. If the point (1, 17) is on the ellipse, find the length of the major and minor axes. Find an equation for the ellipse.

14. Show algebraically that the sum of the distances from (x, y) to (3, 16) and (3, −8) is the same as the sum of the distances from $(x − 3, y − 4)$ to (0, 12) and (0, −12).

15. **Standardized Test Prep** Which of the following is a hyperbola with foci at (3, 4) and (3, −4) and vertices 6 units apart?

    A. $\dfrac{(x − 3)^2}{9} − \dfrac{(y − 4)^2}{16} = 1$

    B. $\dfrac{(x − 3)^2}{9} − \dfrac{y^2}{7} = 1$

    C. $\dfrac{(y − 4)^2}{9} − \dfrac{x^2}{16} = 1$

    D. $\dfrac{y^2}{9} − \dfrac{(x − 3)^2}{7} = 1$

Maintain Your Skills

16. An ellipse has center (2, −1) and one vertex is (6, −1).

    a. Find the coordinates of the other vertex.

    b. Find the foci if (2, 0) is one of the endpoints of the minor axis.

    c. Find the foci if (2, 1) is one of the endpoints of the minor axis.

    d. Find the foci if (2, 2) is one of the endpoints of the minor axis.

    e. Find the foci if (2, 3) is one of the endpoints of the minor axis.

    f. Find the foci if (2, 4) is one of the endpoints of the minor axis.

In this investigation, you sliced a cone to get a conic section—a circle, an ellipse, a parabola, or a hyperbola. You described each conic section verbally as a locus of points, or algebraically by an equation. Then, given an equation, you described its graph as a conic section. The following questions will help you summarize what you have learned.

1. Determine an equation (in the form $y = a(x - h)^2 + k$) for the parabola having focus (1, 2) and directrix the x-axis.

2. Find the center, foci, and the lengths of the major and minor axes of the ellipse having equation $16x^2 - 64x + 25y^2 + 50y = 311$.

3. We know from Theorem 6.6 that the graph of the equation $rx^2 + ty^2 + ux + vy + w = 0$ is a conic. In order for the conic to be a circle, what must be the relationship between r and t?

4. **a.** In order for the graph of the equation $2x^2 + cy^2 + 4x + 4cy + f = 0$ to be an ellipse, what must be true about the value of c?

   b. In order for the graph of the equation $2x^2 + cy^2 + 4x + 4cy + f = 0$ to be a nondegenerate ellipse, what must be true about the value of f?

5. Explain how you know that the graph of the equation $x^2 + y^2 - 2x + 4y + 5 = 0$ is a degenerate conic.

6. How do you slice an infinite double cone with a plane to get a parabola?

7. What is the locus definition of a hyperbola?

8. What kind of conic section do you get when you graph $x^2 + 16y^2 - 8x + 64y + 64 = 0$? How can you identify the conic section from its equation?

Vocabulary

In this investigation, you learned these terms. Make sure you understand what each one means and how to use it.

- center
- conic sections
- directrix
- ellipse
- focus, foci
- hyperbola
- major axis
- minor axis
- parabola
- vertex

Recognizing how to use technology to support your mathematics is an important habit of mind. Although the use of technology in this course is independent of any particular hardware or software, this handbook gives examples of how you can apply the TI-Nspire™ handheld technology.

Graphing an Equation

1. Use the **Text** tool in the **Actions** menu. Write the equation. Press **enter**.

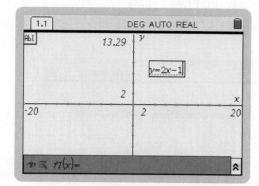

2. Position the cursor on the equation. Press **ctrl** **✺** to grab it. Drag the equation to the axes. Press **enter**.

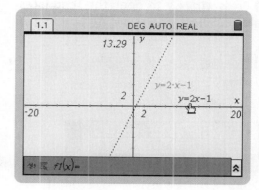

Modeling a Function

1. Choose **Define** from the **Actions** menu (or type **DEFINE**).

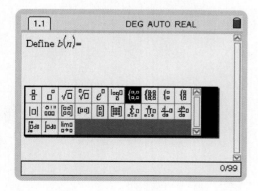

2. Type the function. Press **enter**.

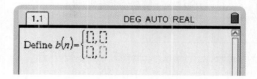

Modeling a Recursive Function I

1. Choose **Define** from the **Actions** menu. Name the function by typing **B**(**N**)**=**. Press **ctrl** **X** to open the Templates palette. Select **⊞**. Press **enter**.

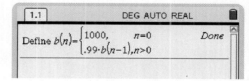

2. Enter the function. Press **tab** to move from box to box. Press **enter** when done.

Modeling a Recursive Function II

1. Choose **Define** from the **Actions** menu. Name the function by typing  ⊜.Press **ctrl** **✕** to open the Templates palette. Select ⊞. Press **enter**.

2. Select the number of pieces in the definition. Press **enter**.

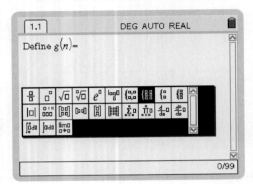

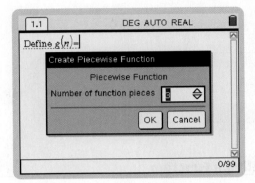

3. Enter the function. Press **tab** to move from box to box. Press **enter** when done.

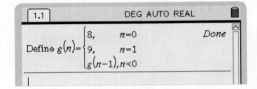

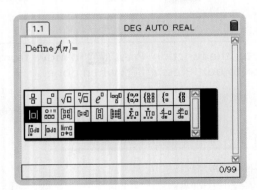

Modeling an Absolute Value Function

1. Choose **Define** from the **Actions** menu. Name the function by typing (**F**)(**N**) ⊜.Press **ctrl** **✕** to open the Templates palette. Select |□|. Press **enter**.

2. Enter the function. Press **enter** when done.

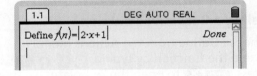

TI-Nspire™ Technology Handbook

Graphing a User-Defined Function by Dragging It Onto the Axes

1. Use the **Text** tool in the **Actions** menu. Type ⓨ ⊜, followed by the function. Press **enter**.

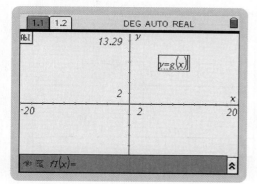

2. Position the cursor on the equation. Press **ctrl** ✹ to grab it. Drag the equation to the axes. Press **enter**.

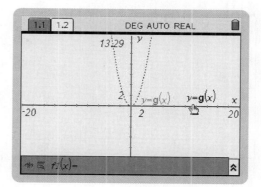

Changing the Graphing Window Settings

1. Choose the **Window Settings** option in the **Window** menu.

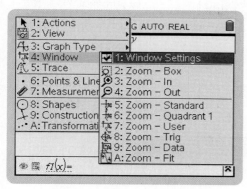

2. Press **tab** to navigate from field to field. Change the window settings as desired. Press **enter** to confirm.

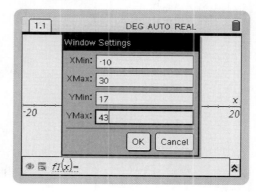

Graphing a Function

1. Tab down to the entry line at the bottom of the screen. Type an expression in x.

2. Press **enter**.

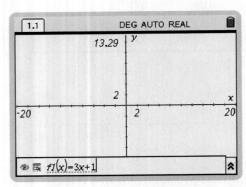

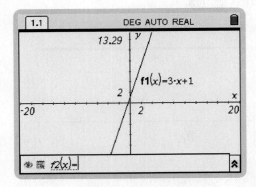

Graphing an Equation in Two Variables

1. Type **SOLVE (**. Type the equation and then **,Y**. Press **enter**.

2. In a graphing screen, graph one of the solutions for y.

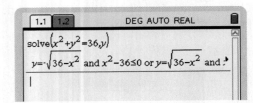

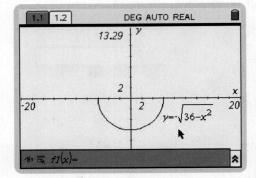

3. In the same screen, graph the other solution for y to complete the graph of

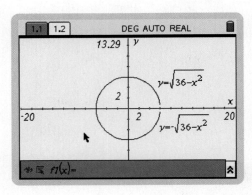

Finding the Intersection of Two Graphs

1. Choose **Intersection Point(s)** from the **Points & Lines** menu.

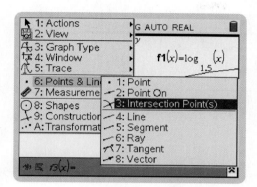

2. Place the cursor on one graph. Press **enter**.

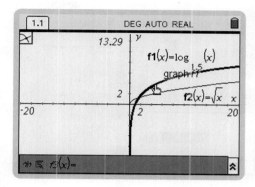

3. Place the cursor on the other graph. Press **enter**.

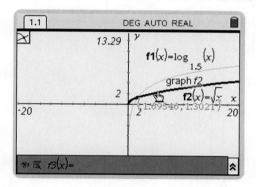

4. Move the cursor to drag the coordinates of the point of intersection. Press **enter** to anchor the coordinates.

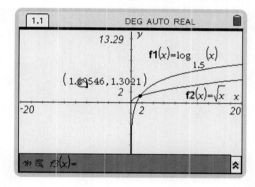

Expanding a Product of Polynomials

1. Choose **Expand** from the **Algebra** menu.

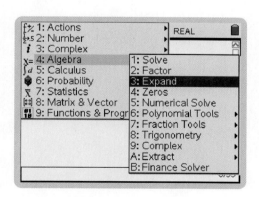

2. Type a product of polynomials. Press **enter**.

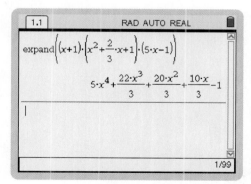

Finding Complex Solutions

1. Choose **Complex** from the **Algebra** menu. Choose **Solve**.

2. Type the equation and then . Type the variable to solve for. Press **enter**

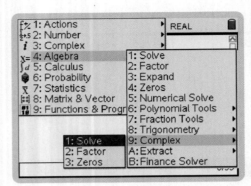

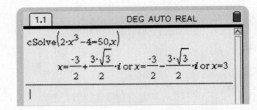

Finding Complex Zeros

1. To find the complex roots of a polynomial, set the polynomial equal to 0. Then find the complex solutions to the equation. (See Finding Complex Solutions, above.)

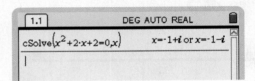

Measuring an Angle (in degrees)

1. Check that the system settings show degree mode.

2. Choose the **Angle** option in the **Measurement** menu.

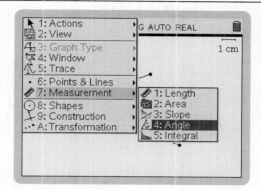

3. Position the pointer on one side of the angle. Press ⊛. Position the pointer on the vertex. Press ⊛. Position the pointer on the other side of the angle. Press ⊛.

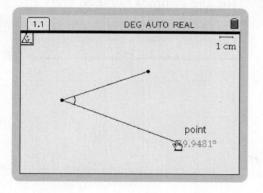

4. Move the pointer to drag the measurement. Press ⊛ to anchor it.

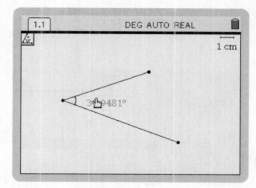

Calculating the Argument of a Complex Number

1. Choose **Polar Angle** from the **Complex** menu.

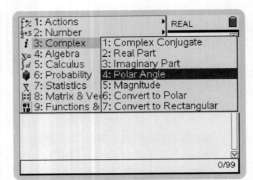

2. Type the complex number. Press **enter**.

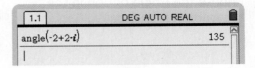

Calculating the Magnitude of a Complex Number

1. Choose **Magnitude** from the **Complex** menu.

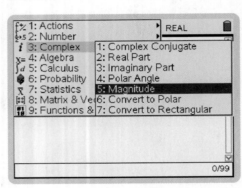

2. Type the complex number. Press **enter**.

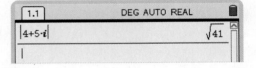

TI-Nspire™ Technology Handbook

Constructing a Line Perpendicular to a Given Line Through a Given Point

1. Choose the **Perpendicular** option in the **Construction** menu.

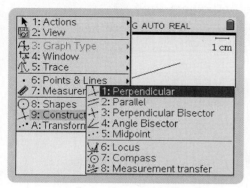

2. Position the pointer on the given line. Press 🔆. Position the pointer on the given point. Press 🔆.

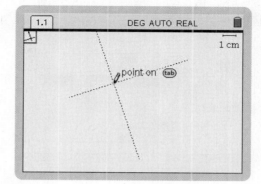

Constructing a Line Parallel to a Given Line Through a Given Point

1. Choose the **Parallel** option in the **Construction** menu.

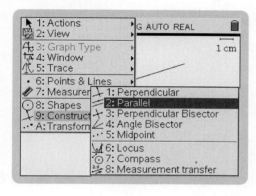

2. Position the pointer on the given line. Press 🔆. Position the pointer on the given point. Press 🔆.

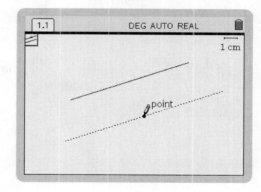

Expanding Expressions

1. Press 🄴🅇🄿🄰🄽🄳 ⟨. Type an expression. Press **enter**.

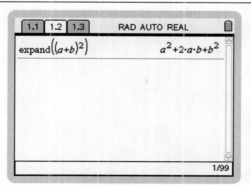

Finding the Intersection(s) of Two Objects

1. Choose the **Intersection Point(s)** option in the **Points & Lines** menu.

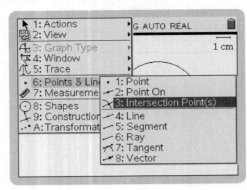

2. Position the pointer on the first object. Press ⊛. Position the pointer on the second object. Press ⊛.

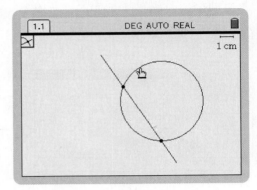

Finding the Area of a Polygon

1. Choose the **Area** option in the **Measurement** menu.

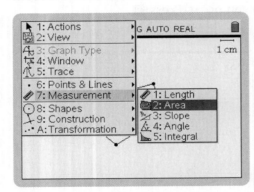

2. Place the pointer on the polygon. Press ⊛.

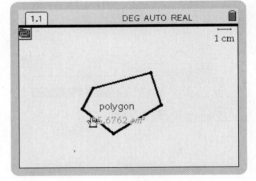

3. Move the pointer to drag the area value. Press ⊛ to anchor it.

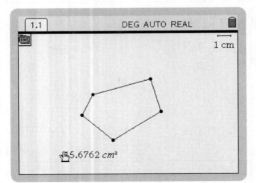

Finding a Dilation—The Ratio Method

1. Choose **Triangle** from the **Shapes** menu. Position the pointer. Press ✖ to anchor one vertex of the triangle. Type Ⓐ to label vertex *A*. Anchor and label vertices *B* and *C* in a similar way.

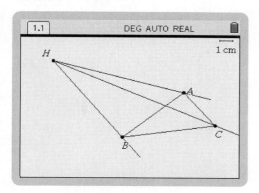

2. Choose **Point** in the **Points & Lines** menu. Position the pointer outside the triangle. Press ✖. Type Ⓗ to label point *H*.

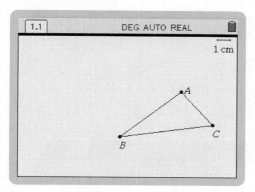

3. Use **Ray** in the **Points & Lines** menu. Draw rays *HA*, *HB*, and *HC*.

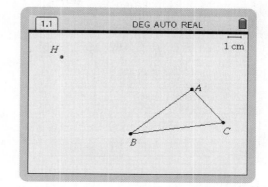

4. Use **Text** in the **Actions** menu. Write the scale factor 0.5.

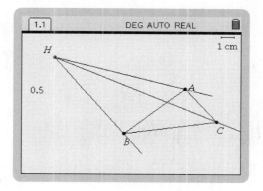

5. Choose **Dilation** in the **Transformation** menu. Click point *H*, point *A*, and the scale factor. The dilated point appears on ray *HA*. Label the dilated point *A'*. Scale points *B* and *C* in a similar way.

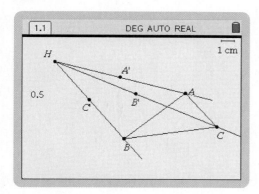

6. Use **Segment** in the **Points & Lines** menu to join points *A'*, *B'*, and *C'*. The dilation of △*ABC* by the factor 0.5 is △*A'B'C'*.

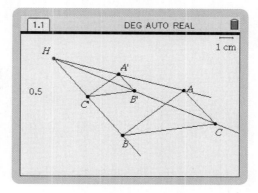

Finding the Maximums, Minimums, and Zeros of a Function

1. Choose the **Graph Trace** option in the **Trace** menu.

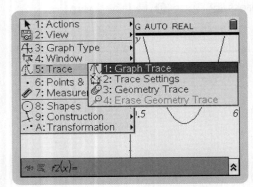

2. Use the ◁ and ▷ keys to move the trace cursor along the graph. Zeros are indicated by the letter z. Press **enter** to set the coordinates.

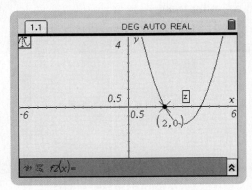

3. Minimums and maximums are indicated by the letters m and M, respectively. Press **enter** to get the coordinates.

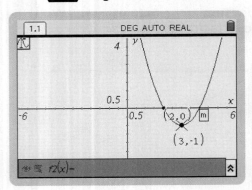

TI-Nspire™ Technology Handbook

Tables

Table 1   Math Symbols

$\ldots$	and so on	$\degree$	degree(s)
$=$	is equal to	$\triangle ABC$	triangle with vertices A, B, and C
$\approx$	is approximately equal to	$\square ABCD$	parallelogram with vertices A, B, C, and D
$\neq$	is not equal to	$n\text{-gon}$	polygon with n sides
$>$	is greater than	s	length of a side
$\geq$	is greater than or equal to	b	base length
$<$	is less than	h	height, length of an altitude
$\leq$	is less than or equal to	a	apothem
$\cdot, \times$	multiplication	P	perimeter
$+$	addition	A	area
$-$	subtraction	B	area of a base
$\pm$	plus or minus	L.A.	lateral surface area
$\mapsto$	which gives, leads to, maps to	S.A.	total surface area
$a_n \to r$	a_n approaches r	ℓ	slant height
n^2	n squared	V	volume
$\sqrt{x}$	nonnegative square root of x	d	diameter
Δ	difference (delta)	r	radius
$\Leftrightarrow$	if and only if	C	circumference
A	point A	π	pi, the ratio of the circumference of a circle to its diameter
A'	image of A, A prime	$\odot A$	circle with center A
$\overleftrightarrow{AB}$	line through A and B	$\overarc{AB}$	arc with endpoints A and B
$\overline{AB}$	segment with endpoints A and B	$\overarc{ABC}$	arc with endpoints A and C and containing B
$\overrightarrow{AB}$	ray with endpoint A through B	$m\overarc{AB}$	measure of $\overarc{AB}$
$\overrightarrow{AB}$	vector with tail A and head B	$a : b, \frac{a}{b}$	ratio of a to b
AB	length of $\overline{AB}$	$\sin A$	sine of $\angle A$
$\parallel$	is parallel to	$\cos A$	cosine of $\angle A$
$\perp$	is perpendicular to	$\tan A$	tangent of $\angle A$
$\cong$	is congruent to	$\sin^{-1} x$	inverse sine of x
$\sim$	is similar to	$\Pi(P)$	power of point P
$\angle A$	angle A		
$\angle ABC$	angle with sides $\overline{BA}$ and $\overline{BC}$		
$m\angle A$	measure of angle A		

Table 2 Formulas

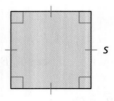

$P = 4s$
$A = s^2$

Square

$P = 2b + 2h$
$A = bh$

Rectangle

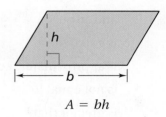

$A = bh$

Parallelogram

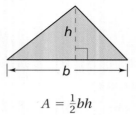

$A = \frac{1}{2}bh$

Triangle

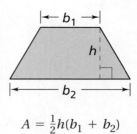

$A = \frac{1}{2}h(b_1 + b_2)$

Trapezoid

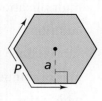

$A = \frac{1}{2}aP$

Regular Polygon

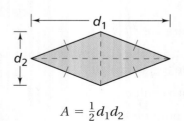

$A = \frac{1}{2}d_1 d_2$

Rhombus

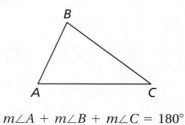

$m\angle A + m\angle B + m\angle C = 180°$

Triangle Angle Sum

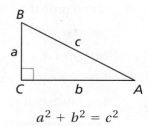

$a^2 + b^2 = c^2$

Pythagorean Theorem

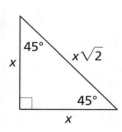

Ratio of sides $= 1 : 1 : \sqrt{2}$

45°-45°-90° Triangle

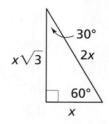

Ratio of sides $= 1 : \sqrt{3} : 2$

30°-60°-90° Triangle

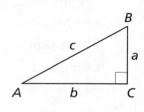

$\tan A = \frac{a}{b}$
$\sin A = \frac{a}{c}$ $\quad \cos A = \frac{b}{c}$

Trigonometric Ratios

Table 2 Formulas (continued)

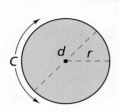

$$C = \pi d \text{ or } C = 2\pi r$$
$$A = \pi r^2$$

Circle

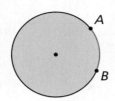

$$\text{Length of } \widehat{AB} = \frac{m\widehat{AB}}{360} \cdot 2\pi r$$

Arc

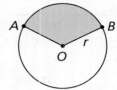

$$\text{Area of } = \frac{m\widehat{AB}}{360} \cdot \pi r^2$$
$$\text{sector } AOB$$

Sector of a Circle

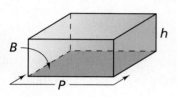

$$\text{L.A.} = Ph$$
$$\text{S.A.} = \text{L.A.} + 2B$$
$$V = Bh$$

Right Prism

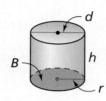

$$\text{L.A.} = 2\pi rh \text{ or } \text{L.A.} = \pi dh$$
$$\text{S.A.} = \text{L.A.} + 2B$$
$$V = Bh$$

Right Cylinder

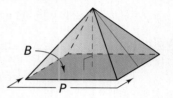

$$\text{L.A.} = \tfrac{1}{2}P\ell$$
$$\text{S.A.} = \text{L.A.} + B$$
$$V = \tfrac{1}{3}Bh$$

Regular Pyramid

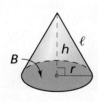

$$\text{L.A.} = \pi r\ell$$
$$\text{S.A.} = \text{L.A.} + B$$
$$V = \tfrac{1}{3}Bh \text{ or } V = \tfrac{1}{3}\pi r^2 h$$

Right Cone

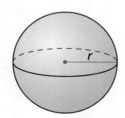

$$\text{S.A.} = 4\pi r^2$$
$$V = \tfrac{4}{3}\pi r^3$$

Sphere

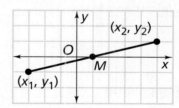

$$d = \sqrt{(x_2 - x_1)^2 + (y_2 - y_1)^2}$$
$$M = \left(\frac{x_1 + x_2}{2}, \frac{y_1 + y_2}{2} \right)$$

Distance and Midpoint

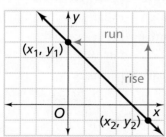
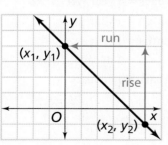

$$m = \frac{\text{rise}}{\text{run}} = \frac{y_2 - y_1}{x_2 - x_1}$$

Slope

Table 3 Measures

United States Customary	Metric

Length

United States Customary	Metric
12 inches (in.) = 1 foot (ft)	10 millimeters (mm) = 1 centimeter (cm)
36 in. = 1 yard (yd)	100 cm = 1 meter (m)
3 ft = 1 yard	1000 mm = 1 meter
5280 ft = 1 mile (mi)	1000 m = 1 kilometer (km)
1760 yd = 1 mile	

Area

United States Customary	Metric
144 square inches (in.^{2}) = 1 square foot (ft^2)	100 square millimeters (mm^2) = 1 square centimeter (cm^2)
9 ft^2 = 1 square yard (yd^2)	10,000 cm^2 = 1 square meter (m^2)
43,560 ft^2 = 1 acre	10,000 m^2 = 1 hectare (ha)
4840 yd^2 = 1 acre	

Volume

United States Customary	Metric
1728 cubic inches (in.^{3}) = 1 cubic foot (ft^3)	1000 cubic millimeters (mm^3) = 1 cubic centimeter (cm^3)
27 ft^3 = 1 cubic yard (yd^3)	1,000,000 cm^3 = 1 cubic meter (m^3)

Liquid Capacity

United States Customary	Metric
8 fluid ounces (fl oz) = 1 cup (c)	1000 milliliters (mL) = 1 liter (L)
2 c = 1 pint (pt)	1000 L = 1 kiloliter (kL)
2 pt = 1 quart (qt)	
4 qt = 1 gallon (gal)	

Weight and Mass

United States Customary	Metric
16 ounces (oz) = 1 pound (lb)	1000 milligrams (mg) = 1 gram (g)
2000 pounds = 1 ton (t)	1000 g = 1 kilogram (kg)
	1000 kg = 1 metric ton

Temperature

United States Customary	Metric
32°F = freezing point of water	0°C = freezing point of water
98.6°F = normal body temperature	37°C = normal body temperature
212°F = boiling point of water	100°C = boiling point of water

Time

United States Customary	Metric
60 seconds (s) = 1 minute (min)	365 days = 1 year (yr)
60 minutes = 1 hour (h)	52 weeks (approx.) = 1 year
24 hours = 1 day (d)	12 months = 1 year
7 days = 1 week (wk)	10 years = 1 decade
4 weeks (approx.) = 1 month (mo)	100 years = 1 century

Table 4 Properties of Real Numbers

Unless otherwise stated, a, b, c, and d are real numbers.

Identity Properties
Addition $a + 0 = a$ and $0 + a = a$
Multiplication $a \cdot 1 = a$ and $1 \cdot a = a$

Commutative Properties
Addition $a + b = b + a$
Multiplication $a \cdot b = b \cdot a$

Associative Properties
Addition $(a + b) + c = a + (b + c)$
Multiplication $(a \cdot b) \cdot c = a \cdot (b \cdot c)$

Inverse Properties
Addition
The sum of a number and its *opposite*, or *additive inverse*, is zero.
$a + (-a) = 0 = -a + a = 0$
Multiplication
The reciprocal, or multiplicative inverse, of a rational number $\frac{a}{b}$ is $\frac{b}{a}$ ($a, b \neq 0$).
$a \cdot \frac{1}{a} = 1$ and $\frac{1}{a} \cdot a = 1$ ($a \neq 0$)

Distributive Properties
$a(b + c) = ab + ac$ $(b + c)a = ba + ca$
$a(b - c) = ab - ac$ $(b - c)a = ba - ca$

Properties of Equality
Addition If $a = b$, then $a + c = b + c$.
Subtraction If $a = b$, then $a - c = b - c$.
Multiplication If $a = b$, then $a \cdot c = b \cdot c$.
Division If $a = b$ and $c \neq 0$, then $\frac{a}{c} = \frac{b}{c}$.
Substitution If $a = b$, then b can replace a in any expression.
Reflexive $a = a$
Symmetric If $a = b$, then $b = a$.
Transitive If $a = b$ and $b = c$, then $a = c$.

Properties of Proportions
$\frac{a}{b} = \frac{c}{d}$ ($a, b, c, d \neq 0$ is equivalent to
(1) $ad = bc$ (2) $\frac{b}{a} = \frac{d}{c}$
(3) $\frac{a}{c} = \frac{b}{d}$ (4) $\frac{a + b}{b} = \frac{c + d}{d}$

Zero-Product Property
If $ab = 0$, then $a = 0$ or $b = 0$.

Properties of Inequality
Addition If $a > b$ and $c \geq d$, then $a + c > b + d$.
Multiplication If $a > b$ and $c > 0$, then $ac > bc$.
If $a > b$ and $c < 0$, then $ac < bc$.
Transitive If $a > b$ and $b > c$, then $a > c$.
Comparison If $a = b + c$ and $c > 0$, then $a > b$.

Properties of Exponents
For any nonzero numbers a and b, any positive number c, and any integers m and n,
Zero Exponent $a^0 = 1$
Negative Exponent $a^{-n} = \frac{1}{a^n}$
Product of Powers $a^m \cdot a^n = a^{m+n}$
Quotient of Powers $\frac{a^m}{a^n} = a^{m-n}$
Power to a Power $(c^m)^n = c^{mn}$
Product to a Power $(ab)^n = a^n b^n$
Quotient to a Power $\left(\frac{a}{b}\right)^n = \frac{a^n}{b^n}$

Properties of Square Roots
For any nonnegative numbers a and b, and any positive number c,
Product of Square Roots $\sqrt{a} \cdot \sqrt{b} = \sqrt{ab}$
Quotient of Square Roots $\frac{\sqrt{a}}{\sqrt{c}} = \sqrt{\frac{a}{c}}$

... Properties, Postulates and Theorems ...

Theorem 3.6, p. 217

If a, b, c, and d are real numbers, then $a + bi = c + di$ only when $a = c$ and $b = d$.

Chapter 4

Theorem 4.1, p. 248

You can match an input-output table having constant differences with a linear function. The slope of the graph of the function is the constant difference in the table.

Theorem 4.2, p. 248

If $f(x) = ax + b$ is a linear function, its differences are constant.

Theorem 4.3, p. 262

For any quadratic function $p(x) = ax^2 + bx + c$, the second differences are constant. The constant second difference is $2a$, twice the coefficient of the squared term.

Theorem 4.4, p. 264

If a table has constant second differences, there is some quadratic function that agrees with the table.

Theorem 4.5, p. 295

Suppose $f: A \rightarrow B$ is one-to-one. Then
- $f^{-1}: B \rightarrow A$ is one-to-one
- $(f^{-1})^{-1} = f$

Lemma 4.1, p. 317

Let $b > 1$ and let x be a positive rational number. Then $b^x > 1$.

Theorem 4.6, p. 317

If $b > 1$, then the function $f(x) = b^x$ is strictly increasing on rational-number inputs. In other words, if s and t are rational numbers such that $s > t$, then $f(s) > f(t)$.

Lemma 4.2, p. 321

Let $0 < b < 1$ and let x be a positive number. Then $b^x < 1$.

Theorem 4.7, p. 321

Let $0 < b < 1$. Then the function $f(x) = b^x$ is strictly decreasing on rational-number inputs.

Chapter 5

Theorem 5.1, p. 375

For $n \geq 0$,

$$(a + b)^n = \binom{n}{0}a^n b^0 + \binom{n}{1}a^{n-1}b^1 + \binom{n}{2}a^{n-2}b^2 + \cdots + \binom{n}{k}a^{n-k}b^k$$

$$+ \cdots + \binom{n}{n-1}a^1 b^{n-1} + \binom{n}{n}a^0 b^n$$

Theorem 5.2, p. 391

Let A and B be events with $P(A) > 0$ and $P(B) > 0$.
- Events A and B are independent if and only if $P(A|B) = P(A)$.
- Events A and B are independent if and only if $P(B|A) = P(B)$.

Chapter 6

Postulate 6.1
The Triangle Congruence Postulates, p. 430

If two triangles share the following triplets of congruent corresponding parts, the triangles are congruent.
- ASA
- SAS
- SSS

Theorem 6.1
Concurrence of Perpendicular Bisectors, p. 446

In any triangle, the perpendicular bisectors of the sides are concurrent.

Theorem 6.2
Concurrence of Angle Bisectors, p. 446

In any triangle, the angle bisectors are concurrent.

Exterior Angle Theorem, Version 1, p. 454

The measure of a triangle's exterior angle is greater than the measures of either of the triangle's two remote interior angles.

Theorem 6.3 The Vertical Angles Theorem, p. 457

Vertical angles are congruent.

Theorem 6.4 The AIP Theorem, p. 463

If two lines form congruent alternate interior angles with a transversal, then the two lines are parallel.

Postulate 6.2 The Parallel Postulate, p. 469

If a point P is not on line ℓ, exactly one line through P exists that is parallel to ℓ.

Theorem 6.5 The PAI Theorem, p. 469

If two parallel lines are cut by a transversal, then the alternate interior angles are congruent.

Theorem 6.6
The Triangle Angle-Sum Theorem, p. 471

The sum of the measures of the angles of a triangle is $180°$.

Theorem 6.7
The Unique Perpendicular Theorem, p. 473

If a point P is not on a line ℓ, there is exactly one line through P that is perpendicular to ℓ.

Exterior Angle Theorem, Version 2, p. 475

The measure of an exterior angle of a triangle is equal to the sum of the measures of the two remote interior angles of the triangle.

Theorem 6.8
Perpendicular Bisector Theorem, pp. 29, 499

Each point on the perpendicular bisector of a segment is equidistant from the two endpoints of the segment.

Theorem 6.9 Isosceles Triangle Theorem, p. 500

The base angles of an isosceles triangle are congruent.

Triangle Inequality Theorem, p. 504

In a triangle, the length of one side is less than the sum of the lengths of the other two sides.

Theorem 6.10, p. 515

Each diagonal of a parallelogram divides the parallelogram into two congruent triangles.

Theorem 6.11, p. 516

The diagonals of a parallelogram bisect each other.

Theorem 6.12, p. 520

If two opposite sides of a quadrilateral are congruent and parallel, then the figure is a parallelogram.

Theorem 6.13 Midline Theorem, p. 520

The segment that joins the midpoints of two sides of a triangle is parallel to the third side and half the length of the third side.

Chapter 7
Theorem 7.1
The Parallel Side-Splitter Theorem, p. 580

If a segment with endpoints on two sides of a triangle is parallel to the third side of the triangle, then

- the segment splits the sides it intersects proportionally
- the ratio of the length of the third side of the triangle to the length of the parallel segment is the common ratio

Theorem 7.2
The Proportional Side-Splitter Theorem, p. 581

If a segment with endpoints on two sides of a triangle splits those sides proportionally, then the segment is parallel to the third side.

Theorem 7.3 AAA Similarity Theorem, p. 601

If three angles of one triangle are congruent to three angles of another triangle, the triangles are similar.

Theorem 7.4 SAS Similarity Theorem, p. 602

If two triangles have two pairs of proportional side lengths and the included angles are congruent, the triangles are similar.

Theorem 7.5 SSS Similarity Theorem, p. 603

If two triangles have all three pairs of side lengths proportional, the triangles are similar.

Theorem 7.6, p. 610

If you scale a polygon by some positive number r, then the ratio of the area of the scaled copy to the area of the original polygon is r^2.

Chapter 8
Theorem 8.1, p. 636

The area A of a regular polygon is equal to half of the product of its perimeter P and its apothem a.

$$A = \tfrac{1}{2}Pa$$

Theorem 8.2, p. 638

The area of a circle is one half its circumference times its radius.

$$A = \tfrac{1}{2}Cr$$

Theorem 8.3, p. 645

If a circle is scaled by a positive number s, then its area is scaled by s^2.

Theorem 8.4, p. 645

If the area of a circle with radius 1 is k, then the area of a circle with radius r is kr^2.

Theorem 8.5, p. 646

The area of a circle of radius r is π times the radius squared.

$$A = \pi r^2$$

Theorem 8.6, p. 650

The circumference of a circle of radius r is 2π times the radius.

$$C = 2\pi r$$

Theorem 8.7, p. 668

Two chords are congruent if and only if their corresponding arcs are congruent.

Theorem 8.8, p. 674

A line through the center of a circle bisects a chord if it is perpendicular to the chord.

Theorem 8.9, p. 675

If a line through the center of a circle bisects a chord, then it is perpendicular to the chord.

Theorem 8.10, p. 675

The center of a circle lies on the line perpendicular to a chord if and only if the line bisects the chord.

Theorem 8.11, p. 675

The measure of an inscribed angle is equal to half the measure of its intercepted arc.

Corollary 8.11.1, p. 676

Inscribed angles are congruent if and only if they intercept the same arc or congruent arcs.

Corollary 8.11.2, p. 676

Any triangle inscribed in a semicircle is a right triangle.

Theorem 8.12, p. 682

In a cyclic quadrilateral, opposite angles are supplementary.

Theorem 8.13, p. 687

If a line intersects a circle in one point (that is, the line is tangent to the circle), it is perpendicular to the radius r drawn to the point of contact.

Theorem 8.14, p. 688

A secant angle with vertex inside a circle is equal in measure to half of the sum of the measures of the arcs it intercepts.

Theorem 8.15, p. 689

A secant angle with vertex outside a circle is equal in measure to half of the difference of the measures of the arcs it intercepts.

Chapter 9

Theorem 9.1, p. 718

In a right triangle, the length of either leg is the geometric mean of the length of its projection on the hypotenuse and the length of the whole hypotenuse.

Theorem 9.2, p. 718

In a right triangle, the length of the altitude relative to the hypotenuse is the geometric mean of the length of the two segments of the hypotenuse.

Theorem 9.3 Distance Formula, p. 730

The distance between two points (x_1, y_1) and (x_2, y_2) can be found using the Pythagorean Theorem. It is the square root of the sum of the square of the difference in the x-coordinates and the square of difference in the y-coordinates.

Theorem 9.4 Midpoint Formula, p. 730

Each coordinate of the midpoint of a line segment is equal to the average of the corresponding coordinates of the endpoints of the line segment.

Postulate 9.1 Cavalieri's Principle, p. 773

Two solids of the same height are cut by a plane so that the resulting cross sections have the same areas. If the solids also have cross-sectional areas equal to each other when cut by any plane parallel to the first, then they have the same volume.

Theorem 9.5, p. 780

The volume of a prism is equal to the product of the area of its base and its height.

$$V_{\text{prism}} = A_{\text{base}} \cdot h$$

Theorem 9.6, p. 781

The volume of a cylinder is equal to the product of the area of its base (a circle) and its height.

$$V_{\text{cylinder}} = A_{\text{base}} \cdot h$$

Theorem 9.7, p. 783

The volume of a pyramid is equal to one third of the product of the area of its base and its height.

$$V_{\text{pyramid}} = \frac{A_{\text{base}} \cdot h}{3}$$

Theorem 9.8, p. 784

The volume of a cone is equal to one third of the product of the area of its base (a circle) and its height.

$$V_{cone} = \frac{A_{base} \cdot h}{3}$$

Theorem 9.9, p. 790

The volume of a sphere with radius r is $\frac{4}{3}\pi r^3$.

Theorem 9.10, p. 790

The surface area of a sphere with radius r is $4\pi r^2$.

Chapter 10

Theorem 10.1 *Power of a Point Theorem*, p. 822

Given a point P and a circle, take any line through P that intersects the circle in two points A and B. Then $PA \cdot PB$ is constant, no matter what line you choose through P. This constant is called the power of the point P. The power is a function of the point, so write the power of P as $\Pi(P)$.

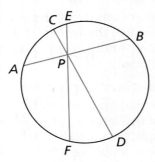

$$PA \cdot PB = PC \cdot PD = PE \cdot PF$$

Corollary 10.1.1, p. 822

Inside a circle, the power of a point d units away from the center of a circle with radius r is $r^2 - d^2$.

Corollary 10.1.2, p. 823

Outside a circle, the power of a point d units away from the center of a circle with radius r is $d^2 - r^2$.

Theorem 10.2, p. 824

The signed power of point $P(x, y)$ with respect to the circle with equation $x^2 + y^2 + Cx + Dy + E = 0$ is

$$\Pi_S(P) = x^2 + y^2 + Cx + Dy + E$$

Honors Appendix

Theorem H.1, p. 843

Suppose $z = a + bi$ and $w = c + di$ are complex numbers. Then, on the complex plane, the numbers $0, z, w$, and $z + w$ form the vertices of a parallelogram.

Theorem H.2 *Multiplication by i*, p. 845

If z is a complex number, iz is obtained from z by rotating it 90° counterclockwise about the origin.

Theorem H.3 *Magnitude and Conjugates*, p. 850

The magnitude $|z|$ of a complex number is given by $|z| = \sqrt{z\bar{z}}$.

Theorem H.4, p. 866

Given complex numbers z and w, the following statements are true.

- $|zw| = |z| \cdot |w|$
- $\arg zw = \arg z + \arg w$

Theorem H.5, p. 873

Suppose that z and w are complex numbers. Then the following statements are true.

$$\bar{z} + \bar{w} = \overline{z + w}$$

When you add conjugates, the result is the conjugate of the sum of the original numbers.

$$\bar{z} \cdot \bar{w} = \overline{zw}$$

When you multiply conjugates, the result is the conjugate of the product of the original numbers.

$$(\bar{z})^2 = \overline{z^2}$$

When you square a conjugate, the result is the conjugate of the square of the original number. If z is a real number, then $\bar{z} = z$.

Theorem H.6 *Polynomials and Conjugates*, p. 874

For any polynomial f with real coefficients and any complex number z, $\overline{f(z)} = f(\bar{z})$.

Corollary H.6.1 *Conjugate Pairs*, p. 874

If f is a polynomial with real coefficients, and $f(z) = 0$, then $f(\bar{z}) = 0$.

Theorem H.7, p. 923

If n is an integer and x is an angle in degrees,

- $\cos(x + 360n) = \cos x$
- $\sin(x + 360n) = \sin x$

Theorem H.8 *The Pythagorean Identity,* p. 928

If α is any angle, then $\cos^2 \alpha + \sin^2 \alpha = 1$.

Theorem H.9 *Angle-Sum Identities,* p. 953

For all α and β,
- $\cos (\alpha + \beta) = \cos \alpha \cos \beta - \sin \alpha \sin \beta$
- $\sin (\alpha + \beta) = \sin \alpha \cos \beta + \cos \alpha \sin \beta$

Theorem H.10, p. 972

An equation for the parabola with focus $(0, c)$ and directrix with equation $y = -c$ is

$$x^2 = 4cy$$

Theorem H.11, p. 974

The ellipse with foci $(c, 0)$ and $(-c, 0)$ and string length $2a$ has equation

$$1 = \frac{x^2}{a^2} + \frac{y^2}{b^2}$$

where $b^2 = a^2 - c^2$.

Theorem H.12, p. 976

The hyperbola with foci $(c, 0)$ and $(-c, 0)$ and constant difference $2a$ has equation

$$1 = \frac{x^2}{a^2} - \frac{y^2}{b^2}$$

where $b^2 = c^2 - a^2$.

Theorem H.13, p. 984

The graph of

$$rx^2 + ty^2 + ux + vy + w = 0$$

is a (possibly degenerate) conic. In fact, the nature of the conic is determined by the sign of rt:
- If $rt > 0$, the graph is an ellipse.
- If $rt = 0$, the graph is a parabola.
- If $rt < 0$, the graph is a hyperbola.

A

alternate exterior angles (p. 463) Alternate exterior angles are nonadjacent exterior angles that lie on opposite sides of a transversal.

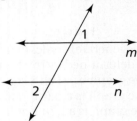

∠1 and ∠2 are
alternate exterior angles.

alternate interior angles (p. 463) Alternate interior angles are nonadjacent interior angles that lie on opposite sides of a transversal.

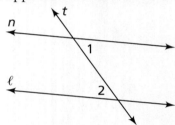

∠1 and ∠2 are
alternate interior angles.

annulus (p. 84) The annulus is the region between two circles with the same center.

apothem (p. 635) An apothem of a regular polygon is the length of the perpendicular segment from the center point of the polygon to one of its sides.

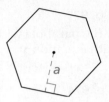

arc (p. 666) An arc is the set of points on a circle that lie in the interior of a particular central angle.

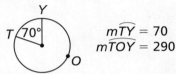

$m\widehat{TY} = 70$
$m\widehat{TOY} = 290$

argument (p. 857) *Argument* is another term used for direction of a complex number vector. The notation is arg z.

arithmetic mean (p. 712) The arithmetic mean of two numbers a and b is $\frac{a + b}{2}$. The arithmetic mean is commonly referred to as the average.

arithmetic sequence (p. 48) A sequence is an arithmetic sequence if its domain is the set of integers $n \geq 0$, and there is a number d, the common difference, for the sequence such that $f(n) = f(n - 1) + d$ for all integers $n > 0$.

B

base (p. 316) In the exponential function $f(x) = a \cdot b^x$, b is the base.

base angles *See* **isosceles trapezoid; isosceles triangle.**

binomial (p. 125) A binomial is a polynomial expression with exactly two terms.

C

center of dilation *See* **dilation.**

central angle (p. 666) A central angle is an angle that has its vertex at the center of a circle.

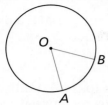

∠AOB is a central angle.

chord (p. 666) A chord is a segment that connects two points on a circle. Any chord through the center of a circle is a diameter.

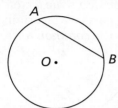

$\overline{AB}$ is a chord.

circumscribe (p. 680) A circle is circumscribed about a polygon if all of the vertices of the polygon are on the circle. A polygon is circumscribed about a circle if all of the sides of the polygon are tangent to the circle.

The circle is circumscribed about the octagon.

closed-form definition (p. 239) A closed-form definition of a function uses direct calculation to find an output for any input.

coefficient (p. 92) The coefficient is the numerical factor in a monomial.

collinear points (p. 447) Collinear points exist on the same line.

Points *A*, *B*, and *C* are collinear.

common ratio *See* **dilation, splits two sides proportionally.**

complex numbers (p. 216) The system of complex numbers ℂ consists of all expressions in the form $a + bi$ with the following properties.

- *a* and *b* are real numbers.
- $i^2 = -1$
- You can use addition and multiplication as if $a + bi$ were a polynomial.

complex plane (p. 837) The complex plane is used to represent a complex number geometrically. The real-number part of the number is located on the horizontal axis and the imaginary part on the vertical axis.

composite function (p. 284) For two functions $f : A \rightarrow B$ and $g : B \rightarrow C$, the composite function meets the following conditions.

- $g \circ f : A \rightarrow C$
- $g \circ f(x) = g(f(x))$

concave polygon (p. 509) A concave polygon has at least one diagonal that contains points outside the polygon.

diagonal outside the quadrilateral

concentric circles (p. 678) Concentric circles are circles that have the same center but not necessarily the same radius.

The two circles both have center *D* and are therefore concentric.

conclusion (p. 487) The conclusion is the part of a statement that you need to prove.

concurrent lines (p. 445) Concurrent lines are three or more lines that meet or intersect at one point.

Lines ℓ, *m*, and *n* are concurrent lines.

concurrent lines (p. 445) Concurrent lines all intersect at the same point.

conditional probability (p. 389) The notation $P(A \mid B)$ denotes the conditional probability that event *B* occurs given that event *A* has occurred.

conic sections (p. 964) Conic sections are curves that result from the intersection of infinite double cones and planes.

conjugate (p. 222) Number pairs of the form $a + bi$ and $a - bi$ are conjugates. The symbol $\bar{z}$ represents the conjugate of z.

consecutive angles (p. 463) Consecutive angles are the angles on the same side of a transversal and between the lines the transversal intersects.

constant (p. 437) A constant is a numerical invariant.

converse (p. 469) The converse of the conditional "if p, then q" is the conditional "if q, then p."

corollary (p. 464) A corollary is a consequence that logically follows from a theorem.

corresponding angles (p. 463) Corresponding angles lie on the same side of a transversal and in corresponding positions relative to the two lines the transversal intersects.

cosine (pp. 747, 907, 918, 922) The cosine function, $y = \cos \theta$, matches the measure θ of an angle in standard position with the x-coordinate of a point on the unit circle. This point is where the terminal side of the angle intersects the unit circle.

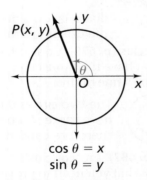

$$\cos \theta = x$$
$$\sin \theta = y$$

cubic function (p. 265) A cubic function is a polynomial in which the highest-degree term is cubed.

cubic polynomial (p. 94) A cubic polynomial is a polynomial of degree 3.

D

degree of a monomial (p. 92) The degree of a monomial is the sum of the exponents of each variable in the monomial.

degree of a polynomial (p. 93) The degree of a polynomial is the largest degree of any of its terms.

diameter (p. 666) A diameter is a chord that passes through the center of a circle.

$\overline{DM}$ is a diameter.

difference table (p. 240) A difference table shows the difference between consecutive outputs. It can help show patterns that lead to recursive definitions.

dilation (p. 561) A dilation is a nonrigid transformation that scales a figure from a *center of dilation* by a *scale factor*. The ratio of corresponding parts of the original figure to the scaled figure is the *common ratio*.

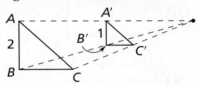

The scale factor of the dilation that maps $\triangle ABC$ to $\triangle A'B'C'$ is $\frac{1}{2}$.

dimension (p. 890) The dimensions of a matrix tell the number of rows and columns. A matrix with m rows and n columns has dimensions $m \times n$.

directrix (p. 968) A parabola can be defined by the set of points equidistant from a fixed point and line. The directrix of the parabola is the fixed line.

disc (p. 447) A disc is a circle and its interior points.

domain (p. 278) The domain of a function is the set of all inputs. *See* **function.**

E

elimination (p. 884) Elimination is a method for solving a system of equations by using addition, subtraction, and multiplication to find an equation in one variable that can be solved.

ellipse (p. 965) An ellipse is an oval shape that has some unique properties, including both vertical and horizontal symmetry.

equal functions (p. 279) Two functions f and g are equal functions if both of these conditions are satisfied.

- f and g have the same domain.
- $f(a) = g(a)$ for every a in the common domain.

equiangular (p. 488) An equiangular polygon is a polygon with angles that are all congruent.

Each angle of the pentagon is a 108° angle.

even function (p. 344) A function f is an even function if it satisfies $f(x) = f(-x)$ for all numbers x in its domain. If point (x, y) is on the graph of f, the point $(-x, y)$ is also on the graph.

event (p. 382) An event is a subset of a sample space, a set of outcomes.

expand an expression (p. 65) To expand an expression, multiply where parentheses indicate multiplication.

expected value (p. 409) The expected value of a random variable X is the sum when each value of X is multiplied by its probability. The typical notation is

$$E(X) = \sum_i x_i \cdot p_i$$

where the x_i are the values of the random variable, and the p_i are the probabilities of each value. An alternative notation is

$$E(X) = \sum_i s_i \cdot P(X = s_i)$$

where $P(X = s_i)$ is the probability that the random variable X takes on the value s_i.

exponential decay (p. 324) Given $f(x) = a \cdot b^x$, if $0 < b < 1$, the function shows exponential decay.

exponential function (p. 316) An exponential function is a function f that you can write in the form $f(x) = a \cdot b^x$, where $a \neq 0$, $b > 0$, and $b \neq 1$.

exponential growth (p. 324) Given $f(x) = a \cdot b^x$, if $b > 1$, the function $f(x)$ shows exponential growth.

exterior angle (p. 454) An exterior angle of a polygon is an angle formed by a side and an extension of an adjacent side.

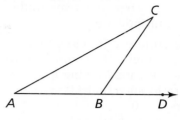

$\angle CBD$ is an exterior angle of $\triangle ABC$.

F

factor an expression (p. 76) To factor an expression, write an expression as a product of two or more expressions.

focus, foci (p. 966) The focus of a parabola is the fixed point in the locus definition of a parabola.

The foci of an ellipse are the two fixed points used in the locus definition of an ellipse.

The foci of a hyperbola are the two fixed points used in the locus definition of a hyperbola.

Focus is the singular of foci.

frequency (p. 398) Let A be an event. The frequency of the event $|A|$ is the number of outcomes in A.

function (p. 278) A function from set A to set B is a pairing between A and B such that each element in A pairs with exactly one element of B. A is the *domain* of f. B is the *target* of f. The set of objects in B that are paired with objects in A is the *range* of f.

Fundamental Theorem of Algebra (p. 219) If $P(x)$ is a polynomial of degree $n \geq 1$ with complex coefficients, then $P(x) = 0$ has at least one complex root.

G

Gaussian Elimination (p. 892) Gaussian elimination is an algorithm that transforms the matrix of any given system of linear equations through a sequence of other matrices, ending in a final matrix form from which the solution to the corresponding system is obvious.

geometric mean (p. 711) The geometric mean of two numbers a and b is c if $c > 0$ and $c^2 = ab$. Equivalently, $c = \sqrt{ab}$. The geometric mean is midway between two numbers with respect to multiplication.

geometric sequence (p. 49) A sequence is a geometric sequence if its domain is the integers $n \geq 0$, and there is a number $r \neq 0$, called the common ratio, such that $f(n) = r \cdot f(n - 1)$ for all integers $n > 0$.

greatest common factor (p. 91) The greatest common factor of an expression is the factor common to all terms that has the greatest coefficient and the greatest exponent.

H

hockey stick property (p. 247) The hockey stick property states that, in a difference table, an output is the sum of all of the differences above it to the right and the single output at the top of the table.

hyperbola (p. 965) A hyperbola is the curve you get by slicing an infinite double cone with a plane that intersects both branches of the cone.

hypothesis (p. 463) The hypothesis of a statement is what you are assuming to be true in order to prove the conclusion.

I

i (p. 208) The imaginary number i is defined as the number with square -1. So $i^2 = -1$ and $i = \sqrt{-1}$.

identity (p. 69) An identity is a statement that two expressions that may seem different are actually equivalent under the basic rules of algebra.

identity function (p. 293) The identity function on a set is the function id that simply returns its input.

identity matrix (p. 894) An identity matrix is a square matrix with all entries 0 except for 1's along the main diagonal from the top left to the bottom right. Multiplying a matrix by an identity matrix will result in the original matrix.

independent (p. 384) Two events A and B are independent if the result from one event has no effect on the other. If A and B are independent, then $P(A \text{ and } B) = P(A) \cdot P(B)$.

inscribe (p. 629) A polygon is inscribed in a circle if all of its vertices are on the circle. A circle is inscribed in a polygon if each side of the polygon is tangent to the circle.

The octagon is inscribed in the circle.

inscribed angle (p. 675) An inscribed angle is an angle with its vertex on a circle and sides that are chords of the circle.

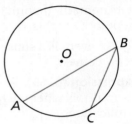

$\angle ABC$ is an inscribed angle.

inscribed circle (p. 680) An inscribed circle of a polygon is a circle that is tangent to all of the polygon's sides. The center of an inscribed circle is the *incenter*, equidistant from the polygon's sides.

invariant (p. 435) An invariant is something that is true for each member of a collection.

inverse function (f^{-1}) (p. 293) Suppose f is a one-to-one function with domain A and range B. The inverse function f^{-1} is a function with these properties:

- f^{-1} has domain B and range A.
- For all x in B, $f(f^{-1}(x)) = x$, or alternatively, $f \circ f^{-1} = \text{id}$.

irrational numbers (pp. 23, 205) Irrational numbers cannot by expressed as the quotient of integers.

isosceles trapezoid (p. 513) An isosceles trapezoid is a trapezoid with opposite nonparallel sides that are congruent. Each angle with vertices that are endpoints of the same base is a *base angle*.

$\angle A$ and $\angle B$ are base angles.
$\angle D$ and $\angle C$ are base angles.

isosceles triangle (p. 484) An isosceles triangle is a triangle with at least two sides congruent. The third side is the *base*. The angles opposite the congruent sides are the *base angles*. The angle between two congruent sides is the *vertex angle*.

K

kite (p. 511) A kite is a quadrilateral in which a pair of adjacent sides are congruent, and the other pair of adjacent sides are congruent as well.

L

leg *See* **isosceles triangle; right triangle; trapezoid.**

limit (p. 627) A limit is the value a sequence of numbers gets increasingly close to.

line of symmetry (p. 186) The line of symmetry of a parabola acts as a mirror for a parabola and passes through the vertex.

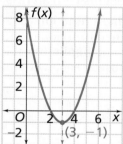

linear approximation (p. 629) Linear approximation is a process devised by Archimedes for approximating the length of a curve using line segments.

linear polynomial (p. 94) A linear polynomial is a polynomial of degree 1.

locus (p. 664) A locus is a set of points that satisfy a given property.

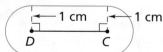

The points in blue are the locus of points in a plane 1 cm from $\overline{DC}$.

M

magnitude (p. 850) The modulus of a complex number z, denoted by $|z|$, is the distance between the complex number and 0 in the complex plane.

major axis (p. 973) The major axis of an ellipse is the longer of the two intersections of the ellipse with the axes of symmetry of the ellipse.

matrix (p. 890) A matrix is a rectangular array of numbers written within brackets. A matrix with m horizontal rows and n vertical columns is an $m \times n$ matrix.

maximum (p. 177) The maximum of a graph is the highest value achieved on the vertical axis.

minimum (p. 177) The minimum of a graph is the lowest value achieved on the vertical axis.

minor axis (p. 973) The minor axis of an ellipse is the shorter of the two intersections of the ellipse with the axes of symmetry of the ellipse.

monic (p. 125) A monic polynomial is a polynomial with a leading coefficient of one.

monic equation (p. 155) A monic equation is an equation that contains a polynomial with a leading coefficient of 1.

monomial (p. 92) A monomial is an expression that you can write as a product of a nonzero number and one or more variables, each raised to a nonnegative integer exponent.

mutually exclusive (p. 384) Two events A and B are mutually exclusive if they do not share any outcomes in the same sample space: whenever $P(A \text{ and } B) = 0$. If A and B are mutually exclusive, then $P(A \text{ or } B) = P(A) + P(B)$.

N

nth root (p. 29) For any real numbers a and b, and any positive integer n, if $a^n = b$, then a is the nth root of b.

natural numbers (p. 205) The natural numbers, or counting numbers, are 1, 2, 3, . . . and are represented by the symbol $\mathbb{N}$.

negative exponent (a^{-m}) (p. 43) If $a \neq 0$ and m is a positive integer, then $a^{-m} = \frac{1}{a^m}$.

nested triangles (p. 577) One triangle is nested inside another triangle if the triangles share a vertex and the sides of the triangles opposite the shared vertex are parallel.

nonmonic quadratic (p. 157) A nonmonic quadratic is a quadratic with a leading coefficient that is a number other than 1.

normal form (p. 101) A polynomial is in normal form if it contains no parenthesis, like terms have been combined, and the degrees of the terms go from highest to lowest.

O

odd function (p. 344) A function f is an odd function if it satisfies $f(-x) = -f(x)$ for all numbers x in its domain. If the point (x, y) is on the graph of f, the point $(-x, -y)$ is also on the graph.

one-to-one (p. 291) A function is one-to-one if its outputs are unique. That is, a function f is one-to-one if $f(r) = f(s)$ only when $r = s$.

outcome (p. 382) An outcome is an element of a sample space.

P

parallel lines (p. 462) Parallel lines are lines in the same plane that do not intersect.

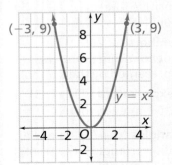

two parallel lines

a plane (for example, a piece of paper)

parallel method (p. 565) The parallel method is a process for dilating a figure by drawing parallel segments.

parallelogram (p. 515) A parallelogram is a quadrilateral with two pairs of parallel sides.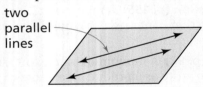

parabola (pp. 183, 965) A parabola is the graph of a quadratic function.

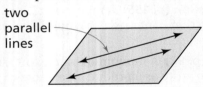

parameter (p. 93) A parameter is an unknown coefficient.

Pascal's Triangle (p. 374) Pascal's triangle is a pattern that can be used to find combinations of n things taken k at a time. Each entry can be labeled $\binom{n}{k}$, where n is the row number and k is the column number.

$$
\begin{array}{ccccccccccccc}
 & & & & & & 1 & & & & & & \\
 & & & & & 1 & & 1 & & & & & \\
 & & & & 1 & & 2 & & 1 & & & & \\
 & & & 1 & & 3 & & 3 & & 1 & & & \\
 & & 1 & & 4 & & 6 & & 4 & & 1 & & \\
 & 1 & & 5 & & 10 & & 10 & & 5 & & 1 & \\
1 & & 6 & & 15 & & 20 & & 15 & & 6 & & 1 \\
\end{array}
$$

perfect square trinomial (p. 134) A perfect square trinomial is a trinomial with identical factors.

period (pp. 15, 945) The period of a periodic function is the smallest value p such that, for all x, $f(x + p) = f(x)$.

pi (p. 645) Pi (π) is the ratio of the circumference of any circle to its diameter. Pi is the numerical value of the area of a circle with radius 1. Pi is an infinite nonrepeating decimal constant that begins with 3.14159.

piecewise-defined function (p. 302) A piecewise-defined function is a function in which the domain is split into at least two non-overlapping subsets, each with its own distinct function definition.

$$\text{Example: } f(x) = \begin{cases} 4, & \text{if } x < -2 \\ 4 - 3x, & \text{if } x \geq -2 \end{cases}$$

polynomial (p. 93) A polynomial is a sum of monomials.

polynomial equation (p. 112) A polynomial equation is an equation in which a polynomial is equal to 0.

power of a point (p. 698) The power of a point with respect to a circle is $(PA)(PB)$, where A and B are the points of intersection of a line through P and the circle.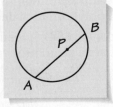

probability of an event (p. 382) The probability of an event A, denoted $P(A)$, is the number of outcomes in A, divided by the number of outcomes in the sample space S.

$$P(A) = \frac{\text{number of outcomes in } A}{\text{number of outcomes in } S} = \frac{|A|}{|S|}$$

projection (p. 718) A projection is the transformation of the points of a geometric figure onto the points of another figure. The projection of a point A onto a line ℓ is the intersection of ℓ with the line perpendicular to ℓ through A.

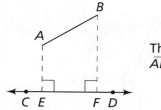

The projection of $\overline{AB}$ onto $\overleftrightarrow{CD}$ is $\overline{EF}$.

proof (p. 479) A proof is an argument in which every statement is supported with a reason.

Q

quadratic function (p. 261) A quadratic function is a function defined by a polynomial of degree 2.

quadratic polynomial (p. 107) A quadratic polynomial is a polynomial of degree 2.

quadrilateral (p. 508) A quadrilateral is a polygon with exactly four sides.

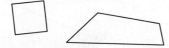

quartic polynomial (p. 93) A quartic polynomial is a polynomial of degree 4.

quintic polynomial (p. 93) A quintic polynomial is a polynomial of degree 5.

R

$\mathbb{R}$ **(p. 277)** $\mathbb{R}$ is the set of all real numbers.

radical (p. 28) A radical is a number such as a square root, a cube root, a fourth root, and so on.

random variable (p. 408) A random variable is function whose inputs are outcomes, and whose outputs are numbers.

range (p. 278) The range of a function is the set of objects that are paired with objects from the domain. *See* **function**.

ratio (p. 549) A ratio is the quotient of two numbers. If only one number is given, the second number is understood to be 1.

ratio method (p. 565) The ratio method is a process for dilating a figure.

rational exponent $\left(a^{\frac{p}{q}}\right)$ **(p. 56)** For integers p and q with $q > 0$, if $a^{\frac{1}{q}}$ is a real number, then $a^{\frac{p}{q}} = \left(a^{\frac{1}{q}}\right)^p = (\sqrt[q]{a})^p$.

rational number (p. 21) A rational number is a number that you can express as $\frac{a}{b}$, where a and b are integers and b is not equal to 0. The symbol $\mathbb{Q}$ denotes the set of rational numbers.

recursive definition (p. 239) A recursive definition of a function gives an output in terms of previous outputs.

rectangle (p. 521) A rectangle is a parallelogram with four right angles.

rhombus (p. 521) A rhombus is a parallelogram with four congruent sides.

row-reduced echelon form (rref) (p. 893) A matrix in row-reduced echelon form is the final matrix in an Gaussian elimination. There will be an identity matrix to the left of the augmentation line.

S

sample space (p. 382) The sample space is a set.

scale a figure (p. 537) When you scale a figure, you draw a new figure, called a *scaled figure*, that is the same shape as the given figure.

scaled figure (p. 537) In a scaled figure, each length is r times the corresponding length in the original figure.

scale factor (p. 536) A scale factor is a number that describes by how much you have reduced or enlarged a map, blueprint, or picture. The scale factor r can be any number, including a fraction.

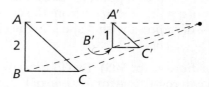

The scale factor of the dilation that maps $\triangle ABC$ to $\triangle A'B'C'$ is $\frac{1}{2}$.

scalene triangle (p. 500) A scalene triangle has no sides of equal length.

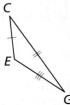

secant (p. 686) A secant line is a line that has two intersections with a circle.

$\overleftrightarrow{AB}$ is a secant of $\odot C$.

secant angle (p. 687) A secant angle is an angle with sides that are two secants of a circle. A secant angle's vertex can be inside or outside the circle.

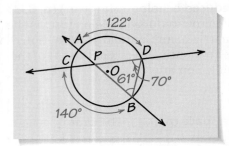

Secants $\overleftrightarrow{AB}$ and $\overleftrightarrow{CD}$ form angle $\angle DPB$.

sector (p. 647) A sector of a circle is a region bounded by two radii and the circle.

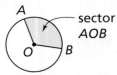

sector AOB

side *See* **quadrilateral.**

signed power of a point (p. 823) The signed power of a point P, d units from the center of a circle of radius r, with respect to the circle is given by $\Pi_S(P) = d^2 - r^2$.

similar figures (p. 595) Two figures are similar if you can rotate and/or flip one of them so that you can dilate it onto the other. Two figures are similar if one is congruent to a dilation of the other

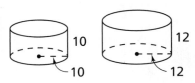

sine (pp. 747, 907, 918, 922) The sine function, $y = \sin\theta$, matches the measure θ of an angle in standard position with the y-coordinate of a point on the unit circle. This point is where the terminal side of the angle intersects the unit circle.

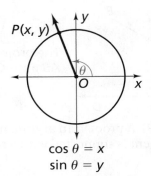

$$\cos\theta = x$$
$$\sin\theta = y$$

skew quadrilateral (p. 509) A skew quadrilateral is a quadrilateral that does not lie completely in one plane.

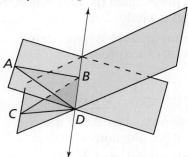

slope (p. 245) Slope is the ratio of the change in the y-coordinates to the change in the x-coordinates.

splits two sides proportionally (p. 580) In a $\triangle ABC$ with D on $\overline{AB}$ and E on $\overline{AC}$, the segment $\overline{DE}$ splits two sides ($\overline{AB}$ and $\overline{AC}$) proportionally if and only if $\frac{AB}{AD} = \frac{AC}{AE}$. The ratio $\frac{AB}{AD}$ is the common ratio.

square (pp. 8, 521) A square is a rectangle with four congruent sides.

square root (p. 8) A square root of a number n is a positive number that you multiply by itself to get the product n.

standard position (of an angle) (p. 920) An angle is in standard position when its vertex is at the origin and one of its sides lies along the positive x-axis. The angle opens counterclockwise from this fixed side.

strictly decreasing (p. 318) A function f is strictly decreasing if for any s and t such that $s > t$, then $f(s) < f(t)$.

strictly increasing (p. 317) A function f is strictly increasing if for any s and t such that $s > t$, then $f(s) > f(t)$.

substitution (p. 884) Substitution is a method for solving a system of equations by replacing one variable with an equivalent expression containing the other variable(s).

supplementary angles (p. 466) Two angles are supplementary if the sum of their measures is 180°.

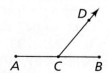

$\angle ACD$ and $\angle DCB$ are supplementary angles.

T

tangent (pp. 686, 747, 907, 922) The tangent of angle θ is $\dfrac{\sin \theta}{\cos \theta}$, whenever $\cos \theta \neq 0$.

target (p. 278) In a function f from A to B, B is the target of f. *See* **function**.

transversal (p. 453) A transversal is a line that intersects two or more lines.

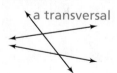

a transversal

trapezoid (p. 511) A trapezoid is a quadrilateral with exactly one pair of parallel sides. The two parallel sides are the *bases* of the trapezoid. The other sides are the *legs* of the trapezoid. The *height* of a trapezoid is the length of a perpendicular segment between the lines containing the bases.

bases

trigonometric equation (p. 933) A trigonometric equation is an equation that involves trigonometric functions.

trigonometry (p. 746) Trigonometry is the study of triangles.

trinomial (p. 130) A trinomial is a polynomial expression with exactly three terms.

trisected (p. 519) A segment is trisected if it is divided into three congruent parts.

U

unit circle (p. 340) The unit circle has a radius of 1 unit and its center at the origin of the coordinate plane.

unit fraction exponent (p. 55) The expression $a^{\frac{1}{n}}$ is defined, when possible, as the real nth root of a.

$$a^{\frac{1}{n}} = \sqrt[n]{a}$$

up-and-over property (p. 247) The up-and-over property states that, in a difference table, an output is the sum of the two numbers above it: the output directly above and the difference above and to the right.

V

vertex (pp. 184, 508) A vertex is the maximum or minimum point of a parabola.

vertex

vertex angle (p. 484) The vertex angle of an isosceles triangle is formed by the two congruent sides of the triangle.

vertex angle

vertical angles (p. 463) Vertical angles are two angles with sides that form two intersecting rays. Vertical angles are congruent.

$\angle 1$ and $\angle 2$ are vertical angles, as are $\angle 3$ and $\angle 4$.

vertex form (p. 185) The vertex form of a quadratic function is $y = a(x - h)^2 + k$.

X

$x \mapsto y$ (p. 274) $x \mapsto y$ is read as "x maps to y." This uses arrow notation to represent a function.

Z

zero exponent (a^0) (p. 43) If $a \neq 0$, then $a^0 = 1$.

Selected Answers

Chapter 1
Lesson 1.01
On Your Own
7. a. not a perfect square **b.** perfect square
8. 1.73; to get more accuracy, you would need a table that breaks the interval between 1.730 and 1.830 into thousandths.

Lesson 1.02
Check Your Understanding
1. a. $x \approx 3.162$ **b.** $x \approx 2.154$ **c.** $x \approx 1.778$
d. $x \approx 1.778$ **2. a.** Since the product of two positive numbers is positive, $\sqrt{2} \cdot \sqrt{3}$ is positive. Square the product to get $(\sqrt{2} \cdot \sqrt{3})^2 = (\sqrt{2})^2 \cdot (\sqrt{3})^2 = 2 \cdot 3 = 6$. So $\sqrt{2} \cdot \sqrt{3}$ is a nonnegative number with a square of 6. There is only one such number, $\sqrt{6}$.
b. Since the quotient of two positive numbers is positive, $\frac{\sqrt{19}}{\sqrt{5}}$ is positive. Square the quotient to get $\left(\frac{\sqrt{19}}{\sqrt{5}}\right)^2 = \frac{(\sqrt{19})^2}{(\sqrt{5})^2} = \frac{19}{5}$. So $\frac{\sqrt{19}}{\sqrt{5}}$ is a nonnegative number with a square of $\frac{19}{5}$. There is only one such number, $\sqrt{\frac{19}{5}}$.
c. Since the product of two positive numbers is positive, $\sqrt{11} \cdot \sqrt{7}$ is positive. Square the product to get $(\sqrt{11} \cdot \sqrt{7})^2 = (\sqrt{11})^2 \cdot (\sqrt{7})^2 = 11 \cdot 7 = 77$. So $\sqrt{11} \cdot \sqrt{7}$ is a nonnegative number with a square of 77. There is only one such number, $\sqrt{77}$. **d.** Since the quotient of two positive numbers is positive, $\frac{\sqrt{12}}{2}$ is positive. Square the quotient to get $\left(\frac{\sqrt{12}}{2}\right)^2 = \frac{(\sqrt{12})^2}{2^2} = \frac{12}{4} = 3$. So $\frac{\sqrt{12}}{2}$ is a nonnegative number with a square of 3. There is only one such number, $\sqrt{3}$.
e. Since the quotient of two positive numbers is positive, $\frac{10}{\sqrt{10}}$ is positive. Square the quotient to get $\left(\frac{10}{\sqrt{10}}\right)^2 = \frac{10^2}{(\sqrt{10})^2} = \frac{100}{10} = 10$. So $\frac{10}{\sqrt{10}}$ is a nonnegative number with a square of 10. There is only one such number, $\sqrt{10}$. **3.** 2

On Your Own
5. Yes, Tony's number is 12. **6. c.** $\sqrt{15}$
7. a. 1 **9. b.** $\sqrt{2}$

Lesson 1.03
Check Your Understanding
1. a. 4 **b.** $2\sqrt{5}$ **c.** 2 **d.** $4\sqrt{5}$ **2. a.** 2 **b.** 2 **c.** 3 **d.** 10 **e.** 3 **f.** In each equation, the number under the radical on the left side of the equation is divisible by a perfect square.
3. a. ± 1.968 **b.** ± 2 **c.** ± 1.627 **d.** no solution **4. a.** $\sqrt{6}$, $\sqrt{22}$, $\sqrt{33}$; 66 **b.** $\sqrt{12}$, $\sqrt{15}$, $\sqrt{20}$; 60 **c.** $\sqrt{35}$, $\sqrt{77}$, $\sqrt{55}$; 385 **d.** The final product is the product of the original numbers under the square root signs. **5.** A

On Your Own
6. a. 3 **8. a.** 1.72 **9. a.** $5\sqrt{2}$
11. $a = 10\sqrt{2} - 10$; $b = 10\sqrt{3} - 10\sqrt{2}$; $c = 20 - 10\sqrt{3}$; 10

Lesson 1.04
Check Your Understanding
1. a. $\frac{\sqrt{2}}{2}$ **b.** $\frac{1}{2}$ **c.** $\frac{\sqrt{31}}{31}$ **2.** If $x > 1$, then $x > \sqrt{x}$. If $0 < x < 1$, then $x < \sqrt{x}$. If $x = 0$ or $x = 1$, then $x = \sqrt{x}$. **3. a.** $\phi^2 - \phi = 1$
b. $\left(\frac{\sqrt{5}+1}{2}\right)^2 - \frac{\sqrt{5}+1}{2} =$
$\frac{5 + 2\sqrt{5} + 1}{4} - \frac{\sqrt{5}+1}{2} =$
$\frac{5 + 2\sqrt{5} + 1}{4} - \frac{2\sqrt{5}+2}{4} =$
$\frac{5 + 2\sqrt{5} + 1 - 2\sqrt{5} + 2}{4} = \frac{4}{4} = 1$
4. a. $\frac{2}{\sqrt{5}-1} = \frac{2}{\sqrt{5}-1} \cdot \frac{\sqrt{5}+1}{\sqrt{5}+1} = \frac{2\sqrt{5}+2}{5-1} = \frac{\sqrt{5}+1}{2}$ **b.** $\phi - 1 = \frac{\sqrt{5}+1}{2} - 1 = \frac{\sqrt{5}+1}{2} - \frac{2}{2} = \frac{\sqrt{5}-1}{2}$ **c.** $\frac{1}{\phi} = \frac{2}{\sqrt{5}+1} = \frac{2}{\sqrt{5}+1} \cdot \frac{\sqrt{5}-1}{\sqrt{5}-1} = \frac{2\sqrt{5}-2}{5-1} = \frac{\sqrt{5}-1}{2} = \phi - 1$

On Your Own
5. a. $2\sqrt{2}$ **6.** Hideki's method
7. a. $2\sqrt{13}$ in. **8. a.** perimeter $= 14\sqrt{3}$ cm; area $= 30$ cm^2

Lesson 1.06
Check Your Understanding
1. a.
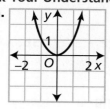
b.
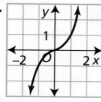

c. d.
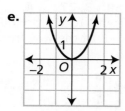 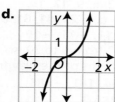

e.

f. Since the graph of $y = x^3$ passes through the graph of $y = -2$, you know that there is a number with cube -2. This number is $\sqrt[3]{-2}$. Since the graph of $y = x^4$ does not pass through the graph of $y = -2$, there is no real number with fourth power -2. Therefore $\sqrt[4]{-2}$ does not exist. **2.** 2.22

3. a. You know that $1 < 2$. Take the square root of each side to get $1 < \sqrt{2}$. You also know that $2 < 4$. Take the square root of both sides to get $\sqrt{2} < 2$. Since the function $f(x) = 2^x$ is continually increasing, and since $2^0 = 1$ and $2^1 = 2$, you know that $0 < a < 1$.

b. $2^{2a} = 2$ **c.** $2a = 1$ **d.** $a = \frac{1}{2}$

e. $\left(2^{\frac{1}{2}}\right)^2 = 2^{\frac{2}{2}} = 2$ **f.** $b = \frac{1}{3}$ **g.** $c = \frac{1}{n}$

On Your Own
5. a. $\sqrt[4]{125}$ and $\sqrt[4]{5}$ are both positive, so their product is positive.
$\left(\sqrt[4]{125} \cdot \sqrt[4]{5}\right)^4 = \left(\sqrt[4]{125}\right)^4 \cdot \left(\sqrt[4]{5}\right)^4$
$= 125 \cdot 5 = 625 = 5^4$. Since $\sqrt[4]{125} \cdot \sqrt[4]{5}$ is a nonnegative number with a fourth power equal to 5^4, the number is 5. **6. a.** 81

7. a. Doubling the length of each side yields 8 times the volume.

Lesson 1.07
On Your Own
6a. no **c.** yes **f.** no **7a.** No; $2^{10} + 2^2 \neq 2^{10+2}$. This sum cannot be written as a single power of 2. **c.** Yes; $2^{10} \cdot 2^2 = 2^{10+2} = 2^{12}$ **h.** Yes; $4 \cdot 2^{10} = 2^2 \cdot 2^{10} = 2^{2+10} = 2^{12}$

Lesson 1.08
Check Your Understanding

1. $(ab)^n = \underbrace{(ab) \cdot (ab) \cdots \cdots (ab)}_{n \text{ copies of } ab}$

$= \underbrace{(a \cdot a \cdots \cdots a)}_{n \text{ copies of } a} \underbrace{(b \cdot b \cdots \cdots b)}_{n \text{ copies of } b}$

$= a^n \cdot b^n$

2. $\dfrac{3^{11}}{3^5} = \dfrac{3 \cdot 3 \cdot 3 \cdot 3 \cdot 3 \cdot 3 \cdot 3 \cdot 3 \cdot 3 \cdot 3 \cdot 3}{3 \cdot 3 \cdot 3 \cdot 3 \cdot 3}$

$= \dfrac{3 \cdot 3 \cdot 3 \cdot 3 \cdot 3}{3 \cdot 3 \cdot 3 \cdot 3 \cdot 3} \cdot \dfrac{3 \cdot 3 \cdot 3 \cdot 3 \cdot 3 \cdot 3}{1}$

$= 1 \cdot 3^6 = 3^6$

3. Corollary 5.1.1:

$\dfrac{a^b}{a^c} = \dfrac{\overbrace{(a \cdot a \cdots \cdots a)}^{b \text{ copies of } a}}{\underbrace{(a \cdot a \cdots \cdots a)}_{c \text{ copies of } a}}$

$= \dfrac{\overbrace{(a \cdot a \cdots \cdots a)}^{c \text{ copies of } a}}{\underbrace{(a \cdot a \cdots \cdots a)}_{c \text{ copies of } a}} \cdot \dfrac{\overbrace{(a \cdot a \cdots \cdots a)}^{b-c \text{ copies of } a}}{1}$

$= 1 \cdot a^{b-c} = a^{b-c}$

Corollary 5.1.2: $(a^b)^c =$

$\underbrace{\overbrace{(a \cdot a \cdots \cdots a)}^{b \text{ copies of } a} \cdot \overbrace{(a \cdot a \cdots \cdots a)}^{b \text{ copies of } a} \cdots \cdots \overbrace{(a \cdot a \cdots \cdots a)}^{b \text{ copies of } a}}_{c \text{ copies of } a^b}$

$= \underbrace{a \cdot a \cdots \cdots a}_{bc \text{ copies of } a} = a^{bc}$

4a. Yes; $3^{14} + 3^{14} + 3^{14} = 3 \cdot 3^{14} = 3^1 + 3^{14} = 3^{1+14} = 3^{15}$ **b.** No; $(3^6)^9 = 3^{6 \cdot 9} = 3^{54} \neq 3^{15}$

c. Yes; $(3^{10})(3^5) = 3^{10+5} = 3^{15}$

d. No; $(3^3)(3^5) = 3^{3+5} = 3^8 \neq 3^{15}$

e. No; $(3^{15})(3^1) = 3^{15+1} = 3^{16} \neq 3^{15}$

f. Yes; $(3^5)(3^5)(3^5) = 3^{5+5+5} = 3^{15}$

g. No; $3^9 + 3^6 \neq 3^{9+6}$. This sum cannot be written as a single power of 3. **h.** Yes; $(3^5)^3 = 3^{5 \cdot 3} = 3^{15}$ **i.** Yes; $(3^3)^5 = 3^{3 \cdot 5} = 3^{15}$ **j.** Yes; $9(3^{13}) = (3^2)(3^{13}) = 3^{2+13} = 3^{15}$ **k**

. No; $(3^5)^{10} = 3^{5 \cdot 10} = 3^{50} \neq 3^{15}$ **l.** Yes; $(3^1)^{15} = 3^{1 \cdot 15} = 3^{15}$ **5.** Answers may vary. Sample: M^3N, $\frac{M^6}{N^3}$ **6.** Each time you multiply a power of x from the first factor by a power of x from the second factor, you can use the Fundamental Law of Exponents to find the exponent to place on x in the resulting term of the product. **7.** 3^{31} **8a.** 3 **b.** 5 **c.** $\frac{6}{5}$ **d.** 3 **9.** $f(n) = 3 \cdot 5^n$ **10.** mean: 11,111; median: $5 \cdot 10^2$ or 500 **11a.** 10 **b.** $\frac{9y^5}{8}$ **c.** $2x^4$ **d.** $\frac{1}{8}$

12a. ± 4 **b.** 2

On Your Own
13a. 1000 **b.** 1,000,000,000,000 **d.** 16

f. 10,000 **17.** about 2,000,000 **18a.** No;
$\frac{2^6}{2^2} = 2^{6-2} = 2^4 \neq 2^3$ **d.** Yes; $\frac{(2^2)^5}{2^7} = \frac{2^{2 \cdot 5}}{2^7} = \frac{2^{10}}{2^7} = 2^{10-7} = 2^3$ **22a.** x^{12} **g.** x^8

Lesson 1.09
Check Your Understanding

1a. Yes; $\left(\frac{1}{7}\right)^{10} = (7^{-1})^{10} = 7^{-1 \cdot 10} = 7^{-10}$
b. No; $7^{-4} \cdot 7^{-3} = 7^{-4+(-3)} = 7^{-7} \neq 7^{-10}$
c. No; $(7^{13})(7^{-6}) = 7^{13+(-6)} = 7^7 \neq 7^{-10}$
d. Yes; $\frac{7^3}{7^{13}} = 7^{3-13} = 7^{-10}$ **e.** No; $\frac{7^2}{7^3 \cdot 7^4 \cdot 7^4}$
$= \frac{7^2}{7^{3+4+4}} = \frac{7^2}{7^{11}} = 7^{2-11} = 7^{-9} \neq 7^{-10}$
f. No; $\frac{1}{7^{-10}} = 7^{-(-10)} = 7^{10} \neq 7^{-10}$
g. No; $7^5 \cdot 7^{-2} = 7^{5+(-2)} = 7^3 \neq 7^{-10}$
h. Yes; $\left(\frac{1}{7^2}\right)^5 = (7^{-2})^5 = 7^{(-2) \cdot 5} = 7^{-10}$
i. No; $(7^5)^{-15} = 7^{5 \cdot (-15)} = 7^{-75} \neq 7^{-10}$
j. Yes; $(7^5)^{-2} = 7^{5 \cdot (-2)} = 7^{-10}$
k. Yes; $(7^{-2})^5 = 7^{-2 \cdot 5} = 7^{-10}$ **l.** Yes; $\frac{1}{7^{10}}$
$= 7^{-10}$ **2.** $10^{-2} \cdot 10^3 = \frac{1}{10^2} \cdot \frac{10^3}{1} = \frac{10^3}{10^2}$
$= 10^{3-2} = 10^1$ **3.** $a^b \cdot a^c = a^{b+c}$:
If $b = 0$, then $a^b \cdot a^c = a^0 \cdot a^c = a^c$
and $a^{b+c} = a^{0+c} = a^c$. $\frac{a^b}{a^c} = a^{b-c}$ $(b > c)$:
If $c = 0$, then $\frac{a^b}{a^c} = \frac{a^b}{a^0} = \frac{a^b}{1} = a^b$ and
$a^{b-c} = a^{b-0} = a^b$. $(a^b)^c = a^{bc}$: If $b = 0$, then
$(a^b)^c = (a^0)^c = 1^c = 1$ and $a^{bc} = a^{0 \cdot c} = a^0 = 1$.

4a. 6 **b.** $\frac{2}{3}$ **c.** 4 **d.** 8 **e.** 1 **f.** $2^{\frac{1}{2}}$ or $\sqrt{2}$ **5.** 1
6. 0.75×10^7h; 1.53×10^9h; 0.89×10^{11}h

7a. 16, 8, 4, **2**, 1, $\frac{1}{2}$,... **b.** 2, **6**, 18, **54**, 162, **486**,... **c.** 1, a, a^2, a^3, a^4, a^5,...
d. b^6, b^3, 1, b^{-3}, b^{-6}, b^{-9},...
e. c^{10}, c^8, c^6, c^4, c^2, 1,...

8a. $h(x) = 2 \cdot 5^x$ **b.** $h(x) = \frac{2}{125}$, $\frac{2}{25}$, $\frac{2}{5}$
9. $(2^3)(2^{-3}) = 2^{3+(-3)} = 2^0 = 1$

On Your Own
10a. 2 **e.** -3 **14a.** $3^{2x} + 2 + 3^{-2x}$ **15b.** z^{-27}
16b. $\frac{1}{9}$ **f.** 3

Lesson 1.10
Check Your Understanding
1a. 0, 3, 6, **9**, **12**, **15**,... **b.** 0, **6**, **12**, **18**, **24**, 30,... **c.** 1, **21**, 41, 61, 81, **101**,... **d.** 5, **1**, -3, -7, -11, -15, -19... **2.** There are five "steps" from 0 to 30, so the third step, 18, is three fifths of the way from 0 to 30. **3a.** 2, -6, 18, -54, **162**, -486,... **b.** 1, $\pm\sqrt{5}$, 5, $\pm 5\sqrt{5}$, **25**, $\pm 25\sqrt{5}$, ... **c.** 1, **5**, **25**, 125, **625**,... **d.** 1, $\pm\sqrt{3}$, 3, $\pm 3\sqrt{3}$, 9, $\pm 9\sqrt{3}$, 27,... **4.** There are three "steps" from 1 to 125, so the second step, 25, is two thirds of the way from 1 to 125. **5a.** $\frac{a+b}{2}$ **b.** $\pm\sqrt{ab}$

6a.

(a, b)	$\dfrac{a+b}{2}$	$\sqrt{ab}$
$(1, 2)$	1.5	1.4142
$(2, 5)$	3.5	3.1623
$(4, 1)$	2.5	2
$(3, 3)$	3	3
$(6, 9)$	7.5	7.3485
$(8, 10)$	9	8.9443
$(7, 7)$	7	7

b. $\frac{a+b}{2}$; Answers may vary. Sample: The square of any real number is positive, so $(a - b)^2 \geq 0$. Then, $a^2 - 2ab + b^2 \geq 0$, $a^2 + 2ab + b^2 \geq 4ab$, $\frac{a^2 + 2ab + b^2}{4} \geq ab$, and $\frac{(a+b)^2}{4} \geq ab$. Taking the square root of each side (since a, $b > 0$) gives $\frac{a+b}{2} \geq \sqrt{ab}$. **7.** Yes; the missing terms could be 2, 4, 8, or -2, 4, -8.

8. $64^{\frac{2}{3}} = 16$, $625^{\frac{1}{4}} = 5$ **9a.** 4 **b.** 3 **c.** 3 **d.** 16
On Your Own
10a. 81 **b.** 27 **12a.** Balance: 546.36, 562.75, 579.64, 597.03 **13a.** 5 **17a.** $\frac{2}{3}$ **b.** 6

Lesson 1.11
Check Your Understanding
1a. a little more than 6 **b.** Answers may vary. Sample: a little more than 222 **2a.** 3 **b.** 32 **c.** 49 **d.** 9 **3a.** Answers may vary. Sample: $a = 32$,

$b = 4$ **b.** Yes; if $a^{\frac{2}{5}} = b$, then $\left(a^{\frac{2}{5}}\right)^5 = b^5$, which simplifies to $a^2 = b^5$.

4. $1^{\frac{p}{q}} = (1^p)^{\frac{1}{q}} = 1^{\frac{1}{q}} = \sqrt[q]{1} = 1$

5. The graph is made up of points from the horizontal lines $y = 1$ and $y = -1$. It consists of the points $(x, 1)$ when x is an even integer and $(x, -1)$ when x is an odd integer. If x is not an integer, the output is sometimes defined (for example, $(-1)^{\frac{1}{3}} = -1$) and sometimes not defined (for example, $(-1)^{\frac{1}{2}}$ is not a real number). **6a.** $a(b(9)) = 9$, $b(a(7)) = 7$ **7.** If $a, b, c, d, \ldots$ is an arithmetic sequence, then $b = a + k, c = a + 2k$, $d = a + 3k, \ldots$, for some number k. Then $10^b = 10^{a+k} = 10^a \cdot 10^k$, $10^c = 10^{a+2k} = 10^a \cdot 10^{2k}$, and $10^d = 10^{a+3k} = 10^a \cdot 10^{3k}$. Thus $10^a, 10^b, 10^c, 10^d, \ldots$ is a geometric sequence with the common ratio 10^k.

On Your Own

10. ± 3, **11a.** 3

15a.

x	$f(x) = x^3$	$g(x) = x^{\frac{1}{3}}$
-8	-512	-2
-2	-8	-1.26
-1	-1	-1
$-\frac{1}{2}$	-0.125	-0.794
$-\frac{1}{8}$	-0.002	-0.5
0	0	0
$\frac{1}{8}$	0.002	0.5
$\frac{1}{2}$	0.125	0.794
1	1	1
2	8	1.26
8	512	2

Chapter 2
Lesson 2.01
On Your Own

5. a. 399 **b.** 2496 **c.** 6313

d. $ab = \frac{(a + b)^2 - (a - b)^2}{4} = \frac{a^2 + 2ab + b^2 - (a^2 - 2ab + b^2)}{4} = \frac{a^2 + 2ab + b^2 - a^2 + 2ab - b^2}{4} = \frac{4ab}{4} = ab$

6. Both sides are equal to $a^2c^2 + a^2d^2 + b^2c^2 + b^2d^2$. **8. a.** The factor $(m + 7)$ is 13 when $m = 6$ since $6 + 7 = 13$, so $m^2 - 4m - 77$ is a multiple of 13. **d.** -7 and 11

Lesson 2.02
Check Your Understanding

1. a. $-2, -1, 0, 1$ **b.** $n, (n + 1), (n + 2)$, $(n + 3)$ **c.** $(n - 1), n, (n + 1)$ **d.** $2n + 1$
2. a. If n is an integer, $2n$ is even, so $2n + 1$ is odd. **b.** $n + (n + 1) + (n + 2) = 3n + 3 = 3(n + 1)$, which is divisible by 3. **c.** No; $n + (n + 1) + (n + 2) + (n + 3) = 4n + 6$. The sum of four consecutive integers is not divisible by 4. **d.** Yes; $n + (n + 1) + (n + 2) + (n + 3) + (n + 4) = 5n + 10 = 5(n + 2)$. The sum of five consecutive integers is divisible by 5. **e.** When k is odd, the sum of k numbers will be divisible by k. **3. a.** Answers may vary. Sample: The product of an even number and an odd number is always even. n must be either even or odd. If n is odd, then $n + 1$ will be even. **b.** Yes; when one of the factors is a multiple of 3, the entire product will be a multiple of 3 as well. **c.** Yes; when one of the factors is a multiple of 4, the entire product will be a multiple of 4 as well. **d.** Yes; when one of the factors is a multiple of 5, the entire product is a multiple of 5. **e.** Yes; when one of the factors is a multiple of k, the entire product is a multiple of k. **4.** $n = 14$ or $n = -15$ **5.** n^3

On Your Own

7. a. -6 **11. a.** $x(x - y)$; $y(x - y)$
b. $x(x - y) \cdot y(x - y) = x^2 - y^2$ in.^{2}
c. 493 in.^{2} **d.** no **12. b.** $(x + y)$ and $(x - y)$
13. c. 493 in.^{2}

Lesson 2.03
Check Your Understanding

1. a. 8 **b.** -17 **c.** $-b$ **d.** $-\frac{13}{27}$ **e.** $\frac{d}{c}$ **f.** 0

2. a. $x = 7$ or $x = -5$ **b.** $x = 3$ or $y = -7$
c. $x = 0$ or $x = -2$ **d.** $x = -3$, $x = -4$, or $x = -5$

3. a. Estimates may vary. Sample: $\frac{5}{3}$, $-\frac{7}{2}$

x	f(x)
−5	60
−4	17
−3	−14
−2	−33
−1	−40
0	−35
1	−18
2	11
3	52
4	105
5	170

b. $(2x + 7)(3x - 5) = 6x^2 + 11x - 35$

	3x	−5
2x	$6x^2$	−10x
+7	21x	−35

c. $x = \frac{5}{3}$ or $-\frac{7}{2}$ **4. a.** $x = -7$, $x = -11$
b. $x \approx -6.8$ or $x \approx -11.2$ **5.** Answers may vary. Sample: Ling is just finding numeric factors, and they do not give her helpful information. **6.** $x = 0$, $x = 1$, or $x = -1$
7. a. Answers may vary. Sample: Apply the Distributive Property to $t(100 - 16t)$.
b. $t = 0$ s or $t = 6.25$ s; $t = 0$ is when the projectile is initially fired and $t = 6.25$ s is when the projectile lands. **c.** $t = 0$ s; $t = 6.25$ s

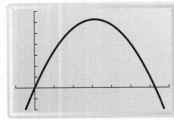

d. At about 3.125 s; you can predict this time because it's halfway between the two values where $s(t) = 0$. **e.** The projectile goes straight u

p to its maximum height and then back down again.

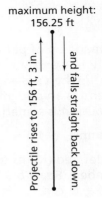

maximum height: 156.25 ft

Projectile rises to 156 ft, 3 in.

and falls straight back down.

On Your Own
8. a. $x = 23$ **9. a.** $x = 8$ or $x = 23$ **10. a.** True; 5 is a prime number. **12.** $(x + 3)(x + 2)$

Lesson 2.04
Check Your Understanding

1. a. $3x^2$ **b.** $9x$ **c.** 3 **d.** 1 **e.** a **f.** 1 **g.** p^2q^4
h. p^2q **i.** p^2q **j.** $3(x + 3)^2$ **2. a.** $3x^2(3x - 5)$
b. $9x(x^2 - 4)$ or $9x(x - 2)(x + 2)$
c. $3(5a^2 + 7b^2)$ **d.** $x^2 + y^2$ **e.** $a(b - c)$
f. $ab + ac + bc$ **g.** $p^2q(pq^3 + q^4 - p^5)$
3. a. $x = 0$ or $x = -\frac{2}{3}$ **b.** $x = 0$ or $x = \frac{5}{3}$
c. $x = 0$, $x = 2$, or $x = -2$ **d.** $a = 0$ or $b = c$
e. $x = 0$ or $x = 100$ **f.** $x = 0$ and $y = 0$
4. $(2x - 3)(3x + 7)$

On Your Own
5. a. $x(3a + 5b)$ **6. a.** $x^3 + x^2 + x + 1$
8. a. Find the area of the two circular bases and add the area of the rectangle.

Lesson 2.05
On Your Own

	1	3	4	5	6	8
1	2	4	5	6	7	9
2	3	5	6	7	8	10
2	3	5	6	7	8	10
3	4	6	7	8	9	11
3	4	6	7	8	9	11
4	5	7	8	9	10	12

7. Observations may vary. Sample: the number of times each value from 2 to 12 occurs is the same as for two standard number cubes. So with these two number cubes, you have the same probability of getting any particular total as you would with standard number cubes.

8. $x^2 + 2x^3 + 3x^4 + 4x^5 + 5x^6 + 6x^7 + 5x^8 + 4x^9 + 3x^{10} + 2x^{11} + x^{12}$ **9. a.** yes
b. no

Lesson 2.06
Check Your Understanding

1. a. Answers may vary. Sample: $x^3 - 2x + 4$, $2x^3 + x^2 + x - 5$ **b.** Not possible; if the sum has degree 4, the product must have degree 4 or greater. **c.** Answers may vary. Sample: x^4, 1 **d.** Not possible; if the sum has degree 2, the product must have degree 2 or greater.

2. Answers may vary. Sample: x^2, $-x^2 + x$
3. a–d. Answers may vary. Samples are given.
a. $2x^2 + 4x + 2$, $x^2 + 3x + 2$
b. $3x^2 + 6x + 1$, $x + 3$ **c.** $x + 5$, $-x - 1$
d. $x + 1$, $x - 1$ **4.** The degree of the squared polynomial is twice the degree of the original; answers may vary.Sample:
$(x + 1)^2 = x^2 + 2x + 1$,
$(x^2 + 2)^2 = x^4 + 4x^2 + 4$,
$(2x^3 + 1)^2 = 4x^6 + 4x^3 + 1$

On Your Own
5. Answers may vary. Samples are given.
a. x, x^5 **6. b.** $s(x) = x^2 - 4x + 5$ **7.** $a = 2$

Lesson 2.07
Check Your Understanding

1. a. $\frac{3}{4}x^5 + x^4 - 13x^2 - 5x + 3$ **b.** 5 **c.** −5
d. −13 **e.** 0 **f.** Answers may vary. Sample:
$-\frac{3}{4}x^5 - x^4 + x^3$ **2. a–d.** Replace x with 10 in each identity to derive the number fact.
3. a. $120 = 2^3 \cdot 3 \cdot 5$; $168 = 2^3 \cdot 3 \cdot 7$ **b.** 24 is the greatest common factor since both have $2^3 \cdot 3$ as factors. **c.** $3^2 \cdot 5^3 = 1125$ **d.** x^2y^3
e. $24x^2y^3$ **4.** $x^4 + 6x^3 + (a + 2)x^2 + (3a - 21)x - 7a$; $a = 7$ **5–8.** Answers may vary. Samples are given.
5. $(1^3 - 1)(1^3 + 1) = 1^6 - 1$
$0 = 0$
$(x^3 - 1)(x^3 + 1) =$
$x^6 + x^3 - x^3 - 1 = x^6 - 1$
6. $2^6 - 1 = (2 - 1)(2 + 1)$
$(2^2 + 2 + 1)(2^2 - 2 + 1)$
$64 - 1 = (1)(3)(4 + 2 + 1)(4 - 2 + 1)$
$63 = 3 \cdot 7 \cdot 3$
$(x - 1)(x + 1)(x^2 + x + 1) \cdot (x^2 - x + 1) =$
$(x - 1)(x^2 + x + 1)(x + 1) \cdot (x^2 - x + 1) =$
$(x^3 - x^2 + x^2 - x + x - 1) \cdot$
$(x^3 + x^2 - x^2 - x + x + 1) =$

$(x^3 - 1)(x^3 + 1) = x^6 - 1$
7. $(2^6 - 1) = (2^2 - 1)(2^4 + 2^2 + 1)$
$64 - 1 = (4 - 1)(16 + 4 + 1); 63 = (3)(21)$
$(x^2 - 1)(x^4 + x^2 + 1) =$
$x^6 + x^4 + x^2 - (x^4 + x^2 + 1) =$
$x^6 + x^4 + x^2 - x^4 - x^2 - 1 =$
$x^6 - 1$
8. $1^3 - 1 = (1 - 1)(1^3 + 1 + 1)$
$1 - 1 = (0)(1 + 1 + 1)$
$0 = 0$
$(x - 1)(x^2 + x + 1) =$
$x^3 + x^2 + x - (x^2 + x + 1) =$
$x^3 + x^2 + x - x^2 - x - 1 =$
$x^3 - 1$ **9.** Answers may vary;
$(s + t)^2 - (s - t)^2 =$
$s^2 + 2st + t^2 - (s^2 - 2st + t^2) =$
$s^2 + 2st + t^2 - s^2 + 2st - t^2 = 4st$
10. Answers may vary; $(n + 1)^2 - (n)^2 =$
$n^2 + 2n + 1 - n^2 = 2n + 1$
11. $(x^3 - 1)(x^3 + 1) = x^6 - 1 =$
$(x^2 - 1)(x^4 + x^2 + 1)$

On Your Own
14. a. $m^2 - n^2 = (m + n)(m - n) =$
$m(m - n) + n(m - n)$ **16. a.** 5

Lesson 2.08
Check Your Understanding

1. a. $k = 4$ **b.** $k = 2$ **c.** $k = -10$ **d.** $k = 5$
e. $k = -\frac{1}{2}$ **f.** $k = 2$ **2. a.** 3 **b.** 5 **c.** 0
3. To get x^3, you must multiply x by itself three times and then multiply the result by 1. There are four ways to do this among the four terms of the product, so the coefficient is 4. **4.** The degrees of the two polynomials are different. **5.** 4 **6.** Answers may vary. Sample: $a = 2$, $b = 2$, and $c = -12$; $a = 1$, $b = -\frac{5}{2}$, and $c = 1$; $a = -\frac{3}{4}$, $b = 1$, and $c = 1$ **7.** When you expand $(h + t)^4$, where h represents heads and t represents tails, you get $h^4 + 4h^3t + 6h^2t^2 + 4ht^3 + t^4$. It shows 6 ways to get two heads and two tails, 4 ways to get 3 heads and one tail, and 6 other tosses that result in a draw. **8.** $x^2 + 3x + 2$
9. a. 84 **b.** $2a^2c^2 + 2a^2b^2 + 2b^2c^2 - a^4 - b^4 - c^4$ **c.** $A = \frac{\sqrt{3}}{4}s^2$ **d.** 0; the sum of the lengths of any 2 sides of a triangle must be greater than the length of the third side.
10. See Figure 1.

Figure 1

$$A = \sqrt{\tfrac{1}{2}(a + b + c)\left(\tfrac{1}{2}(a + b + c) - a\right)\left(\tfrac{1}{2}(a + b + c) - b\right)\left(\tfrac{1}{2}(a + b + c) - c\right)}$$

$$= \sqrt{\tfrac{1}{2}(a + b + c)\left(\tfrac{a}{2} + \tfrac{b}{2} + \tfrac{c}{2} - a\right)\left(\tfrac{a}{2} + \tfrac{b}{2} + \tfrac{c}{2} - b\right)\left(\tfrac{a}{2} + \tfrac{b}{2} + \tfrac{c}{2} - c\right)}$$

$$= \sqrt{\tfrac{1}{2}(a + b + c)\left(-\tfrac{a}{2} + \tfrac{b}{2} + \tfrac{c}{2}\right)\left(\tfrac{a}{2} - \tfrac{b}{2} + \tfrac{c}{2}\right)\left(\tfrac{a}{2} + \tfrac{b}{2} - \tfrac{c}{2}\right)}$$

$$= \sqrt{\tfrac{1}{2}(a + b + c)\tfrac{1}{2}(-a + b + c)\tfrac{1}{2}(a - b + c)\tfrac{1}{2}(a + b - c)}$$

$$= \sqrt{\tfrac{1}{16}(a + b + c)(b + c - a)(a + c - b)(a + b - c)}$$

$$= \tfrac{1}{4}\sqrt{(a + b + c)(a + b - c)(a + c - b)(b + c - a)}$$

On Your Own

12. 20   **15.** −3

Lesson 2.09
On Your Own
6.

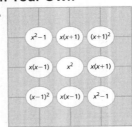

7. b. 43 and 59   **9. a.** yes

11. b. $x^2 - 22x + 120$ **d.** $x^2 - x + \tfrac{2}{9}$

Lesson 2.10
Check Your Understanding
1. a. True; substitute $4x$ for a and $3y$ for b.
b. false **c.** True; substitute 5 for a and t^3 for b. **d.** True: substitute $(x + 3)$ for x and 1 for b. **e.** false **f.** false   **2. a.** 0; since $(50 + x)(50 - x) = 50^2 - x^2$, and because $x^2 \geq 0$, the product is greatest when x^2 is least. **b.** $x = 50$, $y = 50$ **3. a.** $x = 4$, $y = 3$ **b.** $x = 7$, $y = 6$ **c.** $x = 5$, $y = 4$; or $x = 3$, $y = 0$
4. a. 6000 **b.** 5000 **c.** 7400   **5.** no; $(-b)^2 = b^2$
6. The entry that is k away from a^2 is $a^2 - k^2$; moving along the diagonal is the same as moving down k and to the right k, or up k and to the left k. In either case, the product is $(a + k)(a - k)$, or $a^2 - k^2$.   **7. a.** $k = -3$
b. $k = 100$ **c.** $k = 4$
8.

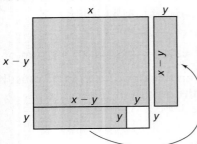

9. No; $(a + 1)^2 - a^2 = a^2 + 2a + 1 - a^2 = 2a + 1$, which is odd for all a.

10. a. $(x + 9.5)^2 - (1.5)^2 = ((x + 9.5) + 1.5)((x + 9.5) - 1.5) = (x + 11)(x - 8)$ **b.** $(x + 10)^2 - (2)^2 = ((x + 10) + 2)((x + 10) - 2) = (x + 12)(x + 8)$
c. $\left(x + \tfrac{27}{2}\right)^2 - \left(\tfrac{1}{2}\right)^2 = \left(\left(x + \tfrac{27}{2}\right) - \left(\tfrac{1}{2}\right)\right) \cdot \left(\left(x + \tfrac{27}{2}\right) + \left(\tfrac{1}{2}\right)\right) = (x + 13)(x + 14)$
11. $r = \tfrac{a + b}{2}$, $s = \pm\tfrac{a - b}{2}$ **12.** 49 cm
13. a. $x = 3$ or $x = -3$ **b.** $x = 7$ or $x = -1$
c. $x = 2$ or $x = 1$ **d.** $x = a + b$ or $x = a - b$

On Your Own
14. a. 9   **15. a.** yes   **16. a.** 48; this is a 7-by-7 square (49 squares) with one missing.
17. $k = 11$ or $k = -11$ **18. a.** 0
21. a. $y(y + 3)(y - 3)$

Lesson 2.11
Check Your Understanding
1. D; D is of the form $x^2 + bx + c = 0$, where the roots sum to $-b$ and have a product of c.
2. a. $x = -9$ and $x = -4$ **b.** $x = -6$ and $x = -7$ **c.** No integer solution; the maximum product of integers that have a sum of 13 is 42, which is less than 224. **d.** $x = 3$ and $x = -16$
e. $x = -2$ and $x = -11$ **f.** $x = -19$ and $x = 6$
g. No integer solution; the maximum product of integers that have a sum of 13 is 42, which is less than 54. **h.** No integer solution; there are no integers that have a sum of 13 and a product of −20. **i.** No integer solution; there are no integers that have a sum of 13 and a product of 17. **j.** $x = 1$ and $x = -14$
3. a. $x = 10$ and $x = 6$ **b.** no solutions
c. $x = 0$ and $x = 16$ **d.** $x = 3$ **e.** $x = 4$ and $x = -4$ **f.** $x = -4$ **g.** $x = -5$ and $x = 2$
h. $x = -7$ and $x = -10$ **i.** no solutions

j. $x = 5$ **4.** A, C, and E **5. a.** The expression $x^2 - 6x + 9$ factors to $(x - 3)^2$, and a square can never be negative.
b. $x^2 + y^2 + 10x - 8y + 42 =$
$(x^2 + 10x + 25) + (y^2 - 8y + 16) + 1 =$
$(x + 5)^2 + (y - 4)^2 + 1$, which is always positive.

On Your Own
8. a. 64 **b.** $(x - 8)(x - 8)$ **11. a.** 25

Lesson 2.12
Check Your Understanding
1. a. $x = 7$ and $x = -1$ **b.** $y = \frac{9}{2}$ and $y = -\frac{11}{2}$
c. $n = -5 + \sqrt{5}$ and $n = -5 - \sqrt{5}$
2. a. $k = 1$ **b.** $k = 2$ **c.** $k = -2$ **d.** $k = 6$
e. $k = 4.5$ **f.** $k = -12.5$ **g.** $k = 8$ and $k = -9$
3. a. $x = -4$ **b.** $y = -5$ **4. a.** 1.06 **b.** 1.01
c. The error is $|1 - x|^2$. **5. a.** $x = 5$ or $x = 1$
b. $x = -9$ or $x = 1$ **c.** $x = 3 - \sqrt{2}$ or
$x = 3 + \sqrt{2}$ **d.** $x = -1$ or $x = 2$
e. $x = -1$ or $x = -5$ **6. a.** 5; 7-by-15
b. 11; 1-by-5 **c.** $-4 + \sqrt{31}$; $(-1 + \sqrt{31})$ by
$(1 + \sqrt{31})$ **7. a.** 60 or -60 **b.** 4 **8. a.** Tony is
referring to adding 1 and subtracting 1, which
have a sum of zero. **b.** $x = -1 - \sqrt{\frac{11}{2}}$ and
$x = -1 + \sqrt{\frac{11}{2}}$ **9.** Answers may vary. Sample:
$x^2 + 2x + 3 = 5$; $x^2 + 2x - 2 = 0$
$x^2 + 2x + 1 - 1 - 2 = 0$
$(x + 1)^2 - 3 = 0$
$(x + 1 + \sqrt{3})(x + 1 - \sqrt{3}) = 0$
The solutions are $x = -1 - \sqrt{3}$ and
$x = -1 + \sqrt{3}$. **10.** Answers may vary.
Sample: $x^2 + 2x + 3 = -15$

On Your Own
13. a. $k = -9$ **14. a.** $x = -11$ or $x = 3$
15. $x = 2$ or $x = 6$ **19. a.** $x = -10$ or $x = -2$

Chapter 3
Lesson 3.01
On Your Own
12. a. $x = 3 \pm \sqrt{5}$ **15. a.** $x = 3$

Lesson 3.02
Check Your Understanding
1. $x = \frac{-7 \pm \sqrt{37}}{6}$ **2.** $x = \frac{-7 \pm \sqrt{145}}{6}$
3. $x = \frac{7 \pm \sqrt{145}}{6}$ **4.** No real solutions; you
get a negative number under the square root
sign. **5.** $x = 2$ or $x = \frac{1}{3}$ **6.** $w = \frac{\sqrt{5} \pm 5}{2}$
7. $z = \sqrt{2} \pm \sqrt{3}$ **8.** $x = 3 \pm k$ **9.** $x = 31$ or
$x = -30$ **10.** $x = 6 \pm \sqrt{65}$ **11. a.** 28 clinks
b. 12 people

On Your Own
12. $x = \frac{3 \pm 2\sqrt{5}}{4}$ **19. a.** $k < 12$ **b.** $k = 12$
c. $k > 12$ **21.** $-\frac{1}{2} < x < \frac{4}{3}$ **24. a.** all real
numbers **25. a.** $x^2 - 12x + 35 = 0$

Lesson 3.03
Check Your Understanding
1. Answers may vary. Samples are given.
a. $x^2 - 20x + 51 = 0$ **b.** $x^2 + 20x + 51 = 0$
c. $x^2 - 40x + 204 = 0$ **d.** $x^2 - 4x + 1 = 0$
e. $x^2 + 4x + 1 = 0$ **f.** $x^2 - 20x + 25 = 0$
2. a. $x^2 + 17x - 78 = 0$
b. $x^2 - 51x - 702 = 0$ **c.** $x^2 + \frac{17}{78}x - \frac{1}{78} = 0$
or $78x^2 + 17x - 1 = 0$
d. $x^2 - 445x + 6084 = 0$ **3. a.** $\frac{-b}{a}$ **b.** $\frac{c}{a}$ **c.** $\frac{-b}{2a}$

On Your Own
4. Answers may vary. Sample:
$x^2 - 2\sqrt{5}x - 4 = 0$ **8.** $\frac{1 \pm \sqrt{5}}{2}$

Lesson 3.04
Check Your Understanding
1. a. $(3x + 7)(3x - 1)$ **b.** $(3x - 5)(2x - 7)$
c. $(5x + 7)(3x - 1)$ **d.** $(9x - 1)(x + 7)$
e. $(9x^2 - 1)(x^2 + 7)$ or
$(3x + 1)(3x - 1)(x^2 + 7)$
2. a. $(3x + 7y)(3x - y)$ **b.** $(2x - 7y)(3x - 5y)$
c. $(3x - a)(5x + 7a)$ **d.** $(9x - b)(x + 7b)$
3. Answers will vary. Sample: Multiply the
constant term by the coefficient of the
x^2-term and change the coefficient of the
x^2-term to 1.

On Your Own
4. a. $-(9x + 1)(2x + 7)$ **8.** $x = 3$ or
$x = -\frac{1}{2}$ **10. a.** $x = -5$ or $x = \frac{7}{3}$

Lesson 3.05
On Your Own
6. -1 **8. a.** $x = -10$ or $x = -4$ **b.** $x = 8$
or $x = -3$ **9.** No; explanations may vary.
Sample: There are no real solutions.

Lesson 3.06
Check Your Understanding
1. a. -16 **b.** -4 **c.** -25 **2.** Answers may vary.
Sample: $f(x) = (x + 5)^2 - 12$ **3.** 10 and 10
4. $\frac{251}{2}$ and $\frac{251}{2}$ **5.** $\frac{c}{2}$ and $\frac{c}{2}$
On Your Own
7. -12 **8.** 45 ft by 45 ft **9.** 45 and 45

Lesson 3.07
Check Your Understanding

1. a.

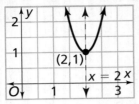

b.

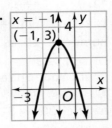

c.

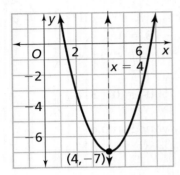

d.

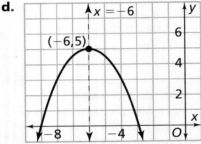

2. a. $(6, 0)$ **b.** $y = -2(x - 3)^2 + 18$

3. a.

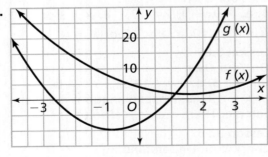

b.

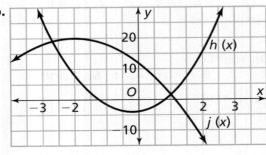

The graphs are also parabolas. **c.** h and j will usually be quadratic. j will be linear if $f(x)$ and $g(x)$ have the same x^2 coefficient and constant if $f(x)$ and $g(x)$ have the same x and x^2 are coefficients. h will be linear if $f(x)$ and $g(x)$ have opposite x^2 coefficients and constant if $f(x)$ and $g(x)$ have opposite x and x^2 coefficients. **4.** 144 ft **5. a.** 16 ft **b.** 64 ft **c.** 256 ft **6. a.** four times as high **b.** nine times as high **c.** Curt: 324 ft; Ryan: 81 ft; Taylor: 9 ft **7.** approximately 282.8 ft/s or about 189 m/h

On Your Own

13. a. $y = x(20 - x)$ **b.** The roots occur when the product is 0. This happens when $x = 0$ or when $x = 20$. The average of the roots gives the line of symmetry, $x = 10$, where the maximum occurs. **c.** $y = -(x - 10)^2 + 100$
15. $(3, 8)$

Lesson 3.08
Check Your Understanding

1. a. $x = -4$ and $x = -6$ **b.** Find the average of the roots or use the rule $x = -\frac{b}{2a}$ to find the x-coordinate, -5. Substitute to find the y-coordinate, -1. **2. a.** $x = \frac{-9 \pm \sqrt{-39}}{2}$ **b.** $\frac{-9}{2}$ **3.** Answers may vary. Samples: $y = x^2 - 8x + 15$; $y = 10x^2 - 80x$; $y = -2x^2 + 16x + 14$ **4. a.** Answers may vary. Sample: The line of symmetry is found by averaging the roots. $x = 5.5$ **b.** Answers may vary. Sample: The minimum y-value is at the vertex, so the vertex is $(5.5, -25)$. **c.** 4

5. a.

Input	Output	Δ
0	0	1
1	1	3
2	4	5
3	9	7
4	16	9
5	25	11
6	36	

b.

Input	Output	Δ
0	0	2
1	2	6
2	8	10
3	18	14
4	32	18
5	50	22
6	72	

c.

Input	Output	Δ
0	−1	−3
1	−4	3
2	−1	9
3	8	15
4	23	21
5	44	27
6	71	

d.

Input	Output	Δ
0	9	−1
1	8	−3
2	5	−5
3	0	−7
4	−7	−9
5	−16	−11
6	−27	

6. a.

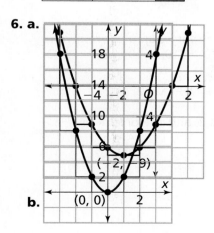

b. (0, 0)

There is a relationship. Starting from the vertex, the next point is across 1 and up 2, then across 1 and up 6, then across 1 and up 10, and so on. Each of the numbers here is twice what it would be for $y = x^2$.

c.

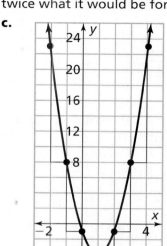

d.

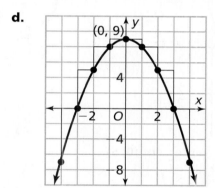

7. Answers may vary. Sample: The numbers in the Δ column of the difference tables are the numbers to go up or down with Linda's method.

On Your Own

9. vertex (5.5, 100); $y = -16(x - 3)(x - 8)$

11. a. (0, −9) **c.** (3, 82)

Lesson 3.09
On Your Own
9a. 102 **14c.** $\frac{3}{2}$ and $\frac{1}{2}$

Lesson 3.2
Check Your Understanding
1a. 4, 6 **b.** 10 **c–g.** no solution **h.** 1 **2a.** no additional solutions **b.** 0 **c.** −6, −4
d–h. no additional solutions **3a–c.** no additional solutions **d.** $\frac{1}{4}, \frac{1}{6}$ **e–h.** no additional solutions **4a–d.** no additional solutions
e. $\sqrt{10}, -\sqrt{10}$ **f–h.** no additional solutions

5a–e. no additional solutions
f. $\sqrt{-10}$, $-\sqrt{-10}$ **g.** $\dfrac{-1 \pm \sqrt{-3}}{2}$ **h.** $\dfrac{-1 \pm \sqrt{-3}}{2}$
6a. 2 **b.** 1 **c.** 0 **d.** 2

7a.

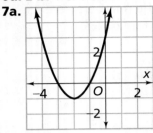

x-intercepts $(-3, 0)$, $(-1, 0)$, y-intercept $(0, 3)$

b.

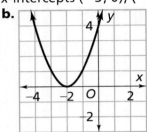

x-intercept $(-2, 0)$, y-intercept $(0, 4)$

c.

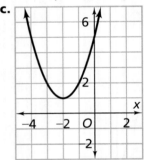

no x-intercept, y-intercept $(0, 5)$

d.

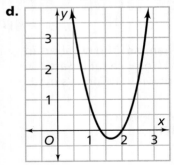

x-intercepts $\left(\frac{4}{3}, 0\right)$, $(2, 0)$, y-intercept $(0, 8)$
8a. 0 **b.** If $f(x) = x^2 - 2x + 2$, then $f(1 + i) = 0$
(by Exercise 8a). **9a.** $a(0) = 2$, $a(1) = 0$,
$a(2) = 6$, $a(3) = 0$, $a(4) = 18$, $a(5) = 0$, $a(6) = 54$
b. $a(10) = 486$, $a(101) = 0$ **c.** No; Answers may

vary. Sample: $a(n) = 0$ for all odd values of n,
and since there are an infinite number of odd
positive integers, $a(n)$ cannot be a polynomial.

10a. rational **b.** irrational **c.** irrational
d. $f(0) = 2$, $f(1) = 2$, $f(2) = 6$, $f(3) = 14$,
$f(4) = 34$, $f(5) = 82$, $f(6) = 198$ **e.** Answers
may vary. Sample: $x^2 - 2x - 1 = 0$ **f.** Answers
may vary. Sample: $2 \cdot f(n - 1) + f(n - 2)$

$$= 2[(1 + \sqrt{2})^{n-1} + (1 - \sqrt{2})^{n-1}]$$
$$\quad + (1 + \sqrt{2})^{n-2} + (1 - \sqrt{2})^{n-2}$$
$$= 2(1 + \sqrt{2})^{n-1} + (1 + \sqrt{2})^{n-2}$$
$$\quad + 2(1 - \sqrt{2})^{n-1} + (1 - \sqrt{2})^{n-2}$$
$$= (1 + \sqrt{2})^{n-2}[2(1 + \sqrt{2}) + 1]$$
$$\quad + (1 + \sqrt{2})^{n-2}[2(1 - \sqrt{2}) + 1]$$
$$= (1 + \sqrt{2})^{n-2}[(3 + 2\sqrt{2})] +$$
$$\quad (1 - \sqrt{2})^{n-2}[(3 - 2\sqrt{2})]$$
$$= (1 + \sqrt{2})^{n-2}(1 + \sqrt{2})^2$$
$$\quad + (1 - \sqrt{2})^{n-2}(1 - \sqrt{2})^2$$
$$= (1 + \sqrt{2})^n + (1 - \sqrt{2})^n$$
$$= f(n)$$

11a. $g(0) = 2$, $g(1) = 4$, $g(2) = 6$, $g(3) = 4$,
$g(4) = -14$, $g(5) = -76$, $g(6) = -234$
b. $(2 + \sqrt{-1})^2 = 4 + (-1) + 4\sqrt{-1} =$
$3 + 4\sqrt{-1}$ **c.** Answers may vary. Sample:
$x^2 - 4x + 5 = 0$ **d.** $4g(n - 1) - 5g(n - 2)$

$$= 4(2 + \sqrt{-1})^{n-1} + 4(2 - \sqrt{-1})^{n-1}$$
$$\quad - 5(2 + \sqrt{-1})^{n-2} - 5(2 - \sqrt{-1})^{n-2}$$
$$= (2 + \sqrt{-1})^{n-2}[4(2 + \sqrt{-1}) - 5]$$
$$\quad + (2 - \sqrt{-1})^{n-2}[4(2 - \sqrt{-1}) - 5]$$
$$= (2 + \sqrt{-1})^{n-2}(8 + 4\sqrt{-1} - 5)$$
$$\quad + (2 - \sqrt{-1})^{n-2}(8 - 4\sqrt{-1} - 5)$$
$$= (2 + \sqrt{-1})^{n-2}(3 + 4\sqrt{-1})$$
$$\quad + (2 - \sqrt{-1})^{n-2}(3 - 4\sqrt{-1})$$
$$= (2 + \sqrt{-1})^{n-2}(2 + \sqrt{-1})^2$$
$$\quad + (2 - \sqrt{-1})^{n-2}(2 - \sqrt{-1})^2$$
$$= (2 + \sqrt{-1})^n + (2 - \sqrt{-1})^n$$
$$= g(n)$$

On Your Own
12. Answers may vary. Samples are given.
a. $(-10) - (-20) = 10$, $(-10)(-20) = 200$
b. $\frac{5}{4} \cdot \frac{4}{5} = 1$, $\frac{5}{4} + \frac{3}{4} = 2$
d. $(1 + \sqrt{-2}) + (1 - \sqrt{-2}) = 2$,
$\sqrt{-1} \cdot \sqrt{-1} = -1$
15c. The sum is 2, and the product is -2.

Lesson 3.11
Check Your Understanding
1a. $a^2 - b^2$ **b.** $a^2 - 2b^2$ **c.** $a^2 - 3b^2$
d. $a^2 - cb^2$ **e.** $a^2 + b^2$
2.

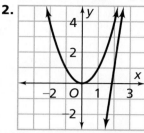

The graphs do not intersect. **3a.** $3 \pm \sqrt{-2}$
b. The sum is 6, and the product is 11. **4.** Yes;
Answers may vary. Sample: The Quadratic
Formula gives the solutions to any quadratic
equation. **5.** $\sqrt{34} = 5.83$ and $-\sqrt{34} = -5.83$
6. No; 0 is nonnegative and has only one
number whose square is 0. **7.** Answers may
vary. Sample: $x^3 - 5x^2 + 8x - 6 =$
$(x - 3)(x^2 - 2x + 2) = 0$, and the solutions to
$x^2 - 2x + 2 = 0$ are $1 + \sqrt{-1}$ and $1 - \sqrt{-1}$.
8a. 5 **b.** 8 **c.** 6

On Your Own
9a. -6 **e.** $-3 + 2\sqrt{-3}$
11b. $7 + 9\sqrt{-1}$ **c.** $23 + 15\sqrt{-1}$
13a. $x^3 - 8 = (x - 2)(x^2 + 2x + 4)$

Lesson 3.12
Check Your Understanding
1a. $12 + i$ **b.** $25 + 21i$ **c.** $10 + 0i$
d. $29 + 0i$ **e.** $6 + 6i$ **f.** $0 + 20i$ **2a.** 6 **b.** 34
c. -14 **d.** 53 **e.** 24 **f.** 169 **3a.** $(a - bi)$
b. $(a + bi) + (a - bi) = a + a + (b - b)i$
$= 2a$, and if a is real, $2a$ is also real.
c. $(a + bi)(a - bi) = a^2 - b^2 i^2 + abi - abi =$
$a^2 + b^2$, and if a and b are real, $a^2 + b^2$ is
also real. **d.** when $a = 0$ in $a + bi$ and $a - bi$
e. when $a = 0$ and $b = 0$ **4.** No; Derman is
wrong because a and b must be real numbers
in $a + bi$. **5.** $4 - 7i$ **6a.** Yes; the opposite of
$2 + 3i$ is $-2 - 3i$. **b.** All complex numbers
have opposites. **7.** If $z = a + bi$,
then $z^2 + \bar{z}^2 = (a + bi)^2 + (a - bi)^2$
$= (a^2 + 2abi - b^2) + (a^2 - 2abi - b^2)$
$= 2a^2 - 2b^2$, which is a real number.
8a. $x^2 - 6x + 13 = 0$ **b.** $x^2 - 6x + 13 = 0$
c. $(x^2 - 6x + 13)(x^2 - 2x + 26) = 0$
d. $(x^2 - 2x + 26)(x^2 + 2x + 26) = 0$
e. $x^2 - 2x + 4 = 0$ **f.** $x - (\sqrt{2} + \sqrt{3}) = 0$, or
$x^4 - 10x^2 + 1 = 0$ **g.** $x^2 - (2\sqrt{2})x + 5 = 0$

On Your Own
10a. $-i$ **b.** 1 **11a.** $3 + 3i$ **d.** $3 \pm 5i$
13. Answers may vary. Samples are given.
a. $1 + i$ **14a.** $(x + i)(x - i) = x^2 - i^2 + xi -$
$xi = x^2 - (-1) = x^2 + 1$

Lesson 3.13
Check Your Understanding
1. $z + \bar{z}$ is a real number. **2a.** $-2i$
b. 7 **c.** $\overline{z + w} = \overline{7 + 2i} = 7 - 2i$, and
$\bar{z} + \bar{w} = -2i + 7 = 7 - 2i$, so they are equal.
3a. $\bar{z} = a - bi$, and $\bar{w} = c - di$
b. $\overline{z + w} = \overline{(a + c) + (b + d)i} =$
$(a + c) - (b + d)i$; $\bar{z} + \bar{w} =$
$(a - bi) + (c - di) = (a + c) - (b + d)i$
4a. $3 - 2i$ **b.** $3 + 2i$ **c.** $7 + 3i$ **d.** $7 + 3i$
e. $22 + 7i$ **f.** $22 + 7i$ **g.** 6 **h.** 41 **5a.** $4 - 7i$
b. $\frac{7}{5} + \frac{6}{5}i$ **c.** $4 + 0i$ **d.** $\frac{4}{5} + \frac{3}{5}i$ **e.** $\frac{4}{5} - \frac{3}{5}i$
f. $\frac{ac + bd}{a^2 + b^2} + \frac{ad - bc}{a^2 + b^2}i$ **6a.** $-9 + 38i$
b. $-9 - 38i$ **c.** $37 + 50i$ **d.** $37 - 50i$ **e.** $1 + 76i$
f. $1 - 76i$ **7.** If $z = a + bi$ and $w = c + di$,
then $\overline{zw} = \overline{(ac - bd) + (ad + bc)i} =$
$(ac - bd) - (ad + bc)i$, and $(\bar{z})(\bar{w}) =$
$(a - bi)(c - di) = (ac - bd) + (-ad - bc)i$
$= (ac - bd) - (ad + bc)i$.
8a. $z + \bar{z} = (a + bi) + (a - bi) = 2a$
b. $z\bar{z} = (a + bi)(a - bi) = a^2 - b^2 i^2 +$
$(ab - ab)i = a^2 + b^2$ **9a.** $a = 7, b = 5$ or
$a = 7, b = -5$ **b.** $7 + 5i, 7 - 5i$

On Your Own
10a. $\frac{1}{2} - \frac{1}{2}i$ **12a.** -1 **g.** $9 - 40i$
16a. $(a + bi)^2 = a^2 + abi + abi + b^2 i^2 =$
$(a^2 - b^2) + (2ab)i$

Chapter 4
Lesson 4.01
On Your Own
3–18. Answers may vary. Samples are given.
3. $E(n) = 2n + 3$ **8.** $J(n) = 2n^2$
12. $N(n) = (n + 3)^2$ **16.** $R(n) = n^3$
18. $T(n) = 3^n$

Lesson 4.02
Check Your Understanding

1.

Input, n	Output, $B(n)$	Δ
0	0	2
1	2	4
2	6	6
3	12	8
4	20	

2a. no **b.** no **c.** yes **d.** no **3a.** no **b.** yes **c.** yes **d.** no

4.

Input	Output	Δ
0	5	6
1	11	8
2	19	10
3	29	15
4	44	

5.

Input	Output	Δ
0	6	3
1	9	3
2	12	3
3	15	3
4	18	

6.

Input	Output	Δ
0	5	−3
1	2	15
2	17	−13
3	4	−5
4	−1	

7a. $f(1) = 1 \cdot f(0) = 1 \cdot 1 = 1$
$f(2) = 2 \cdot f(1) = 2 \cdot 1 = 2$
$f(3) = 3 \cdot f(2) = 3 \cdot 2 = 6$
$f(4) = 4 \cdot f(3) = 4 \cdot 6 = 24$
$f(5) = 5 \cdot f(4) = 5 \cdot 24 = 120$
$f(6) = 6 \cdot f(5) = 6 \cdot 120 = 720$
b. $f(n) = n!$

8a.

Input	Output
0	2
1	6
2	10
3	14
4	18

b–c.

Input	Output
0	2
1	6
2	18
3	54
4	162

d. see part (a) **9.** Answers may vary. Sample: Tables E, F, and G have a constant difference in the difference table; Tables I, J, and K include an x^2 term in the rule.

On Your Own

10.

Side Length	Number of Dots	Δ
0	0	1
1	1	2
2	3	3
3	6	4
4	10	5
5	15	

11a. $T(n) = T(n - 1) + n$
12a. The differences are all a.

Lesson 4.03
Check Your Understanding

1.

Input	Output	Δ
0	−7	3
1	−4	3
2	−1	3
3	2	
4	5	

2. $f(n) = \begin{cases} -7 & \text{if } n = 0 \\ f(n-1) + 3 & \text{if } n > 0 \end{cases}$

3. $g(n) = 3n - 7$ **4a.** 23 **b.** 23.3 for closed form rule; the recursive rule cannot be applied if n is not a nonnegative integer. **5.** The differences are -6, 6, -6, and 6, which are not constant.

6.

n	$p(n)$	Δ
0	3	$-\frac{7}{4}$
1	$\frac{5}{4}$	$-\frac{7}{4}$
2	$-\frac{1}{2}$	$-\frac{7}{4}$
3	$-\frac{9}{4}$	$-\frac{7}{4}$
4	-4	

7. $p(10) = -\frac{29}{2}$; $p(100) = -172$; $p(263) = -\frac{1829}{4}$ **8.** D

9a.

n	$F(n)$	Δ
0	1	0
1	1	1
2	2	1
3	3	2
4	5	3
5	8	5
6	13	

b. The differences are the same as the outputs except that $\Delta_1 = 0$ and $\Delta_n = F(n - 1)$ for $n > 0$. **c.** $F(10) = 89$

On Your Own

14a.

n	$D(n)$	Δ
0	1	1
1	2	2
2	4	4
3	8	8
4	16	16
5	32	32
6	64	

b. The differences are directly related to the output. They are the same. $D(n + 1) - D(n) = D(n)$. They will never get to constant differences
17. -1.5

Lesson 4.04
Check Your Understanding

1a. $\frac{7}{2}$ **b.** $-\frac{1}{2}$ **c.** $f(n) = \frac{7}{2}n - \frac{1}{2}$ **2a.** $\frac{7}{2}$
b. $y = \frac{7}{2}x - \frac{1}{2}$ or $2y = 7x - 1$ **3.** The slope for $(0, -12)$ and $(3, 5)$ is $\frac{17}{3}$, and the slope for $(3, 5)$ and $(4, 10)$ is 5, so one line cannot contain all three points. **4.** No; the difference for the last two outputs is 5, but using that as the constant difference, you would expect the point $(0, -10)$, so the table does not have a constant difference. **5.** $a = -1, b = -26$
6. $f(n) = \frac{n}{2} - 2$ **7a.** 2 **b.** -18
7c. $f(n) = 5n - 33$
8. The differences are 1, 3, 5, and 7. Since those differences are not constant, the table cannot match a linear function.

9.

x	$K(x)$	Δ	Δ^2
0	1	1	2
1	2	3	2
2	5	5	2
3	10	7	
4	17		

On Your Own
10a. -5 **b.** $a = -1$
12a.

b. 0

17.

w	$R(w)$	Δ	Δ^2	Δ^3
0	0	1	6	6
1	1	7	12	6
2	8	19	18	6
3	27	37	24	6
4	64	61	30	6
5	125	91	36	
6	216	127		
7	343			

Lesson 4.05
Check Your Understanding
1. $y(n) = 5n^2 + 3n - 2$

2. $y(n) = -3n^2 + 15n + 10$

3.

w	R(w)	Δ	$Δ^2$	$Δ^3$
0	0	1	6	6
1	1	7	12	6
2	8	19	18	6
3	27	37	24	6
4	64	61	30	6
5	125	91	36	
6	216	127		
7	343			

4.

x	m(x)	Δ	$Δ^2$	$Δ^3$
0	4	−3	34	30
1	1	31	64	30
2	32	95	94	30
3	127	189	124	30
4	316	313	154	30
5	629	467	184	
6	1096	651		
7	1747			

5a. The column for $Δ^3$ should be constant.
b. The constant third difference is 6 times the leading coefficient. **6.** Yes; for any table with constant third differences, calculate $f(x + 1) - f(x)$ and show that the result can be put into Sasha's form. **7.** The Δ column begins $a + b + c$, $7a + 3b + c$, $19a + 5b + c$; the $Δ^2$ column begins $6a + 2b$, $12a + 2b$, $18a + 2b$; the $Δ^3$ column begins $6a$, $6a$, $6a$.
8a. $x = 3$, $x = 5$, $x = 6$
b. $x^3 - 14x^2 + 63x - 90$

9.

x	v(x)	Δ	$Δ^2$	$Δ^3$
0	−90	50	−22	6
1	−40	28	−16	6
2	−12	12	−10	6
3	0	2	−4	6
4	2	−2	2	6
5	0	0	8	
6	0	8		
7	8			

10. $y = 10x^2 - 23x + 7$ **11a.** No, the third differences are not constant. **b.** Except for the left column, each cell is equal to the cell that is one to the right and one down.
12. $f(n) = 2n^3 - 5n^2 + n - 3$

On Your Own
17. None of the first, second, or third differences are constant, so the table is not a linear, quadratic, or cubic function. **18.** The values of Rule 4 match the five input-output pairs in the table.

Lesson 4.06
On Your Own
6a. no **7a.** Answers may vary. Sample: −3 and 3 **8b.** 5 **9b.** 10

Lesson 4.07
Check Your Understanding
1a. all real numbers ≤ 1296
b.

2a. $A(x) = x(72 - x)$ **b.** positive numbers less than 72 **c.** positive numbers less than or equal to 1296

d.
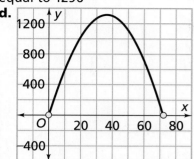

3. No; they have different domains and ranges.

4a.

Input	Output
0	3
1	8
2	13
3	18
4	23
5	28

b. H: all real numbers; K: all nonnegative integers **c.** No; they have different domains and ranges. **5a.** all nonnegative real numbers **b.** all nonnegative real numbers **6a.** domain is $\mathbb{R}^2$ and the target is $\mathbb{R}$ **b.** Answers may vary. Sample: (0, 4), (6, 0), (3, 2), or any solution of $b = \dfrac{12 - 2a}{3}$

c.
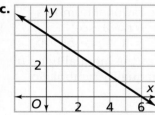

7a. $f(3) = 27$, $f(-3) = 27$ **b.** 2, −2 **c.** 63 **d.** $f(x + 1) = 3(x + 1)^2 = 3(x^2 + 2x + 1) = 3x^2 + 6x + 3$ **e.** $6x + 3$ **f.** 63 **8a.** 5 **b.** 5 **c.** 10 **d.** A **e.** $2x + 1$ **f.** $6x + 3$ **g.** $20x + 10$ **h.** $2x + 11$ **i.** $6x + 13$ **9a.** all real numbers ≤ 6

b.
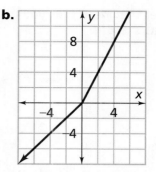

On Your Own
14a. domain: all real numbers; target: all real numbers; range: $f(x) \geq \dfrac{-49}{24}$ **b.** domain: $x \geq 3$; target: all real numbers; range: all nonnegative real numbers **15a.** 12 **d.** $z^2 - 4z - 6$ **16a.** $-\frac{1}{3}$ **17a.** 4096 **18b.** false

Lesson 4.08
Check Your Understanding
1a. 9 **b.** 16 **c.** 35 **d.** 35 **e.** 46 **f.** 144
2a. $g \circ f(x) = 10x + 16$ **b.** $f \circ g(x) = 10x + 5$
3a. $A = \pi r^2$ **b.** $A = 16\pi t^2$ **4a.** $f \circ g(x) = f \circ g(x) = x^2 + 3$; $g \circ f(x) = x^2 + 3$
b. $f \circ g(x) = 2x - 7$; $g \circ f(x) = 2x - 7$
c. $f \circ g(x) = (x - 4)^3$; $g \circ f(x) = (x - 4)^3$
d. Sample: The function takes any input and produces that same value as the output.
5. $g(x) = \dfrac{x + 1}{3}$ **6.** $g(x) = \dfrac{x - 3}{2}$
7a. $g(x) = 2x^2 - 2$ **b.** $g(x) = \dfrac{4x^2 + 1}{2x + 5}$
8a. $f \circ g(x) = acx + ad + b$, $g \circ f(x) = acx + bc + d$ **b.** $ad + b = bc + d$ or $\dfrac{a}{c} = \dfrac{b - 1}{d - 1}$ **9.** $a = 2$, $b = 3$ or $a = -2$, $b = -9$

On Your Own
12c. $a^2 - 9a + 20$ **g.** 4 or 5 **13a.** x^2

Lesson 4.09
Check Your Understanding
1a. Yes; $f^{-1}(x) = x$ **b.** Yes; $g^{-1}(x) = \frac{1}{x}$ **c.** No; $h(x) = x^2$ is not one-to-one. **d.** Yes; $k^{-1}(x) = x$ **e.** No; $l(x) = x^3 - x$ is not one-to-one. **f.** Yes; $m^{-1}(x) = x^2$ with $x \geq 0$. **g.** No; $n(x) = |x|$ is not one-to-one. **2a.** (5, 1) **b.** Answers may vary. Sample: Reflect the graph over the line $y = x$. **c.** Answers may vary. Sample: Each graph represents a one-to-one function, and if you

reflect either graph over the line $y = x$, you get the other graph. **3a.** $x \le 6$

b.
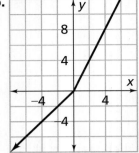

c. Answers may vary. Sample:

$f(x) = \begin{cases} x & \text{if } x < 0 \\ 2x & \text{if } x \ge 0 \end{cases}$ **d.** Answers may vary.

Sample: $f(x) = \begin{cases} x & \text{if } x < 0 \\ 2x & \text{if } 0 \le x \le 6 \\ -x & \text{if } x > 6 \end{cases}$

4a. Answers may vary. Sample: $x > 0$
b. $f^{-1}(x) = \sqrt{x}$ **5a.** the numbers 1, 5, 9, 13
b.

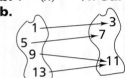

c. Each input is matched to a unique output.
d. $t(x)$ does not have an inverse because it contains (9, 11) and (13, 11). To make it a function, change one of the output 11's to a number other than 3, 7, or 11. **6.** $f^{-1}(x) = \frac{x}{x-1}$ **7.** Yes, $h = j^{-1}$. **8a.** $g \circ f(x) = 25x^2 - 85x + 30$ **b.** $x^2 - 17x + 30$
c. f: parabola opening up with vertex $\left(\frac{17}{10}, -\frac{169}{20}\right)$ and x-intercepts $\left(\frac{2}{5}, 0\right)$ and (3, 0) h: parabola opening up with vertex $\left(\frac{17}{2}, -\frac{169}{4}\right)$ and x-intercepts (2, 0) and (15, 0)
d. f: $\frac{2}{5}$ and 3; h: 2 and 15. **9.** False; Answers may vary. Sample: See Exercise 6, in which $f(x) = f^{-1}(x) = \frac{x}{x-1}$.

On Your Own
10. a and d **14a.** $m^{-1}(x) = \frac{x-3}{5}$

16a. $g \circ f(x) = 125x^3 - 300x^2 - 275x + 150$

Lesson 4.11
On Your Own
11a. $\pm \sqrt{5}$ **b.** 2.32

12.
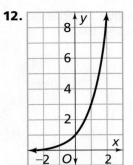

15a. outputs: $\frac{3}{4}$, $\frac{3}{2}$, 3, 6, 12
16b. $L(h) = 100 \cdot \left(\frac{1}{2}\right)^h$

Lesson 4.12
Check Your Understanding

1a. $f(x) = -3 \cdot 2^x$ **b.** $f(x) = 3 \cdot \left(\frac{1}{2}\right)^x$
c. $f(x) = 3 \cdot 2^x$ **d.** $f(x) = 3 \cdot 5^x$

2a. $f(x) = 12 \cdot \left(\frac{1}{2}\right)^x$ **b.** $f(x) = 48 \cdot \left(\frac{1}{2}\right)^x$
3a. Answers may vary. Sample: $f(x) = 2 \cdot 6^x$,

$g(x) = 8 \cdot 3^x$ **b.** $f(x) = a \cdot \left(\sqrt{\frac{72}{a}}\right)^x$

4. Lemma: The proof uses the fact that b^x is strictly decreasing for nonnegative integer inputs. Let $x = \frac{p}{q}$ for some positive integers p and q, and then suppose that $b^{\frac{1}{q}} \ge 1$. Then $b = (b^{\frac{1}{q}})^q \ge 1^q = 1$, which implies $b \ge 1$. But this contradicts the hypothesis of the lemma that $b < 1$. Thus $b^{\frac{1}{q}} < 1$, and therefore $b^x = (b^{\frac{p}{q}}) = (b^{\frac{1}{q}})^p < 1^p = 1$. So, $b^x < 1$.

Theorem: Let s and t be rational numbers such that $s > t$. Then $s - t > 0$, so (using the Lemma) $b^{s-t} < 1$. Since $b^t > 0$, multiplying both sides of the inequality by b^t does not reverse the inequality symbol. So,
$b^{s-t} \cdot b^t < 1 \cdot b^t$
$b^{s-t+t} < b^t$
$b^s < b^t$
Thus, if $s > t$, then $f(s) < f(t)$, which means that f is strictly decreasing on rational number inputs.

5. Answers may vary. Sample: If $f(x) = 2^x$, then $f(-x) = 2^{-x} = \frac{1}{2^x} = \left(\frac{1}{2}\right)^x = g(x)$.
6. 2.807 **7.** 2.807

8a.

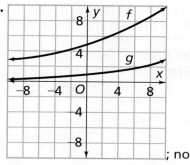

; no

b. one **9a.** 4 **b.** Yes; $\left(2^{\sqrt{2}}\right)^{\sqrt{2}} = 2^{\sqrt{2}\cdot\sqrt{2}} = 2^2 = 4$ **10.** Answers may vary. Sample: A calculator gives error messages because b^a is not defined for $b < 0$.

On Your Own

11. $f(0) = a \cdot b^0 = a \cdot 1 = a$, so the graph contains $(0, a)$. **13a.** $4.11, $4.23 **15.** $2 < \sqrt{6} < 3$, so $3^2 < 3^{\sqrt{6}} < 3^3$ or $9 < 3^{\sqrt{6}} < 27$. **18a.** outputs: $\frac{1}{4}$, $-\frac{1}{2}$, 1, -2, 4, -8

Lesson 4.13
Check Your Understanding

1a. $A(n) = 18 \cdot \left(\frac{1}{3}\right)^n$ **b.** $B(x) = -2 \cdot (4)^n$

c. No exponential function fits the table because the ratio between consecutive outputs is not constant. **d.** $D(z) = \frac{1}{3} \cdot 6^z$

2a. $A(n) = \begin{cases} 18 & \text{if } n = 0 \\ \frac{1}{3} \cdot A(n-1) & \text{if } n > 0 \end{cases}$

b. $B(x) = \begin{cases} -2 & \text{if } x = 0 \\ 4 \cdot B(x-1) & \text{if } x > 0 \end{cases}$

c. not an exponential function

d. $D(z) = \begin{cases} \frac{1}{3} & \text{if } z = 0 \\ 6 \cdot D(z-1) & \text{if } z > 0 \end{cases}$

3. $q(x) = 12{,}500 \cdot \left(\frac{1}{5}\right)^x$ **4.** Disagree; a value of $-\frac{1}{5}$ for b is not possible because the base of an exponential function must be positive.

5. Answers may vary. Sample: $f(x) = 2x + 16$;

$f(x) = (10 \cdot 2^{\frac{3}{5}})(2^{\frac{1}{5}})^x$ **6a.** $a = 100$, $b = 3^{\frac{1}{5}}$

b.

x	T(x)	÷
0	100	≈1.246
1	≈124.57	≈1.246
2	≈155.18	≈1.246
3	≈193.32	≈1.246
4	≈240.82	≈1.246
5	300	

7a. $16,000; $12,800; $10,240
b. $V(n) = 20{,}000 \cdot (0.8)^n$ **c.** Yes; $V(14) = \$879.61$, so after 14 yr the car will be worth less than $1000.

8. $y = y_1^{\frac{-x_2}{x_1-x_2}} \cdot y_2^{\frac{x_1}{x_1-x_2}} \cdot \left(\left(\frac{y_1}{y_2}\right)^{\frac{1}{x_1-x_2}}\right)^x$

On Your Own

10. $M(n) = 24, 36, 54, 81$; $M(n) = 16 \cdot \left(\frac{3}{2}\right)^n$,

$M(n) = \begin{cases} 16 & \text{if } n = 0 \\ \frac{3}{2} \cdot M(n-1) & \text{if } n > 0 \end{cases}$

12b. $y = -5^{\frac{1}{4}} \cdot \left(5^{\frac{1}{4}}\right)^x$ or $y = -5^{\frac{x+1}{4}}$

Lesson 4.14
On Your Own

12a, c.

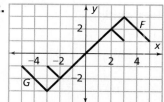

b. Connect $(0, 0)$ and $(-3, -3)$. Connect $(-2, -2)$ and $(-3, -1)$. Connect $(-3, -3)$ and $(-5, -1)$. **d.** Figure G is figure F rotated $180°$ about the origin. **13.** $180°$ rotational symmetry

16b.

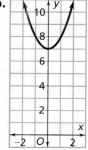

18c.

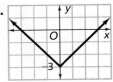

20a.

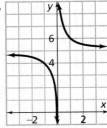

It is the graph of $y = 3^x$ translated 5 units down.

22c.

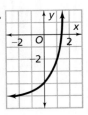

It is the graph of $y = \frac{1}{x}$ translated 5 units up.

Lesson 4.15
Check Your Understanding

1a. $\left(\frac{4}{5}, \frac{3}{5}\right)$, $\left(\frac{4}{5}, -\frac{3}{5}\right)$

b. $\left(-\frac{4}{5}, \frac{3}{5}\right)$, $\left(-\frac{4}{5}, -\frac{3}{5}\right)$, $\left(\frac{3}{5}, \frac{4}{5}\right)$, $\left(\frac{3}{5}, -\frac{4}{5}\right)$, $\left(-\frac{3}{5}, \frac{4}{5}\right)$, $\left(-\frac{3}{5}, -\frac{4}{5}\right)$ **2a.** $\left(\frac{12}{13}, \frac{5}{13}\right)$, $\left(-\frac{12}{13}, \frac{5}{13}\right)$

b. $\left(\frac{8}{17}, \frac{15}{17}\right)$, $\left(\frac{8}{17}, -\frac{15}{17}\right)$ **3.** If a, b, and c form a Pythagorean triple, then a, b, and c are positive integers that satisfy $a^2 + b^2 = c^2$. Dividing both sides of this equation by c^2 gives $\frac{a^2}{c^2} + \frac{b^2}{c^2} = \frac{c^2}{c^2}$, or $\left(\frac{a}{c}\right)^2 + \left(\frac{b}{c}\right)^2 = 1$. Thus, the point $\left(\frac{a}{c}, \frac{b}{c}\right)$ satisfies the equation of the unit circle, $x^2 + y^2 = 1$, and can be used to generate other points that are on the unit circle.

4a. $f(-x) = (-x)^2 = x^2 = f(x)$ **b.** The graph of $y = x^2$ has the y-axis as a line of symmetry, so if (x, y) is on the graph, then $(-x, y)$ is also on the graph. Since opposite inputs have the same output, $f(x) = x^2$ is an even function.

5a. $f(-x) = (-x)^3 + (-x) = -x^3 - x = -(x^3 + x) = -f(x)$ **b.** The graph of $y = x^3 + x$ has 180° rotational symmetry about the

origin, so if (x, y) is on the graph, then $(-x, -y)$ is also on the graph. Since opposite inputs have opposite outputs, $f(x) = x^3 + x$ is an odd function. **6.** even functions: $y = x^2$, $y = |x|$; odd functions: $y = x$, $y = \frac{1}{x}$, $y = x^3$, $y = x^3 - x$, $y = x^3 + x$; both: none; neither: $y = \sqrt{x}$, $y = b^x$, $y = \log_b x$, $x^2 + y^2 = 1$

7. $x^3 + x = 0$, or $x(x^2 + 1) = 0$, has only one real root, 0.

8a.

x	$x - 3$	$(x - 3)^2$
−1	−4	16
0	−3	9
1	−2	4
2	−1	1
3	0	0
4	1	1
5	2	4
6	3	9
7	4	16

b.

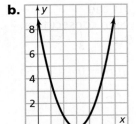

1a. $\left(\frac{4}{5}, \frac{3}{5}\right)$, $\left(\frac{4}{5}, -\frac{3}{5}\right)$

b. $\left(-\frac{4}{5}, \frac{3}{5}\right)$, $\left(-\frac{4}{5}, -\frac{3}{5}\right)$, $\left(\frac{3}{5}, \frac{4}{5}\right)$, $\left(\frac{3}{5}, -\frac{4}{5}\right)$, $\left(-\frac{3}{5}, \frac{4}{5}\right)$, $\left(-\frac{3}{5}, -\frac{4}{5}\right)$ **2a.** $\left(\frac{12}{13}, \frac{5}{13}\right)$, $\left(-\frac{12}{13}, \frac{5}{13}\right)$

b. $\left(\frac{8}{17}, \frac{15}{17}\right)$, $\left(\frac{8}{17}, -\frac{15}{17}\right)$ **3.** If a, b, and c form a Pythagorean triple, then a, b, and c are positive integers that satisfy $a^2 + b^2 = c^2$. Dividing both sides of this equation by c^2 gives $\frac{a^2}{c^2} + \frac{b^2}{c^2} = \frac{c^2}{c^2}$, or $\left(\frac{a}{c}\right)^2 + \left(\frac{b}{c}\right)^2 = 1$. Thus, the point $\left(\frac{a}{c}, \frac{b}{c}\right)$ satisfies the equation of the unit circle, $x^2 + y^2 = 1$, and can be used to generate other points that are on the unit circle.

4a. $f(-x) = (-x)^2 = x^2 = f(x)$ **b.** The graph of $y = x^2$ has the y-axis as a line of symmetry,

so if (x, y) is on the graph, then $(-x, y)$ is also on the graph. Since opposite inputs have the same output, $f(x) = x^2$ is an even function.
5a. $f(-x) = (-x)^3 + (-x) = -x^3 - x = -(x^3 + x) = -f(x)$ **b.** The graph of $y = x^3 + x$ has 180° rotational symmetry about the origin, so if (x, y) is on the graph, then $(-x, -y)$ is also on the graph. Since opposite inputs have opposite outputs, $f(x) = x^3 + x$ is an odd function. **6.** even functions: $y = x^2$, $y = |x|$; odd functions: $y = x$, $y = \frac{1}{x}$, $y = x^3$, $y = x^3 - x$, $y = x^3 + x$; both: none; neither: $y = \sqrt{x}$, $y = b^x$, $y = \log_b x$, $x^2 + y^2 = 1$
7. $x^3 + x = 0$, or $x(x^2 + 1) = 0$, has only one real root, 0.
8a.

x	$x - 3$	$(x - 3)^2$
−1	−4	16
0	−3	9
1	−2	4
2	−1	1
3	0	0
4	1	1
5	2	4
6	3	9
7	4	16

b.

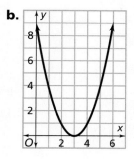

c. The graph of $y = (x - 3)^2$ is the graph of $y = x^2$ translated 3 units to the right.

On Your Own

10a. Near the origin $|x| < 1$, so $|x^3|$ is much less than $|x|$. Thus the x^3-term has very little effect on the value of $x^3 - x$. **11.** $(-1, 0)$, $(0, 0)$, $(1, 0)$

12a.

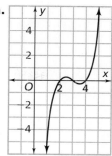

15a. $(x - 6)^2 + y^2 = 25$ **b.** $(x + 3)^2 + y^2 = 16$

Lesson 4.16
Check Your Understanding
1a.

$x = M - 5$	M	$y = \sqrt{M}$
−5	0	0
−4	1	1
−1	4	2
4	9	3
11	16	4
20	25	5

b. The graph of $y = \sqrt{x + 5}$ is the graph of $y = \sqrt{x}$ translated 5 units to the left.
c.

domain: $x \geq -5$, range: $y \geq 0$
2a.

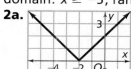

b.

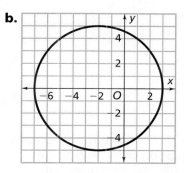

c.

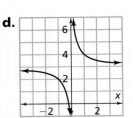

d.

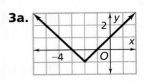

3a.

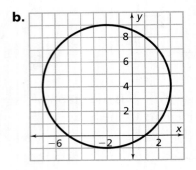

b.

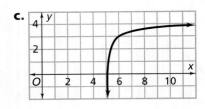

c.

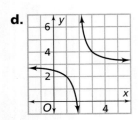

d.

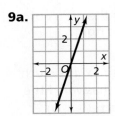

4. Disagree; Walter should have replaced each x in the original equation by $(x - 2)$ to get $y = (x - 2)^3 - (x - 2)$. **5a.** The graph of the

second equation is the graph of the first equation translated 2 units to the right.
b. $x^3 - x + 1$
c.

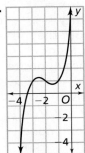

6a. $(-3, 0)$ **b.** $(-3, 2)$ **c.** $(-h, k)$
7a.

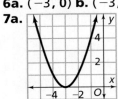

b.

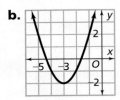

On Your Own
8a.

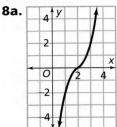

9a.

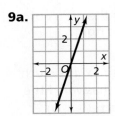

The slope is 3.

11a. $y = 4(x - 3) + 1$ or $y = 4x - 11$

12a. The graph of $y = (x - 3)^2 + 6(x - 3) + 7$ is the graph of $y = x^2 + 6x + 7$ translated 3 units to the right; Answers may vary. Sample: In the equation $y = (x - 3)^2 + 6(x - 3) + 7$, each x in the equation $y = x^2 + 6x + 7$ is replaced by $M = x - 3$, so each point on the graph of $y = M^2 + 6M + 7$ corresponds to the point on the graph of $y = x^2 + 6x + 7$ with x-coordinate 3 units less.

Lesson 4.17
Check Your Understanding

1a.

x	$N = x^2 + 1$	$y = \frac{N}{5}$
-2	5	1
-1	2	$\frac{2}{5}$
0	1	$\frac{1}{5}$
1	2	$\frac{2}{5}$
2	5	1
3	10	2

b. The y-values for the graph of $5y = x^2 + 1$ are smaller by the factor 5 when compared to the corresponding y-values for the graph of $y = x^2 + 1$, so the graph of $5y = x^2 + 1$ is the graph of $y = x^2 + 1$ scaled vertically by the factor $\frac{1}{5}$.

c.

2a.

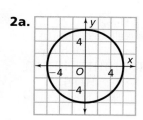

b.

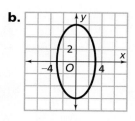

c.

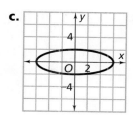

d.

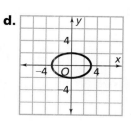

e.

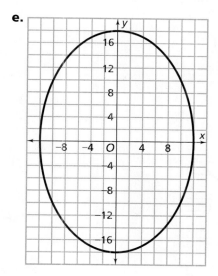

3a.

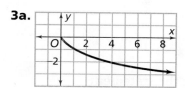

domain: $x \geq 0$, range: $y \leq 0$

b.

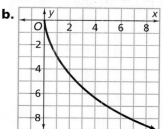

domain: $x \geq 0$, range: $y \leq 0$

c.

domain: $x \leq 0$, range: $y \geq 0$

d.
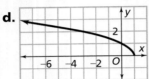

domain: $x \leq 1$, range: $y \geq 0$

4. $y = \left(\frac{1}{2}x - 2\right)^2 + 3$

5a.
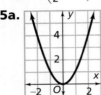

b.
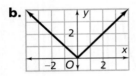

c.
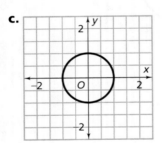

6. Agree with both; the statement $f(-x) = f(x)$ is equivalent to saying the graph of f has the y-axis as a line of symmetry.
7. Because all the exponents are even the y-values for x and $-x$ are the same, so the function is even. **8.** $g(-x) = f(-x) + f(-(-x))$ $= f(-x) + f(x) = g(x)$, so g is an even function.

9a–b.
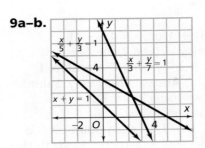

c. Answers may vary. Sample: $(0, 12)$, $(-17, 0)$
d. The intercepts of $\frac{x}{a} + \frac{y}{b} = 1$ are $(0, b)$ and $(a, 0)$.

On Your Own
10a.

11a. the graph of $y = \frac{1}{x}$ reflected over the y-axis **c.** the graph of $y = \frac{1}{x}$ reflected over the y-axis and scaled vertically by the factor 4
13. Answers may vary. Sample: The graph of the second equation is the graph of the first equation after it has been reflected over the y-axis and then over the x-axis.

Chapter 5
Lesson 5.01
On Your Own
7. b. $\frac{19}{25}$ **d.** $\frac{35}{49}$ **8. a.** 120

Lesson 5.02
Check Your Understanding
1. a. $\frac{1}{2}$ **b.** $\frac{1}{4}$ **c.** $\frac{1}{2}$ **d.** $\frac{1}{2}$ **e.** 0 **f.** $\frac{1}{36}$ **g.** $\frac{35}{36}$
2. The results are not equally likely because there are 5 ways to roll a sum of 8 on two dice out of 36 outcomes; $\frac{5}{36}$ **3.** 15; HHTTTT, HTHTTT, HTTHTT, HTTTHT, HTTTTH, THHTTT, THTHTT, THTTHT, THTTTH, TTHHTT, TTHTHT, TTHTTH, TTTHHT, TTTHTH, TTTTHH

4. $\binom{6}{2} = 15$; this represents 15 ways to pick two items from a group of six. **5.** 20; this is the coefficient of the t^3h^3 term; $(t + h)^6 = t^6 + 6t^5h + 15t^4h^2 + 20t^3h^3 + 15t^2h^4 + 6th^5 + t^6$ **6.** $\frac{21}{216}$

On Your Own

9. a. $\frac{1}{6}$ **10. a.** 36

Lesson 5.05

Check Your Understanding

1. a.

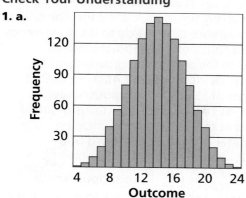

b. To roll a 5, the only possible roll is the four variations of 1-1-1-2. To roll a 23, the only possible roll is the four variations of 6-6-6-5. Also, the frequencies appear symmetric on either side of 14.

2. $\frac{1}{2}$ **3. a.** $x^2 + x^3 + x^4 + x^5 + x^6 + x^{10}$ **b.** 20; $\frac{95}{1296}$ **4. a.** Answers may vary. Sample: $2x^5$ represents the two faces with 5 on them, while the other exponents indicate single faces with 1 through 4 on them. **b.** 13; $\frac{164}{1296}$ **5. a.** $q(x) = 4x^{10} + 4x^9 + 5x^8 + 6x^7 + 7x^6 + 4x^5 + 3x^4 + 2x^3 + x^2$; this represents the frequencies of the sums when the 1-2-3-4-5-5 number cube is rolled twice. **b.** 36 **c.** 4 **d.** 4 **6. a.** $\frac{3}{50}$ or 0.06 **b.** $\frac{425}{1000}$ or 0.425 **c.** $\frac{7760}{10,000}$ or 0.776

On Your Own

7. a. $1 + x + 2x^2 + x^7$ **b.** $\frac{72}{625}$ **8. a.** 0.2; 0.2 **b.** $(0.2)^6 = 0.000064$

Lesson 5.06

Check Your Understanding

1. a. $\frac{1}{24}$ **b.** $\frac{3}{8}$ **2.** 1 **3.** $5719.53 **4.** There is nothing wrong with Daisuke's calculation. His mistake was in the interpretation of his results. Expected value is not a probability and can be greater than 1. $\frac{12}{8}$ represents the number of heads expected when you toss 3 coins.

5. a. $(0.2r + 0.8w)^6 = 0.000064r^6 + 0.001536r^5w + 0.01536r^4w^2 + 0.08192r^3w^3 + 0.24576r^2w^4 + 0.39322rw^5 + 0.26214w^6$; each term is the probability of getting a specific number of questions correct. **b.** 1.2

6. a. $(x^1 + x^2 + x^3 + x^{10})^3 = x^{30} + 3x^{23} + 3x^{22} + 3x^{21} + 3x^{16} + 6x^{15} + 9x^{14} + 6x^{13} + 3x^{12} + x^9 + 3x^8 + 6x^7 + 7x^6 + 6x^5 + 3x^4 + x^3$ **b.** $\frac{27}{64}$ **7.** 16

On Your Own

8. b. $14,925.80 **10. a.** 7 **b.** 10.5 **13.** 0

Lesson 5.07

Check Your Understanding

1.

Matches	Frequency
0 correct	2,118,760
1 correct	1,151,500
2 correct	196,000
3 correct	12,250
4 correct	250
5 correct	1

2. $\frac{5}{11}$ **3.** $\frac{44,800,030}{146,107,962} \approx 0.30662$

4. a. $\frac{1,000,000m + 28,800,030}{146,107,962} = 0.006844m + 0.197115$, where m is the number of millions

b. 0.88154 **c.** greater than $117,308,932

5.

Ticket Type	Frequency	Payout
5 balls + bonus	1	Jackpot
5 balls + no bonus	45	$250,000
4 balls + bonus	255	$10,000
4 balls + no bonus	11,475	$150
3 balls + bonus	12,750	$150
3 balls + no bonus	573,750	$7
2 balls + bonus	208,250	$10
1 ball + bonus	1,249,500	$3
Bonus only	2,349,060	$2
Losing ticket	171,306,450	$0
Total outcomes	175,711,536	

0.25029 **6.** $10.64.

On Your Own

7. $\frac{6}{7}$ **8. a.** $\frac{1,110,353,500}{65,530,000} \approx 16.9468$ **b.** $200,046,500 **11. a.** 720

Chapter 6
Lesson 6.0
Check Your Understanding
1a. Constructions may vary. **b.** not necessarily **c.** one of the side lengths **2a.** Constructions may vary. **b.** not necessarily **c.** Answers may vary. Sample: the length of the third side
3. yes; SSS **4.** yes, though you would need to first deduce that $\overline{AB} \cong \overline{AD}$; SAS **5.** Let the square be $ABCD$, and choose the diagonal $\overline{BD}$. All sides of a square are congruent, and all angles of a square are right angles and hence congruent. The sides $\overline{BA}$ and $\overline{DA}$ and their included right angle in $\triangle BAD$ are congruent, respectively, to sides $\overline{BC}$ and $\overline{DC}$ and their included right angle in $\triangle BCD$. So $\triangle BAD \cong \triangle BCD$ by SAS. Also, $\overline{BD} \cong \overline{BD}$, so $\triangle BAD \cong \triangle BCD$ by SSS.
6. Answers may vary. Sample: SSA is not a valid test for congruence. **7.** Answers may vary. Sample: If SSA were a valid way to prove congruence, then $\triangle COA \cong \triangle COB$, implying that $m\angle COA = m\angle COB$. But $\angle COB$ is entirely contained within $\angle COA$, so these two angles cannot be equal in measure.

On Your Own
9a. yes **b.** $\triangle ABC \cong \triangle DEF$; SSS **11.** no
14. $\triangle ABD$ and $\triangle CBD$; since $\overline{BD}$ is the perpendicular bisector of $\overline{AC}$, $\overline{AD} \cong \overline{CD}$ and $\angle ADB \cong \angle CDB$. $\overline{BD}$ is common to the two triangles. Therefore, $\triangle ABD \cong \triangle CBD$ by SAS.

Lesson 6.01
On Your Own
3. Answers may vary. Sample:

$\frac{z}{w} = 8$

w	z
2	16
3	24
4	32
5	40

$g + h = 8$

g	h
0	8
2	6
4	4
6	2

$m - n = 8$

m	n
10	2
20	12
30	22
40	32

4a. The figure formed by joining the midpoints has four vertices, no three of which are collinear, and when you connect the midpoints in order, the resulting figure will not cross itself. **b.** The quadrilaterals are parallelograms because each midline formed by connecting consecutive midpoints is parallel to a diagonal. Therefore, both pairs of opposite sides are parallel.

Lesson 6.02
Check Your Understanding
1. Call the endpoints of the diameter A and B.
a. Answers may vary. Sample: $m\angle ADB$ is always 90°. In $\triangle ADB$, $\overline{AB}$ is the longest side and $\angle D$ is the largest angle. $m\angle A + m\angle B$ is always 90°. The length of $\overline{AB}$ does not change. $(AD)^2 + (BD)^2 = (AB)^2$ **b.** Answers may vary. Sample: $\angle D$ is the largest angle, and $\overline{AB}$ is the longest side. $m\angle D$ is 90°, as is $m\angle A + m\angle B$. The ratio of any two sides is constant. The ratio of the circumference of the circle to the diameter of the circle is constant. The ratio of the area of $\triangle ABD$ to the area of the circle is constant.
2. b and d **3.** $AC + CB$, $m\angle ACD + m\angle DCB$
4. the area of $\triangle ABC$ **5.** opposite ways; $CE \cdot CD$ **6.** The product $CE \cdot CD$ is greatest when C is at the center of the circle because the diameter is the longest chord of a circle. **7.** Answers may vary. Sample: $\frac{AD}{DC} = \frac{AE}{EB}$, $\frac{\text{area}(\triangle ADE)}{\text{area}(\triangle ACB)} = \left(\frac{DE}{CB}\right)^2$; to support these observations, use the software to measure the lengths and areas, and calculate the quantities in the equations.

On Your Own
8. the circumference **9.** Construct the line through F perpendicular to $\overleftrightarrow{EG}$. Let H be the point where the perpendicular intersects $\overleftrightarrow{EG}$. Construct a segment $\overline{HK}$ on $\overleftrightarrow{EG}$ that has the same length as $\overline{EG}$. $\triangle FHK$ has the same area as $\triangle EFG$. **11a.** yes; $\frac{1}{2}$ **b.** yes; π (or about 3.14) **c.** no

Lesson 6.03
Check Your Understanding
1a. no **b.** yes **c.** yes **2.** yes **3.** Experimentation suggests that concurrence of perpendicular bisectors is an invariant for regular polygons.
4. Experimentation suggests that concurrence of angle bisectors is an invariant for regular polygons. **5.** The five perpendicular bisectors are concurrent at the center of the circle. The five angle bisectors are not concurrent. **6.** The five angle bisectors are concurrent at the center of the circle. The five perpendicular bisectors are not concurrent.
On Your Own
7. Answers may vary. Sample: The medians are concurrent. Any midpoint is collinear with two vertices of the triangle.

Lesson 6.04
On Your Own
3. Constructions and observations may vary.
a. the length of the side that the midline does not intersect (twice the length of the midline) **b.** the area of each of the four triangles formed by the three midlines (one quarter of the area of the original triangle) **6a.** $m\angle BDA = 118°$, $m\angle ADQ = 62°$, $m\angle CDQ = 118°$ **b.** $m\angle BDA = 108°$, $m\angle ADQ = 72°$, $m\angle CDQ = 108°$ **c.** $m\angle BDA = 125°$, $m\angle ADQ = 55°$, $m\angle CDQ = 125°$ **d.** $m\angle BDA = 180° - x°$, $m\angle ADQ = x°$, $m\angle CDQ = 180° - x°$

Lesson 6.05
Check Your Understanding
1a. $m\angle COB = 65°$, $m\angle COD = 25°$
b. $m\angle BOA = 27°$, $m\angle COD = 27°$
c. $m\angle COB = 59°$, $m\angle BOA = 31°$
d. $m\angle DOA = 121°$ **e.** $m\angle COB = 90° - x°$, $m\angle COD = x°$ **2.** Because $m\angle COB + m\angle BOA = 90°$ and $m\angle DOC + m\angle COB = 90°$, $m\angle COB + m\angle BOA = m\angle DOC + m\angle COB$. Therefore $m\angle BOA = m\angle DOC$ (basic rules of algebra).
On Your Own
4b. given **c.** Every figure is congruent to itself. **d.** SAS **e.** CPCTC **6a.** Answers may vary. Sample: $m\angle FCA = m\angle FCB$
b. $\overline{FC} \perp \overline{ED}$ (given). $m\angle FCD = 90°$ and $m\angle FCE = 90°$ (definition of perpendicular lines). $m\angle ACE + m\angle FCA = m\angle FCE$ and $m\angle BCD + m\angle FCB = m\angle FCD$ (the measure of an angle is the sum of the measures of its parts). $m\angle ACE + m\angle FCA = m\angle BCD + m\angle FCB$ (properties of equality). But $m\angle ACE = m\angle DCB$ (given), so $m\angle FCA = m\angle FCB$ (basic rules of algebra).

Lesson 6.06
Check Your Understanding
1. Answers may vary. Samples are given:

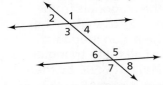

a. A pair of angles are alternate interior angles if they have different vertices, lie between the two lines cut by the transversal, and are on opposite sides of the transversal. $\angle 4$ and $\angle 6$ are alternate interior angles. **b.** A pair of angles are alternate exterior angles if they

have different vertices, lie on opposite sides of the transversal, and are not between the two lines cut by the transversal. $\angle 2$ and $\angle 8$ are alternate exterior angles. **c.** A pair of angles are corresponding angles if they have different vertices and lie on the same side of the transversal, with exactly one of them lying between the two lines cut by the transversal. $\angle 1$ and $\angle 5$ are corresponding angles.
d. A pair of angles are consecutive angles if they have different vertices, lie on the same side of the transversal, and are both between the two lines cut by the transversal. $\angle 3$ and $\angle 6$ are consecutive angles.
2a. $\triangle PXU \cong \triangle UMP$; SSS

b.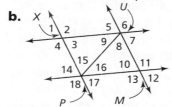

Angles congruent by CPCTC: $\angle 3 \cong \angle 10$, $\angle 9 \cong \angle 16$, $\angle 8 \cong \angle 15$; angles congruent because the parts of one are congruent to the parts of the other: $\angle XUM \cong \angle XPM$; vertical angles: $\angle 1 \cong \angle 3$, $\angle 2 \cong \angle 4$, $\angle 5 \cong \angle 7$, $\angle 6 \cong \angle XUM$, $\angle 10 \cong \angle 12$, $\angle 11 \cong \angle 13$, $\angle 14 \cong \angle 17$, $\angle 18 \cong \angle XPM$ **c.** $\overleftrightarrow{XU} \parallel \overleftrightarrow{PM}$ and $\overleftrightarrow{XP} \parallel \overleftrightarrow{UM}$; AIP Theorem **3a.** $\triangle XUP \cong \triangle MUP$; SSS **b.** Each pair of vertical angles is congruent. (There are two pairs of vertical angles at each of the points X, U, M, and P.) Also, $\angle XPU \cong \angle MPU$, $\angle XUP \cong \angle MUP$, and $\angle UXP \cong \angle UMP$ by CPCTC. **c.** None are necessarily parallel; the conditions that let you use the AIP Theorem are not present.
4. Refer to the figure for parts (a), (b), and (e). Proofs may vary. Samples are given.

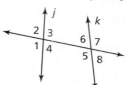

a. Yes; suppose $\angle 1 \cong \angle 5$. $\angle 1 \cong \angle 3$ (vertical angles). So $\angle 3 \cong \angle 5$ (angles congruent to the same angle are congruent). Hence $j \parallel k$ (AIP Theorem). **b.** Yes; suppose $\angle 1 \cong \angle 7$. Since $\angle 1 \cong \angle 3$ and $\angle 5 \cong \angle 7$ (vertical angles), it follows that $\angle 3 \cong \angle 5$. Hence $j \parallel k$ (AIP Theorem). **c.** No; answers may vary. Sample: Let $\triangle PAB$ be an isosceles triangle with

$\overline{PA} \cong \overline{PB}$. If M is the midpoint of $\overline{AB}$, then $\triangle PMA \cong \triangle PMB$ by SSS. Hence $\angle A \cong \angle B$. But $\overleftrightarrow{AB}$ is a transversal of intersecting lines $\overleftrightarrow{PA}$ and $\overleftrightarrow{PB}$. **d.** No; answers may vary. Sample: Consider the situation described in the answer for part (c). For the transversal $\overleftrightarrow{AB}$ of $\overleftrightarrow{PA}$ and $\overleftrightarrow{PB}$, each pair of alternate exterior angles are supplementary, but $\overleftrightarrow{PA}$ and $\overleftrightarrow{PB}$ are not parallel. **e.** Yes; refer to the figure above the answer for part (a), and suppose $\angle 4$ and $\angle 5$ are supplementary. Since $\angle 4$ and $\angle 3$ are supplementary, it follows that $\angle 3 \cong \angle 5$. Hence $j \parallel k$ (AIP Theorem).

On Your Own
5. Yes; the two lines are parallel if they lie in the same plane. They are not parallel if they do not lie in the same plane. **7.** $\overline{MP} \parallel \overline{NQ}$; since O is the midpoint of $\overline{MQ}$ and $\overline{NP}$, $\overline{MO} \cong \overline{QO}$, and $\overline{NO} \cong \overline{PO}$. The vertical angles that have vertex O are congruent. Hence, $\triangle PMO \cong \triangle NQO$ by SAS, and $\angle N \cong \angle P$ by CPCTC. Therefore, $\overline{MP} \parallel \overline{NQ}$ by the AIP Theorem. **10.** $\overline{FI} \parallel \overline{EJ}$ and $\overline{DE} \parallel \overline{FH}$; it is given that $m\angle FGE = m\angle HFI$, so $\overline{FI} \parallel \overline{EJ}$ by the AIP Theorem. $\angle DEG$ is supplementary to $\angle HFI$ and hence is supplementary to the congruent angle $\angle FGE$. Using the corollary proved in Exercise 4e, it follows that $\overline{DE} \parallel \overline{FH}$.

Lesson 6.07
Check Your Understanding
1a. $m\angle 1 = 72°$, $m\angle 2 = 108°$, $m\angle 3 = 108°$, $m\angle 4 = 72°$, $m\angle 5 = 72°$, $m\angle 6 = 108°$, $m\angle 7 = 108°$, $m\angle 8 = 72°$ **b.** $m\angle 1 = 46°$, $m\angle 2 = 134°$, $m\angle 3 = 134°$, $m\angle 4 = 46°$, $m\angle 5 = 46°$, $m\angle 6 = 134°$, $m\angle 7 = 134°$, $m\angle 8 = 46°$ **c.** $m\angle 1 = x°$, $m\angle 2 = 180° - x°$, $m\angle 3 = 180° - x°$, $m\angle 4 = x°$, $m\angle 5 = x°$, $m\angle 6 = 180° - x°$, $m\angle 7 = 180° - x°$, $m\angle 8 = x°$ **d.** $m\angle 1 = 60°$, $m\angle 2 = 120°$, $m\angle 3 = 120°$, $m\angle 4 = 60°$, $m\angle 5 = 60°$, $m\angle 6 = 120°$, $m\angle 7 = 120°$, $m\angle 8 = 60°$ **e.** $m\angle 1 = 60°$, $m\angle 2 = 120°$, $m\angle 3 = 120°$, $m\angle 4 = 60°$, $m\angle 5 = 60°$, $m\angle 6 = 120°$, $m\angle 7 = 120°$, $m\angle 8 = 60°$ **2a.** Yes, $c \parallel d$; dependent on $\angle 2 \cong \angle 3$. **b.** $\angle 2 \cong \angle 3$ **c.** The relationships in parts (a) and (b) would not hold. **3.** Answers may vary. Sample: The measure of $\angle P$ is the sum of the measures of the acute angles at A and B. **4.** Suppose there are two lines perpendicular to ℓ through P, and that they intersect ℓ at M and N. The triangle MNP has two right angles at M and N. These together with the angle at P would give the triangle an

angle sum greater than 180°. Therefore there is only one such perpendicular. **5.** Yes; a diagonal of a quadrilateral divides it into two triangles. The sum of the measures of the angles of the quadrilateral is equal to the sum of the angle measures of the triangles, which is $180° + 180°$, or $360°$. **6.** Answers may vary. Sample: One is the converse of the other. **7a.** Answers may vary. Sample: $\angle CBD \cong \angle CDB$ and $\angle DCE \cong \angle DEC$. **b.** No; suppose $\overline{BC} \parallel \overline{DE}$. Then $\angle ACB \cong \angle AED$ since they are corresponding angles. Since $\overline{BC} \cong \overline{DE}$ and $\angle A \cong \angle A$, you know that $\triangle ABC \cong \triangle ADE$ by AAS. Then $\overline{AC} \cong \overline{AE}$ by CPCTC. But this last statement is impossible given the way the diagram was drawn. Therefore, the assumption that $\overline{BC} \parallel \overline{DE}$ is wrong.

On Your Own
9a. PAI Theorem **b.** Vertical Angles Theorem **c.** $\angle 1 \cong \angle 2$ by part (a), and $\angle 2 \cong \angle 3$ by part (b), so $\angle 1 \cong \angle 3$. **12.** Suppose the exterior angle is at vertex C of $\triangle ABC$. Since the exterior angle is supplementary to $\angle BCA$, $m(\text{exterior angle}) + m\angle BCA = 180°$. But by the Triangle Angle-Sum Theorem, $m\angle A + m\angle B + m\angle BCA = 180°$. It follows by the base moves of algebra that $m(\text{exterior angle}) = m\angle A + m\angle B$.

Lesson 6.08
On Your Own
5. yes; SAS **6.** The pair of congruent angles is not an included pair.

Lesson 6.09
Check Your Understanding
1a. Answers may vary. Sample: Use geometry software to draw convex polygons with different numbers of sides. Use the measurement and calculate features of the software to find the sum of the measures of the angles of each polygon. Check that the sums are the ones predicted by the expression $(n - 2)180°$. **b.** Answers may vary. Sample: Suppose you start with an n-gon. If you select a vertex and draw all the diagonals from that vertex, you get $(n - 2)$ triangles. The sum of the angles of the n-gon is equal to the sum of the angles of all these triangles, or $(n - 2)180°$. **2.** $\angle ABD \cong \angle CBE$ by the Vertical Angles Theorem. Since $\overline{AB} \cong \overline{BC}$ and $\overline{BD} \cong \overline{BE}$, it follows by the SAS Postulate that $\triangle ABD \cong \triangle CBE$. **3.** It is given that $\overline{SV} \cong \overline{TU}$ and $\overline{ST} \cong \overline{VU}$. Since every segment is congruent to itself, $\overline{VT} \cong \overline{VT}$. Therefore, $\triangle STV \cong \triangle UVT$ by SSS. **4.** Since all sides of a square are congruent, $\overline{SW} \cong \overline{EB}$. $\overline{WB} \cong \overline{BW}$ since a segment is congruent to itself. The

angles of a square are right angles and are congruent, so ∠SWB ≅ ∠EBW. Therefore, △SWB ≅ △EBW by SAS.

On Your Own
7. Answers may vary. Sample: It is given that $\overline{XE}$ is a median of △XMY. Hence E is the midpoint of $\overline{MY}$, and consequently $\overline{ME} ≅ \overline{YE}$. It is given that $\overline{XY} ≅ \overline{XM}$. A segment is congruent to itself, so $\overline{XE} ≅ \overline{XE}$. Therefore, △XEM ≅ △XEY by SSS. **9a.** The configuration of the congruent corresponding parts is AAS not ASA. **b.** Yes; change the congruence test used in Timothy's proof from ASA to AAS. **11.** The angles marked in the diagram are given to be congruent. The segments that determine these angles are all congruent because they are radii of the same circle. Therefore, the three triangles are congruent by SAS.

Lesson 6.10
Check Your Understanding
1. The third statement is false; a right triangle with legs of length 1 and 4 has the same area as a right triangle with leg lengths 2 and 2, but they are not congruent. The fifth statement is false; there are people with large hands who do not have large feet. The sixth statement is false; you can keep things in mind even when they are not visible.   **2a.** Hypothesis: Two lines form congruent alternate interior angles with a transversal; conclusion: the two lines are parallel. **b.** Hypothesis: n is a whole number; conclusion: $n^2 + n + 41$ is prime. **c.** Hypothesis: three sides of one triangle are congruent to three sides of another triangle; conclusion: the triangles are congruent. **d.** Hypothesis: two lines are both parallel to a third line; conclusion: the two lines are parallel to each other.

On Your Own
4. True; proofs may vary. Sample: Select two alternate interior angles formed by the two lines and the transversal to which they are perpendicular. These angles are congruent since all the angles formed by perpendicular lines are right angles. By AIP, the lines perpendicular to the transversal are parallel.
5. False; the sketch of the hypothesis shown here provides a counterexample.

Lesson 6.11
Check Your Understanding
1a. The halves of $\overline{AC}$ may not be congruent to the halves of $\overline{BH}$. **b.** The original markings would allow you to conclude that ABCH is a rectangle.
2.

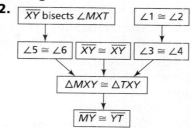

3a.

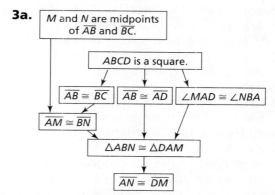

b. Because ABCD is a square, all its sides are congruent. So $\overline{AB} ≅ \overline{BC}$ and $\overline{AB} ≅ \overline{DA}$. Also, all its angles are congruent. So ∠MAD ≅ ∠NBA. Since $\overline{AB} ≅ \overline{BC}$ and M and N are the midpoints of $\overline{AB}$ and $\overline{BC}$, respectively, it follows that $\overline{AM} ≅ \overline{BN}$. Hence △ABN ≅ △DAM by SAS. By CPCTC, $\overline{AN} ≅ \overline{DM}$.

On Your Own
6. Since $\overleftrightarrow{GF} ⊥ \overleftrightarrow{GH}$, m∠HGJ + m∠JGF = 90°. Since $\overleftrightarrow{GJ} ⊥ \overleftrightarrow{GK}$, m∠KGH + m∠HGJ = 90°. By the basic moves of algebra, it follows that m∠JGF = m∠KGH. Therefore, ∠JGF ≅ ∠KGH.
8. It follows from the Triangle Angle-Sum Theorem that each angle of an equilateral triangle has a measure of 60°. Therefore the parts of ∠MLK are congruent to the parts of ∠JLN, which implies ∠MLK ≅ ∠JLN. Sides of an equilateral triangle are congruent, so $\overline{ML} ≅ \overline{JL}$ and $\overline{LK} ≅ \overline{LN}$. So by SAS, △MLK ≅ △JLN. Hence $\overline{MK} ≅ \overline{JN}$ by CPCTC.

Lesson 6.12
Check Your Understanding
1a. Answers may vary. Sample: Let the intersection of the perpendicular bisector and $\overline{AB}$ be C. **Need:** △APB is isosceles.

Use: Isosceles triangles have two congruent sides. **Need:** $\overline{AP} \cong \overline{PB}$ **Use:** CPCTC
Need: $\triangle APC \cong \triangle BPC$ **Use:** SAS
Need: $\overline{PC} \cong \overline{PC}$ **Use:** The triangles share this side. **Need:** $\angle PCB \cong \angle PCA$ **Use:** Both are right angles because $\overrightarrow{PC}$ is a perpendicular bisector. **Need:** $\overline{AC} \cong \overline{BC}$ **Use:** C is a midpoint because $\overrightarrow{PC}$ is a perpendicular bisector. **b.** Since $\overrightarrow{PC}$ is a perpendicular bisector of $\overline{AB}$, C is the midpoint of $\overline{AB}$ and hence $\overline{AC} \cong \overline{BC}$. Also, since $\overrightarrow{PC}$ is a perpendicular bisector of $\overline{AB}$, $m\angle PCB = m\angle PCA = 90°$. Since $\triangle ACP$ and $\triangle BCP$ share side $\overline{PC}$, these triangles are congruent by SAS. Also, by CPCTC, $\overline{AP} \cong \overline{PB}$. Thus $\triangle APB$ has two congruent sides and is isosceles. **2a.** $\triangle AFC$ and $\triangle AFB$ **b.** $\overline{CF} \cong \overline{BF}$ ($\overline{AD}$ bisects $\overline{BC}$). $\overline{AF} \cong \overline{AF}$ (every segment is congruent to itself). $\angle AFC \cong \angle AFB$ ($\overline{AD}$ and $\overline{BC}$ are perpendicular). Therefore, $\triangle AFC \cong \triangle AFB$ by SAS.

On Your Own
5. Let $\triangle ABC$ have altitudes $\overline{BE}$ and $\overline{CD}$, with $\overline{BE} \cong \overline{CD}$. If the triangle is acute, the altitudes lie inside the triangle. Since $\angle A \cong \angle A$, $\overline{BE} \cong \overline{CD}$, and $\angle ADC \cong \angle AEB$ (because all right angles are congruent), you can conclude that $\triangle ADC \cong \triangle AEB$ by AAS. Therefore $\overline{AC} \cong \overline{AB}$, and $\triangle ABC$ is isosceles. If the triangle is a right triangle, the altitudes coincide with two of the sides of the triangle. And since the altitudes are congruent, the sides are congruent as well. Therefore, the triangle is isosceles. If the triangle is obtuse, the altitudes $\overline{CD}$ and $\overline{BE}$ lie outside the triangle. $\angle AEB \cong \angle ADC$ (both are right angles) and $\angle EAB \cong \angle DAC$ (vertical angles). But $\overline{BE} \cong \overline{CD}$ (given). So $\triangle AEB \cong \triangle ADC$ (AAS). Hence $\overline{AB} \cong \overline{AC}$ (CPCTC), which means $\triangle ABC$ is isosceles.

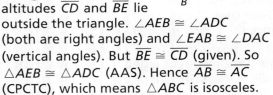

Lesson 6.13
Check Your Understanding
1. Answers may vary. Sample: Since $\overleftrightarrow{ST}$ is the perpendicular bisector of $\overline{RQ}$, it follows from the Perpendicular Bisector Theorem that $\overline{SR} \cong \overline{SQ}$ and $\overline{TR} \cong \overline{TQ}$. Since $\overline{ST} \cong \overline{ST}$, $\triangle SRT \cong \triangle SQT$ (SSS). Therefore, $\angle SRT \cong \angle SQT$ (CPCTC). **2.** The side opposite the included angle for the first triangle is longer than the

side opposite the included angle for the second triangle.

3. •

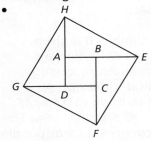

• $m\angle ABC = m\angle BCD = m\angle CDA = m\angle DAB = 90°$; $\overline{AB} \cong \overline{BC} \cong \overline{CD} \cong \overline{DA}$; $\overline{BE} \cong \overline{CF} \cong \overline{DG} \cong \overline{AH}$
• Conjectures may vary.
• Because they are all supplementary to right angles, $m\angle GDH = m\angle HAE = m\angle EBF = m\angle FCG = 90°$. Because $\overline{AB} \cong \overline{BC} \cong \overline{CD} \cong \overline{DA}$ and $\overline{BE} \cong \overline{CF} \cong \overline{DG} \cong \overline{AH}$, it is also true that $\overline{DH} \cong \overline{AE} \cong \overline{BF} \cong \overline{CG}$. Therefore, $\triangle HAE \cong \triangle EBF \cong \triangle FCG \cong \triangle GDH$ by SAS. This means that $\overline{GH} \cong \overline{HE} \cong \overline{EF} \cong \overline{FG}$ by CPCTC. Again by CPCTC, it follows that $\angle AHE \cong \angle BEF$, and hence that $m\angle AHE = m\angle BEF$. By the Triangle Angle-Sum Theorem, we know that $m\angle AHE + m\angle AEH = 90°$. Therefore, $m\angle HEF = m\angle BEF + m\angle AEH = m\angle AHE + m\angle AEH = 90°$. Similarly, $m\angle EFG = m\angle FGH = m\angle GHE = 90°$. Since the sides of $EFGH$ are all congruent, and all the angles of $EFGH$ are right angles, $EFGH$ is a square.

4. •

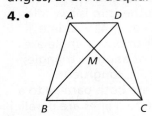

• $\overline{AC} \cong \overline{BD}$; $\overline{AB} \cong \overline{DC}$
• Conjectures may vary.
• $\triangle ABC \cong \triangle DCB$ by SSS. Therefore $\angle MBC \cong \angle MCB$ by CPCTC. It then follows that $\triangle MBC$ is isosceles.

5. •

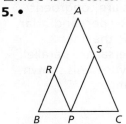

• $\overline{AB} \cong \overline{AC}$; $\overline{AB} \parallel \overline{SP}$, $\overline{AC} \parallel \overline{RP}$
• Conjectures may vary.
• First note that $\angle SCP \cong \angle RPB$ because they

are corresponding angles formed by parallel lines cut by a transversal. Since △ABC is isosceles, ∠RBP ≅ ∠SCP, and therefore, by transitivity, ∠RBP ≅ ∠RPB. This means that △RBP is isosceles and $\overline{RB} \cong \overline{RP}$. Next, draw $\overline{RS}$. By PAI, ∠RSP ≅ ∠ARS and ∠PRS ≅ ∠ASR. Since $\overline{RS} \cong \overline{RS}$, you can conclude that △SRA ≅ △RSP by ASA. So PR = SA and RA = PS. It follows, by substitution, that perimeter ARPS = PR + RA + AS + PS = BR + RA + BR + RA = 2(BR + RA) = 2BA.

6. There are six proofs involved. For the first five, refer to the following figure.

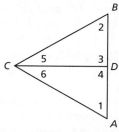

- Assume statements 1 and 2. Then $\overline{AC} \cong \overline{BC}$ and $\overline{DB} \cong \overline{DA}$. Since $\overline{CD} \cong \overline{CD}$, it follows that △ACD ≅ △BCD. By CPCTC, ∠5 ≅ ∠6. Hence $\overline{CD}$ bisects ∠ACB. Again by CPCTC, ∠3 ≅ ∠4. Hence ∠3 ≅ ∠4 (right angles), which implies $\overline{CD}$ is an altitude.
- Assume statements 1 and 3. Then $\overline{AC} \cong \overline{BC}$ and ∠3 and ∠4 are right angles. ∠1 ≅ ∠2 by the Isosceles Triangle Theorem. Therefore, △ACD ≅ △BCD by AAS. By CPCTC, $\overline{DA} \cong \overline{DB}$. So $\overline{CD}$ is a median. Also by CPCTC, ∠5 ≅ ∠6, and hence $\overline{CD}$ bisects ∠ACB.
- Assume statements 1 and 4. Then $\overline{BC} \cong \overline{AC}$ and ∠5 ≅ ∠6. But $\overline{CD} \cong \overline{CD}$, so △ACD ≅ △BCD by SAS. By CPCTC, $\overline{DA} \cong \overline{DB}$. So $\overline{CD}$ is a median. Also by CPCTC, ∠3 ≅ ∠4. Hence $\overline{CD}$ is an altitude.
- Assume statements 2 and 3. Then $\overline{DA} \cong \overline{DB}$ and $\overline{CD} \perp \overline{AB}$. It follows that $\overline{CD}$ is the perpendicular bisector of $\overline{AB}$ and hence, by the Perpendicular Bisector Theorem, AC = BC. Therefore △ABC is isosceles. Since $\overline{CD} \cong \overline{CD}$ and ∠3 ≅ ∠4, △ACD ≅ △BCD by SAS. By CPCTC, ∠5 ≅ ∠6. Thus $\overline{CD}$ bisects ∠ACB.
- Assume statements 3 and 4. Then ∠3 ≅ ∠4 (right angles) and ∠5 ≅ ∠6. Since $\overline{CD} \cong \overline{CD}$, it follows that △ACD ≅ △BCD (ASA). By CPCTC, $\overline{AC} \cong \overline{BC}$ and $\overline{DA} \cong \overline{DB}$. Therefore, △ABC is isosceles and $\overline{CD}$ is a median.
- Assume statements 2 and 4. Then $\overline{DB} \cong \overline{DA}$ and ∠BCD ≅ ∠ACD. First we use an indirect proof that $\overline{AB} \perp \overline{CD}$. Suppose that $\overline{AB}$ is not perpendicular to $\overline{CD}$. Draw the line ℓ that

is perpendicular to $\overline{CD}$ at D. Let M be the point where ℓ intersects $\overrightarrow{CB}$, and let N be the point where ℓ intersects $\overrightarrow{CA}$, as indicated in the figure below.

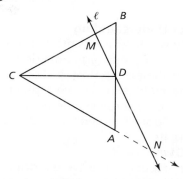

Since ℓ ⊥ $\overline{CD}$, ∠MDC and ∠NDC are right angles and hence are congruent. But ∠BCD ≅ ∠ACD (given) and $\overline{CD} \cong \overline{CD}$. Hence △CMD ≅ △CND by AAS. By CPCTC, $\overline{DM} \cong \overline{DN}$. But $\overline{DB} \cong \overline{DA}$ (given) and ∠BDM ≅ ∠ADN (vertical angles). Hence △BMD ≅ △AND by SAS. By CPCTC, ∠BMD ≅ ∠AND. However, these are alternate interior angles for lines CB and CA and the transversal ℓ. The AIP Theorem implies that lines CB and CA are parallel. This contradicts the fact that lines CB and CA intersect at C. Since the assumption that $\overline{AB}$ is not perpendicular to $\overline{CD}$ has led to a contradiction, these segments are perpendicular. Hence $\overline{CD}$ is an altitude and the perpendicular bisector of $\overline{AB}$. By the Perpendicular Bisector Theorem, CA = CB. So, $\overline{CA}$ and $\overline{CB}$ are legs of isosceles △ABC with base $\overline{AB}$.

On Your Own

9. Answers may vary. Sample: Mark three points A, B, and C on the circle. Draw $\overline{AB}$, $\overline{BC}$, and their perpendicular bisectors. The point of intersection of the bisectors is the center of the circle. **12.** Pick three points A, B, and C on the rim of the blade. Draw the perpendicular bisectors of $\overline{AB}$ and $\overline{BC}$. They will intersect at a point P. Measure $\overline{PA}$ to get the radius of the blade. Double the radius to find the diameter. **15.** Because of the way the folds were made, $\overline{CD}$ is perpendicular to $\overline{AB}$ at the midpoint of $\overline{AB}$. Thus $\overline{CD}$ is the perpendicular bisector of $\overline{AB}$, and it follows from the Perpendicular Bisector Theorem that each point on $\overline{CD}$ is equidistant from A and B.

Lesson 6.14

On Your Own

4. Drawings will vary; rhombus.   **6.** Drawings will vary; yes.   **8.** square

Lesson 6.15

Check Your Understanding

1. no   **2.** yes   **3.** Answers may vary. Samples are given. **a.** The four segments do not intersect at their endpoints. **b.** Some endpoints are not shared by exactly two segments. **c.** There are only three segments in the figure. **d.** Some endpoints are not shared by exactly two segments.

On Your Own

5. You can dissect a concave quadrilateral into two triangles just as you can a convex quadrilateral. The two triangles have angle sums of 180° each, and their combined angle sum is 360°.   **7.** No; answers may vary. Sample: Consider the skew quadrilateral *ABCD* shown at the bottom of p. 144. The four angles of this quadrilateral are ∠*DAB*, ∠*ABC*, ∠*BCD*, and ∠*CDA*. All four of these angles appear to measure less than 90° (and certainly the figure can be drawn so that they are), in which case, the sum of the measures of the angles of *ABCD* is less than 360°.

Lesson 6.16

Check Your Understanding

1. *A*, *B*, *C*, *G*, *H*, *I*, and *L*; each of these figures is a quadrilateral with exactly one pair of sides that appears to be parallel.   **2–8.** Justifications may vary. Samples are given. Figure references are to the figures in Exercise 1.   **2.** always
3. sometimes; figures C and L   **4.** sometimes; figures B and L   **5.** sometimes; figures C and L   **6.** sometimes; draw ∠*DAB* with a ray bisecting it and then draw a parallel to $\overline{AB}$ through *D*. The point where this parallel intersects the angle bisector can be chosen as the fourth vertex of the trapezoid.
7. sometimes; figures L and C   **8.** Never; if one angle of a trapezoid is a right angle, then an angle consecutive to it must also be a right angle, since consecutive angles of parallel lines are supplementary. So if a trapezoid has one right angle, it must in fact have two right angles.   **9.** Answers may vary. Sample: The distance between two parallel lines is the length of any segment perpendicular to both lines and with one endpoint on each line.
10. Let *ABCD* be an isosceles trapezoid with parallel bases $\overline{AB}$ and $\overline{CD}$ (*AB* < *DC*) and $\overline{BC} \cong \overline{AD}$. Draw lines through *A* and *B*

perpendicular to the parallel bases. Let the intersection of $\overline{DC}$ and the perpendicular line through *A* be *X*, and let the intersection of $\overline{DC}$ and the perpendicular line through *B* be *Y*. $\overline{AX} \cong \overline{BY}$ (two segments perpendicular to the same parallel lines are congruent), so △*ADX* ≅ △*CBY* (HL). By CPCTC, ∠*ADX* ≅ ∠*CBY*. Also ∠*CBY* ≅ ∠*DAX* by CPCTC, and ∠*YBA* and ∠*XAB* are right angles. So *m*∠*CBY* + *m*∠*YBA* = *m*∠*DAX* + *m*∠*XAB*. Therefore, *m*∠*CBA* ≅ ∠*DAB*.   **11.** Let *ABCD* be an isosceles trapezoid with parallel bases $\overline{AB}$ and $\overline{CD}$ and $\overline{BC} \cong \overline{AD}$. Draw diagonals $\overline{AC}$ and $\overline{BD}$. Sides $\overline{AD}$ and $\overline{DC}$ in △*ADC* are congruent to sides $\overline{BC}$ and $\overline{CD}$ in △*BCD*. ∠*ADC* ≅ ∠*BCD* (by Exercise 10). Therefore △*ADC* ≅ △*BCD* by SAS, and $\overline{AC} \cong \overline{BD}$ by CPCTC.

On Your Own

12. All appear to be kites except Figure E. Each one appears to have two sets of adjacent congruent sides.   **14.** always   **16.** sometimes   **19.** Let *ABCD* be a kite with $\overline{AB} \cong \overline{BC}$ and $\overline{CD} \cong \overline{DA}$. Draw the diagonal $\overline{BD}$. Since △*DAB* ≅ △*DCB* (SSS), the two parts of ∠*ABC* are congruent, and the two parts of ∠*CDA* are congruent (CPCTC). Therefore, the symmetry diagonal $\overline{BD}$ bisects these angles.

Lesson 6.17

Check Your Understanding

1. If a quadrilateral has its opposite sides congruent, then it is a parallelogram; true; let *ABCD* be a quadrilateral with $\overline{AB} \cong \overline{DC}$ and $\overline{AD} \cong \overline{BC}$. Draw diagonal $\overline{AC}$. By SSS, △*ADC* ≅ △*CBA*. Use AIP to conclude $\overline{AB} \parallel \overline{DC}$ and $\overline{AD} \parallel \overline{BC}$.   **2.** If a quadrilateral has each pair of consecutive angles supplementary, then it is a parallelogram; true; let *ABCD* be a quadrilateral with each pair of consecutive angles supplementary. Since ∠*A* and ∠*B* are supplementary, $\overline{AD} \parallel \overline{BC}$. Since ∠*A* and ∠*D* are supplementary, $\overline{AB} \parallel \overline{DC}$.   **3.** If a quadrilateral has both pairs of opposite angles congruent, then it is a parallelogram; true; let *ABCD* be a quadrilateral with ∠*A* ≅ ∠*C* and ∠*B* ≅ ∠*D*. Hence *m*∠*A* + *m*∠*B* + *m*∠*C* + *m*∠*D* = 2(*m*∠*A* + *m*∠*B*) = 360°, or *m*∠*A* + *m*∠*B* = 180°. Therefore, consecutive angles are supplementary, and, by Exercise 2, *ABCD* is a parallelogram.   **4.** If each diagonal of a quadrilateral divides it into two congruent triangles, then the quadrilateral is a parallelogram; true; match up any two congruent triangles along a congruent side. The opposite angles in the resulting quadrilateral are congruent, so, by Exercise 3, the quadrilateral is a parallelogram. **5.** If a quadrilateral has diagonals that bisect each other, then it is a parallelogram; true; the diagonals divide the parallelogram into four triangles. You can prove that pairs of these are congruent by SAS. Then you know that opposite sides of the quadrilateral are congruent. Therefore the quadrilateral is a parallelogram by Exercise 1. **6.** Answers may vary. Sample: If a pair of consecutive angles of a parallelogram are congruent, then the parallelogram is also a rectangle. To prove this, note that consecutive angles of a parallelogram are supplementary. Then each congruent angle must have measure 90°. The other two angles must then also have measure 90° since they are also consecutive with the first two angles considered. **7a.** Since a diagonal divides a parallelogram into two congruent triangles, opposite sides of the parallelogram are congruent by CPCTC. **b.** Since a diagonal divides a parallelogram into two congruent triangles, opposite angles of the parallelogram are congruent by CPCTC.

8. Let *ABCD* be a parallelogram whose diagonals intersect at *E*, as shown in the diagram. Let ℓ be a line through *E* that does not contain a diagonal. (You can assume ℓ intersects $\overline{AD}$ and $\overline{BC}$, since you can easily modify the proof if ℓ intersects the other pair of parallel sides.) $\overline{AE} \cong \overline{CE}$ because the diagonals of a parallelogram bisect each other. $\angle EAF \cong \angle ECG$ because $\overline{AD}$ is parallel to $\overline{BC}$. Also, $\angle AEF \cong \angle CEG$ because they are vertical angles. Therefore, $\triangle AEF \cong \triangle CEG$ by ASA, and hence $\overline{EF} \cong \overline{EG}$.

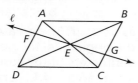

On Your Own
9. always **11.** never **13.** sometimes
17. sometimes **21.** never **23.** always
31. Draw $\overline{AC}$. $\angle DAC \cong \angle BCA$ by PAI, and $\overline{AC} \cong \overline{AC}$. So $\triangle ABC \cong \triangle CDA$ by SAS. Therefore $\angle BAC \cong \angle DCA$ by CPCTC, and $\overline{AB}$ is parallel to $\overline{CD}$ by AIP. Both pairs of opposite sides of *ABCD* are parallel, so *ABCD* is a parallelogram.

Lesson 6.18
Check Your Understanding
1. Let *ABCD* be a rectangle. Opposite sides of *ABCD* are congruent, so $\overline{AD} \cong \overline{BC}$.

All angles of *ABCD* are right angles, so $\angle DAB \cong \angle CBA$ by SAS. $\overline{AB}$ is congruent to itself. Hence $\triangle DAB \cong \triangle CBA$. Therefore, the diagonals $\overline{DB}$ and $\overline{CA}$ are congruent by CPCTC. **2.** Let *ABCD* be a parallelogram with a pair of congruent adjacent sides. Opposite sides of a parallelogram are congruent, so all four sides of *ABCD* are congruent. Therefore, *ABCD* is a rhombus. **3.** sometimes **4.** always
5. sometimes **6.** always **7.** always
8. always **9.** sometimes **10.** sometimes
11. sometimes **12.** sometimes **13.** always
On Your Own
15. If a parallelogram has a right angle, then all its angles are right angles (consecutive angles of a parallelogram are supplementary). A parallelogram with four right angles is a rectangle. **17.** Rhombus; let *ABCD* be a rectangle with *M*, *N*, *P*, and *Q* as the midpoints of $\overline{AB}$, $\overline{BC}$, $\overline{CD}$, and $\overline{DA}$, respectively. $\triangle AMQ \cong \triangle MBN \cong \triangle PCN \cong \triangle PDQ$ by SAS, so $\overline{QM} \cong \overline{MN} \cong \overline{NP} \cong \overline{PQ}$ by CPCTC. Also, *MNPQ* is a parallelogram because it has two pairs of congruent opposite sides. **19.** Since all sides of a rhombus are congruent, the two triangles formed by drawing a diagonal each have two congruent sides. **21.** It follows from the converse of the Perpendicular Bisector Theorem that each diagonal of a rhombus is the perpendicular bisector of the other diagonal. **23.** By PAI, all four angles formed by the diagonal are congruent, so each triangle is isosceles. Moreover, the triangles are also congruent, so all four sides of the parallelogram are congruent by CPCTC.

Chapter 7
Lesson 7.01
On Your Own
8a. 45 mi **b.** 22.5 mi **c.** about 5.6 mi **9.** Answers may vary. Samples are given. **a.** about 241.5 in. by 105 in. **b.** about 25,357.5 in.² **c.** about 20 yd²

Lesson 7.02
Check Your Understanding
1. Answers may vary. Samples: angle measures, congruence of sides, perpendicularity of diagonals **2a.** smaller **b.** same size **c.** larger **d.** smaller **3a.** No; the rectangles are not the same shape. **b.** Yes; the side lengths of the smaller triangle are half the corresponding side lengths of the larger triangle. **c.** No; the diameter of the smaller circle is not half the diameter of the larger circle. **4a.** about $\frac{6}{7}$ **b.** 1 **5.** about $\frac{7}{6}$; 1 **6.** They are reciprocals. **7a.** 4 copies **b.** 9 copies **8a.** 4 **b.** 324 **c.** 16

On Your Own
9a. 0.8, or $\frac{4}{5}$ **b.** 75% **10a.** different
b. different **c.** same **d.** same **13a.** $\frac{1}{3}$; 3; they
are reciprocals. **b.** $\frac{1}{5}$; 5; they are reciprocals.
c. 6; $\frac{1}{6}$; they are reciprocals.

Lesson 7.03
Check Your Understanding
1. Compare ratios of corresponding distances,
such as $\frac{AB}{EF}$ and $\frac{CD}{GH}$. **2.** The choice of unit does
not affect the ratio. **3.** Answers may vary.
Sample: the width of the bottom of each letter,
the length of the horizontal bar in each letter,
the height of each letter, the length of the
"legs" of each letter.
On Your Own
6. The dimensions of the letters in the scaled
copy should be twice the dimensions of the
original letters.

Lesson 7.04
Check Your Understanding
1. 9 **2.** 5 **3.** These triangles are scaled
copies. Explanations may vary. Sample: By
measurement, the lengths of the corresponding
sides are proportional, and the corresponding
angles have equal measures. **4.** no
On Your Own
5. Yes; all the angles are right angles, and in
each rectangle, the ratio $\frac{\text{length of short side}}{\text{length of long side}}$ is $\frac{1}{3}$.
6. 3.2 in.

Lesson 7.05
Check Your Understanding
1. No; explanations may vary. Sample: All
rectangles have 4 right angles, but not all
rectangles are scaled copies of each other.
2. no **3a.** yes **b.** No; explanations may vary.
Sample: In both figures, the polygons have
the same angle measures, but only the first
pair has corresponding side lengths with equal
ratios. **4.** Answers may vary. Sample: Draw
the diagonals and mark the point P where they
intersect. Mark the midpoints of $\overline{PA}$, $\overline{PB}$, $\overline{PC}$,
and $\overline{PD}$. Connect the midpoints, in order, to
get the scaled trapezoid. **5a.** $\frac{3}{4}$ or $\frac{4}{3}$ **b.** 1
6. • No; corresponding sides must have the
same ratio.
 No; corresponding angles must be congruent.
On Your Own
7. No. The angle measures for the first triangle
are 28°, 31°, and 121°. The angle measures for
the second triangle are 31°, 32°, and 117°.
10a. Sample counterexample: a 1-by-2
rectangle and a 1-by-3 rectangle **b.** All angles
measure 90°, and ratios of corresponding sides
are always equal. **d.** Sample counterexample:

an equilateral triangle and a triangle that is
not equilateral **f.** Both triangles have angles
45°, 45°, and 90°. If the legs of the triangles
have measures m and n, then the hypotenuses
have measures $m\sqrt{2}$ and $n\sqrt{2}$. Hence the
ratio of corresponding sides is $\frac{m}{n}$ for all pairs
of corresponding sides. **i.** Each polygon is
equilateral, so the ratio of side lengths does
not vary. If the polygons have n sides, then
each angle measure is $\frac{(n-2)180°}{n}$. **11a.–l.** If no,
a sample counterexample is given. **a.** no;
a 1-by-2 rectangle and a 1-by-3 rectangle
c. no; a trapezoid with bases of lengths 1 and
5 and a trapezoid with bases of lengths 2 and
4 **e.** yes; special case of Exercise 10i **g.** Yes; all
radii of a circle are congruent, so the ratios of
radii of two circles will always be equal. **i.** Yes;
all radii of a sphere are congruent, so the ratios
of radii of two spheres will always be equal. **l.**
no; any cone and a cone with the same base,
but different height

Lesson 7.06
On Your Own
5a.–d. Drawings may vary. Each length in the
scaled copy should have the given relationship
to the corresponding length of the original
hexagon. All angles should measure 120°.
a. $\frac{1}{2}$ as long **b.** the same size **c.** $\frac{3}{2}$ as long **d.** $\frac{3}{4}$
as long **7.** The area A and the perimeter P of
the original rectangle may vary. The areas and
perimeters of the corresponding scaled copies
are **a.** area = $4A$, perimeter = $2P$ **b.** area = $9A$,
perimeter = $3P$ **c.** area = $\frac{1}{4}A$, perimeter = $\frac{1}{2}P$
d. area = $\frac{1}{9}A$, perimeter = $\frac{1}{3}P$ **9.** The area
A and the perimeter P of the original triangle
may vary. The areas and perimeters of the
corresponding scaled copies are **a.** area = $16A$,
perimeter = $4P$ **b.** area = $0.01A$,
perimeter = $0.1P$ **c.** area = $\frac{9}{25}A$,
perimeter = $\frac{3}{5}P$ **d.** area = $\frac{1}{49}A$, perimeter = $\frac{1}{7}P$

Lesson 7.07
Check Your Understanding
1a. Drawings may vary. **b.** The location of the
center of dilation affects where the scaled
copy is located in relation to the original circle.
2a. Drawings may vary. Each side of the
scaled copy should be twice as long as the
corresponding side of the original tilted
square. **b.** They are the same. **c.** no
3. Answers may vary. Sample: To dilate a circle
by the factor $\frac{1}{2}$ using point C as the center of
dilation, select a point A on the circle. Draw
$\overrightarrow{CA}$. Then mark point A' on $\overrightarrow{CA}$ such

that $CA' = \frac{1}{2}CA$. Point A' will be on the scaled copy. Repeat this procedure for several other points of the original circle. Sketch the circle through all the resulting points for the scaled copy. The procedure for dilating the circle by the factor 3 is similar, except this time A' is a point such that $CA' = 3CA$. To dilate a square, find the points on the dilated square that correspond to the vertices of the original square. Connect these points in order to get the dilated square. **4.** Draw the line that passes through the top points of the two figures. Then draw the line that passes through the bottom points of the figures. The point where the two lines intersect is the center of dilation.

On Your Own
5. Choices may vary. The orientation of the two pictures should be the same, but each length in the scaled copy should be twice as long as the corresponding length in the original. **7.** No, the actual measurements on the face are about twice those of the mirror image. **8.** The image you see on "the other side" of the mirror appears the same distance behind the mirror that you are in front of the mirror. Imagine drawing lines from your eyes to the image on the other side of the mirror. Think of your eyes as the center of dilation. The mirror is halfway between, so the image on the mirror appears half the size of your actual face.

Lesson 7.08
Check Your Understanding
1–2. Drawings may vary.
3.

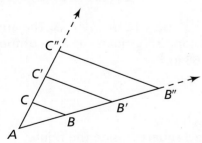

4. 3 times as long; he should have used $DA' = 2$, $DB' = 4$, and $DC' = 3$. **5.** The scale factor is about 1.4. **6a.** The scaled copy should be closer to D than the original, with lengths proportional to the original by the factor $\frac{3}{4}$. **b.** The scaled copy should be farther from D than the original, with lengths 1.5 times as big as those of the original.
7–8. Drawings may vary.

On Your Own
10. Drawings may vary. One of the polygons should have two of its sides contained in the corresponding sides of the other.
12a. $0 <$ scale factor < 1 **b.** scale factor > 1
c. scale factor $= 1$

Lesson 7.09
On Your Own
4. $PQ = 2\sqrt{13}$, $SR = 8$, $QR = 12$, $PR = 10$
6. All will have the same area; they have congruent bases ($\overline{RA}$ and $\overline{GM}$) and equal heights (the distance between $\overleftrightarrow{RA}$ and $\overleftrightarrow{GM}$).

Lesson 7.10
Check Your Understanding
1. 6 **2.** 16 **3.** 8 **4.** 12 **5.** $\frac{1}{4}$
On Your Own
8. Answers may vary. Sample: For the figure in Exercise 6, "whole is to part as whole is to part" means $\frac{AB}{AD} = \frac{AC}{AE}$, "part is to part as part is to part" means $\frac{AD}{DE} = \frac{AE}{DE}$, and "part is to whole as part is to whole" means $\frac{AD}{AB} = \frac{AE}{AC}$.

Lesson 7.11
Check Your Understanding
1. Reverse some of the steps in the proof of the Parallel Side-Splitter Theorem to show that $\frac{SV}{VR} = \frac{SW}{WT}$ implies $\frac{\text{area }(\triangle SVW)}{\text{area }(\triangle RVW)} = \frac{\text{area }(\triangle SVW)}{\text{area }(\triangle TVW)}$ and that this implies area $(\triangle RVW) = $ area$(\triangle TVW)$. Since area$(RVWT)$ is equal to both area$(\triangle RVW) + $ area$(\triangle RWT)$ and area$(\triangle TVW) + $ area$(\triangle RVT)$, it follows that area $(\triangle RVT) = $ area$(\triangle RWT)$. In $\triangle RVT$, draw the altitude $\overline{VM}$ from V to $\overline{RT}$, and in $\triangle RWT$, draw the altitude $\overline{WN}$ from W to $\overline{RT}$. Use the area formula with $\triangle RVT$ and $\triangle RWT$ to get $\frac{1}{2}(RT)(VM) = \frac{1}{2}(RT)(WN)$, from which it follows that $VM = WN$. Conclude that $MVWN$ is a parallelogram (two sides parallel and congruent) and hence that $\overline{VM} \parallel \overline{RT}$. **2a.** $CD = 2$, $AD = 2$, $BC = 2$ **b.** $BC = 4.5$, $CE = 1.5$, $AC = 3$ **c.** $CD = 1$, $CE = 1$, $BC = 2$ **3a.** no
b. yes **c.** yes
On Your Own
5. They cut $\overline{AB}$ and $\overline{BC}$ into four congruent segments. **7.** All the dashed lines are parallel to $\overline{AC}$.

Lesson 7.12
Check Your Understanding
1. $BE = 4$, $EC = 4$, $AD = 3$, $BD = 3$
2. $AD = 1$, $AB = 2$, $EC = 1$, $BC = 2$
3. $AB = 12$, $AD = 4$, $CE = 3$, $BE = 6$

On Your Own

5. Since $\overline{DE} \parallel \overline{BC}$, it follows that corresponding angles of the two triangles are congruent. Use the Parallel Side-Splitter Theorem to show that corresponding sides are proportional. Therefore, the triangles are scaled copies of each other.

Lesson 7.13
On Your Own

7. $\angle D \cong \angle M$, $\angle E \cong \angle A$, $\angle R \cong \angle N$, $\frac{DE}{MA} = \frac{DR}{MN} = \frac{ER}{AN}$, $\frac{DE}{ER} = \frac{MA}{AN}$, $\frac{DE}{DR} = \frac{MA}{MN}$, $\frac{DR}{ER} = \frac{MN}{AN}$
9. No; the sketch should feature two similar polygons that are reflected as well as dilated.

Lesson 7.14
Check Your Understanding

1a. Yes; corresponding angles are congruent, and corresponding sides are proportional.
b. No; corresponding angles are not congruent.
c. No; corresponding angles are not congruent.
2a. yes **b.** yes **c.** no **d.** yes   **3.** Since $\triangle ABC \sim \triangle BDA$, $\angle B \cong \angle D$. Therefore $\overline{AB} \cong \overline{AD}$, and $\triangle BDA$ is isosceles. Any triangle similar to an isosceles triangle must itself be isosceles, so $\triangle ABC$ is isosceles.   **4.** Answers may vary. Sample: By the Midline Theorem, the lengths of the sides of $\triangle GHF$ are half the lengths of the corresponding sides of $\triangle ABC$. Since a midline is parallel to the third side of its triangle, it follows that $AFGH$, $FGCH$, and $FBCH$ are parallelograms. Opposite angles of a parallelogram are congruent, so the corresponding angles of $\triangle GHF$ and $\triangle ABG$ are congruent. Therefore, $\triangle ABC \sim \triangle GHF$.
5. $m\angle BAC = 30°$, $m\angle DAC = 90°$, $m\angle BCA = 120°$, $m\angle ACD = 60°$, $m\angle ADB = 30°$, $BC = 2\sqrt{3}$, $CD = 4\sqrt{3}$, $BD = 6\sqrt{3}$, $AD = 6$

On Your Own

6a. incorrect **b.** correct **c.** incorrect **d.** correct **e.** incorrect **f.** incorrect   **8a.** $\angle D$ **b.** $\angle DTO$
c. $\angle CTA$ **d.** $\angle O$ **e.** $\angle C$ **f.** $\angle A$

Lesson 7.15
Check Your Understanding

1a. Note that $\frac{KM}{KJ} = \frac{KN}{KL} = \frac{1}{4}$, and then use the Proportional Side-Splitter Theorem.
b. • Since $\overline{MN} \parallel \overline{JL}$, $\angle KMN \cong \angle KJL$ and $\angle KNM \cong \angle KLJ$. $\triangle MKN \sim \triangle JKL$ by the AA test.
• From part (a), $\frac{KM}{KJ} = \frac{KN}{KL}$. And since both triangles share a common angle, $\triangle MKN \sim \triangle JKL$ by the SAS Test.
• By the Parallel Side-Splitter Theorem, $\frac{KM}{KJ} = \frac{KN}{KL} = \frac{MN}{JL}$. By the SSS Theorem, $\triangle MKN \sim \triangle JKL$.

2a. 3; AA Similarity Theorem **b.** 3; AA Similarity Theorem **c.** 3; SAS Similarity Test
3. No; answers may vary. Sample: A square with sides of length 1 is not similar to a rectangle that has length 2 and width 1.
4. In quadrilaterals $ABCD$ and $EFGH$, let $\frac{AB}{EF} = \frac{AD}{EH} = \frac{CD}{GH}$, $\angle BAD \cong \angle FEH$, and $\angle ADC \cong \angle EHG$. By the SAS Similarity Theorem, $\triangle ABD \sim \triangle EFH$ and $\triangle CDA \sim \triangle GHE$. Therefore, $\angle CAD \cong \angle GEH$, and $\overline{AC}$ and $\overline{EG}$ are proportional. $\angle BAC \cong \angle FEG$ because each is the difference of congruent angles. By the SAS Similarity Theorem, $\triangle ABC \sim \triangle EFG$ and $\triangle BCD \sim \triangle FGH$. Therefore, BC and FG are proportional to AB and EF. Corresponding angles in similar triangles are congruent, so $\angle ABC \cong \angle EFG$ and $\angle BCD \cong \angle FGH$. All corresponding sides of $ABCD$ and $EFHG$ are proportional and all corresponding angles are congruent, so the quadrilaterals are similar.
5. For parallel lines cut by a transversal, corresponding angles are congruent, so $\angle HFG \cong \angle A$ and $\angle HGF \cong \angle C$. Therefore, $\triangle ABC \sim \triangle FHG$ by the AA Similarity Test.   **6.** B

On Your Own
7. $\frac{15}{4}$ and 6; or $\frac{12}{5}$ and $\frac{24}{5}$; or $\frac{3}{2}$ and $\frac{15}{8}$; yes
9. AA Similarity test (since $\angle A \cong \angle A$ and $\angle ADE \cong \angle C$)   **12.** $\frac{AC}{EC} = \frac{BC}{DC} = 2$, and $\angle C$ is common to the two triangles. Hence $\triangle ABC \sim \triangle EDC$ by the SAS Similarity Theorem; 2.

Lesson 7.16
Check Your Understanding
1. 540   **2.** He needed only 2 bags of seed for the small field.   **3a.** about 31 cm² or 4.8 in.²
b. about 70 cm² or 11 in.²
On Your Own
4a. $\sqrt{12}$ or $\frac{\sqrt{12}}{12}$ **b.** $\sqrt{12}$ or $\frac{\sqrt{12}}{12}$ **5.** The area of the scaled copy is $\frac{1}{16}$ times the area of the original.   **7.** 68 in.²

Chapter 8
Lesson 8.01
On Your Own
4a. There are 5 squares inside the figure.
b. Each square has an area of $\frac{1}{4}$ square inch. The area covered by the squares is $\frac{5}{4}$ square inches, which is definitely less than the area of the blob.

Lesson 8.02
Check Your Understanding
1. The following answers assume that two grid lines pass through the center of the circle.
a. Inner area = 1 in.²; outer area = 4 in.²; area of circle is between these measures.

b. Inner area = 2 in.^{2}; outer area = 3.75 in.^{2}; area of circle is between these measures.
c. Inner area = 2.56 in.^{2}; outer area = 3.5 in.^{2}; area of circle is between these measures.
d. Inner area = 2.86 in.^{2}; outer area = 3.34 in.^{2}; area of circle is between these measures.
2a. Answers may vary. Sample: Place a grid of squares over the shape. To get a low estimate, count grid squares that lie entirely inside the shape and multiply by the area of a grid square. To get a high estimate, count grid squares that lie inside or partially inside the shape and multiply by the area of a grid square. In most cases, the smaller the grid squares, the better the estimates will be.
b. 6 in.^{2} **c.** Answers may vary. Sample: inner area = 5.25 in.^{2}, outer area = 6.75 in.^{2} (You obtain these values by using a grid of $\frac{1}{4}$ in.-by-$\frac{1}{4}$ in. squares, with the perpendicular sides of the triangle lying along grid lines.)
3. ratio of area of smaller to area of larger = $\left(\frac{3.5}{4.5}\right)^2$, or about 0.605 **4a.** The area of the larger circle is 9 times the area of the smaller circle. **b.** The area of the smaller circle is $\frac{1}{4}$ the area of the larger circle. **5–7.** Answers may vary. Samples are given based on drawing a circle with radius 1 in. **5.** The circumference is between 2 in. and 4 in. **6.** The circumference is between 2.8 in. and 3.3 in. **7.** The circumference is between 3.1 in. and 3.2 in.
8. Tables may vary. The following table is based on measuring the figures shown in Exercises 5–7.

Number of Sides	Outer Perimeter	Inner Perimeter	Difference
4	20.4 cm	14.4 cm	6 cm
8	16.8 cm	15.2 cm	1.6 cm
16	16 cm	15.5 cm	0.5 cm

9. Answers may vary. Sample: 15.75 cm
10. As the number of sides of the inscribed and circumscribed polygons increases, the polygons get to be more like the circle.
On Your Own
12a. s-by-$2s$ rectangles, where s is the length of a square of the original grid **b.** twice the area of a square of the original grid **c.** It doubles.
d. No; in a scaled copy, all the lengths change by the same factor. **13.** The curve is approximately $7\frac{1}{8}$ inches long.

Lesson 8.03
Check Your Understanding
1. about 3.125 m^2 **2a.** $\sqrt{2}$ cm **b.** about 6.29 cm^2 **3.** Answers may vary. Sample: Suppose $ABCDEF$ is a regular hexagon and that point O is the center of the circumscribed circle. The sum of the angle measures of $ABCDEF$ is $4 \cdot 180°$, or $720°$. If you draw the radii from O to the vertices of $ABCDEF$, you divide the hexagon into six congruent isosceles triangles (congruent by SSS, isosceles because radii of the same circle are congruent). It follows that the angles of each triangle all have a measure of $60°$. Therefore, the triangles are equilateral, and hence the radii are congruent to the sides of the hexagon.
On Your Own
4a. about 172.8 in.^{2} **6.** about 7.9 cm

Lesson 8.04
On Your Own
4. about 5.57 cm **5.** about 9.1 cm^2

Lesson 8.05
Check Your Understanding
1a. 100π in.^{2} **b.** 25π cm^2 **c.** $\frac{9}{4}\pi$ ft^2
d. 100π in.^{2} **2a.** $\frac{1}{8}$ **b.** π **c.** $\frac{\pi}{8}$ **d.** Answers may vary. Sample: $\frac{11}{28}$ (using $\pi \approx \frac{22}{7}$), 0.3925 (using $\pi \approx 3.14$) **3a.** 25π **b.** $144\pi - 72$
On Your Own
4a. $\frac{25\pi}{6}$ **b.** 20π **6a.** shaded: 9π cm^2; white: $(36 - 9\pi)$ cm^2 **b.** shaded: 9π cm^2; white: $(36 - 9\pi)$ cm^2 **c.** The areas of the shaded regions are the same, and so are the areas of the white regions; if you cut the figure in part (a) vertically through the center and translate the part on the left 6 cm to the right, you get the figure in part (b), provided you ignore the segment down the middle.

Lesson 8.06
Check Your Understanding
1. small arc: $\frac{2\pi}{3}$ cm; large arc: $\frac{10\pi}{3}$ cm **2.** small arc: $\frac{\pi}{3}$ cm; large arc: $\frac{11\pi}{3}$ cm **3.** small arc: $\frac{\pi}{2}$ cm; large arc: $\frac{7\pi}{2}$ cm **4.** True; the formula $C = \pi d$ implies $\frac{c}{d} = \pi$.
On Your Own
6. circumference of canister ($C = 2\pi r$, $h = 6r$, and $2\pi > 6$) **7.** rectangle 5 in. tall and 3π in. wide

Lesson 8.08
On Your Own
7a. right triangle **b.** $\overline{AB}$ (the hypotenuse), midpoint **c.** outside the circle (but not on $\overleftrightarrow{AB}$); inside the circle

Lesson 8.09
Check Your Understanding
1a. chord, diameter **b.** radius **c.** radius **d.** chord **e.** central angle **f.** central angle **g.** minor arc **h.** semicircle   **2.** $m\angle MON = 60°$, $MN = 1$ in., $OH = \dfrac{\sqrt{3}}{2}$ in.   **3a.** 60° **b.** 30° **c.** 45° **d.** 15° **e.** 15° **f.** 15° **g.** 75°   **4.** Yes; given circle O with minor arc and points as described, assume $m\overarc{AC} = x$ and $m\overarc{CB} = y$. Then $m\angle AOC = x$ and $m\angle COB = y$. Therefore $m\angle AOC + m\angle COB = x + y$. And since $\angle AOC$ and $\angle COB$ are adjacent, we know that $m\angle AOC + m\angle COB = m\angle AOB = x + y$. And since the arc associated with $\angle AOB$ is $\overarc{AB}$, we know that $m\overarc{AB} = m\angle AOB = x + y$ $= m\overarc{AC} + m\overarc{CB}$.

On Your Own
5. $\overline{OQ} \cong \overline{OR}$, since radii of the same circle are congruent. Hence $\triangle OQR$ is isosceles. But the bisector of the vertex angle of an isosceles triangle is a median. Thus P is the midpoint of $\overline{QR}$, and so $\overline{QP} \cong \overline{PR}$.   **6.** The angles in question are base angles of congruent isosceles triangles $\triangle FOH$ and $\triangle IOJ$. Since the base angles of an isosceles triangle are congruent, it follows that all four of the angles are congruent.

Lesson 8.10
Check Your Understanding
1. 90°   **2.** If A is at the center of the circle, then all chords through A will have the same length and hence the shortest possible length. If A is not at the center and the center is O, the shortest chord through A will be the chord $\overline{XY}$ perpendicular to $\overline{OA}$ at A. To see why, note that $\overline{XY}$ is shorter than a diameter. Suppose $\overline{PQ}$ is any chord other than $\overline{XY}$ that passes through A. In $\triangle POQ$, let $\overline{OR}$ be the altitude from O. Since $\triangle OAR$ is a right triangle with its right angle at R, it follows that $OA > OR$ (the hypotenuse of a right triangle is longer than each of the legs). $\triangle XOY$ and $\triangle POQ$ are isosceles triangles with legs that are radii of the circle. It follows from the Pythagorean Theorem that the triangle with the greater altitude from O has the shorter base. Hence $XY < PQ$.   **3.** Sketches may vary. Sample:

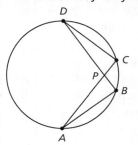

$\angle CAB \cong \angle BDC$, since they intercept the same arc. For the same reason, $\angle ABD \cong \angle DCA$. It is given that $\overline{AB} \cong \overline{CD}$, so $\triangle ABP \cong \triangle DCP$ by ASA. Since they are corresponding parts of congruent triangles, the two segments that form $\overline{AC}$ ($\overline{AP}$ and $\overline{PC}$) are congruent to the two segments that form $\overline{BD}$ ($\overline{DP}$ and $\overline{PB}$). Therefore, $\overline{AC} \cong \overline{BD}$. Similar reasoning applies for other possible diagrams.   **4.** Suppose the adjacent chords are $\overline{AB}$ and $\overline{CB}$ and that $\overline{OB}$ is the radius with which they form congruent angles. $\triangle AOB$ and $\triangle COB$ are isosceles (two sides of each are radii). It is given that $\angle ABO \cong \angle CBO$. So the base angles of $\triangle AOB$ are congruent to the base angles of $\triangle COB$. Since the triangles have $\overline{OB}$ as a common side, $\triangle AOB \cong \triangle COB$ (by AAS). Therefore, $\overline{AB} \cong \overline{BC}$ (by CPCTC).   **5a.** 11.5° **b.** 23° **c.** 23° **d.** 78.5° **e.** 78.5°

On Your Own
7. a circle with the same center as the original circle and lying inside that circle   **8.** 2 ways; $\dfrac{\sqrt{3}}{4} + \dfrac{\pi}{6}$, or $\dfrac{3\sqrt{3} + 2\pi}{12}$ **10a.** 90°, 90°, 90°, 90° **b.** 70° **c.** 140° **d.** 70° **e.** 40°   **12a.** A diameter of a circle that is perpendicular to a chord bisects the chord (Theorem 5.8). $\overline{FZ}$ is perpendicular to $\overline{PQ}$ since it is perpendicular to $\overline{MN}$ and $\overline{MN} \parallel \overline{PQ}$. Hence $\overline{FZ}$ is the perpendicular bisector of $\overline{MN}$ and $\overline{PQ}$. **b.** 5 cm **c.** $5\sqrt{3}$ cm **d.** $\dfrac{5\sqrt{3}}{2}$ cm **e.** 90°   **13.** 45°

Lesson 8.11
Check Your Understanding
1. The radius drawn to the point where a tangent line touches a circle is perpendicular to the tangent line, so $\triangle OPB$ and $\triangle OPA$ are right triangles. The triangles have a common hypotenuse and the legs $\overline{OB}$ and $\overline{OA}$ are congruent. It follows by the Pythagorean Theorem that $PA = PB$ and hence that $\overline{PA} \cong \overline{PB}$.   **2.** $\overline{OB}$ and $\overline{OA}$ are radii, so $OB = OA$. From Exercise 1, $PA = PB$. Since P and O are equidistant from A and B, $\overline{PO}$ is the perpendicular bisector of $\overline{AB}$.   **3.** Suppose the given circle has center O, and let the external point be P. Draw $\overline{OP}$. Construct the midpoint M of $\overline{OP}$. Draw the circle with center M and radius $\overline{MO}$. Let C and D be the points where this circle intersects the given circle. Draw $PCOD$. $\angle C$ and $\angle D$ both intercept a semicircle of the circle with center M. Therefore, $\angle C$ and $\angle D$ are right angles. Hence $\overline{PC}$ and $\overline{PD}$ are tangent to the original circle.   **4a.** 57° **b.** 26° **c.** 65°   **5a.** 14° **b.** 27.5° **c.** Answers may vary. From part (b), $m\angle CAD = 27.5°$. By

Theorem 5.14, $m\angle ADC = \frac{1}{2}(\overset{\frown}{mCBF} - \overset{\frown}{mCE}) = \frac{1}{2}((180° + 14°) - 69°) = 62.5°$. So $m\angle ACD = 180° - 27.5° - 62.5° = 90°$.

On Your Own

6. If $m\angle POQ = 30°$, then $OQ = \frac{2\sqrt{3}}{3}$ in. and $PQ = \frac{\sqrt{3}}{3}$ in.; if $\angle POQ = 45°$, then $OQ = \sqrt{2}$ in. and $PQ = 1$ in.; if $m\angle POQ = 60°$, then $OQ = 2$ in. and $PQ = \sqrt{3}$ in.   **9.** Drawings may vary. Sample:

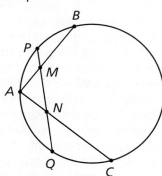

By Theorem 5.13, $m\angle AMN = \frac{1}{2}(\overset{\frown}{mBP} + \overset{\frown}{mAQ})$ and $m\angle ANM = \frac{1}{2}(\overset{\frown}{mAP} + \overset{\frown}{mCQ})$. But $\overset{\frown}{BP} \cong \overset{\frown}{AP}$ and $\overset{\frown}{AQ} \cong \overset{\frown}{CQ}$. Hence $m\angle AMN = m\angle ANM$. Therefore, $\triangle AMN$ is isosceles with legs $\overline{AM}$ and $\overline{AN}$, which means that $\overline{AM} \cong \overline{AN}$.

11a. Exercise 1 shows that $\overline{PA} \cong \overline{PB}$ and $\overline{PC} \cong \overline{PD}$. Radii of the same circle are congruent, so it follows that $PDOC$ and $PBOA$ are kites that have $\overline{PO}$ as a shared axis of symmetry. From this it follows easily that $\angle APC \cong \angle DPB$. **b.** Use the angle congruence proved in part (a) and the facts that $\overline{PA} \cong \overline{PB}$ and $\overline{PC} \cong \overline{PD}$ to conclude that $\triangle PAC \cong \triangle PBD$ (SAS). Hence $\overline{AC} \cong \overline{BD}$ by CPCTC. The diagonals of a kite are perpendicular and $\overline{PO}$ is a shared diagonal of $PDOC$ and $PBOA$. Therefore $\overline{AB}$ and $\overline{CD}$ are both perpendicular to $\overline{PO}$. Hence $\overline{AB} \parallel \overline{CD}$.

Lesson 8.12

Check Your Understanding

1. Construct a circle and a point P inside it such that $\prod(P) = 12$. One such circle and point can be constructed by picking two numbers with a product of 12, such as 2 and 6. Draw a segment of length 8 (that is, $2 + 6$). Mark its midpoint. Then draw the circle that has the segment as a diameter. Mark P on the segment so that P is 2 units from one endpoint. Then $\prod(P) = 12$. Select a stick and place it so that it goes through P and has one end on the circle. Mark the place on the stick that corresponds

to P. Cut off any excess part of the stick that is outside the circle at the other end. Cut the stick in two at the point corresponding to P. Cut another two pieces of these same lengths from another stick. Use the four pieces to build one rectangle. Repeat the process to get rectangles with other dimensions.   **2.** 35.5 in.

3. $\prod(B) = \frac{3}{4}r^2$; $\prod(C) = \frac{7}{16}r^2$; $\prod(D) = \frac{15}{64}r^2$; define $\prod(E)$ to be 0.

On Your Own

6. $PB = 6$ cm, $CP = 7$ cm, $DP = 18$ cm (or $CP = 18$ cm, $DP = 7$ cm)

Lesson 8.13

On Your Own

8. Drawings may vary. The areas for the two colors should be approximately equal.

10. Drawings may vary. The area for one color should be 3 times the area for the other.

Lesson 8.14

Check Your Understanding

1. $\frac{\pi}{4}$ **2.** $\frac{3\pi}{16}$ **3.** $\frac{3\pi}{64}$

On Your Own

5. $\frac{39}{64} \approx 0.609$ **6.** Increase the side length of the squares to about 2.56 in., about 4.09 in., and 5.60 in., respectively.

Lesson 8.14

Check Your Understanding

1. 0; answers may vary. Sample: The squiggly lines have no area.   **2.** $\frac{\pi}{9}$; no; $\frac{4\pi - 9}{18}$; the measure of a set of nonseparate elements is less than or equal to the sum of the measures of the separate elements. The probability of an event can never be greater than 1.   **3.** $P_1 = 1$, $P_2 = \frac{1}{4}$, $P_3 = \frac{1}{16}$, $P_4 = \frac{1}{64}$, $P_5 = \frac{1}{256}$, $P_6 = \frac{1}{1024}$, $P_7 = \frac{1}{4096}$, ..., $P_n = \frac{P_{n-1}}{4}$ (for $n \geq 2$); 0; the measure of the intersection of many elements, each contained in the previous one, is the measure of the smallest one; all of R_n is contained in R_{n-1}.

On Your Own

4a. $\frac{3}{4}$ **b.** $\frac{1}{4}$ **c.** The measure of a set of separate elements is the sum of the measures of the separate elements; there are only two kinds of small squares, white and black.   **6.** $\frac{\pi r^2}{4\ell^2}$; 0, because the drop can be imagined as a circle of radius $r = 0$.

Chapter 8

Lesson 9.01

On Your Own

5a. Nancy; her shadow is longer. **b.** 68 in. **c.** about 60.24 in.   **7.** about 4 in.

9. about 8.08×10^{-9} in.
10. about 6.19 million times

Lesson 9.02
Check Your Understanding
1a. 5; 4 **b.** 7.5; 6 **c.** 5; $2\sqrt{6}$ **d.** 5; 5 **2.** The largest angle with a vertex on the top semicircle intercepts the bottom semicircle and hence has measure $\frac{1}{2} \cdot 180°$, or 90°. **3.** first figure: $AC = 5$, $BD = \sqrt{6}$, $AB = \sqrt{10}$, $BC = \sqrt{15}$; second figure: $AC = 4$, $AD = 3$, $AB = 2\sqrt{3}$, $BD = \sqrt{3}$ **4.** Drawing shows a circle of radius 2 in. with a diameter cut into segments of 1 in. and 3 in. A perpendicular to this diameter at the cut point intersects the circle, and the segment from the cut point to this intersection has length $\sqrt{3}$ in., the geometric mean of 1 and 3.
On Your Own
8a. The perimeters are equal. **b.** the square
9a. No; c is too small. There is no way for the endpoint of c to stretch from P to the edge of the circle. **b.** The small size of the segment of length c makes the construction difficult. **c.** The circle would need to be larger than the circle in Minds in Action so that the chord $a + b$ would be far from the center of the circle such that a very small c would stretch between P and the edge of the circle.

Lesson 9.03
Check Your Understanding
1. Let $\triangle ABC$ be a right triangle with right angle at C. Let $\overline{CH}$ be the altitude from C to $\overline{AB}$. The AA Similarity test shows that $\triangle AHC \sim \triangle CHB$. So $\frac{AH}{CH} = \frac{CH}{BH}$. It follows that $CH^2 = AH \cdot BH$ and hence that $CH = \sqrt{AH \cdot BH}$. **2.** From the given proportion and the fact that the two angles with vertex H are right angles, it follows that $\triangle AHC \sim \triangle CHB$ (you can rotate $\triangle AHC$ so that it can be dilated onto the other triangle). This implies that $\angle A \cong \angle HCB$ and $\angle B \cong \angle ACH$. Since $\angle A$ and $\angle ACH$ are complementary angles, the two small angles with vertex C are complementary. Thus $\angle ACB$ is a right angle. Because $\angle ACB$ is a right angle, $\triangle ABC$ is a right triangle. **3.** If $\overline{CB}$ is the diameter through B, then $\angle CAB$ intercepts a semicircle and hence is a right angle. Theorem 6.1 implies that AB^2 is the product of CB and the length of the projection of $\overline{AB}$ on $\overline{CB}$. **4.** $\sqrt{rs}$
On Your Own
7. Let a and b be the lengths of the legs of a right triangle with hypotenuse of length c. The sum of the areas of the semicircles on the legs is $\frac{1}{2}\left(\frac{a}{2}\right)^2 \pi + \frac{1}{2}\left(\frac{b}{2}\right)^2 \pi$. Simplify to get $\frac{1}{8}\pi(a^2 + b^2)$,

or $\frac{1}{8}\pi c^2$. But the area of the semicircle on the hypotenuse is $\frac{1}{2}\left(\frac{c}{2}\right)^2 \pi$, or $\frac{1}{8}\pi c^2$. **9.** 6
11. $AB = 6$, $AC = 8$

Lesson 9.04
Check Your Understanding
1. P is the midpoint of $\overline{AG}$, so it cuts $\overline{AG}$ into two congruent pieces. Since $\triangle PQG \cong \triangle NMG$, you know that one of those pieces, $\overline{PG}$, is congruent to $\overline{NG}$. So $\overline{AG}$ is composed of two pieces, each congruent to $\overline{NG}$, and it must be twice as long. A similar argument shows that $BG = 2GM$. **2.** $\overline{PQ}$ and $\overline{MN}$ are both parallel to $\overline{AB}$ and hence are parallel to each other. Sasha's reasoning shows that $MN = PQ$. So $PQNM$ is a parallelogram. The diagonals of a parallelogram bisect each other. The desired result follows at once. **3.** Diagrams may vary. For every triangle, the angle bisectors are concurrent, the lines that contain the altitudes are concurrent, and the perpendicular bisectors of the sides of the triangle are concurrent.

Lesson 9.05
Check Your Understanding
1a. $(-33, 561)$ **b.** $\left(3x, \frac{y}{2}\right)$ **2.** $A(2, 4\sqrt{6})$, $B(5, 5\sqrt{3})$, $C(6, 8)$, $D(5\sqrt{2}, 5\sqrt{2})$, $E(10, 0)$, $F(0, -10)$, $G(-8, -6)$ **3a.** $AB = \sqrt{53}$, $BC = 2\sqrt{26}$, $AC = 5$ **b.** length of median from $A = \sqrt{13}$, length of median from $B = 8.5$, length of median from $C = \frac{\sqrt{205}}{2}$
4. $AB = A'B' = \sqrt{34}$, $BC = B'C' = \sqrt{29}$, $AC = A'C' = \sqrt{13}$, so $\triangle ABC \cong \triangle A'B'C'$ by SSS. **5.** $AB = \sqrt{960^2 + 512^2}$ and $A'B' = \sqrt{3840^2 + 2048^2}$, so $AB = \frac{1}{4}A'B'$ because $\sqrt{3840^2 + 2048^2} = \sqrt{(4 \cdot 960)^2 + (4 \cdot 512)^2}$. $BC = \sqrt{897^2 + 496^2}$ and $B'C' = \sqrt{3588^2 + 1984^2}$, so $BC = \frac{1}{4}B'C'$ because $\sqrt{3588^2 + 1984^2} = \sqrt{(4 \cdot 897)^2 + (4 \cdot 496)^2}$. $AC = \sqrt{63^2 + 16^2}$ and $A'C' = \sqrt{252^2 + 64^2}$, so $AC = \frac{1}{4}A'C'$ because $\sqrt{252^2 + 64^2} = \sqrt{(4 \cdot 63)^2 + (4 \cdot 16)^2}$. The lengths of the sides of $\triangle ABC$ are $\frac{1}{4}$ the lengths of the corresponding sides of $\triangle A'B'C'$, so the triangles are similar (SSS Similarity) **6.** Answers may vary. Sample: Use the Distance Formula to calculate the side lengths of each triangle. If the side lengths for the two triangles are the same, then the triangles are congruent by SSS. **7.** Answers may vary.

Sample: Use the Distance Formula to calculate the side lengths of each triangle. If the side lengths of one triangle are proportional to those of the other triangle, then the triangles are similar by SSS Similarity.   **8.** Answers may vary. Sample: Starting with $\overline{ST}$ and going clockwise, let the midpoints of the sides of STAR be P, Q, V, and W. Use the Midpoint Formula to show that these are the points P(3, 5), Q(4, 1), V(−1, −2), and W(−2, 4). Use the Distance Formula to show that $PW = VQ = \sqrt{26}$ and $PQ = WV = \sqrt{37}$. Since the opposite sides of PQVW are congruent, PQVW is a parallelogram.
9. Answers may vary. Sample: Quadrilateral ABCD has vertices A(3, 1), B(4,7), C(11, 3), and D(8, −5). The midpoint of $\overline{AB}$ is E(3.5, 4), of $\overline{BC}$ is F(7.5, 5), of $\overline{CD}$ is G(9.5, −1), and of $\overline{DA}$ is H(5.5, −2). EFGH is a parallelogram because the opposite sides are the same length. $EF = GH = \sqrt{17}$ and $EH = FG + 2\sqrt{10}$.
On Your Own
11a. (−14, 14) **b.** (86, −186)   **13.** E(113, 19), D(116, 15)   **16.** (3, 5)

Lesson 9.06
On Your Own
5. All the ramps are equally steep. The triangles formed by the ramps are similar.   **7.** Ramp C with width 50.9 mm and height 18.5 mm is steepest.   **9.** about 20.4 ft   **10.** about 589 ft

Lesson 9.07
Check Your Understanding
1. A right triangle with legs of lengths a and b has a hypotenuse of length $\sqrt{a^2 + b^2}$. If $c^2 = a^2 + b^2$, this means the hypotenuse has length c. By SSS, a triangle with side lengths a, b, and c is congruent to the right triangle just described and hence is itself a right triangle.
2. $DO = \sqrt{2}$ by the Pythagorean Theorem; $m\angle D = 45°$ because $\triangle DGO$ is isosceles.
3. $m\angle T = 30°$, $m\angle A = 60°$, and $m\angle R = 90°$; the converse of the Pythagorean Theorem tells you that the triangle is a right triangle, and the ratios of the lengths of the sides tell you that its acute angles are 30° and 60°. The larger acute angle is opposite the longer leg.   **4.** Such a triangle may be a 30-60-90 triangle, but it does not have to be. Sketches may vary. Sample:

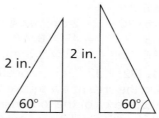

On Your Own
5. $m\angle T = 90°$, $AT = 17$, $AC = 17\sqrt{2}$; $\triangle CTA$ is a 45-45-90 triangle.   **8.** $m\angle S = 60°$, $SI = \frac{4\sqrt{3}}{3}$, $SC = \frac{8\sqrt{3}}{3}$; $\triangle SIC$ is a 30-60-90 triangle.
13. $\frac{16\sqrt{6}}{3}$ cm

Lesson 9.08
Check Your Understanding
1a. sin 40° = 0.64 **b.** cos 70° = 0.34
c. tan 55° = 1.43   **2a.** $\sin A = \frac{4}{5}$, $\cos A = \frac{3}{5}$, $\tan A = \frac{4}{3}$ **b.** $\sin B = \frac{3}{5}$, $\cos B = \frac{4}{5}$, $\tan B = \frac{3}{4}$
c. sin A = cos B, and cos A = sin B; leg adjacent and leg opposite switch roles when you switch from $\angle A$ to $\angle B$.   **3a.** $\sin A = \frac{\sqrt{5}}{5}$, $\cos A = \frac{2\sqrt{5}}{5}$, $\tan A = \frac{1}{2}$ **b.** $\sin B = \frac{2\sqrt{5}}{5}$, $\cos B = \frac{\sqrt{5}}{5}$, $\tan B = 2$ **c.** cos A = sin B and sin A = cos B; leg adjacent and leg opposite switch roles when you switch from $\angle A$ to $\angle B$.   **4.** $\sin B = \frac{12}{13}$, $\cos B = \frac{5}{13}$ **5.** about 4226 ft
On Your Own
6. $m\angle B = 20°$, $UB \approx 23.39$ cm, $BT \approx 21.98$ cm
9. $\sin J = \frac{\sqrt{10}}{10}$, $\cos J = \frac{3\sqrt{10}}{10}$, $\tan J = \frac{1}{3}$, $\sin L = \frac{3\sqrt{10}}{10}$, $\cos L = \frac{\sqrt{10}}{10}$, $\tan L = 3$
13. $\sin \theta = \frac{c}{b}$, $\cos \theta = \frac{a}{b}$, $\tan \theta = \frac{c}{a}$
16. Yes; use the diagram from Exercise 14.
$(\sin \theta)^2 + (\cos \theta)^2 = \left(\frac{c}{d}\right)^2 + \left(\frac{a}{b}\right)^2 = \frac{c^2 + a^2}{b^2} = \frac{b^2}{b^2} = 1$ **18a.** tan 40° ≈ 0.84
b. not possible **c.** sin 40° ≈ 0.64 **d.** not possible
e. cos 40° ≈ 0.77 **f.** not possible
g. tan 50° ≈ 1.19

Lesson 9.09
Check Your Understanding
1. $BC \approx 13.17$; $m\angle B \approx 22.98°$; $m\angle C \approx 17.02°$
2. $AB \approx 5.14$; $m\angle A \approx 48.57°$; $m\angle B \approx 91.43°$
3. $BC \approx 7.51$; $m\angle B \approx 71.62°$; $m\angle C \approx 45.38°$
4a. $A = \frac{1}{2} ab \sin \theta$ **b.** If you scale the given triangle by a factor of r, the lengths of the sides that form the given angle are ar and br. The angle of measure θ still has measure θ. The area of the scaled copy is $\frac{1}{2}(ar)(br) \sin \theta$, or $\left(\frac{1}{2}ab \sin \theta\right) \cdot r^2$.   **5.** area(ABCD) ≈ 16.09

On Your Own

6. $AB = 5$ cm; $BC = 3\sqrt{2}$ cm; $m\angle A \approx 36.87°$; $m\angle B \approx 98.13°$; $m\angle C = 45°$ **8.** $TR \approx 5.00$ in.; $m\angle R \approx 79.96°$; $m\angle T \approx 20.04°$; area($\triangle RAT$) $\approx$ 4.28 in.^{2} **11.** $(32 + 32\sqrt{2})$ in.^{2}, or about 77.25 in.^{2}; find the area of the square and then subtract the total area of the four triangles. **13.** $EG = 10$ in.; $m\angle E \approx 53.13°$; $m\angle G \approx 36.87°$ **16a.** definition of sin 25° (using $\triangle ABD$) and basic moves **b.** definition of sin 35° (using $\triangle BCD$) and basic moves **c.** From parts (a) and (b), $c(\sin 25°) = a(\sin 35°)$. Solve for c. **d.** definition of cos 25° (using $\triangle ABD$) and basic moves **e.** definition of cos 35° (using $\triangle BCD$) and basic moves **f.** $AC = x + y$ together with the equations in parts (d) and (e) **17.** $a \approx 4.39$ in., $c \approx 5.96$ in.

Lesson 9.10
Check Your Understanding
1a. $40\sqrt{3}$ in.^{3} **b.** 4 ft^3 **c.** 1872π cm^3 **d.** 240π cm^3 **2.** The height of the prism is $\frac{13}{3}$ in. **3.** $9\sqrt{3}$ cm
On Your Own
4. $\frac{9}{16}$ in. **5.** $\frac{7}{\pi}$ cm **6.** 213 cans **8.** 192 in.^{3}

Lesson 9.11
On Your Own
4a. about 2.31 cm **b.** about 1.44 cm
7. $\frac{5}{2}\sqrt{\pi}$ in.

Lesson 9.12
Check Your Understanding
1. There is not enough information given to tell how the volumes compare. **2.** No; the bases of the solids are congruent rectangles and hence have the same area. The right prism has a greater height than the new solid, so it has the greater volume. **3a.** 72 cm^3, 72 cm^3 **b.** Yes. Position the first figure so that the 4-cm edges of the two figures are parallel. The cross-sectional area of each prism is 12 cm^2.
On Your Own
4. Answers may vary. Sample: Use a sphere with radius 1 and a cylinder with radius 1 and height $\frac{4}{3}$. Both solids have a volume of $\frac{4\pi}{3}$. A plane that contains a diameter of the sphere has the same cross section as a plane parallel to the base of the cylinder. There are no other cross sections that have equal areas.

6. $3\sqrt{\pi}$ in. **10.** No; answers may vary. Sample: A right triangle with legs of length 1 and 2 has the same area as a square with side length 1, but there can only be one pair of cross sections of each figure that have the same area. **12.** $\frac{64 + \pi}{8\pi}$ in.

Lesson 9.13
Check Your Understanding
1. If r is the radius of the cross section between V and O, and R is the radius of the base, then $\frac{r}{R} = \frac{VO'}{VO}$. Thus $\frac{A_{\text{circle}}}{A_{\text{base}}} = \frac{\pi r^2}{\pi R^2} = \frac{r^2}{R^2} = \left(\frac{r}{R}\right)^2 = \left(\frac{VO'}{VO}\right)^2$. **2.** 96 in.^{3} **3a.** 20 cm^3 **b.** $\frac{2\sqrt{3\pi}}{\pi}$ cm

4a. Answers may vary. Sample: height π and base $2r^2$ **b.** Every pair of cross sections determined by a plane parallel to the bases of the cone and pyramid have the same area. **5.** The cone and the pyramid are the same height and are cut by a plane, so the resulting cross sections have the same area. The cone and the pyramid also have cross-sectional areas that are equal to each other when cut by any plane parallel to the first, therefore the cone and pyramid have the same volume.

On Your Own
6. 8π ft^3 **8.** $\frac{128\sqrt{3}}{3}$ cm^3 **10.** 420

Lesson 9.14
Check Your Understanding
1. Yes; infinitely many ways; yes; infinitely many ways; if the sphere has radius r, then any two planes that are d units from the center of the sphere, where $0 < d < r$, will create two cross sections of equal area. **2.** $\frac{2000\pi}{3}$; 10; $\frac{2000\pi}{3}$
3. $\frac{45\sqrt{5\pi}}{2\pi}$ cm^3
On Your Own
7. $\frac{256\pi}{3}$ mm^3 **9.** $\frac{512\pi\sqrt{2}}{3}$ mm^3
11. about 902.3 in.^{3}

Chapter 10
Lesson 10.01
On Your Own
8. $(\sqrt{13}, 2)$, $(\sqrt{13}, -2)$, $(-\sqrt{13}, 2)$, $(-\sqrt{13}, -2)$
11. d. $AX = \sqrt{2}$, $BX = 4\sqrt{2}$, $CX = 4$, $DX = 2$, **therefore** $AX \cdot BX = CX \cdot DX = 8$

Lesson 10.02
Check Your Understanding

1. a. $|y - 2| = 3$

b.

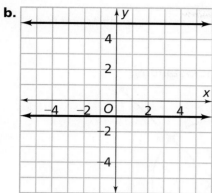

2. a. no **b.** yes **c.** If $a < 0$, this point must be closer to the y-axis than to $(4, 0)$ since $(4, 0)$ will be on the opposite side of the axis. Therefore, the distances could never be equal.
d. $y^2 = 8x - 16$
3. a. No; the distance from $(5, 3)$ to $(15, 0)$ is $\sqrt{109}$, and the distance from $(5, 3)$ to $(6, 0)$ is $\sqrt{10}$.

b. $(9, 0)$ and $(-3, 0)$
c. $36 = (x - 3)^2 + y^2$
d. The graph is a circle with center at $(3, 0)$ and radius 6.
4. a. $y = 2x - 9$ **b.** $y = -\frac{3}{2}x + \frac{19}{2}$ **c.** $x = \frac{37}{7}$
5. a. Answers may vary. Sample:
Any (x, y, z) fitting the equation
$5 = \sqrt{(x - 2)^2 + (y - 3)^2 + (z - 4)^2}$ is in this set. Some examples include: $(7, 3, 4)$, $(2, 3, 9)$, $(2, 0, 0)$, $(-2, 0, 4)$, and $(2, -2, 4)$.
b. Answers may vary. Sample: Any (x, y, z) not fitting the equation in part (a) is not part of this set.
c. $(x - 2)^2 + (y - 3)^2 + (z - 4)^2 = 25$

6. a. a plane **b.** Yes, this point is part of the set.
c. $x + 2y + 3z = 14$ **d.** Yes, this point is part of the set.
e.

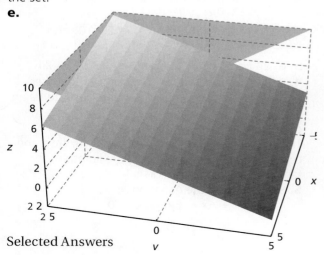

Selected Answers

On Your Own
7. a. $y = -\frac{1}{3}x + \frac{10}{3}$ **11. b.** circle centered at $(0, 0)$ with radius 5

Lesson 10.03
Check Your Understanding
1. a. Answers will vary. One possible answer is $A(0, 0)$, $B(a, 0)$, $C(a, b)$, $D(0, b)$

b. Using the coordinates from part (a), find the length of the diagonal using the distance formula.
$$AC = \sqrt{(a - 0)^2 + (b - 0)^2} = \sqrt{a^2 + b^2}$$
$$BD = \sqrt{(a - 0)^2 + (0 - b)^2} = \sqrt{a^2 + (-b)^2}$$
$$= \sqrt{a^2 + b^2}$$

2.

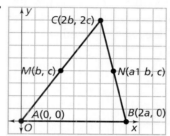

The midpoint of AC is $M(b, c)$ and the midpoint of BC is $N(a + b, c)$.

The length of segment MN, which joins the midpoints of sides AC and BC, is a.

The length of side AB is $2a$, which is twice that of MN.

Both segments are horizontal, therefore parallel, which completes the proof.

3. Assume a quadrilateral has vertices at $A(0, 0)$, $B(2a, 0)$, $C(2b, 2c)$, and $D(2d, 2e)$.

Midpoints of the four sides are $M(a, 0)$, $N(a + b, c)$, $P(b + d, c + e)$, $Q(d, e)$.
The slopes of MN and PQ are both $\frac{c}{b}$ and the slopes of NP and MQ are both $\frac{e}{d - a}$. Therefore, since the slopes of both pairs of opposite sides are equal, this must be a parallelogram.
4. parallelogram

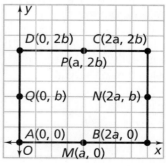

Assume a quadrilateral has vertices at $A(0, 0)$, $B(2a, 0)$, $C(2a, 2b)$, $D(0, 2b)$.

Midpoints of the four sides are $M(a, 0)$, $N(2a, b)$, $P(a, 2b)$, $Q(0, b)$.

Similar to the previous problem, the slopes of MN and PQ are equal and the slopes of NP and MQ are equal. Therefore, since the slopes of both pairs of opposite sides are equal, this must be a parallelogram. Also, since $MN = NP$, $MNPQ$ is a rhombus.

5. Answers may vary. Sample: Joey assumes that the two lines of symmetry of the rhombus are perpendicular. He does this by placing them along the axes. It would be alright for Joey to place one line of symmetry on the axis, then prove the other must lie along the axis as well. But by building the rhombus in this way, Joey has assumed what he is trying to prove, which is invalid.

6.

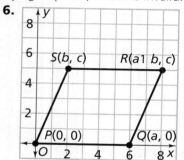

Assume a parallelogram has vertices at $P(0, 0)$, $Q(a, 0)$, $R(a + b, c)$, $S(b, c)$.

The slope of diagonal PR is $\frac{c}{a + b}$, and the slope of diagonal SQ is $\frac{c}{b - a}$.

If these diagonals are perpendicular, then

$$\frac{c}{a + b} \cdot \frac{c}{b - a} = -1$$
$$\frac{c^2}{b^2 - a^2} = -1$$
$$c^2 = a^2 - b^2$$
$$c^2 + b^2 = a^2$$

To prove $PQRS$ is a rhombus, you must show that two consecutive sides are congruent. The length of PQ is a and the length of QR is $\sqrt{b^2 + c^2}$. If the diagonals are perpendicular, then $a^2 = b^2 + c^2$, so $PQ = QR$ and the parallelogram must be a rhombus.

On Your Own

8. Answers may vary. Sample: One way is to use $B(2b, 0)$ and $C(0, 2c)$. Midpoint of BC is $D(b, c)$.
$$AD = \sqrt{b^2 + c^2}$$
$$BD = \sqrt{(2b - b)^2 + (0 - c)^2} = \sqrt{b^2 + c^2}$$
$$CD = \sqrt{(0 - b)^2 + (2c - c)^2} = \sqrt{b^2 + c^2}$$
All three lengths are the same.

11. Answers may vary. Sample: Assume coordinates $A(0, 0)$, $B(2a, 0)$, $C(2b, 2c)$, $D(2d, 2c)$.

The length of AB is $2a$ and the length of CD is $2b - 2d$. The average of these lengths is $a + b - d$.

The midline's endpoints are $M(d, c)$ and $N(a + b, c)$. The distance between M and N is $a + b - d$.

Lesson 10.04

Check Your Understanding

1.

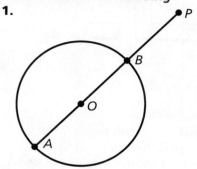

Consider point P outside the circle.

Pick $\overleftrightarrow{OP}$ where O is the center of the circle so that $OP = d$ and AB is a diameter.

$PA = d + r$ and $PB = d - r$, therefore the power of point P with respect to the circle is

$$PA \cdot PB = (d + r)(d - r) = d^2 - r^2$$

2. a. Center is $(-3, 4)$ and radius is 7.

b.

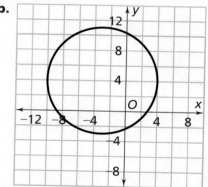

c. The two x-intercepts are $(-3 + \sqrt{33}, 0)$ and $(-3 - \sqrt{33}, 0)$.

The two y-intercepts are $(0, 4 + 2\sqrt{10})$ and $(0, 4 - 2\sqrt{10})$.

3. a. 24 **b.** 24 **c.** $(4, 4)$ and $(-3, -3)$; $P = 24$

4. As the intersection points get closer together, the line through P comes closer and closer to being a tangent of the circle. If PA is the tangent to the circle, then $(PA)^2$ equals the power of point P. This means that if point P is d units away from the center of the circle, and $d > r$, the length of the tangent from P to the circle is $\sqrt{d^2 - r^2}$.

5. Set $y = kx$ in the equation.
$$x^2 + y^2 + 6x - 8y - 24 = 0$$

$$x^2 + (kx)^2 + 6x - 8kx - 24 = 0$$
$$(k^2 + 1)x^2 + (6 - 8k)x - 24 = 0$$
$$x = \frac{8k - 6 \pm \sqrt{(6 - 8k)^2 - 4(k^2 + 1)(-24)}}{2(k^2 + 1)}$$
$$x = \frac{4k - 3 \pm \sqrt{40k^2 - 24k + 33}}{k^2 + 1}$$

Since the values of y are k times the values of x, the two intersections are at
$$\left(\frac{4k - 3 \pm \sqrt{40k^2 - 24k + 33}}{k^2 + 1}, \right.$$
$$\left. k \cdot \frac{4k - 3 \pm \sqrt{40k^2 - 24k + 33}}{k^2 + 1} \right)$$

To determine the power of P, find the distance between $(0, 0)$ and (x, kx).

$$\sqrt{x^2 + (kx)^2} = \sqrt{(k^2 + 1)x^2} = |x|\sqrt{k^2 + 1}$$

The product of the two distances will be $k^2 + 1$ multiplied by the two x-coordinates.

$$\frac{4k - 3 + \sqrt{40k^2 - 24k + 33}}{k^2 + 1} \cdot$$
$$\frac{4k - 3 - \sqrt{40k^2 - 24k + 33}}{k^2 + 1} \cdot (k^2 + 1)$$
$$= \frac{(4k - 3)^2 - (40k^2 - 24k + 33)}{k^2 + 1}$$
$$= \frac{16k^2 - 24k + 9 - (40k^2 - 24k + 33)}{k^2 + 1}$$
$$= \frac{-24k^2 - 24}{k^2 + 1}$$
$$= \frac{-24(k^2 + 1)}{k^2 + 1} = -24$$

(which is independent of k)

On Your Own
6. 20 **8. b.** 20

Honors Appendix
Lesson H.01
On Your Own
7a. $\sqrt{17}$ **8a.** 17 **d.** 85 **9a.** 14.04° **10a.** $4\sqrt{2}$
d. $2\sqrt{2}$ **11a.** $A(8, 0)$, $B(8, 8)$

Lesson H.02
Check Your Understanding
1a–d.

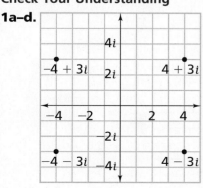

2a. $a > 0$, $b > 0$ **b.** $a < 0$, $b > 0$
c. $a < 0$, $b < 0$ **d.** $a > 0$, $b < 0$
3a.

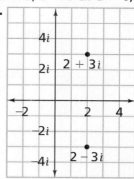

b. The sum is 4, and the product is 13.
4a.

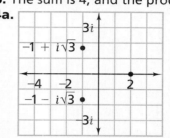

b. Equilateral; the length of each side of the triangle is 2. **c.** The sum is 0, and the product is 8. **5.** Answers may vary. Sample: $1 + i$, $1 - i$, $-1 - i$, $-1 + i$

6a–f.

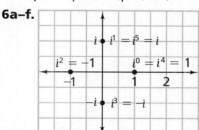

On Your Own
8a–d.

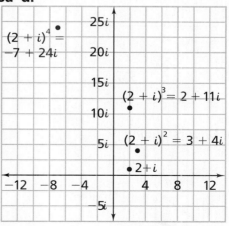

9a.

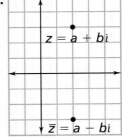

b.

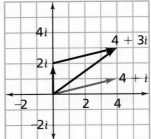

b.

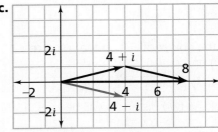

10c. $-3 + i, -3 - i$

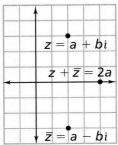

c.

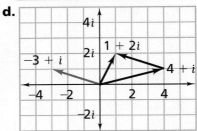

d.

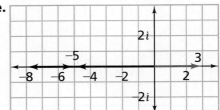

11a. $\pm i, \pm 1$

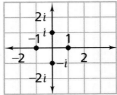

e.

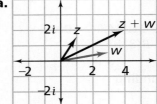

13a. $w = 2 - i,\ 2w = 4 - 2i,\ 3w = 6 - 3i$

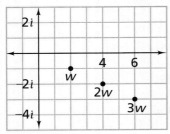

2a.

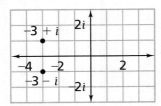

Lesson H.03
Check Your Understanding

1a.

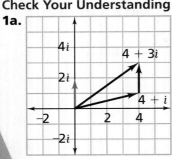

b.

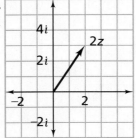

c.

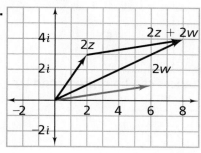

d.

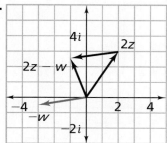

e.

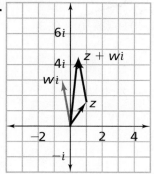

f.

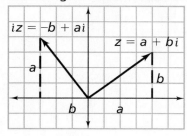

3. $z = a + bi$ is $\sqrt{a^2 + b^2}$ units from the origin, and $iz = -b + ai$ is $\sqrt{b^2 + a^2}$ units from the origin. The distances are equal.

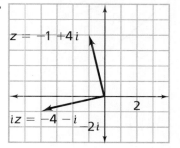

4a. $\sqrt{17}$ **b.** $\sqrt{5}$ **c.** $\sqrt{13}$ **d.** $\sqrt{61}$ **5a.** 17 **b.** 5 **c.** 13 **d.** 61

6a. 65, 17, 80 **b.** rotated 180°

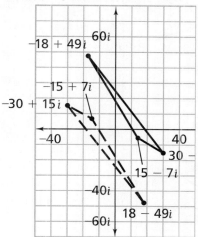

c. rotated 90°

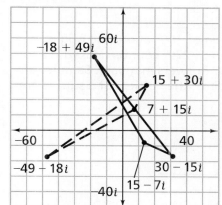

7a.

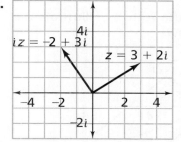

b.

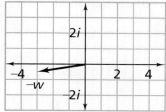

c.

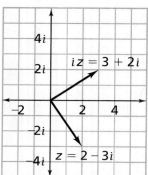

d.

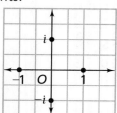

8a. a rotation of 180° about the origin
b. a rotation of 270° counterclockwise about the origin **9.** Answers may vary. Samples are given. **a.** Points; the vertices of a square are points.

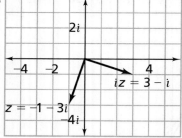

b. Vectors; you use vectors to illustrate the parallelogram law.

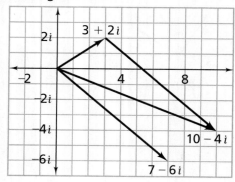

c. Points; the vertices of each triangle are points.

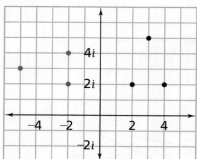

d. Vectors; distances can be represented by vectors.

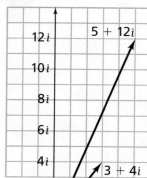

On Your Own

10.

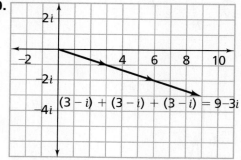

13. $5 + 3i$, $-6 - 4i$, $2 - 7i$, 8

15a. $(1 + i)z = \sqrt{2}i$

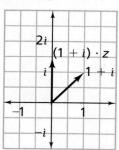

Lesson H.05
On Your Own
8.

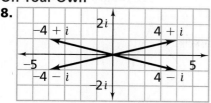

a. 14° **9a.** 30° **10b.** $-1 - 5i$ **d.** $-5 + 12i$

Lesson H.06
Check Your Understanding
1a. magnitude 9, direction 240° **b.** magnitude 27, direction 0° **c.** $x^2 + 3x + 9 = 0$

2. Answers may vary. Sample: For z^2, square the magnitude and double the direction. For z^3, cube the magnitude and triple the direction. For z^n raise the magnitude to the nth power and multiply the direction by n.

3. options b, c, or d

4.

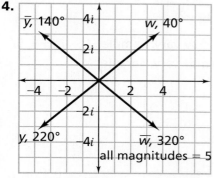

5a. magnitude $5\sqrt{2}$, direction 355°
b. magnitude $5\sqrt{2}$, direction 355°
c. $yz = (-w)(-x) = wx$ **6.** Answers may vary. Sample: The magnitude is about $(3.5)(4.5) = 16$, and the direction is about $50° + 110° = 160°$ **7.** The magnitude of the product is the product of the magnitudes. The direction of the product is the sum of the directions, but subtract 360° if necessary to express the angle between 0° and 360°.

8a.

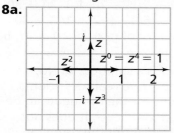

Consecutive powers of i rotate 90° counterclockwise; if you raise $z = i$ to the

nth power, you multiply the direction, 90°, by n, and there is no change to the magnitude. So consecutive powers of i rotate 90° counterclockwise.

b.

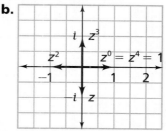

Consecutive powers of $-i$ rotate 90° clockwise; if you raise $z = -i$ to the nth power, you multiply the direction, 270°, by n, and there is no change to the magnitude. So consecutive powers of $-i$ rotate 270° counterclockwise, which is equivalent to rotating by 90° clockwise.

c.

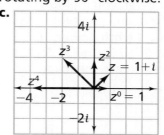

Consecutive powers of $1 + i$ rotate 45° counterclockwise, with the magnitudes increasing by a factor of $\sqrt{2}$; if you raise $z = 1 + i$ to the nth power, you multiply the direction, 45°, by n, and you raise the magnitude, $\sqrt{2}$, to the nth power. So consecutive powers of $1 + i$ rotate 45° counterclockwise, and increase the magnitude by a factor of $\sqrt{2}$.

d.

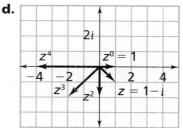

The powers of $1 - i$ rotate 45° clockwise, with the magnitudes increasing by a factor of $\sqrt{2}$; if you raise $z = 1 - i$ to the nth power, you multiply the direction, 315°, by n, and you raise the magnitude, $\sqrt{2}$, to the nth power. So consecutive powers of $1 - i$ rotate 315° counterclockwise (which is equivalent to rotating by 45° clockwise), and increase the magnitude by a factor of $\sqrt{2}$.

e.

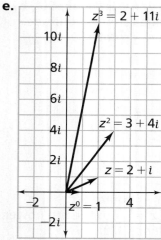

The powers of $2 + i$ rotate about $26.6°$ counterclockwise, with the magnitudes increasing by a factor of $\sqrt{5}$; if you raise $z = 2 + i$ to the nth power, you multiply the direction, $26.6°$, by n, and you raise the magnitude, $\sqrt{5}$, to the nth power. So consecutive powers of $2 + i$ rotate $26.6°$ counterclockwise, and increase the magnitude by a factor of $\sqrt{5}$.

f.

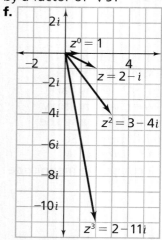

The powers of $2 - i$ rotate about $26.6°$ clockwise, with the magnitudes increasing by a factor of $\sqrt{5}$; if you raise $z = 2 - i$ to the nth power, you multiply the direction, $333.4°$, by n and you raise the magnitude, $\sqrt{5}$, to the nth power. So consecutive powers of $2 - i$ rotate $333.4°$ counterclockwise (which is equivalent to rotating by $26.6°$ clockwise), and increase the magnitude by a factor of $\sqrt{5}$.

9. a, c, d, and e must have magnitude 1.

10a.

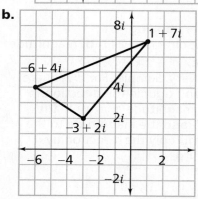

b.

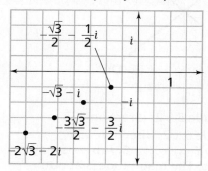

11a. Answers may vary. Sample: $1 + i$, $5 + 5i$

13a. Answers may vary. Sample:

16a. $\frac{7}{5} + \frac{1}{5}i$

Lesson H.07

Check Your Understanding

1a. $x = -2$ **b.** $x = 1 \pm 3i$ **2.** $x^2 - 8x + 17 = 0$

3. $x^3 - 15x^2 + 73x - 119 = 0$ **4a.** $g(-1 + 2i)$
$= (-1 + 2i)^3 - 4(-1 + 2i)^2 - 7(-1 + 2i) - 30$
$= (11 - 2i) - (-12 - 16i) - (-7 + 14i) - 30$
$= 0$ So $(-1 + 2i)$ is a root of $g(x)$. **b.** $-1 - 2i$, 6

5a. $f(3 + i) = (3 + i)^2 - (8 + 6i) = (8 + 6i) - (8 + 6i) = 0$, so $3 + i$ is a solution. **b.** No; The equation does not have real coefficients, which is a requirement for the conjugate to be a root. When you test $x = 3 - i$, it does not make the equation true. **6.** All the complex roots come in pairs, $a + bi$ and $a - bi$, and the product of each pair of complex roots is

$a^2 + b^2$, which is positive. Since the product of all the roots is the product of the complex roots and the real roots, then that product is positive if and only if the product of the real roots is positive.

On Your Own

7a. $|z| = \sqrt{26}$, arg $z \approx 11°$; $|w| = \sqrt{13}$, arg $w \approx 56°$ **10a.** 0 **c.** $1 - 3i$ **13a.** Answers may vary. Sample: $x^3 + 37x + 212 = 0$ **14a.** 0 **b.** 0

Lesson H.08
On Your Own

7. $x = \frac{16}{5}$, $y = -\frac{9}{5}$ **9.** $p(1) = 4$ so $a + b = 4$; $p(3) = 2$ so $3a + b = 2$; $a = -1$ and $b = 5$ so $p(x) = -x + 5$. **12a.** The two equations represent the same line, so any point on $x + 2y = 3$ is a solution to the system. **b.** The two equations represent parallel lines, so the system has no solution.

Lesson H.09
Check Your Understanding

1. $(2, 1, -1)$ **2.** $(2, 1, -1)$ **3.** $(2, 1, -1)$

4. $(2, 1, -1)$ **5.** $a = \frac{1}{2}$, $b = \frac{1}{2}$, $c = 0$.

On Your Own

8. $(-4, 1, -1, 2)$ **9.** The system has no solution.

Lesson H.010
Check Your Understanding

1a. $x - y + 2z = 5$, $2x - 3y + z = 3$, $x + 7z = 16$

b. $\begin{pmatrix} 1 & 0 & 0 & | & 2 \\ 0 & 1 & 0 & | & 1 \\ 0 & 0 & 1 & | & 2 \end{pmatrix}$ or $(x, y, z) = (2, 1, 2)$

2. $\begin{pmatrix} 1 & 0 & 0 & | & -\frac{1}{2} \\ 0 & 1 & 0 & | & \frac{1}{2} \\ 0 & 0 & 1 & | & 1 \end{pmatrix}$

3. Yes, $\begin{pmatrix} 1 & 0 & 0 & | & 1 \\ 0 & 1 & 0 & | & -1 \\ 0 & 0 & 1 & | & 2 \end{pmatrix}$ represents the same solution.

4. $\begin{pmatrix} 1 & 0 & 0 & | & 1 \\ 0 & 1 & 0 & | & -1 \\ 0 & 0 & 1 & | & 2 \end{pmatrix} \xrightarrow[(1)+(3)]{(1)+(2)} \begin{pmatrix} 1 & 1 & 1 & | & 2 \\ 0 & 1 & 0 & | & -1 \\ 0 & 0 & 1 & | & 2 \end{pmatrix}$

$\xrightarrow{(2)+2(3)} \begin{pmatrix} 1 & 1 & 1 & | & 2 \\ 0 & 1 & 2 & | & 3 \\ 0 & 0 & 1 & | & 2 \end{pmatrix}$; then reverse the steps

shown in the middle of page 517 to get

$A = \begin{pmatrix} 1 & 1 & 1 & | & 2 \\ 2 & -1 & 1 & | & 5 \\ 1 & 2 & 3 & | & 5 \end{pmatrix}$.

5. Answers may vary. Sample: Adding a positive multiple is the same as subtracting the same multiple with the opposite sign(s).

6. $\begin{pmatrix} 1 & 0 & | & 1 \\ 0 & 1 & | & -2 \end{pmatrix}$

7. $a = -\frac{7}{2}$, $b = \frac{8}{3}$ **8a.** Each equation in the system is a line in the xy-plane, and the intersection of the lines is the solution to the system. **b.** The solution represents m lines in the xy-plane; if the lines have point(s) in common, that point or points is the solution to the system. **c.** Each equation represents a plane in 3-space; the common intersection of the m planes (if it exists) is the solution to the system.

On Your Own

12. $f(x) = 2x - 2$ **13.** $(2, 0, 4)$
15. $x + 2y + 2z = 3$, $x - \frac{1}{2}y - \frac{1}{2}z = 1$, $x + \frac{1}{3}y + \frac{1}{6}z = 1$ **19.** 4 in. by 6 in. by 8 in.

Lesson H.11
Check Your Understanding

1. $\begin{pmatrix} x \\ y \\ z \end{pmatrix} = \begin{pmatrix} 1 \\ -1 \\ 2 \end{pmatrix}$

2. $\begin{pmatrix} a \\ b \\ c \\ d \end{pmatrix} = \begin{pmatrix} 0 \\ \frac{1}{2} \\ \frac{1}{2} \\ 0 \end{pmatrix}$

3a. The two lines $x + 2y = 1$ and $2x + 4y = 1$ are parallel, so the system has no solution.

b. Gaussian Elimination results in $\begin{pmatrix} 1 & 2 & | & 1 \\ 0 & 0 & | & -1 \end{pmatrix}$, and the second row indicates that the system has no solution. **c.** The inverse does not exist $(ad - bc = 0)$. **4.** Answers may vary. Sample: To solve $AX = B$, find A^{-1} and write $A^{-1}AX = A^{-1}B$ or $X = A^{-1}B$.

5. $MA = \begin{pmatrix} 1 & 0 & 0 \\ 0 & 0 & 1 \end{pmatrix}\begin{pmatrix} 1 & 0 \\ 3 & 4 \\ 0 & 1 \end{pmatrix} = \begin{pmatrix} 1 & 0 \\ 0 & 1 \end{pmatrix}$ and

$$AM = \begin{pmatrix} 1 & 0 \\ 3 & 4 \\ 0 & 1 \end{pmatrix}\begin{pmatrix} 1 & 0 & 0 \\ 0 & 0 & 1 \end{pmatrix} = \begin{pmatrix} 1 & 0 \\ 3 & 4 \\ 0 & 1 \end{pmatrix}, \text{ so}$$

$MA \neq AM$.

6. $AM = \begin{pmatrix} 1 & 2 \\ 3 & 4 \end{pmatrix}\begin{pmatrix} -2 & 1 \\ \frac{3}{2} & -\frac{1}{2} \end{pmatrix} =$

$\begin{pmatrix} -2+3 & 1-1 \\ -6+6 & 3-2 \end{pmatrix} = \begin{pmatrix} 1 & 0 \\ 0 & 1 \end{pmatrix} = I$

7. No, zero is a real number but it does not have an inverse.

8. No; for example, $\begin{pmatrix} 3 & -1 \\ -2 & 2 \end{pmatrix}\begin{pmatrix} 1 \\ 1 \end{pmatrix} = \begin{pmatrix} 2 \\ 0 \end{pmatrix}$ and $\begin{pmatrix} 1 \\ 1 \end{pmatrix} \neq \begin{pmatrix} 2 \\ 0 \end{pmatrix}$.

On Your Own

9. If $\begin{pmatrix} a & b \\ c & d \end{pmatrix}\begin{pmatrix} x \\ y \end{pmatrix} = \begin{pmatrix} x \\ y \end{pmatrix}$, then $ax + by = x$ and $cx + dy = y$. The only values of a, b, c, and d that satisfy both equations simultaneously are $a = 1$, $b = 0$, $c = 0$, and $d = 1$ or $\begin{pmatrix} 1 & 0 \\ 0 & 1 \end{pmatrix}$.

10. $\begin{pmatrix} x & y \\ z & w \end{pmatrix} = \begin{pmatrix} -2 & 1 \\ \frac{3}{2} & -\frac{1}{2} \end{pmatrix}$

Lesson H.12
Check Your Understanding
1. 24.09 **2a.** 210 **b.** 29
c.

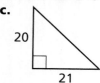

20

21

Each angle measures about 45°. **d.** 46°, 44°
3. $\sin \theta = \frac{15}{17}$, $\tan \theta = \frac{15}{8}$ **4.** $\sin \theta = \frac{\text{opp}}{\text{hyp}}$ and $\cos \theta = \frac{\text{adj}}{\text{hyp}}$, so $\frac{\sin \theta}{\cos \theta} = \frac{\frac{\text{opp}}{\text{hyp}}}{\frac{\text{adj}}{\text{hyp}}} = \frac{\text{opp}}{\text{adj}} = \tan \theta$.
5. $\frac{\sqrt{15}}{4}$ **6.** $72\sqrt{3} \approx 124.71$, $24\sqrt{3} \approx 41.57$, or $18\sqrt{3} \approx 31.2$

On Your Own
9.

θ	$\sin \theta$	$\cos \theta$	$\tan \theta$
30°	$\frac{1}{2}$	$\frac{\sqrt{3}}{2}$	$\frac{\sqrt{3}}{3}$
60°	$\frac{\sqrt{3}}{2}$	$\frac{1}{2}$	$\sqrt{3}$

12a. The largest value is 1 and the smallest is 0. As θ gets close to 90°, $\sin \theta$ gets close to 1,

and as θ gets close to 0, $\sin \theta$ gets close to 0.
13a. $\sin \theta = \frac{4}{5}$, $\cos \theta = \frac{3}{5}$, $\tan \theta = \frac{4}{3}$ **14.** You do not know that $\triangle TRI$ is a right triangle.

Lesson H.13
On Your Own
11.

Angle	Coordinates
0°	(1, 0)
10°	(0.985, 0.174)
20°	(0.940, 0.342)
30°	(0.866, 0.5)
40°	(0.766, 0.643)
50°	(0.643, 0.766)
60°	(0.5, 0.866)
70°	(0.342, 0.940)
80°	(0.174, 0.985)
90°	(0, 1)

12a. magnitude 5, argument $\approx 53°$
15. Answers may vary. Sample: The x-coordinate starts at 1 when Olivia's angle is 0°, decreases to 0 as her angle increases to 90°, decreases to -1 as her angle increases to 180°, increases to 0 as her angle increases to 270°, and increases to 1 as her angle increases to 360°. This pattern will repeat from 360° to 720°, from 720° to 1080°, and so on.
18. $a = -1$, $b = \sqrt{3}$

Lesson H.14
Check Your Understanding
1. Answers may vary. Sample: If Jo's reasoning were correct, then the point $\left(\frac{1}{2}, \frac{1}{2}\right)$ should be on the unit circle and satisfy the equation $x^2 + y^2 = 1$. However, $\left(\frac{1}{2}\right)^2 + \left(\frac{1}{2}\right)^2 \neq 1$, so the point $\left(\frac{1}{2}, \frac{1}{2}\right)$ is not on the circle. **2.** $a = 0.342$, $b = 0.940$ **3.** $-\frac{\sqrt{3}}{2} - \frac{1}{2}i$ $\approx -0.866 - 0.5i$ **4a.** $\cos \theta = -\cos(\theta + 180°)$
b. $\sin \theta = -\sin(\theta + 180°)$
c. $\tan \theta = \tan(\theta + 180°)$ **5a.** 1 **b.** 1 **6.** If the magnitude of a complex number is 1, such as i or $-i$, then it must lie on the unit circle.
7a. $\theta = 0°$ or 180°, or $\theta = 180° \cdot k$, where k is an integer. **b.** $\theta = 90°$ or 270°, or $\theta = 90° + 180° \cdot k$, where k is an integer.
c. $\theta = 0°$ or 180°, or $\theta = 180° \cdot k$, where k is an integer.

On Your Own

8a.

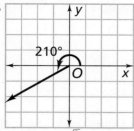

$\sin 210° = -\frac{\sqrt{3}}{2}$, $\cos 210° = -\frac{1}{2}$, $\tan 210° = \frac{\sqrt{3}}{3}$ **11.** Answers may vary. Sample: Since 310° is the same as $-50°$ on the unit circle, we know that $\sin 310° = \sin(-50°)$. And because $-50°$ is in Quadrant IV, where sine is negative, $\sin(-50°) = -\sin 50°$. So, $\sin 310° = -\sin 50°$. **12a.** $-\frac{\sqrt{3}}{2}$

Lesson H.15

Check Your Understanding

1. Answers may vary. Sample: 160° is in Quadrant II and 20° is in Quadrant I. Since $\sin \theta$ is positive in both quadrants, $\sin 160° = \sin 20°$. Since $\cos \theta$ is positive in Quadrant I and negative in Quadrant II, then $\cos 160° = -\cos 20°$. **2a.** I or II **b.** $\cos \theta = \pm\frac{21}{29}$ **c.** $\tan \theta = \pm\frac{20}{21}$ **3.** Answers may vary. Sample: $\theta \approx 89.5°$ **4.** Answers may vary. Sample: Since $-60°$ intersects the unit circle in Quadrant IV, the cosine will be positive. In general, $\cos(-\theta) = \cos \theta$. So $\cos(-60°) = \cos 60° = \frac{1}{2}$. **5.** $\tan 110°$; $\cos 120° = \sin 210°$; $\sin 120°$; $\cos 720°$; $\tan 70°$ **6.** 30°, 150° **7a.** 0.7660 **b.** -0.6428 **c.** -0.6428 **d.** -0.7660 **e.** 1 **f.** 0.6428 **8a.** $\tan^2 \theta = \frac{1}{\cos^2 \theta} - 1$ or $\tan^2 \theta + 1 = \frac{1}{\cos^2 \theta}$ **b.** $\tan^2 \theta + 1 = \frac{\sin^2 \theta}{\cos^2 \theta} + 1 = \frac{\sin^2 \theta}{\cos^2 \theta} + \frac{\cos^2 \theta}{\cos^2 \theta} = \frac{\sin^2 \theta + \cos^2 \theta}{\cos^2 \theta} = \frac{1}{\cos^2 \theta}$. So, $\tan^2 \theta = \frac{1}{\cos^2 \theta} - 1$ or $\tan^2 \theta + 1 = \frac{1}{\cos^2 \theta}$.

On Your Own

9. $\cos(-30°) = \frac{\sqrt{3}}{2}$, $\sin(-30°) = -\frac{1}{2}$, $\tan(-30°) = -\frac{\sqrt{3}}{3}$ **10a.** $\sin 40°$ **d.** $-\sin 45°$ **11a.** $\sin \theta$ **f.** $-\sin \theta$ **13a.** positive **c.** negative **17a.** $-\frac{12}{37}$

Lesson H.16

Check Your Understanding

1. $\cos q \approx -0.69$; $m \angle q \approx 134°$ **2a.** 60°, 300° **b.** $\pm\frac{\sqrt{3}}{2}$ **c.** $\frac{3}{4}$

3.

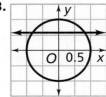

4. (0.8, 0.6), $(-0.8, 0.6)$ **5a.** 53.1°, 306.9° **b.** ± 0.8 **c.** 0.64 **6.** Answers may vary. Sample: $\frac{1}{z} = \frac{1}{\cos 30° + i \sin 30°} = \frac{1}{\frac{\sqrt{3}}{2} + \frac{1}{2}i} = \frac{1}{\frac{\sqrt{3}}{2} + \frac{1}{2}i} \cdot \frac{\frac{\sqrt{3}}{2} - \frac{1}{2}i}{\frac{\sqrt{3}}{2} - \frac{1}{2}i} = \frac{\frac{\sqrt{3}}{2} - \frac{1}{2}i}{\frac{3}{4} + \frac{1}{4}} = \frac{\sqrt{3}}{2} - \frac{1}{2}i = \bar{z}$

On Your Own

8a. 45°, 135° **11a.** Answers may vary. Sample: $\tan 30° = \frac{\sqrt{3}}{3}$ and $\cos 30° = \frac{\sqrt{3}}{2}$, so $\frac{1}{\cos^2 30°} - 1 = \frac{1}{\left(\frac{\sqrt{3}}{2}\right)^2} - 1 = \frac{1}{\frac{3}{4}} - 1 = \frac{4}{3} - \frac{3}{3} = \frac{1}{3} = \frac{3}{9} = \left(\frac{\sqrt{3}}{3}\right)^2 = \tan^2 30°$. **12a.** $\frac{1}{2}$

Lesson H.17

Check Your Understanding

1. $x = 50° + 360° \cdot k$, where k is an integer. **2a.** 37°, 143° **b.** 217°, 323° **3a.** 37°, 323° **b.** no solution **4a.** no solution **b.** 41.8°, 138.2° **c.** 30°, 150°, 210°, 330° **d.** 210°, 330° **5a.** 45°, 225° **b.** 135°, 315° **c.** 0°, 180°, 360° **6.** 30°, 150°, 199.47°, 340.53° **7.** Using the Parallelogram Law from Chapter 3, you find the vertices of the parallelogram formed by za and $\bar{z}$ are (0, 0), (a, b), $(a, -b)$, and $(2a, 0)$. So $z + \bar{z} = 2a$. Also, if $\arg z = \theta$, then $\cos \theta = \frac{a}{|z|}$ (because a is the value of the x-coordinate and $|z|$ is the distance from the origin to z). So $a = |z| \cos \theta$ and $2a = 2|z| \cos \theta$. **8.** Drop a perpendicular from O to $\overline{AB}$ to form two congruent right triangles with acute angles 18° and 72°, legs $\frac{z}{2}$ and $\frac{z\sqrt{3}}{2}$, and hypotenuse 1.

Then $\cos 72° = \frac{\text{adjacent}}{\text{hypotenuse}} = \frac{z}{2}$, so $z = 2 \cdot \cos 72°$.

On Your Own

10b. 45°, 225° **12a.** $0.940 + 0.342i$ **e.** $-0.682 - 0.731i$ **13a.** 36.87°

Lesson H.18

On Your Own

6.

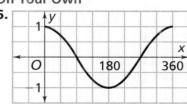

7. $\cos 230° > \cos 190°$

Lesson H.19

Check Your Understanding

1a. The points on the unit circle that represent $\sin 50°$ and $\sin(-50°)$ have opposite y-values. So, $\sin 50° = -\sin(-50°)$. **b.** The y-values for $x = 50°$ and $x = -50°$ on the graph of $y = \sin x$ are opposites. So, $\sin 50° = -\sin(-50°)$. **2.** Answers may vary. Sample: Derman sees only a portion of $y = \sin x$, and all the y-values are close to the x-axis. He should reset his window so that $-360 \le x \le 360$ and $-2 \le y \le 2$.

3.

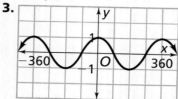

The graph looks like $y = \cos x$ because $\cos (x + 360°) = \cos x$. **4a.** There are infinitely many x-intercepts of $y = \cos x$.
b. A polynomial function must have a finite degree and a finite number of x-intercepts, so the cosine function cannot be written as a polynomial function. **c.** The tangent function, $\frac{\sin \theta}{\cos \theta}$, is undefined when $\cos \theta = 0$, that is when $\theta = 90° + k \cdot 180°$, where k is an integer.

5.

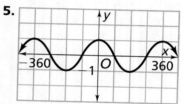

6.

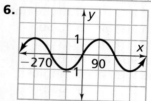

7. 143°, 397°

8.

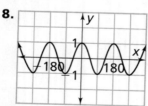

9a.

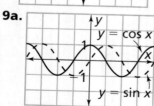

b. Answers may vary. Sample: 45°, 225°. Any angle of the form $45° + k \cdot 180°$, where k is an integer. **10a.** 1 **b.** $\tan \theta = \frac{\sin \theta}{\cos \theta}$ and if $\sin \theta = \cos \theta$, then the tangent must be 1.

11. Answers may vary. Sample:

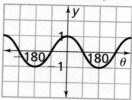

The graph of $y = \cos \theta$ is symmetric about the y-axis, so $\cos (-\theta) = \cos \theta$. **16.** Answers may vary. Samples:
a.

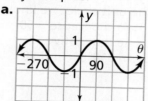

From the graph, $\sin x$ and $\sin (180° - x)$ are equal for any given x, so $\sin (180° - x) = \sin x$.
17. Answers may vary. Sample:

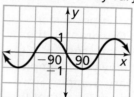

Lesson H.20
Check Your Understanding
1a.

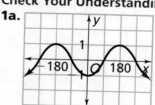

From the graph, $\cos (180° + x)$ and $-\cos x$ are equal for any given x, so $\cos (180° + x) = -\cos x$.
b.

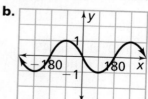

From the graph, $\sin (180° + x)$ and $-\sin x$ are equal for any given x, so $\sin (180° + x) = -\sin x$.
2. $\tan (180° + x) = \frac{\sin (180° + x)}{\cos (180° + x)} = \frac{-\sin x}{-\cos x} = \tan x$

3a.

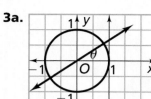

b. $\sin \theta = \dfrac{2\sqrt{13}}{13}$, $\cos \theta = \dfrac{3\sqrt{13}}{13}$

4a. $\tan (90° + \theta) = -\dfrac{3}{2} = -\dfrac{1}{\tan \theta}$ **b.** Answers may vary. Sample: The slope of the line is $\dfrac{y}{x}$, which is the same as the tangent of the angle formed by the line and the positive x-axis.
c. Answers may vary. Sample: If two perpendicular lines intersect at the origin and are not the x- and y-axes, and if (a, b) is a point on one line, then $(-b, a)$ is a point on the other line. So the slopes are $\dfrac{b}{a}$ and $-\dfrac{a}{b}$, which are negative reciprocals. Now suppose two lines have slopes that are negative reciprocals $\dfrac{b}{a}$ and $-\dfrac{a}{b}$. Using the results of Exercise 4a, $\tan (90° + \theta) = -\dfrac{1}{\tan \theta}$. If the line through (a, b) forms an angle of θ with the positive x-axis, then the line through $(-b, a)$ forms an angle of $(\theta + 90°)$, so the two lines are perpendicular. **5.** Answers may vary. Sample: $\cos \theta$ is 0 for $\theta = 90° + k \cdot 180°$, where k is an integer. We can rewrite $90 + 180k$ as $90(1 + 2k)$. The values $2k + 1$ are the odd integers, so the values $90°(1 + 2k)$ are the odd multiples of $90°$. **6a.** $14°$ **b.** $28°$ **c.** $104°$ **d.** $208°$
7a. $14°$ **b.** $28°$ **c.** $104°$ **d.** $208°$
8a. $(x^2 - y^2) + (2xy)i$ **b.** $\dfrac{2xy}{x^2 - y^2}$

On Your Own
10a. All real numbers except $90° + k \cdot 180°$, where k is an integer **11a.** $x \approx 65° + k \cdot 180°$, where k is an integer.

Lesson H.21
Check Your Understanding
1a. $\cos (-x) = \cos x$ and $\sin (-x) = -\sin x$. So, $\cos (a - b) = \cos (a + (-b)) = \cos a \cos (-b) - \sin a \sin (-b) = \cos a \cos b - (\sin a)(-\sin b) = \cos a \cos b + \sin a \sin b$. **b.** If $a = b$, then $\cos (a - b) = \cos 0° = 1$ and $\cos a \cos b + \sin a \sin b = \cos^2 a + \sin^2 a = 1$.
c. $\dfrac{\sqrt{2} + \sqrt{6}}{4}$ **2a.** $\cos (2x) = \cos (x + x) = \cos x \cos x - \sin x \sin x = \cos^2 x - \sin^2 x$
b. $\sin (2x) = \sin (x + x) = \sin x \cos x + \cos x \sin x = 2\sin x \cos x$ **c.** $\cos 2x = \cos^2 x - \sin^2 x = \cos^2 x - (1 - \cos^2 x) = \cos^2 x - 1 + \cos^2 x = 2\cos^2 x - 1$ **3a.** $\dfrac{\sqrt{2} + \sqrt{3}}{2}$
b. Yes; if $A = \dfrac{\sqrt{2} + \sqrt{3}}{2}$, then $4A = 2\sqrt{2 + \sqrt{3}}$ and $(4A)^2 = (4)(2 + \sqrt{3}) = 8 + 4\sqrt{3}$. If $B = \dfrac{\sqrt{2} + \sqrt{6}}{4}$, then $4B = \sqrt{6} + \sqrt{2}$ and $(4B)^2 = 6 + 2\sqrt{12} + 2 = 8 + 2\sqrt{4} \cdot \sqrt{3}$

$= 8 + 4\sqrt{3}$. So, $\dfrac{\sqrt{2 + \sqrt{3}}}{2} = \dfrac{\sqrt{2} + \sqrt{6}}{4}$.
4. $\cos 3x = \cos^3 x - 3 \sin^2 x \cos x$, $\sin 3x = 3 \sin x \cos^2 x - \sin^3 x$ **5.** $\dfrac{\sqrt{3}}{2} + \dfrac{1}{2}i$
6a. $\sin 10° = 0.1736$, $\sin 50° = 0.7660$, and $\sin 70° = 0.9397$; $\sin 10° + \sin 50° = 0.1736 + 0.7660 = 0.9396$, which is about 0.9397. **b.** $80°$ **c.** $65°$
7. $\sin x + \sin (60° - x) = \sin (60° + x)$; to prove that result, the left side is $\sin x + \sin (60° - x) = \sin x + (\sin 60°)(\cos x) - (\cos 60°)(\sin x) = \sin x + \left(\dfrac{\sqrt{3}}{2}\right)(\cos x) - \left(\dfrac{1}{2}\right)(\sin x) = \left(\dfrac{1}{2}\right)(\sin x) + \left(\dfrac{\sqrt{3}}{2}\right)(\cos x)$. The right side is $(\sin 60°)(\cos x) + (\cos 60°)(\sin x) = \left(\dfrac{\sqrt{3}}{2}\right)(\cos x) + \left(\dfrac{1}{2}\right)(\sin x)$. The two sides are equal, so $\sin x + \sin (60° - x) = \sin (60° + x)$.

On Your Own
8. C **11a.** $\sin x$ **d.** $\cos x$ **12.** $x \mapsto 2^x$ matches $f(a + b) = f(a) \cdot f(b)$.

Lesson H.22
On Your Own
6. $x = 16$
8. c.

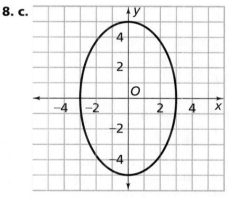

Lesson H.23
Check Your Understanding
1. a. Answers may vary. Sample: The pins should be placed fairly close together. **b.** The pins should be placed far apart, a little shorter than the string length s but larger than $\dfrac{s}{2}$. **c.** If both pins are placed in the same spot, a circle will result. **2. a.** $b = 4, -4$ **b.** $a = 5, -5$ **c.** No; the sum of the distances between this point and the foci does not equal 10.
d. $\sqrt{(x - 3)^2 + y^2} + \sqrt{(x + 3)^2 + y^2} = 10$

3. Your sketch should look like the one on page 471 but points D and E will coincide at the center of the circle. This will also be the point where the two spheres are tangent to the plane of the sliced circle.

4. a. Answers may vary. Sample:
Any point that satisfies the equation
$\left|\sqrt{(x - 3)^2 + y^2} - \sqrt{(x + 3)^2 + y^2}\right| = 4$.

b.

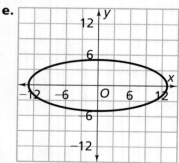

c. $\frac{x^2}{4} - \frac{y^2}{5} = 1$ **5.** If P is any point noncollinear with A and B, then the triangle inequality applies: if the shorter of PA or PB has length x, then the longer cannot be more than $x + 6$. So $|PA - PB| < 6$ is required. If P is collinear with A and B, then $|PA - PB| = 6$ is possible but no more. In the entire plane, no point P can satisfy $|PA - PB| = 10$.

On Your Own

6. a. no **b.** no **c.** yes **d.** no **9.** $x = \frac{1}{4}y^2$

10. a. Answers may vary. Sample: $3x + 25 = 5\sqrt{(x + 3)^2 + y^2}$

Lesson H.24

Check Your Understanding

1. a. $25 \cdot (0)^2 + 169 \cdot (5)^2 = 4225$
$169 \cdot 25 = 4225$

b. Answers may vary. Sample: Any point satisfying the equation $\frac{x^2}{169} + \frac{y^2}{5} = 1$. **c.** The major axis is formed by the points $(13, 0)$ and $(-13, 0)$. The distance between these points is 26. **d.** $c = 12$

e.

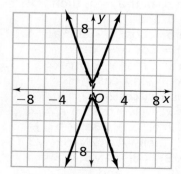

2. a. Answers may vary. Sample: Any points satisfying the equation $\frac{x^2}{9} + \frac{y^2}{25} = 1$. **b.** The major axis is formed by the points $(0, 5)$ and $(0, -5)$. The distance between these points is 10. **c.** $c = 4$

d.

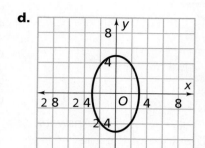

3. The graph will pass through the points $(a, 0)$, $(-a, 0)$, $(0, b)$, and $(0, -b)$.

If $a = b$, then this graph is a circle centered at the origin.

If $a > b$, the graph is an ellipse with major axis along the x-axis with foci points at $(\pm\sqrt{a^2 - b^2}, 0)$.

If $a < b$, the graph is an ellipse with major axis along the y-axis with foci points at $(0, \pm\sqrt{b^2 - a^2})$.

4. a. $y^2 - 9x^2 = 36$
$(\pm 6)^2 - 9 \cdot (0)^2 = 36$

b. $y = \pm 6.7082$ **c.** $y = \pm 16.1555$

d. $y = \pm 300.0600$ **e.** As x grows larger, the ratio of $\frac{y}{x}$ approaches 3 or -3 and the points on the parabola approach asymptotes defined by the lines $y = 3x$ and $y = -3x$.

5. a. This graph is a hyperbola that is a dilation with scale factor $\frac{1}{2}$ from the original in Exercise 5.

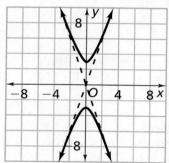

b. This graph is a hyperbola, even closer to the origin.

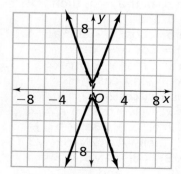

c.

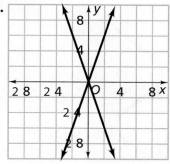

6. a. $x^2 - 2xy + y^2 + 20x + 20y - 100 = 0$
b. $(-5, 5)$ and $(-5, 35)$
c.

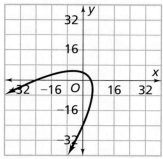

On Your Own
7. $x = -\frac{1}{8}y^2$ **8. c.** The ratio $\frac{y}{x}$ approaches $\frac{3}{4}$.

Lesson H.25
Check Your Understanding
1. a. $(3, 2)$
b.

x	y
6	undefined
7	2
8	4.25
9	5.3541
11	7.1962
13	8.8739
23	16.6969
43	31.8496
103	76.9400
1003	751.9940

c. The graph becomes asymptotic to the line $y - 2 = \frac{3}{4}(x - 3)$.

2. a.

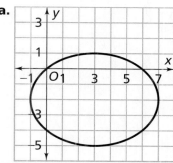

b. no
c.

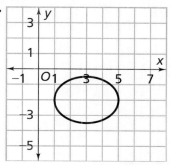

d.

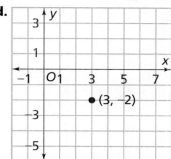

e. No graph, since the equation has no solution.
f. $N = 916$
3. a. Yes; hyperbola
b.

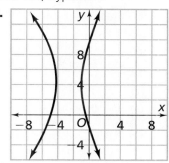

4. a. No; this equation is a single point

b.

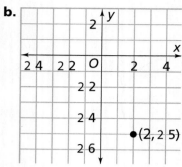

5. a. $(y - 2)^2 = 4(x + 3)^2 - 16$ **b.** The next step in solving this equation is to take a square root, which results in two answers (a positive and negative root).

c. $f_1(x) = 2 + \sqrt{4(x + 3)^2 - 16}$
$f_2(x) = 2 - \sqrt{4(x + 3)^2 - 16}$

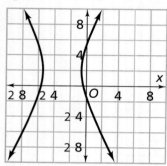

6.

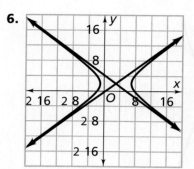

7. $y = \frac{1}{x}$

On Your Own

8. Answers may vary. Sample: The first equation is the sum of squares, and squares can never be negative. The second equation is the difference of squares, and that can be negative. **10. a.** $x \leq -16$ or $x \geq -2$

11. $(4, 10)$ and $(4, 0)$

Index

Index

Index

Index

midpoint, 614–15
parallelograms, 515–20, 518, 615
rectangles, 507, 521, 522, 523, 615
rhombus, 521, 523, 615, 817
sides, 508
skew, 509
squares, 507, 521, 528, 615
trapezoids, 513, 615
vertex of, 508
qualitative facts, 943
quartic polynomials, 111
quintic polynomials, 111
quotient, 225

R

radian, 657, 658, 659, 660
measure, 654
radicals, 4–33, 28–32, 60
expressing with exponents, 31
simplified form of, 18, 33
radius, 17, 345, 346, 350, 360, 630, 636, 640, 644, 645, 647, 650, 651, 654, 669, 679, 691, 699, 700, 712, 732, 783, 790, 795, 802, 804, 821, 824, 827, 828, 829, 913
of spheres, 792
random variables, 408, 409, 415
range, 292, 306, 361
of exponential functions, 318, 320
of functions, 279
ratio, 59, 439, 441, 549, 643, 656, 755
of areas, 608
for circles, 679
common, 580, 613, 679
constant, 438
invariant, 592
special, 746–52
trigonometric, 747, 908
ratio method, 558, 565–71, 571, 616, 770, 790
rational exponents, 42, 56, 60
defining, 54–58
rational numbers, 21–27, 61, 931
decimals, 22
in functions, 315
irrational *versus,* 60
positive, 321
sum of, 24
ratio table, 332
rays, 501, 561, 567, 707
real numbers, 3–61, 203, 217, 219, 220, 230, 838, 851, 941
absolute value, 852

complex numbers as, 216
conjugates as, 225
extension of, 205
nonnegative, 13, 277, 869
positive, 840
real-number solutions, 172
real-world situations, quadratic functions in, 175–76
reciprocals, 858
division and, 222–26
of roots, 166
rectangles, 84, 180, 282, 433, 440, 507, 522, 523, 526, 542, 615, 618, 694, 695, 710, 711, 714, 715
area of, 19, 118, 149, 609
constant-area, 695
defined, 521
dimensions of, 175
geometry software for, 442
maximum area, finding, 182
measuring, 74
perimeter of, 19, 131
scale and, 548, 549, 550, 552
Side-Splitter Theorems and, 589
rectangular prisms, 607
recursive definition, 238–45, 246, 249, 250, 259, 260, 269, 325, 367
defined, 239
function-modeling language and, 240
graph of, 301
recursive functions, 324, 368, 369
recursive rule, 325
reductions, scale and, 572, 593
reflection, of graphs, 300, 301, 356–64
relation, 278
relatively prime pairs, 414
repeated addition, 48
repeated multiplication, 49
restricted domain, 296
reverse list, 489, 495–98
rhombus, 521, 523, 615, 817
diagonal of, 819
Richter, Charles, 3
right angles, 459, 479, 683, 709, 716
right triangles, 19, 617, 692, 713, 718, 719, 720, 721, 729, 736–40, 743, 745, 748, 749, 750, 751, 754, 799, 856, 868, 916
angles, 909
hypotenuse of, 19, 21, 910
isosceles, 836
right triangle trigonometry, 906, 907–12

roots, 28–32, 873–78
average of the, 180
building quadratic formula from, 162–66
comparing, 171
cube, 54
equations with, 171
factoring for, 197, 201
of quadratic equations, 190, 195, 203, 204, 231
of quadratic functions, 199
reciprocals of, 166
sum of, 203
rotated triangles, 953
rounding, decimals, 58
row-reduced echelon form, 893
rules, 146
of algebra, 283, 458
closed-form, 329, 330
of equivalency, 117
finding, 144–45
probability, 381
representing, 113
transformation, 184

S

sample space, 381, 382, 407
SAS Similarity Theorem, 602
scale, 530
testing for, 548–50
scaled copies, 532–37, 596
area and, 627
checking for, 551–56
making, 561–64
of parallelograms, 616, 625
of polygons, 567, 568–70, 610, 625
of triangles, 567, 594, 612
scaled figures, 537
scale factors, 364, 532, 536–43, 557, 564, 572, 593, 595, 612, 616, 634
scalene triangles, 500
scaling, 356–64, 893
horizontal, 368
scaling method, 170
scientific calculators, square root key on, 55
secant angles, 687, 688, 689
secants, 671, 686–92, 701
defined, 686
vertex of, 687, 688
sectors, 647, 703
segments, 520, 571, 715
congruent, 465
diagonals, 507
midpoint of, 730–31, 816, 858
perpendicular, 635
tangent, 690
trisected, 519

Index

Index

Staff Credits

The Pearson people on the CME Project team—representing design, editorial, editorial services, digital product development, publishing services, and technical operations—are listed below. Bold type denotes the core team members.

Ernest Albanese, Scott Andrews, Carolyn Artin, Michael Avidon, Margaret Banker, Suzanne Biron, Beth Blumberg, Stacie Cartwright, Carolyn Chappo, Casey Clark, Bob Craton, Jason Cuoco, Sheila DeFazio, Patty Fagan, **Frederick Fellows**, **Patti Fromkin**, Paul J. Gagnon, Cynthia Harvey, Gillian Kahn, Jonathan Kier, Jennifer King, Elizabeth Krieble, Sara Levendusky, Lisa Lin, Carolyn Lock, Clay Martin, **Carolyn McGuire**, Rich McMahon, Eve Melnechuk, Cynthia Metallides, **Hope Morley**, Jen Paley, Linda Punskovsky, Mairead Reddin, Marcy Rose, Rashid Ross, Carol Roy, Jewel Simmons, Ted Smykal, Laura Smyth, Kara Stokes, Richard Sullivan, Tiffany Taylor-Sullivan, Catherine Terwilliger, Mark Tricca, Lauren Van Wart, Paula Vergith, **Joe Will**, **Kristin Winters**, Allison Wyss

Additional Credits

Niki Birbilis, Gina Choe, Christine Nevola, Jill A. Ort, Lillian Pelaggi, Deborah Savona

Cover Design and Illustration
9 Surf Studios

Cover Photography
Jim Cummins/Corbis; Stockbyte/Getty Images, Inc.

Illustration
Kerry Cashman, Rich McMahon, Jen Paley, Rashid Ross, Ted Smykal

Photography
Chapter 1: Pages 2–3, Randy Faris/Corbis; **4**, Gary Conner/Photo Edit, Inc.; **11**, George Steinmetz/Corbis; **33**, Gary Conner/Photo Edit, Inc.; **34**, Corbis/A. Inden; **47**, Photo Researchers Inc./Andrew Syred; **59**, Corbis/Arctic-Images;

Chapter 2: Pages 62–63, Darrin Zammit Lupi /Reuters/Corbis; **62–63**, Cliff Leight/Getty Images; **64b**, Skyscan/Corbis; **64 inset**, Comstock/Veer; **87**, Skyscan/Corbis; **87 inset**, Comstock/Veer; **88**, Bertrand Collet/Alamy; **98 frame**, Photodisc/SuperStock; **98**, Rob Lewine/Corbis; **105**, Digital Vision Ltd./SuperStock; **111**, ImageDJ/Alamy; **112**, Hope Morley; **123**, EuroStyle Graphics/Alamy; **142**, public domain; **143**, Hope Morley;

Chapter 3: Pages 150–151, Martin Rugner/Age Fotostock; **152**, DAJ/Getty Images, Inc.; **167**, Design Pics, Inc./Alamy; **173**, DAJ/Getty Images, Inc.; **174**, Atlantide Phototravel/Corbis; **177**, Car Culture/Getty Images, Inc.; **183**, R. Ian Lloyd/Masterfile; **189**, Frank Bodenmueller/zefa/Corbis; **195**, Lester Lefkowitz/Getty Images, Inc.; **201**, Robert Glusic/Corbis; **209l**, North Wind; **209r**, Granger; **222**, Carolyn Chappo;

Chapter 4: Pages 232–233, Corbis/William Sallaz; **234**, Visuals Unlimited/Joe McDonald; **239**, Kara Stokes; **250**, Merrill Education; **250r**, Carolyn Chappo; **257**, Photo Researchers, Inc.; **269**, A. & J. Visaoe/Peter Arnold, Inc.; **270**, NewsCom/James Baigrie; **285**, Newscom/Sipa; **286**, Alamy; **312**, Alamy/David Lyons; **323**, Veer; **324**, Dreamstime; **346**, Dreamstime; **351**, John Moore; **365**, Dreamstime;

Chapter 5: Pages 370–371, Paolo Curto/Getty Images; **378–379**, Gallo Images-Anthony/age footstock; **381**, John Gillmoure/CORBIS; **423**, Kevin Schafer/Getty Images;

Chapter 6: Pages 426–427, David Parmenter/www.daveparm.com; **451 inset**, rubberball/Royalty Free; **462**, Jim Cummins/Corbis; **473**, Catherine Booker/Jupiter Images; **477**, Wikimedia; **478**, David Bergman/Corbis; **480**, Kara Stokes; **489**, AP Photo/Timothy D. Easley; **496**, Georgette Douwma/Getty Images, Inc.; **502t**, Elio Ciol/Corbis; **502b**, iStockphoto.com; **505**, David Bergman/Corbis; **506**, Swerve/Alamy; **525**, Rick Friedman/Corbis;

Chapter 7: Pages 530–531, JLImages/Alamy; **532**, Paul Ott; **53l**, Fernando Fernández/age fotostock; **538r**, K-PHOTOS/Alamy; **553 both**, Paul Gagnon; **557**, Paul Ott; **558**, Kavashkin Boris/ITAR-TASS/Corbis; **563**, Michael Newman/Photo Edit; **573**, Deb Nicholls; **574**, Deb Nicholls; **584**, SuperStock Inc.; **587**, Deb Nicholls; **589**, Enrique Algarra/age fotostock; **591**, Deb Nicholls; **592**, Deb Nicholls; **595**, Kara Stokes; **616**, Deb Nicholls;

Chapter 8: Pages 620–621 background, Robert Harding Picture Library Ltd/Alamy; **620–621 inset**, ScotStock/Alamy; **622**, AP Photo/POOL, Mark Wilson; **634**, Big Cheese Photo LLC/Alamy; **634 inset**, Garry Gay/Alamy; **641**, AP Photo/John Gaps III; **642**, Atmosphere Picture Library/Alamy; **653**, AP Photo/Matt Rourke; **661**, www.circlemakers.org; **662**, Allan Munsie/Alamy; **665**, Grigory Dukor/Reuters/Corbis; **673**, ACE STOCK LIMITED/Alamy; **699**, Allan Munsie/Alamy;

Chapter 9: Pages 704–705, ER Productions/Corbis; **705 inset**, Stockbyte/Getty Images, Inc.; **706**, Artist painting a portrait over a grid for accurate proportion, printed Paris 1737 (engraving), Bosse, Abraham (1602–76) (after)/Private Collection, The Stapleton Collection/The Bridgeman Art Library; **710**, Paul Gagnon; **731**, Adam Woolfitt/Corbis; **735**, Foto Marburg/Art Resource, NY; **736**, Ted Pink/Alamy; **738**, David R. Frazier Photolibrary, Inc./Alamy; **761**, Ted Pink/Alamy; **762**, Kara Stokes; **763**, Kara Stokes; **795**, Kara Stokes;

Chapter 10: Pages 800–801, Louie Psihoyos/Getty Images; **803**, Steve Skjold/Alamy; **804**, Dennis Hallinan/Alamy; **818**, Roger Ressmeyer/CORBIS; **824**, Jack Hollingsworth/Getty Images;

Honors Appendix: Pages 830–831, Kris Northern; **832**, Photo Researchers/Mehau Kulyk; **846**, Getty Images/Eric Feferberg; **861**, Photo Researchers/Gregory Sams; **862**, Dr. Bahman Kalantari; **870t**, Photo Researchers/Gusto; **870b**, NewsCom; **877**, Carolyn Chappo; **879**, Dr. Bahman Kalantari; **880**, Getty Images/Al Bello; **889**, Corbis; **905**, Corbis/Anthony John West; **903 both**, AP Images/Dave Bowman; **906**, Getty Images/Joe Sohm; **916**, AP Images/Sue Ogrocki; **931**, Alamy/John Pitcher; **937**, istockphoto; **938**, Photo Researchers; **949**, Getty Images/Grant V. Faint; **959**, Alamy; **960**, Jim West/Alamy; **962**, William Manning/Alamy; **984**, Martin Dohrn/Photo Researchers, Inc.

Note: Every effort has been made to locate the copyright owner of the material reprinted in this book. Omissions brought to our attention will be corrected in subsequent editions.

Additional Credits:

Chapter 1: Lessons 1.01-1.04 taken from lessons 6.6-6.9 from *CME Project: Algebra 1*. Lesson 1.05 taken from lesson 4 of the *CME Project: Algebra 1 Common Core Additional Lessons*. Lesson 1.06 taken from lesson 6.11 from *CME Project: Algebra 2*. Investigation 1B taken from Investigation 5A.

Chapter 2: Whole chapter taken from chapter 7 of *CME Project: Algebra 1*.

Chapter 3: Investigation 3A and 3B taken from Investigation 8A and 8B from *CME Project: Algebra 1*. Investigation 3C taken from Investigation 3A from *CME Project: Algebra 2*.

Chapter 4: Investigation 4A taken from Investigation 1A from *CME Project: Algebra 2*. Investigation 4B taken from Investigation 2A from *CME Project: Algebra 2* except lesson 4.10 which is taken from lesson 1 of the *CME Project: Algebra 2 Common Core Additional Lessons*. Investigation 4C taken from Investigation 5B from *CME Project: Algebra 2*. Investigation 4AD taken from Investigation 6A from *CME Project: Algebra 2*.

Chapter 5: Investigation 5A taken from Investigation 7A from *CME Project: Precalculus*. Lessons 5.03 and 5.04 taken from *CME Project: Precalculus Common Core Additional Lessons, lessons 1 and 2* respectively.

Chapter 6: Lesson 6.0 taken from Investigation *CME Project: Geometry*. Investigation 6A taken from Investigation 1D from *CME Project: Geometry*. Investigations 6B-6D taken from Investigations 2B-2D from *CME Project: Geometry*.

Chapter 7: Whole chapter taken from chapter 4 of *CME Project: Geometry*.

Chapter 8: Investigation 8A taken from Investigation 5A from *CME Project: Geometry*. Lessons 8.04-8.06 taken from lessons 5.4-5.6 of *CME Project: Geometry*. Lessons 8.08-8.10 and Lesson 8.12-8.13 taken from lessons 5.7-5.9 and 5.10-5.11 respectively from *CME Project: Geometry*. Lessons 8.07 and 8.11 taken from lessons 1 and 2 of *CME Project: Geometry Common Core Additional Lessons*.

Chapter 9: Lessons 9.01-9.04 taken from Lessons 6.1-6.4 of *CME Project: Geometry*. Lesson 9.05 taken from lesson 7.6 of *CME Project: Geometry*. Investigation 9B taken from Investigation 6B of *CME Project: Geometry*. Lesson 9.10 and lessons 9.11-9.14 taken from Investigation lesson 3.15 and lessons 6.10-6.13 respectively from *CME Project: Geometry*.

Chapter 10: Investigation 10A taken from Investigation 6A from *CME Project: Precalculus*. Lesson 10.0 taken from Chapter 7 project from *CME Project: Geometry*.

Honors Appendix: Lessons H.01-H.03 taken from *CME Project: Algebra 2*. Lesson H.04 taken from lesson 2 of *CME Project: Algebra 2 Common Core Additional Lessons*. Lessons H.05-H.07 taken from Lessons 3.10-3.12 from *CME Project: Algebra 2*. Lessons H.08-H.11 and lesson H.12 taken from lessons 4.1-4.3 and lesson 4.8 respectively from *CME Project: Algebra 2*. Lessons H.12 - H.21 taken from lessons 8.0-8.9 from *CME Project: Algebra 2*. Lessons H.22-H.25 taken from lessons 6.5-6.8 from *CME Project: Precalculus*.